R"24

COLLINS POCKET GREEK DICTIONARY

GREEK·ENGLISH ENGLISH·GREEK

Harry T. Hionides

New Edition by/Νέα Έκδοση
Niki Watts, Helen George-Papageorgiou

HarperCollins*Publishers*

First published in this edition 1988

© William Collins Sons & Co. Ltd. 1988

Latest reprint 1992

ISBN 0 00 470241 7

Harry T. Hionides

new edition by/νέα έκδοση
Niki Watts, Helen George-Papageorgiou

consultant/σύμβουλος
Roger Green

editorial staff/εκδοτικό προσωπικό
Jeremy Butterfield, Val McNulty, Susan Dunsmore

ISBN 0 00 433209 1 Special edition for Greece and Cyprus

*Printed in Great Britain by
HarperCollins Manufacturing, Glasgow*

ΕΙΣΑΓΩΓΗ

Ο χρήστης που επιθυμεί να διαβάσει και να καταλάβει Αγγλικά θα βρει σ' αυτό το λεξικό έναν περιεκτικό και σύγχρονο κατάλογο λέξεων, καθώς και σημαντικό αριθμό φράσεων που χρησιμοποιούνται σήμερα. Επίσης θα βρει σε αλφαβητική σειρά τους κύριους ανώμαλους τύπους με παραπομπή στο βασικό τους τύπο, καθώς και μερικές από τις συνηθέστερες συντομογραφίες, αρκτικόλεξα και γεωγραφικές ονομασίες.

Ο χρήστης που επιθυμεί να εκφραστεί και να επικοινωνήσει στα Αγγλικά θα βρει όλους τους τρόπους χρήσης των βασικών λέξεων. Όπου μια λέξη έχει πολλές σημασίες, οι αντίστοιχες μεταφράσεις δίνονται κατά σειρά προτεραιότητας ανάλογα με τη συχνότητα των Ελληνικών εννοιών,

INTRODUCTION

The user whose aim is to read and understand Greek will find a comprehensive and up-to-date wordlist which includes the most common scientific and technical terms. The official ("monotonic") accent system has been used throughout, and a high proportion of Demotic words and Demotic versions of words which also have Katharevousa forms have been included.

The user who wants to communicate and express himself in Greek will find clear and detailed treatment of all the basic words, with numerous indicators pointing to the appropriate translation and helping him to use it correctly.

ABBREVIATIONS

επίθετο	**a**	adjective
συντομογραφία	**abbr**	abbreviation
επίρρημα	**ad**	adverb
γεωργία	**AGR**	agriculture
ανατομία	**ANAT**	anatomy
αρχαιολογία	**ARCH**	archaeology
αρχιτεκτονική	**ARCHIT**	architecture
αστρονομία	**ASTR**	astronomy
επίθετο	**attr**	attributive
αυτοκίνητο	**AUT**	automobile
αεροπορία	**AVIAT**	aviation
βιβλικός	**BIBL**	biblical
βιολογία	**BIOL**	biology
βοτανική	**BOT**	botany
Αγγλισμός	**Brit**	British usage
ξυλουργική	**CARP**	carpentry
χημεία	**CHEM**	chemistry
κινηματογράφος	**CINE**	cinema
σύνδεσμος	**cj**	conjunction
κοινός	**col**	colloquial
περιληπτικός	**collect**	collective
εμπορικός	**COMM**	commercial
συγκριτικός	**comp**	comparative
σύνθετος	**compd**	compound
ηλεκτρονικοί υπολογιστές	**COMPUT**	computers
υποκοριστικό	**dim**	diminutive
διπλωματία	**DIP**	diplomacy
εκκλησιαστικός	**ECCL**	ecclesiastical
οικονομία	**ECON**	economics
ηλεκτρισμός	**ELEC**	electricity
ειδικά	**esp**	especially
επιφώνημα	**excl**	exclamation
θηλυκό	**f**	feminine noun
μεταφορικά	**fig**	figuratively
οικονομία	**FIN**	finance
γεωγραφία	**GEOG**	geography
γεωλογία	**GEOL**	geology
γραμματική	**GRAM**	grammar
κυνήγι	**HUNT**	hunting
απρόσωπο	**impers**	impersonal
απαρέμφατο	**infin**	infinitive
επιφώνημα	**interj**	interjection
αμετάβλητος	**inv**	invariable
ανώμαλο	**irreg**	irregular
γλωσσολογία	**LING**	linguistics
κυριολεκτικός	**lit**	literal
λογοτεχνία	**LITER**	literature
αρσενικό	**m**	masculine noun
μαθηματικά	**MATH**	mathematics
μηχανισμός	**MECH**	mechanical

ιατρική	**MED**	medical
στρατιωτικός	**MIL**	military
μουσική	**MUS**	music
ουσιαστικό	**n**	noun
ναυτικός	**NAUT**	nautical, naval
ουδέτερο	**nt**	neuter
ἀριθμός	**num**	numeral
απαρχαιωμένος	**old**	old-fashioned
εαυτός	**o.s.**	oneself
κοινοβούλιο	**PARL**	Parliament
μετοχή	**part**	participle
υποτιμητικός	**pej**	pejorative
προσωπικός	**pers**	personal
φιλοσοφία	**PHIL**	philosophy
φωνητική, φωνολογία	**PHON**	phonetics
φωτογραφία	**PHOT**	photography
φυσική	**PHYS**	physics
πληθυντικός	**pl**	plural
ποίηση	**POET**	poetry
πολιτική	**POL**	politics
κτητικός	**poss**	possessive
μετοχή αορίστου	**pp**	past participle
κατηγορούμενο	**pred**	predicative
πρόθεση	**prep**	preposition
τυπογραφία	**PRINT**	printing/typography
αντωνυμία	**pron**	pronoun
αόριστος, παρατατικός	**pt**	past tense
σήμα κατατεθέν	®	registered trademark
ραδιοφωνία	**RAD**	radio
σιδηρόδρομος	**RAIL**	railways
θρησκεία	**REL**	religion
σχολείο	**SCH**	school
ενικός	**sing**	singular
λαϊκός	**sl**	slang
κάποιος	**s.o.**	someone, somebody
κάτι	**sth**	something
υπερθετικός	**sup**	superlative
τεχνικός	**TECH**	technical
τηλεπικοινωνίες	**TEL**	telecommunications
υφαντά	**TEX**	textiles
θέατρο	**THEAT**	theatre
τηλεόραση	**TV**	television
πανεπιστήμιο	**UNIV**	university
Αμερικανισμός	**US**	American usage
ρήμα	**v**	verb
ρήμα αμετάβατο	**vi**	intransitive verb
ρήμα μεταβατικό	**vt**	transitive verb
ρήμα μεταβατικό και αμετάβατο	**vti**	transitive and intransitive verb
ζωολογία	**ZOOL**	zoology

v

ΣΥΝΤΟΜΟΓΡΑΦΙΕΣ

athletics, sport	αθλητ	αθλητικά
aviation	αερο	αεροπορία
accusative	αιτ	αιτιατική
intransitive verb	αμ, αμετ	ρήμα αμετάβατο
anatomy	ανατ	ανατομία
negative	αρνητ	αρνητικός
architecture	αρχιτεκ	αρχιτεκτονική
astronomy	αστρον	αστρονομία
see (cross-reference)	βλ	βλέπε
botany	βοτ	βοτανική
geography	γεωγρ	γεωγραφία
geometry	γεωμ	γεωμετρία
grammar	γραμμ	γραμματική
religion	εκκλ	εκκλησιαστικός
commerce	εμπόρ	εμπόριο
adjective	επίθ	επίθετο
adverb	επίρ	επίρρημα
exclamation	επιφ	επιφώνημα
zoology	ζωολ	ζωολογία
electricity	πλεκ, πλεκτ	πλεκτρισμός
medicine	ιατρ	ιατρική
et cetera	κτλ	και τα λοιπά
mathematics	μαθημ	μαθηματικά
mechanical	μηχαν	μηχανισμός
figuratively	μεταφ	μεταφορικά
music	μουσ	μουσική
nautical, naval	ναυτ	ναυτικός
law	νομ	νομική
economics	οικ, οικον,	οικονομικά
noun	όνομ, ουσ	όνομα, ουσιαστικό
plural	πλ	πληθυντικός
politics	πολιτ	πολιτική
preposition	πρόθ	πρόθεση
e.g. (for example)	π.χ.	παραδείγματος χάρη
military	στρατ	στρατιωτικός
conjunction	σύνδ	σύνδεσμος
technical	τεχν	τεχνολογία
telecommunications	τηλεπ	τηλεπικοινωνίες
printing, typography	τυπογρ	τυπογραφία
philosophy	φιλοσ	φιλοσοφία
photography	φωτογρ	φωτογραφική
chemistry	χημ	χημεία

PRONUNCIATON OF MODERN GREEK

Each letter in Greek nearly always represents the same sound. The few exceptions are listed below on page viii. The pronunciation system used in the text (given in brackets after each Greek main entry) transcribes the letters of Greek into the English alphabet, with one special character used to represent a less obvious sound. A list of sounds which the English alphabet is used to represent is given below. When you read out the pronunciation you should sound the letters as if you were reading an English word.

GREEK LETTER		CLOSEST ENGLISH SOUND	SHOWN BY	EXAMPLE	PRONOUNCED
Α	α	hand	a	άνθρωπος	anthropos
Β	β	vine	v	βούτυρο	vooteero
Γ	γ	see page viii	g	γάλα	gala
		yes	y	για	ya
Δ	δ	this	ð	δάκτυλος	ðakteelos
Ε	ε	met	e	έτοιμος	eteemos
Ζ	ζ	zone	z	ζώνη	zonee
Η	η	meet	ee*	ήλιος	eeleeos
Θ	θ	thin	th	θέατρο	theatro
Ι	ι	meet	ee*	ίππος	eepos
Κ	κ	key	k	και	ke
Λ	λ	log	l	λάδι	laðee
Μ	μ	mat	m	μάτι	matee
Ν	ν	not	n	νύχτα	neehta
Ξ	ξ	rocks	ks	ξένος	ksenos
Ο	ο	cot	o	όχι	ohee
Π	π	pat	p	πόλη	polee
Ρ	ρ	carrot see page viii	r	ρόδα	roða
Σ	σ,ς	sat	s	σήμα	seema
Τ	τ	top	t	τράπεζα	trapeza
Υ	υ	meet	ee*	ύπνος	eepnos
Φ	φ	fat	f	φούστα	foosta
Χ	χ	see page viii	h	χάνω χέρι	hano heree
Ψ	ψ	lapse	ps	ψάρι	psaree
Ω	ω	cot	o	ώρα	ora

* The letter *i* is used to represent the "ee" sound a) when two such sounds occur together; b) when "ee" is followed by "e"; c) before a stressed vowel e.g.

ικανοποίηση	eekanopieesee
βίαιος	vieos
κριός	krios

COMBINATIONS OF LETTERS

The combinations of letters shown below are pronounced as listed.

GREEK LETTERS	CLOSEST ENGLISH SOUND	SHOWN BY	EXAMPLE	PRONOUNCED
ει	meet	ee	είδος	*ee*ðos
οι			οίκοι	*ee*kee
αι	met	e	αίμα	*e*ma
ου	food	oo	που	p*oo*
μπ	beer	b	μπύρα	*b*eera
	or amber	mb	κάμπος	ka*mb*os
	or ample	mp	σύμπαν	see*mp*an
ντ	door	d	ντομάτα	*d*omata
	or bent	nt	συναντώ	seena*nt*o
	or bend	nd	πέντε	pe*nd*e
γκ, γγ	good	g	γκάζι	*g*azee
	or angle	ng	Αγγλία	a*ng*leea
γξ	links	ks	σφιγξ	sfee*nks*
τζ	friends	dz	τζάμι	*dz*amee

The pairs of vowels shown above are pronounced separately if the first has an acute accent (´) or the second a dieresis (¨); e.g.

παιδάκι	peðakee	παϊδάκι	paeeðakee
καιρός	keros	Κάιρο	kaeero

Some Greek consonant sounds have no English equivalent. The υ of the groups αυ, ευ and ηυ is generally pronounced *v*.

GREEK LETTER	REMARKS	EXAMPLE	PRONOUNCED
Ρ,ρ	slightly trilled *r*	ρόδα	ro*ð*a
Χ,χ	like *ch* in *loch*	χάνω	*h*ano
	or like a rough *h*	χέρι	*h*eree
Γ,γ	like a rough *g*	γάλα	*g*ala
	or like *y*	για	*y*a

STRESS

All Greek words of two or more syllables have an accute accent which indicates where the stress falls. For instance, άγαλμα is pronounced a*gal*ma and αγάπη is pronounced a*ga*pee.

ΑΓΓΛΙΚΗ ΠΡΟΦΟΡΑ

Φωνήεντα και δίφθογγοι		Σύμφωνα	
	Αγγλικό παράδειγμα		Αγγλικό παράδειγμα
ɑː	father	b	bat, baby
ʌ	but, come	d	mended
æ	man, cat	f	fine, raffle
ə	father, ago	g	get, big
ɜː	bird, heard	dʒ	gin, judge
ε	get, bed	ŋ	sing
ɪ	it, big	h	house, he
iː	tea, see	j	young, yes
ɒ	hot, wash	k	come, mock
ɔ	saw, all	l	little, place
ʊ	put, book	m	ram, mummy
uː	too, you	n	ran, nut
aɪ	fly, high	p	pat, pope
aʊː	how, house	r	red, tread
εə	there, bear	s	sand, yes
eɪ	day, obey	t	tab, strut
ɪə	here, hear	v	vine, river
əʊ	go, note	z	rose, zebra
ɔɪ	boy, oil	ʃ	she, machine
ʊə	poor, sure	tʃ	chin, rich
		w	water, which
		ʒ	vision
		θ	think, myth
		ð	this, the

Το σημείο * σημαίνει ότι το τελικό 'r' δεν προφέρεται στα Αγγλικά εκτός αν η λέξη που ακολουθεί αρχίζει με φωνήεντο. Το σημείο ['] καθορίζει την τονιζόμενη συλλαβή.

GREEK-ENGLISH
ΕΛΛΗΝΙΚΑ-ΑΓΓΛΙΚΑ

Α, α

α-, αν- (negative particle) in-, un-, il-, ir-, -less.

αβαθής [avathees] shallow.

αβάπτιστος [avapteestos] unbaptised.

αβάσιμος [avaseemos] groundless || (υποψία) unfounded.

αβάστακτος [avastaktos] unbearable || (δύναμη) uncontrollable.

άβατος [avatos] inaccessible || untrodden.

άβγαλτος [avgaltos] inexperienced.

αβγό, το [avgo] egg.

αβγολέμονο, το [avgolemono] sauce or soup with eggs and lemon.

αβέβαιος [aveveos] doubtful || uncertain.

αβίαστος [aveeastos] unforced, natural.

αβίωτος [aveeotos] unbearable, intolerable.

αβλαβής [avlavees] (έντομο κτλ) harmless.

αβοήθητος [avoeetheetos] without help.

άβολος [avolos] inconvenient || (κάθισμα κτλ) uncomfortable.

άβυσσος, η [aveesos] abyss.

αγαθός [agathos] good, kind || (αφελής) naive || (τίμιος) honest.

άγαλμα, το [agalma] statue.

άγαμος [agamos] unmarried, single.

αγανακτώ [aganakto] be irritated.

αγανάκτηση, η [aganakteesee] indignation, anger.

αγάπη, η [agapee] love, affection.

αγαπημένος [agapeemenos] dear, beloved || (πράγμα) favourite.

αγαπητός [agapeetos] βλ αγαπημένος.

αγαπώ [agapo] love || (μου αρέσει) like.

αγγαρεία, η [angareea] chore || drudgery.

αγγείο, το [angeeo] vase || (πήλινο) pot || (ανατ) blood vessel.

αγγειοπλαστική, η [angeeoplasteekee] pottery.

αγγελία, η [angeleea] announcement || (εμπορ) advertisement.

αγγελιαφόρος, ο, η [angeleeaforos] messenger || (στρατ) orderly.

αγγελικός [angeleekos] angelic(al).

αγγέλω [angelo] announce, declare.

άγγελμα, το [angelma] message, notice.

άγγελος, ο [angelos] angel.

αγγίζω [angeezo] touch.

Αγγλία, η [angleea] England.

αγγλικά, τα [angleeka] English (language).

αγγλικός [angleekos] English.

Αγγλίδα, η [angleeða] Englishwoman.

Άγγλος, ο [anglos] Englishman.

αγγούρι, το [angouree] cucumber.

αγελάδα, η [ayelaða] cow.

αγέλαστος [ayelastos] morose, sullen.

αγέλη, η [ayelee] herd || (προβάτων) flock || (λύκων) pack.

αγένεια, η [ayeneea] rudeness.

αγενής [ayenees] rude, impolite.

αγέραστος [ayerastos] ever young.

αγέρωχος [ayerohos] haughty, arrogant.

αγιάζι [ayazee] hoarfrost, cold || (αύρα) breeze.

αγιάζω [ayazo] (γίνομαι άγιος) become a saint.

αγιασμός, ο [ayasmos] blessing with holy water.

αγιάτρευτος [ayatreftos] incurable.

αγίνωτος [ayeenotos] (φρούτο) unripe, raw.

άγιος [ayos] holy || (πρόσωπο) saint.

αγκαζάρω [angazaro] reserve, book || hire.

αγκαζέ [angaze] arm in arm || (πιασμένο) engaged, taken, occupied.

αγκάθι, το [angathee] thorn, prickle.

αγκαλιά, η [angalia] embrace || (επιρ) armful.

αγκαλιάζω [angaliazo] embrace, hug.

αγκίδα, η [angeeða] splinter, thorn.

αγκινάρα, η [angeenara] artichoke.

αγκίστρι, το [angeestree] hook.

αγκομαχώ [angomaho] gasp, pant.

αγκύλες, οι [angeeles] brackets.

άγκυρα, η [angeera] anchor || σπικώνω ~ weigh anchor.

αγκυροβολία, η [angeerovoleea] mooring.

αγκυροβολώ [angeerovolo] anchor, drop anchor.

αγκώνας, ο [angonas] elbow.

αγναντεύω [agnantevo] see from a distance.

άγνοια, η [agneea] ignorance.

αγνός [agnos] chaste, modest.

αγνοώ [agnoo] be ignorant of || (περιφρονώ) ignore.

αγνωμοσύνη, η [agnomoseenee] ingratitude.

αγνώμων [agnomon] ungrateful.

αγνώριστος [agnoreestos] unrecognizable.

άγνωστος [agnostos] unknown || (ουσ) stranger.

άγονος [agonos] infertile, barren || ~ γραμμή unprofitable shipping line.

αγορά, η [agora] (το μέρος) market || (η πράξη) purchase.

αγοράζω [agorazo] purchase, buy.

αγοραίος [agoreos] for hire || (μεταφ) vulgar, common.

αγορανομία, η [agoranomeea] market inspection police.

αγοραπωλησία, η [agorapoleeseea] transaction.

αγοραστής, ο [agorastees] buyer, purchaser.

αγορεύω [agorevo] make a speech || (με στόμφο) harangue.

αγόρι, το [agoree] boy, lad.

άγουρος [agouros] unripe, green, sour.

αγράμματος [agrammatos] illiterate, uneducated.

άγραφος [agrafos] unwritten.

αγριάδα, η [agriaδa] fierceness, savageness.

αγριεύω [agrievo] be infuriated, become angry.

αγρίμι, το [agreemee] wild animal || (μεταφ) rude fellow.

άγριος [agreeos] wild || savage.

αγροίκος [agreekos] coarse, unrefined.

αγρόκτημα, το [agrokteema] farmland.

αγρός, ο [agros] field || country.

αγρότης, ο [agrotees] farmer || peasant.

αγροφυλακή, η [agrofeelakee] agrarian police.

αγρυπνώ [agreepno] stay awake, lie awake || (επαγρυπνά) be watchful.

αγύμναστος [ageemnastos] untrained, unexercised.

αγχιστεία, η [anghisteea] relationship by marriage.

αγχόνη, η [anghonee] gallows, hanging.

άγχος, το [anghos] anxiety.

άγω [ago] lead, conduct, guide.

αγωγή, η [agoyee] breeding, conduct || (νομ) lawsuit.

αγώγι, το [agoyee] fare.

αγωγός, ο [agogos] conductor || (σωλήνας) pipe, conduit.

αγώνας, ο [agonas] struggle, fight || (αθλητ) game, contest || αγώνες πλ games, sporting events.

αγωνία, η [agoneea] agony || anxiety.

αγωνίζομαι [agoneezome] struggle, fight, strive.

αγωνιστής, ο [agoneestees] contestant, fighter || (πολιτ) militant.

αγωνιώ [agoneeo] be in agony || be anxious.

αγωνιώδης [agoneeoδees] anxious, troubled.

αδαής [aδaees] inexperienced, unfamiliar (with).

αδάμαστος [aδamastos] untamed || (λαός) unconquered || (θάρρος) unbroken.

άδεια, η [aδeea] leave, permission || (γάμου κτλ) licence, permit.

αδειάζω [aδeeazo] empty || (ευκαιρώ) have time.

άδειος [aδeeos] empty, unoccupied.

αδέκαστος [aδekastos] incorruptible || (αμερόληπτος) impartial, unbiased.

αδελφή, η [aδelfee] sister.

αδέλφια, τα [aδelfeea] πλ brothers, brother and sister.

αδελφικός [aδelfeekos] (αγάπη) brotherly || (φίλος) dear.

αδελφός, ο [aδelfos] brother.

αδένας, ο [aδenas] gland.

αδέξιος [aδekseeos] awkward, clumsy.

αδέσμευτος [aδesmeftos] (μεταφ) under no obligation || (χώρα) non-aligned.

αδέσποτος [aδespotos] stray, without an owner.

άδηλος [aδeelos] uncertain, doubtful || άδηλοι πόροι invisible income.

αδήλωτος [aδeelotos] undeclared.

'Αδης, ο [aδees] Hell || Hades.

αδηφάγος [aδeefagos] voracious || (μεταφ) greedy.

αδιάβαστος [aδiavastos] (βιβλίο) unread || (μαθητής) unprepared.

αδιάβατος [aδiavatos] impassable.

αδιάβροχο, το [aδiavroho] raincoat.

αδιάθετος [aδiathetos] (υγεία) unwell || (κεφάλαιο) unspent.

αδιαίρετος [aδieretos] indivisible || undivided.

αδιάκοπος [aδiakopos] uninterrupted, continuous.

αδιάκριτος [aδiakreetos] imperceptible || (χαρακτήρας) indiscreet.

αδιάλλακτος [aδialaktos] implacable, uncompromising.

αδιάλυτος [aδialeetos] indissoluble, undissolved.

αδιάντροπος [aδiantropos] brazen || (ενέργεια) impudent.

αδιαπέραστος [aδeeaperastos] impenetrable.

αδιάρρηκτος [aδeeareektos] unbreakable || (μεταφ) indissoluble.

αδιάσπαστος [aδiaspastos] unbroken || inseparable.

αδιάφορος [aδiaforos] indifferent.

αδιαχώριστος [aδeeahoreestos] inseparable.

αδίδακτος [aδeeδaktos] untaught.

αδιέξοδος, η [aðieksoðos] impasse || (δρόμος) cul de sac, dead end.

αδικία, η [aðeekeea] injustice, wrongdoing, offence.

άδικος [aðeekos] unjust, unfair || **έχω άδικο** I'm in the wrong.

αδικώ [aðeeko] do wrong || (κάποιον) be unjust to.

αδιόρθωτος [aðeeorthotos] irreparable || (χαρακτήρας) incorrigible.

αδίστακτος [aðeestahtos] unhesitating, resolute.

άδολος [aðolos] guileless, innocent.

άδοξος [aðoksos] inglorious.

αδούλευτος [aðouleftos] unwrought, raw || (αγρός) uncultivated.

αδράνεια, η [aðraneea] inertia || (μεταφ) indolence.

αδράχτι, το [aðrahtee] spindle.

αδύνατος [aðoonatos] thin || (όεν γίνεται) impossible.

αδυναμία, η [aðeenameea] (πνεύματος) deficiency || (σώματος) weakness.

αδυνατώ [aðeenato] be unable to.

αδυσώπητος [aðeesopeetos] relentless, implacable.

άδυτο, το [aðeeto] (εκκλ) sanctuary.

αειθαλής [aeethalees] evergreen.

αεικίνητος [aeekeeneetos] in perpetual motion.

αείμνηστος [aeemneestos] late, fondly remembered.

αεράμυνα, η [aerameena] air defence.

αεραγωγός, η [aeragogos] air duct.

αέρας, ο [aeras] air, wind.

αερίζω [aereezo] ventilate, air.

αερισμός, ο [aereesmos] ventilation, airing.

αέριο, το [aereeo] gas.

αεριούχος [aereeouhos] aerated, gaseous.

αεριστήρας, ο [aereesteeras] ventilator.

αεροδρόμιο, το [aeroðromeeo] airport.

αερόλιθος, ο [aeroleethos] meteorite.

αερολιμένας, ο [aeroleemeenas] airport.

αεροπλάνο, το [aeroplano] aeroplane.

αεροπορία, η [aeroporeea] air force.

αεροπορικώς [aeroporeekos] by air.

αερόστατο, το [aerostato] balloon.

αετός, ο [aetos] eagle || (μεταφ) clever person || (χαρταετός) kite.

αζήτητος [azeeteetos] unclaimed || (εμπορ) not in demand.

άζυμος [azeemos] unleavened.

άζωτο, το [azoto] nitrogen.

απδής [aeeðees] loathsome, sickening.

απδία, η [aeeðeea] disgust, loathing.

απδιάζω [aeeðeeazo] feel disgust for, loathe.

απδόνι, το [aeeðonee] nightingale.

απττητος [aeeteetos] undefeated, unbeatable.

αθανασία, η [athanaseea] immortality, eternity.

αθάνατος [athanatos] immortal, deathless.

αθέατος [atheatos] invisible, unseen.

άθελα [athela] unintentionally.

αθέμιτος [athemeetos] illegal, unlawful.

άθεος [atheos] godless || (ουσ) atheist.

αθεόφοβος [atheofovos] impious || (ουσ) rogue.

αθεράπευτος [atherapevtos] incurable || (μεταφ) incorrigible.

αθετώ [atheto] break one's word, violate.

άθικτος [atheektos] untouched, unharmed.

αθλητής, ο [athleetees] athlete.

αθλητικός [athleeteekos] athletic || (σώμα) robust.

αθλητισμός, ο [athleeteesmos] athletics.

άθλιος [athleeos] wretched, miserable.

άθλος, ο [athlos] feat, exploit.

αθόρυβος [athoreevos] quiet, silent.

άθραυστος [athravstos] unbroken || (αντικείμενο) unbreakable.

αθρήσκος [athreeskos] irreligious.

αθροίζω [athreezo] add up, count || (στρατ) gather, assemble.

άθροισμα, το [athreesma] sum, total.

αθυμία, η [atheemeea] dejection, depression.

αθυρόστομος [atheerostomos] indiscreet, impertinent.

αθώος [athoos] innocent.

αθωώνω [athoono] acquit, exonerate.

αίγλη, η [eeglee] splendour || (ονόματος κτλ) grandeur, glory.

αιγόκλημα, το [egokleema] honeysuckle.

Αίγυπτος, η [eeyeeptos] Egypt.

Αιγύπτιος, ο [eeyeepteeos] Egyptian.

αιγυπτιακός [eeyeepteeakos] Egyptian.

αιθέριος [ethereeos] ethereal, essential.

αιθήρας, ο [etheeras] (χημ) ether || air.

αίθουσα, η [ethousa] large room, hall || (σχολική) schoolroom.

αίθριος [ethreeos] clear, bright || (καιρός) fair.

αίμα, το [ema] blood.

αιματηρός [emateeros] bloody, bloodstained.

αιματοχυσία, η [ematoheeseea] bloodshed.

αιμοβόρος [emovoros] bloodthirsty || (μεταφ) ferocious, cruel.

αιμοδοσία, η [emodoseea] blood donation.

αιμομιξία, η [emomeekseea] incest.

αιμορραγία, η [emorayeea] haemorrhage.

αιμοσφαίριο, το [emosfereeo] blood corpuscle.

αίνιγμα, το [eneegma] enigma, riddle.

άιντε [aeede] (έπιφ) come now!, come on!

αίρεση, η [eresee] heresy.

αιρετικός [ereteekos] heretical.

αισθάνομαι [esthanome] feel.

αίσθημα, το [estheema] sensation, feeling || **αισθήματα** πλ feelings.

αισθηματικός [estheemateekos] sentimental.

αίσθηση, η [estheesee] sense, sensation.

αισθητικός [estheeteekos] aesthetic || **ο** ~ beautician.

αισθητός [estheetos] perceptible, noticeable.

αισιόδοξος [eseeoðoksos] optimistic.

αίσχος, το [eshos] shame, disgrace.

αισχροκέρδεια, η [eshrokerðeea] profiteering.

αισχρολογία, η [eshroloyeea] obscenity, filthy talk.

αισχρός [eshros] shameful, infamous.

αίτηση, η [eteesee] application, petition, request.

αιτία, η [eteea] cause, reason, motive.

αιτιατική, η [eteeateekee] (γραμμ) accusative (case).

αίτιο, το [eteeo] cause || (εγκλήματος) motive.

αιτιολογία, η [eteeoloyeea] explanation || (οίκον) particulars.

αίτιος [eteeos] responsible.

αιτώ [eto] request (κάτι) || **αιτούμαι** beg (κάτι).

αιφνιδιασμός, ο [efneeðeeasmos] surprise.

αιχμαλωτίζω [ehmaloteezo] capture || (μεταφ) captivate.

αιχμάλωτος, ο [ehmalotos] captive, prisoner.

αιχμή, η [ehmee] (βελόνας) point || (βέλους) head.

αιώνας, ο [eonas] age, century.

αιώνιος [eoneeos] eternal || perpetual.

ακαδημία, η [akaðeemeea] academy.

ακαθαρσία, η [akatharseea] filth, dirt.

ακάθαρτος [akathartos] dirty, filthy.

ακάθεκτος [akathektos] unrestrained, unchecked.

ακαθόριστος [akathoreestos] undefined.

ακακία, η [akakeea] (δένδρο) acacia.

άκακος [akakos] harmless, innocent.

ακαλαισθησία, η [akalestheeseea] lack of taste.

ακάλεστος [akalestos] uninvited.

ακαλλιέργητος [akalyergeetos] uncultivated || (άνθρωπος) uncultured.

ακαμάτης, ο [akamatees] loafer.

άκαμπτος [akamptos] unbending.

ακανθώδης [akanthoðees] thorny, prickly.

ακανόνιστος [akanoneestos] unregulated || (σχήμα) irregular || (σφυγμός) uneven.

ακαριαίος [akareeayos] instantaneous.

άκαρπος [akarpos] unfruitful || (μεταφ) fruitless.

ακατάβλητος [akatavleetos] indomitable || (χρέη) unpaid.

ακατάδεκτος [akataðektos] disdainful, haughty.

ακατάληπτος [akataleeptos] incomprehensible.

ακατάλληλος [akataleelos] unsuitable, unfit.

ακαταλόγιστος [akatalogeestos] not responsible (for) || irrational.

ακατανόητος [akatanoeetos] inconceivable, unintelligible.

ακατάπαυστος [akatapavstos] unceasing, endless.

ακατάστατος [akatastatos] untidy || (καιρός) changeable.

ακατοίκητος [akateekeetos] uninhabited.

ακατόρθωτος [akatorthotos] unfeasible, impossible.

ακέραιος [akereos] integral, whole || (τίμιος) upright || ~ **αριθμός** integer.

ακεφιά, η [akefia] dejection, gloom.

ακίνδυνος [akeenðeenos] safe, harmless.

ακίνητος [akeeneetos] immovable || (περιουσία) estate, property.

άκλιτος [akleetos] indeclinable.

ακμάζω [akmazo] flourish, thrive.

ακμαίος [akmeos] vigorous, sturdy || (γερός) robust.

ακμή, η [akmee] height, peak || (ιατρ) acne.

ακοή, η [akoee] hearing || **εξ ακοής** by hearsay.

ακοινώνητος [akeenoneetos] unsociable || (εκκλ) not having taken first communion.

ακολασία, η [akolaseea] debauchery, excess.

ακολουθία, η [akoloutheea] retinue, suite || (εκκλ) church service || **κατ'** ~**v** in consequence.

ακόλουθος [akolouthos] (ουσ) attendant || (στρατ) attaché || (επίθ) following, next.

ακολουθώ [akoloutho] follow.

ακολούθως [akolouthos] consequently, afterwards || **ως** ~ as follows.

ακόμα [akoma] yet, more || ~ **και** even if.

ακονίζω [akoneezo] sharpen, whet.

ακόντιο, το [akonteeo] javelin, dart.

άκοπος [akopos] not cut || (εύκολος) easy || (ξεκούραστα) untiring.

ακόρεστος [akorestos] insatiable.

ακουμπώ [akoumbo] lean.

ακούραστος [akourastos] indefatigable, unwearied.

ακούρδιστος [akourðeestos] not tuned || (ρολόι) not wound up.

ακούσιος [akouseeos] unintentional || involuntary.

ακουστικό, το [akousteeko] (τηλεφ) receiver.

ακουστικός [akousteekos] acoustic.

ακουστός [akoustos] famous, celebrated.

ακούω [akouo] hear, listen to || (εισακούω) obey.

άκρα, η [akra] end, tip, extremity.

ακραίος [akreos] extreme, utmost.

ακρατής [akratees] intemperate, incontinent.

ακράτητος [akrateetos] impetuous, rash, unrestrained.

άκρη, η [akree] βλ **άκρα**.

ακριβά [akreeva] dearly.

ακρίβεια, η [akreeveea] (ωρολογίου) accuracy, precision || (μεταφράσεως κτλ) exactness || (τιμής) costliness.

ακριβής [akreevees] exact || (ωρολόγιο κτλ) accurate || (υπολογισμός) correct || (σε ραντεβού) punctual.

ακριβός [akreevos] dear, expensive.

ακριβώς [akreevos] precisely, accurately.

ακρίδα, η [akreeða] locust, grasshopper.

ακρόαση, η [akroasee] hearing, listening || (συνάντηση) audience, interview.

ακροατήριο, το [akroateereeo] audience.

ακροατής, ο [akroatees] listener || (πανεπιστημίου) auditor.

ακροβάτης, ο [akrovatees] acrobat.

ακρογιάλι, το [akroyalee] seashore.

ακρόπολη, η [akropolee] acropolis || citadel.

ακρωτηριάζω [akroteereeazo] maim, mutilate.

ακρωτήριο, το [akroteereeo] cape, promontory.

ακτή, η [aktee] shore, beach, coast.

ακτίνα, η [akteena] ray, beam || (ελπίδος) gleam || (ενεργείας) range || (τροχού) spoke || (κύκλου) radius.

ακτινοβολία, η [akteenovoleea] radiation.

ακτινογραφία, η [akteenografeea] X-ray.

ακτινοθεραπεία, η [akteenotherapeea] radiotherapy.

ακτοπλοΐα, η [aktoploeea] coastal shipping.

άκυρος [akeeros] invalid, void.

ακυρώνω [akeerono] nullify, invalidate || cancel.

αλάβαστρο, το [alavastro] alabaster.

αλάδωτος [alaðotos] (φαγητό) without oil.

αλαζονεία, η [alazoneea] arrogance, boastfulness.

αλάθητος [alatheetos] infallible.

άλαλος [alalos] speechless, dumb.

αλάνθαστος [alanthastos] infallible, certain.

αλάργα [alarga] far off.

αλάτι, το [alatee] salt || **αλατιέρα** saltcellar.

αλατίζω [alateezo] salt.

Αλβανία, η [alvaneea] Albania.

αλβανικός [alvaneekos] Albanian.

Αλβανός, ο [alvanos] Albanian.

άλγεβρα, η [alyevra] algebra.

Αλγερία, η [alyereea] Algeria.

Αλγερινός, ο [alyereenos] Algerian man || α~ (επιθ) Algerian.

αλγερίνικος [alyereeneekos] Algerian.

αλέθω [aletho] grind.

αλείβω [aleevo] coat, smear, rub.

αλείφω [aleefo] βλ **αλείβω**.

αλεξικέραυνο, το [alekseekeravno] lightning conductor.

αλεξιπτωτιστής, ο [alekseeptoteestees] parachutist.

αλεξίπτωτο, το [alekseeptoto] parachute.

αλεπού, η [alepou] fox || (μεταφ) sly person.

άλεσμα, το [alesma] grinding.

αλέτρι, το [aletree] plough.

αλεύρι, το [alevri] flour.

αλήθεια, η [aleetheea] truth || (επιρ) really, indeed.

αληθεύω [aleethevo] be true.

αληθινός [aleetheenos] real, genuine, true.

αλησμόνητος [aleesmoneetos] unforgettable.

αλήτης, ο [aleetees] vagabond, vagrant.

αλιεία, η [alieea] fishing || fishery.

αλιεύς, ο [alievs] fisherman.

αλιεύω [alievo] fish (for).

αλκοολικός [alkooleekos] alcoholic.

αλκυόνα, η [alkeeona] kingfisher, halcyon.

αλλά [ala] but, however, yet.

αλλαγή, η [alayee] change || variation.

αλλάζω [alazo] change, alter.

αλλαντικά, τα [alanteeka] πλ sausages.

αλλεπάλληλος [alepaleelos] repeated, successive.

αλλεργία, η [aleryeea] allergy.

αλληλεγγύη, η [aleelenyiee] mutual help, solidarity.

αλληλένδετος [aleelenðetos] interdependent, bound together.

αλληλογραφία, η [aleelografeea] correspondence.

αλλοδαπός, ο [aloðapos] foreigner, alien.

αλλοίθωρος [aleethoros] cross-eyed.

αλλοίμονο [aleemono] (επιφ) oh dear!

αλλοιώνω [alleeono] alter, change.

αλλοιώς [alios] otherwise, in a different way.

αλλοίωση, η [aliosee] change, alteration || (τροφίμων) adulteration.

αλλοιώτικος [alioteekos] different, unlike || (πρόσωπο) odd, strange.

αλλόκοτος [alokotos] queer, strange, odd.

άλλος [alos] (an)other, else || (επόμενος) next || (διαφορετικός) different || (επί πλέον) more || κάθε άλλο! anything but!

άλλοτε [allote] formerly || sometime.

αλλού [alou] elsewhere.

άλλωστε [aloste] besides, on the other hand.

άλμα, το [alma] jump, leap || ~ τώδης by leaps and bounds.

άλμη, η [almee] brine, pickle.

αλμυρός [almeeros] salty || (μεταφ) costly.

άλογο, το [alogo] horse || αλογόμυγα horsefly.

αλοιφή, η [aleefee] ointment.

αλουμίνιο, το [aloumeeneeo] aluminium.

άλσος, το [alsos] grove, thicket.

αλύγιστος [aleeyeestos] inflexible.

αλύπητος [aleepeetos] pitiless, cruel.

αλυσίδα, η [aleeseeða] chain.

άλυτος [aleetos] (που δεν ελύθη) unsolved || (δεν μπορεί να λυθεί) unsolvable.

άλφα, το [alfa] the letter A.

αλφάβητο, το [alfaveeto] alphabet.

αλώνι, το [alonee] threshing floor || αλωνίζω thresh || (σκορπώ) scatter.

άλωση, η [alosee] fall, capture, conquest.

άμα [ama] as soon as || (εάν) if.

αμαζόνα, η [amazona] amazon.

αμάθεια, η [amatheea] ignorance, illiteracy.

αμαθής [amathees] ignorant, illiterate.

αμάν [aman] (επιφ) for heaven's sake!

αμαξάς, ο [amaksas] coachman, cab driver.

αμάξι, το [amaksee] carriage || (αυτοκίνητο) car.

αμαξοστοιχία, η [amaksosteeheea] train.

αμαρτάνω [amartano] sin.

αμαρτία, η [amarteea] sin || είναι ~ απ' το Θεό it's a pity!

άμαχος [amahos] non-combatant.

άμβωνας, ο [amvonas] pulpit.

αμέ [amme] (επιφ) why not? || of course!

αμείβω [ameevo] reward, compensate.

αμείλικτος [ameeleektos] implacable, inexorable.

αμείωτος [ameeotos] undiminished.

αμέλεια, η [ameleea] negligence, carelessness.

αμελής [amelees] negligent || (μαθητής) lazy.

αμελώ [amelo] neglect.

άμεμπτος [amemptos] irreproachable, blameless.

αμερικάνικος [amereekaneekos] American.

Αμερικανός, ο [amereekanos] American.

Αμερική, η [amereekee] America.

αμέριμνος [amereemnos] carefree, heedless.

αμερόληπτος [ameroleeptos] impartial.

άμεσος [amesos] direct, immediate.

αμέσως [amesos] at once, immediately.

αμετάβλητος [ametavleetos] unchanged || immutable.

αμετάκλητος [ametakleetos] irrevocable.

αμεταχείριστος [ametaheereestos] unused, new.

αμέτοχος [ametohos] exempt, not participating in.

αμέτρητος [ametreetos] countless, immeasurable.

αμήχανος [ameehanos] perplexed, embarrassed.

αμηχανία [ameehaneea] perplexity, confusion.

αμίαντος, ο [ameeantos] asbestos.

αμίλητος [ameeleetos] silent, quiet.

άμιλλα, η [ameela] emulation, rivalry.

αμίμητος [ameemeetos] inimitable.

άμισθος [ameesthos] unsalaried, without pay.

άμμος, η [ammos] sand.

αμμουδιά, η [amouðia] sandy beach.

αμμώδης [amoðees] sandy.

αμμωνία, η [amoneea] ammonia.

αμνησία, η [amneeseea] amnesia.

αμνηστία, η [amneesteea] amnesty.

αμνός, ο [amnos] lamb.

αμοιβαίος [ameeveyos] mutual, reciprocal.

αμοιβή, η [ameevee] reward, recompense.

άμοιρος [ameeros] unfortunate, destitute.

αμόνι, το [amonee] anvil.

άμορφος [amorfos] shapeless.

αμόρφωτος [amorfotos] uneducated, unrefined.

αμπαζούρ, το [ambazour] lampshade.

αμπάρι, το [ambaree] storeroom || (ναυτ) hold.

αμπέλι, το [ambelee] vine || vineyard.
αμπραγιάζ, το [ambrageeaz] clutch.
άμπωτη, η [ambotee] ebb tide.
αμυγδαλές, οι [ameegðales] πλ tonsils.
αμύγδαλο, το [ameegðalo] almond.
αμυδρός [ameeðros] dim, faint.
άμυλο, το [ameelo] starch.
άμυνα, η [ameena] defence.
αμφιβάλλω [amfeevalo] doubt.
αμφίβιος [amfeeveeos] amphibious.
αμφίβολος [amfeevolos] doubtful, dubious.
αμφίεση, η [amfiesee] dress, attire, clothing.
αμφιθέατρο, το [amfeetheatro] amphitheatre.
αμφίρροπος [amfeeropos] undecided, in the balance, wavering.
αμφισβητώ [amfosveetω] dispute.
αμφορέας, ο [amforeas] amphora, pitcher.
αμφότεροι [amfoteree] πλ both.
αν [an] if, whether || ~ **και** although, though.
ανά [ana] along, over || ~ **εις** one by one || ~ **την πόλη** through the city.
αναβαίνω [anaveno] βλ **ανεβαίνω**.
αναβάλλω [anavalo] put off, postpone, delay.
ανάβαση, η [anavasee] ascent.
αναβολή, η [anavolee] postponement, adjournment.
αναβρασμός, ο [anavrasmos] agitation, excitement || fermentation.
ανάβω [anavo] light || (φως κτλ) turn on, switch on || (θυμώνω) get provoked.
αναγγέλλω [anangelo] announce, make known.
αναγγελία, η [anangeleea] announcement, notice.
αναγέννηση, η [anageneesee] revival, renaissance.
αναγκάζω [anangazo] force, compel.
αναγκαίος [anangeyos] necessary, essential, needed.
αναγκαστικός [anangasteekos] compulsory || (προσγείωση κτλ) forced.
ανάγκη, η [anangee] need, necessity, want.
ανάγλυφο, το [anagleefo] bas-relief.
αναγνωρίζω [anagnoreezo] recognize || (παραδέχομαι) admit.
αναγνώριση, η [anagnoreesee] recognition, acknowledgement.
ανάγνωση, η [anagnosee] reading.
αναγνώστης, ο [anagnostees] reader.
αναγούλα, η [anagoula] nausea, disgust.
ανάγω [anago] raise || (μετατρέπω) reduce, convert.
ανάγωγος [anagogos] ill-bred, ill-mannered.

αναδάσωση, η [anaðasosee] reafforestation.
αναδιοργανώνω [anaðeeorganono] reorganize.
αναδιπλασιασμός, ο [anaðeeplaseeasmos] (γραμμ) reduplication.
ανάδοχος, ο [anaðohos] godparent, sponsor.
αναδρομικός [anaðromeekos] retroactive, retrospective.
αναζητώ [anazeeto] search for, seek.
αναζωογονώ [anazoogono] revive, invigorate.
αναζωπυρώ [anazopeero] relight, rekindle || (μεταφ) revive.
ανάθεμα, το [anathema] curse || (εκκλ) excommunication.
αναθέτω [anatheto] commission, entrust || (αφιερώνω) dedicate.
αναθεώρηση, η [anatheoreesee] revision, review.
αναθυμίαση, η [anatheemeeasee] stench, exhalation, fumes.
αναίδεια, η [aneðeea] impudence.
αναιδής [aneðees] impudent, shameless.
αναίμακτος [anemaktos] bloodless.
αναιμία, η [anemeea] anaemia.
αναίρεση, η [aneresee] refutation.
αναισθησία, η [anestheeseea] unconsciousness || (μεταφ) insensibility.
αναισθητικό, το [anestheeteeko] anaesthetic.
αναίσθητος [anestheetos] insensitive || (στους πόνους) unconscious, insensible || (ασυγκίνητος) unmoved.
ανακαινίζω [anakeneezo] renovate, renew.
ανακαλύπτω [anakaleepto] discover, detect.
ανακαλώ [anakalo] recall || (άδεια, διάταγμα) repeal, abrogate || (διαταγή κτλ) cancel, withdraw || (υπόσχεση) retract.
ανακατώνω [anakatono] mix, stir || (συγχέω) confuse.
ανακάτωμα, το [anakatoma] mixing || (φασαρία) confusion || (στομάχου) nausea.
ανακεφαλαίωση, η [anakefaleosee] recapitulation.
ανακηρύσσω [anakeereeso] proclaim, declare.
ανακινώ [anakeeno] stir up || (μεταφ) bring up, raise.
ανάκληση, η [anakleesee] revocation, recalling.
ανακοινώνω [anakeenono] announce.
ανακοπή, η [anakopee] checking || (νομ) reprieve || (ιατρ) heart failure.
ανακουφίζω [anakoufeezo] relieve, alleviate, lighten.
ανακριβής [anakreevees] inaccurate.

ανάκριση, η [anakreesee] interrogation, inquiry.

ακακριτής, ο [anakreetees] examining magistrate.

ανάκτορο, το [anaktoro] palace.

ανακωχή, η [anakohee] armistice, truce.

αναλαμβάνω [analamvano] undertake || recover.

ανάλατος [analatos] (μεταφ) dull.

ανάληψη, η [analeepsee] (εργασίας) resumption, undertaking || (του Χριστού) ascension.

αναλλοίωτος [analeeotos] unchanging, constant, unaltered.

αναλογία, η [analoyeea] relation, proportion, ratio || portion.

αναλογικός [analoyeekos] proportionate.

ανάλογος [analogos] proportionate || (μαθημ) proportional.

αναλόγως [analogos] proportionately, according to.

ανάλυση, η [analeesee] analysis.

αναλυτικός [analeeteekos] analytical || detailed.

αναλφάβητος [analfaveetos] illiterate, ignorant.

αναμένω [anameno] wait for, expect.

ανάμεσα [anamesa] in between, among.

αναμεταξύ [anametaksee] between, among || στο ~ in the meantime, meanwhile.

αναμιγνύω [anameegneeo] mix, blend || implicate.

ανάμικτος [anameektos] mixed.

ανάμιξη, η [anameeksee] mixing, interfering.

άναμμα, το [anama] lighting || (προσώπου) inflammation || (έξαψη) excitement || (μοτέρ κτλ) ignition.

αναμμένος [anamenos] alight, burning.

ανάμνηση, η [anamneesee] recollection, memory.

αναμονή, η [anamonee] expectation, waiting.

αναμφισβήτητος [anamfeesveeteetos] indisputable, unquestionable.

ανανάς, ο [ananas] pineapple.

ανανεώνω [ananeono] renew, renovate.

ανανέωση, η [ananeosee] renewal, renovation.

ανάξιος [anakseeos] unworthy, unfit, inefficient.

αναπαράσταση, η [anaparastasee] representation || (εγκλήματος) reconstruction.

ανάπαυλα, η [anapavla] respite, rest.

ανάπαυση, η [anapavsee] rest, repose || (στρατ) stand easy!

αναπαυτικός [anapavteekos] comfortable, restful.

αναπαύομαι [anapavome] rest, relax.

αναπηδώ [anapeedo] jump up, leap up, start.

ανάπηρος [anapeeros] disabled || (διανοητικώς) deficient.

ανάπλαση, η [anaplasee] reforming, remodelling.

αναπληρώνω [anapleerono] replace || substitute || refill.

αναπνέω [anapneo] breathe.

αναπνοή, η [anapnoee] breath, breathing, respiration.

ανάποδα [anapoda] backwards || (μέσα έξω) inside out, topsy-turvy.

αναποδιά, η [anapodia] reverse, bad luck || contrariness.

αναποδογυρίζω [anapodogeereezo] turn upside down.

ανάποδος, [anapodos] reversed || (άνθρωπος) difficult, cantankerous.

αναπόφευκτος [anapofevktos] inevitable, unavoidable.

αναπτήρας, ο [anapteeras] cigarette lighter.

ανάπτυξη, η [anapteeksee] development || (εξήγηση) explanation.

αναπτύσσω [anapteeso] unfold, develop || (λόγο) expound, explain.

αναρίθμητος [anareethmeetos] countless, innumerable.

ανάρπαστος [anarpastos] quickly bought up.

ανάρρωση, η [anarrosee] convalescence, recovery.

αναρχία, η [anarheea] anarchy.

αναρχικός [anarheekos] anarchical || (ουσ) anarchist.

αναρωτιέμαι [anarotieme] ask o.s., wonder.

ανάσα, η [anasa] breath, breathing || rest, respite.

ανασηκώνω [anaseekono] lift up, raise.

ανασκαφή, η [anaskafee] excavation.

ανάσκελα [anaskela] on one's back.

ανασκόπηση, η [anaskopeesee] review, weighing up.

ανασταίνω [anasteno] revive, restore to life.

ανασταλτικός [anastalteekos] restraining, holding back.

ανάσταση, η [anastasee] resurrection.

ανάστατος [anastatos] in disorder, agitated, excited.

αναστατώνω [anastatono] disturb, upset.

αναστέλλω [anastelo] stop, stay, suspend.

αναστενάζω [anastenazo] sigh, groan.

αναστηλώνω [anasteelono] restore, erect.

αναστήλωση, η [anasteelosee] restoration, erection.

ανάστημα, το [anasteema] height, stature.

αναστολή, η [anastolee] reprieve || suspension || restraint.

ανασυγκρότηση, η [anaseengroteesee] reconstruction.

ανασύρω [anaseero] raise, pull out, pull up, draw up.

αναταράσσω [anataraso] stir up, upset.

ανατέλλω [anatelo] (ήλιος) rise || appear.

ανατίμηση, η [anateemeesee] price rise || revaluation.

ανατινάζω [anateenazo] blow up || spring up.

ανατίναξη, η [anateenaksee] explosion.

ανατοκισμός, ο [anatokeesmos] compound interest.

ανατολή, η [anatolee] east || (ήλιου) sunrise || **'Απω 'Α~** Far East || **Μέση 'Α~** Middle East.

ανατολικός [anatoleekos] eastern || oriental.

ανατομία, η [anatomeea] anatomy.

ανατρέπω [anatrepo] upset || (βάρκα κτλ) overturn, capsize.

ανατρέφω, [anatrefo] rear, bring up, raise.

ανατρέχω [anatreho] refer back to, go back to.

ανατριχιάζω [anatreeheeazo] shiver, shudder.

ανατροπή, η [anatropee] upset, overthrow || (νομ) refutation, reversal.

ανατροφή, η [anatrofee] upbringing, breeding.

ανάτυπο, το [anateepo] offprint, reprint.

άναυδος [anavdos] speechless, dumbfounded.

αναφέρω [anafero] mention, cite || report || relate.

αναφλέγω [anaflego] inflame, ignite.

ανάφλεξη, η [anafleksee] combustion, ignition.

αναφορά, η [anafora] report || (αίτηση) petition.

αναχαιτίζω [anaheteezo] check, restrain || (επίθεση) repel.

αναχρονισμός, ο [anahroneesmos] anachronism.

ανάχωμα, το [anahoma] mound, bank, dyke.

αναχώρηση, η [anahoreesee] departure.

αναχωρώ [anahoro] leave, depart, go.

αναψυκτικά, τα [anapseekteeka] πλ refreshments.

αναψυχή, η [anapseehee] recreation.

ανδρεία, η [anðreea] bravery, valour.

ανδρείος [anðreeos] brave, courageous.

ανδρικός [anðreekos] manly, virile, male.

ανεβάζω [anevazo] raise, lift up || (θέατρο) put on.

ανεβαίνω [aneveno] ascend, climb, go up.

ανέβασμα, το [anevasma] going up || lifting || (έργου) production.

ανεβοκατεβαίνω [anevokateveno] go up and down || (τιμές) fluctuate.

ανέγγιχτος [anengeehtos] untouched, new.

ανέγερση, η [aneyersee] erection || (οίκωμα) getting up.

ανειλικρινής [aneeleekreenees] insincere || false.

ανέκαθεν [anekathen] always, ever, from the beginning.

ανέκδοτο, το [anekðoto] anecdote, funny story.

ανεκμετάλλευτος [anekmetalevtos] unexploited.

ανεκτικός [anekteekos] tolerant, patient, indulgent.

ανεκτίμητος [anekteemeetos] priceless, inestimable.

ανεκτός [anektos] bearable, tolerable.

ανέκφραστος [anekfrastos] inexpressible, indescribable || (ηθοποιός) expressionless || (βλέμμα) vacant.

ανελλιπής [aneleepees] flawless || (οργάνωση) complete || (φοίτηση) continuous.

ανέλπιστος [anelpeestos] unexpected || (γεγονός) unforeseen.

ανεμίζω [anemeezo] ventilate, air || (σίτο) winnow.

ανεμιστήρας, ο [anemeesteeras] fan, ventilator.

ανεμοβλογιά, η [anemovloya] chickenpox.

ανεμόμυλος, ο [anemomeelos] windmill.

άνεμος, ο [anemos] wind.

ανεμοστρόβιλος, ο [anemostroveelos] whirlwind.

ανεμπόδιστος [anembodeestos] unhindered, unimpeded.

ανεμώνα, η [anemona] anemone.

ανένδοτος [anenðotos] unyielding, inflexible.

ανενόχλητος [anenohleetos] undisturbed.

ανεξάντλητος [aneksantleetos] inexhaustible.

ανεξαρτησία, η [aneksarteeseea] independence.

ανεξάρτητος [aneksarteetos] independent.

ανεξέλεγκτος [anekselengtos] unconfirmed || (δαπάνη κτλ) unexamined.

ανεξήγητος [anekseeyeetos] inexplicable.

ανεξίτηλος [anekseeteelos] indelible.

ανεπαίσθητος [anepestheetos] imperceptible, slight.

ανεπαρκής [aneparkees] insufficient, inadequate.

ανέπαφος [anepafos] untouched, intact.

ανεππρέαστος [anepeereastos] unaffected, uninfluenced.

ανεπιθύμητος [anepeetheemeetos] undesirable.

ανεπίσημος [anepeeseemos] unofficial.

ανεπιτυχής [anepeeteehees] unsuccessful.

ανεπιφύλακτος [anepeefeelaktos] unreserved.

ανεπτυγμένος [anepteegmenos] (άνθρωπος) cultured || (σωματικώς) developed.

άνεργος [anergos] unemployed, idle.

ανέρχομαι [anerhome] ascend, climb || (λογαριασμός) amount to.

άνεση, η [annesee] ease, comfort.

ανεστραμμένος [anestramenos] reversed, inverted.

άνετος [anetos] comfortable, easy.

άνευ [anev] without.

ανεύθυνος [anevtheenos] irresponsible.

ανεφάρμοστος [anefarmostos] inapplicable || (μη εφαρμοσθείς) unapplied.

ανέφικτος [anefeektos] unattainable, impossible.

ανεφοδιάζω [anefodeeazo] provision, restock.

ανέχομαι [anehome] tolerate.

ανεψιά, η [anepsia] niece.

ανεψιός, ο [anepsios] nephew.

ανήθικος [aneetheekos] immoral, corrupt.

άνηθο, το [aneetho] dill, anise.

ανήκουστος [aneekoustos] unheard of, incredible.

ανήκω [aneeko] belong (to).

ανήλικος [aneeleekos] under age || minor.

ανήμερα [aneemera] on the same day.

ανήμπορος [aneemboros] indisposed.

ανησυχία, η [aneeseeheea] uneasiness, concern.

ανήσυχος [aneeseehos] uneasy, anxious.

ανησυχώ [aneeseeho] be anxious, be worried.

ανήφορος, ο [aneeforos] uphill road || ascent.

ανθεκτικός [anthekteekos] endurable, resistant.

ανθίζω [antheezo] blossom, flourish.

ανθίσταμαι [antheestame] resist, oppose.

ανθοδέσμη, η [anthodesmee] bouquet, nosegay.

ανθοδοχείο, το [anthodoheeo] flowerpot, vase.

ανθολογία, η [antholoyeea] anthology.

ανθοπώλης, ο [anthopolees] florist.

άνθος, το [anthos] flower.

άνθρακας, ο [anthrakas] coal || (ιατρ) anthrax.

ανθρακικός [anthrakeekos] carbonic.

ανθρακωρυχείο, το [anthrakoreeheeo] coalmine.

ανθρωπιά, η [anthropia] civility || good breeding.

ανθρώπινος [anthropeenos] human.

ανθρωπιστής, ο [anthropeestees] humanist.

ανθρωποκτονία, η [anthropoktoneea] homicide.

ανθρωπολόγος, ο [anthropologos] anthropologist.

άνθρωπος, ο [anthropos] man, person.

ανθρωπότης, η [anthropotees] mankind, humanity.

ανθυγιεινός [antheeyeeinos] unhealthy, unwholesome.

ανία, η [aneea] boredom, weariness, ennui.

ανίατος [aneeatos] incurable.

ανίδεος [aneedeos] unsuspecting || ignorant.

ανικανοποίητος [aneekanopieetos] unsatisfied.

ανίκανος [aneekanos] incapable, unable, unfit || impotent.

ανισόρροπος [aneesoropos] unbalanced.

άνισος [aneesos] unequal, uneven.

ανίσχυρος [aneesheeros] powerless, weak, feeble.

ανίχνευση, η [aneehnevsee] tracking, searching.

άνοδος, η [anodos] ascent, accession.

ανονσία, η [anooeseea] folly, foolishness, nonsense.

ανόητος [anoeetos] foolish, silly, absurd.

ανόθευτος [anothevtos] unadulterated, pure.

άνοιγμα, το [aneegma] opening, aperture.

ανοίγω [aneego] open || (βρύση) turn on || (αύρτη) draw || (ομπρέλλα) put up || (φώτα κτλ) turn on, switch on || (συζήτηση) open, broach || (χάρτη) unfold || (χορό) lead, open || (πηγάδι) dig || (κουρτίνες) draw || (για χρώμα) fade.

ανοίκιαστος [aneekeeastos] unlet, unrented.

ανοικοδομώ [aneekodomo] rebuild.

ανοικτός [aneektos] open || (επί χρωμάτων) light.

άνοιξη, n [aneeksee] spring, springtime.

ανοιχτόκαρδος [aneehtokarðos] open-hearted, cheerful.

ανοιχτοχέρης [aneehtoherees] open-handed, magnanimous.

ανομβρία, n [anomvreea] drought.

ανόμοιος [anomeeos] dissimilar, unlike.

ανοξείδωτος [anokseeðotos] stainless, rustproof.

ανοργάνωτος [anorganotos] unorganized.

ανορεξία, n [anorekseea] loss of appetite || (μεταφ) half-heartedness.

ανορθογραφία, n [anorthografeea] misspelling.

ανοσία, n [anoseea] immunity.

άνοστος [anostos] insipid, unsavoury || (μεταφ) ugly, disagreeable.

ανοχή, n [anohee] forbearance, tolerance || **οίκος ανοχής** brothel.

ανταγωνίζομαι [antagoneezome] compete, vie (with).

ανταγωνισμός, ο [antagoneesmos] competition, contest, rivalry.

ανταλλαγή, n [antalayee] exchange.

αντάλλαγμα, το [antalagma] thing exchanged, recompense.

ανταλλακτικό, το [antalakteeko] spare part, refill.

ανταλλάσσω [antalaso] exchange.

ανταμείβω [antameevo] reward, recompense.

ανταμώνω [antamono] meet, join.

αντάμωση [antamosee] : **καλή ~** goodbye, farewell.

αντανάκλαση, n [antanaklasee] reflection.

αντανακλώ [antanaklo] reflect.

αντάξιος [antakseeos] worthy, deserving.

ανταποδίδω [antapoðeeðo] return, repay.

ανταποκρίνομαι [antapokreenome] be like, correspond to, respond, suit.

ανταπόκριση, n [antapokreesee] correspondence || (εφημερίδας) dispatch.

ανταποκριτής, ο [antapokreetees] correspondent, reporter.

ανταρσία, n [antarseea] rebellion, revolt, mutiny.

αντάρτης, ο [antartees] rebel, insurgent, guerrilla.

άντε [ante] (επιφ) come on!, get a move on!

αντένα, n [antena] aerial, antenna.

αντεπίθεση, n [antepeethesee] counterattack.

αντεπιτίθεμαι [antepeeteetheme] counterattack.

άντερο, το [antero] intestine.

αντέχω [anteho] endure, hold firm, last.

αντζούγια, n [andzouyeea] anchovy.

αντηλιά, n [anteelia] glare.

αντηχώ [anteeho] resound, echo.

αντί [antee] instead of, in exchange for || (τιμή) for || **~ για** instead of || **~ να** instead of.

αντιαεροπορικός [anteeaeroporeekos] anti-aircraft.

αντιγραφή, n [anteegrafee] copy, copying.

αντίγραφο, το [anteegrafo] copy, transcript.

αντιγράφω [anteegrafo] copy, imitate || (στο σχολείο) crib.

αντίδι, το [anteeðee] endive.

αντίδικος, ο [anteeðeekos] opponent.

αντίδοτο, το [anteeðoto] antidote.

αντίδραση, n [anteeðrasee] reaction, opposition.

αντιδραστικός [anteeðrasteekos] reactionary, reactive.

αντιδρώ [anteeðro] react, counteract, oppose.

αντίδωρο, το [anteeðoro] (εκκλ) holy bread.

αντίζηλος [anteezeelos] rival.

αντίθεση, n [anteethesee] contrast || opposition.

αντίθετος [anteethetos] contrary, opposite.

αντίκα, n [anteeka] antique.

αντικαθιστώ [anteekatheesto] replace, substitute || relieve.

αντικανονικός [anteekanoneekos] irregular, against the rules.

αντικατάσταση [anteekatastasee] replacement || substitution.

αντικαταστάτης, ο [anteekatastatees] substitute || successor.

αντίκειμαι [anteekeeme] be opposed to.

αντικειμενικός [anteekeemeneekos] objective.

αντικείμενο, το [anteekeemeno] object, thing || topic.

αντικλείδι, το [anteekleeðee] passkey.

αντικοινωνικός [anteekeenoneekos] unsocial.

αντικρούω [anteekrouo] oppose, refute.

αντίκρυ [anteekree] opposite, face to face.

αντικρύζω [anteekreezo] face, front || meet.

αντίκτυπος, ο [anteekteepos] repercussion, effect, result.

αντίλαλος, ο [anteelalos] echo.

αντιλαμβάνομαι [anteelamvanome] understand || perceive, notice.

αντιλέγω [anteelego] object, contradict.

αντιληπτός [anteeleeptos] perceptible || understandable.

αντίληψη, η [anteeleepsee] understanding, opinion || quickness of mind.

αντιλυσσικός [anteeleeseekos] anti-rabies.

αντιμετωπίζω [anteemetopeezo] confront, face.

αντιμέτωπος [anteemetopos] face to face, facing.

αντιναύαρχος, ο [anteenavarhos] vice-admiral.

αντίο [anteeo] (επιφ) goodbye!

αντιπάθεια, η [anteepatheea] antipathy, aversion.

αντιπαθητικός [anteepatheeteekos] repulsive, repugnant.

αντιπαθώ [anteepatho] dislike.

αντίπαλος, ο [anteepalos] adversary, opponent || (στρατ) enemy.

αντιπερισπασμός, ο [anteepereespasmos] distraction || (στρατ) diversion.

αντίποινα, τα [anteepeena] πλ reprisals.

αντιπολίτευση, η [anteepoleetevsee] opposition.

αντίπραξη, η [anteepraksee] opposition, thwarting.

αντιπρόεδρος, ο [anteeproeðros] vice-president, deputy chairman.

αντιπροσωπεία, η [anteeprosopeea] representation || delegation.

αντιπροσωπεύω [anteeprosopevo] represent, stand for.

αντιπρόσωπος, ο [anteeprosopos] representative || (εμπορικός) agent.

αντίρρηση, η [anteereesee] objection, contradiction.

αντισηπτικός [anteeseepteekos] antiseptic.

αντισταθμίζω [anteestathmeezo] balance || (μηχανική) compensate.

αντίσταση, η [anteestasee] resistance, opposition.

αντιστέκομαι [anteestekome] resist, oppose.

αντίστοιχος [anteesteehos] corresponding, equivalent.

αντιστράτηγος, ο [anteestrateegos] lieutenant-general.

αντιστρέφω [anteestrefo] invert, reverse.

αντίστροφος [anteestrofos] reverse, inverse.

αντισυνταγματικός [anteeseentagmateekos] unconstitutional.

αντιτίθεμαι [anteeteetheme] be opposed.

αντίτιμο, το [anteeteemo] value, price.

αντιτορπιλλικό, το [anteetorpeeleeko] destroyer.

αντίτυπο, το [anteeteepo] copy.

αντίφαση, η [anteefasee] contradiction, discrepancy.

αντιφάσκω [anteefasko] contradict o.s.

αντίχειρας, ο [anteeheeras] thumb.

αντλία, η [antleea] pump.

αντλώ [antlo] pump, draw (off) || derive.

αντοχή, η [antohee] endurance, strength, resistance.

άντρας, ο [antras] man || husband.

αντρίκιος [antreekeeos] βλ ανδρικός.

αντρόγυνο, το [antroyeeno] married couple.

αντωνυμία, η [antoneemeea] pronoun.

ανύπανδρος [aneepanðros] unmarried, single.

ανύπαρκτος [aneeparktos] non-existent.

ανυπαρξία, η [aneeparkseea] non-existence, lack.

ανυπολόγιστος [aneepoloyeestos] incalculable.

ανυπόμονος [aneepomonos] impatient, anxious.

ανυπόπτος [aneepoptos] unsuspecting || not suspect.

ανυπόστατος [aneepostatos] groundless, unfounded || unsubstantial.

ανυπότακτος [aneepotaktos] insubordinate || (λαός) unsubdued.

ανυπόφορος [aneepoforos] intolerable.

ανυψώνω [aneepsono] raise || (μεταφ) praise, elevate, extol.

άνω [ano] up, above || ~ **κάτω** in confusion, upset || (μέρος) above, over.

ανώδυνος [anoðeenos] painless.

ανωμαλία, η [anomaleea] irregularity, unevenness || anomaly.

ανώμαλος [anomalos] (επιφάνεια) irregular, uneven || (άνθρωπος) erratic, eccentric.

ανώνυμος [anoneemos] anonymous || ~ **εταιρεία** limited company.

ανώτατος [anotatos] supreme, uppermost.

ανώτερος [anoteros] superior, higher, upper || ~ **χρημάτων** above money.

άξεστος [aksestos] uncouth, rough, unpolished.

αξέχαστος [aksehastos] unforgotten || unforgettable.

αξία, η [akseea] worth, value, price.

αξιαγάπητος [akseeagapeetos] amiable, lovable.

αξιέπαινος [akseepenos] praiseworthy, laudable.

αξίζω [akseezo] be worth, cost || merit || **αξίζει να τιμωρηθεί** he deserves to be punished.

αξίνα, η [akseena] pickaxe.

αξιοθαύμαστος [akseeothavmastos] wonderful, admirable.

αξιοθέατος [akseeotheatos] worth seeing || **τα αξιοθέατα** the sights.

αξιοθρήνητος [akseeothreeneetos] lamentable, deplorable.

αξιόλογος [akseeologos] remarkable || distinguished.

αξιόπιστος [akseeopeestos] trustworthy, reliable.

αξιοπρεπής [akseeoprepees] dignified, decent.

άξιος [akseeos] capable || deserving || worthy, worth.

αξιοσημείωτος [akseeoseemeeotos] noteworthy, notable, remarkable.

αξιότιμος [akseeoteemos] estimable, honourable.

αξιωματικός, ο [aksecomateekos] officer.

άξονας, ο [aksonas] axis || axle, pivot, shaft.

αξύριστος [akseereestos] unshaven.

άοπλος [aoplos] unarmed.

αόριστος [aoreestos] invisible, indefinite || (γραμμ) aorist.

άοσμος [aosmos] odourless, scentless.

απαγγελία, η [apangeleea] recitation, declamation || diction.

απαγόρευση, η [apagorevsee] prohibition.

απαγορεύω [apagorevo] prohibit, forbid.

απαγωγή, η [apagoyee] abduction || (παιδιού) kidnapping.

απάθεια, η [apatheea] indifference, apathy.

απαισιόδοξος [apeseeoδoksos] pessimist.

απαίσιος [apeseeos] frightful, sinister, horrible.

απαίτηση, η [apeteesee] claim || demand.

απαιτητικός [apeteeteekos] demanding, exacting, importunate.

απαιτώ [apeto] claim, demand, require.

απαλλαγή, η [apalayee] deliverance || release || dismissal.

απαλλάσσω [apalasso] deliver, free || (καθήκοντα) relieve.

απαλλοτριώ [apalotreeo] expropriate, alienate.

απαλός [apalos] soft || gentle.

απάνθρωπος [apanthropos] inhuman, cruel.

άπαντα, τα [apanta] πλ complete works.

απάντηση, η [apanteesee] reply, answer, response.

απαντώ [apanto] answer, reply || meet.

απάνω [apano] up, above || upstairs || ~ **κάτω** approximately || **από πάνω** on top, from above || **έως** ~ to the top || ~ **που** at the moment when || ~ **από**

above, more than || ~ **σε** at the moment of.

απαράδεκτος [aparaδektos] unacceptable, inadmissible.

απαραίτητος [apareteetos] indispensable.

απαράλλακτος [aparalaktos] identical || unchanged.

απαράμιλλος [aparameelos] unrivalled, incomparable, peerless.

απαρατήρητος [aparateereetos] unnoticed, unobserved.

απαρέμφατο, το [aparemfato] (γραμμ) infinitive.

απαρηγόρητος [apareegoreetos] inconsolable.

απαριθμώ [apareethmo] enumerate, count.

απαρνούμαι [aparnoume] renounce, deny, disavow, disown.

απαρτίζω [aparteezo] form, constitute.

απασχόληση, η [apasholeesee] occupation.

απασχολώ [apasholo] occupy, busy.

απατεώνας, ο [apateonas] cheat, deceiver, swindler.

απάτη, η [apatee] deceit, fraud || illusion.

απατηλός [apateelos] deceptive, false, fraudulent.

απατώ [apato] deceive, cheat, defraud.

απεγνωσμένος [apegnosmenos] desperate.

απειθαρχία, η [apeetharheea] insubordination, lack of discipline.

απεικονίζω [apeekoneezo] represent, portray, depict.

απειλή, η [apeelee] threat, menace.

απειλητικός [apeeleeteekos] threatening.

απειρία, η [apeereea] inexperience || (μέτρο) infinity, immensity.

άπειρος [apeeros] inexperienced || (αριθμός) infinite, boundless.

απέλαση, η [apelasee] deportation, expulsion.

απελευθερώνω [apeleftherono] set free, emancipate.

απελευθέρωση, η [apeleftherosee] liberation, emancipation.

απελπίζομαι [apelpeezome] despair.

απελπισία, η [apelpeeseea] despair || **είναι** ~ it's hopeless!

απέναντι [apenante] opposite.

απεναντίας [apenanteeas] on the contrary.

απένταρος [apentaros] penniless, broke.

απέραντος [aperantos] immense, boundless, endless.

απεργία, η [aperyeea] strike.

απερίγραπτος [apereegraptos] indescribable.

απεριόριστος [apereeoreestos] unlimited.

απεριποίητος [apereepieeetos] neglected, untidy.

απερίσκεπτος [apereeskeptos] thoughtless, foolish, heedless.

απερίσπαστος [apereespastos] undistracted.

απέριττος [apereetos] simple, plain, concise.

απεσταλμένος, ο [apestalmenos] envoy, minister, delegate.

απευθύνομαι [apeftheenome] apply, appeal, address.

απεχθάνομαι [apehthanome] detest, abhor.

απεχθής [apehthees] odious, repulsive, detestable.

απέχω [apeho] abstain || be distant, be far from.

απήχηση, η [apeeheesee] effect || echo.

άπιαστος [apeeastos] not caught || intact, intangible.

απίθανος [apeethanos] unlikely, improbable.

απίστευτος [apeestevtos] unbelievable, incredible.

απιστία, [apeesteea] infidelity || incredulity.

άπιστος [apeestos] unbelieving || faithless, infidel.

απιστώ [apeesto] be unfaithful.

άπλα, η [apla] spaciousness.

απλά [apla] simply.

άπλετος [apletos] abundant.

απλήρωτος [apleerotos] unfilled || unpaid.

απλησίαστος [apleeseeastos] unapproachable.

άπληστος [apleestos] insatiable, greedy, avid.

απλοϊκός [aploeekos] naïve, simple.

απλός [aplos] simple || (εισπήριο) single || (ντύσιμο) plain.

απλότητα, η [aploteeta] simplicity, naivety, plainness.

απλούστατα [aploustata] simply.

άπλυτος [apleetos] unwashed || **τα άπλυτα** dirty linen.

άπλωμα, το [aploma] spreading, unfolding || (χεριών) stretching || (ρούχων) hanging out.

απλώνω [aplono] spread, stretch || (ρούχα) hang out.

απλώς [aplos] simply, merely, plainly.

άπνοια, η [apneea] lack of wind.

από [apo] from, of || by || through || than || ~ **καιρού σε καιρόν** from time to time || ~ **φόβο** out of fear || ~ **μνήμης** by heart || ~ **τον ίδιο δρόμο** by the same road || ~ **το παράθυρο** through the window || **ξέρω περισσότερα** ~ **σένα** I know more than you || (προθ) **μέσα** ~ out of || **πριν** ~ before.

αποβάθρα, η [apovathra] pier, wharf.

αποβάλλω [apovalo] reject, expel, dismiss || (μωρό) miscarry.

απόβαση, η [apovasee] disembarkation, landing.

αποβιβάζω [apoveevazo] disembark, unload.

αποβλέπω [apovlepo] consider || aim at, look forward to || regard.

αποβολή, η [apovolee] dismissal || (μωρού) miscarriage, abortion.

αποβραδίς [apovraδees] yesterday evening, since last night.

απογειώνομαι [apoyeeonome] take off.

απογείωση, η [apoyeeosee] takeoff.

απόγεμα, το [apoyema] afternoon.

απόγνωση, η [apognosee] despair, desperation.

απογοήτευση [apogoeetevsee] disappointment, disillusionment.

απογοητεύω [apogoeetevo] disappoint, disillusion.

απόγονος, ο [apogonos] offspring, descendant.

απογραφή, η [apografee] (πληθυσμού) census || (εμπορ) inventory.

αποδεικνύω [apoδeekneeo] prove, demonstrate.

αποδεικτικό, το [apoδeekteeko] certificate.

απόδειξη, η [apoδeeksee] proof || receipt.

αποδεκατίζω [apoδekateezo] decimate.

αποδεκτός [apoδektos] acceptable || accepted.

αποδέχομαι [apoδehome] accept || admit.

απόδημος [apoδeemos] living abroad, migrant.

αποδίδω [apoδeeδo] give back, return || (τιμές) grant, award || (κάτι σε κάτι) attribute || (ελευθερία) restore || (μετάφραση) express || (έργο) produce.

αποδοκιμάζω [apoδokeemazo] disapprove of || demonstrate against.

αποδοκιμασία, η [apoδokeemaseea] disapproval, rejection || booing.

απόδοση, η [apoδosee] (επιστροφή) return, repayment || (μηχανής κτλ) efficiency, capacity || (εργοστασίου) output || (της γης) yield, produce || (έργου) rendering.

αποδοχή, η [apoδohee] acceptance || acceptation || **αποδοχές** πλ salary, fees.

απόδραση, η [apoδrasee] escape.

αποδυτήριο, το [apoδeeteereeo] changing room.

αποζημιώνω [apozeemeeono] compensate, indemnify.

αποζημίωση, η [apozeemeeosee] compensation, indemnity.

αποθαρρύνω [apothareeno] discourage.

απόθεμα, το [apothema] deposit || stock, reserve.

αποθέωση, η [apotheose] apotheosis || (μεταφ) rousing reception.

αποθηκεύω [apotheekevo] store up.

αποθήκη, η [apotheekee] storage room, storehouse, warehouse.

αποθρασύνομαι [apothraseenome] become arrogant.

αποικία, η [apeekeea] colony, settlement.

αποκαθιστώ [apokatheesto] rehabilitate, restore || (κόρη) marry.

αποκαλύπτω [apokaleepto] disclose, unveil, reveal.

αποκάλυψη, η [apokaleepsee] revelation || (θρησκεία) Apocalypse.

αποκαρδιωτικός [apokarδeeoteekos] disheartening.

αποκατάσταση, η [apokatastasee] restoration, resettlement || (κόρης) marriage.

απόκεντρος [apokentros] outlying, remote, out-of-the-way.

αποκέντρωση, η [apokentrosee] decentralization.

αποκεφαλίζω [apokefaleezo] decapitate, behead.

αποκήρυξη, η [apokeereeksee] denunciation, proscription.

αποκηρύσσω [apokeereeso] renounce, disavow || proscribe, outlaw.

αποκλεισμός, ο [apokleesmos] exclusion, blockade, boycott.

αποκλειστικός [apokleesteekos] exclusive.

αποκλείω [apokleeo] exclude || debar || boycott || αποκλείεται it's out of the question.

αποκληρώνω [apokleerono] disinherit.

αποκλίνω [apokleeno] lean, diverge, incline.

αποκοιμίζω [apokeemeezo] lull to sleep.

αποκοιμούμαι [apokeemoume] fall asleep.

αποκομίζω [apokomeezo] carry away || derive.

απόκομμα, το [apokoma] press-cutting || (κομμάτι) bit.

αποκοπή, η [apokopee] cutting off || amputation.

απόκρημνος [apokreemnos] precipitous, steep, abrupt.

αποκριές, οι [apokries] πλ carnival.

αποκρίνομαι [apokreenome] answer, reply.

απόκρουση, η [apokrousee] repulsion || (κατηγορίας) refutation.

αποκρούω [apokrouo] repulse || reject.

αποκρύπτω [apokreepto] conceal, hide, cover.

απόκρυφος [apokreefos] secret || (εκκλ) apocryphal.

απόκτηση, η [apokteesee] acquisition.

αποκτώ [apokto] obtain, get || (παιδί) have.

απολαβή, η [apolavee] gain, profit, income.

απολαμβάνω [apolamvano] gain, earn || (διασκεδάζω) enjoy.

απόλαυση, η [apolavsee] enjoyment.

απολίθωμα, το [apoleethoma] fossil.

απολογία, η [apoloyeea] defence, plea, excuse.

απολογισμός, ο [apoloyeesmos] financial statement, account, report.

απολογούμαι [apologoume] justify o.s., apologize.

απολύμανση, η [apoleemansee] disinfection.

απόλυση, η [apoleesee] release || dismissal.

απολυτήριο, το [apoleeteereeo] discharge certificate || (σχολείου) school leaving certificate, diploma.

απόλυτος [apoleetos] absolute || (αριθμός) cardinal.

απολύτως [apoleetos] absolutely || entirely.

απολύω [apoleeo] release || (διώχνω) dismiss || (από το στρατό) discharge.

απομακρύνω [apomakreeno] remove, send away, keep off.

απόμαχος, ο [apomahos] veteran, pensioner.

απομεινάρια [apomeenaria] πλ remains, left-overs, remnants.

απομένω [apomeno] remain, be left || (κατάπληκτος) be left speechless.

απομίμηση, η [apomeemeesee] imitation, copy.

απομνημονεύματα, τα [apomneemonevmata] πλ memoirs.

απομονώνω [apomonono] isolate || (ηλεκτ) insulate.

απονέμω [aponemo] bestow, allot || confer, award.

απονομή, η [aponomee] award.

αποξενώνω [apoksenono] alienate, estrange.

αποξήρανση, η [apokseeransee] draining, drying.

απόπειρα, η [apopeera] attempt, trial.

αποπεράτωση, η [apoperatosee] completion.

αποπλάνηση, η [apoplaneesee] seduction || (φωτός) aberration.

αποπλέω [apopleo] set sail, sail away.

απορία, η [aporeea] doubt || uncertainty, perplexity.

άπορος [aporos] needy, poor.

απορρέω [aporeo] flow, stem (from), emanate.

απόρρητος [aporeetos] secret.

απορρίματα, τα [aporeemata] πλ rubbish, refuse.

απορρίπτω [aporeepto] cast off || (προσφορά κτλ) reject, refuse || (στις εξετάσεις) fail.

απορροφώ [aporofo] absorb.

απορρυπαντικό, το [aporeepanteeko] detergent.

απορώ [aporo] be at a loss, wonder, be surprised.

απόσβεση, η [aposvesee] extinguishing || (χρέους) liquidation (of debt).

αποσιωπητικά, τα [aposeeopeeteeka] πλ points of omission.

αποσιωπώ [aposeeopo] hush up, pass in silence.

αποσκοπώ [aposkopo] aim, have in view.

απόσπασμα, το [apospasma] extract, excerpt || (στρατ) detachment || **εκτελεστικό ~** firing squad.

αποσπώ [apospo] detach, tear || (στρατ) detach.

απόσταξη, η [apostaksee] distillation.

αποστασία, η [apostaseea] revolt, defection || apostasy.

απόσταση, η [apostasee] distance || remoteness.

αποστειρώνω [aposteerono] sterilize.

αποστέλλω [apostelo] dispatch, send, transmit.

αποστερώ [apostero] deprive.

αποστηθίζω [aposteetheezo] learn by heart.

απόστημα, το [aposteema] abscess.

αποστολέας, ο [apostoleas] sender, shipper.

αποστολή, η [apostolee] sending, consignment || (εμπορική κτλ) mission.

αποστομώνω [apostomono] silence.

αποστράτευση, η [apostratevsee] demobilization.

απόστρατος, ο [apostratos] retired officer, ex-serviceman, veteran.

αποστρέφω [apostrefo] avert, turn away.

αποστροφή, η [apostrofee] repugnance, aversion, abhorrence.

απόστροφος, η [apostrofos] apostrophe.

αποσύνθεση, η [aposeenthesee] decay, decomposition || disorganization.

αποσύρω [aposeero] withdraw || retract.

αποταμιεύω [apotamievo] save, put aside || (τρόφιμα) lay up.

αποτελειώνω [apoteleeono] complete || finish off.

αποτέλεσμα, το [apotelesma] result, effect || **αποτελεσματικός** effective.

αποτελούμαι [apoteloume] consist of, be composed of.

αποτεφρώνω [apotefrono] reduce to ashes, burn down.

απότομος [apotomos] sudden, abrupt || (στροφή) steep, sheer || (τρόπος) curt, gruff.

αποτραβιέμαι [apotravieme] withdraw, give up.

αποτρέπω [apotrepo] avert, turn aside, ward off.

αποτρόπαιος [apotropeos] abominable, hideous, horrible.

αποτροπή, η [apotropee] averting, warding off, dissuasion.

αποτσίγαρο, το [apotseegaro] cigarette end, stub, fag end.

αποτυγχάνω [apoteenghano] fail, fall through, miss.

αποτυπώνω [apoteepono] impress, imprint.

αποτυχία, η [apoteeheea] failure, reverse.

απουσία, η [apouseea] absence || **απουσιάζω** be absent.

αποφασίζω [apofaseezo] decide, resolve, determine.

απόφαση, η [apofasee] decision, resolution || (νομ) verdict || **το παίρνω ~ν** make up one's mind.

αποφασιστικός [apofaseesteekos] decisive, determined.

αποφέρω [apofero] yield, bring in || produce.

αποφεύγω [apofevgo] avoid, keep clear of || (κάπνισμα κτλ) abstain from.

απόφοιτος [apofeetos] school leaver || university graduate.

αποφυγή, η [apofeeyee] avoidance, evasion.

αποφυλακίζω [apofeelakeezo] release from prison.

απόφυση, η [apofeesee] excrescence || protuberance.

αποχαιρετίζω [apohereteezo] wish goodbye, bid farewell.

αποχαιρετισμός, ο [apohereteesmos] farewell, goodbye.

αποχέτευση, η [apohetevsee] draining, drainage.

απόχρωση, η [apohrosee] shade, tone || (χρώματος) fading.

αποχώρηση, η [apohoreesee] withdrawal, retirement, departure.

αποχωρητήριο, το [apohoreeteerio] W.C., lavatory || (στρατ) latrine.

αποχωρίζομαι [apohoreezome] part with, be separated from.

αποχωρισμός, ο [apohoreesmos] separation, parting.

αποχωρώ [apohoro] withdraw, retire, leave.

απόψε [apopse] tonight, this evening.

αποψινός [apopseenos] tonight's.

άποψη, η [apopsee] view, sight || (μεταφ) view, idea.

άπρακτος [apraktos] unsuccessful || unachieved.

απραξία, η [aprakseea] inactivity || (οικ) stagnation, standstill.

απρέπεια, η [aprepeea] indecency, bad manners.

απρεπής [aprepees] indecent, improper, unbecoming.

Απρίλης, ο [apreelees] April.

απρόβλεπτος [aprovleptos] unforeseen, unexpected.

απροετοίμαστος [aproeteemastos] unprepared, unready.

απροθυμία, η [aprotheemeea] reluctance, hesitancy.

απρόθυμος [aprotheemos] unwilling, reluctant, hesitant.

απρόοπτος [aprooptos] unforeseen, unexpected.

απρόσβλητος [aprosvleetos] unassailable || invulnerable.

απροσδόκητος [aprosδokeetos] unexpected, unforeseen, sudden.

απρόσεκτος [aprosektos] inattentive, careless, remiss.

απροσεξία, η [aprosekseea] inattention, inadvertence.

απρόσιτος [aproseetos] inaccessible, unapproachable.

απροστάτευτος [aprostatevtos] unprotected || forlorn.

απρόσωπος [aprosopos] impersonal.

αποχώρπτο, το [aprohoreeto] limit, dead end.

άπτερος [apteros] wingless.

απτόπτος [aptoeetos] undaunted, intrepid.

απύθμενος [apeethmenos] bottomless.

απωθώ [apotho] repel, repulse, thrust back || (μεταφ) reject.

απώλεια, η [apoleea] loss || (θάνατος) bereavement.

απώλητος [apoleetos] unsold.

απών [apon] absent, missing.

απώτατος [apotatos] furthest, remotest, most distant.

απώτερος [apoteros] farther, further || ~ σκοπός ulterior motive.

άρα [ara] so, thus, therefore, consequently.

άρα [ara] I wonder if, can it be that?

αραβικός [araveekos] Arabian, Arabic.

αραβόσιτο, ο [aravoseeto] maize, corn.

άραγε [araye] is it?, can it be?, I wonder if.

άραγμα, το [aragma] anchoring, mooring.

αραδιάζω [araδeeazo] put in a row, line up || (ονόματα κτλ) enumerate.

αράζω [arazo] moor, anchor, drop anchor.

αραιός [areos] sparse, scattered || (επισκέψεις) infrequent, rare.

αραιώνω [areono] (σάλτσα κτλ) thin down || (γραμμές κτλ) spread out || (επισκέψεις) lessen, cut down.

αρακάς, ο [arakas] (common) pea.

αράπης, ο [arapees] negro, dark person || (φόβητρο) bogey.

αραπίνα, η [arapeena] negress, dark woman.

αράχνη, η [arahnee] spider || cobweb.

'Άραβας, ο [aravas] Arab.

αργά [arga] slowly || late.

αργαλειός, ο [argalios] loom.

αργία, η [aryeea] holiday, closing day || idleness.

άργιλλος, η [aryeelos] clay.

αργοκίνητος [argokeeneetos] slow-moving, sluggish.

αργομισθία, η [argomeestheea] sinecure.

αργοπορία, η [argoporeea] slowness, delay.

αργός [argos] slow || idle, inactive.

αργόσχολος [argosholos] idle, unoccupied.

αργότερα [argotera] later, then.

άργυρος, ο [aryeeros] silver.

αργώ [argo] be late || (μαγαζί) be closed.

άρδευση, η [arδevsee] irrigation.

'Άρειος [areeos] : ~ Πάγος Supreme Court.

αρεστός [arestos] agreeable, pleasing, gratifying.

αρέσω [areso] please, delight, like || μου αρέσει I like it.

αρετή, η [aretee] virtue.

αρετσίνωτος [aretseenotos] unresinated.

αρθρίτιδα, η [arthreeteeδa] arthritis.

αρθρογράφος, ο [arthrografos] journalist.

άρθρο, το [arthro] article, clause, term.

άρθρωση, η [arthrosee] articulation, joint || good articulation.

αρίθμηση, η [areethmeesee] numbering, counting, pagination.

αριθμητική, η [areethmeeteekee] arithmetic.

αριθμός, ο [areethmos] number.

αριθμώ [areethmo] count, enumerate.

άριστα [areesta] very well || (βαθμολογία) excellent.

αριστερά [areestera] left hand || (επιρ) on the left, to the left.

αριστερός [areesteros] left, left-handed || left-wing.

αριστοκρατία, η [areestokrateea] aristocracy.

αριστούργημα, το [areestouryeema] masterpiece.

αρκετά [arketa] enough, sufficiently.

αρκετός [arketos] enough, sufficient, adequate.

αρκούδα, η [arkouδa] bear.

αρκτικός [arkteekos] Arctic, northern.

αρκώ [arko] be enough, suffice || **αρκεί να** as long as.

αρλούμπα, η [arloumba] foolish talk, nonsense.

άρμα, το [arma] chariot || (στρατ) ~ **μάχης** tank.

αρματώνω [armatono] arm || equip.

αρμέγω [armego] milk || (μεταφ) fleece.

Αρμένης, ο [armenees] Armenian.

αρμενίζω [armeneezo] set sail, sail.

άρμη, η [armee] brine.

αρμόδιος [armoδeeos] qualified, competent || propitious.

αρμοδιότης, η [armoδeeotees] province, jurisdiction.

αρμόζω [armozo] fit || befit, be becoming, be proper.

αρμονία, η [armoneea] harmony, concord.

αρμός, ο [armos] joint.

αρμοστής, ο [armostees] high commissioner, governor.

αρμύρα, η [armeera] saltiness.

αρμυρός [armeeros] salty.

άρνηση, η [arneesee] refusal || denial || negation.

αρνί, το [arnee] lamb || (μεταφ) docile person.

αρνούμαι [arnoume] refuse, deny, decline || disown.

άροτρο, το [arotro] plough.

αρουραίος, ο [aroureos] field mouse, rat.

άρπα, η [arpa] harp.

αρπαγή, η [arpayee] rapine || rape || stealing.

αρπάζομαι [arpazome] take hold of || come to blows.

αρπάζω [arpazo] grab, snatch || steal, pinch || (ευκαιρία) seize || (λέξεις) catch, pick up.

αρπακτικός [arpakteekos] greedy || (ζώο) rapacious, predatory.

αρραβώνες, οι [aravones] engagement.

αρραβωνιάζω [aravoneeazo] betroth (old), engage.

αρραβωνιαστικιά, η [aravoneeasteekia] fiancée.

αρραβωνιαστικός, ο [aravoneeasteekos] fiancé.

αρρενωπός [arenopos] manly, masculine.

άρρην [areen] male.

αρρωσταίνω [arosteno] make sick || fall ill.

αρρώστια, η [arosteea] illness, sickness.

άρρωστος [arostos] ill, sick, unwell.

αρσενικός [arseneekos] male || (γραμμ) masculine.

άρση, η [arsee] removal, lifting || (μεταφ) raising, abrogation.

αρτηρία, η [arteereea] artery || (οδός) thoroughfare.

άρτιος [arteeos] whole, entire || (αριθμός) even.

αρτοποιείο, το [artopieeo] bakery, baker's shop.

αρτοπωλείο, το [artopoleeo] baker's shop.

άρτος, ο [artos] bread.

άρτυμα, το [arteema] seasoning, sauce.

αρχαιοκαπηλία, η [arheokapeeleea] illicit trade in antiquities.

αρχαιολόγος, ο [arheologos] archeologist.

αρχαιολογία, η [arheoloyeea] archeology.

αρχαίος [arheos] ancient || antiquated.

αρχαιότης, η [arheotees] antiquity || (στα γραφεία) seniority.

αρχάριος [arhareeos] beginner, novice, apprentice.

αρχείο, το [arheeo] archives, records.

αρχέτυπο, το [arheteepo] archetype, original.

αρχή, η [arhee] beginning, start || (φιλοσ) principle || (διοίκ) authority || **κατ' αρχήν** in principle.

αρχηγείο, το [arheeyo] headquarters.

αρχηγία, η [arheeyeea] command, leadership.

αρχηγός, ο [arheegos] commander, leader, chief || (οικογενείας) head.

αρχιεπίσκοπος, ο [arhiepeeskopos] archbishop.

αρχιερέας, ο [arhiereas] prelate, high priest.

αρχίζω [arheezo] begin, start, commence.

αρχικός [arheekos] initial, first, original.

αρχιστράτηγος, ο [arheestrateegos] commander-in-chief, generalissimo.

αρχισυντάκτης, ο [arheeseentaktees] editor-in-chief.

αρχιτέκτων, ο [arheetekton] architect.

άρχοντας, ο [arhontas] lord, master, elder.

αρχοντιά, η [arhontia] distinction, nobility || wealth.

αρχοντικός [arhonteekos] fine, of distinction, lordly.

αρωγή, η [aroyee] help, assistance, aid.

άρωμα, το [aroma] aroma, perfume, odour || **αρωματικός** scented.

ας [as] let, may || ~ **είναι** so be it, let it be.

ασανσέρ, το [asanser] lift, elevator.

ασαφής [asafees] obscure, vague.

ασβέστης, ο [asvestees] lime.

ασβεστώνω [asvestono] whitewash.

αοέβεια, n [aseveea] disrespect || impiety.

ασεβής [asevees] disrespectful || impious.

αοέλγεια, n [aselya] lewdness, debauchery.

άσεμνος [asemnos] indecent, obscene, immodest.

ασήκωτος [aseekotos] unraised || (βαρύς) impossible to lift.

ασήμαντος [aseemantos] insignificant, unimportant.

ασημένιος [aseemeneeos] silver(y).

ασήμι, το [aseemee] silver || ασημικά πλ silverware.

άσημος [aseemos] obscure, insignificant, unimportant.

ασθένεια, n [astheneea] sickness, illness.

ασθενής [asthenees] ill, weak || (ο άρρωστος) patient.

ασθενικός [astheneekos] sickly.

ασθενώ [astheno] be ill, fall sick, get sick.

άσθμα, το [asthma] asthma.

ασιτία, n [aseeteea] undernourishment.

άσκηση, n [askeesee] exercise, practice || drill.

ασκητής, ο [askeetees] hermit.

άσκοπος [askopos] pointless, aimless, purposeless.

ασκός, ο [askos] (skin) bag || wineskin.

ασκούμαι [askoume] exercise, practise.

ασκώ [asko] exercise, practise.

ασπάζομαι [aspazome] kiss, embrace || (μεταφ) adopt, espouse.

ασπασμός, ο [aspasmos] embrace, kiss || greeting.

άσπαστος [aspastos] unbroken || unbreakable.

άσπιλος [aspeelos] immaculate, spotless.

ασπιρίνη, n [aspeereenee] aspirin.

ασπίδα, n [aspeeδa] shield.

άσπλαγχνος [asplanghnos] hard-hearted, pitiless, unmerciful.

άσπονδος [asponδos] irreconcilable, relentless.

ασπούδαστος [aspouδastos] uneducated, ignorant.

ασπράδι, το [aspraδee] white spot || (ματιού, αυγού) white.

ασπρειδερός [aspreeδeros] whitish.

ασπρίζω [aspreezo] whiten, bleach || (γίνομαι άσπρος) turn white.

ασπρομάλλης [aspromalees] white-haired.

ασπροπρόσωπος [asproprosopos] uncorrupted || successful.

ασπρόρουχα, τα [asprorouha] πλ underclothes, linen.

άσπρος [aspros] white.

άσσος, ο [assos] ace.

αστάθεια, n [astatheea] instability, inconstancy, fickleness.

άσταθής [astathees] unsteady, fickle, unstable.

άστακός, ο [astakos] lobster.

άστατος [astatos] fickle, unstable.

άστεγος [astegos] homeless || roofless.

αστειεύομαι [astievome] joke, jest.

αστείο, το [asteeo] joke, pleasantry.

αστείος [asteeos] humorous, funny.

αστείρευτος [asteerevtos] inexhaustible, limitless.

αστέρι, το [asteree] star.

αστερισμός, ο [astereesmos] constellation.

αστεροσκοπείο, το [asteroskopeeo] observatory.

αστήρικτος [asteereektos] unsupported || (μεταφ) untenable.

αστιγματισμός, ο [asteegmateesmos] astigmatism.

αστικός [asteekos] urban || civic || ~ κώδικας civil code.

αστοιχείωτος [asteeheeotos] unlearned, ignorant.

αστόχαστος [astohastos] thoughtless, imprudent.

αστοχία, n [astoheea] failure || carelessness.

αστοχώ [astoho] miss the mark, fail || (λησμονώ) forget.

αστράγαλος, ο [astragalos] anklebone.

αστραπή, n [astrapee] lightning.

αστραπιαίος [astrapieos] lightning, quick.

αστράπτω [astrapto] lighten || flash, glitter.

αστρικός [astreekos] stellar, astral.

άστριφτος [astreeftos] not twisted.

άστρο, το [astro] star.

αστρολογία, n [astroloyeea] astrology.

αστρολόγος, ο [astrologos] astrologer.

αστροναύτης, ο [astronaftees] astronaut.

αστρονομία, n [astronomeea] astronomy.

αστρονόμος, ο [astronomos] astronomer.

αστροπελέκι, το [astropelekee] thunderbolt.

αστροφεγγιά, n [astrofengia] starlight.

άστρωτος [astrotos] (κρεββάτι) unmade || (τραπέζι) unlaid || (πάτωμα) bare || (δρόμος) unpaved.

άστυ, το [astee] city.

αστυνομία, n [asteenomeea] police.

αστυνομικός [asteenomeekos] policeman, of the police.

αστυνόμος, ο [asteenomos] police officer.

αστυφύλακας, ο [asteefeelakas] police constable.

ασυγκίνητος [aseengkeeneetos] unmoved, unfeeling.

ασυγκράτητος [aseengkrateetos] unsuppressible.

ασύγκριτος [aseengkreetos] incomparable.

ασουγύριστος [aseeyeereestos] untidy, disarranged.

ασυγχώρητος [aseenghoreetos] inexcusable, unforgivable.

ασυζήτητος [aseezeeteetos] unquestionable, incontrovertible.

ασυλία, η [aseeleea] asylum, immunity, inviolability.

ασύλληπτος [aseeleeptos] elusive, not caught || (μεταφ) inconceivable.

ασυλλόγιστος [aseeloyeestos] rash, thoughtless.

άσυλο, το [aseelo] shelter, refuge, asylum.

ασυμβίβαστος [aseemveevastos] irreconcilable, incompatible.

ασύμμετρος [aseemetros] disproportionate.

ασυμπλήρωτος [aseembleerotos] uncompleted, incomplete.

ασύμφορος [aseemforos] disadvantageous, not profitable.

ασυναγώνιστος [aseenagoneestos] unbeatable, unrivalled.

ασυναίσθητος [aseenestheetos] unconscious, inconsiderate.

ασυναρτησία, η [aseenarteeseea] incoherence || inconsistency.

ασυνάρτητος [aseenarteetos] incoherent || inconsistent.

ασυνείδητος [aseeneedeetos] unscrupulous, unconscionable.

ασυνέπεια, η [aseenepeea] inconsequence, inconsistency.

ασυνεπής [aseenepees] inconsistent.

ασυνήθιστος [aseeneetheestos] unusual, uncommon.

ασυρματιστής, ο [aseermateestees] wireless operator.

ασύρματος, ο [aseermatos] wireless || **σταθμός ασυρμάτου** wireless station.

ασύστολος [aseestolos] impudent, brazen.

άσφαιρος [asferos] blank.

ασφάλεια, η [asfaleea] security, safety || (ζωής κτλ) insurance || (αστυνομία) police || (ηλεκτ) fuse || (όπλου) safety catch.

ασφαλής [asfalees] safe, secure, sure.

ασφαλίζω [asfaleezo] secure, assure || (ζωήκ κτλ) insure.

ασφαλιστήριο, το [asfaleesteereeo] insurance policy.

ασφάλιστρο, το [asfaleestro] insurance premium.

άσφαλτος, η [asfaltos] asphalt || (δρόμος) tarred road.

ασφαλώς [asfalos] surely, certainly || safely.

ασφυκτικός [asfeekteekos] suffocating.

ασφυξία, η [asfeekseea] suffocation, asphyxia.

άσχετος [ashetos] irrelevant, unrelated, unconnected.

ασχήμια, η [asheemeea] ugliness, deformity.

άσχημος [asheemos] ugly || unsightly || bad.

ασχολία, η [asholeea] occupation, business, job.

ασχολούμαι [asholoume] be occupied with, keep busy.

άσωτος [asotos] dissolute || prodigal, wasteful.

αταίριαστος [atereeastos] incompatible || dissimilar.

άτακτος [ataktos] irregular || disorderly || (παιδί) naughty, unruly.

αταξία, η [atakseea] confusion, disorder || unruliness.

ατάραχος [atarahos] calm, composed, quiet.

αταραξία, η [atarakseea] composure, calmness, serenity.

άταφος [atafos] unburied.

άτεκνος [ateknos] childless.

ατέλεια, η [ateleea] defect || (δασμού) exemption || (χαρακτήρος) imperfection.

ατελείωτος [ateleeotos] endless || unfinished, incomplete.

ατελής [atelees] incomplete || defective || (φόρου) tax-free.

ατελώνιστος [ateloneestos] duty-free || not cleared through customs.

ατενίζω [ateneezo] gaze, stare at, look fixedly at.

ατζαμής [adzamees] unskilled || awkward, clumsy.

ατίθασος [ateethasos] stubborn || (άλογο) difficult to tame.

ατιμάζω [ateemazo] dishonour, disgrace || (βιάζω) rape, ravish.

ατιμία, η [ateemeea] dishonour, disgrace, infamy.

άτιμος [ateemos] dishonest, infamous, disreputable || (συμπεριφορά) disgraceful.

ατιμώρητος [ateemoreetos] unpunished.

ατμάκατος, η [atmakatos] small steamboat.

ατμάμαξα, η [atmamaksa] locomotive.

ατμοκίνητος [atmokeeneetos] steam-driven.

ατμομηχανή, η [atmomeehanee] steam engine, locomotive.

ατμοπλοία, η [atmoploeea] steam navigation.

ατμόπλοιο, το [atmopleeo] steamship.

ατμός, ο [atmos] steam, vapour || (κρασιον) fume.

ατμόσφαιρα, η [atmosfera] atmosphere.

άτοκος [atokos] without interest.

άτολμος [atolmos] timid, faint-hearted.

ατομικιστής [atomeekeestees] egoist.

ατομικός [atomeekos] personal || (ενέργεια κτλ) atomic.

ατομικότητα, η [atomeekoteeta] individuality.

άτομο, το [atomo] (θυσική) atom || (άνθρωπος,) individual, person.

ατονία, η [atoneea] langour, weakness, dejection.

άτονος [atonos] languid, dull || (γραμμ) unaccented.

ατού, το [atoo] trump.

ατόφυος [atofeeos] solid, massive.

άτριφτος [atreeftos] not rubbed, not grated.

ατρόμητος [atromeetos] bold, dauntless, daring.

ατροφία, η [atrofeea] atrophy.

ατροφικός [atrofeekos] atrophied, emaciated.

ατρύγητος [atreeyeetos] ungathered, unharvested.

άτρωτος [atrotos] unwounded, unhurt || invulnerable.

ατσαλένιος [atsaleneeos] of steel, steely.

ατσάλι, το [atsalee] steel.

άτσαλος [atsalos] untidy, disorderly, unkempt || (ζωή) riotous, lawless.

ατσίδα, η [atseeda] alert person, wide-awake person.

ατύχημα, το [ateeheema] mishap, accident, misfortune, injury.

ατυχής [ateehees], άτυχος [ateehos] unfortunate, unlucky, wretched.

ατυχία, η [ateeheea] misfortune, bad luck.

ατυχώ [ateeho] fail, have bad luck, meet with misfortune.

αυγερινός, ο [avgereenos] morning star.

αυγή, η [avyee] dawn, daybreak.

αυγό, το [avgo] egg.

αυγολέμονο, το [avgolemono] lemon and egg sauce or soup.

αυγοτάραχο, το [avgotaraho] botargo.

αυγουλιέρα, η [avgouliera] eggcup.

Αύγουστος, ο [avgoustos] August.

αυθάδεια, η [avthadeea] audacity, insolence.

αυθάδης [avthadees] impertinent, saucy.

αυθαιρεσία, η [avthereseea] high-handed act.

αυθαίρετος [avtheretos] arbitrary, high-handed.

αυθεντία, η [avthenteea] authority, authenticity.

αυθεντικός [avthenteekos] authentic, authoritative.

αυθημερόν [avtheemeron] on the very same day.

αυθόρμητος [avthormeetos] spontaneous.

αυθυποβολή, η [avtheepovolee] auto-suggestion.

αυλαία, η [avlea] curtain.

αυλάκι, το [avlakee] channel, ditch, trench || (ξύλου κτλ) groove.

αυλακωτός [avlakotos] grooved, furrowed, scored.

αυλή, η [avlee] yard, courtyard || (βασιλέως) court.

αυλόγυρος, ο [avloyeeros] enclosure, surrounding wall.

αυλός, ο [avlos] pipe, flute, reed.

άυλος [aeelos] immaterial, incorporeal.

αυξάνω [avksano] increase, augment || (ταχύτητα) accelerate.

αύξηση, η [avkseesee] increase || (γραμμ) augment.

αυξομείωση, η [avksomeeosee] fluctuation, variation.

αύξων [avkson] increasing || ~ αριθμός serial number.

αϋπνία, η [aeepneea] sleeplessness, insomnia.

άυπνος [aeepnos] sleepless, wakeful.

αύρα, η [avra] breeze.

αυριανός [avreeanos] of tomorrow.

αύριο [avreeo] tomorrow.

αυστηρός [avsteeros] severe, rigorous, austere.

αυστηρότητα, η [avsteeroteeta] severity, strictness, austerity.

Αυστραλία, η [avstraleea] Australia.

αυστραλιακός [avstraleeakos] Australian.

Αυστραλός, ο [avstralos] Australian.

Αυστρία, η [avstreea] Austria.

Αυστριακός, ο [avstreeakos] Austrian.

αυταπάρνηση, η [avtaparneesee] self-abnegation.

αυταπάτη, η [avtapatee] self-delusion, self-deception.

αυταρέσκεια, η [avtareskeea] complacency.

αυτάρκεια, η [avtarkeea] contentment.

αυτάρκης [avtarkees] self-sufficient, satisfied.

αυταρχικός [avtarheekos] authoritative, dictatorial.

αυτί, το [avtee] ear.

αυτοβιογραφία, η [avtoveeografeea] autobiography.

αυτόγραφο, το [avtografo] autograph.

αυτοδημιούργητος [avtoðeemeeouryeetos] self-made.

αυτοδιάθεση, η [avtoðeeathesee] self-determination.

αυτοδικαίως [avtoðeekeos] of right, de jure.

αυτοδιοίκηση, η [avtoðieekeesee] self-government.

αυτοθυσία, η [avtotheeseea] self-sacrifice.

αυτοκέφαλος [avtokefalos] independent || (εκκλ) autocephalous.

αυτοκινητιστής, ο [avtokeeneeteestees] motorist.

αυτοκίνητο, το [avtokeeneeto] car, automobile (US).

αυτοκινητόδρομος, ο [avtokeeneetoðromos] motorway, highway.

αυτοκρατορία, η [avtokratoreea] empire.

αυτοκράτωρας, ο [avtokratoras] emperor.

αυτοκτονία, η [avtoktoneea] suicide.

αυτοκτονώ [avtoktono] commit suicide.

αυτόματος [avtomatos] automatic.

αυτονόητος [avtonoeetos] self-explanatory, obvious.

αυτοπεποίθηση, η [avtopepeetheesee] self-confidence, self-reliance.

αυτοπροσώπως [avtoprosopos] personally.

αυτόπτης, ο [avtoptees] eyewitness.

αυτός [avtos] he || **ο ~** the same.

αυτοσυντήρηση [avtoseenteereesee] self-preservation.

αυτοσυντήρητος [avtoseenteereetos] self-supporting.

αυτοσχεδιάζω [avtosheðeeazo] improvise, extemporize.

αυτοσχέδιος [avtosheðeeos] improvised, impromptu, makeshift.

αυτοτελής [avtotelees] self-sufficient || independent.

αυτού [avtou] there.

αυτουργός, ο [avtourgos] perpetrator.

αυτοφυής [avtofiees] indigenous, natural.

αυτόφωρος [avtoforos] in the very act, red-handed.

αυτόχειρας, ο [avtoheeras] suicide.

αυτόχθων, ο [avtohthon] indigenous, aboriginal, native.

αυτοψία, η [avtopseea] (ιατρ) autopsy || (νομ) local inspection.

αυχένας, ο [avhenas] nape of the neck || cervix || (μεταφ) neck.

αφάγωτος [afagotos] uneaten || not having eaten || untouched.

αφαίμαξη, η [afemaksee] bloodletting.

αφαίρεση, η [aferesee] deduction, subtraction || (φιλοσ) abstraction.

αφαιρούμαι [aferoume] be absent-minded.

αφαιρώ [afero] deduct, subtract || (κλέβω) steal, rob.

αφαλός, ο [afalos] navel.

αφάνεια, η [afaneea] obscurity, oblivion.

αφανής [afanees] obscure, unknown || invisible.

αφανίζω [afaneezo] ruin, destroy.

αφάνταστος [afantastos] unimaginable.

άφαντος [afantos] invisible, unseen.

αφασία, η [afaseea] muteness, aphasia.

αφειδής [afeeðees] lavish, extravagant.

αφελής [afelees] simple, ingenuous, guileless.

αφέντης, ο [afentees] master, boss || owner.

αφεντικό, το [afenteeko] governor, boss, employer.

αφερέγγυος [aferengeeos] insolvent.

άφεση, η [afesee] remission || discharge.

αφετηρία, η [afeteereea] starting point || beginning.

αφή, η [afee] sense of touch || (αίσθηση) feeling.

αφήγηση, η [afeeyeesee] narration, account.

αφηγούμαι [afeegoume] narrate, relate, tell.

αφηνιάζω [afeeneeazo] bolt || (για ανθρώπους) run amok.

αφήνω [afeeno] let, permit || (μόνος) let alone || (ελευθερώνω) let go of || (εγκαταλείπω) abandon.

αφηρημάδα, η [afeereemaða] absentmindedness.

αφηρημένος [afeereemenos] absentminded || (φίλος) abstract.

αφθαρσία, η [aftharseea] indestructibility, incorruptibility.

άφθαρτος [afthartos] incorruptible, indestructible.

άφθαστος [afthastos] unsurpassed, incomparable, unexcelled.

αφθονία, η [afthoneea] abundance, profusion.

άφθονος [afthonos] abundant, plentiful, profuse.

αφθονώ [afthono] abound with, teem with, be plentiful in.

αφιέρωμα, το [afieroma] offering, dedication.

αφιερώνω [afierono] dedicate, devote || (βιβλίο κτλ) inscribe.

αφιέρωση, n [afierosee] dedication, devotion.

αφιλοκερδής [afeelokerðees] disinterested, selfless.

αφιλότιμος [afeeloteemos] wanting in self-respect, mean.

αφίνω [afeeno] βλ **αφήνω**.

άφιξη, n [afeeksee] arrival, coming.

αφιόνι, το [afonee] poppy || opium.

άφλεκτος [aflektos] nonflammable.

άφοβος [afovos] intrepid, fearless, bold.

αφομοιώνω [afomeeono] assimilate.

αφομοίωση, n [afomeeosee] assimilation.

αφοπλίζω [afopleezo] disarm || (φρούριο κτλ) dismantle.

αφοπλισμός, ο [afopleesmos] disarmament.

αφόρετος [aforetos] unworn, new.

αφόρητος [aforeetos] intolerable, insufferable.

αφορίζω [aforeezo] excommunicate.

αφορισμός, ο [aforeesmos] excommunication.

αφορμή, n [aformee] motive, pretext, cause.

αφορολόγητος [aforoloyeetos] untaxed, free from taxation.

αφορώ [aforo] concern || regard || όσον αφορά as regards.

αφοσιώνομαι [afoseeonome] devote o.s., be attached to.

αφοσίωση, n [afoseeosee] devotion, attachment, affection.

αφότου [afotou] since, as long as.

αφού [afou] since, after.

άφρακτος [afraktos] unfenced, unwalled.

αφράτος [afratos] light and crisp || frothy, foamy || (δέρμα) soft.

αφρίζω [afreezo] foam || (μεταφ) be furious.

αφρικανικός [afreekaneekos] African.

Αφρικανός, ο [afreekanos] African.

Αφρική, n [afreekee] Africa.

αφροδισιολόγος, ο [afroðeeseeologos] venereal disease specialist.

αφροδίσιος [afroðeeseeos] venereal.

αφρόντιστος [afronteestos] neglected, uncared for.

αφρός, ο [afros] foam || (κοινωνίας) cream || (σαπουνιού) lather.

αφρώδης [afroðees] frothy, foamy.

άφρων [afron] foolish, thoughtless, rash.

αφυδάτωση, n [afeeðatosee] dehydration.

αφύπνιση, n [afeepneesee] awakening || (μεταφ) dawning.

αφύσικος [afeeseekos] unnatural || (προσποιητός) affected.

άφωνος [afonos] mute, speechless, silent.

αφώτιστος [afoteestos] dark || (άνθρωπος) unenlightened.

αχ [ah] (επιφ) ah!, oh!, alas!

αχαΐρευτος [ahaeerevtos] scoundrel.

αχανής [ahanees] immense, enormous, vast.

αχαρακτήριστος [aharakteereestos] unprincipled, indescribable.

αχαριστία, n [ahareesteea] ingratitude.

αχάριστος [ahareestos] ungrateful.

άχαρος [aharos] ungraceful, awkward, unsightly || unpleasant.

αχηβάδα, n [aheevaða] cockle, sea shell, shellfish.

αχθοφόρος, ο [ahthoforos] porter.

αχινός, ο [aheenos] sea urchin.

αχλάδι, το [ahlaðee] pear.

άχνα, n [ahna] βλ **αχνός**.

αχνάρι, το [ahnaree] footprint || (μεταφ) pattern.

άχνη, n [ahnee] mist, evaporation || (χημ) corrosive sublimate.

αχνίζω [ahneezo] evaporate || steam.

αχνός, ο [ahnos] vapour, steam || (χρώμα) pale, colourless.

αχόρταγος [ahortagos] insatiable, greedy || (ζώο) voracious.

αχούρι, το [ahouree] stable, stall || (μεταφ) untidy place, pigsty.

αχρείαστος [ahreeastos] unnecessary, needless.

αχρείος [ahreeos] wicked, vile.

αχρησιμοποίητος [ahreeseemopieetos] unused.

αχρηστεύω [ahreestevo] make useless.

αχρηστία, n [ahreesteea] obsoleteness, uselessness.

άχρηστος [ahreestos] useless, worthless.

αχρονολόγητος [ahronoloyeetos] undated.

αχρωμάτιστος [ahromateestos] unpainted, uncoloured, plain.

άχρωμος [ahromos] colourless, uncoloured.

άχτι, το [ahtee] yearning, longing.

αχτίδα, n [ahteeða] ray, beam.

αχτένιστος [ahteneestos] uncombed, unkempt || (λόγος κτλ) unpolished.

άχυρο, το [aheero] straw, hay.

αχυρώνας, ο [aheeronas] barn, hayloft.

αχώνευτος [ahonevtos] undigested || indigestible.

αχώριστος [ahoreestos] inseparable.

άψητος [apseetos] not cooked, underdone.

αψηφώ [apseefo] disregard, disdain, scorn.

αψιμαχία, n [apseemaheea] skirmish.

αψίδα, n [apseeða] arch, vault || apse.

άψογος [apsogos] faultless, irreproachable.

αψυχολόγητος [apseeholoyeetos] ill-considered, impolitic.

άψυχος [apseehos] lifeless || (δειλός) cowardly, timid.

άωτον, το [aoton]: άκρον ~ acme, height of.

B, β

βαγόνι, το [vagonee] carriage || (εμπορικό) wagon, truck || (βαγκόν-λι) sleeping car.

βάδην [vaδeen] at a walking pace.

βαδίζω [vaδeezo] walk || (στρατ) march || (πηγαίνω) go.

βάδισμα, το [vaδeesma] step, walk, gait.

βαζελίνη, η [vazeleenee] vaseline.

βάζο, το [vazo] vase.

βάζω [vazo] put, set, place || (φορώ) put on || (φόρους κτλ) impose, lay || ~ εμπρός start, begin || ~ χέρι lay hands on || ~ τα δυνατά μου do my best.

βαθαίνω [vatheno] deepen || βλ και βαθύνω.

βαθειά [vatheea] deep(ly), profoundly.

βαθμηδόν [vathmeeδon] by degrees, gradually.

βαθμιαίος [vathmieos] gradual, progressive.

βαθμίδα, η [vathmeeδa] step, stair || (μεταφ) rank.

βαθμολογία, η [vathmologeea] (οργάνου) graduation || (μαθήματος) grades, marks.

βαθμός, ο [vathmos] degree || (στρατ) grade, rank || (μαθήματος) mark.

βάθος, το [vathos] depth, bottom || (φόντο) back, background.

βαθούλωμα, το [vathouloma] hollow, depression.

βαθουλώνω [vathoulono] hollow out || become hollow.

βάθρο, το [vathro] (βάση) basis, foundation || (αγάλματος κτλ) pedestal || (γεφύρας) pillar.

βαθύνω [vatheeno] deepen, hollow out, become deeper.

βαθύπλουτος [vatheeploutos] opulent.

βαθύς [vathees] deep || (σκότος κτλ) heavy, deep || (ύπνος) sound || (αίσθημα) profound || (πνεύμα) penetrating, sagacious.

βαθύτητα, η [vatheeteeta] depth, profundity, deepness.

βαθύφωνος [vatheefonos] bass, deep-voiced.

βάιο, το [vaeeo] palm branch.

βακαλάος, ο [vakalaos] cod.

βάκιλλος, ο [vakeelos] bacillus.

βακτηρίδιο, το [vakteereeδeeo] bacillus.

βαλανίδι, το [valaneeδee] acorn || βαλανιδιά oak tree.

βάλανος, ο [valanos] acorn.

βαλβίδα, η [valveeδa] valve.

βαλές, ο [vales] knave (in cards).

βαλίτσα, η [valeetsa] suitcase, (hand)bag.

βαλκάνια, τα [valkaneea] πλ the Balkans.

βάλς, το [vals] waltz.

βάλσαμο, το [valsamo] balsam, balm || (μεταφ) consolation.

βαλσαμώνω [valsamono] embalm || (μεταφ) console, comfort.

βάλσιμο, το [valseemo] placing, setting, laying.

βάλτος, ο [valtos] marsh, fen, bog.

βαλτός [valtos] instigated, planted.

βαμβακερός [vamvakeros] of cotton.

βαμβάκι, το [vamvakee] cotton.

βάμμα, το [vamma] tincture, dye.

βαμμένος [vamenos] dyed, painted.

βάναυσος [vanavsos] rough, coarse, rude.

βάνδαλος, ο [vandalos] vandal.

βανίλ(λ)ια, η [vaneeleea] vanilla.

βαπόρι, το [vaporee] steamship.

βαπτίζω [vapteezo] baptize, christen || dip, plunge.

βάπτιση, η [vapteesee] βλ βάπτισμα.

βάπτισμα, το [vapteesma] baptism, christening.

βαπτιστικός [vapteesteekos] baptismal || (ουσ) godchild.

βάπτω [vapto] (χάλυψ) temper || (μπογιά) paint || (παπούτσια) polish.

βάραθρο, το [varathro] abyss, gulf, chasm.

βαραίνω [vareno] weigh down, make heavier || (κουράζω) weary || (αισθάνομαι βάρος) feel heavy || (μεταφ) carry weight.

βαράω [varao] βλ βαρώ.

βαρβαρικός [varvareekos] barbaric.

βάρβαρος [varvaros] barbarous, brutal, savage.

βάρδια, η [varδeea] watch, duty, shift.

βαρέλι, το [varelee] barrel, cask.

βαρετός [varetos] annoying, boring, tedious.

βαρήκοος [vareekoos] hard of hearing.

βαριά, η [varia] (σφυρί) hammer || (επιρ) seriously.

βαρίδι, το [vareeδee] (counter)weight.

βαριέμαι [varieme] be bored, be tired (of) || (δε θέλω) not want (to) || δε βαριέσαι never mind!, don't bother!

βάρκα, η [varka] small boat, rowing boat, dinghy.

βαρκάρης, ο [varkarees] boatman.

B

βαρόμετρο, το [varometro] barometer.

βάρος, το [varos] weight, load, burden || σε ~ του at his expense.

βαρύθυμος [vareetheemos] sad, depressed.

βαρύνω [vareeno] weigh down, lie heavy || βλ και βαραίνω.

βαρύς [varees] heavy || (ποινή) severe, harsh || (σφάλμα) serious || (ύπνος) deep, heavy || (ζυγός) oppressive || (ευθύνη) grave || (άνθρωπος) slow, dull-witted.

βαρυσήμαντος [vareeseemantos] significant, grave, momentous.

βαρύτιμος [vareeteemos] precious, costly, valuable.

βαρύτονος [vareetonos] baritone || (γραμμ) with a grave accent.

βαρύφωνος [vareefonos] deep-voiced, bass.

βαρώ [varo] beat, hit, shoot || (σάλπιγγα) sound || (καμπάνα) toll.

βασανίζω [vasaneezo] torture, torment || (ένα θέμα κτλ) examine thoroughly, go into || (το μυαλό) rack.

βασανιστήριο, το [vasaneesteereeo] rack, torture chamber.

βάσανο, το [vasano] pain, trial, ordeal || (μεταφ) nuisance.

βασίζω [vaseezo] base.

βασικός [vaseekos] primary, basic, fundamental.

βασιλεία, η [vaseeleea] kingdom || reign.

βασίλειο, το [vaseeleeo] kingdom.

βασιλέας, ο [vaseeleas] king.

βασιλεύω [vaseelevo] reign, rule.

βασιλιάς, ο [vaseelias] βλ βασιλέας.

βασιλική, η [vaseeleekee] basilica.

βασιλικός [vaseeleekos] royal, royalist || (ούσ) basil.

βασίλισσα, η [vaseeleesa] queen.

βασιλομήτωρ, η [vaseelomeetor] queen mother.

βασιλόπιττα, η [vaseelopeeta] New Year's cake.

βασιλόφρων [vaseelofron] royalist.

βάσιμος [vaseemos] sound, trustworthy.

βάση, η [vasee] base, foundation || (βαθμόν) pass mark.

βασκανία, η [vaskaneea] evil eye.

βαστώ [vasto] (φέρω) bear, hold, support || (συγκρατώ) hold, control || (ύφασμα κτλ) keep, wear || (κρατώ) carry, hold.

βατ(τ), το [vat] watt.

βατόμουρο, το [vatomouro] blackberry.

βατός [vatos] (δρόμος) passable || (ποτάμι) fordable || (ύψωμα) accessible.

βάτραχος, ο [vatrahos] frog, toad.

βαυκαλίζω βαφή, η [vafee] dyeing || shoe polish || dye.

βάφομαι [vafome] make-up.

βαφτίσια, τα [vafteeseea] πλ christening.

βαφτισιμιός, ο [vafteeseemios] godson.

βάφω [vafo] βλ βάπτω.

βάψιμο, το [vapseemo] painting, make-up.

βγάζω [vgazo] take off, raise, draw out || (εξαλείφω) get out, wash out || (λάδι, χυμό κτλ) press, squeeze || (πόδι, χέρι) dislocate || (καπνό κτλ) give off || (παράγω) produce || (χρήματα) make, earn || (βουλευτή κτλ) elect || (διακρίνω) make out, read || (δίδω όνομα) name, call || (αποδεικνύω) prove || (αφαιρώ) take from || (εφημερίδα κτλ) publish || (περίπατο) take for a walk.

βγαίνω [vgeno] go out, come out, get out || (ανατέλλω) rise || (κυκλοφορά) be out || (εκλέγομαι) be elected || (εξαλείφομαι) fade, come out.

βγαλμένος [vgalmenos] taken off, removed.

βγάλσιμο, το [vgalseemo] extraction, removal || (κοκκάλου) dislocation.

βδέλλα, η [vðella] leech.

βέβαιος [veveos] certain, sure, convinced.

βεβαιώνω [veveono] confirm, affirm, assure || certify.

βεβαίως [veveos] certainly, surely.

βεβαίωση, η [veveosee] confirmation || (χαρτί) certificate.

βεβαρημένος [vevareemenos] marked || (συνείδηση) heavy.

βέβηλος [veveelos] profane, sacrilegious, impious.

βεβιασμένος [veveeasmenos] forced.

βελάζω [velazo] bleat.

βελανίδι, το [velaneeðee] acorn.

βελγικός [velyeekos] Belgian.

Βέλγιο, το [velyo] Belgium.

Βέλγος ο [velgos] Belgian.

βέλο, το [velo] veil.

βελόνα, η [velona] needle.

βελονιά, η [velonia] stitch.

βέλος, το [velos] arrow, dart.

βελούδο, το [velouðo] velvet.

βελτιώνω [velteeono] improve, better.

βελτίωση, η [velteeosee] improvement.

βενζινάκατος, η [venzeenakatos] small motorboat.

βενζίνη, η [venzeenee] petrol.

βεντάλια, η [ventaleea] fan.

βεντέττα, η [venteta] vendetta || (ηθοποιός) star.

βέρα, η [vera] wedding ring.

βεράντα, η [veranta] veranda, porch.

βέργα, η [verga] stick, rod, switch, twig.

βερεσέ [verese] on credit, on trust.

βερίκοκκο, το [vereekoko] apricot.

βερνίκι, το [verneekee] varnish, polish || (μεταφ) veneer.

βέρος [veros] genuine, true, real.

βέτο, το [veto] veto.

βήμα, το [veema] step, pace || (βίδας) pitch, thread || (έλικος) twist || (έδρα) rostrum.

βηματίζω [veemateezo] step, pace, walk.

βήτα, το [veeta] the letter B.

βήχας, ο [veehas] cough.

βήχω [veeho] cough.

βία, η [veea] force, violence || hurry || (μετά βίας) with difficulty.

βιάζομαι [veeazome] be in a hurry, be rushed.

βιάζω [veeazo] force, compel || (παραβιάζω) break open || (παραβαίνω) violate || (ασελγώ) rape, ravish.

βίαιος [vieos] violent, forcible || fiery, passionate.

βιαιότητες, οι [vieoteetes] πλ acts of violence.

βιαίως [vieos] violently, forcibly.

βιασμός, ο [veeasmos] rape, violation.

βιαστής, ο [veeastees] ravisher, rapist.

βιαστικός [veeasteekos] urgent, pressing, hurried.

βιασύνη, η [veeaseenee] haste, urgency.

βιβλιάριο, το [veevleeareeo] booklet, card, bank book.

βιβλικός [veevleekos] biblical.

βιβλιογραφία, η [veevleeografeea] bibliography.

βιβλιοθηκάριος, ο [veevleeotheekareeos] librarian.

βιβλιοθήκη, η [veevleeotheekee] bookcase || library.

βιβλίο, το [veevleeo] book.

βιβλιοπώλης, ο [veevleeopolees] bookseller.

βίβλος, η [veevlos] Bible.

βίδα, η [veeða] screw || (μεταφ) whim, caprice.

βιδώνω [veeðono] screw.

βίζα, η [veeza] visa.

βίζιτα, η [veezeeta] visit, call || visitor.

βίλλα, η [veela] villa.

βιογραφία, η [veeografeea] biography.

βιολέττα, η [veeoleta] violet.

βιολί, το [veeolee] violin, fiddle || αλλάζω ~ change one's tune.

βιολόγος, ο [veeologos] biologist.

βιομηχανία, η [veeomeehaneea] industry || manufacture.

βιομηχανικός [veeomeehaneekos] industrial.

βιοπαλαιστής, ο [veeopalestees] breadwinner.

βιοπάλη, η [veeopalee] working hard to make a living.

βίος, ο [veeos] life.

βιός, το [veeos] wealth, property.

βιοτεχνία, η [veeotehneea] handicraft.

βιοχημεία, η [veeoheemeea] biochemistry.

βιταμίνη, η [veetameenee] vitamin.

βιτρίνα, η [veetreena] shop window, showcase.

βίτσιο, το [veetseeo] bad habit.

βιώσιμος [veeoseemos] viable, feasible.

βλαβερός [vlaveros] harmful || (έντομο) noxious.

βλάβη, η [vlavee] harm, damage || (μηχανής) motor trouble, breakdown.

βλάκας, ο [vlakas] blockhead, fool, idiot.

βλακεία, η [vlakeea] nonsense, silliness.

βλακώδης [vlakoðees] stupid, silly.

βλάπτω [vlapto] harm, injure, damage.

βλαστάρι, το [vlastaree] sprout, bud || (οικογενείας) scion.

βλάστηση, η [vlasteesee] sprouting || (φυτεία) vegetation.

βλαστός, ο [vlastos] shoot, sprout || (μεταφ) scion, offspring.

βλασφημία, η [vlasfeemeea] blasphemy, curse.

βλασφημώ [vlasfeemo] curse, revile.

βλάχος, ο [vlahos] (μεταφ) bumpkin, boor.

βλέμμα, το [vlemma] look, glance, eye.

βλεννόρροια, η [vlenoreea] gonorrhoea.

βλέπω [vlepo] see, look at.

βλεφαρίδα, η [vlefareeða] eyelash.

βλέφαρο, το [vlefaro] eyelid.

βλήμα, το [vleema] projectile.

βλογιά, η [vloya] smallpox.

βλοσυρός, ο [vloseeros] fierce, stern, grim.

βόας, ο [voas] boa.

βογγητό, το [vongeeto] groan, moan.

βογγώ [vongo] moan, groan || roar.

βόδι, το [voðee] ox.

βοδινό, το [voðeeno] beef.

βοή, η [voee] shout, cry, humming, roaring || (όχλου) clamour.

βοήθεια, η [voeetheea] help, aid, assistance.

βοήθημα, το [voeetheema] help, assistance, relief.

βοηθητικός [voeetheeteekos] auxiliary || (άνεμος) favourable, fair.

βοηθός, ο [voeethos] assistant, helper, collaborator.

βοηθώ [voeetho] help, aid, give a hand, relieve.

βόθρος, ο [vothros] cesspool, ditch.

βολάν, το [volan] steering wheel, driving wheel.

βολβός, ο [volvos] bulb, kind of onion || (ματιού) eyeball.

βολεύομαι [volevome] get comfortable || get fixed up.

βολεύω [volevo] accommodate, fit in, suit || τα ~ get along, do well.

βολή, η [volee] throw, blow, stroke, shot || (απόσταση) range.

βόλι, το [volee] ball, bullet.

βολιδοσκοπώ [voleeδoskopo] sound.

βολικός [voleekos] convenient, handy, easy.

βολίδα, η [voleeδa] sounding lead || (αστρο) meteor || (σφαίρα) bullet, ball.

βόλτα, η [volta] walk || (στροφή) revolution || (κοχλίου) thread || κόβω βόλτες I stroll about.

βόμβα, η [vomva] bomb.

βομβαρδίζω [vomvarδeezo] bomb, bombard || (μεταφ) assail.

βομβαρδισμός, ο [vomvarδeesmos] bombing.

βομβαρδιστικό, το [vomvarδeesteeko] (αερο) bomber.

βόμβος, ο [vomvos] hum, buzz, buzzing.

βορειοανατολικός [voreeoanatoleekos] north-east(ern).

βορειοδυτικός [voreeoδeeteekos] northwest(ern).

βόρειος [voreeos] north(ern).

βορείως [voreeos] northwards, to the north, north.

βοριάς, ο [vorias] north wind.

βορράς, ο [vorras] north.

βοσκή, η [voskee] pasture.

βοσκός, ο [voskos] shepherd.

βοσκοτόπι, το [voskotopee] pasture land.

βόσκω [vosko] graze || (μεταφ) drift.

βοτάνι, το [votanee] plant, herb.

βοτανικός [votaneekos] botanic(al).

βότανο, το [votano] herb, plant.

βοτανολόγος, ο [votanologos] botanist.

βότρυς, ο [votrees] bunch of grapes.

βότσαλο, το [votsalo] pebble.

βουβάλι, το [vouvalee] buffalo.

βουβός [vouvos] dumb, mute.

βουδδιστής, ο [vouδeestees] Buddhist.

βουή [vouee] βλ βοή.

βουίζω [voueezo] buzz, hum.

Βουλγαρία, η [voulgareea] Bulgaria.

Βουλγαρικός [voulgareekos] Bulgarian.

Βουλγαρός, ο [voulgaros] Bulgarian.

βούλευμα, το [voulevma] decision, ordinance, decree.

βουλευτής, ο [voulevtees] member of parliament, deputy.

βουλή, η [voulee] parliament, chamber || (θέληση) will, volition.

βούληση, η [vouleesee] desire, will || κατά ~ at will.

βούλιαγμα, το [vouleeagma] sinking, submergence || collapse.

βουλιάζω [vouleeazo] sink || (μεταφ) ruin, be ruined.

βουλιμία, η [vouleemeea] insatiable appetite.

βουλλοκέρι, το [voulokeree] sealing wax.

βούλλωμα, το [vouloma] sealing, stamping || (το αντικείμενο) cork, stopper.

βουλλώνω [voulono] seal || (πωματίζω) stop, choke up, fill.

βουνήσιος [vouneeseeos] mountainous || (ουσ) highlander.

βουνό, το [vouno] mountain.

βούρδουλας, ο [vourδoulas] whip, lash.

βούρκος, ο [vourkos] mud, mire || (μεταφ) mire, gutter.

βουρκώνω [vourkono] fill with tears.

βούρλο, το [vourlo] (bul)rush.

βούρτσα, η [vourtsa] (hair)brush || (ρούχων) clothes brush || (δοντιών) toothbrush.

βουρτσίζω [vourtseezo] brush, brush down.

βουστάσιο, το [voustaseeo] ox stall, cowshed.

βούτηγμα, το [vouteegma] plunging, dipping || (μεταφ) plundering, stealing.

βούτημα, το [vouteema] hard biscuit.

βουτηχτής, ο [vouteehtees] diver || (μεταφ) thief.

βουτιά, η [voutia] dive || (μεταφ) snatching, stealing.

βούτυρο, το [vouteero] butter.

βουτώ [vouto] plunge, dip || (κλέβω) steal, snatch.

βραβείο, το [vraveeo] prize.

βραβεύω [vravevo] award, reward.

βράγχια, τα [vrangheea] πλ gills || (ιατρ) branchiae.

βραδιά, η [vraδia] evening.

βραδιάζω [vraδeeazo]: βραδιάζει it's getting dark.

βραδινός [vraδeenos] evening.

βράδυ, το [vraδee] evening.

βραδύνω [vraδeeno] be late, be slow.

βραδύς [vraδees] slow, sluggish, tardy.

βραδύτης, η [vraδeetees] slowness, tardiness.

βράζω [vrazo] boil, ferment, seethe.

βρακί, το [vrakee] trousers || underpants.

βράσιμο, το [vraseemo] boiling, fermentation.

βράση, η [vrasee] boiling || (μούστου κτλ) fermentation.

βρασμός, ο [vrasmos] boiling || (μεταφ) agitation, excitement.

βραστός [vrastos] boiled || boiling, hot.

βραχιόλι, το [vraheeolee] bracelet.

βραχίονας, ο [vraheeonas] arm, forearm || branch.

βραχνιάζω [vrahneeazo] become hoarse.

βραχνός [vrahnos] hoarse.

βράχος, ο [vrahos] rock.

βραχυκύκλωμα, το [vraheekeekloma] short circuit.

βραχυπρόθεσμος [vraheeprothesmos] short-dated || short-term.

βραχύτητα, η [vraheeteeta] shortness, brevity, conciseness.

βραχώδης [vrahoðees] rocky.

βρε [vre] (επιφ) you there!, hey, you!

βρεγμένος [vregmenos] wet, moist.

βρέξιμο, το [vrekseemo] wetting, watering, moistening.

βρεφοκομείο, το [vrefokomeeo] foundling hospital, public nursery.

βρέφος, το [vrefos] baby, infant.

βρέχω [vreho] water, wet, dampen, rain.

βρίζω [vreezo] abuse, swear at, insult || outrage.

βρισιά, η [vreesia] abuse, insult, outrage.

βρισίδι, το [vreeseeðee] stream of abuse.

βρίσκομαι [vreeskome] be, find o.s.

βρίσκω [vreesko] find || (τυχαίως) come across, discover || (σκέπτομαι) think, deem || (παίρνω) get, procure || (μαντεύω) guess.

βρογχίτιδα, η [vrongheeteeða] bronchitis.

βροντερός [vronteros] thundering, noisy.

βροντή, η [vrontee] thunder.

βρόντος, ο [vrontos] noise, roar || heavy fall || στο βρόντο in vain.

βροντώ [vronto] (μεταφ) knock, make a noise.

βροχερός [vroheros] wet, rainy.

βροχή, η [vrohee] rain || ~ ψιλή drizzle.

βρυκόλακας, ο [vreekolakas] vampire, ghost.

βρύο, το [vreeo] moss || seaweed.

βρύση, η [vreesee] fountain, spring || (μεταλλική) tap.

βρυχώμαι [vreehome] roar, bellow.

βρώμα, η [vroma] filth, stink || (για πρόσωπο) hussy, bitch, slut.

βρωμερός [vromeros] stinking, smelly || (υπόθεση) nasty, odious, vile || (άτομο) stinking, dirty, slovenly.

βρώμη, η [vromee] oats.

βρωμιά, η [vromia] filth, dirt || (μεταφ) nasty business, corruption.

βρωμίζω [vromeezo] stink, dirty, sully.

βρώμικος [vromeekos] dirty, grubby || (μεταφ) nasty, odious, vile.

βρωμώ [vromo] give off a stench, smell badly, stink.

βυζαίνω [veezeno] suckle || (μεταφ) suck.

βυζαντινός [veezanteenos] Byzantine.

βυζί, το [veezee] breast.

βυθίζω [veetheezo] sink, plunge, dip.

βύθιση, η [veetheesee] sinking, submersion.

βύθισμα, το [veetheesma] (ναυτ) draught || sinking.

βυθοκόρος, η [veethokoros] dredger, dredge.

βυθός, ο [veethos] bottom of the sea.

βυρσοδεψείο, το [veersoðepseeo] tannery.

βύσσινο, το [veeseeno] sour cherry.

βυτίο, το [veeteeo] cask, barrel.

βωβός [vovos] dumb, mute, silent.

βώλος, ο [volos] clod || βώλοι πλ marbles.

βωμολοχία, η [vomoloheea] obscenity, scurrility.

βωμός, ο [vomos] altar.

Γ, γ

γαβάθα, η [gavatha] earthenware vessel || wooden bowl.

γάγγλιο, το [gangleeo] ganglion.

γάγγραινα, η [gangrena] gangrene || (μεταφ) canker.

γάδος, ὁ [gaðos] cod(fish).

γάζα, η [gaza] gauze.

γαζί, το [gazee] stitch || (της χειρός) handstitch || (της μηχανής) machine-stitch.

γάζωμα, το [gazoma] stitching.

γάιδαρος, ο [gaeeðaros] ass, donkey || (μεταφ) boor, ass.

γαϊδουράγκαθο, το [gaeeðourangatho] thistle.

γαϊδουριά, η [gaeeðouria] rudeness.

γαιοκτήμονας, η [geokteemonas] landowner.

γάλα, το [gala] milk.

γαλάζιος [galazeeos] azure, blue.

γαλαζοαίματος [galazoematos] blue-blooded.

γαλαζόπετρα, η [galazopetra] turquoise.

γαλακτερός [galakteros] milky, of milk.

γαλακτικός [galakteekos] lactic.

γαλακτοκομείο, το [galaktokomeeo] dairy farm.

γαλακτοπωλείο, το [galaktopoleeo] dairy.

γαλακτώδης [galaktoðees] milky, milk-white.

γαλάκτωμα, το [galaktoma] emulsion.

γαλανόλευκος, η [galanolevkos] the Greek flag.

γαλανομμάτης [galanomatees] blue-eyed.

γαλανός [galanos] blue.

Γαλαξίας, ο [galakseeas] Milky Way.

γαλαρία, η [galareea] gallery.
γαλατάς, ο [galatas] milkman.
γαλβανίζω [galvaneezo] galvanize || (μεταφ) electrify, rouse, stimulate.
γαλέρα, η [galera] galley.
γαλέττα, η [galeta] hard tack.
γαληνεύω [galeenevo] calm, quieten down.
γαλήνη, η [galeenee] calm, peace, serenity.
γαλήνιος [galeeneeos] calm, composed, serene.
Γαλλία, η [galeea] France.
γαλλικός [galeekos] French.
Γάλλος, ο [galos] Frenchman.
γαλόνι, το [galonee] (μέτρο) gallon || (στρατ) stripe, pip.
γαλοπούλα, η [galopoula] turkey hen.
γάμα, το [gama] the letter G.
γαμήλιος [gameeleeos] nuptial, bridal || **γαμήλιο ταξίδι** honeymoon.
γάμπα, η [gamba] calf, leg.
γαμπρός, ο [gambros] bridegroom || son-in-law || brother-in-law.
γαμψός [gampsos] hooked, crooked.
γάντζος, ο [ganĎzos] hook, grapple.
γαντζώνω [ganĎzono] hook.
γάντι, το [gantee] glove.
γαργαλίζω [gargaleezo] tickle || (μεταφ) tempt, allure.
γαργάρα, η [gargara] gargle.
γαρδένια, η [garĎeneea] gardenia.
γαρίδα, η [gareeĎa] shrimp, prawn.
γαρνίρισμα, το [garneereesma] adornment, garnishing, decoration.
γαρνίρω [garneero] garnish, trim.
γαρνιτούρα, η [garneetoura] garniture, trimming.
γαρυφαλιά, η [gareefalia] carnation || (μπαχαρικό) clove tree.
γαρύφαλλο, το [gareefalo] carnation || (μπαχαρικό) clove.
γαστραλγία, η [gastralyeea] stomachache.
γαστρικός [gastreekos] gastric.
γαστρίτιδα, η [gastreeteeĎa] gastritis.
γαστρονομία, η [gastronomeea] gastronomy.
γάτα, η [gata] cat.
γαυγίζω [gavyeezo] bark.
γαύγισμα, το [gavyeesma] barking, baying.
γδάρσιμο, το [gĎarseemo] (πράξη) flaying || (αποτέλεσμα) scratch.
γδέρνω [gĎerno] flay, skin || (μεταφ) fleece.
γδύνομαι [gĎeenome] get undressed, strip.
γδύνω [gĎeeno] undress || (μεταφ) rob.
γεγονός, το [yegonos] event, fact.
γειά, η [ya] health || ~ **σας** hello || so long, goodbye.

γείσο, το [yeeso] (αρχιτεκ) eaves || cornice || (κασκέτου) peak.
γειτονεύω [yeetonevo] be close to, be adjoining.
γειτονιά, η [yeetonia] neighbourhood, vicinity.
γελαστός [yelastos] smiling, pleasant, cheerful.
γελάω [yelao] βλ **γελώ**.
γελιέμαι [yelieme] be deceived, be mistaken.
γέλιο, το [yeleeo] laugh, laughter.
γελοιογραφία, η [yeleeografeea] caricature, cartoon.
γελοιοποίηση, η [yeleeopieesee] ridicule, derision.
γελοιοποιούμαι [yeleeopeeoume] make o.s. ridiculous.
γελοιοποιώ [yeleeopeeo] make ridiculous, ridicule.
γελοίος [yeleeos] ludicrous, ridiculous.
γελώ [yelo] laugh || (μάτια κτλ) smile, twinkle || (εξαπατώ) deceive, take in.
γεμάτος [yematos] full || (δρόμος κτλ) crowded, swarming || (όπλο, δένδρο κτλ) loaded || (δωμάτιο κτλ) packed, crammed || (παχύς) stout, plump.
γεμίζω [yemeezo] fill up || (πλοίο) load || (μαξιλάρι κτλ) stuff || (συμπληρώνω) fill out.
γέμισμα, το [yemeesma] filling || (στρώματος) stuffing || (φεγγαριού) waxing || (όπλου) charging, loading.
γεμιστός [yemeestos] stuffed.
Γενάρης [yenarees] January.
γενεά, η [yenea] race, generation, breed.
γενεαλογία, η [yenealoyeea] genealogy, lineage, pedigree.
γενέθλια, τα [yenethleea] πλ birthday, anniversary.
γενειάς, η [yenias] beard.
γενειοφόρος, ο [yeneeoforos] bearded.
γένεση, η [yenesee] origin, birth || (εκκλ) Genesis.
γενέτειρα, η [yeneteera] native country, birthplace.
γενετή, η [yenetee]: **εκ γενετής** from birth.
γενετήσιος [yeneteeseeos] productive, generative, sexual.
γενίκευση, η [yeneekevsee] generalization.
γενικεύω [yeneekevo] generalize.
γενική [yeneekee] general, universal, wide || (γραμμ) genitive (case) || βλ και **γενικός**.
γενικός [yeneekos] general || βλ και **γενική**.
γενικότητα, η [yeneekoteeta] generality.
γέννα, η [yena] birth, childbirth || (μεταφ) breed.

γενναιοδωρία, η [yeneodoreea] generosity.

γενναιόδωρος [yeneodoros] generous, magnanimous.

γενναίος [yeneos] courageous, brave.

γενναιότητα, η [yeneoteeta] courage, bravery.

γενναιοφροσύνη, η [yeneofroseenee] generosity, liberality.

γενναιόφρων, ο [yeneofron] magnanimous, liberal.

γενναιόψυχος [yeneopseehos] generous, brave.

γέννημα, το [yeneema] offspring, product || (μωρό) progeny.

γέννηση, η [yeneesee] birth.

γεννητικός [yeneeteekos] genital, sexual.

γεννήτρια, η [yeneetreea] generator.

γεννώ [yeno] (για γυναίκα) give birth to, bring forth || (για άλογα) drop a foal || (για κουνέλια, γουρούνια) litter || (για πτηνά) lay || (μεταφ) create, breed, cause.

γεννώμαι [yenome] be born.

γένος, το [yenos] race, family, line || το ανθρώπινο ~ mankind || (ζώων, φυτών) kind, species || (γραμμ) gender.

γερά [yera] strongly, hard, vigorously.

γεράκι, το [yerakee] hawk.

γεράματα, τα [yeramata] πλ old age.

γεράνι, το [yeranee] geranium.

γερανός, ο [yeranos] (πτηνό) crane || (μηχάνημα) crane, winch.

γερατειά [yeratia] βλ **γεράματα.**

Γερμανία, η [yermaneea] Germany.

γερμανικός [yermaneekos] German.

Γερμανός, ο [yermanos] German.

γέρνω [yerno] lean, bend || (για βάρκα κτλ) lean, tilt || (για ήλιο κτλ) go down, sink.

γερνώ [yerno] age, grow old.

γεροντικός [yeronteekos] senile.

γεροντοκόρη, η [yerontokoree] old maid, spinster.

γεροντοπαλήκαρο, το [yerontopaleekaro] old bachelor.

γέρος, ο [yeros] old man.

γερός [yeros] (άνθρωπος) vigorous, sturdy || (κράση) sound, healthy || (τροφή) solid, substantial, hearty || (ξύλο) sound || (πάτωμα) solid, firm || (τοίχος) strong || (επιχείρημα) strong, valid.

γερουσία, η [yerouseea] senate.

γερουσιαστής, ο [yerouseeastees] senator.

γεύμα, το [yevma] meal, dinner.

γεύομαι [yevome] taste, try.

γεύση, η [yevsee] taste, flavour.

γέφυρα, η [yefeera] bridge.

γεφυρώνω [yefeerono] bridge || build a bridge.

γεωγραφία, η [yeografeea] geography.

γεωγράφος, ο [yeografos] geographer.

γεώδης [yeodees] earthy.

γεωλογία, η [yeoloyeea] geology.

γεωλόγος, ο [yeologos] geologist.

γεωμετρία, η [yeometreea] geometry.

γεωμετρικός [yeometreekos] geometric(al).

γεωπονία, η [yeoponeea] agriculture.

γεωργία, η [yeoryeea] agriculture, farming.

γεωργικός [yeoryeekos] agricultural.

γεωργός, ο [yeorgos] farmer.

γεώτρηση, η [yeotreesee] drilling.

γεωτρύπανο, το [yeotreepano] drill.

γη, η [yee] earth, land, ground.

γηγενής [yeegenees] native, indigenous.

γήινος [yeeinos] earthly, terrestrial.

γήπεδο, το [yeepedo] ground, sportsground.

γήρας, το [yeeras] old age.

για [ya] for, because of, on behalf of || γι' αυτό therefore || ~ καλά for certain, for good || ~ την ώρα for the time being || ~ πού whither? || ~ το Θεο for God's sake || (επίρ) as, for || (συνδ) ~ να in order to || ~ φαντάσου! fancy that! || ~ πες μου tell me.

γιαγιά, η [yayia] grandmother.

γιακάς, ο [yakas] collar.

γιαλός, ο [yalos] seashore.

γιαούρτι, το [yaourtee] yoghurt.

γιασεμί, το [yasemee] jasmine.

γιατί [yatee] why? || (συνδ) because.

γιατρεύω [yatrevo] cure, heal, treat.

γιατρός, ο [yatros] doctor.

γιγάντιος [yeeganteeos] gigantic.

γιγαντόσωμος [yeegandosomos] huge (in size).

γίγας, ο [yeegas] giant.

γίδα, η [yeeda] goat.

γιδοβοσκός, ο [yeedovoskos] goatherd.

γιλέκο, το [yeeleko] waistcoat.

γίνομαι [yeenome] be done, become || (μεγαλώνω) grow || (στρέφω) turn || (γεγονός κτλ) happen, occur || (ωριμάζω) ripen || ~ καλά recover || τι γίνεσαι; how are you?

γινόμενο, το [yeenomenon] product.

Γιουγκοσλαβία, η [yougoslaveea] Yugoslavia.

γιουγκοσλαβικός [yougoslaveekos] Yugoslavian.

Γιουγκοσλάβος, ο [yougoslavos] Yugoslav.

γιουχαΐζω [youhaeezo] hoot, jeer.

γιρλάντα, η [yeerlanta] garland, wreath.

γιωτ, το [yot] yacht.

γκαβός [gavos] cross-eyed || (κατ επέκτασιν) blind.

γκάζι, το [gazee] gas || πατώ ~ step on the gas.

γκαζιέρα, η [gaziera] cooking stove, primus stove.

γκαζόζα, η [gazoza] lemonade.

γκαρίζω [gareezo] bray.

γκαρσόνι, το [garsonee] waiter.

γκαρσονιέρα, η [garsoniera] bachelor flat.

γκάφα, η [gafa] blunder.

γκέμι, το [gemee] bridle, reins.

γκίνια, η [geeneea] bad luck.

γκιώνης, ο [geeonees] (scops) owl.

γκουβερνάντα, η [gouvernanta] governess.

γκρεμίζω [gremeezo] demolish, pull down, wreck.

γκρεμίζομαι [gremeezvome] fall, crumble, collapse.

γκρεμνός [gremnos] sheer drop, crag.

γκρίζος [greezos] grey.

γκρίνια, η [greeneea] grumble, nag, murmur.

γκρινιάζω [greeneeazo] complain, nag, grumble.

γλάρος, ο [glaros] seagull.

γλάστρα, η [glastra] flowerpot.

γλαύκωμα, το [glavkoma] glaucoma.

γλαφυρός [glafeeros] elegant, graceful.

γλείφω [gleefo] lick.

γλεντζές, ο [glenõzes] fun-loving person, reveller.

γλέντι, το [glenδee] party, feast.

γλεντώ [glenδo] amuse || (απολαμβάνω) enjoy || (επί χρημάτων) squander.

γλεύκος, το [glevkos] must.

γλιστερός [gleesteros] slippery.

γλίστρημα, το [gleestreema] slide, slip || (μεταφ) blunder, mistake.

γλιστρώ [gleestro] slide, slip || (μεταφ) slip away.

γλοιώδης [gleeoδes] slimy, sticky || (πρόσωπο) slippery.

γλόμπος, ο [glombos] globe.

γλουτός, ο [gloutos] buttock, rump.

γλύκα, η [gleeka] sweetness.

γλυκά, τα [gleeka] πλ pastries, confectionery.

γλυκαίνω [gleekeno] sweeten, make mild, soften.

γλυκάνισο, το [gleekaneeso] anise.

γλύκισμα, το [gleekeesma] cake, pastry.

γλυκομίλητος [gleekomeeleetos] soft-spoken, affable.

γλυκομιλώ [gleekomeelo] speak tenderly, speak kindly.

γλυκό, το [gleeko] jam, sweetmeat.

γλυκόξινος [gleekokseenos] bittersweet.

γλυκοχάραγμα, το [gleekoharagma] daybreak, twilight.

γλυκός [gleeko] affable, sweet ||

(καιρός) mild || (φως) subdued, mellow || (χρώμα) delicate || (ήχος) soft, sweet || (κρασί) sweet || (όνειρα) pleasant.

γλύπτης, ο [gleeptees] sculptor.

γλυπτική, η [gleepteekee] sculpture.

γλυπτός [gleeptos] sculptured, carved.

γλυτώνω [gleetono] save, deliver || (αμεταβ) escape.

γλύφω [gleefo] βλ γλείφω.

γλώσσα, η [glossa] tongue, language || (ψάρι) sole.

γλωσσάς, ο [glossas] chatterbox, gossip.

γλωσσικός [glosseekos] linguistic.

γλωσσολογία, η [glossologeea] linguistics.

γλωσσολόγος, ο [glossologos] linguist.

γλωσσομαθής [glossomathees] polyglot, linguist.

γνάθος, ο [gnathos] jaw.

γνέθω [gnetho] spin.

γνήσιος [gneeseeos] genuine, real || (παιδί) legitimate.

γνησίως [gneeseeos] genuinely, authentically.

γνωμάτευση, η [gnomatevsee] opinion, adjudication.

γνώμη, η [gnomee] opinion, view.

γνωμικό, το [gnomeeko] maxim, saying, adage.

γνωμοδότης, ο [gnomoδotees] adviser, councillor.

γνωμοδοτώ [gnomoδoto] give one's opinion, judge.

γνώμων, ο [gnomon] set square, level || (μεταφ) criterion, model.

γνωρίζω [gnoreezo] let it be known, inform || (έχω γνώση) know, be aware of || (αναγνωρίζω) discern, distinguish || (έχω σχέσεις) know, be acquainted with || (παρουσιάζω κάποιο) introduce.

γνωριμία, η [gnoreemeea] acquaintance, familiarity.

γνώριμος [gnoreemos] known, intimate.

γνώρισμα, το [gnoreesma] sign, mark, indication.

γνώση, η [gnosee] knowledge, notion || γνώσεις πλ knowledge, learning.

γνώστης, ο [gnostees] expert, connoisseur, specialist.

γνωστικός [gnosteekos] prudent.

γνωστοποίηση, η [gnostopieesee] notification, announcement.

γνωστοποιώ [gnostopeeo] notify, inform, advise.

γνωστός [gnostos] known || (φίλος) acquaintance.

γογγύλη, η [gongeelee] turnip.

γοερός [goeros] plaintive, woeful.

γόης, ο [goees] charmer.

γοητεία, η [goeeteea] charm || attractiveness.

γοπτευτικός [goeetevteekos] charming, captivating.

γοπτεύω [goeetevo] charm, attract.

γόπτρο, το [goeetro] prestige, reputation.

γομάρι, το [gomaree] load || (μεταφ) simpleton, beast.

γόμμα, η [gomma] gum || (σβυσήματος) india rubber, eraser.

γόμωση, η [gomosee] stuffing || (όπλο) charge.

γονατίζω [gonateezo] (make to) kneel || (μεταφ) humble || (αμεταβ) kneel down || (μεταφ) give way, yield.

γονατιστά [gonateesta] on one's knees, kneeling.

γόνατο, το [gonato] knee.

γονεάς, ο [goneas] father || γονείς πλ parents.

γονιμοποίηση, η [goneemopieesee] fertilization, impregnation.

γονιμοποιώ [goneemopeeo] fecundate, fertilize.

γόνιμος [goneemos] fertile, prolific || (μεταφ) inventive.

γονιμότητα, η [goneemoteeta] fecundity, fertility.

γόνος, ο [gonos] child, offspring || (σπέρμα) sperm, seed.

γόπα, η [gopa] bogue (fish) || (τσιγάρου) cigarette butt.

γοργός [gorgos] rapid, quick.

γορίλλας, ο [goreelas] gorilla.

γούβα, η [gouva] cavity, hole.

γουδί, το [goudee] mortar.

γουδοχέρι, το [goudoheree] pestle.

γουλί, το [goulee] stalk, stump || (μεταφ) bald.

γουλιά, η [goulia] sip.

γούνα, η [gouna] fur.

γουργουρητό, το [gourgoureeto] rumbling, rumble.

γούρι, το [gouree] good luck.

γουρλώνω [gourlono] open (eyes) wide, goggle.

γουρούνι, το [gourounee] pig, hog.

γουρσούζης, ο [goursouzees] luckless person, unlucky person.

γουρσουζιά, η [goursoozia] bad luck.

γουστάρω [goustaro] desire, feel like || (ευχαριστούμαι) delight in, enjoy.

γούστο, το [gousto] taste || (φιλοκαλία) good taste || για ~ for the hell of it.

γοφός, ο [gofos] haunch, hip.

Γραικός, ο [grekos] Greek.

γράμμα, το [gramma] letter, character.

γραμμάριο, το [grammareeo] gram(me).

γραμματεία, η [grammateea] secretariat, secretary's office.

γραμματέας, ο [grammateas] secretary.

γραμματική, η [grammateekee] grammar.

γραμμάτιο, το [grammateeo] bill of exchange || (χρεωστικό) promissory note.

γραμματοκιβώτιο, το [grammatokeevoteeo] letterbox, postbox.

γραμματόσημο, το [grammatoseemo] (postage) stamp.

γραμμένος [grammenos] written || (μεταφ) destined.

γραμμή, η [grammee] line, row || (έπιρ) straight, in a row || πρώτης ~ς first-class.

γραμμικός [grameekos] linear.

γραμμόφωνο, το [grammofono] gramophone.

γρανίτης, ο [graneetees] granite.

γραπτός [graptos] written.

γραπτώς [graptos] in writing.

γραπώνω [grapono] seize, snatch.

γρασίδι, το [graseedee] grass.

γρατσουνίζω [gratsouneezo] scratch.

γρατσούνισμα, το [gratsouneesma] scratch.

γραφειοκράτης, ο [grafeeokratees] bureaucrat.

γραφειοκρατία, η [grafeeokrateea] bureaucracy.

γραφείο, το [grafeeo] desk, bureau || (δωμάτιο) study || (ίδρυμα) office, bureau.

γραφικός [grafeekos] of writing, clerical || (μεταφ) picturesque, colourful.

γραφικότης, η [grafeekotees] picturesqueness, vividness.

γραφίτης, ο [grafeetees] graphite.

γραφομηχανή, η [grafomeehanee] typewriter.

γράφω [grafo] write, record, compose || enrol.

γράψιμο, το [grapseemo] writing.

γρήγορα [greegora] quickly, promptly.

γρηγορώ [greegoro] watch, be alert || be awake.

γριά, η [grea] old woman.

γρίλλια, η [greeleea] grille.

γρίππη, η [greepee] influenza.

γρίφος, ο [greefos] riddle, puzzle, enigma.

γριφώδης [greefodees] enigmatic(al), obscure.

γροθιά [grothia] fist || punch.

γρονθοκόπημα, το [gronthokopeema] boxing, punch.

γρονθοκοπώ [gronthokopo] punch, pound.

γρουσούζης [groosoozees] βλ γουρσούζης.

γρυλισμός, ο [greeleesmos] grunting, snorting.

γρυλλίζω [greeleezo] grunt, squeal.

γρύλλος, ο [greelos] piglet || (έντομο) cricket || (μηχάνημα) jack.

γυάλα, η [yeeala] glass, jar || (ψαριών) bowl.

γυαλάδα, η [yeealaδa] brilliance, shine, gloss.

γυαλάδικο, το [yeealaδeeko] glassware || glass works.

γυαλένιος [yeealeneeos] glass.

γυαλί, το [yeealee] glass || πλ spectacles, glasses.

γυαλίζω [yeealeezo] polish, shine.

γυάλισμα, το [yeealeesma] polishing, glazing.

γυαλιστερός [yeealeesteros] polished, glossy.

γυαλόχαρτο, το [yeealoharto] glasspaper, sandpaper.

γυιός, ο [yos] son.

γυμνάζομαι [yeemnazome] train o.s., exercise, practise.

γυμνάζω [yeemnazo] exercise, train, drill.

γυμνασιάρχης, ο [yeemnaseearhees] secondary school headmaster.

γυμνάσια, τα [yeemnaseea] πλ manoeuvres.

γυμνάσιο, το [yeemnaseeo] secondary school, high school.

γυμναστήριο, το [yeemnasteereeo] gymnasium.

γυμναστής, ο [yeemnastees] P.T. instructor.

γυμναστική, η [yeemnasteekee] πλ gymnastics || exercise.

γύμνια, η [yeemneea] nudity, nakedness || poverty.

γυμνιστής, η [yeemneestees] nudist.

γυμνός [yeemnos] naked, bare, nude.

γυμνώνω [yeemnono] bare, expose || (μεταφ) strip.

γύμνωση, η [yeemnosee] disrobing || denudation || fleecing.

γυναίκα, η [yeeneka] woman || (σύζυγος) wife.

γυναικάς, ο [yeenekas] woman-chaser, rake.

γυναικείος [yeenekeeos] womanly, feminine.

γυναικολογία, η [yeenekologeea] gynaecology.

γυναικολόγος, ο [yeenekologos] gynaecologist.

γυναικόπαιδα, τα [yeenekopeδa] πλ women and children.

γυναικοπρεπής [yeenekoprepees] womanly, effeminate, womanish.

γυναικωνίτης, ο [yeenekoneetees] harem.

γυνή [yeenee] βλ γυναίκα.

γύπος, ο [yeepas] vulture.

γυρεύω [yeerevo] ask for, call for || (ελεημοσύνη) beg for || (να βρω κάτι) look for, seek || (αποζημίωση κτλ) claim || (διαζύγιο) apply for || (βοήθεια) request.

γυρίζω [yeereezo] turn, rotate, revolve || (σβούρα) spin || (στρέφω) turn || (αναστρέφω) turn || (επιστρέφω) return || (αμεταβ) turn, rotate || (ταινία) shoot.

γύρισμα, το [yeereesma] turn, revolution || (δρόμου, ποταμού) turn, twist, winding.

γυρισμός, ο [yeereesmos] return, coming back.

γυριστός [yeereestos] curved, turned up, crooked.

γυρνάω [yeernao] βλ γυρίζω.

γυρολόγος, ο [yeerologos] hawker, pedlar.

γύρος, ο [yeeros] circle, circumference || (φορέματος) hem || (περιστροφή) turn, revolution || (περπάτημα) walk || (βαρελιού) hoop.

γυρτός [yeertos] bent, inclined, curved.

γύρω [yeero] round, around, about, round about.

γυφτιά, η [yeeftia] stinginess, avarice, shabbiness.

γύφτος, ο [yeeftos] gipsy.

γύψινος [yeepseenos] plaster.

γύψος, ο [yeepsos] plaster of Paris.

γυψώνω [yeepsono] plaster.

γωνία, η [goneea] angle, corner || (εργαλείο) square, set square || (απόμερος τόπος) nook, den || (ψωμιού) crust of bread.

γωνιακός [goneeakos] angular || (της γωνίας) corner.

γωνιόλιθος, ο [goneeoleethos] cornerstone.

γωνιώδης [goneeoδees] angular.

Δ, δ

δα [δa] (indeclinable particle) όχι ~ certainly not! || τόσος ~ only so tall, so small.

δάγκωμα, το [δangoma] bite.

δαγκώνω [δangono] bite.

δαδί, το [δaδee] pinewood, firewood.

δαίδαλος, ο [δeδalos] labyrinthine, intricate, complicated.

δαιμονίζω [δemoneezo] enrage, infuriate.

δαιμονισμένος [δemoneesmenos] (μεταφ) mischievous || possessed.

δαιμόνιο, το [δemoneeo] genius || (διάβολος) demon, fiend.

δαιμόνιος [δemoneeos] very clever, marvellous, divine.

δαίμων, ο [δemon] demon, devil, fiend.

δάκρυ, το [δakree] tear.

δακρύζω [δakreezo] shed tears, weep || (επί φυτών) sweat.

δακτυλήθρα, η [δakteeleethra] thimble.

δακτυλίδι, το [δakteeleeδee] ring.

δακτυλικός [δakteeleekos] digital, dactylic.

δάκτυλο, το [δakteelo] βλ δάκτυλος.

δακτυλογράφος, ο, η [δakteelografos] typist.

δάκτυλος, ο [δakteelos] finger || (ποδιού) toe || (μονάς μήκους) inch.

δαμάζω [δamazo] tame, subdue.

δαμαλισμός, ο [δamaleesmos] vaccination.

δαμάσκηνο, το [δamaskeeno] plum || (ξηρό) prune.

δανείζομαι [δaneezome] borrow.

δανείζω [δaneezo] lend, loan.

δάνειο, το [δaneeo] loan.

δανειστής, ο [δaneestees] lender, creditor.

Δανία, η [δaneea] Denmark.

δανικός [δaneekos] Danish.

Δανός, ο [δanos] Dane.

δαντέλλα, η [δantella] lace.

δαπάνη, η [δapanee] expenditure, expense, cost.

δαπανηρός [δapaneeros] costly, expensive.

δαπανώ [δapano] spend, consume.

δάπεδο, το [δapeδo] floor || ground.

δαρμός, ο [δarmos] βλ δάρσιμο.

δάρσιμο, το [δarseemo] beating || (γάλακτος) churning.

δασκάλα, η [δaskala] teacher, schoolmistress.

δασκαλεύω [δaskalevo] coach, teach.

δάσκαλος, ο [δaskalos] teacher, schoolmaster.

δασμολόγιο, το [δasmoloyeeo] tariff.

δασμός, ο [δasmos] tax, (customs) duty.

δάσος, το [δasos] forest, woodland.

δασύς, ο [δasees] thick, bushy, hairy.

δασώδης [δasoδees] wooded, woody.

δαυλί, το [δavlee] torch, firebrand.

δάφνη, η [δafnee] laurel, bay tree, bay.

δε [δe] and || but || on the other hand || ο μεν... ο ~ the one... the other.

δεδομένα, τα [δeδomena] πλ data, facts.

δεδουλεμένος [δeδoulemenos]: ~ τόκος accrued interest.

δέηση, η [δeesee] prayer, supplication.

δείγμα, το [δeegma] sample, specimen || (ένδειξη) token, sign.

δειγματολόγιο, το [δeegmatoloyeeo] sample, collection.

δεικνύω [δeekneeo] show, point out || (επί οργάνων) mark, indicate.

δείκτης, ο [δeektees] indicator || (χειρός) forefinger || (ωρολογίου) hand || (ζυγού) index, cock || (πυξίδος) needle.

δεικτικός [δeekteekos] indicative || (γραμμ) demonstrative.

δειλά [δeela] timidly, faint-heartedly.

δείλι, το [δeelee] (late) afternoon.

δειλία, η [δeeleea] timidity, cowardice.

δειλιάζω [δeeleeazo] lose courage, be afraid.

δειλινό, το [δeeleeno] (late) afternoon.

δειλός [δeelos] timid || cowardly, fainthearted.

δεινός [δeenos] horrid || (ικανός) able, clever, expert.

δεισιδαιμονία, η [δeeseeδemoneea] superstition.

δεισιδαίμων [δeeseeδemon] superstitious.

δείχνω [δeehno] βλ δεικνύω.

δέκα [δeka] ten.

δεκάδα, η [δekaδa] set of ten.

δεκαδικός [δekaδeekos] decimal.

δεκαετηρίδα, η [δekaeteereeδa] decade || (εορτή) tenth anniversary.

δεκαετής, ο, η [δekaetees] ten-year-old.

δεκαετία, η [δekaeteea] ten years, decade.

δεκάζω [δekazo] corrupt, bribe.

δεκάλογος, ο [δekalogos] Decalogue, Ten Commandments.

δεκανέας, ο [δekaneas] corporal.

δεκανίκι, το [δekaneekee] crutch.

δεκαπενθήμερο, το [δekapentheemero] fortnight.

δεκαπλάσιος [δekaplaseeos] tenfold.

δεκάρα [δekara] one tenth of a drachma.

δεκάρι, το [δekaree] ten-drachma piece || (στα χαρτιά) ten.

δεκασμός, ο [δekasmos] bribery, corruption.

δέκατος [δekatos] tenth.

Δεκέμβριος, ο [δekemvreeos] December.

δέκτης, ο [δektees] receiver.

δεκτικός [δekteekos] capable of, susceptible to, receptive to.

δεκτός [δektos] accepted || (γνώμη) admissible.

δελεάζω [δeleazo] tempt, entice, bait.

δελεαστικός [δeleasteekos] tempting, attractive.

δέλτα, το [δelta] (γράμμα) delta || (ποταμού) delta.

δελτίο, το [δelteeo] bulletin || (υγείας) report || (ψηφοδέλτιο) ballot.

δελφίνι, το [δelfeenee] dolphin.

δέμα, το [δema] (πάκο) bale, bundle || (ταχυδρομικό) parcel.

δεμάτι, το [δematee] bundle || (καρότων κτλ) bunch || (φρυγάνων) faggot.

δε(ν) [δe(n)] (negative particle) no, not.

δενδρολίβανο, το [δenδroleevano] rosemary.

δένδρο, το [δenδro] tree.

δενδρόφυτος [δenδrofeetos] full of trees, wooded.

δένω [δeno] bind, tie || (με αλυσίδα) chain, link || (γραβάτα κτλ) tie || (βιβλίο) bind || (προσδένω) fasten, fix || (καράβι) moor, berth || (γλυκό κτλ) thicken || (μεταφ) bind.

δεξαμενή, η [δeksamenee] tank, reservoir || (ναυτ) dock, basin.

δεξιά, η [δeksia] right hand || (πολιτ) right wing || (έπιρ) to the right.

δεξιός [δekseeos] right || right-handed || (πολιτ) right-wing || (επιτήδειος) clever.

δεξιότητα, η [δekseeoteeta] skilfulness, cleverness.

δεξιόχειρας, ο [δekseeoheeras] right-handed (person).

δεξιώνομαι [δekseeonome] receive, welcome.

δεξίωση, η [δekseeosee] reception.

δέον, το [δeon] what is necessary.

δεόντως [δeondos] suitably, fitly, properly.

δέος, το [δeos] awe, fear, fright.

δέρας, το [δeras]: **το χρυσόμαλλον ~** the golden fleece.

δέρμα, το [δerma] skin, pelt || leather.

δερμάτινος [δermateenos] of leather.

δερματίτιδα, η [δermateeδa] dermatitis.

δέρνω [δerno] beat, flog || (γάλα) churn.

δέσιμο, το [δeseemo] tying, binding || bandage.

δεσμά, τα [δesma] πλ chains, fetters, bonds.

δέσμευση, η [δesmevsee] tying, binding.

δεσμεύω [δesmevo] bind by a promise, pledge.

δέσμη, η [δesmee] bunch || (φύλλων) bundle.

δέσμιος, ο [δesmeeos] prisoner, captive.

δεσμός, ο [δesmos] tie, bond.

δεσμοφύλακας, ο [δesmofeelakas] prison warder.

δεσπόζω [δespozo] dominate, rule || (υπέρκειμαι) tower above, overlook || (μεταφ) rise above.

δεσποινίς, η [δespeenees] young lady || Miss.

δεσπότης, ο [δespotees] ruler, master || (έκκλ) (arch)bishop.

δεσποτικός [δespoteekos] despotic.

δετός [δetos] tied, bound.

Δευτέρα, η [δevtera] Monday.

δευτερεύων [δevterevon] secondary || subordinate.

δευτεροβάθμιος [δevterovathmeeos] second-degree.

δευτερόλεπτο, το [δevterolepto] second.

δεύτερος [δevteros] second || (σε ποιότητα) inferior.

δευτερότοκος [δevterotokos] second-born.

δέχομαι [δehome] accept, receive || (παραδέχομαι) approve || (δεξιούομαι)

welcome, greet || (υφίσταμαι) receive || (ανέχομαι) tolerate.

δήθεν [δeethen] apparently, as if, so-called.

δηκτικός [δeekteekos] biting, scathing.

δηλαδή [δeelaδee] that is to say, namely, viz.

δηλητηριάζω [δeeleeteereeazo] poison || (μεταφ) corrupt, taint.

δηλητηρίαση [δeeleeteereeasee] poisoning || (μεταφ) corruption.

δηλητήριο, το [δeeleeteereeo] poison, venom.

δηλώνω [δeelono] declare, state || (γέννηση κτλ) register, give notice || (αμπόρευμα) enter (goods).

δήλωση, η [δeelosee] declaration, statement || (γέννηση κτλ) register.

δημαγωγία, η [δeemagoyeea] demagogy.

δημαρχείο, το [δeemarheeo] town hall || city hall (US).

δήμαρχος, ο [δeemarhos] mayor.

δήμευση, η [δeemevsee] confiscation.

δημεύω [δeemevo] confiscate, seize.

δημητριακός [δeemeetreeakos]: **τα δημητριακά** cereals, crops.

δήμιος, ο [δeemeeos] executioner, hangman.

δημιουργία, η [δeemeeouryeea] creation.

δημιουργικός [δeemeeouryeekos] creative.

δημιουργός, ο [δeemeeourgos] creator.

δημιουργώ [δeemeeourgo] create || establish.

δημοδιδάσκαλος, ο [δeemoδeeδaskalos] primary schoolteacher.

δημοκράτης, ο [δeemokratees] democrat.

δημοκρατία, η [δeemokrateea] democracy || republic.

δημοκρατικός [δeemokrateekos] democratic, republican.

δημοπρασία, η [δeemopraseea] auction.

δήμος, ο [δeemos] municipality.

δημοσία [δeemoseea] (επιρ) publicly.

δημοσίευμα, το [δeemosievma] newspaper article, publication.

δημοσίευση, η [δeemosievsee] publication.

δημοσιεύω [δeemosievo] publish, make known.

δημοσιογράφος, ο [δeemoseeografos] journalist, reporter.

δημόσιο, το [δeemoseeo] the state, the public.

δημόσιος [δeemoseeos] public || (κρατικός) national.

δημοσιότητα, η [δeemoseeoteeta] publicity.

δημότης, ο [deemotees] citizen.

δημοτική, η [deemoteekee] demotic (Greek).

δημοτικός [deemoteekos] municipal || (δημοφιλής) popular.

δημοτικότητα, η [deemoteekoteeta] popularity.

δημοφιλής [deemofeelees] popular, well-liked.

δημοψήφισμα, το [deemopseefeesma] plebiscite.

δημώδης [deemoðees] popular, folk.

διά [ðia] for, by, with, about || (μετά γενικής) through, across, by means of || ~ **παντός** forever || ~ **μιας** at one go || ~ **θαλάσσης** by sea.

διαβάζω [ðeeavazo] read, study || (μετά προσοχής) peruse.

διαβάθμιση, η [ðeeavathmeesee] grading, graduation.

διαβάλλω [ðeeavalo] slander, defame, calumniate.

διάβαση, η [ðeeavasee] crossing, passage || (στενό) pass, ford.

διάβασμα, το [ðeeavasma] reading, lecture || studying.

διαβασμένος [ðeevasmenos] learned, prepared (for examination).

διαβατήριο, το [ðeevateereeo] passport.

διαβάτης, ο [ðeeavatees] passer-by.

διαβατός [ðeeavatos] passable || (ποταμού) fordable.

διαβεβαιώνω [ðeeaveveono] assure, assert, affirm.

διαβεβαίωση, η [ðeeaveveosee] assurance, affirmation.

διάβημα, το [ðeeaveema] step, measure, move.

διαβήτης, ο [ðeeaveetees] pair of compasses || (ιατρ) diabetes.

διαβιβάζω [ðeeaveevazo] transmit, forward, convey.

διαβίβαση, η [ðeeaveevasee] transmission, forwarding.

διαβιβρώσκω [ðeeaveevrosko] corrode || (σκουλίκι) eat into || (θάλασσα κτλ) erode.

διαβίωση, η [ðeeaveeosee] living.

διαβλέπω [ðeeavlepo] discern, penetrate, foresee.

διαβόητος [ðeeavoeetos] notorious.

διαβολεμένος [ðeeavolemenos] shrewd, cunning || (μεταφ) devilish.

διαβολή, η [ðeeavolee] slander, calumny.

διαβολικός [ðeeavoleekos] satanic, diabolical.

διάβολος, ο [ðeeavolos] devil, satan || (φασαρίας) noisy, boisterous.

διαβουλεύομαι [ðeeavoulevome] deliberate, confer || (μηχανορραφώ) plot.

διαβρέχω [ðeeavreho] wet, soak, steep.

διάβρωση, η [ðeeavrosee] corrosion.

διαγγέλλω [ðeeangelo] announce, notify.

διάγνωση, η [ðeeagnosee] diagnosis.

διάγραμμα, το [ðeeagrama] diagram, drawing, plan.

διαγραφή, η [ðeeagrafee] cancellation.

διαγράφω [ðeeagrafo] trace out || (σβήνω) efface, cancel.

διάγω [ðeeago] live, pass one's time.

διαγωγή, η [ðeeagoyee] behaviour, conduct, deportment.

διαγωνίζομαι [ðeeagoneezome] compete, contend.

διαγώνιος [ðeeagoneeos] diagonal.

διαγωνισμός, ο [ðeeagoneesmos] competition || (εξετάσεις) examination.

διαδέχομαι [ðeeaðehome] succeed, follow.

διάδηλος [ðeeaðeelos] manifest, evident.

διαδήλωση, η [ðeeaðeelosee] demonstration, manifestation.

διάδημα, το [ðeeaðeema] crown, diadem.

διαδίδω [ðeeaðeeðo] spread, circulate, propagate.

διαδικασία, η [ðeeaðeekaseea] procedure, legal inquiry.

διάδικος, ο [ðeeaðeekos] litigant.

διάδοση, η [ðeeaðosee] spreading || rumour.

διαδοχή, η [ðeeaðohee] succession.

διάδοχος, ο, η [ðeeaðohos] successor, crown prince.

διαδραματίζω [ðeeaðramateezo] play (a role), act.

διαδρομή, η [ðeeaðromee] course, distance || (εμβόλου) stroke.

διάδρομος, ο [ðeeaðromos] passage, corridor, hall.

διαζευκτικός [ðeeazevkteekos] (γραμμ) disjunctive.

διάζευξη, η [ðeeazevksee] separation, severance.

διαζύγιο, το [ðeeazeeyeeo] divorce.

διάζωμα, το [ðeeazoma] frieze.

διαθέσιμος [ðeeatheseemos] available, free.

διάθεση, η [ðeeathesee] arrangement, disposal || (κέφι) mood, humour.

διαθέτω [ðeeatheto] dispose, arrange || (χρησιμοποιώ) employ, use, make available || (διανέμω) allot.

διαθήκη, η [ðeeatheekee] will, testament.

διάθλαση, η [ðeeathlasee] refraction.

διαίρεση, η [ðieresee] division, separation || (μεταφ) discord, difference.

διαιρέτης, ο [ðieretees] divisor, divider.

διαιρώ [ðiero] divide, separate.

διαισθάνομαι [δiesthanome] feel, have a presentiment.
διαίσθηση, η [δiestheesee] presentiment.
δίαιτα, η [δieta] diet.
διαιτησία, η [δieteeseea] arbitration.
διαιτητής, ο [δieteetees] arbiter || (ποδοσφαίρου) referee || umpire.
διαιωνίζω [δieoneezo] perpetuate || protract.
διαιώνιση, η [δieoneesee] perpetuation.
διακαής [δeeakaees] ardent, fervent, eager.
διακανονίζω [δeeakanoneezo] regulate, adjust, settle.
διακατέχω [δeeakateho] possess.
διάκειμαι [δeeakeeme] be disposed, be inclined.
διακεκριμένος [δeeakekreemenos] distinguished, eminent.
διάκενος [δeeakenos] empty, hollow, vacant || το διάκενο void, vacuum.
διακήρυξη, η [δeeakeereeksee] declaration, proclamation.
διακηρύττω [δeeakeereeto] declare, proclaim, announce.
διακινδυνεύω [δeeakeenδeenevo] risk, endanger, hazard.
διακλάδωση, η [δeeakλaδosee] fork || (δρόμου κτλ) branch.
διακομίζω [δeeakomeezo] transport, carry.
διάκονος, ο [δeeakonos] deacon.
διακοπή, η [δeeakopee] suspension, interruption, recess || (ρεύματος) cut.
διακόπτης, ο [δeeakoptees] switch, stopcock.
διακόπτω [δeeakopto] suspend, cut off, interrupt, discontinue.
διάκος, ο [δeeakos] deacon.
διακόσμηση, η [δeeakosmeesee] decoration, embellishment.
διακοσμητής, ο [δeeakosmeetees] decorator.
διάκοσμος, ο [δeeakosmos] ornamentation, decoration.
διακοσμώ [δeeakosmo] decorate, adorn.
διακρίνω [δeeakreeno] discern, discriminate.
διάκριση, η [δeeakreesee] distinction || (κρίση) discretion.
διακύμανση, η [δeeakeemansee] fluctuation, undulation.
διακωμωδώ [δeeakomoδo] ridicule, satirize.
διαλαλώ [δeealalo] proclaim, cry out, broadcast.
διαλεγμένος [δeealegmenos] selected, chosen.
διαλέγω [δeealego] choose, select, pick out.
διάλειμμα, το [δeealeema] interval, recess || intermission.

διάλειψη, η [δeealeepsee] irregularity.
διαλεκτική, η [δeealekteekee] dialectics.
διαλεκτός [δeealektos] chosen, select.
διάλεκτος, η [δeealektos] dialect, idiom.
διάλεξη [δeealeksee] lecture || conversation.
διαλεύκανση, η [δeealevkansee] elucidation.
διαλλακτικός [δeealakteekos] conciliatory.
διαλογή, η [δeealoyee] sorting.
διαλογίζομαι [δeealoyeezome] meditate, consider.
διαλογισμός, ο [δeealoyeesmos] reflection, thought.
διάλογος, ο [δeealogos] dialogue, conversation.
διάλυμα, το [δeealeema] solution.
διάλυση, η [δeealeesee] dissolution, decomposition || (εντός υγρού) solution || (εταιρείας κτλ) liquidation || (στρατ) disbanding.
διαλυτός [δeealeetos] soluble, dissolvable.
διαλύω [δeealeeo] dissolve || (εταιρεία) liquidate || (συμβόλαιο κτλ) annul, cancel || (εχθρό) disband, defeat, scatter || (αμφιβολία κτλ) dispel.
διαμάντι, το [δeeamantee] diamond || διαμαντικά πλ jewellery, gems.
διαμαρτυρόμενος [δeeamarteeromenos] Protestant.
διαμαρτυρώ [δeeamarteero] protest.
διαμάχη, η [δeeamahee] dispute, fight.
διαμελίζω [δeeameleezo] dismember.
διαμένω [δeeameno] reside, live, stay.
διαμέρισμα, το [δeeamereesma] region, constituency, district || (οικία) apartment, flat.
διάμεσος [δeeamesos] intermediary, intermediate.
διαμέτρημα, το [δeeametreema] bore, calibre.
διάμετρος, η [δeeametros] diameter || gauge.
διαμοιράζω [δeeameerazo] distribute, share.
διαμονή, η [δeeamonee] stay, residence, sojourn.
διαμορφώνω [δeeamorfono] model, shape, form.
διανέμω [δeeanemo] distribute || divide.
διανόηση, η [δeeanoeesee] thought || intelligence.
διανοητικώς [δeeanoeeteekos] intellectually.
διάνοια, η [δeeaneea] intellect, mind.
διανοίγω [δeeaneego] open (up).
διανομέας, ο [δeeanomeas] distributor || (ταχυδρομικός) postman.

διανομή, n [ðeeanomee] distribution.

διανοούμενοι, οι [ðeeanooumenee] πλ intellectuals.

διανυκτερεύω [ðeeaneekterevo] spend the night || stay open all night.

διανύω [ðeeaneeo] go through, cover, terminate.

διαξιφισμός, ο [ðeeakseefeesmos] sword-thrust || fencing.

διαπασών, n, το [ðeeapason] tuning fork || (μουσ) octave.

διαπεραστικός [ðeeaperasteekos] piercing, sharp || (βροχή) drenching.

διαπερνώ [ðeeaperno] pierce, penetrate, pass through.

διαπιστευτήρια, τα [ðeeapeestevteereea] credentials.

διαπιστώνω [ðeeapeestono] ascertain, find out, confirm.

διαπίστωση, n [ðeeapeestosee] ascertainment.

διάπλαση, n [ðeeaplasee] (con)formation || moulding.

διαπλάσσω [ðeeaplaso] form, shape || (μεταφ) educate, train.

διάπλατα [ðeeaplata] wide-open.

διαπλάτυνση, n [ðeeaplateensee] widening.

διαπλέω [ðeeapleo] cross over, sail through.

διαπληκτισμός, ο [ðeeapleekteesmos] dispute, quarrel.

διαπνοή, n [ðeeapnoee] respiration.

διαποτίζω [ðeeapoteezo] soak, saturate.

διαπραγματεύομαι [ðeeapragmatevome] negotiate || discuss.

διαπραγμάτευση, n [ðeeapragmatevsee] negotiation.

διαπράττω [ðeeaprato] perpetrate, commit.

διαπρεπής [ðeeaprepees] eminent, distinguished.

διαπρέπω [ðeeaprepo] excel.

διάπυρος [ðeeapeeros] red-hot || (μεταφ) fervent, eager.

διάρθρωση, n [ðeearthrosee] articulation, joint, structure.

διάρκεια, n [ðeearkeea] duration.

διαρκώ [ðeearko] last, endure || continue.

διαρκώς [ðeearkos] continually, constantly, always.

διαρρέω [ðeeareo] traverse || (δοχείο) leak || (υγρού, νέα κτλ) leak out || (χρόνος) elapse, pass.

διαρρηγνύω [ðeeareegneeo] tear, burst open, break.

διάρρηξη, n [ðeeareeksee] breaking, rupture || (κλοπή) burglary.

διαρροή, n [ðeearoee] flow || (σωλήνος) leakage.

διάρροια, n [ðeeareea] diarrhoea.

διαρρυθμίζω [ðeeareethmeezo] arrange, regulate.

διαρρύθμιση, n [ðeeareethmeesee] arrangement, regulation.

διασαφηνίζω [ðeeasafeeneezo] clarify, elucidate.

διασαφήνιση, n [ðeeasafeeneesee] clarification, elucidation.

διασάφηση, n [ðeeasafeesee] βλ **διασαφήνιση**.

διάσειση, n [ðeeaseesee] concussion, shock.

διάσελο, το [ðeeaselo] pass.

διάσημος [ðeeaseemos] famous, celebrated, renowned.

διασκεδάζω [ðeeaskeðazo] scatter, dispel || (ψυχαγωγώ) divert, amuse || (αμεταβ) amuse o.s.

διασκέδαση, n [ðeeaskeðasee] dispersion || (ψυχαγωγία) entertainment.

διασκεδαστικός [ðeeaskeðasteekos] diverting, entertaining.

διασκευάζω [ðeeaskevazo] arrange, modify, alter.

διασκευή, n [ðeeaskevee] arrangement, adaptation, modification.

διάσκεψη, n [ðeeaskepsee] deliberation || conference.

διασκορπίζω [ðeeaskorpeezo] scatter, disperse || (χρήμα) waste.

διάσπαση, n [ðeeaspasee] distraction || (ατόμου) splitting.

διασπείρω [ðeeaspeero] disseminate, disperse, scatter || (μεταφ) circulate.

διασπορά, n [ðeeaspora] dispersion, scattering.

διασπώ [ðeeaspo] sever, rupture.

διασταλτικός [ðeeastalteekos] dilating, dilative.

διάσταση, n [ðeeastasee] separation, disagreement || (μέτρο) dimension.

διασταυρώνω [ðeeastavrono] cross || meet.

διασταύρωση, n [ðeeastavrosee] crossing || (δρόμων) intersection.

διαστέλλω [ðeeastelo] distinguish || (διανοίγω) distend, expand.

διάστημα, το [ðeeasteema] space, interval, period || **κατά διαστήματα** from time to time || at intervals.

διαστολή, n [ðeeastolee] distinction || (καρδιάς) diastole || (γραμμ) comma.

διαστρεβλώνω [ðeeastrevlono] twist, bend || (μεταφ) alter, distort.

διαστρέφω [ðeeastrefo] twist, bend || (μεταφ) pervert, corrupt.

διαστροφή, n [ðeeastrofee] perversion, distortion.

διασύρω [ðeeaseero] (μεταφ) defame, slander, backbite.

διασχίζω [ðeeasheezo] tear || (μεταφ) cross, travel through.

διασώζω [ðeeasozo] preserve, rescue, deliver.

διάσωση, η [δeeasosee] deliverance, rescue, preservation.

διαταγή, η [δeeatayee] order, command, instruction.

διάταγμα, το [δeeatagma] order, decree, edict.

διάταξη, η [δeeataksee] arrangement || (νόμου κτλ) provision.

διατάραξη, η [δeeataraksee] disturbance, upheaval.

διαταράσσω [δeeataraso] disturb, agitate.

διατάσσω [δeeataso] arrange || order, command.

διατείνομαι [δeeateenome] maintain, declare.

διατελώ [δeeatelo] be, stand.

διατέμνω [δeeatemno] intersect, split.

διατήρηση [δeeatereese] maintenance, preservation, conservation.

διατηρώ [δeeateero] hold, maintain || preserve, conserve || (ψυχραιμία) keep.

διατίμηση, η [δeeateemeesee] tariff, rate, price list.

διατιμώ [δeeateemo] fix the price of, regulate the sale of.

διατομή [δeeatomee] cross-cut, cut.

διατρέφω [δeeatrefo] keep, feed, support.

διατρέχω [δeeatreho] run through || (απόσταση) cover, traverse.

διάτρηση, η [δeeatreesee] perforation, drilling, cutting.

διάτρητος [δeeatreetos] perforated, drilled.

διατριβή, η [δeeatreevee] stay || (μελέτη) study, thesis || (ασχολία) pastime.

διατροφή, η [δeeatrofee] food, board || (επί διαζυγίου) alimony.

διατρυπώ [δeeatreepo] pierce, bore through.

διάττων, ο [δeeaton] shooting star.

διατυμπανίζω [δeeateembaneezo] divulge, let out, give away.

διατυπώνω [δeeateepono] formulate, state.

διαύγεια, η [δeeavyeea] clearness, transparency.

διαφαίνομαι [δeeafenome] show through, appear, come in sight.

διαφανής [δeeafanees] clear, transparent.

διαφέρω [δeeafero] be different from, differ.

διαφεύγω [δeeafevgo] escape, get away, evade.

διαφημίζω [δeeafeemeezo] advertise.

διαφήμιση, η [δeeafeemeesee] advertisement, advertising.

διαφθείρω [δeeaftheero] spoil, damage || (μεταφ) corrupt.

διαφθορά, η [δeeafthora] corruption, depravity.

διαφορά, η [δeeafora] difference || dissension, contention.

διαφορετικός [δeeaforeteekos] different, dissimilar.

διαφορικό, το [δeeaforeeko] differential.

διαφορικός [δeeaforeekos] differential.

διάφορο, το [δeeaforo] profit, interest, gain.

διαφοροποίηση, η [δeeaforopieesee] differentiation.

διάφορος [δeeaforos] different, various, mixed || τα διάφορα miscellaneous.

διάφραγμα, το [δeeafragma] partition || (ανατ) diaphragm.

διαφυγή η [δeeafeeyee] escape, evasion || (υγρού κτλ) leak, leakage.

διαφύλαξη, η [δeeafeelaksee] preservation, protection.

διαφυλάσσω [δeeafeelaso] preserve, protect, keep.

διαφωνία, η [δeeafoneea] discord, disagreement.

διαφωνώ [δeeafono] disagree, differ.

διαφωτίζω [δeeafoteezo] clear up || enlighten.

διαφώτιση, η [δeeafoteesee] enlightenment.

διαχειρίζομαι [δeeaheereezome] administer, manage, handle.

διαχείριση, η [δeeaheereesee] management, handling, administration.

διαχειριστής, ο [δeeaheereestees] administrator || (στρατ) pay corps officer.

διαχέω [δeeaheo] diffuse, give out.

διάχυση, η [δeeaheesee] diffusion || (μεταφ) effusiveness, gaiety.

διαχυτικός [δeeaheeteekos] effusive, gushing, demonstrative.

διάχυτος [δeeaheetos] diffuse.

διαχωρίζω [δeeaheoreezo] separate, divide.

διαχώριση, η [δeeaheoreesee] separation.

διαψεύδομαι [δeeapsevδome] contradict o.s., fail.

διαψεύδω [δeeapsevδo] deny, give the lie to || disappoint.

διάψευση, η [δeeapsevsee] denial, contradiction || disappointment.

διγαμία, η [δeegameea] bigamy.

δίγαμος, ο [δeegamos] bigamist.

δίγλωσσος [δeeglosos] bilingual.

δίδαγμα, το [δeeδagma] teaching, moral || (εκκλ) lesson.

διδακτικός [δeeδakteekos] instructive, didactic.

διδακτορική, η [δeeδaktoreekee] (διατριβή) doctorate.

δίδακτρα, τα [δeeδaktra] πλ tuition fees.

διδάκτωρ, ο [δeeδaktor] doctor.

διδασκαλία, η [δeeδaskeleea] teaching, instruction.

διδάσκω [δeeδasko] teach, instruct.

δίδυμος [δeeδeemos] twin.

διεγείρω [δieyeero] excite, rouse, incite.

διέγερση, η [δieyersees] excitation, stimulation.

διεζευγμένος [δiezevgmenos] divorced.

διεθνής [δiethnees] international.

διείσδυση, η [δieesδeesee] penetration, piercing.

διεισδύω [δieesδeeo] penetrate, enter, advance.

διεκδίκηση, η [δiekδeekeesee] claim, vindication.

διεκδικώ [δiekδeeko] claim, contest.

διεκπεραιώνω [δiekpereono] bring to a conclusion || (στέλλω) forward.

διεκπεραίωση, η [δiekpereosee] forwarding, consignment.

διεκφεύγω [δiekfevgo] slip away, escape.

διέλευση, η [δielevsee] crossing, passing.

διένεξη, η [δieneksee] dispute, quarrel.

διενεργώ [δienergo] operate, effect, hold.

διεξάγω [δieksago] conduct, accomplish, carry out.

διεξέρχομαι [δiekserhome] traverse, travel through || (μεταφ) look into.

διεξοδικός [δieksoδeekos] lengthy, extensive, detailed.

διέξοδος, η [δieksoδos] issue, outlet || (μεταφ) way out, alternative.

διέπω [δiepo] govern, rule.

διερεύνηση [δierevneesee] investigation, research.

διερευνητικός [δierevneeteekos] searching, exploratory.

διερευνώ [δierevno] search, explore, examine.

διερμηνέας, ο [δiermeeneas] interpreter, translator.

διερμηνεύω [δiermeenevo] interpret, translate.

διέρχομαι [δierhome] pass by, cross.

διερωτώμαι [δierotome] ask o.s., wonder.

διεσπαρμένος [δiesparmenos] dispersed.

διεστραμμένος [δiestramenos] perverse, wicked.

διετής [δietees] lasting two years || (επί φυτών) biennial.

διετία, η [δieteea] (space of) two years.

διευθέτηση, η [δievtheteesee] arrangement, settlement.

διευθετώ [δievtheto] arrange, settle || adjust.

διεύθυνση, η [δievtheensee] address || direction || (εταιρείας) management.

διευθυντής, ο [δievtheentees] director || (σχολής) principal || (μους) conductor || (θεάτρου) manager || (εφημερίδος) editor || (φυλακών) governor, warden || (σωματείου) president || (προσωπικού) personnel manager.

διευθύνω [δievtheeno] direct, guide || (επιχείρηση) manage || (εφημερίδα) edit || (βιομηχανία) handle, manage, direct || (έργα) superintend, oversee || (ορχήστρα) lead, conduct.

διευκόλυνση, η [δievkoleensee] easing, help.

διευκολύνω [δievkoleeno] facilitate, help forward.

διευκρινίζω [δievkreeneezo] clear up, explain.

διευκρίνιση, η [δievkreeneesee] elucidation, explanation.

διεύρυνση, η [δievreensee] widening, broadening, enlargement.

διεφθαρμένος [δieftharmenos] corrupt, immoral, dissolute.

δίζυγο, το [δeezeego] parallel bars.

διήγημα, το [δieegeema] story, tale.

διήγηση, η [δieegeesee] narration.

διηγούμαι [δieegoume] narrate, relate, tell.

διήθηση, η [δieetheesee] filtration, percolation.

διηρημένος [δieereemenos] divided, separated.

διίσταμαι [δieestame] (μεταφ) stand apart || (μεταφ) disagree.

διισχυρίζομαι [δieesheereezome] maintain.

δικάζω [δeekazo] try, judge.

δικαιόγραφο, το [δeekeografo] title deed.

δικαιοδοσία, η [δeekeoδoseea] jurisdiction, province.

δικαιολόγηση, η [δeekeoloyeesee] justification, excuse.

δικαιολογητικά, τα [δeekeoloyeeteeka] πλ documentary proof.

δικαιολογία, η [δeekeoloyeea] justification, excuse.

δικαιολογώ [δeekeologo] justify, excuse, vindicate.

δίκαιο, το [δeekeo] justice, right || law.

δίκαιος [δeekeos] fair, just, righteous.

δικαιοσύνη, η [δeekeoseenee] justice, fairness.

δικαιούχος, ο [δeekeouhos] beneficiary.

δικαιώνω [δeekeono] side with || justify, vindicate.

δικαίωμα, το [δeekeoma] right, claim.

δικαίωση, η [δeekeosee] justification, vindication.

δίκανο, το [δeekano] double-barrelled shotgun.

δικάσιμος, η [δeekaseemos] day of trial.

δικαστήριο, το [δeekasteereeo] law court, court of justice, tribunal.

δικαστής, ο [δeekastees] judge, justice, magistrate.

δικαστικός [δeekasteekos] judicial, judiciary.

δικέφαλος [δeekefalos] two-headed.

δίκη, η [δeekee] trial, suit, lawsuit, case.

δικηγόρος, ο, [δeekeegoros] lawyer, barrister, attorney.

δικηγορώ [δeekeegoro] practise as a lawyer, plead.

δικογραφία, η [δeekografeea] file of proceedings || (δικηγόρου) brief.

δικονομία, η [δeekonomeea] procedure.

δίκταμο, το [δeektamo] dittany.

δικτατορία, η [δeektatoreea] dictatorship.

δικτατορικός [δeektatoreekos] dictatorial.

δίκτυο, το [δeekteeo] net, network || (μεταφ) snare, trap.

δικτυωτό, το [δeekteeoto] wire netting, lattice, grille, trellis.

δίλημμα, το [δeeleema] dilemma.

διμερής [δeemerees] bipartite.

διμοιρία, η [δeemeereea] platoon, section.

δίνη, η [δeenee] whirlpool, whirlwind.

δίνω [δeeno] give, grant || (τιμή) offer || (παράγω) produce, yield || (μάχη) give battle || (γροθιά) deal a blow to.

διογκώνω [δeeongono] swell, inflate.

διόγκωση, η [δeeongosee] swelling, inflation.

διόδια, τα [δeeoδeea] πλ toll || (ναυτ) port toll.

δίοδος, η [δeeoδos] passage, pass, defile.

διοίκηση, η [δieekeesee] administration, command.

διοικητήριο, το [δieekeeteereeo] prefecture, commissioner's office.

διοικητής, ο [δieekeetees] governor, commissioner, commandant.

διοικητικός [δieekeeteekos] administrative.

διοικώ [δieeko] administer, govern, rule, command.

διόλου [δeeolou] (επιρ) not at all || όλως ~ entirely, quite.

διοξείδιο, το [δeeokseeδeeo] dioxide.

διοπτεύω [δeeoptevo] observe with binoculars || (ναυτ) take bearings of.

διόπτρα, η [δeoptra] binoculars.

διόραση, η [δeeorasee] perspicuity.

διορατικός [δeeorateekos] clear-sighted || (πνεύμα) shrewd, keen.

διορατικότητα, η [δeeorateekoteeta] perspicacity.

διοργανώνω [δeeorganono] organize, form, arrange.

διοργάνωση, η [δeeorganosee] organization, arrangement.

διορθώνω [δeeorthono] correct, put straight || (πανταλόνι) patch, mend || (μεταφ) remedy, make good.

διόρθωση, η [δeeorthosee] correction, putting right.

διορθωτής, ο [δeeorthotees] (τυπογρ) proofreader.

διορία, η [δeeoreea] time limit, term, delay.

διορίζω [δeeoreezo] appoint || order, fix.

διορισμένος [δeeoreesmenos] appointed.

διορισμός, ο [δeeoreesmos] appointment.

διόροφος [δeeorofos] two-storeyed.

διόρυξη, η [δeeoreeksee] digging, excavation.

διότι [δeeotee] because.

διουρητικός [δeeoureeteekos] diuretic.

διοχέτευση, η [δeeohetevsee] (ηλεκ) conduct || (ύδατος) conveyance.

διοχετεύω [δeeohetevo] conduct, convey || (μεταφ) transmit, divert.

δίπατος [δeepatos] two-storeyed.

δίπλα, η [δeepla] fold, pleat, wrinkle.

δίπλα [δeepla] (επιρ) by, near, next door, close.

διπλά [δeepla] twice as much.

διπλανός [δeeplanos] nearby, next-door, adjacent.

διπλαρώνω [δeeplarono] accost || (ναυτ) come alongside.

διπλασιάζω [δeeplaseeazo] double.

διπλασιασμός, ο [δeeplaseeasmos] reduplication.

διπλάσιος [δeeplaseeos] double, twice as much.

διπλός [δeeplos] double.

διπλότυπο, το [δeeploteepo] duplicate, stub, counterfoil.

δίπλωμα, το [δeeploma] diploma, degree || (τύλιγμα) folding, wrapping.

διπλωμάτης, ο [δeeplomatees] diplomat.

διπλωματία, η [δeeplomateea] diplomacy.

διπλωματικός [δeeplomateekos] diplomatic.

διπλωματούχος [δeeplomatouhos] having a diploma, holding a degree.

διπλώνω [δeeplono] fold.

δίπλωση, η [δeeplosee] folding, wrapping.

δίποδος [δeepoδos] two-legged, two-footed.

διπρόσωπος [δeeprosopos] two-faced, deceitful.

δίς [δees] twice.

δισάκκι, το [δeesakee] saddlebag, travelling bag.

δισέγγονο, το [δeesengono] great-grandchild.

δισεκατομμύριο, το [δeesekatomeereeo] billion.

δίσεκτο, το [δeesekto]: ~ έτος leap year.

δισκίο, το [δeeskeeo] (ιατρ) tablet.

δισκοβόλος, ο [δeeskovolos] discus thrower.

δίσκος, ο [δeeskos] tray || (ζυγού) pan, scale || (αθλητ) discus || (πλίου κτλ) disk || (εκκλ) collection plate || (γραμμοφώνου) record.

δισταγμός, ο [δeestagmos] hesitation, doubt.

διστάζω [δeestazo] hesitate, doubt.

διστακτικός [δeestakteekos] hesitant, irresolute.

δίστηλος [δeesteelos] two-columned.

δίστιχο, το [δeesteeho] distich, couplet.

δισύλλαβος [δeeseelavos] of two syllables.

δίτροχος [δeetrohos] two-wheeled.

διυλίζω [δeeleezo] filter, distil, strain.

διύλιση [δeeleesee] filtering, straining.

διυλιστήριο, το [δeeleesteereeo] filter, strainer || (πετρελαίου) refinery.

διφθερίτιδα, η [δeefthereeteeδa] diphtheria.

δίφθογγος, η [δeefthongos] diphthong.

διφορούμενος [δeeforoumenos] ambiguous.

δίφραγκο, το [δeefrango] two-drachma piece.

δίφυλλος [δeefeelos] two-leaved.

διχάζομαι [δeehazome] (μεταφ) become disunited, disagree.

διχάζω [δeehazo] divide, split || (μεταφ) estrange, disunite.

διχάλη, η [δeehalee] pitchfork.

διχαλωτός [δeehalotos] forked, cloven.

διχασμός, ο [δeehasmos] division || disagreement.

διχόνοια, η [δeehoneea] dissension, discord.

διχοτόμος [δeehotomos] bisector.

διχοτομώ [δeehotomo] bisect.

δίχρονος [δeehronos] (μηχανή) two-stroke (engine).

δίχως [δeehos] without || ~ άλλο without fail.

δίψα, η [δeepsa] thirst.

διψασμένος [δeepsasmenos] thirsty, eager (for).

διψώ [δeepso] feel thirsty || thirst for, be eager for.

διωγμός, ο [δeeogmos] persecution.

διώκω [δeeoko] pursue, chase, expel, persecute || (μεταφ) banish, dispel.

δίωξη, η [δeeoksee] persecution, hunting.

διώρυγα, η [δeeoreega] canal.

διώχνω [δeeohno] βλ διώκω.

δόγμα, το [δogma] dogma, creed, doctrine.

δογματικός [δogmateekos] dogmatic(al).

δόκανο, το [δokano] trap || (μεταφ) lure, snare.

δοκάρι, το [δokaree] beam, rafter, girder.

δοκιμάζω [δokeemazo] taste, try out || (αυτοκίνητο) test, try || (ρούχα) fit || (υποφέρω) undergo, suffer.

δοκιμασία, η [δokeemaseea] suffering.

δοκιμαστικός [δokeemasteekos] trial, test || ~ σωλήνας test tube.

δοκιμή, η [δokeemee] trial, test, testing || (θέατρο) rehearsal || (ρούχα) fitting.

δοκίμιο, το [δokeemeeo] treatise || (τυπογρ) printer's proof.

δόκιμος [δokeemos] esteemed, first-rate || ο ~ cadet.

δοκός, η [δokos] girder, beam.

δόλιος [δoleeos] fraudulent, crafty.

δόλιος [δoleeos] wretched, unlucky, poor.

δολιότης, η [δoleeotees] deceit, fraudulence, fraud.

δολοπλόκος [δoloplokos] treacherous, artful.

δόλος, ο [δolos] fraud, deceit, guile.

δολοφονία, η [δolofoneea] murder.

δολοφονικός [δolofoneekos] murderous.

δολοφόνος, ο, η [δolofonos] assassin, murderer.

δολοφονώ [δolofono] murder, assassinate.

δόλωμα, το [δoloma] bait, decoy.

δόνηση, η [δoneesee] vibration || (σεισμός) tremor, shock.

δόντι, το [δontee] tooth || (ελέφαντος) tusk || (μηχαν) cog.

δονώ [δono] vibrate, shake.

δόξα, η [δoksa] glory.

δοξάζω [δoksazo] glorify, celebrate, extol.

δοξάρι, το [δoksaree] (μουσ) bow.

δοξολογία, η [δoksologeea] doxology, Te Deum.

δόρυ, το [δoree] spear.

δορυφόρος, ο [δoreeforos] satellite.

δοσίλογος [δoseelogos] quisling.

δόση, η [δosee] portion || dose || (πληρωμή) instalment.

δοσοληψία, η [δosoleepseea] transaction.

δοτική, η [δoteekee] (γραμμ) dative (case).

δούκας, ο [δoukas] duke.
δούκισσα, η [δoukeesa] duchess.
δουλεία, η [δouleea] slavery,
servitude.
δουλειά, η [δoulia] work, affair,
business.
δούλεμα, το [δoulema] teasing.
δουλευτής, ο [δoulevtees] hard
worker, industrious worker.
δουλεύω [δoulevo] work, operate ||
(έχω δουλειά) have a job || (ρολόι κτλ)
work, operate || (περιπαίζω) tease.
δούλη, η [δoulee] slave.
δουλικός [δouleekos] servile, slavish.
δουλοπρεπής [δouloprepees] servile,
mean.
δούλος, ο [δoulos] slave || servant.
δουλώνω [δoulono] enslave, subjugate.
δούπος, ο [δoupos] thump, bump.
δοχείο, το [δoheeo] receptacle,
vessel, pot.
δρακόντειος [δrakonteeos] (μεταφ)
severe, harsh.
δράκος, ο [δrakos] ogre, dragon.
δράμα, το [δrama] drama || (μεταφ)
trouble.
δραματική, η [δramateekee] πλ
dramatics.
δραματικός [δramateekos] dramatic,
tragic.
δράμι, το [δrameeo] dram || (μεταφ)
tiny amount.
δραπετεύω [δrapetevo] escape.
δραπέτης [δrapetees] fugitive.
δράση, η [δrasee] activity, action ||
άμεσος ~ flying squad.
δραστήριος [δrasteereeos] active,
energetic, vigorous.
δραστηριότητα, η
[δrasteereeoteeta] activity, energy,
effectiveness.
δράστης, ο, η [δrastees] perpetrator,
culprit.
δραστικός [δrasteekos] efficacious,
drastic, effective.
δραχμή, η [δrahmee] drachma.
δρεπάνι, το [δrepanee] sickle.
δριμύς [δreemees] sharp, bitter,
severe, keen.
δρομάς, η [δromas] dromedary.
δρομέας, ο [δromeas] runner.
δρομολόγιο, το [δromoloyeeo]
itinerary || timetable.
δρόμος, ο [δromos] road, street ||
(αθλητ) race || (απόσταση) distance.
δροσερός [δroseros] cool, fresh.
δροσιά, η [δrosia] freshness || dew.
δροσίζομαι [δroseezome] refresh o.s.,
cool down.
δροσίζω [δroseezo] cool, refresh || get
cool.
δροσιστικός [δroseesteekos]
refreshing.
δρυμός, ο [δreemos] forest, wood.

δρυοκολάπτης, ο [δreeokolaptees]
woodpecker.
δρύς, η [δrees] oak.
δρω [δro] act, do, take effect.
δυάδα, η [δeeaδa] couple, pair.
δυαδικός [δeeaδeekos] binary || dual.
δυϊκός [δieekos] (γραμμ) dual
(number).
δύναμαι [δeename] can, may || be able
to.
δυναμική, η [δeenameekee]
dynamics.
δυναμικός [δeenameekos] energetic,
dynamic.
δύναμη, η [δeenamee] strength,
might, power, force.
δυναμίτιδα, η [δeenameeteeδa]
dynamite.
δυναμό, το [δeenamo] dynamo.
δυνάμωμα, το [δeenamoma]
intensification, strengthening.
δυναμώνω [δeenamono] strengthen,
make stronger || (υγεία) become
stronger.
δυναμωτικός [δeenamoteekos]
fortifying, strengthening || (ιατρ) tonic.
δυναστεία, η [δeenasteea] dynasty,
regime, rule.
δυνάστης, ο [δeenastees] ruler,
potentate || (μεταφ) oppressor, despot.
δυνατά [δeenata] strongly, hard ||
loudly.
δυνατός [δeenatos] strong, powerful ||
(κυβέρνηση) powerful || (φωνή) loud ||
(ένδοχος) possible || δυνατό! possibly!,
maybe!
δυνατότητα, η [δeenatoteeta]
possibility.
δύο [δeeo] two.
δυόσμος, ο [δeeosmos] mint,
spearmint.
δυσανάγνωστος [δeesanagnostos]
illegible.
δυσανάλογος [δeesanalogos]
disproportionate.
δυσανασχετώ [δeesanasheto] be
anxious, be indignant, get angry.
δυσαρέσκεια, η [δeesareskeea]
displeasure, discontent.
δυσάρεστος [δeesarestos]
unpleasant, disagreeable.
δυσαρεστημένος
[δeeasaresteemenos] displeased,
dissatisfied.
δυσαρεστώ [δeesaresto] displease,
dissatisfy.
δυσβάστακτος [δeesvastaktos]
unbearable, heavy, overwhelming.
δύσβατος [δeesvatos] inaccessible,
rough.
δυσειδής [δeeseeδees] ugly, unsightly.
δυσεντερία, η [δeesentereea]
dysentery.
δισεπίλυτος [δeesepeeleetos] difficult
to solve.

δισεύρετος [δeesevretos] difficult to find.

δυσθυμία, η [δeestheemeea] sadness, depression.

δύσθυμος [δeestheemos] depressed, sad.

δύση, η [δeesee] west || (ηλίου) setting || (μεταφ) decline.

δύσκαμπτος [δeeskambtos] rigid, stiff, inflexible.

δυσκινησία, η [δeeskeeneeseea] sluggishness.

δυσκοιλιότητα, η [δeeskeeleeoteeta] constipation.

δυσκολεύομαι [δeeskolevome] find difficult, find hard, be hard put (to).

δυσκολεύω [δeeskolevo] make difficult, make hard.

δυσκολία, η [δeeskoleea] difficulty.

δυσκολο- [δeeskolo] (first component) difficult, hard.

δύσκολος [δeeskolos] difficult || (άνθρωπος) hard to please.

δυσμένεια, η [δeesmeneea] disfavour, disgrace.

δυσμενής [δeesmenees] adverse, unfavourable.

δύσμορφος [δeesmorfos] deformed, ugly.

δυσνόητος [δeesnoeetos] difficult to understand.

δυσοίωνος [δeeseeonos] inauspicious, ill-omened.

δυσοσμία, η [δeesosmeea] bad smell, stench, offensive odour.

δύσπεπτος [δeespeptos] indigestible.

δυσπιστία, η [δeespeesteea] mistrust, incredulity.

δύσπιστος [δeespeestos] incredulous, distrustful, unbelieving.

δυσπιστώ [δeespeesto] distrust, mistrust.

δύσπνοια, η [δeespneea] difficult breathing.

δυσπρόσιτος [δeesproseetos] inaccessible.

δυστοκία, η [δeestokeea] difficult birth || (μεταφ) indecision.

δύστροπος [δeestropos] perverse, peevish.

δυστροπώ [δeestropo] behave peevishly.

δυστύχημα, το [δeesteeheema] accident, stroke of bad luck.

δυστυχής [δeesteehees] unhappy, unfortunate.

δυστυχία, η [δeesteeheea] unhappiness, adversity, poverty.

δυστυχισμένος [δeesteeheesmenos] βλ δυστυχής.

δυστυχώ [δeesteeho] be unhappy, be unfortunate, be poor.

δυσφημίζω [δeesfeemeezo] defame, slander.

δυσφήμιση, η [δeesfeemeesee] calumny, slander.

δυσφόρητος [δeesforeetos] hard to endure.

δυσφορώ [δeesforo] be displeased || (με κάτι) be discontented.

δυσχεραίνω [δeeshereno] impede, make difficult.

δυσχέρεια, η [δeeshereea] difficulty || hardship.

δυσχερής [δeesherees] difficult.

δύσχρηστος [δeeshreestos] unwieldy, inconvenient, awkward.

δυσωδία, η [δeesoδeea] stench, stink.

δύτης, ο [δeetees] diver.

δυτικός [δeeteekos] west(ern).

δύω [δeeo] set || (μεταφ) decline, wane.

δώδεκα [δoδeka] twelve.

δωδεκάγωνο, το [δoδekagono] dodecagon.

δωδεκαδάκτυλο, το [δoδekaδakteelo] duodenum.

δωδεκάδα, η [δoδekaδa] dozen.

δωδεκαετής [δoδekaetees] twelve years old.

δωδεκαπλάσιος [δoδekaplaseeos] twelve-fold.

δωδέκατος [δoδekatos] twelfth.

δώμα, το [δoma] flat roof, terrace || apartment.

δωμάτιο, το [δomateeo] room || (ύπνου) bedroom.

δωρεά, η [δorea] bequest, present, gift || ~ν (επιρ) gratis, free, for nothing.

δωροδοκία, η [δoroδokeea] bribery, corruption.

δωροδοκώ [δoroδoko] bribe, corrupt.

δώρο, το [δoro] gift, present.

δωσίαλογος [δoseealogos] responsible, answerable.

Ε, ε

έ [e] (επιφ) well!, hey!, hallo!

εάν [ean] βλ αν.

έαρ, το [ear] spring.

εαυτός [eaftos] oneself || καθ'εαυτού really, exactly, precisely.

εβδομάδα, η [evδomaδa] week.

εβδομαδιαίος [evδomaδieos] weekly.

έβδομος [evδomos] seventh.

εβραϊκός [evraeekos] Jewish.

Εβραίος, ο [evreos] Hebrew, Jew.

έγγαμος [engamos] married.

εγγίζω [engeezo] draw near || (μεταφ) touch.

εγγλέζικος [englezeekos] English.

Εγγλέζος, ο [englezos] Englishman.

εγγόνι, το [engonee] grandchild.

εγγονός, ο [engonos] grandson.

εγγραφή, η [engrafee] registration, record, entry.

έγγραφο, το [engrafo] document.
εγγράφω [engrafo] register, enrol || (μαθημ) inscribe.
εγγύηση, η [engieesee] security, guarantee, bail.
εγγύς [engees] near, at hand.
εγγυώμαι [engeeome] guarantee, vouch for.
εγείρω [eyeero] raise, build.
έγερση, η [eyersee] raising, building || (από ύπνο) awakening.
εγκαθίσταμαι [engkatheestame] settle, put up, settle o.s.
εγκαθιστώ [engkatheesto] set up, settle, establish.
εγκαίνια, τα [engkeeneea] πλ inauguration, opening.
έγκαιρος [engkeros] timely, opportune.
εγκάρδιος [engkarδeeos] cordial, affectionate.
εγκάρσιος [engkarseeos] transverse, slanting, oblique.
εγκαταλείπω [engkataleepo] abandon, desert.
εγκατάσταση, η [engkatastasee] installation, establishing.
έγκαυμα, το [engkavma] burn.
έγκειται [engkeete]: σε σας ~ it rests with you.
εγκέφαλος, ο [engkefalos] brain.
εγκλείω [engkleeo] enclose || confine || lock up.
έγκλημα, το [engkleema] crime || sin || ~τίας, ο criminal || ~τικός criminal || ~τικότης, η delinquency, wrongdoing, crime.
εγκοπή, η [engkopee] incision, notch, groove.
εγκόσμιος [engkosmeeos] mundane, worldly || social.
εγκράτεια, η [engkrateea] sobriety, moderation, temperance.
εγκρίνω [engkreeno] approve, ratify.
έγκριση, η [engkreesee] approval, sanction.
εγκύκλιος, η [engkeekleeos] circular letter.
εγκυκλοπαίδεια, η [engkeeklopeδeea] encyclopaedia.
έγκυος [engkeeos] pregnant.
έγκυρος [engkeeros] valid, sound, well-grounded.
εγκώμιο, το [engkomeeo] praise.
έγνοια, η [egneea] care, anxiety, concern.
εγχείρηση, η [engheereesee] operation.
εγχειρίδιο, το [engheereeδeeo] manual.
έγχρωμος [enghromos] coloured.
εγχώριος [enghoreeos] local, native, domestic.
εγώ [ego] I || (ουσ) το ~ ego ||

εγωισμός, ο [egoeesmos] pride, conceit, selfishness.
έδαφος, το [eδafos] ground, earth, soil.
έδρα, η [eδra] seat, chair || (ανατ) bottom || (εκκλ) see.
εδραιώνω [eδreono] establish, strengthen, make firm.
εδρεύω [eδrevo] reside, have one's seat.
εδώ [eδo] here || ~ και τρία χρόνια three years ago.
εδώλιο, το [eδoleeo] bench, seat.
εθελοντής, ο [ethelontees] volunteer.
εθελουσίως [ethelouseeos] voluntarily.
έθιμο, το [etheemo] custom, tradition || habit.
εθιμοτυπία, η [etheemoteepeea] formality, etiquette.
εθνάρχης, ο [ethnarhees] national leader.
εθνικός [ethneekos] national.
εθνικότητα, η [ethneekoteeta] nationality.
εθνικόφρων [ethneekofron] patriotic, nationalistic.
έθνος, το [ethnos] nation.
ειδάλλως [eeδalos] if not, otherwise.
ειδεμή [eeδemee] otherwise.
ειδήμων [eeδeemon] expert, skilled, well-informed.
ειδήσεις, οι [eeδeesees] πλ news.
ειδικός [eeδeekos] special, particular || (άνθρωπος) specialist.
ειδοποίηση, η [eeδopieesee] notification, notice.
ειδοποιώ [eeδopeeo] notify, inform, advise.
είδος, το [eeδos] sort, kind, type || (βοτ) species || τα είδη goods, wares || kinds.
ειδύλλιο, το [eeδeeleeo] love affair || idyll.
ειδωλολάτρης, ο [eeδololatrees] pagan, heathen.
είδωλο, το [eeδolo] idol || image.
είθισται [eetheeste] it is the custom.
εικασία, η [eekaseea] conjecture, guess.
εικαστικός [eekasteekos] conjectural || εικαστικαί τέχναι fine arts.
εικόνα [eekona] image, picture || (εκκλ) icon.
εικονίζω [eekoneezo] portray, depict, represent.
εικονικός [eekoneekos] figurative || (επίθεση) sham || (πράξη) bogus || (τιμή) conventional.
εικόνισμα, το [eekoneesma] portrait || (αγιογραφία) icon.
εικονογραφία, η [eekonografeea] illustration || (εκκλ) iconography.

εικονοστάσι(ο), το [eekonostasee(o)] (εκκλ) shrine, screen.

είκοσι [eekosee] twenty.

εικοστός [eekostos] twentieth.

ειλικρίνεια, η [eeleekreeneea] sincerity, frankness.

ειλικρινής [eeleekreenees] sincere, candid.

είμαι [eeme] I am, I'm.

είναι [eene] be, is, it is || το ~ being.

ειρήνη, η [eereenee] peace.

ειρηνικός [eereeneekos] peaceful.

ειρηνοδικείο, το [eereenoδeekeeo] magistrate's court.

ειρμός, ο [eermos] train of thought, continuity.

ειρωνεύομαι [eeronevome] speak derisively, speak ironically.

ειρωνεία, η [eeroneea] irony, mockery.

εις [ees] in, among, at || (χρόνος) within || to, into, on.

εισαγγελέας, ο [eesangeleas] public prosecutor || district attorney (US).

εισάγω [eesago] import || (νομοσχέδιο) introduce || (φέρω πρώτα) introduce for the first time || (παρουσιάζω) present ||

εισαγωγέας, ο importer ||

εισαγωγή, η importation || (παρονύαση) introduction ||

εισαγωγικά, τα inverted commas.

εισβάλλω [eesvalo] invade || (ποταμός) flow into.

εισβολή, η [eesvolee] invasion.

εισέρχομαι [eeserhome] come in, enter, go in.

εισήγηση, η [eeseeyeesee] report || suggestion.

εισηγούμαι [eeseegoume] propose, move || introduce.

εισιτήριο, το [eeseeteereeo] ticket.

εισόδημα, το [eesoδeema] income, revenue.

είσοδος, η [eesoδos] entry, entrance || admission.

εισπνέω [eespneo] inhale, breathe in.

εισπράκτορας, ο [eespraktoras] conductor || collector.

είσπραξη, η [eespraksee] collection || receipt.

εισπράττω [eesprato] collect.

εισφορά, η [eesfora] contribution.

εισχωρώ [eeshoro] penetrate, intrude, get in.

είτε [eete]: ~ ... ~ either ... or, whether ... or.

εκ [ek] from, out of, by, of || εξ ανάγκης of necessity || ~ νέου again || εξ ίσου equally.

εκ-, εξ- [ek, eks] out, off || completely, wholly.

έκαστος [ekastos] each, every one || καθ' εκάστην every day || τα καθ'έκαστα the details.

εκάστοτε [ekastote] each time.

εκατέρωθεν [ekaterothen] on both sides, mutually.

εκατό [ekato] hundred || τά ~ per cent.

εκατομμύριο, το [ekatomeereeo] million.

εκατομμυριούχος, ο [ekatomeereeouhos] millionaire.

εκατονταετηρίδα, η [ekatontaeteereeδa] century || centenary.

εκατονταπλάσιος [ekatontaplaseeos] hundredfold.

εκατοστάρι, το [ekatostaree] hundred-drachma note.

εκατοστόμετρο, το [ekatostometro] centimetre.

εκατοστός [ekatostos] hundredth.

εκβάλλω [ekvalo] take out, extract || (απομακρύνω) repudiate || (εχθρό) drive out || (επί ποταμών) flow into.

έκβαση, η [ekvasee] issue, outcome, result.

εκβιάζω [ekveeazo] (κάποιο) force, compel || blackmail || (διάβαση κτλ) force.

εκβολή η [ekvolee] ejection || (ποταμού) mouth, estuary.

έκδηλος [ekδeelos] manifest, evident, obvious.

εκδηλώνω [ekδeelono] show, reveal.

εκδίδω [ekδeeδo] issue, publish || (απόφαση) pronounce || (συναλλαγματική) draw || (εγκληματία κτλ) extradite.

εκδίκηση, η [ekδeekeesee] vengeance, revenge.

εκδικητικός [ekδeekeeteekos] revengeful, vindictive.

εκδικούμαι [ekδeekoume] take revenge on, get even with.

εκδιώκω [ekδeeoko] expel, oust || (στρατ) dislodge, drive out.

εκδορά, η [ekδora] abrasion || skinning.

έκδοση, η [ekδosee] publication, edition || (χαρτονομίσματος) issue || (παραλλαγή) version, story || (εγκληματία κτλ) extradition.

εκδότης, ο [ekδotees] publisher, editor.

εκδοτικός [ekδoteekos] publishing || ~ οίκος publishing house.

εκδοχή, η [ekδohee] interpretation, version.

εκδρομή η [ekδromee] excursion, outing, trip.

εκεί [ekee] there || ~ που instead of, while, whereas.

εκείνος [ekeenos] he, that one there.

εκεχειρία, η [ekeheereea] truce, armistice.

έκθαμβος [ekthamvos] dazzled, astounded.

έκθεμα, το [ekthema] exhibit.

έκθεση, η [ekthesee] (στο ύπαιθρο) exposure || (ανθέων κτλ) exhibition || (εμπορευμάτων) display, exposition || (γραπτή) composition.

εκθέτης, ο [ekthetees] exhibitor || (μαθημ) exponent.

έκθετος [ekthetos] exposed.

εκθέτω [ektheto] expose, display, exhibit || (την ζωή) expose, imperil || (τέκνο) abandon || (σχέδια) state, disclose || (μεταφ) lay bare, expose.

εκθρονίζω [ekthroneezo] dethrone.

εκκαθαρίζω [ekathareezo] clear out, clean || (λογαριασμό) liquidate, settle.

εκκεντρικός [ekentreekos] eccentric.

εκκενώ [ekeno] empty (out), vacate || (ποτήρι κτλ) drain || (όπλο) fire || (οικία) leave.

εκκένωση, η [ekenose] evacuation, emptying || (ηλεκ) discharge.

εκκίνηση, η [ekeeneese] departure, starting off.

εκκλησία, η [ekleeseea] church || **εκκλησιαστικός** ecclesiastic(al).

έκκληση, η [ekleesee] appeal.

εκκρεμής [ekremees] unsettled, pending.

εκκωφαντικός [ekofanteekos] deafening.

εκλέγω [eklego] choose, pick out || elect.

έκλειψη, η [ekleepsee] eclipse || (μεταφ) disappearance.

εκλεκτικός [eklekteekos] choosy, selective.

εκλεκτός [eklektos] choice, select, picked || **οι εκλεκτοί** élite.

εκλιπαρώ [ekleeparo] entreat, implore.

εκλογέας, ο [eklogeas] elector, voter.

εκλογή, η [eklogee] choice, selection || election.

εκλογές, οι [ekloges] πλ elections.

εκλογικός [eklogeekos] electoral.

εκμαγείο, το [ekmayeeo] (plaster) cast.

εκμαιεύω [ekmeyevo] extract, elicit.

εκμεταλλεύομαι [ekmetalevome] exploit.

εκμηδενίζω [ekmeeðeneezo] annihilate.

εκμίσθωση, η [ekmeesthosee] leasing, lease.

εκμισθωτής, ο [ekmeesthotees] lessor, hirer.

εκμυστηρεύομαι [ekmeesteerevome] confide a secret, confess.

εκνευρίζω [eknevreezo] annoy, exasperate.

εκούσιος [ekouseeos] voluntary || willing.

εκπαίδευση, η [ekpeðevsee] education, training.

εκπαιδευτήριο, το [ekpeðevteereeo] school, institute.

εκπαιδευτικός [ekpeðevteekos] educational || (δάσκαλος) schoolteacher.

εκπαιδεύω [ekpeðevo] educate, train, instruct.

εκπατρίζω [ekpatreezo] expatriate.

εκπέμπω [ekpembo] send forth, emit || (από ραδιοφώνου) broadcast.

εκπίπτω [ekpeepto] decline, fall || (μεταφ) deduct, reduce, lower.

εκπληκτικός [ekpleekteekos] astonishing, surprising.

έκπληξη, η [ekpleeksee] surprise, astonishment.

εκπληρώ [ekpleero] fulfil, perform.

εκπλήσσω [ekpleeso] surprise, astonish.

εκπνέω [ekpneo] exhale || (πεθαίνω) die || (μεταφ) expire, terminate.

εκποιώ [ekpeeo] sell, dispose of.

εκπομπή, η [ekpombee] emission || (ραδιοφώνου) broadcast.

εκπρόθεσμος [ekprothesmos] overdue.

εκπρόσωπος, ο [ekprosopos] representative.

εκπροσωπώ [ekprosopo] represent.

έκπτωση, η [ekptosee] decline, fall || (δικαιωμάτων) loss || (τιμής κτλ) reduction, rebate, discount, deduction.

εκρήγνυμαι [ekreegneeme] explode, erupt, burst.

εκρηκτικός [ekreekteekos] explosive.

έκρηξη, η [ekreeksee] explosion, eruption, outburst.

εκσκαφή, η [ekskafee] excavation, cutting.

έκσταση, η [ekstasee] ecstasy, rapture.

εκστρατεία, η [ekstrateea] expedition, campaign.

εκσφενδονίζω [eksfenðoneezo] fling, throw, hurl.

έκτακτος [ektaktos] temporary, emergency || (ειδικός) special, exceptional, excellent.

εκτάκτως [ektaktos] temporarily || extraordinarily, unusually.

έκταση, η [ektasee] extent, stretch.

εκτεθειμένος [ektetheemenos] exposed || compromised.

εκτείνω [ekteeno] stretch, extend, prolong.

εκτέλεση, η [ektelesee] execution || performance, fulfilment.

εκτελεστικός [ektelesteekos] executive.

εκτελώ [ektelo] execute || perform, carry out.

εκτενής [ektenees] extensive, lengthy.

εκτεταμένος [ektetamenos] extensive, long.

εκτίθεμαι [ekteetheme] be embarrassed || display.

εκτίμηση, η [ekteemeesee] esteem, estimation, appreciation.

εκτιμώ [ekteemo] esteem, value, appreciate, estimate.

εκτοξεύω [ektoksevo] shoot, cast, hurl.

εκτοπίζω [ektopeezo] displace, dislodge || (εξορίζω) exile.

εκτόπισμα, το [ektopeesma] displacement.

έκτος [ektos] sixth.

εκτός [ektos] outside, save (for) || ~ της πόλεως outside the city || ~ από apart from, besides, except for || ~ αν unless || ~ κινδύνου out of danger.

έκτοτε [ektote] ever since, since then.

εκτρέπομαι [ektrepome] deviate from || (μεταφ) go astray.

εκτρέπω [ektrepo] deflect, turn aside, divert.

εκτροχιάζομαι [ektroheeazome] become derailed || (μεταφ) go astray.

έκτρωμα, το [ektroma] monster, freak.

έκτρωση, η [ektrosee] abortion, miscarriage.

εκτυλίσσομαι [ekteeleesome] develop, evolve.

εκτυπώνω [ekteepono] print || emboss.

εκτυφλωτικός [ekteefloteekos] blinding.

εκφέρω [ekfero] express.

εκφοβίζω [ekfoveezo] intimidate, frighten.

εκφορά, η [ekfora] funeral, burial.

εκφορτωτής, ο [ekfortotees] unloader, docker.

εκφράζω [ekfrazo] express, reveal.

έκφραση, η [ekfrasee] expression.

εκφραστικός [ekfrasteekos] expressive.

εκφυλισμός, ο [ekfeeleesmos] degeneration.

εκφωνώ [ekfono] deliver a speech || read aloud.

εκχύλισμα, το [ekheeleesma] extract.

εκχωρώ [ekhoro] transfer, assign, cede || (θέση) make way.

έλα [ela] (επιφ) come, come now.

ελαιογραφία, η [eleografeea] oil painting.

ελαιόλαδο, το [eleolaðo] olive oil.

έλαιο, το [eleo] olive oil, oil.

ελαιοτριβείο, το [eleotreeveeo] olive press.

ελαιόχρωμα, το [eleohroma] oil paint.

ελαιώνας, ο [eleonas] olive grove.

έλασμα, το [elasma] metal plate, sheet iron.

ελαστικό, το [elasteeko] tyre || rubber, elastic.

ελαστικός [elasteekos] flexible, elastic.

ελατήριο, το [elateereeo] spring || (μεταφ) incentive, motive.

έλατο, το [elato] fir, fir tree.

ελάττωμα, το [elatoma] defect, fault.

ελαττώνω [elatono] diminish, lessen, decrease.

ελάττωση, η [elatosee] decrease, curtailment.

ελάφι, το [elafee] deer.

ελαφρόπετρα, η [elafropetra] pumice stone.

ελαφρός [elafros] light, slight || (καφές κτλ) mild, thin, weak.

ελαφρώνω [elafrono] reduce, lighten || feel relieved.

ελάχιστα [elaheesta] very little.

ελάχιστος [elaheestos] least, very little || του' λάχιστο(ν) at least.

Ελβετία, η [elveteea] Switzerland.

Ελβετίδα, η [elveteeða] Swiss woman.

ελβετικός [elveteekos] Swiss.

Ελβετός, ο [elvetos] Swiss man.

ελεγκτής, ο [elengtees] inspector, auditor.

έλεγχος, ο [elenghos] inspection, examination || (λογαριασμού) verification, control, auditing || (μηχανής) testing, overhauling || (μεταφ) censure, check, reproach.

ελέγχω [elengho] check, control, test.

ελεεινός [eleeenos] pitiful, wretched, vile.

ελεημοσύνη, η [eleyeemoseenee] alms, charity.

έλεος, το [eleos] mercy, pity.

ελευθερία, η [eleesthereea] liberty, freedom.

ελεύθερος [eleftheros] free || (εργένης) unmarried.

ελευθερώνω [eleftherono] redeem, set free, release, rid.

ελεφαντόδοντο, το [elefantoðonto] tusk || ivory.

ελέφας, ο [elefas] elephant.

ελεώ [eleo] give alms to, commiserate with || Κύριε ελέησον (επιφ) Lord have mercy!, for Heaven's sake!

ελιά, η [elia] olive, olive tree || (προσώπου κτλ) mole.

ελιγμός, ο [eleegmos] twisting, winding || (στρατ) manoeuvre, movement.

έλικα(ς), η, ο [eleeka(s)] coil, spiral || (προπέλλα) screw, propeller || (βοτ) tendril.

ελικόπτερο, το [eleekoptero] helicopter.

ελίσσομαι [eleesome] wind, coil, twist || (στρατ) manoeuvre.

έλκηθρο, το [elkeethro] sledge, sled.

ελκυστικός [elkeesteekos] attractive, winsome.

ελκύω [elkeeo] charm, attract || draw, pull.

έλκω [elko] draw, pull, haul.

Ελλάδα, η [elaða] Greece.

Ελλάς, η [elas] Greece.

έλλειμμα, το [eleema] deficit, shortage.

έλλειψη, η [eleepsee] lack, want, deficiency || (μαθημ) ellipse.

Έλλην(ας), ο [eleen(as)] Greek (person).

Ελληνίδα, η [eleeneeða] Greek woman.

ελληνικά, τα [eleeneeka] πλ Greek (language).

ελληνικός [eleeneekos] Greek.

ελληνισμός, ο [eleeneesmos] the Greek people.

ελληνιστί [eleeneestee] in Greek.

ελλιπής [eleepees] defective, wanting.

έλξη, η [elksee] pulling, traction, drawing, attraction.

ελονοσία, η [elonoseea] malaria.

έλος, το [elos] marsh, swamp, morass.

ελπίδα, η [elpeeða] hope, expectation || (παρ' ~ contrary to expectation.

ελώδης [eloðees] marshy, swampy.

εμβαδό, το [emvaðo] area.

εμβαθύνω [emvatheeno] (μεταφ) examine thoroughly, probe deeply.

έμβασμα, το [emvasma] remittance (of money).

εμβατήριο, το [emvateereeo] march.

έμβλημα, το [emvleema] emblem, crest, symbol.

εμβολιάζω [emvoleeazo] (φυτό) graft || (άνθρωπο) vaccinate, inoculate.

εμβόλιο, το [emvoleeo] vaccine || (φυτό) graft.

έμβολο, το [emvolo] piston, rod || (πλοίου) ram.

εμβρόντητος [emvronteetos] thunderstruck, stupefied.

έμβρυο, το [emvreeo] embryo, foetus.

εμένα [emena] me.

εμείς [emees] we.

εμετικός [emeteekos] emetic.

εμετός, ο [emetos] vomiting.

εμμένω [emeno] adhere to || persist, insist.

έμμεσος [emesos] indirect.

έμμηνα, τα [emeena] πλ menstruation.

έμμισθος [emeesthos] salaried, paid.

έμμονος [emonos] persistent, obstinate, persevering.

εμπάθεια, η [empatheea] animosity, ill feeling.

εμπαίζω [empezo] tease, mock, deceive.

εμπειρία, η [embeereea] experience, skill.

εμπειρογνώμων, ο, η [embeerognomon] expert, specialist.

έμπειρος [embeeros] experienced, skilled (in), able.

εμπιστεύομαι [embeestevome] (en)trust, confide.

εμπιστευτικός [embeestevteekos] confidential.

έμπιστος [embeestos] trustworthy, reliable, faithful || **εμπιστοσύνη, η** trust, confidence.

εμπλοκή, η [emblokee] (στρατ) engagement || (μηχανής) jamming || gear of car.

εμπλουτίζω [emblouteezo] enrich.

εμπνέομαι [embneome] feel inspired.

έμπνευση, η [embnevsee] inspiration.

εμπνέω [embneo] inspire.

εμποδίζω [emboðeezo] hinder, obstruct, prevent || hold back, impede.

εμπόδιο, το [emboðeeo] obstacle, impediment, obstruction.

εμπόρευμα, το [emborevma] merchandise.

εμπορεύομαι [emborevome] engage in commerce || deal in, trade in.

εμπορικός [emboreekos] commercial, mercantile.

εμπόριο, το [emboreeo] trade, commerce.

έμπορος, ο [emboros] merchant, trader, vendor.

εμποροϋπάλληλος, ο, η [emboroeepaleelos] shop assistant || clerk (US).

εμπρησμός, ο [embreesmos] arson.

εμπρηστικός [embreesteekos] incendiary || (μεταφ) fiery.

εμπρόθεσμος [embrothesmos] within the time limit.

εμπρός [embros] forward(s), before, in front of || ~ σε compared with || πηγαίνω ~ to succeed || ~ από in front of || το ρολόι πάει ~ the clock is fast || ~ μου in front of me || ~! hallo, come in || βάζω ~ to start.

εμφανής [emfanees] apparent, obvious, clear.

εμφανίζομαι [emfaneezome] appear, present o.s., make an appearance.

εμφανίζω [emfaneezo] exhibit, reveal || (φωτογρ) develop.

εμφάνιση, η [emfaneesee] appearance, presentation || (φωτογρ) development.

έμφαση, η [emfasee] stress, emphasis.

εμφύλιος [emfeeleeos]: ~ πόλεμος civil war.

έμφυτος [emfeetos] innate, inherent, intuitive.

εμψυχώνω [empseehono] encourage, stimulate.

εν [en] in, at, within || ~ τούτοις

however, nevertheless || ~ **τάξει** all right.

έν(α), το [en(a)] one || a, an.

εναγόμενος [enagomenos] defendant.

ενάγω [enago] sue, bring action against.

εναγωνίως [enagoneeos] anxiously, with anguish.

εναέριος [enaereeos] aerial, overhead || airy.

εναλλαγή, η [enalayee] permutation, exchange, interchange.

εναλλάξ [enalaks] alternately, in turn.

εναλλάσσω [enalaso] alternate, exchange.

έναντι [enantee] towards, against || βλ και **απέναντι**.

ενάντια [enanteea] adversely, contrarily || ~ **σε** against.

εναντίο(ν) [enanteeo(n)] against || contrary to.

εναντίο(ν), το [enanteeo(n)] the contrary.

ενάντιος [enanteeos] adverse, contrary, opposite || **απ' εναντίας** on the contrary.

εναπόκειται [enapokeete]: **σε σένα ~** it's up to you.

ενάρετος [enaretos] virtuous, upright.

έναρθρος [enarthros] articulate, jointed.

εναρκτήριος [enarkteereeos] inaugural.

εναρμονίζω [enarmoneezo] harmonize.

έναρξη, η [enarksee] opening, beginning, inauguration.

ένας, ο [enas] one || a, an || ~ ~ one by one || ~ **κι** ~ especially good, very bad || **ο ~ τον άλλο** one another.

ενασχόληση, η [enasholeesee] occupation, employment.

ένατος [enatos] ninth.

ένδεια, η [endeea] deficiency || poverty.

ενδεικνύομαι [endeekneeome] be called for, be necessary.

ενδεικνύω [endeekneeo] indicate.

ενδεικτικό, το [endeekteeko] certificate.

ενδεικτικός [endeekteekos] indicative.

ένδειξη, η [endeeksee] indication, sign.

ένδεκα [endeka] eleven.

ενδέχεται [endehete] it is possible, it is likely.

ενδεχόμενο, το [endehomeno] eventuality, possibility.

ενδιάμεσος [endeeamesos] intermediate, in-between.

ενδιαφέρομαι [endeeaferome] be interested in.

ενδιαφέρον, το [endeeaferon] interest, concern.

ενδιαφέρω [endeeafero] concern, interest || ~**ν** interesting.

ενδίδω [endeedo] give way to || give way, bend.

ένδικος [endeekos] legal, judicial.

ενδοιάζω [endeeazo] hesitate, waver.

ένδο- [endo] (combining form) within, in.

ένδοξος [endoksos] celebrated, glorious, illustrious.

ενδότερος [endoteros] inner, interior.

ενδοχώρα, η [endohora] hinterland.

ένδυμα, το [endeema] dress, garment, clothes || ~**σία, η** suit, dress, garb.

ενέδρα, η [enedra] ambush.

ένεκα [eneka] on account of, because of.

ενενήντα [eneneenta] ninety.

ενέργεια, η [enerya] energy, action || (φαρμάκου) efficacy.

ενεργητικός [eneryeeteekos] energetic, active || (φάρμακο) effective.

ενεργός [energos] active || effective.

ενεργούμαι [energoume] move the bowels || take place.

ενεργώ [energo] act, take steps || (φάρμακο κτλ) take effect, work || (καθαρτικό) purge.

ένεση, η [enesee] injection.

ενεστώς, ο [enestos] (γραμμ) present tense.

ενετικός [eneteekos] Venetian.

ενεχυροδανειστής, ο [eneheerodaneestees] pawnbroker.

ενήλικας [eneeleekas] of age, adult.

ενηλικιούμαι [eneeleekeeoume] come of age, reach majority.

ενήμερος [eneemeros] aware, informed.

ενημερώνω [eneemerono] inform, bring up to date.

ενθάρρυνση, η [enthareensee] encouragement, cheering up.

ενθαρρύνω [enthareeno] encourage, cheer up, hearten.

ένθερμος [enthermos] ardent, warm, hearty.

ενθουσιάζομαι [enthouseeazome] be enthusiastic about.

ενθουσιασμός, ο [enthouseeasmos] enthusiasm.

ενθύμιο, το [entheemeeo] keepsake, souvenir, memento.

ενθυμούμαι [entheemoume] recall, remember, recollect.

ενιαίος [enieos] single, uniform.

ενικός [eneekos] (γραμμ) singular (number).

ενίσχυση, η [eneesheesee] reinforcement, strengthening || (ηλεκ) amplification.

ενισχύω [eneesheeo] support, reinforce, assist.

εννέα [ennea] nine || ~ **κόσιοι** nine hundred.

εννιά [ennia] nine.

έννοια, η [enneea] sense, concept, meaning, interpretation.

έννοια, η [enyeea] concern, worry || (σκοτούρα) anxiety || ~ **σου** (επιφ) take care!, don't worry!

έννομος [ennomos] lawful, legal, legitimate.

εννοείται [ennoeete] it is understood, certainly.

εννοώ [ennoo] understand, mean, intend.

'ΓΝΟΙΚΙΆΖΕΤΑΙ' [eneekeeazete] 'to let', 'for rent'.

ενοικιάζω [eneekeeazo] rent, let, hire.

ενοικιαστής, ο [eneekeeastees] tenant || (νομ) lessee.

ενοίκιο, το [eneekeeo] rent.

ένοικος, ο [eneekos] tenant, lodger.

ένοπλος [enoplos] armed, in arms.

ενορία, η [enoreea] parish.

ενόρκως [enorkos] under oath, on oath.

ενόσω [enoso] as long as.

ενότητα, η [enoteeta] unity, concord.

ενοχή, η [enohee] guilt, culpability.

ενόχληση, η [enohleesee] trouble, annoyance, inconvenience.

ενοχλητικός [enohleeteekos] troublesome, inconvenient, annoying.

ενοχλώ [enohlo] trouble, annoy, pester, inconvenience.

ενσάρκωση, η [ensarkosee] incarnation, embodiment.

ένσημο, το [enseemo] stamp.

ενσκήπτω [enskeepto] happen suddenly, break out || break into.

ένσταση, η [enstasee] objection.

ένστικτο, το [ensteekto] instinct.

ένταλμα, το [entalma] warrant, writ.

ένταση, η [entasee] strain, tension || intensity, intensification.

εντατικός [entateekos] intensive.

ενταύθα [entavtha] here || (ένδειξη επιστολής) in town, local.

εντείνω [enteeno] stretch || (τις προσπάθειες) intensify || (τις σχέσεις) overstrain.

έντεκα [enteka] eleven.

εντέλεια, η [enteleea] perfection.

εντελώς [entelos] completely, entirely, totally.

εντερικός [entereekos] intestinal.

έντερο, το [entero] intestine.

εντεταλμένος [entetalmenos] responsible for, charged with || (ουσ) delegate.

έντεχνος [entehnos] skilful, artistic, ingenious.

έντιμος [enteemos] honest || (οικογένεια κτλ) respectable, honourable.

έντοκος [entokos] with interest.

εντολή, η [entolee] order, mandate || authorization, commission.

εντομοκτόνο, το [entomoktono] insecticide.

έντομο, το [entomo] insect.

έντονος [entonos] (προσπάθεια) strenuous, intense || (φως) strong || (χρώμα) bright, deep.

εντοπίζω [entopeezo] localize || (πυρκαγιά) restrict, confine.

εντόπιος [entopeeos] local, native, indigenous.

εντός [entos] within, inside, in, into || ~ **ολίγου** soon.

εντόσθια, τα [entostheea] πλ entrails, intestines.

εντριβή, η [entreevee] massage || (μηχανική) friction.

έντυπο, το [enteepo] printed matter.

έντυπος [enteepos] printed.

εντυπωσιακός [enteeposeeakos] impressive, striking.

εντύπωση, η [enteeposee] impression, sensation, feeling.

ενώ [eno] while, whereas, since.

ενώνω [enono] unite, join, connect.

ενώπιο [enopeeo] in the presence of, in front of.

ένωση, η [enosee] union || (πλεκτ) short circuit.

εξ [eks] βλ εκ.

εξαγοράζω [eksagorazo] buy off, redeem, ransom, obtain by bribery.

εξαγριώνω [eksagreeono] infuriate, enrage.

εξάγω [eksago] take out, extract || (εμπόριο) export || (φίλοσ) deduce.

εξαγωγή, η [eksagoyee] export || (οδόντος) extraction.

εξάδελφος, ο [eksadelfos] cousin.

εξαερίζω [eksaereezo] ventilate, air.

εξαεριστήρας, ο [eksaereesteeras] ventilator.

εξαίρεση, η [ekseresee] exception, exemption (from), immunity (from).

εξαιρετικός [eksereteekos] exceptional, unusual, excellent, remarkable.

εξαίρετος [ekseretos] excellent, remarkable.

εξαιρώ [eksero] except, exempt.

εξαίσιος [ekseseeos] excellent, splendid.

εξακολουθώ [eksakoloutho] continue.

εξακόσιοι [eksakosiee] six hundred.

εξακριβώνω [eksakreevono] verify, ascertain, establish, clear up.

εξαλείφω [eksaleefo] efface, rub out, remove, obliterate.

έξαλλος [eksalos] beside o.s., frenzied.

εξάμβλωμα, το [eksamvloma] monstrosity.

εξαναγκάζω [eksanangazo] compel, force, coerce.

εξάνθημα, το [eksantheema] rash, pimples.

εξανίσταμαι [eksaneestame] rebel, protest.

εξαντλώ [eksantlo] exhaust.

εξαπατώ [eksapato] cheat, deceive, delude || be unfaithful to.

εξάπλωση, η [eksaplosee] spreading out, extension.

εξαπολύω [eksapoleeo] let loose, hurl.

εξάπτω [eksapto] excite, provoke || (περιέργεια κτλ) rouse, stir.

εξαργυρώνω [eksargeerono] cash, turn into money.

εξάρθρωση, η [eksarthrosee] dislocation.

έξαρση, η [eksarsee] (μεταφ) elevation, exaltation.

εξαρτήματα, τα [eksarteemata] πλ gear, tackle, rigging, accessories.

εξάρτηση, η [eksarteesee] dependence.

εξαρτώμαι [eksartome] depend on, turn on.

εξασθένηση, η [eksastheneesee] weakening, enfeeblement.

εξάσκηση, η [eksaskeesee] exercise, practice, training.

εξασκώ [eksasko] exercise, practise || (πίεση) exert.

εξασφαλίζω [eksasfaleezo] assure || (θέση) book, reserve.

εξατμίζω [eksatmeezo] evaporate || (μεταφ) vanish, melt away.

εξάτμιση, η [eksatmeesee] evaporation || (αυτοκινήτου) exhaust.

εξαφανίζομαι [eksafaneezome] disappear, vanish.

εξαφανίζω [eksafaneezo] eliminate, wipe out, destroy.

έξαφνα [eksafna] all of a sudden.

έξαψη, η [eksapsee] fit of anger || excitement, elation.

εξεγείρομαι [ekseyeerome] rise, rebel.

εξέδρα, η [eksedra] platform, stand || (λιμανιού) pier.

εξελιγμένος [ekseleegmenos] developed, evolved.

εξέλιξη, η [ekseleeksee] evolution, development.

εξελίσσομαι [ekseleesome] unfold, evolve, develop.

εξερευνητής, ο [ekserevneetees] explorer.

εξερευνώ [ekserevno] investigate, explore.

εξέρχομαι [ekserhome] go out, leave || βλ και **βγαίνω**.

εξετάζω [eksetazo] examine, interrogate, investigate.

εξέταση, η [eksetasee] examination, inspection.

εξεύρεση, η [eksevresee] discovery, finding out, invention.

εξευτελίζω [eksevteleezo] cheapen, lower, humiliate.

εξέχω [ekseho] stand out, project || excel.

έξη, η [eksee] habit, custom, use.

εξήγηση, η [ekseeyeesee] explanation, interpretation.

εξηγούμαι [ekseegoume] explain, make clear, give an explanation.

εξηγώ [ekseego] explain || interpret.

εξή(κο)ντα [eksee(ko)nta] sixty.

εξημερώνω [ekseemerono] tame.

εξηντλημένος [ekseentleemenos] exhausted, used up.

εξής [eksees]: **ως** ~ as follows || **τα** ~ the following || **στο** ~ henceforth || **και ούτω καθ'** ~ and so on.

εξιλεώνω [ekseeleono] appease, pacify || atone for.

εξίσταμαι [ekseestame] be astonished, wonder at.

εξίσωση, η [ekseesosee] balancing, equalizing || (μαθημ) equation.

εξόγκωμα, το [eksongoma] swelling, tumour, bulge.

εξογκώνω [eksongono] swell || (μεταφ) exaggerate.

έξοδο, το [eksodo] expense.

έξοδος, η [eksodos] opening, emergence || (πόρτα) exit || (στρατ) sortie || (εκκλ) exodus.

εξοικειώνω [ekseekeeono] familiarize, accustom.

εξολοθρεύω [eksolothrevo] exterminate, destroy.

εξομαλύνω [eksomaleeno] smooth down || level.

εξομοιώνω [eksomeeono] assimilate to, liken to, rank together.

εξομολόγηση, η [eksomoloyeesee] confession, acknowledgement.

εξομολογώ [eksomologo] confess.

εξοντόνω [eksontono] annihilate, exterminate.

εξοπλίζω [eksopleezo] arm, equip.

εξοργίζω [eksoryeezo] enrage, make angry.

εξορία, η [eksoreea] banishment, exile.

εξορίζω [eksoreezo] exile, banish.

εξορκίζω [eksorkeezo] conjure, exorcise.

εξουδετερώνω [eksoudeterono] neutralize.

εξουσία, η [eksouseea] power, authority, government.

εξουσιοδοτώ [eksouseeodoto] give authority to, authorise, empower.

εξοφλώ [eksoflo] (λογαριασμό) pay off, liquidate || (μεταφ) fulfil.

εξοχή, η [eksohee] countryside || (εδαφική) eminence, protrusion || **κατ'** ~ preeminently, par excellence.

εξοχικός [eksoheekos] country, rural, rustic.

έξοχος [eksohos] excellent, eminent, notable.

εξοχότης, η [eksohotees] excellence || **η αυτού** ~ His Excellency.

εξύβριση, η [ekseevreesee] abuse, insult, offence.

εξυμνώ [ekseemno] praise, celebrate.

εξυπακούεται [ekseepakouete] it is understood, it follows.

εξυπηρέτηση, η [ekseepeereteesee] assistance, service, attendance.

εξυπηρετικός [ekseepeereteekos] helpful, useful.

εξυπηρετώ [ekseepeereto] serve, assist, attend upon.

εξυπνάδα, η [ekseepnaδa] cleverness, shrewdness.

έξυπνος [ekseepnos] clever, intelligent, smart, witty.

εξυψώνω [ekseepsono] elevate, raise || (μεταφ) exalt, extol, glorify.

έξω [ekso] out, outside, without, abroad || **απ'** ~ from outside || (μάθημα) by heart || ~ **από** outside, except for || **μια και** ~ at one go.

εξώγαμος [eksogamos] illegitimate, bastard.

εξώθυρα, η [eksotheera] outside door, gateway.

εξωθώ [eksotho] drive, push, force.

εξωκκλήσι, το [eksokleesee] chapel, (country) church.

εξώπορτα, η [eksoporta] βλ **εξώθυρα**.

εξωραΐζω [eksoraeezo] beautify, decorate, embellish.

έξωση, η [eksosee] eviction, expulsion.

εξώστης, ο [eksostees] balcony.

εξωτερικό, το [eksotereeko] exterior || foreign country, abroad.

εξωτερικός [eksotereekos] external || foreign.

εξωτικό, το [eksoteeko] spook, spectre, wraith.

εξωτικός [eksoteekos] exotic || outlandish.

εξωφρενικός [eksofreneekos] crazy || maddening || unreasonable, absurd.

εξώφυλλο, το [eksofeelo] cover, flyleaf || (παραθύρου) shutter.

εορτάζω [eortazo] celebrate.

εορτή, η [eortee] holiday || name day || festival.

επάγγελμα, το [epangelma] profession, vocation || **επαγγελματίας, ο** craftsman, businessman.

έπαθλο, το [epathlo] prize, trophy.

έπαινος, ο [epenos] praise.

επαινώ [epeno] praise, speak highly of.

επακόλουθα, τα [epakoloutha] πλ consequences.

επακολουθώ [epakoloutho] follow, come after.

έπακρο, το [epakro]: **στο** ~ extremely, to the extreme.

επαλείφω [epaleefo] smear (with), anoint (with).

επαληθεύω [epaleethevo] establish, verify.

επάλληλος [epaleelos] successive, one after another.

επανάγω [epanago] bring back (again).

επανακτώ [epanakto] recover.

επαναλαμβάνω [epanalamvano] repeat, resume.

επανάληψη, η [epanaleepsee] resumption, repetition.

επανάσταση, η [epanastasee] revolution.

επαναστάτης, ο [epanastatees] revolutionary, rebel.

επαναστατικός [epanastateekos] revolutionary.

επαναστατώ [epanastato] revolt, rebel.

επαναφέρω [epanafero] restore, bring back.

επανειλημμένος [epaneeleemenos] repeatedly.

επανέρχομαι [epanerhome] return.

επάνοδος, η [epanoδos] return.

επανόρθωση, η [epanorthosee] reparation, restoration.

επαξίως [epakseeos] deservedly, worthily.

επάρατος [eparatos] (μεταφ) hateful, abominable.

επάρκεια, η [eparkeea] sufficiency, adequacy.

έπαρση, η [eparsee] conceit, haughtiness.

επαρχία, η [eparheea] province, district.

επαρχιώτης, ο [eparheeotees] provincial.

έπαυλη, η [epavlee] villa || country house.

επαφή, η [epafee] contact, touch.

επείγομαι [epeegome] be in a hurry, make haste.

επειγόντως [epeegontos] urgently.

επείγων [epeegon] urgent, pressing.

επειδή [epeeδee] because, as, for, since.

επεισόδιο, το [epeesoδeeo] episode, incident || (καυγάς) quarrel, dispute.

έπειτα [epeeta] next, then, afterwards || moreover || ~ **από** after.

επέκταση, η [epektasee] extension.

επεκτείνω [epekteeno] extend, prolong.

επεμβαίνω [epemveno] interfere, intervene.

επέμβαση, η [epemvasee] intervention, interference || (ιατρ) operation.

επένδυση, η [epenδeesee] lining, covering || (οικον) investment.

επεξεργασία, η [epeksergaseea] processing, elaboration.

επεξήγηση, η [epekseeyeesee] explanation, elucidation.

επέρχομαι [eperhome] come suddenly, occur, happen.

επέτειος, η [epeteeos] anniversary.

επευφημώ [epefeemo] cheer, applaud.

επηρεάζω [epeereazo] influence, affect.

επί [epee] on, upon, over, above || (διάρκεια) for || ~ πλέον furthermore || ~ τέλους at last.

επιβάλλομαι [epeevalome] assert o.s. || be indispensable.

επιβάλλω [epeevalo] impose, inflict.

επιβαρύνω [epeevareeno] burden.

επιβατηγό, το [epeevateego] passenger ship.

επιβάτης, ο [epeevatees] passenger.

επιβατικό, το [epeevateeko] passenger vehicle, passenger ship.

επιβεβαιώνω [epeeveveono] confirm, corroborate.

επιβιβάζομαι [epeeveevazome] embark, go on board.

επιβιβάζω [epeeveevazo] put aboard.

επιβλαβής [epeevlavees] harmful.

επιβλέπω [epeevlepo] supervise.

επιβλητικός [epeevleeteekos] imposing.

επιβολή, η [epeevolee] imposition, infliction.

επιβουλεύομαι [epeevoulevome] plot against.

επιβραδύνω [epeevraδeeno] retard, delay.

επίγειος [epeeyeeos] earthly, worldly.

επίγνωση, η [epeegnosee] knowledge, understanding.

επίγραμμα, το [epeegrama] epigram.

επιγραφή, η [epeegrafee] inscription || (βιβλίου) title.

επιδεικνύομαι [epeeδeekneeome] show off, be pompous.

επιδεικνύω [epeeδeekneeo] display || show off.

επιδεικτικός [epeeδeekteekos] showy.

επιδείνωση, η [epeeδeenosee] aggravation.

επίδειξη, η [epeeδeeksee] display || showing off.

επιδέξιος [epeeδekseeos] skilful.

επιδερμίδα, η [epeeδermeeδa] complexion || epidermis.

επίδεσμος, ο [epeeδesmos] bandage.

επιδέχομαι [epeeδehome] allow, be susceptible to, tolerate.

επιδημία, η [epeeδeemeea] epidemic.

επιδιόρθωση, η [epeeδeeorthosee] repair, mending.

επιδιώκω [epeeδeeoko] aim at, pursue, seek.

επιδοκιμάζω [epeeδokeemazo] approve.

επίδομα, το [epeeδoma] allowance, extra pay.

επίδοση, η [epeeδosee] presentation, delivery || (νομ) deposit || (μεταφ) progress, development || (αθλητ) record.

επίδραση, η [epeeδrasee] effect, influence.

επιδρομή, η [epeeδromee] invasion, raid.

επιδρώ [epeeδro] influence, act upon.

επιεικής [epieekees] lenient, indulgent.

επιζήμιος [epeezeemeeos] harmful, injurious.

επιζώ [epeezo] survive, outlive.

επίθεση, η [epeethesee] attack || application.

επιθετικός [epeetheteekos] aggressive.

επίθετο, το [epeetheto] adjective || surname.

επιθεώρηση, η [epeetheoreesee] inspection || (περιοδικό) review || (θέατρο) revue.

επιθυμία, η [epeetheemeea] desire, wish.

επιθυμώ [epeetheemo] wish for, desire.

επίκαιρος [epeekeros] timely, opportune || topical.

επικαλούμαι [epeekaloume] invoke.

επίκειμαι [epeekeeme] be imminent || impend.

επικερδής [epeekerδees] profitable.

επικεφαλίδα, η [epeekefaleeδa] headline || title.

επικίνδυνος [epeekeenδeenos] dangerous, hazardous.

επικοινωνία, η [epeekeenoneea] contact, communication.

επικοινωνώ [epeekeenono] communicate.

επικός [epeekos] epic.

επικράτεια, η [epeekrateea] state, dominion.

επικρατώ [epeekrato] prevail, predominate.

επικρίνω [epeekreeno] criticize, censure.

επικροτώ [epeekroto] approve.

επικυρώνω [epeekeerono] ratify, confirm, sanction.

επιλαχών, ο [epeelahon] runner-up.

επιληψία, η [epeeleepseea] epilepsy.

επιλογή, η [epeeloyee] selection, choice.

επίλογος, ο [epeelogos] epilogue || conclusion.

επιλοχίας, ο [epeeloheeas] sergeant-major.

επίμαχος [epeemahos] disputed || controversial.

επιμελής [epeemelees] diligent, industrious, careful.

επιμελητήριο, το [epeemeleeteereeo] (εμπορικό) chamber of commerce.

επιμελητής, ο [epeemeleetees] superintendent || (university) tutor.

επιμελούμαι [epeemeloume] take care of.

επιμένω [epeemeno] insist, persist.

επιμήκης [epeemeekees] oblong, elongated.

επιμονή, η [epeemonee] insistence, perseverance.

επίμονος [epeemonos] persistent, stubborn, obstinate.

επινοώ [epeenoo] invent, contrive, devise.

επίπεδο, το [epeepeδo] level || (βιοτικό) standard of living.

επίπεδος [epeepeδos] plane, level, flat || even.

επιπίπτω [epeepeepto] fall upon.

έπιπλα, τα [epeepla] πλ furniture.

επιπλέω [epeepleo] float || (μεταφ) keep afloat.

επίπληξη, η [epeepleeksee] reproach, rebuke.

επιπλήττω [epeepleeto] reproach, chide.

επιπλοκή, η [epeeplokee] complication.

επιπλώνω [epeeplono] furnish.

επίπλωση, η [epeeplosee] furnishing.

επιπόλαιος [epeepoleos] superficial || frivolous.

επίπονος [epeeponos] laborious, toilsome.

επίρρημα, το [epeereema] adverb.

επιρροή, η [epeeroee] influence.

επίσημος [epeeseemos] official, formal.

επίσης [epeesees] likewise, also, too.

επισιτισμός, ο [epeeseeteesmos] provisioning, provisions.

επισκεπτήριο, το [epeeskepteereeo] visiting card || visiting hour.

επισκέπτης, ο [epeeskeptees] visitor.

επισκέπτομαι [epeeskeptome] visit, call upon.

επισκευάζω [epeeskevazo] repair, mend.

επισκευή, η [epeeskevee] repairing, mending.

επίσκεψη, η [epeeskepsee] visit, call.

επίσκοπος, ο [epeeskopos] bishop.

επισπεύδω [epeespevδo] hasten, rush.

επιστάτης, ο [epeestatees] supervisor || overseer || attendant.

επιστήθιος [epeesteetheeos]: ~ φίλος bosom friend.

επιστήμη, η [epeesteemee] science.

επιστημονικός [epeesteemoneekos] scientific.

επιστήμων, ο, η [epeesteemon] scientist, professional (person) || expert.

επιστολή, η [epeestolee] letter.

επιστράτευση, η [epeestratevsee] mobilization, call-up.

επιστρέφω [epeestrefo] return.

επιστροφή, η [epeestrofee] return.

επίστρωμα, το [epeestroma] covering.

επισυνάπτω [epeeseenapto] annex, attach.

επισύρω [epeeseero] attract, draw, catch one's eye.

επισφαλής [epeesfalees] precarious, risky || unstable.

επιταγή, η [epeetayee] order || cheque.

επιτακτικός [epeetakteekos] imperative.

επίταξη, η [epeetaksee] requisition.

επιτάφιος, ο [epeetafeeos] Good Friday procession.

επιταχύνω [epeetaheeno] accelerate, speed up.

επιτελείο, το [epeeteleeo] (general) staff.

επιτετραμμένος, ο [epeetetramenos] chargé d'affaires.

επίτευγμα, το [epeetevgma] achievement.

επίτευξη, η [epeetevksee] attainment || obtaining.

επιτήδειος [epeeteeδeeos] suitable for || clever, skilful.

επίτηδες [epeeteeδes] on purpose, purposely.

επιτηδευμένος [epeeteeδevmenos] affected.

επιτηρώ [epeeteero] supervise, oversee, watch.

επιτίθεμαι [epeeteetheme] attack, assail, assault.

επίτιμος [epeeteemos] honorary.

επιτόκιο, το [epeetokeeo] compound interest.

επίτομος [epeetomos] abridged, shortened, condensed.

επί τόπου [epeetopou] on the spot.

επιτρέπω [epeetrepo] allow, permit.

επιτροπή, η [epeetropee] committee, commission.

επίτροπος, ο [epeetropos] guardian, trustee || commissioner.

επιτυγχάνω [epeeteenghano] attain, get || get right || (κατά τύχην) meet, find || (στη δουλειά) succeed.

επιτυχής [epeeteehees] successful.

επιτυχία, η [epeeteeheea] success.

επιφάνεια, η [epeefaneea] surface.

επιφανής [epeefanees] eminent, prominent.

Επιφάνια, τα [epeefaneea] πλ Epiphany.

επιφέρω [epeefero] bring about, cause.

επιφυλακή, η [epeefeelakee]: σε ~ at the ready, on the alert.

επιφύλαξη, η [epeefeelaksee] circumspection || reservation.

επιφυλάσσομαι [epeefeelasome] reserve, intend.

επιφώνημα, το [epeefoneema] (γραμμ) interjection.

επιχείρημα, το [epeeheereema] argument || attempt.

επιχειρηματίας, ο [epeeheereemateeas] businessman.

επιχείρηση, η [epeeheereesee] undertaking || (οικον) enterprise, business || (στρατ) operation.

επιχρυσώνω [epeehreesono] gild.

εποικοδομητικός [epeekoδomeeteekos] constructive, edifying.

επόμενος [epomenos] next, following.

επομένως [epomenos] consequently, therefore.

επονομάζω [eponomazo] surname, name.

εποπτεύω [epoptevo] supervise, oversee, inspect.

επουλώνω [epoulono] heal.

εποχή, η [epohee] epoch, era || (του έτους) season.

επτά [epta] seven.

επτακόσιοι [eptakosiee] seven hundred.

επώδυνος [epoδeenos] painful.

επωμίδα, η [epomeeδa] epaulette.

επωμίζομαι [epomeezome] shoulder (a burden).

επωνυμία, η [eponeemeea] (nick)name || surname || (εταιρείας) title.

επώνυμο, το [eponeemo] surname, family name.

επωφελής [epofelees] profitable, beneficial, useful.

επωφελούμαι [epofeloume] take advantage, avail o.s., profit.

έρανος, ο [eranos] fund, collection.

ερασιτέχνης, ο [eraseetehnees] amateur.

εραστής, ο [erastees] lover.

εργάζομαι [ergazome] work || function.

εργαλείο, το [ergaleeo] tool, implement.

εργασία, η [ergaseea] work, job, business || (επιδεξιότητα) workmanship.

εργαστήριο, το [ergasteereeo] laboratory || studio || workshop.

εργάτης, ο [ergatees] labourer, worker || (ναυτ) windlass.

εργατιά, η [ergateea] working class.

εργατικός [ergateekos] industrious, of the working class.

εργένης, ο [ergenees] bachelor.

εργοδηγός, ο [ergoδeegos] foreman.

εργοδότης, ο [ergoδotees] employer.

εργολάβος, ο [ergolavos] contractor.

έργο, το [ergo] work || act, deed || (βιβλίο) book || (σινεμά) film.

εργοστάσιο, το [ergostaseeo] factory || works.

εργόχειρο, το [ergoheero] handiwork || (κέντημα) embroidery.

ερεθίζω [eretheezo] irritate, excite.

ερεθισμός, ο [eretheesmos] irritation.

ερείπιο, το [ereepeeo] ruin, wreck.

έρευνα, η [erevna] (re)search, investigation.

ερευνητής, ο [erevneetees] researcher || explorer.

ερευνώ [erevno] search, investigate.

ερημιά, η [ereemeea] solitude || wilderness.

έρημος, η [ereemos] desert || (επιθ) desolate, deserted.

ερημώνω [ereemono] lay waste, devastate.

έριδα, η [ereeδa] dispute, quarrel.

ερίφι, το [ereefee] kid.

έρμαιο, το [ermeo] prey || victim.

ερμηνεία, η [ermeeneea] interpretation.

ερμηνεύω [ermeenevo] interpret.

ερμητικός [ermeeteekos] hermetic.

ερπετό, το [erpeto] reptile.

έρπω [erpo] crawl, creep.

ερυθρόδερμος, ο [ereethroδermos] redskin.

ερυθρός [ereethros] red.

έρχομαι [erhome] come.

ερχόμενος [erhomenos] coming, next.

ερχομός, ο [erhomos] coming, arrival.

ερωμένη, η [eromenee] mistress.

ερωμένος, ο [eromenos] lover.

έρωτας, ο [erotas] love, passion.

ερωτευμένος [erotevmenos] in love.

ερωτεύομαι [erotevome] fall in love.

ερώτημα, το [eroteema] question, problem.

ερωτηματικό, το [eroteemateeko] question mark.

ερωτηματολόγιο, το [eroteematoloyeeo] questionnaire.

ερώτηση, η [eroteesee] question, query.

ερωτικός [eroteekos] erotic || amatory.

ερωτύλος [eroteelos] amorous.

ερωτώ [eroto] ask, inquire || question.

εσκεμμένος [eskemenos] premeditated || deliberately.

εσοδεία, η [esoδeea] crop, harvest.

έσοδο, το [esodo] income, revenue, receipt.

εσοχή, η [esohee] recess, indentation.

εσπεριδοειδή, τα [espereedoeedee] πλ citrus fruits.

εσπερινός, ο [espereenos] vespers.

εσπευσμένος [espevsmenos] hasty, hurried.

εστία, η [esteea] hearth, fireplace || (σπίτι) home || (λίκνος) cradle || (σόμπας) burner.

εστιατόριο, το [esteeatoreeo] restaurant.

έστω [esto] so be it || ~ **και** even, if.

ευ [..xo] you

εσχάρα, η [eshara] grill, gridiron, grid.

έσχατος [eshatos] extreme, utmost, last.

έσω [eso] within, inside.

εσωκλείω [esokleeo] enclose.

εσώρρουχα, τα [esorouha] πλ underclothes, underwear.

εσωτερικός [esotereekos] interior, inner, internal || domestic.

εταιρεία, η [etereea] company, society, firm, partnership.

ετερογενής [eterogenees] heterogeneous.

έτερος [eteros] (an)other || **αφ' ετέρου** on the other hand.

ετήσιος [eteeseeos] annual, yearly.

ετικέττα, η [eteeketa] label, price tag.

ετοιμάζομαι [eteemazome] get ready, prepare.

ετοιμάζω [eteemazo] prepare, make ready.

ετοιμασία, η [eteemaseea] preparation.

έτοιμος [eteemos] ready.

έτος, το [etos] year.

έτσι [etsee] thus, so, like this, like that, in this way || ~ **κι** ~ middling || in any case, || ~ **κι αλλοιώς** in any case, either way.

ετυμηγορία, η [eteemeegoreea] verdict.

ετυμολογία, η [eteemoloyeea] etymology.

ευ- [ev] well, easily.

ευαγγέλιο, το [evangeleeo] gospel.

Ευαγγελισμός, ο [evangeleesmos] Annunciation.

ευάερος [evaeros] well-ventilated, airy.

ευαισθησία, η [evestheeseea] sensitivity.

ευαίσθητος [evestheetos] sensitive.

ευανάγνωστος [evanagnostos] legible.

εύγε [evye] (επιφ) bravo!, good show!

ευγένεια, η [evgeneea] courtesy, politeness.

ευγενικός [evyeneekos], **ευγενής** [evyenees] polite, courteous.

εύγευστος [evyevstos] palatable, tasty.

ευγλωττία, η [evgloteea] eloquence.

ευγνωμοσύνη, η [evgnomoseenee] gratitude.

ευγνώμων [evgnomon] grateful, thankful.

ευδαιμονία, η [evðemoneea] prosperity || happiness.

ευδιάθετος [evðeeathetos] in good humour.

ευδιάκριτος [evðeeakreetos] discernible, distinct.

ευδοκιμώ [evðokeemo] succeed || thrive || prosper.

ευδοκώ [evðoko] be pleased to, deign, consent.

ευέξαπτος [eveksaptos] irritable, excitable.

ευεργέτης, ο [everyetees] benefactor.

ευεργετικός [everyeteekos] beneficial, beneficent, charitable.

εύζωνας, ο [evzonas] evzone.

ευήλιος [eveeleeos] sunny.

ευημερώ [eveemero] prosper.

ευθεία, η [evthea] straight line || **κατ'** ~ direct, straight.

εύθετος [evthetos] suitable, proper, convenient.

εύθικτος [evtheektos] touchy, sensitive.

εύθραυστος [evthravstos] fragile, brittle.

ευθύγραμμος [evtheegramos] straight, rectilinear.

ευθυμία, η [evtheemeea] gaiety, cheerfulness.

εύθυμος [evtheemos] merry, gay, cheerful.

ευθύνη, η [evtheenee] responsibility.

ευθύνομαι [evtheenome] be responsible, be accountable.

ευθύς [evthees] (επιρ) immediately, at once.

ευθύς [evthees] straight, upright || (τίμιος) honest, straightforward.

ευκαιρία, η [evkereea] opportunity, chance || (εμπόριο) bargain.

εύκαιρος [evkeros] opportune || (ελεύθερος) available, free.

ευκάλυπτος [evkaleeptos] eucalyptus.

εύκαμπτος, ο [evkambtos] flexible, pliable.

ευκατάστατος [evkatastatos] well-to-do, well-off.

ευκίνητος [evkeeneetos] agile, nimble.

ευκοιλιότητα, η [evkeeleeoteeta] diarrhoea.

ευκολία, η [evkoleea] ease, convenience || (χάρη) favour.

εύκολος [evkolos] easy || convenient.

ευκολύνω [evkoleeno] facilitate.

ευκρατής [evkratees] temperate, mild.

ευλαβής [evlavees] devout, pious.

ευλογία, η [evloyeea] blessing, benediction.

ευλογιά, η [evloya] smallpox.

ευλογώ [evlogo] bless.

ευλύγιστος [evleeyeestos] flexible, supple, pliant.

ευμενής [evmenees] benevolent, kind, well-disposed.

ευμετάβλητος [evmetavleetos] changeable, inconstant.

ευνόητος [evnoeetos] easily understood || intelligible.

εύνοια, η [evneea] favour, goodwill.

ευνοϊκός [evnoeekos] propitious, favourable.

ευνοούμενος [evnooumenos] favourite.

ευνοώ [evnoo] favour.

ευπαθής [evpathees] sensitive, delicate.

ευπαρουσίαστος [evparouseea- stos] presentable, imposing.

εύπιστος [evpeestos] credulous, gullible.

εύπορος [evporos] well-off, prosperous.

ευπρέπεια, η [evprepeea] propriety || decency.

ευπρεπίζω [evprepeezo] put in order || adorn, embellish.

ευπρόσδεκτος [evprosδektos] welcome, acceptable.

ευπρόσιτος [evproseetos] accessible, approachable.

ευρετήριο, το [evreteereeo] index, catalogue.

ευρέως [evreos] widely, largely.

εύρημα, το [evreema] find, discovery.

ευρίσκω [evreesko] βλ βρίσκω.

ευρύς [evrees] wide, extended, broad.

ευρύχωρος [evreehoros] spacious, roomy.

ευρωπαϊκός [evropaeekos] European.

Ευρώπη, η [evropee] Europe.

ευσέβεια, η [evseveea] piety, devoutness.

ευσεβής [evsevees] pious, devout.

ευσπλαγχνία, η [evsplanghneea] compassion, pity.

ευστάθεια, η [evstatheea] stability, firmness.

εύστοχος [evstohos] well-aimed, proper.

εύστροφος [evstrofos] agile, nimble, versatile.

ευσυνείδητος [evseeneeδetos] conscientious || scrupulous.

εύσωμος [evsomos] well-built, stout, sturdy.

ευτέλεια, η [evteleea] meanness, baseness, cheapness.

ευτελής [evtelees] cheap, mean, worthless.

ευτύχημα, το [evteeheema] good luck, lucky thing.

ευτυχής [evteehees] lucky, fortunate, happy.

ευτυχία, η [evteeheea] happiness, good fortune.

ευτυχισμένος [evteeheesmenos] βλ ευτυχής.

ευτυχώς [evteehos] luckily, happily, fortunately.

ευυπόληπτος [eveepoleeptos] reputable, esteemed.

εύφλεκτος [evflektos] inflammable.

ευφορία, η [evforeea] fruitfulness, fertility.

ευφράδεια, η [evfraδeea] eloquence.

ευφυής [evfiees] intelligent, witty, clever.

ευφυΐα, η [evfieea] intelligence, wit, ingenuity.

ευχαρίστηση, η [evhareesteesee] satisfaction, pleasure.

ευχαριστίες, οι [evhareesties] πλ thanks.

ευχάριστος [evhareestos] pleasant, agreeable.

ευχαρίστως [evhareestos] gladly, with pleasure.

ευχαριστώ [evhareesto] thank || please, gratify || thank you.

ευχέρεια, η [evhereea] ease, facility.

ευχή, η [evhee] prayer || wish || blessing.

εύχομαι [evhome] wish, hope.

εύχρηστος [evhreestos] useful, handy || in general use.

εφ [ef] βλ επί.

εφάμιλλος [efameelos] equal to, on a par with, a match for.

εφάπαξ [efapaks] in a lump sum, once only.

εφαπτόμενη, η [efaptomenee] tangent.

εφαρμογή, η [efarmoyee] application, fitting.

εφαρμόζω [efarmozo] fit || apply || enforce.

έφεδρος, ο [efeδros] reservist.

εφεξής [efeksees] henceforth, hereafter.

έφεση, η [efesee] (νομ) appeal.

εφετείο, το [efeteeo] court of appeal.

εφέτος [efetos] this year.

εφεύρεση, [efevresee] invention.

εφευρετικός [efevreteekos] inventive, ingenious.

έφηβος, ο [efeevos] youth, adolescent.

εφηβικός [efeeveekos] of youth, of puberty || εφηβική ηλικία adolescence.

εφημερεύω [efeemerevo] be on duty.

εφημερίδα, η [efeemereeða] newspaper, journal, gazette.

εφιάλτης, ο [efeealtees] nightmare.

εφικτός [efeektos] possible, attainable, feasible.

εφιστώ [efeesto]: ~ **την προσοχή** draw attention to.

εφόδια, τα [efoðeea] πλ supplies, equipment || **εφοδιάζω** supply, equip, furnish.

έφοδος [efoðos] charge, assault, attack.

εφοπλιστής, ο [efopleestees] shipowner.

εφορεία, η [eforeea] tax office, revenue department.

έφορος, ο [eforos] inspector, director, keeper, curator.

εφτά [efta] βλ **επτά.**

εφτακόσιοι [eftakosiee] βλ **επτακόσιοι.**

εχεμύθεια, η [ehemeetheea] secrecy, discretion || **υπό ~ν** under pledge of secrecy.

εχθές [ehthes] yesterday.

έχθρα, η [ehthra] enmity, hostility.

εχθρεύομαι [ehthrevome] hate, dislike.

εχθρικός [ehthreekos] hostile, (of the) enemy, inimical.

εχθρικότητα, η [ehthreekoteeta] hostility.

εχθροπραξίες, οι [ehthropraksies] πλ hostilities.

εχθρός, ο [ehthros] enemy, foe.

έχιδνα, η [eheeðna] viper, adder.

έχω [eho] have, keep || consider || cost, be worth || ~ **δίκιο I** am right || **τι έχεις;** what's wrong?, what's the matter?

εψιλο, το [epseelo] the letter E.

έως [eos] till, until, to || as far as.

Z, ζ

ζαβολιά, η [zavolia] cheating, trickery.

ζαβός [zavos] crooked, perverse || clumsy.

ζακέτα, η [zaketa] jacket.

ζαλάδα, η [zalaða] giddiness, dizziness || headache.

ζάλη, η [zalee] dizziness.

ζαλίζομαι [zaleezome] become dizzy, become confused.

ζαλίζω [zaleezo] make dizzy, confuse, daze, stun.

ζαμπό, το [zambo] ham.

ζάπλουτος [zaploutos] very rich, opulent.

ζάρα, η [zara] crease, wrinkle.

ζάρια, τα [zareea] πλ dice.

ζαρκάδι, το [zarkaðee] roe(buck).

ζάρωμα, το [zaroma] creasing, wrinkling || crease, wrinkle.

ζαρώνω [zarono] crease, wrinkle || shrink.

ζαφείρι, το [zafeeree] sapphire.

ζαχαρένιος [zahareneeos] sugary || (μεταφ) honeyed.

ζάχαρη, η [zaharee] sugar.

ζαχαροκάλαμο, το [zaharokalamo] sugar cane.

ζαχαροπλαστείο, το [zaharoplasteeo] confectioner's (shop), cake shop.

ζαχαρωτά, τα [zaharota] πλ sweets.

ζεματίζω [zemateezo] scald || be very hot.

ζεμάτισμα [zemateestos] scalding, boiling.

ζενίθ, το [zeneeth] zenith.

ζερβός [zervos] left-handed || left.

ζέση, η [zesee] boiling || (μεταφ) warmth, fervour.

ζεσταίνομαι [zestenome] get warm, feel hot.

ζεσταίνω [zesteno] heat up, warm.

ζεστασιά, η [zestasia] warmth, heat.

ζέστη, η [zestee] heat, warmth || **κάνει ~** it's hot, it's warm.

ζεστός [zestos] hot, warm.

ζευγαράκι, το [zevgarakee] pair (of lovers).

ζευγάρι, το [zevgaree] pair, couple || (βοδιών) yoke.

ζευγνύω [zevgneeo] yoke, harness, link.

ζεύγος, το [zevgos] pair, couple.

ζεύξη, η [zevksee] yoking || bridging, junction.

ζέφυρος, ο [zefeeros] light breeze.

ζήλεια, η [zeeleea] envy, jealousy.

ζηλευτός [zeelevtos] enviable, desirable || much desired.

ζηλεύω [zeelevo] envy, be jealous of.

ζηλιάρης [zeeleearees] envious, jealous.

ζήλος, ο [zeelos] zeal, ardour, eagerness.

ζηλότυπος [zeeloteepos] βλ **ζηλιάρης.**

ζημία, η [zeemeea] damage, loss, injury || harm.

ζημιώνω [zeemeeono] damage, cause a loss, injure.

ζήτα, το [zeeta] the letter Z.

ζήτημα, το [zeeteema] question, subject, matter || **είναι ~** it's doubtful (whether).

ζήτηση, η [zeeteesee] demand || search, pursuit.

ζητιανεύω [zeeteeanevo] beg, ask for alms.

ζητιάνος, ο [zeeteeanos] beggar.

ζήτω [zeeto] (επιφ) long live!, up with!

ζητώ [zeeto] seek, ask for, look for, demand || beg.

ζητωκραυγή, η [zeetokravgee] cheer.

ζιζάνιο, το [zeezaneeo] (μεταφ) naughty person || (βοτ) weed.

ζόρι, το [zoree] force, violence || difficulty || **με το ~** against one's will.

ζορίζω [zoreezo] force, exert pressure on.

ζόρικος [zoreekos] hard, difficult || (επι ανθρωπος) hard to please, irksome.

ζούγκλα η [zoungla] jungle.

ζουζούνι, το [zouzounee] insect.

ζούλισμα, το [zouleesma] squeezing, crushing.

ζουμερός [zoumeros] juicy, succulent.

ζουμί, το [zoumee] juice || broth || (ψητού) gravy.

ζουμπούλι, το [zoumboulee] hyacinth.

ζούρλα, η [zourla] lunacy, folly.

ζουρλομανδύας, ο [zourlomandeeas] strait jacket.

ζοφερός [zoferos] dark, gloomy.

ζοχάδα, η [zohada] peevishness, sourness, sullenness.

ζυγαριά, η [zeegaria] pair of scales, balance.

ζυγίζομαι [zeeyeezome] hover over.

ζυγίζω [zeeyeezo] weigh.

ζυγός, ο [zeegos] yoke || (παλάντζας) scale, beam.

ζυγός [zeegos] even (number) || **μονά ζυγά** odd or even.

ζυγώνω [zeegono] draw near.

ζύθος, ο [zeethos] beer, ale.

ζυμάρι, το [zeemaree] dough || **ζυμαρικά** pastry, pies, cakes.

ζύμη, η [zeemee] leaven, dough.

ζύμωμα, το [zeemoma] kneading.

ζυμώνομαι [zeemonome] ferment.

ζυμώνω [zeemono] knead || ferment.

ζύμωση, η [zeemosee] fermentation.

ζω [zo] live, experience || lead a life.

ζωγραφιά, η [zografia] painting, drawing.

ζωγραφική, η [zografeekee] painting.

ζωγραφιστός [zografeestos] painted.

ζωγράφος, ο [zografos] painter, artist.

ζώδιο, το [zodeeo] sign of the zodiac.

ζωέμπορος, ο [zoemboros] cattle dealer.

ζωή, η [zoee] life, living || lifetime.

ζωηρεύω [zoeerevo] become lively || brighten up.

ζωηρός [zoeeros] lively, vivid || (θερμός) warm, animated || (χρώματος) bright || (εύθυμος) gay, full of life.

ζωηρότητα, η [zoeeroteeta] heat, warmth || (κινήσεως) quickness, promptness || (βλέμματος) vivacity, brightness.

ζωικός [zoeekos] animal || vital, necessary.

ζωμός, ο [zomos] broth, soup.

ζωνάρι, το [zonaree] belt, sash, girdle, waistband.

ζώνη, η [zonee] zone || βλ και **ζωνάρι**.

ζωντανεύω [zontanevo] revive, return to life.

ζωντάνια, η [zontaneea] liveliness, alertness.

ζωντανός [zontanos] living, live, vivid || lively.

ζωντοχήρα, η [zontoheera] divorced woman, divorcée.

ζωντοχήρος, ο [zontoheeros] divorced man, divorcé.

ζωογονώ [zoogono] animate || (μεταφ) stimulate, excite.

ζωοκλοπή, η [zooklopee] cattle rustling, sheep stealing.

ζωολογία, η [zooloyeea] zoology.

ζώο, το [zoo] animal || (μεταφ) fool, ass.

ζωοτροφές, οι [zootrofes] πλ animal fodder, food stuffs.

ζωόφιλος [zoofeelos] fond of animals.

ζωπυρώ [zopeero] rekindle, revive.

ζωτικός [zoteekos] vital.

ζωτικότητα, η [zoteekoteeta] vitality || (μεταφ) vital importance.

ζωύφιο, το [zoeefeeo] insect, louse || πλ vermin.

Η, η

η [ee] the.

ή [ee] or || **~ ... ~** either ... or || (συγκριτικός) than.

ήβη, η [eevee] puberty.

ηγεμόνας, ο [eeyemonas] prince, sovereign || governor.

ηγεσία, η [eeyeseea] leadership.

ηγέτης, ο [eeyetees] leader, chief.

ηγούμαι [eegoume] lead, command.

ηγούμενος, ο [eegoumenos] abbot.

ήδη [eedee] already, even now.

ηδονή, η [eedonee] delight, sensual pleasure, lust.

ηδονικός [eedoneekos] delightful || sensual.

ηθική, η [eetheekee] ethics || morality.

ηθικό, το [eetheeko] morale || morality, morals.

ηθικός [eetheekos] ethical, moral || virtuous, modest.

ηθογραφία, η [eethografeea] folk customs, folklore.

ηθοποιία, η [eethopieea] acting.

ηθοποιός, ο, η [eethopeeos] actor, actress.

ήθη, τα [eethee] πλ manners, habits, customs.

ήθος, το [eethos] character, nature, manner.

ηλεκτρίζω [eelektreezo] electrify.

ηλεκτρικό, το [eelektreeko] electricity.

πλεκτρικός [eelektreekos] electric.
πλεκτρισμός, ο [eelektreesmos] electricity.
πλεκτρολόγος, ο [eelektrologos] electrician.
πλεκτρονική, η [eelektroneekee] ηλ electronics.
πλεκτρόνιο, το [eelektroneeo] electron.
πλεκτροπληξία, η [eelektropleekseea] electric shock.
πλιακός [eeleeakos] of the sun, solar.
πλίαση, η [eeleeasee] sunstroke.
πλίθιος [eeleetheeos] idiotic, stupid, silly.
πλικία, η [eeleekeea] age.
πλικιωμένος [eeleekeeomenos] aged, advanced in years.
πλιοβασίλεμα, το [eelecovaseelema] sunset.
πλιοθεραπεία, η [eeleeotherapeea] sunbathing.
πλιοκαμένος [eeleeokamenos] sunburnt, tanned.
ήλιος, ο [eeleeos] sun || (φυτό) sunflower.
ημέρα, η [eemera] day || **της ~ς** fresh, today's.
ημερεύω [eemerevo] tame, domesticate || calm down, appease.
ημερήσιος [eemereeseeos] daily, everyday.
ημερολόγιο, το [eemeroloyo] calendar, almanac || (πλοίου) logbook || (ατόμου) diary.
ημερομηνία, η [eemeromeeneea] date.
ημερομίσθιο, το [eemeromeestheeo] daily wage.
ήμερος [eemeros] domesticated || tame, gentle.
ημερώνω [eemerono] tame || calm down, pacify.
ημιαργία, η [eemeearyeea] half-day (holiday).
ημιεπίσημος [eemiepeeseemos] semi-official.
ημιθανής [eemeethanees] half-dead.
ημίθεος, ο [eemeetheos] demigod.
ημικύκλιο, το [eemeekeekleeo] semicircle.
ημιμαθής [eemeemathees] half-learned (person), having a smattering of learning.
ημίμετρα, τα [eemeemetra] ηλ half-measures.
ημιπληγία, η [eemeepleeyeea] stroke, paralysis.
ημισέληνος, η [eemeeseleenos] crescent.
ήμισυ, το [eemeesee] half.
ημισφαίριο, το [eemeesfereeo] hemisphere.
ημιτελής [eemeetelees] half-finished.

ημίφως, το [eemeefos] twilight || dim light.
ημίχρονο, το [eemeehrono] (αθλητ) half-time.
ημίωρο, το [eemeeoro] half-hour.
ηνίο, το [eeneeo] rein, bridle.
ηνωμένος [eenomenos] united, joint || **Ηνωμένο Βασίλειο** United Kingdom || **Ηνωμένες Πολιτείες (Αμερικής)** United States (of America).
ήπαρ, το [eepar] liver.
ήπειρος, η [eepeeros] continent || mainland, land.
ηπειρωτικός [eepeeroteekos] continental.
ήπιος [eepeeos] mild, indulgent || (ασθένεια) benign.
ηρεμία, η [eeremeea] quietness, tranquility, serenity.
ήρεμος [eeremos] calm, tranquil, peaceful, still.
ηρεμώ [eeremo] be calm || keep quiet, keep still.
ηρωικός [eeroeekos] heroic.
ηρωίνη, η [eeroeenee] heroin.
ήρωας, ο [eeroas] hero.
ηρωίδα, η [eeroeeδa] heroine.
ηρωισμός, ο [eeroeesmos] heroism.
ησυχάζω [eeseehazo] grow quiet, rest, calm down.
ησυχία, η [eeseeheea] quietness, peace, serenity.
ήσυχος [eeseehos] quiet, peaceful, composed.
ήτα, το [eeta] the letter Η.
ήττα, η [eeta] defeat, beating.
ηττοπάθεια, η [eetopatheea] defeatism.
ήττον, το [eeton] less.
ηττώμαι [eetome] be defeated, succumb.
ηφαίστειο, το [eefesteeo] volcano.
ηχηρός [eeheeros] loud, ringing, resonant.
ηχητικός [eeheeteekos] producing sound, resounding.
ήχος, ο [eehos] sound.
ηχώ, η [eeho] echo, sound || (μεταφ) repercussion.
ηχώ [eeho] ring, sound, strike, reverberate.

Θ, θ

θα [tha] shall, will, should, would.
θάβω [thavo] bury, inter || (μεταφ) hide.
θαλαμηγός, η [thalameegos] yacht.
θάλαμος, ο [thalamos] room || (νοσοκομείου) ward || (ποπλάτου κτλ) inner tube || (όπλου) chamber.
θάλασσα η [thalassa] sea || **τα κάνω ~** mess up, fail

θαλασσινά, τα [thalaseena] πλ shellfish.

θαλασσοδέρνω [thalassoðerno] buffet || (μεταφ) struggle against (adversity).

θαλασσόλυκος, ο [thalasoleekos] sea dog, mariner.

θαλασσοπόρος, ο [thalasoporos] navigator, seafarer.

θαλασσώνω [thalasono]: τα ~ turn things topsy-turvy, mess it up.

θαλερός [thaleros] green, in bloom || (μεταφ) fresh, vigorous.

θάμβος, το [thamvos] astonishment, wonder.

θάμνος, ο [thamnos] bush, shrub, scrub.

θαμπός [thambos] (χρώμα) lifeless, without lustre || dim, cloudy.

θάμπωμα, το [thamboma] dazzle || astonishment || (ματιού) dimness || (μυαλού) confusion.

θαμπώνω [thambono] dazzle || tarnish, blur, dim || grow dim.

θαμώνας, ο [thamonas] habitué, regular customer, frequent visitor.

θανάσιμος [thanaseemos] deadly, fatal.

θανατηφόρος [thanateeforos] deadly, murderous.

θανατικός [thanateekos] capital, of death.

θάνατος, ο [thanatos] death.

θανατώνω [thanatono] execute.

θανή, η [thanee] death || funeral.

θαρραλέος [tharaleos] plucky, daring, bold.

θαρρετός [tharetos] βλ **θαρραλέος**.

θαρρεύω [tharevo] venture, dare, hazard.

θάρρος, το [tharos] daring, courage, spunk, mettle.

θαρρώ [tharo] believe, think.

θαύμα, το [thavma] miracle, wonder.

θαυμάζω [thavmazo] wonder at, admire, be amazed at.

θαυμάσιος [thavmaseeos] admirable, marvellous, superb.

θαυμασμός, ο [thavmasmos] wonder, admiration, astonishment.

θαυμαστής, ο [thavmastees] admirer, fan.

θαυμαστικό, το [thavmasteeko] exclamation mark.

θαυμαστικός [thavmasteekos] admiring.

θαυμαστός [thavmastos] admirable, astonishing.

θαυματουργός [thavmatourgos] wondrous, miracle-making, miraculous.

θάψιμο, το [thapseemo] burial.

θεά, η [thea] goddess.

θέα, η [thea] view, sight, aspect.

θέαμα, το [theama] spectacle, show || **θεαματικός** spectacular, wonderful.

θεατής, ο [theatees] spectator, onlooker.

θεατός [theatos] visible, perceptible.

θεατρικός [theatreekos] theatrical || (μεταφ) pompous, showy.

θεατρίνος, ο [theatreenos] actor.

θέατρο, το [theatro] theatre, stage.

θεία, η [theea] aunt.

θειάφι, το [theeafee] sulphur.

θεϊκός [theyeekos] divine.

θείος, ο [theeos] uncle.

θείος [theeos] divine, holy, sacred.

θέλγητρο, το [thelyeetro] charm, enchantment, attraction.

θέλγω [thelgo] charm, enchant, fascinate.

θέλημα, το [theleema] will, wish, desire || **θεληματικός** voluntary || willing.

θέληση, η [theleesee] will, volition, will power.

θελκτικός [thelkteekos] seductive, attractive, captivating.

θέλω [thelo] wish, want, require, need || be willing || ~ να πω I mean to say || **θέλει δεν θέλει** whether he likes it or not.

θέμα, το [thema] subject, point, topic || (γραμμ) stem, theme.

θεμέλιο, το [themeleeo] foundation || (μεταφ) basis, groundwork.

θεμιτός [themeetos] lawful, legal || permissible.

θεόγυμνος [theoyeemnos] stark naked.

θεοκρατία, η [theokrateea] theocracy.

θεολογία, η [theoloyeea] theology.

θεολογικός [theoloyeekos] theological.

θεολόγος, ο [theologos] theologian.

θεομηνία, η [theomeeneea] natural disaster, calamity.

θεοποιώ [theopeeo] (μεταφ) idolize, praise, laud.

θεόρατος [theoratos] enormous, colossal.

θεός, ο [theos] god.

θεοσεβής [theosevees] pious, devout.

θεότητα, η [theoteeta] deity.

Θεοτόκος, η [theotokos] the Virgin Mary.

θεοφάνεια, τα [theofaneea] πλ the Epiphany.

θεοφοβούμενος [theofovoumenos] godly, pious.

θεραπεία, η [therapeea] cure, treatment || recovery.

θεραπευτήριο, το [therapevteereeo] hospital, clinic || (σχολής) infirmary.

θεραπευτικός [therapevteekos] curative.

θεραπεύω [therapevo] cure, treat || (μεταφ) satisfy.

θεράπων, ο [therapon] servant || attendant.

θέρετρο, το [theretro] resort || country house.

θερίζω [thereezo] mow, cut || reap || (μεταφ) annihilate.

θερινός [thereenos] summer, summery.

θεριό, το [therio] beast.

θερισμός, ο [threesmos] reaping, mowing, cutting.

θεριστής, ο [thereestees] reaper, mower.

θεριστικός [thereesteekos] of reaping, for mowing || sweeping.

θερμαίνομαι [thermenome] be feverish.

θερμαίνω [thermeno] heat up, warm up || (μεταφ) revive.

θέρμανση, η [thermansee] heating, warming.

θερμαστής, ο [thermastees] stoker.

θερμάστρα, η [thermastra] (heating) stove, furnace.

θέρμες, οι [therme] πλ hot springs.

θέρμη, η [thermee] fever || (μεταφ) ardour, zeal.

θερμίδα, η [thermeeδa] calorie.

θερμόαιμος [thermoemos] hot-blooded, irritable, touchy.

θερμοκήπιο, το [thermokeepeeo] hot house, greenhouse.

θερμοκρασία, η [thermokraseea] temperature.

θερμόμετρο, το [thermometro] thermometer.

θερμός [thermos] warm || (μεταφ) passionate, fervent, heated.

θερμοσίφωνας, ο [thermoseefonas] water heater.

θερμοστάτης, ο [thermostatees] thermostat.

θερμότητα, η [thermoteeta] heat, warmth || (μεταφ) zeal, earnestness.

θερμοφόρος, η [thermoforos] hot-water bottle.

θέρος, ο [theros] harvest.

θέρος, το [theros] summer.

θέση, η [thesee] place, seat || position || (στρατ) emplacement, location || (εργασίας) employment, job, office || (χώρος) room, space || (κατηγορία) class.

θεσμός, ο [thesmos] institution, law, decree.

θεσπίζω [thespeezo] decree, legislate, enact (laws).

θετικός [theteekos] positive, real, actual || (πληροφορία) definite.

θετός [thetos] adopted || foster.

θέτω [theto] put, set || impose.

θεωρείο, το [theoreeo] (θεάτρου) box || (τύπου κτλ) gallery.

θεώρημα, το [theoreema] theorem.

θεώρηση, η [theoreesee] visa || (εγγράφου) certification.

θεωρητικός [theoreeteekos] theoretical || imposing.

θεωρία, η [theoreea] theory.

θεωρώ [theoro] consider, regard, look at || certify, visa.

θήκη, η [theekee] box, case || (εργαλείων) toolbag.

θηλάζω [theelazo] suckle, nurse.

θηλαστικό, το [theelasteeko] mammal.

θηλειά, η [theelia] noose, loop, slipknot || buttonhole.

θηλή, η [theelee] nipple, teat.

θηλυκό, το [theeleeko] female.

θηλυκός [theeleekos] female || (γραμμ) feminine.

θηλυκότητα, η [theeleekoteeta] femininity.

θηλυπρεπής [theeleeprepees] effeminate, womanish.

θημωνιά, η [theemonia] stack, pile || (σανού) haystack.

θήρα, η [theera] chase, hunt || (κυνήγι) game, quarry.

θήραμα, το [theerama] game, prey.

θηρίο, το [theereeo] wild beast, brute || (μεταφ) monster, fiend.

θηριώδης [theereeoδees] fierce, savage, brutal, bestial.

θησαυρίζω [theesavreezo] hoard up, accumulate || become wealthy.

θησαυρός, ο [theesavros] treasure || (μεταφ) storehouse, thesaurus.

θησαυροφυλάκιο, το [theesavrofeelakeeo] treasury.

θήτα, το [theeta] the letter Θ.

θητεία, η [theeteea] military service || term of office.

θιασάρχης, ο [theeasarhees] manager, impresario.

θίασος, ο [theeasos] cast, troupe.

θίγω [theego] touch (upon) || (μεταφ) offend, insult.

θλάση, η [thlasee] breaking || (ιατρ) fracture, bruise.

θλιβερός [thleeveros] sad || (γεγονότα) deplorable, painful.

θλίβω [thleevo] press, crush || (μεταφ) afflict, distress.

θλιμμένος [thleemenos] distressed, afflicted || in mourning.

θλίψη, η [thleepsee] crushing || (μεταφ) grief, sorrow.

θνησιμότητα, η [thneeseemoteeta] death rate, mortality.

θνητός [thneetos] mortal.

θόλος, ο [tholos] (αρχιτεκ) vault, dome || (ουρανίσκου) roof.

θολός [tholos] dull, blurred || (κρασί) turbid || (κατάσταση) confused.

θολώνω [tholono] make dull || (το μυαλό) confuse, disturb || (νερό κτλ) muddy || (ουρανός) get overcast.

θολωτός [tholotos] vaulted.
θόρυβος, ο [thoreevos] noise, turmoil, clamour.
θορυβούμαι [thoreevoume] worry, be uneasy.
θορυβώ [thoreevo] create a disturbance || disturb.
θορυβώδης [thoreevoðees] noisy, boisterous.
θρανίο, το [thraneeo] (school) desk, bench, seat.
θράσος, το [thrasos] impudence, insolence.
θρασύς [thrasees] impudent, brazen, saucy, bold.
θραύση, η [thravsee] fracture || destruction, ruin.
θραύσμα, το [thravsma] fragment || (λίθου) splinter.
θραύω [thravo] break, smash, crack.
θρεμμένος [thremenos] well-fed.
θρεπτικός [threpteekos] nourishing, nutritious.
θρέφω [threfo] βλ τρέφω.
θρέψη, η [threpsee] feeding, nourishing.
θρήνος, ο [threenos] lamentation, wailing.
θρηνώ [threeno] lament, mourn || complain.
θρησκεία, η [threeskeea] religion.
θρησκευτικός [threeskevteekos] religious || (ακρίβεια) scrupulous.
θρησκόληπτος [threeskoleeptos] fanatically religious.
θρήσκος [threeskos] religious.
θριαμβευτικός [threeamvefteekos] triumphant, triumphal.
θριαμβεύω [threeamvevo] triumph || (μεταφ) excel, prevail.
θρίαμβος, ο [threeamvos] triumph, victory.
θρόισμα, το [throeesma] rustle.
θρόμβωση, η [thromvosee] thrombosis.
θρόνος, ο [thronos] throne.
θρούμπα, η [throumba] ripe olive.
θρυλικός [threeleekos] legendary.
θρύλος, ο [threelos] legend || rumour.
θρύμμα, το [threema] fragment, scrap || θρυμματίζω break to pieces, shatter.
θυγατέρα, η [theegatera] daughter.
θυγατρικός [theegatreekos]: ~ ή εταιρεία subsidiary.
θύελλα, η [thiela] storm.
θυελλώδης [thieloðees] stormy.
θύλακας, ο [theelakas] satchel, pouch.
θύμα, το [theema] victim.
θυμάμαι [theemame] βλ θυμούμαι.
θυμάρι, το [theemaree] thyme.
θύμηση, η [theemeesee] memory, remembrance.

θυμητικό, το [theemeeteeko] memory.
θυμίαμα, το [theemeeama] incense.
θυμιατό, το [theemeeato] censer.
θυμίζω [theemeezo] remind, recall.
θυμός, ο [theemos] anger, rage.
θυμούμαι [theemoume] remember, recall.
θυμώνω [theemono] make angry, infuriate || get angry, flare up.
θύρα, η [theera] door, gate, doorway.
θυρίδα, η [theereða] small window || (θεάτρου) box office || (τραπέζης) counter.
θυρωρός, ο [theeroros] hall porter, concierge.
θύσανος, ο [theesanos] crest, tuft || tassel.
θυσία, η [theeseea] sacrifice || θυσιάζω sacrifice.
θωπεία, η [thopeea] petting, patting, stroking, caress(ing).
θωρακίζω [thorakeezo] plate with steel.
θώρακας, ο [thorakas] cuirass, breastplate || thorax.
θωρηκτό, το [thoreekto] battleship.
θωριά, η [thoria] air, appearance || colour, complexion.
θωρώ [thoro] see, look.

Ι, ι

ιαματικός [yamateekos] curative, medicinal.
ίαμβος, ο [eeamvos] iambus.
Ιανουάριος, ο [yanouareeos] January.
Ιάπωνας, ο [yaponas] Japanese (man).
ιαπωνέζικος [yaponezeekos] Japanese.
Ιαπωνία, [yaponeea] Japan.
ιάσιμος [yaseemos] curable.
ίαση, η [eeasee] cure, healing, recovery.
ιατρείο, το [yatreeo] doctor's surgery, clinic || infirmary.
ιατρική, η [yatreekee] medicine.
ιατρικός [yatreekos] medical.
ιατρός, ο, η [yatros] doctor, physician.
ιβίκος, ό [eeveeskos] hibiscus.
ιδανικό, το [eeðaneeko] ideal.
ιδανικός [eeðaneekos] ideal.
ιδέα, η [eeðea] idea || notion, thought.
ιδεαλιστής, ο [eeðealeestees] idealist.
ιδεολογία, η [eeðeoloyeea] ideology.
ιδεολόγος, ο, η [eeðeologos] idealist.
ιδεώδης [eeðeoðees] ideal.
ιδιάζων [eeðeeazon] typical, singular.
ιδιαίτερος [eeðieteros] special,

characteristic || **ο ~** private secretary || **τα ιδιαίτερα** private affairs.
ιδιαιτέρως [eeðieteros] in particular || privately.
ιδιοκτησία, η [eeðeeokteeseea] ownership || property, estate.
ιδιοκτήτης, ο [eeðeeokteetees] owner, proprietor || landlord.
ιδιόκτητος [eeðeeokteetos] privately owned.
ιδιοποιούμαι [eeðeeopeeoume] appropriate, usurp.
ιδιόρρυθμος [eeðeeoreethmos] peculiar, original, eccentric.
ίδιος [eeðeeos] same || own, oneself || particular || **~ με** same as || **εγώ ο ~** I myself.
ιδιοσυγκρασία, η [eeðeeoseengkraseea] temperament, idiosyncrasy.
ιδιοτελής [eeðeeotelees] selfish, self-centred.
ιδιότητα, η [eeðeeoteeta] property, quality, characteristic.
ιδιότροπος [eeðeeotropos] peculiar, eccentric || singular.
ιδιοφυής [eeðeeofiees] talented, gifted.
ιδίωμα, το [eeðeeoma] idiom, dialect || property, characteristic || **ιδιωματικός** idiomatic.
ιδιωματισμός, ο [eeðeeomateesmos] idiom.
ιδίως [eeðeeos] specially, particularly.
ιδιωτικός [eeðeeoteekos] private, particular.
ιδιώτης, ο [eeðeeotees] individual, layman.
ιδού [eeðou] (επιφ) look!, behold!, here it is!
ίδρυμα, το [eeðreema] institution, foundation || establishment.
ίδρυση, η [eeðreesee] establishment, founding.
ιδρυτής, ο [eeðreetees] founder.
ιδρύω [eeðreeo] found, establish.
ιδρώνω [eeðrono] perspire, sweat.
ιδρώτας, ο [eeðrotas] sweat.
ιεραπόστολος, ο [ierapostolos] missionary.
ιερέας, ο [iereas] priest.
ιεροκήρυκας, ο [ierokeereekas] preacher, missionary.
ιερό, το [iero] sanctuary, holy of holies.
ιερός [ieros] holy, sacred.
ιεροσυλία, η [ieroseeleea] sacrilege.
ίζημα, το [eezeema] sediment.
ιθαγένεια, η [eethageneea] nationality, citizenship.
ιθαγενής [eethagenees] native, indigenous.
ικανοποίηση, η [eekanopieesee] satisfaction, contentment.

ικανοποιητικός [eekanopieeteekos] satisfactory, sastisfying.
ικανοποιώ [eekanopeeo] satisfy, please || (τα πάθη) satiate || (πείνα) appease.
ικανός [eekanos] capable, able || sufficient || (εργάτης) skilful.
ικανότητα, η [eekanoteeta] capacity, competence, skill.
ικετεύω [eeketevo] implore, beg.
ίκτερος, ο [eekteros] jaundice.
ιλαρά, η [eelara] measles.
ιλιγγιώδης [eeleengeeoðees] giddy, dizzy.
ίλιγγος, ο [eeleengos] giddiness, dizziness.
ιμάντας, ο [eemandas] strap || (μηχανής) belt, band.
ιματιοθήκη, η [eemateeotheekee] wardrobe || cloakroom.
ίνα, η [eena] fibre, filament.
ινδαλμα, το [eenðalma] ideal || illusion, fancy.
Ινδία, η [eenðeea] India.
Ινδιάνος, ο [eenðeeanos] (Red) Indian || **ι~** turkey.
ινδικός [eenðeekos] Indian.
**Ινδονησία, [eenðoneeseea] Indonesia.
ινδονησιακός [eenðoneeseeakos] Indonesian.
Ινδονήσιος, ο [eenðoneeseeos] Indonesian.
Ινδός, ο [eenðos] Indian.
ινστιτούτο, το [eensteetouto] institute || **~ καλλονής** beauty salon.
ίντσα, η [eentsa] inch.
ινώδης [eenoðees] fibrous || (κρέας) stringy.
ιξώδης [eeksoðees] glutinous, sticky, gummy.
ιός, ο [yos] venom || (ιατρ) virus || (μεταφ) malice, spite.
Ιούλιος, ο [youleeos] July.
Ιούνιος, ο [youneeos] June.
ιππασία, η [eepaseea] horsemanship || riding.
ιππέας, ο [eepeas] rider, horseman || (σκακιού) knight.
ιππικό, το [eepeeko] cavalry.
ιπποδρομίες, οι [eepoðromies] πλ races.
ιππόδρομος, ο [eepoðromos] racecourse || hippodrome.
ιπποδύναμη, η [eepoðeenamee] horsepower.
ιπποπόταμος, ο [eepopotamos] hippopotamus.
ίππος, ο [eepos] horse.
ιππότης, ο [eepotees] knight, chevalier.
ίπταμαι [eeptame] fly, soar.
ιπταμένη, η [eeptamenee] air hostess.
ιπτάμενος, ο [eeptamenos] flyer.
Ιράν, το [eeran] Iran.

ίριδα, η [eereeδa] rainbow || (ματιού) iris.
ιριδισμός, ο [eereeδeesmos] iridescence.
Ιρλανδία, η [eerlanδeea] Ireland.
ιρλανδικός [eeerlanδeekos] Irish.
Ιρλανδός, ο [eerlanδos] Irishman.
ίσα [eesa] equally, as far as || straight, directly || ~ ~ exactly, precisely || ~ με up to, until.
ίσαμε [eesame] βλ **ίσα με.**
ισάξιος [eesakseeos] equivalent (to).
ισάριθμος [eesareethmos] equal in number.
ισημερία, η [eeseemereea] equinox.
ισημερινός, ο [eeseemereenos] equinoctial || (ουσ) equator.
ισθμός, ο [eesthmos] isthmus.
ίσια [eeseea] βλ **ίσα.**
ίσιος [eeseeos] straight, erect || honest || equal to.
ισ(ι)ώνω [ees(ee)ono] straighten || make even, smooth.
ίσκιος, ο [eeskeeos] shade, shadow.
ισόβιος [eesoveeos] for life, lifelong.
ισόγειο, το [eesoyeo] ground floor.
ισοδύναμος [eesoδeenamos] equivalent || equal in force.
ισοδυναμώ [eesoδeenamo] be equivalent to.
ισοζύγιο, το [eesozeeyo] balancing, balance || ~ πληρωμών balance of payments.
ισολογισμός, ο [eesoloyeesmos] balance sheet.
ισόπαλος [eesopalos] evenly matched, of equal strength.
ισοπεδώνω [eesopeδono] level up, level down, smooth.
ισόπλευρος [eesoplevros] equilateral.
ισορροπημένος [eesoropeemenos] well-balanced.
ισορροπία, η [eesoropeea] balance, equilibrium.
ισορροπώ [eesoropo] balance.
ίσος [eesos] equal to, the same as || εξ ίσου likewise.
ισότητα, η [eesoteeta] equality.
ισότιμος [eesoteemos] equal in rank || equal in value.
ισοφαρίζω [eesofareezo] equal, make equal || be equal to.
Ισπανία, η [eespaneea] Spain.
ισπανικός [eespaneekos] Spanish.
Ισπανός, ο [eespanos] Spaniard.
Ισραήλ, η [eesraeel] Israel.
ισραηλινός [eesraeeleenos] Israeli.
Ισραηλίτη, ο [eesraeeleetee] Israeli.
ιστιοπλοΐα, η [eesteeoploeea] sailing.
ιστιοφόρο, το [eesteeoforo] sailing ship.
ιστορία, η [eestoreea] history || story, tale.
ιστορίες, οι [eestories] πλ trouble, scene, quarrel.

ιστορικός [eestoreekos] historic(al) || (ουσ) historian.
ιστός, ο [eestos] mast, pole || (βιολ) tissue.
ισχιαλγία, η [eesheealyeea] sciatica.
ισχίο, το [eesheeo] hip.
ισχνός [eeshnos] lean, thin || (βλάστηση) scanty, sparse.
ισχυρίζομαι [eesheereezome] assert, maintain, declare.
ισχυρισμός, ο [eesheereesmos] assertion, contention, allegation.
ισχυρογνώμων [eesheerognomon] stubborn, headstrong, obstinate.
ισχυρός [eesheeros] strong, sturdy || (φωνή) loud || (άνεμος) stiff, strong.
ισχύς, η [eeshees] strength, power, force || (νόμου κτλ) validity.
ισχύω [eesheeo] have validity || be in force.
ισώνω [eesono] βλ **ισ(ι)ώνω.**
ίσως [eesos] perhaps, probably, maybe.
Ιταλία, η [eetaleea] Italy.
ιταλικός [eetaleekos] Italian.
Ιταλός, ο [eetalos] Italian (person).
ιτιά, η [eetia] willow tree.
ιχθυοπωλείο, το [eehtheeopoleeo] fishmonger's shop.
ιχθύς, ο [eehthees] fish.
ιχνογραφία, η [eehnografeea] sketching, drawing.
ίχνος, το [eehnos] footprint, track || trace, vestige || (μεταφ) mark, sign.
ιώδιο, το [yoδeeo] iodine.
ιωνικός [yoneekos] Ionic, Ionian.
ιώτα, το [yota] the letter I.

Κ, κ

κάβα, η [kava] wine cellar.
καβαλιέρος, ο [kavalieros] escort, partner.
καβάλλα, η [kavala] riding || (επιρ) on horseback || (σε τοίχο κτλ) astride.
καβαλλάρης, ο [kavalarees] rider, horseman || (εγχόρδου) bridge.
καβαλλέτο, το [kavaleto] easel.
καβαλλικεύω [kavaleekevo] mount a horse || (μεταφ) dominate.
καβαλλώ [kavalo] βλ **καβαλλικεύω.**
καβγαδίζω [kavgaδeezo] quarrel, wrangle, squabble.
καβγάς, ο [kavgas] row, quarrel.
καβγατζής, ο [kavgatzees] grouch, wrangler.
κάβος, ο [kavos] cape, headland || (ναυτ) cable.
καβούκι, το [kavoukee] shell.
κάβουρας, ο [kavouras] crab || crawfish.
καβουρδίζω [kavourδeezo] roast, brown || scorch.

καβούρι, το [kavouree] βλ κάβουρας.

καγκελάριος, ο [kangelareeos] chancellor.

κάγκελο, το [kangelo] (παραθύρου κτλ) bar || (σκάλας) balustrade || (κήπου) railings || (δικτυωτό) grille.

καγχάζω [kanghazo] guffaw.

κάδος, ο [kaðos] bucket, vat, tub, small barrel.

κάδρο, το [kaðro] (πλαίσιο) frame || (πίνακα) frame || (χάρτου) border || (φωτογραφία) framed picture.

καημένος [kaeemenos] (μεταφ) miserable, wretched.

καημός, ο [kaeemos] longing, yearning.

καθαίρεση, η [katheresee] dismissal, degradation.

καθαιρώ [katherο] dismiss, discharge || (ιερέα) unfrock.

καθαρεύουσα, η [katharevousa] formal Greek (language).

καθαρίζω [kathareezo] clean, clear || (κουκιά, φρούτα) peel, pare, shell || (μεταλλικά είδη) burnish || (ποτήρια) polish || (εξηγώ) explain, clarify || (λογαριασμούς) settle, clear up.

καθαριότητα, η [kathareeoteeta] cleanness, cleanliness || brightness.

καθάρισμα, το [kathareesma] cleaning || peeling || polishing.

καθαριστήριο, το [kathareesteereeo] dry cleaner's.

καθαρίστρια, η [kathareestria] charwoman, cleaning lady.

κάθαρμα, το [katharma] (μεταφ) rogue, rascal, scamp.

καθαρόαιμος [katharoemos] thoroughbred.

καθαρός [katharos] (πρόσωπο κτλ) neat, tidy || (φωνή) clear, distinct || (χρυσός) pure || (ουρανός) clear || (απάντηση) plain, straightforward || (ιδέα) clear, distinct || (κέρδος) clear, net || (έννοια) obvious, manifest, evident.

καθαρότητα, η [katharoteeta] cleanness, purity || clearness.

κάθαρση, η [katharsee] cleansing, refining || catharsis || quarantine.

καθαυτό [kathavto] exactly, precisely || really.

κάθε [kathe] each, every || ~ άλλο far from it || το ~ τι everything.

κάθειρξη, η [katheerksee] βλ φυλάκιση.

καθέκαστα, τα [kathekasta] πλ details, particulars.

καθελκύω [kathelkeeo] (ναυτ) launch.

καθένας [kathenas] everyone, each one, everybody.

καθεξής [katheksees] so forth, so on.

καθεστώς, το [kathestos]: το ~ regime, status quo.

κάθετος [kathetos] vertical, perpendicular, upright.

καθηγητής, ο [katheeyeetees] professor, teacher.

καθήκι, το [katheekee] chamberpot || (μεταφ) rogue, vicious person.

καθήκον, το [katheekon] duty, task || καθήκοτα πλ functions, duties.

καθηλώνω [katheelono] pin down, fix || immobilize.

καθημερινός [katheemereenos] daily, everyday.

καθημερινώς [katheemereenos] daily.

καθησυχάζω [katheeseehazo] (ένα φόβο) calm, reassure, pacify || become calm.

καθιερώνω [kathierono] consecrate, dedicate || establish, validate.

καθίζηση, η [katheezeesee] subsidence, landslide.

καθίζω [katheezo] seat, place || (πλοίο) run aground.

καθισιό, το [katheesio] idleness, unemployment, inactivity.

κάθισμα, το [katheesma] chair, seat || (πλοίο) stranding.

καθίσταμαι [katheestame] become, get, grow.

καθιστός [katheestos] sitting (down).

καθιστώ [katheesto] (εγκαθιστώ) establish, install || (κάποιο) make, render || (διορίζω) appoint.

καθοδηγώ [kathoðeego] instruct, guide, lead.

κάθοδος, η [kathoðos] descent || alighting.

καθολικός [katholeekos] catholic || (γνώμη) unanimous || universal.

καθόλου [katholou] generally || (διόλου) not at all, no way.

κάθομαι [kathome] be seated, sit down, sit.

καθομιλουμένη, η [kathomeeloumenee] the spoken language.

καθορίζω [kathoreezo] determine, define, fix, decide.

καθορισμός, ο [kathoreesmos] defining, fixing, determination.

καθόσο [kathoso] as || according to what || being.

καθρέφτης, ο [kathreftees] mirror, looking-glass.

καθρεφτίζω [kathrefteezo] reflect, mirror.

καθυστερημένος [katheestereemenos] backward || late.

καθυστέρηση, η [katheestereesee] delay, lateness.

καθυστερούμενα, τα [katheesteroumena] πλ arrears.

καθώς [kathos] as well as, like, as || ~ πρέπει proper.

και [ke] and, also, too || ~ ... ~ both ... and || ~ να even if.

καΐκι, το [kaeekee] caique, sailing boat.

καϊμάκι, το [kaeemakee] cream || (του καφέ) froth.

καινοτομία, η [kenotomeea] innovation.

καινούργιος [kenouryos] new, fresh.

καιρικός [kereeos] of the weather.

καίριος [kereeos] timely || (πλήγμα) deadly, mortal || (σημείο) vital, important.

καιρός, ο [keros] time, period || weather || με τον καιρό in course of time.

καιροσκοπώ [keroskopo] wait for an opportunity, be an opportunist.

καισαρικός [kesareekos] Caesarean.

καίτοι [ketee] though, although.

καίομαι [keome] be on fire.

καίω [keo] burn.

κακά [kaka] badly, ill || bad things.

κακάο, το [kakao] cocoa.

κακαρίζω [kakareezo] cluck, gobble.

κακεντρέχεια, η [kakentreheea] malevolence, spite.

κακία, η [kakeea] wickedness, malice.

κακίζω [kakeezo] reproach, blame, reprimand.

κακοβαλμένος [kakovalmenos] untidy || badly placed.

κακόβουλος [kakovoulos] malicious.

κακογλωσσιά, η [kakogloseea] slander, calumny || gossip.

κακοήθης [kakoeethees] dishonest, vile || (ιατρ) malignant, serious.

κακόηχος [kakoeehos] dissonant, unpleasant to hear.

κακοκαιρία, η [kakokereea] bad weather.

κακοκεφιά, η [kakokefia] depression, bad mood.

κακομαθαίνω [kakomatheno] (μωρό κτλ) spoil || acquire bad habits.

κακομαθημένος [kakomatheemenos] ill-bred, spoilt, rude.

κακομεταχειρίζομαι [kakometaheereezome] maltreat, abuse.

κακομοίρης [kakomeerees] hapless, wretched.

κακό, το [kako] evil, harm, wrong, bad, mischief.

κακοπέραση, η [kakoperasee] privation, hardship.

κακοπιστία, η [kakopeesteea] perfidy, faithlessness.

κακοποιός [kakopeeos] criminal, ill-doer.

κακοποιώ [kakopeeo] maltreat || rape.

κακός [kakos] bad, wicked || (παιδί) mischievous || nasty, serious.

κακοσμία, η [kakosmeea] stench, stink.

κακοσυνηθίζω [kakoseeneetheezo] πλ κακομαθαίνω.

κακοτυχία, η [kakoteeheea] misfortune, bad luck.

κακούργημα, το [kakouryeema] crime, villainy, felony.

κακουργιοδικείο, το [kakouryodeekeeo] criminal court.

κακούργος, ο [kakourgos] criminal || (μεταφ) villain, rogue.

κακουχία, η [kakouheea] hardship, privation.

κακοφαίνεται [kakofenete]: μου ~ it displeases me, it offends me.

κακοφτιαγμένος [kakofteeagmenos] badly made, badly wrought.

κακόφωνος [kakofonos] discordant, dissonant.

κάκτος, ο [kaktos] cactus.

κακώς [kakos] badly, wrongly.

κάκωση, η [kakosee] ill treatment || (αποτέλεσμα) suffering, hardship.

καλά [kala] well, all right || properly, thoroughly.

καλάθι, το [kalathee] basket || ~ αχρήστων wastepaper bin.

καλαισθησία, η [kalestheeseea] good taste, elegance.

καλαμάρι, το [kalamaree] inkstand, inkpot || (ψάρι) cuttlefish, squid.

καλαματιανός [kalamateeanos] (dance) of Kalamata.

καλάμι, το [kalamee] reed, cane || (ψαρέματος) fishing rod || (ἀνατ) shinbone.

καλαμοζάχαρο, το [kalamozakharo] cane sugar.

καλαμπόκι, το [kalambokee] maize, corn.

καλαμπούρι, το [kalambouree] joke, pun.

κάλαντα, τα [kalanta] πλ carols.

καλαπόδι, το [kalapodee] (shoemaker's) last, shoe last.

καλαφατίζω [kalafateezo] caulk.

κάλεσμα, το [kalesma] invitation.

καλεσμένος [kalesmenos] invited || (ουσ) guest.

καλημαύκι, το [kaleemavkee] priest's high hat.

καλημέρα [kaleemera] (επιφ) good morning.

καληνύχτα [kaleeneehta] (επιφ) good night.

καληνυχτίζω [kaleeneehteezo] bid good night.

καλησπέρα [kaleespera] (επιφ) good afternoon || good evening.

κάλι, το [kalee] potash.

καλιακούδα, η [kaleeakouda] crow.

καλλιέργεια, η [kalierya] cultivation, tilling || (μεταφ) cultivation.

καλλιεργώ [kaliergo] cultivate, till, grow.

καλλικάντζαρος, ο
[kaleekandzaros] sprite, spook, goblin.
καλλιστεία, τα [kaleesteea] πλ beauty
competition.
καλλιτέχνης, ο [kaleetehnees] artist.
καλλιτεχνικός [kaleetehneekos] of
art, of artists, artistic.
καλλονή, η [kalonee] beauty.
κάλλος, το [kalos] beauty, charm.
καλλυντικά, τα [kaleenteeka] πλ
cosmetics, make-up.
καλλωπίζω [kalopeezo] beautify,
decorate, adorn.
καλμάρω [kalmaro] become calm,
relax.
καλντερίμι, το [kalntereemee]
cobbled street, paving stone.
καλό, το [kalo] good, benefit || favour ||
blessing || στο ~! so long!
καλοαναθρεμμένος
[kaloanathremenos] well brought up.
καλοβαλμένος [kalovalmenos] well
turned out, well-groomed, tidy.
καλόβολος [kalovolos]
accommodating, easy-going,
complaisant.
καλόγερος, ο [kaloyeros] monk ||
(σπυρί) boil, carbuncle || (παιχνίδι)
hopscotch.
καλόγρια, η [kalogreea] nun.
καλοζώ [kalozo] live well || support
comfortably.
καλοήθης [kaloeethees] moral,
virtuous || (ιατρ) benign.
καλοθρεμμένος [kalothremenos]
well-nourished || well-bred.
καλοκάγαθος [kalokagathos] kind-
natured, good.
καλοκαίρι, το [kalokeree] summer ||
καλοκαιρία fine weather ||
καλοκαιρινός summer, summery.
καλοκαμωμένος [kalokamomenos]
well-made || handsome.
καλόκαρδος [kalokarðos] good-
hearted, cheerful.
καλοκοιτάζω [kalokeetazo] look
closely at || look after well || ogle.
καλομαθαίνω [kalomatheno] spoil,
pamper, pet || develop good habits.
καλομαθημένος [kalomatheemenos]
pampered.
καλοντυμένος [kalonteemenos]
well-dressed.
καλοπέραση, η [kaloperasee]
comfort, happy life, good life.
καλοπερνώ [kaloperno] lead a
pleasant life || be well treated.
καλοπιάνω [kalopeeano] coax, treat
gently.
καλοπροαίρετος [kaloproeretos]
well-disposed, obliging.
καλοριφέρ, το [kaloreefer] central
heating || radiator, heater.
καλορρίζικος [kaloreezeekos] lucky.
κάλος, ο [kalos] corn.

καλός [kalos] (άνθρωπος) kind, good ||
(εργάτης) skilful || (υπάλληλος) able,
efficient || (νέα) good, favourable ||
(τροφή) wholesome || (καρδιά) kind.
καλοσυνηθίζω [kaloseeneetheezo]
βλ καλομαθαίνω.
καλούπι, το [kaloupee] form, mould.
καλούτσικος [kaloutseekos] not bad,
passable, adequate.
καλπάζω [kalpazo] gallop || walk fast,
run.
κάλπη, η [kalpee] ballot box.
κάλπικος [kalpeekos] counterfeit,
false || (μεταφ) worthless.
κάλτσα, η [kaltsa] sock, stocking.
καλύβι, το [kaleevee] hut, cabin,
hovel.
κάλυμμα, το [kaleema] wrapper,
cover || (κρεββατιού) blanket, coverlet ||
(κεφαλής) cap, headdress || (τραπεζιτικό)
margin, cover.
κάλυκας, ο [kaleekas] (βοτ) calyx ||
(στρατ) cartridge || (ανατ) calix.
καλύπτω [kaleepto] cover, veil, hide ||
(προθέσεις) cloak, mask, conceal.
καλύτερα [kaleetera] better.
καλυτερεύω [kaleeterevo] improve ||
get better.
καλύτερος [kaleeteros] better.
κάλυψη, η [kaleepsee] covering.
καλώ [kalo] call, beckon, name || (σε
δείπνο) invite || (νομ) summon.
καλώδιο, το [kaloðeeo] rope || cable.
καλώς [kalos] well || rightly, properly ||
έχει ~ good, agreed || ~ ωρίσατε
(επιφ) welcome!
καλωσορίζω [kalosoreezo] welcome.
καλωσύνη, η [kaloseenee] goodness,
kindness || (καιρός) fine weather.
καμάκι, το [kamakee] harpoon, fish
spear.
κάμαρα, η [kamara] room.
καμάρα, η [kamara] arch, archway,
arcade || (θόλου) vault.
καμάρι, το [kamaree] pride, boast.
καμαριέρα, η [kamariera]
chambermaid, parlourmaid.
καμαρότος, ο [kamarotos] steward,
cabin boy.
καμαρώνω [kamarono] take pride in,
glory in.
καμαρωτός [kamarotos] (αρχιτεκ)
arched, vaulted || (υπερηφάνεια) proud,
haughty.
καμέλια, η [kameleea] camellia.
καμήλα, η [kameela] camel.
καμηλοπάρδαλη, η
[kameeloparðalee] giraffe.
καμινάδα, η [kameenaða] chimney,
smokestack || funnel.
καμινέτο, το [kameeneto] spirit
lamp.
καμίνι, το [kameenee] furnace, kiln.
καμιόνι, το [kameeonee] lorry, truck.
καμμιά [kamia] βλ κανένας.

καμουτσίκι, το [kamoutseekee] whip.

καμουφλάζ, το [kamouflaz] camouflage, disguise.

καμουφλάρω [kamouflaro] camouflage, disguise.

καμπάνα, η [kambana] bell.

καμπαναριό, το [kambanario] belfry, steeple.

καμπαρντίνα, η [kambarndeena] gabardine.

καμπή, η [kambee] bend, turn || (σωλήνα κτλ) elbow, knee.

κάμπια, η [kambeea] caterpillar.

καμπίνα, η [kambeena] cabin.

καμπινές, ο [kambeenes] toilet, rest room, W.C.

κάμπος, ο [kambos] plain, flat country.

κάμποσος [kambosos] considerable, some.

καμπούρα, η [kamboura] hump, hunch.

καμπούρης, ο [kambourees] hunchback.

καμπουριάζω [kamboureeazo] hunch || stoop.

κάμπτομαι [kambtome] bow || yield, sag || (τιμές) go down.

κάμπτω [kambto] bend, turn, curve.

καμπύλη, η [kambeelee] curve, bend.

καμπύλος [kambeelos] curved, rounded || crooked.

καμφορά, η [kamfora] camphor.

κάμψη, η [kampsee] bending, flexion || (τιμών) fall, drop.

καμώματα, τα [kamomata] πλ affected manners, antics.

καμώνομαι [kamonome] pretend, feign.

καν [kan] at least, even || **ούτε** ~ not even || ~ ... ~ either ... or.

Καναδάς, ο [kanaðas] Canada.

καναδικός [kanaðeekos] Canadian.

Καναδός, ο [kanaðos] Canadian.

κανακάρης [kanakarees] petted, spoilt || (ουσ) only child.

κανάλι, το [kanalee] channel, canal.

καναπές, ο [kanapes] sofa.

καναρίνι, το [kanareenee] canary.

κανάτα, η [kanata] jug, pitcher.

κανείς [kanees] someone, anyone || no one, nobody.

κανέλλα, η [kanela] cinnamon.

κανένας [kanenas] anyone, one, some || no, no one.

καννάβατσο, το [kanvatso] canvas, pack cloth.

καννάβι, το [kanavee] hemp.

κάννη, η [kanee] barrel of a gun.

καννίβαλος, ο [kaneevalos] cannibal.

κανόνας, ο [kanonas] rule || (εκκλ) canon.

κανόνι, το [kanonee] cannon.

κανονίζω [kanoneezo] regulate ||

(υποθέσεις) settle, arrange || (λογαριασμούς) settle, close, pay off.

κανονικός [kanoneekos] regular, usual, ordinary || (εκκλ) canonical.

κανονισμός, ο [kanoneesmos] regulation, rule(s), by-laws.

κάνουλα, η [kanoula] tap || faucet (US).

καντάδα, η [kantaða] serenade.

καντήλι, το [kanteelee] small olive-oil light, nightlight.

καντίνα, η [kanteena] canteen.

κάνω [kano] do, make, create, build || (υποκρίνομαι) play, sham || **τα ~ θάλασσα** (η σαλάτα) to make a mess of it || ~ **παιδί** to have a child || ~ **νερά** to leak || (μεταφ) to hedge || ~ **πως** to pretend that || **τι κάνετε;** how are you?

κάπα, η [kapa] peasant's cloak.

καπάκι, το [kapakee] lid, cover.

καπάρο, το [kaparo] deposit.

καπαρώνω [kaparono] give a deposit || book, engage.

καπέλλο, το [kapelo] hat.

καπετάνιος, ο [kapetaneeos] captain, skipper, chief.

καπηλεία, η [kapeeleea] (μεταφ) huckstering, exploiting.

καπηλειό, το [kapeelio] wine shop, taverna.

καπίστρι, το [kapeestree] bridle, halter.

καπλαμάς, ο [kaplamas] veneer.

καπνέμπορος, ο [kapnemboros] tobacco dealer, tobacconist.

καπνιά, η [kapnia] soot, lampblack.

καπνίζω [kapneezo] smoke || cure.

κάπνισμα, το [kapneesma] smoking.

καπνιστής, ο [kapneestees] smoker || (κρέατος) curer.

καπνιστός [kapneestos] smoked, smoke-cured.

καπνοδόχος, η [kapnoðohos] chimney || (πλοίου) funnel.

καπνοπώλης, ο [kapnopolees] tobacconist.

καπνός, ο [kapnos] smoke || tobacco || (μεταφ) **έγινε** ~ he vanished (into thin air).

κάποιος [kapeeos] someone || a certain.

καπότα, η [kapota] shepherd's cloak.

κάποτε [kapote] from time to time, now and again, sometimes || once.

κάπου [kapou] somewhere || ~ ~ once in a while || ~ **δέκα** about ten.

κάππα, το [kapa] the letter K.

κάππαρη, η [kaparee] caper.

καπρίτσιο, το [kapreetseeo] caprice, whim, fancy.

κάπως [kapos] somehow, somewhat.

καραβάνα, η [karavana] mess tin || platter.

καραβάνι, το [karavanee] caravan.

καράβι, το [karavee] ship, boat, vessel.

καραβίδα, η [karaveeða] crawfish.

καραβοκύρης, ο [karavokeerees] owner of a vessel || captain.

καραγκιόζης, ο [karangeeozees] (μεταφ) comical person, comedian.

καραδοκώ [karoðoko] watch for, look out for || waylay.

καρακάξα, η [karakaksa] magpie.

καραμέλα, η [karamela] sweet || caramel.

καραμούζα, η [karamouza] toy flute || (αυτοκινήτου) horn.

καραμπίνα, η [karambeena] carbine.

καραντίνα, η [karanteena] quarantine.

καράτι, το [karatee] carat.

καρατομώ [karatomo] behead, decapitate.

καράφα, η [karafa] carafe || (κρασιού) decanter.

καράφλα, η [karafla] baldness.

καρβέλι, το [karvelee] (round) loaf.

καρβουνιάρης, ο [karvouneearees] coal merchant || coalman.

κάρβουνο, το [karvouno] coal, charcoal.

κάργα [karga] quite full || tightly, closely.

κάρδαμο, το [karðamo] cress.

καρδιά, η [karðia] heart || (φρούτου) core, centre.

καρδιακός [karðiakos] affected with heart disease.

καρδιολόγος, η [karðiologos] heart specialist.

καρδιοχτύπι, το [karðiohteepee] heartbeat || (μεταφ) anxiety.

καρέκλα, η [karekla] chair, seat.

καρίνα, η [kareena] keel.

καρκίνος, η [karkeenos] cancer || crab.

καρκίνωμα, το [karkeenoma] carcinoma.

καρμανιόλα, η [karmaneeola] guillotine || (στα χαρτιά) dishonest card game.

καρμπόν, το [karbo] carbon paper.

καρναβάλι, το [karnavalee] carnival.

καρότο, το [karoto] carrot.

καρούλι, το [karoulee] reel, spool || pulley.

καρούμπαλο, το [karoumbalo] bump (on the head).

καρπαζιά, η [karpazia] clout on the head.

καρπός, ο [karpos] fruit || (ανατ) wrist.

καρπούζι, το [karpouzee] watermelon.

καρπούμαι [karpoume] reap the fruits of || (μεταφ) benefit by.

καρποφόρος [karpoforos] fruitful || effective || lucrative.

καρποφορώ [karpoforo] produce fruit || (μεταφ) succeed.

καρρέ, το [karre] (στα χαρτιά) foursome || (φουστανιού) open neck of dress.

καρρό, το [karo] (στα χαρτιά) diamond || (σχεδίου) check.

κάρρο, το [karo] cart, wagon.

καρροτσάκι, το [karotsakee] handcart, barrow || (μωρού) pram.

κάρτα, η [karta] postcard || visiting card.

καρτέρι, το [karteree] βλ **ενέδρα.**

καρτερώ [kartero] persevere, persist || wait for, expect.

καρύδι, το [kareeðee] walnut || Adam's apple || **καρυδιά, η** walnut tree, walnut (ξύλο).

καρύκευμα, το [kareekevma] seasoning || (το μπαχαρικό) condiment, spice.

καρυοθραύστης, ο [kareeothravstees] nutcracker.

καρυοφύλλι, το [kareeofeelee] clove || (όπλου) flintlock.

καρφί, το [karfee] nail.

καρφίτσα, η [karfeetsa] pin || (κόσμημα) brooch.

καρφώνω [karfono] nail, pin || (μεταφ) fix.

καρχαρίας, ο [karhareeas] shark.

κασετίνα, η [kaseteena] (σχολική) pencil box || (κοσμημάτων) jewellery box.

κάσ(σ)α, η [kasa] case, box || (χρηματοκιβώτιο) safe || (μεταφ) coffin, bier.

κασέλα, η [kasela] wooden chest, trunk.

κασκέτο, το [kasketo] cap.

κασμήρι, το [kasmeeree] cashmere.

κασόνι, το [kasonee] packing case.

κασσίτερος, ο [kaseeteros] tin.

καστανιά, η [kastania] chestnut tree.

κάστανο, το [kastano] chestnut.

καστανός [kastanos] chestnut-coloured, maroon.

καστόρι, το [kastoree] beaver || felt.

κάστρο, το [kastro] castle, fortress.

κατά [kata] against, upon, during, according to, by, about || ~ **τύχη** by chance || ~ **βάθος** at bottom || **καθ' εκάστην** every day || ~ **διαβόλου** to the devil, to hell.

καταβαίνω [kataveno] βλ **κατεβαίνω.**

καταβάλλω [katavalo] overthrow, overcome, exhaust || (προσπάθειες) strive, endeavour || (χρήματα) pay, put down.

κατάβαση, η [katavasee] descent, alighting, getting off.

καταβιβάζω [kataveevazo] let down, take down || (ύψος) lower, reduce.

καταβολή, η [katavolee] (χρημάτων) paying in, deposit.

καταβρέχω [katavreho] sprinkle, soak, water.

καταβροχθίζω [katavrohtheezo] devour, eat ravenously, gulp down.

καταγγελία, η [katangeleea] denunciation || annulment, revocation.

καταγής [katayees] on the ground, on the floor.

καταγίνομαι [katayeenome] busy o.s. with, see to.

κάταγμα, το [katagma] fracture.

κατάγομαι [katagome] be descended from, come from.

καταγωγή, η [katagoyee] descent, origin, lineage.

καταγώγιο, το [katagoyo] hovel, hideout, den of vice.

καταδέχομαι [kataðehome] deign, condescend.

κατάδηλος [kataðeelos] evident, clear.

καταδίδω [kataðeeðo] denounce, betray.

καταδικάζω [kataðeekazo] condemn, sentence || (μεταφ) doom, proscribe.

καταδίκη, η [kataðeekee] sentence, conviction || censure, blame.

κατάδικος, ο, η [kataðeekos] prisoner, condemned person.

καταδιωκτικό, το [kataðeeokteeko] fighter (plane).

καταδιώκω [kataðeeoko] pursue, chase || (πολιτικώς) persecute, oppress.

κατάδοση, η [kataðosee] betrayal, denunciation.

καταδρομή, η [kataðromee] pursuit.

καταδρομικό, το [kataðromeeko] cruiser.

καταδυναστεύω [kataðeenastevo] oppress.

καταδύομαι [kataðeeome] dive, plunge.

καταζητώ [katazeeto] pursue, chase.

καταθέτω [katatheto] deposit, lay down || (σαν μάρτυρας) give evidence || (οπλα) lay down || (σχέδιο) introduce.

καταθλιπτικός [katathleepteekos] crushing, overwhelming.

καταιγίδα, η [kateyeeða] tempest, storm, hurricane.

κατάιφι, το [kataeefee] kind of oriental cake.

κατακάθι, το [katakathee] residue, sediment, dregs.

κατάκειμαι [katakeeme] lie flat, lie down.

κατάκαρδα [katakarða] deeply, seriously, profoundly, to heart.

κατακέφαλα [katakefala] headlong, on the head.

κατακλύζω [katakleezo] flood, inundate || (μεταφ) invade, overrun.

κατακλυσμός, ο [katakleesmos] flood.

κατάκοιτος [katakeetos] bedridden.

κατάκοπος [katakopos] exhausted, deadbeat, dog-tired.

κατακόβω [katakovo] cut to pieces, cut up, lacerate.

κατακόρυφο, το [katakoreefo] zenith || (μεταφ) acme.

κατακόρυφος [katakoreefos] vertical, perpendicular.

κατακρατώ [katakrato] withhold, keep illegally.

κατακραυγή, η [katakravyee] outcry || protestation.

κατακρεουργώ [katakreourgo] butcher, massacre.

κατακρημνίζω [katakreemneezo] demolish, pull down.

κατακρίνω [katakreeno] blame, criticize, condemn.

κατάκτηση, η [katakteesee] conquest, subjugation.

κατακτώ [katakto] conquer, subjugate.

καταλαβαίνω [katalaveno] understand.

καταλαμβάνω [katalamvano] take, lay hold of, seize || (χώρο) take up.

καταλήγω [kataleego] end in, come to, result in, come to an end.

κατάληξη, η [kataleeksee] termination, ending.

καταληπτός [kataleeptos] comprehensible, intelligible, clear.

κατάληψη, η [kataleepsee] occupation, capture || (ιδέας) understanding, comprehension.

κατάλληλος [kataleelos] suitable, appropriate, fit, proper.

καταλογίζω [kataloyeezo] attribute, impute, ascribe.

κατάλογος, ο [katalogos] catalogue, list || (φαγητών) menu || (τιμών) inventory, register, roll.

κατάλοιπα, τα [kataleepa] waste || **ραδιενεργά** ~ radioactive waste.

κατάλυμα, το [kataleema] lodging, housing || (στρατ) barracks, billeting.

κατάλυση, η [kataleesee] abolition || (χημ) catalysis.

καταλύω [kataleeo] abolish, do away with || take up lodging.

καταμερίζω [katamereezo] share out, distribute, apportion.

καταμεσής [katamesees] in the very middle.

κατάμεστος [katamestos] quite full, crowded.

καταμετρώ [katametro] measure, survey, gauge.

κατάμουτρα [katamoutra] point-blank.

καταναλίσκω [katanaleesko] consume, spend, use up || (ποτά) drink.

κατανάλωση, η [katanalosee] consumption.

καταναλωτής, ο [katanalotees] consumer, customer.

κατανέμω [katanemo] distribute || (ευθύνες) allot, assign, share.

κατανόηση, η [katanoeesee] understanding, comprehension.

κατανοώ [katanoo] understand, comprehend.

κατάντημα, το [katanteema] wretched state.

καταντώ [katanto] be reduced to, bring to, end up as.

κατάνυξη, η [kataneeksee] compunction, piety.

καταπακτή, η [katapaktee] trap, pitfall.

καταπατώ [katapato] violate, encroach upon.

κατάπαυση, η [katapavsee] cessation, stopping, halting.

καταπέλτης, ο [katapeltees] catapult.

καταπέτασμα, το [katapetasma]: **τρώω το ~** to eat to bursting point.

καταπιάνομαι [katapeeanome] undertake, enter upon, engage upon.

καταπιέζω [katapiezo] oppress, crush, harass.

καταπίνω [katapeeno] swallow, gobble up || (για κύματα) engulf.

καταπίπτω [katapeepto] fall down, come down || collapse || (λιγοστεύω) diminish.

καταπλακώνω [kataplakono] flatten, crush.

κατάπλασμα, το [kataplasma] poultice.

καταπλέω [katapleo] sail in, sail down.

καταπληκτικός [katapleekteekos] amazing, wonderful, marvellous, astonishing.

κατάπληκτος [katapleektos] stupefied, amazed.

κατάπληξη, η [katapleeksee] surprise, astonishment.

καταπλήσσω [katapleeso] astonish, surprise, amaze, stupefy.

καταπνίγω [katapneego] strangle, throttle, suffocate || (εξέγερση) suppress, put down.

καταποντίζομαι [kataponteezome] go down, sink.

καταπραΰνω [katapraeeno] pacify, mollify, appease, calm, assuage.

κατάπτυστος [katapteestos] despicable, abject, low, villainous.

κατάπτωση, η [kataptosee] downfall || (εδάφους) landslide || (μεταφ) prostration, exhaustion || dejection, depression.

κατάρα, η [katara] curse, imprecation || (μεταφ) hell, woe, damnation.

καταραμένος [kataramenos] cursed, damned.

καταργώ [katargo] abolish, annul, cancel.

καταριέμαι [katarieme] curse, damn, call down curses on.

καταρράκτης, ο [kataraktees] cascade, waterfall || (τεχν) sluice.

καταρρέω [katareo] collapse, fall down || (μεταφ) give out.

καταρρίπτω [katareepto] (κάποιο) knock down || (τοίχο) pull down, demolish || (επιχείρημα) prove to be wrong || (ρεκόρ) beat, break || (αερο) shoot down.

καταρροή, η [kataroee] catarrh, head cold.

κατάρτι, το [katartee] mast.

καταρτίζω [katarteezo] organize, establish, form, prepare, construct.

καταρώμαι [katarome] βλ **καταριέμαι.**

κατάσβεση, η [katasvesee] extinction, blowing out || (μεταφ) suppression || (δίψας) slaking, quenching.

κατασκευάζω [kataskevazo] construct, make, erect, build || (ιστορία κτλ) invent, concoct, fabricate || (έργο τέχνης) fashion, model.

κατασκεύασμα, το [kataskevasma] fabrication, concoction || construction, creation.

κατασκευή, η [kataskevee] making, construction || (έργο) structure, edifice, building || (εφεύρεση) invention, fabrication.

κατασκήνωση, η [kataskeenosee] camp, encampment || camping.

κατάσκοπος, ο [kataskopos] spy, secret agent.

κάτασπρος [kataspros] pure white, white as a sheet.

κατασταλάζω [katastalazo] (μεταφ) end in, conclude, settle on.

κατάσταση, η [katastasee] situation, condition, state || (περιουσία) wealth, property || (ονομαστική) register, list.

καταστατικό, το [katastateeko] (εταιρείας) statute.

καταστέλλω [katastelo] suppress, overcome || curb, control, contain.

κατάστημα, το [katasteema] establishment, institution || shop, store || **καταστηματάρχης** shopkeeper.

κατάστιχο, το [katasteeho] accounts book || register.

καταστολή, η [katastolee] suppression || checking, bridling, controlling.

καταστρεπτικός [katastrepteekos] destructive, devastating, ruinous.

καταστρέφω [katastrefo] destroy, ruin, devastate || spoil, damage.

καταστροφή, η [katastrofee] destruction, ruin, disaster, catastrophe.

κατάστρωμα, το [katastroma] deck.

καταστρώνω [katastrono] draw up, make up, frame || lay down.

κατάσχεση, η [katashesee] seizure, confiscation || (λόγω χρέους) attachment.

κατάταξη, η [katataksee] classification, sorting, grading || (στρατ) induction.

κατατάσσομαι [katatasome] enlist.

κατατομή, η [katatomee] profile || vertical section, cutoff.

κατατόπια, τα [katatopeea] πλ locality, every nook and cranny.

κατατοπίζομαι [katatopeezome] find one's bearings.

κατατοπίζω [katatopeezo] direct, explain, inform.

κατατρέχω [katatreho] persecute, harass.

καταφανής [katafanees] obvious, evident, manifest.

καταφατικός [katafateekos] affirmative, positive.

καταφέρνω [kataferno] persuade, convince, manage, accomplish, succeed || τα ~ succeed, manage.

καταφέρω [katafero] deal, strike || βλ και **καταφέρνω**.

καταφθάνω [katafthano] arrive || overtake, catch up, overhaul.

κατάφορτος [katafortos] overloaded.

καταφρονώ [katafrono] scorn, despise.

καταφύγιο, το [katafeeyo] refuge, hiding place.

κατάφυτος [katafeetos] covered with vegetation.

κατάφωτος [katafotos] profusely illuminated.

κατάχαμα [katahama] on the ground, on the floor.

καταχθόνιος [katahthoneeos] infernal, fiendish, devilish.

καταχραστής, ο [katahrastees] embezzler, defaulter.

καταχρεωμένος [katahreomenos] deep in debt.

κατάχρηση, η [katahreesee] abuse, misuse, breach of trust.

καταχρώμαι [katahrome] abuse, take advantage of, presume upon.

καταχωρώ [katahoro] enter in a register, insert, register, record.

καταψηφίζω [katapseefeezo] vote against, oppose.

κατάψυξη, η [katapseeksee] refrigeration.

κατεβάζω [katevazo] let down || (αποσκευές) take or bring down || (θερμοκρασία κτλ) lower, reduce || (κόστος) lessen, decrease || (αυλαία) drop.

κατεβαίνω [kateveno] come down, go down, descend.

κατέβασμα, το [katevasma] descent, lowering, taking down.

κατεβασμένος [katevasmenos] (τιμή) reduced || (κατηφής) depressed.

κατεδαφίζω [katedafeezo] demolish, pull down, raze.

κατειλημμένος [kateeleemenos] occupied, reserved.

κατεργάζομαι [katergazome] elaborate, work out, shape, fashion.

κατεργάρης, ο [katergarees] rascal, rogue || (επιθ) cunning, tricky.

κατέρχομαι [katerhome] βλ **κατεβαίνω**.

κατεύθυνση, η [kateftheensee] direction, line, course.

κατευθύνομαι [kateftheenome] turn, head (for).

κατευθύνω [kateftheeno] direct, guide, aim, turn.

κατευνάζω [katevnazo] calm, pacify, appease, mollify.

κατέχω [kateho] possess, own, have, hold || (θέση) occupy || (γνωρίζω) know.

κατεψυγμένος [katepseegmenos] frozen, icy, frigid, polar.

κατηγορηματικός [kateegoreemateekos] categorical, explicit.

κατηγορητήριο, το [kateegoreeteereeo] indictment.

κατηγορία, η [kateegoreea] accusation, charge || category, class, division.

κατήγορος, ο [kateegoros] plaintiff, accuser || δημόσιος ~ public prosecutor.

κατηγορούμενο, το [kateegoroumeno] (γραμμ) complement || attribute.

κατηγορούμενος [kateegoroumenos] the accused || defendant.

κατηγορώ [kateegoro] accuse, charge || blame, criticize.

κατηφής [kateefees] gloomy, depressed.

κατήφορος, ο [kateeforos] descent, slope.

κατηχώ [kateeho] (εκκλ) catechize || (σε οργάνωση) initiate.

κάτι [katee] something || some.

κατοικία, η [kateekeea] dwelling, residence, home.

κατοικίδιος [kateekeeðeeos] domesticated.

κατοικώ [kateeko] live in, dwell in, inhabit, reside.

κατολίσθηση, η [katoleestheesee] landslide.

κατόπι(ι) [katop(i)ee] after, close after || then || behind || ~ν από after.

κατοπτρίζω [katoptreezo] reflect, mirror || (μεταφ) represent.

κατόρθωμα, το [katorthoma] achievement, feat.

κατορθώνω [katorthono] succeed in, perform well.

κατορθωτός [katorthotos] feasible, possible, practicable.

κατουρλιό, το [katourlio] urine, piss (col).

κατουρώ [katouro] piss (col), urinate.

κατοχή, η [katohee] possession || (στρατ) occupation || (νομ) detention.

κάτοχος, ο [katohos] possessor, occupier || experienced person.

κατοχυρώνω [katoheerono] fortify || (μεταφ) secure, safeguaru.

κατρακυλώ [katrakeelo] bring down, tumble down, come down.

κατράμι, το [katramee] tar, asphalt.

κατσαβίδι, το [katsaveedee] screwdriver.

κατσάδα, η [katsaδa] scolding, dressing-down, reprimand.

κατσαρίδα, η [katsareeδa] cockroach.

κατσαρόλα, η [katsarola] saucepan.

κατσαρός [katsaros] curly, curled, fuzzy.

κατσίκα, η [katseeka] goat.

κατσικήσιος [katseekeeseeos] of a goat.

κατσίκι, το [katseekee] kid.

κατσουφιάζω [katsoufeeazo] look sour, look sullen, frown.

κάτω [kato] down, under, underneath, below || on the ground || **στο ~** ~ after all || **απάνω ~** approximately, about || **άνω ~** upset, in a turmoil.

κατώτατος [katotatos] lowest, least, undermost.

κατώτερος [katoteros] lower || poorer (quality), inferior.

κατώφλι, το [katoflee] threshold, doorstep || (μεταφ) eve.

καυγάς, ο [kavgas] quarrel, wrangle, squabble, argument.

καύκαλο, το [kavkalo] skull || shell, carapace.

καύσιμα, τα [kavseema] πλ fuel.

καύσιμος [kavseemos] combustible, inflammable.

καύση, η [kavsee] burning || (χημ) combustion.

καυστικός [kavsteekos] caustic.

καύσωνας, ο [kavsonas] heatwave.

καυτερός [kavteros] hot || (υγρό) scalding || (μεταφ) caustic, biting.

καυτηριάζω [kavteereeazo] cauterize || (ζώα) brand || (μεταφ) stigmatize.

καυτός [kavtos] scalding, boiling, hot.

καύχημα, το [kavheema] boast, pride, glory.

καυχιέμαι [kavhieme] boast of, be proud of.

καφάσι, το [kafasee] trellis, lattice || (για φρούτα) crate.

καφενείο, το [kafeneeo] coffee house.

καφές, ο [kafes] coffee.

καφετζής, ο [kafetsees] coffee-house keeper.

καφετιέρα, η [kafetiera] coffee pot.

καχεκτικός [kahekteekos] sickly (person), weakly (person).

καχύποπτος [kaheepoptos] suspicious, distrustful.

κάψα, η [kapsa] excessive heat.

καψαλίζω [kapsaleezo] singe, broil || toast.

κάψιμο, το [kapseemo] burning || scald.

καψούλι, το [kapsoulee] (ιατρ) capsule.

κέδρος, ο [keδros] cedar tree, cedar (wood).

κείμενο, το [keemeno] text.

κειμήλιο, το [keemeeleeo] heirloom, treasure.

κελαϊδώ [kelaeeδo] sing, warble, chirp.

κελεπούρι, το [kelepouree] bargain || windfall, godsend.

κελευστής, ο [kelevstees] petty officer.

κελλάρι, το [kelaree] cellar || larder.

κελλί, το [kelee] cell || honeycomb.

κέλυφος, το [keleefos] shell, husk, bark.

κενό, το [keno] void, empty space, vacuum || (μεταφ) gap.

κενός [kenos] empty || (οικία) unoccupied, vacant.

κέντημα, το [kenteema] sting, bite || embroidery || (μεταφ) exhortation.

κεντρί, το [kentree] sting || thorn.

κεντρίζω [kentreezo] (βόδι) prick, goad || (άλογο) spur || (δένδρο) graft || (μεταφ) rouse, stir up.

κεντρικός [kentreekos] central, middle || principal.

κεντρομόλος [kentromolos] centripetal.

κέντρο, το [kentro] (πόλης) centre || (γεωμ) centre || (διασκέδασης) (night) club, taverna || **τηλεφωνικό ~** telephone exchange.

κεντρόφυγος [kentrofeegos] centrifugal.

κεντώ [kento] embroider || (μεταφ) incite, rouse, awaken, stir up.

κενώνω [kenono] empty || (δρόμο) drain || (συρτάρι) clean out || (σπίτι) evacuate.

κένωση, η [kenosee] emptying, clearing out || bowel movement.

κεραία, η [kerea] antenna, feeler || (ασυρμάτου) aerial.

κεραμίδι, το [kerameeδee] tile, slate || **κεραμίδα** roof.

κεραμική, η [kerameekee] ceramics.

κεράσι, το [kerasee] cherry ||
κερασιά, η cherry tree.
κέρασμα, το [kerasma] treat.
κερατάς, ο [keratas] cuckold.
κέρατο, το [kerato] horn || (για
άνθρωπο) obstinate, perverse.
κεραυνοβόλος [keravnovolos] like
lightning.
κεραυνός, ο [keravnos] thunderbolt.
κερδίζω [kerðeezo] win, earn || get,
gain || profit by.
κέρδος, το [kerðos] earnings,
winnings || advantage.
κερδοσκοπώ [kerðoskopo] speculate.
κερένιος [kereneeos] wax, waxen.
κερί, το [keree] wax || taper, wax
candle.
κερκίδα, η [kerkeeða] tier of seats.
κέρμα, το [kerma] fragment || coin ||
(για μηχάνημα) token.
κερνώ [kerno] treat || stand or buy a
drink.
κετσές, ο [ketses] felt.
κεφαλαιοκρατία, η [kefaleokrateea]
capitalism.
κεφάλαια, τα [kefalea] πλ funds,
capital.
κεφάλαιο, το [kefaleo] capital, funds
|| (βιβλίου) chapter.
κεφαλαίο, το [kefaleo] capital
(letter).
κεφαλαιώδης [kefaleoðees] essential,
fundamental.
κεφαλή, η [kefalee] head || leader,
chief.
κεφάλι, το [kefalee] head || (μεταφ)
brains.
κεφάτος [kefatos] well-disposed,
merry, jovial.
κέφι, το [kefee] good humour, gaiety ||
στο ~ merry, mellow.
κεφτές, ο [keftes] meatball, rissole.
κεχρί, το [kehree] millet.
κεχριμπάρι, το [kehreembaree]
amber.
κηδεία, η [keeðeea] funeral
(procession).
κηδεμώνας, ο [keeðemonas]
guardian || curator.
κήλη, η [keelee] hernia, rupture.
κηλιδώνω [keeleeðono] stain, dirty ||
(μεταφ) sully, tarnish.
κηλίδα, η [keeleeða] spot, stain ||
(μεταφ) slur, blemish.
κήπος, ο [keepos] garden.
κηπουρική, η [keepoureekee]
gardening, horticulture.
κηπουρός, ο [keepouros] gardener.
κηρήθρα, η [keereethra] honeycomb.
κηροπήγιο, το [keeropeeyo]
candlestick, taper-stand.
κήρυγμα, το [keereegma]
proclamation || (εκκλ) sermon,
preaching.

κήρυκας, ο [keereekas] herald ||
(εκκλ) preacher.
κηρύσσω [keereeso] proclaim,
announce || (εκκλ) preach.
κήτος, το [keetos] cetacean, whale.
κηφήνας, ο [keefeenas] drone ||
(μεταφ) idler, loafer.
κιάλια, τα [kialeea] πλ binoculars,
opera glasses.
κίβδηλος [keevðeelos] adulterated,
counterfeit || (μεταφ) fraudulent.
κιβώτιο, το [keevoteeo] chest, box ||
~ ταχύτητων gearbox.
κιγκλίδωμα, το [keengleeðoma]
(φράκτης) barrier, fence || (σιδερένιο)
grating || (ξύλινο) lattice work ||
(παραθύρου) bar.
κιθάρα, η [keethara] guitar.
κιλό, το [keelo] kilogram.
κιμάς, ο [keemas] minced meat.
κιμωλία, η [keemoleea] chalk.
Κίνα, η [keena] China.
κινδυνεύω [keenðeenevo] endanger ||
be in danger, risk, venture.
κίνδυνος, ο [keenðeenos] danger,
peril, hazard, jeopardy.
κινέζικα, τα [keenezeeka] πλ Chinese
language.
κινέζικος [keenezeekos] Chinese.
Κινέζος, ο [keenezos] Chinese,
Chinaman || οι κινέζοι the Chinese.
κίνημα, το [keeneema] movement ||
(μεταφ) rebellion, revolt.
κινηματογράφος, ο
[keeneematografos] cinema.
κίνηση, η [keeneesee] movement ||
(κυκλοφορίας) flow of traffic || (αξιών)
transactions.
κινητήρας, ο [keeneeteeras] motor.
κινητός [keeneetos] movable.
κίνητρο, το [keeneetro] motive.
κινίνη, η [keeneenee] quinine.
κινούμαι [keenoume] move.
κινώ [keeno] set in motion, move,
rouse, make go, set going.
κιόλα(ς) [keeola(s)] already, also,
even.
κιονοστοιχία, η [keeonosteeheea]
colonnade.
κιόσκι, το [keeoskee] kiosk.
κίσσα, η [keesa] magpie.
κισσός, ο [keesos] ivy.
κιτρινίζω [keetreeneezo] go yellow,
make yellow, pale.
κίτρινος [keetreenos] yellow || sallow,
pale.
κίτρο, το [keetro] citron.
κλαδευτήρι, το [klaðevteeree]
pruning hook, pruning scissors.
κλαδεύω [klaðevo] prune, trim.
κλάδος, ο [klaðos] branch, sector.
κλαίγομαι [klegome] complain, gripe.
κλαίω [kleo] cry, weep || feel sorry for,
weep for.

κλάμα, το [klama] crying, wailing, weeping.

κλάνω [klano] break wind, fart (col).

κλαρί, το [klaree] small branch.

κλάση, η [klasee] class, age group, category.

κλάσμα, το [klasma] fraction || fragment.

κλασσικός [klaseekos] classic(al) || (μεταφ) standard, standing.

κλαψιάρης [klapseearees] given to complaining || tearful, plaintive.

κλάψιμο, το [klapseemo] crying, grumbling.

κλέβω [klevo] βλ **κλέπτω.**

κλειδαριά, η [kleeðaria] lock || (ασφαλείας) safety lock || (κρεμαστή) padlock.

κλειδαρότρυπα, η [kleeðarotreepa] keyhole.

κλειδί, το [kleeðee] key.

κλειδώνω [kleeðono] lock up || (περιορίζω) confine, coop up.

κλείδωση, η [kleeðosee] joint.

κλείνω [kleeno] close, shut, shut up, seal || (με σύρτη) bolt || (βρύση) turn off || ~ **το μάτι** wink || ~ **τα εξήντα** I'm nearing sixty.

κλείσιμο, το [kleeseemo] closing, locking up || (μεταφ) conclusion.

κλεισούρα, η [kleesoura] pass || mustiness.

κλειστός [kleestos] shut, closed.

κλέπτης, ο [kleptees] thief, burglar || (πορτοφολιών) pickpocket.

κλέπτω [klepto] (κάτι) steal || (κάποιο) rob || (με απάτη) cheat, swindle.

κλεφτά [klefta] furtively, stealthily || hurriedly.

κλέφτης, ο [kleftees] thief || klepht.

κλεφτοπόλεμος, ο [kleftopolemos] guerrilla warfare.

κλεφτός [kleftos] stolen || furtive, stealthy.

κλεψιά, η [klepseea] βλ **κλοπή.**

κλέψιμο, το [klepseemo] theft, robbery, burglary.

κλεψύδρα, η [klepseeðra] water clock, sandglass.

κλήμα, το [kleema] vine || **κληματαριά, η** vine arbour, climbing vine || bower || **κληματόφυλλο, το** vine leaf.

κληρικός [kleereekos] clerical, of the clergy.

κληροδότημα, το [kleeroðoteema] legacy, bequest.

κληρονομιά, η [kleeronomeea] inheritance || heritage, legacy.

κληρονομικός [kleeronomeekos] hereditary.

κληρονόμος, ο, η [kleeronomos] heir, heiress.

κληρονομώ [kleeronomo] inherit, come into an estate.

κλήρος, ο [kleeros] lot, fate || (εκκλ) clergy || (μεταφ) lot, fortune.

κλήρωση, η [kleerosee] drawing of lottery, prize drawing.

κλήση, η [kleesee] call, calling || writ of summons.

κλητήρας, ο [kleeteeras] clerk || (δικαστικός) bailiff.

κλίβανος, ο [kleevanos] oven, kiln, furnace.

κλίμα, το [kleema] climate || (μεταφ) atmosphere.

κλίμακα, η [kleemaka] staircase, stairs, ladder || scale || (μουσ) gamut, scale.

κλιμακωτός [kleemakotos] graduated.

κλιματισμός, ο [kleemateesmos] air conditioning.

κλινήρης [kleeneerees] bedridden.

κλινική, η [kleeneekee] clinic, (private) hospital.

κλίνω [kleeno] lean, bend || (έχω τάση προς) tend || (γραμμ) decline, conjugate.

κλίση, η [kleesee] inclination, slope || proneness, tendency || (γραμμής) slope || (γραμμ) declension, conjugation || (στέγης) slant.

κλονίζομαι [kloneezome] stagger || (μεταφ) hesitate, falter, waver.

κλονίζω [kloneezo] shake, unsettle || (υγεία) damage, ruin.

κλονισμός, ο [kloneesmos] shaking, concussion || (μεταφ) hesitation, wavering.

κλοπή, η [klopee] theft, robbery, burglary.

κλοπιμαίος [klopeemeos] stolen || furtive, stealthy.

κλουβί, το [klouvee] cage.

κλούβιος [klouveeos] bad, rotten || (μεταφ) empty-headed, stupid.

κλύσμα, το [kleesma] enema.

κλώθω [klotho] spin.

κλωνάρι, το [klonaree] branch (of tree) || shoot.

κλώσιμο, το [kloseemo] spinning.

κλώσσα, η [klosa] (brooding) hen.

κλωστή, η [klostee] thread, string.

κλωτσιά, η [klotsia] kick.

κλωτσώ [klotso] kick.

κνήμη, η [kneemee] shin || leg.

κόβομαι [kovome] cut o.s.

κόβω [kovo] (ψωμί) cut, slice || (μαλλιά) cut, trim || (νύχια) pare || (κρέας) carve || (νομίσματα) coin, mint || (νερό) turn off || (καφέ, σιτάρι) grind, mill || (κεφάλι) behead || (εφόδια) cut off || ~ **μονέδα** make money || ~ **εισιτήριο** buy a ticket || ~ **δεξιά** turn right.

κόγχη, η [konghee] marine shell || (ματιού) eye socket || (αρχιτεκ) niche.

κοιλάδα, η [keelaða] valley, vale.

κοιλιά, η [keelia] belly, abdomen || (τοίχου) bulge.

κοίλος [keelos] hollow, sunken.

κοιλότητα, η [keeloteeta] hollowness || concavity.

κοιμάμαι [keemame] sleep, be asleep.

κοίμηση, η [keemeesee] (εκκλ) Assumption || sleeping.

κομητήριο, το [keemeeteereeo] cemetery, graveyard.

κοιμίζω [keemeezo] put to sleep || quiet, lull, beguile.

κοιμισμένος [keemeesmenos] (μεταφ) sluggish, stupid, dull.

κοιμούμαι [keemoume] βλ κοιμάμαι.

κοινοβουλευτικός [keenovoulevteekos] parliamentary, parliamentarian.

κοινοβούλιο, το [keenovouleeo] parliament || (στην Αγγλία) Houses of Parliament.

κοινό, το [keeno] the public.

κοινοποιώ [keenopeeo] notify, inform, announce || serve (a notice).

κοινοπολιτεία, η [keenopoleeteea] commonwealth.

κοινός [keenos] common || ordinary, vulgar || (εργασία κτλ) collective || (γραμμ) common (noun) || κοινή γνώμη public opinion || από κοινού in common, together.

κοινότητα, η [keenoteeta] community || parish || Βουλή των Κοινοτήτων House of Commons.

κοινοτοπία, η [keenotopeea] commonplace || banality.

κοινωνία, η [keenoneea] society, community, association || (εκκλ) Holy Communion.

κοινωνικός [keenoneekos] social, sociable || κοινωνικός λειτουργός social worker.

κοινωνώ [keenono] receive Holy Communion || administer Holy Communion.

κοιτάζω [keetazo] look at, pay attention to || consider, see || attend.

κοίτασμα, το [keetasma] layer, deposit, stratum.

κοιτίδα, η [keeteeδa] cradle || (μεταφ) origin, birthplace.

κοιτώνας, ο [keetonas] bedroom || dormitory.

κοκεταρία, η [koketareea] smartness, coquetry, stylishness.

κόκκαλο, το [kokalo] bone || (παπουτσιού) shoehorn || έμεινε ~ he was astounded.

κοκκινέλι, το [kokeenelee] red wine.

κοκκινίζω [kokeeneezo] redden, blush, turn red.

κοκκινογούλι, το [kokeenogoulee] beetroot, beet.

κοκκινομάλλης [kokeenomalees] red-haired.

κόκκινος [kokeenos] red, scarlet || (μάγουλα) ruddy, rosy.

κόκκος, ο [kokos] grain || (καφέ) bean || (σκόνης) speck.

κοκκύτης, ο [kokeetees] whooping cough.

κόκορας, ο [kokoras] cock, rooster.

κοκορέτσι, το [kokoretsee] sheep's entrails.

κολάζω [kolazo] punish, chastise.

κολακεία, η [kolakeea] flattery, softsoaping.

κολακευτικός [kolakevteekos] complimentary.

κολακεύω [kolakevo] flatter, fawn upon.

κόλακας, ο [kolakas] flatterer, wheedler.

κόλαση, η [kolasee] hell.

κολατσιό, το [kolatsio] snack.

κολικός, ο [koleekos] colic.

κολιός, ο [kolios] kind of mackerel.

κόλλα, η [kola] glue, gum, paste || (κολλαρίσματος) starch || (χαρτιού) sheet of paper.

κολλάρο, το [kolaro] collar.

κολλέγιο, το [koleyo] college.

κόλλημα, το [koleema] glueing, sticking || soldering.

κολλητικός [koleeteekos] contagious, infectious.

κολλητός [koleetos] soldered || close-fitting || (εφαπτόμενος) contiguous.

κολλιέ, το [kolie] necklace.

κόλλυβα, τα [koleeva] πλ boiled wheat (given after funerals).

κολλώ [kolo] glue, stick, paste || solder, fuse || (αρρώστια) get, catch || (σε κάποιο) stick to, attach to.

κολοκύθι, το [kolokeethee] vegetable marrow, pumpkin.

κολόνα, η [kolona] βλ κολώνα.

κολόνια, η [koloneea] eau de Cologne.

κολοσσιαίος [kolosieos] colossal, enormous.

κολοσσός, ο [kolosos] colossus, giant.

κόλπο, το [kolpo] trick, artifice, deceit.

κόλπος, ο [kolpos] breast, bosom || (γεωγραφικός) gulf, bay.

κολυμβήθρα, η [koleemveethra] font.

κολυμβητής, ο [koleemveetees] swimmer.

κολύμπι, το [koleembee] swimming.

κολυμπώ [koleembo] swim.

κολώνα, η [kolona] pillar, column.

κόμβος, ο [komvos] knot || junction.

κόμης, ο [komees] count, earl.

κομητεία, η [komeeteea] county, shire.

κομήτης, ο [komeetees] comet.

κομιστής, ο [komeestees] carrier, bearer.

κόμιστρα, τα [komeestra] πλ carriage fees.

κόμμα, το [koma] (πολιτικό) party || (γραμμ) comma || (μαθημ) decimal point.

κομματάρχης, ο [komatarhees] party leader.

κομμάτι, το [komatee] piece || (ψωμί) slice || (ζάχαρη) lump || fragment, chip || (επιρ) a bit.

κομματιάζω [komateeazo] cut up, parcel out, tear, break.

κομμένος [komenos] sliced, cut || (κουρασμένος) exhausted.

κομ(μ)οδίνο, το [komoδeeno] bedside table.

κομμουνιστής, ο [komouneesteos] communist.

κόμμωση, η [komosee] hairdressing, hair style.

κομμωτήριο, το [komoteereeo] hairdressing salon.

κομπιάζω [kombeeazo] (μεταφ) hesitate.

κομπίνα, η [kombeena] racket (col).

κομπιναιζό, το [kombeenezo] slip, petticoat.

κομπόδεμα, το [komboδema] hoard of money, savings.

κομπολό(γ)ι, το [kombolo(y)ee] string of beads, worry beads.

κόμπος, ο [kombos] βλ **κόμβος**.

κομπόστα, η [kombosta] compote.

κομπρέσσα, η [kombresa] compress.

κομφόρ, τα [komfor] πλ home comforts, necessities.

κομψός [kompsos] fashionable, stylish, smart.

κονδύλιο, το [konδeeleeo] item, entry.

κονιάκ, το [koneeak] cognac, brandy.

κονίαμα, το [koneeama] mortar || plaster.

κονσέρβα, η [konserva] tinned food, canned food, preserve(s).

κονσέρτο, το [konserto] concert.

κοντά [konta] close to, close by, near || almost, nearly || ~ **σε** near, next to || ~ **στα άλλα** moreover.

κονταίνω [konteno] shorten, curtail || get shorter.

κοντάρι, το [kontaree] pole || (σημαίας) staff || (ναυτ) mast.

κοντεύω [kontevo] be about to, be nearly finished, be on the verge (of) || (πλησιάζω) approach, come near, draw near.

κόντημα, το [konteema] shortening, shrinking.

κοντινός [konteenos] neighbouring, near(by) || (δρόμος) short, quick.

κοντός [kontos] short || (ουσ) pole, post, stake.

κοντοστέκω [kontosteko] pause || hesitate, waver.

κόντρα [kontra] against, opposite.

κοπάδι, το [kopaδee] flock || herd, drove || (λύκων) pack || (ανθρώπων) crowd, throng.

κοπάζω [kopazo] calm down, grow quiet, subside.

κοπανίζω [kopaneezo] beat, pound, grind.

κόπανος, ο [kopanos] pestle, crusher || (μεταφ) fool, idiot.

κοπέλλα, η [kopela] girl || (υπηρεσίας) servant, maid.

κοπή, η [kopee] cutting || stoppage.

κόπια, η [kopeea] copy, transcript.

κοπιάζω [kopeeazo] labour, toil || take the trouble (to).

κοπιαστικός [kopeeasteekos] wearisome, hard, fatiguing, troublesome.

κοπίδι, το [kopeeδee] chisel.

κόπος, ο [kopos] fatigue, toil, labour, trouble, effort.

κόπρανα, τα [koprana] πλ excrement.

κοπριά, η [kopreea] dung, manure.

κοπρόσκυλο, το [koproskeelo] (μεταφ) worthless person, scoundrel.

κοπτήρας, ο [kopteeras] incisor || (χαρτοκοπτήρας) cutter.

κοπτική, η [kopteekee] cutting, tailoring.

κόπτω [kopto] βλ **κόβω**.

κόπωση, η [koposee] fatigue, weariness, toil.

κόρακας, ο [korakas] crow, raven.

κοράλλι, το [koralee] coral.

κορδέλλα, η [korδela] ribbon, band, tape || (μεταφ) zigzag, twist and turn.

κορδόνι, το [korδonee] cord, string.

κορδώνομαι [korδonome] strut, swagger, put on airs.

κορδώνω [korδono] tighten, stretch, extend.

κορεσμός, ο [koresmos] satisfaction, satiety.

κόρη, η [koree] girl || (παρθένα) virgin || (παιδί) daughter || (οφθαλμού) pupil.

κοριός, ο [korios] bedbug.

κοριτσάκι, το [koreetsakee] little girl.

κορίτσι, το [koreetsee] girl || virgin.

κορμί, το [kormee] body || trunk.

κορμός, ο [kormos] trunk.

κορμοστασιά, η [kormostasia] stature, bearing, figure.

κορνάρω [kornaro] sound one's horn, hoot.

κορνίζα, η [korneeza] frame || cornice.

κοροϊδεύω [koroeeδevo] scoff at, laugh at, ridicule || deceive.

κορόιδο, το [koroeeδo] laughing stock, butt, scapegoat.

κορσές, ο [korses] corset.

κορτάρω [kortaro] flirt, court.

κορυδαλλός, ο [koreeðalos] skylark, lark.

κορυφαίος, ο [koreefeos] leader, chief.

κορυφή, η [koreefee] top || κορφή, η [korfee] top || (όρους) top, peak || (γωνίας) vertex || (μεταφ) leading person, outstanding person.

κόρφος, ο [korfos] bosom.

κορώνα, η [korona] crown, coronet || ~ γράμματα heads or tails.

κοσκινίζω [koskeeneezo] sift, screen || (μεταφ) sift carefully.

κόσκινο, το [koskeeno] sieve, sifter.

κοσμάκης, ο [kosmakees] the man in the street.

κόσμημα, το [kosmeema] decoration, jewel || κοσμήματα πλ jewellery.

κοσμήτορας, ο [kosmeetoras] dean (of university).

κοσμικός [kosmeekos] lay || mundane || (γεγονός) social.

κόσμιος [kosmeeos] decent, modest, proper.

κόσμος, ο [kosmos] universe, world || (άνθρωποι) people || (στόλισμα) embellishment.

κοσμώ [kosmo] adorn, embellish.

κοστίζω [kosteezo] cost, be expensive.

κόστος, το [kostos] cost, price.

κοστούμι, το [kostoumee] suit.

κότερο, το [kotero] sailboat, yacht || (ναυτ) cutter.

κοτέτσι, το [kotetsee] hen coop.

κοτόπουλο, το [kotopoulo] chicken.

κοτρώνι, το [kotronee] large stone, boulder.

κοτσάνι, το [kotsanee] stem, stalk.

κότσι, το [kotsee] anklebone.

κότσια, τα [kotseea] πλ guts, strength.

κοτσίδα, η [kotseeða] tress, braid, pigtail.

κότσυφας, ο [kotseefas] blackbird.

κότ(τ)α, η [kota] hen || fowl.

κουβαλώ [kouvalo] carry, bring, transport.

κουβάρι, το [kouvaree] ball.

κουβαριάζω [kouvareeazo] wind into a ball || crumple || (μεταφ) cheat.

κουβαρίστρα, η [kouvareestra] bobbin, spool.

κουβάς, ο [kouvas] bucket, pail.

κουβέντα, η [kouventa] conversation, chat.

κουβεντιάζω [kouventeeazo] converse, discuss, chat.

κουβέρ, το [kouver] service charge, cover charge.

κουβέρτα, η [kouverta] blanket, coverlet || (ναυτ) deck.

κουδούνι, το [kouðounee] bell || (εισόδου) doorbell.

κουδουνίζω [kouðouneezo] ring, tinkle, jingle.

κουδουνίστρα, η [kouðouneestra] rattle.

κουζίνα, η [kouzeena] kitchen || (για μαγείρευμα) stove.

κουκέτα, η [kouketa] berth.

κουκί, το [koukee] broad bean || grain.

κούκλα, η [koukla] doll || (ράφτη) dummy || (καλαμποκιού) corn cob || (μεταφ) lovely child || pretty woman.

κούκος, ο [koukos] cuckoo || bonnet, cap.

κουκουβάγια, η [koukouvaya] owl.

κουκούλα, η [koukoula] cowl, hood || (τσαγιού) tea cosy.

κουκούλι, το [koukoulee] cocoon.

κουκουλώνω [koukoulono] keep secret || bury || wrap warmly.

κουκουνάρι, το [koukounaree] pine cone || seed of pine cone.

κουκούτσι, το [koukoutsee] stone, kernel, pip || (μεταφ) morsel, scrap.

κουλούρα, η [kouloura] roll, French roll || (ναυτ) lifebuoy.

κουλούρι, το [koulouree] ring-shaped biscuit.

κουλουριάζω [kouloureeazo] coil, roll up, fold.

κουμάντο, το [koumanto] order, control.

κουμπάρα, η [koumbara] godmother || matron of honour.

κουμπαράς, ο [koumbaras] moneybox, piggy bank.

κουμπάρος, ο [koumbaros] godfather || (σε γάμο) best man.

κουμπί, το [koumbee] button, stud || (φώτων) switch.

κουμπότρυπα, η [koumbotreepa] buttonhole.

κουμπώνω [koumbono] button up, fasten.

κουνάβι, το [kounavee] marten, ferret.

κουνέλι, το [kounelee] rabbit.

κούνημα, το [kouneema] shaking, swinging, wagging || (μεταφ) swaying.

κούνια, η [kouneea] cradle, cot, crib || (κήπου) swing.

κουνιάδα, η [kouneeaða] sister-in-law.

κουνιάδος, ο [kouneeaðos] brother-in-law.

κουνιστός [kouneestos] rocking || (μεταφ) swaying.

κουνούπι, το [kounoupee] mosquito.

κουνουπίδι, το [kounoupeeðee] cauliflower.

κουνιέμαι [kounieme] move, shake || get moving.

κουνώ [kouno] move, shake || (μαντήλι) wave || (ουρά) wag || (μωρό) rock || (κεφάλι) shake.

κούπα, η [koupa] cup, bowl, glass || (σε χαρτιά) heart.

κουπί, το [koupee] oar || **τραβώ** ~ to row.

κούρα, η [koura] cure || medical attendance.

κουράγιο, το [kourayo] bravery, fearlessness.

κουράζομαι [kourazome] get tired, tire o.s.

κουράζω [kourazo] tire, weary || bore || (όραση) strain.

κούραση, η [kourasee] weariness, fatigue || (μηχανής) wear and tear.

κουρασμένος [kourasmenos] tired, weary || (πρόσωπο) drawn.

κουραστικός [kourasteekos] tiresome, trying, troublesome.

κουραφέξαλα, τα [kourafeksala] πλ bullshit (col), balls (col).

κουρδίζω [kourdeezo] wind up || (βιολί) tune || (μεταφ) stir up, incite.

κουρέας, ο [koureas] barber.

κουρείο, το [koureeo] barber's shop.

κουρέλι, το [kourelee] rag, tatter, shred.

κούρεμα, το [kourema] haircut || shearing, clipping.

κουρεύω [kourevo] cut the hair of, trim, clip || (πρόβατο) shear || (χλόη) mow.

κουρκούτι, το [kourkoutee] batter || pap.

κούρσα, η [koursa] race || (διαδρομή) ride || (αμάξι) car.

κουρσάρος, ο [koursaros] pirate.

κουρσεύω [koursevo] plunder, raid.

κουρτίνα, η [kourteena] curtain.

κουσούρι, το [kousouree] defect, fault.

κουτάβι, το [koutavee] puppy.

κουτάλι, το [koutalee] spoon.

κουταμάρα, η [koutamara] foolishness, nonsense.

κούτελο, το [koutelo] forehead.

κουτί, το [koutee] box, case || (σπίρτων) matchbox || (κονσέρβας) tin.

κουτός [koutos] silly, foolish, slow-witted.

κουτουλώ [koutoulo] nod drowsily || butt.

κουτουρού [koutourou]: **στα** ~ heedlessly, haphazardly, by chance.

κουτρουβάλα, η [koutrouvala] somersault.

κουτσαίνω [koutseno] limp || cripple.

κουτσομπολεύω [koutsombolevo] gossip, spread reports, tittle-tattle.

κουτσομπολιό, το [koutsombolio] gossip, tittle-tattle.

κουτσός [koutsos] crippled, limping.

κούτσουρο, το [koutsouro] log, stump.

κουφαίνομαι [koufenome] go deaf.

κουφαίνω [koufeno] deafen, make deaf.

κουφαμάρα, η [koufamara] deafness.

κουφάρι, το [koufaree] body || corpse.

κουφέτο, το [koufeto] sugared almond.

κούφιος [koufeos] hollow, empty || (δόντι) decayed || (ήχος) muffled || (άνθρωπος) not serious, frivolous.

κουφόβρααη, η [koufovrasee] sweltering heat.

κουφός [koufos] hard of hearing.

κούφωμα, το [koufoma] hollow, cavity || opening.

κοφίνι, το [kofeenee] basket, hamper, pannier.

κοφτά [kofta]: **ορθά** ~ frankly, categorically.

κοφτερός [kofteros] sharp, cutting.

κόφτω [kofto] βλ **κόβω.**

κόχη, η [kohee] βλ **κώχη.**

κοχλάζω [kohlazo] boil, bubble || (μεταφ) seethe.

κοχλίας, ο [kohleeas] snail || (ήλος) screw.

κοχύλι, το [koheelee] sea shell.

κόψη, η [kopsee] cutting, slicing, clipping || edge.

κόψιμο, το [kopseemo] cut, gash || cutting || (ασθένια) bellyache (col).

κραγιόν, το [krayon] crayon || lipstick.

κραδαίνω [kradeno] flourish, wave, vibrate.

κράζω [krazo] croak, caw || cry out || call.

κραιπάλη, η [krepalee] riot, orgy || drunkenness.

κράμα, το [krama] mixture, blend || alloy, amalgam.

κρανίο, το [kraneeo] cranium || skull.

κράνος, το [kranos] helmet.

κράξιμο, το [krakseemo] crowing, cawing.

κρασί, το [krasee] wine.

κράση, η [krasee] (σώματος) temperament, make-up.

κράσπεδο, το [kraspedo] (λόφου) foot || (πεζοδρομίου) kerb || curb (US).

κρατήρας, ο [krateeras] crater.

κράτηση, η [krateesee] confinement, arrest || (μισθού) deduction(s).

κρατιέμαι [kratieme] hold one's own, be well preserved.

κρατικοποίηση, η [krateekopieesee] nationalization.

κρατικός [krateekos] national.

κράτος, το [kratos] influence, power, authority || the state.

κρατώ [krato] last, keep || (επιβάλλομαι) hold in check, rule || (κατάγομαι) be descended from || (βαστώ) have, hold || (υποβαστώ) support.

κραυγάζω [kravgazo] cry, howl, shout, scream.

κραυγή, η [kravyee] shout, cry, outcry.

κρέας, το [kreas] meat, flesh.

κρεββάτι, το [krevatee] bed.

κρεββατοκάμαρα, η [krevatokamara] bedroom.

κρεββατώνω [krevatono] confine to bed, lay up.

κρέμα, η [krema] cream.

κρεμάζω [kremazo] hang, suspend.

κρεμάλα, η [kremala] gallows, gibbet.

κρέμασμα, το [kremasma] suspension, hooking on || hanging.

κρεμαστός [kremastos] suspended.

κρεμάστρα, η [kremastra] hanger || hat rack || portmanteau.

κρεμιέμαι [kremieme] hang, be suspended.

κρεμμύδι, το [kremeeδee] onion.

κρεμ(ν)ώ [krem(n)o] hang, hook up, suspend.

κρεοπώλης, ο [kreopolees] butcher.

κρεουργώ [kreourgo] butcher || massacre.

κρεπ, το [krep] crêpe rubber || crape.

κρημνίζομαι [kreemneezome] fall, crumble, collapse.

κρημνίζω [kreemneezo] hurl down, pull down, wreck.

κρήνη, η [kreenee] fountain.

κρηπίδωμα, το [kreepeeδoma] foundation, base, groundwork || (ναυτ) breakwater || (σταθμού) railway platform.

κρησφύγετο, το [kreesfeeyeto] hideaway, retreat.

κριάρι, ο [kreearee] ram.

κριθαράκι, το [kreetharakee] barley-shaped noodle || (ματιού) stye.

κριθάρι, το [kreetharee] barley.

κρίκος, ο [kreekos] link, buckle, ring || (ανυψώσεως) jack.

κρίμα, το [kreema] sin, guilt || pity, misfortune || τι ~! what a pity!, what a shame!

κρίνος, ο [kreenos] lily.

κρίνω [kreeno] judge, consider || (αποφασίζω) decide.

κριός, ο [krios] ram.

κρίσιμος [kreeseemos] critical, grave, momentous || trying.

κρίση, η [kreesee] judgment, view || (οικονομική) crisis, depression || (έλλειψη) deficiency, shortage || (πνεύματος) judgment.

κριτήριο, το [kreeteereeo] criterion, test.

κριτής, ο [kreetees] judge.

κριτική, η [kreeteekee] criticism, review.

κριτικός [kreeteekos] discerning, critical || (ουσ) critic.

κροκόδειλος, ο [krokoδeelos] crocodile.

κρόκος, ο [krokos] crocus || (αυγού) yolk.

κρόσσι, το [krosee] fringe.

κρόταφος, ο [krotafos] (ανατ) temple.

κρότος, ο [krotos] crash, bang, noise || (μεταφ) sensation.

κρουαζιέρα, η [krouaziera] cruise.

κρούση, η [krousee] striking, sounding || (στρατ) encounter.

κρούσμα, το [krousma] (ιατρ, νομ) case.

κρούστα, η [krousta] crust, rind || scab.

κρούω [krouo] strike, sound || knock on || (κουδούνι) ring.

κρυάδα, η [kreeaδa] cold, chill.

κρύβομαι [kreevome] go into hiding.

κρύβω [kreevo] βλ κρύπτω.

κρυμμένος [kreemenos] concealed.

κρύο, το [kreeo] cold.

κρυολόγημα, το [kreeoloyeema] (ιατρ) cold.

κρυοπάγημα, το [kreeopayeema] frostbite.

κρύος [kreeos] cold || indifferent, phlegmatic, cool.

κρύπτω [kreepto] hide, conceal || cover, screen || (μεταφ) withhold, hold back.

κρυστάλλινος [kreestaleenos] like crystal, very clear.

κρύσταλλο, το [kreestalo] crystal (glass).

κρυφά [kreefa] secretly, clandestinely, stealthily.

κρυφός [kreefos] private, secluded || (χαρά) secret, inner || (άνθρωπος) discreet, reticent.

κρύψιμο, το [kreepseemo] concealing, hiding.

κρυψίνους [kreepseenous] deceitful, underhand, sneaky.

κρυψώνας, ο [kreepsonas] hideout, lurking place.

κρυώνω [kreeono] grow cold, feel cold || cool down, chill.

κτένι, το [ktenee] comb || (τσουγκράνα) rake || κτενίζω to comb || (μεταφ) brush up, finish in detail || ~σμα combing || hair-dressing.

κτήμα, το [kteema] estate, land || κτηματίας, ο landowner, proprietor.

κτηνίατρος, ο [kteeneeeatros] veterinary surgeon.

κτήνος, το [kteenos] brute, beast, animal || κτήνη cattle.

κτηνοτροφία, η [kteenotrofeea] stockbreeding.

κτηνώδης [kteenoδees] beastly, bestial || (όρεξη) hoggish.

κτήση, η [kteesee] acquisition, occupation, occupancy.

κτητικός [kteeteekos] (γραμμ) possessive || acquisitive.

κτίζω [kteezo] construct, erect, build.

κτίριο, το [kteereeo] building, edifice.

κτίσιμο, το [kteeseemo] building, erection.

κτίστης, ο [kteestees] builder, mason.

κτυπώ [kteepo] beat, strike, flog, thrash.

κυάνιο, το [keeaneeo] cyanide.

κυβέρνηση, η [keeverneesee] government, management.

κυβερνήτης, ο [keeverneetees] governor || (ναυτ) commander.

κυβερνητικός [keeverneeteekos] governmental.

κυβερνώ [keeverno] govern || (πλοίο) steer || (σπίτι) manage, direct.

κύβος, ο [keevos] cube || die.

κυδώνι, το [keedonee] quince || (όστρακο) kind of shellfish.

κύηση, η [kieesee] pregnancy || gestation.

κυκλάμινο, το [keeklameeno] cyclamen.

κυκλικός [keekleekos] circular.

κύκλος, ο [keeklos] circle || (ηλιακός κτλ) cycle, period || (προσώπων) set.

κυκλοφορία, η [keekloforeea] circulation || (αυτοκινήτων) traffic flow.

κυκλοφορώ [keekloforo] put into circulation, spread || go about.

κύκλωμα, το [keekloma] electric circuit || encirclement.

κυκλώνας, ο [keeklonas] cyclone.

κυκλώνω [keeklono] surround, encircle, envelop.

κύκνος, ο [keeknos] swan.

κυλάω [keelao] roll.

κυλιέμαι [keelieme] roll over || (χοίρος) wallow.

κυλικείο, το [keeleekeeo] buffet, sideboard || refreshment room.

κύλινδρος, ο [keeleenoros] cylinder || roller, barrel.

κυλότα, η [keelota] panties.

κύμα, το [keema] wave.

κυμαίνομαι [keemenome] undulate, wave, ripple || (μεταφ) fluctuate, waver, hesitate.

κυματίζω [keemateezo] wave, flutter || ripple.

κυματοθραύστης, ο [keematothravstees] breakwater.

κύμινο, το [keemeeno] cumin.

κυνήγι, το [keeneeyee] hunting, shooting, chase || game.

κυνηγός, ο [keeneegos] hunter, shooter.

κυνηγώ [keeneego] hunt, chase, run after || go shooting.

κυνικός [keeneekos] cynic(al).

κυοφορώ [keeoforo] be pregnant.

κυπαρίσσι, το [keepareessee] cypress tree.

κύπελλο, το [keepelo] cup, goblet, tumbler.

κυπριακός [keepreeakos] Cypriot.

Κύπριος, ο [keepreeos] Cypriot.

Κύπρος, η [keepros] Cyprus.

κύπτω [keepto] bend, bow || slant || (μεταφ) give way.

κυρά, η [keera] missus (col).

κυρία, η [keereea] lady, mistress || Mrs.

Κυριακή, η [keereeakee] Sunday.

κυριαρχία, η [keereearheea] sovereignty, dominion.

κυριαρχώ [keereearho] dominate, exercise authority || be sovereign.

κυριεύω [keerievo] subjugate, capture, dominate || (πάθος) seize, possess.

κυριολεκτικώς [keereeolekteekos] exactly, precisely, to the letter.

κύριος, ο [keereeos] master, sir, gentleman || Mr.

κύριος [keereeos] essential, vital || main, chief, leading.

κυριότητα, η [keereeoteeta] ownership.

κυρίως [keereeos] principally, chiefly, mainly, especially.

κύρος, το [keeros] authority, power || validity, weight.

κυρτός [keertos] bent, crooked || convex, bulging.

κυρώνω [keerono] confirm || (νόμο) sanction, approve || (απόφαση) ratify, validate.

κύρωση, η [keerosee] confirmation, sanction || penalty.

κύστη, η [keestee] bladder, cyst.

κύτος, το [keetos] (ναυτ) hold.

κυττάζω [keetazo] βλ **κοιτάζω.**

κύτταρο, το [keetaro] cell.

κυψέλη, η [keepselee] swarm (of bees) || beehive || (αυτιού) earwax.

κώδικας, ο [kodeekas] code || codex.

κωδωνοκρουσία, η [kodonokrouseea] chiming, ringing, pealing.

κωδωνοστάσιο, το [kodonostaseeo] belfry, church steeple.

κωκ, το [kok] coke.

κώλος, ο [kolos] arse (col), bottom, backside (col) || ~ **και βρακί** intimate.

κωλοφωτιά, η [kolofotia] glow-worm.

κώλυμα, το [koleema] obstacle, impediment.

κωλυσιεργώ [koleesiergo] obstruct, hinder.

κωλύω [koleeo] stop, prevent, hinder.

κώμα, το [koma] coma.

κωματώδης [komatodees] comatose, lethargic.

κωμικός [komeekos] comic(al), funny || (ουσ) comedian.

κωμόπολη, η [komopolee] market town.

κωμωδία, η [komodeea] comedy.

κώνος, ο [konos] cone.

κωπηλασία, η [kopeelaseea] rowing.
κωπηλάτης, ο [kopeelatees] rower.
κωφάλαλος [kofalalos] deaf-and-dumb.
κώχη, η [kohee] corner, nook, recess || (πανταλονιού) crease.

Λ, λ

λάβα, η [lava] lava.
λαβαίνω [laveno] βλ λαμβάνω.
λάβαρο, το [lavaro] banner, standard.
λαβείν, το [laveen] credit || δούναι και ~ debit and credit.
λαβή, η [lavee] handle, grip || pretext, excuse, reason.
λαβίδα, η [laveeδa] grip, nippers, hold || (χειρουργική) forceps.
λάβρα, η [lavra] excessive heat, suffocating heat.
λαβράκι, το [lavrakee] bass fish.
λαβύρινθος, ο [laveereenthos] labyrinth.
λαβωματιά, η [lavomatia] wound.
λαβώνω [lavono] wound.
λαγάνα, η [lagana] unleavened bread.
λαγκάδι, το [langaδee] ravine, narrow valley, defile.
λάγνος [lagnos] lewd, lascivious, wanton.
λαγός, ο [lagos] hare.
λαγωνικό, το [lagoneeko] hunting dog || greyhound, pointer.
λαδερός [laδeros] oily, greasy || cooked with oil.
λάδι, το [laδee] olive oil.
λαδομπογιά, η [laδomboya] oil paint.
λαδόχαρτο, το [laδoharto] greaseproof paper.
λαδώνω [laδono] apply oil || lubricate || (μεταφ) bribe.
λαδωτήρι, το [laδoteeree] cruet stand.
λάθος, το [lathos] error, mistake, slip, fault || κατά ~ by mistake.
λαθραίος [lathreos] furtive, clandestine, secret.
λαθραίως [lathreos] secretly, furtively, stealthily.
λαθρεμπόριο, το [lathremboreeo] smuggling || contraband.
λαθρέμπορος, ο [lathremboros] smuggler, contrabandist.
λαθρεπιβάτης, ο [lathrepeevatees] stowaway.
λαίδη, η [leδee] (τίτλος) lady.
λαϊκός [laeekos] popular, familiar, vulgar || current, common || lay.
λαίμαργος [lemargos] gluttonous, greedy || (ουσ) gourmand.
λαιμός, ο [lemos] neck, throat, gullet || (μεταξύ βουνών) gorge, pass.
λακέρδα, η [lakerδa] salted tunny fish.

λακές, ο [lakes] lackey, flunkey.
λακκάκι, το [lakakee] dimple.
λάκκος, ο [lakos], λακκούβα, η [lakouva] hole, pit || grave.
λακτίζω [lakteezo] kick, boot, lash out.
λακωνικός [lakoneekos] laconic, terse, brief.
λαλιά, η [lalia] voice || speech || (για πουλιά) singing, warbling.
λαλώ [lalo] speak, talk || crow || sing.
λάμα, η [lama] sheet, thin plate || (μαχαιριού) blade.
λαμαρίνα, η [lamareena] sheet iron, iron plate.
λαμβάνω [lamvano] take hold of, take || receive, obtain || ~ την τιμή I have the honour || ~ χώρα to take place, occur.
λάμδα, το [lamδa] the letter Λ.
λάμπα, η [lamba] lamp || (ηλεκτρική) electric lamp, bulb.
λαμπάδα, η [lambaδa] torch || candle, taper.
λαμποκοπώ [lambokopo] shine, gleam.
Λαμπρή, η [lambree] Easter.
λαμπρός [lambros] brilliant, splendid, excellent, superb.
λαμπρώς [lambros] (επιφ) splendid!, excellent! || (επίρ) brilliantly.
λαμπτήρας, ο [lambteeras] βλ λάμπα.
λάμπω [lambo] shine, glitter, gleam || (μεταφ) excel.
λάμψη, η [lampsee] brightness, brilliance || glaze.
λανθάνω [lanthano] be latent || escape notice.
λανθασμένος [lanthasmenos] mistaken, wrong.
λανσάρω [lansaro] launch, advertise, present.
λαξεύω [laksevo] hew, chisel, carve.
λαογραφία, η [laografeea] folklore.
λαός, ο [laos] people, multitude, masses.
λαούτο, το [laouto] lute.
λαπάς, ο [lapas] pap, boiled rice || poultice || (μεταφ) indolent person.
λαρδί, το [larδee] lard, fat.
λαρύγγι, το [lareengee] throat, larynx, windpipe, gullet.
λαρυγγίτιδα, η [lareengeeteeδa] laryngitis.
λαρυγγολόγος, ο [lareengologos] throat specialist.
λασκάρω [laskaro] slacken, loosen || (ναυτ) cast off.
λάσπη, η [laspee] mud, mire || mortar || έκοψε ~ he escaped || he disappeared.
λασπώνω [laspono] cover with mud, dirty, soil.
λαστιχένιος [lasteeheneeos] rubber || elastic.

λάστιχο, το [lasteeho] rubber || elastic || rubber band || (αυτοκινήτου) tyre || (παιδιού) catapult, sling.

λατέρνα, η [laterna] barrel organ.

λατινικά, τα [lateeneeka] πλ Latin.

λατινικός [lateeneekos] Latin.

λατομείο, το [latomeeo] quarry.

λατρεία, η [latreea] adoration, worship || (αγάπη) fervent love.

λατρευτός [latrevtos] adorable, adored.

λατρεύω [latrevo] adore || idolize.

λάτρης, ο [latrees] worshipper || fan.

λάφυρο, το [lafeero] booty, spoils, loot.

λαχαίνω [laheno] meet, come across || (συμβαίνω) happen, occur || (στον κλήρο) fall to, win.

λαχαναγορά, η [lahanagora] vegetable market.

λαχανιάζω [lahaneeazo] pant, gasp.

λαχανικό, το [lahaneeko] vegetable, green.

λάχανο, το [lahano] cabbage.

λαχείο, το [laheeo] lottery, raffle.

λαχνός, ο [lahnos] lot, chance || prize, share.

λαχτάρα, η [lahtara] anxiety || (επιθυμία) yearning || (φόβος) dread, fright.

λαχταρώ [lahtaro] be impatient || (επιθυμώ) yearn, desire || (φοβάμαι) be frightened.

λέαινα, η [layena] lioness.

λεβάντα, η [levanta] lavender.

λεβέντης, ο [leventees] fine man, gentleman || brave man.

λεβεντιά, η [leventia] manliness.

λέβητας, ο [leveetas] cauldron || boiler.

λεβιές, ο [levies] lever.

λεγάμενος [legamenos]: **ο ~** you know who || the so-called.

λεγεώνα, η [leyeona] legion || great number.

λέγω [lego] say, tell, speak || (πιστεύω) think || (εννοώ) mean || **δεν σου ~** I do not deny it, but || **τι λες** (επιφ) you don't say!, fancy that! || **που λες** well! || **λες και** as if.

λεηλασία, η [leyeelaseea] plundering, looting, pillage.

λεηλατώ [leyeelato] plunder, loot.

λεία, η [leea] prey || booty, loot.

λειαίνω [lieno] smooth, level, plane, polish.

λειβάδι, το [leevadee] pasture land, meadow.

λείος [leeos] smooth, even, level.

λείπω [leepo] be absent, be missing, want, lack || **μου λείπει** I am missing, I lack || **μας έλειψες** we missed you || **λίγο έλειψε να** he nearly, he almost.

λειρί, το [leeree] cockscomb, crest.

λειτουργία, η [leetouryeea] function, operation || (εκκλ) mass, liturgy.

λειτουργός, ο, η [leetourgos] officer, official, civil servant.

λειτουργώ [leetourgo] function, work || (εκκλ) celebrate mass.

λείψανα, τα [leepsana] πλ remnants, remains || (εκκλ) relics.

λειψός [leepsos] deficient, defective.

λειώνω [leeono] melt, liquefy || (συνθλίβω) crush, smash || (διαλύω) dissolve || (παθαίνω φθορά) wear out, spoil.

λεκάνη, η [lekanee] basin, washbowl || pan.

λεκές, ο [lekes] stain, splash, spot || (μελάνης) blot.

λεκιάζω [lekeeazo] stain, soil, spot.

λελέκι, το [lelekee] stork || (μεταφ) tall person.

λεμβοδρομία, η [lemvodromeea] regatta, boat race.

λέμβος, η [lemvos] rowboat || launch.

λεμονάδα, η [lemonada] lemonade.

λεμόνι, το [lemonee] lemon || **λεμονιά** lemon tree.

λεξικογραφία, η [lekseekografeea] lexicography.

λεξικό, το [lekseeko] lexicon, dictionary.

λεξιλόγιο, το [lekseeloyo] vocabulary || glossary.

λέξη, η [leksee] word.

λεοντάρι, το [leontaree] lion.

λεοπάρδαλη, η [leopardalee] leopard.

λέπι, το [lepee] (ψαριού) scale (of fish).

λεπίδα, η [lepeeda] blade.

λέπρα, η [lepra] leprosy.

λεπρός [lepros] leprous.

λεπτά, τα [lepta] πλ money.

λεπταίνω [lepteno] thin, make slender || refine.

λεπτομέρεια [leptomereea] detail, particular || **λεπτομερειακός** detailed, of detail.

λεπτομερώς [leptomeros] minutely, closely, in detail.

λεπτό, το [lepto] (της ώρας) minute || (νόμισμα) lepton (one hundredth of a drachma).

λεπτός [leptos] thin, fine, slight, slim || (στη σκέψη) subtle || (ρουχισμός) light || (των αισθήσεων) keen.

λεπτότητα, η [leptoteeta] delicacy, weakness || tactfulness, tact || subtlety.

λέρα, η [lera] dirt, filth || (άνθρωπος) rogue, rascal.

Λ

λερωμένος [leromenos] dirty, filthy, grubby, grimy.

λερώνομαι [leronome] get dirty.

λερώνω [lerono] dirty, soil, stain || (μεταφ) tarnish, taint.

λέσχη, η [leshee] club || casino.

λεύκα, η [levka] poplar.

λευκαίνω [levkeno] whiten || bleach || (τοίχο) whitewash.

λευκός [levkos] white, clean || blank.

λευκοσίδηρος [levkoseeðeeros] tin.

λευκόχρυσος, ο [levkohreesos] platinum.

λεύκωμα, το [levkoma] album || (ιατρ) albumin.

λευτεριά, η [levteria] freedom, liberty.

λευχαιμία, η [levhemeea] leukaemia.

λεφτά [lefta] βλ **λεπτά**.

λεφτό [lefto] βλ **λεπτό**.

λεχώνα, η [lehona] woman who has just given birth.

λέω [leo] βλ **λέγω**.

λεωφορείο, το [leoforeeo] bus, omnibus, coach.

λεωφόρος, η [leoforos] avenue, boulevard.

λήγω [leego] come to an end, terminate || (οικο) mature, fall due.

λήθαργος, ο [leethargos] lethargy, drowsiness, stupor.

λήθη, η [leethee] forgetfulness, forgetting, oversight.

λημέρι, το [leemeree] retreat, hiding place, hideout, den.

ληξιαρχείο, το [leekseearheeo] registry office, parish register.

λήξη, η [leeksee] termination, conclusion || expiration date.

λησμονώ [leesmono] forget, neglect, omit.

ληστεία, η [leesteea] holdup, robbery.

ληστεύω [leestevo] rob, hold up.

ληστής, ο [leestees] brigand, bandit, robber.

λήψη, η [leepsee] receipt, receiving.

λιάζομαι [leeazome] sunbathe, lie in the sun.

λιακάδα, η [leeakaða] sunshine.

λίαν [leean] much, very much, too.

λιανίζω [leeaneezo] cut to pieces, mince.

λιανικός [leeaneekos] retail.

λιανός [leeanos] thin, slender.

λιβάδι, το [leevaðee] βλ **λειβάδι**.

λιβανέζικος [leevanezeekos] Lebanese.

Λιβανέζος, ο [leevanezos] Lebanese.

λιβάνι, το [leevanee] incense, frankincense.

λιβανίζω [leevaneezo] burn incense || (μεταφ) flatter basely.

Λίβανο, το [leevano] Lebanon.

λίβρα, η [leevra] pound.

Λιβύη, η [leeviee] Libya.

λιβυκός [leeveekos] Libyan.

Λίβυος, ο [leeveeos] Libyan.

λιγάκι [leegakee] a little, a bit.

λίγδα, η [leegða] fat, grease || dirt, stain.

λιγνίτης, ο [leegneetees] lignite.

λιγνός [leegnos] skinny, thin, slim.

λίγο [leego] a little, a bit || ~ **πολύ** more or less.

λίγος [leegos] a little, a bit || **παρά λίγο** nearly, almost.

λιγοστεύω [leegostevo] lessen, decrease.

λιγοστός [leegostos] very little, hardly enough.

λιγότερος [leegoteros] less.

λιγούρα, η [leegoura] nausea || faintness from hunger.

λιγοψυχία, η [leegopseeheea] faintheartedness || faintness.

λιγώνομαι [leegonome] long for, be impatient || be faint from desire.

λιγώνω [leegono] nauseate || make faint.

λιθάρι, το [leetharee] stone.

λίθινος [leetheenos] of stone.

λιθοβολώ [leethovolo] pelt with stones, stone.

λιθογραφία, η [leethografeea] lithography.

λιθόκτιστος [leethokteestos] built in stone.

λίθος, ο, η [leethos] stone || (ιατρ) calculus.

λιθόστρωτο, το [leethostroto] pavement, paved way.

λιθόστρωτος [leethostrotos] paved with stones.

λικέρ, το [leeker] liqueur.

λικνίζω [leekneezo] rock, lull to sleep || swing.

λίκνο, το [leekno] cradle, cot, crib.

λίμα, η [leema] (εργαλείο) file.

λιμάνι, το [leemanee] port, harbour.

λιμάρω [leemaro] file || chatter, gossip.

λιμενάρχης, ο [leemenarhees] harbour master.

λιμενικός [leemeneekos] of the port, of the harbour.

λιμήν, ο [leemeen] βλ **λιμάνι**.

λίμνη, η [leemnee] lake.

λιμνοθάλασσα, η [leemnothalasa] lagoon.

λιμοκτονώ [leemoktono] starve, famish.

λινάρι, το [leenaree] flax.

λινάτσα, η [leenatsa] sacking.

λινέλαιο, το [leeneleo] linseed oil.

λινός [leenos] linen.

λιοντάρι, το [leeontaree] lion.

λιπαίνω [leepeno] lubricate, grease || (με λίπασμα) manure, fertilize.

λιπαρός [leeparos] greasy, fatty || (γόνιμος) fat, rich.

λίπασμα, το [leepasma] fertilizer, manure.

λιποθυμία, η [leepotheemeea] faint(ing), swooning.

λιποθυμώ [leepotheemo] faint, lose consciousness.

λίπος, το [leepos] fat, lard || grease.

λιποτάκτης, ο [leepotaktees] deserter.

λίρα, η [leera] pound, sovereign.

λιρέττα, η [leereeta] Italian lira.

λίστα, η [leesta] list, catalogue.

λιτανεία, η [leetaneea] religious procession.

λιτός [leetos] temperate, frugal || plain.

λιτότητα, η [leetoteeta] temperance, moderation || (οίκον) austerity.

λίτρα, η [leetra] (βάρος) pound || litre.

λίτρο, το [leetro] βλ λίτρα.

λιχουδιά, η [leehouδia] titbit || appetizer.

λοβός, ο [lovos] lobe || husk || (αρχιτεκ) foil.

λογαριάζω [logareeazo] count, measure, compute || rely on, look to || (λαμβάνω υπόψη) consider || (πρόθεση να) count on, aim to, mean to.

λογαριασμός, ο [logareeasmos] count, calculation, computation || bill || accounts.

λογάριθμος, ο [logareethmos] logarithm.

λογάς, ο [logas] gossip, babbler, longwinded talker.

λόγγος, ο [longos] thicket.

λόγια, τα [loya] πλ words.

λογιάζω [loyazo] take into consideration.

λογική, η [loyeekee] logic.

λογικός [loyeekos] rational, logical, sensible || right, fair.

λόγιος, ο [loyos] scholar, man of letters.

λογισμός, ο [loyeesmos] reasoning, thought || reckoning || (μαθημ) calculus.

λογιστήριο, το [loyeesteereeo] bursar's office || bursary.

λογιστής, ο [loyeestees] accountant, bookkeeper || (ναυτ) purser.

λογιστική, η [loyeesteekee] accountancy.

λογοδιάρροια, η [logoδeeareea] unrestrained talkativeness, chattering.

λογοδοτώ [logoδoto] give an account, account for.

λογοκρισία, η [logokreeseea] censorship.

λογομαχία, η [logomaheea] dispute, wrangle, controversy.

λογοπαίγνιο, το [logopegneeo] pun.

λόγος, ο [logos] (ομιλία) speech || (φράση κτλ) word, saying || (μνεία) mention || rumour || (αίτιο) cause,

reason, purpose || (παράδειγμα) instance, supposition || (αγόρευση) speech, discourse || (λογοδοσία) explanation, account || (υπόσχεση) promise || (αναλογία) ratio, proportion.

λογοτέχνης, ο [logotehnees] author, writer.

λογοτεχνία, η [logotehneea] literature.

λόγχη, η [longhee] bayonet || spear, lance.

λοιμός, ο [leemos] pestilence, pest, plague.

λοιμώδης [leemoδees] contagious.

λοιπόν [leepon] then, thus, and so || well!, what then!

λοιπός [leepos] left, remaining || και τα λοιπά and so forth, and so on.

λόξα, η [loksa] whim, mania, fancy.

λοξά [loksa] on the slant, obliquely || in an underhand way.

λοξοδρομώ [loksoδromo] shift course, deviate || (ναυτ) tack || (μεταφ) go astray.

λοξός [loksos] oblique, slanting, inclined.

λόξυγγας, ο [lokseengas] hiccup.

λόρδος, ο [lorδos] lord.

λοσιόν, η [losion] lotion.

λοστός, ο [lostos] crowbar, iron bar.

λοστρόμος, ο [lostromos] boatswain.

λούζομαι [louzome] wash one's hair.

λούζω [louzo] wash, bathe || (μεταφ) reproach severely.

λουκάνικο, το [loukaneeko] sausage, hot dog, frankfurter.

λουκέτο, το [louketo] padlock.

λούκι, το [loukee] pipe, conduit || gutter.

λουκούμι, το [loukoumee] Turkish delight || (μεταφ) delicious (attr).

λουλάκι, το [loulakee] indigo.

λουλούδι, το [loulouδee] flower, blossom.

λουξ [louks] luxurious, posh.

Λουξεμβούργο, το [louksemvourgo] Luxembourg.

λουρί, το [louree] strap || (μηχανής) belt, band.

λουρίδα, η [loureeδa] strip, belt, band.

λούσιμο, το [louseemo] washing one's hair || (μεταφ) reprimanding.

λούσο, το [louso] smart clothes || sumptuousness, luxury.

λουστράρω [loustraro] gloss, glaze || (παπούτσια) polish.

λουστρίνια, τα [loustreeneea] πλ patent leather shoes.

λούστρος, ο [loustros] shoeblack, boot black.

λουτρά, τα [loutra] πλ baths, hot springs.

λουτρό, το [loutro] bath || (δωμάτιο) bathroom.

λουτρόπολη, η [loutropolee] bathing resort, spa.

λουφάζω [loufazo] remain silent || cringe with fear.

λοφίο, το [lofeeo] plume || (πτηνού) tuft, crest || (στρατ) pompom.

λόφος, ο [lofos] hill, height.

λοχαγός, ο [lohagos] captain.

λοχίας, ο [loheeas] sergeant.

λόχος, ο [lohos] company.

λυγερός [leeyeros] slim, lithe, graceful.

λυγίζω [leeyeezo] bend, curve || yield.

λυγμός, ο [leegmos] sob, sobbing.

λύκειο, το [leekeeo] private secondary school, lyceum.

λύκος, ο [leekos] wolf.

λυκόφως, το [leekofos] evening twilight, dusk.

λυμαίνομαι [leemenome] ravage, devastate, lay waste.

λυντσάρω [leentsaro] lynch.

λύνω [leeno] βλ **λύω.**

λύομαι [leeome] come undone.

λυπάμαι [leepame] be sorry, regret || pity.

λύπη, η [leepee] grief, chagrin, sorrow || pity, commiseration.

λυπημένος [leepeemenos] sad, grieved, distressed.

λυπούμαι [leepoume] βλ **λυπάμαι.**

λύσιμο, το [leeseemo] undoing, loosening || solution, solving || taking to pieces.

λύση, η [leesee] answer, solution || untying || dismantling.

λύσσα, η [leesa] rabies || (μεταφ) rage, fury, wrath.

λυσσά(ζ)ω [leesa(z)o] rage, go mad.

λυσσώ [leeso] (μεταφ) be furious.

λυτός [leetos] loose, untied, unfastened.

λύτρα, τα [leetra] πλ ransom money.

λυτρώνω [leetrono] deliver, free, set free.

λυτρωτής, ο [leetrotees] liberator, redeemer, rescuer.

λύω [leeo] unloose || (δεσμό κτλ) untie, unfasten || (διαλύω) dismantle || (βρίσκω λύση) resolve || (παύω) close, discharge || (καταργώ) annul, break off.

λυώνω [leeono] βλ **λειώνω.**

λωλαίνω [loleno] drive mad, bewilder.

λωλός [lolos] foolish, crazy, mad.

λωποδύτης, ο [lopoδeetees] thief, blackleg.

λωρίδα, η [loreeδa] strip, band, belt.

Μ, μ

μα [ma] but || by || ~ **το Θεό** by God!, God be witness!

μαγαζί, το [magazee] shop, store.

μαγγάνι, το [manganee] (εργαλείο) tool, vice || (πηγαδιού) wheel || winch.

μαγγάνιο, το [manganeeo] manganese.

μαγγανοπήγαδο, το [manganopeegaδo] wheel well (for water).

μαγγώνω [mangono] grip, squeeze, clip.

μαγεία, η [mayeea] sorcery, witchcraft, magic || charm, fascination.

μάγειρας, ο [mayeeras] cook.

μαγειρεύω [mayeerevo] cook || (μεταφ) plot, manipulate.

μαγειρική, η [mayeereekee] cooking, cookery.

μαγευτικός [mayevteekos] charming, enchanting, delightful.

μαγεύω [mayevo] charm, fascinate, delight, attract.

μάγια, τα [maya] πλ witchcraft, spell, charm.

μαγιά, η [maya] yeast, leaven.

μαγικός [mayeekos] magic(al), fascinating, bewitching.

μαγιό, το [mayo] bathing suit, swimsuit.

μαγιονέζα, η [mayoneza] mayonnaise.

μάγισσα, η [mayeesa] witch, enchantress.

μαγκάλι, το [mangalee] brazier, firepan.

μάγκας, ο [mangas] urchin, rascal, bum.

μαγκούρα, η [mangoura] crook, heavy stick.

μαγνήσιο, το [magneeseeo] magnesium.

μαγνήτης, ο [magneetees] magnet.

μαγνητίζω [magneeteezo] magnetize || attract, captivate.

μαγνητικός [magneeteekos] magnetic || attractive.

μαγνητισμός, ο [magneeteesmos] magnetism.

μαγνητόφωνο, το [magneetofono] tape recorder.

μάγος, ο [magos] magician, wizard.

μαγουλάδες, οι [magoulaδes] mumps.

μάγουλο, το [magoulo] cheek (of face).

μάδημα, το [maδeema] plucking, depilation || (μεταφ) fleecing.

μαδώ [maδo] pluck, pluck off, remove the hair || (μεταφ) fleece.

μαέστρος, ο [maestros] conductor || (μεταφ) authority.

μάζα, η [maza] paste || lump || (ανθρώπων) mass, crowd.

μάζεμα, το [mazema] collecting, gathering || (υφάσματος) shrinking.

μαζεύομαι [mazevome] collect || nestle || settle down.

μαζεύω [mazevo] gather, collect || (μαλλί) wind || (για ρούχα) shrink.

μαζί [mazee] together, with, in one lot, jointly.

μαζικός [mazeekos] of the mass, collective.

Μάης, ο [maees] May.

μαθαίνω [matheno] learn || teach, train || (νέα) hear || learn.

μάθημα, το [matheema] lesson.

μαθηματικά, τα [matheemateeka] πλ mathematics.

μαθηματικός [matheemateekos] mathematical || (ουσ) mathematician.

μαθημένος [matheemenos] used to.

μάθηση, η [matheesee] learning, education.

μυθητευόμενος [matheetevomenos] apprentice, novice.

μαθητής, ο [matheetees] student, pupil || (φιλοσόφου) disciple.

μαία, η [mea] midwife.

μαίανδρος, ο [meanðros] meander, in-and-out.

μαιευτήρας, ο [mayevteeras] obstetrician.

μαιευτήριο, το [mayevteereeo] maternity hospital.

μαιευτική, η [mayevteekee] obstetrics.

μαϊμού, η [maeemou] monkey, ape.

μαίνομαι [menome] rage, be furious.

μαϊντανός, ο [maeentanos] parsley.

Μάιος, ο [maeeos] May.

μακάβριος [makavreeos] macabre, gruesome, ghastly.

μακάρι [makaree] (επιφ) would to God!

μακαρίζω [makareezo] regard as fortunate, envy.

μακάριος [makareeos] happy, fortunate, blessed || calm, serene.

μακαρίτης [makareetees] late, deceased.

μακαρόνια, τα [makaroneea] πλ macaroni.

μακελειό, το [makelio] (μεταφ) slaughter, massacre.

μακέτα, η [maketa] model, drawing, plan.

μακραίνω [makreno] make longer || grow taller.

μακριά [makria] (a)far, far off, at a distance.

μακρινός [makreenos] far distant, far off || (ταξίδι) long.

μακρόβιος [makroveeos] long-lived.

μάκρος, το [makros] length || duration.

μακρύνω [makreeno] βλ μακραίνω.

μακρύς [makrees] long, lengthy, extensive.

μαλάζω [malazo] massage, knead || soften, mollify, pacify || (πόνο) alleviate.

μαλάκιο, το [malakeeo] mollusc.

μαλακός [malakos] soft || mild, gentle || (κλίμα) genial.

μαλάκυνση, η [malakeensee] softening, enervation.

μαλακώνω [malakono] soften, get milder || assuage || become calmer.

μάλαμα, το [malama] gold.

μαλάσσω [malaso] βλ μαλάζω.

μαλθακός [malthakos] soft, effeminate, delicate.

μάλιστα [maleesta] more especially, particularly || yes, indeed || even.

μαλλί, το [malee] wool, fleece || hair.

μαλλιά, τα [malia] πλ hair (of the head) || ~ κουβάρια upside down.

μαλλιαρός [maleearos] hairy, long-haired || woolly.

μάλλινος [maleenos] woollen.

μάλλον [malon] more, better, rather.

μαλώνω [malono] argue || chide, reprimand, rebuke.

μαμά, η [mama] mother, mummy.

μάμμη, η [mamee] grandmother.

μαμμή, η [mamee] midwife.

μαμμούνι, το [mamounee] small insect, grub.

μανδύας, ο [manðeeas] mantle, cloak || (στρατ) greatcoat.

μάνι μάνι [maneemanee] quickly, in a jiffy.

μανία, η [maneea] fury, passion, mania || whim, fancy || έχω ~ με to be crazy about.

μανιακός [maneeakos] raving, frenzied || (ποίκτης) inveterate.

μανιβέλλα, η [maneevela] starting handle || lever, bar.

μανικέτι, το [maneeketee] cuff.

μανίκι, το [maneekee] sleeve.

μανιτάρι, το [maneetaree] mushroom.

μανιώδης [maneeoðees] passionate, inveterate || furious, raging.

μάνα, η [mana] mother, mamma.

μανούλα, η [manoula] mummy || mom (US).

μανουάλιο, το [manoualeeo] candelabrum.

μανούβρα, η [manouvra] manoeuvre.

μανούρι, το [manouree] kind of white cheese.

μανταλάκι, το [mantalakee] clothes peg.

μάνταλο, το [mantalo] latch, bolt, bar.

μανταλώνω [mantalono] latch, lock up, bolt.

μανταρίνι, το [mantareenee] tangerine.

μαντάρισμα, το [mantareesma] darning || (υφάσματος) mending.

μαντάρω [mantaro] darn, mend.

μαντάτο, το [mantato] information, news.

μαντείο, το [manteeo] oracle.

μαντεύω [mantevo] foretell || guess || find out, fathom.

μαντήλι, το [manteelee] handkerchief.

μάντης, ο [mantees] wizard, prophet.

μαντινάδα, η [manteenaða] rhyming couplet.

μάντρα, η [mantra] pen, fold, sty || (περίφραγμα) enclosure, wall || yard.

μαντράχαλος, ο [mantrahalos] lanky fellow.

μαξιλάρι, το [makseelaree] pillow, cushion.

μάππας, ο [mapas] stupid fellow, imbecile.

μαραγκός, ο [marangos] carpenter || joiner.

μαράζι, το [marazee] pining, depression, languor.

μάραθ(ρ)ο, το [marath(r)o] fennel.

μαραίνομαι [marenome] fade, wither away, shrivel || (μεταφ) waste away.

μαραίνω [mareno] wither, dry up, fade.

μαρασμός, ο [marasmos] withering, fading away || (μεταφ) decay.

μαργαρίνη, η [margareenee] margarine.

μαργαρίτα, η [margareeta] daisy.

μαργαριτάρι, το [margareetaree] pearl.

μαρίδα, η [mareeða] whitebait, small fry.

μάρκα, η [marka] (εμπορ) make || (αυτοκινήτου) model || (νόμισμα) mark || (μεταφ) cunning fellow.

μαρμαρένιος [marmareneeos] of marble.

μάρμαρο, το [marmaro] marble.

μαρμελάδα, η [marmelaða] marmalade.

Μαροκινός, ο [marokeenos] Moroccan || μ~ (επιθ) Moroccan.

Μαρόκο, το [maroko] Morocco.

μαρούλι, το [maroulee] lettuce.

Μάρτης, ο [martees] March.

μαρτυρία, η [marteereea] deposition, giving of evidence || proof, token.

μαρτυρικός [marteereekos] insufferable, unbearable.

μαρτύριο, το [marteereeo] torment, suffering.

μαρτυρώ [marteero] give evidence, testify || (προδίδω) betray, inform against || (ενδεικνύω) show, indicate || (γίνομαι μάρτυς) suffer martyrdom (*for Christ*).

μάρτυς, ο [martees] witness || (εκκλ) martyr.

μας [mas] us || our.

μασέλα, η [masela] false teeth.

μασιά, η [masia] πλ tongs, fire-tongs || pincers.

μάσκα, η [maska] mask ||

μασκαράς, ο [maskaras] masquerader || (μεταφ) impostor, rascal, scoundrel.

μασόνος, ο [masonos] freemason.

μασουλώ [masoulo] chew, munch.

μασούρι, το [masouree] spool, bobbin || tube.

μάστιγα, η [masteega] whip || (μεταφ) curse, plague.

μαστίγιο, το [masteeyo] whip || switch.

μαστιγώνω [masteegono] whip, lash, flog.

μαστίζω [masteezo] infest, devastate, desolate.

μαστίχα, η [masteeha] mastic || (ποτό) mastic brandy.

μάστορας, ο [mastoras] artisan, workman || (μεταφ) expert, skilful person.

μαστορεύω [mastorevo] work || mend, repair.

μαστός, ο [mastos] breast || (μεταφ) hillock.

μαστροπός, ο, η [mastropos] procurer, procuress, pimp.

μασχάλη, η [mashalee] armpit.

μασώ [maso] chew, masticate || (τα λόγια) stammer.

ματαιόδοξος [mateoðoksos] vain, self-conceited.

μάταιος [mateos] vain, useless, unavailing || conceited.

ματαιώνω [mateono] frustrate, foil, cancel, stop.

μάτι, το [matee] eye || (φύλλου κτλ) bud || αυγό ~ fried egg (sunny-side up) || βάζω στο ~ to set one's heart on || έχω στο ~ to covet || κλείνω το ~ to wink || μάτια μου! my darling!

ματιά, η [matia] glance, gaze, eye, look || ~ζω cast an evil eye on, bewitch.

ματόκλαδο, το [matoklaðo] eyelash, lash.

ματόφυλλο, το [matofeelo] eyelid.

μάτσο, το [matso] truss, bunch, bundle || (ξύλων) faggot.

ματσούκα, η [matsouka] club, cudgel.

ματώνω [matono] bleed.

μαυραγορίτης, ο [mavragoreetees] black marketeer.

μαυρειδερός [mavreeðeros] blackish || brown.

μαυρίζω [mavreezo] blacken, darken || (από ήλιο) get tanned || (μεταφ) blackball, vote against.

μαυρίλα, η [mavreela] blackness, darkness, gloominess.

μαυροδάφνη, η [mavroðafnee] kind of sweet wine.

μαυροπίνακας, ο [mavropeenakas] blackboard || blacklist.

μαύρος [mavros] black || brown || (νέγρος) negro || (μεταφ) miserable, luckless.

μαχαίρι, το [maheree] knife || στα ~α at loggerheads.

μαχαιριά, η [maheria] stab.

μαχαιροβγάλτης, ο [maherovgaltees] cut-throat || bully.

μαχαιροπήρουνα, τα [maheropeerouna] πλ cutlery.

μαχαιρώνω [maherono] stab.

μαχαλάς, ο [mahalas] quarter, district, neighbourhood.

μάχη, η [mahee] battle, combat || struggle, fight.

μαχητής, ο [maheetees] combatant, fighter, soldier.

μαχητικός [maheeteekos] warlike, martial || combative, ready to fight.

μάχομαι [mahome] fight, combat, struggle || hate, abhor.

με [me] with, by, through, by means of, on, of || ~ τα πόδια on foot || ~ το καλό God willing || ~ το μήνα by the month || δύο ~ τρία two by three (feet etc) || ~ τον καιρό eventually, in the course of time || δύο ~ τρεις between two and three o'clock || έχω μανία ~ το to be mad on, be crazy about || γελώ ~ to laugh at || ~ τη σειρά in turn || ανάλογα ~ according to whether.

μεγάθυμος [megatheemos] generous, magnanimous.

μεγαλείο, το [megaleeo] splendour, grandeur || (μεταφ) splendid.

μεγαλειότητα, η [megaleeoteeta] majesty, grandeur || η Αυτού ~ His Majesty.

μεγαλειώδης [megaleeodees] magnificent, superb, majestic.

μεγαλέμπορος, ο [megalemboros] wholesaler.

μεγαλεπήβολος [megalepeevolos] grandiose, imposing.

μεγαλοποιώ [megalopeeo] magnify, exaggerate, overdo.

μεγαλοπρεπής [megaloprepees] majestic, stately, splendid, magnificent.

μεγάλος [megalos] great, large, big, long.

μεγαλουργώ [megalourgo] achieve great things.

μεγαλόφρονας [megalofronas] generous, magnanimous || boastful, arrogant.

μεγαλοφυής [megalofiees] gifted, ingenious.

μεγαλόψυχος [megalopseehos] magnanimous, generous.

μεγαλύνω [megaleeno] magnify, exalt.

μεγαλώνω [megalono] increase, enlarge || (ανατρέφω) bring up, raise || (μεγαλοποιώ) magnify, exaggerate || grow up.

μέγαρο, το [megaro] mansion, palace, imposing building.

μέγας [megas] βλ μεγάλος.

μεγάφωνο, το [megafono] (ραδιοφώνου) loudspeaker || megaphone.

μέγγενη, η [mengenee] (εργαλείο) vice.

μέγεθος, το [meyethos] size, greatness, height, magnitude, extent, length.

μεγέθυνση, η [meyetheensee] enlargement, increase, extension.

μεγιστάνας, ο [meyeestanas] magnate, seigneur.

μέγιστος [meyeestos] greatest, largest || enormous, colossal.

μεδούλι, το [medoulee] marrow.

μέδουσα, η [medousa] kind of jellyfish.

μεζές, ο [mezes] titbit, snack.

μεζούρα, η [mezoura] tape measure.

μεθαύριο [methavreeo] the day after tomorrow.

μέθη, η [methee] intoxication, drunkenness || (μεταφ) enthusiasm.

μεθοδικός [methodeekos] systematic, methodical.

μέθοδος, η [methodos] method, system, process.

μεθόριος, η [methoreeos] boundary, frontier.

μεθύσι, το [metheesee] βλ μέθη.

μεθυσμένος [metheesmenos] drunk.

μεθώ [metho] make drunk, intoxicate || get drunk.

μειδίαμα, το [meedeeama] smile.

μείζων [meezon] larger, greater || (μουσ) major.

μειοδοτώ [meeodoto] bid the lowest price.

μείον [meeon] less, minus.

μειονέκτημα, το [meeonekteema] disadvantage, inconvenience.

μειονότητα, η [meeonoteeta] minority.

μειοψηφία, η [meeopseefeea] minority of votes.

μειώνω [meeono] lessen, diminish, reduce, decrease.

μείωση, η [meeosee] decrease, reduction || (μεταφ) humiliation.

μελαγχολία, η [melangholeea] melancholy, dejection, gloominess.

μελαγχολικός [melangholeekos] sad, depressed, gloomy.

μελαγχολώ [melangholo] become sad.

μελάνη, η [melanee] ink.

μελανιά, η [melania] inkstain || bruise || ~ζω bruise || turn blue with cold.

μελανοδοχείο, το [melanodoheeo] inkstand, inkpot.

μελάτος [melatos] (αυγό) soft-boiled.

μελαχροινός [melahreenos] dark, brown, swarthy.

μελαψός [melapsos] dark-skinned, swarthy.

μέλει [melee]: **δεν με ~** I don't care, I'm not interested.

μελέτη, η [meletee] (πραγματεία) treatise || study || (κτιρίου) plan, design || mediation, contemplation.

μελετηρός [meleteeros] studious.

μελετώ [meleto] study || (ερευνώ) search, investigate || (σκοπεύω) have in mind, intend || (πιάνο) practise.

μέλημα, το [meleema] concern, care, solicitude, duty.

μέλι, το [melee] honey.

μελίγγι, το [meleengee] (ανατ) temple.

μέλισσα, η [meleesa] bee.

μελίσσι, το [meleesee] beehive || swarm.

μελισσοκομία, η [meleesokomeea] beekeeping.

μελιτζάνα, η [meleedzana] eggplant.

μέλλον, το [melon] future || outlook.

μελλόνυμφος, ο, η [meloneemfos] husband/wife-to-be.

μέλλω [melo] intend, be about to.

μέλλων [melon] future || **ο ~** (γραμμ) future tense.

μέλος, το [melos] member || (μους) melody, air || (του σώματος) member, limb.

μελτέμι, το [meltemee] north wind, trade wind.

μελωδία, η [meloðeea] melody, tune.

μελωδικός [meloðeekos] melodious, tuneful.

μεμβράνη, η [memvranee] membrane || (χαρτί) parchment.

μεμονωμένος [memonomenos] isolated, lonely, alone.

μεν [men] on the one hand || **οι ~** ... **οι δε** some ... others.

μενεξές, ο [menekses] violet.

μένος, το [menos] fervour, zeal, eagerness || wrath, anger, fury.

μέντα, η [menta] mint, peppermint.

μένω [meno] remain, stop, stay || (απομένω) be left, survive || (διαμένω) reside, live || **~ από** run out of, be short of.

μέρα, η [mera] βλ **ημέρα**.

μεράκι, το [merakee] ardent desire, yearning || (λύπη) regret, sorrow.

μεραρχία, η [merarheea] division.

μεριά, η [meria] place || side.

μερίδα, η [mereeða] ration, portion, helping.

μερίδιο, το [mereeðeeo] share, portion.

μερικός [mereekos] partial, some, a few || **μερικά** πλ some, certain, a few.

μέριμνα, η [mereemna] care, anxiety, solicitude, concern.

μεριμνώ [mereemno] look after, care for, be anxious about.

μέρισμα, το [mereesma] dividend || allotment, part.

μερμήγκι, το [mermeengee] ant.

μεροκάματο, το [merokamato] day's wages.

μεροληπτώ [meroleepto] take sides, be partial, be one-sided.

μέρος, το [meros] part, party || (μερίδα) portion, share || (τόπος) place, spot || (πλευρά) side || (ρόλος) role || (γραμμ) part of speech || (αποχωρητήριο) W.C. || **κατά ~** aside, apart.

μέσα [mesa] in(to) || inside || within || among || (πολιτ) means || **~ σε** inside, within || in, into.

μεσάζω [mesazo] mediate, intercede.

μεσαίος [meseos] middle.

μεσαίωνας, ο [meseonas] Middle Ages || **μεσαιωνικός** medieval.

μεσάνυχτα, τα [mesaneehta] πλ midnight.

μέση, η [mesee] middle || (σώματος) waist || **αφήνω στη ~** to leave incomplete, leave undone.

μεσήλικας [meseeleekas] middle-aged.

μεσημβρινός [meseemvreenos] of noon || (νότιος) southern || (ουσ) meridian.

μεσημέρι, το [meseemeree] noon || **μέρα ~** in broad daylight || **μεσημεριανός** midday || **μεσημεριανός ύπνος** siesta.

μεσίστιος [meseesteeos] half-mast.

μεσιτεύω [meseetevo] intercede, intervene || be a broker.

μεσίτης, ο [meseetees] mediator || agent, broker.

μεσιτικό [meseeteeko]: **~ γραφείο** house agency.

μεσογειακός [mesoyakos] Mediterranean.

Μεσόγειος, η [mesoyos] the Mediterranean.

μεσόκοπος [mesokopos] βλ **μεσήλικας.**

μεσολαβώ [mesolavo] intercede, intervene || (σε χρόνο) come between.

μέσο, το [meso] middle, midst || (τρόπος) method, means, way || **μέσα** πλ influence, pull, power.

μέσος [mesos] middle || medium || (όρος) mean, average.

μεσοφόρι, το [mesoforee] petticoat, underskirt.

μεστός [mestos] full, replete, crammed with || (ώριμος) ripe.

μεστώνω [mestono] mature, ripen, mellow.

μέσω [meso] through, via.

μετά [meta] with || after, in || (επίρ) afterwards.

μεταβαίνω [metaveno] go, proceed.

μεταβάλλω [metavalo] change, convert, transform.

μετάβαση, η [metavasee] going, passage, transference.

μεταβατικός [metavateekos] transitional, provisory || (γραμμ) transitive (verb).

μεταβιβάζω [metaveevazo] (διαταγή) transmit, hand on || (μεταφέρω) transport || (ιδιοκτησία) transfer, hand over.

μεταβλητός [metavleetos] variable, unsettled, changeable.

μεταβολή, η [metavolee] alteration, change || (στρατ) about-turn, half-turn.

μετάγγιση, η [metangeesee] transfusion, drawing off || (κρασιού κτλ) decanting.

μεταγενέστερος [metayenesteros] posterior, subsequent, later.

μεταγραφή, η [metagrafee] transfer.

μεταγωγικό, το [metagoyeeko] (ναυτ) transport ship.

μεταδίδω [metadeedo] impart, transmit || (ραδιοφωνία) broadcast || (αρρώστια) infect.

μετάδοση, η [metadosee] transmission || (αρρώστιας) contagion, spreading || αγία ~ Holy Communion.

μεταδοτικός [metadoteekos] contagious, infectious.

μετάθεση, η [metathesee] transfer, removal.

μεταθέτω [metatheto] transpose, transfer, remove, move.

μετακινώ [metakeeno] move, shift, displace.

μετακομίζω [metakomeezo] transport, transfer, remove || (σπίτι) move, change residence, move out.

μεταλλείο, το [metaleeo] mine.

μετάλλευμα, το [metalevma] ore.

μεταλλικός [metaleekos] metallic || mineral.

μετάλλινος [metaleenos] of metal.

μετάλλιο, το [metaleeo] medal.

μέταλλο, το [metalo] metal.

μεταμέλεια, η [metameleea] repentance, regrets.

μεταμόρφωση, η [metamorfosee] transformation, reformation || (εκκλ) transfiguration.

μεταμόσχευση, η [metamoshevsee] transplantation.

μεταμφίεση, η [metamfiesee] disguise, masquerade.

μεταμφιεσμένος [meemfiesmenos] disguised.

μετανάστευση, η [metanastevsee] emigration, (im)migration.

μεταναστεύω [metanastevo] (e)migrate, immigrate.

μετανάστης, ο [metanastees] (e)migrant, immigrant.

μετάνοια, η [metaneea] repentance, regret || (εκκλ) penance || (γονυκλισιά) genuflexion.

μετανοώ [metanoo] repent, regret, be sorry (for).

μετάξι, το [metaksee] silk.

μεταξοσκώληκας, ο [metaksoskoleekas] silkworm.

μεταξύ [metaksee] between, among, amongst, amid(st) || ~ μας between ourselves, between you and me || εν τω ~ meanwhile.

μεταξωτό, το [metaksoto] silk material, silk stuff.

μεταπείθω [metapeetho] dissuade, prevail upon.

μεταποιώ [metapeeo] transform, alter, convert.

μεταπολεμικός [metapolemeekos] postwar.

μετάπτωση, η [metaptosee] change, relapse.

μεταπωλώ [metapolo] resell, sell again.

μεταρρυθμίζω [metareethmeezo] reform, rearrange.

μετασχηματιστής, ο [metasheemateestees] transformer.

μετατοπίζω [metatopeezo] shift, displace.

μετατόπιση, η [metatopeesee] shifting || displacement.

μετατρέπω [metatrepo] transform, turn, change, alter || (για ποινή) commute.

μεταφέρω [metafero] transport, carry, convey || (οίκον) transfer, carry over.

μεταφορά, η [metafora] transportation, conveyance || (γραμμ) metaphor.

μεταφορικά, τα [metaforeeka] πλ carriage fees.

μεταφράζω [metafrazo] translate.

μετάφραση, η [metafrasee] translation.

μεταφραστής, ο [metafrastees] translator.

μεταφυτεύω [metafeetevo] transplant.

μεταχειρίζομαι [metaheereezome] use, employ || treat, behave towards.

μεταχειρισμένος [metaheereesmenos] worn, used || (δεύτερο χέρι) secondhand.

μετεκπαίδευση, η [metekpedevsee] postgraduate study.

μετέπειτα [metepeeta] after, afterwards, subsequently || οι ~ posterity, the descendants.

μετέχω [meteho] take part, participate || partake.

μετέωρο, το [meteoro] meteor, shooting star.

μετέωρος [meteoros] dangling, in the air || (μεταφ) hesitant, undecided || in suspense.

μετοικώ [meteeko] emigrate || (σπίτι) move house.
μετόπισθεν [metopeesthen]: τα ~ the rear.
μετοχή, η [metohee] (οικον) stock, share || (γραμμ) participle.
μετοχικός [metoheekos] (οικον) of a share, of joint stock || (γραμμ) participial.
μέτοχος, ο [metohos] participant, sharer || (οικον) shareholder.
μέτρα, τα [metra] πλ measurements || proceedings, steps || λαμβάνω ~ to take measures.
μέτρημα, το [metreema] measuring, mensuration || counting, numbering.
μετρημένος [metreemenos] measured, limited || (άνθρωπος) temperate, discreet, moderate.
μετρητά, τα [metreeta] πλ: τα ~ cash, money || τοις μετρητοίς in cash, (for) ready money.
μετρητής, ο [metreetees] meter, counter, gauge.
μετρητός [metreetos] measurable, calculable.
μετριάζω [metreeazo] moderate, diminish, slacken, lessen.
μετρικός [metreekos] metric(al).
μετριοπάθεια, η [metreeopatheea] moderation, temperance.
μετριοπαθής [metreeopathees] moderate, sober, temperate.
μέτριος [metreeos] ordinary, moderate || mediocre || (καφές) semi-sweetened.
μετριόφρονας [metreeofronas] modest, unassuming, decent, retiring.
μετριοφροσύνη, η [metreeofroseenee] modesty, decency.
μέτρο, το [metro] measure, metre || (μεταφ) measure, step || (μουσ) bar, measure || (ποιητικό) metre, foot.
μετρώ [metro] measure, count, number, gauge.
μέτωπο, το [metopo] forehead, brow || (πρόσοψη) face, front, facade || (μάχη) front, battlefront.
μέχρι(ς) [mehree(s)] till, until, down to, up to || as far as || ~ ενός to the last man || ~ τούδε until now.
μη [mee] don't || not, no || lest.
μηδαμινός [meeδameenos] worthless, of no account, insignificant, trivial.
μηδέν, το [meeδen] nothing || zero || cipher.
μηδενίζω [meeδeneezo] nullify || mark with a zero.
μηδενικό, το [meeδeneeko] zero || cipher.
μηδενιστής, ο [meeδeneestees] nihilist.
μήκος, το [meekos] length || (γεωγραφικό) longitude || κατά ~ in length, lengthwise.

μπλίγγι, το [meeleengee] (ανατ) temple.
μήλο, το [meelo] apple || (πρόσωπο) cheekbone || μηλίτης cider.
μηλόπηττα, η [meelopeeta] apple pie.
μην, ο [meen], μήνας, ο [meenas] month.
μηνιαίος [meenieos] monthly || month's.
μηνιάτικο, το [meeniateeko] month's wages || month's rent.
μηνίγγι, το [meeneengee] βλ μηλίγγι.
μηνιγγίτιδα, η [meeneengeeteeδa] meningitis.
μήνις, η [meenees] rage, anger, fury, wrath.
μήνυμα, το [meeneema] message, notice, announcement.
μήνυση, η [meeneesee] summons, charge.
μηνυτής, ο [meeneetees] plaintiff, complainant.
μηνύω [meeneeo] give notice || bring a charge against.
μήπως [meepos] lest in any way, in case || I wonder if.
μηρός, ο [meeros] thigh, leg.
μηρυκάζω [meereekazo] chew the cud, ruminate.
μήτε [meete] βλ ούτε.
μητέρα, η [meetera] mother.
μήτρα, η [meetra] uterus, womb || (χυτηρίου) mould, matrix, form.
μητρική [meetreekee]: ~ γλώσσα mother tongue, native language.
μητρόπολη, η [meetropolee] metropolis, capital || (εκκλ) cathedral.
μητροπολιτικός [meetropoleeteekos] metropolitan.
μητροπολίτης, ο [meetropoleetees] metropolitan bishop.
μητρότητα, η [meetroteeta] motherhood.
μητρυιά, η [meetria] stepmother.
μητρυιός, ο [meetrios] stepfather.
μητρώο, το [meetroo] register, roll, official list of names.
μηχανεύομαι [meehanevome] contrive, engineer, plot, bring about.
μηχανή, η [meehanee] machine, engine, works || (μεταφ) typewriter || camera.
μηχάνημα, το [meehaneema] machine, apparatus, contrivance.
μηχανική, η [meehaneekee] engineering, mechanics.
μηχανικός [meehaneekos] mechanical || (ουσ) engineer || mechanic || architect.
μηχανισμός, ο [meehaneesmos] mechanism, machinery.
μηχανοκίνητος

[meehanokeeneetos] motorized || machine-operated.

μηχανοποιώ [meehanopeeo] mechanize.

μηχανορραφία, η [meehanorafeea] machination || intrigue.

μία, μια [meea, mia] one || a, an || ~ **και** since, seeing that || ~ **που** as, since.

μίασμα, το [meeasma] miasma, infection.

μιγάδας, ο [meegaðas] half-caste, mulatto || hybrid.

μίγμα, το [meegma] mixture, blend.

μίζα, η [meeza] (μηχανής) self-starter || (στα χαρτιά) stake.

μιζέρια, η [meezerteea] misery, wretchedness || (τσιγγουνιά) meanness.

μικραίνω [meekreno] curtail, lessen || shorten, grow smaller.

μικρόβιο, το [meekroveeo] microbe.

μικρογραφία, η [meekrografeea] miniature.

μικροπρά(γ)ματα, τα [meekropra(g)mata] πλ trifles.

μικροπρεπής [meekroprepees] mean, base.

μικρός [meekros] small, little || short || young || (διαφορά) trivial.

μικροσκοπικός [meekroskopeekos] minute.

μικροσκόπιο, το [meekroskopeeo] microscope.

μικρόφωνο, το [meekrofono] microphone.

μικρόψυχος [meekropseehos] faint-hearted.

μικρύνω [meekreeno] βλ **μικραίνω.**

μικτό [meekto]: ~ **βάρος** gross weight.

μικτός [meektos] mixed, composite || (σχολείο) coeducational.

μιλιά, η [meelia] speech, word.

μίλι, το [meelee] mile.

μιλώ [meelo] speak.

μίμηση, η [meemeesee] imitation.

μιμητής, ο [meemeetees] imitator.

μιμητικός [meemeeteekos] imitative.

μιμόζα, η [meemoza] mimosa.

μίμος, ο [meemos] mimic, jester.

μιμούμαι [meemoume] imitate, copy, mimic.

μινιατούρα, η [meeneeatoura] miniature.

μίξη, η [meeksee] mixing, mixture, blend.

μισαλλόδοξος [meesaloðoksos] intolerant.

μισάνθρωπος, ο [meesanthropos] misanthrope.

μισητός [meeseetos] hated, hateful, odious.

μισθοδοτώ [meesthoðoto] pay a salary to, hire.

μισθολόγιο, το [meestholoyo] payroll || rate of pay.

μισθός, ο [meesthos] salary, wages, pay.

μισθοφόρος, ο [meesthoforos] mercenary, hired man.

μισθώνω [meesthono] hire, rent || let out, hire out.

μισθωτής, ο [meesthotees] tenant || hirer.

μισθωτός [meesthotos] salaried, paid.

μισό, το [meeso] half || **στα μισά** halfway, in the middle.

μισογύνης, ο [meesoyeenees] woman-hater, misogynist.

μίσος, το [meesos] hatred, aversion.

μισός [meesos] half.

μισοφέγγαρο, το [meesofengaro] halfmoon, crescent.

μίσχος, ο [meeshos] stalk (of leaf).

μισώ [meeso] hate, detest, loathe.

μίτρα, η [meetra] mitre.

μνεία, η [mnea] mention.

μνήμα, το [mneema] grave, tomb, sepulchre.

μνημείο, το [mneemeeo] monument, cenotaph.

μνήμη, η [mneemee] memory, mind, recollection.

μνημονεύω [mneemonevo] celebrate, commemorate || quote, mention || learn by heart.

μνημονικό, το [mneemoneeko] βλ **μνήμη.**

μνημόσυνο, το [mneemoseeno] requiem.

μνησίκακος [mneeseekakos] spiteful, vindictive.

μνηστεύομαι [mneestevome] get engaged.

μνηστή, η [mneestee] fiancée.

μνηστήρας, ο [mneesteeras] fiancé || (μεταφ) claimant.

μόδα, η [moða] fashion, custom, habit, way || **της** ~**ς** fashionable.

μοδίστρα, η [moðeestra] dressmaker, seamstress.

μοιάζω [meeazo] look like.

μοίρα, η [meera] fate, destiny, fortune || (αερο) squadron || (γεωμ) degree.

μοιράζομαι [meerazome] share with.

μοιράζω [meerazo] share out, divide, distribute || (ρόλους) allot, assign || (διανέμω) deliver || (χαρτιά) deal || ~ **τη διαφορά** to split the difference.

μοιραίος [meereos] unavoidable || fatal, deadly.

μοιραίως [meereos] inevitably, fatally.

μοίραρχος, ο [meerarhos] captain of the gendarmerie.

μοιρολατρία, η [meerolatreea] fatalism.

μοιρολόγι, το [meeroloyee] dirge, lamentation.

μοιρολογώ [meerologo] lament, mourn.

μοιχεία, η [meeheea] adultery.

μολαταύτα [molatavta] nevertheless, yet, still.

μόλη [molee] barely, hardly, scarcely || as soon as.

μολονότι [molonotee] although, though.

μόλυβδος, ο [moleevðos] lead.

μολύβι, το [moleevee] lead || pencil.

μόλυνση, η [moleensee] contamination, infection, pollution.

μολύνω [moleeno] infect, contaminate, pollute.

μόλυσμα, το [moleesma] infection, contagion.

μομφή, η [momfee] blame, reproach, reprimand.

μονάδα, η [monaða] unit.

μοναδικός [monaðeekos] unique, singular, only.

μοναξιά, η [monaksia] solitude, isolation, loneliness.

μονάρχης, ο [monarhees] monarch, sovereign.

μοναρχία, η [monarheea] monarchy.

μοναρχικός, ο [monarheekos] monarchist.

μοναστήρι, το [monasteeree] monastery.

μονάχα [monaha] only.

μοναχή, η [monahee] nun.

μοναχικός [monaheekos] monastic || (ερημικός) isolated, solitary, lonely.

μοναχοπαίδι, το [monahopeðee] only child.

μονάχος [monahos] alone, single, only, sole || real, authentic.

μοναχός, ο [monahos] monk.

μονή, η [monee] βλ **μοναστήρι**.

μόνιμος [moneemos] permanent, lasting, durable, fixed.

μονογαμία, η [monogameea] monogamy.

μονογενής [monoyenees] one and only.

μονόγραμμα, το [monograma] monogram, initials.

μονογραφή, η [monografee] initials.

μονόδρομος, ο [monoðromos] one-way street.

μονοιάζω [moneeazo] agree with, get on well with || reconcile.

μονοκατοικία, η [monokateekeea] one-family house.

μονοκόμματος [monokomatos] in one piece || stiff || forthright || massive.

μονομαχία, η [monomaheea] duel.

μονομερής [monomerees] one-sided, partial.

μονομιάς [monomias] all at once.

μόνο [mono] only, alone, solely, merely, nothing but || ~ **που** except that || ~ **να** provided that.

μονοπάτι, το [monopatee] footpath, pathway.

μονόπλευρος [monoplevros] one-sided, partial.

μονοπώλιο, το [monopoleeo] monopoly.

μονοπωλώ [monopolo] monopolize.

μόνος [monos] alone, single, by o.s., apart || ~ **μου** of my own accord, by myself.

μονός [monos] single || simple || (αριθμός) odd.

μονότονος [monotonos] monotonous, unvaried || (μεταφ) wearisome.

μονόφθαλμος [monofthalmos] one-eyed.

μοντέλο, το [montelo] model.

μοντέρνος [monternos] modern, up-to-date.

μονώνω [monono] set apart, cut off || insulate.

μόνωση, η [monosee] insulation || solitude, isolation.

μονωτικός [monoteekos] insulating.

μόριο, το [moreeo] particle || molecule.

μόρτης, ο [mortees] hooligan, blackguard.

μορφάζω [morfazo] grimace, make faces || (από πόνο) wince.

μορφασμός, ο [morfasmos] grimace || wince.

μορφή, η [morfee] shape, form || look, face, aspect || phase.

μορφίνη, η [morfeenee] morphine.

μορφολογία, η [morfoloyeea] morphology.

μορφώνω [morfono] shape, form || (εκπαιδεύω) train, educate, teach.

μόρφωση, η [morfosee] education, learning.

μορφωτικός [morfoteekos] cultural || instructive.

μόστρα, η [mostra] shop window, display || specimen, sample.

μοσχάρι, το [mosharee] calf || veal.

μοσχοβολώ [moshovolo] smell sweetly, be fragrant.

μοσχοκάρυδο, το [moshokareeðo] nutmeg.

μοσχολίβανο, το [mosholeevano] frankincense.

μοτοσυκλέτα, η [motoseekleta] motorbike, motorcycle.

μου [mou] me || my.

μουγγός [moungos] dumb, mute.

μουγγρίζω [moungreezo] roar, bellow || (άνεμος) howl, wail || (από πόνο) moan, groan.

μουδιάζω [mouðeeazo] become numb.

μουλάρι, το [moularee] mule.

μούμια, η [moumeea] mummy || shrivelled person.

μουντζούρα, η [mountzoura] smudge, stain, smear || (μεταφ) blemish.

μουντός [mountos] dull, dim.
μούρη, η [mouree] face || snout.
μούρλια, η [mourleea] madness ||
είναι ~ it's perfect!, it's a dream!
μουρλός [mourlos] mad, insane ||
bewildered.
μουρμουρητό, το [mourmoureeto]
murmuring || grumbling.
μουρμουρίζω [mourmoureezo]
mutter, murmur || (μεταφ) whisper ||
babble.
μούρο, το [mouro] mulberry ||
μουριά, η mulberry tree.
μουρούνα, η [mourouna] codfish.
μούσα, η [mousa] muse.
μουσακάς, ο [mousakas] moussaka,
minced meat with vegetables.
μουσαμάς, ο [mousamas] oilcloth,
linoleum || mackintosh.
μουσαφίρης, ο [mousafeerees]
guest, visitor.
μουσείο, το [mouseeo] museum.
μούσι, το [mousee] beard, goatee.
μουσική, η [mouseekee] music.
μουσικός [mouseekos] musical || (ουσ)
musician.
μούσκεμα, το [mouskema] wetting,
soaking || τα κάνω ~ to make a mess
of.
μουσκεύω [mouskevo] soak, wet,
damp || get wet.
μούσμουλο, το [mousmoulo] loquat.
μουσουργός, ο, η [mousourgos]
composer.
μουστάκι, το [moustakee]
moustache.
μουστάρδα, η [moustarða] mustard.
μούστος, ο [moustos] must.
μούτρα, τα [moutra] πλ: έχω ~ να I
dare to || πέφτω με τα ~ to apply
o.s. enthusiastically || to tuck in.
μούτρο [moutro]: είναι ~ he's a thief,
he's deceitful.
μούτσος, ο [moutsos] cabin boy.
μούχλα, η [mouhla] mould, mildew.
μουχλιάζω [mouhleeazo] make
mouldy || become mouldy.
μοχθηρός [mohtheeros] wicked,
mischievous, malicious.
μόχθος, ο [mohthos] pains, fatigue,
trouble.
μοχλός, ο [mohlos] lever, (crow)bar ||
(μεταφ) promoter, instigator.
μπαγιάτικος [bayateekos] (ψωμί)
stale || rancid.
μπάγκος, ο [bangos] bench || counter.
μπάζα, τα [baza] πλ debris, rubble.
μπάζω [bazo] usher in, thrust ||
(συμμαζεύομαι) shrink.
μπαίνω [beno] go into, get in, enter ||
(υφάσματ) shrink || (μεταφ) catch on,
understand || ~ μέσα to fall into debt ||
~ σε μια σειρά to settle down, fall
into line.
μπακάλης, ο [bakalees] grocer.

μπακάλικο, το [bakaleeko] grocer's
shop || grocery (US).
μπακαλιάρος, ο [bakaleearos] salted
codfish.
μπακίρι, το [bakeeree] copper.
μπακλαβάς, ο [baklavas] pastry of
almonds and honey.
μπαλαντέρ, ο [balanðer] (στα χαρτιά)
joker.
μπαλκόνι, το [balkonee] balcony.
μπάλα, η [bala] ball || bullet.
μπαλέτο, το [baleto] ballet.
μπαλόνι, το [balonee] balloon.
μπαλντάς, ο [balntas] axe, hatchet.
μπάλωμα, το [baloma] mending,
patching, repairing.
μπαλώνω [balono] patch, mend, repair
|| τα ~ to make excuses || to make up.
μπάμιες, οι [bamies] πλ okra, gumbo,
lady's fingers.
μπαμπάκι, το [bambakee] cotton.
μπαμπάς, ο [bambas] daddy, papa.
μπαμπούρας, ο [bambouras] hornet.
μπανάνα, η [banana] banana.
μπανιέρα, η [baniera] bathtub.
μπάνιο, το [baneeo] bath || bathing,
swimming || (λεκάνη) tub || (δωμάτιο)
bathroom.
μπάντα, η [banta] (ήσυχη γωνιά)
corner || (πλευρά) side || (μουσ) band ||
(συμμορία) gang, band || βάζω στη ~
to save || κάνε στη ~ make room,
stand aside.
μπαντιέρα, η [bantiera] banner,
standard.
μπαξές, ο [bakses] garden.
μπαούλο, το [baoulo] trunk, chest.
μπαρκάρω [barkaro] go on board ||
ship.
μπάρμπας, ο [barbas] old man ||
uncle.
μπαρμπούνι, το [barbounee] red
mullet.
μπαρούτι, το [baroutee] gunpowder ||
έγινε ~ he got furious.
μπάρρα, η [bara] bar, crowbar.
μπασμένος [basmenos] aware ||
knowledgeable || (ρούχα) shrunk.
μπάσταρδος, ο [bastarðos] bastard.
μπαστούνι, το [bastounee] walking
stick, cane || (χαρτιά) club.
μπαταρία, η [batareea] battery.
μπατζανάκης, ο [batzanakees]
brother-in-law.
μπάτσος, ο [batsos] slap, smack || (sl)
policeman.
μπαχαρικό, το [bahareeko] spice.
μπεζ [bez] beige.
μπεκάτσα, η [bekatsa] woodcock.
μπεκρής, ο [bekrees] drunkard,
tippler, boozer.
μπελάς, ο [belas] trouble,
embarrassment, annoyance.
μπέμπης, ο [bembees] baby.

μπενζίνα, n [benzeena] petrol || (πλοιάριο) motorboat.

μπέρδεμα, το [berðema] tangle, entanglement, confusion, disorder.

μπερδεύομαι [berðovme] get implicated, become entangled || be confused.

μπερδεύω [berðevo] involve || confuse, make a muddle of || entangle.

μπερμπάντης, ο [bermbantees] rascal, scoundrel.

μπετό, το [beto] concrete.

μπετούγια, n [betouya] latch, catch.

μπήζω [beezo] drive in, hammer in || (βελόνα) stick in, thrust in.

μπιζέλι, το [beezelee] pea.

μπίρα, n [beera] beer.

μπισκότο, το [beeskoto] biscuit.

μπίτ(ι) [beet(ee)] entirely || not in the least.

μπιφτέκι, το [beeftekee] hamburger, steak.

μπλάστρι, το [blastree] plaster.

μπλε [ble] blue.

μπλέκω [bleko] complicate, perplex || get implicated.

μπλέξιμο, το [blekseemo] entanglement, involvement, complication.

μπλοκάρω [blokaro] blockade || block.

μπλούζα, n [blouza] blouse.

μπλόφα, n [blofa] bluff, deception.

μπογιά, n [boya] paint, dye || (παπουτσιών) boot polish.

μπόγιας, ο [boyas] dog-catcher || hangman.

μπογιατζής, ο [boyadzees] painter || polisher.

μπογιατίζω [boyateezo] paint, colour, coat || polish.

μπόι, το [boee] height, size.

μπόλι, το [bolee] graft || μπολιάζω vaccinate, inoculate || graft.

μπόλικος [boleekos] plentiful, abundant, numerous.

μπόμπα, n [bomba] bomb.

μπόρα, n [bora] rain squall, shower, storm.

μπορώ [boro] can, be able, may.

μπόσικος [boseekos] loose, slack || (μεταφ) trifling || unreliable.

μποστάνι, το [bostanee] melon field.

μποτίλια, n [boteeleea] bottle || μποτιλιάρω bottle || (μεταφ) block up, jam.

μπότα, n [bota] boot.

μπουγάδα, n [bougaða] family wash, washing.

μπουζί, το [bouzee] spark plug.

μπουζούκι, το [bouzoukee] kind of mandolin, bouzouki.

μπούκα, n [bouka] hole, mouth, entrance || muzzle.

μπουκάλα, n [boukala] big bottle || έμεινε ~ he was left in the lurch.

μπουκάλι, το [boukalee] bottle.

μπουκιά, n [boukia] mouthful.

μπουκώνω [boukono] fill the mouth || (μεταφ) bribe.

μπουλούκι, το [bouloukee] crowd || band, troop.

μπουμπούκι, το [boumboukee] bud, sprout.

μπουμπουνητό, το [boumbouneeto] thundering, roll of thunder, rumble.

μπουνάτσα, n [bounatsa] fine weather || calm sea.

μπουνιά, n [bounia] punch, blow with the fist.

μπούρδα, n [bourða] rubbish, hot air.

μπουρμπουλήθρα, n [bourmbouleethra] bubble.

μπουσουλώ [bousoulo] crawl.

μπούστος, ο [boustos] bust.

μπούτι, το [boutee] thigh || (αρνήσιο) leg of lamb.

μπουφές, ο [boufes] sideboard || buffet.

μπούφος, ο [boufos] horned owl || (μεταφ) booby.

μπουχτίζω [bouhteezo] have enough of || eat one's fill.

μπόχα, n [boha] stink, foul smell.

μπράβο [bravo] (επιφ) good show!, bravo!, good for you!

μπράτσο, το [bratso] arm.

μπριζόλα, n [breezola] chop, cutlet.

μπρίκι, το [breekee] coffee pot.

μπρος [bros] forward(s), in front of || βλ και εμπρός.

μπροστινός [brosteenos] in front || former.

μπρούμυτα [broumeeta] flat on one's face.

μπρούντζος, ο [broundzos] bronze, brass.

μπύρα, n [beera] βλ μπίρα.

μυ, το [mee] the letter M.

μυαλό, το [meealo] brain(s) || (γνώση) mind, intellect.

μυαλωμένος [meealomenos] learned, wise.

μύγα, n [meega] fly.

μύδι, το [meeðee] mussel.

μυελός, ο [mielos] marrow (of bone).

μυζήθρα, n [meezeethra] kind of white soft cheese.

μύηση, n [mieesee] initiation.

μυθικός [meetheekos] mythical, legendary || incredible.

μυθιστόρημα, το [meetheestoreema] novel, romance, story.

μυθιστοριογράφος, ο [meetheestoreeografos] novelist.

μυθολογία, n [meetholoyeea] mythology.

μύθος, ο [meethos] fable || myth || legend.

μυθώδης [meethoðees] fabled, legendary || untrue || incredible.
μυϊκός [mieekos] muscular.
μυκηθμός, ο [meekeethmos] bellowing, howling || lowing.
μύκητας, ο [meekeetas] fungus, mushroom.
μύλος, ο [meelos] mill || (ανεμόμυλος) windmill.
μυλωνάς, ο [meelonas] miller.
μύξα, η [meeksa] snot || mucus.
μυρίζω [meereezo] smell.
μύριοι [meeriee] ten thousand || (μεταφ) numberless.
μυρμήγκι, το [meermeengee] ant.
μυρτιά, η [meertia] myrtle.
μυρωδάτος [meeroðatos] aromatic, fragrant.
μυρωδιά, η [meeroðia] smell, scent, odour || (αρωματικό) fragrance, perfume || **παίρνω** ~ to get wind of.
μυς, ο [mees] muscle.
μυσαρός [meesaros] abominable, detestable, odious.
μυσταγωγία, η [meestagoyeea] initiation || holy ceremony.
μυστήριο, το [meesteereeo] mystery, secret.
μυστήριος [meesteereeos] mysterious, inexplicable.
μυστηριώδης [meesteereeoðees] mysterious, dark.
μυστικιστής, ο [meesteekeestees] mystic.
μυστικό, το [meestecko] secret.
μυστικός [meesteekos] secret(ive) || reticent, discreet || (αστυνομικός) undercover man || ~ **δείπνος** Last Supper.
μυστικότητα, η [meesteekoteeta] secrecy, discretion.
μυστρί, το [meestree] trowel.
μυτερός [meeteros] pointed.
μύτη, η [meetee] nose || (άκρη) tip || (παπουτσιού) toe || (πένας) nib || (βελόνας) point.
μυώ [meeo] initiate into, admit into.
μυώδης [meeoðees] muscular, brawny, powerful.
μύωπας [meeopas] near-sighted, short-sighted.
μωαμεθανός, ο [moamethanos] Mohammedan.
μώβ [mov] mauve.
μώλος, ο [molos] mole, jetty, pier.
μωλωπίζω [molopeezo] bruise, contuse.
μώλωπας, ο [molopas] bruise, contusion.
μωρέ [more] (επιφ) hey you!, you!, I say!
μωρία, η [moreea] stupidity, foolishness.
μωρό, το [moro] baby, infant.
μωσαϊκό, το [mosaeeko] mosaic.

N, ν

να [na] that, to, in order to, so as to || here it is!
ναι [ne] yes, indeed, certainly.
νάιλον, το [naeelon] nylon.
νάνος, ο [nanos] dwarf.
νανουρίζω [nanoureezo] lull to sleep || (στην κούνια) rock || (στην αγκαλιά) nurse.
νανούρισμα, το [nanoureesma] lullaby || rocking to sleep.
ναός, ο [naos] church || temple.
ναργιλές, ο [naryeeless] hubble-bubble, hookah.
νάρθηκας, ο [nartheekas] (εκκλ) nave, narthex || (βοτ) fennel.
ναρκαλιευτικό, το [narkalievteeko] minesweeper.
νάρκη, η [narkee] numbness, torpor || (ναυτ) mine || (πνεύματος) sluggishness.
νάρκισσος, ο [narkeesos] narcissus.
ναρκώνω [narkono] numb || (μεταφ) dull, stupefy.
νάρκωση, η [narkosee] numbness || torpidity, sluggishness.
ναρκωτικά, τα [narkoteeka] πλ drugs, narcotics.
νάτριο, το [natreeo] sodium.
ναυάγιο, το [navayo] shipwreck || (μεταφ) wreck.
ναυαγός, ο [navagos] shipwrecked person.
ναυαρχείο, το [navarheeo] admiralty.
ναύαρχος, ο [navarhos] admiral.
ναύκληρος, ο [navkleeros] boatswain.
ναύλα, τα [navla] πλ fare, passage money.
ναυλώνω [navlono] charter, freight.
ναυμαχία, η [navmaheea] sea battle, naval action.
ναυπηγείο, το [navpeeyeeo] shipyard, dockyard.
ναυσιπλοΐα, η [navseeploeea] sailing, shipping || navigation.
ναύσταθμος, ο [navstathmos] dockyard, naval arsenal.
ναύτης, ο [navtees] sailor, seaman, mariner.
ναυτία, η [navteea] seasickness || nausea.
ναυτικό, το [navteeko] navy.
ναυτικός [navteekos] maritime || nautical || (άνδρας) seafarer.
ναυτιλία, η [navteeleea] navigation || shipping || **ναυτιλιακός** marine, naval, nautical.
ναυτολογώ [navtologo] enlist a crew, muster seamen.
νέα, η [nea] girl.
νέα, τα [nea] πλ news.

νεανικός [neaneekos] youthful, juvenile.

νεαρός [nearos] young || youthful, juvenile.

νέγρος, ο [negros] negro.

νέκρα, η [nekra] dead silence, stagnation.

νεκρικός [nekreekos] of death, funereal || gloomy.

νεκροθάπτης, ο [nekrothaptees] gravedigger.

νεκροκεφαλή, η [nekrokefalee] skull.

νεκρολογία, η [nekroloyeea] obituary.

νεκρός [nekros] dead, lifeless || (ουσ) **ο ~** dead person.

νεκροταφείο, το [nekrotafeeo] cemetery, graveyard.

νεκροτομείο, το [nekrotomeeo] mortuary, morgue.

νεκροφόρα, η [nekrofora] hearse.

νεκροψία, η [nekropseea] autopsy, post-mortem.

νεκρώνω [nekrono] deaden || (τα πάθη) subdue.

νεκρώσιμος [nekroseemos] funeral.

νέκταρ, το [nektar] nectar.

νέμω [nemo] distribute, share.

νέο, το [neo] piece of news.

νεογέννητος [neoyeneetos] newborn.

νεογνό, το [neogno] newborn animal || newborn baby.

νεοελληνικά, τα [neoeleeneeka] πλ modern Greek (language).

νεοελληνικός [neoeleeneekos] of modern Greece.

νεόκτιστος [neokteestos] newly constructed.

νεολαία, η [neolea] youth.

νεόνυμφος, ο, η [neoneemfos] recently married man or woman.

νεόπλουτος [neoploutos] nouveau riche, parvenu.

νέος [neos] young || (καινούργιο) new, fresh || (επιπρόσθετο) further, additional || (σύγχρονος) modern || (ουσ) a young man.

νεοσσός, ο [neosos] nestling, chick.

νεοσύλλεκτος, ο [neoseelektos] recruit.

νεοσύστατος [neoseestatos] newly-established, newly-founded.

νεότητα, η [neoteeta] βλ **νεολαία**.

νεράιδα, η [neraeeða] fairy, Nereid.

νεράντζι, το [nerandzee] bitter orange.

νερό, το [nero] water || urine.

νερόβραστος [nerovrastos] boiled in water || (μεταφ) insipid, tasteless.

νερομπογιά, η [neromboya] watercolour.

νεροποντή, η [neropontee] shower of rain, downpour.

νερουλός [neroulos] watery, thin.

νεροχύτης, ο [neroheetees] kitchen sink.

νερώνω [nerono] mix with water.

νέτα σκέτα [netasketa] frankly, flatly.

νέτος [netos] net || (μεταφ) done, finished, completed.

νεύμα, το [nevma] sign, nod, wink, beckoning.

νευραλγία, η [nevralyeea] neuralgia.

νευραλγικός [nevralyeekos]: **νευραλγικό σημείο** weak spot.

νευριάζω [nevreeazo] make angry, irritate, vex || become angry.

νευρικός [nevreekos] nervous || excitable, highly strung.

νεύρο, το [nevro] nerve || muscle || vigour.

νευρόσπαστος, ο [nevrospastos] (μεταφ) nervous person.

νευρώδης [nevroðees] sinewy || nervous || (μεταφ) strong, spirited.

νευρωτικός [nevroteekos] neurotic.

νεύω [nevo] nod, make a sign, beckon, wink.

νεφελώδης [nefeloðees] cloudy, nebulous || (μεταφ) vague, hazy.

νέφος, το [nefos] cloud || (μεταφ) gloom, shadow.

νεφοσκεπής [nefoskepees] cloudy, overcast.

νεφρό, το [nefro] kidney.

νέφτι, το [neftee] turpentine, turps.

νεώριο, το [neoreeo] dry dock, dockyard.

νεωτερισμός, ο [neotereesmos] innovation || novelty, fashion.

νεώτερα, τα [neotera] πλ latest news.

νεώτερος [neoteros] younger || (γεγονός) recent, later || (νέα) fresh.

νήμα, το [neema] thread || (βαμβακερό) cotton thread || (μάλλινο) yarn.

νηνεμία, η [neenemeea] calmness, stillness.

νηολόγιο, το [neeoloyo] register of merchant shipping.

νηοπομπή, η [neeopombee] convoy, escort of ships.

νηπιαγωγείο, το [neepeeagoyeeo] kindergarten.

νήπιο, το [neepeeo] infant, baby, newborn child.

νησί, το [neesee] island.

νησιώτης, ο [neeseeotees] islander.

νήσος, η [neesos] βλ **νησί**.

νηστεία, η [neesteea] fast, fasting.

νηστεύω [neestevo] fast.

νηστικός [neesteekos] hungry.

νηφάλιος [neefaleeos] sober || (μεταφ) calm, cool, composed.

νιαουρίζω [neeaoureezo] miaow, mew.

νιάτα, τα [neeata] πλ youth.

νικέλιο, το [neekeleeo] nickel.

νίκη, η [neekee] victory, triumph.
νικητής, ο [neekeetees] victor || (σε παιχνίδι) winner.
νικηφόρος [neekeeforos] victorious, triumphant.
νικώ [neeko] (τον εχθρό) defeat, vanquish || (ανταγωνιστή) beat, surpass || (εμπόδια κτλ) surmount, overcome.
νίλα, η [neela] practical joke || calamity, ruin.
νιπτήρας, ο [neepteeras] washbasin, washstand.
νίπτω [neepto] wash || (μεταφ) wash out.
νισάφι, το [neesafee] mercy, compassion, pity.
νιφάδα, η [neefaða] snowflake.
Νοέμβρης, ο [noemvrees], **Νοέμβριος, ο** [noemvreeos] November.
νοερός [noeros] mental, intellectual.
νόημα, το [noeema] reflection, thought || (έννοια) sense, meaning || (νεύμα) sign, wink.
νοημοσύνη, η [noeemoseenee] intelligence, intellect.
νοήμων [noeemon] intelligent, smart.
νόηση, η [noeesee] understanding, intellect || mind, wit.
νοητός [noeetos] comprehensible, conceivable.
νοθεία, η [notheea] falsification, adulteration.
νόθευση, η [nothevsee] adulteration, forgery.
νοθεύω [nothevo] falsify, forge, adulterate.
νόθος [nothos] bastard || (για ζώα κτλ) hybrid || (μεταφ) unstable.
νοιάζει [neeazee]: **με ~** I care, I am anxious about.
νοιάζομαι [neeazome] care about, look after || be anxious about.
νοίκι, το [neekee] rent || **νοικιάζω** rent, hire, let out || **νοικάρης, ο** tenant.
νοικοκυρά, η [neekokeera] housewife, mistress of the house || landlady.
νοικοκύρης, ο [neekokeerees] landlord || owner || (αυτεξούσιος) independent || be anxious about.
νοικοκυριό, το [neekokeerio] housekeeping.
νοιώθω [neeotho] understand || feel, perceive || know.
νομαδικός [nomaðeekos] nomadic, roving.
νομαρχείο, το [nomarheeo] prefecture.
νομάρχης, ο [nomarhees] prefect, governor.
νομίζω [nomeezo] believe, think || suppose, presume.

νομικά, τα [nomeeka] πλ law studies, jurisprudence.
νομική, η [nomeekee] law.
νομικός [nomeekos] of the law, legal, lawful.
νομιμοποιώ [nomeemopeeo] legitimize, legalize, validate.
νόμιμος [nomeemos] legal, lawful, rightful.
νομιμότητα, η [nomeemoteeta] legitimacy, legality.
νομιμόφρονας [nomeemofronas] law-abiding, obedient, loyal.
νόμισμα, το [nomeesma] money, coin, currency.
νομοθεσία, η [nomotheseea] legislation, law-making.
νομοθέτης, ο [nomothetees] legislator, lawgiver.
νομομαθής, ο [nomomathees] jurist, legist.
νομός, ο [nomos] prefecture, province.
νόμος, ο [nomos] law, act (of Parliament), enactment.
νομοσχέδιο, το [nomosheðeeo] bill, draft of a law.
νομοταγής [nomotayees] law-abiding, loyal.
νονός, ο [nonos] godfather, sponsor.
νοοτροπία, η [nootropeea] mentality, mental character.
Νορβηγία, η [norveeyeea] Norway.
νορβηγικός [norveeyeekos] Norwegian.
Νορβηγός, ο [norveegos] Norwegian.
νοσηλεία, η [noseeleea] nursing, treatment, care of the sick.
νοσηλεύω [noseelevo] treat, tend, nurse.
νοσηρός [noseeros] unhealthy, sickly, weakly || (περιέργεια) morbid.
νοσοκομείο, το [nosokomeeo] hospital, infirmary.
νοσοκόμος, ο, η [nosokomos] nurse || (στρατ) hospital orderly.
νόσος, η [nosos] illness, disease, sickness.
νοσταλγία, η [nostalyeea] nostalgia || homesickness.
**νοσταλγικός, [nostalyeekos] nostalgic || homesick.
νοσταλγώ [nostalgo] feel nostalgic for || crave for || be homesick.
νοστιμάδα, η [nosteemaða] tastiness || prettiness || piquancy.
νοστιμεύω [nosteemevo] flavour, make tasty || make attractive.
νόστιμος [nosteemos] tasty || attractive, charming.
νότα, η [nota] (διπλωματική) note || (μουσ) note.
νοτιά, η [notia] south || south wind.

νοτίζω [noteezo] moisten, dampen || become damp.

νοτιοανατολικός [noteeoanatoleekos] south-eastern.

νοτιοδυτικός [noteeoδeeteekos] south-western.

νότιος [noteeos] southern.

νότος, ο [notos] south.

νουθεσία, η [noutheseea] admonition, advice, counsel.

νουθετώ [noutheto] admonish, advise, give advice to.

νούμερο, το [noumero] number || (θεάτρου) act || odd character.

νουνός, ο [nounos] godfather, sponsor.

νους, ο [nous] mind, wit, intelligence, sense.

νούφαρο, το [noufaro] water lily.

νοώ [noo] comprehend, understand || think, reflect.

ντάης, ο [daees] bully, ruffian.

ντάμα, η [dama] lady || partner || (στα χαρτιά) queen || (παιχνίδι) game of draughts.

νταμιτζάνα, η [dameedzana] demijohn.

νταμπλάς, ο [damblas] apoplexy || (μεταφ) amazement, stupefaction.

νταντά, η [danda] child's nurse, nanny.

νταντέλα, η [dantela] lace.

νταούλι, το [daoulee] drum.

νταραβέρι, το [daraveree] relation, dealing || (φασαρία) fuss, trouble.

ντε [de]: **έλα ~** (επιφ) come on!, hurry up!

ντεπόζιτο, το [depozeeto] cistern || tank.

ντέρτι, το [dertee] regret, pain, sorrow || longing, yearning.

ντιβάνι, το [deevanee] divan.

ντολμάς, ο [dolmas] stuffed vine or cabbage leaves.

ντομάτα, η [domata] tomato.

ντόμπρος [dombros] sincere, candid, frank, honest.

ντόπιος [dopeeos] local, native.

ντόρος, ο [doros] trouble, din || (μεταφ) sensation.

ντουβάρι, το [douvaree] wall || (μεταφ) fool.

ντουέτο, το [doueto] duet.

ντουζίνα, η [douzeena] dozen.

ντουλάπα, η [doulapa] wardrobe.

ντουλάπι, το [doulapee] cupboard.

ντουνιάς, ο [dounias] people, mankind, humanity.

ντους, το [dous] shower bath.

ντρέπομαι [drepome] be bashful || be ashamed.

ντροπαλός [dropalos] shy, modest, timid.

ντροπή, η [dropee] shame || modesty, bashfulness.

ντροπιάζω [dropeeazo] shame.

ντυμένος [deemenos] dressed.

ντύνομαι [deenome] get dressed.

ντύνω [deeno] dress || (έπιπλα) upholster.

ντύσιμο, το [deeseemo] dressing || attire, outfit, dress.

νυ, το [nee] the letter N.

νυκτερινός [neektereenos] of night, nocturnal.

νυκτόβιος [neektoveeos] living by night.

νυκτοφύλακας, ο [neektofeelakas] night watchman.

νυμφεύω [neemfevo] marry, wed.

νύμφη, η [neemfee] bride || (μυθολογία) nymph || (ζωολ) larva.

νύξη, η [neeksee] hint, allusion.

νύστα, η [neesta] sleepiness, drowsiness.

νυστάζω [neestazo] be sleepy, feel sleepy.

νυσταλέος [neestaleos] sleepy || (μεταφ) dull, sluggish.

νύφη, η [neefee] βλ **νύμφη.**

νυφικός [neefeekos] bridal, nuptial.

νυφίτσα, η [neefeetsa] weasel.

νυχθημερόν [neehtheemeron] day and night.

νύχι, το [neehee] nail || (ποδιών) toenail || (ζώου) claw, talon || **νύχια** πλ clutches.

νύχτα, η [neehta] night, darkness || (επιρ) at night, by night.

νυχτερίδα, η [neehtereeδa] bat.

νυχτικό, το [neehteeko] nightgown.

νυχτώνω [neehtono]: **νυχτώνει** night falls.

νωθρός [nothros] sluggish, lazy, slothful.

νωπός [nopos] fresh, new, recent || (για ρούχα) still damp.

νωρίς [norees] early.

νώτα, τα [nota] πλ back || (στρατ) rear.

νωχελής [noheelees] indolent, idle, slothful.

Ξ, ξ

ξαγρυπνώ [ksagreepno] stay awake || watch over || burn the midnight oil.

ξαδέρφη, η [ksaδerfee] cousin.

ξάδερφος, ο [ksaδerfos] cousin.

ξακουστός [ksakoustos] renowned, celebrated, famous.

ξαλαφρώνω [ksalafrono] lighten the load of, help || (μεταφ) relieve || relieve one's mind.

ξανά [ksana] again, afresh, anew.

ξαναβάζω [ksanavazo] put back again, replace.

ξανάβω [ksanavo] irritate || become annoyed, get furious.

ξαναγυρίζω [ksanayeereezo] return, send back || turn again.

ξανακάνω [ksanakano] redo, remake, repeat.

ξαναλέω [ksanaleo] repeat, reiterate.

ξανανιώνω [ksananeeono] rejuvenate || become young again.

ξαναπαθαίνω [ksanapatheno] be taken in again || suffer again.

ξαναπαίρνω [ksanaperno] take again || (θάρρος) pluck up again || (υπάλληλος) take on again, rehire || (θέση) go back to.

ξαναπαντρεύομαι [ksanapanðrevome] remarry.

ξανασαίνω [ksanaseno] recover, refresh ό.s., relax.

ξαναφορτώνω [ksanafortono] reload.

ξανθίζω [ksantheezo] become fairer.

ξανθομάλλης [ksanthomalees] fair-haired.

ξανθός [ksanthos] blond, fair, light || (στάχυ) yellow, golden.

ξάνοιγμα, το [ksaneegma] clearing up, brightening || launching out.

ξανοίγομαι [ksaneegome] confide one's secrets || spend freely.

ξανοίγω [ksaneego] (μεταφ) look, see || clear up.

ξάπλα, η [ksapla] sprawling around || lying down.

ξάπλωμα, το [ksaploma] lying down || stretching out, spreading.

ξαπλώνομαι [ksaplonome] spread || lie down.

ξαπλώνω [ksaplono] spread out || lie down.

ξαποσταίνω [ksaposteno] rest, relax.

ξαποστέλνω [ksapostelno] send off, forward || dismiss.

ξασπρίζω [ksaspreezo] whiten || blanch, pale, fade.

ξάστερα [ksastera] frankly, flatly, categorically.

ξάστερος [ksasteros] cloudless, bright || (μεταφ) lucid, clear.

ξαφνιάζομαι [ksafneeazome] be taken by surprise, be frightened.

ξαφνιάζω [ksafneeazo] startle, surprise, frighten, scare.

ξαφνικά [ksafneeka] all of a sudden.

ξαφνικό, το [ksafneeko] surprise || accident, mishap.

ξαφρίζω [ksafreezo] skim || (μεταφ) steal.

ξάφρισμα, το [ksafreesma] skimming || frothing.

ξεβάφω [ksevafo] fade || lose colour, discolour.

ξεβγάζω [ksevgazo] wash out || (προπέμπω) show out, get rid of.

ξεβράκωτος [ksevrakotos] trouserless || (μεταφ) penniless.

ξεγελώ [kseyelo] cheat, dupe, deceive.

ξεγεννώ [kseyeno] deliver a child || be delivered of.

ξεγνοιάζω [ksegneeazo] be free from care.

ξεγράφω [ksegrafo] efface, strike out || (μεταφ) wipe out || write off.

ξεδιαλέγω [kseðeealego] select, choose, sort.

ξεδιαλύνω [kseðeealeeno] get to the bottom of, unravel.

ξεδιάντροπος [kseðeeantropos] immodest, brazen.

ξεδιπλώνω [kseðeeplono] unfurl, open out, spread.

ξεδιψώ [kseðeepso] quench one's thirst || refresh.

ξεθαρρεύω [ksetharevo] become too bold.

ξεθεώνω [ksetheono] wear out, exhaust, harass, worry.

ξεθυμαίνω [ksetheemeno] escape, leak out || (μεταφ) calm down, abate.

ξεθωριάζω [ksethoreeazo] fade || lose colour, discolour.

ξεκαθαρίζω [ksekathareezo] liquidate, settle accounts || elucidate || kill off.

ξεκάνω [ksekano] sell off || kill, exterminate.

ξεκαρδίζομαι [ksekarðeezome] burst out laughing.

ξεκάρφωτος [ksekarfotos] (μεταφ) unconnected, irrelevant.

ξεκινώ [ksekeeno] set off, start, depart || drive off.

ξεκλείδωτος [ksekleeðotos] unlocked.

ξεκοκκαλίζω [ksekokaleezo] eat to the bone || (μεταφ) spend foolishly.

ξεκομμένα [ksekomena] to the point, frankly.

ξεκουμπώνω [ksekoumbono] unbutton, unfasten.

ξεκουράζομαι [ksekourazome] relax, rest.

ξεκουράζω [ksekourazo] rest, relieve, refresh, repose.

ξεκουφαίνω [ksekoufeno] deafen, stun.

ξελιγωμένος [kseleegomenos] be hungry for, hunger for.

ξελιγώνω [kseleegono] (μεταφ) wear o.s. out, tire.

ξελογιάζω [kseloyazo] seduce, lead astray, fascinate.

ξεμαλλιασμένος [ksemaleeasmenos] dishevelled.

ξεμοναχιάζω [ksemonaheeazo] take aside.

ξεμπαρκάρω [ksembarkaro] land || unload.

ξεμπερδεύω [ksemberðevo] unravel, disentangle || get clear of, get rid of.

ξεμπλέκω [ksembleko] free o.s. || ~ από get free of.

ξεμυαλίζω [ksemeealeezo] infatuate, turn the head of, lead astray.

ξένα, τα [ksena] πλ foreign parts.

ξεναγός, ο, η [ksenagos] tourist guide.

ξενπτειά, η [kseneetia] foreign parts, foreign country.

ξενπτεύομαι [kseneetevome] live abroad.

ξενίζω [kseneezo] surprise, astonish.

ξενικός [kseneekos] foreign, alien, outlandish.

ξενοιάζω [kseneeazo] be free from cares.

ξενοδοχείο, το [ksenodoheeo] hotel.

ξενοδόχος, ο [ksenodohos] hotelier, innkeeper.

ξενοικιάζομαι [kseneekeeazome] become vacant.

ξένος [ksenos] foreign, strange, unfamiliar || (ουσ) ~ foreigner, stranger || visitor.

ξενοφοβία, η [ksenofoveea] xenophobia.

ξενόφωνος [ksenofonos] foreign-speaking.

ξεντύνω [ksenteeno] undress, disrobe.

ξενυχτώ [kseneehto] stay up late, stay out all night.

ξενώνας, ο [ksenonas] spare room, guest room.

ξεπαγιάζω [ksepayazo] freeze || get frozen.

ξεπαστρεύω [ksepastrevo] exterminate, wipe out.

ξεπερασμένος [kseperasmenos] out-of-date, old-fashioned.

ξεπερνώ [kseperno] surpass, overtake || (σε δρόμο) outrun || (σε ύψος) be taller.

ξεπεσμός, ο [ksepesmos] decay, decline || (τιμών) fall || (νομίσματος) depreciation.

ξεπετιέμαι [ksepetieme] jump up suddenly, shoot up.

ξεπέφτω [ksepefto] reduce, abate || (τιμών) fall || (μεταφ) fall into disrepute.

ξεπλένω [ksepleno] rinse.

ξεπληρώνω [ksepleerono] pay off, discharge (a debt).

ξεπούλημα, το [ksepouleema] sale, sellout, liquidation || fire sale (US).

ξεπουλώ [ksepoulo] sell off || sell out, liquidate.

ξεπροβοδίζω [kseprovodeezo] escort off, say goodbye to.

ξέρα, η [ksera] (θάλασσας) rock, reef || (καιρού) drought, dryness.

ξεραΐλα, η [kseraeela] aridity, dryness, drought.

ξεραίνομαι [kserenome] dry up, wither, get parched.

ξεραίνω [ksereno] dry up || parch, bake || (φυτά) wither.

ξερνώ [kserno] vomit, bring up || belch out.

ξερόβηχας, ο [kseroveehas] dry cough.

ξεροκαταπίνω [kserokatapeeno] swallow with embarrassment.

ξεροκέφαλος [kserokefalos] thickheaded || obstinate, stubborn.

ξερονήσι, το [kseroneesee] barren island, desert island.

ξερός [kseros] arid, dry, barren || (γλώσσα) parched || (ύφος) curt, snappish || έμεινε ~ he was stumped || he dropped dead || έπεσε ~ στον ύπνο he dropped off to sleep.

ξεριζώνω [ksereezono] pull up, uproot || root out, wipe out.

ξέρω [ksero] know how to, understand, be aware of.

ξεσηκώνω [kseseekono] rouse, excite || (σχέδιο) transfer, copy.

ξεσκάζω [kseskazo] refresh o.s., relax.

ξεσκεπάζω [kseskepazo] unveil, uncover || reveal, disclose, let out.

ξεσκίζω [kseskeezo] rip up.

ξεσκονίζω [kseskoneezo] dust, give a dusting to.

ξεσκονόπανο, το [kseskonopano] duster, dust rag.

ξεσπάζω [ksespazo] (μεταφ) burst into, burst out.

ξεσπαθώνω [ksespathono] unsheathe one's sword || (μεταφ) speak out.

ξεστομίζω [ksestomeezo] utter, launch, hurl.

ξεστραβώνω [ksestravono] straighten out || become straight.

ξεστρώνω [ksestrono] take up, remove || (τραπέζι) clear away.

ξεσχίζω [ksesheezo] tear to pieces, lacerate.

ξετινάζω [kseteenazo] toss, shake, beat || (μεταφ) reduce to poverty.

ξετρελαίνω [ksetreleno] drive mad, bewilder || (από έρωτα) bewitch.

ξετρυπώνω [ksetreepono] appear suddenly, crop up.

ξετσίπωτος [ksetseepotos] shameless.

ξεύρω [ksevro] βλ ξέρω.

ξεφαντώνω [ksefantono] live fast, feast, revel.

ξεφεύγω [ksefevgo] elude || slip out.

ξεφλουδίζω [kseflou deezo] peel || pare || shell || (το δέρμα) lose the skin.

ξεφορτώνομαι [ksefortonome] get rid of, shake off.

ξεφορτώνω [ksefortono] unload || (μεταφ) get rid of.

ξεφτέρι, το [ksefteree] sharp person, witty person.

ξεφτίζω [ksefteezo] fray out || (νήμα) pull out, unweave.

ξεφυλλίζω [ksefeeleezo] skim over, run through || strip the leaves, pluck.

ξεφυτρώνω [ksefeetrono] sprout, shoot up || appear suddenly.
ξεφωνητό, το [ksefoneeto] yell, shout, outcry, scream.
ξεφωνίζω [ksefoneezo] shout, bawl, yell, scream.
ξεχαρβαλωμένος [kseharvalomenos] shaky, loose, falling apart.
ξεχασμένος [ksehasmenos] forgotten.
ξεχειλίζω [kseheeleezo] overflow, run over.
ξεχειμωνιάζω [kseheemoneeazo] pass the winter, winter.
ξεχνώ [ksehno] forget, leave out, neglect.
ξεχρεώνω [ksehreono] pay up, discharge || settle, fulfil.
ξεχύνομαι [kseheenome] overflow.
ξεχύνω [kseheeno] pour out, overflow.
ξέχωρα [ksehora] apart, separately || ~ από apart from.
ξεχωρίζω [ksehoreezo] separate || single out || distinguish, discern || make one's mark.
ξεχωριστά [ksehoreesta] separately.
ξεχωριστός [ksehoreestos] separate || distinct, peculiar || distinguished, exceptional.
ξεψυχώ [ksepseeho] die, expire, give up the ghost.
ξηλώνω [kseelono] take apart, unstitch.
ξημερώματα [kseemeromata] πλ daybreak, dawn.
ξημερώνομαι [kseemeronome] stay awake till morning.
ξηρά, η [kseera] dry land, mainland.
ξηραίνω [kseereno] dry, drain.
ξηραντήριο, το [kseeranteereeo] drier.
ξηρασία, η [kseeraseea] aridity || drought.
ξηροί [kseeree]: ~ καρποί πλ dried fruit and nuts.
ξι, το [ksee] the letter Ξ.
ξινίζω [kseeneezo] turn sour, get sour.
ξινίλα, η [kseeneela] bitterness, acidity, tartness, sharpness.
ξινός [kseenos] sour, acid, sharp || (για φρούτα) unripe, green.
ξιπασμένος [kseepasmenos] vain, conceited.
ξιφασκία, η [kseefaskia] fencing, swordplay.
ξιφίας, ο [kseefeeas] swordfish.
ξιφολόγχη, η [kseefolonghee] bayonet.
ξιφομαχώ [kseefomaho] fence.
ξίφος, το [kseefos] sword.
ξοδεύομαι [ksodevome] spend, incur expenses.
ξοδεύω [ksodevo] spend, use up, consume, expend.

ξόρκι, το [ksorkee] exorcism || entreaty.
ξύγκι, το [kseengee] fat, lard, grease, tallow.
ξυδάτος [kseeðatos] pickled.
ξύδι, το [kseeðee] vinegar.
ξυλάνθρακας, ο [kseelanthrakas] charcoal.
ξυλεία, η [kseeleea] timber, lumber.
ξύλινος [kseeleenos] wooden, wood.
ξύλο, το [kseelo] wood || τρώω ~ to receive a beating || έπεσε ~ there was a fight.
ξυλοκάρβουνο, το [kseelokarvouno] charcoal.
ξυλοκόπος, ο [kseelokopos] woodcutter, lumberjack.
ξυλοκοπώ [kseelokopo] thrash, beat soundly.
ξυλοπόδαρο, το [kseelopoðaro] stilt.
ξυλουργική, η [kseelouryeekee] joinery, carpentry.
ξυλουργός, ο [kseelourgos] joiner, carpenter.
ξυλοφορτώνω [kseelofortono] thrash, leather, lick.
ξύνομαι [kseenome] scratch (o.s.).
ξύνω [kseeno] scratch, scrape || (μολύβι) sharpen || scrape off.
ξύπνημα, το [kseepneema] awakening, waking up.
ξυπνητήρι, το [kseepneeteeree] alarm clock.
ξύπνιος [kseepneeos] wakeful, awake || (μεταφ) alert, clever, intelligent.
ξυπνώ [kseepno] wake up, rouse.
ξυπόλυτος [kseepoleetos] barefooted, shoeless.
ξυράφι, το [kseerafee] razor.
ξυραφάκι, το [kseerafakee] razor blade.
ξυρίζομαι [kseereezome] shave, get shaved, have a shave.
ξυρίζω [kseereezo] shave.
ξύρισμα, το [kseereesma] shave, shaving.
ξυριστική [kseereesteekee]: ~ μηχανή safety razor.
ξύσιμο, το [kseeseemo] scratching, scraping || rubbing, erasing || sharpening.
ξυστός [kseestos] grated, scratched.
ξύστρα, η [kseestra] grater, scraper, rasp || pencil sharpener.
ξωκκλήσι, το [ksokleesee] country chapel.
ξωτικό, το [ksoteeko] ghost, spirit, goblin.
ξώφυλλο, το [ksofeelo] book cover || (παραθύρου) outside shutter.

O, o

O [n] the.

όαση, η [oasee] oasis.

οβελίας, ο [oveleeas] lamb on the spit.

οβίδα, η [oveeδa] explosive shell.

οβολός, ο [ovolos] mite, contribution.

ογδόντα [ogδonda] eighty.

ογδοηκοστός [ogδoeekostos] eightieth.

ογδοντάρης, ο [ogδontarees] octogenarian.

όγδοος [ogδoos] eighth.

ογκόλιθος, ο [ongoleethos] block of stone.

όγκος, ο [ongos] volume, mass, bulk, lump || (ιατρ) tumour.

ογκούμαι [ongoume] swell, grow fatter || (μεταφ) increase, swell.

ογκώδης [ongoδees] voluminous, massive || (άτομο) stout, portly.

οδεύω [oδevo] walk, tramp, trudge || accompany || (προς) proceed, advance.

οδηγητής, ο [oδeeyeetees] guide.

οδηγία, η [oδeeyeea] direction, guidance || instruction, directions, orders.

οδηγός, ο [oδeegos] guide, conductor || (αυτοκινήτου) driver, chauffeur.

οδηγώ [oδeego] guide, lead || (αυτοκίνητο κτλ) drive || show how to, instruct.

οδοιπορία, η [oδeeporeea] walk, journey || march.

οδοιπορικά, τα [oδeeporeeka] πλ: ~ έξοδα travelling expenses.

οδοιπόρος, ο, η [oδeeporos] traveller, voyager.

οδοιπορώ [oδeeporo] walk, tramp || march || travel.

οδοκαθαριστής, ο [oδokathareestees] street sweeper.

οδοντιατρείο, το [oδonteeatreeo] dentist's surgery, dental clinic.

οδοντιατρική, η [oδonteeatreekee] dentistry.

οδοντίατρος, ο, η [oδonteeatros] dentist.

οδοντόβουρτσα, η [oδontovourtsa] toothbrush.

οδοντογλυφίδα, η [oδontogleefeeδa] toothpick.

οδοντόπαστα, η [oδontopasta] dentifrice, toothpaste.

οδοντοστοιχία, η [oδontosteeheea] (set of) false teeth.

οδοντωτός [oδontotos] toothed, jagged, cogged || ~ σιδηρόδρομος funicular railway.

οδοποιία, η [oδopieea] road construction, roadmaking.

οδός, η [oδos] street || (ευρεία) main street, thoroughfare || (εθνική) state highway || (εμπορική) trade route || καθ' οδόν on the way, along the road.

οδόστρωμα, το [oδostroma] road surface.

οδοστρωτήρας, ο [oδostroteeras] steamroller.

οδόφραγμα, το [oδofragma] barricade, roadblock, barrier.

οδύνη, η [oδeenee] pain, suffering || (ηθική) grief || affliction.

οδυνηρός [oδeeneeros] (πληγή) painful || (μέρος) sore || (θέαμα) harrowing.

οδυρμός, ο [oδeermos] lamentation, wailing.

οδύρομαι [oδeerome] lament, complain, moan.

όζον, το [ozon] ozone.

όζος, ο [ozos] knot || (των δακτύλων) knuckles.

οζώδης [ozoδees] knotty, gnarled.

οθόνη, η [othonee] screen.

Οθωμανός, ο [othomanos] Ottoman.

οίδημα, το [eeδeema] swelling.

οικειοθελώς [eekeeothelos] (υπακούω) voluntarily || (κάνω κάτι) purposely, wilfully.

οικειοποίηση, η [eekeeopieesee] appropriation.

οικειοποιούμαι [eekeeopeeoume] appropriate to o.s., usurp.

οικείος [eekeeos] intimate, familiar || sociable, affable || οι οικείοι relatives, close relations.

οικειότητα, η [eekeeoteeta] familiarity, closeness.

οίκημα, το [eekeema] dwelling, lodging, habitation.

οικία, η [eekeea] house, home.

οικιακός [eekeeakos] domestic, home || (ζώο) domesticated.

οικίζω [eekeezo] inhabit, colonize, settle.

οικισμός, ο [eekeesmos] settling, colonizing.

οικογένεια, η [eekoyeneea] family.

οικογενειακός [eekoyeneeakos] of the family.

οικογενειακώς [eekoyeneeakos] with the entire family.

οικοδέσποινα, η [eekoδespeena] lady of the house, hostess.

οικοδεσπότης, ο [eekoδespotees] master of the house, host.

οικοδομή, η [eekoδomee] construction, act of building || building under construction.

οικοδόμημα, το [eekoδomeema] building, structure.

οικοδόμηση, η [eekoδomeesee] construction, building, erection.

οικοδομική, η [eekoδomeekee] building.

οικοδομικός [eekoδomeekos] constructive.

οικοδομώ [eekoδomo] build, construct, raise.

οικοκυρά [eekokeera] βλ
νοικοκυρά.

οικοκύρης [eekokeerees] βλ
νοικοκύρης.

οίκον [eekon]: κατ' ~ at home.

οικονομία, η [eekonomeea]
economy, husbandry, thrift || saving.

οικονομικά, τα [eekonomeeka] πλ
finances || (επιρ) reasonably, cheaply.

οικονομικός [eekonomeekos]
economic, financial || (φθηνά)
reasonable, cheap.

οικονόμος, ο, η [eekonomos]
steward, stewardess || (μεταφ) thrifty
person.

οικονομώ [eekonomo] save,
economize || find, get hold of || τα ~
make ends meet, make money.

οικόπεδο, το [eekopeðo] building
site, plot.

οίκος, ο [eekos] house || business
house.

οικοτροφείο, το [eekotrofeeo]
boarding school.

οικότροφος, ο, η [eekotrofos]
boarder.

οικουμένη, η [eekoumenee] world,
universe.

οικουμενικός [eekoumeneekos]
ecumenical.

οικτείρω [eekteero] feel compassion
for, pity || despise, scorn.

οίκτος, ο [eektos] compassion, pity ||
contempt, scorn.

οικτρός [eektros] deplorable ||
wretched, miserable.

οινόπνευμα, το [eenopnevma]
alcohol || οινοπνευματώδης
alcoholic.

οίνος, ο [eenos] wine.

οιοσδήποτε [eeosðeepote] any(body)
|| any kind of, whoever, whichever.

οισοφάγος, ο [eesofagos]
oesophagus.

οίστρος, ο [eestros] gadfly || (μεταφ)
inspiration, goading.

οιωνός, ο [eeonos] omen, presage,
portent.

οκνηρός [okneeros] lazy, idle,
sluggish.

οκνός [oknos] nonchalant, languid,
slack.

οκρίβαντας, ο [okreevantas] easel.

οκτάγωνος [oktagonos] octagonal.

οκτακόσιοι [oktakosiee] eight
hundred.

οκταπόδι, το [oktapoðee] octopus.

οκτώ [octo] eight.

Οκτώβριος, ο [oktovreeos] October.

όλα, τα [ola] πλ everything || ~ κι ~
anything else but.

ολάκερος [olakeros] whole, entire,
total, complete.

ολέθριος [olethreeos] ominous,
disastrous, destructive.

όλεθρος, ο [olethros] calamity,
destruction, ruin.

ολημερίς [oleemerees] all day long.

ολιγάριθμος [oleegareethmos] few in
number, a few.

ολιγαρκής [oleegarkees] temperate,
frugal, moderate.

ολιγαρχία, η [oleegarheea] oligarchy.

ολιγόλογος [oleegologos] concise,
succinct || taciturn.

ολίγο [oleego] (a) little.

ολίγος [oleegos] short, a little, a few ||
ολίγον κατ' ολίγον gradually ||
παρ' ολίγο να nearly, almost.

ολιγοστεύω [oleegostevo] diminish,
decrease, lessen.

ολιγοστός [oleegostos] scarcely
enough, scanty, inconsiderable.

ολιγοψυχία, η [oleegopseeheea]
timidity.

ολιγωρία, η [oleegoreea] negligence,
neglect, indifference.

ολικός [oleekos] total, whole,
complete.

ολικώς [oleekos] totally, utterly.

ολισθαίνω [oleestheno] slip, slide ||
(μεταφ) lapse into, slip into.

ολίσθημα, το [oleestheema]
slip(ping), slide || mistake, fault.

ολισθηρός [oleestheeros] slippery,
greasy.

ολκή, η [olkee] attraction, pull, weight
|| calibre, bore.

Ολλανδέζος, ο [olanðezos]
Dutchman.

Ολλανδία, η [olanðeea] Holland.

ολλανδικός [olanðeekos] Dutch.

όλμος, ο [olmos] mortar.

όλο [olo] all || ~ και περισσότερο
more and more, always.

ολογράφως [olografos] written in full.

ολόγυρα [oloyeera] all round, in a
circle.

ολοένα [oloena] incessantly,
constantly.

ολοήμερος [oloeemeros] lasting a
whole day.

ολοίδιος [oloeeðeeos] the spitting
image.

ολοίσιος [oloeeseeos] direct, straight ||
upright.

ολοκαύτωμα, το [olokavtoma]
holocaust || sacrifice.

ολόκληρος [olokleeros] entire, whole,
full, complete.

ολοκληρώνω [olokleerono] complete,
finish || (μαθημ) integrate.

ολοκληρωτικός [olokleeroteekos]
full, entire, complete || totalitarian ||
(μαθημ) integral.

ολόμαλλος [olomalos] all wool, pure
wool.

ολομέλεια, η [olomeleea] total
membership, all members present.

ολομερής [olomerees] entire, whole, complete.

ολομόναχος [olomonahos] quite alone.

ολονυχτίς [oloneehtees] the whole night long.

ολόρθος [olorthos] straight, upright, standing.

όλος [olos] all, whole || όλοι everyone, everybody || όλοι μας all of us, altogether || όλα όλα altogether, the total.

ολοσχερής [olosherees] utter, complete, full, entire.

ολοταχώς [olotahos] at full speed, at top speed.

ολότελα [olotela] entirely, altogether, completely.

ολοφάνερος [olofaneros] obvious, plain, clear.

ολόχαρος [oloharos] joyful, happy.

ολόχρυσος [olohreesos] all gold, solid gold.

ολόψυχος [olopseehos] wholeheartedly.

Ολυμπιακός [oleembeeakos] Olympic.

όλως [olos] wholly, altogether, totally || ~ διόλου completely, wholly || ~ υμέτερος yours truly.

ομάδα, η [omaða] group, company, band, gang || (αθλητική) team.

ομαδικός [omaðeekos] collective.

ομαδικώς [omaðeekos] in a body, collectively.

ομαλός [omalos] even || level || smooth, regular || (βίος) uneventful || flat.

ομαλότητα, η [omaloteeta] regularity, smoothness, evenness.

ομελέτα, η [omeleta] omelette.

ομήγυρη, η [omeeyeeree] party, meeting, assembly, circle.

όμηρος, ο [omeeros] hostage.

όμικρο, το [omeekro] the letter O.

ομιλητής, ο [omeeleetees] speaker, lecturer.

ομιλητικός [omeeleeteekos] sociable, affable.

ομιλία, η [omeeleea] talk, conversation || speech, lecture.

όμιλος, ο [omeelos] company, group, club.

ομιλώ [omeelo] speak, talk.

ομίχλη, η [omeehlee] fog, mist.

ομιχλώδης [omeehloðees] foggy, misty.

ομοβροντία, η [omovronteea] salvo, volley.

ομογένεια, η [omoyeneea] homogeneity || fellow Greeks.

ομογενής [omoyenees] similar || of the same race || expatriate Greek.

ομοεθνής [omoethnees] of the same nation, fellow (countryman).

ομοειδής [omoeeðees] of the same kind || uniform, similar.

ομόθρησκος [omothreeskos] of the same religion.

ομόθυμος [omotheemos] unanimous.

ομοιάζω [omeeazo] resemble, look like || be like.

ομοιογενής [omeeoyenees] homogeneous || uniform.

ομοιοκαταληξία, η [omeeokataleekseea] rhyme, rime.

ομοιόμορφος [omeeomorfos] uniform, unvarying.

ομοιοπαθής [omeeopathees] fellow (sufferer), in the same boat.

όμοιος [omeeos] similar, (a)like, same, in conformity with.

ομοιότητα, η [omeeoteeta] resemblance, similarity, likeness.

ομοίωμα, το [omeeoma] likeness, image || effigy.

ομοιωματικά, τα [omeeomateeka] πλ ditto marks.

ομόκεντρος [omokentros] concentric.

ομολογία, η [omoloyeea] confession, avowal, acknowledgement, admission || (οικον) bond, share.

ομόλογο, το [omologo] bond, promissory note, obligation.

ομολογουμένως [omologoumenos] avowedly, admittedly.

ομολογώ [omologo] acknowledge, confess, admit.

ομόνοια, η [omoneea] concord, agreement, accord, peace.

ομόρρυθμος [omoreethmos]: ~ εταιρεία partnership (in business).

ομορφαίνω [omorfeno] beautify || become beautiful.

ομορφιά, η [omorfia] beauty, handsomeness.

όμορφος [omorfos] handsome, beautiful, nice.

ομοσπονδία, η [omosponðeea] federation, confederacy.

ομότιμος [omoteemos]: ~ καθηγητής professor emeritus.

ομόφρονας [omofronas] having the same ideas, thinking alike.

ομοφυλοφιλία, η [omofeelofeeleea] homosexuality.

ομοφωνία, η [omofoneea] unanimity.

ομόφωνος [omofonos] unanimous.

ομπρέλλα, η [ombrella] umbrella.

ομφαλός, ο [omfalos] navel || (μεταφ) centre.

ομώνυμος [omoneemos] having the same name.

όμως [omos] yet, nevertheless, but, however.

ον, το [on] creature, being.

ονειρεύομαι [oneerevome] dream, have visions.

ονειροκρίτης, ο [oneerokreetees] dream interpreter.

όνειρο, το [oneero] dream || vision, imagination.

ονειροπολώ [oneeropolo] daydream || dream (of), build castles in the air.

ονειρώδης [oneerodees] dreamlike, fantastic || grand.

όνομα, το [onoma] name || (γραμμ) noun || fame, reputation || **βγάζω ~** gain renown, become famous || **~ και πράμα** in every sense || **ονόματι** by name of.

ονομάζω [onomazo] name, call || appoint.

ονομασία, η [onomaseea] name, appellation || designation, appointment.

ονομαστική, η [onomasteekee] (γραμμ) nominative (case) || **~ εορτή** name day.

ονομαστικός [onomasteekos] nominal.

ονομαστός [onomastos] famous, famed, celebrated.

ονοματεπώνυμο, το [onomateponeemo] name and surname.

ονοματολογία, η [onomatoloyeea] nomenclature, terminology.

οντότητα, η [ontoteeta] entity, being || personality.

όντως [ontos] really, truly, in truth.

οξεία, η [okseea] (γραμμ) acute accent.

οξείδιο, το [okseedeeo] oxide.

οξείδωση, η [okseedosee] oxidation || corrosion, rusting.

οξικός [okseekos] acetic.

όξινος [okseenos] sour, bitter, acid.

οξύ, το [oksee] acid.

οξυά, η [oksia] beech tree || beech.

οξυγονοκόλληση, η [okseegonokoleesee] oxyacetylene welding.

οξυγόνο, το [okseegono] oxygen.

οξυδέρκεια, η [okseederkeea] perspicacity, acumen || (μεταφ) discernment.

οξύθυμος [okseetheemos] irritable, touchy.

οξύνους [okseenous] sagacious, acute, keen, clever.

οξύνω [okseeno] sharpen, whet || (το νου) sharpen || (αισθήματα) stir up, arouse, provoke.

οξύς [oksees] sharp, pointed || piercing, shrill || (γεύση) sour, strong.

οξύτητα, η [okseeteeta] sharpness || keenness, acuteness.

οξύφωνος, ο [okseefonos] (μουσ) tenor.

όξω [okso] βλ **έξω**.

οπαδός, ο, η [opados] adherent, partisan, supporter.

όπερα, η [opera] opera.

οπή, η [opee] opening, aperture, hole, gap.

όπιο, το [opeeo] opium.

όπισθεν [opeesthen] behind, in the rear || **κάνω ~** go backwards, put in reverse.

οπίσθιος [opeestheeos] hind, posterior, back.

οπισθογραφώ [opeesthografo] endorse (a cheque).

οπισθοδρομικός [opeesthodromeekos] retrogressive || (στις απόψεις) reactionary.

οπισθοφυλακή, η [opeesthofeelakee] rearguard.

οπισθοχώρηση, η [opeesthohoreesee] retreat, withdrawal.

οπίσω [opeeso] behind, back || again.

όπλα, τα [opla] βλ arms.

οπλή, η [oplee] hoof.

οπλίζω [opleezo] arm || (μεταφ) reinforce, strengthen.

οπλισμός, ο [opleesmos] armament, equipment || (καλωδίου) sheathing.

οπλιταγωγό, το [opleetagogo] troopship.

οπλίτης, ο [opleetees] soldier.

όπλο, το [oplo] arm, weapon || rifle || (αμύνης) branch of army.

οπλοπολυβόλο, το [oplopoleevolo] light machine gun.

οπλοστάσιο, το [oplostaseeo] arsenal, armoury.

οπλοφορία, η [oploforeea] carrying of arms.

όποιος [opeeos] whoever, whichever || **~ κι'** whosoever, anybody.

οποίος [opeeos] of what kind || **ο ~** who, which.

οποιοσδήποτε [opeeosdeepote] whoever, whatsoever.

οπόταν [opotan] whenever, when.

όποτε [opote] whenever, at any time.

οπότε [opote] at which time, when.

όπου [opou] where, wherever.

οπουδήποτε [opoudeepote] wheresoever, wherever.

οπτασία, η [optaseea] vision, apparition.

οπτική, η [opteekee] optics.

οπτικός [opteekos] optic(al) || (ουσ) optician.

οπωρικά, τα [oporeeka] πλ fruit.

οπωροπωλείο, το [oporopoleeo] fruit market.

οπωροφόρος [oporoforos] bearing fruit, fruit-producing.

όπως [opos] as, like || **~** somehow or other, after a fashion || (συνδ) in order that, so as.

οπωσδήποτε [oposdeepote] howsoever, anyway, without fail || definitely.

όραμα, το [orama] vision ||

οραματίζομαι have visions, visualize.

όραση, n [orasee] sense of sight, vision.

ορατός [oratos] visible, perceptible.

ορατότητα, n [oratoteeta] visibility.

οργανικός [organeekos] organic.

οργανισμός, ο [organeesmos] organism || organization.

όργανο, το [organo] organ || (μουσ) instrument || implement, tool || (κατασκοπείας) agent.

οργανώνω [organono] organize, constitute, form.

οργάνωση, n [organosee] organization, arranging.

οργασμός, ο [orgasmos] orgasm, heat || (μεταφ) feverish activity.

οργή, n [oryee] anger, rage || **να πάρει n ~** damn it!, damnation!

όργια, τα [orya] πλ orgies || (μεταφ) corrupt practices || **οργιάζω** revel, debauch.

οργίζω [oryeezo] anger, enrage, irritate.

οργυιά, n [orya] fathom.

όργωμα, το [orgoma] ploughing, tilling, tillage.

οργώνω [orgono] plough, till, furrow.

ορδή, n [ordee] horde, host, rabble.

ορειβασία, n [oreevaseea] mountain climbing.

ορειβάτης, ο [oreevatees] mountain climber.

ορειβατικός [oreevateekos] of climbing, of mountaineering.

ορεινός [oreenos] mountainous, hilly || of the mountains.

ορείχαλκος, ο [oreehalkos] brass, bronze.

ορεκτικό, το [orekteeko] appetizer, titbit || drink.

ορεκτικός [orekteekos] appetizing, savoury || tempting.

όρεξη, n [oreksee] appetite || desire, liking.

ορθά [ortha] right, rightly || upright || **~ κοφτά** flatly, frankly.

ορθάνοιχτος [orthaneehtos] wide open.

όρθιος [ortheeos] on end, upright, erect, standing.

ορθογραφία, n [orthografeea] spelling, orthography || dictation.

ορθογώνιο, το [orthogoneeo] rectangle.

ορθογώνιος [orthogoneeos] right-angled || rectangular.

ορθοδοξία, n [orthoðokseea] orthodoxy.

ορθόδοξος [orthoðoksos] orthodox.

ορθολογισμός, ο [ortholoyeesmos] rationalism.

ορθοπεδική, n [orthopeðeekee] orthopaedics.

ορθοποδώ [orthopoðo] walk straight || stand on sure ground, thrive.

ορθός [orthos] light || correct || proper || upright, erect, standing.

ορθοστασία, n [orthostaseea] standing.

ορθότητα, n [orthoteeta] accuracy || soundness || aptness.

όρθρος, ο [orthros] (εκκλ) matins || dawn, daybreak.

ορθώνομαι [orthonome] rise, get up || (άλογο) rear up.

ορθώνω [orthono] raise, pull up, lift up || redress.

ορθώς [orthos] βλ **ορθά**.

οριζόντιος [oreezonteeos] horizontal, level.

ορίζω [oreezo] mark, bound, delimit || fix, settle, define || rule, control, govern.

ορίζων, ο [oreezon] horizon.

όριο, το [oreeo] boundary, limit, border || (μεταφ) scope, boundary.

ορισμένος [oreesmenos] defined, fixed || certain, special.

ορισμός, ο [oreesmos] designation, fixing || definition || order, instruction.

ορίστε [oreeste] I beg your pardon? || come in, take a seat || may I help you? || **καλώς ορίσατε** (επιφ) welcome!

οριστική, n [oreesteekee] (γραμμ) indicative (mood).

οριστικός [oreesteekos] definitive, final.

ορκίζομαι [orkeezome] swear, take the oath.

ορκίζω [orkeezo] put on oath, swear in.

όρκος, ο [orkos] oath || vow.

ορκωμοσία, n [orkomoseea] swearing (in).

ορκωτός [orkotos] sworn || **οι ορκωτοί** the jury.

ορμή, n [ormee] vehemence || impulse, impetus || passion.

ορμητήριο, το [ormeeteereeo] starting place || motive.

ορμητικός [ormeeteekos] impetuous, hot-tempered, fiery.

ορμόνη, n [ormonee] hormone.

όρμος, ο [ormos] bay, inlet.

ορμώ [ormo] dash, rush || **~μαι** be urged || come from.

όρνεο, το [orneo] bird of prey.

όρνιθα, n [orneetha] hen, chicken, fowl.

ορνιθοσκαλίσματα, τα [orneethoskaleesmata] πλ scrawl, scribble.

ορνιθοτροφείο, το [orneethotrofeeo] poultry farm.

ορνιθώνας, ο [orneethonas] chicken coop, henhouse, hen roost.

όρνιο, το [orneeo] bird of prey || (μεταφ) dullard, dolt.

οροθεσία, η [orotheseea] fixing of boundaries.

ορολογία, η [oroloyeea] terminology.

οροπέδιο, το [oropeδeeo] plateau, tableland.

όρος, το [oros] mountain.

όρος, ο [oros] term, condition, stipulation, proviso || limit, end || (επιστημονικός) term, definition.

ορρός, ο [oros] serum.

οροσειρά, η [oroseera] mountain range, mountain chain.

ορόσημο, το [oroseemo] boundary mark, boundary stone.

οροφή, η [orofee] ceiling, roof.

όροφος, ο [orofos] floor, storey.

ορτύκι, το [orteekee] quail.

όρυζα, η [oreeza] rice.

ορυκτέλαιο, το [oreekteleo] petroleum || lubricant.

ορυκτολογία, η [oreektoloyeea] mineralogy.

ορυκτό, το [oreekto] mineral, ore.

ορυκτός [oreektos] mineral, dug-up.

ορύσσω [oreeso] dig, excavate || (πηγάδι) bore, sink.

ορυχείο, το [oreeheeo] mine.

ορφανός [orfanos] orphan.

ορφανοτροφείο, το [orfanotrofeeo] orphanage.

όρχης [orhees] testicle || (λουλούδι) orchid.

ορχήστρα, η [orheestra] orchestra.

όσιος [oseeos] holy, blessed || saint.

οσμή, η [osmee] odour, smell, scent.

όσο [oso] as, as far as, as long as || ~ για as for || ~ αφορά as regards, with regard to || εφ ~ as long as, inasmuch as || ~ νάρθει until he comes || ~ νάναι nevertheless.

όσος [osos] as much as, as many as, all.

όσπριο, το [ospreeo] pulse, legume.

οστούν, το [ostoun] bone.

οστρακιά, η [ostrakia] scarlet fever.

όστρακο, το [ostrako] shell || (αρχαιολογία) potsherd.

οσφραίνομαι [osfrenome] smell, scent || (μεταφ) feel.

όσφρηση, η [osfreesee] sense of smell.

οσφύς, η [osfees] waist, loins, haunches.

όταν [otan] when, at the time when, whenever.

ότι [otee] (συνδ) that || (επιρ) as soon as || just (now).

ό, τι [otee] what(ever).

οτιδήποτε [oteeδeepote] whatsoever || anything at all.

ότου [otou] έως ~ until || μέχρις ~ until || αφ ~ since.

Ουγγαρία, η [oungareea] Hungary.

ουγγιά, η [oungia] ounce.

ουγγρικός [oungreekos] Hungarian.

Ούγγρος, ο [oungros] Hungarian.

ουδέ [ouδe] βλ ούτε.

ουδείς [ouδees] no(body), no one, none.

ουδέποτε [ouδepote] never.

ουδέτερος [ouδeteros] neither || (επίθ) neutral || (γραμμ) neuter.

ουδόλως [ouδolos] by no means, no wise, by no manner of means.

ούζο, το [ouzo] ouzo.

ουλή, η [oulee] scar.

ούλο, το [oulo] (ανατ) gum.

ούρα, τα [oura] πλ urine, piss (col).

ουρά, η [oura] tail || train of dress || queue || (φάλαγγας) rear || λεφτά με ~ loads of money.

ουραγός, ο [ouragos] person bringing up the rear, the last one.

ουρανής [ouranees] sky blue.

ουράνιο, το [ouraneeo] uranium.

ουράνιο [ouraneeo]: ~ τόξο rainbow.

ουράνιος [ouraneeos] heavenly, celestial.

ουρανίσκος, ο [ouraneeskos] palate.

ουρανοκατέβατος [ouranokatevatos] heaven-sent || (μεταφ) unexpected.

ουρανοξύστης, ο [ouranokseestees] skyscraper.

ουρανός, ο [ouranos] sky, heaven || canopy.

ουρητήριο, το [oureeteereeo] urinal, john (col).

ουρικός [oureekos] uric, urinary.

ούριος [oureeos] (άνεμος) tail, favourable, fair.

ουρλιάζω [ourleeazo] howl, roar || (από πόνο) yell, scream || (από θυμό) bellow.

ούρλιασμα, το [ourleeasma] howl(ing), bellowing, yelling.

ουρώ [ouro] urinate.

ους, το [ous] ear.

ουσία, η [ouseea] matter, substance || essence || (μεταφ) gist, main point.

ουσιαστικό, το [ouseeasteeko] (γραμμ) substantive, noun.

ουσιαστικός [ouseeasteekos] substantial, essential.

ουσιώδης [ouseeoδees] essential, vital, indispensable, capital.

ούτε [oute] not even || ~ ... ~ neither ... nor.

ουτοπία, η [outopeea] Utopia.

ούτω(ς) [outo(s)] so, such, thus || ~ ώστε so that, in order that.

ουχί [ouhee] βλ όχι.

οφειλέτης, ο [ofeeletees] debtor.

οφειλή, η [ofeelee] debt, sum due || (μεταφ) obligation, duty.

οφείλομαι [ofeelome] be due.

οφείλω [ofeelo] owe || be obliged to || ~ να πάω I should go.

όφελος, το [ofelos] profit, advantage, benefit.

οφθαλμαπάτη, η [ofthalmapatee] optical illusion.

οφθαλμίατρος, ο, η [ofthalmeeatros] eye specialist, oculist.

οφθαλμός, ο [ofthalmos] eye || (βιολ) bud.

οφθαλμοφανής [ofthalmofanees] obvious, manifest, evident.

όφις, ο [ofees] snake, serpent.

όχεντρα, η [ohentra] βλ οχιά.

οχέτευση, η [ohetevsee] drainage.

οχετός, ο [ohetos] drain, sewer || conduit, pipe.

όχημα, το [oheema] vehicle, carriage, coach.

όχθη, η [ohthee] (ποταμού) bank || (λίμνης) shore.

όχι [ohee] no || not.

οχιά, η [ohia] viper.

οχλαγωγία, η [ohlagoyeea] disturbance, riot, tumult.

οχληρός [ohleeros] tiresome, unpleasant, burdensome.

οχλοβοή, η [ohlovoee] uproar, din, hubbub.

οχλοκρατία, η [ohlokrateea] mob rule.

όχλος, ο [ohlos] populace, mob, crowd, rabble.

οχυρό, το [oheero] strong point, fort, stronghold.

οχυρώνομαι [oheeronome] (μεταφ) find an excuse, justify.

οχυρώνω [oheerono] fortify, entrench.

όψη, η [opsee] aspect, appearance, look || view, sight || countenance || face || λαμβάνω υπ ~ take into account || εξ όψεως by sight || εν όψει in view of || in view.

οψιγενής [opseeyenees] posthumous || late, belated.

όψιμος [opseemos] tardy, late, of a late season.

Π, π

παγανισμός, ο [paganeesmos] paganism.

παγερός [payeros] icy cold, freezing || (μεταφ) chilly, frigid.

παγετός, ο [payetos] frost.

παγετώδης [payetoδees] icy, icy cold, freezing.

παγετώνας, ο [payetonas] glacier.

παγίδα, η [payeeδa] trap, snare || (τάφρος) pitfall.

παγίδευμα, το [payeeδevma] ensnaring, trapping.

παγιδεύω [payeeδevo] snare, catch, entice.

πάγιος [payos] fixed, stable, firm || (καθεστώς) secure, durable || (δάνειο) consolidated loan || (πρόσοδος) steady income.

παγιώνω [payono] consolidate, make secure.

παγίως [payeeos] firmly, securely.

πάγκος, ο [pangkos] bench, seat.

παγκόσμιος [pangkosmeeos] universal, world-wide.

πάγκρεας, το [pangkreas] pancreas.

παγόβουνο, το [pagovouno] iceberg.

παγόδα, η [pagoδa] pagoda.

παγοδρομία, η [pagoδromeea] skating.

παγοθραύστης, ο [pagothravstees] icebreaker.

παγοπέδιλο, το [pagopeδeelo] iceskate.

πάγος, ο [pagos] ice, frost.

παγούρι, το [pagouree] can, tin, flask || (στρατ) canteen.

παγωμένος [pagomenos] frozen, frostbitten.

παγώνι, το [pagonee] peacock.

παγωνιά, η [pagonia] frost.

παγώνω [pagono] freeze, congeal, frost.

παγωτό, το [pagoto] ice cream.

παζαρεύω [pazarevo] haggle over, bargain for.

παζάρι, το [pazaree] market, bazaar || bargaining, haggling.

παθαίνω [patheno] undergo, suffer, be injured.

πάθημα, το [patheema] mishap, accident.

πάθηση, η [patheesee] complaint, sickness, affliction.

παθητικός [patheeteekos] passive, submissive || (γραμμ) passive (voice) || charged with passion || (οικ) debit.

παθολογία, η [patholoyeea] pathology.

παθολογικός [patholoyeekos] pathological.

παθολόγος, ο [pathologos] general practitioner.

πάθος, το [pathos] illness, passion || suffering || (έχθρα) animosity.

παιδαγωγείο, το [peδagoyeeo] children's school.

παιδαγωγία, η [peδagoyeea] education, pedagogy.

παιδαγωγικός [peδagoyeekos] educational, pedagogical.

παιδαγωγός, ο, η [peδagogos] tutor, preceptor, pedagogue.

παιδαγωγώ [peδagogo] educate, instruct, teach.

παιδάκι, το [peδakee] little child.

παιδαριώδης [peδareeoδees] puerile, childish || (εύκολο) quite simple, trivial.

παιδεία, η [peδeea] education, learning, instruction, culture.

παίδεμα, το [peδema] torture, trial, ordeal.

παιδεύομαι [peδevome] try hard, struggle.

παιδεύω [peðevo] pester, torture, torment.

παιδί, το [peðee] child, boy || chap.

παιδιαρίζω [peðeeareezo] act like a child.

παιδίατρος, ο, η [peðeeatros] paediatrician, child specialist.

παιδικός [peðeekos] child's, of children || childish || ~ **σταθμός** day nursery.

παίζω [pezo] play || (παιχνίδι) speculate, gamble || (μεταφ) swing, sway.

παίκτης, ο [pektees] player || gambler, gamester.

παινεύω [penevo] βλ **επαινώ**.

παίξιμο, το [pekseemo] playing || (με κάτι) toying with || (θεάτρου) performance || (παιχνίδι) gaming, gambling.

παίρνω [perno] receive, take hold of, get, contain || (πόλη κτλ) capture || (διά της βίας) wrench from || (υπηρέτη) hire, take on || (καφέ κτλ) take, have || (κρύο κτλ) catch, get || (σαν παράδειγμα) take, draw || (σημείωση) take (a note) || (κάτι για κάτι) take for, consider (as) || (με κάποια έννοια) understand, interpret || (χρήματα) be paid, draw, receive || (για γυναίκα) marry, wed || **τον** ~ fall asleep || ~ **από πίσω** follow closely.

παιχνίδι, το [pehneeðee] play, game, sport || (για παιδιά) toy, plaything.

παιχνιδιάρης [pehneeðeearees] playful, gay, mirthful.

πακετάρω [paketaro] pack, box.

πακέτο, το [paketo] pack, packet, parcel, box, bundle.

παλαβομάρα, η [palavomara] madness, lunacy, foolish act.

παλαβός [palavos] mad, insane, stupid || (παράτολμος) foolhardy.

παλαίμαχος [palemahos] veteran.

παλαιογραφία, η [paleografeea] pal(a)eography.

παλαιοπωλείο, το [paleopoleeo] secondhand shop, antique shop.

παλαιοπώλης, ο [paleopolees] secondhand dealer.

παλαιός [paleos] old || (μνημείο κτλ) ancient, old || (άλλοτε) former.

παλαιστής, ο [palestees] wrestler.

παλαίστρα, η [palestra] arena, ring.

παλαιώνω [paleono] wear out, become antiquated.

παλαμάκια, τα [palamakeea] πλ clapping, applause.

παλαμάρι, το [palamaree] (ναυτ) cable, mooring line.

παλάμη, η [palamee] palm || (μέτρο) span.

παλάτι, το [palatee] palace || mansion.

παλεύω [palevo] wrestle, struggle, fight.

πάλη, η [palee] wrestling || (μεταφ) struggle, strife, contest.

παλιανθρωπιά, η [palianthropia] villainy, meanness, roguery.

παλιάνθρωπος, ο [palianthropos] rogue, rascal, scamp.

παλιάτσος, ο [paliatsos] clown, buffoon.

πάλι [palee] again, once more, over again.

παλινδρομικός [paleenðromeekos] alternating, reciprocating, recoiling.

παλινόρθωση, η [paleenorthosee] restoration, re-establishment.

παλιόπαιδο, το [paliopeðo] bad boy, young scamp.

παλίρροια, η [paleereea] tide, floodtide.

παλληκαράς, ο [paleekaras] bully.

παλληκάρι, το [paleekaree] young man, brave person || (εργένης) bachelor.

παλληκαρίσια [paleekareeseea] boldly, bravely.

πάλλω [palo] throb, beat, palpitate || (ηλεκτ) vibrate.

παλμός, ο [palmos] oscillation, vibration || palpitation, throbbing || (ενθουσιασμού) feeling, eagerness.

παλούκι, το [paloukee] stake, pole || (μεταφ) difficulty.

παλτό, το [palto] overcoat.

παμπάλαιος [pampaleos] ancient || out-of-date.

πάμπλουτος [pamploutos] extremely wealthy.

παμπόνηρος [pamponeeros] very cunning, very sly.

πάμπτωχος [pamptohos] very poor, very needy.

πάμφθηνος [pamftheenos] very cheap, extremely cheap.

παμψηφεί [pampseefee] unanimously.

παν, το [pan] the whole world || (το κεφαλαιώδες) essentials, everything.

πανάγαθος [panagathos] merciful || extremely virtuous.

Παναγία, η [panayeea] the Virgin Mary.

πανάδα, η [panaða] brown patch, freckle.

πανάθλιος [panathleeos] wretched, miserable.

πανάκεια, η [panakeea] panacea.

πανάρχαιος [panarheos] very ancient.

πανδαιμόνιο, το [panðemoneeo] pandemonium.

πάνδεινος [panðeenos] disastrous, most terrible.

πανδοχείο, το [panðoheeo] inn.

πανδρειά, η [panðria] marriage, matrimony.

πανδρεύω [panðrevo] marry.

πανελλήνιος [paneleeneeos] panhellenic.

πανεπιστημιακός

[panepeesteemeeakos] of the university.

πανεπιστήμιο, το
[panepeesteemeeo] university.

πανέρι, το [paneree] wide basket.

πανευτυχής [paneftechees] very happy.

πανηγυρίζω [paneeyeereezo] celebrate, fête.

πανηγυρικός [paneeyeereekos] festive || (ουσ) oration, panegyric.

πανηγύρι, το [paneeyeeree] festival, festivity || (εμπορικό) fair.

πανηγυρισμός, ο [paneeyeereesmos] celebration.

πάνθηρας, ο [pantheeras] panther.

πανί, το [panee] cloth, linen || (ναυτ) sail.

πανίδα, η [paneeδa] fauna.

πανικόβλητος [paneekovleetos] panic-stricken.

πανικός, ο [paneekos] panic.

πανίσχυρος [paneesheeros] all-powerful.

πάνινος [paneenos] of cloth, of linen, of cotton.

πανόμοιος [panomeeos] similar, alike.

πανομοιότυπο, το [panomeeoteepo] facsimile.

πανοπλία, η [panopleea] arms, armour.

πανόραμα, το [panorama] panorama.

πανούκλα, η [panoukla] plague, pestilence.

πανουργία, η [panouryeea] ruse, trick, cunning.

πανούργος [panourgos] malicious, tricky, wily, cunning.

πανσέληνος, η [panseleenos] full moon.

πανσές, ο [panses] pansy.

πάντα [panta] forever, always || anyway, in any case.

πανταλόνι, το [pantalonee] trousers || pants, knickers.

πανταχού [pantahoo] everywhere.

παντελής [pantelees] complete, absolute, entire.

παντελώς [pantelos] utterly, absolutely, totally.

παντζάρι, το [pandzaree] beetroot.

παντιέρα, η [pantiera] banner, flag.

παντοδύναμος [pantoδeenamos] omnipotent, all-powerful.

παντοειδώς [pantoeeδos] in every way.

παντοιοτρόπως [panteeotropos] in every way, by every means.

Παντοκράτορας, ο [pantokratoras] the Almighty.

παντομίμα, η [pantomeema] pantomime.

παντοπωλείο, το [pantopoleeo] grocer's shop || grocery (US).

παντοπώλης, ο [pantopolees] grocer.

πάντοτε [pantote] always, at all times, forever.

παντοτεινά [pantoteena] perpetually, everlastingly.

παντού [pantou] everywhere.

παντούφλα, η [pantoufla] slipper.

παντρειά, η [pantria] βλ **πανδρειά**.

παντρεύω [pantrevo] βλ **πανδρεύω**.

πάντως [pantos] anyhow, in any case, at any rate.

πανωλεθρία, η [panolethreea] heavy loss, total ruin.

πανώλη, η [panolee] plague, pestilence.

πανωφόρι, το [panoforee] overcoat.

παξιμάδι, το [pakseemaδee] rusk || (για βίδα) nut (of screw).

παπαδιά, η [papaδia] priest's wife.

παπάκι, το [papakee] duckling.

παπαρούνα, η [paparouna] poppy.

Πάπας, ο [papas] Pope.

παπάς, ο [papas] priest.

παπί, το [papee] young duck || **γίνομαι ~** get wet to the skin.

πάπια, η [papeea] duck || bedpan || **κάνω την ~** to act the innocent.

πάπλωμα, το [paploma] cotton quilt.

παπουτσάδικο, το [papoutsaδeeko] shoemaker's shop.

παπουτσής, ο [papoutsees] shoemaker, bootmaker.

παπούτσι, το [papoutsee] shoe.

παππούς, ο [papoos] grandfather.

παρά [para] than || but || (προθ) near, close, by || (προσθήκη) in spite of, against my will || (αντίθεση) against, contrary to || (αφαίρεση) by, almost, nearly.

παραβαίνω [paraveno] break, violate, infringe.

παραβάλλω [paravalo] compare.

παραβάν, το [paravan] (folding) screen.

παραβαρύνω [paravareeno] overload, overburden || become very heavy.

παράβαση, η [paravasee] violation, transgression, breach.

παραβάτης, ο [paravatees] violator, transgressor.

παραβιάζω [paraveeazo] (πόρτα κτλ) force entry, break open || (νόμο) violate, infringe.

παραβλέπω [paravlepo] neglect, omit || turn a blind eye (to), ignore.

παραβολή, η [paravolee] comparison, collation || (εκκλ) parable || (μαθημ) parabola.

παράβολο, το [paravolo] fee, deposit.

παραγάδι, το [paragaδee] large fishing net.

παραγγελία, η [parangeleea]

command, commission, order ||
(μήνυμα) message || επί ~ made to
order.

παραγγέλω [parangelo] order,
command || inform.

παραγεμίζω [parayemeezo] fill up ||
become too full || (μαγειρική) stuff ||
cram.

παραγίνομαι [parayeenome] grow
too much || go too far || get overripe || ~
χοντρός grow too fat.

παράγκα, η [paranga] wooden hut,
shack.

παραγκωνίζω [parangoneezo] elbow,
thrust aside.

παραγνωρίζω [paragnoreezo] ignore
|| misinterpret || mistake identity of.

παράγομαι [paragome] be derived
from.

παράγοντας, ο [paragontas] βλ
παράγων.

παράγραφος, ο [paragrafos]
paragraph.

παράγω [parago] produce, bear ||
derive.

παραγωγή, η [parayoyee] production
|| output, generation || (γραμμ)
derivation.

παραγωγικός [parayoyeekos]
productive.

παραγωγός, ο [parayogos] producer,
grower.

παράγων, ο [paragon] agent, factor ||
(μαθημ) factor.

παράδειγμα, το [paraδeegma]
example || **παραδείγματος χάρη**
for example, for instance.

παραδειγματίζω [paraδeegmateezo]
set an example, exemplify.

παράδεισος, ο [paraδeesos] paradise.

παραδεκτός [paraδektos] admitted,
accepted || acceptable, admissible.

παραδέχομαι [paraδehome] admit,
acknowledge, confess, allow.

παραδίδομαι [paraδeeδome]
surrender, submit, yield.

παραδίδω [paraδeeδo] hand over ||
surrender || (μάθημα) teach, give
lessons.

παράδοξος [paraδoksos] peculiar,
odd, singular || unusual.

παραδόπιστος [paraδopeestos]
greedy, extremely fond of money.

παράδοση, η [paraδosee] delivery,
surrender || (της χώρας) tradition ||
(μαθήματος) teaching.

παραδουλεύτρα, η [paraδoulevtra]
charwoman.

παραδρομή, η [paraδromee]
carelessness, oversight.

παραείμαι [paraeeme] be beyond
measure, be too much.

παραζάλη, η [parazalee] confusion,
agitation, turmoil.

παραθαλάσσιος [parathalaseeos] by
the sea, coastal.

παραθερίζω [parathereezo] spend the
summer.

παραθεριστής, ο [parathereestees]
summer holidaymaker.

παραθέτω [paratheto] contrast,
compare || (αναφέρω) cite, quote.

παράθυρο, το [paratheero] window.

παραθυρόφυλλο, το
[paratheerofeelo] shutter.

παραίσθηση, η [parestheesee]
hallucination, illusion.

παραίτηση, η [pareteesee]
resignation, renunciation || abdication.

παραιτούμαι [paretoume] resign, give
up || (αποφεύγω) avoid.

παρατώ [parato] give up, leave,
desert.

παράκαιρος [parakeros]
unseasonable, inopportune, untimely.

παρακάλια, τα [parakaleea] πλ
supplications, pleading.

παρακαλώ [parakalo] ask, beg,
entreat || ~! don't mention it!, please!, a
pleasure!

παρακάμπτω [parakampto] get
round, surpass || (ένα θέμα) evade.

παρακάνω [parakano] exaggerate, go
too far.

παρακαταθήκη, η
[parakatatheekee] consignment,
deposit || stock || provisions ||
(παράδοση) heritage.

παρακάτω [parakato] lower down || at
a lower price.

παρακείμενος [parakeemenos]
adjoining, adjacent || ο ~ (γραμμ)
perfect tense.

παρακινώ [parakeeno] exhort, urge ||
instigate.

παρακλάδι, το [parakladee] shoot,
bough || (ποταμού) branch.

παράκληση, η [parakleesee] request,
plea || (εκκλ) prayer.

παρακμή, η [parakmee] decay,
decline.

παρακοή, η [parakoee] disobedience,
insubordination.

παρακολουθώ [parakoloutho] follow,
come behind || watch || go after || (την
έννοια) understand.

παρακούω [parakouo] hear wrongly ||
(απειθαρχώ) disobey.

παρακρατώ [parakrato] retain || keep
back || (για χρόνο) last too long.

παράκτιος [parakteeos] coastal,
inshore.

παραλαβή, η [paralavee] receipt,
receiving, delivery.

παραλαμβάνω [paralamvano]
receive, take delivery of || take
possession of.

παραλείπω [paraleepo] leave out,
miss, neglect, omit.

παράλειψη, η [paraleepsee] omission, neglect(ing).

παραλέω [paraleo] exaggerate, overcolour.

παραλήπτης, ο [paraleeptees] payee, addressee, consignee.

παραλήρημα, το [paraleereema] delirium, frenzy.

παραλία, η [paraleea] seashore, shore, coast, beach || **παραλιακός** of the seashore, of the coast.

παραλλαγή, η [paralayee] change, variation || (αστρον) deviation.

παράλληλος [paraleelos] parallel.

παραλογίζομαι [paraloyeezome] talk irrationally, rave.

παράλογος [paralogos] illogical, absurd, foolish.

παράλυση, η [paraleesee] paralysis || helplessness.

παράλυτος [paraleetos] paralytic, stiff, crippled || (ιατρ) paralyzed.

παραλύω [paraleeo] make loose, make shaky || slacken, relax || (ιατρ) paralyze.

παραμάνα, η [paramana] nurse, nanny || (καρφίτσα) safety pin.

παραμελώ [paramelo] neglect, leave undone, disregard.

παραμένω [parameno] stay by || remain, continue to exist || sojourn.

παράμερα [paramera] out of the way, apart.

παραμερίζω [paramereezo] set aside || get out of the way || fend off.

παραμιλώ [parameelo] speak too much || rave.

παραμονεύω [paramonevo] watch for, waylay.

παραμονή, η [paramonee] stay || eve.

παραμορφώνω [paramorfono] deform, disfigure, twist.

παραμύθι, το [parameethee] fable, story, fairy tale.

παρανόηση, η [paranoeesee] misunderstanding.

παρανομία, η [paranomeea] illegality || breach of the law.

παράνομος [paranomos] illegal, unlawful.

παρανομώ [paranomo] transgress a law.

παρανοώ [paranoo] misunderstand.

παρανύμφος, η [paraneemfos] bridesmaid.

παρανυχίδα, η [paraneeheeða] hangnail.

παράξενα [paraksena] oddly, strangely.

παραξενεύομαι [paraksenevome] be astonished, be amazed (at).

παραξενιά, η [parakseneea] caprice, fancy, whim.

παράξενος [paraksenos] peculiar, singular, odd.

παραξηλώνω [parakseelono] unsew, unstitch || **το ~** I go too far, I exaggerate.

παραπανήσιος [parapaneeseeos] superfluous, to spare || (τιμή) excess, overly much.

παραπάνω [parapano] higher up || (επιπρόσθετα) in addition || **με το ~** enough and to spare || **~ από** over, more than, greater than.

παραπάτημα, το [parapateema] false step || (μεταφ) misconduct.

παραπατώ [parapato] slip, stumble || stagger.

παραπέμπω [parapembo] refer to || send, hand over.

παραπέρα [parapera] further on, over there.

παραπεταμένος [parapetamenos] thrown away || (μεταφ) disdained, scorned.

παραπέτασμα, το [parapetasma] curtain || (πολιτ) Iron Curtain.

παραπέτο, το [parapeto] parapet, breastwork.

παράπηγμα, το [parapeegma] wooden hut, shack, shanty.

παραπλανώ [paraplano] seduce, mislead, lead astray.

παραπλεύρως [paraplevros] next door || next to, beside.

παραπλήσιος [parapleeseeos] next to, nearby || (όμοιος) very like, similar.

παραποιώ [parapeeo] counterfeit || forge, tamper with.

παραπομπή, η [parapombee] referring || (σε βιβλίο) reference, footnote.

παραπονετικός [paraponeteekos] doleful, whining.

παραπονιάρης [paraponeearees] grumbling, grousing.

παραπονιέμαι [paraponieme] complain, grumble.

παράπονο, το [parapono] complaint, grievance.

παράπτωμα, το [paraptoma] fault, mistake || breach.

παράρτημα, το [pararteema] annexe, supplement || outbuilding || (τράπεζας) branch || (εφημερίδας) special edition, extra.

παράς, ο [paras] money, cash.

παράσημο, το [paraseemo] decoration, medal, order, insignia.

παρασημοφορώ [paraseemoforo] decorate, invest with an order.

παράσιτα, τα [paraseeta] πλ atmospherics || parasites.

παράσιτος, ο [paraseetos] sponger, hanger-on, parasite.

παρασιωπώ [paraseeopo] pass over in silence.

παρασκευάζω [paraskevazo] prepare, get ready, arrange.

παρασκεύασμα, το [paraskevasma] substance prepared, preparation.

παρασκευή, η [paraskevee] preparation || (ημέρα) Friday.

παρασκήνια, τα [paraskeeneea] πλ (θέατρο)wings || **παρασκνιακός** behind the scenes.

παράσταση, η [parastasee] representation, portrayal || (παρουσία) presence, demeanour || (θεάτρου) show, performance || (νομ) appearance.

παραστατικός [parastateekos] expressive, descriptive, vivid.

παραστέκω [parasteko] assist, help, support.

παράστημα, το [parasteema] carriage, bearing, figure.

παραστράτημα, το [parastrateema] straying, misconduct.

παρασύνθημα, το [paraseentheema] password.

παρασύρω [paraseero] drag along, sweep away || run over || (σε σφάλμα) lead astray, carry away.

παράταξη, η [parataksee] array, parade, order || pomp, ceremony || (πολιτ) political party.

παράταση, η [paratasee] extension, protraction || renewal.

παρατάσσω [parataso] arrange, set in order, line up.

παρατατικός, ο [paratateekos] (γραμμ) imperfect tense.

παρατείνω [parateeno] prolong, lengthen || extend, defer.

παρατήρηση, η [parateereesee] observation, remark || (κουβέντα) comment || reproach, reprimand.

παρατηρητής, ο [parateereetees] observer, watcher, spotter.

παρατηρητικός [parateereeteekos] observing, keen || reproachful.

παρατηρώ [parateero] observe, perceive, notice || (επιτιμώ) reproach, blame.

παράτολμος [paratolmos] reckless, audacious, bold.

παρατραβώ [paratravo] draw out, prolong || last too long || (μεταφ) go too far.

παρατράγουδο, το [paratragoudo] untoward incident.

παρατσούκλι, το [paratsouklee] nickname.

παρατυπία, η [parateepeea] breach of formalities || irregularity.

πάραυτα [paravta] immediately, at once, forthwith.

παραφέρνω [paraferno] carry more than necessary || resemble.

παραφέρομαι [paraferome] flare up, lose one's temper.

παραφθορά, η [parafthora] alteration, corruption, change.

παραφορά, η [parafora] frenzy, outburst || rage.

παράφορος [paraforos] hotheaded, hasty, furious.

παραφορτώνω [parafortono] overload, overburden || (μεταφ) drive too hard.

παράφραση, η [parafrasee] paraphrase, free translation.

παραφρονώ [parafrono] become insane, go mad.

παραφροσύνη, η [parafroseenee] madness, insanity, foolish act.

παραφυάδα, η [parafiaða] sprout, shoot.

παραφυλάω [parafeelao] lie in wait for || be on the watch for.

παραφωνία, η [parafoneea] dissonance || (μεταφ) discord, disagreement.

παραχαράκτης, ο [paraharaktees] forger, counterfeiter.

παραχωρώ [parahoro] grant, yield, concede || (παραδίδω) surrender, resign.

παρδαλός [parðalos] spotted || multicoloured, gaudy.

παρέα, η [parea] company, set, party || **κάνω ~ με** keep company with.

παρειά, η [paria] cheek || (μεταφ) wall.

παρείσακτος [pareesaktos] intrusive, intruding.

παρέκβαση, η [parekvasee] digression.

παρέκει [parekee] further on, a little further.

παρεκκλήσι, το [parekleesee] chapel.

παρεκκλίνω [parekleeno] deviate from, turn aside from || diverge.

παρεκτείνω [parekteeno] prolong, extend.

παρεκτός [parektos] except, save, besides.

παρεκτροπή, η [parektropee] aberration, deviation || (ηθική) misconduct, dissoluteness.

παρέλαση, η [parelasee] parade, march-past, procession.

παρελαύνω [parelavno] march past, parade.

παρέλευση, η [parelevsee] passage of time, passing.

παρελθόν, το [parelthon] the past.

παρεμβαίνω [paremveno] interfere, intervene, meddle with.

παρεμβάλλω [paremvalo] insert, interpose.

παρέμβαση, η [paremvasee] intervention, mediation.

παρεμβολή, η [paremvolee] insertion.

παρεμπιπτόντως [parempeeptontos] by the way.

παρεμφερής [paremferees] similar, of the same nature, resembling.

παρενέργεια, η [parenerya] side effect.

παρένθεση, η [parenthesee] insertion || (γραμμ) parenthesis.

παρενοχλώ [parenohlo] inconvenience, trouble, harass.

παρεξήγηση, η [parekseeyeesee] misunderstanding.

παρεξηγώ [parekseego] misunderstand, misinterpret, misconstrue.

παρεπόμενα, τα [parepomena] πλ consequences, issues.

παρερμηνεία, η [parermeeneea] misinterpretation.

παρέρχομαι [parerhome] elapse, pass || (τελειώνω) come to an end || (ππδώ) pass over || omit.

παρευρίσκομαι [parevreeskome] be present at, attend.

παρεφθαρμένος [pareftharmenos] defective (linguistically).

παρέχω [pareho] procure || give, supply || (ευκαιρία) occasion, bring about.

παρηγοριά, η [pareegoreea] consolation, comfort, solace.

παρηγορώ [pareegoro] console, comfort.

παρθενία, η [partheneea] virginity, maidenhood || chastity.

παρθενικός [partheneekos] virginal || (μεταφ) pure || maiden.

παρθένος, η [parthenos] virgin, maiden.

Παρθενώνας, ο [parthenonas] Parthenon.

παρίσταμαι [pareestame] be present at, assist (at) || arise.

παριστάνω [pareestano] represent, portray, depict || (ρόλο) perform || pretend to be.

πάρκο, το [parko] park.

παρμπρίζ, το [parbreez] (αυτοκινήτου) windscreen.

παρντόν [parnton] pardon me!

παροδικός [paroðeekos] passing, fleeting, momentary.

πάροδος, η [paroðos] side street || (χρόνου κτλ) passing, course.

παροικία, η [pareekeea] colony, quarter.

παροιμία, η [pareemeea] proverb, adage, saying.

παροιμιώδης [pareemeeoðees] proverbial || famous, renowned.

παρομοιάζω [paromeeazo] compare, liken || resemble, be similar.

παρόμοιος [paromeeos] similar, alike.

παρόν, το [paron] the present.

παρονομαστής, ο [paronomastees] (μαθημ) denominator.

παροξυσμός, ο [parokseesmos] fit, attack || incitement.

παρόρμηση, η [parormeesee] prompting, instigation || stimulation, exhortation.

παροτρύνω [parotreeno] βλ **παρακινώ**.

παρουσία, η [parouseea] presence, attendance || **δευτέρα** ~ second coming, doomsday.

παρουσιάζομαι [parouseeazome] appear || introduce o.s.

παρουσιάζω [parouseeazo] present, show, introduce.

παρουσιαστικό, το [parouseeasteeko] presence, demeanour, bearing.

παροχή, η [parohee] furnishing || contribution, donation || granting.

παρρησία, η [pareeseea] frankness, candour.

πάρσιμο, το [parseemo] capture, taking || (ελάττωση) trimming, lessening.

παρτέρι, το [parteree] flower bed.

παρτίδα, η [parteeða] part, portion || (παιγνιδιού) game (of cards).

παρωδία, η [paroðeea] parody, farce, travesty.

παρών [paron] present, actual.

παρωνυμία, η [paroneemeea] nickname || surname.

παρωπίδα, η [paropeeða] blinker, blind.

παρωχημένος [paroheemenos] past, gone by.

πας [pas] any, all, every || (οι πάντες) everybody, everyone.

πασαλείβομαι [pasaleevome] be smeared || get a smattering of knowledge.

πασαλείβω [pasaleevo] smear, daub || smudge.

πασάς, ο [pasas] pasha.

πασίγνωστος [paseegnostos] well-known, notorious.

πασιέντζα, η [pasiendza] patience, solitaire (card game).

πασπαλίζω [paspaleezo] sprinkle, powder (with).

πασπατεύω [paspatevo] pry about, feel, finger.

πάσσαλος, ο [passalos] stake, post, pole.

πάσσο, το [passo] stride, step || **πάω** ~ (στα χαρτιά) pass (at cards).

πάστα, η [pasta] dough, paste || (γλυκό) pastry, cake || (χαρακτήρας) character, sort.

παστέλι, το [pastelee] concoction of honey and sesame.

παστίτσιο, το [pasteetseeo] baked macaroni.

παστός [pastos] salted.

παστουρμάς, ο [pastourmas] seasoned cured meat.

παστρεύω [pastrevo] clean, cleanse || (μεταφ) destroy, exterminate.

παστρικός [pastreekos] clean, neat || (μεταφ) dishonest, depraved.

Πάσχα, το [pasha] Easter.

πασχαλιά, η [pashalia] lilac.

πασχίζω [pasheezo] try hard to, strive, endeavour.

πάσχω [pasho] be ill, suffer || ο πάσχων the patient, the sufferer.

πάταγος, ο [patagos] din, noise, bang || (μεταφ) sensation, stir.

παταγώδης [patagodees] uproarious, noisy, loud.

πατάρι, το [pataree] loft, attic.

πατάτα, η [patata] potato.

πατέρας, ο [pateras] father.

πατερίτσα, η [patereetsa] crook, crutch || bishop's staff.

πατηκώνω [pateekono] press down, crush, compress.

πάτημα, το [pateema] step, footstep || (ίχνος) footprint || (σταφυλιών) treading, pressing || excuse.

πατημασιά, η [pateemasia] footprint, trace, track.

πατινάρω [pateenaro] skate.

πάτος, ο [patos] bottom.

πατούσα, η [patousa] (ανατ) sole.

πατριάρχης, ο [patreearhees] patriarch.

πατριαρχείο, το [patreearheeo] patriarchate.

πατρίδα, η [patreeda] native country, birthplace.

πατρικός [patreekos] paternal || fatherly.

πάτριος [patrecos] paternal, ancestral || native.

πατριώτης, ο [patreeotees] compatriot || patriot.

πατριωτικός [patreeoteekos] patriotic.

πατριωτισμός, ο [patreeoteesmos] patriotism.

πατρόν, το [patron] pattern (in dressmaking).

πατροπαράδοτος [patroparadotos] usual, customary, traditional || hereditary.

πατρυιός, ο [patreeos] stepfather.

πατσαβούρα, η [patsavoura] dish cloth, rag || (μεταφ) rag (newspaper).

πατσάς, ο [patsas] (soup of) tripe.

πάτσι [patsee] even, quits.

πατώ [pato] step on || (κουδούνι κτλ) press || press down || (μεταφ) violate || run over || ~ πόδι I put my foot down.

πάτωμα, το [patoma] floor, ground || storey.

πατώνω [patono] lay a floor || touch bottom, reach bottom.

παύλα, η [pavla] dash (punctuation).

παύση, η [pavsee] stoppage, cessation, discharge || (μουσ) rest, pause.

παύω [pavo] cease, stop || cause to cease || (απολύω) dismiss || (σταματώ) stop, finish, give up.

παφλασμός, ο [paflasmos] splashing, gushing || bubbling up.

παχαίνω [paheno] βλ παχύνω.

παχιά [pahia] πλ: ~ λόγια empty words, empty promises.

πάχνη, η [pahnee] hoarfrost, rime.

παχνί, το [pahnee] manger, crib.

πάχος, το [pahos] plumpness || thickness || (λίπος) fat, grease || (στρώματος) depth.

παχουλός [pahoulos] plump, chubby.

παχύδερμος [paheedermos] (μεταφ) insensitive.

παχύνω [paheeno] fatten || grow fat.

παχύς [pahees] trick || fleshy, fat || (σε λίπος) rich in fat || (λειβάδι) rich.

παχύσαρκος [paheesarkos] fat, stout, obese.

πάω [pao] go || take || carry || τα ~ καλά I get along well with || ~ περίπατο it's a washout || I go for a walk || ~ να σκάσω I'm ready to burst.

πεδιάδα, η [pedeeada] plain, flat country.

πέδιλο, το [pedeelo] sandal.

πεδινός [pedeenos] flat, level || (έδαφος) even, smooth.

πεδίο, το [pedeeo] plain, flat country, ground || (μάχης) field of battle || (οπτικό) field.

πεζεύω [pezevo] dismount.

πεζή [pezee] on foot.

πεζικό, το [pezeeko] infantry.

πεζογραφία, η [pezografeea] prose.

πεζογράφος, ο, η [pezografos] prose writer, novelist.

πεζοδρόμιο, το [pezodromeeo] pavement || sidewalk (US).

πεζοναύτης, ο [pezonavtees] marine.

πεζοπορία, η [pezoporeea] walking, walk || (στρατ) march.

πεζός [pezos] pedestrian || (της πρόζας) in prose || (μεταφ) banal, trivial, common.

πεζούλι, το [pezoulee] parapet || bench || (σε λόφο) terrace.

πεθαίνω [petheno] die || (μεταφ) perish || be fond of, be mad about.

πεθερά, η [pethera] mother-in-law.

πεθερικά, τα [pethereeka] πλ in-laws.

πεθερός, ο [petheros] father-in-law.

πειθαρχία, η [peetharheea] discipline.

πειθαρχικός [peetharheekos] disciplinary || (υπάκουος) obedient, docile, submissive.

πειθαρχώ [peetharho] be obedient, obey one's superiors.

πειθήνιος [peetheeneeos] docile, obedient, submissive.

πείθω [peetho] convince, persuade.

πειθώ, η [peetho] persuasion, conviction.

πείνα, η [peena] hunger, famine, starvation || πειναλέος starving, famished, ravenous || πεινασμένος hungry, famished.

πεινώ [peeno] be hungry, be starving.

πείρα, η [peera] experience, background.

πείραγμα, το [peeragma] teasing || annoyance || (ασθένεια) malady.

πειραγμένος [peeragmenos] hurt, offended || (κρέας) tainted, spoilt.

πειράζει [peerazee]: ~; is it all right?, is it important?

πειράζω [peerazo] trouble, anger, annoy || tease || (την υγεία) upset, be bad for || (ενοχλώ) disturb.

πειρακτικός [peerakteekos] irritating, offensive, cutting.

πείραμα, το [peerama] experiment || trial, test || πειραματικός experimental.

πειρασμός, ο [peerasmos] temptation.

πειρατής, ο [peeratees] pirate, corsair || pirate taxi.

πείσμα, το [peesma] obstinacy, stubbornness || πεισματάρης obstinate, stubborn || πεισματώδης headstrong, stubborn || πεισματώνομαι be unyielding || πεισματώνω make obstinate, irritate || become obdurate.

πειστήριο, το [peesteereeo] proof.

πειστικός [peesteekos] convincing, persuasive.

πέλαγος, το [pelagos] open sea.

πελαγώνω [pelagono] (μεταφ) lose one's way, be at a loss, feel at sea.

πελαργός [pelargos] stork.

πελατεία, η [pelateea] clientèle, customers, patronage.

πελάτης, ο [pelatees] customer, patron, client || (ξενοδοχείου) guest.

πελεκάνος, ο [pelekanos] pelican.

πελεκούδι, το [pelekouðee] chip, paring, shaving.

πελεκώ [peleko] axe, hew, cut into shape, carve || (μεταφ) thrash.

πέλμα, το [pelma] sole || (ανατ) shoe, flange. (τεχνική)

Πελοπόννησος, η [peloponeesos] the Peloponnese.

πελτές, ο [peltes] tomato purée || (φρούτων) jelly.

πελώριος [peloreeos] enormous, mammoth || (σφάλμα) gross.

Πέμπτη, η [pemptee] Thursday.

πέμπτος [pemptos] fifth.

πενήντα [peneenta] fifty.

πενηνταριά, η [peneentaria]: καμιά ~ about fifty.

πενθήμερος [pentheemeros] of five days.

πένθιμος [pentheemos] sorrowful, mournful, dismal || in mourning.

πένθος, το [penthos] bereavement || mourning.

πενθώ [pentho] lament, mourn || be in mourning.

πενία, η [peneea] poverty, want.

πενιχρός [peneehros] poor, mean || (γεύμα) poor, scant || paltry.

πέννα, η [pena] pen || (μουσ) plectrum || (νόμισμα) penny.

πένσα, η [pensa] tweezers, forceps || (ραπτικής) dart.

πεντάγραμμο, το [pentagramo] (μουσ) stave, staff.

πεντακόσιοι [pentakosiee] five hundred.

πεντάμορφος [pentamorfos] extremely beautiful.

πεντάρα, η [pentara] (μεταφ) farthing || nickel (US).

πεντάρι, το [pentaree] figure 5 || (στα χαρτιά) five (at cards).

πέντε [pente] five.

Πεντηκοστή, η [penteekostee] Whit Sunday.

πέος, το [peos] penis.

πεπειραμένος [pepeeramenos] experienced, versed in.

πεπεισμένος [pepeesmenos] convinced, certain, sure.

πέπλο, το [peplo] veil.

πεποίθηση, η [pepeetheesee] conviction, certainty, assurance.

πεπόνι, το [peponee] melon.

πεπτικός [pepteekos] digestive, peptic.

πέρα [pera] beyond, over, on the other side, over there || εκεί ~ yonder || ~ για ~ through and through || εδώ ~ here || ~ από beyond, across || τα βγάζω ~ manage, make out.

περαιτέρω [peretero] further || moreover.

πέραμα, το [perama] passage, ford || ferry.

πέρας, το [peras] end, extremity || completion, close.

πέρασμα, το [perasma] crossing, passage || (βελόνας) threading || (ασθενείας) passing || (τόπος) much-visited spot.

περασμένος [perasmenos] past, gone, last, by.

περαστικά [perasteeka]: ~! get well soon!

περαστικός [perasteekos] passing by || transient, transitory || (δρόμος) frequented, busy.

περατώνω [peratono] finish, bring to an end, complete.

περβάζι, το [pervazee] doorframe, frame, cornice.

περγαμηνή, η [pergameenee] parchment.

πέρδικα, η [perðeeka] partridge.
πέρδομαι [perðome] fart (col), break wind.
περηφάνεια, η [pereefaneea] βλ **υπερηφάνεια.**
περηφανεύομαι [pereefanevome] βλ **υπερηφανεύομαι.**
περήφανος [pereefanos] βλ **υπερήφανος.**
περί [peree] about, concerning, regarding, of || (με απ) round, near || round about, approximately || ~ τίνος πρόκειται; what's it all about?
περιαυτολογία, η [pereeavtoloyeea] boasting, bragging.
περιαυτολογώ [pereeavtologo] boast.
περιβάλλον, το [pereevalon] environment, surroundings.
περιβάλλω [pereevalo] encircle, surround || (ρούχα) clothe, dress.
περίβλημα, το [pereevleema] wrapper || (καρπού) shell, husk || casing.
περιβόητος [pereevoeetos] famous, renowned, infamous.
περιβολάρης, ο [pereevolarees] gardener.
περιβολή, η [pereevolee] garment, dress || surrounding.
περιβόλι, το [pereevolee] garden, orchard.
περίβολος, ο [pereevolos] enclosure, yard || (τοίχος) surrounding wall || park.
περιβρέχω [pereevreho] bathe, wash.
περίγελος, ο [pereeyelos] laughing stock.
περιγελώ [pereeyelo] mock, ridicule, derive || dupe, trick.
περιγιάλι, το [pereeyalee] seashore, coast.
περιγραφή, η [pereegrafee] description, account.
περιγράφω [pereegrafo] describe, portray.
περίδοξος [pereeðoksos] illustrious, famous.
περιεκτικός [periekteekos] capacious || (τροφή) substantial || (λόγος) comprehensive, concise, succinct.
περιεργάζομαι [periergazome] examine carefully.
περιέργεια, η [perierya] curiosity.
περίεργος [periergos] curious, strange, inquiring.
περιεχόμενο, το [periehomeno] contents || (σημασία) meaning.
περιέχω [perieho] contain, hold.
περιζήτητος [pereezeeteetos] in great demand, greatly prized.
περιηγητής, ο [perieeyeetees] tourist, traveller.
περιθάλπω [pereethalpo] attend, look after, treat.
περίθαλψη, η [pereethalpsee] attendance, care, relief.

περιθώριο, το [pereethoreeo] margin, room.
περικάλυμμα, το [pereekaleema] wrapper, covering, shell.
περικεφαλαία, η [pereekefalea] helmet.
περικλείω [pereekleeo] enclose, include.
περικοκλάδα, η [pereekoklaða] climbing plant || convolvulus.
περικοπή, η [pereekopee] cutting off, deduction || (από βιβλίο) extract, passage.
περικυκλώνω [pereekeeklono] surround.
περιλαίμιο, το [pereelemeeo] animal's collar || necklace.
περιλάπτος [pereelalectos] celebrated, famous, renowned.
περιλαμβάνω [pereelamvano] contain, have, hold || (περιέχω) include, comprise.
περιληπτικός [pereeleepteekos] comprehensive || concise, succinct.
περίληψη, η [pereeleepsee] summary, précis, résumé.
περίλυπος [pereeleepos] sad, sorrowful || (έκφραση) gloomy, doleful.
περιμαζεύω [pereemazevo] gather up || (από τον δρόμο) rescue, harbour || (περιορίζω) check, control.
περιμένω [pereemeno] wait || wait for, expect.
περίμετρος, η [pereemetros] circumference, perimeter.
πέριξ [pereeks] about, round || τα ~ the environs, suburb.
περιοδεία, η [pereeoðeea] tour, travelling, trip.
περιοδικό, το [pereeoðeeko] magazine, periodical.
περιοδικός [pereeoðeekos] periodic(al).
περίοδος, η [pereeoðos] period, era, age || season || (γυναικών) (menstrual) period.
περίοπτος [pereeoptos] overlooking, rising, conspicuous || noticeable.
περιορίζω [pereeoreezo] limit, restrict || (ελέγχω) control || (ελαττώνω) reduce, cut down, curtail.
περιορισμός, ο [pereeoreesmos] limitation || detention, restriction || (ελάττωση) reduction.
περιουσία, η [pereeouseea] property, estate || (πλούτη) fortune, wealth.
περιοχή, η [pereeohee] area, region, district || extent, expanse.
περιπαίζω [pereepezo] ridicule, mock || dupe, trick, take in.
περίπατο [pereepato]: πάω ~ go for a stroll || (μεταφ) be a failure.
περίπατος, ο [pereepatos] walk, ride, drive, spin.
περιπέτεια, η [pereepeteea]

adventure || (μεταφ) misadventure, incident.

περιπετειώδης [pereepeteeodees] full of adventures || (ιστορία) of adventure.

περιπλανώ [pereeplano] send long way round || ~ **μαι** wander, rove, lose one's way.

περιπλέκω [pereepleko] interlace, entangle || complicate, confuse, muddle.

περιπλέω [pereepleo] circumnavigate.

περιπλοκή, η [pereeplokee] complication, complexity, intricacy.

περίπλοκος [pereeplokos] complex, involved.

περιποίηση, η [pereepieesee] care, attendance, looking after.

περιποιητικός [pereepieeteekos] considerate, obliging.

περιποιούμαι [pereepeeoume] take care of || (ασθενή) nurse.

περίπολος, η [pereepolos] patrol.

περίπου [pereepou] about, nearly, almost.

περίπτερο, το [pereeptero] pavilion, kiosk.

περιπτώσει [pereeptosee]: **εν πάσει** ~ in any case, anyway.

περίπτωση, η [pereeptosee] case, condition, circumstance.

περίσκεψη, η [pereeskepsee] prudence, caution, discretion.

περισπασμός, ο [pereespasmos] diversion, distraction.

περίσεια, η [pereeseea] excess, superabundance.

περίσσευμα, το [pereesevma] surplus, excess.

περισσεύω [pereesevo] be in excess, be left over.

περίσσιος [pereeseeos] (άφθονος) abundant || (περιττός) unnecessary.

περισσότερο [pereesotero] more.

περισσότερος [pereesoteros] more || ο ~ most.

περίσταση, η [pereestasee] circumstance, event, fact, occasion, situation.

περιστατικό, το [pereestateeko] incident, event.

περιστέλλω [pereestelo] repress, check, restrain, reduce.

περιστέρι, το [pereesteree] pigeon, dove.

περιστοιχίζω [pereesteeheezo] surround, encircle.

περιστολή, η [pereestolee] limitation, decrease, restriction, checking.

περιστρέφομαι [pereestrefome] revolve, spin, turn.

περιστρέφω [pereestrefo] (ρόδα κτλ) turn, rotate || (κλειδί) turn, twist.

περιστροφή, η [pereestrofee] revolution, turn, rotation.

περίστροφο, το [pereestrofo] revolver.

περισυλλέγω [pereeseelego] collect, gather.

περιτειχίζω [pereeteeheezo] build a wall round.

περιτομή, η [pereetomee] circumcision.

περίτρανος [pereetranos] obvious, clear, evident.

περιτριγυρίζω [pereetreeyeereezo] surround, encircle, border.

περίτρομος [pereetromos] terrified, frightened.

περιτροπή, η [pereetropee]: **εκ περιτροπής** by turns, in turn.

περιττός [pereetos] (προσπάθεια) useless, unavailing || superfluous, unnecessary, needless || ~ **αριθμός** odd number.

περιτύλιγμα, το [pereeteeleegma] wrapper, wrapping.

περιτυλίσσω [pereeteeleeso] wrap up || roll up.

περιφέρεια, η [pereefereea] (δένδρου) girth || (γεωμ) circumference || (χώρος) district, region.

περιφέρομαι [pereeferome] stroll, walk up and down, hang about || (η γη κτλ) turn round, rotate.

περιφέρω [pereefero] turn, revolve, rotate.

περίφημος [pereefeemos] famous, admirable, celebrated.

περίφραγμα, το [pereefragma] enclosure, hedge, fencing.

περίφραξη, η [pereefraksee] enclosing, fencing.

περιφραστικός [pereefrasteekos] periphrastic(al).

περιφρόνηση, η [pereefroneesee] contempt, scorn.

περιφρονητικός [pereefroneeteekos] disdainful, contemptuous, haughty.

περιφρονώ [pereefrono] hold in contempt, despise, spurn.

περιχαρής [pereeharees] cheerful, merry, joyful, gay.

περίχωρα, τα [pereehora] πλ neighbourhood, environs || (πόλη) suburb, outskirts.

περιωπή, η [pereeopee] eminence || (μεταφ) importance.

περνώ [perno] (ποτάμι, γέφυρα κτλ) pass, cross, go over || (κάτι σε κάποιο) pass, hand over || (κάτι μέσα σε κάτι) pass through || (τον καιρό) spend || (βελόνα) thread (a needle) || (υγρό από φίλτρο) filter, strain || (νόμο) get voted, pass || (στο δρόμο) pass, leave behind || ~ **για** mistake for || ~ **από** call at, go via.

περονιάζω [peroneeazo] pierce, go through.

περονόσπορος, ο [peronosporos] mildew.

περούκα, η [perouka] wig.

περπάτημα, το [perpateema] walking || gait.

περπατώ [perpato] walk || go across || (σκύλο κτλ) take for a walk.

Πέρσης, ο [persees] Iranian.

Περσία, η [perseea] Iran.

περσικός [perseekos] Iranian.

πέρ(υ)σι [per(ee)see] last year || περ(υ)σινός of last year.

πέσιμο, το [peseemo] falling, fall.

πεσμένος [pesmenos] fallen || impaired, worsened.

πέστροφα, η [pestrofa] trout.

πέταγμα, το [petagma] flying, flight || throwing away, casting.

πετάγομαι [petagome] fly up || rush || butt in.

πετάλι, το [petalee] pedal.

πεταλίδα, η [petaleeda] limpet.

πέταλο, το [petalo] petal || (αλόγου) horseshoe.

πεταλούδα, η [petalouda] butterfly || (λαιμοδέτου) bow, bow tie.

πεταλώνω [petalono] shoe (a horse).

πέταμα [petama] βλ πέταγμα.

πεταχτά [petahta]: στα ~ hastily, hurriedly, quickly.

πεταχτός [petahtos] nimble || sticking out.

πετεινός, ο [peteenos] cock || (ένπλου) hammer.

πετ(ι)μέζι, το [pet(ee)mezee] must turned into syrup || (επίθ, μεταφ) very sweet.

πέτο, το [peto] lapel.

πετονιά, η [petonia] fishing line.

πέτρα, η [petra] stone, rock || precious stone.

πετράδι, το [petradee] pebble || precious stone.

πετρέλαιο, το [petreleo] petroleum, oil || (ακάθαρτο) crude oil.

πετρελαιοπηγή, η [petreleopeeyee] oil well.

πετρελαιοφόρο, το [petreleoforo] oil tanker.

πέτρινος [petreenos] made of stone.

πετροβολώ [petrovolo] pelt with stones.

πέτσα, η [petsa] skin || (γάλακτος) cream.

πετσέτα, η [petseta] table napkin || towel.

πετσί, το [petsee] skin, pelt, hide || leather, dressed skin.

πέτσινος [petseenos] leather.

πετσοκόβω [petsokovo] cut up, carve || cut badly, butcher.

πετυχαίνω [peteeheno] βλ επιτυγχάνω.

πετώ [peto] fly || (από χαρά) jump for joy || (στα σκουπίδια) throw away || ~ έξω throw out || kick out (col).

πεύκο, το [pefko] pine.

πέφτει [peftee]: δε σου ~ λόγος you've got no say in the matter.

πέφτω [pefto] tumble, fall || drop, come down, subside || come off || occur || ~ στο κρεββάτι I go to bed || ~ έξω make a mistake || (ναυτ) run aground || ~ δίπλα make up to || ~ με τα μούτρα apply o.s., take up eagerly.

πέψη, η [pepsee] digestion.

πηγάδι, το [peegadee] well.

πηγάζω [peegazo] spring from, originate, emanate.

πηγαινοέρχομαι [peeyenoerhome] go to and fro.

πηγαίνω [peeyeno] go || escort, take || βλ και πάω.

πηγή, η [peeyee] spring, source || (μεταφ) origin, cause.

πηγούνι, το [peegounee] chin.

πηδάλιο, το [peedaleeo] rudder || helm || wheel.

πηδαλιούχος, ο [peedaleeouhos] helmsman.

πήδημα, το [peedeema] jump(ing), spring || sudden rise.

πηδώ [peedo] leap, jump, vault || jump over || (παραλείπω) skip, leave out.

πήζω [peezo] coagulate, thicken, curdle.

πηκτός [peektos] coagulated, thick, curdled.

πηλάλα, η [peelala] quick running || (επίρ) at full speed.

πηλίκο, το [peeleeko] quotient.

πήλινος [peeleenos] earthen, of clay.

πηλός, η [peelos] clay || mud, slime, sludge.

πηνίο, το [peeneeo] bobbin, spool || (ηλεκ) coil.

πήξη, η [peeksee] coagulation, congealing || sticking in.

πηρούνι, το [peerounee] fork.

πήχη, η [peehee] measure of length (0.46 m).

πηχτός [peehtos] coagulated, jellied || thick.

πήχυς, ο [peehees] cubit || ell.

πι, το [pee] the letter Π || στο ~ και φι in two shakes of a lamb's tail.

πια [pia] not any longer || now, finally, at last, at long last.

πιάνο, το [peeano] piano.

πιάνομαι [peeanome] be caught at, be paralyzed || (τσακώνομαι) quarrel with.

πιάνω [peeano] take hold of, catch || occupy || (συζήτηση) engage || (περιέχω) contain, hold || (λιμάνι) land || ~ σπίτι rent a house || ~ τόπο come in useful || ~ κουβέντα get into conversation || ~ δουλειά start a job, find a job.

πιάσιμο, το [peeaseemo] hold, grasp ||

catching || (αφή) feeling, touch || (φυτού κτλ) taking root || (σώματος) stiffness, paralysis.

πιασμένος [peeasmenos] occupied, taken || (στο σώμα) cramped, (feeling) stiff.

πιατέλα, η [peeatela] large dish, flat dish.

πιατικά, τα [peeateeka] πλ crockery, earthenware.

πιάτσα, η [peeatsa] market || (ταξί) taxi rank.

πιέζω [piezo] press, squeeze, compress || oppress, force.

πίεση, η [piesee] pressure, oppression || (αίματος) blood pressure.

πιεστήριο, το [piesteereeo] press || (ελιών) oil press.

πιεστικός [piesteekos] pressing, oppressive || urgent.

πιέτα, η [pieta] pleat.

πιθαμή, η [peethamee] span of hand.

πιθανός [peethanos] probable, likely.

πιθανότητα, η [peethanoteeta] likelihood, probability.

πιθανώς [peethanos] probably, likely, in all likelihood.

πίθηκος, ο [peetheekos] ape.

πιθάρι, το [peetharee] jar.

πίκα, η [peeka] umbrage, pique || (στα χαρτιά) spade.

πικάντικος [peekanteekos] piquant, spicy.

πίκρα, η [peekra] grief, bitterness, affliction.

πικραίνομαι [peekrenome] be grieved, be embittered.

πικραίνω [peekreno] render bitter || grieve, distress.

πικροδάφνη, η [peekroðafnee] oleander.

πικρός [peekros] bitter || biting, harsh.

πικρόχολος [peekroholos] (μεταφ) touchy, irritable, snappy.

πιλάφι, το [peelafee] pilaf, rice dish.

πιλότος, ο [peelotos] pilot.

πίνακας, ο [peenakas] list, table || (του τείχου) notice board || (σχολείου) blackboard || (περιεχομένων) table of contents.

πινακίδα, η [peenakeeða] nameplate || (αυτοκινήτου) licence plate, number plate.

πινακοθήκη, η [peenakotheekee] picture gallery, art gallery.

πινέζα, η [peeneza] drawing pin.

πινέλο, το [peenelo] artist's paintbrush.

πίνω [peeno] drink, take in || (τσιγάρο) smoke.

πιο [pio] more, greater.

πιοτό, το [pioto] drinking || liquor.

πίπα, η [peepa] pipe || cigarette holder.

πιπεράτος [peeperatos] peppery || biting, caustic, piquant.

πιπέρι, το [peeperee] pepper.

πιπεριά, η [peeperia] pepper || (δένδρο) pepper tree.

πιπιλίζω [peepeeleezo] suck, sip.

πισίνα, η [peeseena] swimming pool.

πισινός [peeseenos] back, posterior || ο ~ backside (col), arse (col), bum (col).

πίσσα, η [peesa] pitch, tar, asphalt.

πισσώνω [peesono] tar, pitch.

πίστα, η [peesta] ring || racetrack || (χορού) dance floor.

πιστευτός [peestevtos] trustworthy || credible.

πιστεύω [peestevo] believe, have faith in || suppose, fancy, think.

πίστη, η [peestee] faith, confidence, trust || fidelity || (οικον) credit, trustworthiness.

πιστόλι, το [peestolee] pistol.

πιστοποιητικό, το [peestopieeteeko] certificate.

πιστοποιώ [peestopieeo] certify, guarantee, vouch for.

πιστός [peestos] faithful, loyal, devoted || accurate.

πιστώνω [peestono] (οικον) credit with, give credit.

πίστωση, η [peestosee] credit, trust.

πιστωτής, ο [peestotees] creditor.

πίσω [peeso] behind || back || over again || πάει ~ το ρολόι the clock is slow || κάνω ~ move back || ~ μου behind me || ~ από behind, following.

πίτα, η [peeta] kind of cake, pie.

πίτουρο, το [peetouro] bran.

πιτσιλίζω [peetseeleezo] splash, sprinkle, dash (with).

πιτσιρίκος, ό [peetseereekos] small boy || kid (col).

πιτυρίδα, η [peeteereeða] scurf, dandruff.

πιωμένος [piomenos] drunk, tipsy.

πλά(γ)ι, το [pla(y)ee] side || στο πλάι close by, near, beside.

πλαγιά, η [playa] slope of hill, hillside.

πλαγιάζω [playazo] go to bed || lie down || put to bed.

πλαγιαστός [playiastos] lying down, reclining.

πλάγιος [playeeos] oblique || indirect || crooked, dishonest.

πλαγίως [playeeos] indirectly || next door.

πλαδαρός [plaðaros] flabby, soft || (προσπάθεια) feeble, ineffective.

πλάζ, η [plaz] bathing beach.

πλάθω [platho] mould, create, fashion.

πλάι [plaee] alongside, next door || ~ ~ side by side || ~ σε next to, along with.

πλαϊνός [plaeenos] adjoining, next door.

πλαίσιο, το [pleseeo] frame, framework || chassis || (μεταφ) scope, range.

πλαισιώνω [pleseeono] border, surround, frame, encircle.

πλάκα, η [plaka] slab, plate, paving stone || plaque || (σχολική) slate || (σαπούνι) cake || (γραμμοφώνου) record || (φωτογραφική) plate || σπάσαμε ~ we had a lot of fun || έχει ~ it's funny, it's hilarious.

πλακάκι, το [plakakee] floor tile, wall tile.

πλακόστρωτος [plakostrotos] paved, laid with tiles.

πλάκωμα, το [plakoma] pressure, crush || unexpected arrival.

πλακώνω [plakono] crush, press down || happen unexpectedly || come suddenly.

πλάνη, η [planee] mistake, delusion || (εργαλείο) plane.

πλανήτης, ο [planeetees] planet.

πλανίζω [planeezo] plane, smooth down.

πλανόδιος [planoδeeos] travelling || ~ έμπορος pedlar, hawker.

πλαντάζω [plantazo] be furious, fume, be enraged.

πλανώμαι [planome] ramble, wander || (κάνω λάθος) be mistaken, delude o.s.

πλασιέ, ο [plasie] commercial traveller, salesman.

πλάση, η [plasee] foundation, creation || moulding, formation.

πλάσμα, το [plasma] creature, being || invention, fiction || beauty.

πλάστιγγα, η [plasteenga] weighing machine, balance.

πλαστικός [plasteekos] plastic || comely.

πλαστογραφώ [plastografo] counterfeit || falsify.

πλαστός [plastos] false, forged || artificial, fictitious.

πλαταίνω [plateno] βλ πλατύνω.

πλάτανος, ο [platanos] plane tree.

πλατεία, η [plateea] town square || (θεάτρου) pit.

πλάτη, η [platee] back || shoulder blade.

πλατιά [platia] widely.

πλάτος, το [platos] width, broadness, breadth || (γεωγραφική) latitude.

πλατύνω [plateeno] make wider, stretch, let out || become wider, broaden.

πλατύς [platees] wide, broad, large, ample || (μεταφ) far-reaching.

πλέγμα, το [plegma] network.

πλειοδοτώ [pleeoδoto] make highest offer or bid.

πλειονότητα, η [pleeonoteeta] majority.

πλειοψηφία, η [pleeopseefeea] majority (of votes).

πλειστηριασμός, ο [pleesteereeasmos] auction.

πλεκτός [plektos] knitted, plaited, woven.

πλέκω [pleko] plait, weave || (κάλτσες) knit.

πλεμόνι, το [plemonee] lung.

πλένω [pleno] βλ πλύνω.

πλέξιμο, το [plekseemo] knitting || braiding || (σε υπόθεση) involvement.

πλεξούδα, η [pleksouδa] plait, braid, tress.

πλέον [pleon] more || επί ~ in addition || not any longer || moreover || now.

πλεονάζω [pleonazo] abound, be plentiful || exceed, be superfluous.

πλεόνασμα, το [pleonasma] surplus, excess || (βάρους) overweight.

πλεονέκτημα, το [pleonekteema] advantage, benefit || gift, quality, merit.

πλεονέκτης, ο [pleonektees] greedy person, covetous person.

πλεονεκτώ [pleonekto] have the advantage || be greedy.

πλεονεξία, η [pleonekseea] cupidity, greed, avidity.

πλευρά, η [plevra] side || rib || (όρους) slope, declivity || (μεταφ) point of view.

πλευρίζω [plevreezo] (ναυτ) come alongside.

πλευρίτιδα, η [plevreeteeδa] pleurisy.

πλευρό, το [plevro] side || rib || (στρατ) flank.

πλεχτό, το [plehto] pullover || knitted article.

πλέω [pleo] navigate, sail || float || (μεταφ) wade, wallow.

πληγή, η [pleeyee] wound, injury, sore || (μεταφ) plague, evil, sore.

πλήγμα, το [pleegma] blow || wound.

πληγώνω [pleegono] wound, injure || offend, hurt.

πλήθη, τα [pleethee] πλ the masses.

πλήθος, το [pleethos] crowd || mass || great number.

πληθυντικός, ο [pleetheenteekos] (γραμμ) plural.

πληθύνω [pleetheeno] multiply, increase || augment.

πληθυσμός, ο [pleetheesmos] population.

πληθώρα, η [pleethora] abundance, excess, plenitude.

πληθωρισμός, ο [pleethoreesmos] inflation || plenitude.

πληκτικός [pleekteekos] boring, tiresome, irksome, dull, trying.

πλήκτρο, το [pleektro] (πιάνο κτλ) key || plectrum || drumstick.

πλημμέλημα, το [pleemeleema] misdemeanour, offence.

πλημμύρα, η [pleemeera] flood, inundation || (μεταφ) plenitude.

πλημμυρίζω [pleemeereezo] inundate, overflow || (μεταφ) swarm.

πλην [pleen] except, save || (επίρ) unless, except that || (συνδ) but || (μαθημ) minus || ~ **τούτου** besides, moreover.

πλήξη, n [pleeksee] tedium, weariness, boredom.

πληρεξούσιο, το [pleereksouseeo] power of attorney.

πληρεξούσιος, ο, n [pleereksouseeos] representative, proxy || plenipotentiary, deputy.

πλήρης [pleerees] full, complete, whole || swarming, teeming, packed.

πληροφορία, n [pleeroforeea] information, report.

πληροφορίες, οι [pleerofories] πλ information.

πληροφορική, n [pleeroforeekee] informatics, computer science.

πληροφορούμαι [pleeroforoume] learn, discover.

πληροφορώ [pleeroforo] inform, notify.

πληρώ [pleero] fill || fulfil, perform.

πλήρωμα, το [pleeroma] crew || fullness || filling, completion.

πληρωμή, n [pleeromee] payment, reward || salary, wages.

πληρώνω [pleerono] pay, settle || (μεταφ) pay up, discharge.

πληρωτής [pleerotees] payer.

πλησιάζω [pleeseeazo] approach, go near, put near, draw near.

πλησιέστερος [pleesiesteros] closer || ο ~ the nearest.

πλησίον [pleeseeon] near, close by || ο ~ neighbour.

πλήττω [pleeto] strike, hit, wound, afflict || (παθαίνω πλήξη) be bored, be weary.

πλινθόκτιστος [pleenthokteestos] built of bricks.

πλίνθος, n [pleenthos] brick, firebrick.

πλοηγός, ο [ploeegos] (ναυτ) pilot.

πλοιάριο, το [pleeareeo] small boat, launch.

πλοίαρχος, ο [pleearhos] (ναυτ) captain || (εμπορικού) master, skipper.

πλοίο, το [pleeo] ship, vessel, boat.

πλοκάμι, το [plokamee] tress, braid, plait || (χταποδιού) tentacle.

πλοκή, n [plokee] plot (of play).

πλους, ο [plous] sailing, passage || navigating.

πλουσιοπάροχος [plouseeoparohos] copious, generous, abundant.

πλούσιος [plouseeos] rich, wealthy || splendid, magnificent.

πλουτίζω [plouteezo] make rich || get rich.

πλούτη, τα [ploutee] πλ riches, wealth.

πλούτος, ο [ploutos] opulence, wealth || richness || (εδάφους) fertility.

πλυντήριο, το [pleenteereeo] laundry room || washing machine.

πλύνω [pleeno] wash, clean || brush || scrub.

πλύσιμο, το [pleeseemo] wash(ing).

πλυσταριό, το [pleestario] laundry room.

πλύστρα, n [pleestra] washerwoman || wash-board.

πλώρη, n [ploree] prow || **βάζω** ~ set sail (for).

πλωτάρχης, ο [plotarhees] lieutenant-commander.

πλωτός [plotos] navigable || floating || (γέφυρα) pontoon bridge.

πνεύμα, το [pnevma] ghost, soul, breath of life || mind || genius, spirit || (γραμμ) breathing || **Άγιο** ~ Holy Ghost.

πνευματικός [pnevmateekos] spiritual || intellectual, mental || pneumatic.

πνευμονία, n [pnevmoneea] pneumonia.

πνεύμονας, ο [pnevmonas] lung.

πνευστός [pnevstos] blown, wind (instrument).

πνέω [pneo] blow || ~ **τα λοίσθια** I breathe my last.

πνιγηρός [pneeyeeros] stifling, suffocating, choking.

πνιγμός, ο [pneegmos] suffocation, choking || drowning || throttling.

πνίγω [pneego] drown || stifle, suffocate || choke, throttle.

πνίξιμο, το [pneekseemo] drowning || strangulation.

πνοή, n [pnoee] breath(ing) || (μεταφ) inspiration.

ποδήλατο, το [podeelato] bicycle.

ποδηλατώ [podeelato] cycle, pedal.

πόδι, το [podee] foot, leg || (μέτρο) foot || (ποτηριού) stem || **στο** ~ standing || on the go || **σηκώνω στο** ~ cause a commotion.

ποδιά, n [podia] apron, overall || (παραθύρου) windowsill.

ποδόγυρος, ο [podoyeeros] border, hem.

ποδοπατώ [podopato] tread on, trample on, trample underfoot.

ποδοσφαιριστής, ο [podosfereestees] football player.

ποδόσφαιρο, το [podosfero] game of football.

πόζα, n [poza] pose, affectation.

ποζάρω [pozaro] pose, sit for || put on.

πόθος, ο [pothos] desire, wish, yearning.

ποθώ [potho] desire, long for, wish, be eager for.

ποίημα, το [pieema] poem.

ποίηση, n [pieesee] poetry.

ποιητής, ο [pieetees] poet || creator, maker.

ποιπτικός [pieeteekos] poetic.

ποικιλία, η [peekeeleea] variety, diversity, assortment.

ποικίλλω [peekeelo] embellish, adorn || vary, change.

ποικίλος [peekeelos] varied, diverse, different || miscellaneous.

ποιμένας, ο [peemenas] shepherd, herdsman.

ποίμνιο, το [peemneeo] flock, herd, drove || (εκκλ) flock.

ποινή, η [peenee] penalty, punishment, pain.

ποινικός [peeneekos] penal, criminal, felonious.

ποιόν, το [peeon] quality, property, attribute, nature.

ποιος [peeos] who?, which?, what?

ποιότητα, η [peeoteeta] quality, property.

πολεμικό, το [polemeeko] warship.

πολεμικός [polemeekos] warlike, bellicose || of war, martial.

πολέμιος [polemeeos] unfriendly, hostile || ο ~ enemy, adversary.

πολεμιστής, ο [polemeestees] fighter, warrior, combatant.

πόλεμος, ο [polemos] war, warfare.

πολεμοφόδια, τα [polemofoδeea] nλ munitions, ammunition.

πολεμώ [polemo] fight, make war against || contend, strive (to).

πολεοδομία, η [poleoδomeea] town planning.

πόλη, η [polee] city, town.

πολικός [poleekos] polar.

πολιορκία, η [poleeorkeea] siege, blockade.

πολιορκώ [poleeorko] besiege, surround || invest.

πολιτεία, η [poleeteea] state, government || country, nation || town.

πολίτευμα, το [poleetevma] system of government, regime.

πολιτεύομαι [poleetevome] go into politics, meddle in politics.

πολιτευτής, ο [poleetevtees] politician, statesman.

πολιτικά, τα [poleeteeka] nλ politics.

πολίτης, ο [poleetees] citizen || civilian.

πολιτική, η [poleeteekee] politics || policy.

πολιτικός [poleeteekos] civic, civilian || political || (ουο) politician.

πολιτισμένος [poleeteesmenos] civilized, cultured.

πολιτισμός, ο [poleeteesmos] civilization, culture.

πολιτογραφώ [poleetografo] naturalize (as citizen).

πολιτοφυλακή, η [poleetofeelakee] militia, civil guard || national guard (US).

πολλαπλασιάζω [polaplaseeazo] multiply || propagate, increase.

πολλαπλασιασμός, ο [polaplaseeasmos] multiplication || increase.

πολλαπλάσιο, το [polaplaseeo] multiple.

πολλοί [polee] nλ many.

πόλο, το [polo] polo.

πόλος, ο [polos] pole.

πολτός, ο [poltos] pap || purée || rag pulp.

πολύ [polee] much || numerous, several || great, a lot || το ~ at the most.

πολυάνθρωπος [poleeanthropos] populous, crowded.

πολυάριθμος [poleeareethmos] numerous.

πολυάσχολος [poleeasholos] very busy, very occupied.

πολυβόλο, το [poleevolo] machine gun.

πολυγαμία, η [poleegameea] polygamy.

πολύγλωσσος [poleeglosos] polyglot.

πολυγράφος, ο [poleegrafos] duplicator.

πολυέλαιος, ο [polieleos] chandelier.

πολυζήτητος [poleezeeteetos] much sought-after.

πολυθρόνα, η [poleethrona] armchair.

πολυκατοικία, η [poleekateekeea] block of flats, apartment building.

πολυκοσμία, η [poleekosmeea] crowds of people.

πολύκροτος [poleekrotos] causing a commotion.

πολυλογάς, ο [poleelogas] chatterbox, babbler, gossip.

πολυλογία, η [poleeloyeea] loquacity, garrulity, babble.

πολυμελής [poleemelees] having many members, numerous.

πολυμερής [poleemerees] varied, diversified.

πολυμήχανος [poleemeehanos] very ingenious || cunning, crafty.

πολυπληθής [poleepleethees] very numerous, crowded.

πολύπλοκος [poleeplokos] intricate, complicated, very involved.

πολύπους, ο [poleepous] polyp || (ιατρ) polypus.

πολύπτυχος [poleepteehos] with many folds, many-pleated.

πολύς [polees] much, numerous, many, great || (χρόνος) long.

πολυσύνθετος [poleeseenthetos] very complex || compound.

πολυτέλεια, η [poleeteleea] luxury.

πολυτελής [poleetelees] sumptuous, splendid, rich.

πολυτεχνείο, το [poleetehneeo]

Polytechnic, National Technical School.

πολύτιμος [poleeteemos] valuable, precious, priceless.

πολυφαγία, η [poleefayeea] gluttony, voracity, greediness.

πολύχρωμος [poleehromos] multicoloured, variegated.

πολύωρος [poleeoros] lasting many hours, long-drawn-out.

Πολωνία, η [poloneea] Poland.

πολωνικός [poloneekos] Polish.

πόμολο, το [pomolo] door knob, handle.

πομπή, η [pompee] procession, parade || shame, stigma.

πομπός, ο [pompos] transmitter.

πομπώδης [pompoδees] pompous, bombastic.

πονεμένος [ponemenos] in distress || sad, hurt.

πονηρεύομαι [poneerevome] employ cunning, use wiles || become suspicious.

πονηρεύω [poneerevo] rouse suspicions of || make suspicious || become cunning.

πονηρία, η [poneereea] ruse, trick, guile || suspicion, slyness.

πονηρός [poneeros] cunning, wily, crafty || suspicious, distrustful || diabolical.

πονόδοντος, ο [ponoδontos] toothache.

πονοκέφαλος, ο [ponokefalos] headache.

πονόλαιμος, ο [ponolemos] sore throat.

πόνος, ο [ponos] suffering, pain || (τοκετού) labour || compassion, pity, sympathy.

ποντάρω [pontaro] punt || back, bet on.

ποντικός, ο [ponteekos] mouse, rat || (ανατ) muscle.

πόντος, ο [pontos] sea || (παιχνιδιού) point || (μέτρο) centimetre || (πλέξιμο) stitch || **Εύξεινος** ~ Black Sea.

πονώ [pono] feel compassion for, sympathize with || hurt, pain || (αμετ) feel pain, suffer.

πορδή, η [porδee] fart (col).

πορεία, η [poreea] march, route || course, run.

πορεύομαι [porevome] proceed, go, walk, march.

πορθμείο, το [porthmeeo] ferry (boat).

πορθμός, ο [porthmos] strait, sound, channel.

πόρισμα, το [poreesma] deduction, inference, conclusion || finding || (μαθημ) corollary.

πορνείο, το [porneeo] brothel || whorehouse (US).

πόρνη, η [pornee] prostitute, whore.

πόρος, ο [poros] passage, ford || (του σώματος) pore || πλ means, income, resources.

πόρπη, η [porpee] buckle, clasp, brooch.

πορσελάνη, η [porselanee] china, porcelain.

πόρτα, η [porta] door, gate, doorway, gateway.

Πορτογαλία, η [portogaleea] Portugal.

πορτογαλικός [portogaleekos] Portuguese.

Πορτογάλος, ο [portogalos] Portuguese man.

πορτοκαλάδα, η [portokalaδa] orangeade.

πορτοκάλι, το [portokalee] orange.

πορτοκαλιά, η [portokalia] orange tree.

πορτοφολάς, ο [portofolas] pickpocket.

πορτοφόλι, το [portofolee] wallet.

πορτραίτο, το [portreto] portrait.

πορφύρα, η [porfeera] purple.

πορώδης [poroδees] porous.

πόσιμο [poseemo]: ~ **νερό** drinking water.

πόσιμος [poseemos] drinkable.

ποσό, το [poso] quantity, amount || (χρήματος) sum.

πόσο [poso] how much.

πόσος [posos] how much?, how many?, how large?, how great?

ποσοστό, το [pososto] percentage, share, quota.

ποσότητα, η [posoteeta] quantity, amount.

πόστο, το [posto] strategic position.

ποσώς [posos] not at all, in no way, by no means.

ποτάμι, το [potamee], **ποταμός, ο** [potamos] river.

πότε [pote] when? || ~ ~ sometimes, from time to time || ~ ... ~ sometimes... sometimes.

ποτέ [pote] once, formerly || ever || (μετά από αρνητ) never || ~ **πλέον** never again.

ποτήρι, το [poteeree] drinking glass.

πότης, ο [potees] heavy drinker, boozer.

ποτίζω [poteezo] water, irrigate || become damp, become saturated.

πότισμα, το [poteesma] watering, irrigation.

ποτιστήρι, το [poteesteeree] watering can.

ποτό, το [poto] drink, beverage.

πού [pou] where?, whither? || ~ –; where are you going? || ~ **να ξέρω**; how should I know? || ~ **και** ~ once in a while, now and then.

που [pou] who, whom, which, that ||

when || (συνδ) that || (επίρ) somewhere, where.

πουγγί, το [poungee] purse, bag || money.

πούδρα, η [pouðra] powder.

πουθενά [pouthena] not anywhere || nowhere.

πουκάμισο, το [poukameeso] shirt.

πουλάκι, το [poulakee] little bird || ~ μου my darling, my pet.

πουλάρι, το [poularee] foal, colt.

πουλερικά, τα [poulereeka] πλ poultry.

πούλημα, το [pouleema] βλ πώληση.

πουλί, το [poulee] bird.

πούλμαν, το [poulman] (motor) coach.

πουλώ [poulo] βλ πωλώ.

πούντα, η [pounda] cold, pleurisy.

πουντιάζω [pounteeazo] cool, chill || feel very cold.

πούπουλο, το [poupoulo] down, plume, feather.

πουρές, ο [poures] purée.

πουρμπουάρ, το [pourbouar] gratuity, tip.

πουρνάρι, το [pournaree] evergreen oak.

πούρο, το [pouro] cigar.

πούσι, το [pousee] mist, fog.

πούστης, ο [poustees] bugger, queen (col), queer (col).

πουτάνα, η [poutana] whore.

πράγμα, το [pragma] thing, object || matter, business, affair || (προϊόντα) goods || (ύφασμα) cloth.

πράγματι [pragmatee] in fact, actually.

πραγματεύομαι [pragmatevome] deal with, treat, handle || negotiate.

πραγματικός [pragmateekos] real, actual, substantial, authentic.

πραγματικότητα, η [pragmateekoteeta] reality, fact, truth.

πραγματογνώμονας, ο [pragmatognomonas] assessor, valuer || expert.

πραγματοποιώ [pragmatopeeo] carry out, realize, fulfil, work out.

πρακτικά, τα [prakteeka] πλ records, minutes, proceedings.

πρακτικός [prakteekos] useful, practical || vocational.

πρακτορείο, το [praktoreeo] agency, travel agency.

πράκτορας, ο [praktoras] agent || μυστικός ~ secret agent.

πραμάτεια, η [pramateea] goods, commodities.

πράξη, η [praksee] action, act || practice, experience || (γεννήσεως κτλ) certificate, registration || (οικον) deal, transaction || (μαθημ) operation.

πραξικόπημα, το [prakseekopeema] coup d'état.

πράος [praos] affable, gentle, kind.

πρασιά, η [prasia] flower bed or lawn round house.

πρασινάδα, η [praseenaða] verdure, greenery || green colour.

πράσινος [praseenos] green, verdant || unripe.

πράσο, το [praso] leek.

πρατήριο, το [prateereeo] specialist shop || ~ βενζίνης petrol station.

πράττω [prato] perform, act || do.

πραΰνω [praeeno] appease, calm, soothe, pacify.

πρέζα, η [preza] pinch.

πρέπει [prepee] it is necessary, it is proper that || ~ να πάω I must go || καθώς ~ decent, honourable, a gentleman.

πρέπων [prepon] suitable, fitting, proper || decent, correct.

πρεσβεία, η [presveea] embassy, legation || delegation.

πρεσβευτής, ο [presvevtees] ambassador, minister || representative.

πρεσβεύω [presvevo] profess, avow, affirm, represent.

πρεσβυωπία, η [presveeopeea] long-sightedness.

πρέφα, η [prefa] card game || το πήρε ~ he smelt a rat.

πρήζομαι [preezome] become swollen, swell.

πρήζω [preezo] (μεταφ) infuriate.

πρήξιμο, το [preekseemo] swelling, tumour.

πρίγκηπας, ο [preengkeepas] prince.

πρίζα, η [preeza] plug, socket.

πριν [preen] before, previously, prior to || ~ από μένα ahead of me, in front of me || ~ τον πόλεμο before the war.

πριόνι, το [preeonee] saw, handsaw, hacksaw.

πριονίζω [preeoneezo] saw.

πρίσμα, το [preesma] prism.

προ [pro] before, in front of, ahead of, in the face of || ~ ημερών a few days ago || ~ παντός especially, above all.

προαγγέλλω [proangelo] predict, prophesy.

προάγω [proago] put forward, promote, advance || speed up, further || η προαγωγή (ουσ) advancement, promotion || ο προαγωγός (ουσ) pimp, pander.

προαίρεση, η [proeresee] intention, purpose || bent, bias.

προαιρετικός [proereteekos] optional || voluntary.

προαίσθηση, η [proestheesee] presentiment, foreboding.

προάλλες [proales]: τις ~ just the other day, recently.

προαναφερθείς [proanaferthees] above-mentioned.

προασπίζω [proaspeezo] defend, protect, guard.

προάστειο, το [proasteeo] suburb.

προαύλιο, το [proavleeo] forecourt, courtyard.

πρόβα, η [prova] fitting of clothes || trial, rehearsal.

προβάδισμα, το [provaðeesma] precedence, priority.

προβαίνω [proveno] advance, move forward || proceed, make || ~ σε carry out, make.

προβάλλω [provalo] project, further || (σκιά) cast || (φιλμ) project, show || (αντίσταση) offer resistance || (αντίρρηση) raise || (δικαιολογία) put forward an excuse || (αμετ) appear suddenly in view.

προβάρω [provaro] try on, go for a fitting.

προβατίνα, η [provateena] ewe, lamb.

πρόβατο, το [provato] sheep.

προβιά, η [provia] animal's skin.

προβιβάζω [proveevazo] promote, push forward.

πρόβιος [proveeos] of a sheep.

προβλέπω [provlepo] foresee, forecast || prepare for, provide.

πρόβλεψη, η [provlepsee] forecast, anticipation.

πρόβλημα, το [provleema] problem || (μεταφ) riddle, puzzle.

προβλήτα, η [provleeta] jetty, mole.

προβολέας, ο [provoleas] searchlight, headlight || (σινεμά) projector.

προβολή, η [provolee] projection || (προϊόντος) promotion.

προβοσκίδα, η [provoskeeða] trunk || (εντόμου) proboscis.

προγενέστερος [proyenesteros] anterior, previous, former || (ουσ) precursor.

πρόγευμα, το [proyevma] breakfast.

προγνωστικό, το [prognosteeko] prediction, forecast || tip.

πρόγονος, ο [progonos] ancestor, forefather, forebear.

προγονός, ο, η [progonos] stepson, stepdaughter.

πρόγραμμα, το [programa] programme, plan, schedule.

προγράφω [prografo] proscribe, outlaw.

προγυμνάζω [proyeemnazo] exercise, train || tutor.

προδιαγράφω [proðeeagrafo] prearrange.

προδιάθεση, η [proðeeathesee] predisposition, liability (to), prejudice (against).

προδιαθέτω [proðeeatheto] predispose, forewarn, influence, prejudice.

προδίδω [proðeeðo] reveal, betray || denounce, inform.

προδοσία, η [proðoseea] betrayal || treachery.

προδότης, ο [proðotees] traitor, informer.

πρόδρομος, ο [proðromos] forerunner, precursor || herald.

προεδρεία, η [proeðreea] presidency, chairmanship.

προεδρεύω [proeðrevo] preside, chair.

πρόεδρος, ο, η [proeðros] president, chairman || presiding judge.

προειδοποίηση, η [proeeðopieesee] previous warning, premonition.

προειδοποιώ [proeeðopeeo] let know || warn.

προεισαγωγή, η [proeesagoyee] introduction, preface.

προεκλογικός [proekloyeekos] pre-election.

προέκταση, η [proektasee] extension, prolongation.

προέλαση, η [proelasee] advance, forward movement.

προελαύνω [proelavno] advance, move forward.

προέλευση, η [proelevsee] provenance, place of origin.

προεξέχω [proekseho] jut out, project, protrude.

προεξοφλώ [proeksoflo] (χρέος) pay off in advance || receive in advance || take for granted, rely on.

προεξοχή, η [proeksohee] projection, protrusion, prominence.

προεργασία, η [proergaseea] preliminary work.

προέρχομαι [proerhome] originate, come from, issue from.

προετοιμάζω [proeteemazo] prepare, fit for, train for.

προετοιμασία, η [proeteemaseea] preparation.

προέχω [proeho] jut out || surpass || predominate.

πρόζα, η [proza] prose.

προηγούμαι [proeegoume] surpass, be ahead || precede, come before.

προηγούμενο, το [proeegoumeno] precedent.

προηγούμενος [proeegoumenos] preceding, previous, earlier.

προηγουμένως [proeegoumenos] previously, beforehand.

προθάλαμος, ο [prothalamos] anteroom, antechamber, waiting room.

πρόθεση, η [prothesee] purpose, design, intention || (γραμμ) preposition, prefix.

προθεσμία, η [prothesmeea] time limit, delay, term, option.

προθήκη, η [protheekee] shop window || showcase.

προθυμία, η [protheemeea] eagerness, readiness, alacrity.

πρόθυμος [protheemos] eager, willing, ready || obliging.

πρόθυρα, τα [protheera] πλ gates, approach || (μεταφ) verge, eve, threshold.

προίκα, η [preeka] dowry, marriage portion.

προικίζω [preekeezo] dower || endow (with), equip (with).

προικοθήρας, ο [preekotheeras] fortune hunter, dowry hunter.

προικοσύμφωνο, το [preekoseemfono] marriage contract.

προϊόν, το [proeeon] πλ product, production || proceeds.

προϊόντα, τα [proeeonta] πλ produce, articles, products.

προΐσταμαι [proeestame] direct, manage, supervise.

προϊστάμενος, ο [proeestamenos] superior, chief, supervisor.

πρόκα, η [proka] nail, tack.

προκαλώ [prokalo] challenge || provoke, incite.

προκαταβολή, η [prokatavolee] prepayment, advance payment || deposit.

προκαταβολικώς [prokatavoleekos] in advance, beforehand.

προκαταλαμβάνω [prokatalamvano] forestall, occupy beforehand.

προκατάληψη, η [prokataleepsee] bias, prejudice.

προκαταρκτικός [prokatarkteekos] preliminary, preparatory.

προκατειλημμένος [prokateeleemenos] biased, prejudiced.

προκάτοχος, ο [prokatohos] predecessor || previous holder, previous occupant.

πρόκειται [prokeete] it's a matter of || it's a question of || **περί τίνος ~;** what's it all about? || **~ να έλθω** I am due to come.

προκήρυξη, η [prokeereeksee] proclamation, announcement || manifesto.

πρόκληση, η [prokleesee] affront, challenge || provocation, instigation.

προκλητικός [prokleeteekos] provocative, provoking || seductive.

προκόβω [prokovo] progress, succeed, prosper, make good.

προκομμένος [prokomenos] hard-working, diligent.

προκοπή, η [prokopee] progress || industry || success.

προκρίνω [prokreeno] prefer, choose || predetermine.

προκυμαία, η [prokeemea] quay, pier, jetty.

προκύπτω [prokeepto] arise || result, ensue.

προλαβαίνω [prolaveno] get a start on, forestall || catch, overtake || (σε χρόνο) be on time, manage || have enough time for.

προλεγόμενα, τα [prolegomena] πλ preface, foreword.

προλέγω [prolego] forecast, predict || say previously.

προλετάριος [proletareeos] proletarian.

προληπτικός [proleepteekos] precautionary, preventive || superstitious.

πρόληψη, η [proleepsee] prevention || superstition.

πρόλογος, ο [prologos] prologue, preface, preamble.

προμαντεύω [promantevo] prophesy, foretell, predict.

πρόμαχος, ο [promahos] champion, defender, protector.

προμελέτη, η [promeletee] preliminary study || premeditation || **εκ προμελέτης** deliberately || premeditated.

προμεσημβρία, η [promeseemvreea] forenoon, morning.

προμήθεια, η [promeetheea] supply, provision, supplying, victualling || (ποσοστό) commission, brokerage.

προμηθευτής, ο [promeethevtees] provider, purveyor, supplier.

προμηθεύομαι [promeethevome] get, supply o.s. with.

προμηθεύω [promeethevo] supply, provide, furnish.

προμηνύω [promeeneeo] portend, presage, foretell.

προνοητικός [pronoeeteekos] having foresight, provident, careful.

πρόνοια, η [pronea] care, concern, precaution || providence, welfare.

προνόμιο, το [pronomeeo] privilege, advantage || gift, talent.

προνομιούχος [pronomeeouhos] privileged, favoured.

προνοώ [pronoo] foresee, forecast || provide for, think of.

προξενείο, το [prokseneeo] consulate.

προξενητής, ο [prokseneetees] intermediary, matchmaker.

προξενιά, η [proksenia] matchmaking.

πρόξενος, ο [proksenos] (διπλωμάτης) consul.

προξενώ [prokseno] cause, occasion, inflict, bring about.

προοδευτικός [prooδevteekos] progressive, forward || gradual.

προοδεύω [prooδevo] progress, make headway || develop.

πρόοδος, η [prooδos] advance,

progress || development, improvement || (μαθημ) progression.
προοίμιο, το [preemeeo] preface, prelude, preamble.
προοπτική, η [proopteekee] perspective || prospect in view.
προορίζω [prooreezo] destine, intend, foreordain.
προορισμός, ο [prooreesmos] end, intention || destination.
προπαγάνδα, η [propaganda] propaganda.
προπαρασκευή, η [proparaskevee] preparation || coaching.
προπέλα, η [propela] propeller.
πρόπερσι [propersee] two years ago.
προπέτασμα, το [propetasma] screen || ~ **καπνού** smoke screen.
προπληρώνω [propleerono] pay in advance.
πρόποδες, οι [propodes] πλ foot of mountain.
προπολεμικός [propolemeekos] prewar.
προπόνηση, η [proponeesee] training, coaching.
πρόποση, η [proposee] toast (*drink*).
προπύλαια, τα [propeelea] πλ propylaea.
προπύργιο, το [propeeryo] rampart, bulwark, bastion.
προς [pros] towards || (για) for || at || in || ~ **όφελός μου** to my advantage, to my good || ~ **τιμή του** in his honour, for his sake || ~ **το παρόν** for the present || **ένα ~ ένα** one by one || **ως ~ εμέ** as far as I am concerned || ~ **Θεού!** for God's sake! || ~ **τούτοις** moreover || ~ **δε** in addition, furthermore.
προσάγω [prosago] put forward, exhibit, produce.
προσάναμα, το [prosanama] tinder, firewood || fuel.
προσανατολίζομαι [prosanatoleezome] find one's bearings.
προσανατολίζω [prosanatoleezo] orientate || direct, guide.
προσαράσσω [prosaraso] run aground, be stranded.
προσαρμογή, η [prosarmoyee] adaptation, accommodation || adjustment.
προσαρμόζω [prosarmozo] fit to || adapt, adjust, apply.
προσάρτημα, το [prosarteema] accessory, annexe, addition.
προσάρτηση, η [prosarteesee] annexation.
προσαρτώ [prosarto] append, attach || annex.
προσβάλλω [prosvalo] assail, attack || (υγεία) harm, injure || (δυσαρεστώ) hurt, offend || (διαθήκη) challenge.

προσβλητικός [prosvleeteekos] offensive, abusive, insolent.
προσβολή, η [prosvolee] onset, attack || (υγείας) fit, stroke || offence, insult.
προσγειώνομαι [prosyonome] land.
προσγείωση, η [prosyeeosee] landing, alighting.
προσδίδω [prosdeedo] lend, add to, give.
προσδιορίζω [prosdeeoreezo] determine, define, fix || allocate, assign.
προσδοκώ [prosdoko] hope, expect, anticipate.
προσεγγίζω [prosengeezo] put near || approach, come near || (κατά προσέγγιση) approximate || (ναυτ) put in at, land at.
προσεκτικός [prosekteekos] attentive, heedful, mindful || careful.
προσέλευση, η [proselevsee] arrival, approach.
προσελκύω [proselkeeo] (προσοχή) attract, win, draw, catch || (υποστηρικτές) gain, win over.
προσέρχομαι [proserhome] attend, present o.s. || apply for.
προσευχή, η [prosevhee] prayer.
προσεύχομαι [prosevhome] pray, say one's prayers.
προσεχής [prosehees] next || forthcoming.
προσέχω [proseho] pay attention to, notice || be attentive, be mindful || (κάποιο) take care of.
προσεχώς [prosehos] shortly, soon, in a short time.
προσηλυτίζω [proseeleeteezo] convert, proselytize.
προσηλωμένος [proseelomenos] attached to, devoted to, devoted in.
προσηλώνω [proseelono] nail, fix || (μεταφ) look fixedly (at).
πρόσθεση, η [prosthesees] addition, increase.
πρόσθετος [prosthetos] additional, extra.
προσθέτω [prostheto] add, sum up || mix with.
προσθήκη, η [prostheekee] addition, increase.
πρόσθιος [prostheeos] front, fore.
προσιτός [proseetos] attainable, accessible || (τιμή) reasonable, within one's means.
πρόσκαιρος [proskeros] transitory, passing, momentary.
προσκαλώ [proskalo] call, send for || (νομ) summon, subpoena || (σε γεύμα κτλ) invite.
προσκεκλημένος [proskekleemenos] invited.
προσκέφαλο, το [proskefalo] pillow, cushion.
πρόσκληση, η [proskleesee] call,

προσκλητήριο, το [proskleeteereeo] invitation (card) || (στρατ) call, roll call || (ναυτ) muster roll.

προσκόλληση, η [proskoleesee] adherence, attaching || fidelity.

προσκολλώ [proskolo] stick, attach, paste on || second, attach.

προσκομίζω [proskomeezo] bring forward, bring || offer.

πρόσκοπος, ο [proskopos] scout || boy scout.

προσκρούω [proskrouo] crash || strike (against) || be opposed to.

προσκύνημα, το [proskeeneema] adoration || submission || place of pilgrimage.

προσκυνητής, ο [proskeeneetees] pilgrim.

προσκυνώ [proskeeno] adore, worship || pay homage to, yield.

προσλαμβάνω [proslamvano] take on, engage, employ.

προσμένω [prosmeno] wait for, hope for.

πρόσμειξη, η [prosmeeksee] blending, mixing.

πρόσοδος, η [prosodos] income, revenue || (εμπόριο) profit || yield.

προσοδοφόρος [prosodoforos] productive, profitable, lucrative.

προσόν, το [prason] aptitude, fitness, qualification || advantage.

προσοχή, η [prosohee] attention, notice || caution, precaution, care.

πρόσοψη, η [prosopsee] façade, front(age).

πρόσοψι, το [prosopsee] towel.

προσπάθεια, η [prospatheea] endeavour, effort, attempt, labour.

προσπαθώ [prospatho] try, attempt.

προσπερνώ [prosperno] overtake || (μεταφ) surpass.

προσποίηση, η [prospieesee] pretence, sham.

προσποιητός [prospieetos] affected, assumed, feigned.

προσποιούμαι [prospeeoume] affect, put on || pretend.

προσταγή, η [prostayee] order, ordering, command.

προστάζω [prostazo] order, direct, command.

προστακτική, η [prostakteekee] (γραμμ) imperative (mood).

προστασία, η [prostaseea] protection, defence.

προστατευόμενος, ο [prostatevomenos] protégé.

προστατευτικός [prostatevteekos] protecting || condescending.

προστατεύω [prostatevo] defend, protect || extend patronage to.

προστάτης, ο [prostatees] protector, patron || prostate.

προστίθεμαι [prosteetheme] be added, be mixed (with).

πρόστιμο, το [prosteemo] fine, penalty.

προστρέχω [prostreho] rush up, run up || resort to, turn to.

προστριβή, η [prostreevee] friction, rubbing || (μεταφ) dispute.

προστυχιά, η [prosteehia] vulgarity, rudeness, contemptible act.

πρόστυχος [prosteehos] vile, rude, ill-mannered || of bad quality.

προσύμφωνο, το [proseemfono] preliminary agreement, draft agreement.

πρόσφατος [prosfatos] recent, new || (μόδα) modern.

προσφέρομαι [prosferome] offer || be appropriate, be fitting.

προσφέρω [prosfero] offer, present, give.

προσφεύγω [prosfevgo] have recourse to, turn to.

προσφιλής, η [prosfeelees] dear, loved, precious.

προσφορά, η [prosfora] offer, offering, proposal, bid || thing offered.

πρόσφορος [prosforos] convenient, opportune, suitable.

πρόσφυγας, ο [prosfeegas] refugee.

προσφυγή, η [prosfeeyee] recourse, resort || (νομ) legal redress, appeal.

προσφυής [prosfiees] suitable, well-adapted, fitting.

πρόσχαρος [prosharos] cheerful, lively, merry, gay.

προσχέδιο, το [prosheδeeo] rough draft, sketch.

πρόσχημα, το [prosheema] pretext, excuse.

προσχωρώ [proshoro] join, go over (to) || cleave (to), adhere (to).

προσωδία, η [prosoδeea] prosody.

προσωνυμία, η [prosoneemeea] nickname, name.

προσωπάρχης, ο [prosoparhees] personnel officer, staff manager.

προσωπείο, το [prosopeeo] mask.

προσωπικό, το [prosopeeko] personnel, staff || (σπιτιού) servants.

προσωπικός [prosopeekos] personal.

προσωπικότητα, η [prosopeekoteeta] personality, individuality.

προσωπικώς [prosopeekos] personally.

προσωπίδα, η [prosopeeδa] mask.

πρόσωπο, το [prosopo] face, visage || person || (θεάτρου) role, character, part.

προσωπογραφία, η

[prosopografeea] portrait painting, portrait.

προσωποποίηση, n [prosopopieesee] personification || impersonation.

προσωρινός [prosoreenos] provisional, passing, fleeting.

πρόταση, n [protasee] proposal, suggestion, offer, motion || (γραμμ) sentence || clause.

προτείνω [proteeno] extend, stretch out, put forward || propose, suggest.

προτελευταίος [protelevteos] last but one.

προτεραιότητα, n [protereoteeta] priority, primacy.

προτέρημα, το [protereema] gift, faculty, advantage, talent.

πρότερος [proteros] earlier, previous to, prior (to).

προτέρων [proteron]: εκ των ~ beforehand.

προτεσταντισμός, o [protestanteesmos] Protestantism.

προτίθεμαι [proteetheme] intend, propose, mean, think.

προτίμηση, n [proteemeesee] preference, predilection.

προτιμότερος [proteemoteros] preferable to.

προτιμώ [proteemo] prefer, like better.

προτομή, n [protomee] bust.

προτού [protou] before || previously.

προτρέπω [protrepo] exhort, instigate, incite.

προτροπή, n [protropee] exhortation, prompting.

πρότυπο, το [proteepo] original, pattern, model, example || mould.

πρότυπος [proteepos] model.

προϋπαντώ [proeepanto] go to meet.

προϋπάρχω [proeeparho] pre-exist || (σε χρόνο) come before.

προϋπόθεση, n [proeepothesee] assumption, presumption.

προϋποθέτω [proeepotheto] presuppose, presume.

προϋπολογίζω [proeepoloyeezo] estimate, compute beforehand.

προϋπολογισμός, o [proeepoloyeesmos] estimate || budget.

προφανής [profanees] obvious, evident, plain, clear.

προφανώς [profanos] obviously, evidently, manifestly.

πρόφαση, n [profasee] pretext, excuse, pretence.

προφέρ(ν)ω [profer(n)o] pronounce, utter, articulate.

προφητεία, n [profeeteea] prophecy, prophetic utterance.

προφητεύω [profeetevo] prophesy, predict.

προφήτης, o [profeetees] prophet.

προφητικός [profeeteekos] prophetic.

προφθάνω [profthano] anticipate, forestall || catch, overtake, overhaul || (σε χρόνο) be in time for, have the time to.

προφορά, n [profora] pronunciation, accent.

προφτάνω [proftano] βλ προφθάνω.

προφυλακή, n [profeelakee] vanguard, outpost.

προφυλακίζω [profeelakeezo] hold in custody, detain.

προφυλακτήρας, o [profeelakteeras] bumper (AUT).

προφυλακτικός [profeelakteekos] wary, careful || precautionary, preventive.

προφύλαξη, n [profeelaksee] precaution, cautiousness.

προφυλάσσομαι [profeelasome] take precautions, protect o.s.

προφυλάσσω [profeelaso] protect, preserve (from), defend.

πρόχειρος [proheeros] ready, handy || impromptu.

προχθές [prohthes] the day before yesterday.

προχωρώ [prohoro] go forward, advance || progress, gain ground.

προωθώ [prootho] impel || push forward, urge on.

πρόωρος [prooros] premature, untimely, hasty.

πρύμ(ν)η, n [preem(n)ee] stern, poop.

πρύτανης, o [preetanees] head of university, dean.

πρώην [proeen] former, ex-.

πρωθυπουργός, o [protheepourgos] prime minister, premier.

πρωί [proee] in the morning || (ουσ) morning.

πρώιμος [proeemos] untimely, premature || (για φυτά) precocious, early.

πρωινός [proeenos] morning || rising early.

πρωινό, το [proeeno] morning || (πρόγευμα) breakfast.

πρωκτός, o [proktos] anus.

πρώρα, n [prora] prow, bows.

πρώτα [prota] first, at first || before, formerly, once.

πρωταγωνιστής, o [protagoneestees] protagonist, hero.

πρωτάθλημα, το [protathleema] championship.

πρωτάκουστος [protakoustos] unheard-of, unprecedented.

πρωταρχικός [protarheekos] most important.

πρωτεία, τα [proteea] πλ first place, primacy, precedence.

πρωτεργάτης, ο [protergatees] perpetrator, pioneer, cause.

πρωτεύουσα, η [protevousa] capital, metropolis.

πρωτεύω [protevo] be first, lead, surpass, triumph (over).

πρωτοβάθμιος [protovathmeeos] of the first degree.

πρωτοβουλία, η [protovouleea] initiative.

πρωτοβρόχια, τα [protovroheea] πλ first rains in autumn.

πρωτόγονος [protogonos] primitive || (ήθη) rough, rude, unpolished.

πρωτοδικείο, το [protodeekeeo] court of first instance.

πρωτοετής [protoetees] first-year.

πρωτόκολλο, το [protokolo] register, record || protocol, etiquette.

Πρωτομαγιά, η [protomaya] May Day.

πρωτομηνιά, η [protomeenia] first day of month.

πρώτο [proto] first, firstly, in the first place, to start with.

πρωτοπορεία, η [protoporeea] vanguard.

πρωτοπόρος, ο [protoporos] pioneer, forerunner, innovator.

πρώτος [protos] first, foremost || best, top || initial, elementary || (αριθμός) prime.

πρωτοστατώ [protostato] lead.

πρωτότοκος [prototokos] first-born, oldest.

πρωτοτυπία, η [prototeepeea] originality || eccentricity.

πρωτότυπο, το [prototeepo] original, pattern, model.

πρωτότυπος [prototeepos] original, novel, singular.

πρωτοφανής [protofanees] new, fresh || astonishing.

Πρωτοχρονιά, η [protohronia] New Year's Day.

πρωτύτερα [proteetera] earlier on, at first, before.

πταισματοδικείο, το [ptesmatodeekeeo] police court.

πτέρυγα, η [ptereega] wing.

πτερύγιο, το [ptereeyo] fin || aileron, wing flap.

πτερωτός [pterotos] winged.

πτηνό, το [pteeno] bird, fowl.

πτηνοτροφία, η [pteenotrofeea] poultry farming.

πτήση, η [pteesee] flight, flying.

πτοώ [ptoo] intimidate, frighten, browbeat.

πτυχή, η [pteehee] fold, pleat || wrinkle || (πανταλονιού) crease.

πτυχίο, το [pteeheeo] diploma, certificate.

πτυχιούχος [pteeheeouhos] graduate, holding a diploma.

πτώμα, το [ptoma] corpse, dead body || (ζώου) carcass.

πτώση, η [ptosee] fall, tumble || collapse || drop || (γραμμ) case.

πτώχευση, η [ptohevsee] bankruptcy, failure, insolvency.

πτωχεύω [ptohevo] go bankrupt || become poor.

πτωχοκομείο, το [ptohokomeeo] poorhouse.

πτωχός [ptohos] poor, needy.

πυγμαχία, η [peegmaheea] boxing, pugilism.

πυγμή, η [peegmee] fist || (μεταφ) vigour, determination.

πυγολαμπίδα, η [peegolampeeδa] glow-worm, firefly.

πυθμένας, ο [peethmenas] bottom.

πυκνά [peekna] closely, densely, thickly.

πυκνός [peeknos] thick, dense, closely-packed, close || (γένεια) bushy.

πυκνότητα, η [peeknoteeta] density, compactness, thickness || (κυμάτων) frequency.

πυκνώνω [peeknono] thicken, condense, grow thick || make more frequent.

πυκνωτής, ο [peeknotees] (ηλεκ) condenser.

πύλη, η [peelee] gate, gateway.

πυξίδα, η [peekseeδa] (mariner's) compass || box.

πύο, το [peeo] pus, matter.

πυρ, το [peer] fire, firing.

πυρά, η [peera] fire || (μεταφ) sensation of burning.

πυρακτώνω [peeraktono] make red-hot, glow.

πυραμίδα, η [peerameeδa] pyramid.

πύραυλος, ο [peeravlos] rocket.

πύργος, ο [peergos] tower || castle, palace || (ναυτ) bridge house.

πυρετός, ο [peeretos] high temperature, fever || (μεταφ) activity, energy.

πυρετώδης [peeretoδees] feverish || (μεταφ) restless, feverish.

πυρήνας, ο [peereenas] stone, pip || centre, core || nucleus.

πυρηνέλαιο, το [peereeneleo] oil from stones || seed oil.

πυρηνικός [peereeneekos] nuclear.

πύρινος [peereenos] burning, fiery, red-hot || (μεταφ) ardent, fervent.

πυρίτης, ο [peereetees] pyrites, flint.

πυρίτιδα, η [peereeteeδa] gunpowder, powder.

πυρκαϊά, η [peerkaeea] fire, burning, conflagration.

πυροβολητής, ο [peerovoleetees] gunner.

πυροβολικό, το [peerovoleeko] artillery.

πυροβολισμός, ο [peerovoleesmos] firing, shot.
πυροβολώ [peerovolo] fire || shoot at || shell.
πυρομαχικά, τα [peeromaheeka] πλ munitions || ammunition.
πυροσβέστης, ο [peerosvestees] fireman.
πυροσβεστική [peerosvesteekee]: ~ **υπηρεσία** fire brigade.
πυροτέχνημα, το [peerotehneema] firework, cracker.
πυρπολικό, το [peerpoleeko] fire ship.
πυρπολώ [peerpolo] set on fire, burn down, consume by fire.
πυρσός, ο [peersos] torch, brand || beacon.
πυρώνω [peerono] get red-hot, heat.
πυτζάμα, η [peedzama] pyjamas.
πυώδης [peeoðees] full of pus.
πωλείται [poleete]: ' ~ ' 'for sale'.
πώληση, η [poleesee] sale, selling.
πωλητής, ο [poleetees] seller || salesman || shop assistant.
πωλήτρια, η [poleetreea] seller || saleswoman.
πωλώ [polo] sell || (μεταφ) sell, betray.
πώμα, το [poma] stopper, plug || (μποτίλιας) cork || lid, cover.
πωρόλιθος, ο [poroleethos] porous stone.
πώρωση, η [porosee] hardening || (μεταφ) insensibility, callousness.
πώς [pos] how?, what? || ~ **όχι**; and why not? || ~! yes, certainly.
πως [pos] that.
πως [pos] somewhat, somehow, in any way.

Ρ, ρ

ραββίνος, ο [raveenos] rabbi.
ραβδί, το [ravðee] cane, stick.
ραβδίζω [ravðeezo] flog, thrash, cane.
ράβδος, η [ravðos] stick, staff || (μαγική) wand || (εκκλ) pastoral staff || (σιδηροδρομική) rail.
ράβδωση, η [ravðosee] stripe || (αρχιτεκτονική) fluting || groove.
ραβδωτός [ravðotos] striped || fluted || lined, ruled.
ράβω [ravo] sew up, sew on || stitch || (κοστούμι) have a suit made.
ραγάδα, η [ragaða] crack, fissure, chink.
ραγδαίος [ragðeos] violent, turbulent || (πτώση) rapid, headlong || (πρόοδος) rapid, speedy.
ραγδαίως [ragðeos] violently, impetuously, swiftly.
ραγίζω [rayeezo] crack, split.
ράγισμα, το [rayeesma] crack, fissure, split.

ραδιενέργεια, η [raðienerya] radioactivity.
ραδιενεργός [raðienergos] radioactive.
ραδίκι, το [raðeekee] chicory, dandelion.
ραδιογραφία, η [raðeeografeea] X-ray photography.
ραδιοθεραπεία, η [raðeeotherapeea] X-ray treatment.
ραδιολογία, η [raðeeoloyeea] radiology.
ράδιο, το [raðeeo] radium.
ραδιοτηλεγράφημα, το [raðeeoteelegrafeema] radiotelegram.
ραδιοτηλεγραφία, η [raðeeoteelegrafeea] radiotelegraphy.
ραδιοτηλεφωνία, η [raðeeoteelefoneea] radiotelephony.
ραδιουργία, η [raðiouryeea] intrigue, machination.
ραδιούργος, ο [raðiourgos] scheming, intriguing, plotting.
ραδιόφωνο, το [raðeeofono] radio.
ράθυμος [ratheemos] languid, listless, lazy.
ραίνω [reno] sprinkle, scatter, spread.
ράϊσμα, το [raeesma] βλ **ράγισμα**.
ρακένδυτος [rakenðeetos] in rags, tattered.
ρακί, το [rakee] kind of spirit.
ράκος, το [rakos] rag, tatters || (μεταφ) physical wreck.
ράμμα, το [rama] stitch, thread.
ραμμένος [ramenos] sewn.
ραμολής, ο [ramolees] imbecile, half-wit.
ραμφίζω [ramfeezo] peck at, pick up.
ράμφος, το [ramfos] (μεγάλων πουλιών) bill, beak || (μεταφ) burner, jet.
ρανίδα, η [raneeða] drop, blob.
ραντεβού, το [rantevou] meeting, engagement, rendezvous.
ραντίζω [ranteezo] sprinkle, spray, water.
ράντισμα, το [ranteesma] sprinkling, watering.
ραντιστήρι, το [ranteesteeree] watering can || (εκκλ) sprinkler.
ράντσο, το [rantso] campbed.
ραπάνι, το [rapanee] radish.
ραπίζω [rapeezo] slap or smack in the face.
ράπισμα, το [rapeesma] clout, slap.
ραπτάδικο, το [raptaðeeko] βλ **ραφτάδικο**.
ράπτης, ο [raptees] tailor.
ραπτικά, τα [rapteeka] πλ fees for tailoring, fees for sewing.
ραπτική, η [rapteekee] βλ **ραφτική**.
ραπτομηχανή, η [raptomeehanee] sewing machine.
ράπτρια, η [raptreea] dressmaker.
ράπτω [rapto] βλ **ράβω**.
ράσο, το [raso] frock, cassock.

ρασοφόρος, ο [rasoforos] priest, monk.

ράτσα, η [ratsa] race, generation, breed || από ~ thoroughbred.

ραφείο, το [rafeeo] tailor's shop.

ραφή, η [rafee] dressmaking || stitching, seam.

ράφι, το [rafee] shelf || (τοίχου) bracket || μένω στο ~ be left on the shelf, be an old maid.

ραφινάρισμα, το [rafeenareesma] refinement.

ραφινάρω [rafeenaro] refine || purify, polish.

ραφτάδικο, το [raftaδeeko] tailor's shop.

ράφτης [raftees] βλ ράπτης.

ραφτικά, τα [rafteeka] βλ ραπτικά.

ραφτική, η [rafteekee] dressmaking, sewing, tailoring.

ραχάτι, το [rahatee] lazing about, idling, leisure.

ράχη, η [rahee] back, backbone || (βιβλίου) spine || (βουνού) crest, ridge.

ραχιτικός [raheeteekos] suffering from rickets.

ραχοκοκκαλιά, η [rahokokalia] backbone, spine.

ράψιμο, το [rapseemo] sewing, stitching || tailoring, dressmaking.

ραψωδία, η [rapsoδeea] rhapsody.

ρεαλισμός, ο [realeesmos] realism.

ρεαλιστής, ο [realeestees] realist.

ρεβεγιόν, το [reveyon] midnight supper.

ρεβίθι, το [reveethee] chickpea.

ρέγγα, η [renga] herring.

ρέγουλα, η [regoula] order, regular arrangement || moderation, measure.

ρεζέρβα, η [rezerva] stock || (λάστιχου κτλ) spare wheel.

ρεζιλεύω [rezeelevo] ridicule, make a fool of || humiliate.

ρεζίλι, το [rezeelee] shame, derision, object of ridicule || γίνομαι ~ become a laughing stock.

ρεζιλίκι [rezeeleekee] βλ ρεζίλι.

ρείθρο, το [reethro] watercourse, rivulet || ditch, gutter (of street).

ρεκλάμα, η [reklama] advertisement || show, display.

ρεκλαμάρω [reklamaro] advertise.

ρεκόρ, το [rekor] record.

ρεμάλι, το [remalee] worthless person.

ρεματιά, η [rematia] ravine, torrent, riverbed.

ρεμβάζω [remvazo] muse, daydream, be in a reverie.

ρεμβασμός, ο [remvasmos] musing, reverie.

ρέμπελος [rembelos] lazy, sluggish || disorderly.

ρεπάνι, το [repanee] radish.

ρεπερτόριο, το [repertoreeo] repertoire.

ρεπό, το [repo] time off, break, rest period, rest.

ρέπω [repo] lean, incline, slope || (μεταφ) tend towards.

ρεσιτάλ, το [reseetal] recital.

ρέστα, τα [resta] πλ change.

ρετάλι, το [retalee] remnant.

ρετσίνα, η [retseena] resinated wine.

ρετσινόλαδο, το [retseenolaδo] castor oil.

ρεύμα, το [revma] current, stream, flow || (αέρος) draught.

ρευματισμός, ο [revmateesmos] rheumatism.

ρεύομαι [revome] belch.

ρεύση, η [revsee] outflow, flowing || emission.

ρευστοποιώ [revstopeeo] liquefy.

ρευστός [revstos] fluid, liquid || (μεταφ) fickle, inconstant, changeable.

ρευστότητα, η [revstoteeta] fluidity || (μεταφ) inconstancy.

ρεφενές, ο [refenes] share, quota.

ρεφορμιστής, ο [reformeestees] reformist.

ρέψιμο, το [repseemo] belching || decay.

ρέω [reo] flow, stream || (σταγόνες) trickle || (δάκρυα) fall.

ρήγας, ο [reegas] (χαρτιά) king.

ρήγμα, το [reegma] crack, breach, fissure, hole || (μεταφ) rupture.

ρήμα, το [reema] word, saying || (γραμμ) verb.

ρημάδι, το [reemaδee] ruin || wreckage, derelict || κλείσ' το ~ shut the blooming thing!

ρημάζω [reemazo] ruin, destroy || fall into ruins.

ρήξη, η [reeksee] rupture, breach || conflict, quarrel, dispute.

ρητίνη, η [reeteenee] resin.

ρητό, το [reeto] maxim, saying, motto.

ρητορεύω [reetorevo] make speeches, harangue.

ρητορική, η [reetoreekee] oratory.

ρητός [reetos] formal, explicit, flat, positive.

ρήτρα, η [reetra] clause, proviso, provision.

ρήτορας, ο [reetoras] orator.

ρητώς [reetos] explicitly, expressly, flatly.

ρηχά, τα [reeha] πλ shallows.

ρίγα, η [reega] ruler, measuring rule || line, stripe.

ρίγανη, η [reeganee] origanum.

ριγέ [reeye] striped.

ρίγος, το [reegos] shiver || thrill.

ριγώ [reego] shiver, tremble, thrill.

ριγωτός [reegotos] (χάρτης) lined, ruled || (ύφασμα) striped.

ρίζα, n [reeza] root || (βουνού) foot, base || (μεταφ) origin, source, cause.

ριζικό, το [reezeeko] destiny, fortune, lot, fate.

ριζικός [reezeekos] radical, fundamental.

ριζόγαλο, το [reezogalo] rice pudding.

ριζόνερο, το [reezonero] rice water.

ριζοσπάστης, ο [reezospastees] radical.

ριζοσπαστικός [reezospasteekos] radical.

ριζώνω [reezono] become established, become fixed, take root, grow.

ρίμα, n [reema] rhyme.

ρινικός [reeneekos] nasal.

ρινίσματα, τα [reeneesmata] nλ filings.

ρινόκερος, ο [reenokeros] rhinoceros.

ριξιά, n [reeksia] throw, cast(ing) || (όπλου) charge || shot, firing.

ρίξιμο, το [reekseemo] casting, throwing || dropping || (όπλου) firing, shooting.

ριπή, n [reepee] burst of firing, throwing || (ανέμου) gust, blast.

ρίπτω [reepto] βλ ρίχνω.

ρίχνομαι [reehnome] fling o.s., rush || (στο νερό) plunge.

ρίχνω [reehno] throw, fling, cast || (βόμβα) drop || (όπλο) shoot, fire || (ανατρέπω) overthrow, defeat || (τοίχο) pull down, demolish || (δένδρο) hew, fell || ρίχνει βροχή it's raining.

ριψοκινδυνεύω [reepsokeenδeenevo] risk, endanger || take risks.

ρόγχος, ο [ronghos] rattle, blowing || death rattle.

ρόδα, n [roδa] wheel.

ροδάκινο, το [roδakeeno] peach.

ροδαλός [roδalos] rosy, light pink.

ροδέλα, n [roδela] washer.

ρόδι, το [roδee] pomegranate.

ρόδινος [roδeenos] rosy || (μεταφ) rose-coloured, bright.

ροδίτης, ο [roδeetees] kind of pink grape.

ροδοδάφνη, n [roδoδafnee] oleander.

ροδοκόκκινος [roδokokeenos] ruddy, rose-red.

ρόδο, το [roδo] rose.

ροζ [roz] pink.

ροζιάρικος [rozeeareekos] gnarled.

ρόζος, ο [rozos] knot, node || (δακτύλων) knuckle.

ροή, n [roee] flow, flood || (nύου) discharge, running.

ρόκα, n [roka] distaff || (χόρτο) rocket.

ροκάνα, n [rokana] (παιχνίδι) rattle.

ροκάνι, το [rokanee] plane.

ροκανίδι, το [rokaneeδee] chip, shaving.

ροκανίζω [rokaneezo] plane || (μεταφ) gnaw, crunch.

ροκέτα, n [roketa] rocket.

ρολό, το [rolo] cylindrical roll || shutter.

ρολογάς, ο [rologas] watchmaker, clockmaker.

ρολόι, το [roloee] (τοίχου) clock || (χεριού) watch || (μετρητής) meter || πάει ~ it's going smoothly.

ρόλος, ο [rolos] roll || (θεατρικός) part, role || (μεταφ) part || δεν παίζει ρόλο it's not important.

ρομάντζο, το [romantzo] romance.

ρομαντικός [romanteekos] romantic.

ρομαντικότητα, n [romanteekoteeta] romanticism.

ρόμβος, ο [romvos] rhombus.

ρόμπα, n [romba] dressing gown.

ρόπαλο, το [ropalo] club.

ροπή, n [ropee] inclination, propensity || (μηχανής) momentum.

ρουζ, το [rouz] rouge.

ρουθούνι, το [routhounee] nostril.

ρουθουνίζω [routhouneezo] snort, sniff, snuffle.

ρουκέτα, n [rouketa] βλ ροκέτα.

ρουλεμάν, το [rouleman] ball bearings, roller bearings.

ρουλέτα, n [rouleta] roulette.

Ρουμανία, n [roumaneea] Rumania.

ρουμανικός [roumaneekos] Rumanian.

Ρουμάνος, ο [roumanos] Rumanian.

ρούμι, το [roumee] rum.

ρουμπίνι, το [roumbeenee] ruby.

ρούπι, το [roupee] measure of length (.08 m) || δεν το κουνάω ~ I refuse to move.

ρους, ο [rous] βλ ροή.

ρουσφέτι, το [rousfetee] favour, string pulling, political favour.

ρουτίνα, n [routeena] routine.

ρούφη(γ)μα, το [roufee(g)ma] noisy sipping, gulp, sucking in.

ρουφηξιά, n [roufeeksia] mouthful, sip || (nίπας κτλ) puff.

ρουφήχτρα, n [roufeehtra] whirlpool.

ρουφιάνος, ο [roufeeanos] pimp || schemer.

ρουφώ [roufo] draw in, suck up, absorb, sip.

ρουχικά, τα [rouheeka] nλ clothing, garments.

ρούχο, το [rouho] cloth, stuff, material || (φόρεμα) dress, attire.

ρόφημα, το [rofeema] hot drink.

ροχαλητό, το [rohaleeto] snore, snoring.

ροχαλίζω [rohaleezo] snore.

ρόχαλο, το [rohalo] phlegm, spit.

ρυάκι, το [reeakee] stream, brook, rivulet.

ρύγχος, το [reenghos] muzzle, nose, snout || nozzle.

ρύζι, το [reezee] rice.

ρυζόγαλο, το [reezogalo] rice pudding.

ρυθμίζω [reethmeezo] (ρολόι) regulate, set right || (τα του σπιτιού) manage || (υποθέσεις) settle || (λογαριασμούς) close, make up.

ρυθμικός [reethmeekos] rhythmical.

ρύθμιση, η [reethmeesee] regulating, adjusting.

ρυθμιστής, ο [reethmeestees] regulator.

ρυθμός, ο [reethmos] rhythm, rate || (μουσ) cadence || (αρχιτεκτονική) order, style.

ρυμοτομία, η [reemotomeea] street plan, roadmaking.

ρυμούλκα, η [reemoulka] trailer.

ρυμούλκηση, η [reemoulkeesee] towing, dragging.

ρυμουλκό, το [reemoulko] tugboat, steam tug || (τρακτέρ) tractor.

ρυμουλκώ [reemoulko] tow, tug, drag, pull || (μεταφ) drag by the nose.

ρυπαίνω [reepeno] make dirty, soil || (μεταφ) defile, tarnish.

ρύπανση, η [reepansee] dirtying, blemishing, defiling || pollution.

ρύπος, ο [reepos] filth, dirt || (μεταφ) disgrace, shame.

ρυτίδα, η [reeteeða] wrinkle, seam, line || (της θάλασσας) ripple.

ρυτιδώνω [reeteeðono] wrinkle, line || get wrinkled.

ρω, το [ro] the letter P.

ρώγα, η [roga] nipple.

ρωγμή, η [rogmee] crack, split, cleft, crevice.

ρωμαίικα, τα [romeika] Modern Greek, Demotic Greek || **μίλα ~!** come to the point!

ρωμαϊκός [romaeekos] Roman.

Ρωμαίος, ο [romeos] Roman.

ρωμαλέος [romaleos] robust, strong, vigorous, sturdy.

ρώμη, η [romee] vigour, strength, force, robustness.

Ρώμη, η [romee] Rome.

Ρωμιός, ο [romios] modern Greek.

Ρωμιοσύνη, η [romioseenee] the modern Greek people.

Ρωσία, η [roseea] Russia.

Ρώσος, ο [rosos] Russian (person).

ρωτώ [roto] βλ **ερωτώ.**

Σ, σ

σα [sa] βλ **σαν.**

σάβανο, το [savano] winding sheet, shroud.

σάββατο, το [savato] Saturday.

σαββατοκύριακο, το [savatokeereeako] weekend.

σαβούρα, η [savoura] rubbish, junk, trash || ballast.

σαγανάκι, το [saganakee] frying pan || (φαγητό) dish of fried cheese.

σαγή, η [sayee] harness.

σαγηνεύω [sayeenevo] seduce, charm, attract.

σαγήνη, η [sayeenee] fascination, enchantment.

σαγόνι, το [sagonee] chin.

σαδισμός, ο [saðeesmos] sadism.

σαδιστής, ο [saðeestees] sadist.

σαθρός [sathros] rotted, decayed, rotten || (μεταφ) groundless.

σαιζόν, η [sezon] season.

σαΐτα, η [saeeta] arrow, dart || weaver's shuttle.

σάκα, η [saka] (μαθητική) satchel || (κυνηγού) game pouch, gamebag || briefcase.

σακάκι, το [sakakee] jacket, coat.

σακαράκα, η [sakaraka] (μεταφ) tin lizzie (col), old motorcar, old bike.

σακατεύω [sakatevo] cripple, mutilate, maim || (μεταφ) wear out, exhaust.

σακάτης, ο [sakatees] cripple, maimed person.

σακί, το [sakee] sack, bag.

σακίδιο, το [sakeeðeeo] haversack, satchel, small bag.

σακοράφα, η [sakorafa] sack needle, packing needle.

σάκος, ο [sakos] sack, bag, sackful || (ταχυδρομικός) mailbag || kitbag.

σακούλα, η [sakoula] sack, bag || paper bag.

σακούλι, το [sakoulee] sack, small bag.

σακουλιάζω [sakouleeazo] put into a bag, put into a sack, pocket || (για ρούχα) be loose-fitting, not fit well.

σαλάμι, το [salamee] sausage, salami.

σαλαμούρα, η [salamoura] brine.

σαλάτα, η [salata] salad || **τα κάνω ~** make a muddle of it, foul up the works.

σάλεμα, το [salema] moving, stirring, shaking.

σαλεύω [salevo] move, stir, shake || budge.

σάλι, το [salee] shawl.

σάλιαγκας, ο [saleeangas] snail.

σαλιάζω [saleeazo] salivate.

σαλιάρα, η [saleeara] baby's bib.

σαλιαρίζω [saleeareezo] chatter, prattle.

σαλιγκάρι [saleengaree] βλ **σάλιαγκας.**

σάλιο, το [saleeo] saliva, spittle.

σαλιώνω [saleeono] lick, moisten, dampen, wet.

Σ

σαλόνι, το [salonee] drawing room || (πλοίου) saloon.

σάλος, ο [salos] swell, surge || (πλοίου) rolling || (μεταφ) disturbance || tumult.

σαλπάρω [salparo] weigh anchor.

σάλπιγκα, η [salpeenga] trumpet, bugle || (ανατ) tube.

σαλπίζω [salpeezo] sound the trumpet.

σάλπισμα, το [salpeesma] trumpet call.

σαλτάρω [saltaro] jump, leap.

σαλτιμπάγκος, ο [salteembangos] fairground acrobat || (μεταφ) charlatan, buffoon.

σάλτος, ο [saltos] jump, leap, bound.

σάλτσα, η [saltsa] gravy, sauce.

σαμάρι, το [samaree] packsaddle.

σαμαρώνω [samarono] saddle, pack.

σαματάς, ο [samatas] (φασαρία) noise, din, roar || fight.

σάματι(ς) [samatee(s)] as though.

σαμπάνια, η [sampaneea] champagne.

σαμποτάζ, το [sampotaz] sabotage.

σαμποτάρω [sampotaro] sabotage.

σαμπρέλα, η [sambrela] inner tube.

σάμπως [sambos] as though || it appears that.

σαν [san] when, as soon as, if || like, as if || ~ σήμερα πέρσυ about a year ago today || ~ τι; like what? || ~ να as though.

σανατόριο, το [sanatoreeo] sanatorium.

σανδάλι, το [sanδalee] sandal.

σανίδα, η [saneeδa] board, beam, plank || (σιδερώματος) ironing board.

σανιδώνω [saneeδono] floor, plank, cover with board.

σανός, ο [sanos] hay, fodder.

σαντιγύ, το [santeeyee] chantilly.

σάντουιτς, το [santoueets] sandwich.

σαντούρι, το [santouree] kind of string instrument.

σαπίζω [sapeezo] rot, spoil, decompose, decay.

σαπίλα, η [sapeela] decay, putridity || (μεταφ) corruption, dishonesty.

σάπιος [sapeeos] decomposed, rotten || corrupt, depraved, wicked.

σαπουνάδα, η [sapounaδa] soapsuds, lather.

σαπούνι, το [sapounee] soap || (ξυρίσματος) shaving soap.

σαπουνίζω [sapouneezo] soap || lather.

σαπουνόφουσκα, η [sapounofouska] soap bubble.

σαπωνοποιός, ο [saponopeeos] soap manufacturer.

σάρα, η [sara]: η ~ και η μάρα rabble.

σαράβαλο, το [saravalo] ruin, wreck || sickly person.

σαράκι, το [sarakee] woodworm || (μεταφ) remorse, prick of conscience.

σαρακοστή, η [sarakostee] Lent.

σαράντα [saranta] forty.

σαρανταποδαρούσα, η [sarantapoδarousa] centipede.

σαρανταριά, η [sarantaria] forty.

σαραντίζω [saranteezo] become forty || be forty days since.

σαράφης, ο [sarafees] moneychanger.

σαρδέλα, η [sarδela] anchovy || sardine.

σαρδόνιος [sarδoneeos] sardonic, sarcastic.

σαρίκι, το [sareekee] turban.

σάρκα, η [sarka] flesh.

σαρκασμός, ο [sarkasmos] derision, raillery, sarcasm.

σαρκαστικός [sarkasteekos] sarcastic, jeering, mocking.

σαρκικός [sarkeekos] carnal, fleshy, sensual.

σαρκοβόρος [sarkovoros], **σαρκοφάγος** [sarkofagos] carnivorous, flesh-eating || n **σαρκοφάγος** sarcophagus.

σαρκώδης [sarkoδees] fleshy || (φρούτο) pulpy.

σάρκωμα, το [sarkoma] sarcoma, fleshy growth.

σάρπα, η [sarpa] scarf.

σάρωμα, το [saroma] sweeping.

σαρώνω [sarono] (δωμάτιο) sweep || (δρόμο) scavenge || (μεταφ) rake.

σας [sas] you || your.

σασ(σ)ί, το [sasee] chassis.

σαστίζω [sasteezo] disconcert, embarrass, confuse || get disconcerted.

σατανάς, ο [satanas] Satan || (μεταφ) devilish person.

σατανικός [sataneekos] devilish, satanical, fiendish.

σατέν, το [saten] satin.

σατράπης, ο [satrapees] satrap || (μεταφ) tyrant.

σάτυρα, η [sateera] satire, skit, lampoon.

σατυρίζω [sateereezo] satirize, ridicule.

σατυρικός [sateereekos] satirical.

σάτυρος, ο [sateeros] satyr || (μεταφ) debauchee.

σαύρα, η [savra] lizard.

σαφήνεια, η [safeeneea] clearness, distinctness, lucidity.

σαφηνίζω [safeeneezo] clarify, elucidate, explain.

σαφής [safees] clear, obvious, plain.

σαφώς [safos] clearly, obviously.

σαχλαμάρα, η [sahlamara] nonsense, rubbish.

σαχλός [sahlos] flat, flabby || stupid.

σβάρνα, η [svarna] harrow.

σβέλτος [sveltos] nimble || slim, slender.

σβέρκος, ο [sverkos] nape of neck, scruff.

σβήνω [sveeno] extinguish, quench, put out || (γράμματα) erase || (διά τριβής) rub out || (με πένα κτλ) strike out || (φωτιά) die out || (χρώμα) fade || (ενθουσιασμός) subside, die down.

σβήσιμο, το [sveeseemo] extinction || erasure, rubbing out.

σβηστός [sveestos] put out, extinguished, switched off.

σβούρα, η [svoura] spinning top.

σβύνω [sveeno] βλ σβήνω.

σβώλος, ο [svolos] lump (of earth) || ball, clod.

σγουραίνω [sgoureno] curl || become curly.

σγουρός [sgouros] curly, fuzzy, curled || curly-haired.

σε [se] you || to, at, in.

σέβας, το [sevas], σεβασμός, ο [sevasmos] regard, reverence, deference.

σεβάσμιος [sevasmeeos] venerable, respectable, reverend.

σεβαστός [sevastos] respected || respectable, considerable.

σέβη, τα [sevee] πλ respects.

σεβντάς, ο [sevntas] love, yearning.

σέβομαι [sevome] respect, venerate, admire, esteem.

σειρά, η [seera] series, succession || row, line, rank || (στην τάξη) turn || sequence, order || με τη ~ in turn, in order || μπαίνω σε ~ settle down.

σειρήνα, η [seereena] siren, enchantress || hooter, buzzer, alarm.

σειρήτι, το [seereetee] stripe, ribbon, braid.

σεισμικός [seesmeekos] seismic.

σεισμογράφος, ο [seesmografos] seismograph.

σεισμόπληκτος [seesmopleektos] struck by earthquake.

σεισμός, ο [seesmos] earthquake.

σείω [seeo] move, shake, wave.

σέλα, η [sela] saddle.

σέλας, το [selas] brightness, brilliance, radiance || βόρειο ~ northern lights, aurora borealis.

σελάχι, το [selahee] gun belt || (ψάρι) ray.

σελήνη, η [seleenee] moon.

σεληνιασμός, ο [seleeneeasmos] epilepsy.

σεληνόφως, το [seleenofos] moonlight.

σελίδα, η [seleeδa] page (of book).

σελίνι, το [seleenee] shilling.

σέλινο, το [seleeno] celery.

σελώνω [selono] saddle.

σεμινάριο, το [semeenareeo] seminary.

σεμνός [semnos] decent, unassuming, modest || (ενδυμασία) simple, plain.

σεμνότητα, η [semnoteeta] dignity, modesty, decency.

σεμνότυφος [semnoteefos] prudish, demure, priggish.

σένα [sena] you.

σεντόνι, το [sentonee] sheet.

σεντούκι, το [sentoukee] linen closet || box, chest.

σέξ, το [seks] sex.

σεξουαλικότητα, η [seksoualeekoteeta] sexual instinct, sexuality.

Σεπτέμβρης, ο [septemvrees], Σεπτέμβριος, ο [septemvreeos] September.

σέρα, η [sera] greenhouse, glasshouse.

σερβίρισμα, το [serveereesma] waiting on, serving.

σερβίρω [serveero] wait at table, serve.

σερβιτόρα, η [serveetora] waitress.

σερβιτόρος, ο [serveetoros] waiter.

σερβίτσιο, το [serveetseeo] dinner service || place setting.

σεργιάνι, το [seryanee] walk, promenade.

σερμπέτι, το [sermbetee] sherbet, syrup.

σέρνομαι [sernome] creep, crawl, drag || drag o.s. along.

σέρνω [serno] draw, pull, drag || (βαρύ πράγμα) haul || (χορό) lead || ~ φωνή scream, shriek, cry out.

σεσημασμένος [seseemasmenos] criminal.

σεφτές, ο [seftes] first sale (of a day).

σήκωμα, το [seekoma] raising, lifting || getting out of bed.

σηκωμός, ο [seekomos] rising, rebellion.

σηκώνομαι [seekonome] rise, stand up, get up || (επαναστατώ) rebel.

σηκώνω [seekono] raise, hoist, pick up, lift up || (μεταφέρω) carry || (αφυπνίζω) get up || (ανέχομαι) bear, tolerate || ~ το τραπέζι clear the table || ~ στο πόδι incite, rouse, disturb || ~ κεφάλι become arrogant, rebel.

σηκώτι, το [seekotee] liver.

σήμα, το [seema] signal, sign, mark, badge || ~ κατατεθέν trademark, registration mark.

σημαδεμένος [seemaδemenos] marked || maimed, scarred.

σημαδεύω [seemaδevo] mark || aim at, take aim at.

σημάδι, το [seemaδee] trace, scar, spot || (ένδειξη) sign, mark, indication.

σημαδούρα, η [seemaδoura] buoy.

σημαία, η [seemea] flag, ensign, colours, standard.

σημαίνω [seemeno] mean, be a sign

of, signify || (καμπάνα κτλ) ring, strike, sound, signal || (έχων σημασία) matter, be of consequence.

σημαιοφόρος, ο [seemeoforos] standard bearer || (ναυτ) ensign, sublieutenant || (μεταφ) leader.

σήμανση, η [seemansee] marking, stamping || noting of details.

σημαντικός [seemanteekos] important, significant || (πρόσωπο) remarkable, considerable || momentous.

σήμαντρο, το [seemantro] stamp, seal || (εκκλ) special monastery bell.

σημασία, η [seemaseea] sense, meaning || importance, gravity, significance.

σημείο, το [seemeeo] sign, mark, proof, indication || (θέση, βαθμός) stage, point || (μαθημ) symbol, sign || ~ **του ορίζοντος** point of the compass.

σημείωμα, το [seemeeoma] written note, memorandum, record.

σημειωματάριο, το [seemeeomatareeo] notebook, agenda, diary.

σημείωση, η [seemeeosee] written note || remark, comment.

σημειωτέος [seemeeoteos] to be noted || noticeable, noteworthy.

σήμερα [seemera] today || ~ **το απόγευμα** this evening, this afternoon.

σήπομαι [seepome] rot, decay, decompose.

σηπτικός [seepteekos] septic.

σήραγγα, η [seeranga] tunnel.

σηψαιμία, η [seepsemeea] septicaemia, blood poisoning.

σήψη, η [seepsee] decay, putrefaction || (ιατρ) sepsis.

σθεναρός [sthenaros] sturdy, strong, vigorous, powerful, robust.

σθένος, το [sthenos] vigour, strength, energy || courage, pluck.

σιαγώνα, η [seeagona] jaw || (ανατ) jawbone.

σιάζω [seeazo] arrange, set in order, straighten, tidy || (επισκευάζω) repair, mend, patch.

σίαλος, ο [seealos] saliva, spittle.

σιάξιμο, το [seeakseemo] tidying.

σιγά [seega] softly, lightly, gently, slowly || ~ ~ carefully, by degrees.

σιγαλός [seegalos] silent, quiet, gentle, still || (επίρ) slowly.

σιγανός [seeganos] βλ **σιγαλός**.

σιγαρέτο, το [seegareto] cigarette.

σιγή, η [seeyee] silence, hush.

σίγμα, το [seegma] the letter Σ.

σιγοβράζω [seegovrazo] simmer.

σίγουρα [seegoura] for certain, for sure.

σίγουρος [seegouros] certain, assured, sure || (φάρμακο) infallible.

σιγώ [seego] keep quiet, remain silent || die down.

σίδερα, τα [seedera] πλ ironwork || (γραμμές) railway lines || (φυλακή) irons, fetters.

σιδεράς, ο [seederas] blacksmith, ironmonger.

σιδερένιος [seedereneeos] of iron.

σιδερικά, τα [seedereeka] πλ scrap iron || ironware.

σίδερο, το [seedero] iron || (σιδερώματος) flatiron || (μαλλιών) curling tongs.

σιδέρωμα, το [seederoma] ironing, pressing.

σιδερώνω [seederono] iron.

σιδηροδρομικός [seedeeroðromeekos] of railways.

σιδηροδρομικώς [seedeeroðromeekos] by rail, by train.

σιδηρόδρομος, ο [seedeeroðromos] railway, railroad.

σιδηροπυρίτης, ο [seedeeropeereetees] pyrites.

σίδηρος, ο [seedeeros] iron.

σιδηροτροχιά, η [seedeerotrohia] railway track.

σιδηρουργείο, το [seedeerouryeeo] forge, smithy.

σιδηρουργός, ο [seedeerourgos] blacksmith.

σιδηρωρυχείο, το [seedeeroreeheeo] iron mine.

σίελος, ο [sielos] βλ **σίαλος**.

σικ [seek] chic, stylishness || (επίθ) smart, stylish.

σίκαλη, η [seekalee] rye.

σιλό, το [seelo] silo.

σιλουέτα, η [seeloueta] silhouette, figure.

σιμά [seema] near, close by.

σιμιγδάλι, το [seemeegðalee] semolina.

σιμώνω [seemono] approach, draw near.

σινάπι, το [seenapee] mustard, mustard seed.

σινιάλο, το [seeneealo] βλ **σήμα**.

σινικός [seeneekos]: **σινική μελάνη** India ink.

σιντριβάνι, το [seentreevanee] fountain.

σιρόκος, ο [seerokos] south-east wind.

σιρόπι, το [seeropee] syrup.

σιταρένιος [seetareneeos] wheaten, of wheat.

σιτάρι, το [seetaree] wheat, grain.

σιτεύω [seetevo] fatten || (το κρέας) hang, make tender.

σιτηρά, τα [seeteera] πλ cereals.

σιτίζω [seeteezo] feed, nurture, nourish.

σιτοβολώνας, ο [seetovolonas] granary, barn.

σίτος, ο [seetos] βλ **σιτάρι**.

σιφόνι, το [seefonee] siphon.

σιφονιέρα, η [seefoniera] chest of drawers.

σίφουνας, ο [seefounas] waterspout, whirlwind.

σιχαίνομαι [seehenome] loathe, detest, feel disgust for.

σιχαμένος [seehamenos] loathsome, sickening.

σιχαμερός [seehameros] disgusting, repulsive.

σιωπή η [seeopee] silence.

σιωπηλός [seeopeelos] silent, quiet, noiseless.

σιωπηρός [seeopeeros] tacit.

σιωπώ [seeopo] remain silent || hold one's tongue.

σκάβω [skavo] βλ **σκάπτω**.

σκάγι, το [skayee] small shot, pellet.

σκάζω [skazo] burst, open, split, crack || (ξύλο κτλ) split, splinter || (οβίδα) burst, explode || be exasperated, be infuriated (by) || **το ~** make off || **σκάσε!** shut up!

σκαθάρι, το [skatharee] scarab(ee).

σκάκι, το [skakee] chess.

σκάλα, η [skala] stairs, staircase, flight, ladder || (υπηρεσίας) backstairs || (αποβάθρα) wharf, landing stage || (λιμάνι) port || (μουσ) scale || (μαλλιών) wave.

σκαλί, το [skalee] step, flight, rung || grade.

σκαλίζω [skaleezo] hoe, weed, dig || (μέταλλο) chisel || (πέτρα κτλ) sculpture || (ξύλο) carve || (φωτιά) stir, poke || (βιβλιοθήκη κτλ) rummage, seek, search.

σκάλισμα, το [skaleesma] weeding, hoeing || searching || carving, sculpting.

σκαλιστήρι, το [skaleesteeree] hoe, weeding fork.

σκαλιστής, ο [skaleestees] carver, engraver, chiseller.

σκαλιστός, [skaleestos] engraved, carved, chiselled, sculptured.

σκαλοπάτι, το [skalopatee] step, rung.

σκάλωμα, το [skaloma] scaling || (μεταφ) hitch, impediment.

σκαλώνω [skalono] climb, mount || (μεταφ) get held up, meet with an obstacle.

σκαλωσιά, η [skalosia] scaffolding.

σκαμνί, το [skamnee] stool || chair.

σκαμπίλι, το [skambeelee] slap, smack.

σκαμπιλίζω [skambeeleezo] slap.

σκανδάλη, η [skanðalee] trigger.

σκανδαλιάρης, ο [skanðaliarees] unruly or muddled or mischievous person.

σκανδαλίζομαι [skanðaleezome] be tempted || be shocked.

σκανδαλίζω [skanðaleezo] intrigue, allure || scandalize, shock, offend.

σκάνδαλο, το [skanðalo] scandal || intrigue.

σκανδαλώδης [skanðaloðees] scandalous, disgraceful.

σκαντζόχοιρος, ο [skandzoheeros] hedgehog.

σκαπάνη, η [skapanee] mattock, pickaxe, pick.

σκαπουλάρω [skapoularo] escape from, elude.

σκάπτω [skapto] dig up, scoop out || (τάφρο) excavate || (χαράσσω) engrave, carve, chisel.

σκάρα [skara] βλ **εσχάρα**.

σκαρί, το [skaree] slipway || (μεταφ) character, make-up, idiosyncrasy.

σκαρλατίνα, η [skarlateena] scarlet fever.

σκαρπίνι, το [skarpeenee] lace-up shoe.

σκάρτος [skartos] defective, useless, unserviceable.

σκαρφάλωμα, το [skarfaloma] climbing up, scrambling up.

σκαρφαλώνω [skarfalono] climb, clamber up, scramble up.

σκάρωμα, το [skaroma] (μεταφ) fabrication, invention.

σκαρώνω [skarono] (μεταφ) fabricate, invent.

σκασίλα, η [skaseela] chagrin, spite, vexation, distress || **σκασίλα μου!** I couldn't care less!

σκάσιμο, το [skaseemo] fissure, cracking || (δέρματος) chap || (διαφυγή) desertion, escape || (μαθήματος) playing truant.

σκασμός, ο [skasmos] suffocation || resentment || ~! shut up!, hold your tongue!

σκαστός [skastos] noisy || loud || (στρατ) AWOL || (μαθητής) playing truant.

σκατά, τα [skata] πλ shit (col).

σκάφανδρο, το [skafanðro] diving suit.

σκάφη, η [skafee] trough, tub.

σκαφή, η [skafee] digging.

σκάφος, το [skafos] hull || ship, vessel, boat.

σκάψιμο, το [skapseemo] digging, ploughing || carving.

σκάω [skao] βλ **σκάζω**.

σκεβρός [skevros] crooked, warped, deformed.

σκεβρώνω [skevrono] warp, twist || get warped.

σκέλεθρο, το [skelethro], **σκελετός, ο** [skeletos] skeleton || framework, shape || (αυτοκινήτου) chassis.

σκελετώδης [skeletoðees] bony, emaciated.

σκελίδα, η [skeleeða] clove of garlic.

σκέλος, το [skelos] leg || side.

σκεπάζω [skepazo] cover || protect || hide.

σκεπάρνι, το [skeparnee] adze.

σκέπασμα, το [skepasma] roofing, covering || blanket || lid.

σκεπαστά [skepasta] secretly, on the quiet.

σκεπαστός [skepastos] covered in, veiled, roofed || (μεταφ) secret.

σκέπη, η [skepee] shelter, cover || (μεταφ) protection.

σκεπή, η [skepee] roof.

σκεπτικιστής, ο [skepteekeestees] sceptic, doubtful person.

σκεπτικός [skepteekos] sceptical || pensive, engrossed.

σκέπτομαι [skeptome] think, reflect || contemplate (doing).

σκέρτσα, τα [skertsa] πλ flirtatious ways.

σκέρτσο, το [skertso] charm || jesting, playfulness.

σκέτος [sketos] plain, simple || (καφές) without sugar.

σκεύος, το [skevos] utensil, implement || (εκκλ) vessel.

σκευοφόρος, ο [skevoforos] luggage van, baggage cart.

σκευωρία, η [skevoreea] scheme, machination, intrigue.

σκέψη, η [skepsee] thought, consideration || concern.

σκηνή, η [skeenee] scene, trouble, quarrel || (θεάτρου) action, stage || (τέντα) tent.

σκηνικά, τα [skeeneeka] πλ (stage) scenery.

σκηνικός [skeeneekos] of the stage, theatrical.

σκηνογραφία, η [skeenografeea] stage designing.

σκηνοθεσία, η [skeenotheseea] stage production || (μεταφ) fabrication.

σκηνοθέτης, ο [skeenothetees] stage manager.

σκήπτρο, το [skeeptro] sceptre || (μεταφ) superiority, prevalence.

σκήτη, η [skeetee] small monastery, cloister.

σκιά, η [skia] shade, shadow || phantom.

σκιαγραφώ [skeeagrafo] sketch, line.

σκιάδι, το [skeeaðee] straw hat || sunshade.

σκιάζομαι [skeeazome] be scared, take fright (at).

σκιάζω [skeeazo] shade || conceal the sun || veil, hide || (φοβίζω) frighten || (μεταφ) overshadow.

σκιάχτρο, το [skeeahtro] scarecrow || bogey.

σκιερός [skieros] shady, shadowy.

σκίζομαι [skeezome] struggle.

σκίζω [skeezo] split, cleave, tear, rip || ~ τα ρούχα μου I swear I'm innocent.

σκίουρος, ο [skeeouros] squirrel.

σκιρτώ [skeerto] bound, leap, bounce, hop.

σκίσιμο, το [skeeseemo] tear, rent, laceration || crack.

σκίτσο, το [skeetso] sketch, cartoon.

σκιώδης [skeeoðees] βλ **σκιερός**.

σκλαβιά, η [sklavia] servitude, slavery || (μεταφ) obligation, drudgery.

σκλάβος, ο [sklavos] slave || captive.

σκλαβώνω [sklavono] subjugate, enslave || (μεταφ) put under obligation.

σκληραγωγώ [skleeragogo] accustom to hardship, season, toughen.

σκληραίνω [skleereno] harden, make hard || become callous.

σκληρός [skleeros] hard, tough || cruel, heartless.

σκληροτράχηλος [skleerotraheelos] opinionated, headstrong, obstinate.

σκληρύνω [skleereeno] βλ **σκληραίνω**.

σκνίπα, η [skneepa] gnat, midge || (μεταφ) drunk as a lord.

σκοινί, το [skeenee] βλ **σχοινί**.

σκόλη, η [skolee] holiday, feast day.

σκολίωση, η [skoleeosee] scoliosis.

σκολνώ [skolno] repose || get off (work), leave.

σκόνη, η [skonee] dust, powder || (για δόντια) tooth powder.

σκονίζω [skoneezo] coat with dust.

σκοντάφτω [skontafto] knock against, stumble || come up against an obstacle.

σκόντο, το [skonto] discount, deduction.

σκόπελος, ο [skopelos] reef, rock, shoal || (μεταφ) stumbling block, danger.

σκοπευτήριο, το [skopevteereeo] shooting gallery, shooting range.

σκοπεύω [skopevo] take aim at || (με όπλο) take aim || (έχω σκοπό) intend, propose, plan.

σκοπιά, η [skopia] lookout || sentry box || (σιδηροδρομική) signal box.

σκόπιμος [skopeemos] opportune, convenient, expedient || intentional, deliberate.

σκοπίμως [skopeemos] intentionally, deliberately.

σκοποβολή, η [skopovolee] target practice, shooting.

σκοπός, ο [skopos] purpose, intent, intention || aim, goal || (φρουρός) sentinel || (στόχος) mark, target || (ήχος) tune, air.

σκορβούτο, το [skorvouto] scurvy.

σκορδαλιά, η [skorðalia] garlic sauce.

σκόρδο, το [skorðo] garlic.

σκόρος, ο [skoros] moth.

σκοροφαγωμένος
[skorofagomenos] moth-eaten.

σκορπίζω [skorpeezo] scatter,
disperse || (περιουσία) dissipate, waste ||
(φως) shed, spread || disintegrate, melt
away.

σκόρπιος [skorpeeos] dispersed.

σκορπιός, ο [skorpios] scorpion.

σκορπώ [skorpo] βλ **σκορπίζω.**

σκοτάδι, το [skotaδee] darkness,
obscurity || gloom.

σκοτεινιάζω [skoteeneeazo] darken,
become overcast || cloud over.

σκοτεινός [skoteenos] dark, dismal,
gloomy || (ουρανός) overcast || (νύχτα)
murky || (χαρακτήρας) sombre,
melancholy || (προθέσεις) underhand,
sinister || (λόγια) obscure, abstruse.

σκοτίζομαι [skoteezome] worry,
trouble o.s. || care for.

σκοτίζω [skoteezo] darken, obscure ||
worry, annoy, vex.

σκοτοδίνη, η [skotoδeenee] dizziness,
vertigo.

σκότος, το [skotos] darkness,
obscurity, gloom.

σκοτούρα, η [skotoura] (μεταφ) care,
nuisance || dizziness.

σκοτωμός, ο [skotomos] massacre,
killing || (μεταφ) hustle, jostle.

σκοτώνομαι [skotonome] hurt o.s.
seriously || (μεταφ) work o.s. to death.

σκοτώνω [skotono] kill || while away
(the time), kill time.

σκούζω [skouzo] howl, yell, scream.

σκουλαρίκι, το [skoulareekee]
earring.

σκουλήκι, το [skouleekee] worm ||
maggot, mite.

σκουντουφλώ [skountouflo] stumble,
bump against.

σκουντώ [skounto] push, jostle, shove.

σκούπα, η [skoupa] broom.

σκουπιδαριό, το [skoupeeδario]
rubbish dump.

σκουπίδι, το [skoupeeδee] rubbish,
garbage, refuse.

σκουπιδιάρης, ο [skoupeeδeearees]
dustman, garbage collector.

σκουπίζω [skoupeezo] sweep, wipe,
mop, dust, clean.

σκούρα, η [skoura]: **τα βρήκα ~** I
found things difficult.

σκουριά, η [skouria] rust || **~ζω** rust,
corrode.

σκούρος [skouros] dark-coloured,
brown.

σκούφια, η [skoufeea] cap, baby's
bonnet.

σκούφος, ο [skoufos] cap, beret,
bonnet.

σκύβαλα, τα [skeevala] πλ (μεταφ)
grain siftings || refuse.

σκύβω [skeevo] bend, lean, bow,
incline.

σκυθρωπός [skeethropos] sullen,
sulky, surly || (ύφος) morose.

σκύλα, η [skeela] bitch || (μεταφ) cruel
woman.

σκυλί, το [skeelee] dog || **έγινε ~** he
got furious.

σκυλιάζω [skeeleeazo] infuriate ||
become enraged.

σκυλοβρίζω [skeelovreezo] berate
rudely.

σκυλολόι, το [skeeloloee] rabble,
mob, riffraff.

σκύλος, ο [skeelos] βλ **σκυλί.**

σκυλόψαρο, το [skeelopsaro]
dogfish || shark.

σκυταλοδρομία, η
[skeetaloδromeea] relay race.

σκυφτός [skeeftos] bending, stooping.

σκωληκοειδίτιδα, η
[skoleekoeeδeeteeδa] appendicitis.

σμάλτο, το [smalto] enamel.

σμαράγδι, το [smaragδee] emerald.

σμέουρο, το [smeouro] raspberry.

σμηναγός, ο [smeenagos] (αερο)
flight lieutenant.

σμήναρχος, ο [smeenarhos] group
captain || colonel (US).

σμηνίας, ο [smeeneeas] sergeant.

σμηνίτης, ο [smeeneetees] airman.

σμήνος, το [smeenos] swarm || (αερο)
flight, squadron || crowd.

σμίγω [smeego] mingle, mix || meet,
come face to face with || join.

σμίκρυνση, η [smeekreensee]
reduction, diminution, decrease.

σμίλη, η [smeelee] chisel.

σμίξιμο, το [smeekseemo] mixing,
meeting, mating, joining.

σμόκιν, το [smokeen] dinner jacket.

σμπαράλια, τα [smbaraleea] πλ tiny
pieces.

σμπάρο, το [smbaro] shot.

σμύρη, η [smeeree] emery.

σνομπαρία, η [snombareea]
snobbishness.

σοβαρεύομαι [sovarevome] look
serious, speak seriously.

σοβαρό [sovaro]: **~ ποσό** a
substantial sum.

σοβαρός [sovaros] serious, grave,
solemn.

σοβάς, ο [sovas] wall plaster.

σοβατίζω [sovateezo] plaster.

σόδα, η [soδa] soda water ||
bicarbonate of soda.

σοδειά, η [soδia] βλ **εσοδεία.**

σόι [soee] lineage, breed || sort, kind ||
από ~ from a good family.

σοκάκι, το [sokakee] narrow street,
lane, alley.

σοκάρω [sokaro] shock, upset.

σόκιν [sokeen] shocking, suggestive.

σοκολάτα, η [sokolata] chocolate.

σόλα, η [sola] sole (of shoe).

σόλοικος [soleekos] incorrect, ungrammatical || (μεταφ) improper.

σολομός, ο [solomos] salmon.

σόμπα, η [somba] heater, heating stove.

σορός, ο [soros] bier, coffin || the dead (person).

σοσιαλιστής, ο [soseealeestees] socialist.

σου [sou] your.

σούβλα, η [souvla] skewer.

σουβλάκια, τα [souvlakeea] πλ meat on a skewer.

σουβλερός [souvleros] sharp, pointed.

σουβλί, το [souvlee] awl || spit.

σουβλιά, η [souvlia] injury from a pointed object || (πόνος) acute pain.

σουβλίζω [souvleezo] run through, pierce || (ψήνω) skewer || (πονώ) cause pain.

σουγιάς, ο [souyas] penknife.

σούζα [souza]: **στέκομαι** ~ obey blindly || (μεταφ) fawn.

Σουηδία, η [soueedeea] Sweden.

σουηδικός [soueedeekos] Swedish.

Σουηδός, ο [soueedos] Swede.

σουλατσάρω [soulatsaro] wander about, loaf.

σουλούπι, το [souloupee] outline, cut, contour.

σουλτανίνα, η [soultaneena] sort of seedless grape, sultana.

σουλτάνος, ο [soultanos] sultan.

σουμιές, ο [soumies] spring mattress.

σούπα, η [soupa] soup.

σουπιά, η [soupia] cuttlefish || (μεταφ) sneaky person.

σούρα, η [soura] fold, wrinkle, crease, pleat.

σουραύλι, το [souravlee] pipe, reed, flute.

σούρουπο, το [souroupo] dusk, nightfall.

σουρτούκης, ο [sourtoukees] gadabout.

σουρωμένος [souromenos] intoxicated.

σουρώνω [sourono] strain, filter || fold, pleat, crease || (αδυνατίζω) lose weight, grow thin || get drunk.

σουρωτήρι, το [souroteeree] strainer.

σουσάμι, το [sousamee] sesame.

σούσουρο, το [sousouro] noise, din || rustle || (μεταφ) scandal.

σούστα, η [sousta] spring (of seat) || (όχημα) cart || clasp, clip.

σουτ [sout] (επιφ) hush!, shut up!

σουτζουκάκια, τα [soutzoukakeea] πλ meatballs.

σουτιέν, το [soutien] bra(ssiere).

σούφρα, η [soufra] pleat, crease, fold || (μεταφ) theft.

σουφρώνω [soufrono] fold, pleat, crease || (μεταφ) pinch, steal.

σοφία, η [sofeea] wisdom, learning || erudition.

σοφίζομαι [sofeezome] devise.

σοφίτα, η [sofeeta] attic, garret.

σοφός [sofos] wise || learned, lettered.

σπαγγοραμένος [spangoramenos] mean, tight-fisted.

σπάγγος, ο [spangos] twine, string || (μεταφ) mean person.

σπάζω [spazo] break, shatter, smash || ~ **το κεφάλι μου** think hard || ~ **στο ξύλο** beat.

σπαθί, το [spathee] sabre, sword || (στα χαρτιά) spade.

σπαθιά, η [spathia] sword stroke.

σπανάκι, το [spanakee] spinach.

σπάνη, η [spanee] rarity, shortage.

σπανίζω [spaneezo] become rare, be exceptional, be scarce.

σπάνιος [spaneeos] few and far between, uncommon.

σπανιότητα, η [spaneeoteeta] rarity, rareness, scarcity.

σπανίως [spaneeos] rarely.

σπανός [spanos] smooth-faced, beardless || raw, very young.

σπαράγγι, το [sparangee] asparagus.

σπαραγμός, ο [sparagmos] tearing || heartbreak, anguish.

σπαρακτικός [sparakteekos] heartbreaking, agonizing || (θέαμα) harrowing.

σπάραχνα, το [sparahna] πλ gills.

σπάργανα, τα [spargana] πλ swaddling clothes.

σπαρμένος [sparmenos] spread || strewn, sown.

σπαρτά, τα [sparta] πλ crops.

σπαρταριστός [spartareestos] (ψάρι) fresh || (κορίτσι) beautiful || vivid, very descriptive.

σπαρταρώ [spartaro] throb, palpitate, jump.

σπαρτός [spartos] βλ **σπαρμένος**.

σπάσιμο, το [spaseemo] break, fracture.

σπασμός, ο [spasmos] convulsion, twitching.

σπασμωδικός [spasmoδeekos] spasmodic || hasty.

σπατάλη, η [spatalee] lavishness, extravagance, waste.

σπάταλος [spatalos] wasteful, extravagant.

σπαταλώ [spatalo] waste, lavish, squander.

σπάτουλα, η [spatoula] spatula.

σπείρα, η [speera] coil, spiral || (ομάδα) band, gang, clique.

σπείρω [speero] sow || propagate.

σπεκουλάρω [spekoularo] speculate.

σπέρμα, το [sperma] seed, germ ||

semen, sperm || (μεταφ) offspring || cause, motive.

σπερμολογία, η [spermologeea] spreading of rumours.

σπέρνω [sperno] βλ **σπείρω**.

σπεύδω [spevδo] hurry, make haste.

σπήλαιο, το [speeleo], **σπηλιά, η** [speelia] cave, cavern, lair.

σπίθα, η [speetha] spark, flash.

σπιθαμή, η [speethamee] span.

σπιθοβολώ [speethovolo] sparkle, spark || gleam, glitter.

σπιθούρι, το [speethouree] pimple.

σπινθήρας, ο [speentheeras] (αυτοκινήτου) ignition spark.

σπιούνος, ο [speeounos] spy || stool pigeon.

σπιρούνι, το [speerounee] spur.

σπιρτάδα, η [speertaδa] pungency || (μεταφ) wit, intelligence.

σπίρτο, το [speerto] match || alcohol.

σπιρτόζος [speertozos] witty, clever, ingenious.

σπιτήσιος [speeteeseeos] home-made, domestic.

σπίτι, το [speetee], **σπιτικό, το** [speeteeko] house, home || (μεταφ) family || **από ~** wellborn.

σπιτικός [speeteekos] βλ **σπιτήσιος**.

σπιτονοικοκύρης, ο [speetoneekokokeerees] householder, landlord.

σπιτώνω [speetono] lodge, house || (μεταφ) keep (a woman).

σπλάχνα, τα [splahna] πλ entrails, innards || (μεταφ) feelings || offspring.

σπλαχνικός [splahneekos] merciful, sympathetic.

σπλάχνο, το [splahno] offspring, child.

σπλήνα, η [spleena] spleen.

σπογγαλιεία, η [spongalieea] sponge fishing.

σπογγίζω [spongeezo] sponge up || mop up, wipe away.

σπόγγος, ο [spongos] sponge.

σπογγώδης [spongoδees] spongy.

σπονδή, η [sponδee] libation.

σπονδυλική [sponδeeleekee]: **~ στήλη** spine, backbone.

σπονδυλικός [sponδeeleekos] vertebral.

σπόνδυλος, ο [sponδeelos] vertebra || (κίονος) drum.

σπονδυλωτός [sponδeelotos] vertebrate.

σπορ, το [spor] sport, games, pastime.

σπορά, η [spora] sowing || seed time || (μεταφ) generation.

σποραδικός [sporaδeekos] dispersed, scanty.

σπορέλαιο, το [sporeleo] seed oil.

σπόρια, τα [sporeea] πλ seeds.

σπόρος, ο [sporos] seed, germ || semen.

σπουδάζω [spouδazo] study, attend school.

σπουδαίος [spouδeos] serious, important || exceptional.

σπουδασμένος [spouδasmenos] learned, educated.

σπουδαστής, ο [spouδastees] student.

σπουδή, η [spouδee] haste, keenness || (μελέτη) study.

σπουργίτης, ο [spouryeetees] sparrow.

σπρωξιά, η [sproksia] push, hustle, jostle, shoving.

σπρώξιμο, το [sprokseemo] pushing || encouraging.

σπρώχνω [sprohno] push, thrust, shove || encourage, incite.

σπυρί, το [speeree] grain || (εξάνθημα) pimple || boil.

σπυρωτός [speerotos] granular, granulated.

στάβλος, ο [stavlos] stable || cowshed.

σταγόνα, η [stagona] drop, dash.

σταγονόμετρο, το [stagonometro] dropper || **με το ~** in small doses, little by little.

σταδιοδρομία, η [staδeeoδromeea] career, course.

στάδιο, το [staδeeo] stadium, athletic ground || (μεταφ) career, vocation.

στάζω [stazo] trickle, dribble, drip, leak.

σταθεροποίηση, η [statheropieesee] stabilization, steadying down.

σταθερός [statheros] stable, firm, steadfast, secure.

σταθμά, τα [stathma] πλ weights.

σταθμάρχης, ο [stathmarhees] station master.

στάθμευση, η [stathmevsee] stopping, waiting, parking || stationing.

σταθμεύω [stathmevo] stop, wait, stand, camp, park.

στάθμη, η [stathmee] level, plumbline || (νερού) water level.

σταθμίζω [stathmeezo] weigh, level || (μεταφ) appreciate, calculate.

σταθμός, ο [stathmos] station, halting place || (αυτοκινήτου) garage || parking lot (US) || (ταξί) taxi rank || stop, stay, wait || (στην ιστορία) landmark, stage.

στάκτη, η [staktee] ash, ashes, cinders.

σταλα(γ)ματιά, η [stala(g)matia] drop, dash.

σταλάζω [stalazo] drip, dribble, trickle.

σταλακτίτης, ο [stalakteetees] stalactite.

σταμάτημα, το [stamateema] stop, halting, checking || pause || block.

σταματώ [stamato] stop (working), check.

στάμνα, η [stamna] pitcher, jug.

στάμπα, η [stampa] stamp, seal || impression.

στάνη, η [stanee] sheepfold, pen.

στανιό, το [stanio]: με το ~ against one's will, involuntarily.

στάξιμο, το [stakseemo] dripping, trickling.

στάση, η [stasee] halt, stop, bus stop, station || (εργασίας) suspension, stoppage || (τρόπος) posture, position || (ιατρ) retention || (εξέγερση) revolt, rebellion || (μεταφ) behaviour, attitude.

στασιάζω [staseeazo] mutiny, rebel.

στασίδι, το [staseeδee] pew, stall.

στάσιμος [staseemos] motionless, stationary || (νερό) stagnant.

στατήρας, ο [stateeras] hundredweight.

στατική, η [stateekee] statics.

στατικός [stateekos] static(al).

στατιστική, η [stateesteekee] statistics.

σταυλάρχης, ο [stavlarhees] stable master.

σταύλος, ο [stavlos] stable || cowshed || (χοίρων) pig sty.

σταυροδρόμι, το [stavroδromee] crossroads || crossing.

σταυροειδής [stavroeeδees] cruciform, crosslike.

σταυροκοπιέμαι [stavrokopieme] cross o.s. over and over again.

σταυρόλεξο, το [stavrolekso] crossword puzzle.

σταυροπόδι [stavropoδee] cross-legged.

σταυρός, ο [stavros] cross, crucifix || stake, pale.

σταυροφορία, η [stavroforeea] crusade.

σταυρώνω [stavrono] crucify || (τα χέρια) cross || (διασταυρούμαι) cross, meet and pass, cut across.

σταυρωτός [stavrotos] crossways, crosswise || (σακάκι) double-breasted.

σταφίδα, η [stafeeδa] raisin || (σμυρναίκή) sultana || κορινθιακή ~ currant || γίνομαι ~ get intoxicated.

σταφυλή, η [stafeelee] grapes || (ανατ) uvula.

σταφύλι, το [stafeelee] grape.

σταφυλόκοκκος, ο [stafeelokokos] staphylococcus.

στάχι, το [stahee] ear of corn, ear of wheat.

στάχτη, η [stahtee] βλ στάκτη.

σταχτής [stahtees] ashen, pale.

σταχτόνερο, το [stahtonero] lye.

στεγάζω [stegazo] roof || cover, house, shelter.

στεγανός [steyanos] airtight, hermetical, waterproof.

στέγαση, η [stegasee] housing, sheltering.

στέγασμα, το [steyasma] roof || cover, shelter.

στέγη, η [steyee] roof || (μεταφ) house, dwelling.

στεγνός [stegnos] dry || (μεταφ) skinny, spare.

στεγνώνω [stegnono] dry, become dry.

στείρος [steeros] barren, unproductive || (προσπάθεια) vain.

στέκα, η [steka] billiard cue || (μεταφ) woman as thin as a rake.

στέκει [stekee]: ~ καλά he is well-off || he is fit and well.

στέκομαι [stekome] stand up || come to a standstill, stop || (μεταφ) prove to be || happen.

στέκω [steko] stand, stand still, come to a stop.

στελέχη, τα [stelehee] πλ cadres, management staff.

στέλεχος, το [stelehos] stalk, stem || shank, rod || (τσεκ) counterfoil || (χερούλι) handle.

στέλλω [stelo], στέλνω [stelno] send, direct, dispatch, forward.

στέμμα, το [stema] crown, diadem.

στεναγμός, ο [stenagmos] sigh, sighing || moan, groan.

στενάζω [stenazo] sigh, heave a sigh || (μεταφ) moan.

στενεύω [stenevo] narrow down, take in, tighten || shrink, get narrow.

στενογραφία, η [stenografeea] shorthand, stenography.

στενοκέφαλος [stenokefalos] narrow-minded, strait-laced.

στενόμακρος [stenomakros] long and narrow, oblong.

στενό, το [steno] strait || (οροσειράς) pass, gorge.

στενός [stenos] narrow || tight-fitting || (μεταφ) close, intimate || (φίλος) dear.

στενότητα, η [stenoteeta] tightness, closeness || narrowness || χρήματος lack of money.

στενοχωρημένος [stenohoreemenos] upset, sad || hard-up || ill at ease.

στενοχώρια, η [stenohoreea] lack of room || (δυσκολία) difficulty, inconvenience, discomfort.

στενόχωρος [stenohoros] narrow, limited, tight || troublesome.

στενοχωρώ [stenohoro] worry, embarrass, annoy.

στενωπός, η [stenopos] narrow street, back street || defile, pass.

στερεά, η [sterea] mainland || ~ Ελλάδα central Greece.

στερεοποιώ [stereopeeo] solidify.

στερεός [stereos] firm, compact, well-built || solid, substantial || (χρώμα) fast.

στερεότυπος [stereoteepos] stereotyped, invariable.

στερεύω [sterevo] dry up || stop, cease.

στερέωμα, το [stereoma] consolidation || support, fastening || (ουρανός) firmament.

στερεώνω [stereono] consolidate || make secure || ~ **σε μια δουλειά** settle down to one job.

στερήσεις, οι [stereesees] πλ privation, want, loss.

στέρηση, η [stereesee] deprivation || shortage, absence.

στεριά, η [steria] terra firma.

στερλίνα, η [sterleena] pound sterling.

στέρνα, η [sterna] cistern, tank.

στέρνο, το [sterno] breastbone, chest.

στερνός [sternos] later, last.

στερούμαι [steroume] go without, lack || (φτώχεια) be needy.

στερώ [stero] deprive of, take away.

στέφανα, τα [stefana] πλ marriage wreaths.

στεφάνη, η [stefanee] crown || (αγγείου) brim || (βαρελιού) hoop || (άνθους) corolla || ring, band || (τροχού) tyre.

στεφάνι, το [stefanee] garland, wreath || (βαρελιού) hoop, band.

στεφανώνομαι [stefanonome] marry, get married.

στεφανώνω [stefanono] crown || be the best man at a wedding.

στέψη, η [stepsee] coronation || wedding ceremony.

στηθόδεσμος, ο [steethoðesmos] βλ **σουτιέν.**

στήθος, το [steethos] chest, breast || (γυναικός) bosom.

στηθοσκοπώ [steethoskopo] examine with a stethoscope.

στήλη, η [steelee] staff, pillar, column || (μπαταρία) electric battery || (εφημερίδας) column.

στηλώνω [steelono] prop up, support || bolster up.

στημόνι, το [steemonee] warp.

στήνω [steeno] raise, hold up, erect, put up || ~ **παγίδα** lay a trap.

στήριγμα, το [steereegma] prop, support, stay.

στηρίζομαι [steereezome] lean on, rely on || be based on.

στηρίζω [steereezo] support || prop || base on, reckon on.

στητός [steetos] standing, upright.

στιβαρός [steevaros] strong, robust, steady, firm.

στιβάδα, η [steevaða] pile, heap, mass.

στίβος, ο [steevos] track, ring, racetrack.

στίγμα, το [steegma] spot, brand, stain, stigma || disgrace || position, fix.

στιγμή, η [steegmee] instant, moment

|| (τυπογραφικό) dot, point || **τελεία** ~ full stop || **άνω** ~ colon.

στιγμιαίος [steegmieos] instantaneous || momentary, temporary.

στιγμιότυπο, το [steegmeeoteepo] snapshot, snap.

στίλβω [steelvo] shine, glitter, sparkle.

στιλβώνω [steelvono] polish, varnish, burnish.

στιλβωτήριο, το [steelvoteereeo] shoe shine parlour.

στιλέτο, το [steeleto] stiletto, dagger.

στιλπνός [steelpnos] brilliant, polished, bright.

στίξη, η [steeksee] punctuation || dot, spot, speckle.

στιφάδο, το [steefaðo] meat stew with onions.

στίφος, το [steefos] crowd, horde, throng || rabble, gang.

στιχομυθία, η [steehomeetheea] vivid dialogue.

στίχος, ο [steehos] line, row, file || verse.

στιχουργός, ο [steehourgos] rhymester, versifier.

στοά, η [stoa] colonnade, portico, arcade || passage || (ορυχείου) gallery || (μασωνική) (masonic) lodge.

στοίβα, η [steeva] pile, stack, mass.

στοιβάζω [steevazo] stack, pile up || crowd, squeeze.

στοιχεία, τα [steeheea] πλ elements, rudiments || (τυπογραφείου) printing types.

στοιχειό, το [steehio] ghost, phantom.

στοιχείο, το [steeheeo] component, element || (νομ) piece of evidence || (αλφαβήτου) letter || (πλεκτ) cell || (μεταφ) factor.

στοιχειοθεσία, η [steeheeotheseea] typesetting.

στοιχειώδης [steeheeoðees] elementary, rudimentary || essential, capital.

στοιχειωμένος [steeheeoomenos] haunted.

στοιχειώνω [steeheeoono] become haunted, haunt.

στοίχημα, το [steeheema] bet, wager || stake || **βάζω** ~ lay a bet, wager.

στοιχηματίζω [steeheemateezo] bet, wager.

στοιχίζω [steeheezo] cost || (μεταφ) pain, grieve.

στοίχος, ο [steehos] row, line, rank.

στόκος, ο [stokos] putty, stucco.

στολή, η [stolee] uniform || costume.

στολίδι, το [stoleeðee] jewellery || (στόλισμα) adornment, decoration.

στολίζω [stoleezo] adorn, decorate, deck, trim, embellish.

στολισμός, ο [stoleesmos] ornamenting, decoration, embellishing.

στόλος, ο [stolos] navy, fleet.

στόμα, το [stoma] mouth || lips.

στομάχι, το [stomahee] stomach.

στομαχιάζω [stomaheeazo] suffer from indigestion.

στόμιο, το [stomeeo] mouth, opening, aperture, entrance || muzzle.

στόμφος, ο [stomfos] boast, declamation.

στομώνω [stomono] blunt || temper, harden.

στορ, το [stor], στόρι, το [storee] blind, roller blind.

στοργή, η [storyee] affection, tenderness, love.

στουμπώνω [stoumbono] stuff, pad, plug || become stuffed.

στουπί, το [stoupee] oakum, wad, tow || (μεταφ) drunk as a lord.

στουπόχαρτο, το [stoupoharto] blotting paper.

στουρνάρι, το [stournaree] flint, gun flint.

στοχάζομαι [stohazome] think, meditate (on) || consider.

στοχασμός, ο [stohasmos] thought, meditation.

στοχαστικός [stohasteekos] thoughtful || discreet, wise.

στόχαστρο, το [stohastro] front sight (of gun).

στόχος, ο [stohos] mark, target, objective || aim, end.

στραβά [strava] obliquely, crookedly || wrongly, amiss || τόβαλε ~ he doesn't give a damn.

στραβισμός, ο [straveesmos] squinting.

στραβοκάνης [stravokanees] bandy-legged.

στραβομάρα, η [stravomara] blindness || (κακοτυχία) bad luck, mischance || (μεταφ) blunder, gross mistake, howler.

στραβόξυλο, το [stravokseelo] obstinate person, contrary fellow.

στραβοπάτημα, το [stravopateema] staggering || false step.

στραβός [stravos] crooked, awry, twisted || (λοξός) slanting || (ελαττωματικός) faulty || (τυφλός) blind.

στραβώνομαι [stravonome] go blind.

στραβώνω [stravono] bend, distort || make a mess of || spoil || (τυφλώνω) blind || (λυγίζω) become twisted.

στραγάλια, τα [stragaleea] πλ roasted chickpeas.

στραγγαλίζω [strangaleezo] strangle, throttle || stifle.

στραγγαλιστής, ο [strangaleestees] strangler.

στραγγίζω [strangeezo] drain, filter, press out, wring out || (κουράζομαι) get exhausted.

στραγγιστήρι, το [strangeesteeree] strainer, filter, colander.

στραμπουλίζω [strambouleezo] sprain, twist.

στραπατσάρω [strapatsaro] harm, damage || ruffle || (ταπεινώνω) humiliate.

στραπάτσο, το [strapatso] maltreatment || humiliation.

στράτα, η [strata] way, street, road.

στρατάρχης, ο [stratarhees] (field) marshal.

στράτευμα, το [stratevma] army, troops, forces.

στρατεύματα, τα [stratevmata] πλ troops.

στρατεύομαι [stratevome] serve in the army.

στρατεύσιμος [stratevseemos] subject to conscription.

στρατηγείο, το [strateeyeeo] headquarters.

στρατήγημα το [strateeyeema] stratagem || trick, ruse.

στρατηγία, η [strateeyeea] generalship.

στρατηγική, η [strateeyeekee] strategy.

στρατηγικός [strateeyeekos] strategic.

στρατηγός, ο [strateegos] general.

στρατί, το [stratee] βλ στράτα.

στρατιά, η [stratia] army, force.

στρατιώτης, ο [strateeotees] soldier, private || warrior.

στρατιωτικό, το [strateeoteeko] military service.

στρατιωτικός [strateeoteekos] military || ~ νόμος martial law.

στρατοδικείο, το [stratoδeekeeo] court-martial.

στρατοκρατία, η [stratokrateea] militarism, military government.

στρατολογία, η [stratoloyeea] conscription, call-up.

στρατόπεδο, το [stratopeδo] camp, encampment || side, party.

στρατός, ο [stratos] army, troops, forces.

στρατόσφαιρα, η [stratosfera] stratosphere.

στρατώνας, ο [stratonas] barracks.

στρεβλός [strevlos] crooked, deformed, twisted || (μεταφ) rough, difficult.

στρείδι, το [streeδee] oyster.

στρέμμα, το [strema] (approx) quarter of an acre.

στρέφομαι [strefome] turn, rotate || revolve.

στρέφω [strefo] turn, turn about || rotate, revolve.

στρεψοδικία, η [strepsoδeekeea] chicanery, quibbling, pettifoggery.

στρίβω [streevo] twist, rotate, turn || το ~ slip away, slip off.

στρίγ(γ)λα, n [stree(n)gla] witch, sorceress, shrew.

στριγ(γ)λιά, n [stree(n)glia] wickedness, shrewishness || (κραυγή) shrill cry, shriek.

στριμμένος [streemenos] twisted || ill-humoured, wicked, malicious.

στριφογυρίζω [streefoyeereezo] move round, turn round || whirl, spin.

στρίφωμα, το [streefoma] hemming.

στρίψιμο, το [streepseemo] twisting, turning.

στροβιλίζω [stroveeleezo] whirl, turn round, twirl.

στρόβιλος, ο [stroveelos] spinning top, peg top || (άνεμος) whirlwind || (χιόνι) eddying, swirling || (μηχανή) turbine || (σκόνης) whirling cloud.

στρογγυλεύω [strongeeievo] make round || grow plump, get stout.

στρογγυλός [strongeelos] round(ed) || (πρόσωπο) full || (αριθμός) round, even.

στρουθοκάμηλος, n [strouthokameelos] ostrich.

στρουμπουλός [stroumboulos] plump.

στρόφαλος, ο [strofalos] crank, handle || (αυτοκινήτου) starting handle.

στροφή, n [strofee] turn, revolution || (οδού) twist, bend || (κατευθύνσεως) detour, change of direction || (ποίηση) stanza || (μουσ) ritornello.

στρόφιγγα, n [strofeenga] hinge, pivot || tap.

στριμώ(χ)νω [streemo(h)no] squeeze, crowd, cram || press hard, oppress, annoy.

στρυφνός [streefnos] harsh || peevish || (χαρακτήρας) crabbed || (ύφος κτλ) obscure, difficult || (γεύση) sharp, biting.

στρώμα, το [stroma] couch, bed, mattress || (γεωλογίας) bed, layer, stratum || στο ~ ill in bed.

στρώνομαι [stronome] apply o.s. || install o.s.

στρώνω [strono] spread, lay || (κρεβάτι) make || (δρόμο) pave || (μεταφ) be well under way || ~ το κρεβάτι make the bed.

στρώση, n [strosee] layer || strewing || paving, flooring.

στρωσίδι, το [stroseedee] carpet || bedding.

στρωτός [strotos] strewn || paved || (ζωή) even, normal, regular.

στύβω [steevo] squeeze, wring, press || (μεταφ) rack one's brains || (στειρεύω) dry up, run dry.

στυγερός [steeyeros] abominable, heinous, horrible.

στυγνός [steegnos] doleful, despondent, gloomy.

στυλό, το [steelo] fountain pen.

στυλοβάτης, ο [steelovatees] pedestal, base || (μεταφ) pillar, founder.

στύλος, ο [steelos] pillar, column, pole || (μεταφ) prop, mainstay, breadwinner.

στυλώνω [steelono] support, prop up || fix.

στυπτικός [steepteekos] binding, styptic.

στυφός [steefos] sour, acrid, bitter.

στύψη, n [steepsee] alum.

στύψιμο, το [steepseemo] squeezing, pressing, wringing.

στωικός [stoeekos] stoic(al).

συ [see] you.

σύγγαμβρος, ο [seengamvros] brother-in-law.

συγγένεια, n [seengeneea] relationship, kinship || affinity, relation, connection.

συγγενής [seengenees] connected, related || (ουσ) relation, kinsman.

συγγενολό(γ)ι, το [seengenolo(y)ee] relations, relatives, kindred.

συγγνώμη, n [seengnomee] pardon, excuse || forgiveness.

σύγγραμμα, το [seengrama] work (of writing), treatise.

συγγραφέας, ο [seengrafeas] author, writer.

συγγράφω [seengrafo] write a work, compose.

συγκαίομαι [seengkeome] be chafed, be galled.

σύγκαλα, τα [seengkala] πλ: στα ~ μου normal, in good health.

συγκαλύπτω [seengkaleepto] hide, cloak, hush up, cover.

συγκαλώ [seengkalo] convene, convoke || (πρόσωπα) assemble, call together.

συγκαταβατικός [seengkatavateekos] accommodating || (τιμή) moderate, reasonable.

συγκατάθεση, n [seengkatathesee] assent, consent, acquiescence.

συγκαταλέγω [seengkatalego] include, number among || consider, regard.

συγκατανεύω [seengkatanevo] consent, assent, adhere to.

συγκατοικώ [seengkateeko] cohabit, live together.

συγκεκριμένος [seengkekreemenos] concrete, positive, clear, specific.

συγκεκριμένως [seengkekreemenos] plainly, concretely, actually.

συγκεντρώνομαι [seengkentronome] concentrate.

συγκεντρώνω [seengkentrono] collect, bring togther, concentrate || centralize.

συγκέντρωση, n [seengkentrosee] crowd, gathering, assembly || concentration || centralization.

συγκερασμός, ο [seengkerasmos] mixing, mingling || compromise.

συγκεχυμένος [seengkeheemenos] confused, jumbled || (ήχος) indistinct || (φήμες) vague || (ιδέες) hazy, dim || (λόγοι) imprecise, obscure.

συγκίνηση, n [seengkeeneesee] emotion, sensation.

συγκινητικός [seengkeeneeteekos] moving, touching, stirring.

συγκινούμαι [seengkeenoume] be excited || be touched.

συγκινώ [seengkeeno] move, affect, touch || excite.

σύγκληση, n [seengkleesee] convocation, calling together.

σύγκλητος, n [seengkleetos] senate.

συγκλίνω [seengkleeno] converge, concentrate.

συγκλονίζω [seengkloneezo] shake, excite, stir up, shock.

συγκοινωνία, n [seengkeenoneea] communications || means of transport.

συγκοινωνώ [seengkeenono] communicate, be connected.

συγκολλώ [seengkolo] glue, join together || (μέταλλα) weld, solder || ~ **σαμπρέλα** mend a puncture.

συγκομιδή, n [seengkomeedee] harvest, crop.

συγκοπή, n [seengkopee] syncopation || (ιατρ) heart failure || (γραμμ) contraction.

συγκράτηση, n [seengkrateesee] containing, bridling, restraining.

συγκρατούμαι [seengkratoume] control o.s., contain o.s.

συγκρατώ [seengkrato] check || (πάθη) govern || (θυμό) contain, control, suppress || (τα πλήθη) restrain.

συγκρίνω [seengkreeno] compare (with), liken (to).

σύγκριση, n [seengkreesee] comparison, parallel.

συγκριτικός [seengkreeteekos] comparative, compared (to).

συγκρότημα, το [seengkroteema] group, cluster || (κτίρια) complex || (μουσ) group, band.

συγκροτώ [seengkroto] form, compose || convoke, convene.

συγκρούομαι [seengkrouome] bump into, collide || clash, come to blows.

σύγκρουση, n [seengkrousee] collision, clash, fight, engagement.

σύγκρυο, το [seengkreeo] shivering, trembling.

συγκυρία, n [seengkeereea] coincidence, occurrence, chance || (οικον) conjuncture.

συγυρίζω [seeyeereezo] tidy up, arrange || (μεταφ) ill-treat.

συγχαίρω [seenghero] congratulate, compliment.

συγχαρητήρια, τα [seenghareeteereea] πλ congratulations.

συγχέω [seengheo] confound, confuse, perplex.

συγχορδία, n [seenghorδeea] harmony of sounds, accord.

συγχρονίζω [seenghroneezo] modernize, bring up to date.

σύγχρονος [seenghronos] contemporary || simultaneous || contemporaneous.

συγχύζω [seengheezo] get mixed up || worry, confound, harass.

σύγχυση, n [seengheesee] confusion, disorder || chaos, commotion.

συγχωνεύω [seenghonevo] amalgamate, blend, merge.

συγχώρηση, n [seenghoreesee] remission, pardon.

συγχωρητέος [seenghoreeteos] pardonable, excusable.

συ(γ)χωρείτε [see(ng)horeete]: **με ~** excuse me, I beg your pardon.

συγχωρώ [seenghoro] pardon, forgive, excuse || tolerate, permit.

συζήτηση, n [seezeeteesee] discussion, debate || **ούτε ~** it's out of the question.

συζητώ [seezeeto] discuss, argue, debate.

συζυγικός [seezeeyeekos] conjugal, marital.

σύζυγος, ο, n [seezeegos] consort, spouse, husband, wife.

συζώ [seezo] live together, cohabit.

συκιά, n [seekia] fig tree.

σύκο, το [seeko] fig.

συκοφάντης, ο [seekofantees] slanderer.

συκοφαντώ [seekofanto] slander.

συκώτι, το [seekotee] liver.

σύληση, n [seeleesee] spoliation, sacking.

συλλαβή, n [seelavee] syllable.

συλλαλητήριο, το [seelaleeteereeo] mass meeting, demonstration.

συλλαμβάνω [seelamvano] catch, lay hold of, capture, seize, arrest || (ιδέες) conceive.

συλλέγω [seelego] collect, gather.

συλλέκτης, ο [seelektees] collector.

σύλληψη, n [seeleepsee] capture, arrest, seizure || (ιδέας) conception.

συλλογή, n [seeloyee] set, assortment, collection || (σκέψη) thought, concern.

συλλογίζομαι [seeloyeezome] think out, reflect about, consider, reason (out).

συλλογικός [seeloyeekos] collective.

συλλογισμένος [seeloyeesmenos] pensive, thoughtful, absorbed (in).

συλλογισμός, ο [seeloyeesmos] thought, reflection || reasoning, syllogism.

σύλλογος, ο [seelogos] society, club, association.

συλλυπητήρια, τα
[seeleepeeteereea] πλ condolences, sympathy.

συλλυπούμαι [seeleepoume] offer condolence || feel sorry for.

συμβαδίζω [seemvaδeezo] keep up with || go together, coexist.

συμβαίνω [seemveno] happen, take place, come about.

συμβάλλομαι [seemvalome] contract, enter into an agreement.

συμβάλλω [seemvalo] contribute to, pay one's share || (ποτάμι) meet, join, unite.

συμβάν, το [seemvan] event, accident, occurrence.

σύμβαση, η [seemvasee] agreement, contract, treaty, pact.

συμβία, η [seemveea] wife, consort.

συμβιβάζομαι [seemveevazome] compromise, agree with || be compatible with.

συμβιβάζω [seemveevazo] reconcile, arrange, adjust.

συμβιβασμός, ο [seemveevasmos] compromise, accommodation, adjustment, settlement.

συμβίωση, η [seemveeoosee] living together, cohabitation.

συμβόλαιο, το [seemvoleo] contract, agreement.

συμβολαιογράφος, ο [seemvoleografos] notary public.

συμβολή, η [seemvolee] contribution || (ποταμών) confluence, junction.

συμβολίζω [seemvoleezo] symbolize, represent.

σύμβολο, το [seemvolo] symbol, mark, sign, emblem, token.

συμβουλεύομαι [seemvoulevome] consult, refer to, take advice.

συμβουλεύω [seemvoulevo] advise, recommend.

συμβουλή, η [seemvoulee] advice, counsel.

συμβούλιο, το [seemvouleeo] council, board, committee.

σύμβουλος, ο [seemvoulos] adviser, counsellor || councillor.

συμμαζεύω [seemazevo] tidy up, collect, assemble, gather together || (ελέγχω) restrain, check, hold.

συμμαχία, η [seemaheea] alliance, coalition.

σύμμαχος [seemahos] allied || (ουσ) ally.

συμμερίζομαι [seemereezome] share, have a part (in).

συμμετέχω [seemeteho] participate in, take part in, be a party to.

συμμετοχή, η [seemetohee] participation || sharing.

συμμετρία, η [seemetreea] symmetry, proportion.

συμμετρικός [seemetreekos] symmetrical || well-proportioned.

συμμορία, η [seemoreea] gang, band, body.

συμμορφώνομαι [seemorfonome] comply, conform, agree with, adapt to.

συμμορφώνω [seemorfono] adapt, conform || bring to heel.

συμπαγής [seembayees] solid, firm, compact, close.

συμπάθεια, η [seempatheea] compassion, sympathy || weakness (for) || favourite.

συμπαθής [seempathees] likeable, lovable.

συμπαθητικός [seempatheeteekos] likeable, lovable || sympathetic.

συμπάθιο, το [seempatheeo]: με το ~ begging your pardon.

συμπαθώ [seempatho] feel compassion for || have a liking for.

σύμπαν, το [seempan] universe || everything, all, everybody.

συμπατριώτης, ο [seempatreeotees] compatriot, fellow countryman.

συμπεθεριά, η [seempetheria] relationship by marriage.

συμπέθεροι, οι [seempetheree] πλ fathers-in-law || relations by marriage.

συμπεραίνω [seempereno] conclude, presume, infer, surmise.

συμπέρασμα, το [seemperasma] conclusion, inference, end.

συμπεριλαμβάνω [seempereelamvano] include, contain, comprise.

συμπεριφέρομαι [seempereeferome] behave, conduct o.s.

συμπεριφορά, η [seempereefora] behaviour, conduct.

συμπίεση, η [seempiesee] compression, squeezing.

συμπίπτω [seempeepto] coincide, concur, converge || happen, change.

σύμπλεγμα, το [seemplegma] tangle || cluster || network.

συμπλέκομαι [seemplekome] come to blows, quarrel || fight.

συμπλέκτης, ο [seemblektees] (μηχαν) clutch.

συμπλήρωμα, το [seempleeroma] complement || supplement, addition.

συμπληρωματικός [seempleeromateekos] complementary, further || supplementary.

συμπληρώνω [seempleerono] complete, complement, finish || (θέση) fill || (φόρμα) fill in.

συμπλήρωση, η [seempleerosee] completion, filling, achievement.

συμπλοκή, η [seemplokee] fight, engagement, clash, brawl.

σύμπνοια, η [seempneea] harmony, agreement, understanding.

συμπολιτεία, η [seempoleeteea] confederation, confederacy.

συμπολίτης, ο [seempoleetees] fellow citizen, fellow countryman.

συμπονώ [seempono] feel compassion for, sympathize with.

συμπόσιο, το [seemposeeo] banquet, feast.

συμποσούμαι [seemposoume] come to, run (to).

σύμπραξη, η [seempraksee] cooperation, contribution.

συμπτύσσομαι [seempteesome] fall back, shorten.

συμπτύσσω [seempteeso] shorten, abridge, abbreviate, cut short.

σύμπτωμα, το [seemptoma] symptom || sign, indication.

σύμπτωση, η [seemptosee] coincidence, accident, chance.

συμπυκνώνω [seempeeknono] condense, compress.

συμπυκνωτής, ο [seempeeknotees] condenser.

συμφέρει [seemferee] it's worth it, it's to one's advantage.

συμφέρον, το [seemferon] advantage, interest, profit, benefit.

συμφεροντολογία, η [seemferontoloyeea] self-interest.

συμφιλιώνω [seemfeeleeono] reconcile, restore friendship, make up.

συμφορά, η [seemfora] calamity, disaster, misfortune.

συμφόρηση, η [seemforeesee] traffic jam, congestion || (ιατρ) stroke.

σύμφορος [seemforos] advantageous, profitable, useful.

συμφύρω [seemfeero] confuse, mingle, mix, jumble.

σύμφωνα [seemfona]: ~ **με** according to, in conformity with.

συμφωνητικό, το [seemfoneeteeko] agreement, deed of contract.

συμφωνία, η [seemfoneea] agreement, convention || accord, consent || (μουσ) symphony.

σύμφωνο, το [seemfono] (γράμμα) consonant || compact, agreement, pact.

σύμφωνος [seemfonos] in accord, in conformity with.

συμφωνώ [seemfono] concur, agree || match, go well together.

συμψηφίζω [seempseefeezo] counterbalance, make up for.

συν [seen] together, with || (μαθημ) plus || ~ **τω χρόνω** in time, gradually, eventually || ~ **τοις άλλοις** moreover, in addition.

συναγερμός, ο [seenayermos] alarm, call to arms, alert || (πολιτικός) rally, mass meeting.

συναγρίδα, η [seenagreeδa] kind of sea bream.

συνάγω [seenago] assemble, collect, bring together || (συμπεραίνω) infer, conclude, deduce.

συναγωγή, η [seenagoyee] collection, gathering, assembly || (εβραίων) synagogue.

συναγωνίζομαι [seenagoneezome] rival, compete || fight together.

συναγωνιστής, ο [seenagoneestees] rival, competitor || (συμπολεμιστής) brother in arms || (ανταγωνιστής) rival.

συνάδελφος, ο [seenaδelfos] colleague, fellow member.

συναινώ [seeneno] consent to, agree to, acquiesce.

συναίρεση, η [seeneresee] (γραμμ) contraction.

συναισθάνομαι [seenesthanome] become aware of, be conscious of, feel.

συναίσθημα, το [seenestheema] sentiment, feeling, sensation.

συναισθήματα, τα [seenestheemata] πλ emotions, feelings.

συναισθηματικός [seenestheemateekos] emotional, sentimental.

συναίσθηση, η [seenestheesee] feeling, sense, appreciation, consciousness.

συναλλαγή, η [seenalayee] exchange, dealings, trade || **ελεύθερη** ~ free trade.

συνάλλαγμα, το [seenalagma] foreign currency || draft, bill || **τιμή συναλλάγματος** rate of exchange.

συναλλαγματική, η [seenalagmateekee] bill of exchange.

συναλλάσσομαι [seenalasome] deal, trade, traffic || (συναναστρέφομαι) associate with.

συνάμα [seenama] together, in one lot, at the same time, at once.

συναναστρέφομαι [seenanastrefome] consort with, mix with.

συναναστροφή, η [seenanastrofee] association, company || party, reception.

συνάντηση, η [seenanteesee] falling in with, meeting || encounter.

συναντώ [seenanto] meet, happen (upon), run across.

συναντώμαι [seenantome] meet, come together.

σύναξη, η [seenaksee] concentration, meeting || collecting, receipts.

συναπτός [seenaptos] consecutive, successive || annexed, tied, appended.

συνάπτω [seenapto] annex, attach || (συμμαχία) contract, form || (δάνειο) incur || (ειρήνη) conclude || (μάχη) join, give battle || ~ **σχέσεις** make friends.

συναρμολογώ [seenarmologo] fit

together || join || make up, piece together.

συναρπάζω [seenarpazo] carry away, enrapture, entrance.

συνάρτηση, η [seenarteesee] attachment, connection || cohesion.

συνασπισμός, ο [seenaspeesmos] coalition, alliance, league.

συναυλία, η [seenavleea] concert.

συνάφεια, η [seenafeea] connection, link, reference.

συναφής [seenafees] adjacent (to) || linked, connected || like.

συνάχι, το [seenahee] cold (in the head), catarrh.

σύναψη, η [seenapsee] conclusion, arrangement || contraction || joining.

συνδεδεμένος [seenðeðemenos] closely associated with, having ties with.

σύνδεση, η [seenðesee] joining, binding together.

σύνδεσμος, ο [seenðesmos] bond, union || (στρατ) liaison || relationship, affinity || (γραμμ) conjunction.

συνδετήρας, ο [seenðeteeras] clip, paper clip.

συνδετικός [seenðeteekos] joining, connective || (γραμμ) copulative.

συνδέω [seenðeo] bind together, unite || (μεταφ) join, link, bind.

συνδιαλέγομαι [seenðeealegome] converse (with), talk (to).

συνδιάσκεψη, η [seenðeeaskepsee] deliberation || conference.

συνδικάτο, το [seenðeekato] syndicate || (εργατών) trade union.

συνδράμω [seenðramo] support, help || contribute to.

συνδρομή, η [seenðromee] coincidence, conjunction || (βοήθεια) help, assistance || subscription, contribution.

συνδρομητής, ο [seenðromeetees] subscriber.

σύνδρομο, το [seenðromo] syndrome.

συνδυάζομαι [seenðeeazome] harmonize, go together, match.

συνδυάζω [seenðeeazo] unite, combine || match, pair || arrange.

συνδυασμός, ο [seenðeeasmos] combination, arrangement || matching.

συνεδριάζω [seeneðreeazo] meet, be in session.

συνέδριο, το [seeneðreeo] congress, convention, council.

σύνεδρος, ο [seeneðros] delegate || councillor || (δικαστηρίου) judge.

συνείδηση, η [seeneeðeesee] conscience.

συνειδητός [seeneeðeetos] conscious, wilful.

συνειρμός, ο [seeneermos] coherence, order, sequence.

συνεισφέρω [seeneesfero] contribute, subscribe.

συνεκτικός [seenekteekos] cohesive, binding, tenacious.

συνέλευση, η [seenelevsee] meeting, assembly.

συνεννόηση, η [seenenoeesee] understanding, concert, concord, agreement || exchange of views.

συνεννοούμαι [seenenooume] agree, come to an agreement || exchange views.

συνενοχή, η [seenenohee] complicity, abetment, connivance.

συνέντευξη, η [seenentevksee] interview, appointment, rendezvous.

συνενώ [seeneno] unite, join together.

συνεπάγομαι [seenepagome] lead to, involve, have as consequence, call for.

συνεπαίρνω [seeneperno] transport, carry away.

συνέπεια, η [seenepeea] result, outcome, consequence || consistency || κατά ~ consequently.

συνεπής [seenepees] true, in keeping with, consistent || punctual.

συνεπώς [seenepos] consequently, accordingly.

συνεπτυγμένος [seenepteegmenos] compact, succinct, brief.

συνεργάζομαι [seenergazome] cooperate, collaborate || contribute.

συνεργάτης, ο [seenergatees] collaborator || contributor.

συνεργείο, το [seeneryeeo] workroom, workshop || gang, shift, team of workers || repair shop.

συνεργία, η [seeneryeea] complicity, abetment, confederacy.

σύνεργο, το [seenergo] implement, tool, instrument.

συνεργός, ο [seenergos] accessary, accomplice, abettor, party (to).

συνερίζομαι [seenereezome] heed, take into account, keep up rivalry with.

συνέρχομαι [seenerhome] get over, recover || come together, meet, assemble.

σύνεση, η [seenesee] caution, good sense, prudence, judgment.

συνεσταλμένος [seenestalmenos] shy, modest, timid, circumspect.

συνεταιρισμός, ο [seenetereesmos] cooperative, association.

συνέταιρος, ο [seeneteros] partner, associate, colleague, co-partner.

συνετός [seenetos] wise, discreet, prudent, sensible, cautious.

συνεφέρνω [seeneferno] revive, bring round || come to.

συνέχεια, η [seeneheea] continuity || continuation, outcome || (επίρ) continuously, successively.

συνεχής [seenehees] continuous,

incessant, unceasing, continual ||
successive || adjacent.

συνεχίζω [seeneheezo] continue, keep
on, go on.

συνεχώς [seenehos] continually,
endlessly.

συνήγορος, ο [seeneegoros]
advocate, defender, counsel.

συνήθεια, η [seeneetheea] habit,
custom, practice, use.

συνήθης [seeneethees] habitual,
customary, usual, common, ordinary.

συνηθίζεται [seeneetheezete] it is
usual, it is the fashion.

συνηθίζω [seeneetheezo] accustom to
|| get accustomed to || be in the habit of.

συνηθισμένος [seeneetheesmenos]
accustomed, familiar || habitual,
customary.

συνημμένος [seeneemenos]
attached, connected, annexed,
enclosed.

σύνθεση, η [seenthese] mixture,
composition || collocation || structure,
synthesis.

συνθέτης, ο [seenthetees] composer
|| compositor.

συνθετικό, το [seentheteeko]
component, constituent.

συνθετικός [seentheteekos]
constituent, component || artificial,
synthetic.

σύνθετος [seenthetos] compound,
composite || intricate.

συνθέτω [seentheto] compose, make
up.

συνθήκες, οι [seentheekes] πλ
conditions, circumstances, situation.

συνθήκη, η [seentheekee] treaty,
agreement, pact || convention.

συνθηκολογώ [seentheekologo]
surrender, capitulate || negotiate a
treaty.

σύνθημα, το [seentheema] signal,
sign, password, watchword.

συνθηματικός [seentheemateekos]
symbolic || in code.

συνθλίβω [seenthleevo] squeeze,
compress, crush.

συνίσταμαι [seeneestame] consist of,
be composed of.

συνιστώ [seeneesto] advise,
recommend || (επιτροπή) establish, set
up, form || (γνωρίζω) introduce.

συννεφιά, η [seenefia] cloudy
weather || ~ζω become cloudy ||
(μεταφ) look sullen.

σύννεφο, το [seenefo] cloud.

συννυφάδα, η [seeneefaða] wife of
one's brother-in-law.

συνοδ(ε)ία η [seenoðeea] escort,
retinue, suite, convoy, procession ||
(μουσ) accompaniment.

συνοδεύω [seenoðevo] accompany,
go with, escort || (ναυτ) convoy.

συνοδοιπόρος, ο, η [seenoðeeporos] fellow traveller.

σύνοδος, η [seenoðos] congress,
sitting, assembly || (εκκλ) synod.

συνοδός, ο, η [seenoðos] steward,
escort || **ιπτάμενη** ~ air hostess.

συνοικέσιο, το [seeneekeseeo]
arranged marriage, match.

συνοικία, η [seeneekeea] quarter,
neighbourhood, ward.

συνοικιακός [seeneekeeakos] local,
suburban.

συνοικισμός, ο [seeneekeesmos]
settlement || colonization || quarter.

συνολικός [seenoleekos] total, whole.

σύνολο, το [seenolo] total, entirety.

συνομήλικος [seenomeeleekos] of
the same age.

συνομιλητής, ο [seenomeeleetees]
interlocutor.

συνομιλία, η [seenomeeleea]
conversation, chat, talk || interview.

συνομοταξία, η [seenomotakseea]
branch, group, class.

συνονόματος [seenonomatos]
namesake, having the same name.

συνοπτικός [seenopteekos]
summary, brief, synoptic, concise.

σύνορα, τα [seenora] πλ frontier,
boundaries.

συνορεύω [seenorevo] have a
common frontier, border on.

σύνορο, το [seenoro] boundary,
border, frontier.

συνουσία, η [seenouseea] coition,
intercourse, copulation.

συνοφρυόνομαι [seenofreeonome]
frown, scowl || look sullen.

συνοχή, η [seenohee] coherence,
cohesion || (ιδεών) sequence, chain.

σύνοψη, η [seenopsee] summary,
compendium, synopsis || (εκκλ) prayer
book, breviary.

συνταγή, η [seentayee] formula,
prescription || recipe.

σύνταγμα, το [seentagma]
constitution, charter || (στρατ)
regiment.

συνταγματάρχης, ο
[seentagmatarhees] colonel.

συνταγματικός [seentagmateekos]
constitutional.

συντάκτης, ο [seentaktees] author,
writer || (εφημερίδας) editor ||
(συνθήκης) drafter, framer.

συντακτικός [seentakteekos]
component, constituent || (εφημερίδας)
editorial || (γραμμ) syntactic(al).

σύνταξη, η [seentaksee] compilation
|| wording, writing || organization ||
(εφημερίδας) editing, editorial staff ||
pension || (γραμμ) construction, syntax.

συνταξιούχος, ο, η
[seentaksiouhos] pensioner || retired
officer.

συνταράσσω [seentaraso] agitate, shake, disturb, trouble || (μεταφ) disconcert.

συντάσσω [seentaso] arrange, compile || write, draft, draw up || (γραμμ) construe || constitute, form, organize || (νόμο) frame || (εφημερίδα) edit.

συνταυτίζω [seentavteezo] identify, regard as the same.

συντείνω [seenteeno] contribute to, concur.

συντέλεια, n [seenteleea]: ~ του κόσμου end of the world.

συντελεστής, ο [seentelestees] factor, component, contributor || (μαθημ) coefficient.

συντελώ [seentelo] finish, complete || contribute to, conduce to.

συντεταγμένη, n [seentetagmenee] coordinate.

συντετριμμένος [seentetreemenos] deeply afflicted, crushed.

συντεχνία, n [seentehneea] guild, fellowship, confraternity || trade union.

συντήρηση, n [seenteereesee] preservation, conservation || (μηχανής) maintenance.

συντηρητικός [seenteereeteekos] conservative, preserving.

συντηρώ [seenteero] preserve, conserve || keep up, maintain || (διατρέφω) maintain, support.

σύντομα [seentoma] in short, briefly || soon, at once, immediately.

συντομεύω [seentomevo] shorten, curtail, abridge.

συντομία, n [seentomeea] shortness, brevity || terseness.

σύντομος [seentomos] short, succinct, brief.

συντονίζω [seentoneezo] coordinate, harmonize, tune together.

συντρέχω [seentreho] help || meet, converge || contribute.

συντριβή, n [seentreevee] ruin || crushing, smashing.

συντρίβω [seentreevo] shatter, break, crush, smash || ruin, wear out.

συντρίμια, τα [seentreemeea] πλ debris, fragments, wreckage.

συντριπτικός [seentreepteekos] (μεταφ) crushing, overwhelming.

συντροφιά, n [seentrofia] companionship, company || gathering, society || (επίρ) together.

σύντροφος, ο, n [seentrofos] companion, mate, comrade || (εμπορ) associate, partner.

συνύπαρξη, n [seeneeparksee] coexistence.

συνυπάρχω [seeneeparho] coexist.

συνυπεύθυνος [seeneepevtheenos] jointly liable.

συνυφαίνω [seeneefeno] entwine || (μεταφ) conspire, intrigue.

συνωμοσία, n [seenomoseea] conspiracy, plot.

συνωμοτώ [seenomoto] conspire, plot.

συνώνυμο, το [seenoneemo] synonym.

συνωστισμός, ο [seenosteesmos] jostle, crush, scramble.

σύξυλος [seekseelos] with crew and cargo || έμεινε ~ he was amazed, he was speechless.

Συρία, n [seereea] Syria.

συριακός [seereeakos] Syrian.

σύριγγα, n [seereenga] pan pipes || syringe, tube.

Σύριος, ο [seereeos] Syrian.

σύρμα, το [seerma] wire.

συρματόπλεγμα, το [seermatoplegma] barbed wire || wire netting.

σύρραξη, n [seeraksee] clash, collision, shock, conflict.

συρρέω [seereo] crowd, throng, flock || flow into.

σύρριζα [seereeza] by the root, root and branch || very closely.

συρροή, n [seeroee] crowd, throng || inflow, influx || abundance, profusion.

συρτάρι, το [seertaree] drawer.

σύρτης, ο [seertees] bolt, bar.

συρτός [seertos] dragged || listless, drawling || (πόρτα) sliding || (ουσ) kind of circular dance.

συρφετός, ο [seerfetos] mob, populace, common people.

σύρω [seero] βλ σέρνω.

συσκέπτομαι [seeskeptome] confer, deliberate, take counsel.

συσκευάζω [seeskevazo] pack, box, wrap, parcel.

συσκευασία, n [seeskevaseea] wrapping up, packing || (φαρμακευτική) preparation.

συσκευή, n [seeskevee] apparatus, contrivance.

σύσκεψη, n [seeskepsee] discussion, deliberation || conference, consultation.

συσκοτίζω [seeskoteezo] obscure, darken, black out || (μεταφ) confuse.

συσκότιση, n [seeskoteesee] blackout || confusion.

σύσπαση, n [seespasee] contraction, writhing, shrinking.

συσπειρούμαι [seespeeroume] roll into a ball, coil || (μεταφ) snuggle.

συσσίτιο, το [seeseeteeo] mess, common meal || soup kitchen.

σύσσωμος [seesomos] all together, entire, united, in a body.

συσσωρευτής, ο [seesorevtees] accumulator.

συσσωρεύω [seesorevo] accumulate, collect, pile up || amass.

συσταίνω [seesteno] βλ συνιστώ.

συστάδα, η [seestaða] clump of trees, cluster, grove.

συστάσεις, οι [seestasees] πλ references, advice || recommendation, introductions.

σύσταση, η [seestasee] address.

σύσταση, η [seestasee] composition, structure || (πάχος) consistency || (σχηματισμός) formation, creation, setting up || (πρόταση) recommendation, recommending || (συμβουλή) advice, counsel.

συστατικά, τα [seestateeka] πλ component parts, ingredients || references, recommendations.

συστατική [seestateekee]: ~ επιστολή letter of introduction, letter of reference.

συστατικός [seestateekos] component, essential, constituent.

συστέλλομαι [seestelome] shrink, contract || feel shy, be timid.

συστέλλω [seestelo] contract, shrink, shrivel.

σύστημα, το [seesteema] method, system, plan || custom, habitude.

συστηματικός [seesteemateekos] systematic, methodical.

συστημένο [seesteemeno]: ~ γράμμα registered letter.

συστήνω [seesteeno] βλ συνιστώ.

συστολή, η [seestolee] shrinking, contraction || modesty, shame, bashfulness.

συσφίγγω [seesfeengo] tighten, constrict, draw tighter, grasp.

συσχετίζω [seesheteezo] compare, relate, put together.

σύφιλη, η [seefeelee] syphilis.

συχνά [seehna] often, frequently.

συχνάζω [seehnazo] frequent, haunt, resort.

συχνός [seehnos] frequent, repeated.

συχνότητα, η [seehnoteeta] frequency.

συχωράω [seehorao] forgive, tolerate.

σφαγείο, το [sfayeeo] slaughterhouse || butchery, slaughter.

σφαγή, η [sfayee] slaughter, carnage, massacre.

σφάγιο, το [sfayo] victim, animal for slaughter.

σφαδάζω [sfaðazo] writhe, jerk, squirm.

σφάζω [sfazo] slaughter, kill, massacre, murder.

σφαίρα, η [sfera] globe, sphere || ball || (όπλου) bullet || (μεταφ) sphere, field.

σφαλιάρα, η [sfaleeara] slap in the face || smack.

σφαλίζω [sfaleezo] enclose, shut in || (κλείνω) close, lock, bolt.

σφάλλω [sfalo] be wrong, make a mistake || misfire.

σφάλμα, το [sfalma] wrong act, fault || error, blunder, slip.

σφάχτης, ο [sfahtees] twinge, sharp pain.

σφενδόνη, η [sfenðonee] sling.

σφετερίζομαι [sfetereezome] purloin, embezzle || appropriate, usurp.

σφήκα, η [sfeeka] wasp.

σφην, η [sfeen)], σφήνα, η [sfeena] wedge.

σφηνώνω [sfeenono] push in, thrust in between || wedge.

σφίγγα, η [sfeenga] sphinx || (μεταφ) enigmatic.

σφίγγομαι [sfeengome] squeeze together || endeavour, try hard.

σφίγγω [sfeengo] squeeze, press || tighten, pull tighter || (σκληρύνω) become tight, stick.

σφίξη, η [sfeeksee] urgency, necessity.

σφίξιμο, το [sfeekseemo] pressing, tightening, squeezing || pressure, squeeze.

σφιχτός [sfeehtos] tight, hard, thick || stingy, tight-fisted.

σφοδρός [sfoðros] violent, wild, strong, severe, sharp.

σφοδρότητα, η [sfoðroteeta] violence, vehemence, wildness.

σφουγγάρι, το [sfoungaree] sponge.

σφουγγαρόπανο, το [sfoungaropano] mop, floorcloth.

σφραγίζω [sfrayeezo] set one's seal to, stamp || (μπουκάλι) cork || (δόντι) fill.

σφραγίδα, η [sfrayeeða] seal, signet, stamp || (μεταφ) impression.

σφρίγος, το [sfreegos] youthful exuberance, vigour, pep.

σφυγμός, ο [sfeegmos] pulse || (μεταφ) caprice, whim.

σφύζω [sfeezo] throb, beat violently, pulsate.

σφύξη, η [sfeeksee] pulsation, throbbing, throb.

σφυρηλατώ [sfeereelato] hammer, batter, forge, pound away || trump up.

σφυρί, το [sfeeree] hammer.

σφύριγμα, το [sfeereegma] whistling, hissing.

σφυρίζω [sfeereezo] whistle, hiss, boo.

σφυρίχτρα, η [sfeereehtra] whistle || (ναυτ) pipe.

σφυροκοπώ [sfeerokopo] hammer || pound away.

σχεδία, η [sheðeea] raft, float.

σχεδιάγραμμα, το [sheðeeagrama] sketch, outline, draft.

σχεδιάζω [sheðeeazo] sketch, outline, design, draw || plan, intend, mean.

σχεδιαστής, ο [sheðeeastees] draughtsman, designer.

σχέδιο, το [sheðeeo] plan, design || sketch, outline || scheme || ~ πόλεως town planning.

σχεδόν [sheðon] almost, nearly, all but || not much, scarcely.

σχέση, η [shesee] relation, connection, reference || intercourse, relations.

σχετίζομαι [sheteezome] be intimate with, get acquainted with, make friends with.

σχετίζω [sheteezo] put side by side, connect, compare.

σχετικά [sheteeka] relative to, relatively || ~ με with reference to, regarding, referring to.

σχετικός [sheteekos] relative, pertinent.

σχετικότητα, η [sheteekoteeta] relativity.

σχήμα, το [sheema] form, shape || (μέγεθος) format, size || (ιερατικό) cloth || gesture || ~ λόγου figure of speech.

σχηματίζω [sheemateezo] form, model, shape || create, produce || constitute.

σχηματισμός, ο [sheemateesmos] forming, formation, fashioning, construction.

σχίζομαι [sheezome] crack, tear || fork.

σχίζω [sheezo] split, cleave || tear, rend, fissure.

σχίσμα, το [sheesma] crack || schism, dissension, breach.

σχισμάδα, η [sheesmaða] crack, split, fissure.

σχισμή, η [sheesmee] crack, fissure, split.

σχιστόλιθος, ο [sheestoleethos] schist, slate.

σχιστός [sheestos] split, slit, torn, open.

σχοινί, το [sheenee] rope, cord || clothes line.

σχοινοβάτης, ο [sheenovatees] acrobat, rope dancer.

σχολάω [sholao] stop work || rest, be on vacation || (από σχολείο) let out || (από εργασία) dismiss, discharge.

σχολαστικός [sholasteekos] pedantic, scholastic.

σχολείο, το [sholeeo] school.

σχολή, η [sholee] school, academy || free time, leisure.

σχολιάζω [sholeeazo] comment on, pass remarks (on), criticize || annotate, edit.

σχολιαστής, ο [sholeeastees] commentator || editor, annotator, scholiast.

σχολικός [sholeekos] of school, scholastic, educational.

σχόλιο, το [sholeeo] comment, commentary, annotation.

σώβρακο, το [sovrako] pants, drawers.

σώζομαι [sozome] escape || remain in existence.

σώζω [sozo] save, rescue || preserve, keep.

σωθικά, τα [sotheeka] πλ entrails, bowels, intestines, innards.

σωλήνας, ο [soleenas] pipe, tube, conduit || hose.

σωληνάριο, το [soleenareeo] small tube.

σώμα, το [soma] body, corpse || corps || ~ στρατού army corps, armed force, army.

σωματείο, το [somateeo] guild, association.

σωματέμπορος, ο [somatemboros] white slaver || pimp.

σωματικός [somateekos] of the body, physical.

σωματοφυλακή, η [somatofeelakee] bodyguard.

σωματώδης [somatoðees] corpulent, stout, portly.

σώνει [sonee]: ~ και καλά with stubborn insistence.

σώνω [sono] save, rescue, preserve || use up, consume || attain, reach || be enough, be sufficient.

σώος [soos] safe, entire, whole, unharmed || intact || ~ κι αβλαβής safe and sound.

σωπαίνω [sopeno] keep silent, say nothing.

σωριάζομαι [soreeazome] collapse, fall in.

σωρός, ο [soros] heap, mass, pile || a lot of, a stack of.

σωσίας, ο [soseeas] living image, double || stand-in.

σωσίβιο, το [soseeveeo] lifebelt, life jacket.

σώσιμο, το [soseemo] saving || finishing up, eating.

σωστά [sosta]: με τα ~ του in his right mind, in earnest.

σωστά [sosta] correctly, precisely, rightly, exactly, absolutely.

σωστός [sostos] correct, just, right || whole, entire || absolute.

σωτήρας, ο [soteeras] saviour, liberator, rescuer.

σωτηρία, η [soteereea] safety, security || salvation, deliverance, saving.

σωφέρ, ο [sofer] chauffeur, driver.

σώφρονας [sofronas] wise, sensible, prudent || moderate, sober, temperate.

σωφρονίζω [sofroneezo] reform, chastise, correct, bring to reason, render wise.

σωφροσύνη, η [sofroseenee] wisdom, prudence, sense, judgment || moderation, composure.

T, τ

τα [ta] πλ the || them.

ταβάνι, το [tavanee] ceiling.

ταβέρνα, η [taverna] tavern, inn, eating house.

τάβλα, η [tavla] board, plank || table || ~ **στο μεθύσι** dead drunk.

τάβλι, το [tavlee] backgammon.

ταγάρι, το [tagaree] bag, sack, wallet.

ταγγός [tangos] rancid, rank.

ταγή, η [tayee] fodder.

ταγιέρ, το [tayier] woman's suit.

τάγμα, το [tagma] order || (στρατ) battalion.

ταγματάρχης, ο [tagmatarhees] major.

τάδε [taδe] as follows, the following, this, that || **ο ~ Mr** so and so || such.

τάζω [tazo] promise, dedicate, vow.

ταΐζω [taeezo] feed || (μωρό) nurse.

ταινία, η [teneea] band, stretch, strip, ribbon || (κινηματογράφου) strip, film || (μηχανής) tape, ribbon || (ιατρ) tapeworm || (μετρήσεως) tape measure.

ταίρι, το [teree] helpmate, partner, mate || one of two || match, equal.

ταιριάζει [tereeazee]: **δεν ~** it's not fitting, it's not proper.

ταιριάζω [tereeazo] match, pair, suit, harmonize.

ταιριαστός [tereeastos] well-suited, matched.

τάκος, ο [takos] wooden fixing block, stump.

τακούνι, το [takounee] heel.

τακτ, το [takt] tact.

τακτικά [takteeka] regularly, frequently.

τακτική, η [takteekee] tactics, strategy || method, regularity.

τακτικός [takteekos] regular || orderly, settled, quiet || fixed || (αριθμός) ordinal.

τακτοποίηση, η [taktopieesee] arrangement, accommodation || compromise.

τακτοποιώ [taktopeeo] arrange, set in order || settle, fix up.

τακτός [taktos] fixed, appointed, settled.

ταλαιπωρία, η [taleeporeea] torment, hardship, pain, adversity.

ταλαίπωρος [taleeporos] miserable, wretched, unfortunate.

ταλαιπωρούμαι [taleeporoume] suffer, toil, labour.

ταλαιπωρώ [taleeporo] harass, pester, torment.

ταλαντεύομαι [talantevome] swing, sway, rock || waver, hesitate.

ταλέντο, το [talento] talent, gift, faculty.

τάλιρο, το [taleero] coin of five drachmas.

τάμα, το [tama] βλ **τάξιμο.**

ταμείο, το [tameeo] cashier's office, booking office, cash desk || treasury, pension fund.

ταμίας, ο [tameeas] cashier, teller, treasurer.

ταμιευτήριο, το [tamievteereeo] savings bank.

ταμπακιέρα, η [tambakiera] cigarette case || snuff box.

ταμπέλα, η [tambela] nameplate, bill || registration plate.

ταμπλό, το [tamblo] painting, picture || (αυτοκινήτου) dashboard || switchboard || instrument panel.

ταμπούρλο, το [tambourlo] drum || (παιδικό) side drum.

τανάλια, τα [tanaleea] πλ pliers, tongs, tweezers.

τανκ, το [tank] (στρατ) tank.

τάξη, η [taksee] order, succession, regularity || class, rank, grade || (σχολείου) form || **εντάξει** O.K., all right || **τάξεις** πλ ranks || **πρώτης τάξεως** first-rate, first-class.

ταξί, το [taksee] taxi (cab).

ταξιάρχης, ο [takseearhees] brigadier || (εκκλ) archangel.

ταξιαρχία η [takseearheea] brigade.

ταξιδεύω [takseeδevo] travel, journey.

ταξίδι, το [takseeδee] trip, journey, travel, voyage.

ταξιδιώτης, ο [takseeδeeotees] traveller.

ταξιθέτρια, η [takseethetreea] theatre attendant, usher.

ταξικός [takseekos] class.

ταξίμετρο, το [takseemetro] taximeter.

τάξιμο, το [takseemo] vow, promise.

ταξινομώ [takseenomo] classify, class, arrange || grade.

τάπα, η [tapa] plug, cork, stopper || ~ **στο μεθύσι** dead drunk.

ταπεινός [tapeenos] modest, humble || abject, vile, base.

ταπεινοφροσύνη, η [tapeenofroseenee] humility, modesty.

ταπεινώνομαι [tapeenonome] be humiliated || lower o.s.

ταπεινώνω [tapeenono] humble, humiliate, mortify, embarrass.

ταπέτο, το [tapeto] carpet, rug.

ταπετσαρία, η [tapetsareea] tapestry, wall covering || upholstery.

ταπητουργία, η [tapeetouryeea] carpet-making.

τάραγμα, το [taragma] agitation, shaking.

ταράζω [tarazo] shake || disturb, upset.

ταραμάς, ο [taramas] preserved roe.

ταραξίας, ο [tarakseeas] rowdy person, agitator, noisy person.

ταράτσα, η [taratsa] flat roof, terrace.

ταραχή, η [tarahee] agitation, disturbance || upset.

ταραχοποιός, ο [tarahopeeos] βλ **ταραξίας.**

ταρίφα, η [tareefa] scale of charges, price list, rates.

ταριχεύω [tareehevo] embalm || preserve, cure, smoke.

ταρσανάς, ο [tarsanas] boatbuilder's yard.

τάρταρα, τα [tartara] πλ bowels of the earth.

τασάκι, το [tasakee] saucer || ashtray.

τάση, η [tasee] tension, strain || (ηλεκτ) voltage || (μεταφ) inclination, proclivity, tendency.

τάσι, το [tasee] shallow bowl, goblet.

τάσσομαι [tasome] place o.s. || (μεταφ) support.

τάσσω [taso] place, put || post, set || marshal || assign, fix.

ταυ, το [tav] the letter T.

ταυρομαχία, η [tavromaheea] bullfight.

ταύρος, ο [tavros] bull.

ταύτα [tavta] πλ these || **μετά ~** afterwards.

ταυτίζω [tavteezo] identify, regard as same.

ταυτόσημος [tavtoseemos] equivalent, synonymous.

ταυτότητα, η [tavtoteeta] identity, sameness || identity card.

ταυτόχρονος [tavtohronos] simultaneous.

ταφή, η [tafee] burial, interment.

τάφος, ο [tafos] grave, tomb, vault.

τάφρος, η [tafros] ditch, trench, drain || (οχυρού) moat.

τάχα(τες) [taha(tes)] perhaps, apparently, supposedly || as if.

ταχεία, η [taheea] express train.

ταχίνι, το [taheenee] ground sesame.

ταχυδακτυλουργία, η [taheeðakteelouryeea] conjuring trick, juggling.

ταχυδρομείο, το [taheeðromeeo] post, mail || post office.

ταχυδρομικώς [taheeðromeekos] by post, by mail.

ταχυδρόμος, ο [taheeðromos] postman.

ταχυδρομώ [taheeðromo] mail, post.

ταχύνω [taheeno] quicken, speed up, accelerate || hasten, push forward.

ταχυπαλμία, η [taheepalmeea] palpitation.

ταχύς [tahees] quick, brisk, rapid, fleet, swift, fast || prompt, speedy.

ταχύτητα, η [taheeteeta] swiftness, speed, rapidity || promptness || velocity, rate.

ταψί, το [tapsee] large shallow baking pan.

τέζα [teza] stretched, spread, tight ||

έμεινε ~ he kicked the bucket (col) || **~ στο μεθύσι** dead drunk.

τεθλασμένη, η [tethlasmenee] zigzag line, broken line.

τεθλασμένος [tethlasmenos] broken.

τεθλιμμένος [tethleemenos] grief-stricken, heartbroken.

τείνω [teeno] tighten, stretch out || strain || tend (to), lead (to), be inclined (to).

τείχος, το [teehos] wall, high wall.

τεκμήριο, το [tekmeereeo] sign, token, mark, clue, indication.

τεκτονισμός, ο [tektoneesmos] freemasonry.

τελάρο, το [telaro] embroidery frame || (θύρας) doorframe || (πίνακα) frame.

τελεία, η [teleea] full stop || **άνω ~** semicolon.

τελειοποιώ [teleeopeeo] perfect, improve, make better.

τέλειος [teleeos] perfect, faultless || ideal || accomplished.

τελειότητα, η [teleeoteeta] perfection, faultlessness.

τελειόφοιτος [teleeofeetos] final-year (student) || graduate.

τελειωμός, ο [teleeomos] end, finish || **τελειωμό δεν έχει** it is interminable, it is inexhaustible.

τελειώνω [teleeono] exhaust, finish up || end, conclude, finish || (μεταφ) die, be exhausted.

τελείως [teleeos] faultlessly, perfectly || completely, fully, entirely, utterly.

τελειωτικός [teleeoteekos] definitive, decisive, final, conclusive.

τελεσίγραφο, το [teleseegrafo] ultimatum.

τελεσίδικος [teleseeðeekos] final, irrevocable, decisive.

τέλεση, η [telesee] ceremony || perpetration || completion.

τελετάρχης, ο [teletarhees] master of ceremonies.

τελετή, η [teletee] celebration, rite || feast, festival.

τελευταίος [televteos] last || most recent.

τελευταίως [televteos] of late, recently.

τέλι, το [telee] thin wire.

τελικά [teleeka] in the end, finally.

τέλμα, το [telma] swamp, marsh, bog.

τέλος, το [telos] end || (φόρος) tax, duty || expiration, close || **~ πάντων** after all, at all events, finally || **επί τέλους** at last, at long last || **στο ~** at the end, finally || **εν τέλει** in the end, finally.

τελούμαι [teloume] happen, take place.

τελωνείο, το [teloneeo] customs house.

τελώνης, ο [telonees] customs officer.

τεμαχίζω [temaheezo] cut into pieces, separate, break up.

τεμάχιο, το [temaheeon] piece, parcel, bit, fragment, chunk.

τέμενος, το [temenos] temple, shrine, mosque, house of worship.

τέμνω [temno] cut, divide, open.

τεμπέλης [tembelees] lazy, indolent, idle.

τεμπελιάζω [tembeleeazo] loaf, get lazy, idle.

τέμπλο, το [templo] iconostasis, reredos.

τενεκεδένιος [tenekeðeneeos] made of tin.

τενεκές, ο [tenekes] tin || large can || (μεταφ) good-for-nothing.

τένις, το [tenees] tennis.

τένοντας, ο [tenontas] tendon.

τενόρος, ο [tenoros] tenor.

τέντα, η [tenta] tent || marquee.

τέντζερες, ο [tendzeres] cooking pot, kettle, casserole.

τεντώνω [tentono] stretch, tighten, bend || (μεταφ) strain.

τέρας, το [teras] monster, abortion, freak || (μεταφ) terror.

τεράστιος [terasteeos] prodigious, enormous, huge, vast.

τερατούργημα, το [teratouryeema] monstrosity || atrocious deed.

τερατώδης [teratoðees] prodigious, monstrous || ugly, frightful.

τέρμα, το [terma] extremity, terminus, end || (αθλητ) goal.

τερματίζω [termateezo] finish, put an end to, terminate, end.

τερματικό, το [termateeko] computer terminal.

τερματοφύλακας, ο [termatofeelakas] goalkeeper.

τερπνός [terpnos] delightful, agreeable, pleasing.

τερτίπι, το [terteepee] trick.

τέρψη, η [terpsee] delight, pleasure, amusement.

τέσσαρα [tessara] four || **με τα** ~ on all fours.

τέσσερις [tesserees] four.

τεταμένος [tetamenos] stretched, extended, strained.

τέτανος, ο [tetanos] tetanus.

Τετάρτη, η [tetartee] Wednesday.

τέταρτο, το [tetarto] quarter of an hour || quarto.

τέταρτος [tetartos] fourth.

τετελεσμένος [tetelesmenos] accomplished, achieved, done || **τετελεσμένο γεγονός** fait accompli || ~ **μέλλων** (γραμμ) future perfect tense.

τέτοιος [teteeos] similar, alike, such || **ο** ~ what's-his-name.

τεταγωνικός [tetragoneekos] square, quadrangular.

τετράγωνο, το [tetragono] (γεωμ) square, quadrangle || (πόλης) block.

τετράγωνος [tetragonos] square || (μεταφ) well-grounded, reasonable.

τετράδιο, το [tetraðeeo] exercise book, copybook.

τετρακόσιοι [tetrakosiee] four hundred.

τετράπαχος [tetrapahos] very stout, very fat, corpulent.

τετραπέρατος [tetraperatos] very clever, shrewd.

τετραπλάσιος [tetraplaseeos] four times as much.

τετράποδο, το [tetrapoðo] quadruped || (μεταφ) beast, brute.

τετράδα, η [tetraða] set of four.

τετράτροχος [tetratrohos] four-wheeled.

τετριμμένος [tetreemenos] worn-out || (μεταφ) hackneyed.

τεύτλο, το [tevtlo] beetroot, beet.

τεύχος, το [tevhos] issue (of a publication).

τέφρα, η [tefra] ashes, cinders.

τεφτέρι, το [tefteree] notebook || account book.

τέχνες, οι [tehnes] πλ: **καλές** ~ fine arts.

τέχνασμα, το [tehnasma] ruse, artifice, trick, device.

τέχνη, η [tehnee] art || profession || dexterity || (πολεμική) stratagem.

τεχνητός [tehneetos] sham, false, artificial || simulated, affected.

τεχνική, η [tehneekee] technique, means.

τεχνικός [tehneekos] technical, professional || (ουσ) technician.

τεχνίτης, ο [tehneetees] professional, craftsman || technician, mechanic || (μεταφ) specialist, expert.

τεχνολογία, η [tehnoloyeea] technology || (γραμμ) grammatical analysis.

τεχνοτροπία, η [tehnotropeea] artistic style.

τέως [teos] formerly, former, late || **ο** ~ **πρόεδρος** the ex-president.

τζάκι, το [dzakee] fireplace || heating range.

τζάμι, το [dzamee] window pane, pane of glass.

τζαμί, το [dzamee] mosque.

τζάμπα [dzamba] free, gratis, for nothing || to no purpose, wantonly.

τζαναμπέτης, ο [dzanambetees] peevish person || wicked person.

τζελατίνα, η [dzelateena] gelatine || celluloid holder.

τζίρος, ο [dzeeros] business turnover.

τζίτζικας, ο [dzeedzeekas] cicada.

τζίφρα, η [dzeefra] cipher || initial, monogram.

τζόγος, ο [dzogos] gambling.

τζόκεϋ, ο [dzokey] jockey.
τήβεννος, η [teevenos] toga || gown, robe.
τηγανητός [teeganeetos] fried.
τηγάνι, το [teeganee] frying pan.
τηγανίζω [teeganeezo] fry.
τήκομαι [teekome] thaw, melt || wither, pine, languish.
τήκω [teeko] melt, thaw.
τηλεβόας, ο [teelevoas] loudhailer, loudspeaker.
τηλεβόλο, το [teelevolo] cannon.
τηλεγράφημα, το [teelegrafeema] telegram, cable.
τηλέγραφος, ο [teelegrafos] telegraph.
τηλεγραφώ [teelegrafo] telegraph, wire.
τηλεόραση, η [teeleorasee] television.
τηλεπάθεια, η [teelepatheea] telepathy.
τηλεπικοινωνία, η [teelepeekeeononeea] telecommunications.
τηλεσκόπιο, το [teeleskopeeo] telescope.
τηλεφώνημα, το [teelefoneema] telephone call.
τηλεφωνητής, ο [teelefoneetees] telephone operator.
τηλέφωνο, το [teelefono] telephone, phone.
τηλεφωνώ [teelefono] telephone, call up.
τήξη, η [teeksee] melting, thawing || casting.
τήρηση, η [teereesee] observance || maintenance, keeping.
τηρώ [teero] keep, observe, follow, maintain.
τι [tee] what || what, how.
τι [tee] something || a bit.
τίγρη, η [teegree] tiger, tigress.
τιθασεύω [teethasevo] tame, domesticate.
τίθεμαι [teetheme] be arranged, be placed, be imposed.
τίλιο, το [teeleeo] infusion of lime flowers.
τιμαλφή, τα [teemalfee] πλ jewellery, jewels.
τιμάριθμος, ο [teemareethmos] cost of living.
τιμή, η [teemee] respect, honour || rate, price || value, worth.
τίμημα, το [teemeema] cost, price || value.
τιμητικός [teemeeteekos] honorary || honouring.
τίμιος [teemeeos] honest, upright || precious, valuable.
τιμιότητα, η [teemeeoteeta] honesty.
τιμοκατάλογος, ο [teemokatalogos] price list, tariff.

τιμολόγιο, το [teemoloyo] invoice, bill.
τιμόνι, το [teemonee] helm, rudder || tiller, wheel || (αυτοκινήτου) steering wheel || (ποδηλάτου) handlebars.
τιμονιέρης, ο [teemonierees] steersman, helmsman.
τιμώ [teemo] honour, respect, venerate, do honour to.
τιμώμαι [teemome] cost, be worth || be honoured.
τιμωρία, η [teemoreea] punishment, chastisement, penalty.
τιμωρώ [teemoro] punish, chastise || fine.
τινάζομαι [teenazome] leap, spring, start || brush one's clothes.
τινάζω [teenazo] shake off, shake || (πετώ) hurl, toss || (φτερουγίζω) flap || ~ στον αέρα blow up.
τίποτα [teepota] any, anything || nothing || ~! I don't mention it!, forget it!
τιποτένιος [teepoteneeos] mean, trivial, trifling, worthless.
τιράντες, οι [teerantes] πλ pair of braces.
τιρμπουσόν, το [teermbouson] corkscrew.
τίτλος, ο [teetlos] title, right, claim || certificate.
τιτλοφορώ [teetloforo] entitle, confer a title.
τμήμα, το [tmeema] part, segment, section || (υπουργείου) branch, department || (αστυνομίας) police station.
τμηματάρχης, ο [tmeematarhees] chief of a department.
το [to] the || it.
τοιούτος [teeoutos] such || (μεταφ) homosexual.
τοιχογραφία, η [teehografeea] fresco, wall painting.
τοιχοκόλληση, η [teehokoleesee] bill posting, bill sticking.
τοίχος, ο [teehos] wall.
τοίχωμα, το [teehoma] inner wall, partition wall || inner surface.
τοκετός, ο [toketos] childbirth, confinement.
τοκίζω [tokeezo] lend at interest, invest.
τοκογλύφος, ο [tokogleefos] usurer.
τοκομερίδιο, το [tokomereedeeo] dividend coupon.
τόκος, ο [tokos] interest, rate.
τόλμη, η [tolmee] daring, audacity.
τολμηρός [tolmeeros] bold, courageous, daring, venturesome.
τολμώ [tolmo] dare, risk, hazard.
τομάρι, το [tomaree] hide, skin, leather.
τομέας, ο [tomeas] sector || incisor, chisel.

τομή, η [tomee] cut, gash, incision || (διαγράμματος) section.

τόμος, ο [tomos] volume, tome.

τονίζω [toneezo] accent || accentuate, stress, lay emphasis on || tone up.

τονισμός, ο [toneesmos] accentuation || emphasizing.

τόνος, ο [tonos] ton || (ψάρι) tuna fish || accent, tone || (γραμμ) accent || (μουσ) key || **μιλώ με τόνο** raise one's voice || **δίνω ~ σε** brighten up.

τονώνω [tonono] fortify, invigorate, brace up.

τονωτικός [tonoteekos] bracing, invigorating, tonic.

τοξικομανής, ο, η [tokseekomanees] drug addict.

τοξικός [tokseekos] toxic || poisonous.

τοξοειδής [toksoeeδees] bowed, arched, curved, bow-shaped.

τόξο, το [tokso] bow || (κτιρίου) arch || (γεωμ) arc, curve.

τοπίο, το [topeeo] landscape || site, locality.

τόπι, το [topee] ball || (υφάσματος) roll of cloth || (κανονιού) cannonball.

τοπικός [topeekos] local.

τοπογραφία, η [topografeea] topography.

τοποθεσία, η [topotheseea] location, site, position, place.

τοποθέτηση, η [topotheteesee] putting, placing || (οικον) investment, investing.

τοποθετώ [topotheto] place, set, put || (οικον) invest.

τόπος, ο [topos] place, position, site || (χώρα) country || (χώρος) space, room || (μαθημ) locus || **πιάνω τόπο** have effect, be of use || **έμεινε στον τόπο** he died suddenly.

τοπωνυμία, η [toponeemeea] place name.

τορνευτός [tornevtos] well-turned, turned.

τορνεύω [tornevo] turn a lathe, work a lathe || (μεταφ) give fine shape to.

τόρνος, ο [tornos] lathe.

τορπίλη, η [torpeelee] torpedo.

τορπιλίζω [torpeeleezo] torpedo.

τόσο [toso] so much || ~ ... **όσο** as much ... as, both ... and || **όχι και ~** not so much.

τόσος [tosos] so big, so large, so great || so much, so many || ~ **δα** very little, very small, only so small || **άλλοι τόσοι** as many again || **κάθε τόσο** every now and again || **εκατόν τόσα** a hundred odd.

τότε [tote] then, at that time || in that case, therefore, thereupon || ~ **που** when.

τουαλέτα, η [toualeta] toilet || (γυναίκας) dress || (αίθουσα) dressing room || (τραπέζι) dressing table || (αποχωρητήριο) lavatory.

τούβλο, το [touvlo] brick || (μεταφ) simpleton.

τουλάχιστον [toulaheeston] at least, at all events.

τούλι, το [toulee] tulle.

τουλίπα, η [touleepa] tulip.

τουλούμι, το [touloumee] goatskin bottle || **βρέχει με το ~** it's raining cats and dogs.

τούμπα, η [toumba] somersault, fall || mound || **κάνω τούμπες κοωτοω** fall head over heels.

τούμπανο, το [toumbano] drum.

τουμπάρω [toumbaro] overturn, upset || (μεταφ) persuade || reverse.

τουναντίο(ν) [tounanteeo(n)] on the contrary.

τουπέ, το [toupe] cheek, audacity, nerve.

τουρισμός, ο [toureesmos] tourism, touring.

τουρίστας, ο [toureestas] tourist.

Τουρκία, η [tourkeea] Turkey.

τουρκικός [tourkeekos] Turkish.

τουρκοκρατία, η [tourkokrateea] Turkish domination of Greece.

Τούρκος, ο [tourkos] Turk || **γίνομαι ~** get angry.

τουρλώνω [tourlono] pile up || swell out, become round.

τουρλωτός [tourlotos] piled up || rounded, bulging.

τουρνέ, η [tourne] theatrical tour.

τουρσί, το [toursee] pickle, brine.

τούρτα, η [tourta] gateau, layer cake, tart.

τουρτουρίζω [tourtoureezo] shiver, tremble, shudder.

τούτος [toutos] this one.

τούφα, η [toufa] tuft, bunch, cluster.

τουφέκι, το [toufekee] rifle, musket, gun.

τουφεκιά, η [toufekia] gunshot, rifle shot.

τουφεκίζω [toufekeezo] shoot, fire || execute.

τράβηγμα, το [traveegma] pulling, dragging, tug || (υγρού) drawing off.

τραβώ [travo] pull, drag, heave, haul || ~ **το δρόμο μου** go my own way || (όπλο, χρήματα κτλ) draw || **το τραβάει** he imbibes || (απορροφάω) absorb || (τουφεκιά) fire, shoot || (ταχύτητα) reach distance of || (προσελκύω) entice, attract || **δε με τραβάει** it doesn't attract me || (ζητώ) ask for, want || **ο καιρός τραβάει πανωφόρι** the weather calls for a coat || **η καρδιά μου ~ τσιγάρο** I need a smoke || (υποφέρω) undergo, endure, bear || (αμετ) make towards, head for || move on || (συνεχίζω) last, go on || (τσιμπούκι κτλ) suck, draw ||

τραβιέμαι (αμετ) draw back, leave || (εμπόριο) be in demand || (δεν υποφέρεται) it's unbearable.

τραγανίζω [traganeezo] crunch, munch, grind.

τραγανό, το [tragano] cartilage, grist.

τραγανός [traganos] crisp, brittle.

τραγί, το [trayee] kid.

τραγικός [trayeekos] calamitous, tragic || (ποιητής) tragic poet.

τράγος, ο [tragos] goat.

τραγούδι, το [tragoudee] song, air, tune.

τραγουδιστής, ο [tragoudeestees] singer, vocalist.

τραγουδιστός [tragoudeestos] sung || (φωνή) tuneful.

τραγουδώ [tragoudo] sing, chant || (σιγά) hum.

τραγωδία, η [tragodeea] tragedy.

τραγωδός, ο, η [tragodos] tragic actor, tragedian, tragic actress.

τραίνο, το [treno] railway train || (επιβατικό) passenger train.

τρακ, το [trak] stage fright.

τρακάρισμα, το [trakareesma] crash, collision || unexpected meeting.

τρακάρω [trakaro] knock against, collide with || meet by accident || (μεταφ) touch for a loan.

τρακατρούκα, η [trakatrouka] firecracker.

τράκο, το [trako], **τράκος, ο** [trakos] collision || (μεταφ) attack, assault.

τρακτέρ, το [trakter] farm tractor.

τραμ, το [tram] tram, tramcar, tramway.

τραμπούκος, ο [tramboukos] out-and-out rascal, scoundrel, rotter.

τρανός [tranos] powerful || large, grand || important, weighty.

τράνταγμα, το [trantagma] jolting, shake, shaking || jolt, jerk.

τραντάζω [trantazo] jolt, shake up and down.

τράπεζα, η [trapeza] table || (εμπορ) bank || αγία ~ altar.

τραπεζαρία, η [trapezareea] dining room.

τραπέζι, το [trapezee] table || dinner || στρώνω ~ set the table || τους είχαμε ~ we invited them to dinner.

τραπεζίτης, ο [trapezeetees] banker || (δόντι) molar.

τραπεζιτικός [trapezeeteekos] banking || (υπάλληλος) bank employee.

τραπεζομάντηλο, το [trapezomanteelo] tablecloth.

τράπουλα, η [trapoula] pack of cards.

τράτα, η [trata] seine || fishing boat.

τρατάρω [trataro] regale || pay for, offer.

τραυλίζω [travleezo] stammer, stutter, lisp.

τραυλός [travlos] stammering, stuttering.

τραύμα, το [travma] wound, hurt, injury || (μεταφ) wound, sore.

τραυματίας, ο [travmateeas] casualty, wounded person.

τραυματίζω [travmateezo] wound, hurt, injure.

τραχεία, η [traheea] trachea, windpipe.

τραχηλιά, η [traheelia] collar, collarette || bib.

τράχηλος, ο [traheelos] neck.

τραχύνω [traheeno] make harsh, make rough || irritate.

τραχύς [trahees] harsh, rough || (γεύση) tart, sharp || (στην ακοή) harsh, grating || (χαρακτήρας) sour, crabbed.

τρεις [trees] three.

τρέλα, η [trela] madness, insanity || folly || (ιατρ) mania || (μεταφ) anything pleasing.

τρελαίνομαι [trelenome] go insane || be driven mad || be mad about.

τρελαίνω [treleno] drive mad, bewilder.

τρελοκομείο, το [trelokomeeo] madhouse.

τρελός [trelos] insane, mad || (ουσ) madman || (μωρό) mischievous.

τρεμοσβήνω [tremosveeno] flicker, sparkle.

τρεμούλα, η [tremoula] shivering, trembling || (φωνής) quiver || (από κρύο) shivering || scare.

τρέμω [tremo] tremble || (από κρύο) shiver || (από φόβο) shake || (το φως) flicker, waver || (φωνή) quiver.

τρέξιμο, το [trekseemo] running || (υγρού) flowing || (αίματος) flow, gush.

τρέπω [trepo] change, convert || turn, translate || ~ δε φυγή put to flight.

τρέφω [trefo] nourish, nurture || (ελπίδα) cherish, foster || (γένια) grow || support, keep.

τρεχάλα, η [trehala] running || (σαν επίρ) at full speed.

τρεχάματα, τα [trehamata] πλ running about || (μεταφ) cares.

τρεχάμενος [trehamenos] running.

τρεχαντήρι, το [trehanteeree] small sailing boat.

τρεχάτος [trehatos] running, hasty.

τρέχω [treho] run, race, hurry || (για υγρά) flow || leak || τι τρέχει; what's happening?, what's the matter?

τρεχούμενος [trehoumenos] (λογαριασμός) current.

τρία [treea] three.

τριάδα, η [treeada] trinity || trio.

τρίαινα, η [treena] trident.

τριακόσιοι [treeakosiee] three hundred.

τριανδρία, η [treeanδreea] triumvirate.

τριάντα [treeanta] thirty.

τριαντάφυλλο, το [treeantafeelo] rose.

τριάρι, το [treearee] figure 3 || three at cards || (διαμέρισμα) three-room apartment.

τριάδα, η [treeaδa] trinity || trio.

τριβή, η [treevee] friction, chafing, rubbing || wear and tear || (μεταφ) practice, use, experience.

τρίβομαι [treevome] wear out || disintegrate || (μεταφ) get experienced, get practice in.

τρίβω [treevo] rub || polish up || grate || (το σώμα) massage.

τριγμός, ο [treegmos] crackling, creaking || (δοντιών) grinding, gnashing.

τριγυρίζω [treeyeereezo], **τριγυρνώ** [treeyeerno] encircle || roam, hang about.

τριγωνικός [treegoneekos] triangular.

τριγωνομετρία, η [treegonometreea] trigonometry.

τρίγωνο, το [treegono] triangle.

τρίδυμα, τα [treeδeema] πλ triplets.

τριετής [trietees] of three years || (ηλικία) three years old || (φοιτητής) third-year.

τρίζω [treezo] crackle, crack, creak, squeak || (δόντια) grind, gnash, grit.

τριήρης, η [trieerees] trireme.

τρικαντό, το [treekanto] three-cornered hat, cocked hat.

τρικλίζω [treekleezo] stagger, totter, wobble, reel.

τρίκλωνος [treeklonos] three-stranded.

τρικούβερτος [treekouvertos] (μεταφ) splendid, terrific, wonderful.

τρικυμία, η [treekeemeea] storm, tempest, hurricane.

τρικυμιώδης [treekeemeeoδees] stormy, tempestuous, rough.

τρίλια, η [treeleea] trill.

τριμελής [treemelees] of three members.

τριμερής [treemerees] tripartite.

τριμηνία, η [treemeeneea] quarter of a year || quarter's rent.

τριμηνιαίος [treemeenieos] of three months, quarterly.

τρίμηνο, το [treemeeno] βλ **τριμηνία.**

τρίμηνος [treemeenos] βλ **τριμηνιαίος.**

τρίμμα, το [treema] fragment, morse, chip, particle.

τριμμένος [treemenos] showing signs of wear and tear || ground.

τρίξιμο, το [treekseemo] gnashing, grinding.

τρίπατος [treepatos] three-storeyed.

τριπλασιάζω [treeplaseeazo] treble, triple, triplicate.

τριπλάσιος [treeplaseeos] threefold, triple, treble.

τριποδίζω [treepoδeezo] trot.

τρίποδο, το [treepoδo] tripod || easel || three-legged support.

τρίπτυχο, το [treepteeho] triptych.

τρισδιάστατος [treesδeeastatos] three-dimensional.

τρισέγγονο, το [treesengono] great-great-grandchild.

τρισκατάρατος [treeskataratos] thrice-cursed || abominable.

Τρίτη, η [treetee] Tuesday.

τρίτο, το [treeto] third || (επίρ) thirdly.

τρίτος [treetos] third || third-party.

τρίφτης, ο [treeftees] grater, rasp.

τριφύλλι, το [treefeelee] clover, trefoil.

τρίχα, η [treeha] hair || bristle || fur || **στην ~** spruced up || **παρά ~** nearly.

τρίχες, οι [treehes] πλ nonsense, rubbish.

τριχιά, η [treehia] rope.

τριχοειδής [treehoeeδees] capillary.

τρίχωμα, το [treehoma] fur || (σώματος) hair.

τριχωτός [treehotos] hairy, shaggy.

τρίψιμο, το [treepseemo] chafing, massage, rubbing, friction || (στίλβωμα) polishing || grating, grinding, crushing.

τρίωρος [treeoros] of three hours.

τρόλλεϋ [troley] trolley bus.

τρόμαγμα, το [tromagma] fright, scare.

τρομάζω [tromazo] terrify, frighten || get scared.

τρομακτικός [tromakteekos] fearful, awful, frightening || (μεταφ) terrific.

τρομάρα, η [tromara] dread, fright, fear.

τρομερός [tromeros] terrible, dreadful, frightful || (μεταφ) terrific, astonishing.

τρομοκρατία, η [tromokrateea] terrorism || terror.

τρομοκρατώ [tromokrato] terrorize.

τρόμος, ο [tromos] trembling, shaking || dread, fright.

τρόμπα, η [tromba] pump.

τρομπέτα, η [trompeta] trumpet.

τρομπόνι, το [tromponee] trombone.

τρόπαιο, το [tropeo] trophy || triumph.

τροπάριο, το [tropareeo] (εκκλ) hymn || (μεταφ) same old refrain.

τροπή, η [tropee] change || turn || (μαθημ) conversion.

τροπικός [tropeekos] tropical || (γραμμ) of manner.

τροπολογία, η [tropoloyeea] amendment, alteration, change, modification.

τροποποίηση, η [tropopieesee] modification, alteration, change.

τρόποι, οι [tropee] πλ manners, behaviour.

τρόπος, ο [tropos] way, manner, method || behaviour, conduct || (μουσ) mode || ~ **του λέγειν** so to speak.

τρούλλος, ο [troulos] dome, cupola.

τρουλλωτός [troulotos] domed, dome-shaped.

τροφή, η [trofee] food, nutrition || (ζώων) pasture, fodder || sustenance.

τρόφιμα, τα [trofeema] πλ provisions, food, victuals.

τρόφιμος, ο, η [trofeemos] lodger, boarder || paying guest || inmate || (μεταφ) nursling.

τροφοδοσία, η [trofoδoseea] provisioning, supplying || supply.

τροφοδότης, ο [trofoδotees] caterer, purveyor, provider, supplier.

τροφοδοτώ [trofoδoto] feed, provision, keep supplied, supply, serve.

τροχάδην [trohaδeen] hurriedly, hastily, at full speed || (μεταφ) fluently.

τροχαία [trohea]: ~ **κίνηση** traffic || **η** ~ traffic police.

τροχαίο [troheo]: ~ **υλικό** rolling stock.

τροχαίος, ο [troheos] trochee || (επίθ) wheeled, rolling.

τροχαλία, η [trohaleea] pulley, block.

τροχιά, η [trohia] track, groove, rut || (σιδηροδρόμου) track, rail || (δορυφόρου κτλ) orbit, trajectory.

τροχίζω [troheezo] sharpen, whet, grind || (μεταφ) train, exercise.

τρόχισμα, το [troheesma] sharpening, whetting, grinding || (μεταφ) exercising.

τροχονόμος, ο [trohonomos] traffic policeman.

τροχοπέδη, η [trohopeδee] brake, skid, wheel brake.

τροχός, ο [trohos] wheel || grindstone, whetstone.

τροχοφόρο, το [trohoforo] vehicle.

τρυγητής, ο [treeyeetees] grape harvester, vintager.

τρυγητός, ο [treeyeetos] grape harvest, vintage.

τρυγόνι, το [treegonee] turtledove.

τρύγος, ο [treegos] βλ **τρυγητός**.

τρυγώ [treego] gather grapes || (μεταφ) loot, fleece.

τρύπα, η [treepa] hole || (βελόνας) eye || (μεταφ) den, lair.

τρυπάνι, το [treepanee] drill, drilling machine.

τρύπημα, το [treepeema] perforating, boring, piercing || prick, punch.

τρυπητήρι, το [treepeeteeree] awl, punch, drill.

τρυπητό, το [treepeeto] strainer, colander.

τρύπιος [treepeeos] with holes, perforated, holed, riddled.

τρυπητός [treepeetos] perforated, holed, riddled.

τρυπώ [treepo] bore, make a hole, pierce || prick, punch.

τρυπώνω [treepono] hide, conceal || squeeze in || take refuge.

τρυφερός [treeferos] tender, soft || affectionate, affable, mild.

τρυφερότητα, η [treeferoteeta] tenderness, softness || affection, kindness.

τρώγλη, η [troglee] hole, lair, den || hovel, shack.

τρώγομαι [trogome] be edible || (μεταφ) be tolerable || **τρώγονται** they are quarrelling.

τρώγω [trogo] eat, bite || **με τρώει** it itches || ~ **ξύλο** get a beating || ~ **το κόσμο** look everywhere.

τρωκτικό, το [trokteeko] rodent.

τρωτός [trotos] vulnerable.

τρώω [troo] βλ **τρώγω**.

τσαγιέρα, η [tsayera] teapot.

τσαγκάρης, ο [tsangarees] shoemaker.

τσάι, το [tsaee] tea.

τσακάλι, το [tsakalee] jackal.

τσακίζομαι [tsakeezome] strive, struggle || (διπλώνω) fold.

τσακίζω [tsakeezo] break, shatter, smash || (μεταφ) weaken, wear out, enfeeble.

τσάκιση, η [tsakeesee] crease, pleat.

τσάκισμα, το [tsakeesma] breaking, shattering, smashing.

τσακμάκι, το [tsakmakee] tinderbox || cigarette lighter.

τσάκωμα, το [tsakoma] seizing, catching || quarrelling, dispute.

τσακώνομαι [tsakonome] quarrel.

τσακώνω [tsakono] catch in the act.

τσαλαβουτώ [tsalavouto] flounder, wallow, splash about || (μεταφ) do a sloppy job.

τσαλακώνω [tsalakono] crease, crumple, wrinkle.

τσαλαπατώ [tsalapato] trample underfoot, tread over.

τσαμπί, το [tsambee] bunch (of grapes), cluster.

τσάντα, η [tsanta] pouch || handbag || briefcase || (φωνίσματος) shopping bag || (ταχυδρόμου) satchel.

τσάπα, η [tsapa] hoe, pickaxe.

τσαπατσούλης [tsapatsoulees] untidy in one's work.

τσαπί, το [tsapee] βλ **τσάπα**.

τσάρκα, η [tsarka] walk, promenade, stroll.

τσαρούχι, το [tsarouhee] rustic shoe with pompom.

τσατσάρα, η [tsatsara] comb.

τσαχπινιά, η [tsahpeenia] coquetry, roguery, trickery.

τσεκ, το [tsek] cheque || check (US).

τσεκούρι, το [tsekouree] axe, hatchet.

τσελίγκας, ο [tseleengas] chief shepherd.

τσεμπέρι, το [tsemberee] kerchief, veil.

τσέπη, η [tsepee] pocket || pocketful.

τσεπώνω [tsepono] pocket || (μεταφ) filch, swipe.

τσευδίζω [tsevðeezo] lisp, stammer, falter.

τσευδός [tsevðos] lisping, stammering.

τσεχικός [tseheekos] Czech.

Τσέχος, ο [tsehos] Czech.

Τσεχοσλοβακία, η [tsehoslovakeea] Czechoslovakia.

τσιγαρίζω [tseegareezo] fry lightly, brown, roast brown.

τσιγάρο, το [tseegaro] cigarette.

τσιγαροθήκη, η [tseegarotheekee] cigarette case.

τσιγαρόχαρτο, το [tseegaroharto] tissue paper.

τσιγγάνος, ο [tseenganos] gipsy.

τσιγγούνης [tseengounees] miserly, stingy || (ουσ) miser.

τσιγκέλι, το [tseengelee] meat hook.

τσιγκλώ [tseenglo] goad, prick, spur.

τσίγκος, ο [tseengos] zinc.

τσίκνα, η [tseekna] smell of burning meat.

τσικνίζω [tseekneezo] scorch, burn || have a burnt smell.

τσικουδιά, η [tseekouðia] terebinth || (ποτό) kind of spirit.

τσίμα [tseema]: ~ ~ scarcely || on the brink of.

τσιμέντο, το [tseemento] cement.

τσιμουδιά, η [tseemouðia]: δεν έβγαλε ~ he remained speechless || ~! not a word!, mum's the word!

τσίμπημα, το [tseembeema] prick, sting, pinch || bite, peck.

τσιμπιά, η [tseembia] pinch.

τσιμπίδα, η [tseembeeða] nippers, tongs, forceps, pincers.

τσιμπιδάκι, το [tseembeeðakee] tweezers || hairclip.

τσίμπλα, η [tseembla] mucus of eyes.

τσιμπούκι, το [tseemboukee] tobacco pipe.

τσιμπούρι, το [tseembouree] (έντομο) tick || (μεταφ) troublesome or bothersome person, pest.

τσιμπούσι, το [tseembousee] spread, repast, regalement, feast.

τσιμπώ [tseembo] prick, pinch, sting || (δαγκώνω) bite, peck || (φαγητό) nibble || (μεταφ) cadge || (συλλαμβάνω) seize, collar.

τσίνορο, το [tseenoro] eyelash.

τσίπα, η [tseepa] thin skin, crust || (μεταφ) shame.

τσιπούρα, η [tseepoura] gilthead.

τσίπουρο, το [tseepouro] kind of spirit.

τσιρίζω [tseereezo] screech, shriek, scream.

τσίρκο, το [tseerko] circus.

τσίρλα, η [tseerla] diarrhoea.

τσίρος, ο [tseeros] dried mackerel || (μεταφ) skinny person.

τσιρότο, το [tseeroto] sticking plaster.

τσίτα [tseeta] very tight || ~ ~ scarcely.

τσιτσίδι [tseetseeðee] stark naked.

τσιτσιρίζω [tseetseereezo] sizzle.

τσιτώνω [tseetono] stretch, tighten, strain.

τσιφλίκι, το [tseefleekee] large country estate, farm, ranch.

τσίχλα, η [tseehla] thrush || (αδύνατος) skinny person.

τσόκαρο, το [tsokaro] wooden shoe.

τσολιάς, ο [tsolias] evzone, kilted soldier.

τσο(μ)πάνης, ο [tso(m)panees] shepherd.

τσοντάρω [tsontaro] join on.

τσουβάλι, το [tsouvalee] sackful || sack.

τσουγκράνα, η [tsoungrana] rake.

τσουγκρανίζω [tsoungraneezo] scratch, rake.

τσουγκρίζω [tsoungreezo] strike against || clink glasses, touch glasses.

τσούζω [tsouzo] smart, sting, hurt.

τσουκάλι, το [tsoukalee] jug, pot || chamberpot.

τσουκνίδα, η [tsoukneeða] nettle.

τσούλα, η [tsoula] loose-living woman, whore.

τσουλάω [tsoulao] slip along, slide along || (όχημα) push.

τσουλούφι, το [tsouloufee] lock of hair.

τσουρέκι, το [tsourekee] bun, brioche.

τσούρμο, το [tsourmo] throng || band, troop.

τσουρουφλίζω [tsouroufleezo] grill brown, scorch.

τσουχτερός [tsouhteros] keen, smart, sharp || (κρύο) biting || harsh.

τσούχτρα, η [tsouhtra] jellyfish.

τσόφλι, το [tsoflee] shell || rind.

τσόχα, η [tsoha] felt.

τυγχάνω [teenghano] happen to be || obtain, attain.

τύλιγμα, το [teeleegma] winding, rolling, coiling, wrapping.

τυλίγω [teeleego] roll up, wind, coil || wrap up, fold round, twist.

τυλώνω [teelono] fill up.

τύμβος, ο [teemvos] grave, tomb.

τύμπανο, το [teembano] drum, tambour || (αυτιού) || eardrum || tympanum.

Τυνησία, η [teeneeseea] Tunisia.

τυνησιακός [teeneeseeakos] Tunisian.

Τυνήσιος, ο [teeneeseeos] Tunisian.

τυπικός [teepeekos] usual, conventional || typical.

τυπικότητα, η [teepeekoteeta] formality.

τυπογραφείο, το [teepografeeo] printing press, printer's.

τυπογραφία, η [teepografeea] printing.

τυπογράφος, ο [teepografos] printer.

τύποι, οι [teepee] πλ conventions, form.

τυποποίηση, η [teepopieesee] standardization.

τύπος, ο [teepos] print, imprint, stamp || (καλούπι) mould, matrix, form || (υπόδειγμα) model, type || (συμπεριφοράς) formality, rule of procedure || (οικίας) type, kind of || (μαθημ) formula || (εφημερίδες) the press || (για άνθρωπο) figure, character.

τυπώνω [teepono] print, stamp.

τυραννία, η [teeraneea] tyranny, oppression || torment, torture.

τύραννος, ο [teeranos] oppressor, tyrant.

τυραννώ [teerano] oppress || torture, harass.

τυρί, το [teeree] cheese.

τυροκομία, η [teerokomeea] cheese-making.

τυρόπιτα, η [teeropeeta] cheese pie || cheesecake.

τύρφη, η [teerfee] peat.

τύφλα, η [teefla] blindness || ~ στο μεθύσι dead drunk.

τυφλοπόντικας, ο [teefloponteekas] mole.

τυφλός [teeflos] blind.

τυφλώνομαι [teeflonome] grow blind, blind o.s.

τυφλώνω [teeflono] blind || (φως) dazzle || (μεταφ) deceive, hoodwink.

τύφος, ο [teefos]: εξανθηματικός ~ typhus || κοιλιακός ~ typhoid fever.

τυφώνας, ο [teefonas] typhoon, hurricane, cyclone.

τυχαίνω [teeheno] βλ **τυγχάνω**.

τυχαίος [teeheos] casual, fortuitous, chance.

τυχαίως [teeheos] by chance, by accident.

τυχερά [teehera] πλ casual profits, tips, perks.

τυχερό, το [teehero] fortune, destiny.

τυχερός [teeheros] fortunate, lucky.

τύχη, η [teehee] destiny, chance, fortune, lot, fate || (καλή) good luck || στην ~ haphazard, at random.

τυχοδιώκτης, ο [teehoδeeoktees] adventurer, opportunist.

τυχόν [teehon] by chance || τα ~ έξοδα incidental expenses.

τυχών [teehon]: ο ~ the first comer, anyone.

τύψη, η [teepsee] remorse, prick of conscience.

τώρα [tora] nowadays, at present, now || this minute || at once.

τωρινός [toreenos] present-day, contemporary, of today.

Υ, υ

ύαινα, η [iena] hyena.

υάκινθος, ο [yakeenthos] hyacinth.

ύαλος, η [eealos] glass.

υαλουργία, η [yalouryeea] glassmaking.

υαλουργός, ο [yalourgos] glassmaker.

υάρδα, η [yarδa] yard.

ύβος, ο [eevos] hump.

υβρεολόγιο, το [eevreologyo] volley of abuse, tirade.

υβρίζω [eevreezo] insult, abuse, swear at.

ύβρη, η [eevree] insult, injury || oath.

υβριστικός [eevreesteekos] insulting, rude.

υγεία, η [eeyeea] health.

υγειονομικός [eeyonomeekos] sanitary.

υγιαίνω [eeyeno] be healthy.

υγιεινός [eeyeenos] healthy || wholesome.

υγιής [ecyees] healthy || (μεταφ) sound.

υγραίνω [eegreno] moisten, dampen, wet.

υγρασία, η [eegraseea] moisture, moistness, humidity.

υγροποιώ [eegropeeo] liquefy.

υγρός [eegros] fluid, liquid || humid, damp || watery.

υδαταγωγός, ο [eeδatagogos] water pipe.

υδατάνθρακας, ο [eeδatanthrakas] carbohydrate.

υδατοστεγής [eeδatosteyees] watertight, waterproof.

υδατοφράκτης, ο [eeδatofraktees] dam, weir.

υδραγωγείο, το [eeδragoyeeo] aqueduct.

υδραντλία, η [eeδrantleea] water pump.

υδράργυρος, ο [eeδraryeeros] mercury, quicksilver.

υδρατμός, ο [eeδratmos] vapour, steam.

υδραυλική, η [eeðravleekee] hydraulics.

υδραυλικός [eeðravleekos] hydraulic || (ουσ) plumber.

ύδρευση, η [eeðrevsee] water supply, drawing of water.

υδρόβιος [eeðroveeos] aquatic.

υδρόγειος, η [eeðroyos] earth.

υδρογόνο, το [eeðrogono] hydrogen.

υδρογραφία, η [eeðrografeea] hydrography.

υδροηλεκτρικός [eeðroeelektreekos] hydroelectric.

υδροκέφαλος [eeðrokefalos] hydrocephalous.

υδροκίνητος [eeðrokeeneetos] waterpowered.

υδροκυάνιο, το [eeðrokeeaneeo] prussic acid.

υδρόμυλος, ο [eeðromeelos] water mill.

υδροπλάνο, το [eeðroplano] seaplane.

υδρορρόη, η [eeðroroee] (στη στέγη) gutter.

υδροστάθμη, η [eeðrostathmee] water level.

υδροστατικός [eeðrostateekos] hydrostatic.

υδροστρόβιλος, ο [eeðrostroveelos] water turbine || whirlpool.

υδροφοβία, η [eeðrofoveea] rabies, hydrophobia.

υδροφόρος [eeðroforos] water-carrying || (ουσ) water carrier.

υδροχαρής [eeðroharees] water-loving.

υδροχλωρικός [eeðrohloreekos] hydrochloric.

υδρόχρωμα, το [eeðrohroma] whitewash.

υδρόψυκτος [eeðropseektos] water-cooled.

υδρωπικία, η [eeðropeekeea] dropsy.

ύδωρ, το [eeðor] water.

υιοθεσία, η [yotheseea] adoption.

υιοθετώ [yotheto] adopt, accept, support.

υιός, ο [yos] son.

ύλη, η [eelee] material, matter, stuff.

υλικό, το [eeleeko] material, stuff || element, ingredient.

υλικός [eeleekos] material, real.

υλισμός, ο [eeleesmos] materialism.

υλιστής, ο [eeleestees] materialist.

υλοτομία, η [eelotomeea] woodcutting, timber-felling.

υμένας, ο [eemenas] membrane || tissue, hymen.

ύμνος, ο [eemnos] hymn || anthem.

υμνώ [eemno] celebrate, praise, eulogize.

υνί, το [eenee] ploughshare.

υπάγομαι [eepagome] belong, be dependent || be answerable.

υπαγόρευση, η [eepagorevsee] dictation || (μεταφ) suggestion.

υπαγορεύω [eepagorevo] dictate || (μεταφ) inspire, suggest.

υπάγω [eepago] go || go under, rank.

υπαίθριος [eepethreeos] outdoor, in the open air || field.

ύπαιθρο, το [eepethro] open air, open country.

ύπαιθρος, η [eepethros] (χώρα) countryside.

υπαινιγμός, ο [eepeneegmos] hint, allusion, intimation.

υπαινίσσομαι [eepeneesome] hint at, allude to.

υπαίτιος [eepeteeos] responsible, culpable.

υπακοή, η [eepakoee] obedience || submission.

υπάκουος [eepakouos] obedient || submissive.

υπακούω [eepakouo] obey.

υπάλληλος, ο, η [eepaleelos] employee, clerk || (υπουργείου) official, functionary || **δημόσιος ~** civil servant, government employee.

υπαξιωματικός, ο [eepakseeomateekos] non-commissioned officer.

υπαρκτός [eeparktos] existent || subsisting || real.

ύπαρξη, η [eeparksee] existence || being, life.

υπαρχηγός, ο [eeparheegos] deputy commander.

υπάρχω [eeparho] exist, be || live || **υπάρχει** there is || **τα υπαρχοντά μου** my possessions, my things.

υπασπιστής, ο [eepaspeestees] aide-de-camp || (στρατ) adjutant.

ύπατος, ο [eepatos] consul || (επίθ) highest, supreme.

υπέδαφος, το [eepeðafos] subsoil.

υπεισέρχομαι [eepeeserhome] enter secretly || glide into.

υπεκφεύγω [eepekfevgo] escape, avoid || slip away.

υπεκφυγή, η [eepekfeeyee] escape, subterfuge || evasion.

υπενθυμίζω [eepentheemeezo] remind of, call to mind || allude to.

υπενοικιάζω [eepeneekeeazo] sublet, rent from a tenant.

υπεξαίρεση, η [eepekseresee] pilfering, taking away.

υπέρ [eeper] over, upwards, above || (για) for, on behalf of || **τα ~ και τα κατά** pros and cons, for and against.

υπεραιμία, η [eeperemeea] excess of blood.

υπεραμύνομαι [eeperameenome] defend, support.

υπεράνθρωπος [eeperanthropos] superhuman || (ουσ) superman.

υπεράνω [eeperano] above, beyond, over.

υπερασπίζομαι [eeperaspeezome] defend o.s.

υπερασπίζω [eeperaspeezo] defend, protect || maintain.

υπεράσπιση, η [eeperaspeesee] defence || protection || the defendants.

υπεραστικός [eeperasteekos] long-distance.

υπερβαίνω [eeperveno] cross, surmount || exceed, go beyond, overdo.

υπερβάλλω [eepervalo] surpass, outdo, exceed || exaggerate, overdo, magnify.

υπέρβαση, η [eepervasee] exceeding || (traffic) violation || trespass.

υπερβολή, η [eepervolee] exaggeration || (γεωμ) hyperbola.

υπερβολικός [eepervoleekos] excessive || exaggerated, exaggerating.

υπέργηρος [eeperyeeros] extremely old, very old.

υπερδιέγερση, η [eeperðieyersee] over-excitement.

υπερένταση, η [eeperentasee] overstrain, overstress.

υπερευαίσθητος [eeperevestheetos] over-sensitive, hypersensitive.

υπερέχω [eepereho] excel, surpass, exceed.

υπερήλικος/κη [eepereeleekas] elderly person, very old person.

υπερηφάνεια, η [eepereefaneea] pride || haughtiness.

υπερηφανεύομαι [eepereefanevome] pride o.s. || be proud.

υπερήφανος [eepereefanos] proud || haughty.

υπερθεματίζω [eeperthemateezo] make higher bid || (μεταφ) outdo.

υπερθετικός [eepertheteekos] superlative.

υπερίπταμαι [eepereeptame] fly over, fly above.

υπερισχύω [eepereesheeo] predominate, prevail over || overcome, triumph.

υπεριώδης [eepereeoðees] ultraviolet.

υπερκόπωση, η [eeperkoposee] overwork, breakdown.

υπέρμαχος, ο, η [eepermahos] champion, defender.

υπέρμετρος [eepermetros] excessive, huge.

υπερνικώ [eeperneeko] overcome || subdue, master.

υπέρογκος [eeperongos] colossal, enormous || outrageous.

υπεροπτικός [eeperopteekos] haughty, presumptuous, arrogant.

υπεροχή, η [eeperohee] superiority, predominance.

υπέροχος [eeperohos] superior, excellent, eminent.

υπεροψία, η [eeperopsea] arrogance, disdain, haughtiness.

υπερπέραν, το [eeperperan] the beyond, afterlife.

υπερπηδώ [eeperpeeðo] surmount || jump over.

υπερπόντιος [eeperponteeos] overseas || transmarine.

υπέρταση, η [eepertasee] high blood pressure.

υπέρτατος [eepertatos] highest, greatest, supreme.

υπερτερώ [eepertero] excel, exceed, surpass || outnumber.

υπερτίμηση, η [eeperteemeesee] overestimation || (οικ) rise in price, increase in value.

υπερτιμώ [eeperteemo] overvalue, overestimate || (οικ) raise price of.

υπερτροφία, η [eepertrofeea] (ιατρ) hypertrophy.

υπέρυθροι [eepereethree] πλ: ~ ακτίνες infrared rays.

υπέρυθρος [eepereethros] reddish.

υπερύψηλος [eepereepseelos] very high, exceedingly high.

υπερυψώνω [eepereepsono] raise up || exalt.

υπερφυσικός [eeperfeeseekos] supernatural || (μεταφ) extraordinary, prodigious.

υπερωκεάνειο, το [eeperokeaneeo] liner.

υπερωρία, η [eeperoreea] overtime.

υπεύθυνος [eepevtheenos] responsible, answerable.

υπήκοος [eepeekoos] submissive, obedient || (ουσ) subject of state.

υπηκοότητα, η [eepeekooteeta] nationality, citizenship.

υπηρεσία, η [eepeereseea] service, attendance || duty, employ || (οικίας) domestic servant.

υπηρεσιακή [eepeereseeakee]: ~ κυβέρνηση caretaker government]

υπηρεσιακός [eepeereseeakos] of service.

υπηρέτης, ο [eepeeretees] servant.

υπηρέτρια, η [eepeeretreea] maid.

υπηρετώ [eepeereto] serve || do one's military service.

υπναλέος [eepnaleos] drowsy, sleepy.

υπναράς, ο [eepnaras] person who enjoys sleeping.

υπνοβάτης, ο [eepnovatees] sleepwalker.

ύπνος, ο [eepnos] sleep.

ύπνωση, η [eepnosee] hypnosis.

υπνωτίζω [eepnoteezo] hypnotize.

υπνωτικό, το [eepnoteeko] soporific drug, sleeping pill.

υπνωτισμός, ο [eepnoteesmos] hypnotism.

υπό [eepo] below, beneath || (μέσο) by, with.

υπόβαθρο, το [eepovathro] base, pedestal, stand.

υποβάλλω [eepovalo] submit, hand in || (υποτάσσω) subject || suggest, propose.

υποβαστάζω [eepovastazo] support, prop up, bear.

υποβιβάζω [eepoveevazo] lower || reduce, diminish || demote.

υποβλέπω [eepovlepo] suspect || cast glances at, leer.

υποβλητικός [eepovleeteekos] evocative.

υποβοηθώ [eepovoeetho] assist, back up, support.

υποβολέας, ο [eepovoleas] prompter || instigator.

υποβολή, η [eepovolee] submission, presentation || prompting, instigation.

υποβόσκω [eepovosko] smoulder || lie hidden.

υποβρύχιο, το [eepovreeheeo] submarine || (μεταφ) kind of sweet.

υπόγειο, το [eepoyo] basement, cellar.

υπόγειος [eepoyos] underground.

υπογραμμίζω [eepogrameezo] underline, emphasize.

υπογραφή, η [eepografee] signature.

υπογράφω [eepografo] sign || (μεταφ) approve, subscribe.

υποδαυλίζω [eepoðavleezo] fan the flame || (μεταφ) foment, excite.

υποδεέστερος [eepoðeesteros] inferior, lower.

υπόδειγμα, το [eepoðeegma] model, example, specimen || sample.

υποδειγματικός [eepoðeegmateekos] exemplary, representative.

υποδεικνύω [eepoðeekneeo] indicate || suggest, propose.

υπόδειξη, η [eepoðeeksee] indication || recommendation.

υποδέχομαι [eepoðehome] receive, welcome, greet.

υποδηλώ [eepoðeelo] convey, indicate, hint at.

υποδηματοποιείο, το [eepoðeematopieeo] shoemaker's shop.

υποδιαίρεση, η [eepoðieresee] subdivision.

υποδιαιρώ [eepoðiero] subdivide.

υποδιαστολή, η [eepoðeeastolee] decimal point || (γραμμ) comma.

υποδιευθυντής, ο [eepoðieftheendees] assistant director, vice-principal, deputy manager.

υπόδικος, ο [eepoðeekos] the accused.

υπόδουλος [eepoðoulos] enslaved.

υποδουλώνω [eepoðoulono] subjugate, enslave, subdue.

υποδοχή, η [eepoðohee] reception.

υποδύομαι [eepoðeeome] play the part, assume a role.

υποζύγιο, το [eepozeeyo] beast of burden.

υποθάλπω [eepothalpo] foment || protect, maintain || entertain, harbour.

υπόθεση, η [eepothesee] conjecture, supposition || matter, affair, business || (δικαστηρίου) case, action || (θεατρικού έργου κτλ) subject, plot, matter, theme.

υποθετικός [eepotheteekos] hypothetical, speculative || imaginary || (γραμμ) conditional.

υπόθετο, το [eepotheto] suppository.

υποθέτω [eepotheto] suppose, assume.

υποθηκεύω [eepotheekevo] mortgage.

υποθήκη, η [eepotheekee] mortgage.

υποκαθιστώ [eepokatheesto] replace, substitute.

υποκατάσταση, η [eepokatastasee] replacement, substitution.

υποκατάστημα, το [eepokatasteema] branch office || chain store (US).

υπόκειμαι [eepokeeme] be subject, be liable || lie under.

υποκειμενικός [eepokeemeneekos] subjective.

υποκείμενο, το [eepokeemeno] subject || individual || scamp.

υποκινώ [eepokeeno] stir up, excite, incite.

υποκλέπτω [eepoklepto] purloin, pilfer.

υποκλίνομαι [eepokleenome] bow, bend || yield.

υπόκλιση, η [eepokleesee] bow, curtsy.

υποκοριστικό, το [eepokoreesteeko] diminutive.

υπόκοσμος, ο [eepokosmos] underworld.

υποκρίνομαι [eepokreenome] act, play the part of, impersonate || dissemble.

υπόκριση, η [eepokreesee] pretending, acting || dissembling.

υποκρισία, η [eepokreeseea] hypocrisy.

υποκριτής, ο [eepokreetees] actor || hypocrite.

υποκριτικός [eepokreeteekos] feigned, insincere.

υπόκρουση, η [eepokrousee] accompaniment.

υποκύπτω [eepokeepto] bend, submit, succumb || yield.

υπόκωφος [eepokofos] hollow, deep || smothered.

υπόλειμμα, το [eepoleema] residue, remnant, rest.

υπολείπομαι [eepoleepome] be left || be inferior to.

υπόληψη, η [eepoleepsee] esteem || credit, reputation.

υπολογίζω [eepoloyeezo] estimate, calculate || consider.

υπολογισμός, ο [eepoloyeesmos] calculation, estimate || account.

υπολογιστής, ο [eepoloyeestees] : **(ηλεκτρονικός)** ~ computer.

υπόλογος [eepologos] responsible, accountable, liable.

υπόλοιπο, το [eepoleepo] remainder, balance.

υπόλοιπος [eepoleepos] remaining, rest of.

υπολοχαγός, ο [eepolohagos] lieutenant.

υπομένω [eepomeno] endure, tolerate.

υπόμνημα, το [eepomneema] memorandum.

υπόμνηση, η [eepomneesee] reminder || suggestion.

υπομονεύω [eepomonevo] be patient || endure.

υπομονή, η [eepomonee] patience, endurance.

υπομονητικός [eepomoneeteekos] patient, enduring.

υπόνοια, η [eeponeea] suspicion || surmise.

υπονομεύω [eeponomevo] undermine, sabotage.

υπόνομος, ο, η [eeponomos] sewer || (στρατ) mine.

υπονοώ [eeponoo] infer, mean.

υποπίπτω [eepopeepto] commit, fall into || come to the notice of.

υποπροϊόν, το [eepoproeeon] by-product.

υποπρόξενος, ο [eepoproksenos] vice-consul.

υποπτεύομαι [eepoptevome] suspect, have an idea.

ύποπτος [eepoptos] suspect, suspicious, suspected.

υποσημείωση, η [eeposeemeeosee] footnote, annotation.

υποσιτισμός, ο [eeposeeteesmos] undernourishment, malnutrition.

υποσκάπτω [eeposkapto] undermine, sabotage.

υποσκελίζω [eeposkeleezo] upset || supplant.

υποστάθμη, η [eepostathmee] dregs, sediment, residue.

υπόσταση, η [eepostasee] existence || foundation, basis || (ιατρ) hypostasis.

υπόστεγο, το [eepostego] shed, hangar || shelter.

υποστέλλω [eepostelo] strike, lower || slow down, reduce.

υποστήριγμα, το [eeposteereegma] support, prop.

υποστηρίζω [eeposteereezo] prop up, support || second, back || maintain.

υποστήριξη, η [eeposteereeksee] prop, support || backing.

υπόστρωμα, το [eepostroma] substratum || saddlecloth.

υποσυνείδητο, το [eeposeeneeδeeto] subconscious.

υπόσχεση, η [eeposhesee] promise, pledge, engagement.

υπόσχομαι [eeposhome] promise, pledge.

υποταγή, η [eepotayee] obedience, subjection, submission.

υποτακτική, η [eepotakteekee] subjective.

υποτακτικός [eepotakteekos] obedient, submissive.

υπόταση, η [eepotasee] low blood pressure.

υποτάσσομαι [eepotasome] submit, give in.

υποτάσσω [eepotaso] subjugate, subdue.

υποτείνουσα, η [eepoteenousa] hypotenuse.

υποτελής [eepotelees] subordinate, tributary, vassal.

υποτίθεμαι [eepoteetheme] be supposed || suppose, consider.

υποτίμηση, η [eepoteemeesee] reduction in price, depreciation || underestimation.

υποτιμώ [eepoteemo] underestimate || lower the price of, depreciate.

υποτροπή, η [eepotropee] relapse, deterioration.

υποτροφία, η [eepotrofeea] scholarship.

υποτυπώδης [eepoteepoδees] sketchy, imperfectly formed.

ύπουλος [eepoulos] shifty, underhand, cunning.

υπουργείο, το [eepouryeeo] ministry.

υπουργικός [eepouryeekos] ministerial.

υπουργός, ο [eepourgos] minister || secretary (US).

υποφαινόμενος [eepofenomenos]: **ο** ~ the undersigned.

υποφερτός [eepofertos] tolerable || passable.

υποφέρω [eepofero] bear, support, endure || feel pain, suffer.

υποχθόνιος [eepohthoneeos] infernal, subterranean.

υποχονδρία, η [eepohonδreea] hypochondria || obsession.

υπόχρεος [eepohreos] obliged.

υποχρεώνω [eepohreono] oblige || compel.

υποχρέωση, η [eepohreosee] obligation, duty.

υποχρεωτικός [eepohreoteekos] obligatory || compulsory.

υποχώρηση, η [eepohoreesee] withdrawal, yielding || subsidence.

υποχωρώ [eepohoro] withdraw, give way || fall in, cave in.

υποψήφιος, ο [eepopseefeeos] candidate, applicant.

υποψηφιότητα, η [eepopseefeeoteeta] candidature, application.

υποψία, η [eepopseea] suspicion, misgiving.

υποψιάζομαι [eepopseeazome] suspect, have suspicions.

ύπτιος [eepteeos] lying on one's back.

ύστατος [eestatos] last, final.

ύστερα [eestera] afterwards, then, later || furthermore || ~ **από** after, following (this).

υστέρημα, το [eestereema] shortage, deficiency || small savings.

υστερία, η [eestereea] hysteria.

υστερικός [eestereekos] hysterical.

υστερισμός, ο [eestereesmos] hysteria, hysterics.

υστεροβουλία, η [eesterovouleea] afterthought || deceit.

υστερόγραφο, το [eesterografo] postscript.

ύστερος [eesteros] later || inferior || **εκ των υστέρων** on second thoughts, looking back.

υστερώ [eestero] come after || be inferior || deprive.

υφαίνω [eefeno] weave, spin || (μεταφ) plot.

ύφαλα, τα [eefala] πλ beam || part below waterline.

υφαλοκρηπίδα, η [eefalokreepeeδa] continental shelf.

ύφαλος, η [eefalos] reef, shoal.

ύφανση, η [eefansee] weaving || weave.

υφαντός [eefandos] woven.

υφαντουργία, η [eefandouryea] textile industry, weaving industry.

υφαρπάζω [eefarpazo] obtain by fraud.

ύφασμα, το [eefasma] cloth, fabric, stuff, material || **υφάσματα** textiles.

ύφεση, η [eefesee] decrease, abatement || (βαρομέτρου) depression || (μουσ) flat (note).

υφή, η [eefee] texture, web, weave.

υφηγητής, ο [eefeeyeetees] lecturer || assistant professor (US).

υφήλιος, η [eefeeleeos] earth, world, globe.

υφίσταμαι [eefeestame] bear, undergo, sustain || (είμαι) exist, be in force.

υφιστάμενος, το [eefeestamenos] subordinate, inferior.

ύφος, το [eefos] style || air, look, tone.

υφυπουργός, ο [eefeepourgos] undersecretary of state.

υψηλός [eepseelos] high, towering, tall || (μεταφ) lofty, great.

υψηλότητα, η [eepseeloteeta] Highness || **η Αυτού ~** His Royal Highness.

υψηλόφρονας [eepseelofronas] generous || highminded, haughty.

υψικάμινος, η [eepseekameenos] blast furnace.

ύψιλον, το [eepseelon] the letter Y.

υψίπεδο, το [eepseepeδo] plateau.

ύψιστος [eepseestos] highest || (ουσ) God.

υψίφωνος, ο, η [eepseefonos] tenor || soprano.

υψόμετρο, το [eepsometro] altitude.

ύψος, το [eepsos] height, altitude || (μουσ) pitch.

ύψωμα, το [eepsoma] height, elevation || hillock.

υψώνω [eepsono] raise, elevate || increase || hoist.

ύψωση, η [eepsosee] raising, lifting, elevation || rise in price.

Φ, φ

φάβα, η [fava] yellow pea || pea purée.

φαγάς, ο [fagas] glutton, gourmand.

φαγγρί, το [fangree] sea bream.

φαγητό, το [fayeeto] meal, dish, food || dinner.

φαγκότο, το [fangoto] bassoon.

φαγοπότι, το [fagopotee] revel, eating and drinking.

φαγούρα, η [fagoura] itching, irritation.

φάγωμα, το [fagoma] corrosion, disintegration || (τσακωμός) quarrel, dispute, wrangling.

φαγωμάρα, η [fagomara] itch, irritation || (τσακωμός) arguing, dispute.

φαγωμένος [fagomenos] eaten || eroded || **είμαι ~** I've eaten.

φαγώσιμα, τα [fagoseema] πλ provisions, victuals.

φαγώσιμος [fagoseemos] eatable, edible.

φαεινή [faeenee]: **~ ιδέα** brainwave, bright idea.

φαΐ, το [faee] food, meal.

φαιδρός [feδros] merry, cheerful || (μεταφ) ridiculous.

φαίνομαι [fenome] appear, come in sight || seem, look || show o.s. to be.

φαινόμενα, τα [fenomena] πλ: **κατά τα ~** judging by appearances.

φαινομενικώς [fenomeneekos] apparently, outwardly.

φαινόμενο, το [fenomeno] wonder, prodigy || phenomenon.

φάκα, η [faka] mousetrap || snare.

φάκελος, ο [fakelos] envelope || file, cover, dossier, record.

φακή, η [fakee] lentils.

φακίδα, η [fakeeða] freckle.

φακός, ο [fakos] lens || magnifying glass, magnifier.

φάλαγγα, η [falanga] phalanx || (στρατ) column || (στοίχος) row.

φάλαινα, η [falena] whale.

φαλάκρα, η [falakra] baldness || bald head.

φαλακραίνω [falakreno] go bald.

φαλακρός [falakros] bald(-headed) || bare.

φαλλός, ο [falos] phallus.

φάλτσο, το [faltso] wrong note, dissonance || (μεταφ) mistake, fault, error.

φαμίλια, η [fameeleea] family.

φάμπρικα, η [fambreeka] factory || fabrication, device, artifice.

φανάρι, το [fanaree] lamp, light, lantern || (αυτοκινήτου) headlamp || (φάρου) lighthouse.

φαναρτζής, ο [fanardzees] tinsmith || lampmaker.

φανατίζω [fanateezo] make fanatical, fanaticize.

φανατικός [fanateekos] overzealous, fanatical || (ουσ) fanatic, zealot.

φανατισμός, ο [fanateesmos] fanaticism.

φανέλα, η [fanela] flannel || vest || woollen cloth.

φανερός [faneros] clear, plain, evident, certain.

φανερώνω [fanerono] reveal, make plain.

φαντάζομαι [fandazome] imagine, fancy, think || (πιστεύω) believe.

φαντάζω [fandazo] make an impression, stand out || look glamorous.

φαντάρος, ο [fandaros] infantryman.

φαντασία, η [fandaseea] imagination || illusion || (υπερηφάνεια) vanity, pride || (μουσ) fantasia.

φαντασιοπληξία, η [fandaseeopleekseea] extravagant notion || caprice, whim.

φάντασμα, το [fandasma] phantom, ghost, spirit.

φαντασμαγορία, η [fandasmagoreea] phantasmagoria.

φαντασμένος [fandasmenos] presumptuous, vain.

φανταστικός [fandasteekos] illusory, imaginary || fantastic, extravagant.

φανταχτερός [fandahteros] showy, bright || gaudy, glaring.

φάντης, ο [fandees] (στα χαρτιά) knave.

φανφαρόνος, ο [fanfaronos] braggart, boaster, blusterer.

φάπα, η [fapa] slap, box on the ear, smack.

φάρα, η [fara] race, progeny, breed || crew.

φαράγγι, το [farangee] gorge, gully, precipice, ravine.

φαράσι, το [farasee] dustpan.

φαρδαίνω [farðeno] widen, broaden, become wider || stretch, extend.

φάρδος, το [farðos] width, breadth.

φαρδύς [farðees] wide, large, broad, ample.

φαρέτρα, η [faretra] quiver.

φαρμακείο, το [farmakeeo] chemist shop.

φαρμακερός [farmakeros] venomous || spiteful, bitter.

φαρμάκι, το [farmakee] poison || (μεταφ) anything bitter.

φάρμακο, το [farmako] drug, medicine, remedy.

φαρμακοποιός, ο [farmakopeeos] pharmacist, chemist || druggist (US).

φαρμακώνω [farmakono] poison || (μεταφ) cause grief || mortify.

φάρος, ο [faros] lighthouse, beacon.

φάρσα, η [farsa] trick, farce || practical joke.

φάρυγγας, ο [fareengas] pharynx, windpipe.

φασαρία, η [fasareea] disturbance || fuss, noise, bustle.

φασιανός, ο [faseeanos] pheasant.

φάση, η [fasee] phase || change, turn || aspect.

φασισμός, ο [faseesmos] fascism.

φασιστικός [faseesteekos] fascist.

φασκιά, η [faskia] swaddling band, swaddling clothes.

φασκόμηλο, το [faskomeelo] sage || sage tea.

φάσκω [fasko]: ~ και αντιφάσκω contradict o.s.

φάσμα, το [fasma] ghost, spirit || (φυσική) spectrum.

φασματοσκόπιο, το [fasmatoskopeeo] spectroscope.

φασόλι, το [fasolee] haricot bean, kidney bean.

φασο(υ)λάδα, η [faso(u)laða] bean soup.

φασο(υ)λάκια, τα [faso(u)lakeea] πλ green beans.

φάτνη, η [fatnee] manger, crib, stall.

φατρία, η [fatreea] faction, clique, gang.

φατριάζω [fatreeazo] form factions, be factious.

φάτσα, η [fatsa] face || front || (επίρ) opposite.

φαυλοκρατία, η [favlokrateea] political corruption.

φαύλος [favlos] wicked, depraved || ~ κύκλος vicious circle.

φαφλατάς, ο [faflatas] chatterer, mumbler.

Φεβρουάριος, ο [fevrouareeos] February.

φεγγάρι, το [fengaree] moon.

φεγγίτης, ο [fengeetees] skylight, fanlight, garret window.

φεγγοβολώ [fengovolo] shine brightly.

φέγγω [fengo] shine, give light.

φείδομαι [feedome] save, spare || be sparing of, be stingy.

φειδωλός [feeδolos] sparing, thrifty || stingy, mean, niggardly.

φελλός, ο [felos] cork.

φεουδαρχικός [feouδarheekos] feudal.

φέουδο, το [feouδo] fief.

φερέγγυος [ferengeeos] solvent, trustworthy.

φέρελπις [ferelpees] full of promise || hopeful.

φερετζές, ο [feredzes] veil (of a Moslem woman).

φέρετρο, το [feretro] coffin, bier.

φερμένος [fermenos] arrived, brought, imported.

φερμουάρ, το [fermouar] zip fastener.

φέρνω [ferno] βλ **φέρω**.

φέρομαι [ferome] conduct, behave || be reputed, be held as.

φέρσιμο, το [ferseemo] behaviour, conduct.

φέρω [fero] bring, carry, support || (στέλλω) fetch || (έχω πάνω μου) carry, have || (προξενώ) cause || (παράγω) bear, bring forth, bring in, yield || (φορώ) wear || (κατευθύνω) lead, conduct || ~ **αντιρρήσεις** protest || **φερ' ειπείν** for example.

φέσι, το [fesee] fez || **γίνομαι** ~ get dead drunk.

φέτα, η [feta] slice || (τυρί) kind of white cheese.

φετινός [feteenos] of this year.

φέτος [fetos] this year.

φευγάλα, η [fevgala] flight, escape, stampede.

φευγαλέος [fevgaleos] fleeting.

φευγατίζω [fevgateezo] help to escape.

φευγάτος [fevgatos] gone, fled, run away, left.

φεύγω [fevgo] leave, depart, get away || escape, flee || run away from, shun.

φήμη, η [feemee] report, rumour || reputation || renown, repute || fame.

φημίζομαι [feemeezome] be well-known.

φθάνω [fthano] catch, overtake, attain || (μεταφ) equal, be equal to || arrive, reach || draw near || ~ **σε** reach the point of, be reduced to || **φθάνει να** provided that.

φθαρτός [fthartos] perishable, destructible, liable to decay.

φθείρομαι [theerome] decay, wash away || (μεταφ) lose importance.

φθείρω [theero] damage, spoil || corrupt, pervert, taint.

φθινόπωρο, το [ftheenoporo] autumn.

φθίνω [ftheeno] pine away || decay || decline, fail.

φθισικός [ftheeseekos] consumptive, tubercular.

φθίση, η [ftheesee] consumption || decline.

φθόγγος, ο [fthongos] voice, sound || (μουσ) note.

φθονερός [fthoneros] envious, jealous.

φθόνος, ο [fthonos] malicious envy, jealousy.

φθονώ [fthono] be envious of, begrudge.

φθορά, η [fthora] deterioration, damage, destruction || decay || loss.

φθορισμός, ο [fthoreesmos] fluorescence.

φι, το [fee] the letter Φ.

φιάλη, η [feealee] bottle, flagon, flask.

φιγούρα, η [feegoura] figure, image || (μεταφ) expression, air || **κάνω** ~ cut a fine figure.

φιγουράρω [feegouraro] show off, appear.

φίδι, το [feeδee] snake, serpent.

φιδωτός [feeδotos] winding, twisting.

φίλαθλος, ο, η [feelathlos] sports fan.

φιλαλήθης [feelaleethees] truthful.

φιλάνθρωπος, ο, η [feelanthropos] philanthropist, charitable person.

φιλαράκος, ο [feelarakos] beau || chum, pal || scoundrel, rascal.

φιλάργυρος [feelaryeeros] niggardly, miserly || (ουσ) miser.

φιλάρεσκος [feelareskos] coquettish, spruce.

φιλαρμονική, η [feelarmoneekee] (musical) band.

φιλαρχία, η [feelarheea] love of authority.

φιλάσθενος [feelasthenos] sickly, weakly, puny.

φιλελευθερισμός, ο [feelelevthereesmos] liberalism.

φιλελεύθερος, ο [feelelevtheros] liberal.

φιλέλληνας, ο, η [feeleleenas] philhellene.

φιλενάδα, η [feelenaδa] girlfriend || (μεταφ) mistress.

φιλές, ο [feeles] hairnet.

φιλέτο, το [feeleto] fillet of meat.

φιλεύω [feelevo] make a present || entertain.

φίλη, η [feelee] friend.

φιλήδονος [feeleeδonos] sensual, voluptuous.

φίλημα, το [feeleema] kiss.

φιλήσυχος [feeleeseehos] peace-loving, calm, quiet, serene.

φιλί, το [feelee] βλ φίλημα.

φιλία, η [feeleea] friendship.

φιλικός [feeleekos] friendly || of a friend.

φίλιππος, ο, η [feeleepos] horse lover || racegoer.

φιλιστρίνι, το [feeleestreenee] porthole.

φιλμ, το [feelm] film.

φίλντισι, το [feelnteesee] mother-of-pearl || ivory.

φιλόδοξος [feeloðoksos] ambitious || pretentious, showy.

φιλοδοξώ [feeloðokso] be ambitious || aspire to, desire strongly.

φιλοδώρημα, το [feeloðoreema] || tip, gratuity.

φιλοκερδής [feelokerðees] greedy, covetous, eager for gain.

φιλολογία, η [feeloloyeea] literature || philology.

φιλόλογος, ο [feelologos] man of letters, philologist || scholar.

φιλομαθής [feelomathees] fond of learning.

φιλόμουσος [feelomousos] lover of music || fond of learning.

φιλονικία, η [feeloneekeea] dispute, wrangle.

φιλονικώ [feeloneeko] quarrel,wrangle.

φινοξενία, η [feeloksenea] hospitality.

φιλόξενος [feeloksenos] hospitable.

φιλοξενώ [feelokseno] entertain, give hospitality, receive.

φιλοπατρία, η [feelopatreea] patriotism.

φιλοπόλεμος [feelopolemos] warlike, martial.

φιλόπονος [feeloponos] assiduous, diligent, industrious.

φιλοπονώ [feelopono] prepare assiduously.

φίλος, ο [feelos] friend || (επιθ) dear, friendly.

φιλοσοφία, η [feelosofeea] philosophy.

φιλοσοφικός [feelosofeekos] philosophical.

φιλόσοφος, ο, η [feelosofos] philosopher.

φιλόστοργος [feelostorgos] loving, affectionate.

φιλοτελισμός, ο [feeloteleesmos] philately.

φιλοτέχνημα, το [feelotehneema] work of art.

φιλότεχνος [feelotehnos] art lover || artistic, skilful.

φιλοτιμία, η [feeloteemeea], φιλότιμο, το [feeloteemo] sense of honour, pride, self-respect, dignity.

φιλότιμος [feeloteemos] eager to excel || obliging || having a sense of pride and honour || generous.

φιλοτιμούμαι [feeloteemoume] make it a point of honour.

φιλοτιμώ [feeloteemo] put s.o. on his dignity.

φιλοφρόνηση, η [feelofroneesee] compliment, courtesy.

φίλτατος [feeltatos] dearest, most beloved.

φίλτρο, το [feeltro] filter || philtre.

φιλύποπτος [feeleepoptos] distrustful, suspicious.

φιλώ [feelo] kiss, embrace.

φιμώνω [feemono] muzzle, gag || (μεταφ) silence, hush.

φίμωτρο, το [feemotro] muzzle, gag.

Φινλανδία, η [feenlanðeea] Finland.

φινλανδικός [feenlanðeekos] Finnish.

Φινλανδός, ο [feenlanðos] Finn.

φίνος [feenos] fine.

φιόγκος, ο [feeongos] knot, bow.

φίρμα, η [feerma] firm || trade name.

φίσα, η [feesa] filing slip || gambling chip.

φίσκα [feeska] brimming over.

φιστίκι, το [feesteekee] pistachio nut || ~ αράπικο monkey nut, peanut.

φιτίλι, το [feeteelee] wick || (δυναμίτιδας) fuse.

φλάμπουρο, το [flambouro] pennon, standard.

φλάουτο, το [flaouto] flute.

φλέβα, η [fleva] vein || (μεταλλεύματος) lode || (μεταφ) talent.

Φλεβάρης, ο [flevarees] February.

φλέγμα, το [flegma] phlegm, mucus || (μεταφ) coolness, unconcern.

φλεγματικός [flegmateekos] phlegmatic || stolid.

φλεγμονή, η [flegmonee] inflammation, soreness.

φλέγομαι [flegome] burn, ignite || (μεταφ) flare up.

φλέγον [flegon]: ~ ζήτημα topical problem.

φλερτάρω [flertaro] flirt with.

φλυναφώ [fleenafo] prate, babble, prattle.

φλιτζάνι, το [fleedzanee] cup.

φλόγα, η [floga] flame, blaze || (μεταφ) passion, ardour.

φλογέρα, η [floyera] shepherd's pipe, reed.

φλογερός [floyeros] burning, flaming || (μεταφ) ardent, fervent.

φλογίζω [floyeezo] inflame, kindle.

φλόγωση, η [flogosee] inflammation, soreness.

φλοιός, ο [flees] peel, rind || (φυστικιού) shell || (δένδρου) bark || (γης) crust.

φλοίσβος, ο [fleesvos] rippling of waves || babbling.

φλοκάτη, η [flokatee] thick blanket, peasant's cape.

φλόκος, ο [flokos] jib.

φλομώνω [flomono] stun || grow wan.

φλούδα, η [flouda] βλ **φλοιός**.

φλουρί, το [flouree] gold coin.

φλυαρία, η [fleeareea] gossiping, chatter, prattle.

φλύαρος [fleearos] talkative.

φλυαρώ [fleearo] chatter, tattle, prattle.

φλυτζάνι, το [fleedzanee] cup.

φοβάμαι [fovame] be afraid.

φοβέρα, η [fovera] threat, menace, intimidation.

φοβερίζω [fovereezo] threaten, menace, intimidate.

φοβερός [foveros] terrible, frightful || amazing, formidable.

φόβητρο, το [foveetro] scarecrow || bogey || fright.

φοβητσιάρης [foveetseearees] fearful, timid, timorous.

φοβία, η [foveea] fear, phobia.

φοβίζω [foveezo] frighten || menace, threaten, intimidate.

φόβος, ο [fovos] fear, dread, fright.

φόδρα, η [fodra] lining.

φοίνικας, ο [feeneekas] palm tree || (καρπός) date || phoenix.

φοίτηση, η [feeteesee] attendance (at school).

φοιτητής, ο [feeteetees] student.

φοιτώ [feeto] be a student, attend a course of studies.

φόλα, η [fola] dog poison.

φονεύω [fonevo] murder, kill.

φονιάς, ο [fonias] murderer.

φονικό, το [foneeko] murder, homicide, carnage.

φόνος, ο [fonos] murder, homicide.

φόντο, το [fonto] bottom, base, back || (ζωγραφιάς) background || (κεφάλαιο) capital.

φόρα, η [fora] impulse, impetus || force || **βγάζω στη ~** bring into the open, uncover.

φορά, η [fora] force || course, run, impetus || (κατεύθυνση) direction || (ευκαιρία) time || **άλλη ~** another time || **άλλη μια ~** once again || **μια ~** once, only once.

φοράδα, η [forada] mare.

φορατζής, ο [foradzees] tax collector.

φορβή, η [forvee] fodder, forage.

φορείο, το [foreeo] stretcher, litter.

φόρεμα, το [forema] dress, garment.

φορεσιά, η [foresia] dress, suit of clothes || attire.

φορέας, ο [foreas] carrier, porter || (οικον) agent, body.

φορητός [foreetos] portable, easy to carry.

φόρμα, η [forma] form, shape || mould, matrix || (εργάτη) overall || (ντοκουμέντο) form, document || **σε ~** in good form, in tiptop shape.

φοροδιαφυγή, η [forodeeafeeyee] tax evasion.

φορολογία, η [foroloyeea] taxation || tax, rate.

φορολογούμενος, ο [forologoumenos] taxpayer, ratepayer.

φορολογώ [forologo] tax, put a tax on.

φόρος, ο [foros] tax, rate, duty.

φορτηγό, το [forteego] lorry || truck (US) || (ναυτ) cargo vessel.

φορτίζω [forteezo] charge with electricity.

φορτικός [forteekos] intrusive, importunate || troublesome.

φορτίο, το [forteeo] cargo, load || burden, charge, weight.

φορτοεκφορτωτής, ο [fortoekfortotees] stevedore.

φόρτος, ο [fortos] burden, heavy load.

φορτσάρω [fortsaro] force || intensify || (ανέμου) increase, strengthen.

φόρτωμα, το [fortoma] loading || (μεταφ) burden, care.

φορτώνομαι [fortonome] pester, annoy, bother.

φορτώνω [fortono] load, pile (on) || take on cargo.

φορτωτική, η [fortoteekee] bill of lading.

φορώ [foro] wear || put on, get into || carry.

φουγάρο, το [fougaro] funnel, flue, tall chimney, smokestack.

φουκαράς, ο [foukaras] poor devil || unfortunate fellow.

φουμάρω [foumaro] smoke.

φούμος, ο [foumos] soot || lampblack.

φούντα, η [founta] tassel || tuft, crest.

φουντάρω [fountaro] (ναυτ) sink || cast anchor.

φουντούκι, το [fountoukee] hazelnut.

φουντώνω [fountono] become bushy || stretch out, spread || expand.

φουντωτός [fountotos] bushy, thick.

φούρια, η [foureea] haste.

φούρκα, η [fourka] rage, anger || (κρεμάλα) gallows, gibbet.

φουρκέτα, η [fourketa] hairpin.

φουρκίζω [fourkeezo] vex, harass.

φούρναρης, ο [fournarees] baker.

φουρνέλο, το [fournelo] grid || blasting charge.

φουρνιά, η [fournia] ovenful || (μεταφ) batch.

φούρνος, ο [fournos] oven || bakery || kiln, furnace.

φουρτούνα, η [fourtouna] tempest, storm || rough sea || (μεταφ) calamity, misfortune.

φούσκα, η [fouska] bladder || (παιχνίδι) balloon || blister || soap bubble.

φουσκάλα, η [fouskala] blister || bubble.

φουσκοθαλασσιά, η [fouskothalasia] surge of sea.

φούσκωμα, το [fouskoma] inflation, swelling || swaggering.

φουσκωμένος [fouskomenos] swollen, inflated, puffed up.

φουσκώνω [fouskono] swell, inflate, blow up || (λάστιχο) pump || (μεταφ) exaggerate || (ενοχλώ) irritate || (ζύμη) rise || (αναπνοή) puff, pant || (μεταφ) puff o.s. up.

φουσκωτός [fouskotos] puffed, inflated || curved.

φούστα, η [fousta] skirt.

φουστανέλα, η [foustanela] kind of kilt worn as part of the Greek national costume.

φουστάνι, το [foustanee] gown, dress, frock.

φούχτα, η [fouhta] handful || hollow of hand.

φράγκο, το [frango] franc || drachma.

φραγκοστάφυλο, το [frangostafeelo] redcurrant.

φραγκόσυκο, το [frangoseeko] prickly pear.

φράγμα, το [fragma] enclosure, fence || barrage, dam || barrier.

φραγμός, ο [fragmos] fence, barrier || (στρατ) barrage.

φράζω [frazo] surround, hedge || bar, block up, stop, obstruct.

φράκο, το [frako] dress coat, tails.

φράκτης, ο [fraktees] fence, enclosure, fencing.

φραμπαλάς, ο [frambalas] furbelow.

φράντζα, η [frandza] fringe.

φραντζόλα, η [frandzola] long loaf.

φράξιμο, το [frakseemo] enclosing, fencing || stopping up, blockage.

φράουλα, η [fraoula] strawberry.

φράπα, η [frapa] kind of large citrus fruit, grapefruit.

φρασεολογία, η [fraseoloyeea] phraseology.

φράση, η [frasee] phrase || period.

φράσσω [fraso] βλ **φράζω.**

φράχτης, ο [frahtees] fence, enclosure, fencing, hedge.

φρέαρ, το [frear] well || (μεταλλείο) pit, shaft.

φρεάτιο, το [freateeo] small well.

φρεγάδα, η [fregaða] frigate.

φρένα, τα [frena] πλ reason, senses || brakes.

φρενάρισμα, το [frenareesma] braking.

φρενάρω [frenaro] brake || (μεταφ) check.

φρένες, οι [frenes] πλ mind, reason, wits || **έξω φρενών** off one's head, enraged || unbelievable.

φρενιάζω [freneeazo] get furious, fret and fume.

φρένο, το [freno] brake.

φρενοβλαβής [frenovlavees] mentally disturbed.

φρενοκομείο, το [frenokomeeo] madhouse, lunatic asylum.

φρενολογία, η [frenoloyeea] phrenology.

φρεσκάδα, η [freskaða] freshness || coolness, chilliness.

φρεσκάρω [freskaro] freshen, cool || (ο καιρός) become worse.

φρέσκο, το [fresko] fresco || coolness, freshness, chilliness || **στο ~** in prison.

φρέσκος [freskos] fresh, new, recent || cool.

φρικαλέος [freekaleos] horrible, hideous, ghastly.

φρίκη, η [freekee] terror, horror || (επιφ) frightful.

φρικιάζω [freekeeazo] shiver, shudder || be disgusted.

φρικτός [freektos], **φρικώδης** [freekoðees] (θέαμα) horrible, ghastly || (εμφάνιση) hideous || (καιρός) horrid, vile || awful.

φρόκαλο, το [frokalo] sweepings, rubbish || broom.

φρόνημα, το [froneema] opinion, sentiment, morale || **φρονήματα** political convictions.

φρονηματίζω [froneemateezo] inspire self-confidence, render self-confident.

φρόνηση, η [froneesee] prudence, wariness, circumspection.

φρόνιμα [froneema] (επιφ) behave yourself.

φρονιμάδα, η [froneemaða] wisdom, prudence || moderation || (παιδιού) quietness, good behaviour || (γυναίκας) modesty, chastity.

φρονιμεύω [froneemevo] become prudent, grow wise, be well-behaved.

φρονιμίτης, ο [froneemeetees] wisdom tooth.

φρόνιμος [froneemos] reasonable, sound, well-behaved || virtuous, wise.

φροντίζω [fronteezo] look after, care for || see to.

φροντίδα, η [fronteeða] concern, care, anxiety.

φροντίδες, οι [fronteeðes] πλ things to do, cares.

φροντιστήριο, το [fronteesteereeo] coaching school || prep school.

φρονώ [frono] think, suppose, believe, consider.

φρουρά, η [froura] lookout, guard || garrison.

φρούριο, το [froureeo] fortress, stronghold.

φρουρός, ο [frouros] guard, sentinel, sentry || (μεταφ) guardian.

φρουρώ [frouro] guard, keep watch, stand sentry.

φρούτο, το [frouto] fruit, dessert.

φρυγανιά n [freegania] toast.

φρύδι, το [freedee] eyebrow.

φταίξιμο, το [ftekseemo] fault, error, mistake, blame.

φταίχτης, ο [ftehtees] person responsible, culprit.

φταίω [fteo] be responsible, be to blame || make a mistake.

φτάνω [ftano] βλ **φθάνω.**

φτέρη, n [fteree] fern.

φτέρνα, n [fterna] heel.

φτερνίζομαι [fterneezome] sneeze.

φτέρνισμα, το [fterneesma] sneeze, sneezing.

φτερό, το [ftero] feather, plume || wing || (ξεσκονίσματος) feather duster || (αυτοκινήτου) mudguard || fender (US).

φτερούγα, n [fterouga] wing.

φτερουγίζω [fterouyeezo] flutter, flap.

φτηναίνω [fteeneno] cheapen, become cheaper, go down.

φτήνεια, n [fteeneea] cheapness, low price.

φτηνός [fteenos] cheap.

φτιά(χ)νομαι [fteea(h)nome] make up one's face || look better.

φτιά(χ)νω [fteea(h)no] arrange, tidy up, correct || (κατασκευάζω) make || have made || do.

φτιαχτός [fteeahtos] fabricated, affected.

φτυάρι, το [fteeaaree] shovel, spade, scoop.

φτύνω [fteeno] spit, expectorate || spit out.

φτύσιμο, το [fteeseemo] spitting.

φτυστός [fteestos]: ~ **ο πατέρας του** the spitting image of his father.

φτωχαίνω [ftoheno] impoverish, make poor || become poor.

φτώχεια, n [ftoheea] poverty, destitution.

φτωχεύω [ftohevo] become poor || go bankrupt.

φτωχικό, το [ftoheeko] humble abode.

φτωχικός [ftoheekos] poor, mean, scant || shabby.

φτωχός [ftohos] poor, needy, penniless.

φυγαδεύω [feegaδevo] help to escape.

φυγάδας, ο [feegaδas] runaway, deserter, fugitive, renegade.

φυγή, n [feeyee] escape, fleeing, flight.

φυγοδικία, n [feegoδeekeea] default.

φυγόδικος/κn [feegoδeekos] defaulter.

φυγόκεντρος [feegokentros] centrifugal.

φυγόπονος [feegoponos] lazy || (ουσ) slacker, shirker.

φύκια, τα [feekeea] πλ seaweed.

φυλάγομαι [feelagome] take precautions, take care.

φυλάγω [feelago] guard, protect || mind, tend || (αντικείμενο) keep, lay aside || lie in wait for.

φύλακας, ο [feelakas] keeper, guardian, watchman, guard, caretaker.

φυλακή, n [feelakee] prison, jail.

φυλακίζω [feelakeezo] incarcerate, imprison.

φυλάκιο, το [feelakeeo] guardhouse, post.

φυλάκιση, n [feelakeesee] imprisonment.

φυλακισμένος, ο [feelakeesmenos] prisoner.

φυλαχτό, το [feelahto] talisman, amulet, charm.

φυλετικός [feeleteekos] tribal, racial.

φυλή, n [feelee] race, tribe, line.

φυλλάδα, n [feelaδa] booklet, pamphlet, brochure.

φυλλάδιο, το [feelaδeeo] pamphlet || instalment, issue, part.

φυλλοκάρδια, τα [feelokarδeea] πλ bottom of one's heart.

φυλλομετρώ [feelometro] turn pages of, skim over, run through.

φύλλο, το [feelo] leaf || (λουλουδιού) petal || (χαρτιού κτλ) sheet || (σελίδα) page || (πόρτας κτλ) shutter, leaf || (χαρτοπαιξίας) (playing) card || (εφημερίδα) newspaper || ~ **πορείας** marching orders.

φυλλοξήρα, n [feelokseera] phylloxera.

φύλλωμα, το [feeloma] foliage.

φύλο, το [feelo] sex || race.

φυματικός [feemateekos] consumptive, tubercular.

φυματίωση, n [feemateeosee] tuberculosis, consumption.

φύομαι [feeome] grow, bud, sprout.

φύρα, n [feera] loss of weight, waste.

φυραίνω [feereno] shorten, shrink || lose weight, lose volume.

φύραμα, το [feerama] paste, dough || blend || (μεταφ) character, sort.

φύρδην [feerδeen]: ~ **μίγδην** pell-mell, helter-skelter.

φυσαλίδα, n [feesaleeδa] bubble || blister.

φυσαρμόνικα, n [feesarmoneeka] accordion || mouth organ.

φυσέκι, το [feesekee] cartridge.

φυσερό, το [feesero] bellows.

φύση, n [feesee] nature.

φύσημα, το [feeseema] breath || puff || breathing.

φυσίγγιο, το [feeseengeeo] cartridge.

φυσικά, τα [feeseeka] πλ physics.

φυσικά [feeseeka] naturally, as a matter of fact.

φυσική, η [feeseekee] physics, natural philosophy.

φυσικό, το [feeseeko] custom, habit.

φυσικός [feeseekos] natural || physical || (ουσ) physicist.

φυσικότητα, η [feeseekoteeta] naturalness, artlessness.

φυσιογνωμία, η [feeseeognomeea] cast of features || countenance || well-known person.

φυσιολάτρης, ο [feeseeolatrees] lover of nature.

φυσιολογία, η [feeseeoloyeea] physiology.

φυσιολογικός [feeseeoloyeekos] physiological || (κανονικό) normal.

φύση, η [feesee] nature || character, temper || **φύσει** by nature.

φυσομανώ [feesomano] rage.

φυσώ [feeso] blow up || puff, blow out || pant || **φυσάει** it's windy.

φυτεία, η [feeteea] plantation || vegetation, bed of vegetables.

φύτεμα, το [feetema] planting.

φυτεύω [feetevo] plant, lay out || (μεταφ) lodge, stick.

φυτικός [feeteekos] vegetable.

φυτοζωώ [feetozoo] live in poverty, scrape through.

φυτοκομία, η [feetokomeea] horticulture.

φυτολογία, η [feetoloyeea] botany.

φυτό, το [feeto] plant, vegetable.

φύτρα, η [feetra] germ, embryo || (μεταφ) lineage, origin.

φυτρώνω [feetrono] grow, germinate, sprout.

φυτώριο, το [feetoreeo] nursery, plantation, seedbed.

φώκια, η [fokeea] seal.

φωλιά, η [foleea] nest, den, lair, hole || (μεταφ) hovel.

φωλιάζω [foleeazo] nestle, nest.

φωνάζω [fonazo] shout, call, summon || cry, scream, shriek.

φωνακλάς, ο [fonaklas] loud talker, noisy talker.

φωνή, η [fonee] sound || voice || cry, shout, scream.

φωνήεν, το [fonien] vowel.

φωνητική, η [foneeteekee] phonetics.

φωνητικός [foneeteekos] vocal || phonetic, phonic.

φως, το [fos] light || (μεταφ) sight || knowledge, illumination.

φωστήρ(ας), το [fosteer(as)] luminary || (μεταφ) learned, erudite person.

φωσφόρος, ο [fosforos] phosphorus.

φώτα, τα [fota] πλ lights || (μεταφ) knowledge, learning || (εκκλ) Epiphany.

φωταγωγός, ο [fotagogos] light well, skylight.

φωταγωγώ [fotagogo] illuminate.

φωταέριο, το [fotaereeo] gas (lighting).

φωταψία, η [fotapseea] illumination.

φωτεινός [foteenos] luminous, light, bright || clear, lucid.

φωτιά, η [fotia] fire || (καπνιστού) light || (μεταφ) great heat || fury || (σε τιμή) costliness.

φωτίζω [foteezo] illuminate, light up, light || enlighten, inform.

φώτιση, η [foteesee] enlightenment || inspiration.

φωτισμός, ο [foteesmos] lighting, illumination.

φωτοβολίδα, η [fotovoleeδa] flare.

φωτογενής [fotogenees] photogenic.

φωτογραφείο, το [fotografeeo] photographic studio.

φωτογραφία, η [fotografeea] photograph || photography.

φωτογραφική, η [fotografeekee] photography || ~ **μηχανή** camera.

φωτογράφος, ο [fotografos] photographer.

φωτόμετρο, το [fotometro] light meter.

φωτοσκίαση, η [fotoskeeasee] shading, light and shade.

φωτοστέφανος, ο [fotostefanos] halo || (μεταφ) glory, prestige.

φωτοτυπία, η [fototeepeea] photocopy.

φωτοχυσία, η [fotoheeseea] illumination.

Χ, χ

χαβάς, ο [havas] tune, air, melody.

χαβιάρι, το [haviaree] caviar.

χαβούζα, η [havouza] cistern, reservoir.

χαγιάτι, το [hayiatee] upper gallery round courtyard.

χάδια, τα [haδeea] πλ petting, cajolery.

χαζεύω [hazevo] gape || idle about, loiter.

χάζι, το [hazee] pleasure, delight || **το κάνω** ~ it entertains me.

χαζός [hazos] stupid, silly, foolish.

χαΐβάνι, το [haeevanee] beast || (μεταφ) jackass.

χάΐδεμα, το [haeeδema] caressing, pat, stroke || (μεταφ) cajolery.

χαΐδευτικός [haeeδevteekos] caressing, affectionate || (άνεμος) soft.

χαΐδεμένος [haeeδemenos] spoilt.

χαΐδεύομαι [haeeδevome] nuzzle, cuddle || seek attention.

χαΐδεύω [haeeδevo] caress, fondle, pat || pet, spoil || fawn upon.

χαιρέκακος [herekakos] malicious, mischievous.

χαίρετε [herete] (επιφ) hello, good day || be seeing you.

χαιρετίζω [hereteezo] hail, greet || salute.

χαιρέτισμα, το [hereteesma] salute, greeting, salutation, bow.

χαιρετισμός, ο [hereteesmos] βλ **χαιρέτισμα**.

χαιρετώ [hereto] βλ **χαιρετίζω**.

χαίρομαι [herome] be happy || enjoy.

χαίρω [hero] be pleased || ~ **άκρας υγείας** be in tiptop shape.

χαίτη, η [hetee] mane, shock of hair.

χακί, το [hakee] khaki.

χαλάζι, το [halazee] hail.

χαλάλι [halalee]: ~ **σου** you merit it, you can have it.

χαλαρός [halaros] relaxed, slack, loose.

χαλαρώνω [halarono] unbend || (σχοινί) loosen, slacken || (μεταφ) relax || (προσπάθεια) abate, ease up || (ζήλο) cool.

χάλασμα, το [halasma] ruin, demolition || (μηχανής) putting out of order || ruin.

χαλασμένος [halasmenos] rotten, turned bad || broken, not working || damaged, demolished.

χαλασμός, ο [halasmos] demolition, destruction || (μεταφ) disturbance, storm, excitement || catastrophe.

χαλάστρα, η [halastra]: **μου κάνουν** ~ they foiled my plans, they cramped my style.

χαλβάς, ο [halvas] halva || (μεταφ) indolent person, silly fellow.

χαλί, το [halee] carpet, rug.

χάλια, τα [haleea] πλ bad condition, sad plight.

χαλίκι, το [haleekee] pebble, small stone, gravel.

χαλιναγωγώ [haleenagogo] lead by the bridle || (μεταφ) check, curb || (πάθη) control, curb.

χαλινάρι, το [haleenaree] bridle, bit, rein || (μεταφ) curbing, holding back.

χαλκάς, ο [halkas] ring, link.

χάλκινος [halkeenos] of copper.

χαλκογραφία, η [halkografeea] copperplate engraving, art of copperplating.

χαλκομανία, η [halkomaneea] transfer design.

χαλκός, ο [halkos] copper, brass, bronze.

χαλνώ [halno] βλ **χαλώ**.

χάλυβας, ο [haleevas] steel.

χαλύβδινος [haleevðeenos] made of steel.

χαλώ [halo] demolish, break, ruin, spoil || (φθείρω) wear out || (νεύρα) fret || (υγεία) break down || (δαπανώ) spend, consume || (διαφθείρω) corrupt, pervert || (νόμισμα) change || (δόντι) decay ||

(κρέας) taint, go bad || ~ **τον κόσμο** move heaven and earth, make a fuss.

χαμαιλέοντας, ο [hameleondas] chameleon || (βοτ) thistle.

χαμάλης, ο [hamalees] porter || (μεταφ) vulgar fellow, scoundrel.

χαμάμι, το [hamamee] Turkish bath.

χαμένα [hamena]: **τα έχω** ~ be mixed up, be bewildered.

χαμένος [hamenos] lost, disappeared || (ουσ: στα χαρτιά) loser || (μεταφ) scoundrel, rascal || scatterbrain.

χαμηλός [hameelos] low || (φωνή) gentle, soft, subdued.

χαμηλόφωνα [hameelofona] in an undertone, softly.

χαμηλώνω [hameelono] lower, reduce, bring down || subside.

χαμίνι, το [hameenee] street urchin, mischievous youngster.

χαμόγελο, το [hamoyelo] smile.

χαμογελώ [hamoyelo] smile.

χαμόκλαδο, το [hamoklaðo] shrub.

χαμομήλι, το [hamomeelee] camomile.

χαμός, ο [hamos] loss, destruction, ruin || death.

χάμουρα, τα [hamoura] πλ harness, trappings.

χαμπάρι, το [hambaree] piece of news || **παίρνω** ~ become aware, perceive.

χάμω [hamo] down, on the ground.

χάνι, το [hanee] country inn, lodging house.

χανούμισσα, η [hanoumeesa] Turkish lady.

χαντάκι, το [hantakee] ditch, drain, trench || (οχυρού) moat.

χαντακώνω [hantakono] (μεταφ) destroy, ruin.

χάντρα, η [hantra] bead.

χάνομαι [hanome] lose o.s., get lost || **να χαθείς!** go to hell! || **χάσου** get out of my sight!

χάνω [hano] lose, go astray || (ευκαιρία) let slip || (καιρό) waste time || (τραίνο) lose, miss || become disconcerted, get confused.

χάος, το [haos] chaos, wild disorder || bottomless pit.

χάπι, το [hapee] pill.

χαρά, η [hara] joy || (υπερβολική) delight, glee || pleasure, enjoyment || ~ **θεού** delight || **μια** ~ very well, splendidly || **γεια** ~ so long!, goodbye! || hello! || ~ **στο πράμα** wonderful!, it's nothing! (ironic).

χάραγμα, το [haragma] tracing, engraving || incision, cut.

χαράδρα, η [haraðra] ravine, gorge, gully.

χαράζω [harazo] cut, engrave || rule lines || trace || (δρόμο κτλ) mark out, lay out.

χάρακας, ο [harakas] straight edge, ruler.

χαρακιά, η [harakia] scratch, incision, mark || groove || (γραμμή) line, stroke.

χαρακτήρας, ο [harakteeras] character, letter || temper, nature.

χαρακτηρίζω [harakteereezo] define, qualify || characterize.

χαρακτηριστικά, τα [harakteereesteeka] πλ person's features.

χαρακτηριστικός [harakteereesteekos] typical, distinctive, characteristic.

χαράκτης, ο [haraktees] engraver, carver.

χαρακτική, η [harakteekee] art of engraving.

χαράκωμα, το [harakoma] trench || (γραμμών) ruling.

χαραμάδα, η [haramaδa] fissure, crack, crevice.

χαράματα, τα [haramata] πλ dawn, daybreak.

χαραματιά, η [haramatia] incision, crack || (επιφάνειας) scratch, trace, engraving.

χαραμίζω [harameezo] waste, spend uselessly.

χάραξη, η [haraksee] engraving, tracing, incision || (δρόμου) laying out.

χαράσσω [harasso] engrave, carve || (γραμμές) rule || map out, trace || (δρόμο) lay out.

χαράτσι, το [haratsee] (μεταφ) oppressive tax.

χαρατσώνω [haratsono] exact money from || tax oppressively.

χαραυγή, η [haravyee] daybreak, dawn.

χαρέμι, το [haremee] harem.

χάρη, η [haree] grace, charm || good point || favour || gratitude || (ποινής) remittance, pardon || ~ σε σένα thanks to you || λόγου ~ for instance || χάριν του for, on behalf of || παραδείγματος ~ for example, for instance || για ~ σου for your sake, on your behalf.

χαριεντίζομαι [harienteezome] be in a teasing mood, jest || become very charming.

χαρίζω [hareezo] give, donate, present || (χρέος κτλ) remit.

χάρισμα, το [hareesma] talent, gift || accomplishment || (επιρ) free, gratis, for nothing.

χαριστική [hareesteekee]: ~ βολή coup de grace.

χαριστικός [hareesteekos] prejudiced, partial.

χαριτολογώ [hareetologo] jest, speak wittily, speak amusingly.

χαριτωμένος [hareetomenos] charming, enchanting.

χάρμα, το [harma] delight, source of joy.

χαρμάνι, το [harmanee] mixture, blend.

χαρμόσυνος [harmoseenos] cheerful, glad.

χαροκόπος, ο [harokopos] pleasure-loving person, rake.

χάρος, ο [haros] death.

χαρούμενος [haroumenos] cheerful, joyful, happy.

χαρούπι, το [haroupee] carob.

χαρταετός, ο [hartaetos] kite.

χαρτζιλίκι, το [hardzeeleekee] pocket money.

χάρτης, ο [hartees] paper || (γεωγραφικός) map || (συνταγματικός) charter.

χαρτί, το [hartee] paper || (χαρτοπαιξίας) playing card || ~ υγείας toilet paper.

χάρτινος [harteenos] of paper.

χαρτοκόπτης, ο [hartokoptees] paper knife.

χαρτόνι, το [hartonee] cardboard, pasteboard.

χαρτονόμισμα, το [hartonomeesma] banknote || bill (US) || paper money.

χαρτοπαίκτης, ο [hartopektees] gambler, card player.

χαρτοπαιξία, η [hartopekseea] gambling, card playing.

χαρτοπόλεμος, ο [hartopolemos] confetti throwing.

χαρτοπώλης, ο [hartopolees] stationer, paper merchant.

χαρτόσημο, το [hartoseemo] stamp tax.

χαρτοφύλακας, ο [hartofeelakas] briefcase || (εκκλ) archivist.

χαρτοφυλάκιο, το [hartofeelakeeo] letter-case, briefcase || (μεταφ) portfolio.

χαρωπός [haropos] cheerful, happy.

χασάπης, ο [hasapees] butcher.

χασάπικο, το [hasapeeko] butcher's shop.

χάση, η [hasee]: στη ~ και στη φέξη once in a blue moon.

χάσιμο, το [haseemo] loss.

χασίσι, το [haseesee] hashish.

χάσκω [hasko] yawn, gape || stand ajar.

χάσμα, το [hasma] abyss, pit || lacuna, gap.

χασμουρητό, το [hasmoureeto] yawning, yawn.

χασμουριέμαι [hasmourieme] yawn.

χασμωδία, η [hasmoδeea] hiatus || disorder, confusion.

χασομερώ [hasomero] be idle || hang around, linger.

χασούρα, η [hasoura] loss.

χαστούκι, το [hastoukee] slap, smack, clout.

χατίρι, το [hateeree] favour, good turn || για το ~ σου for your sake.

χαυλιόδοντας, ο [havleeoðondas] tusk.

χαύνος [havnos] slack, indolent || faint-hearted.

χαφιές, ο [hafies] stool, nark, agent, informer.

χάφτω [hafto] swallow, gobble down || (μεταφ) take in.

χαχανίζω [hahaneezo] burst into laughter, laugh loudly.

χάχας, ο [hahas] moron, idiot.

χαψιά, η [hapsia] mouthful.

χαώδης [haoðees] chaotic, confused.

χέζομαι [hezome] be in a fright, be scared || χέστηκα I don't give a damn.

χέζω [hezo] defecate || (μεταφ) send to the devil.

χείλι, το [heelee] χείλος, το [heelos] lip || (μεταφ) brink, verge || (ποτηριού) brim, rim.

χείμαρρος, ο [heemaros] torrent, torrent bed.

χειμερινός [heemereenos] winter, wintry.

χειμώνας, ο [heemonas] winter.

χειμωνιάτικος [heemoneeateekos] βλ χειμερινός.

χειραφετώ [heerafeto] liberate, emancipate || manumit.

χειραψία, η [heerapseea] shake of the hand.

χειρίζομαι [heereezome] handle, manipulate, manage || (μηχανή) drive.

χειρισμός, ο [heereesmos] manipulation, working, driving || (υποθέσεως) handling, management.

χειριστήρια, τα [heereesteereea] πλ controls of a machine.

χειριστής, ο [heereestees] operator || pilot.

χειροβομβίδα, η [heerovomveeða] grenade.

χειρόγραφο, το [heerografo] manuscript.

χειροκίνητος [heerokeeneetos] hand-operated.

χειροκρότημα, το [heerokroteema] clapping, applause.

χειροκροτώ [heerokroto] applaud, cheer, clap.

χειρομαντεία, η [heeromandeea] palm reading.

χειρονομία, η [heeronomeea] flourish, gesture || gesticulation.

χειροπέδες, οι [heeropeðes] πλ pair of handcuffs.

χειροπιαστός [heeropeeastos] tangible.

χειροπόδαρα [heeropoðara] hand and foot.

χειροποίητος [heeropieetos] handmade.

χειρότερα [heerotera] worse.

χειροτερεύω [heeroterevo] worsen, deteriorate.

χειρότερος [heeroteros] worse || ο ~ the worst.

χειροτεχνία, η [heerotehneea] handicraft.

χειροτονία, η [heerotoneea] ordination, consecration.

χειρουργείο, το [heerouryeeo] operating theatre.

χειρουργική, η [heerouryeekee] surgery.

χειρουργικός [heerouryeekos] surgical.

χειρουργός, ο [heerourgos] surgeon.

χειροφίλημα, το [heerofeeleema] kissing of the hand.

χειρωνακτικός [heeronakteekos] manual.

χέλι, το [helee] eel.

χελιδόνι, το [heleeðonee] (ζωολ) swallow.

χελώνα, η [helona] tortoise, turtle.

χεράκι, το [herakee] tiny hand.

χέρι, το [heree] hand || arm || (χειρολαβή) handle || (μπογιάς) coat || (στο πλύσιμο) treatment, going-over || ~ ~ hand-in-hand || ~ με ~ quickly, directly || βάζω ένα ~ give a hand || βάζω ~ lay hands on, fondle || από πρώτο ~ at first hand.

χερούλι, το [heroulee] handle, haft || (στάμνας) ear.

χερσαίος [herseos] terrestrial || (κλίμα) continental.

χερσόνησος, η [hersoneesos] peninsula.

χέρσος [hersos] uncultivated, fallow, waste.

χέσιμο, το [heseemo] defecation || (μεταφ) fright, terror || volley of abuse.

χημεία, η [heemeea] chemistry.

χημικός [heemeekos] chemical || (ουσ) chemist.

χήνα, η [heena] goose.

χήρα, η [heera] widow.

χηρεύω [heerevo] become widowed || (θέση) be unoccupied, be vacant.

χήρος, ο [heeros] widower.

χθές [hthes] yesterday.

χθεσινός [htheseenos] of yesterday || (πρόσφατος) latest, recent.

χι, το [hee] the letter X.

χιαστί [heeastee] crossways, crosswise, diagonally.

χίλια [heeleea]: ~ δυο a thousand and two.

χιλιάδα, η [heeleeaða] thousand.

χιλιάρικο, το [heeleeareeko] thousand-drachma note.

χιλιετηρίδα, η [heelieteereeða], χιλιετία, η [heelietea] millenium.

χιλιόγραμμο, το [heeliogramo] kilogramme.

χίλιοι [heeliee] thousand.

χιλιόμετρο, το [heeleeometro] kilometre.

χιλιοστό, το [heeleeosto] millimetre || thousandth part.

χιλιοστός [heeleeostos] thousandth.

χίμαιρα, η [heemera] chimera || (μεταφ) illusion.

χιμπαντζής, ο [heempandzees] chimpanzee.

χιονάνθρωπος, ο [heeonanthropos] snowman.

χιονάτος [heeonatos] snow-white, snowy.

χιόνι, το [heeonee] snow.

χιονιά, η [heeonia] snowy weather || snowball.

χιονίζει [heeoneezee] it is snowing.

χιονίστρα, η [heeoneestra] chilblain.

χιονοδρομία, η [heeonoðromeea] skiing.

χιονοθύελλα, η [heeonothiela] snowstorm, blizzard.

χιονόνερο, το [heeononero] sleet, melted snow.

χιονοστιβάδα, η [heeonosteevaða] avalanche, snowdrift.

χιούμορ, το [heeoumor] wit, humour || χιουμοριστικός humorous, humoristic.

χιτώνας, ο [heetonas] robe, tunic || (ματιού) cornea.

χλαίνη, η [hlenee] greatcoat || (ναυτ) duffel coat || cloak, capote.

χλαμύδα, η [hlameeða] mantle.

χλευάζω [hlevazo] mock, scoff at, make fun of.

χλευαστικός [hlevasteekos] mocking, sarcastic, derisive.

χλιαρός [hleearos] tepid, lukewarm || (άνεμος) mild || (μεταφ) weak, lax.

χλιδή, η [hleeðee] luxury, voluptuousness.

χλιμιντρίζω [hleemeendreezo] neigh, whinny.

χλοερός [hloeros] green, fresh, verdant.

χλόη, η [hloee] grass, turf, lawn || greenness, verdure.

χλωμιάζω [hlomeeazo] (go) pale || blanch.

χλωμός [hlomos] pale, pallid, wan.

χλώριο, το [hloreeo] chlorine, chloride.

χλωρίδα, η [hloreeða] flora.

χλωρός [hloros] green, unseasoned || fresh.

χλωροφόρμιο, το [hloroformeeo] chloroform.

χλωροφύλλη, η [hlorofeelee] chlorophyll.

χνάρι, το [hnaree] pattern, model || track.

χνούδι, το [hnouðee] down, fuzz, fluff.

χνουδωτός [hnouðotos] downy, fluffy.

χνώτο, το [hnoto] breath.

χόβολη, η [hovolee] embers, burning charcoal.

χοιρινό, το [heereeno] pork.

χοιρομέρι, το [heeromeree] ham, bacon.

χοίρος, ο [heeros] pig, hog, swine.

χολέρα, η [holera] cholera.

χολή, η [holee] bile || (ζώου) gall || (μεταφ) rancour, bitterness.

χολιάζω [holeeazo] get irritated || irritate || lose one's temper.

χολοσκάω [holoskao] afflict, grieve, exasperate || get riled.

χονδρικός [honðreekos] wholesale.

χονδροειδής [honðroeeðees] rough, clumsy, coarse || (ψεύδος) flagrant || vulgar.

χόνδρος, το [honðros] cartilage || grit.

χονδρός [honðros] big, fat, stout, thick || (σε τρόπους) vulgar, unpolished || (αστείο) coarse.

χοντραίνω [hondreno] become fat, make thicker, put on weight.

χοντροκέφαλος [hondrokefalos] stupid, thickheaded || obstinate, headstrong.

χοντροκοπιά, η [hondrokopia] clumsy job of work.

χοντρός [hondros] βλ χονδρός.

χορδή, η [horðee] chord, string || (ανατ) cord.

χορευτής, ο [horevtees] dancer || partner.

χορευτικός [horevteekos] for dancing, of dancing.

χορεύω [horevo] dance || dance with.

χορήγηση, η [horeeyeesee] granting, giving, supplying.

χορηγώ [horeego] provide, allocate, supply, grant.

χορογραφία, η [horografeea] choreography.

χοροδιδάσκαλος, ο [horoðeeðaskalos] dancing master.

χοροπηδώ [horopeeðo] leap about, gambol, caper.

χορός, ο [horos] dancing, dance || chorus, choir.

χοροστατώ [horostato] conduct divine service.

χόρτα, τα [horta] πλ green vegetables, wild greens.

χορταίνω [horteno] have enough, satiate || satisfy || (βαριέμαι) get bored with.

χορτάρι, το [hortaree] grass.

χορταρικά, τα [hortareeka] πλ vegetables, greens.

χορτασμός, ο [hortasmos] satisfaction, satiety.

χορταστικός [hortasteekos] satisfying, substantial, filling || abundant.

χορτάτος [hortatos] satisfied, satiated.

χόρτο, το [horto] grass, herb || (άγριο) weed.

χορτοφάγος [hortofagos] vegetarian || (ζώο) herbivorous.

χορωδία, η [horoðeea] choir, chorus.

χουζούρι, το [houzouree] rest, idleness, leisure.

χουρμάς, ο [hourmas] (βοτ) date.

χούφτα, η [houfta] handful || hollow of hand.

χουφτιά, η [houftia] handful.

χρειάζομαι [hreeazome] lack, want, require || be necessary, be useful.

χρεόγραφο, το [hreografo] security, debenture, bond.

χρέος, το [hreos] debt || obligation.

χρεωκοπία, η [hreokopeea] bankruptcy, failure.

χρεωκοπώ [hreokopo] go bankrupt, break.

χρεωλυσία, η [hreoleeseea] amortization, sinking fund.

χρεώνομαι [hreonome] get into debt.

χρεώνω [hreono] debit, charge.

χρεωστάσιο, το [hreostaseeo] moratorium.

χρεώστης, ο [hreostees] debtor.

χρεωστώ [hreosto] be in debt, owe, be indebted (to) || be obliged.

χρήμα, το [hreema] money.

χρηματίζομαι [hreemateezome] take bribes || hoard up money.

χρηματίζω [hreemateezo] serve as, be.

χρηματικός [hreemateekos] of money, monetary.

χρηματιστήριο, το [hreemateesteereeo] stock exchange.

χρηματιστής, ο [hreemateestees] stockbroker.

χρηματοδοτώ [hreematoðoto] finance, invest.

χρηματοκιβώτιο, το [hreematokeevoteeo] safe, strong-box, cash box.

χρήση, η [hreesee] use, usage, employment || enjoyment || application || (οικον) financial year || **προς** ~ for the use || **εν χρήσει** in use, used.

χρησιμεύω [hreeseemevo] be useful || be good for, serve.

χρησιμοποίηση, η [hreeseemopieesee] employment, utilization.

χρησιμοποιώ [hreeseemopieo] use, utilize, make use of.

χρήσιμος [hreeseemos] useful, handy.

χρησιμότητα [hreeseemoteeta] usefulness, utility, benefit.

χρησμός, ο [hreesmos] oracle, divination.

χρηστός [hreestos] honourable, upright, virtuous.

χρίζω [hreezo] βλ **χρίω**.

χρίσμα, το [hreesma] chrism, unction || anointing.

χριστιανικός [hreesteeaneekos] Christian.

χριστιανισμός, ο [hreesteeaneesmos] Christianity.

χριστιανός, ο [hreesteeanos] Christian.

χριστιανοσύνη, η [hreesteeanoseenee] Christendom.

Χριστός, ο [hreestos] Christ.

Χριστούγεννα, τα [hreestouyena] πλ Christmas.

χρίω [hreeo] anoint || plaster.

χροιά, η [hreea] complexion, colour || shade, tone, nuance.

χρονιά, η [hroneea] year.

χρονικά, τα [hroneeka] πλ annals.

χρονικογράφος, ο [hroneekografos] chronicler.

χρονικό, το [hroneeko] chronicle.

χρονικός [hroneekos] of time, temporal.

χρόνιος [hroneeos] chronic, enduring, lasting.

χρονογράφημα, το [hronografeema] newspaper leader article.

χρονογράφος, ο [hronografos] leader writer.

χρονολογία, η [hronoloyeea] date || chronology.

χρονολογούμαι [hronologoume] date from, be dated.

χρονόμετρο, το [hronometro] chronometer.

χρόνος, ο [hronos] time, duration || age, period || (γραμμ) tense, quantity || **ο** ~ year || **προ χρόνων** some years ago || **του χρόνου** next year || **χρόνια πολλά!** happy name day!, happy birthday!, many happy returns!

χρονοτριβώ [hronotreevo] linger, loiter.

χρυσαλλίδα, η [hreesaleeða] chrysalis.

χρυσάνθεμο, το [hreesanthemo] chrysanthemum.

χρυσάφι, το [hreesafee] gold.

χρυσαφικά, τα [hreesafeeka] πλ jewellery.

χρυσή, η [hreesee] jaundice.

χρυσικός, ο [hreeseekos] goldsmith || jeweller.

χρυσόδετος [hreesoðetos] mounted in gold.

χρυσοθήρας, ο [hreesotheeras] gold-digger, prospector.

χρυσόμαλλο [hreesomalo] ~ **δέρας** golden fleece.

χρυσός, ο [hreesos] gold || (επίθ) golden || (μεταφ) kind-hearted, adorable.

χρυσοχοείο, το [hreesohoeeo] jeweller's shop, goldsmith's shop.

χρυσοχόος, ο [hreesohoos] goldsmith || jeweller.

χρυσόψαρο, το [hreesopsaro] goldfish.

χρυσώνω [hreesono] gild, gold-plate.

χρυσωρυχείο, το [hreesoreeheeo] gold mine.

χρώμα, το [hroma] colour, tint, hue || (μπογιά) paint, dye || complexion.

χρωματίζω [hromateezo] colour, paint, dye, tint.

χρωματικός [hromateekos] chromatic || of colour.

χρωματισμός, ο [hromateesmos] colouring, painting.

χρωματιστός [hromateestos] coloured.

χρώμιο, το [hromeeo] chromium, chrome.

χρωστικός [hrosteekos] colouring.

χρωστώ [hrosto] βλ χρεωστώ.

χταπόδι, το [htapoðee] octopus.

χτένα, η [htena] βλ χτένι.

χτένι, το [htenee] comb.

χτενίζω [hteneezo] comb || (ομιλία κτλ) polish up.

χτένισμα, το [hteneesma] combing || hairstyle.

χτες [htes] βλ χθές.

χτεσινός [hteseenos] βλ χθεσινός.

χτήμα, το [hteema] βλ κτήμα.

χτίζω [hteezo] βλ κτίζω.

χτικιό, το [hteekio] tuberculosis || (μεταφ) torture, anguish.

χτίστης, ο [hteestees] bricklayer, builder.

χτυπάω [hteepao] βλ χτυπώ.

χτύπημα, το [hteepeema] blow, punch, kick, hit, knock || bruise, wound.

χτυπητός [hteepeetos] beaten || tawdry, garish, loud, striking.

χτυποκάρδι, το [hteepokarðee] rapid beating of the heart.

χτύπος, ο [hteepos] blow, stroke || (καρδιάς) throb, beat || (ρολογιού) tick(ing).

χτυπώ [hteepo] knock, thrash, hit, beat, strike || hurt o.s. || (χέρια) clap || (πόδια) stamp || (χρόνο) beat || (συγά κτλ) whisk || (ρολογιού κτλ) peal, strike, sound || χτυπάει άσχημα it jars, it looks bad || μου χτυπάει στα νεύρα it gets on my nerves || χτυπιέμαι come to blows || feel sorry, repent.

χυδαίος [heeðeos] vulgar, trivial, crude, rude, coarse.

χυδαιότητα, η [heeðeoteeta] vulgarity, coarseness, foul language.

χυλόπιτα, η [heepoleeta] kind of macaroni || (μεταφ) failure in love.

χυλός, ο [heelos] pap, liquid paste.

χύμα [heema] confusedly, pell-mell || loose, unpacked, unbottled.

χυμός, ο [heemos] sap, juice.

χυμώ [heemo] rush upon, charge.

χυμώδης [heemoðees] juicy, sappy.

χύνομαι [heenome] overflow, pour out || flow out || (μεταφ) charge against, rush upon.

χύνω [heeno] spill, tip over, pour out || (δάκρυα) shed || (μέταλλο) cast.

χύσιμο, το [heeseemo] discharge, pouring out, spilling || casting, moulding.

χυτήριο, το [heeteereeo] foundry, smelting works.

χυτός [heetos] moulded, cast || (σκορπισμένος) dispersed, scattered || (μυλλιά) flowing, loose || (ρούχα) tight-fitting.

χυτοσίδηρος, ο [heetoseeðeeros] cast iron.

χύτρα, η [heetra] cooking pot, pot, porridge pot.

χωλ, το [hol] hall.

χωλαίνω [holeno] limp, be lame || (μεταφ) halt, hobble, move slowly.

χώμα, το [homa] soil, dust, earth || ground.

χωματένιος [homateneeos] earthen.

χώνευση, η [honevsee] digestion || (μετάλλων) casting, founding.

χωνευτήριο, το [honevteereeo] crucible, melting pot.

χωνευτικός [honevteekos] digestible, digestive.

χωνεύω [honevo] digest || (μέταλλο) cast, smelt || (μεταφ) tolerate, endure.

χωνί, το [honee] funnel, horn || (παγωτού) cone.

χώνομαι [honome] squeeze in || hide || (μεταφ) interfere.

χώνω [hono] thrust, force || bury || (κρύβω) hide.

χώρα, η [hora] country, place || chief town || (ανατ) region || λαμβάνω ~ happen.

χωρατεύω [horatevo] joke.

χωρατό, το [horato] joke, jest, witticism.

χωράφι, το [horafee] field, land.

χωράω [horao] βλ χωρώ.

χωρητικότητα, η [horeeteekoteeta] volume, capacity || (ναυτ) tonnage.

χώρια [horeea] βλ χωριστά.

χωριανός, ο [horeeanos] fellow villager, countryman.

χωριάτης, ο [horeeatees] peasant, villager, countryman || (μεταφ) ill-mannered person, unpolished person.

χωριάτικος [horeeateekos] peasant, of the village || rustic.

χωρίζομαι [horeezome] leave, part from.

χωρίζω [horeezo] separate, disconnect, part, split || (δρόμοι) branch off ||

(ζεύγος) get a divorce || ~ **με** break up with, part from.

χωρικός [horeekos] village, rural, country || (ουσ) peasant, villager.

χωριό, το [horio] village, hamlet || (μεταφ) hometown.

χωρίς [horees] without, apart from || not including || ~ **άλλο** without fail || **με** ~ without.

χώρισμα, το [horeesma] sorting, separation || (δωματίου) wall, partition || compartment.

χωρισμένος [horeesmenos] divided || separated, divorced.

χωρισμός, ο [horeesmos] separation || partition || separating || divorce.

χωριστά [horeesta] apart, individually || (προθ) not counting, apart from, not including.

χωριστός [horeestos] separate, different, distinct, isolated.

χωρίστρα, η [horeestra] parting of hair.

χώρος, ο [horos] space, area, room || interval, distance.

χωροφύλακας, ο [horofeelakas] gendarme.

χωροφυλακή, η [horofeelakee] gendarmerie.

χωρώ [horo] fit into, have room || (περιέχω) hold, contain || **δε χωράει αμφιβολία** there's no doubt, undoubtedly.

χώσιμο, το [hoseemo] driving in, burying || hiding.

Ψ, ψ

ψάθα, η [psatha] straw, cane || (χαλί) rush mat || (καπέλο) straw hat || **στη** ~ penniless.

ψάθινος [psatheenos] made of straw.

ψαλίδα, η [psaleeδa] shears || centipede.

ψαλίδι, το [psaleeδee] scissors, pruning scissors || curling tongs.

ψαλιδίζω [psaleeδeezo] cut, trim || (μεταφ) reduce, cut down.

ψάλλω [psalo] sing, chant || extol, celebrate.

ψαλμός, ο [psalmos] psalm, chant.

ψαλμωδία, η [psalmoδeea] chanting of psalms || monotonous delivery.

ψάλτης, ο [psaltees] chorister, singer, chanter.

ψάξιμο, το [psakseemo] searching, quest, search.

ψαράδικο, το [psaraδeeko] fishing boat || fishmonger's shop.

ψαράδικος [psaraδeekos] of a fisherman.

ψαράς, ο [psaras] fisherman || fishmonger.

ψάρεμα, το [psarema] fishing, angling, netting.

ψαρεύω [psarevo] fish || sound, fish for information.

ψάρι, το [psaree] fish.

ψαρόβαρκα, η [psarovarka] fishing boat.

ψαροκόκαλο, το [psarokokalo] fish bone || (σχέδιο) herringbone.

ψαρόκολλα, η [psarokola] fish glue.

ψαρομάλλης, ο [psaromalees] grey-haired person.

ψαρονέφρι, το [psaronefree] fillet of meat.

ψαρός [psaros] grey, grizzled.

ψαύση, η [psavsee] touching, feeling, light touch.

ψαχνό, το [psahno] lean meat.

ψάχνομαι [psahnome] look through one's pockets.

ψάχνω [psahno] search for, look for || seek, rummage.

ψαχουλεύω [psahoulevo] search for, grope for, fumble around for.

ψεγάδι, το [psegaδee] fault, failing, shortcoming.

ψέγω [psego] blame, reprove, censure.

ψείρα, η [pseera] louse || vermin.

ψειριάζω [pseereeazo] get lousy.

ψειρίζω [pseereezo] delouse || (μεταφ) examine in great detail.

ψεκάζω [psekazo] spray.

ψεκαστήρας, ο [psekasteeras] spray, vapourizer || scent sprayer.

ψελλίζω [pseleezo] stammer, stutter.

ψέλνω [pselno] βλ **ψάλλω.**

ψέμα, το [psema] lie, falsehood, fib.

ψες [pses] last night.

ψευδαίσθηση, η [psevδestheesee] delusion, hallucination.

ψευδάργυρος, ο [psevδaryeeros] zinc.

ψευδής [psevδees] untrue, false || artificial, sham, fictitious || deceptive.

ψευδίζω [psevδeezo] βλ **ψελλίζω.**

ψευδολογώ [psevδologo] tell lies, tell stories, fib.

ψεύδομαι [psevδome] lie, fib.

ψευδομάρτυρας, ο, η [psevδomarteeras] false witness, perjurer.

ψευδομαρτυρώ [psevδomarteero] give false witness, commit perjury.

ψευδορκία, η [psevδorkeea] perjury.

ψευδορκώ [psevδorko] commit perjury, perjure.

ψευδός [psevδos] lisping, stammering, stuttering.

ψευδώνυμο, το [psevδoneemo] pseudonym, assumed name.

ψεύτης, ο [psevtees] liar, fibber || cheat, impostor.

ψευτιά, η [psevtia] untruth, lie.

ψευτίζω [psevteezo] adulterate || become adulterated.

ψεύτικος [psevteekos] false, untrue || artificial || (σε ποιότητα) inferior.

ψήγμα, το [pseegma] filings, shavings, chips.

ψηλά [pseela] high up, aloft.

ψηλαφώ [pseelafo] feel, touch, finger || (ψάχνω) feel one's way, grope.

ψηλομύτης [pseelomeetees] haughty, overbearing.

ψηλός [pseelos] high, tall, lofty, great.

ψήλωμα, το [pseeloma] eminence, elevation || making taller, growing.

ψηλώνω [pseelono] make taller, make higher || grow taller.

ψήνομαι [pseenome] become very hot || (στη δουλειά) become broken in.

ψήνω [pseeno] bake, roast, cook || (μεταφ) torture, worry, pester.

ψήσιμο, το [pseeseemo] baking, broiling, roasting, cooking, frying.

ψησταριά, η [pseestaria] barbecue apparatus.

ψητό, το [pseeto] roast meat, grilled meat || (μεταφ) the main point.

ψητός [pseetos] roast, baked, roasted.

ψηφιδωτό, το [pseefeedoto] mosaic.

ψηφίζω [pseefeezo] vote || (νόμο) pass, carry.

ψηφίο, το [pseefeeo] cipher, figure || (αλφαβήτου) letter, character.

ψήφισμα, το [pseefeesma] decree, enactment, edict.

ψηφοδέλτιο, το [pseefoδelteeo] ballot paper.

ψηφοδόχος, η [pseefoδohos] ballot box.

ψηφοθηρώ [pseefotheero] solicit votes, canvass for votes.

ψήφος, ο, η [pseefos] vote, voting, suffrage.

ψηφοφορία, η [pseefoforeea] voting, ballot(ting).

ψι, το [psee] the letter Ψ.

ψιθυρίζω [pseetheereezo] mutter, murmur, whisper.

ψιθύρισμα, το [pseetheereesma] whisper(ing), muttering, murmuring.

ψίθυρος, ο [pseetheeros] murmur, whisper, mutter, growl.

ψιλά, τα [pseela] πλ small change || (μεταφ) cash, money.

ψιλικά, τα [pseeleeka] πλ haberdashery || small wares.

ψιλικαντζήδικο, το [pseeleekandzeeδeeko] haberdashery.

ψιλολογώ [pseelologo] examine carefully, sift.

ψιλός [pseelos] fine, slender, thin || shrill.

ψιλοτραγουδώ [pseelotragouδo] hum.

ψίχα, η [pseeha] kernel, crumb || (καρδιού) edible part of nut || (μεταφ) bit, scrap.

ψιχάλα, η [pseehala] drizzle.

ψιχαλίζει [pseehaleezee] it's drizzling.

ψίχουλο, το [pseehoulo] crumb.

ψόγος, ο [psogos] blame, reproach.

ψοφίμι, το [psofeemee] carcass, carrion.

ψόφιος [psofeeos] (για ζώα) dead || (μεταφ) worn-out || ~ στην κούραση dead tired.

ψόφος, ο [psofos] noise, tumult || (θάνατος) death || (μεταφ) freezing cold.

ψοφώ [psofo] die || (μεταφ) ~ για yearn for, be mad on.

ψυγείο, το [pseeyeeo] refrigerator, icebox || (αυτοκινήτου) radiator.

ψυκτικός [pseekteekos] cooling.

ψύλλος, ο [pseelos] flea || (μεταφ) trifle.

ψύξη, η [pseeksee] refrigeration || chill, chilling.

ψυχαγωγία, η [pseehagoyeea] recreation, amusement, diversion, entertainment.

ψυχαγωγικός [pseehagoyeekos] recreational, entertaining.

ψυχανάλυση, η [pseehanaleesee] psychoanalysis.

ψυχή, η [pseehee] soul, ghost || heart, core || (θάρρος) energy, spirit.

ψυχιατρείο, το [pseeheeatreeo] mental hospital, asylum.

ψυχιατρική, η [pseeheeatreekee] psychiatry.

ψυχίατρος, ο [pseeheeatros] psychiatrist.

ψυχικό, το [pseeheeko] act of charity || alms, charity.

ψυχικός [pseeheekos] psychical || **ψυχική διάθεση** humour, mood, disposition || **ψυχική οδύνη** mental stress.

ψυχογιός, ο [pseehoyos] adopted son.

ψυχολογία, η [pseeholoyeea] psychology.

ψυχολογικός [pseeholoyeekos] psychological.

ψυχολόγος, ο [pseehologos] psychologist.

ψυχολογώ [pseehologo] read mind of || psychoanalyse.

ψυχομαχώ [pseehomaho] be at the last gasp.

ψυχοπαθής [pseehopathees] psychopath(ic).

ψυχοπαίδι, το [pseehopeδee] adopted child.

ψυχοπόνια, η [pseehoponeea] commiseration, pity.

ψυχορραγώ [pseehorago] βλ **ψυχομαχώ.**

ψύχος, το [pseehos] cold, chilliness.

ψυχοσύνθεση, η [pseehoseenthesee] person's psychological make-up.

ψύχρα, η [pseehra] chilly weather, cold.

Ψ

ψυχραιμία, η [pseehremeea] self-control, sangfroid, coolness.

ψύχραιμος [pseehremos] cool, cool-headed.

ψυχραίνομαι [pseehrenome] be on bad terms with.

ψυχραίνω [pseehreno] cool, chill, make cold || (μεταφ) cool off.

ψυχρολουσία, η [pseehrolouseea] (μεταφ) telling off, rebuke.

ψυχρός [pseehros] cold || (μεταφ) indifferent, apathetic.

ψυχρότητα, η [pseehroteeta] coldness || indifference.

ψύχω [pseeho] freeze, chill, make cold.

ψύχωση, η [pseehosee] psychosis || craze, complex.

ψωμάκι, το [psomakee] roll, piece of bread.

ψωμάς, ο [psomas] baker.

ψωμί, το [psomee] bread || loaf || (μεταφ) living.

ψωμοζώ [psomozo] eke out one's living, live scantily.

ψωμοτύρι, το [psomoteeree] bread and cheese.

ψώνια, τα [psonea] πλ provisions, shopping, purchases.

ψωνίζω [psoneezo] buy, purchase || go shopping || την ~ become queer, go mad.

ψώνιο, το [psoneeo] purchase || (μεταφ) mania.

ψώρα, η [psora] scabies, itch, mange || (μεταφ) pest.

ψωριάζω [psoreeazo] become itchy, be mangy.

ψωριάρης [psoreearees] mangy || (μεταφ) beggar, ragamuffin.

ψωρίαση, η [psoreeasee] psoriasis, itch(ing).

ψωροκώσταινα, η [psorokostena] poverty-stricken Greece, poor Greece.

ψωροπερηφάνεια, η [psoropereefaneea] pretensions, stupid pride.

Ω, ω

ω [o] (επιφ) oh!, ah!, aha!

ωάριο, το [oareeo] ovum.

ωδείο, το [odeeo] conservatory.

ωδή, η [odee] ode, song.

ωδική, η [odeekee] singing lesson || art of singing.

ωδικός [odeekos] singing, melodious.

ωδίνες, οι [odeenes] πλ childbirth pains || (μεταφ) difficulties.

ώθηση, η [otheesee] push, pushing, thrust, impulsion.

ωθώ [otho] push, thrust, impel || incite, urge.

ωκεανός, ο [okeanos] ocean.

ωλένη, η [olenee] forearm.

ωμέγα, το [omega] the letter Ω.

ωμοπλάτη, η [omoplatee] shoulder blade.

ώμος, ο [omos] shoulder.

ωμός [omos] uncooked, raw || hard, cruel, unrelenting.

ωμότητα, η [omoteeta] cruelty, ferocity.

ωμότητες, οι [omoteetes] πλ outrages, atrocities.

ωοειδής [ooeedees] oval, egg-shaped.

ωοθήκη, η [ootheekee] ovary || egg cup.

ωοτόκος [ootokos] oviparous, egg-laying.

ώρα, η [ora] hour, time || με την ~ on the hour || ~ με την ~ any minute || με τις ώρες for hours || στην ~ at the right time, on the dot, on time || της ώρας fresh, cooked to order.

ωραία [orea] beautiful || very well, perfectly, good.

ωραίος [oreos] handsome, comely, lovely || fine, good.

ωραιότητα, η [oreoteeta] beauty, good looks.

ωράριο, το [orareeo] working hours, timetable.

ωριαίος [orieos] hourly || lasting an hour.

ωριμάζω [oreemazo] become ripe, mature, mellow.

ωρίμανση, η [oreemansee] ripening, maturity.

ώριμος [oreemos] ripe, mature, mellow.

ωριμότητα, η [oreemoteeta] ripeness, maturity, full growth.

ωροδείκτης, ο [orodeektees] hour hand.

ωροσκόπιο, το [oroskopeeo] horoscope.

ωρύομαι [oreeome] howl, roar || yell, scream.

ως [os] until, till, down to, up to, as far as || (επίρ) about || ~ ότου να until.

ως [os] as, for, like, just as, such as || (συνδ) as, while, as soon as || βλ και ως.

ωσότου [osotou] until, by the time.

ώσπου [ospou] until.

ώστε [oste] thus, and so, so, accordingly, therefore || that || ούτως ~ thereby.

ωστόσο [ostoso] nevertheless || meanwhile.

ωτακουστής, ο [otakoustees] eavesdropper.

ωτομοτρίς, η [otomotrees] railcar.

ωτορινολαρυγγολόγος, ο [otoreenolareengologos] ear, nose and throat doctor.

ωφέλεια, η [ofeleea] benefit, utility, usefulness, profit, advantage || είδα ~ I benefited.

ωφέλημα, το [ofeleema] benefit, gain, particular profit, advantage.

ωφέλιμος [ofeleemos] beneficial, useful, of use, advantageous.

ωφελούμαι [ofeloume] benefit, profit from, turn to good account.

ωφελώ [ofelo] do good to, be useful to, benefit, aid.

ώχρα, η [ohra] ochre.

ωχριώ [ohreeo] become pale, make wan.

ωχρός [ohros] pallid, pale || (μεταφ) indistinct, dim.

ωχρότητα, η [ohroteeta] pallor, paleness.

ENGLISH–GREEK
ΑΓΓΛΙΚΑ–ΕΛΛΗΝΙΚΑ

A

a, an [ei,æn] *indefinite article* ένας, μια, ένα.

A.A. *n. abbr of* Automobile Association; *abbr of* Alcoholics Anonymous.

aback [ə'bæk] *ad:* **to be taken ~** ξαφνιάζομαι, σαστίζω.

abandon [ə'bændən] *vt* εγκαταλείπω, αφήνω.

abash [ə'bæʃ] *vt* ξεφτελίζω, ντροπιάζω.

abate [ə'beit] *vi* μειώνομαι, κοπάζω, καταργούμαι.

abbey ['æbi] *n* μονή, μοναστήρι.

abbot ['æbət] *n* ηγούμενος, αββάς.

abbreviate [ə'bri:vieit] *vt* συντομεύω.

abbreviation [əbri:vi'eiʃən] *n* σύντμηση, συντετμημένη λέξη.

abdicate ['æbdikeit] *vi* παραιτούμαι, εγκαταλείπω.

abdication [æbdi'keiʃən] *n* παραίτηση.

abdomen ['æbdəmən] *n* κοιλιά.

abduction [æb'dʌkʃən] *n* απαγωγή.

aberration [æbə'reiʃən] *n* παρέκκλιση, παρεκτροπή.

abet [ə'bet] *vt* υποκινώ, παρακινώ.

abeyance [ə'beiəns] *n:* **in ~** εκκρεμώ, αχρηστεύομαι.

abhor [əb'hɔː*] *vt* απεχθάνομαι, σιχαίνομαι || **~rent** *a* απεχθής.

abide [ə'baid] *(irreg v) vt* ανέχομαι, αντέχω ♦ *vi* εμμένω, τηρώ || **to ~ by** τηρώ, συμμορφούμαι.

ability [ə'biliti] *n* ικανότητα, επιδεξιότητα, δύναμη.

ablaze [ə'bleiz] *a* φλεγόμενος, λάμπων.

able ['eibl] *a* ικανός, επιτήδειος.

ably ['eibli] *ad* επιδέξια, προκομμένα.

abnormal [æb'nɔːməl] *a* ανώμαλος || **~ity** *n* ανωμαλία || (BIOL) τερατωδία, δυσμορφία.

aboard [ə'bɔːd] *ad:* **to go ~** επιβιβάζομαι || **to be ~** ευρίσκομαι επί.

abode [ə'bəud] *n* διαμονή, κατοικία.

abolish [ə'bɒliʃ] *vt* καταργώ.

abolition [æbə'liʃən] *n* κατάργηση.

abominable [ə'bɒminəbl] *a* αποτρόπαιος, απαίσιος.

abominably [ə'bɒminəbli] *ad* απαίσια.

aborigines [æbə'ridʒiniːz] *npl* ιθαγενείς.

abort [ə'bɔːt] *vt* αποβάλλω, διακόπτω ♦ *vi* αποβάλλομαι, ματαιούμαι.

abortion [ə'bɔːʃən] *n* έκτρωση, αποβολή.

abortive [ə'bɔːtiv] *a* αποτυχημένος, πρόωρος, ανεπιτυχής.

abound [ə'baund] *vi* αφθονώ, βρίθω.

about [ə'baut] *prep* περί, γύρω από, κοντά ♦ *ad* (τρι)γύρω, κοντά || (estimate)
περίπου || **to be ~ to** το μόλις πρόκειται να.

above [ə'bʌv] *prep* πάνω από, πέρα από || (in rank) ανώτερος από, μεγαλύτερος από ♦ *ad* επάνω, στους ουρανούς || **~board** *a* τίμια και ειλικρινή, άψογα || **~ ground** επιφανειακός.

abrasion [ə'breiʒən] *n* φθορά, (εκ)τριβή, γδάρσιμο.

abrasive [ə'breisiv] *a* υποξυστικός || **~ material** μέσον λειάνσεως.

abreast [ə'brest] *ad* παραπλεύρως, μαζί.

abridge [ə'bridʒ] *vt* συντομεύω, συντέμνω.

abroad [ə'brɔːd] *ad* στο εξωτερικό, στα ξένα.

abrupt [ə'brʌpt] *a* απότομος, ξαφνικός, αγενής.

abscess ['æbsis] *n* απόστημα *nt.*

abscond [əb'skɒnd] *vi* φυγοδικώ, δραπετεύω, φεύγω κρυφά.

absence ['æbsəns] *n* απουσία || (lack of) έλλειψη, ανυπαρξία || (of mind) αφηρημάδα.

absent ['æbsənt] *a* απών, απουσιάζων ♦ [æb'sent] *vt:* **he ~ed himself** απουσίαζε || **~ee** *n* απών *m*, απουσιάζων *m* || **~eeism** *n* απουσία || **~-minded** *a* αφηρημένος.

absolute ['æbsəluːt] *a* απόλυτος, τέλειος, απεριόριστος || **~ly** *ad* τελείως.

absolve [əb'zɒlv] *vt* απαλλάσσω, αθωώνω.

absorb [əb'zɔːb] *vt* απορροφώ.

absorbent [əb'zɔːbənt] *a, n* απορροφητικός || **~ cotton** (US) *n* απορροφητικό βαμβάκι.

absorbing [əb'zɔːbiŋ] *a* ενδιαφέρων.

abstain [əb'stein] *vi* απέχω, συγκρατούμαι || **to ~ from** αποφεύγω.

abstinence ['æbstinəns] *n* αποχή, εγκράτεια.

abstract ['æbstrækt] *a* αφηρημένος ♦ *n* το αφηρημένο || (summary) περίληψη || (excerpt) απόσπασμα *nt* ♦ [æb'strækt] *vt* (remove) αφαιρώ.

abstruse [æb'struːs] *a* ασαφής, δυσνόητος.

absurd [əb'sɜːd] *a* γελοίος, παράλογος || **~ity** *n* παραλογισμός.

abundance [ə'bʌndəns] *n* αφθονία, περίσσευμα *nt.*

abundant [ə'bʌndənt] *a* άφθονος, πλούσιος.

abuse [ə'bjuːz] *vt* (misuse) κακομεταχειρίζομαι, καταχρώμαι || (speak harshly) βρίζω ♦ [ə'bjuːs] *n*

κακομεταχείριση, κατάχρηση ||
(swearing) βρισιές fpl.
abusive [ə'bju:sɪv] a υβριστικός.
abut [ə'bʌt] vi συνορεύω με.
abysmal [ə'bɪzml] a φοβερός,
απερίγραπτος.
abyss [ə'bɪs] n άβυσσος.
academic [ækə'dɛmɪk] n, a
ακαδημαϊκός.
academy [ə'kædəmɪ] n ακαδημία.
accede [æk'si:d] vi (agree) συμφωνώ,
προσχωρώ || (to throne) ανέρχομαι.
accelerate [æk'sɛləreɪt] vt επιταχύνω,
επισπεύδω ♦ vi επιταχύνομαι.
acceleration [ækselə'reɪʃən] n
επιτάχυνση.
accelerator [ək'seləreɪtə*] n (AUT)
γκάζι.
accent [ˈæksɛnt] n τόνος || (of speech)
προφορά ♦ [æk'sɛnt] vt τονίζω || ~**uate**
vt τονίζω.
accept [ək'sept] vt (gift etc) δέχομαι ||
(agree) παραδέχομαι || ~**able** a
(απο)δεκτός, ευπρόσδεκτος,
παραδεκτός || ~**ance** n αποδοχή,
παραδοχή.
access [ˈæksɛs] n (entrance) είσοδος f ||
(COMPUT) πρόσβαση || ~ **time** (COMPUT)
χρόνος προσπέλασης || ~**ible** a
προσιτός, ευπρόσιτος.
accessories [æk'sɛsərɪz] npl
εξαρτήματα ntpl, συμπληρώματα ntpl ||
(toilet) είδη ntpl τουαλέτας.
accessory [æk'sɛsərɪ] n (to a crime etc)
συνένοχος || (part) εξάρτημα nt.
accident [ˈæksɪdənt] n (mishap)
δυστύχημα nt, ατύχημα nt || (chance) τύχη
|| by ~ κατά τύχη || ~**ally** ad τυχαία.
acclaim [ə'kleɪm] vt επευφημώ,
ζητωκραυγάζω, αναφωνώ ♦ n
ζητωκραυγή.
acclimatize [ə'klaɪmətaɪz] vt: to
become ~d εγκλιματίζομαι.
accommodate [ə'kɒmədeɪt] vt (be
suitable for) εξοικονομώ, διευθετώ,
προσαρμόζω || (lodge) στεγάζω, παρέχω
κατάλυμα || (supply etc) εξοικονομώ,
εφοδιάζω.
accommodating [ə'kɒmədeɪtɪŋ] a
εξυπηρετικός, πρόθυμος.
accommodation [əkɒmə'deɪʃən] n
(lodging) κατάλυμα nt, στέγαση || (loan)
δάνειο || (adjustment) προσαρμογή.
accompaniment [ə'kʌmpənɪmənt] n
συνοδεία || (MUS) ακομπανιαμέντο.
accompany [ə'kʌmpənɪ] vt συνοδεύω,
συντροφεύω.
accomplice [ə'kʌmplɪs] n συνένοχος,
συνεργός.
accomplish [ə'kʌmplɪʃ] vt περατώνω,
συμπληρώνω || ~**ed** a (skilled) τέλειος ||
~**ment** n (ability) ικανότητα, προσόντα
ntpl || (completion) εκπλήρωση.
accord [ə'kɔːd] n συμφωνία, ομοφωνία
|| of my own ~ αυθόρμητα ♦ vt (grant)
παρέχω, χορηγώ || (agree with) συμφωνώ

|| ~**ance** n συμφωνία || in ~ with
σύμφωνα με || ~**ing to** prep σύμφωνα
με, κατά τον || ~**ingly** ad επομένως.
accordion [ə'kɔːdɪən] n ακορντεόν nt
inv.
accost [ə'kɒst] vt πλησιάζω, πλευρίζω.
account [ə'kaunt] n (bill) λογαριασμός,
υπολογισμός || (credit) λογαριασμός ||
(story) αφήγηση, περιγραφή || (financial
report) ανάλυση, έκθεση || on no ~ για
κανένα λόγο || on ~ of εξαιτίας || to ~
for vt εισηγώ || to take into ~ λαμβάνω
υπόψη || ~**able** a υπόλογος, υπεύθυνος
|| (explicable) ευεξήγητος.
accountant [ə'kauntənt] n λογιστής.
accumulate [ə'kju:mjuleɪt] vt
συσσωρεύω, μαζεύω ♦ vi
συσσωρεύομαι.
accumulation [əkju:mju'leɪʃən] n
συσσώρευση, μάζεμα nt.
accuracy [ˈækjurəsɪ] n ακρίβεια.
accurate [ˈækjurɪt] a ακριβής, ορθός ||
~**ly** ad με ακρίβεια, σωστά.
accusation [ækju:'zeɪʃən] n κατηγορία.
accuse [ə'kju:z] vt κατηγορώ || ~**d** n
κατηγορούμενος || ~**r** n ενάγων m,
μηνυτής, κατήγορος.
accustom [ə'kʌstəm] vt συνηθίζω,
εθίζω || ~**ed** a συνηθισμένος.
ace [eɪs] n άσσος.
ache [eɪk] vi πονώ.
achieve [ə'tʃiːv] vt κατορθώνω,
επιτυγχάνω, φθάνω || ~**ment** n
κατόρθωμα, επίτευξη.
acid [ˈæsɪd] a οξύς, ξινός ♦ n (CHEM) οξύ
nt || ~ **test** n αποφασιστική δοκιμασία,
τελικό κριτήριο || ~**ity** n (CHEM) οξύτητα,
ξινίλα.
acknowledge [ək'nɒlɪdʒ] vt (admit)
αναγνωρίζω, παραδέχομαι || (thank) είμαι
ευγνώμων, απαντώ || ~**ment** n
αναγνώριση, παραδοχή || (of letter etc)
βεβαίωση.
acne [ˈæknɪ] n ακμή, σπυράκια ntpl.
acorn [ˈeɪkɔːn] n βαλανίδι.
acoustic [ə'kuːstɪk] a ακουστικός || ~**s**
npl ακουστική.
acquaint [ə'kweɪnt] vt γνωρίζω,
πληροφορώ || ~**ance** n (person)
γνωριμία, γνωστός/ή m/f || (knowledge)
γνώση, εξοικείωση.
acquiesce [ækwɪ'es] vi συναινώ,
συγκατατίθεμαι, δέχομαι.
acquire [ə'kwaɪə*] vt αποκτώ.
acquisition [ækwɪ'zɪʃən] n απόκτημα nt,
απόκτηση.
acquisitive [ə'kwɪzɪtɪv] a πλεονέκτης,
αρπακτικός.
acquit [ə'kwɪt] vt (free from accusation)
απαλλάσσω, αθωώνω || (conduct o.s.)
εκπληρώ, καταφέρνω || ~**tal** n αθώωση,
απαλλαγή.
acre [ˈeɪkə*] n 4 στρέμματα ntpl.
acrobat [ˈækrəbæt] n ακροβάτης.
across [ə'krɒs] prep (through) δια μέσου
♦ ad (crosswise) εγκάρσια, λοξά,

σταυρωτά || (distance) πλάτος, μήκος || ~ the road (στο δρόμο) απέναντι.

act [ækt] n (deed) πράξη, ενέργεια || (law or decree) νόμος, νομοθέτημα nt || (of play) πράξη (έργου) ♦ vti (take action) ενεργώ, δρω, πράττω || (part) παίζω, παριστάνω, κάνω || (pretend) προσποιούμαι, υποκρίνομαι, υποδύομαι || ~ing n (THEAT) ηθοποιία, παίξιμο ♦ a αναπληρωματικός.

action ['ækʃən] n (deed) πράξη || (motion) λειτουργία, ενέργεια || (battle) μάχη || to bring an ~ against κάνω αγωγή κατά || naval ~ ναυμαχία || to take ~ ενεργώ.

active ['æktɪv] a (lively) ενεργητικός, ζωηρός || (working) δραστήριος, ενεργός || (GRAM) ενεργητικός || on ~ service εν ενεργεία.

activity [æk'tɪvɪtɪ] n δραστηριότητα, δράση.

actor ['æktə*] n ηθοποιός.

actress ['æktrɪs] n ηθοποιός f, θεατρίνα.

actual ['æktjʊəl] a πραγματικός, αληθινός || ~ly ad πράγματι.

acumen ['ækjumen] n οξύνοια, ευφυΐα.

acute [ə'kjuːt] a οξύς, διαπεραστικός || ~ly ad έντονα || ~ accent n οξεία.

ad [æd] abbr of advertisement.

A.D. ad (abbr of Anno Domini) μ.Χ.

Adam ['ædəm] n Αδάμ || ~'s apple n καρύδι του λαιμού.

adamant ['ædəmənt] a αμετάπειστος, άκαμπτος.

adapt [ə'dæpt] vt προσαρμόζω, εναρμόζω ♦ vi: to ~ to προσαρμόζομαι || ~able a προσαρμόσιμος, ευάρμοστος || ~ation n προσαρμογή || (of play etc) διασκευή || ~er n (ELEC) προσαρμοστής.

add [æd] vt προσθέτω, αθροίζω || to ~ up vt προσθέτω.

adder ['ædə*] n (snake) οχιά, όχεντρα.

addict ['ædɪkt] n: drug ~ ναρκομανής ♦ [ə'dɪkt] vt αφοσιώνω, παραδίδω || ~ed to επιρρεπής σε || ~ion n ροπή προς, εθισμός.

adding machine ['ædɪŋməʃiːn] n αθροιστική μηχανή.

addition [ə'dɪʃən] n πρόσθεση, προσθήκη || in ~ επί πλέον, επιπροσθέτως || ~al a πρόσθετος.

address [ə'dres] n διεύθυνση || (speech) προσφώνηση, λόγος || (manners) συμπεριφορά || (COMPUT) διεύθυνση || vt απευθύνω || (speak) προσφωνώ || (envelope) γράφω διεύθυνση.

addressee [ædre'siː] n παραλήπτης.

adenoids ['ædɪnɔɪdz] npl κρεατάκια.

adept ['ædept] a: ~ at έμπειρος σε, ικανός σε.

adequate ['ædɪkwɪt] a επαρκής, ικανός.

adhere [əd'hɪə*] vi (stick to) προσκολλώμαι || (support) εμμένω, προσχωρώ || to ~ to προσχωρώ, εμμένω.

adhesive [əd'hiːzɪv] a συγκολλητικός,

κολλώδης ♦ n κολλητική ουσία || ~ tape n λευκοπλάστης.

adjacent [ə'dʒeɪsənt] a παρακείμενος, γειτονικός, συνορεύων.

adjective ['ædʒektɪv] n επίθετο.

adjoin [ə'dʒɔɪn] vi γειτονεύω, συνορεύω με, συνάπτω || ~ing a συνεχόμενος, παρακείμενος.

adjourn [ə'dʒɜːn] vt (postpone) αναβάλλω ♦ vi αναβάλλομαι, διακόπτομαι.

adjudicator [ə'dʒuːdɪkeɪtə*] n διαιτητής, δικαστής.

adjust [ə'dʒʌst] vt (put right) ρυθμίζω, κανονίζω || (to fit) προσαρμόζω, εφαρμόζω || ~able a ρυθμιζόμενος, ρυθμιστός || ~ment n ρύθμιση, τακτοποίηση.

adjutant ['ædʒətənt] n υπασπιστής.

ad lib [æd'lɪb] ad κατά βούληση ♦ ad-lib vi αυτοσχεδιάζω.

administer [əd'mɪnɪstə*] vt (manage) διευθύνω, διαχειρίζομαι, διοικώ || (dispense) απονέμω || (medicine) παρέχω, δίνω.

administration [ədmɪnɪs'treɪʃən] n διοίκηση, διαχείριση, διεύθυνση || ~ of justice απονομή δικαιοσύνης.

administrative [əd'mɪnɪstrətɪv] a διοικητικός.

administrator [əd'mɪnɪstreɪtə*] n διευθυντής, διοικητής || (of will) εκτελεστής.

admirable ['ædmərəbl] a θαυμαστός, θαυμάσιος.

admiral ['ædmərəl] n ναύαρχος.

Admiralty ['ædmərəltɪ] n ναυαρχείο.

admiration [ædmə'reɪʃən] n θαυμασμός, κατάπληξη.

admire [əd'maɪə*] vt θαυμάζω || ~r n θαυμαστής.

admission [əd'mɪʃən] n (entrance) είσοδος f, εισαγωγή || (fee) τιμή εισιτηρίου || (confession) παραδοχή, αναγνώριση.

admit [əd'mɪt] vt (let in) επιτρέπω την είσοδο, εισέρχομαι || (confess) παραδέχομαι, αναγνωρίζω || (receive as true) (επι)δέχομαι || ~tance n είσοδος, είσοδος f || ~tedly ad ομολογουμένως.

ado [ə'duː] n: without more ~ χωρίς περισσότερη φασαρία.

adolescence [ædəʊ'lesns] n εφηβική ηλικία.

adolescent [ædəʊ'lesnt] a, n έφηβος.

adopt [ə'dɒpt] vt υιοθετώ || (accept) παραδέχομαι, αποδέχομαι || ~ed son n θετός || ~ion n υιοθεσία || (of idea etc) αποδοχή, έγκριση.

adore [ə'dɔː*] vt λατρεύω, υπεραγαπώ.

adorn [ə'dɔːn] vt κοσμώ, στολίζω, καλλωπίζω.

adrenalin [ə'drenəlɪn] n αδρεναλίνη.

Adriatic [eɪdrɪ'ætɪk] n Αδριατική.

adrift [ə'drɪft] ad έρμαιο || (col) τα έχω χαμένα.

adult ['ædʌlt] *a, n* ενήλικος, έφηβος || (*LAW*) ενήλικος.

adulterate [ə'dʌltəreit] *vt* νοθεύω, αλλοιώνω, νερώνω.

adultery [ə'dʌltəri] *n* μοιχεία.

advance [əd'vɑːns] *n* πρόοδος *f*, προχώρηση || (*money*) προκαταβολή, πίστωση || (*in prices*) αύξηση, ύψωση ♦ *vi* προχωρώ || (*MIL*) προελαύνω || (*price*) ανατιμώμαι, ανεβαίνω || **~d** *a* προχωρημένος || (*ideas*) προοδευτικός || (*study etc*) ανώτερος || **~d ignition** *n* προανάφλεξη || **in ~** προκαταβολικά || **in ~ of** πριν από, (ε)νωρίτερα || **~ booking** *n*: **to make an ~ booking** κλείνω θέση.

advantage [əd'vɑːntidʒ] *n* πλεονέκτημα *nt*, προτέρημα *nt* || **to take ~ of** (*profit by*) επωφελούμαι από, εκμεταλλεύομαι || (*misuse*) καταχρώμαι || **~ over** υπεροχή.

advantageous [ædvən'teidʒəs] *a* επωφελής, λυσιτελής.

advent ['ædvənt] *n* έλευση, εμφάνιση || (*REL*) σαραντάμερο || **the Second A~** *n* Δευτέρα Παρουσία.

adventure [əd'ventʃə*] *n* περιπέτεια || (*bold undertaking*) τόλμημα *nt* || **~r** *n* τολμηρός || (*in bad sense*) τυχοδιώκτης.

adventurous [əd'ventʃərəs] *a* ριψοκίνδυνος, τυχοδιωκτικός.

adverb ['ædvəːb] *n* επίρρημα *nt*.

adversary ['ædvəsəri] *n* αντίπαλος, ανταγωνιστής.

adverse ['ædvəːs] *a* αντίθετος, ενάντιος, δυσμενής.

adversity [əd'vəːsiti] *n* ατυχία, αναποδιά.

advertise ['ædvətaiz] *vt* διαφημίζω, ρεκλαμάρω.

advertisement [əd'vəːtismənt] *n* διαφήμιση, ρεκλάμα || (*poster*) αφίσα.

advertiser ['ædvətaizə*] *n* διαφημιστής.

advertising ['ædvətaiziŋ] *n* διαφήμιση, ρεκλάμα || **~ agency** *n* διαφημιστικό γραφείο.

advice [əd'vais] *n* συμβουλή || (*information*) πληροφορία, είδηση.

advisable [əd'vaizəbl] *a* φρόνιμος, σκόπιμος.

advise [əd'vaiz] *vt* συμβουλεύω, συνιστώ || (*apprise*) ειδοποιώ || **~r** *n* σύμβουλος.

advisory [əd'vaizəri] *a* συμβουλευτικός.

advocate ['ædvəkit] *n* (*LAW*) δικηγόρος, συνήγορος || (*supporter*) υποστηρικτής ♦ ['ædvəkeit] *vt* υποστηρίζω, συνιστώ || (*LAW*) συνηγορώ.

aerial ['eəriəl] *a* εναέριος ♦ *n* κεραία || **~ photograph** *n* εναέριος φωτογραφία.

aeroplane ['eərəplein] *n* αεροπλάνο.

aerosol ['eərəsɒl] *n* αεροζόλ *nt inv*.

aesthetic [iːs'θetik] *a* αισθητικός || (*artistic*) καλαίσθητος.

afar [ə'fɑː*] *ad*: **from ~** από μακριά.

affable ['æfəbl] *a* προσηνής, γλυκομίλητος, καταδεκτικός.

affair [ə'fɛə*] *n* υπόθεση, δουλειά || (*matter*) πράγμα *nt*.

affect [ə'fekt] *vt* (*influence*) θίγω, επηρεάζω || (*feign*) προσποιούμαι, κάνω τον || **~ation** *n* προσποίηση || **~ed** *a* προσποιητός || (*moved*) συγκινημένος || (*MED*) προσβλημένος.

affection [ə'fekʃən] *n* αγάπη, στοργή || **~ate** *a* φιλόστοργος.

affiliate [ə'filieit] *vt* εισάγω, συνεργάζομαι.

affinity [ə'finiti] *n* συγγένεια.

affirmation [æfə'meiʃən] *n* (δια)βεβαίωση || (*assent*) κατάφαση.

affirmative [ə'fəːmətiv] *a* καταφατικός, βεβαιωτικός ♦ *n* κατάφαση || **in the ~** καταφατικά.

affix [ə'fiks] *vt* επισυνάπτω, προσαρτώ, θέτω.

afflict [ə'flikt] *vt* θλίβω, πικραίνω || (*MED*) προσβάλλω || **~ion** *n* θλίψη, λύπη || (*misfortune*) ατύχημα *nt*, συμφορά.

affluence ['æfluəns] *n* (*abundance*) αφθονία || (*wealth*) πλούτος.

affluent ['æfluənt] *a* πλούσιος.

afford [ə'fɔːd] *vt* (*have the means*) δύναμαι, έχω τα μέσα || (*provide*) παρέχω, προσφέρω.

affront [ə'frʌnt] *vt* προσβάλλω, ντροπιάζω ♦ *n* προσβολή.

Afghanistan [æf'gænistæn] *n* Αφγανιστάν *nt*.

afield [ə'fiːld] *ad*: **far ~** μακριά.

afloat [ə'fləut] *ad*: **I am ~** επιπλέω.

afraid [ə'freid] *a* έμφοβος, φοβισμένος || **to be ~ of** φοβούμαι || **to be ~ to** δεν τολμώ || **~ that** φοβούμαι ότι.

afresh [ə'freʃ] *ad* από την αρχή, πάλι.

Africa ['æfrikə] *n* Αφρική || **~n** *n* Αφρικανός/n *m/f* ♦ *a* αφρικανικός.

aft [ɑːft] *ad* προς την πρύμνη, προς τα πίσω.

after ['ɑːftə*] *prep* μετά, ύστερα από || (*according to*) κατά ♦ *ad* έπειτα, ύστερα ♦ *a* επόμενος || *cj* αφού || **some time ~** λίγο αργότερα || **what is he ~?** τι ζητά; || τι ψάχνει; || **~ all** τέλος πάντων, επί τέλους || **~ five (o'clock)** περασμένες πέντε || **~ you, sir!** παρακαλώ!, περάστε!

after- ['ɑːftə*] (*in compds*) *a* μετά, μέλλων.

aftermath ['ɑːftəmæθ] *n* συνέπεια, επακόλουθο.

afternoon ['ɑːftə'nuːn] *n* απόγευμα *nt* || **good ~!** χαίρετε!

afterthought ['ɑːftəθɔːt] *n* μεταγενεστέρα σκέψη.

afterwards ['ɑːftəwədz] *ad* αργότερα, στη συνέχεια.

again [ə'gen] *ad* πάλι, ξανά || **~ and ~** επανειλημμένως, πάλι και πάλι.

against [ə'genst] *prep* κατά, εναντίον.

age [eidʒ] *n* ηλικία || (*generation*) γενεά || (*period*) εποχή || (*century*) αιώνας *m* ♦ *vti* γερνώ || (*wine etc*) ωριμάζω || **of ~** ενηλικιωμένος, ενήλικος || **~d** *a*

ηλικιωμένος, γέρος || ~**d 20 (years)**
ηλικίας 20 ετών || ~**less** a αγέραστος,
αιώνιος.

agency ['eidʒənsi] n, a (επί)δράση,
ενέργεια || (factor) παράγοντας, αίτιο ||
(intervention) υπηρεσία, οργανισμός ||
(office) πρακτορείο, αντιπροσωπεία.

agenda [ə'dʒɛndə] n ημερησία διάταξη ||
(notebook) ατζέντα, σημειωματάριο.

agent ['eidʒənt] n πράκτορας,
αντιπρόσωπος || (cause) παράγοντας,
συντελεστής.

aggravate ['ægrəveit] vt επιδεινώνω,
χειροτερεύω || (provoke) εντείνω,
ερεθίζω.

aggregate ['ægrigit] n άθροισμα nt,
σύνολο ♦ a συνολικός.

aggression [ə'greʃən] n επίθεση,
επιδρομή.

aggressive [ə'gresiv] a επιθετικός ||
(vigorous) ρωμαλέος.

aggrieved [ə'griːvd] a θλιμμένος,
πικραμένος.

aghast [ə'gɑːst] a κατάπληκτος,
εμβρόντητος.

agile ['ædʒail] a ευκίνητος, ελαφρός.

agitate ['ædʒiteit] vt (set in motion)
(ανα)ταράσσω || (excite) ταράσσω,
ανησυχώ || (POL) κινούμαι, κάνω κίνηση ||
to ~ **for** δημιουργώ κίνηση για.

agitation [ædʒi'teiʃən] n αναταραχή.

agitator ['ædʒiteitə*] n υποκινητής,
ταραχοποιός.

agnostic [æg'nɒstik] a, n αγνωστικός.

ago [ə'gəu] ad περασμένος, πριν, από
πριν || **long** ~ προ πολλού || **some time**
~ προ καιρού.

agog [ə'gɒg] a ανυπόμονος.

agonizing ['ægənaizin] a σπαρακτικός,
φρικτός.

agony ['ægəni] n αγωνία, βάσανο.

agree [ə'griː] vti (consent)
συγκατατίθεμαι, αποδέχομαι || (have
same opinion) συμφωνώ, είμαι σύμφωνος
|| (of climate etc) ταιριάζω, ωφελώ || (come
to an agreement) συμβιβάζομαι || **it does
not** ~ **with me** με πειράζει, με ενοχλεί,
δεν μου ταιριάζει || ~**d** a (of persons)
είμαι σύμφωνος || (of things) εγκρίνεται!,
σύμφωνοι! || ~**ment** n συμφωνία ||
(formal) σύμβαση, συνθήκη.

agricultural [ægri'kʌltʃərəl] a
γεωργικός.

agriculture ['ægrikʌltʃə*] n γεωργία.

aground [ə'graund] ad (NAUT) στη
στεριά || **to run** ~ προσαράσσω,
καθίζω, εξοκέλλω.

ahead [ə'hed] ad εμπρός, προ || **to get**
~ προχωρώ, προηγούμαι || ~ **of** μπρος
από.

A.I. n (abbr of artificial intelligence) T.N.

aid [eid] n βοήθεια, συνδρομή || (assistant)
βοηθός ♦ vt βοηθώ, συντρέχω.

ailment ['eilmənt] n αδιαθεσία,
αρρώστια.

aim [eim] n (point) σκόπευση || (target)
στόχος || (purpose) σκοπός, αντικείμενο

♦ vti (throw) ρίχνω, κτυπώ || (point)
σκοπεύω || (intend) επιδιώκω || ~**less** a
άσκοπος, ασυνάρτητος.

air [εə*] n αέρας m || (tune) μέλος nt,
σκοπός, ήχος || (appearance)
παρουσιαστικό, αέρας, ύφος ♦ vt αερίζω
|| (question) εκθέτω, ανακινώ || (opinions)
επιδεικνύω, αποκαλύπτω || ~**borne** a
αεροφερόμενος || ~ **conditioning** n
κλιματισμός || ~**craft** n αεροσκάφος nt,
αεροπλάνο || ~**craft carrier** n
αεροπλανοφόρο || ~**force** n (πολεμική)
αεροπορία || ~**gun** n αεροβόλο || ~
hostess n αεροσυνοδός || ~**line** n
αεροπορική γραμμή || ~**liner** n
επιβατικό αεροπλάνο || ~**mail** n: **by**
~**mail** αεροπορικώς || ~**plane** n (US)
αεροπλάνο || ~**pocket** n κενόν nt
αέρος || ~ **port** n αεροδρόμιο || ~ **raid**
n αεροπορική επιδρομή || ~**tight** a
αεροστεγής, ερμητικός.

aisle [ail] n διάδρομος || (of church)
πτέρυγα.

ajar [ə'dʒɑː*] ad μισοανοιγμένος.

akin [ə'kin] a συγγενεύων.

à la carte [ælæ'kɑːt] ad α-λα-κάρτ.

alarm [ə'lɑːm] n (of danger) συναγερμός,
κραυγή κινδύνου || (device) σύστημα
ειδοποίησης || (fright) φόβος, αναταραχή
♦ vt τρομάζω, φοβίζω, ταράσσω || ~
clock n ξυπνητήρι.

Albania [æl'beiniə] n Αλβανία || ~**n** n
Αλβανός/ίδα m/f ♦ a αλβανικός.

album ['ælbəm] n λεύκωμα nt, άλμπουμ
nt inv.

alcohol ['ælkəhɒl] n αλκοόλ nt inv,
οινόπνευμα nt || ~**ic** a, n αλκοολικός.

alcove ['ælkəuv] n παστάς, αλκόβα || (of
wall) σηκός, αχιβάδα.

alderman ['ɔːldəmən] n δημοτικός
σύμβουλος.

ale [eil] n μπύρα.

alert [ə'lɜːt] a άγρυπνος, προσεκτικός ||
(nimble) ευκίνητος, σβέλτος ♦ n
επιφυλακή, συναγερμός.

algebra ['ældʒibrə] n άλγεβρα.

Algeria [æl'dʒiəriə] n Αλγερία ||
Algerian a αλγερίνικος ♦ n
Αλγερινός/ή m/f.

alias ['eiliæs] ad άλλως ♦ n ψευδώνυμο,
πλαστό όνομα nt.

alibi ['ælibai] n άλλοθι || (col) δικαιολογία.

alien ['eiliən] n, a ξένος, αλλοδαπός ||
~**ate** vt (turn away) αποσπώ, αποξενώ ||
~**ation** n αποξένωση.

alight [ə'lait] a αναμμένος, φλεγόμενος
♦ vi κατέρχομαι, κατεβαίνω || (of birds)
κάθομαι.

align [ə'lain] vt ευθυγραμμίζω || ~**ment**
n ευθυγράμμιση.

alike [ə'laik] a όμοιος, παρόμοιος, ίδιος
♦ ad ομοίως, ίδια.

alive [ə'laiv] a ζωντανός || (lively) ζωηρός
|| (teeming) βρίθων, γεμάτος.

alkali ['ælkəlai] n άλκαλι.

all [ɔːl] a, pron πας, όλος, όλοι, πάντες ♦ n
όλο, σύνολο, ολότητα ♦ ad εντελώς,

τελείως, όλο || **after** ~ στο κατω-κάτω ||
~ **in** ~ στο σύνολο || **above** ~
προπαντός.
all- ['ɔːl] *(in compds)* α ολο-, παν-, παντο-,
τελείως.
allay [ə'leɪ] *vt* καταπραΰνω, γλυκαίνω ||
(lessen) καθησυχάζω, ανακουφίζω.
allegation [ælɛ'geɪʃən] *n* ισχυρισμός,
υπαινιγμός.
allege [ə'lɛdʒ] *vt* ισχυρίζομαι,
επικαλούμαι || ~**dly** *ad* δήθεν.
allegiance [ə'liːdʒəns] *n* πίστη, υπακοή.
allegory ['ælɪɡərɪ] *n* αλληγορία.
allergic [ə'lɜːdʒɪk] α αλλεργικός.
allergy ['ælədʒɪ] *n* αλλεργία.
alleviate [ə'liːvɪeɪt] *vt* ελαφρώνω,
ανακουφίζω.
alley ['ælɪ] *n* δρομίσκος, πάροδος *f*,
δρομάκος.
alliance [ə'laɪəns] *n* συμμαχία ||
(marriage) επιγαμία, συμπεθεριά.
allied ['ælaɪd] α: ~ **to** συγγενεύω με.
alligator ['ælɪɡeɪtə*] *n* αλλιγάτορας.
all-in ['ɔːlɪn] α *(exhausted)* εξαντλημένος.
alliteration [ə'lɪtə'reɪʃən] *n* παρήχηση.
all-night ['ɔːl'naɪt] α *(café etc)*
ολονύκτιος, διανυκτερεύων.
allocate ['æləʊkeɪt] *vt* διαθέτω,
παραχωρώ || *(for special purpose)*
κατανέμω, αναθέτω.
allocation [æləʊ'keɪʃən] *n* εκχώρηση,
απονομή.
allot [ə'lɒt] *vt* παραχωρώ, διαθέτω,
κατανέμω || ~**ment** *n (share)* μερίδιο,
τμήμα *nt.*
all-out ['ɔːl'aʊt] *ad* με όλες τις δυνάμεις.
allow [ə'laʊ] *vt* επιτρέπω || *(grant)*
παρέχω, δίδω || *(acknowledge)*
αναγνωρίζω, (παρα)δέχομαι || **to** ~ **for**
αφήνω περιθώριο για || ~**ance** *n*
επίδομα *nt,* εισόδημα *nt.*
alloy ['ælɔɪ] *n* κράμα *nt* ♦ *vt* αναμιγνύω,
συντήκω || *(fig)* νοθεύω.
all-round ['ɔːl'raʊnd] α τελειότατος,
αρτιότατος.
all-time ['ɔːl'taɪm] α παντοτινός.
allude [ə'luːd] *vi:* **to** ~ **to** εννοώ,
υπονοώ, υπαινίσσομαι.
alluring [ə'ljʊərɪŋ] α δελεαστικός,
γοητευτικός.
allusion [ə'luːʒən] *n* υπαινιγμός, νύξη.
ally ['ælaɪ] *n* σύμμαχος ♦ [ə'laɪ] *vt*
συνδέω, ενώνω ♦ *vi* συμμαχώ,
συνδέομαι.
almighty [ɔːl'maɪtɪ] α: **the A**~ ο
Παντοδύναμος.
almond ['ɑːmənd] *n* αμύγδαλο || *(tree)*
αμυγδαλιά.
almost ['ɔːlməʊst] *ad* σχεδόν, περίπου.
alms [ɑːmz] *npl* ελεημοσύνη, ψυχικό.
alone [ə'ləʊn] α μόνος, μονάχος,
μοναχός ♦ *ad* μόνο.
along [ə'lɒŋ] *ad:* **move** ~ προχωρώ,
βηματίζω || εμπρός!, έλα λοιπόν! ♦ *prep*
κατά μήκος || ~**side** *ad, prep*
πλευρισμένος, πλάι-πλάι || **all** ~ από
καιρό, απ' την αρχή.

aloof [ə'luːf] α, *ad* μακριά, σε απόσταση.
aloud [ə'laʊd] *ad* μεγαλοφώνως,
φωναχτά, δυνατά.
alphabet ['ælfəbɛt] *n* αλφάβητο || ~**ical**
α αλφαβητικός.
alpine ['ælpaɪn] α αλπικός.
Alps [ælps] *npl:* **the** ~ οι 'Αλπεις.
already [ɔːl'rɛdɪ] *ad* ήδη, κιόλας.
alright [ɔːl'raɪt] = **all right** || *see*
right.
also ['ɔːlsəʊ] *ad* επίσης, ακόμη και.
altar ['ɒltə*] *n* βωμός, θυσιαστήριο ||
(church) Αγία Τράπεζα.
alter ['ɒltə*] *vt* μεταβάλλω, τροποποιώ,
μεταποιώ ♦ *vi* μεταβάλλομαι || ~**ation** *n*
μεταβολή, αλλαγή, αλλοίωση.
alternate [ɒl'tɜːnɪt] α εναλλάσσων,
εναλλασσόμενος ♦ ['ɒltɜːneɪt] *vt*
εναλλάσσω, χρησιμοποιώ εναλλάξ ♦ *vi*
εναλλάσσομαι *(with* με) || ~**ly** *ad*
εναλλάξ, αλληλοδιαδόχως.
alternative [ɒl'tɜːnətɪv] *n* εκλογή, λύση
|| ~**ly** *ad* εναλλάξ.
alternator ['ɒltɜːneɪtə*] *n (ELEC)*
εναλλάκτης.
although [ɔːl'ðəʊ] *cj* αν και, μολονότι,
καίτοι.
altitude ['æltɪtjuːd] *n* ύψος, υψόμετρο.
alto ['æltəʊ] *n (male)* οξύφωνος || *(female)*
κοντράλτο.
altogether [ɔːltə'gɛðə*] *ad* τελείως,
ολοσχερώς, εντελώς.
aluminium [æljʊ'mɪnɪəm], *(US)*
aluminum [ə'luːmɪnəm] *n* αλουμίνιο,
αργίλιο.
always ['ɔːlweɪz] *ad* πάντα, πάντοτε,
διαρκώς.
am [æm] *see* **be.**
a.m. *ad (abbr of ante meridiem)* π.μ.
amass [ə'mæs] *vt* συσσωρεύω, μαζεύω.
amateur ['æmətə*] *n* ερασιτέχνης ♦ α
ερασιτεχνικός.
amaze [ə'meɪz] *vt* εκπλήσσω,
καταπλήσσω, θαμπώνω || ~**ment** *n*
κατάπληξη, έκπληξη, ξάφνιασμα *nt.*
amazing [ə'meɪzɪŋ] α καταπληκτικός,
απίστευτος.
ambassador [æm'bæsədə*] *n*
πρεσβευτής, πρέσβυς *m.*
ambiguity [æmbɪ'gjuɪtɪ] *n* αμφιλογία,
ασάφεια, διφορούμενο.
ambiguous [æm'bɪgjʊəs] α αμφίβολος,
αβέβαιος, ασαφής.
ambition [æm'bɪʃən] *n* φιλοδοξία.
ambitious [æm'bɪʃəs] α φιλόδοξος.
amble ['æmbl] *vi* βαδίζω ήρεμα.
ambulance ['æmbjʊləns] *n*
ασθενοφόρο αυτοκίνητο.
ambush ['æmbʊʃ] *n* ενέδρα, καρτέρι ♦
vt παρασύρω σε ενέδρα.
amenable [ə'miːnəbl] α υπάκουος,
πρόθυμος.
amend [ə'mɛnd] *vt* διορθώνω,
τροποποιώ ♦ *vi* διορθώνομαι ♦ *n:* **to**
make ~**s** επανορθώνω, αποζημιώνω ||
~**ment** *n* τροποποίηση, διόρθωση.

amenity [ə'miːnɪtɪ] n χάρη, ομορφιά, άνεση.

America [ə'mɛrɪkə] n Αμερική.

American [ə'mɛrɪkən] a αμερικανικός ♦ n Αμερικανός/ίδα m/f.

amiable ['eɪmɪəbl] a ευγενικός, φιλόφρων.

amicable ['æmɪkəbl] a φιλικός || ~ **settlement** n συμβιβασμός.

amid(st) [ə'mɪd(st)] prep ανάμεσα, αναμεταξύ.

amiss [ə'mɪs] a, ad εσφαλμένα, κακά, στραβά || **to take ~** παίρνω στραβά, παρεξηγώ.

ammunition [æmju'nɪʃən] n πολεμοφόδια ntpl, πυρομαχικά ntpl.

amnesia [æm'niːzɪə] n αμνησία.

amnesty ['æmnɪstɪ] n αμνηστία.

amok [ə'mɒk] ad = **amuck.**

among(st) [ə'mʌŋ(st)] prep μεταξύ, μέσα, ανάμεσα.

amoral [æ'mɒrəl] a άσχετος με την ηθική.

amorous ['æmərəs] a ερωτόληπτος, ερωτιάρης.

amount [ə'maʊnt] n ποσό, σύνολο, ποσότητα ♦ vi ανέρχομαι, ισοδυναμώ || **to ~ to** το ανέρχομαι.

ampere ['æmpɛə*] n αμπέρ nt inv.

amphibious [æm'fɪbɪəs] a αμφίβιος.

amphitheatre ['æmfɪθɪətə*] n αμφιθέατρο.

ample ['æmpl] a (enough) αρκετός, πλήρης || (big) ευρύς, πλατύς || (abundant) άφθονα, πλούσια.

amplifier ['æmplɪfaɪə*] n ενισχυτής.

amputate ['æmpjʊteɪt] vt αποκόπτω, ακρωτηριάζω.

amuck [ə'mʌk] ad: **to run ~** παθαίνω αμόκ, παραφέρομαι.

amuse [ə'mjuːz] vt διασκεδάζω, ξεκουράζω || ~**ment** n διασκέδαση, θέαμα nt, αναψυχή.

amusing [ə'mjuːzɪŋ] a διασκεδαστικός, ξεκαρδιστικός.

an [æn] see **a.**

anaemia [ə'niːmɪə] n αναιμία.

anaemic [ə'niːmɪk] a αναιμικός.

anaesthetic [ænɪs'θɛtɪk] n αναισθητικό.

analgesic [ænæl'dʒiːsɪk] a, n αναλγητικός.

analogy [ə'nælədʒɪ] n αναλογία.

analyse ['ænəlaɪz] vt αναλύω.

analysis [ə'nælɪsɪs] n ανάλυση.

anarchist ['ænəkɪst] n αναρχικός.

anarchy ['ænəkɪ] n αναρχία.

anatomy [ə'nætəmɪ] n ανατομία.

ancestor ['ænsɪstə*] n πρόγονος, προπάτορας.

ancestry ['ænsɪstrɪ] n καταγωγή.

anchor ['æŋkə*] n άγκυρα ♦ vi αγκυροβολώ, ρίχνω άγκυρα, αράζω.

anchovy ['æntʃəvɪ] n αντσούγια, χαμψί.

ancient ['eɪnʃənt] a αρχαίος, παλαιός.

and [ænd, ənd] cj και.

anecdote ['ænɪkdəʊt] n ανέκδοτο.

anew [ə'njuː] ad πάλι, ξανά.

angel ['eɪndʒəl] n άγγελος, αγγελούδι.

anger ['æŋgə*] n οργή, θυμός, παραφορά ♦ vt εξοργίζω, θυμώνω.

angle ['æŋgl] n γωνία || (viewpoint) άποψη ♦ vt ψαρεύω || ~**r** n ψαράς (με καλάμι).

Anglican ['æŋglɪkən] n Αγγλικανός.

angling ['æŋglɪŋ] n ψάρεμα nt.

Anglo- ['æŋgləʊ] prefix αγγλο-.

angrily ['æŋgrɪlɪ] ad οργισμένα, θυμωμένα.

angry ['æŋgrɪ] a οργισμένος, θυμωμένος.

anguish ['æŋgwɪʃ] n αγωνία, αδημονία, πόνος.

angular ['æŋgjʊlə*] a γωνιακός, γωνιώδης.

animal ['ænɪməl] n ζώο ♦ a ζωικός.

animate ['ænɪmɪt] a έμψυχος, ζωντανός ♦ ['ænɪmeɪt] vt ζωογονώ, δίδω κίνηση || ~**d** a ζωντανός, ζωηρός.

animosity [ænɪ'mɒsɪtɪ] n εχθρότητα, έχθρα.

aniseed ['ænɪsiːd] n γλυκάνισο.

ankle ['æŋkl] n αστράγαλος.

annex ['ænɛks] n (also: **annexe**) παράρτημα nt ♦ [ə'nɛks] vt προσαρτώ.

annihilate [ə'naɪəleɪt] vt εκμηδενίζω, εξαφανίζω.

anniversary [ænɪ'vɜːsərɪ] n επέτειος f.

annotate ['ænəʊteɪt] vt σχολιάζω.

announce [ə'naʊns] vt (αν)αγγέλλω, ανακοινώ || ~**ment** n αναγγελία, ανακοίνωση || ~**r** n εκφωνητής.

annoy [ə'nɔɪ] vt ενοχλώ, πειράζω || ~**ance** n ενόχληση, μπελάς || ~**ing** a ενοχλητικός, οχληρός.

annual ['ænjʊəl] a ετήσιος, χρονιάρικος ♦ n (book) επετηρίδα, ημερολόγιο || ~**ly** ad ετησίως.

annuity [ə'njuːɪtɪ] n πρόσοδος f, επίδομα nt.

annul [ə'nʌl] vt ακυρώνω, διαλύω, καταγγέλλω || ~**ment** n ακύρωση, κατάργηση.

annum ['ænəm] see **per.**

anoint [ə'nɔɪnt] vt χρίω, αλείφω.

anomaly [ə'nɒməlɪ] n ανωμαλία.

anonymous [ə'nɒnɪməs] a ανώνυμος.

another [ə'nʌðə*] a, pron άλλος (ένας), ακόμη (ένας) || **one ~** ο ένας τον άλλο.

answer ['ɑːnsə*] n απάντηση || (solution) λύση ♦ vi απαντώ || (suit) ανταποκρίνομαι || **to ~ for** vt εγγυούμαι για || ~**able** a υπεύθυνος, υπόλογος.

ant [ænt] n μυρμήγκι.

antagonist [æn'tægənɪst] n ανταγωνιστής, αντίπαλος || ~**ic** a εχθρικός, ανταγωνιστικός.

antagonize [æn'tægənaɪz] vt προκαλώ ανταγωνισμό, προκαλώ εχθρότητα.

Antarctic [ænt'ɑːktɪk] a ανταρκτικός.

antelope ['æntɪləʊp] n αντιλόπη.

antenatal ['æntɪ'neɪtl] a πριν τη γέννηση.

antenna [æn'tɛnə] n κεραία.

anthem ['ænθəm] n ύμνος.

anthology [æn'θɒlədʒi] n ανθολογία.
anthropologist [ænθrə'pɒlədʒist] n ανθρωπολόγος.
anthropology [ænθrə'pɒlədʒi] n ανθρωπολογία.
anti-aircraft ['ænti'ɛəkrɑːft] a αντιαεροπορικός.
antibiotic ['æntibai'ɒtik] n αντιβιοτικό.
anticipate [æn'tisipeit] vt προλαμβάνω || (foresee) προβλέπω, προοδοκώ.
anticipation [æntisi'peiʃən] n πρόληψη, πρόβλεψη || (expectation) προσδοκία.
anticlimax ['ænti'klaimæks] n αντικλίμακα, κατάπτωση, παρακμή.
anticlockwise ['ænti'klɒkwaiz] ad αριστεράστροφα.
antics ['æntiks] npl κόλπα ntpl, αστεία ntpl.
anticyclone ['ænti'saiklɒun] n αντικυκλώνας.
antidote ['æntidɒut] n αντίδοτο.
antifreeze ['ænti'friːz] n αντιψυκτικό, αντιπηκτικό.
antiquarian [ænti'kwɛəriən] n αρχαιοδίφης, αρχαιόφιλος.
antiquated ['æntikweitid] a αρχαϊκός, απηρχαιωμένος, πεπαλαιωμένος.
antique [æn'tiːk] n αρχαίο, παλιό, αντίκα || ~s npl αρχαιότητες, αντίκες.
antiquity [æn'tikwiti] n αρχαιότητα.
antiseptic [ænti'septik] a, n αντισηπτικό.
antisocial ['ænti'sɒuʃəl] a αντικοινωνικός.
antlers ['æntləz] npl κέρατα (ελαφιού).
anus ['einəs] n δακτύλιος, έδρα.
anvil ['ænvil] n άκμονας, αμόνι.
anxiety [æŋ'zaiəti] n ανησυχία, φόβος.
anxious ['æŋkʃəs] a ανήσυχος, στενοχωρημένος || (impatient) ανυπόμονος || ~ly ad ανήσυχα, ανυπόμονα.
any ['eni] pron, a κανείς, καμμιά, κανένα || (whosoever) οποιοσδήποτε, κάθε ♦ ad καθόλου, πια || ~body pron κανείς, καμμιά, οποιοσδήποτε, καθένας || ~how ad οπωσδήποτε, όπως κι αν είναι || ~one pron οποιοσδήποτε, καθένας, όλοι || ~thing pron τίποτε, κάτι, οτιδήποτε || ~way ad οπωσδήποτε ♦ cj οπωσδήποτε, εν πάση περιπτώσει || ~where ad οπουδήποτε, πουθενά.
apart [ə'pɑːt] ad χωριστά, κατά μέρος || ~ from εκτός του ότι.
apartheid [ə'pɑːteit] n φυλετική διάκριση.
apartment [ə'pɑːtmənt] n (flat) διαμέρισμα nt.
apathetic [æpə'θetik] a απαθής, αδιάφορος.
apathy ['æpəθi] n απάθεια, αδιαφορία.
ape [eip] n πίθηκος, μαϊμού f ♦ vt μιμούμαι.
aperitif [ə'peritiv] n ορεκτικό.
aperture ['æpətjuə*] n άνοιγμα nt, οπή, σχισμή.
apex ['eipeks] n κορυφή.

apologetic [əpɒlə'dʒetik] a απολογητικός.
apologize [ə'pɒlədʒaiz] vi ζητώ συγγνώμη.
apology [ə'pɒlədʒi] n απολογία, συγγνώμη.
apostle [ə'pɒsl] n απόστολος.
apostrophe [ə'pɒstrəfi] n απόστροφος.
appal [ə'pɔːl] vt τρομάζω, προκαλώ φρίκη || ~ling a τρομερός, φρικτός.
apparatus [æpə'reitəs] n συσκευή, μηχάνημα nt.
apparent [ə'pærənt] a φαινόμενος, εμφανής, φανερός || ~ly ad προφανώς, όπως φαίνεται.
apparition [æpə'riʃən] n φάντασμα nt.
appeal [ə'piːl] n έκκληση, κλήση προσφυγή || (LAW) κλήση, έφεση || (charm) γοητευτική, ελκυστικά ♦ vi προσφεύγω, απευθύνομαι || ~ing a συγκινητικός, συμπαθητικός.
appear [ə'piə*] vi φαίνομαι, εμφανίζομαι || ~ance n εμφάνιση, παρουσία, παρουσιαστικό || to put in or make an ~ance εμφανίζομαι, παρουσιάζομαι.
appease [ə'piːz] vt κατευνάζω, ικανοποιώ.
appendicitis [əpendi'saitis] n σκωληκοειδίτιδα.
appendix [ə'pendiks] n παράρτημα nt, εξάρτημα nt || (ANAT) σκωληκοειδής απόφυση.
appetite ['æpitait] n όρεξη || loss of ~ n ανορεξία.
appetizing ['æpitaiziŋ] a ορεκτικός, ελκυστικός.
applaud [ə'plɔːd] vt χειροκροτώ, επευφημώ.
applause [ə'plɔːz] n χειροκροτήματα ntpl, επιδοκιμασία.
apple ['æpl] n μήλο || ~ pie n μηλόπιτα || ~ tree n μηλιά.
appliance [ə'plaiəns] n όργανο, μηχάνημα nt, εργαλείο.
applicable [ə'plikəbl] a εφαρμόσιμος, κατάλληλος.
applicant ['æplikənt] n υποψήφιος, αιτητής.
application [æpli'keiʃən] n (request) αίτηση || (hard work) επιμέλεια, προσοχή, προσήλωση || (putting into practice) εφαρμογή, χρήση.
apply [ə'plai] vi εφαρμόζω || (place on) επιθέτω, βάζω || (for job etc) απευθύνομαι, υποβάλλω αίτηση || to ~ the brake πατώ φρένο, φρενάρω || to ~ o.s. προσηλούμαι, αφοσιώνομαι.
appoint [ə'pɔint] vt (δι)ορίζω, ονομάζω || ~ment n συνάντηση, ραντεβού nt inv.
apportion [ə'pɔːʃən] vt κατανέμω, διανέμω, μοιράζω.
appreciable [ə'priːʃəbl] a υπολογίσιμος, αισθητός.
appreciate [ə'priːʃieit] vt εκτιμώ, υπολογίζω, αποδίδω σημασία ♦ vi (ECON) ανατιμούμαι, υπερτιμούμαι.

appreciation [əpriːʃiˈeiʃən] n εκτίμηση || (ECON) υπερτίμηση, ανατίμηση.

apprehend [æpriˈhend] vt συλλαμβάνω, αντιλαμβάνομαι.

apprehension [æpriˈhenʃən] n (fear) φόβος, ανησυχία || (understanding) αντίληψη, νόηση || (arrest) σύλληψη.

apprehensive [æpriˈhensiv] a (worried) ανήσυχος, φοβισμένος.

apprentice [əˈprentis] n μαθητευόμενος ♦ vt τοποθετώ σαν μαθητευόμενο || ~ship n μαθητεία, μαθήτευση.

approach [əˈprəutʃ] n προσέγγιση, πλησίασμα nt || (path) είσοδος f, οδός f || (GOLF) κτύπημα nt ♦ vti πλησιάζω, προσεγγίζω || ~able a ευπρόσιτος, προσηνής, προσιτός.

appropriate [əˈprəuprɪit] a κατάλληλος, αρμόδιος, προσφορότερος, ♦ [əˈprəuprieit] vt οικειοποιούμαι, ιδιοποιούμαι, παίρνω.

approval [əˈpruːvəl] n έγκριση.

approve [əˈpruːv] vti εγκρίνω, επιδοκιμάζω, επικυρώνω || ~d a εγκριθείς, εγκεκριμένος.

approximate [əˈprɒksimit] a κατά προσέγγιση ♦ [əˈprɒksimeit] vt προσεγγίζω, πλησιάζω.

approximation [əprɒksiˈmeiʃən] n προσέγγιση, εγγύτητα.

apricot [ˈeiprikɒt] n βερύκκοκο.

April [ˈeiprəl] n Απρίλιος.

apron [ˈeiprən] n ποδιά.

apt [æpt] a (suitable) κατάλληλος, αρμόζων || (ready) υποκείμενος σε.

aptitude [ˈæptitjuːd] n ικανότητα.

aqualung [ˈækwʌlʌŋ] n συσκευή καταδύσεως, ακουαλάγκ nt inv.

aquarium [əˈkweəriəm] n ενυδρείο, ακουάριο.

aquatic [əˈkwætik] a υδρόβιος || ~ sports npl θαλάσσια σπόρ nt inv.

aqueduct [ˈækwidʌkt] n υδραγωγείο.

Arab [ˈærəb] a αραβικός.

Arabia [əˈreibiə] n Αραβία || ~n a άραβας, αραβικός ♦ n ΄Αραβας, Αράπης/ίνα m/f.

Arabic [ˈærəbik] a αραβικός ♦ n αραβική γλώσσα.

arable [ˈærəbl] a καλλιεργήσιμος.

arbitrary [ˈɑːbitrəri] a αυθαίρετος.

arbitration [ɑːbiˈtreiʃən] n διαιτησία || ~ court n διαιτητικό δικαστήριο.

arbitrator [ˈɑːbitreitə*] n διαιτητής.

arc [ɑːk] n τόξο.

arcade [ɑːˈkeid] n στοά, καμάρα.

arch [ɑːtʃ] n αψίδα, καμάρα ♦ a (chief) αρχι- ♦ vt (bend) λυγίζω, καμπουριάζω.

archaeologist [ɑːkiˈɒlədʒist] n αρχαιολόγος.

archaeology [ɑːkiˈɒlədʒi] n αρχαιολογία.

archaic [ɑːˈkeiik] a αρχαϊκός.

archbishop [ˈɑːtʃˈbiʃəp] n αρχιεπίσκοπος.

archer [ˈɑːtʃə*] n τοξότης || ~y n τοξοβολία.

archetype [ˈɑːkitaip] n αρχέτυπο.

archipelago [ɑːkiˈpeligəu] n αρχιπέλαγος nt.

architect [ˈɑːkitekt] n αρχιτέκτονας ||~ural a αρχιτεκτονικός || ~ure n αρχιτεκτονική.

archives [ˈɑːkaivz] npl αρχεία ntpl, έγγραφα ntpl.

archway [ˈɑːtʃwei] n στοά, αψιδωτή είσοδος.

Arctic [ˈɑːktik] a αρκτικός.

ardent [ˈɑːdənt] a φλογερός, ζωηρός.

ardour [ˈɑːdə*] n ζέση, μανία, πόθος.

arduous [ˈɑːdjuəs] a τραχύς, δύσκολος, κοπιώδης.

are [ɑː*] see be.

area [ˈɛəriə] n περιοχή, έκταση, χώρος || (MATH) εμβαδό.

arena [əˈriːnə] n παλαίστρα, κονίστρα, αρένα.

aren't [ɑːnt] = are not || see be.

argue [ˈɑːgjuː] vti (discuss) συζητώ, πραγματεύομαι || (prove) (απο)δεικνύω || (reason) φέρω επιχειρήματα, παρατάσσω.

argument [ˈɑːgjumənt] n επιχείρημα nt, συζήτηση || (dispute) φιλονικία, λογομαχία || (of play) σύνοψη, περίληψη || ~ative a συζητητικός.

aria [ˈɑːriə] n σκοπός, άρια.

arid [ˈærid] a ξηρός, άνυδρος.

arise [əˈraiz] (irreg v) vi σηκώνομαι || (appear) εμφανίζομαι, απορρέω.

aristocracy [ærisˈtɒkrəsi] n αριστοκρατία.

aristocrat [ˈæristəkræt] n αριστοκράτης.

arithmetic [əˈriθmətik] n αριθμητική.

arm [ɑːm] n βραχίονας, μπράτσο || (hand) χέρι || (weapon) όπλο ♦ vt (εξ)οπλίζω, αρματώνω || ~s npl όπλα ntpl || ~ed forces npl ένοπλες δυνάμεις.

armchair [ˈɑːmtʃɛə*] n πολυθρόνα.

armful [ˈɑːmful] n αγκαλιά.

armistice [ˈɑːmistis] n ανακωχή.

armour, (US) **armor** [ˈɑːmə*] n θωράκιση || (panoply) αρματωσιά || ~ed car n τεθωρακισμένο άρμα μάχης.

armoury [ˈɑːməri] n οπλοστάσιο, οπλαποθήκη.

armpit [ˈɑːmpit] n μασχάλη.

army [ˈɑːmi] n στρατός || (of people etc) πλήθος nt.

aroma [əˈrəumə] n άρωμα nt, μυρωδιά || ~tic a αρωματικός.

around [əˈraund] ad (τρι)γύρω, ολόγυρα || (about) περίπου ♦ prep περί, γύρω.

arouse [əˈrauz] vt διεγείρω, αφυπνίζω, ξυπνώ.

arrange [əˈreindʒ] vt τακτοποιώ, διαρρυθμίζω, διευθετώ, κανονίζω || ~ment n τακτοποίηση, ρύθμιση, διευθέτηση.

arrears [əˈriəz] npl καθυστερούμενα ntpl, εκπρόθεσμος || in ~ καθυστερούμενα.

arrest [ə'rest] n (making prisoner) σύλληψη, κράτηση || (halt) ανακαίτηση, σταμάτημα nt ♦ vt σταματώ, ανακαιτίζω || (LAW) συλλαμβάνω.

arrival [ə'raɪvl] n άφιξη, ερχομός || **new ~** n νεοαφιχθείς/ίσα m/f|| (baby) νεογέννητο.

arrive [ə'raɪv] vi αφικνούμαι, φθάνω (at σε)|| (at a conclusion) καταλήγω.

arrogance ['ærəgəns] n αλαζονεία, έπαρση, αυθάδεια.

arrogant ['ærəgənt] a αλαζόνας, υπερόπτης, αυθάδης.

arrow ['ærəʊ] n βέλος nt, σαΐτα.

arsenal ['ɑːsɪnl] n οπλοστάσιο.

arsenic ['ɑːsnɪk] n αρσενικό.

arson ['ɑːsn] n εμπρησμός.

art [ɑːt] n τέχνη || **~ gallery** n πινακοθήκη.

artery ['ɑːtərɪ] n αρτηρία.

artful ['ɑːtful] a (person) επιδέξιος, εφευρετικός || (crafty) πονηρός, δόλιος.

arthritis [ɑː'θraɪtɪs] n αρθρίτιδα.

artichoke ['ɑːtɪtʃəʊk] n αγκινάρα.

article ['ɑːtɪkl] n (of agreement etc) άρθρο, όρος || (GRAM) άρθρο || (newspaper etc) άρθρο || (items) είδος nt, αντικείμενο.

articulate [ɑː'tɪkjulɪt] a αρθρωτός, έναρθρος || (in expression) σαφής, ευκρινής || ~**d** a έναρθρος.

artificial [ɑːtɪ'fɪʃl] a τεχνητός, ψεύτικος || ~ **intelligence (A.I.)** (COMPUT) τεχνητή νοημοσύνη (T.N.) || ~ **respiration** n τεχνητή αναπνοή.

artillery [ɑː'tɪlərɪ] n πυροβολικό.

artisan ['ɑːtɪzæn] n τεχνίτης, βιοτέχνης, εργάτης.

artist ['ɑːtɪst] n καλλιτέχνης/ιδα m/f|| (painter) ζωγράφος || ~**ic** a καλλιτεχνικός.

artless ['ɑːtlɪs] a άτεχνος || (natural) απέριττος, φυσικός || (naive) αφελής, απονήρευτος.

as [æz, əz] ad (in main clause) επίσης, εξίσου, τόσο ... όσο || ~ **regards** όσο για || cj (in subject clause) όσο, τόσο ... όσο, σαν || (time) ενώ, καθώς || (because) επειδή || (manner) do ~ **you like** κάμετε όπως σας αρέσει || ~ **is** όπως είναι.

asbestos [æz'bestəs] n αμίαντος, άσβεστος.

ascend [ə'send] vi ανέρχομαι, ανεβαίνω.

ascension [ə'senʃən] n ανάβαση, άνοδος f, ανάληψη || **A~ Day** n της Αναλήψεως.

ascent [ə'sent] n άνοδος f, ανάβαση || (incline) ανήφορος, ανωφέρεια, κλίση.

ascertain [æsə'teɪn] vt διαπιστώνω, εξακριβώνω.

ascetic [ə'setɪk] a ασκητικός.

ash [æʃ] n τέφρα, στάχτη || (tree) μελία, φλαμούρι.

ashamed [ə'ʃeɪmd] a: **to be ~** είμαι ντροπιασμένος, ντρέπομαι.

ashen ['æʃən] a σταχτής || (person) ωχρός, κίτρινος.

ashore [ə'ʃɔː*] ad στην ξηρά, προσαραγμένος.

ashtray ['æʃtreɪ] n στακτοδοχείο.

Asia ['eɪʃə] n Ασία || ~**n** a ασιατικός || ~**tic** a ασιατικός || ~ **Minor** n Μικρά Ασία.

aside [ə'saɪd] ad κατά μέρος, πλάι, παράμερα || ~ **from** εκτός, πέρα.

ask [ɑːsk] vt (ε)ρωτώ, ζητώ, προσκαλώ || **to ~ a question** υποβάλλω ερώτηση.

askance [ə'skɑːns] ad: **to look at s.o. ~** κοιτάζω με δυσπιστία.

askew [ə'skjuː] ad λοξά, στραβά.

asleep [ə'sliːp] a, ad κοιμισμένος || (foot) μουδιασμένος || **to fall ~** αποκοιμιέμαι.

asparagus [əs'pærəgəs] n σπαράγγι.

aspect ['æspekt] n θέα, όψη, προσανατολισμός.

asphalt ['æsfælt] n άσφαλτος f|| ~ **road** n ασφαλτοστρωμένος (δρόμος).

asphyxiate [æs'fɪksɪeɪt] vt πνίγω.

aspiration [æspə'reɪʃən] n φιλοδοξία, βλέψη || (GRAM) δασεία προφορά.

aspire [əs'paɪə*] vt: **to ~** το φιλοδοξώ, αποβλέπω.

aspirin ['æsprɪn] n ασπιρίνη.

ass [æs] n γάιδαρος.

assailant [ə'seɪlənt] n επιτιθέμενος.

assassin [ə'sæsɪn] n δολοφόνος || ~**ate** vt δολοφονώ || ~**ation** n δολοφονία.

assault [ə'sɔːlt] n έφοδος, επίθεση ♦ vt επιτίθεμαι, εξορμώ || (person) βιάζω.

assemble [ə'sembl] vt συγκεντρώνω, συναθροίζω || (machine etc) ενώνω, συναρμολογώ ♦ vi συγκεντρούμαι, συγκεντρώνομαι.

assembly [ə'semblɪ] n συνέλευση, συγκέντρωση || (machines) συναρμολόγηση, συγκρότημα nt || ~ **line** n τράπεζα συναρμολογήσεως, αλυσίδα.

assent [ə'sent] n συγκατάθεση, έγκριση ♦ vi συγκατατίθεμαι, συναινώ, επικυρώ.

assert [ə'sɜːt] vt επιβάλλω, διεκδικώ || (ascertain) βεβαιώ, υποστηρίζω || ~**ion** n ισχυρισμός, υποστήριξη.

assess [ə'ses] vt καταλογίζω, υπολογίζω, επιβάλλω (φόρο) || (property) εκτιμώ, φορολογώ || ~**ment** n καταλογισμός, εκτίμηση || (tax) φόρος || ~**or** n ελεγκτής (εφοριακός).

asset ['æset] n περιουσιακό στοιχείο || (qualities) προσόν nt, αξία, ατού nt inv || ~**s** npl περιουσία || (ECON) ενεργητικό.

assiduous [ə'sɪdjuəs] a επιμελής, προσεκτικός.

assign [ə'saɪn] vt προορίζω, παρέχω, παραχωρώ, δίδω || ~**ment** n ανατιθεμένη εργασία.

assimilate [ə'sɪmɪleɪt] vt εξομοιώνω || (food) αφομοιώνω.

assist [ə'sɪst] vt βοηθώ, συντρέχω, μετέχω || ~**ance** n βοήθεια, αρωγή || ~**ant** n βοηθός m/f ♦ a βοηθητικός, αναπληρωματικός.

assizes [ə'saɪzɪz] npl: **court of ~** ορκωτό δικαστήριο.

associate [ə'səʊ∫ɪɪt] n εταίρος, συνέταιρος, συνεργάτης ♦ [ə'səʊ∫ɪeɪt] vti: **to ~ with** συνδέω, συνεταιρίζω, συνεργάζομαι, συναναστρέφομαι.

association [əsəʊsɪ'eɪ∫ən] n (club) εταιρεία, οργανισμός, σωματείο || (keeping company) συναναστροφή, σχέση || ~ **football** n ποδόσφαιρο.

assorted [ə'sɔ:tɪd] a ταιριασμένος.

assortment [ə'sɔ:tmənt] n συλλογή || (arrangement) τακτοποίηση, ταξινόμηση.

assume [ə'sju:m] vt (take for granted) υποθέτω, θεωρώ || (duty) αναλαμβάνω, αναδέχομαι || ~**d name** n ψευδώνυμο.

assumption [ə'sʌmp∫ən] n (supposition) υπόθεση, εικασία.

assurance [ə'∫ʊərəns] n (certainty) βεβαιότητα || (confidence) διαβεβαίωση, υπόσχεση || (insurance) ασφάλεια (ζωής).

assure [ə'∫ʊə*] vt (δια)βεβαιώ, εξασφαλίζω || ~**d** a βέβαιος.

asterisk [ˈæstərɪsk] n αστερίσκος.

astern [ə'stɜ:n] ad πίσω, προς τα πίσω.

asthma [ˈæsmə] n άσθμα nt || ~**tic** a ασθματικός.

astonish [ə'stɒnɪ∫] vt εκπλήσσω, καταπλήσσω || ~**ment** n έκπληξη, κατάπληξη.

astound [ə'staʊnd] vt καταπλήσσω.

astray [ə'streɪ] ad: **to go ~** περιπλανώμαι, παραστρατίζω, ξεστρατίζω.

astride [ə'straɪd] a, prep καβάλλα, ασεβάλ.

astrologer [əs'trɒlədʒə*] n αστρολόγος.

astrology [əs'trɒlədʒɪ] n αστρολογία.

astronaut [ˈæstrənɔ:t] n αστροναύτης.

astronomer [əs'trɒnəmə*] n αστρονόμος.

astronomy [əs'trɒnəmɪ] n αστρονομία.

astute [əs'tju:t] a έξυπνος, τετραπέρατος || (crafty) πανούργος, πονηρός.

asunder [ə'sʌndə*] ad χωριστά, κομματιαστά.

asylum [ə'saɪləm] n (refuge) άσυλο, καταφύγιο || (for insane) ψυχιατρείο.

at [æt] prep (of place) σε || (of time) σε, κατά, περί || ~ **six o'clock** στις έξι || ~ **first** στην αρχή || ~ **home** στο σπίτι || ~ **least** τουλάχιστο || ~ **last** επί τέλους || (of cause) για || ~ **all** καθόλου || **not** ~ **all** καθόλου.

ate [eɪt] pt of **eat**.

atheist [ˈeɪθɪɪst] n άθεος, αθεϊστής.

athlete [ˈæθli:t] n αθλητής/τρια m/f.

athletic [æθˈletɪk] a αθλητικός || ~**s** n αθλητισμός, σπορ nt inv.

Atlantic [ət'læntɪk] n Ατλαντικός.

atlas [ˈætləs] n άτλας.

atmosphere [ˈætməsfɪə*] n ατμόσφαιρα.

atmospheric [ætməs'ferɪk] a ατμοσφαιρικός.

atom [ˈætəm] n άτομο || ~**ic bomb** n

ατομική βόμβα || ~**ic energy** n ατομική ενέργεια.

atonement [ə'təʊnmənt] n έκτιση, επανόρθωση.

atrocious [ə'trəʊ∫əs] a φρικτός, φρικαλέος.

atrocity [ə'trɒsɪtɪ] n αγριότητα, φρίκη (εγκλήματος).

attach [ə'tæt∫] vt συνδέω, προσαρτώ, (επι)συνάπτω || **to ~ importance to** δίνω σημασία σε || ~**ed** a αποσασμένος, προσαρτημένος || ~**ment** n προσάρτηση, προσκόλληση || (devotion to) αφοσίωση, στοργή.

attaché [ə'tæ∫eɪ] n ακόλουθος || ~ **case** n χαρτοφύλακας.

attack [ə'tæk] n επίθεση, προσβολή ♦ vt επιτίθεμαι, προσβάλλω || ~**er** n επιτιθέμενος.

attain [ə'teɪn] vt φθάνω, κατορθώνω || ~**ment** n επίτευξη, πραγματοποίηση || (learning) γνώση, προσόν nt.

attempt [ə'tempt] n απόπειρα, προσπάθεια, δοκιμή ♦ vt αποπειρώμαι, προσπαθώ.

attend [ə'tend] vt (be present) παρευρίσκομαι || (visit) επισκέπτομαι, συχνάζω || (wait on) υπηρετώ ♦ vi (listen) εισακούω || (look after) ασχολούμαι || **to ~ to** προσέχω, φροντίζω || ~**ance** n (presence) συμμετοχή, παρουσία || ~**ant** n ακόλουθος, υπηρέτης/τρια m/f ♦ a συνοδεύων.

attention [ə'ten∫ən] n προσοχή || (care) περιποίηση, φροντίδα.

attentive [ə'tentɪv] a προσεκτικός, περιποιητικός.

attest [ə'test] vt επικυρώ, βεβαιώ, καταθέτω σαν μάρτυρας.

attic [ˈætɪk] n σοφίτα.

attitude [ˈætɪtju:d] n στάση.

attorney [ə'tɜ:nɪ] n δικηγόρος, πληρεξούσιος || **district ~** n εισαγγελέας || **A~ general** n γενικός εισαγγελέας || **power of ~** n πληρεξούσιο.

attract [ə'trækt] vt ελκύω, έλκω, τραβώ, γοητεύω || ~**ion** n (PHYS) έλξη || (of person) γοητεία || (THEAT) ατραξιόν f inv || ~**ive** a ελκυστικός, γοητευτικός.

attribute [ˈætrɪbju:t] n χαρακτηριστικό γνώρισμα nt || (GRAM) επίθετο ♦ [ə'trɪbju:t] vt: **to ~ to** αποδίδω (σε).

auburn [ˈɔ:bən] a πυρόξανθος.

auction [ˈɔ:k∫ən] n πλειστηριασμός, δημοπρασία ♦ vt πλειστηριάζω, βγάζω στο σφυρί || ~**eer** n προϊστάμενος δημοπρασιών.

audacious [ɔ:'deɪ∫əs] a τολμηρός, παράτολμος || (insolent) θρασύς, αναιδής.

audacity [ɔ:'dæsɪtɪ] n τόλμη, θάρρος nt || (insolence) αναίδεια.

audible [ˈɔ:dɪbl] a ακουστός, ακουόμενος.

audience [ˈɔ:dɪəns] n (formal interview)

ακρόαση || (gathering) ακροατήριο ||
(THEAT) θεατές mpl.

audit ['ɔːdɪt] n έλεγχος, επαλήθευση ♦
vt ελέγχω || ~**or** n ελεγκτής || (student)
ακροατής.

audition [ɔː'dɪʃən] n ακρόαση
(τραγουδιστού κτλ).

auditorium [ɔːdɪ'tɔːrɪəm] n αίθουσα,
θέατρο.

augment [ɔːg'mɛnt] vt (επ)αυξάνω,
μεγαλώνω.

augur ['ɔːgə*] vi προοιωνίζομαι,
προβλέπω.

August ['ɔːgəst] n Αύγουστος.

aunt [ɑːnt] n θεία || ~**y**, ~**ie** n θείτσα.

aura ['ɔːrə] n ατμόσφαιρα,
φωτοστέφανος.

auspices ['ɔːspɪsɪz] npl αιγίδα || (omens)
οιωνοί || **under the ~ of** υπό την αιγίδα
του.

auspicious [ɔːs'pɪʃəs] a ευνοϊκός,
ευοίωνος.

austere [ɒs'tɪə*] a αυστηρός.

austerity [ɒs'tɛrɪtɪ] n αυστηρότητα || (of
habits etc) λιτότητα.

Australia [ɒs'treɪlɪə] n Αυστραλία || ~**n**
n Αυστραλός/ίδα m/f ♦ a αυστραλιακός.

Austria ['ɒstrɪə] n Αυστρία || ~**n** n
Αυστριακός/ή m/f ♦ a αυστριακός.

authentic [ɔː'θɛntɪk] a αυθεντικός,
γνήσιος.

author ['ɔːθə*] n συγγραφέας || (cause)
δημιουργός, πρωταίτιος.

authoritarian [ɔːθɒrɪ'tɛərɪən] a
απολυταρχικός.

authority [ɔː'θɒrɪtɪ] n εξουσία, άδεια,
εντολή || (specialist) αυθεντία || (POL)
υπηρεσία.

authorize ['ɔːθəraɪz] vt εξουσιοδοτώ,
επιτρέπω.

auto ['ɔːtəu] n (US) = **automobile.**

autobiography [ɔːtəubaɪ'ɒɡrəfɪ] n
αυτοβιογραφία.

autograph ['ɔːtəɡrɑːf] n αυτόγραφο.

automatic [ɔːtə'mætɪk] a αυτόματος.

automation [ɔːtə'meɪʃən] n
αυτοματοποίηση.

automaton [ɔː'tɒmətən] n αυτόματο.

automobile ['ɔːtəməbiːl] n (US)
αυτοκίνητο, αμάξι.

autonomous [ɔː'tɒnəməs] a
αυτόνομος.

autopsy ['ɔːtɒpsɪ] n νεκροψία.

autumn ['ɔːtəm] n φθινόπωρο.

auxiliary [ɔːɡ'zɪlɪərɪ] a βοηθητικός,
επικουρικός.

avail [ə'veɪl] n χρησιμότητα, ωφέλεια,
όφελος ♦ vti ωφελώ, βοηθώ, εξυπηρετώ.

availability [əveɪlə'bɪlɪtɪ] n
διαθεσιμότητα.

available [ə'veɪləbl] a διαθέσιμος,
προσιτός.

avalanche ['ævəlɑːnʃ] n χιονοστιβάδα ||
(fig) συρροή, πλημμύρα.

avant-garde ['ævɑːŋ'ɡɑːd] n
προφυλακή.

Ave. abbr of **Avenue.**

avenge [ə'vɛndʒ] vt εκδικούμαι.

avenue ['ævənjuː] n λεωφόρος f.

average ['ævərɪdʒ] n μέσο, μέσος όρος
|| (NAUT) αβαρία ♦ a μέσος, μέτριος ♦ vti
εξάγω το μέσο όρο.

averse [ə'vɜːs] a αντίθετος ενάντιος ||
to be ~ to εναντιούμαι σε.

aversion [ə'vɜːʃən] n αποστροφή,
απέχθεια || (col) αντιπάθεια.

avert [ə'vɜːt] vt αποστρέφω || (prevent)
αποτρέπω, απομακρύνω.

aviary ['eɪvɪərɪ] n πτηνοτροφείο.

aviation [eɪvɪ'eɪʃən] n αεροπορία.

avid ['ævɪd] a: ~ **for** άπληστος,
αχόρταγος για || ~**ly** ad άπληστα.

avocado [ævə'kɑːdəu] n αβοκάντο.

avoid [ə'vɔɪd] vt αποφεύγω || ~**able** a
αποφευκτός || ~**ance** n αποφυγή.

await [ə'weɪt] vt αναμένω, περιμένω.

awake [ə'weɪk] (irreg v) vti ξυπνώ,
αφυπνίζω, εφυπνίζομαι ♦ a ξύπνιος,
άγρυπνος.

awakening [ə'weɪknɪŋ] n αφύπνιση,
ξύπνημα nt.

award [ə'wɔːd] n βραβείο || (LAW)
διαιτησία ♦ vt επιδικάζω || (reward)
απονέμω.

aware [ə'wɛə*] a: ~ **(of)**
πληροφορημένος, γνώστης || ~**ness** n
συνείδηση.

away [ə'weɪ] ad μακριά || (absent)
απουσιάζω, λείπω.

awe [ɔː] n φόβος, τρόμος || (deep respect)
σεβασμός ♦ vt τρομάζω || ~-**inspiring** a
επιβλητικός.

awful ['ɔːfəl] a (very bad) τρομερός,
φοβερός || ~**ly** ad τρομερά, τρομακτικά.

awhile [ə'waɪl] ad για λίγο, μια στιγμή.

awkward ['ɔːkwəd] a αδέξιος,
ανεπιτήδειος.

awning ['ɔːnɪŋ] n σκηνή, τέντα.

awoke [ə'wəuk] pt, pp of **awake.**

awry [ə'raɪ] ad λοξός, στραβός || **to go
~** πηγαίνω στραβά.

ax [æks] (US) = **axe.**

axe [æks] n τσεκούρι ♦ vt περιορίζω ||
(dismiss) απολύω.

axiom ['æksɪəm] n αξίωμα nt.

axle ['æksl] n άξονας.

ay(e) [aɪ] interj (yes) ναι || **the ~es** npl τα
ναι, τα υπέρ.

B

B.A. see **bachelor.**

babble ['bæbl] n μωρολογία, τραύλισμα
nt ♦ vi τραυλίζω, φλυαρώ.

babe [beɪb] n μωρό, μπέμπης.

baboon [bə'buːn] n μπαμπουίνος.

baby ['beɪbɪ] n βρέφος nt, νήπιο, μωρό ||
~ **carriage** n (US) καροτσάκι μωρού ||
~**ish** a μωρουδίστικος || ~-**sit** vi
μπέιμπισιτ, φυλάω νήπιο, προσέχω μωρό
|| ~-**sitter** n φύλακας νηπίων,
μπέιμπισιτερ.

bachelor ['bætʃələ*] n άγαμος, εργένης

B

|| **B~ of Arts (B.A.)** n ≈ πτυχιούχος πανεπιστημίου (θεωρητικών επιστημών) || **B~ of Science (B.Sc.)** n ≈ πτυχιούχος πανεπιστημίου (θετικών επιστημών).

back [bæk] n (person, horse) ράχη, πλάτη, νώτα ntpl || (house etc) το πίσω μέρος || (SPORT) μπάκ nt inv ♦ vt (support) υποστηρίζω || (movement) κάνω πίσω || (SPORT) ποντάρω ♦ vi (go backwards) οπισθοχωρώ, κάνω πίσω ♦ a οπίσθιος, πισινός ♦ ad πίσω, προς τα πίσω || (again) πάλι || (in time) εδώ και λίγα χρόνια || **to ~ out** vi ανακαλώ, αποσύρομαι || (col) το σκάω || **to ~ up** vt (COMPUT) εξασφαλίζω || **~biting** n κουτσομπολιό || **~bone** n ραχοκοκκαλιά || (firmness) θάρρος nt, κουράγιο || **~-cloth** n φόντο || **~er** n (SPORT) οπαδός || (COMM) χρηματοδότης || **~fire** n πρόωρη έκρηξη || **~ground** n (scene) βάθος nt, φόντο || (information) προϊστορία, το ιστορικό || (education etc) προσόντα ntpl || **~hand** n (blow) ανάποδη καρπαζιά || **~handed** a ύπουλος || **~handed compliment** διφορούμενο κομπλιμέντο, διφορούμενη φιλοφρόνηση || **~ing** n υποστήριξη || (movement) οπισθοδρόμηση || **~ number** n (newspaper etc) παληό φύλλο || **~ pay** n καθυστερούμενος μισθός |||| **~side** n (col) πισινός || **~up disk** n (COMPUT) εφεδρικός δίσκος **~ward** a οπίσθιος, προς τα πίσω || (child etc) καθυστερημένο || **~wards** ad προς τα πίσω || (flow) αντίθετα || **~ yard** n πίσω αυλή.

bacon ['beɪkən] n καπνιστό χοιρινό, μπέικον nt inv.

bacteria [bæk'tɪərɪə] npl μικρόβια ntpl.

bad [bæd] a κακός, άσχημος.

badge [bædʒ] n διακριτικό, σήμα nt, έμβλημα nt.

badger ['bædʒə*] n ασβός ♦ vt παρενοχλώ, βασανίζω.

badly ['bædlɪ] ad κακά, άσχημα || **~ off** σε δύσκολη οικονομική κατάσταση φτωχός.

bad-tempered ['bæd'tempəd] a δύστροπος, γκρινιάρης.

baffle ['bæfl] vt (puzzle) ματαιώνω, τα χάνω.

bag [bæg] n σάκκος, σακκούλα || (handbag) τσάντα ♦ vt σακκουλιάζω || (capture etc) σκοτώνω, πιάνω || **~ful** n σακκουλιά.

baggage ['bægɪdʒ] n αποσκευές fpl, βαλίτσες pl.

bagpipes ['bægpaɪps] npl γκάϊντα.

bail [beɪl] n εγγύηση ♦ vt (prisoner) ελευθερώνω με εγγύηση || **to ~ out** (boat) βγάζω τα νερά, αδειάζω || see also **bale**.

bailiff ['beɪlɪf] n δικαστικός κλητήρας.

bait [beɪt] n δόλωμα nt ♦ vt δελεάζω, δολώνω || (harass) βασανίζω.

bake [beɪk] vt ψήνω σε φούρνο ♦ vi

ψήνομαι || **~r** n φούρναρης || **~ry** n φουρνάρικο.

baking ['beɪkɪŋ] n ψήσιμο.

balance ['bæləns] n ζυγός, ζυγαριά || (equilibrium) ισορροπία || (of account) υπόλοιπο || (ECON) ισολογισμός ♦ vt ζυγίζω, σταθμίζω || (counterbalance) ισορροπώ, ισοζυγίζω || **~d** a ισορροπημένος || (equal) ίσος, ισοδύναμος || **~ sheet** n ισολογισμός.

balcony ['bælkənɪ] n εξώστης, μπαλκόνι.

bald [bɔːld] a φαλακρός || (plain) γυμνός, ξηρός.

bale [beɪl] n δέμα nt, μπάλα, κόλος || **to ~ or bail out** (AVIAT) πηδώ με αλεξίπτωτο.

Balkan ['bɔːlkən] a Βαλκανικός.

ball [bɔːl] n σφαίρα, μπάλα, τόπι || (dance) χοροεσπερίδα, χορός.

ballad ['bæləd] n μπαλάντα.

ballast ['bæləst] n έρμα, σαβούρα.

ball bearing [bɔːl'beərɪŋ] n σφαιροτριβέας, ρουλεμάν nt inv.

ballerina [bælə'riːnə] n μπαλαρίνα.

ballet ['bæleɪ] n μπαλέτο.

balloon [bə'luːn] n αερόστατο, μπαλόνι.

ballot ['bælət] n ψηφοδέλτιο.

ballpoint (pen) ['bɔːlpɔɪnt (pen)] n στυλό, πένα διαρκείας.

ballroom ['bɔːlrʊm] n αίθουσα χορού.

balmy ['bɑːmɪ] a γλυκός, κατευναστικός || (col) παλαβός.

balustrade [bæləs'treɪd] n κιγκλίδωμα nt, κάγκελα ntpl.

bamboo [bæm'buː] n μπαμπού nt inv, καλάμι.

ban [bæn] n απαγόρευση || (church) αφορισμός ♦ vt απαγορεύω.

banal [bə'nɑːl] a κοινός, χυδαίος.

banana [bə'nɑːnə] n μπανάνα.

band [bænd] n δεσμός, δέσιμο, στεφάνι || (group) ομάδα, συντροφιά || (MUS) ορχήστρα, μπάντα ♦ vi (+ together) συνασπίζομαι ♦ vt (tie) δένω.

bandage ['bændɪdʒ] n επίδεσμος, φασκιά.

bandit ['bændɪt] n ληστής.

bandy(-legged) ['bændɪ('legd)] a στραβοπόδης, στραβοκάνης.

bang [bæŋ] n (blow) κτύπημα nt || (noise) θόρυβος ♦ vti κτυπάω, κρούω.

banish ['bænɪʃ] vt εξορίζω, εκτοπίζω.

banister(s) ['bænɪstə*(z)] n(pl) κιγκλίδωμα nt, κάγκελα ntpl.

banjo ['bændʒəʊ] n μπάντζο.

bank [bæŋk] n τράπεζα || (ground) ανάχωμα nt, ύψωμα nt || (of river) όχθη ♦ vt (tilt) κλίνω, στρέφω || (pile up) σωριάζω || (money) καταθέτω, βάζω || **~ account** n τραπεζιτικός λογαριασμός || **~er** n τραπεζίτης || **~ holiday** n αργία τραπεζών || **~note** n τραπεζογραμμάτιο, μπαγκανότα.

bankrupt ['bæŋkrʌpt] n πτωχεύσας, χρεωκοπημένος ♦ vt πτωχεύω || **~cy** n πτώχευση, χρεωκοπία.

banner ['bænə*] n σημαία, μπαντιέρα.

banns [bænz] *npl* αγγελία γάμου.

banquet ['bæŋkwit] *n* συμπόσιο, γλέντι, τσιμπούσι.

baptism ['bæptizəm] *n* βάφτισμα *nt*.

baptize [bæp'taiz] *vt* βαφτίζω.

bar [ba:*] *n* (rod) ράβδος f, κοντάρι || (of soap etc) κομμάτι, πλάκα || (pub) μπάρ *nt inv*, ποτοπωλείο || (obstacle) φραγμός, εμπόδιο || (in court) εδώλιο || (MUS) μπάρα ♦ *vt* (fasten) κλείνω, αμπαρώνω, κιγκλιδώνω || (hinder) φράσσω, εμποδίζω || (exclude) απαγορεύω, αποκλείω || the B~ δικηγορικό επάγγελμα *nt*.

barbaric [ba:'bærik] *a* βάρβαρος, αγροίκος.

barbarity [ba:'bæriti] *n* βαρβαρότητα, αγριότητα.

barbarous ['ba:bərəs] *a* βάρβαρος.

barbecue ['ba:bikju:] *n* σχάρα.

barbed wire ['ba:bd'waiə*] *n* συρματόπλεγμα *nt*.

barber ['ba:bə*] *n* κουρέας, μπαρμπέρης.

barbiturate [ba:'bitjurit] *n* βαρβιτουρικό.

bare [bɛə*] *a* γυμνός || (living etc) λιγοστός ♦ *vt* γυμνώνω || (reveal) αποκαλύπτω || ~**back** *ad* χωρίς σέλλα || ~**faced** *a* ξεδιάντροπος, αναιδής || ~**foot** *a* ξυπόλητος || ~**ly** *ad* μόλις.

bargain ['ba:gin] *n* συναλλαγή, αγορά || (bought cheaply) ευκαιρία || **into the** ~ επί πλέον, από πάνω.

barge [ba:dʒ] *n* φορτηγίδα, μαούνα || **to** ~ **in** *vi* επεμβαίνω.

baritone ['bæritəun] *n* βαρύτονος.

bark [ba:k] *n* (tree) φλοιός, φλούδα || (dog) γαύγισμα *nt* ♦ *vi* (dog) γαυγίζω.

barley ['ba:li] *n* κριθάρι.

barmaid ['ba:meid] *n* σερβιτόρα του μπαρ.

barman ['ba:mən] *n* μπάρμαν *m inv*.

barn [ba:n] *n* (αιτ)αποθήκη || (US) σταύλος.

barnacle ['ba:nəkl] *n* ανατίφη, στρειδόνι.

barometer [bə'rɒmitə*] *n* βαρόμετρο.

baron ['bærən] *n* βαρώνος || ~**ess** *n* βαρώνη.

barracks ['bærəks] *npl* στρατώνας, μπαράκα.

barrage ['bæra:ʒ] *n* (dam) φράγμα *nt* || (MIL) πυρ *nt* φραγμού, μπαρράζ *nt inv*.

barrel ['bærəl] *n* βυτίο, βαρέλι || (measure) βαρέλι || (gun) κάννη.

barren ['bærən] *a* στείρος, άγονος.

barricade [bæri'keid] *n* προπέτασμα *nt* φράγμα *nt* ♦ *vt* φράσσω.

barrier ['bæriə*] *n* φραγμός || (obstruction) εμπόδιο.

barrister ['bæristə*] *n* δικηγόρος *m/f*.

barrow ['bærəu] *n* (cart) μονότροχο, χειράμαξα.

bartender ['ba:tendə*] *n* (US) = **barman**.

base [beis] *n* βάση ♦ *vt* βασίζω, στηρίζω ♦ *a* ταπεινός, πρόστυχος || (inferior)

φθηνός || ~**ball** *n* μπέιζ-μπώλ *nt inv* || ~**ment** *n* υπόγειο.

bash [bæʃ] *vt* (col) κτυπώ, τσακίζω.

bashful ['bæʃful] *a* ντροπαλός.

basic ['beisik] *a* βασικός, θεμελιώδης || ~**ally** *ad* βασικά.

basilica [bə'zilikə] *n* βασιλική.

basin ['beisn] *n* λεκάνη || (NAUT) νεωδόχος f, δεξαμενή.

basis ['beisis] *n* βάση.

bask [ba:sk] *vi* λιάζομαι.

basket ['ba:skit] *n* καλάθι, πανέρι || ~**ball** *n* καλαθόσφαιρα, μπάσκετ *nt inv*.

bass [beis] *n* (MUS) βαθύφωνος, μπάσος.

bassoon [bə'su:n] *n* φαγκότο.

bastard ['ba:stəd] *n* νόθος *n m/f*, μπάσταρδος.

baste [beist] *vt* (sewing) παρραράβω, ξυλίζω, ραβδίζω || (cooking) βουτυρώνω.

bastion ['bæstiən] *n* (stronghold) προμαχώνας.

bat [bæt] *n* (SPORT) ρόπαλο, μαγγούρα || (ZOOL) νυκτερίδα ♦ *vi* κτυπώ με το ρόπαλο || **off one's own** ~ εξ ιδίας πρωτοβουλίας.

batch [bætʃ] *n* φουρνιά (ψωμί) || (set) σωρός, ομάδα.

bath [ba:θ] *n* λουτρό, μπάνιο || (tub) λουτήρας, μπανιέρα ♦ *vt* λούω, μπανιαρίζω || ~**s** *npl* δημόσια λουτρά *ntpl*, μπάνια *ntpl*, χαμάμ *nt inv* || ~**chair** *n* καροτσάκι (αναπήρων), αναπηρική καρέκλα.

bathe [beið] *vi* λούομαι, κάνω μπάνιο ♦ *vt* λούω, πλένω || ~**r** *n* κολυμβητής/ήτρια *m/f*, λουόμενος/η *m/f*.

bathing ['beiðiŋ] *n* κολύμπι || ~ **cap** *n* σκούφος του μπάνιου || ~ **costume** *n* μπανιερό, μαγιό *nt inv*.

bathmat ['ba:θmæt] *n* ψάθα του μπάνιου.

bathroom ['ba:θrum] *n* λουτρό.

bath towel ['ba:θtauəl] *n* πετσέτα του μπάνιου.

baton ['bætən] *n* ράβδος f || (conductor's) μπαγκέτα || (truncheon) γκλώμπ *nt inv*.

battalion [bə'tæliən] *n* τάγμα *nt*.

batter ['bætə*] *n* κουρκούτι ♦ *vt* κτυπώ, κοπανίζω.

battery ['bætəri] *n* (MIL) πυροβολαρχία || (cell) συστοιχία.

battle ['bætl] *n* μάχη ♦ *vi* μάχομαι, πολεμώ || ~**field** *n* πεδίο μάχης || ~**ments** *npl* επάλξεις fpl, παραπέτο, πολεμίστρες fpl || ~**ship** *n* θωρηκτό.

bawdy ['bɔ:di] *a* ασελγής, αισχρός.

bawl [bɔ:l] *vi* κραυγάζω, σκούζω.

bay [bei] *n* (of sea) κόλπος, κόρφος || (tree) δάφνη || **at** ~ σε δύσκολη θέση, στα στενά.

bayonet ['beiənit] *n* ξιφολόγχη, μπαγιονέττα.

bay window ['bei'windəu] *n* παράθυρο σε προεξοχή τοίχου.

bazaar [bə'za:*] *n* παζάρι || (for charity) φιλανθρωπική αγορά.

B.B.C. *abbr of British Broadcasting Corporation.*

B.C. *ad (abbr of before Christt)* π.Χ.

be [bi:] *(irreg v) vi (exist)* είμαι, υπάρχω || *(live)* είμαι, ζω, κατοικώ || *(stay)* είμαι, κάνω || *(cost)* είμαι, κοστίζω || *(location)* είμαι, ευρίσκομαι || *(visit)* είμαι, επισκέπτομαι || *(take place)* είμαι, γίνομαι.

beach [bi:tʃ] *n* παραλία, ακρογιαλιά ♦ *vt* προσγιαλώ, αράζω || *(run aground)* προσαράσσω.

beacon ['bi:kən] *n* φάρος, φανάρι.

bead [bi:d] *n* χάντρα, πέρλα || *(perspiration)* σταγονίδι.

beak [bi:k] *n* ράμφος *nt,* μύτη.

beaker ['bi:kə*] *n* γυάλινο ποτήρι.

beam [bi:m] *n* δοκός *f,* δοκάρι || *(of balance)* ζυγοστάτης, μπράτσο || *(of light)* ακτίνα, δέσμη || *(smlk.)* λάμψη, ακτινοβολία ♦ *vi* ακτινοβολώ, λάμπω.

bean [bi:n] *n (broad)* κουκί || *(kidney)* φασόλι || *(string)* φασολάκι.

bear [beə*] *(irreg v) n* αρκούδα ♦ *vt (carry)* φέρω, βαστώ, σηκώνω || *(support)* υποβαστάζω, στηρίζω || *(put up with)* υποφέρω, αντέχω, ανέχομαι || *(produce)* γεννώ, παράγω || ~**able** *a* υποφερτός, ανεκτός.

beard [biəd] *n* γένι, μούσι || ~**ed** *a* με γένεια.

bearing ['bεərɪŋ] *n (behaviour)* συμπεριφορά, ύφος *nt* || *(relation)* σχέση, έννοια || ~**s** *npl*: **I lose my** ~**s** χάνω τον προσανατολισμό.

beast [bi:st] *n* ζώο, κτήνος *nt,* θηρίο || *(person)* ζώο, παλιάνθρωπος || ~**ly** *a* κτηνώδης, βρώμικος.

beat [bi:t] *(irreg v) n (stroke)* κτύπημα *nt* || *(pulsation)* σφυγμός, παλμός || *(of policeman)* περιπολία || *(MUS)* χρόνος, μέτρο ♦ *vt* κτυπώ, δέρνω, ματσουκώνω || *(defeat)* υπερτερώ, νικώ || **to** ~ **about the bush** γυρίζω γύρω-γύρω από ένα θέμα || **to** ~ **time** κρατώ το χρόνο || **to** ~ **off** *vt* διώκνω, απωθώ || **to** ~ **up** *vt* σπάζω στο ξύλο || ~**en track** *n* πεπατημένη || ~**er** *n (for eggs, cream)* κτυπητήρι.

beautiful ['bju:tɪful] *a* ωραίος, εξαίσιος, υπέροχος || ~**ly** *ad* θαυμάσια, υπέροχα.

beauty ['bju:tɪ] *n* ομορφιά || *(woman)* καλλονή.

beaver ['bi:və*] *n* κάστορι, κάστορας.

because [bɪ'kɒz] *cj* διότι, γιατί, επειδή || ~ **of** εξαιτίας (+ *genitive).*

beckon ['bεkən] *vt* γνεύω, κάνω νόημα.

become [bɪ'kʌm] *vt (befit)* αρμόζω, ταιριάζω ♦ *vi* γίνομαι, καταντώ.

becoming [bɪ'kʌmɪŋ] *a* αρμόζων || *(dress etc)* ταιριαστός, που πηγαίνει.

bed [bεd] *n* κρεββάτι || *(of river)* κοίτη || *(foundation)* στρώμα *nt,* στρώση || *(garden)* πρασιά || ~ **and breakfast** *n* δωμάτιο με πρωινό || ~**clothes** *npl* σεντόνια *ntpl* και κουβέρτες *fpl* || ~**ding** *n* στρώματα *ntpl.*

bedlam ['bεdləm] *n (uproar)* φασαρία, θόρυβος.

bedraggled [bɪ'drægld] *a* κουρελιασμένος.

bedridden ['bεdrɪdn] *a* κρεββατωμένος, κατάκοιτος.

bedroom ['bεdrʊm] *n* υπνοδωμάτιο, κρεββατοκάμαρα.

bed-sitter ['bεd'sɪtə*] *n* υπνοδωμάτιο.

bee [bi:] *n* μέλισσα.

beech [bi:tʃ] *n* οξιά.

beef [bi:f] *n* βωδινό.

beehive ['bi:haɪv] *n* κυψέλη.

beeline ['bi:laɪn] *n:* **to make a** ~ **for** πηγαίνω κατ, ευθείαν.

been [bi:n] *pp of* **be.**

beer [bɪə*] *n* μπύρα.

beetle ['bi:tl] *n* σκαθάρι.

beetroot ['bi:tru:t] *n* πατζάρι, κοκκινογούλι.

befall [bɪ'fɔ:l] *vti* συμβαίνω, τυχαίνω.

before [bɪ'fɔ:*] *prep (in place)* προ, εμπρός, ενώπιον || *(of time)* πριν, προ ♦ *cj* προ, πριν, πριν να ♦ *ad (of place)* εμπρός, προ, μπροστά || *(of time)* πριν, πρωτύτερα, προτού.

befriend [bɪ'frεnd] *vt* βοηθώ, προστατεύω.

beg [bεg] *vti* ζητώ, παρακαλώ || *(for alms)* ζητιανεύω.

began [bɪ'gæn] *pt of* **begin.**

beggar ['bεgə*] *n* ζητιάνος/α *m/f,* επαίτης.

begin [bɪ'gɪn] *(irreg v) vti* αρχίζω, αρχινώ || **to** ~ **with** πρώτα-πρώτα, πριν ν'αρχίσουμε || ~**ner** *n* αρχάριος/α *m/f,* πρωτάρης/α *m/f* || ~**ning** *n* αρχή.

begrudge [bɪ'grʌdʒ] *vt* δίνω με το ζόρι, λυπούμαι.

begun [bɪ'gʌn] *pp of* **begin.**

behalf [bɪ'ha:f] *n* εκ μέρους, υπέρ || **on** ~ **of** για λογαριασμό του, εκ μέρους.

behave [bɪ'heɪv] *vi* (συμπερι)φέρομαι.

behaviour, *(US)* **behavior** [bɪ'heɪvjə*] *n* συμπεριφορά, φέρσιμο.

behind [bɪ'haɪnd] *prep* πίσω από || *(time)* καθυστερημένος ♦ *ad* όπισθεν, πίσω από ♦ *n* πισινός.

behold [bɪ'həʊld] *vt* βλέπω, αντικρύζω.

beige [beɪʒ] *a* μπεζ.

being ['bi:ɪŋ] *n* ύπαρξη, γέννηση || *(person)* ον *nt,* είναι *nt inv.*

belch [bεltʃ] *vti* ρεύομαι.

belfry ['bεlfrɪ] *n* καμπαναριό.

Belgian ['bεldʒən] *n* Βέλγοβ/Βελγίδα *m/f* ♦ *a* βελγικός.

Belgium ['bεldʒəm] *n* Βέλγιο.

belie [bɪ'laɪ] *vt* διαψεύδω, ξεγελώ.

belief [bɪ'li:f] *n (trust)* πίστη || *(idea)* γνώμη, δοξασία.

believable [bɪ'li:vəbl] *a* πιστευτός.

believe [bɪ'li:v] *vt* πιστεύω, δέχομαι ♦ *vi* πιστεύω, έχω εμπιστοσύνη || ~**r** *n* πιστός/ή *m/f.*

belittle [bɪ'lɪtl] *vt* υποτιμώ, περιφρονώ.

bell [bεl] *n* καμπάνα || *(in house)* κουδούνι.

belligerent [bɪ'lɪdʒərənt] a (fig) καυγατζής.

bellow ['beləʊ] vti μουγγρίζω, μουγκαρίζω ♦ μουγκρητό.

bellows ['beləʊz] npl φυσερό.

belly ['belɪ] n κοιλιά.

belong [bɪ'lɒŋ] vi ανήκω || it does not ~ here δεν ανήκει εδώ || to ~ to vt ανήκω, μετέχω σε || (a place) κατάγομαι από || ~ings npl περιουσία, υπάρχοντα ntpl.

beloved [bɪ'lʌvɪd] a πολυαγαπημένος ♦ n αγαπητός.

below [bɪ'ləʊ] prep υπό, κάτω από, κάτω θεν ♦ ad από κάτω.

belt [belt] n ζώνη, ταινία || (round waist) ζωνάρι, λουρί ♦ vt ζώνω || (beat) δέρνω με λουρί.

bench [bentʃ] n κάθισμα nt, πάγκος || (workshop) τεζάκι, πάγκος || (of judge) έδρα.

bend [bend] (irreg v) n καμπή, στροφή, γωνία ♦ vt κάμπτω, λυγίζω || (NAUT) δένω ♦ vi (stoop) σκύβω.

beneath [bɪ'niːθ] prep κάτωθεν, χαμηλότερα, υπό ♦ ad από κάτω.

benefactor ['benɪfæktə*] n ευεργέτης, δωρητής.

beneficial [benɪ'fɪʃəl] a ωφέλιμος, χρήσιμος.

benefit ['benɪfɪt] n όφελος nt, ωφέλεια ♦ vt ωφελώ ♦ vi επωφελούμαι.

benevolent [bɪ'nevələnt] a αγαθοεργός, καλοπροαίρετος.

bent [bent] n (inclination) κλίση, ροπή ♦ a: to be ~ on αποφασισμένος να ♦ pt, pp of bend.

bequeath [bɪ'kwiːð] vt κληροδοτώ, αφήνω.

bequest [bɪ'kwest] n κληροδότημα.

bereaved [bɪ'riːvd] n (person) τεθλιμμένος.

bereavement [bɪ'riːvmənt] n απώλεια, πένθος nt.

beret ['bereɪ] n μπερέ nt inv, σκούφος.

berry ['berɪ] n ρόγα, μούρο.

berserk [bə'sɜːk] a: to go ~ γίνομαι έξω φρενών.

berth [bɜːθ] n (anchoring) όρμος || (ship, train) κλίνη, καμπίνα ♦ vt προσορμίζω, πλευρίζω ♦ vi αγκυροβολώ, πλευρίζω.

beseech [bɪ'siːtʃ] (irreg v) vt ικετεύω, εκλιπαρώ.

beset [bɪ'set] vt κυκλώνω, περισφίγγω.

beside [bɪ'saɪd] prep πλάι, κοντά, δίπλα || to be ~ o.s. είμαι εκτός εαυτού.

besides [bɪ'saɪdz] prep εκτός από ♦ ad εκτός αυτού, ακόμη, άλλωστε.

besiege [bɪ'siːdʒ] vt πολιορκώ.

best [best] a καλύτερος ♦ ad καλύτερα || at ~ το καλύτερο, ακόμα και || to make the ~ of it όσο μπορώ καλύτερα || ~ man n παράνυμφος, κουμπάρος.

bestow [bɪ'stəʊ] vt παρέχω, απονέμω.

bestseller ['best'selə*] n βιβλίο μεγάλης κυκλοφορίας.

bet [bet] (irreg v) n στοίχημα nt ♦ vt στοιχηματίζω, βάζω στοίχημα.

betray [bɪ'treɪ] vt προδίδω, αποκαλύπτω || (be false) εξαπατώ || ~al n προδοσία.

better ['betə*] a καλύτερος ♦ ad καλύτερα ♦ vt καλυτερεύω, βελτιώνω ♦ n: to get the ~ of νικώ κάποιο, υπερέχω || he thought ~ of it άλλαξε γνώμη || ~ off a (richer) πιο εύπορος, πλουσιότερος.

betting ['betɪŋ] n στοίχημα(τα) nt.

between [bɪ'twiːn] prep μεταξύ, ανάμεσα ♦ ad ανάμεσα.

beverage ['bevərɪdʒ] n ποτό.

beware [bɪ'weə*] vti προσέχω, φοβούμαι || '~ of the dog' 'προσοχή, σκύλος'.

bewildered [bɪ'wɪldəd] a ζαλισμένος, χαμένος.

bewitching [bɪ'wɪtʃɪŋ] a γοητευτικός, μαγευτικός.

beyond [bɪ'jɒnd] prep (of place) πέρα από || (of time) πέραν του || (in addition) εκτός, πέρα από ♦ ad πέρα από, εκεί κάτω.

bias ['baɪəs] n (slant) λοξότητα || (prejudice) προκατάληψη, συμπάθεια || ~(s)ed a προκατειλημμένος, επηρεασμένος.

bib [bɪb] n σαλιάρα, μπούστος.

Bible ['baɪbl] n Βίβλος f, Ευαγγέλιο.

bibliography [bɪblɪ'ɒgrəfɪ] n βιβλιογραφία.

bicker ['bɪkə*] vi καυγαδίζω || ~ing n καυγάς.

bicycle ['baɪsɪkl] n ποδήλατο.

bid [bɪd] (irreg v) n προσφορά || (CARDS) δήλωση ♦ vt (command) διατάσσω, προστάζω || (offer) προσφέρω, πλειοδοτώ || (greeting) χαιρετώ || (goodbye) αποχαιρετώ || ~der n (person) πλειοδότης || ~ding n (order) εντολή, παραγγελία || (offer) πλειοδοσία.

bidet ['biːdeɪ] n μπιντέ nt inv.

big [bɪg] a μεγάλος, σπουδαίος.

bigamy ['bɪgəmɪ] n διγαμία.

bigot ['bɪgət] n στενοκέφαλος, φανατικός || ~ed a στενοκέφαλος || ~ry n μισαλλοδοξία.

bike [baɪk] n ποδήλατο.

bikini [bɪ'kiːnɪ] n μπικίνι nt inv.

bile [baɪl] n χολή.

bilingual [baɪ'lɪŋgwəl] a δίγλωσσος.

bill [bɪl] n (notice) αγγελία, αφίσα || (account) λογαριασμός || (law) νομοσχέδιο || (note) γραμμάτιο || (beak) ράμφος nt, μύτη || (US) χαρτονόμισμα nt.

billet ['bɪlɪt] n (MIL) κατάλυμα nt || (job) θέση.

billfold ['bɪlfəʊld] n (US) πορτοφόλι.

billiards ['bɪlɪədz] n μπιλιάρδο.

billion ['bɪlɪən] n (Brit) τρισεκατομμύριο || (US) δισεκατομμύριο.

billy goat ['bɪlɪgəʊt] n τράγος.

bin [bɪn] n κασέλα, κασόνι, κιβώτιο.

bind [baɪnd] (irreg v) vt (tie) δένω || (together) προσδένω || (a book) δένω ||

(oblige) δεσμεύω, δένω || ~**ing** n σύνδεση, δέση, δέσιμο || *(book)* βιβλιοδεσία.

binoculars [bɪˈnɒkjʊləz] npl κιάλια ntpl.

biochemistry [ˈbaɪəʊˈkemɪstrɪ] n βιοχημεία.

biography [baɪˈɒɡrəfɪ] n βιογραφία.

biological [baɪəˈlɒdʒɪkəl] a βιολογικός.

biology [baɪˈɒlədʒɪ] n βιολογία.

birch [bɜːtʃ] n *(tree)* σημύδα || *(for whipping)* βέργα.

bird [bɜːd] n πουλί || ~**'s-eye view** n θέα από ψηλά.

birth [bɜːθ] n γέννα, τοκετός || *(beginning)* γέννηση || **of good** ~ καλής καταγωγής || ~ **certificate** n πιστοποιητικό γεννήσεως || ~ **control** n έλεγχος γεννήσεων || ~**day** n γενέθλια ntpl || **place** n τόπος γεννήσεως || ~ **rate** n γεννήσεις fpl.

biscuit [ˈbɪskɪt] n παξιμάδι, μπισκότο.

bisect [baɪˈsekt] vt διχοτομώ.

bishop [ˈbɪʃəp] n επίσκοπος, δεσπότης.

bit [bɪt] n *(piece)* κομμάτι || *(of tool)* τρυπάνι || *(of horse)* στομίδα, χαβιά, χαλινάρι || *(COMPUT)* bit n inv.

bitch [bɪtʃ] n *(dog)* σκύλα || *(unpleasant woman)* παλιοθήλυκο.

bite [baɪt] *(irreg v)* n δάγκωμα nt || *(mouthful)* μπουκιά ♦ vti δαγκώνω || *(insect)* τσιμπώ || **a** ~ **to eat** μπουκιά, λίγο φαγητό.

biting [ˈbaɪtɪŋ] a δηκτικός.

bitter [ˈbɪtə*] a πικρός || *(feeling)* φαρμακερός, δηκτικός, πικρός ♦ n *(beer)* πικρή μπύρα || **to the** ~ **end** μέχρι τέλους, μέχρι εσχάτων || ~**ness** n πικρία, πίκρα || ~**sweet** a γλυκόπικρος.

bizarre [bɪˈzɑː*] a παράξενος, αλλόκοτος.

blab [blæb] vti τα λέω όλα, προδίδω.

black [blæk] n μαύρος || *(without light)* σκοτεινός ♦ vt *(shoes)* βάφω, λουστράρω || *(eye)* μαυρίζω || ~ **and blue** γεμάτος σημάδια, καταμαυρισμένος || ~**berry** n βατόμουρο || ~**bird** n κότσυφας || ~**board** n πίνακας, μαυροπίνακας || ~**currant** n μαύρο φραγκοστάφυλλο || ~**en** vt μαυρίζω, λερώνω || ~**leg** n απεργοσπάστης || ~**list** n μαύρος πίνακας || ~**mail** vt εκβιάζω || ~**mailer** n εκβιαστής || ~ **market** n μαύρη αγορά || ~**out** n *(MIL)* συσκότιση || *(ELEC)* διακοπή ρεύματος || *(faint)* σκοτοδίνη, λιποθυμία || ~**smith** n σιδεράς.

bladder [ˈblædə*] n κύστη || *(of football etc)* σαμπρέλλα.

blade [bleɪd] n *(leaf etc)* φύλλο || *(of tool etc)* λεπίδα, λάμα || *(of oar etc)* πτερύγιο, φτερό.

blame [bleɪm] n μομφή, ψόγος, φταίξιμο ♦ vt κατηγορώ, ψέγω || ~**less** a άψογος, ανεύθυνος.

bland [blænd] a ήπιος, μειλίχιος.

blank [blæŋk] a *(page)* λευκός, άγραφος || *(vacant)* ανέκφραστος, χαμένα,

συγχισμένος ♦ n κενό || *(cartridge)* άσφαιρο φυσίγγι.

blanket [ˈblæŋkɪt] n κλινοσκέπασμα nt, κουβέρτα.

blare [blɛə*] n δυνατός ήχος, ούρλιασμα nt ♦ vi αντηχώ, διασαλπίζω.

blasphemy [ˈblæsfɪmɪ] n βλαστήμια.

blast [blɑːst] n *(gust)* φύσημα nt, ριπή || *(NAUT)* σφύριγμα nt || *(MINING)* φουρνέλο ♦ vt βάζω φουρνέλο || ~**-off** n *(SPACE)* εκτόξευση.

blatant [ˈbleɪtənt] a κραυγαλέος, ολοφάνερος.

blaze [bleɪz] n *(fire)* φλόγα, ανάφλεξη, φωτιά ♦ vi παίρνω φωτιά || *(person)* εξάπτομαι ♦ vt: **to** ~ **a trail** χαράσσω δρόμο.

blazer [ˈbleɪzə*] n σπορ σακάκι.

bleach [bliːtʃ] n άσπρισμα nt, μπουγάδα ♦ vt ασπρίζω, ξεβάφω || *(hair)* αποχρωματίζω.

bleak [bliːk] a ψυχρός, μελαγχολικός.

bleary-eyed [ˈblɪərˈaɪd] a με θολωμένα μάτια.

bleat [bliːt] n βέλασμα nt ♦ vt βελάζω.

bled [bled] pt, pp of **bleed**.

bleed [bliːd] *(irreg v)* vi χύνω αίμα, χάνω αίμα ♦ vt φλεβοτομώ, παίρνω αίμα.

bleeding [ˈbliːdɪŋ] a ματωμένος.

blemish [ˈblemɪʃ] n ελάττωμα nt, κηλίδα ♦ vt κηλιδώνω || *(reputation)* καταστρέφω.

blend [blend] n χαρμάνι, μίγμα nt ♦ vt ανακατεύω, συγχωνεύω ♦ vi *(colours etc)* ταιριάζω.

bless [bles] vt ευλογώ, δοξάζω || ~**ing** n ευλογία, ευτύχημα nt.

blew [bluː] pt of **blow**.

blight [blaɪt] n *(disease)* ερυσίβη, συρίκι, συναπίδι || *(fig)* πληγή ♦ vt καταστρέφω.

blimey [ˈblaɪmɪ] excl *(col)* να με πάρει ο διάβολος.

blind [blaɪnd] a τυφλός, στραβός || *(alley etc)* αδιέξοδος ♦ n τέντα || *(excuse)* πρόσχημα nt, υποκρισία ♦ vt τυφλώνω, στραβώνω || ~**fold** a με δεμένα μάτια ♦ vt δένω τα μάτια || ~**ly** ad στα τυφλά, στα στραβά || ~**ness** n τυφλότητα, στραβομάρα.

blink [blɪŋk] vti ανοιγοκλείνω τα μάτια, μισοκλείνω τα μάτια || ~**ers** npl παρωπίδες fpl.

blinking [ˈblɪŋkɪŋ] a *(col)* = **bloody**.

bliss [blɪs] n μακαριότητα, ευδαιμονία.

blister [ˈblɪstə*] n *(on skin)* φυσαλίδα, φουσκάλα || *(on surfaces etc)* φουσκάλα ♦ vti φουσκαλιάζω, φλυκταινούμαι.

blithe [blaɪð] a χαρούμενος, εύθυμος.

blitz [blɪts] n μπλίτς nt inv, βίαιη επίθεση.

blizzard [ˈblɪzəd] n χιονοθύελλα.

bloated [ˈbləʊtɪd] a φουσκωμένος, πρησμένος.

bloc [blɒk] n *(POL)* συνασπισμός, μπλόκ nt inv.

block [blɒk] n *(piece)* τεμάχιο, μεγάλο κομμάτι || *(for chopping)* επικόπανο, πικόπι || *(traffic)* συνωστισμός, διακοπή || *(obstacle)* εμπόδιο || *(city)* τετράγωνο ♦ vt φράσσω, εμποδίζω || ~**ade** n αποκλεισμός, μπλόκο ♦ vt αποκλείω, μπλοκάρω || ~**age** n εμπλοκή, μπλοκάρισμα nt.

bloke [blǝuk] n (col) άνθρωπος.

blond(e) [blɔnd] a ξανθός, ξανθή ♦ n ξανθός, ξανθιά.

blood [blʌd] n αίμα nt || (kinship) συγγένεια || (descent) καταγωγή || ~ **donor** n αιμοδότης/τρια m/f || ~ **group** n ομάδα αίματος || ~ **pressure** n πίεση αίματος || ~**shed** n αιματοχυσία || ~**shot** a κόκκινος || ~**stained** a αιματοσταγής, ματωμένος || ~**stream** n κυκλοφοριακό σύστημα nt || ~**thirsty** a αιμοβόρος || ~ **transfusion** n μετάγγιση αίματος || ~**y** a (col) παλιο-, βρωμο- || (lit) αιματηρός || ~**y-minded** a τζαναμπέτης.

bloom [blu:m] n (flower) λουλούδι || (perfection) άνθηση, ακμή ♦ vi ανθίζω || **in** ~ στην άνθησή του.

blossom ['blɔsǝm] n άνθος nt ♦ vi ανθίζω.

blot [blɔt] n λεκές m || (disgrace) κηλίδα ♦ vt (stain) λεκιάζω || (dry ink) στυπώνω, τραβώ || **to** ~ **out** n εξαφανίζω, σβήνω.

blotchy ['blɔtʃi] a γεμάτος κοκκινίλες.

blotting paper ['blɔtɪŋpeɪpǝ*] n στυπόχαρτο.

blouse [blauz] n μπλούζα.

blow [blǝu] (irreg v) n (with fist) κτύπημα nt, γροθιά || (with stick) ραβδισμός || (of air) φύσημα nt || (of fate) πλήγμα nt ♦ vt φυσάω || (a fuse) καίομαι || (col: squander) σπαταλάω || **at a single** ~ μ'ένα κτύπημα || **to** ~ **one's top** ξεσπάω || **to** ~ **over** vi περνώ, ξεθυμαίνω || **to** ~ **up** vi σκάω, ανατινάσσω ♦ vt (tyre) φουσκώνω || ~**lamp** n καμινευτήρ || ~**out** n (AUT) κλατάρισμα nt || ~**y** a ανεμώδης.

blubber ['blʌbǝ*] n λίπος nt φάλαινας.

blue [blu:] a γαλάζιος, γαλανός || (paint) μπλέ || (with cold etc) μελανιασμένος ♦ n: **to have the** ~**s** μελαγχολώ || ~**bell** n ζυμπούλι || ~**bottle** n κρεατόμυγα || ~**print** n κυανοτυπία, σχέδιο.

bluff [blʌf] n (deception) μπλόφα, απάτη ♦ vt μπλοφάρω, εξαπατώ ♦ a ντόμπρος.

blunder ['blʌndǝ*] n μεγάλο λάθος nt, χοντροκοπιά ♦ vi κάνω γκάφα.

blunt [blʌnt] a αμβλύς, στομωμένος || (person) μονοκόμματος ♦ vt αμβλύνω, στομώνω || ~**ly** ad απότομα, ντόμπρα.

blur [blǝ:*] n θολούρα, θαμπάδα || (stain) μουτζούρα ♦ vti θολώνω, θαμπώνω.

blurt [blǝ:t]: **to** ~ **out** vt λέω κάτι απερίσκεπτα, αποκαλύπτω.

blush [blʌʃ] vi κοκκινίζω ♦ n κοκκίνισμα nt.

bluster ['blʌstǝ*] vi (of wind) φυσώ δυνατά || (of person) κάνω φασαρία, κομπάζω.

boar [bɔ:*] n γουρούνι αρσενικό, καπρί.

board [bɔ:d] n (of wood) σανίδα, τάβλα || (notice) πινακίδα, ταμπλώ nt inv || (of paper) χαρτόνι || (meal) φαΐ || (of men) συμβούλιο, επιτροπή ♦ vt (feed) δίνω τροφή || (ship, train) επιβαίνω, μπαρκάρω || (with planks) σανιδώνω || ~ **and lodging** φαΐ και ύπνος || **to** ~ **up** vt (περι)φράσσω με σανίδες || ~**er** n οικότροφος || (lodger) ένοικος || ~**ing house** n πανσιόν f inv || ~**ing school** n σχολή με οικοτροφείο || ~**ing school pupil** n εσωτερικός.

boast [bǝust] vi καυχώμαι, κομπορρημονώ ♦ n κομπασμός, καυχησιολογία || ~**ful** a καυχησιάρης, φανφαρόνος.

boat [bǝut] n βάρκα, καΐκι || (ship) καράβι || ~**er** (hat) ναυτική ψάθα || ~**ing** n λεμβοδρομία με βάρκα || ~**swain** ['bǝusǝn] n λοστρόμος.

bob [bɔb] vi ανεβοκατεβαίνω.

bobbin ['bɔbɪn] n πηνίο, κουβαρίστρα || (ELEC) μπομπίνα.

bobsleigh ['bɔbsleɪ] n μπομπολέτ nt inv, έλκηθρο.

bodice ['bɔdɪs] n στήθος nt φορέματος, μπούστος.

bodily ['bɔdɪli] ad σωματικά || (together) συλλογικά, όλοι μαζί.

body ['bɔdi] n σώμα nt, κορμί || (legislative etc) σώμα, σωματείο || (collection) μεγάλο πλήθος nt, μάζα || (of car etc) σώμα, κύριο μέρος nt || ~**guard** n σωματοφύλακας || ~**work** n καρότσα.

bog [bɔg] n έλος nt ♦ vi: **to get** ~**ged down** βουλιάζω.

boggle ['bɔgl] vi διστάζω.

bogus ['bǝugǝs] a ψεύτικος.

boil [bɔil] vt (potatoes etc) βράζω ♦ vi βράζω, κοχλάζω ♦ n (MED) καλόγερος || **to come to the** ~ παίρνω βράση || ~**er** n λέβης, καζάνι || ~**ing point** n σημείο βρασμού.

boisterous ['bɔistǝrǝs] a θορυβώδης, ταραχώδης.

bold [bǝuld] a τολμηρός, θαρραλέος || ~**ness** n τολμηρότητα, θάρρος nt.

bollard ['bɔlǝd] n δέστρα.

bolster ['bǝulstǝ*] n μαξιλάρα || **to** ~ **up** vt (υπο)στηρίζω.

bolt [bǝult] n (of door etc) σύρτης, μάνταλο || (rush away) εξόρμηση, φυγή ♦ vt (a door etc) μανταλώνω, κλειδώνω || (food) καταβροχθίζω ♦ vi (rush away) φεύγω, εξορμώ || (escape) δραπετεύω.

bomb [bɔm] n βόμβα ♦ vt βομβαρδίζω || ~**ard** [bɔm'ba:d] vt βομβαρδίζω, σφυροκοπώ || ~**ardment** n βομβαρδισμός || ~**er** n (person) βομβαρδιστής || (AVIAT) βομβαρδιστικό || ~**ing** n βομβαρδισμός || ~**shell** n (fig) κατάπληξη, σαν βόμβα.

bona fide ['bǝunǝ'faidi] a καλής πίστεως.

bond [bɔnd] n (link) δεσμός, συνάφεια || (promise) υπόσχεση, σύμβαση || (ECON) ομολογία.

bone [bǝun] n κόκκαλο ♦ vt ξεκοκκαλίζω || ~**-dry** a εντελώς ξηρός, κατάξερος.

bonfire ['bɒnfaɪə*] n φωτιά.

bonnet ['bɒnɪt] n γυναικείο καπέλλο || (child's) σκουφίτσα || (cap) σκούφος, μπερές m || (Brit: of car) καπό.

bonus ['bəʊnəs] n επιμίσθιο, επίδομα nt.

bony ['bəʊnɪ] a κοκκαλιάρης.

boo [buː] vt αποδοκιμάζω, γιουχαΐζω.

book [bʊk] n βιβλίο, κιτάπι ♦ vt (ticket etc) βγάζω εισιτήριο || (a room) κλείνω δωμάτιο || (person) πληρώνω, τιμωρούμαι || ~case n βιβλιοθήκη || ~ing office n πρακτορείο εισιτηρίων || ~-keeping n λογιστική || ~let n φυλλάδιο, βιβλιαράκι || ~maker n (RACING) μπουκμέικερ m inv || ~seller n βιβλιοπώλης || ~shop n βιβλιοπωλείο || ~stall n πάγκος βιβλιοπώλου || ~store n = ~shop.

boom [buːm] n (noise) κρότος, βόμβος || (NAUT) απόφρυγμα || (iii iii iii ii) μηγχνι οι || (busy period) μπουμ nt inv, κύμα nt ευημερίας, αιχμή ευημερίας ♦ vi ανέρχομαι, ανεβαίνω.

boon [buːn] n (blessing) όφελος nt.

boorish ['bʊərɪʃ] a άξεστος, αγροίκος.

boost [buːst] n προώθηση ♦ vt προωθώ, ενισχύω.

boot [buːt] n μπότα || (Brit: of car) πορτμπαγκάζ nt inv ♦ vt (kick) λακτίζω, κλωτσάω || to ~ (in addition) επί πλέον.

booze [buːz] n ποτό ♦ vi ξεφαντώνω, μεθοκοπώ.

border ['bɔːdə*] n (frontier) σύνορο, μεθόριος f || (edge) γύρος, σειρήτι, μπορντούρα || (page etc) πλαίσιο, βινιέτα || to ~ on vt συνορεύω με || ~line n (fig) εγγίζω τα όρια.

bore [bɔː*] pt of bear || n (person or thing) πληκτικός, ενοχλητικός, αφόρητος || (of gun etc) διαμέτρημα nt ♦ vt τρυπώ, ανοίγω τρύπα || (weary) πλήττω, λιμάρω || ~dom n πλήξη, ανία.

boring ['bɔːrɪŋ] a ανιαρός, βαρετός.

born [bɔːn] pp: to be ~ γεννιέμαι.

borough ['bʌrə] n (διοικητική) περιφέρεια.

borrow ['bɒrəʊ] vt δανείζομαι.

bosom ['bʊzəm] n στήθος nt, κόρφος.

boss [bɒs] n κύφωμα nt, καμπούρα || (master) το αφεντικό ♦ vt διευθύνω, κάνω το διευθυντή || ~y a αυταρχικός.

bosun ['bəʊsn] n = **boatswain** || see **boat**.

botanical [bə'tænɪkəl] a βοτανικός.

botanist ['bɒtənɪst] n βοτανολόγος m/f.

botany ['bɒtənɪ] n βοτανική.

botch [bɒtʃ] vt φτιάνω τσαπατσούλικα, κουτσοφτιάχνω || (patch) κουτσομπαλώνω.

both [bəʊθ] a, pron αμφότεροι, και οι δύο ♦ ad και... και... || (j) όχι μόνο... αλλά και....

bother ['bɒðə*] n ενόχληση, μπελάς ♦ vt ενοχλώ, πειράζω, σκοτίζω ♦ vi στενοχωριέμαι, νοιάζομαι.

bottle ['bɒtl] n φιάλη, μπουκάλι, μποτίλια ♦ vt εμφιαλώνω, μπουκαλάρω, μποτιλιάρω || ~neck n (production)

δυσχέρεια || (traffic) συνωστισμός || ~-opener n ανοιχτήρι για μπουκάλες.

bottom ['bɒtəm] n κάτω μέρος nt, βάθος nt || (of sea etc) πυθμένας, βυθός || (seat) πισινός, ποπός || (ship) πλοίο || κάτω μέρος nt, κάτω-κάτω || (lowest) κατώτατος || ~less a απύθμενος.

bough [baʊ] n κλάδος, κλαδί.

bought [bɔːt] pt, pp of buy.

boulder ['bəʊldə*] n λίθος, λιθάρι, ογκόλιθος.

bounce [baʊns] n (rebound) αναπήδηση, γκελ nt inv ♦ vi κάνω γκελ, αναπηδώ || (col: person) μπαίνω-βγαίνω ξαφνικά ♦ vt κάνω μπάλα να κάνει γκέλ.

bound [baʊnd] pt, pp of bind || n όριο, σύνορο || (restriction) όρια ntpl || (leap) πήδημα nt ♦ vi (spring, leap) πηδώ, σκιρτώ || (limit) περιορίζω ♦ a προσηλωμένος, για, κατευθυνόμενος προς.

boundary ['baʊndərɪ] n όριο, σύνορο.

bouquet ['bʊkeɪ] n μπουκέτο.

bout [baʊt] n (contest) γύρος, αγώνας, συνάντηση || (of illness) προσβολή.

bow [bəʊ] n (curve) καμπή || (ribbon) φιόγκος || (weapon) τόξο, δοξάρι || (MUS) δοξάρι βιολιού.

bow [baʊ] vi υποκλίνομαι, σκύβω το κεφάλι ♦ vt κλίνω, κάμπτω || (submit) υποκύπτω, υποτάσσομαι ♦ n υπόκλιση, κλίση (της κεφαλής) || (of ship) πλώρη.

bowels [baʊəlz] npl έντερα ntpl, σπλάχνα ntpl || (fig) σπλάχνα ntpl.

bowl [bəʊl] n (basin) λεκάνη, γαβάθα || (of pipe) λουλάς || (wooden ball) σφαίρα ♦ vti παίζω μπάλα, ρίχνω μπάλα || ~s npl παιχνίδι της μπάλας.

bow-legged ['bəʊlɛgɪd] a στραβοπόδης, στραβοκάνης.

bowler ['bəʊlə*] n παίκτης της μπάλας || (hat) μελόν nt.

bowling ['bəʊlɪŋ] n (game) παιχνίδι της μπάλας, μπόλιγκ nt inv.

bow tie ['bəʊ'taɪ] n παπιγιόν nt inv, πεταλούδα.

box [bɒks] n κιβώτιο || (small) κουτί || (THEAT) θεωρείο ♦ vt (s.o.'s ears) καρπαζώνω || (package) πακετάρω ♦ vi πυγμαχώ, παίζω μποξ || ~er n (person) πυγμάχος, μποξέρ m inv || (dog) μπόξερ m inv || ~ing n (SPORT) πυγμαχία, μποξ nt inv || ~ office n ταμείο (θεάτρου) || ~ room n αποθήκη οικίας.

boy [bɔɪ] n αγόρι, παιδί.

boycott ['bɔɪkɒt] n μπουκοτάρισμα ♦ vt αποκλείω, μπουϊκοτάρω.

boyfriend ['bɔɪfrɛnd] n φίλος, αγαπημένος.

boyish ['bɔɪɪʃ] a παιδιάστικος, αγορίστικος.

bra [brɑː] n σουτιέν nt inv, στηθόδεσμος.

brace [breɪs] n (clamp) δεσμός || (pair) ζευγάρι || (support) στύλωμα nt || (tool) ματικάπι ♦ vt συνδέω, στερεώνω || (o.s.) τονώνω, δυναμώνω || ~s npl τιράντες fpl.

bracelet ['breɪslɪt] n βραχιόλι.

bracing ['breɪsɪŋ] a τονωτικός.

bracken ['brækən] n φτέρη.

bracket ['brækɪt] n (support) υποστήριγμα nt, ωτίδα, κρεμάθρα || (round) παρένθεση || (square) αγκύλη || (group) ομάδα ♦ vt βάζω σε παρένθεση || (associate) συνδέω.

brag [bræg] vi καυχώμαι.

braid [breɪd] n (of hair) πλεξίδα, πλεξούδα || (officer's etc) σειρήτι, κορδόνι.

Braille [breɪl] n Μπράιλ nt inv.

brain [breɪn] n εγκέφαλος, μυαλό || (person) διάνοια || ~s npl μυαλά ntpl || ~**washing** n πλύση εγκεφάλου || ~**wave** n έμπνευση, επινόηση || ~**y** a ευφυής.

braise [breɪz] vt ψήνω στην κατσαρόλα.

brake [breɪk] n (on vehicle) τροχοπέδη, φρένο ♦ vti φρενάρω, πατώ φρένο.

bramble ['bræmbl] n βάτος.

branch [brɑːntʃ] n (of tree) κλάδος, κλαδί || (division) κλάδος || (office) υποκατάστημα nt ♦ vi διακλαδούμαι, χωρίζομαι.

brand [brænd] n (trademark) μάρκα || (on cattle) σφράγισμα με αναμμένο σίδηρο.

brand-new ['brænd'njuː] a κατακαίνουργιος, ολοκαίνουργιος, του κουτιού.

brandy ['brændɪ] n κονιάκ nt inv.

brash [bræʃ] a αναιδής, αδιάντροπος.

brass [brɑːs] n μπρούτζος || ~ **band** n μπάντα, φανφάρα.

brat [bræt] n κουτσούβελο, διαβολάκι.

bravado [brə'vɑːdəʊ] n παλληκαρισμός.

brave [breɪv] a γενναίος || (show) περίφημος ♦ n ερυθρόδερμος πολεμιστής ♦ vt αψηφώ || ~**ry** n θάρρος nt, ανδρεία.

brawl [brɔːl] n καυγάς ♦ vi καυγαδίζω.

brawn [brɔːn] n μυϊκή δύναμη, δύναμη || (COOKING) πηκτή.

brazen ['breɪzn] a (metal) μπρούτζινος || (shameless) αναιδής, ξετσίπωτος ♦ vt: to ~ it out καυχώμαι ξετσίπωτα.

brazier ['breɪzɪə*] n μαγκάλι, φουφού f inv.

Brazil [brə'zɪl] n Βραζιλία || ~**ian** a βραζιλιανός ♦ n Βραζιλιάνος/n m/f|| ~**nut** n Βραζιλιανό καρύδι.

breach [briːtʃ] n (gap) ρήγμα nt, τρύπα || (of trust, duty) παραβίαση, παράβαση || (quarrel) ρήξη, τσάκωμα nt ♦ vt γκρεμίζω.

bread [bred] n ψωμί || (living) καθημερινό ψωμί || ~ **and butter** n μέσα συντηρήσεως || ~**crumbs** npl ψίχουλα ntpl || ~**winner** n στήριγμα nt της οικογενείας.

break [breɪk] (irreg v) vt (crush) συντρίβω, τσακίζω || (apart) σπάω || (promise) αθετώ || (silence etc) διακόπτω || (habit) κόβω || (the law) παραβιάζω ♦ vi θραύομαι, τσακίζομαι || (friendship etc) τα χαλώ || (dissolve) διαλύομαι ♦ n (gap) ρήξη, άνοιγμα nt, χάσμα nt || (rest) διακοπή, διάλειμμα nt || (chance) ευκαιρία, τύχη || (fracture) ρωγμή || to ~

free or **loose** vi δραπετεύω, απελευθερώνομαι || to ~ **in** vt (a horse etc) δαμάζω || (conversation) διακόπτω ♦ vi (burglar) κάνω διάρρηξη || to ~ **out** vi ξεσπώ || (of prison) δραπετεύω || to ~ **up** vi διαλύομαι ♦ vt χωρίζω, συντρίβω, τεμαχίζω || ~**able** a εύθραυστος || ~**age** n σπάσιμο, ράγισμα nt || ~**down** n (in discussions) διακοπή || (of health) κατάρρευση || (mental) χάσιμο του μυαλού || ~**er** n (NAUT) κύμα nt.

breakfast ['brekfəst] n πρωινό, κολατσιό.

breakthrough ['breɪkθruː] n δίοδος f, ρήγμα nt.

breakwater ['breɪkwɔːtə*] n κυματοθραύστης.

breast [brest] n (of woman) μαστός, βυζί || (of man, animal) στήθος nt || ~**stroke** n απλωτή.

breath [breθ] n πνοή, αναπνοή || out of ~ λαχανιασμένος.

breathe [briːð] vti αναπνέω || ~**r** n ανάσα.

breathless ['breθlɪs] a λαχανιασμένος.

bred [bred] pt, pp of **breed**.

breed [briːd] (irreg v) n γενεά, ράτσα ♦ vt γεννώ, φέρνω || (animals) τρέφω ♦ vi αναπαράγομαι || ~**er** n (person) αναπαραγωγός m/f, κτηνοτρόφος m/f|| ~**ing** n ανατροφή.

breeze [briːz] n αύρα, αεράκι.

breezy ['briːzɪ] a ευάερος || (person) γεμάτος ζωή.

brevity ['brevɪtɪ] n βραχύτητα, συντομία.

brew [bruː] vt (drinks) παρασκευάζω (μπύρα) αποστάζω || (tea) βράζω || (plot) μηχανορραφώ ♦ vi βράζομαι || (storm etc) έρχεται || ~**ery** n ζυθοποιία, ποτοποιία.

bribe [braɪb] n δωροδοκία ♦ vt δωροδοκώ, λαδώνω || ~**ry** n δωροδοκία, μπούκωμα nt.

brick [brɪk] n πλίνθος, τούβλο || ~**layer** n τουβλάς || ~**work** n πλινθοδομή.

bridal ['braɪdl] a νυφικός, γαμήλιος.

bride [braɪd] n νύφη || ~**groom** n γαμπρός || ~**smaid** n παράνυφη.

bridge [brɪdʒ] n γεφύρι, γιοφύρι || (NAUT) γέφυρα || (CARDS) μπριτζ nt inv || (of nose) ράχη της μύτης ♦ vt γεφυρώνω.

bridle ['braɪdl] n χαλινάρι, γκέμι ♦ vt (a horse) χαλινώνω || (control) χαλιναγωγώ.

brief [briːf] a σύντομος, βραχύς ♦ n (LAW) δικογραφία, φάκελος ♦ vt δίδω οδηγίες, ενημερώνω || ~**s** npl κοντή κυλόττα || ~**case** n χαρτοφύλακας || ~**ing** n κατατόπισμα, οδηγίες fpl.

brigade [brɪ'geɪd] n (MIL) ταξιαρχία || see **fire**.

brigadier [brɪgə'dɪə*] n ταξίαρχος.

bright [braɪt] a (as light) φωτεινός, λαμπερός, γυαλιστερός || (weather) φωτεινός, καθαρός || (clever) έξυπνος, ευφυής || (colour) ζωηρός, λαμπρός ||

~ **en** *vti* ζωηρεύω, φωτίζομαι, αστράφτω.

brilliance ['brɪljəns] *n* λαμπρότητα, εξυπνάδα || *(of surface etc)* φωτεινότητα || *(of style)* ζωηρότητα.

brilliant ['brɪljənt] *a* φωτεινός, λαμπρός || *(person)* σπουδαίος, λαμπρός || *(splendid)* έξοχος.

brim [brɪm] *n (of cup)* χείλος *nt* || *(of hat)* γύρος, μπορ *nt inv* ♦ *vi* ξεχειλίζω || ~**ful** a ξέχειλος.

brine [braɪn] *n* σαλαμούρα, άρμη.

bring [brɪŋ] *(irreg v) vt* φέρω, φέρνω || **to ~ about** *vt* επιτυγχάνω, καταφέρνω || **to ~ off** *vt* φέρω σε πέρας || **to ~ round** *or* **to** *vt* επαναφέρω, συνεφέρω || **to ~ up** *vt (raise)* ανατρέφω, μεγαλώνω || *(introduce)* προβάλλω, θέτω.

brisk [brɪsk] *a* ζωηρός.

bristle ['brɪsl] *n* γουρουνότριχα ♦ *vi* ανατριχιάζω.

Britain ['brɪtən] *n* Βρεττανία.

British ['brɪtɪʃ] *a* βρετανικός, αγγλικός || **the ~** *npl* οι Άγγλοι *mpl* || ~ **Isles** *npl* Βρεττανικαί Νήσοι *fpl*.

Briton ['brɪtən] *n* Βρεττανός/ίδα *m/f*.

brittle ['brɪtl] *a* εύθραυστος.

broach [brəʊtʃ] *vt (subject)* θίγω (ζήτημα).

broad [brɔːd] *a* ευρύς, φαρδύς, πλατύς || *(daylight)* το φως της ημέρας || *(general)* απλό, γενικό || *(accent)* χωριάτικη προφορά || ~**cast** *n* εκπομπή ♦ *vti* μεταδίδω ραδιοφωνικώς || ~ **casting** *n* εκπομπή, μετάδοση || ~**en** *vt* ευρύνω, πλαταίνω ♦ *vi* ευρύνομαι, ανοίγω || ~**ly** *ad* ευρέως, πλατειά || ~-**minded** *a* με ανοικτό μυαλό, ανεκτικός, ευρείας αντιλήψεως.

broccoli ['brɒkəlɪ] *n* μπρόκολο.

brochure ['brəʊʃjʊə*] *n* φυλλάδιο, μπροσούρα.

broke [brəʊk] *pt of* **break** ♦ *a* απένταρος || ~**n** *pp of* **break** || ~**n-hearted** *a* με ραγισμένη καρδιά.

broker ['brəʊkə*] *n* μεσίτης, χρηματιστής.

bronchitis [brɒŋˈkaɪtɪs] *n* βρογχίτιδα.

bronze [brɒnz] *n* μπρούντζος || ~**d** *a* ηλιοψημένος, μαυρισμένος.

brooch [brəʊtʃ] *n* καρφίτσα.

brood [bruːd] *n* κλώσσισμα *nt*, γενιά ♦ *vi* κλωσσώ || *(meditate)* μελαγχολώ.

brook [brʊk] *n (stream)* ρυάκι, ρέμα *nt*.

broom [brʊm] *n* σκούπα || ~**stick** *n* σκουπόξυλο.

Bros. *(abbr of Brothers)* Αφοι (Αδελφοί *mpl)*.

broth [brɒθ] *n* ζουμί κρέατος, σούπα.

brothel ['brɒθl] *n* μπορντέλο, οίκος ανοχής.

brother ['brʌðə*] *n* αδελφός || ~-**in-law** *n* γαμπρός, κουνιάδος.

brought [brɔːt] *pt, pp of* **bring**.

brow [braʊ] *n (forehead)* κούτελο, μέτωπο || *(eyebrow)* φρύδι || *(of hill etc)* χείλος *nt*, φρύδι.

brown [braʊn] *a* καστανός, καφετής ♦ *n* καφετής ♦ *vti* σκουραίνω, μαυρίζω || *(cooking)* καβουρδίζω || ~**ie** *n (girl guide)* προσκοπίνα.

browse [braʊz] *vi (examine casually)* ξεφυλλίζω, βόσκω, τριγυρίζω.

bruise [bruːz] *n* μώλωπας, κτύπημα *nt* ♦ *vti* κτυπώ, κτυπιέμαι.

brunette [bruːˈnɛt] *n* μελαχροινή.

brunt [brʌnt] *n* ορμή, φόρα.

brush [brʌʃ] *n* βούρτσα || *(paint)* πινέλο || *(fight)* σύγκρουση ♦ *vt* βουρτσίζω || *(lightly)* ξεσκονίζω || **to ~ aside** *vt* παραμερίζω || ~-**wood** *n* θάμνοι *mpl*, χαμόκλαδα *ntpl*.

brusque [bruːsk] *a* απότομος, τραχύς.

Brussels sprout ['brʌslz'spraʊt] *n* (Βελγικό) λαχανάκι, πετί-πουά

brutal ['bruːtl] *a* κτηνώδης || ~**ity** *n* κτηνωδία.

brute [bruːt] *n* κτήνος *nt*, θηρίο.

B.Sc. *abbr see* **bachelor.**

bubble ['bʌbl] *n* μπουρμπουλήθρα, φουσκάλα ♦ *vi* κοχλάζω || *(river, wine)* αφρίζω || **to ~ over** *(fig)* ξεχειλίζω.

buck [bʌk] *n* ελάφι αρσενικό || *(rabbit)* κούνελος ♦ *vt* ενθαρρύνω, δίνω κουράγιο || **to ~ up** *vi* ενθαρρύνομαι, (ξανα) παίρνω κουράγιο.

bucket ['bʌkɪt] *n* κουβάς, κάδος.

buckle ['bʌkl] *n* πόρπη, φιούμπα ♦ *vt* κουμπώνω, θηλυκώνω || *(bend)* λυγίζω, στραβώνω.

bud [bʌd] *n* μπουμπούκι.

Buddhism ['bʊdɪzəm] *n* Βουδδισμός.

budding ['bʌdɪŋ] *a* που μπουμπουκιάζει.

buddy ['bʌdɪ] *n* φιλαράκος.

budge [bʌdʒ] *vti* κινούμαι, υποχωρώ.

budgerigar ['bʌdʒərɪga:*] *n* παπαγαλάκι.

budget ['bʌdʒɪt] *n* προϋπολογισμός.

buff [bʌf] *a (colour)* σαμουά, κρεατί.

buffalo ['bʌfələʊ] *n* βουβάλι.

buffer ['bʌfə*] *n* αποσβεστήρας, αμορτισέρ *nt inv*.

buffet ['bʌfɪt] *n* πλήγμα *nt*, κτύπημα *nt* || ['bʊfeɪ] *(bar)* αναψυκτήριο || *(food)* μπουφές *m inv* ♦ *vt* πλήττω, κτυπώ.

buffoon [bəˈfuːn] *n* παλιάτσος, καραγκιόζης.

bug [bʌg] *n (insect)* κοριός || *(US)* ζωύφιο || *(spy device)* κρυφό μικρόφωνο || *(COMPUT)* λάθος *nt*, σφάλμα *nt*.

bugle ['bjuːgl] *n* σάλπιγγα.

build [bɪld] *(irreg v) vt* οικοδομώ, χτίζω || ~**er** *n* οικοδόμος, κατασκευαστής || ~**ing** *n* κτίριο, οικοδομή || ~**ing society** *n* οικοδομικός συνεταιρισμός || ~-**up** *n* διαφήμιση.

built [bɪlt] *pt, pp of* **build** || **well-~** *a (person)* γεροδεμένος || ~-**in** *a (cupboard)* εντοιχισμένος.

bulb [bʌlb] *n (BOT)* βολβός || *(ELEC)* λάμπα, γλόμπος.

Bulgaria [bʌlˈgɛərɪə] *n* Βουλγαρία.

bulge [bʌldʒ] *n* διόγκωση, φούσκωμα *nt* ♦ *vti* προεξέχω, εξογκούμαι, φουσκώνω.

bulk [bʌlk] n μέγεθος nt, όγκος || (greater part) μεγαλύτερο μέρος nt || ~**head** n διάφραγμα nt || ~**y** a ογκώδης, χοντρός.

bull [bul] n ταύρος || (rubbish) ψέματα ntpl, αρλούμπες fpl || ~**dog** n μπουλντόγκ m inv.

bulldozer ['buldəuzə*] n μπουλντόζα.

bullet ['bulit] n σφαίρα, βόλι.

bulletin ['bulitin] n δελτίο, ανακοινωθέν nt.

bullfight ['bulfait] n ταυρομαχία.

bullion ['buljən] n χρυσός (άργυρος) σε ράβδους.

bullock ['bulək] n βόδι, μοσχάρι.

bull's-eye ['bulzai] n κέντρο (στόχου).

bully ['buli] n τύραννος ♦ vt απειλώ, τρομοκρατώ.

bum [bʌm] n (col) πιοινός || (tramp) αλήτης, ακαμάτης || **to** ~ **around** vi κοπροσκυλιάζω.

bump [bʌmp] n (blow) κτύπημα nt, τίναγμα nt || (bruise) πρήξιμο, καρούλα, καρούμπαλο ♦ vti κτυπώ, σκοντάφτω || ~**er** n (car) προφυλακτήρας ♦ a: ~**er harvest** πλούσια (σοδειά).

bumpy ['bʌmpi] a ανώμαλος (δρόμος).

bun [bʌn] n σταφιδόψωμο, κουλουράκι.

bunch [bʌntʃ] n μάτσο, φούχτα, χούφτα, δέμα nt.

bundle ['bʌndl] n δέμα nt, μπόγος ♦ vt πακετάρω, δένω || (also: ~ **off**) ξεφορτώνομαι.

bung [bʌŋ] n πώμα nt, τάπα ♦ vt (throw) ρίχνω, χώνω.

bungalow ['bʌŋgəlou] n μπάγκαλο, εξοχικό σπίτι.

bungle ['bʌŋgl] vt τα κάνω θάλασσα, είμαι αδέξιος.

bunion ['bʌnjən] n κάλος.

bunk [bʌŋk] n κλίνη, κουκέτα.

bunker ['bʌŋkə*] n αποθήκη καυσίμων, καρβουνιέρα.

bunny ['bʌni] n κουνελάκι.

bunting ['bʌntiŋ] n ύφασμα nt για σημαίες, σημαιοστολισμός.

buoy [bɔi] n (NAUT) σημαδούρα || (lifebuoy) σωσσίβιο || ~**ant** a (of person) εύθυμος, κεφάτος || **to** ~ **up** vt ενισχύω, αναθαρρύνω, ενθαρρύνω.

burden ['bɜːdn] n φόρτωμα nt, βάρος nt, δυσβάστακτο βάρος ♦ vt (επι)βαρύνω, φορτώνω.

bureau [bjuə'rəu] n γραφείο που κλείνει || (for information etc) υπηρεσία πληροφοριών.

bureaucracy [bjuə'rɒkrəsi] n γραφειοκρατία.

burglar ['bɜːglə*] n διαρρήκτης/τρια m/f || ~ **alarm** n κουδούνι ασφαλείας || ~**ize** vt (US) διαρρηγνύω || ~**y** n διάρρηξη.

burgle ['bɜːgl] vt διαρρηγνύω.

burial ['beriəl] n ταφή || ~ **ground** n νεκροταφείο.

burlesque [bɜː'lesk] n επιθεώρηση, μπυρλέσκ nt inv.

burly ['bɜːli] a γεροδεμένος.

burn [bɜːn] (irreg v) n έγκαυμα nt ♦ vt καίω ♦ vi φλέγομαι || **to** ~ **one's fingers** (fig) βρίσκω το μπελά μου || ~**ing question** n φλέγον ζήτημα nt.

burnt [bɜːnt] pt, pp of **burn** ♦ a καμένος, ψημένος.

burrow ['bʌrəu] n φωλιά, τρύπα, λαγούμι ♦ vti σκάβω λαγούμι, ανοίγω τρύπα.

burst [bɜːst] (irreg v) n έκρηξη, ριπή ♦ vt (explode) προκαλώ έκρηξη || (break) σπάζω || (break out) διαρρηγνύω, σπάω ♦ vi (tank etc) διαρρηγνύομαι, σπάζω || (flower) σκάζω, ανοίγω || (into pieces) γίνομαι κομμάτια.

bury ['beri] vt (inter) θάβω || (hide) κρύβομαι, χώνω, βυθίζομαι.

bus [bʌs] n λεωφορείο.

bush [buʃ] n θάμνος, χαμόκλαδο.

bushy ['buʃi] a δασύς, πυκνός.

busily ['bizili] ad δραστήρια.

business ['biznis] n επιχείρηση, δουλειά || (concern) δουλειά || ~**man** n επιχειρηματίας.

bus stop ['bʌsstɒp] n στάση λεωφορείου.

bust [bʌst] n (statue) προτομή, μπούστος || (of woman) στήθος nt.

bustle ['bʌsl] n (θορυβώδης) κίνηση, πάταγος ♦ vi πηγαινοέρχομαι, βιάζομαι.

busy ['bizi] a απασχολημένος, πολυάσχολος ♦ vt ασχολούμαι, φροντίζω || ~**body** n πολυπράγμονας, παπατρέχας.

but [bʌt] cj (still, yet, besides) αλλά, μα ♦ ad (only, except, as) μόνο, μόλις, δεν... παρά ♦ prep (except) εκτός, παρά.

butane ['bjuːtein] n βουτάνιο.

butcher ['butʃə*] n χασάπης || (savage) σφαγέας ♦ vt σφάζω.

butler ['bʌtlə*] n μπάτλερ m inv, αρχιυπηρέτης.

butt [bʌt] n (cask) βαρέλι, βουτσί || (target) στόχος || (of cigarette) αποτσίγαρο, γόπα || (thick end) χοντρό άκρο ♦ vt κτυπώ με το κεφάλι.

butter ['bʌtə*] n βούτυρο ♦ vt βουτυρώνω || **to** ~ **up** vt (fig) κολακεύω, ξεσκονίζω.

butterfly ['bʌtəflai] n πεταλούδα.

buttocks ['bʌtəks] npl γλουτοί mpl, τα οπίσθια ntpl.

button ['bʌtn] n κουμπί ♦ vti κουμπώνω || ~**hole** n κουμπότρυπα.

buttress ['bʌtris] n αντέρεισμα nt.

buy [bai] (irreg v) vt αγοράζω || **to** ~ **up** vt αγοράζω χονδρικώς || ~**er** n αγοραστής.

buzz [bʌz] n βούισμα nt ♦ vi βουίζω.

buzzard ['bʌzəd] n ικτίνος.

buzzer ['bʌzə*] n βομβητής, ψιθυριστής.

by [bai] prep (near, beside) παρά, πλάι, δίπλα, κοντά || (through) διά, από || (with) από, με || ~ **and large** κατά κανόνα || ~**far** κατά πολύ || ~ **name** κατ' όνομα.

by-election ['baiilekʃn] n αναπληρωματικές εκλογές fpl.

bygone ['baigɒn] a περασμένος, παλιός ♦ n: let ~s be ~s περασμένα, ξεχασμένα.

bypass ['baipɑːs] n (MECH) βοηθητική δίοδος.

byproduct ['baiprɒdʌkt] n υποπροϊόν.

bystander ['baistændə*] n παριστάμενος.

byte [bait] n (COMPUT) byte.

C

C. abbr of **centigrade**.

cab [kæb] n αμάξι, ταξί || (of train, truck) θέση οδηγού.

cabaret ['kæbərei] n καμπαρέ nt inv.

cabbage ['kæbidʒ] n λάχανο.

cabin ['kæbin] n καλύβα || (NAUT) καμπίνα || ~ **cruiser** n θαλαμηγός f χωρίς κατάρτια.

cabinet ['kæbinit] n κομό || (POL) υπουργικό συμβούλιο || ~**maker** n επιπλοποιός.

cable ['keibl] n καλώδιο || (message) τηλεγράφημα nt ♦ vti τηλεγραφώ || ~ **railway** n κρεμαστός σιδηρόδρομος.

cackle ['kækl] n κακάρισμα nt ♦ vi κακαρίζω.

cactus ['kæktəs] n κάκτος.

caddie, caddy ['kædi] n κάντι.

cadet [kə'det] n (NAUT) δόκιμος || (MIL) εύελπις || (AVIAT) ίκαρος.

cadge [kædʒ] vt ζητιανεύω, σελεμίζω.

Caesarean [siː'zɛəriən] a: ~ **(section)** καισαρική (τομή).

café ['kæfei] n καφενείο || (with food) καφεστιατόριο || (bar) καφεμπάρ nt inv.

cafeteria n [kæfi'tiəriə] n καφετηρία.

cage [keidʒ] n κλουβί ♦ vt εγκλουβίζω.

cagey ['keidʒi] a (col) πονηρός.

cajole [kə'dʒəul] vt καλοπιάνω.

cake [keik] n κέικ nt inv, γλύκισμα nt|| (pie) πίτα || (of soap etc) πλάκα.

calamity [kə'læmiti] n συμφορά, καταστροφή.

calcium ['kælsiəm] n ασβέστιο.

calculate ['kælkjuleit] vti υπολογίζω, λογαριάζω.

calculating ['kælkjuleitiŋ] a υπολογιστικός, εσκεμμένος.

calculation [kælkju'leiʃən] n υπολογισμός.

calculus ['kælkjuləs] n λογισμός.

calendar ['kæləndə*] n ημερολόγιο.

calf [kɑːf] n (cow) μοσχάρι || (skin) βιδέλο || (ANAT) κνήμη, γάμπα.

calibre, (US) caliber ['kælibə*] n διαμέτρημα nt || (fig) αξία ικανότητα.

call [kɔːl] vt καλώ, φωνάζω || (meeting) συγκαλώ || (TEL) κλήση, πρόσκληση ♦ vi (visit) επισκέπτομαι, έρχομαι ♦ n (shout) φωνή, κραυγή || (visit) επίσκεψη || ~**box** n τηλεφωνικός θάλαμος || ~**er** n (visitor) επισκέπτης/τρια m/f || ~ **girl** n κοκότα || ~**ing** n (profession) επάγγελμα nt || to ~ **for** vt καλώ, έρχομαι || to ~ **off** vt

ακυρώνω, σταματώ, διακόπτω || to ~ **on** vt (visit) επισκέπτομαι || to ~ **up** vt (MIL) (επι)στρατεύω || (TEL) (προς)καλώ, τηλεφωνώ.

callous ['kæləs] a σκληρός, άκαρδος.

calm [kɑːm] n αταραξία ♦ vti καθησυχάζω ♦ a ήρεμος, ατάραχος || ~**ness** n ηρεμία, κάλμα || to ~ **down** vi καταπραΰνω, καλμάρω ♦ vt ηρεμώ, καθησυχάζω.

calorie ['kæləri] n θερμίδα.

camber ['kæmbə*] n καμπυλότητα, κυρτότητα.

came [keim] pt of **come**.

camel ['kæməl] n καμήλα.

cameo ['kæmiəu] n καμέα.

camera ['kæmərə] n φωτογραφική μηχανή || ~**man** n οπερατέρ m inv.

camouflage ['kæməflɑːʒ] n καμουφλάρισμα nt ♦ vt καμουφλάρω.

camp [kæmp] n κατασκήνωση || (MIL.) στρατόπεδο ♦ vi κατασκηνώνω || (MIL) στρατοπεδεύω.

campaign [kæm'pein] n εκστρατεία ♦ vi (also fig) εκστρατεύω, κάνω καμπάνια.

campbed ['kæmp'bed] n κρεββάτι εκστρατείας, ράντσο.

camper ['kæmpə*] n σκηνίτης, εκδρομέας.

camping ['kæmpiŋ] n: to go ~ πηγαίνω σε κατασκήνωση.

campsite ['kæmpsait] n τόπος κατασκηνώσεως.

can [kæn] auxiliary v (be able) δύναμαι, μπορώ || (be allowed) επιτρέπεται, μπορώ || (know how) γνωρίζω, ξέρω ♦ n τενεκές m, κουτί ♦ vt κονσερβοποιώ.

Canada ['kænədə] n Καναδάς.

Canadian [kə'neidiən] a καναδικός ♦ n Καναδός/n m/f.

canal [kə'næl] n (waterway) διώρυγα, κανάλι || (ANAT) σωλήνας, πόρος.

canary [kə'nɛəri] n καναρίνι ♦ a καναρινί (χρώμα).

cancel ['kænsəl] vt (check etc) ακυρώνω || (strike out) διαγράφω || (MATH) εξαλείφω || ~**lation** n ακύρωση, ματαίωση.

cancer ['kænsə*] n καρκίνος.

candid ['kændid] a ειλικρινής.

candidate ['kændideit] n υποψήφιος/a m/f.

candle ['kændl] n κερί || ~**stick** n κηροπήγιο.

candour ['kændə*] n ευθύτητα, ντομπροσύνη.

candy ['kændi] n καραμέλα.

cane [kein] n (bamboo etc) καλάμι || (stick) μπαστούνι ♦ vt (beat) ραβδίζω.

canine ['kænain] a σκυλίσιος.

canister ['kænistə*] n τενεκεδάκι, κουτί.

cannabis ['kænəbis] n κάνναβη f.

canned ['kænd] a (food) κονσερβοποιημένος.

cannibal ['kænibəl] n κανίβαλος m/f, ανθρωποφάγος m/f || ~**ism** n ανθρωποφαγία.

cannon ['kænən] n (gun) πυροβόλο, κανόνι.

cannot ['kænɒt] = can not || see can.

canoe [kə'nuː] n μονόξυλο, κανό || ~ing n κανό.

canon ['kænən] n κανόνας || (criterion) κριτήριο || (clergyman) εφημέριος.

can opener ['kænəupnə*] n ανοιχτήρι.

canopy ['kænəpi] n σκιάδα, προστέγασμα nt.

can't [kænt] = can not || see can.

cantankerous [kæn'tæŋkərəs] a διεστραμμένος, καυγατζής.

canteen [kæn'tiːn] n (shop) καντίνα || (MIL) παγούρι.

canter ['kæntə*] n τριποδισμός ♦ vi καλπάζω ελαφρά.

canvas ['kænvəs] n κανναβάτσο || (NAUT) πανιά ntpl || (ART) μουσαμάς || under ~ σε σκηνές.

canvass ['kænvəs] vt (election) ψηφοθηρώ || (discuss) συζητώ, ερευνώ.

canyon ['kænjən] n φαράγγι, χαράδρα.

cap [kæp] n (hat) σκούφος, τραγιάσκα || (top) κάλυμμα nt ♦ vt στέφω, στεφανώνω || (bottle etc) πωματίζω, σφραγίζω || (outdo) υπερβάλλω.

capability [keipə'biləti] n ικανότητα.

capable ['keipəbl] a ικανός || ~ of ικανός να.

capacity [kə'pæsiti] n (space) χωρητικότητα || (ability) ικανότητα || (position) ιδιότητα.

cape [keip] n (garment) κάπα, μπελερίνα || (GEOG) ακρωτήρι.

capital ['kæpitl] n (city) πρωτεύουσα || (ECON) κεφάλαιο || (letter) κεφαλαίο γράμμα || ~ism n καπιταλισμός, κεφαλαιοκρατία || ~ist a καπιταλιστής || ~ punishment n θανατική ποινή.

capitulate [kə'pitjuleit] vi συνθηκολογώ.

capitulation [kəpitju'leiʃən] n συνθηκολόγηση.

capricious [kə'priʃəs] a ιδιότροπος, ασταθής.

capsize [kæp'saiz] vti ανατρέπω, μπατάρω.

capstan ['kæpstən] n εργάτης.

capsule ['kæpsjuːl] n (ANAT) κάψα || (MED) καψούλια.

captain ['kæptin] n (leader) αρχηγός || (MIL) λοχαγός || (NAUT) πλοίαρχος ♦ vt οδηγώ, διευθύνω.

caption ['kæpʃən] n επικεφαλίδα || (of picture) λεζάντα.

captivate ['kæptiveit] vt γοητεύω, σαγηνεύω, δελεάζω.

captive ['kæptiv] n, a αιχμάλωτος.

captivity [kæp'tiviti] n αιχμαλωσία.

capture ['kæptʃə*] vt συλλαμβάνω, αιχμαλωτίζω || (fort etc) κυριεύω ♦ n σύλληψη || (objective) κατάληψη.

car [kaː*] n (motor) αυτοκίνητο, αμάξι || (railway) βαγόνι.

carafe [kə'ræf] n καράφα.

caramel ['kærəməl] n καραμέλα.

carat ['kærət] n καράτι.

caravan ['kærəvæn] n καραβάνι || (house on wheels) τροχόσπιτο.

caraway ['kærəwei]: ~ seed n κύμινο.

carbon ['kaːbən] n άνθρακας || (paper) καρμπό nt inv || ~ copy n καρμπό nt inv || ~ ribbon n ταινία καρμπόν.

carburettor [kaːbju'retə*] n καρμπυρατέρ nt inv.

carcass ['kaːkəs] n πτώμα nt, κουφάρι, ψοφίμι.

card [kaːd] n (playing) τραπουλόχαρτο || (visiting) επικεπτήριο || (general) δελτάριο || ~board n χαρτόνι || ~ game n χαρτοπαιξία.

cardiac ['kaːdiæk] a καρδιακός.

cardigan ['kaːdigən] n πλεκτή ζακέτα.

cardinal ['kaːdinl] a: ~ number απόλυτος αριθμός.

care [kɛə*] n (worry, attention) φροντίδα, μέριμνα, προσοχή ♦ vi φροντίζω, με νοιάζει || ~ of (abbr c/o) φροντίδι του || to ~ about vt με ενδιαφέρει, με νοιάζει || to take ~ προσέχω || to take ~ of vt ενδιαφέρομαι για, φροντίζω για || to ~ for vt ενδιαφέρομαι || (love) αγαπώ, αρέσω.

career [kə'riə*] n σταδιοδρομία, καριέρα ♦ vi τρέχω, ορμώ.

carefree ['kɛəfriː] a αμέριμνος, ξένοιαστος.

careful ['kɛəful] a προσεκτικός, επιμελής || ~ly ad προσεκτικά.

careless ['kɛəlis] a απρόσεκτος, απερίσκεπτος || ~ness n απροσεξία, αμέλεια.

caress [kə'rɛs] n θωπεία, χάδι ♦ vt θωπεύω, χαϊδεύω.

caretaker ['kɛəteikə*] n επιστάτης.

car-ferry ['kaːfɛri] n πορθμείο οχημάτων, φέρρυ-μποτ nt inv.

cargo ['kaːgəu] n φορτίο.

caricature ['kærikətjuə*] n γελοιογραφία, καρικατούρα.

carnation [kaː'neiʃən] n γαρύφαλλο.

carnival ['kaːnivəl] n (public celebration) αποκριές fpl, καρναβάλι.

carol ['kærəl] n (Christmas) κάλαντα ntpl.

carp [kaːp] n (fish) κυπρίνος, σαζάνι || to ~ at vt επικρίνω, κατσαδιάζω, αντιλέγω.

car park ['kaːpaːk] n χώρος παρκαρίσματος.

carpenter ['kaːpintə*] n μαραγκός.

carpentry ['kaːpintri] n ξυλουργική.

carpet ['kaːpit] n τάπης, χαλί ♦ vt στρώνω με χαλί.

carriage ['kæridʒ] n (vehicle) άμαξα, όχημα nt || (carrying) μεταφορά || (fees) μεταφορικά ntpl || (bearing) συμπεριφορά, ύφος nt || ~ return n επαναφορά κυλίνδρου || ~way n (part of road) αμαξιτή οδός.

carrier ['kæriə*] n (μετα)φορέας, κομιστής || ~-bag n μεγάλη χαρτοσακκούλα.

carrot ['kærət] n καρότο.

carry ['kæri] vt (transport, hold)

(μετα)φέρω, βαστάζω, κουβαλώ ||
(responsibility) έχω ευθύνες || **to be**
carried away *(fig)* παρασύρομαι || **to ~**
on *vti* συνεχίζω, επιμένω || **to ~ out** *vt*
(orders) εκτελώ.

cart [kɑːt] *n* κάρο ♦ *vt* μεταφέρω με
κάρο.

cartilage ['kɑːtɪlɪdʒ] *n* χόνδρος,
τραγανό.

carton ['kɑːtən] *n* κουτί από χαρτόνι.

cartoon [kɑːˈtuːn] *n* *(PRESS)*
γελοιογραφία, σκίτσο || *(CINE)*
κινούμενες εικόνες *fpl*, μίκυ-μάους *nt inv*.

cartridge ['kɑːtrɪdʒ] *n* *(for gun)* φυσίγγι,
φυσέκι.

carve [kɑːv] *vti* σκαλίζω, χαράσσω,
κόβω.

carving ['kɑːvɪŋ] *n* *(in wood etc)* γλυπτική,
σκάλισμα *nt* || **~ knife** *n* μαχαίρι για
κόψιμο.

car wash ['kɑːwɒʃ] *n* πλύσιμο
αυτοκινήτου.

cascade [kæsˈkeɪd] *n* καταρράκτης.

case [keɪs] *n* *(box)* θήκη, κιβώτιο, κασόνι ||
(instance) περίπτωση || *(state)* κατάσταση,
ζήτημα *nt* || *(GRAM)* πτώση || *(LAW)*
υπόθεση || **in ~** σε περίπτωση που || **in**
any ~ εν πάσει περιπτώσει.

cash [kæʃ] *n* μετρητά (χρήματα) *ntpl* ♦ *vt*
εξαργυρώνω || **~ desk** *n* ταμείο.

cashier [kæˈʃɪə] *n* ταμίας, κασιέρης.

cashmere [kæʃˈmɪə*] *n* κασμήρι.

cash register ['kæʃˈredʒɪstə*] *n*
μηχανή ταμείου, ταμειακή μηχανή.

casing ['keɪsɪŋ] *n* περίβλημα *nt*, πλαίσιο,
θήκη.

casino [kəˈsiːnəʊ] *n* καζίνο.

cask [kɑːsk] *n* βαρέλι.

casket ['kɑːskɪt] *n* *(box)* κουτί, κασετίνα
|| *(US)* φέρετρο.

casserole ['kæsərəʊl] *n* *(pot)* τσουκάλι,
νταβάς || *(meal)* γιουβέτσι.

cassock ['kæsɒk] *n* ράσο.

cast [kɑːst] *(irreg v)* *vt* *(throw)* ρίχνω, πετώ
|| *(shed)* βγάζω, απορρίπτω || *(THEAT)*
διανέμω ρόλους, αναθέτω ρόλο || *(metal)*
χύνω, καλουπώνω ♦ *n* *(THEAT)* θίασος ||
to ~ off *vti* βγάζω || *(NAUT)* απονλέω.

caste [kɑːst] *n* κοινωνική τάξη, κάστα.

cast iron ['kɑːstˈaɪən] *n* χυτοσίδηρος.

castle ['kɑːsl] *n* *(fortress)* φρούριο ||
(mansion) πύργος.

castor ['kɑːstə*] *n* *(wheel)* καρούλι, ρόδα
|| **~ oil** *n* ρετσινόλαδο || **~ sugar** *n* ψιλή
ζάχαρη.

castrate [kæsˈtreɪt] *vt* μουνουχίζω.

casual ['kæʒjʊl] *a* *(occasional)* τυχαία ||
(work, attitude) τυχαίος, απερίσκεπτος ||
(meeting) τυχαίος || **~ly** *ad* αδιάφορα.

casualty ['kæʒjʊltɪ] *n* τραυματίας.

cat [kæt] *n* γάτα.

catalogue, *(US)* **catalog** ['kætəlɒg] *n*
κατάλογος ♦ *vt* εγγράφω σε κατάλογο.

catalyst ['kætəlɪst] *n* καταλύτης.

catapult ['kætəpʌlt] *n* καταπέλτης.

cataract ['kætərækt] *n* *(waterfall)*
καταρράκτης || *(MED)* καταρράκτης.

catarrh [kəˈtɑː*] *n* κατάρρους *m*.

catastrophe [kəˈtæstrəfɪ] *n*
καταστροφή, συμφορά.

catch [kætʃ] *(irreg v)* *n* *(for window etc)*
δόντι, μπετούγια, ασφάλεια || *(SPORT,*
breath) πιάσιμο || *(fish)* πιάνω (πολλά
ψάρια) || *(HUNT)* θήραμα *nt* || *vt* *(seize)*
πιάνω, αρπάζω || *(surprise)* συλλαμβάνω ||
(in time) (προ)φθάνω, πιάνω στα πράσα ||
to ~ a cold αρπάζω κρύο.

catching ['kætʃɪŋ] *a* *(MED)* μεταδοτικός,
κολλητικός.

catch phrase ['kætʃfreɪz] *n* σύνθημα *nt*.

catchy ['kætʃɪ] *a* *(tune)* ελκυστικός.

categorical [kætɪˈgɒrɪkəl] *a*
κατηγορηματικός.

category ['kætɪgərɪ] *n* κατηγορία, τάξη.

cater ['keɪtə*] *vi* *(food)* τροφοδοτώ,
σερβίρω || ~ **ing** n τροφοδότηση,
τροφοδοσία || **to ~ for** *(fig)* φροντίζω,
ικανοποιώ.

caterpillar ['kætəpɪlə*] *n* κάμπια.

cathedral [kəˈθiːdrəl] *n* καθεδρικός
ναός, μητρόπολη.

catholic ['kæθəlɪk] *a* καθολικός,
παγκόσμιος, ευρύς || **C~** *n* καθολικός/η
m/f ♦ *a* *(REL)* καθολικός.

cattle ['kætl] *npl* κτήνη *ntpl*, ζώα *ntpl*.

catty ['kætɪ] *a* δηκτικός, πονηρός.

cauliflower ['kɒlɪflaʊə*] *n* κουνουπίδι.

cause [kɔːz] *n* *(reason)* αιτία, αφορμή,
λόγος || *(object)* υπόθεση, χάρη ♦ *vt*
προξενώ, κάνω να.

causeway ['kɔːzweɪ] *n* υψωμένος
δρόμος.

caustic ['kɔːstɪk] *a* *(burning)* καυστικός ||
(sarcastic) σαρκαστικός.

caution ['kɔːʃən] *n* *(care)* προσοχή ||
(warning) προειδοποίηση ♦ *vt*
προειδοποιώ.

cautious ['kɔːʃəs] *a* προσεκτικός.

cavalry ['kævəlrɪ] *npl* ιππικό.

cave [keɪv] *n* σπηλιά || **~man** *n*
τρωγλοδύτης ♦ **to ~ in** *vi* καταρρέω,
σωριάζομαι.

cavern ['kævən] *n* σπηλιά.

caviar(e) ['kævɪɑː*] *n* χαβιάρι.

cavity ['kævɪtɪ] *n* κοίλωμα *nt*, τρύπα.

C.B.I. *abbr of Confederation of British*
Industry Συνομοσπονδία Βρεττανών
Βιομηχάνων.

cc *abbr of cubic centimetres; carbon copy.*

cease [siːs] *vti* παύω, σταματώ, τελειώνω
|| **~fire** *n* ανακωχή || **~less** *a*
ακατάπαυστος, αδιάκοπος.

cedar ['siːdə*] *n* κέδρος.

ceiling ['siːlɪŋ] *n* ταβάνι || *(fig)* ανώτατο
ύψος.

celebrate ['selɪbreɪt] *vt* γιορτάζω ||
(wedding etc) τελώ || **~d** *a* διάσημος.

celebration [selɪˈbreɪʃən] *n* γιορτασμός,
τελετή.

celebrity [sɪˈlebrɪtɪ] *n* *(person)*
διασημότητα.

celery ['selərɪ] *n* σέλινο.

celestial [sɪˈlestɪəl] *a* ουράνιος.

cell [sel] *n* *(in monastery)* κελλί || *(in jail)*

φυλακή || (ELEC) στοιχείο || (BIOL) κύτταρο.

cellar ['sɛlə*] n υπόγειο, κελλάρι || (wine) κάβα.

cello ['tʃɛləʊ] n βιολοντσέλο.

cellophane ['sɛləfeɪn] n (R) σελοφάν nt inv.

cellular ['sɛljʊlə*] a κυτταρικός, κυψελοειδής.

cellulose ['sɛljʊləʊs] n κελλουλόζη, κυτταρίνη.

cement [sə'mɛnt] n τσιμέντο ♦ vt (lit) συγκολλώ με τσιμέντο || (fig) στερεώνω, κατοχυρώνω.

cemetery ['sɛmɪtrɪ] n νεκροταφείο.

cenotaph ['sɛnətɑːf] n κενοτάφιο.

censer ['sɛnsə*] n θυμιατήρι, λιβανιστήρι.

censor ['sɛnsə*] n λογοκριτής, ελεγκτής || ~ship n λογοκρισία.

censure ['sɛnʃə*] vt επικρίνω, ψέγω.

census ['sɛnsəs] n απογραφή.

cent [sɛnt] n αέντ || (col) πεντάρα.

centenary [sɛn'tiːnərɪ] n εκατονταετηρίδα.

center ['sɛntə*] n (US) = **centre**.

centigrade ['sɛntɪgreɪd] a εκατονταβάθμιος.

centilitre, (US) **centiliter** ['sɛntɪliːtə*] n εκατοστόλιτρο.

centimetre, (US) **centimeter** ['sɛntɪmiːtə*] n εκατοστόμετρο.

centipede ['sɛntɪpiːd] n σαρανταποδαρούσα.

central ['sɛntrəl] a κεντρικός || ~ **heating** n κεντρική θέρμανση || ~**ize** vt συγκεντρώνω || ~ **processing unit (CPU)** (COMPUT) κεντρική μονάδα επεξεργασίας (ΚΜΕ).

centre ['sɛntə*] n κέντρο.

century ['sɛntjʊrɪ] n αιώνας.

ceramic [sɪ'ræmɪk] a κεραμικός.

cereal ['sɪərɪəl] n (any grain) δημητριακά ntpl, σιτηρά ntpl.

ceremony ['sɛrɪmənɪ] n εθιμοτυπία (religious) τελετή.

certain ['sɜːtən] a (sure) βέβαιος, σίγουρος, ασφαλής || (some, one) ωρισμένος, κάποιος || **for** ~ σίγουρα || ~**ly** ad ασφαλώς, σίγουρα || ~**ty** n βεβαιότητα, σιγουριά.

certificate [sə'tɪfɪkɪt] n πιστοποιητικό, βεβαίωση.

certify ['sɜːtɪfaɪ] vti πιστοποιώ, βεβαιώ, κυρώνω.

cf. abbr = compare.

chafe [tʃeɪf] vti τρίβω, ερεθίζομαι, φθείρομαι.

chaffinch ['tʃæfɪntʃ] n σπίνος.

chain [tʃeɪn] n αλυσίδα, καδένα || (mountains) σειρά ♦ vt (also: ~ **up**) δένω με αλυσίδα, δεσμεύω || ~ **reaction** n αλυσωτή αντίδραση || ~ **store** n υποκατάστημα nt.

chair [tʃɛə*] n καρέκλα || (UNIV etc) έδρα ♦ vt (preside) προεδρεύω || ~**man** n πρόεδρος || (director) διευθυντής.

chalet ['ʃæleɪ] n σαλέ nt inv.

chalice ['tʃælɪs] n δισκοπότηρο.

chalk [tʃɔːk] n (GEOL) ασβεστόλιθος || (crayon) κιμωλία.

challenge ['tʃælɪndʒ] n πρόκληση ♦ vt προκαλώ || (dispute) αμφισβητώ || ~**r** n διεκδικητής.

challenging ['tʃælɪndʒɪŋ] a προκλητικός.

chamber ['tʃeɪmbə*] n (compartment) δωμάτιο || (of gun etc) θαλάμη (όπλου) || ~ **of commerce** n Εμπορικό Επιμελητήριο || ~**maid** n καμαριέρα || ~ **music** n μουσική δωματίου.

chamois ['ʃæmwɑː] n: ~ **leather** n σαμουά nt inv.

champagne [ʃæm'peɪn] n σαμπάνια.

champion ['tʃæmpɪən] n (SPORT) πρωταθλητής/τρια m/f || (of cause) πρόμαχος || ~**ship** n πρωτάθλημα nt.

chance [tʃɑːns] n (opportunity) ευκαιρία || (possibility) ελπίδα, πιθανότητα ♦ a τυχαίος ♦ vt: **to** ~ **it** διακινδυνεύω, παίζω στην τύχη || **to take a** ~ δοκιμάζω.

chancel ['tʃɑːnsəl] n ιερό (ναού).

chancellor ['tʃɑːnsələ*] n (UNIV) πρύτανης m || **C**~ **of the Exchequer** n Υπουργός Οικονομικών.

chandelier [ʃændə'lɪə*] n πολύφωτο, πολυέλαιος.

change [tʃeɪndʒ] vt αλλάζω, τροποποιώ || (exchange) ανταλλάσσω || (trains) αλλάζω ♦ vi αλλάζω, μεταβάλλομαι ♦ n (alteration) αλλαγή, μεταβολή || (coins) ψιλά ntpl || (balance) ρέστα ntpl || ~**able** a (weather) άστατος || ~**over** n (to new system) αλλαγή συστήματος.

changing ['tʃeɪndʒɪŋ] a ευμετάβλητος, αλλάζων || ~-**room** n (in shop) βεστιάριο.

channel ['tʃænl] n (of stream) κοίτη || (of bay etc) δίαυλος, μπούκα || (strait) πορθμός, στενό || (of communication) οδός f, δρόμος || (RAD etc) ζώνη συχνοτήτων || (TV) κανάλι ♦ vt αυλακώνω || **the (English) C**~ n Μάγχη || **C**~ **Islands** npl νησιά της Μάγχης.

chant [tʃɑːnt] n τραγούδι || (church) ψαλμός ♦ vt τραγουδώ || (church) ψάλλω.

chaos ['keɪɒs] n χάος nt.

chap [tʃæp] n ρωγμή, σκάσιμο, τύπος ♦ vt (skin) σκάζω από το κρύο.

chapel ['tʃæpəl] n παρεκκλήσι.

chaperon ['ʃæpərəʊn] n συνοδός κοριτσιού ♦ vt συνοδεύω.

chaplain ['tʃæplɪn] n εφημέριος.

chapter ['tʃæptə*] n (of book) κεφάλαιο.

char [tʃɑː*] vt (burn) μαυρίζω με κάψιμο ♦ n (cleaner) παραδουλεύτρα.

character ['kærɪktə*] n (qualities) χαρακτήρας || (LITER, THEAT etc) πρόσωπο, χαρακτήρας || (peculiar person) τύπος, χαρακτήρας || (letter, sign, COMPUT) χαρακτήρας, στοιχείο, γράμμα || ~**s per second (c.p.s.)** χαρακτήρες mpl ανά δευτερόλεπτο (χ.α.δ.) || ~**istic** a χαρακτηριστικός ♦ n χαρακτηριστικό γνώρισμα nt.

charade [ʃə'rɑːd] n συλλαβόγριφος, φαρσα.

charcoal ['tʃɑːkəul] n ξυλοκάρβουνο.

charge [tʃɑːdʒ] n (price) τίμημα nt, τιμή || (accusation) κατηγορία || (load for gun) γόμωση || (attack) έφοδος f, προσβολή ♦ vt (fill, load) γεμίζω, φορτίζω || (a price) ζητώ (τιμή), χρεώνω || (a battery) επιφορτίζω || (attack) εφορμώ || (accuse) κατηγορώ ♦ vi επιπίπτω, προσβάλλω || in ~ of φροντίζω, που φροντίζει || to take ~ αναλαμβάνω, είμαι υπεύθυνος.

charitable ['tʃærɪtəbl] a φιλάνθρωπος, ελεήμονας.

charity ['tʃærɪtɪ] n (institution) φιλανθρωπικό ίδρυμα || αγαθοεργία.

charlady ['tʃɑːleɪdɪ] n παραδουλεύτρα.

charm [tʃɑːm] n (attractiveness) γοητεία || (for luck) φυλαχτό ♦ vt μαγεύω, γοητεύω || ~ing a γοητευτικός.

chart [tʃɑːt] n (of information) γραφική παράσταση, διάγραμμα nt || (NAUT) χάρτης.

charter ['tʃɑːtə*] vt ναυλώνω ♦ n καταστατικός χάρτης || ~ flight n ναυλωμένη πτήση || ~ed accountant n λογιστής.

charwoman ['tʃɑːwumən] n = charlady.

chase [tʃeɪs] vt (run after) κυνηγώ, (κατα)-διώκω ♦ n (act of chasing) κυνήγι, καταδίωξη.

chasm ['kæzəm] n χάσμα nt, κενό.

chassis ['ʃæsɪ] n σασσί nt inv.

chastity ['tʃæstɪtɪ] n αγνότητα, παρθενία.

chat [tʃæt] vi κουβεντιάζω ♦ n (friendly, casual talk) φιλική κουβεντούλα.

chatter ['tʃætə*] vi φλυαρώ || (of teeth) τρέμω, κτυπώ ♦ n φλυαρία, τερετισμός || ~box n (esp child) φλύαρος.

chatty ['tʃætɪ] a (style) ομιλητικός, πολυλογάς.

chauffeur ['ʃəufə*] n οδηγός, σωφέρ m inv.

cheap [tʃiːp] a (joke) άνοστο (αστείο) || (poor quality) φτηνός, πρόστυχος, μικρής αξίας || ~en vt (person) υποτιμώ, ξευτελίζω || ~ly ad φτηνά.

cheat [tʃiːt] vti (εξ)απατώ, κοροϊδεύω ♦ n αγύρτης, κατεργάρης || ~ing n (at cards) κλέψιμο || (general) παγανοντιά.

check [tʃek] vt (examine) ελέγχω || (halt) σταματώ, αναχαιτίζω ♦ n (examination) έλεγχος, επαλήθευση || (restraint) περιορισμός || (restaurant bill) λογαριασμός || (pattern) καρρώ nt inv || (US) = **cheque** || ~ers npl (US) ντάμα || ~mate n ματ nt inv || ~point n σημείο ελέγχου || ~up n (MED) γενική εξέταση.

cheek [tʃiːk] n παρειά, μάγουλο || (impudence) αναίδεια || ~bone n μήλο (παρειάς) || ~y a αναιδής.

cheer [tʃɪə*] n (joy) ευθυμία || (shout) ζητωκραυγή ♦ vt (shout) επευφημώ,

ζητωκραυγάζω || (comfort) χαροποιώ || (encourage) ενθαρρύνω ♦ vi: to ~ up κάνω κέφι || **good** ~ n φαγητά ntpl || ~**ful** a χαρωπός καλόκεφος || ~**fulness** n ευθυμία || (of fireplace etc) ζεστασιά || ~**ing** n ζητοκραυγές fpl, χειροκροτήματα ntpl ♦ a ενθαρρυντικός, προκαλών το κέφι || ~**io** interj (in departure) γεια χαρά || (greeting) γεια σου || ~**less** a μελαγχολικός, κακόκεφος.

cheese [tʃiːz] n τυρί.

chef [ʃef] n αρχιμάγειρας.

chemical ['kemɪkəl] a χημικός.

chemist ['kemɪst] n (MED) φαρμακοποιός m/f || (scientist) χημικός m/f || ~**ry** n χημεία || ~**'s (shop)** n φαρμακείο.

cheque [tʃek] n επιταγή || ~ **book** n βιβλιάριο επιταγών.

chequered ['tʃekəd] a (fig) περιπετειώδης.

cherish ['tʃerɪʃ] vt (a hope) τρέφω || (love) λατρεύω || (look after) περιποιούμαι.

cherry ['tʃerɪ] n (tree) κερασιά || (fruit) κεράσι.

chess [tʃes] n σκάκι || ~**board** n σκακιέρα || ~**man** n πιόνι, πεσσός.

chest [tʃest] n (ANAT) στήθος nt || (box) κιβώτιο, μπαούλο || **to get sth off one's** ~ ξελαφρώνω || ~ **of drawers** n σιφονιέρα, κομό.

chestnut ['tʃesnʌt] n κάστανο || ~ **(tree)** n καστανιά.

chew [tʃuː] vti μασώ || ~**ing gum** n τσίχλα.

chic [ʃiːk] a κομψός, σικ.

chick [tʃɪk] n πουλάκι.

chicken ['tʃɪkɪn] n (bird, food) κοτόπουλο.

chickenpox ['tʃɪkɪnpɒks] n ανεμοβλογιά.

chicory ['tʃɪkərɪ] n κιχώρι, αντίδι.

chief [tʃiːf] n αρχηγός m/f, διευθυντής/διευθύντρια m/f ♦ a κύριος, πρωτεύων, πρώτος || ~**ly** ad κυρίως, προπάντων.

chilblain ['tʃɪlbleɪn] n χιονίστρα.

child [tʃaɪld] n παιδί || ~**birth** n τοκετός, γέννα || ~**hood** n παιδικά χρόνια ntpl || ~**ish** a παιδαριώδης, παιδιάστικος || ~**like** a αφελής, παιδιάστικος || ~**ren** ['tʃɪldrən] npl of child παιδιά, παιδάκια ntpl.

chill [tʃɪl] n (coldness) ψυχρότητα, κρυάδα || (cold) κρυολόγημα nt ♦ a ψυχρός κρύος || ~**y** a ψυχρός, κρύος.

chime [tʃaɪm] n κωδωνοκρουσία ♦ vi ηχώ αρμονικά.

chimney ['tʃɪmnɪ] n καπνοδόχος f, καμινάδα.

chimpanzee [tʃɪmpæn'ziː] n χιμπαντζής.

chin [tʃɪn] n πηγούνι.

china ['tʃaɪnə] n πορσελάνη || (dishes, cups) πιάτα ntpl.

China ['tʃaɪnə] n Κίνα.

Chinese ['tʃaɪ'niːz] a κινέζικος ♦ n

(person) Κινέζος/α m/f|| *(language)*
κινεζική.
chink [tʃɪŋk] n *(opening)* ρωγμή, σκάσιμο ||
(noise) ήχος (μετάλλου κτλ).
chip [tʃɪp] n απόκομμα nt, θρύμμα nt ♦ vt
θραύω, θρυμματίζω, αποκόπτω || to ~
in vi *(CARDS)* ποντάρω || *(interrupt)*
παρεμβαίνω || συνεισφέρω.
chiropodist [kɪˈrɒpədɪst] n
πεντικιουρίστας.
chirp [tʃəːp] n τερετισμός, τιτίβισμα nt,
κελάδημα nt ♦ vi τερετίζω, τιτιβίζω,
κελαϊδώ.
chisel [ˈtʃɪzl] n σμίλη.
chit [tʃɪt] n σημείωμα nt, γραπτή άδεια.
chitchat [ˈtʃɪttʃæt] n κουβέντα.
chloride [ˈklɔːraɪd] n χλωρίδιο.
chlorine [ˈklɔːriːn] n χλώριο.
chloroform [ˈklɒrəfɔːm] n
χλωροφόρμιο.
chock [tʃɒk] n μόρσος, τάκος.
chocolate [ˈtʃɒklɪt] n σοκολάτα.
choice [tʃɔɪs] n εκλογή, προτίμηση ||
(variety) ποικιλία ♦ a εκλεκτός.
choir [ˈkwaɪə*] n χορός || ~boy n παιδί
χορωδίας.
choke [tʃəʊk] vi *(be unable to breathe)*
πνίγομαι ♦ vt *(stop breathing of)*
ασφυκτιώ, στραγγαλίζω || *(block)*
εμφράσσω ♦ n *(AUT)* διαχύτης,
εμφράκτης.
cholera [ˈkɒlərə] n χολέρα.
choose [tʃuːz] *(irreg v)* vt διαλέγω,
προτιμώ || *(decide)* αρέσω, προτιμώ.
chop [tʃɒp] vt *(cut with a blow)* κόβω,
αποκόβω || *(into pieces)* κατακόβω,
διαμελίζω, λιανίζω ♦ vi: to ~ and
change πωλώ και αγοράζω ♦ n *(blow)*
κτύπημα nt|| *(meat)* μπριζολάκι || ~py a
ταραγμένος, κυματώδης || ~sticks npl
ξυλαράκια ntpl *(για το πιλάφι)*, κινέζικο
πιρούνι.
choral [ˈkɔːrəl] a χορικός.
chord [kɔːd] n χορδή.
chore [tʃɔə*] n βαρετή δουλειά.
choreographer [kɒrɪˈɒɡrəfə*] n
χορογράφος m/f.
chortle [ˈtʃɔːtl] vi καγχάζω, κακαρίζω.
chorus [ˈkɔːrəs] n *(choir etc)* χορός,
χορωδία || *(many voices)* τραγούδι εν
χορώ || ~ of praise n *(fig)* συναυλία
επαίνων.
chose [tʃəʊz] pt of choose.
chosen [ˈtʃəʊzn] pp of choose.
Christ [kraɪst] n Χριστός.
christen [ˈkrɪsn] vt βαπτίζω || ~ing n
βάπτισμα nt.
Christian [ˈkrɪstɪən] n Χριστιανός/n m/f
♦ a χριστιανικό || ~ name n όνομα nt||
~ity n χριστιανισμός.
Christmas [ˈkrɪsməs] n Χριστούγεννα
ntpl|| ~ card n χριστουγεννιάτικη
κάρτα.
chrome [krəʊm] n επιχρωμίωση.
chromium [ˈkrəʊmɪəm] n χρώμιο.
chronic [ˈkrɒnɪk] a *(MED)* χρόνιος.

chronicle [ˈkrɒnɪkl] n χρονικό,
χρονογράφημα nt.
chronological [krɒnəˈlɒdʒɪkəl] a
χρονολογικός.
chrysanthemum [krɪˈsænθəməm] n
χρυσάνθεμο.
chubby [ˈtʃʌbɪ] a παχουλός,
στρουμπουλός.
chuck [tʃʌk] vt πετώ, ρίχνω ♦ n
σφιγκτήρας, τσόκ nt inv.
chuckle [ˈtʃʌkl] vi γελώ χαμηλόφωνα.
chum [tʃʌm] n στενός φίλος.
chunk [tʃʌŋk] n χοντρό κομμάτι.
church [tʃəːtʃ] n *(building)* εκκλησία, ναός
|| ~yard n αυλόγυρος εκκλησίας,
νεκροταφείο.
churlish [ˈtʃəːlɪʃ] a άξεστος, δύστροπος.
churn [tʃəːn] n *(for butter)* βουτίνα,
καρδάρα, ντουρβάνι.
chute [ʃuːt] n τσουλήθρα.
chutney [ˈtʃʌtnɪ] n τσάτνυ nt inv
(αρωματικό).
CID n *(abbr of Criminal Investigation
Department)* ≈ Ανακριτικό Τμήμα.
cider [ˈsaɪdə*] n μηλίτης *(οίνος)*.
cigar [sɪˈɡɑː*] n πούρο.
cigarette [sɪɡəˈret] n τσιγάρο,
σιγαρέττο || ~ case n τσιγαροθήκη,
ταμπακιέρα || ~ end n γόπα,
αποτσίγαρο || ~ holder n πίπα.
cinder [ˈsɪndə*] n ανθρακιά, θράκα,
στάκτη.
cine [ˈsɪnɪ]: ~-camera n
κινηματογραφική μηχανή || ~-film n
κινηματογραφική ταινία.
cinema [ˈsɪnəmə] n *(THEAT)* σινεμά nt inv
|| *(motion pictures)* κινηματογράφος.
cinnamon [ˈsɪnəmən] n κανέλα.
cipher [ˈsaɪfə*] n *(zero)* μηδενικό || *(code)*
κρυπτογράφηση || *(person)* μηδενικός.
circle [ˈsəːkl] n *(ring, figure)* κύκλος,
γύρος || *(of friends)* κύκλος, συντροφιά ♦
vi περιστρέφομαι, στριφογυρίζω ♦ vt
(surround) περικυκλώνω ♦ vi *(move in a
circle)* κάνω τον κύκλο, κάνω κύκλους.
circuit [ˈsəːkɪt] n *(moving around)*
κυκλικός δρόμος, περιστροφή || *(tour by
judges)* περιοδεία *(δικαστού)* || *(ELEC)*
κύκλωμα nt|| ~ous a κυκλικός, έμμεσος.
circular [ˈsəːkjʊlə*] a κυκλικός || *(in a
circle)* κυκλοτερής ♦ n εγκύκλιος,
διαφημιστικό γράμμα.
circulate [ˈsəːkjʊleɪt] vi κυκλοφορώ ♦
vt θέτω σε κυκλοφορία.
circulation [səːkjʊˈleɪʃən] n
κυκλοφορία.
circumcise [ˈsəːkəmsaɪz] vt περιτέμνω.
circumference [səˈkʌmfərəns] n
περιφέρεια.
circumspect [ˈsəːkəmspekt] a
προσεκτικός, μετρημένος.
circumstances [ˈsəːkəmstənsɪz] npl
(facts connected with sth) περιστάσεις fpl,
συνθήκες fpl, συμβάντα ntpl|| *(financial
condition)* οικονομική κατάσταση.
circus [ˈsəːkəs] n τσίρκο.
cistern [ˈsɪstən] n δεξαμενή, ντεπόζιτο.

cite [sait] vt (mention, quote) αναφέρω, παραπέμπω.

citizen ['sitizn] n (city dweller) αστός/η m/f|| πολίτης/ισσα m/f|| ~ship n πολιτικά δικαιώματα ntpl.

citrus fruit ['sitrəs 'fruːt] n εσπεριδοειδή ntpl.

city ['siti] n πόλη || the C~ το εμπορικόν κέντρο του Λονδίνου.

civic ['sivik] a αστικός, πολιτικός.

civil ['sivl] a πολιτικός || (polite) ευγενικός || ~ engineer n πολιτικός μηχανικός m/f || ~ian n πολίτης/ισσα m/f, ιδιώτης m/f ♦ a πολιτικός || ~ law n αστικόν δίκαιο || ~ servant n δημόσιος m/f/ υπάλληλος || C~ Service n Δημόσιες Υπηρεσίες fpl || ~ war n εμφύλιος πόλεμος.

civilization [sivilai'zeiʃən] n πολιτισμός.

civilized ['sivilaizd] a πολιτισμένος.

claim [kleim] vt απαιτώ, ζητώ, διεκδικώ ♦ n αίτησn, απαίτηση, αξίωση || ~ant n απαιτητής/τήτρια m/f || (LAW) ενάγων/ουσα m/f, δικαιούχος/α m/f.

clam [klæm] n αχιβάδα.

clamber ['klæmbə*] vi σκαρφαλώνω.

clammy ['klæmi] a ιδρωμένος, κολλώδης.

clamp [klæmp] n σφιγκτήρας, σύνδεσμος ♦ vt (συσ)σφίγγω.

clang [klæŋ] n κλαγγή, κρότος ♦ vti αντηχώ, κροτώ.

clap [klæp] vti κτυπώ, χειροκροτώ || ~ping n χειροκρότημα nt.

claret ['klærət] n μαύρο κρασί, μπορντώ nt inv.

clarification [klærifi'keiʃən] n (fig) διευκρίνιση.

clarify ['klærifai] vt διευκρινίζω.

clarinet [klæri'net] n κλαρίνο.

clarity ['klæriti] n διαύγεια.

clash [klæʃ] n σύγκρουση, αντίθεση || (sound) δυνατό και πχηρό κτύπημα ♦ vi συγκρούομαι.

clasp [klaːsp] n πόρπη, κόπιτσα ♦ vt αγκαλιάζω, σφίγγω.

class [klaːs] n (rank) τάξη || (sort) τάξη, είδος nt, κατηγορία || (SCH) τάξη ♦ vt ταξινομώ, βαθμολογώ.

classic ['klæsik] n κλασσικός ♦ a (traditional) κλασσικός || ~al a κλασσικός.

classification [klæsifi'keiʃən] n ταξινόμηση, κατάταξη.

classify ['klæsifai] vt ταξινομώ, κατατάσσω.

classroom ['klaːsrum] n αίθουσα παραδόσεων, τάξη.

clatter ['klætə*] n θόρυβος, γδούπος ♦ vi κροτώ, θορυβώ.

clause [klɔːz] n (of contract etc) όρος, άρθρο, διάταξη || (GRAM) πρόταση.

claustrophobia [klɔːstrə'fəubiə] n κλειστοφοβία.

claw [klɔː] n νύχι || (of quadrupeds) χηλή, οπλή ♦ vt νυχιάζω, γρατσουνίζω.

clay [klei] n άργιλος, πηλός.

clean [kliːn] a (free from dirt) καθαρός,

παστρικός || (guiltless) καθαρός, τίμιος || (lines) καθαρές (γραμμές), σαφές περίγραμμα ♦ vt καθαρίζω, παστρεύω || ~er n (person) καθαριστής/ρια m/f || ~ing n κάθαρση, καθάρισμα nt || ~liness n καθαριότητα, πάστρα || ~-up n καθαρισμός || to ~ out vt καθαρίζω || (col) ξεπεναρίζω || to ~ up vt κάνω καθαρισμό, σιάζω || (col) κερδίζω.

cleanse [klenz] vt αποκαθαίρω, καθαρίζω, πλένω.

clear [kliə*] a (water etc) καθαρός, διαυγής || (sound) καθαρός (ήχος) || (meaning) σαφής, καθαρός || (certain) σαφής || (road) ανοικτός ♦ vt καθαρίζω, ξεκαθαρίζω ♦ vi (become clear) διευκρινίζεται || ~ance n (in sale) εκποίηση, ξεπούλημα nt || (free space) απελευθέρωση, εκκένωση || (permission) άδεια || ~-cut a σαφής, συγκεκριμένος || ~ing n καθάρισμα nt || ~ly ad σαφώς, προφανώς, ασφαλώς || ~way n (Brit) εθνικ όδος χωρίς στάθμευση || to ~ up vi διαλύω, ξεκαθαρίζω ♦ vt τακτοποιώ, σιάζω || ξεκαθαρίζω.

clench [klentʃ] vt (teeth etc) σφίγγω.

clergy ['kləːdʒi] n κλήρος, ιερατείο || ~man n κληρικός, ιερωμένος, παπάς.

clerical ['klerikəl] a κληρικός, ιερατικός || του γραφείο.

clerk [klaːk, (US) klзːrk] n (US) (salesman, woman) υπάλληλος m/f || (in office) γραφέας m.

clever ['klevə*] a (with hands) επιδέξιος, καπάτσος || (in mind) ευφυής, σπιρτόζος || ~ly ad ευφυώς, έξυπνα.

cliché ['kliːʃei] n στερεότυπο, κλισέ nt inv.

click [klik] vi κτυπώ, κάνω τικ-τάκ ♦ n κλικ nt inv, ξηρός κρότος.

client ['klaiənt] n πελάτης/ισσα m/f || ~ele [kliːaːn'tel] n πελατεία.

cliff [klif] n γκρεμός.

climate ['klaimit] n κλίμα nt.

climax ['klaimæks] n αποκορύφωμα nt.

climb [klaim] vti ανέρχομαι, ανεβαίνω, σκαρφαλώνω ♦ n ανέβασμα nt, ανηφοριά || ~er n (of mountains) ορειβάτης m/f || ~ing n: to go ~ ing κάνω ορειβασία.

clinch [klintʃ] vt (fig: decide) συνάπτω, κλείνω.

cling [kliŋ] vi προσκολλιέμαι, πιάνομαι.

clinic ['klinik] n κλινική || ~al a κλινικός.

clink [kliŋk] n κτύπημα nt (ποτηριών) ♦ vti κτυπώ, πχώ.

clip [klip] n συνδετήρας, τσιμπιδάκι ♦ vt (papers) συνδέω || (hair) κουρέβω, ψαλιδίζω || (hedge) κόβω || ~pers npl (instrument) κουρευτική μηχανή.

clique [kliːk] n κλίκα.

cloak [kləuk] n πανωφόρι || (fig) κάλυμμα nt, πέπλο || ~-room n (for coats etc) γκαρνταρόπα || (W.C.) αποχωρητήριο, μέρος nt, καμπινέτο.

clock [klɔk] n ρολόι || ~wise ad

δεξιόστροφος || ~work n μηχανισμός ρολογιού.

clog [klɒg] n (shoe) τσόκαρο ♦ vti εμποδίζω, κωλύω, φράσσω.

close [kləʊs] a (near) κοντινός, εγγύς, διπλανός || (atmosphere etc) ασφυκτικός, πνιγηρός, στενός || (mean) σφικτός || (weather) κλειστός, βαρύς ♦ ad (near) κοντά, από κοντά, σφικτά || ~ly ad προσεκτικά, στενά, κατά πόδας.

close [kləʊz] vt (shut) κλείνω || (end) τελειώνω, τερματίζω ♦ vi κλείομαι || (end) τερματίζομαι ♦ n (end) τέλος nt || to ~ down vti κλείνω, διακόπτω || ~d a (road) απαγορεύεται η διάβαση || ~d shop n κλειστό κατάστημα nt.

closet ['klɒzit] n μικρό δωμάτιο || (store-room) αποθήκη.

close-up ['kləʊsʌp] n λεπτομέρεια.

closure ['kləʊzə*] n κλείσιμο, τερματισμός.

clot [klɒt] n (esp blood) θρόμβος, σβώλος ♦ vi θρομβούμαι, πήζω.

cloth [klɒθ] n (material) ύφασμα nt, πανί || (for cleaning) πατσαβούρα.

clothe [kləʊð] vt ντύνω, καλύπτω || ~s npl ρούχα ntpl || ~s brush n βούρτσα || ~s line n σχοινί απλώματος ρούχων || ~s peg n μανταλάκι.

clothing ['kləʊðiŋ] n = clothes || see clothe.

cloud [klaʊd] n σύννεφο || (of dust etc) νέφος nt, σύννεφο || ~burst n μπόρα || ~y a συνεφιασμένος || (wine etc) θολωμένο.

clout [klaʊt] n κτύπημα nt ♦ vt κτυπώ, καρπαζώνω.

clove [kləʊv] n γαρύφαλο.

clover ['kləʊvə*] n τριφύλλι || ~ leaf n τριφύλλι.

clown [klaʊn] n παλιάτσος, κλάουν nt inv ♦ vi κάνω τον παλιάτσο.

club [klʌb] n (stick) ρόπαλο, ματσούκα || (society) λέσχη || (golf) κλόμπ nt inv || (CARDS) σπαθί ♦ vt κτυπώ με ρόπαλο, με κλόμπ ♦ vi: to ~ together συνειοφέρω, βάζω ρεφενέ || ~house n λέσχη.

cluck [klʌk] vi κακαρίζω.

clue [klu:] n νύξη, ένδειξη || he hasn't a ~ δεν έχει ιδέα.

clump [klʌmp] n συστάδα (δένδρων), μεγάλο κομμάτι.

clumsy ['klʌmzi] a (person) αδέξιος, ατζαμής || (object) βαρύς, άκομψος.

clung [klʌŋ] pt, pp of cling.

cluster ['klʌstə*] n συστάδα, ομάδα || (of grapes) τσαμπί || (of stars) σύμπλεγμα nt ♦ vi συγκεντρώνομαι, μαζεύομαι.

clutch [klʌtʃ] n (grip, grasp) άρπαγμα nt, σφικτό πιάσιμο || (AUT) αμπραγιάζ nt inv, συμπλέκτης ♦ vt αρπάζω, πιάνω σφικτά.

clutter ['klʌtə*] nt παραγεμίζω, κάνω ανωκάτω.

coach [kəʊtʃ] n (bus) λεωφορείο, πούλμαν nt inv || (teacher) φροντιστής || (RAIL) άμαξα, βαγόνι || (trainer)

προγυμναστής/άστρια m/f || vt προγυμνάζω.

coagulate [kəʊˈægjʊleit] vti πήζω.

coal [kəʊl] n άνθρακας, κάρβουνο, γαιάνθρακας.

coalfield ['kəʊlfi:ld] n ανθρακοφόρος περιοχή.

coalition [kəʊəˈliʃən] n συνασπισμός.

coalmine ['kəʊlmain] n ανθρακωρυχείο.

coarse [kɔ:s] a (lit) τραχύς, ακατέργαστος || (fig) άξεστος, χυδαίος.

coast [kəʊst] n παραλία, ακτή || ~al a παράκτιος, παραλιακός || ~er n ακτοπλοϊκό || ~guard n ακτοφυλακή || ~line n ακτή, παραλία.

coat [kəʊt] n (garment) σακάκι || (of animal) προβιά || (layer etc) στρώμα nt, χέρι ♦ vt (with paint etc) επιχρίω || ~ of arms n οικόσημο || ~ hanger n κρεμάστρι || ~ing n επίστρωμα nt, χέρι.

coax [kəʊks] vt καλοπιάνω, καταφέρνω.

cobbler ['kɒblə*] n μπαλωματής.

cobble(stone)s ['kɒbl(stəʊn)z] npl βότσαλα ntpl, καλντερίμι.

cobra ['kəʊbrə] n κόμπρα.

cobweb ['kɒbweb] n ιστός αράχνης, αραχνιά.

cocaine [kəˈkein] n (MED) κοκαΐνη.

cock [kɒk] n (poultry) κόκορας, πετεινός || (bird etc) αρσενικό πουλί || (tap, faucet etc) κρουνός, κάνουλα ♦ vt σηκώνω, βάζω στραβά (το καπέλο) || (a gun) σηκώνω το λύκο || ~erel n κοκοράκι.

cockle ['kɒkl] n κοχύλι.

cockney ['kɒkni] n Λονδρέζος κατωτέρας τάξης, κόκνυ inv.

cockpit ['kɒkpit] n (AVIAT) θέση χειριστού.

cockroach ['kɒkrəʊtʃ] n κατσαρίδα.

cocktail ['kɒkteil] n (drink) κοκτέιλ nt inv || ~ cabinet n μπάρ nt inv || ~ party n πάρτυ κοκτέιλ nt inv.

cocoa ['kəʊkəʊ] n κακάο.

coconut ['kəʊkənʌt] n καρύδα.

cocoon [kəˈku:n] n κουκούλι.

cod [kɒd] n μουρούνα.

code [kəʊd] n (of laws) κώδικας || (signals) σύστημα nt κρυπτογραφίας.

codify ['kəʊdifai] vt κωδικοποιώ.

coerce [kəʊˈɜ:s] vt πιέζω, αναγκάζω.

coercion [kəʊˈɜ:ʃən] n καταπίεση.

coexistence ['kəʊigˈzistəns] n συνύπαρξη.

coffee ['kɒfi] n καφές m.

coffin ['kɒfin] n φέρετρο, κάσα.

cog [kɒg] n (of wheel etc) δόντι.

cognac ['kɒnjæk] n κονιάκ nt inv.

coherent [kəʊˈhiərənt] a (consistent) συναφής, συνεπής.

coil [kɔil] n κουλούρα, σπείρωμα nt || (ELEC) πηνίο ♦ vt συσπειρώνω, τυλίγω, κουλουριάζω.

coin [kɔin] n νόμισμα nt, κέρμα nt || ~age n (system) νομισματικό σύστημα nt || νόμισμα nt.

coincide [kəʊinˈsaid] vt συμπίπτω,

συμφωνώ || ~nce [kəu'ınsıdəns] n
σύμπτωση.

coke [kəuk] n κώκ nt inv.

colander ['kʌləndə*] n τρυπητό,
σουρωτήρι.

cold [kəuld] a ψυχρός, κρύος ♦ n ψύχος
nt, κρύο || (illness) κρυολόγημα nt || to
have ~ feet (γ)κιοτέβω || **to give the
~ shoulder** φέρομαι ψυχρά || ~**ly** ad
ψυχρά, κρύα.

coleslaw ['kəulslɔː] n λαχανοσαλάτα.

colic ['kɒlık] n κωλικόπονος.

collaborate [kə'læbəreıt] vi
συνεργάζομαι.

collaboration [kəlæbə'reıʃən] n
συνεργασία.

collapse [kə'læps] vi καταρρέω ♦ n
κατάρρευση.

collapsible [kə'læpsəbl] a
πτυσσόμενος, πτυκτός.

collar ['kɒlə*] n (of coat, shirt) κολλάρο,
γιακάς || ~**bone** n κλειδί του ώμου.

collate [kɒ'leıt] vt (αντι)παραβάλλω.

colleague ['kɒliːg] n συνάδελφος m/f,
συνεργάτης m/f.

collect [kə'lekt] vt συλλέγω, μαζεύω ♦
vi συναθροίζομαι || ~**ion** n συλλογή ||
(money) είσπραξη || ~**ive** a συλλογικός ||
(POL) κολλεκτίβο.

collector [kə'lektə*] n (of art etc)
συλλέκτης/τρια m/f || (of money)
εισπράκτορας.

college ['kɒlıdʒ] n (non-specialized)
κολλέγιο || (esp Oxford and Cambridge)
πανεπιστήμιο.

collide [kə'laıd] vi συγκρούομαι,
τρακάρω.

collision [kə'lıʒən] n σύγκρουση.

colloquial [kə'ləukwıəl] a της
καθομιλουμένης.

colon ['kəulən] n (GRAM) διπλή στιγμή.

colonel ['kɜːnl] n συνταγματάρχης.

colonial [kə'ləunıəl] a αποικιακός.

colonize ['kɒlənaız] vt αποικίζω.

colony ['kɒlənı] n αποικία || (of
immigrants etc) παροικία.

color ['kʌlə*] n (US) = **colour**.

colossal [kə'lɒsl] a κολοσσιαίος.

colour ['kʌlə*] n χρώμα nt || (paints etc)
βαφή, μπογιά || (of skin) χρώμα nt ♦ vt
χρωματίζω, βάφω || (news) χρωματίζω,
γαρνίρω || ~**s** npl χρώματα ntpl || (NAUT)
σημαία || ~**-blind** a δαλτωνικός || ~**ed** a
χρωματιστός, έγχρωμος || (fig)
εξογκωμένος || ~ **film** n (for camera)
έγχρωμο φίλμ || ~**ful** a ζωντανός || ~
television n έγχρωμη τηλεόραση.

colt [kəult] n πώλος, πουλάρι.

column ['kɒləm] n (pillar) κίονας,
στύλος, κολώνα || (of troops) φάλαγγα ||
(of page) στήλη || ~**ist** a αρθρογράφος
m/f.

coma ['kəumə] n κώμα nt, λήθαργος.

comb [kəum] n (for hair) κτένι, χτένα || (of
cock) λειρί || (honey) κηρήθρα ♦ vt (hair)
κτενίζω || (search) ερευνώ, ψάχνω.

combat ['kɒmbæt] n πάλη, διαμάχη ♦ vt
(κατα)πολεμώ.

combination [kɒmbı'neıʃən] n
συνδυασμός, ένωση.

combine [kəm'baın] vti συνδυάζω,
συνεργάζομαι, ενούμαι ♦ ['kɒmbaın] n
συνδυασμός, εταιρεία, συνδικάτο || ~
harvester n θεριστική και αλωνιστική
μηχανή.

combustion [kəm'bʌstʃən] n καύση,
ανάφλεξη.

come [kʌm] (irreg v) vi (approach)
έρχομαι, φθάνω || (reach) τελειώνω,
φθάνω, βρίσκομαι || (become) γίνομαι,
συμβαίνω || (result) καταλήγω || **to ~
about** vi συμβαίνω, γίνομαι || **to ~
across** vt συναντώ || **to ~ by** (visit)
περνώ || (find) βρίσκω, αποκτώ || **to ~ in
for** vt έχω μερίδιο, υπόκειμαι || **to** into vt
(enter) μπαίνω μέσα, εμφανίζομαι ||
(inherit) κληρονομώ || (fashion) γίνομαι
της μόδας || **to ~ out with** vt βγαίνω,
βγάζω || **to ~ to** vt (bill) φθάνω || (grief)
μού συμβαίνει δυστύχημα || (nothing)
αποτυγχάνω || (notice) αντιλαμβάνομαι ||
to ~ up to vt ανεβαίνω || (amount)
φθάνω || **to ~ up with** vt προφταίνω ||
~**back** n επάνοδος f.

comedian [kə'miːdıən] n κωμικός.

comedown ['kʌmdaun] n ξεπεσμός.

comedy ['kɒmıdı] n κωμωδία.

comet ['kɒmıt] n κομήτης.

comfort ['kʌmfət] n (of body) άνεση || (of
mind) παρηγοριά ♦ vt παρηγορώ ||
~**able** a αναπαυτικός, άνετος.

comic ['kɒmık] n (actor) κωμικός ||
(magazine) κόμικς ntpl inv ♦ a (also: ~**al**)
κωμικός, αστείος.

comma ['kɒmə] n (GRAM) κόμμα nt.

command [kə'mɑːnd] n (order) διαταγή
|| (control) εξουσία, κυριαρχία, διοίκηση ||
(COMPUT) εντολή ♦ vt (order) διατάζω ||
(be in charge) διοικώ, εξουσιάζω , ελέγχω
|| (be able to get) κατέχω, διαθέτω ♦ vi
προστάζω || ~**eer** [kɒmən'dıə*] vt
επιτάσσω || ~**er** n (MIL) διοικητής ||
(NAUT) πλωτάρχης.

commandment [kə'mɑːndmənt] n
εντολή.

commando [kə'mɑːndəu] n κομμάντο
m inv, καταδρομέας.

commemorate [kə'meməreıt] vt
γιορτάζω.

commemoration [kəmemə'reıʃən] n:
in ~ of εις μνήμην του.

commemorative [kə'memərətıv] a
αναμνηστικός.

commence [kə'mens] vti αρχίζω.

commend [kə'mend] vt συνιστώ,
επαινώ || ~**ation** [kɒmən'deıʃən] n
έπαινος.

commensurate [kə'menʃərıt] a
ανάλογος.

comment ['kɒment] n σχόλιο, εξήγηση
♦ vi (+ on) σχολιάζω, επεξηγώ || ~**ary** n
(SPORT) ρεπορτάζ nt inv || σχόλιο || ~**ator**
n σχολιαστής/σχολιάστρια m/f.

commerce ['kɔmɜ:s] n εμπόριο.

commercial [kə'mɜ:ʃəl] a εμπορικός ♦ n (TV) διαφήμιση || ~**ize** vt εμπορεύομαι.

commiserate [kə'mɪzəreɪt] vi: **to ~ with** συμπονώ, συλλυπούμαι.

commission [kə'mɪʃən] n (duty) εντολή, παραγγελία || (fee) προμήθεια || (MIL) βαθμός αξιωματικού || (reporting body) επιτροπή ♦ vt αναθέτω, επιφορτίζω || **out of ~** εκτός ενεργείας, χαλασμένο || ~**aire** n θυρωρός || ~**er** n μέλος nt επιτροπής, αρμοστής.

commit [kə'mɪt] vt (a crime) διαπράττω (έγκλημα) || (to paper) καταγράφω || (to memory) απομνημονεύω || (entrust) εμπιστεύομαι, αναθέτω || ~**ment** n δέσμευση, υποχρέωση.

committee [kə'mɪtɪ] n επιτροπή.

commodity [kə'mɔdɪtɪ] n εμπόρευμα nt.

common ['kɔmən] a (shared) κοινός || (knowledge etc) κοινός, συνήθης || (ordinary, usual) συνήθης, συνηθισμένος || (mean, low) χυδαίος, πρόστυχος || (frequent) συνήθης ♦ n: **in ~** από κοινού || ~**ly** ad συνήθως || **C~ Market** n Κοινή Αγορά || ~**place** a κοινοτοπία, πεζός || ~**room** n αίθουσα καθηγητών || ~**sense** n κοινός νούς || **the C~wealth** n Κοινοπολιτεία.

commotion [kə'məuʃən] n ταραχή.

communal [kɔmju:nl] a κοινοτικός.

commune [kɔmju:n] n (group of people living communally) κοινότητα ♦ [kə'mju:n] vi (+ with) συναναστρέφομαι.

communicate [kə'mju:nɪkeɪt] vt (transmit) ανακοινώνω, μεταδίδω ♦ vi (connect) συγκοινωνώ || (be in touch) (+ with)επικοινωνώ.

communication [kəmju:nɪ'keɪʃən] n ανακοίνωση, μετάδοση || συγκοινωνία, επικοινωνία || ~**s** npl (transport etc) συγκοινωνία || ~ **cord** n κώδων m κινδύνου.

communion [kə'mju:nɪən] n κοινότητα || (REL) θρησκευτική ομάδα || (Holy) **C~** n (Αγία) Μετάληψη.

communiqué [kə'mju:nɪkeɪ] n ανακοινωθέν nt.

communism ['kɔmjunɪzəm] n κομμουνισμός.

communist ['kɔmjunɪst] n κομμουνιστής/ίστρια m/f ♦ a κομμουνιστικός.

community [kə'mju:nɪtɪ] n κοινότητα || (the public) κοινωνία, το κοινό || ~ **centre** n αίθουσα αναψυχής.

commutation ticket [kɔmju'teɪʃəntɪkɪt] n (US) εισιτήριο διαρκείας.

compact [kəm'pækt] a συμπαγής, σφικτός ♦ ['kɔmpækt] n (agreement) σύμβαση, συμφωνία || (powder) πουδριέρα.

companion [kəm'pænɪən] n σύντροφος m/f, συνάδελφος m/f, ταίρι || ~**ship** n συντροφιά.

company ['kʌmpənɪ] n (business)

εταιρεία || (of people) παρέα, συντροφιά || (MIL) λόχος || (guests) κόσμος || **to keep s.o. ~** κάνω παρέα.

comparable ['kɔmpərəbl] a συγκρίσιμος, ανάλογος, παραβλητός.

comparative [kəm'pærətɪv] a συγκριτικός, σχετικός.

compare [kəm'pɛə*] vt συγκρίνω, παραβάλλω || (+ with) παρομοιάζω ♦ vi συγκρίνομαι.

comparison [kəm'pærɪsn] n σύγκριση || παρομοίωση || **in ~ (with)** συγκρινόμενος (με).

compartment [kəm'pɑ:tmənt] n (NAUT) διαμέρισμα nt || (RAIL) βαγκόν-λι nt inv.

compass ['kʌmpəs] n (instrument) πυξίδα || ~**es** npl διαβήτης.

compassion [kəm'pæʃən] n ευσπλαχνία, οίκτος || ~**ate** a φιλεύσπλαχνος.

compatible [kəm'pætɪbl] a συμβιβάσιμος, σύμφωνος.

compatibility [kəmpætɪ'bɪlɪtɪ] n (COMPUT) συμβατότητα.

compel [kəm'pel] vt αναγκάζω, υποχρεώνω.

compendium [kəm'pendɪəm] n σύνοψη, επιτομή.

compensate ['kɔmpenseɪt] vt αποζημιώνω ♦ vi: **to ~ for** αντισταθμίζω.

compensation [kɔmpen'seɪʃən] n (money) αποζημίωση || (satisfaction) ικανοποίηση.

compere ['kɔmpɛə*] n κομπέρ m/f inv.

compete [kəm'pi:t] vi συναγωνίζομαι, ανταγωνίζομαι || (for prize) διαγωνίζομαι.

competence ['kɔmpɪtəns] n ικανότητα, επιδεξιότητα.

competent ['kɔmpɪtənt] a ικανός, επιδέξιος || (office etc) αρμόδιος.

competition [kɔmpɪ'tɪʃən] n άμιλλα || (rivalry) ανταγωνισμός, συναγωνισμός.

competitive [kəm'petɪtɪv] a ανταγωνιστικός, συναγωνιστικός.

competitor [kəm'petɪtə*] n ανταγωνιστής/ίστρια m/f, αντίπαλος m/f.

compile [kəm'paɪl] vt συλλέγω, συναθροίζω.

complacency [kəm'pleɪsnsɪ] n αυταρέσκεια.

complacent [kəm'pleɪsənt] a αυτάρεσκος, αυταρεστημένος.

complain [kəm'pleɪn] vi παραπονιέμαι, γκρινιάζω || ~**t** n παράπονο, γκρίνια || (illness) αρρώστια.

complement ['kɔmplɪmənt] n πληρότητα || (MATH) συμπλήρωμα nt || (esp ship's crew etc) πλήρες πλήρωμα nt || ~**ary** a συμπληρωματικός.

complete [kəm'pli:t] a πλήρης, συμπληρωμένος, τέλειος ♦ vt συμπληρώνω, αποτελειώνω || ~**ly** πλήρως, εντελώς.

completion [kəm'pli:ʃən] n συμπλήρωση, αποπεράτωση.

complex ['kɔmpleks] a πολύπλοκος, πολυσύνθετος ♦ n (mental) σύμπλεγμα nt, κόμπλεξ nt inv|| (of buildings) σύμπλεγμα nt.

complexion [kəm'plekʃən] n χρώμα nt, χροιά.

complexity [kəm'pleksitɪ] n περιπλοκή.

complicate ['kɔmplikeɪt] vt περιπλέκω || ~d a μπλεγμένος.

complication [kɔmplɪ'keɪʃən] n περιπλοκή.

compliment ['kɔmplimənt] n φιλοφρόνηση, κομπλιμέντο ♦ ['kɔmpliment] vt κομπλιμεντάρω, συγχαίρω || ~s npl ευχές fpl, χαιρετισμοί mpl|| ~ary a φιλοφρονητικός, κομπλιμεντόζικος.

comply [kəm'plaɪ] vi: to ~ with συμμορφούμαι, ενδίδω, εκπληρώ.

component [kəm'pəunənt] a συνθετικός, συστατικός ♦ n συστατικό || (PHYS) συνιστώσα δύναμη.

compose [kəm'pəuz] vt συντάσσω, γράφω || (MUS) μελοποιώ, συνθέτω || (calm) ηρεμώ|| ~d a ατάραχος, ήρεμος || ~r n (MUS) μουσουργός, συνθέτης.

composite ['kɔmpəzɪt] a σύνθετος, μικτός.

composition [kɔmpə'zɪʃən] n σύνθεση || (structure) σύσταση.

compost ['kɔmpɔst] n (fertilizer) φουσκί.

composure [kəm'pəuʒə*] n ηρεμία αταραξία.

compound ['kɔmpaund] n (GRAM) σύνθετος λέξη || (enclosure) κλειστός χώρος || (CHEM) ένωση ♦ a σύνθετος.

comprehend [kɔmprɪ'hend] vt (understand) καταλαβαίνω || (include) συμπεριλαμβάνω.

comprehension [kɔmprɪ'henʃən] n κατανόηση, αντίληψη.

comprehensive [kɔmprɪ'hensɪv] a περιεκτικός.

compress [kəm'pres] vt συμπιέζω ♦ ['kɔmpres] n (MED) επίθεμα nt, κομπρέσσα || ~ion n (συμ) πίεση, σύμπτυξη.

comprise [kəm'praɪz] vi αποτελούμαι από.

compromise ['kɔmprəmaɪz] n συμβιβασμός ♦ vt (expose) εκθέτω ♦ vi (agree) συμβιβάζομαι.

compulsion [kəm'pʌlʃən] n βία, καταναγκασμός.

compulsory [kəm'pʌlsərɪ] a (obligatory) υποχρεωτικός.

computer [kəm'pju:tə*] n υπολογιστής.

comrade ['kɔmrɪd] n σύντροφος/φισσα m/f, συνάδελφος m/f || ~ship n καμαραντερί.

concave ['kɔn'keɪv] a κοίλος, βαθουλός.

conceal [kən'si:l] vt (απο) κρύπτω.

concede [kən'si:d] vt (admit) παραδέχομαι ♦ vi (yield) παραχωρώ.

conceit [kən'si:t] n ματαιοδοξία, ξιπασιά || ~ed a φαντασμένος, ξιπασμένος.

conceivable [kən'si:vəbl] a διανοητός, δυνατός.

conceive [kən'si:v] vt (imagine) φαντάζομαι || (child) συλλαμβάνω.

concentrate ['kɔnsəntreɪt] vi (+ on) συγκεντρώνομαι ♦ vt συγκεντρώνω.

concentration [kɔnsən'treɪʃən] n συγκέντρωση || ~ camp n στρατόπεδο συγκεντρώσεως.

concept ['kɔnsept] n ιδέα, έννοια.

conception [kən'sepʃən] n σύλληψη, αντίληψη.

concern [kən'sɜːn] n (affair) ενδιαφέρον, συμφέρον || (business) επιχείρηση || (anxiety) ανησυχία ♦ vt ενδιαφέρομαι, ενδιαφέρω|| ~ed a (anxious) ανήσυχος || ~ing prep όσο αφορά.

concert ['kɔnsət] n συνεννόηση, συμφωνία || (MUS) συναυλία || in ~ από συμφώνου, μαζί || ~ hall n αίθουσα συναυλιών.

concertina [kɔnsə'ti:nə] n ακορντεό nt inv.

concerto [kən'tʃeɪtəu] n κονσέρτο.

concession [kən'seʃən] n παραχώρηση, εκχώρηση.

conciliation [kənsɪlɪ'eɪʃən] n συμφιλίωση.

concise [kən'saɪs] a σύντομος, συνοπτικός.

conclude [kən'klu:d] vt (end) τελειώνω, περαίνω || (settle) συνάπτω, κλείνω || (decide) συμπεραίνω, καταλήγω ♦ vi τερματίζω.

conclusion [kən'klu:ʒən] n συμπέρασμα nt, τέλος nt|| in ~ εν τέλει.

conclusive [kən'klu:sɪv] a αποφασιστικός, πειστικός.

concoct [kən'kɔkt] vt (drink etc) κατασκευάζω || (plan etc) εφευρίσκω, καταστρώνω.

concrete ['kɔnkri:t] n σκυροκονίαμα nt, μπετό ♦ a συγκεκριμένος.

concur [kən'kɜː*] vi συμπίπτω, συμφωνώ.

concurrently [kən'kʌrəntlɪ] ad από κοινού.

concussion [kən'kʌʃən] n τράνταγμα nt || (MED) διάσειση.

condemn [kən'dem] vt καταδικάζω || ~ation n καταδίκη, μομφή.

condensation [kɔnden'seɪʃən] n συμπύκνωση.

condense [kən'dens] vi συμπυκνούμαι ♦ vt συμπυκνώνω || ~d milk n συμπυκνωμένο γάλα.

condescend [kɔndɪ'send] vi καταδέχομαι || ~ing a καταδεκτικός, ευπροσήγορος.

condition [kən'dɪʃən] n (state) κατάσταση, συνθήκη || (term) όρος ♦ vt

ρυθμίζω, καθορίζω || on ~ that υπό τον
όρο να || ~al a υπό όρους,
προϋποθετικός.

condolences [kən'dəʊlənsɪz] npl
συλλυπητήρια ntpl.

condone [kən'dəʊn] vt συγχωρώ,
παραβλέπω.

conducive [kən'djuːsɪv] a
συντελεστικός.

conduct ['kɒndʌkt] n (behaviour)
διαγωγή || (management) διεξαγωγή ♦
[kən'dʌkt] vt (people) οδηγώ, φέρω ||
(affairs) διευθύνω, εκτελώ || (MUS)
διευθύνω || ~ed tour n ξεναγηση || ~or
n (orchestra) μαέστρος || (bus)
εισπράκτορας || ~ress n (bus)
εισπράκτόρισσα.

cone [kəʊn] n (MATH) κώνος || (ice cream)
παγωτό χωνάκι || (pine) κουκουνάρι.

confectioner [kən'fekʃənə*] n
ζαχαροπλάστης || ~'s (shop) n
ζαχαροπλαστείο || ~y n
ζαχαροπλαστείο.

confederation [kənfedə'reɪʃən] n
συνομοσπονδία.

confer [kən'fɜː*] vt (grant) απονέμω,
παρέχω ♦ vi (consult) συζητώ,
διασκέπτομαι || ~ence ['kɒnfərəns] n
(συν)διάσκεψη, συμβούλιο.

confess [kən'fes] vti (admit)
(εξ)ομολογώ || (REL) εξομολογούμαι ||
~ion n ομολογία || (REL) εξομολόγηση.

confetti [kən'fetɪ] n χαρτοπόλεμος,
κονφετί nt inv.

confide [kən'faɪd] vi: to ~ in
εμπιστεύομαι.

confidence ['kɒnfɪdəns] n (trust)
εμπιστοσύνη || (secret) μυστικό || ~ trick
n κόλπο, απάτη.

confident ['kɒnfɪdənt] a βέβαιος,
σίγουρος || ~ial a (secret) εμπιστευτικός
|| (trusted) της εμπιστοσύνης.

confine [kən'faɪn] vt περιορίζω || (shut
up) εγκλείω || ~d a (space)
περιορισμένος || ~ment n (limiting)
περιορισμός || (birth) λοχεία, τοκετός.

confirm [kən'fɜːm] vt (report)
επιβεβαιώνω || (appointment) επικυρώνω ||
~ation n (general) επιβεβαίωση || (REL)
χρίσμα nt, μύρωση || ~ed a έμμονος,
αμετάπειστος.

confiscate ['kɒnfɪskeɪt] vt δημεύω.

confiscation [kɒnfɪs'keɪʃən] n δήμευση.

conflict ['kɒnflɪkt] n σύγκρουση,
διαμάχη, αντίθεση ♦ [kən'flɪkt] vi
συγκρούομαι, διαφέρω, αντιμάχομαι ||
~ing a αντιφατικός, συγκρουόμενος.

conform [kən'fɔːm] vi (+ to)
συμμορφώνομαι, προσαρμόζομαι.

confront [kən'frʌnt] vt αντιμετωπίζω ||
~ation n αντιμετώπιση.

confuse [kən'fjuːz] vt συγχύζω,
ταράσσω.

confusing [kən'fjuːzɪŋ] a συγκεχυμένος.

confusion [kən'fjuːʒən] n (disorder)
σύγχυση || (tumult) αναστάτωση,

αναμπουμπούλα || (embarrassment)
σάστισμα nt.

congeal [kən'dʒiːl] vi πήζω.

congenial [kən'dʒiːnɪəl] a ταιριαστός,
ευχάριστος.

congested [kən'dʒestɪd] a (overcrowded)
συνωστισμένος.

congestion [kən'dʒestʃən] n (of traffic
etc) συμφόρηση, συνωστισμός.

conglomeration [kənglɒmə'reɪʃən] n
σύμφυρμα nt, σύμπηγμα nt.

congratulate [kən'grætjuleɪt] vt (+ on)
συγχαίρω.

congratulations [kəngrætju'leɪʃənz]
npl συγχαρητήρια ntpl.

congregate ['kɒngrɪgeɪt] vi
συναθροίζομαι.

congregation [kɒngrɪ'geɪʃən] n
συνάθροιση, εκκλησίασμα nt.

congress ['kɒngres] n συνέλευση,
συνέδριο || (US) Κογκρέσσο || ~man n
(US) μέλος nt του Κογκρέσσου.

conical ['kɒnɪkəl] a κωνικός, κωνοειδής.

conifer ['kɒnɪfə*] n κωνοφόρο
(δένδρο).

conjecture [kən'dʒektʃə*] n εικασία,
συμπερασμός ♦ vti εικάζω, συμπεραίνω.

conjugal ['kɒndʒugəl] a συζυγικός.

conjunction [kən'dʒʌŋkʃən] n
σύνδεσμος || in ~ with από κοινού με.

conjure ['kʌndʒə*] vti πλέκω, μηχανεύω
|| to ~ up vt επινοώ, επικαλούμαι || ~r n
ταχυδακτυλουργός.

conjuring ['kʌndʒərɪŋ] n: ~ trick n
ταχυδακτυλουργία.

conk [kɒŋk]: to ~ out vi (col) σβήνω.

connect [kə'nekt] vti (train) συνδέω,
συνδέομαι, συνδυάζω || ~ion n (joining)
σύνδεση, συνάφεια || (relation) σχέση,
συσχετισμός || in ~ion with σχετικά
με.

connexion [kə'nekʃən] n =
connection || see **connect**.

connoisseur [kɒnə'sɜː*] n ειδήμονας,
τεχνοκρίτης.

conquer ['kɒŋkə*] vt (overcome)
υπερνικώ, υποτάσσω || (by war) κατακτώ,
κυριεύω || ~or n κατακτητής/ήτρια m/f,
νικητής/ήτρια m/f.

conquest ['kɒŋkwest] n κατάκτηση.

conscience ['kɒnʃəns] n συνείδηση.

conscientious [kɒnʃɪ'enʃəs] a
ευσυνείδητος.

conscious ['kɒnʃəs] a συνειδητός,
συναισθανόμενος || ~ness n
συναίσθηση.

conscript ['kɒnskrɪpt] n στρατεύσιμος,
κληρωτός || ~ion [kən'skrɪpʃən] n
στρατολογία.

consecrate ['kɒnsɪkreɪt] vt εγκαινιάζω,
χειροτονώ || (devote) αφιερώνω.

consecutive [kən'sekjutɪv] a
διαδοχικός.

consensus [kən'sensəs] n κοινή
συναίνεση, επικρατούσα γνώμη.

consent [kən'sent] n συγκατάθεση,
συναίνεση ♦ vi (+ to) συγκατατίθεμαι.

consequence ['kɒnsɪkwəns] n (importance) σπουδαιότητα || (result, effect) συνέπεια, επακόλουθο.

consequently ['kɒnsɪkwəntlɪ] ad επομένως, συνεπώς.

conservation [kɒnsə'veɪʃən] n συντήρηση, διατήρηση.

conservative [kən'sɜːvətɪv] a συντηρητικός, μετριοπαθής || C~ a (party) συντηρητικός || n Συντηρητικός/ή m/f.

conservatory [kən'sɜːvətrɪ] n (greenhouse) θερμοκήπιο, σέρρα || (MUS) ωδείο.

conserve [kən'sɜːv] vt συντηρώ, διατηρώ.

consider [kən'sɪdə*] vt (think over) μελετώ || (take into account) λαμβάνω υπόψιν || (deem) θεωρώ.

considerable [kən'sɪdərəbl] a σημαντικός, αξιόλογος.

considerate [kən'sɪdərɪt] a διακριτικός, αβρός.

consideration [kənsɪdə'reɪʃən] n (thoughtfulness) αβροφροσύνη, διακριτικότητα || (serious thought) μελέτη, σκέψη || (reason) λόγος || (reward) αμοιβή.

considering [kən'sɪdərɪŋ] prep λαμβανομένου υπόψιν.

consign [kən'saɪn] vt αποστέλλω, παραδίδω || ~ment n αποστολή.

consist [kən'sɪst] vi (+ of) συνίσταμαι, αποτελούμαι.

consistency [kən'sɪstənsɪ] n (firmness) συνοχή, συνέπεια, σταθερότητα || (density) πυκνότητα, στερεότητα.

consistent [kən'sɪstənt] a σταθερός, συνεπής, σύμφωνος.

consolation [kɒnsə'leɪʃən] n παρηγορία.

console [kən'səul] vt παρηγορώ || (COMPUT) πληκτρολόγιο.

consolidate [kən'sɒlɪdeɪt] vt συγκεντρώνω, παγιώνω.

consommé [kən'sɒmeɪ] n ζωμός κρέατος, κονσομέ nt inv.

consonant ['kɒnsənənt] n (GRAM) σύμφωνο.

consortium [kən'sɔːtɪəm] n κοινοπραξία, κονσόρτιουμ nt inv.

conspicuous [kən'spɪkjʊəs] a καταφανής, περίβλεπτος || (prominent) αξιοσημείωτος, σημαντικός.

conspiracy [kən'spɪrəsɪ] n συνωμοσία.

conspire [kən'spaɪə*] vi συνωμοτώ, συνεργώ.

constable ['kʌnstəbl] n αστυφύλακας, χωροφύλακας.

constabulary [kən'stæbjulərɪ] n αστυνομία.

constant ['kɒnstənt] a σταθερός, συνεχής || ~ly ad σταθερά, συνεχώς.

constellation [kɒnstə'leɪʃən] n αστερισμός.

consternation [kɒnstə'neɪʃən] n κατάπληξη.

constipated ['kɒnstɪpeɪtɪd] a δυσκοίλιος.

constituency [kən'stɪtjuənsɪ] n εκλογική περιφέρεια.

constituent [kən'stɪtjuənt] n (elector) ψηφοφόρος m/f || (essential part) συστατικό.

constitute ['kɒnstɪtjuːt] vt (amount to) συνιστώ, αποτελώ.

constitution [kɒnstɪ'tjuːʃən] n (laws) σύνταγμα nt || (health) κράση || ~al a συνταγματικός.

constrain [kən'streɪn] vt εξαναγκάζω || ~t n εξαναγκασμός || (feelings) ταραχή, τράκ nt inv.

constrict [kən'strɪkt] vt συσφίγγω || ~ion n σύσφιγξη, σφίξιμο.

construct [kən'strʌkt] vt κατασκευάζω, οικοδομώ || ~ion n κατασκευή, οικοδόμηση || (GRAM) σύνταξη, ερμηνεία || ~ive a εποικοδομητικός, δημιουργικός.

construe [kən'struː] vt ερμηνεύω.

consul ['kɒnsəl] n πρόξενος || ~ate ['kɒnsjulɪt] n προξενείο.

consult [kən'sʌlt] vt συμβουλεύομαι || ~ant n (MED) ειδικός γιατρός || (other specialist) σύμβουλος m/f || ~ation n συμβούλιο, συνδιάσκεψη || ~ing room n ιατρείο.

consume [kən'sjuːm] vt καταναλίσκω || ~r n καταναλωτής.

consumption [kən'sʌmpʃən] n κατανάλωση || (MED) φθίση, φυματίωση.

contact ['kɒntækt] n επαφή ♦ vt έρχομαι σε επαφή με || ~ lenses npl φακοί mpl επαφής.

contagious [kən'teɪdʒəs] a μεταδοτικός, κολλητικός.

contain [kən'teɪn] vt περιέχω || to ~ o.s. συγκρατούμαι || ~er n (small) δοχείο || (TRANSPORT) (εμπορευματικό) κιβώτιο.

contaminate [kən'tæmɪneɪt] vt μολύνω, μιαίνω.

contamination [kəntæmɪ'neɪʃən] n μόλυνση, μίανση.

contemplate ['kɒntempleɪt] vt (look at) κυττάζω, παρατηρώ || (meditate) μελετώ, αναπολώ || (intend) σχεδιάζω.

contemplation [kɒntem'pleɪʃən] n σκέψη, συλλογή.

contemporary [kən'tempərərɪ] a σύγχρονος ♦ n σύγχρονος/η m/f, συνομήλικος/η m/f.

contempt [kən'tempt] n περιφρόνηση || ~ible a αξιοκαταφρόνητος || ~uous a περιφρονητικός.

contend [kən'tend] vt (strive) (συν)αγωνίζομαι || (argue) ισχυρίζομαι || ~er n (competitor) ανταγωνιστής/ίστρια m/f.

content [kən'tent] a ικανοποιημένος, ευχαριστημένος ♦ vt ικανοποιώ ♦ ['kɒntent] n (of article etc) περιεχόμενο || ~s npl (of room) περιεχόμενα ntpl || (of book) (πίνακας) περιεχομένων || (of *barrel)* περιεκτικότητα || ~**ed** *a* ικανοποιημένος.

contention [kənˈtenʃən] *n (dispute)* αγώνας, διαμάχη || *(opinion)* ισχυρισμός.

contentment [kənˈtentmənt] *n* ικανοποίηση.

contest [ˈkɒntest] *n* αγώνας, πάλη ♦ [kənˈtest] *vt* διαμφισβητώ, διεκδικώ, αγωνίζομαι || ~**ant** *n* αγωνιζόμενος/η *m/f*, διεκδικητής/ήτρια *m/f*.

context [ˈkɒntekst] *n* συμφραζόμενα *ntpl.*

continent [ˈkɒntinənt] *n* ήπειρος *f*|| **the** **C**~ Ευρώπη || ~**al** *a* ηπειρωτικός.

contingency [kənˈtindʒənsi] *n* ενδεχόμενο, σύμπτωση.

contingent [kənˈtindʒənt] *n* ενδεχόμενος || *(MIL)* τμήμα στρατού ή ναυτικού ♦ *a* (+ *(up)on)* εξαρτώμενος από.

continual [kənˈtinjuəl] *a (endless)* συνεχής, αδιάκοπος || *(often repeated)* συχνός || ~**ly** *ad* συνεχώς.

continuation [kəntinjuˈeiʃən] *n* συνέχεια, συνέχιση.

continue [kənˈtinjuː] *vi* συνεχίζομαι || *(remain)* (παρα)μένω || συνεχίζω || *(resume)* εξακολουθώ.

continuity [kɒntiˈnjuːiti] *n* συνέχεια.

continuous [kənˈtinjuəs] *a* συνεχής, αδιάκοπος.

contort [kənˈtɔːt] *vt* συστρίβω, παραμορφώνω || ~**ion** *n* στρίψιμο || *(of face)* μορφασμός || ~**ionist** *n* ακροβάτης/ισσα *m/f*.

contour [ˈkɒntuə*] *n (shape)* περίγραμμα *nt* || *(of map)* ισοϋψείς καμπύλες *fpl.*

contraband [ˈkɒntrəbænd] *n* λαθρεμπόριο, κοντραμπάντο.

contraception [kɒntrəˈsepʃən] *n* πρόληψη συλλήψεως.

contraceptive [kɒntrəˈseptiv] *n* αντισυλληπτικό.

contract [ˈkɒntrækt] *n* συμβόλαιο, συμφωνία ♦ [kənˈtrækt] *vi (to do sth)* συμφωνώ, συμβάλλομαι || *(become smaller)* συστέλλομαι, στενεύω || ~**ion** *n* συστολή, μάζεψια *nt* || ~**or** *n* εργολάβος, προμηθευτής.

contradict [kɒntrəˈdikt] *vt (say the opposite)* αντιλέγω || *(deny)* διαψεύδω || ~**ion** *n (in terms)* αντίφαση || *(denial)* διάψευση.

contralto [kənˈtræltəu] *n* μεσόφωνος, κοντράλτο.

contraption [kənˈtræpʃən] *n* μηχανή, μαραφέτι.

contrary [ˈkɒntrəri] *a (opposite)* εναντίος, αντίθετος || *(unfavourable)* αντίθετος, δυσμενής || **on the** ~ τουναντίον.

contrast [ˈkɒntrɑːst] *n* σύγκριση, αντίθεση ♦ [kənˈtrɑːst] *vt* συγκρίνω, αντιπαραβάλλω.

contravene [kɒntrəˈviːn] *vt (a rule etc)* παραβαίνω, καταπατώ || *(conflict with)* διαφεύδω, προσκρούω.

contribute [kənˈtribjuːt] *vi (help)* συμβάλλω, βοηθώ || *(subscribe)* συνεισφέρω ♦ *vt* καταβάλλω.

contribution [kɒntriˈbjuːʃən] *n* συνεισφορά, συνεργασία.

contributor [kənˈtribjutə*] *n* συνεισφέρων/ουσα *m/f* συνεργάτης/ιδα *m/f.*

contrite [ˈkɒntrait] *a* συντριμμένος, μετανοών.

contrive [kənˈtraiv] *vt (bring about)* καταφέρνω.

control [kənˈtrəul] *vt (check)* συγκρατώ, χαλιναγωγώ || *(direct)* διευθύνω, εξουσιάζω ♦ *n (check)* έλεγχος, επίβλεψη || *(restraint)* χαλινός || ~**s** *npl* χειριστήριο, έλεγχος || ~ **key** *n (COMPUT)* πλήκτρο ελέγχου.

controversial [kɒntrəˈvɜːʃəl] *a* συζητήσιμος.

controversy [kənˈtrɒvəsi] *n* συζήτηση, διαφωνία.

convalesce [kɒnvəˈles] *vi* αναρρωνύω || ~**nce** *n* ανάρρωση || ~**nt** *a, n* αναρρωνύων.

convene [kənˈviːn] *vti* συγκαλώ, συνέρχομαι.

convenience [kənˈviːniəns] *n (being convenient)* καταλληλότητα, συμφωνία || *(thing)* ευκολία, άνεση.

convenient [kənˈviːniənt] *a* κατάλληλος, βολικός, χρήσιμος.

convent [ˈkɒnvənt] *n* μονή γυναικών.

convention [kənˈvenʃən] *n (assembly)* συνέδριο, συνέλευση || *(custom)* έθιμο, συνήθεια || ~**al** *a (traditional)* εθιμοτυπικός, συνηθισμένος.

converge [kənˈvɜːdʒ] *vi* συγκλίνω.

conversant [kənˈvɜːsənt] *a* (+ *with)* οικείος, γνωστός.

conversation [kɒnvəˈseiʃən] *n* συνδιάλεξη, συνομιλία, κουβέντα || ~**al** *a* ομιλητικός, καθομιλούμενος.

converse [kənˈvɜːs] *vi* συνομιλώ, συνδιαλέγομαι ♦ [ˈkɒnvɜːs] *a* αντίθετος || ~**ly** *ad* αντίστροφα, αντιθέτως.

conversion [kənˈvɜːʃən] *n* μετατροπή || *(esp REL)* προσηλύτιση || ~ **table** *n* πίνακας μετατροπών.

convert [kənˈvɜːt] *vt (change)* μετατρέπω || *(esp REL)* προσηλυτίζω ♦ [ˈkɒnvɜːt] *n* προσήλυτος || ~**ible** *n (AUT)* καμπριολέ *nt inv.*

convex [ˈkɒnˈveks] *a* κυρτός.

convey [kənˈvei] *vt (carry)* μεταφέρω || *(communicate)* μεταβιβάζω, μεταδίδω || ~**or belt** *n* μεταφορέας.

convict [kənˈvikt] *vt* καταδικάζω ♦ [ˈkɒnvikt] *n* καταδικος/η *m/f* || ~**ion** *n (verdict)* καταδίκη || *(belief)* πεποίθηση.

convince [kənˈvins] *vt* πείθω.

convincing [kənˈvinsiŋ] *a* πειστικός.

convoy [ˈkɒnvɔi] *n* συνοδεία, νπομπή.

convulse [kənˈvʌls] *vt (esp with laughter)* ξεραίνομαι στα γέλια.

convulsion [kənˈvʌlʃən] *n* σπασμός.

coo [ku:] vi (dove) τερετίζω σαν περιστέρι.

cook [kuk] vt μαγειρεύω ♦ vi ψήνομαι ♦ n μάγειρας || ~**book** n βιβλίο μαγειρικής || ~**er** n συσκευή μαγειρέματος || ~**ery** n μαγειρική || ~**ery book** n = **cookbook** || ~**ie** n (US) μπισκότο || ~**ing** n μαγειρική.

cool [ku:l] a (fairly cold) δροσερός || (calm) ψύχραιμος || (unfriendly) ψυχρός, αδιάφορος || (impudent) αναιδής, θρασύς ♦ vti δροσίζω, κρυώνω || ~**ness** n ψύχρα, ψυχρότητα.

coop [ku:p] n κοτέτσι, κλούβα ♦ vt: to ~ up (fig) περιορίζω, κλείνω.

co-op ['kəu'ɒp] n = **cooperative**.

cooperate [kəu'ɒpəreit] vi συνεργάζομαι.

cooperation [kəuɒpə'reiʃən] n συνεργασία.

cooperative [kəu'ɒpərətiv] a συνεργατικός ♦ n (farmers) συνεταιρισμός || ~ **store** n (retail) πρατήριο συνεταιρισμού.

coordinate [kəu'ɔ:dineit] vt συνδυάζω, συντονίζω.

coordination [kəuɔ:di'neiʃən] n συντονισμός.

coot [ku:t] n φαλαρίδα, λούφα.

cope [kəup] vi (+ with) αντιμετωπίζω, αντεπεξέρχομαι.

co-pilot ['kəu'pailət] n δεύτερος χειριστής.

copper ['kɒpə*] n χαλκός, μπακίρι || (coin) δεκάρα || (sl: policeman) αστυφύλακας.

coppice ['kɒpis] n, **copse** [kɒps] n δασύλλιο, λόχμη.

copulate ['kɒpjuleit] vi συνουσιάζομαι, γαμώ.

copy ['kɒpi] n (imitation) αντίγραφο, αντιγραφή || (of book) αντίτυπο ♦ vt αντιγράφω, απομιμούμαι || (COMPUT) αντιγράφω || ~**book** n τετράδιο || ~**cat** n μιμητής/τρια m/f || ~**right** n πνευματική ιδιοκτησία || ~**right reserved** απαγορεύεται η αναδημοσίευση.

coral ['kɒrəl] n κοράλλιο || ~ **reef** n κοραλλιογενές νησί.

cord [kɔ:d] n σχοινί, χορδή || see **vocal**.

cordial ['kɔ:diəl] a εγκάρδιος || ~**ly** ad (invite) εγκάρδια, θερμά.

cordon ['kɔ:dn] n (ornamental) κορδόνι || (of police etc) ζώνη.

corduroy ['kɔ:dərɒi] n κοτλέ nt inv.

core [kɔ:*] n πυρήνας, καρδιά ♦ vt αφαιρώ το πυρήνα.

cork [kɔ:k] n φελλός || (of bottle) πώμα nt || ~**screw** n τιρ-μπουσόν nt inv.

cormorant ['kɔ:mərənt] n φαλακροκόρακας, καλικατζού f inv.

corn [kɔ:n] n σιτηρά ntpl, δημητριακά ntpl || (US: maize) καλαμπόκι || (on foot) κάλος.

cornea ['kɔ:niə] n κερατοειδής.

corned ['kɔ:nd] ~ **beef** n βοδινό κρέας σε κονσέρβα.

corner ['kɔ:nə*] n (of street) γωνία || (of room) γωνία, κώχη || (fig) δύσκολη θέση ♦ vt φέρνω σε δύσκολη θέση, στριμώχνω || (ECON) μονοπωλώ ♦ vi (turn) παίρνω στροφή || ~ **kick** n κόρνερ nt inv || ~**stone** n ακρογωνιαίος λίθος, βάση.

cornet ['kɔ:nit] n (MUS) κορνέττα || (ice cream) χωνάκι.

cornflour ['kɔ:nflauə*] n καλαμποκάλευρο, κορνφλάουερ nt inv.

cornice ['kɔ:nis] n κορνίζα.

cornstarch ['kɔ:nstɑ:tʃ] n (US) = **cornflour**.

corny ['kɔ:ni] a (joke) σαχλός.

coronary ['kɒrənəri] a στεφανιαίος ♦ n στεφανιαία || ~ **thrombosis** n θρόμβωση της στεφανιαίας.

coronation [kɒrə'neiʃən] n στέψη.

coroner ['kɒrənə*] n ιατροδικαστής m/f.

corporal ['kɔ:pərəl] n (MIL) δεκανέας || (AVIAT) υποσμηνίας ♦ a σωματικός.

corporation [kɔ:pə'reiʃən] n σωματείο || (esp business) εταιρεία.

corps [kɔ:*] n (στρατιωτικό) σώμα nt.

corpse [kɔ:ps] n πτώμα nt, κουφάρι.

corpulent ['kɔ:pjulənt] a παχύσαρκος.

corpuscle ['kɔ:pʌsl] n σωματίδιο || (blood corpuscle) αιμοσφαίριο.

corral [kə'rɑ:l] n μάντρα.

correct [kə'rɛkt] a (accurate) ακριβής, ορθός, διορθωμένος || (proper) άψογος, όπως πρέπει ♦ vt (papers etc) διορθώνω || (make right) επανορθώνω || ~**ion** n διόρθωση || ~**ly** ad ορθά, σωστά.

correlate ['kɒrileit] vt σχετίζομαι, συσχετίζω.

correlation [kɒri'leiʃən] n συσχετισμός, συσχέτιση.

correspond [kɒris'pɒnd] vi (agree with) ανταποκρίνομαι, ταιριάζω || (write) αλληλογραφώ || ~**ence** n (letters) αλληλογραφία || (similarity) αντιστοιχία, αντιστοίχιση || ~**ence course** n μάθημα nt αλληλογραφίας || ~**ent** n (reporter) ανταποκριτής/τρια m/f || ~**ing** a αντίστοιχος.

corridor ['kɒridɔ:*] n διάδρομος.

corroborate [kə'rɒbəreit] vt επιβεβαιώνω, ενισχύω.

corroboration [kərɒbə'reiʃən] n επιβεβαίωση, επίρρωση.

corrode [kə'rəud] vti διαβρώνω, σκουριάζω.

corrosion [kə'rəuʒən] n διάβρωση, σκωρίαση.

corrugated ['kɒrəgeitid] a κυματοειδής || ~ **cardboard** n κυματοειδές χαρτόνι || ~ **iron** n αυλακωτό έλασμα nt.

corrupt [kə'rʌpt] a διεφθαρμένος ♦ vt διαφθείρω || ~**ion** n διαφθορά, δεκασμός.

corset ['kɔ:sit] n κορσές m.

cortège [kɔ:'teiʒ] n νεκρώσιμος πομπή.

cortisone ['kɔ:tizəun] n κορτιζόνη.

cosh [kɒʃ] n μαγκούρα, βούρδουλας ♦ vt κτυπώ με βούρδουλα.

cosiness ['kɔuzinis] n άνεση.
cosmetic [kɔz'metik] n καλλυντικό.
cosmic ['kɔzmik] a κοσμικός.
cosmonaut ['kɔzmənɔːt] n αστροναύτης, κοσμοναύτης.
cosmopolitan [kɔzmə'pɔlitən] a κοσμοπολιτικός.
cosmos ['kɔzmɔs] n κόσμος, σύμπαν nt.
cost [kɔst] (irreg v) n κόστος nt, τιμή, δαπάνη ♦ vt κοστίζω, || it ~s £5 στοιχίζει πέντε λίρες || it ~s too much στοιχίζει πολλά || it ~ him his life τού κόστισε τη ζωή || at all ~s πάση θυσία.
costly ['kɔstli] a (expensive) δαπανηρός || (jewellery etc) πολύτιμος.
cost price [kɔstprais] n τιμή κόστους.
costume ['kɔstjuːm] n (style of dress) ένδυμα nt, φορεσιά, μόδα || (woman's outer clothes) ενδυμασία, κοστούμι || (for bathing) μπανιερό, μαγιώ nt inv.
cosy ['kɔuzi] a αναπαυτικός, ζεστός.
cot [kɔt] n (child's bed) κρεββατάκι.
cottage ['kɔtidʒ] n εξοχικό σπιτάκι || ~ cheese n άσπρο τυρί.
cotton ['kɔtn] n βαμβάκι, μπαμπάκι || ~ wool n ακατέργαστο βαμβάκι.
couch [kautʃ] n ντιβάνι, καναπές m ♦ vt εκφράζω, συγκαλύπτω.
cough [kɔf] vi βήχω ♦ n βήχας || ~ drop n παστίλια για το βήχα.
could [kud] pt of can || ~n't = could not || see can.
council ['kaunsl] n συμβούλιο || ~lor n σύμβουλος m/f.
counsel ['kaunsəl] n (LAW) δικηγόρος m/f|| (opinion) συμβουλή || ~lor n σύμβουλος.
count [kaunt] vt (add up) μετρώ, αριθμώ || (include) υπολογίζω, συμπεριλαμβάνω ♦ vi (be of importance) υπολογίζομαι, στηρίζομαι ♦ n (reckoning) αρίθμηση, μέτρηση, λογαριασμός || (nobleman) κόμης || to ~ on vt υπολογίζω, στηρίζομαι σε || to ~ up vt προσθέτω.
counter ['kauntə*] n θυρίδα, γκισέ nt inv || (machine that counts) μετρητής ♦ vt αντιτίθεμαι, ανταπαντώ || ad εναντίον, αντιθέτως || ~act vt αντιδρώ, εξουδετερώνω || ~-attack n αντεπίθεση || ~balance vt αντισταθμίζω || ~-espionage n αντικατασκοπεία.
counterfeit ['kauntəfit] a πλαστός, κίβδηλος ♦ n παραποίηση, απάτη ♦ vt πλαστογραφώ.
counterfoil ['kauntəfɔil] n στέλεχος nt.
counterpart ['kauntəpaːt] n αντίστοιχο, ταίρι.
countess ['kauntis] n κόμισσα, κοντέσσα.
countless ['kauntlis] a αναρίθμητος, αμέτρητος.
country ['kʌntri] n (land) χώρα || (of birth) πατρίδα || (rural district) ύπαιθρος f, εξοχή, επαρχία || (region) περιοχή || ~ dancing n εθνικός χορός, λαϊκός χορός || ~ house n εξοχικό σπίτι || ~man n

(national) (συμ)πατριώτης || (rural) επαρχιώτης, χωριάτης || ~side n ύπαιθρος f.
county ['kaunti] n κομητεία, επαρχία || ~ town n πρωτεύουσα κομητείας.
coup [kuː] n (also: ~ d'état) πραξικόπημα nt.
coupé ['kuːpei] n κουπέ nt inv.
couple ['kʌpl] n ζευγάρι, δύο ♦ vt ενώνω, ζευγαρώνω.
couplet ['kʌplit] n δίστοιχο.
coupling ['kʌpliŋ] n σύζευξη.
coupon ['kuːpɔn] n κουπόνι, απόκομμα nt.
courage ['kʌridʒ] n θάρρος nt, γενναιότητα || ~ous a θαρραλέος.
courier ['kuriə*] n αγγελιοφόρος.
course [kɔːs] n (path, track) διαδρομή || (line of action) πορεία, δρόμος || (series, procedure) μάθημα nt, κουρ nt inv || (career, journey) πορεία || (part of meal) φαγητό, πιάτο || of ~ φυσικά, και βέβαια || in the ~ of κατά τη διάρκεια του || in due ~ εν καιρώ δέοντι || see golf.
court [kɔːt] n (attendants of sovereign) αυλή || (residence of sovereign) (βασιλική) αυλή || (of justice) δικαστήριο ♦ vt κορτάρω, προσκαλώ, επιδιώκω || see tennis.
courteous ['kɜːtiəs] a ευγενής.
courtesy ['kɜːtisi] n ευγένεια.
courthouse ['kɔːthaus] n (US) δικαστικό μέγαρο.
courtier ['kɔːtiə*] n αυλικός.
court-martial ['kɔːt'mɑːʃəl] n στρατοδικείο.
court room ['kɔːtrum] n αίθουσα δικαστηρίου.
courtyard ['kɔːtjɑːd] n αυλή.
cousin ['kʌzn] n ξάδελφος/n m/f.
cove [kəuv] n όρμος.
cover ['kʌvə*] vt (place over) καλύπτω, σκεπάζω || (shield, screen) καλύπτω, προστατεύω, κρύβω || (deal with) καλύπτω, περιλαμβάνω || (protect) προστατεύω ♦ n κάλυμμα nt, σκέπασμα nt || ~age n (of news) ρεπορτάζ nt inv || ~ charge n κουβέρ nt inv || ~ing n κάλυψη, σκέπασμα nt, επένδυση || ~ing letter n επιβεβαιωτική επιστολή.
covet ['kʌvit] vt εποφθαλμιώ.
cow [kau] n αγελάδα.
coward ['kauəd] n άνανδρος/n m/f, δειλός/n m/f|| ~ice n δειλία || ~ly a άνανδρος, δειλός.
cowboy ['kaubɔi] n καουμπόι nt inv.
cower ['kauə*] vi μαζεύομαι, τρέμω.
cowshed ['kauʃed] n βουστάσιο.
coxswain ['kɔksn] n (abbr: cox) πηδαλιούχος.
coy [kɔi] a ντροπαλός, σεμνός.
c.p.s. abbr see character.
CPU abbr see central.
crab [kræb] n κάβουρας || ~ apple n αγριόμηλο.
crack [kræk] n (sharp noise) κρότος, τριγμός || (of whip) στράκα || (split) ρωγμή,

σκάσιμο ♦ vt (noise) κροτώ || (split)
θραύω, ραγίζω ♦ a λαμπρός, εκλεκτός ||
~er n (firework) βαρελότο, στράκα ||
(biscuit) ναξιμαδάκι, μπισκότο || to ~ up
vi κομματιάζω || (fig) καταρρέω.

crackling ['kræklɪŋ] n κροταλισμός,
τρίξιμο || (of pig) πέσα ψημένου
γουρουνιού.

cradle ['kreɪdl] n κοιτίδα, λίκνο, κούνια.

craft [krɑ:ft] n (skill) τέχνη, χειροτεχνία,
επάγγελμα nt || (cunning) πανουργία,
δόλος || (boat) σκάφος nt, βάρκα ||
~sman n τεχνίτης || ~smanship n
τέχνη || ~y a πανούργος, πονηρός,
πολυμήχανος.

crag [kræg] n κατσάβραχο, γκρεμός ||
~gy a απόκρημνος, βραχώδης.

cram [kræm] vt μπάζω, χώνω.

cramp [kræmp] n (MED) σπασμός,
κράμπα ♦ vt εμποδίζω, περιορίζω.

crane [kreɪn] n γερανός, κρένι.

crank [kræŋk] n (lever)
(χειρο)στρόφαλος, μανιβέλα || (person)
ιδιότυπος, εκκεντρικός ♦ vt βάζω μπρος
με μανιβέλλα || ~shaft n
στροφαλοφόρος (άξωνας).

cranny ['krænɪ] n σχισμή, ρωγμή.

crash [kræʃ] n κρότος, βρόντος || (AVIAT)
συντριβή, πτώση || (AUT) σύγκρουση ||
(ECON) κράχ nt inv ♦ vti πέφτω,
συντρίβομαι || ~ helmet n
προστατευτικό κράνος || ~ landing n
αναγκαστική προσγείωση.

crate [kreɪt] n κασόνι, κοφίνι, καφάσι.

crater ['kreɪtə*] n κρατήρας.

cravat(e) [krə'væt] n γραβάτα.

crave [kreɪv] vi (+ for) εκλιπαρώ, ποθώ.

craving ['kreɪvɪŋ] n πόθος, λαχτάρα.

crawl [krɔ:l] vi έρπω, σέρνομαι ♦ n
σύρσιμο, βραδυπορία || (swimming)
κρώουλ nt inv.

crayon ['kreɪən] n κραγιόνι, παστέλ nt
inv.

craze [kreɪz] n μανία, λόξα.

crazy ['kreɪzɪ] a (foolish) ανόητος ||
(insane) παράφρονας, τρελλός, μουρλός.

creak [kri:k] n τρίγμός ♦ vi τρίζω.

cream [kri:m] n καϊμάκι, κρέμα, σαντιγί f
inv || (polish) αλοιφή || (cosmetic) κρέμα ||
(colour) ιβουάρ nt inv, κρεμ || ~ cake n
πάστα, τούρτα || ~y a καϊμακλίδικος,
βουτιρένιος.

crease [kri:s] n πτυχή, τσάκισμα nt,
τσαλάκωμα nt ♦ vti διπλώνω, ζαρώνω,
τσαλακώνω.

create [kri:'eɪt] vt (bring into being)
δημιουργώ || (cause) προξενώ || (COMPUT:
file) δημιουργώ.

creation [kri:'eɪʃən] n δημιούργημα nt.

creative [kri:'eɪtɪv] a δημιουργικός.

creator [kri'eɪtə*] n δημιουργός.

creature ['kri:tʃə*] n πλάσμα nt, ον nt.

credentials [krɪ'denʃəlz] npl (papers)
διαπιστευτήρια ntpl, πιστοποιητικά ntpl.

credibility [kredə'bɪlɪtɪ] n αξιοπιστία,
(το) πιστευτό.

credible ['kredɪbl] a πιστευτός,
αξιόπιτος.

credit ['kredɪt] n πίστη, πίστωση ||
(recognition) αναγνώριση ♦ vt πιστεύω ||
~able a έντιμος, αξιέπαινος || ~ card n
κάρτα πιστώσεως || ~or n πιστωτής.

creed [kri:d] n πίστη, θρήσκευμα nt.

creek [kri:k] n κολπίσκος || (US) ρέμα nt.

creep [kri:p] (irreg v) vi έρπω, σύρομαι ||
~er n (animal) ερπετό || (plant)
αναρριχητικό || ~y a (frightening)
ανατριχιαστικός.

cremate [krɪ'meɪt] vt αποτεφρώνω,
καίω.

cremation [krɪ'meɪʃən] n καύση
(νεκρού).

crematorium [kremə'tɔ:rɪəm] n
κρεματόριο.

crêpe [kreɪp] n κρεπ(ι) nt inv.

crept [krept] pt, pp of **creep**.

crescent ['kresnt] n ημισέληνος f || (esp
street) ημικυκλικός δρόμος.

cress [kres] n κάρδαμο.

crest [krest] n (tuft) λοφίο, λειρί || (of
wave) κορυφή || (badge) κορωνίδα,
οικόσημο || ~fallen a κατηφής,
αποθαρρημένος.

Crete [kri:t] n Κρήτη.

crevasse [krɪ'væs] n σχισμή.

crevice ['krevɪs] n ρωγμή, χαραμάδα.

crew [kru:] n πλήρωμα nt || ~-cut n
πολύ κοντό μαλλί.

crib [krɪb] n (child's bed) παιδικό κρεβάτι ||
(copy) αντιγραφή.

crick [krɪk] n πιάσιμο.

cricket ['krɪkɪt] n (insect) γρύλλος,
τριζόνι || (game) κρίκετ nt inv.

crime [kraɪm] n (wicked act) κακούργημα
nt || (lawbreaking) έγκλημα nt.

criminal ['krɪmɪnl] n εγκληματίας,
κακούργος ♦ a εγκληματικός, ποινικός.

crimson ['krɪmzn] n πορφυρό, βυσσινί
♦ a κατακόκκινος.

cringe [krɪndʒ] vi φέρομαι
δουλοπρεπώς, σκύβω.

crinkle ['krɪŋkl] vt ζαρώνω, τσαλακώνω
|| (rustle) τρίβω.

cripple ['krɪpl] n ανάπηρος, χωλός ♦ vt
τραυματίζω, σακατεύω, παραλύω.

crisis ['kraɪsɪs] n (time of danger etc)
κρίση.

crisp [krɪsp] a τραγανός, αφράτος,
φρέσκος ♦ n ξεροτηγανισμένη πατάτα.

criss-cross ['krɪskrɒs] a σταυρωτός,
καφασωτός.

criterion [kraɪ'tɪərɪən] n κριτήριο.

critic ['krɪtɪk] n (THEAT etc) τεχνοκρίτης,
κριτικός || επικριτής || ~al a (like a critic)
κριτικός || (danger) κρίσιμος || (severe)
αυστηρός || ~ally ad με κριτική
διάθεση, κρίσιμος || ~ism ['krɪtɪsɪzəm] n
(judgment) κριτική || (finding fault) επίκριση
|| ~ize ['krɪtɪsaɪz] vt (επι)κρίνω,
κατακρίνω.

croak [krəuk] vi (crow) κρώζω || (frog)
κοάζω ♦ n (of crow) κρωγμός || (of frog)
κοασμός.

crochet ['krəʊʃeɪ] n κροσέ nt.

crockery ['krɒkərɪ] n πήλινα σκεύη ntpl.

crocodile ['krɒkədaɪl] n κροκόδειλος.

crocus ['krəʊkəs] n κρόκος.

crook [krʊk] n (criminal) λωποδύτης, απατεώνας || (of shepherd) γκλίτσα || ~ed a αγκυλωτός.

crop [krɒp] n συγκομιδή, σοδιά || to ~ up vi (fig) παρουσιάζομαι, προκύπτω.

croquet ['krəʊkeɪ] n κροκέ nt.

croquette [krəʊˈket] n κροκέτα, κεφτές m.

cross [krɒs] n (of Christ) σταυρός || (mark) σταυρός || (breed) διασταύρωση || (misfortune) εμπόδιο, δυσκολία ♦ vt (pass over) διασχίζω, περνώ || (make sign) σταυροκοπιέμαι || (place across) σταυρώνω || (mix breeds) διασταυρώνω || (cheque) διαγραμμίζω ♦ a θυμωμένος, κακόκεφος || ~-country (race) n ανώμαλος δρόμος || ~-examination n εξέταση κατ'αντιπαράσταση || ~-examine vt εξετάζω κατ'αντιπαράσταση || ~-eyed a αλλοίθωρος || ~ing n (of road etc) διάβαση, πέρασμα nt || (sea passage) διάπλους m || (place for crossing) διάβαση || at ~-purposes παρεξηγημένοι, σε αντίθεση || ~-reference n παραπομπή || ~roads n σταυροδρόμι || ~section n εγκάρσια τομή || ~ wind n πλάγιος άνεμος || ~word (puzzle) n σταυρόλεξο.

crotch [krɒtʃ] n διακλάδωση δέντρου, καβάλος του πανταλονιού.

crotchet ['krɒtʃɪt] n ιδιοτροπία, βίδα.

crotchety ['krɒtʃɪtɪ] a (person) ιδιότροπος.

crouch [kraʊtʃ] vi σκύβω, μαζεύομαι.

crow [krəʊ] n κορώνη, κουρούνα ♦ vi κράζω, λαλώ || (fig) κομπάζω.

crowbar ['krəʊbɑː*] n λοστός.

crowd [kraʊd] n πλήθος nt, όχλος, συρροή ♦ vt (fill) γεμίζω ♦ vi (flock together) συναθροίομαι, συνωστίζομαι || ~ed a γεμάτος.

crown [kraʊn] n (royal headdress) στέμμα nt, κορώνα || (of tooth) κορώνα || (top of head etc) κορυφή, κορφή || (of flowers) στεφάνι ♦ vt (put crown on) στεφανώνω || (be at top of) πάνω απ'όλα, αποκορυφώνω || ~ jewels npl κοσμήματα του Στέμματος ntpl || ~ prince n διάδοχος του θρόνου.

crucial ['kruːʃəl] a αποφασιστικός, κρίσιμος.

crucifix ['kruːsɪfɪks] n εσταυρωμένος || ~ion n σταύρωση.

crucify ['kruːsɪfaɪ] vt σταυρώνω, βασανίζω.

crude [kruːd] a (unfinished) ακατέργαστος || (petroleum) αργό πετρέλαιο || (harsh) ωμός, άξεστος || (humour) χοντρό χιούμορ.

cruel ['krʊəl] a (vicious) αιμοβόρος, αμείλικτος || (severe, distressing) σκληρός, ωμός || (hard-hearted) σκληρόκαρδος ||

~ty n σκληρότητα, ασπλαχνία || (to wife) κακοποίηση.

cruise [kruːz] n περίπλους m, κρουαζιέρα ♦ vi κάνω κρουαζιέρα, περιπλέω || ~r n καταδρομικό.

crumb [krʌm] n ψίχουλο || (fig) απομεινάρι.

crumble ['krʌmbl] vti καταρρέω, θρυμματίζομαι.

crumbly ['krʌmblɪ] a εύθρυπτος.

crumpet ['krʌmpɪt] n είδος τηγανίτας.

crumple ['krʌmpl] vt τσαλακώνω, ζαρώνω.

crunch [krʌntʃ] n τραγάνισμα nt || (sound) τρίξιμο ♦ vt μασώ, τραγανίζω || ~y a τραγανιστός.

crusade [kruːˈseɪd] n σταυροφορία.

crush [krʌʃ] n σύνθλιψη, συνωστισμός ♦ vt συνθλίβω || (a rebellion) συντρίβω, καταβάλλω ♦ vt (material) τσαλακώνω || ~ing a συντριπτικός.

crust [krʌst] n (of bread) κόρα || (of cake etc) κρούστα || (of earth etc) φλοιός, κρούστα.

crutch [krʌtʃ] n δεκανίκι, πατερίτσα.

crux [krʌks] n ουσία, κεντρικό σημείο.

cry [kraɪ] vi (sell etc) διαλαλώ || (shout) φωνάζω, βάζω τις φωνές || (weep) κλαίω, θρηνώ ♦ n φωνή, κλάμα nt.

crypt [krɪpt] n κρύπτη.

cryptic ['krɪptɪk] a μυστικός, δυσνόητος.

crystal ['krɪstl] n (natural form) κρύσταλλος || (clear glass) κρύσταλλο || ~-clear a κρυστάλλινος || ~-lize vti (lit) (απο)κρυσταλλώνω || (fig) (απο)κρυσταλλούμαι.

cu. abbr: ~ ft. = cubic feet; ~ in. = cubic inches.

cub [kʌb] n νεογνό ζώο.

cube [kjuːb] n (figure) κύβος.

cubic ['kjuːbɪk] a κυβικός.

cubicle ['kjuːbɪkəl] n θαλαμίσκος.

cuckoo ['kʊkuː] n κούκος.

cucumber ['kjuːkʌmbə*] n αγγούρι.

cuddle ['kʌdl] vti αγκαλιάζω, κουκουλώνομαι ♦ n αγκάλιασμα nt.

cue [kjuː] n (hint) νύξη, υπαινιγμός || (in billiards) στέκα.

cuff [kʌf] n (of shirt, coat etc) μανικέτι || (US) = turn-up || ~link n μανικετόκουμπο ntpl.

cuisine [kwɪˈziːn] n μαγειρική.

cul-de-sac ['kʌldəˈsæk] n αδιέξοδο.

culinary ['kʌlɪnərɪ] a μαγειρικός.

culminate ['kʌlmɪneɪt] vi αποκορυφώνομαι, μεσουρανώ.

culmination [kʌlmɪˈneɪʃən] n μεσουράνημα nt, κολοφών m.

culprit ['kʌlprɪt] n ένοχος.

cult [kʌlt] n (religious) λατρεία || (mode) μόδα, λόξα.

cultivate ['kʌltɪveɪt] vt καλλιεργώ.

cultivation [kʌltɪˈveɪʃən] n καλλιέργεια.

cultural ['kʌltʃərəl] a πνευματικός, μορφωτικός.

culture ['kʌltʃə*] n (refinement)

καλλιέργεια || *(intellectual development)*
ανάπτυξη, κουλτούρα || ~**d** a
μορφωμένος, καλλιεργημένος.
cumbersome ['kʌmbəsəm] a
ενοχλητικός, βαρύς, δυσκίνητος.
cumulative ['kjuːmju:lətɪv] a
επισωρευτικός, αθροιστικός.
cunning ['kʌnɪŋ] n πανουργία,
καπατσοσύνη ♦ a πονηρός,
τετραπέρατος.
cup [kʌp] n κούπα, φλυτζάνι || *(prize)*
κύπελλο.
cupboard ['kʌbəd] n ντουλάπι, αρμάρι.
cupful ['kʌpful] n φλυτζανιά.
cupola ['kjuːpələ] n θόλος, τρούλλος.
curable ['kjuərəbl] a ιάσιμος, που
γιατρεύεται.
curator [kjuə'reɪtə*] n έφορος
(μουσείου).
curb [kɜːb] vt χαλιναγωγώ, ελέγχω ♦ n
χαλινός, φραγμός || *see* **kerb(stone)**.
curfew ['kɜːfjuː] n απαγόρευση της
κυκλοφορίας.
curiosity [kjuərɪ'ɒsɪtɪ] n περιέργεια ||
(strange object) περίεργο αντικείμενο.
curious ['kjuərɪəs] a (φιλο)περίεργος ||
(strange) περίεργος, παράξενος.
curl [kɜːl] n βόστρυχος, μπούκλα || *(of lips
etc)* στρίψιμο ♦ vti *(hair etc)* σγουραίνω ||
(lips) στρίβω, στραβώνω || *(wrap)* τυλίγω ||
~**er** n ρολά ntpl, μπικουτί nt inv.
curly ['kɜːlɪ] a κατσαρός, σγουρός.
currant ['kʌrənt] n Κορινθιακή
σταφίδα.
currency ['kʌrənsɪ] n νόμισμα nt || *(of
ideas)* κυκλοφορία, πέραση.
current ['kʌrənt] n ρεύμα nt, ροή, ρέμα
nt ♦ a κυκλοφορών, εν χρήσει || ~
account n τρεχούμενος λογαριασμός ||
~ **affairs** npl επίκαιρα ntpl || ~**ly** ad
γενικώς, σήμερα.
curriculum [kə'rɪkjuləm] n κύκλος
μαθημάτων || ~ **vitae** n περίληψη
προσόντων.
curry ['kʌrɪ] n κάρρι nt inv || ~ **powder** n
σκόνη κάρρι.
curse [kɜːs] vi βλαστημώ, υβρίζω ♦ vt
καταριέμαι, αναθεματίζω ♦ n κατάρα,
ανάθεμα nt || *(bad language)* βλαστήμια.
cursor ['kɜːsə*] n *(COMPUT)* δείκτης
θέσεως.
cursory ['kɜːsərɪ] a γρήγορος,
βιαστικός.
curt [kɜːt] a απότομος, κοφτός.
curtail [kɜː'teɪl] vt περικόπτω,
περιορίζω.
curtain ['kɜːtn] n *(esp at window)*
κουρτίνα || *(THEAT)* αυλαία,
παραπέτασμα nt.
curtsy ['kɜːtsɪ] n υπόκλιση ♦ vi κάνω
υπόκλιση.
curve [kɜːv] n καμπή.
cushion ['kuʃən] n μαξιλαράκι.
custard ['kʌstəd] n ψημένη κρέμα.
custodian [kʌs'təudɪən] n φύλακας,
επιστάτης.

custody ['kʌstədɪ] n επιτήρηση,
κηδεμονία || *(under arrest)* κράτηση.
custom ['kʌstəm] n *(fashion)* έθιμο,
συνήθεια || *(business)* πελατεία || ~**ary** a
συνηθισμένος || ~-**made** a καμωμένο
επί παραγγελία.
customer ['kʌstəmə*] n πελάτης/τισσα
m/f.
customs ['kʌstəmz] n *(taxes)* δασμοί mpl
|| **C**~ *(place)* τελωνείο || **C**~ **officer** n
τελωνειακός υπάλληλος.
cut [kʌt] vt *(irreg v)* *(divide)* κόβω, χαράζω
|| *(wound)* πληγώνω || *(reduce)* κατεβάζω
(τιμές) ♦ n *(sharp stroke)* κόψη, κόψιμο ||
(wound) τομή, κόψιμο, πληγή || *(reduction)*
περικοπή, μείωση || *(share)* μερίδιο.
cute [kjuːt] a χαριτωμένος.
cuticle ['kjuːtɪkl] n *(on nail)* επιδερμίδα,
cutlery ['kʌtlərɪ] n μαχαιροπήρουνα
ntpl.
cutlet ['kʌtlɪt] n κοτολέττα.
cutout ['kʌtaut] n *(ELEC)* διακόπτης.
cutprice ['kʌtpraɪs] n τιμή ελαττωμένη.
cutting ['kʌtɪŋ] n αιχμή, κόψη.
cwt *abbr of* **hundredweight(s)**.
cyanide ['saɪənaɪd] n κυανίδη.
cycle ['saɪkl] n *(bicycle)* ποδήλατο ||
(series) κύκλος, περίοδος f || *(of poems etc)*
κύκλος ♦ vi πηγαίνω με ποδήλατο.
cycling ['saɪklɪŋ] n ποδηλατοδρομία,
ποδήλατο.
cyclist ['saɪklɪst] n ποδηλατιστής.
cyclone ['saɪkləun] n κυκλώνας.
cygnet ['sɪgnɪt] n μικρός κύκνος.
cylinder ['sɪlɪndə*] n κύλινδρος || *(of gas
etc)* φιάλη, μπουκάλα || ~ **block** n
συγκρότημα nt κυλίνδρου || ~ **capacity**
n όγκος κυλίνδρου || ~ **head** n κεφαλή
κυλίνδρου.
cymbals ['sɪmbəlz] npl κύμβαλα ntpl.
cynic ['sɪnɪk] n κυνικός || ~**al** a κυνικός,
δύσπιστος || ~**ism** ['sɪnɪsɪzəm] n
κυνισμός, χοτηροκουβέντα.
cypress ['saɪprɪs] n κυπαρίσσι.
Cyprus ['saɪprəs] n Κύπρος f.
cyst [sɪst] n κύστις.
czar [zɑː] n τσάρος || ~**ina** n τσαρίνα.
Czech [tʃek] a τσεχικός || n Τσέχος/α
m/f.
Czechoslavakia ['tʃekəuslɒu'vækɪə] n
Τσεχοσλοβακία.

D

dab [dæb] vt επαλείφω ♦ n *(tap)* ελαφρό
κτύπημα nt || *(smear)* μικρή ποσότητα,
λίγο.
dad(dy) ['dæd(ɪ)] n μπαμπάς,
μπαμπάκας || **daddy-long-legs** n
τιπούλη, αλογατάκι.
daffodil ['dæfədɪl] n ασφόδελος.
daft [dɑːft] a ανόητος, τρελλός.
dagger ['dægə*] n εγχειρίδιο, στιλέττο.
dahlia ['deɪlɪə] n ντάλια.
daily ['deɪlɪ] a ημερήσιος ♦ n
καθημερινή *(εφημερίδα)*.

dainty ['deɪntɪ] a κομψός, νόστιμος.
dairy ['dɛərɪ] n (shop) γαλακτοπωλείο, γαλατάδικο || (on farm) γαλακτοκομείο ♦ a γαλακτοκομικό.
daisy ['deɪzɪ] n μαργαρίτα || ~ **wheel** n (on printer) μαργαρίτα || ~ **wheel printer** n εκτυπωτής μαργαρίτας.
dam [dæm] n (for water) φράγμα nt, ανάχωμα nt ♦ vt φράσσω.
damage ['dæmɪdʒ] n βλάβη, ζημιά ♦ vt βλάπτω, ζημιώνω || ~s npl (LAW) αποζημίωση.
dame [deɪm] n κυρία, κυρά.
damn [dæm] vt καταδικάζω ♦ a (col) διάβολος || ~ **it** να πάρει ο διάβολος!, να πάρει η ευχή! || ~ing a καταδικαστικός, επιβαρυντικός.
damp [dæmp] a υγρός, νοτερός ♦ n υγρασία, υγρότητα ♦ vt (also: ~en) υγραίνω, μουσκεύω || (discourage) μειώνω, ελαττώνω, κόβω || ~ness n υγρασία, υγρότητα.
damson ['dæmzən] n δαμάσκηνο.
dance [dɑːns] n χορός || (party) χορευτική συγκέντρωση, πάρτυ nt inv ♦ vi χορεύω || ~ **hall** n χορευτικό κέντρο || ~r n χορευτής, χορεύτρια.
dancing ['dɑːnsɪŋ] n χορός.
dandelion ['dændɪlaɪən] n αγριοραδίκι.
dandruff ['dændrəf] n πιτυρίδα.
dandy ['dændɪ] n κομψευόμενος, δανδής.
Dane [deɪn] n Δανός/έζα m/f.
danger ['deɪndʒə*] n κίνδυνος || ~! (sign) προσοχή || **in** ~ διατρέχω κίνδυνο || ~ous a επικίνδυνος.
dangle ['dæŋgl] vti αιωρούμαι, ταλαντεύομαι, κρέμομαι.
Danish ['deɪnɪʃ] a δανικός ♦ n Δανική γλώσσα.
dare [dɛə*] vt τολμώ ♦ vi: **to** ~ **(to) do sth** τολμώ να κάνω κάτι || **I** ~ **say** ασφαλώς, πιθανώς.
daring ['dɛərɪŋ] a τολμηρός, άφοβος.
dark [dɑːk] a (dim) σκοτεινός, μαύρος || (gloomy) σκοτεινός, μελαγχολικός || (colour) μελαχροινός, μελαψός ♦ n σκοτάδι || (ignorance) σε άγνοια || **after** ~ αφού νυχτώσει || ~en vti σκοτεινιάζω || ~ness n σκότος nt, σκοτάδι || ~ **room** n σκοτεινός θάλαμος.
darling ['dɑːlɪŋ] n πολυαγαπημένος.
darn [dɑːn] n μαντάρισμα nt ♦ vt μπαλώνω, καρικώνω.
dart [dɑːt] n (quick move) ορμή || (weapon) βέλος nt, σαΐτα ♦ vi εξακοντίζω, ορμώ || ~s σαΐτα || ~board n στόχος σαΐτας.
dash [dæʃ] n (rush) εξόρμηση || (waves) χτύπημα nt, σπάσιμο || (mark) παύλα ♦ vt (lit) ρίχνω, χτυπώ, καταστρέφω ♦ vi εφορμώ, πέφτω || ~board n ταμπλό nt inv || ~ **a** (person) ορμητικός, ζωηρός.
data ['deɪtə] npl δεδομένα ntpl, στοιχεία ntpl || ~**base** n βάση δεδομένων || ~ **processing** n κατεργασία στοιχείων.
date [deɪt] n (point in time) χρονολογία, ημερομηνία || (with person) ραντεβού nt

inv || (fruit) χουρμάς ♦ vt (letter etc) βάζω ημερομηνία || (person) δίνω ραντεβού || ~d a με χρονολογία.
daub [dɔːb] vt (smear) πασαλείβω, αλείφω || (paint badly) μουντζουρώνω.
daughter ['dɔːtə*] n θυγατέρα, κόρη || ~-in-law n νύφη.
dawdle ['dɔːdl] vi χασομερώ, τεμπελιάζω.
dawn [dɔːn] n αυγή ♦ vi υποφώσκω, χαράζω || (become apparent) αποκαλύπτω.
day [deɪ] n ημέρα, μέρα || (24 hours) εικοσιτετράωρο || (date, time) ημερομηνία || (daylight) φως nt της ημέρας || ~ **by** ~ ημέρα με την ημέρα || ~break n αυγή, χάραμα nt || ~dream n ονειροπόλημα nt, ρεμβασμός ♦ vi ονειροπολώ, ρεμβάζω || ~light n φως nt της ημέρας || ~time n ημέρα.
daze [deɪz] vt θαμπώνω, ζαλίζω ♦ n θάμπωμα nt, ζάλη.
dazzle ['dæzl] vt θαμπώνω, τυφλώνω ♦ n θάμπωμα nt, τύφλωμα nt.
dead [dɛd] a νεκρός, πεθαμένος || (without feeling) αναίσθητος || (exact) πλήρης, ακριβής ♦ ad τελείως, ακριβώς, απολύτως || **the** ~ npl οι νεκροί mpl, οι πεθαμένοι mpl || ~en vt νεκρώνω, κατασιγάζω || ~ **end** n αδιέξοδο || ~ **heat** n ισοπαλία || ~line n (χρονικό) όριο || ~lock n αδιέξοδο || ~ly a θανατηφόρος, θανάσιμος || (fig) αδυσώπητος, αφόρητος || ~ **pan** a (πθοποιός) χωρίς έκφραση.
deaf [dɛf] a κουφός || ~-aid n ακουστικό κωφών || ~en vt (ξε)κουφαίνω || ~ening a εκκωφαντικός || ~-mute n κωφάλαλος/η m/f || ~ness n κουφαμάρα.
deal [diːl] n (irreg v) n συμφωνία, δουλειά ♦ vti (CARDS) μοιράζω, δίνω || **a great** ~ **of** n ποσότητα, πολύ || **to** ~ **with** vt αντιμετωπίζω, λαμβάνω μέτρα || ~er n έμπορος, αντιπρόσωπος || (CARDS) μοιραστής.
dear [dɪə*] a (beloved) αγαπητός, προσφιλής || (expensive) ακριβός, δαπανηρός ♦ n προσφιλής, αγαπημένος || ~ **me** Θεέ μου || **D**~ **Sir** αξιότιμε, αγαπητέ κύριε || **D**~ **John** αγαπητέ Γιάννη || ~ly ad (love) με αγάπη || (pay) ακριβά.
death [dɛθ] n θάνατος || ~bed n νεκροκρέββατο || ~ **certificate** n πιστοποιητικό θανάτου || ~ **duties** npl (Brit) φόρος κληρονομίας || ~ly a νεκρικός, ωχρός || ~ **penalty** n ποινή θανάτου || ~ **rate** n θνησιμότητα.
debase [dɪ'beɪs] vt ξευτελίζω, υποβιβάζω.
debate [dɪ'beɪt] n συζήτηση ♦ vt συζητώ || (consider) σκέφτομαι.
debauchery [dɪ'bɔːtʃərɪ] n ακολασία.
debit ['dɛbɪt] n δούναι, παθητικό ♦ vt χρεώνω.
debris ['dɛbriː] n συντρίμματα ntpl, μπάζα.

debt [dɛt] *n* χρέος *nt*, οφειλή || **to be in ~** χρωστώ || **~or** *n* οφειλέτης, χρεώστης.

debug [diː'bʌg] *vt (COMPUT)* αφαιρώ λάθη *or* σφάλματα.

début ['deɪbuː] *n* πρώτη εμφάνιση, ντεμπούτο.

decade ['dɛkeɪd] *n* δεκαετία.

decadence ['dɛkədəns] *n* παρακμή.

decay [dɪ'keɪ] *n* παρακμή, φθορά, κατάπτωση ♦ *vi* παρακμάζω, μαραίνομαι.

decease [dɪ'siːs] *n* θάνατος || **~d** *n* μακαρίτης/ισσα *m/f.*

deceit [dɪ'siːt] *n* απάτη, δόλος || **~ful** *a* δόλιος, απατηλός.

deceive [dɪ'siːv] *vt* εξαπατώ, κοροϊδεύω.

decelerate [diː'sɛləreɪt] *vti* επιβραδύνω, κόβω ταχύτητα.

December [dɪ'sɛmbə*] *n* Δεκέμβρης, Δεκέμβριος.

decency ['diːsənsɪ] *n (fit behaviour)* ευπρέπεια, σεμνότητα || *(respectability)* κοσμιότητα.

decent ['diːsənt] *a (respectable)* ευπρεπής, συμμαζεμένος || *(pleasant)* αρκετά καλός.

deception [dɪ'sɛpʃən] *n* εξαπάτηση, τέχνασμα *nt.*

deceptive [dɪ'sɛptɪv] *a* απατηλός.

decibel ['dɛsɪbɛl] *n* ντεσιμπέλ *nt inv.*

decide [dɪ'saɪd] *vt (settle)* κρίνω, αποφασίζω ♦ *vi (determine)* αποφασίζω, καταλήγω || **to ~ to do** αποφασίζω να κάνω || **~d** *a* αποφασισμένος, οριστικός || **~dly** *ad* αποφασιστικά, βεβαίως.

deciduous [dɪ'sɪdjʊəs] *a* φυλλοβόλος.

decimal ['dɛsɪməl] *a* δεκαδικός ♦ *n* δεκαδικό || **~ point** *n* υποδιαστολή.

decimate ['dɛsɪmeɪt] *vt* αποδεκατίζω.

decipher [dɪ'saɪfə*] *vt* ξεδιαλύνω, βγάζω.

decision [dɪ'sɪʒən] *n* απόφαση.

decisive [dɪ'saɪsɪv] *a* αποφασιστικός.

deck [dɛk] *n (NAUT)* κατάστρωμα *nt,* κουβέρτα || *(of bus)* όροφος || *(of cards)* τράπουλα || **~chair** *n* σαιζ-λογκ *f inv.*

declaration [dɛklə'reɪʃən] *n* δήλωση, διακήρυξη.

declare [dɪ'klɛə*] *vt (state)* δηλώνω || *(war)* κηρύσσω || *(in customs)* δηλώνω.

decline [dɪ'klaɪn] *n (decay)* παρακμή, πτώση, πέσιμο || *(lessening)* πέσιμο, κατάπτωση ♦ *vt (refuse)* αρνούμαι || *(GRAM)* κλίνω ♦ *vi* φθίνω, εξασθενίζω, αδυνατίζω.

declutch ['diː'klʌtʃ] *vi* ντεμπραγιάρω.

decode ['diː'kəʊd] *vt* αποκρυπτογραφώ.

decompose [diːkəm'pəʊz] *vi (rot)* αποσυντίθεμαι, σαπίζω.

decontaminate [diːkən'tæmɪneɪt] *vt* απολυμαίνω.

décor ['deɪkɔː*] *n* διακόσμηση, ντεκόρ *nt inv.*

decorate ['dɛkəreɪt] *vt (renew paint etc)* χρωματίζω, βάφω || *(adorn)* (δια)κοσμώ, στολίζω || *(give medal etc)* παρασημοφορώ.

decoration [dɛkə'reɪʃən] *n (of house)* διακόσμηση || *(MIL)* παράσημο.

decorator ['dɛkəreɪtə*] *n* διακοσμητής/ήτρια *m/f.*

decoy ['diːkɔɪ] *n* δέλεαρ *nt inv,* δόλωμα *nt.*

decrease [diː'kriːs] *n* μείωση, ελάττωση ♦ *vti* μειώνω, ελαττώνομαι.

decree [dɪ'kriː] *n* διάταγμα *nt,* βούλευμα *nt.*

decrepit [dɪ'krɛpɪt] *a* παραγηρασμένος || *(furniture etc)* ξεχαρβαλωμένος.

dedicate ['dɛdɪkeɪt] *vt* αφιερώνω.

dedication [dɛdɪ'keɪʃən] *n* αφιέρωση.

deduce [dɪ'djuːs] *vt* συμπεραίνω.

deduct [dɪ'dʌkt] *vt* αφαιρώ || **~ion** *n* αφαίρεση, συμπέρασμα *nt || (fin price etc)* έκπτωση.

deed [diːd] *n* πράξη, έργο || *(LAW)* έγγραφο.

deep [diːp] *a (water)* βαθύς || *(breath)* βαθειά || *(voice)* βαθειά, βαρειά || **in ~ water** σε μεγάλη δυσκολία || **~en** *vt* εμβαθύνω, βαθαίνω || **~freeze** *n* κατάψυξη || **~seated** *a* βαθειά ριζωμένος.

deer [dɪə*] *n* ελάφι.

deface [dɪ'feɪs] *vt* παραμορφώνω.

defamation [dɛfə'meɪʃən] *n* δυσφήμηση.

default [dɪ'fɔːlt] *n* παράλειψη, αθέτηση || *(LAW)* απουσία || *(COMPUT)* παράλειψη ♦ *vi* παραλείπω καθήκον, φυγοδικώ || **by ~** ερήμην || **~er** *n* φυγόδικος.

defeat [dɪ'fiːt] *n (overthrow)* ανατροπή, ματαίωση || ήττα, συντριβή ♦ *vt* νικώ, ανατρέπω || **~ist** *a* ηττοπαθής.

defect ['diːfɛkt] *n* ατέλεια, ελάττωμα *nt* ♦ [dɪ'fɛkt] *vi* λιποτακτώ || **~ive** *a* ελλιπής, ελαττωματικός.

defence [dɪ'fɛns] *n (MIL, SPORT)* άμυνα, υπεράσπιση || δικαιολογία || **~less** *a* ανυπεράσπιστος.

defend [dɪ'fɛnd] *vt* υπερασπίζω || **~ant** *n* εναγόμενος || **~er** *n* υπερασπιστής, υπέρμαχος.

defensive [dɪ'fɛnsɪv] *a* αμυντικός ♦ *n* άμυνα.

defer [dɪ'fɜː*] *vt* αναβάλλω.

deference ['dɛfərəns] *n* σεβασμός.

defiance [dɪ'faɪəns] *n* αψηφισιά, περιφρόνηση.

defiant [dɪ'faɪənt] *a* προκλητικός, αψηφών.

deficiency [dɪ'fɪʃənsɪ] *n* έλλειψη, ατέλεια.

deficient [dɪ'fɪʃənt] *a* ατελής, ελλιπής.

deficit ['dɛfɪsɪt] *n* έλλειμμα *nt.*

define [dɪ'faɪn] *vt* (καθ)ορίζω || *(explain)* εξηγώ, καθορίζω.

definite ['dɛfɪnɪt] *a (fixed)* (καθ)ορισμένος || *(clear)* σαφής || *(GRAM)* οριστικό || **~ly** *ad* σαφώς.

definition [dɛfɪ'nɪʃən] *n* (καθ)ορισμός.

definitive [dɪ'fɪnɪtɪv] a οριστικός, τελικός.

deflate [diː'fleɪt] vt ξεφουσκώνω || (currency) υποτιμώ.

deflation [diː'fleɪʃən] n (FIN) υποτίμηση.

deflect [dɪ'flɛkt] vt εκτρέπω, παρεκκλίνω.

deform [dɪ'fɔːm] vt παραμορφώνω, ασχημίζω || ~ed a δύσμορφος παραμορφωμένος || ~ity n δυσμορφία, παραμόρφωση.

defraud [dɪ'frɔːd] vt εξαπατώ, κλέβω.

defrost [diː'frɒst] vt (fridge) ξεπαγώνω.

deft [dɛft] a επιτήδειος, επιδέξιος.

defunct [dɪ'fʌŋkt] a μακαρίτης.

defy [dɪ'faɪ] vt (challenge) προκαλώ || (ignore) αψηφώ.

degenerate [dɪ'dʒɛnəreɪt] vi εκφυλίζομαι ♦ [dɪ'dʒɛnərɪt] a εκφυλισμένος.

degradation [dɛgrə'deɪʃən] n ξεφτελισμός, υποβιβασμός.

degrading [dɪ'greɪdɪŋ] a ξεφτελιστικός, ταπεινωτικός.

degree [dɪ'griː] n (step, stage) βαθμός || (UNIV) πτυχίο || (measurement) μοίρα || by ~s βαθμηδόν.

dehydrated [diːhaɪ'dreɪtɪd] a αφυδατωμένος.

de-ice [diː'aɪs] vt (windscreen) ξεπαγώνω.

deign [deɪn] vi καταδέχομαι, ευαρεστούμαι.

deity ['diːɪtɪ] n θεότητα.

dejected [dɪ'dʒɛktɪd] a κατηφής, άκεφος.

dejection [dɪ'dʒɛkʃən] n κατήφεια, ακεφιά.

delay [dɪ'leɪ] vt αναβάλλω, καθυστερώ ♦ vi βραδύνω, αργώ ♦ n αργοπορία, αναβολή, επιβράδυνση || without ~ χωρίς καθυστέρηση.

delegate ['dɛlɪgɪt] n αντιπρόσωπος, απεσταλμένος ♦ ['dɛlɪgeɪt] vt εντέλλομαι, εξουσιοδοτώ.

delegation [dɛlɪ'geɪʃən] n αντιπροσωπεία.

delete [dɪ'liːt] vt αφαιρώ, σβήνω.

deliberate [dɪ'lɪbərɪt] a (intentional) εσκεμμένος || (slow) αργός, επιφυλακτικός ♦ [dɪ'lɪbəreɪt] vi διαλογίζομαι, συνδιασκέπτομαι || ~ly ad εσκεμμένα.

delicacy ['dɛlɪkəsɪ] n (daintiness) ευαισθησία, λεπτότητα || (refinement) λεπτότητα || (choice food) λιχουδιές fpl.

delicate ['dɛlɪkɪt] a (fine) λεπτός, απαλός || (fragile) λεπτός || (situation) λεπτός, δύσκολος || (MED) λεπτή, ευπαθής.

delicious [dɪ'lɪʃəs] a νόστιμος, ευχάριστος.

delight [dɪ'laɪt] n ευχαρίστηση, τέρψη ♦ vt χαιροποιώ, τέρπω || ~ful a γοητευτικός, πολύ ευχάριστος.

delinquency [dɪ'lɪŋkwənsɪ] n εγκληματικότητα, αδίκημα nt.

delinquent [dɪ'lɪŋkwənt] n εγκληματίας,
παραπτωματίας ♦ a παραπτωματικός || (ECON) εκπρόθεσμος.

delirium [dɪ'lɪrɪəm] n παραλήρημα nt.

deliver [dɪ'lɪvə*] vt (distribute) (παρα)δίδω, διανέμω || (pronounce) εκφωνώ, μεταδίδω || (free) απαλλάσσω, ελευθερώνω, σώζω || ~y n παράδοση, διανομή || (of speech) παράδοση, εκφώνηση.

delta ['dɛltə] n δέλτα nt.

delude [dɪ'luːd] vt εξαπατώ.

deluge ['dɛljuːdʒ] n κατακλυσμός.

delusion [dɪ'luːʒən] n (αυτ)απάτη.

de luxe [dɪ'lʌks] a ντε λουξ.

demand [dɪ'mɑːnd] vt απαιτώ, αξιώνω ♦ n αξίωση, απαίτηση || (call for a commodity) ζήτηση || in ~ ζητούμαι || on ~ επί τη εμφανίσει || ~ing a απαιτητικός, διεκδικητικός.

demarcation [diːmɑː'keɪʃən] n οροθεσία.

demented [dɪ'mɛntɪd] a παράφρονας, τρελλός.

demise [dɪ'maɪz] n αποβίωση.

demobilization ['diːməubɪlaɪ'zeɪʃən] n αποστράτευση.

democracy [dɪ'mɒkrəsɪ] n δημοκρατία.

democrat ['dɛməkræt] n δημοκράτης || ~ic a δημοκρατικός.

demolish [dɪ'mɒlɪʃ] vt (lit) κατεδαφίζω, κατακρημνίζω || (fig) συντρίβω.

demolition [dɛmə'lɪʃən] n κατεδάφιση.

demonstrate ['dɛmənstreɪt] vt αποδεικνύω || (protest) διαδηλώνω.

demonstration [dɛmən'streɪʃən] n απόδειξη, επίδειξη || (POL) διαδήλωση.

demonstrator ['dɛmənstreɪtə*] n (POL) διαδηλωτής.

demoralize [dɪ'mɒrəlaɪz] vt εξαχρειώνω, αποθαρρύνω.

demote [dɪ'məut] vt υποβιβάζω.

demure [dɪ'mjuə*] a σοβαρός, μετριόφρονας.

den [dɛn] n τρώγλη, φωλιά || (room) καμαρούλα.

denial [dɪ'naɪəl] n άρνηση.

Denmark ['dɛnmɑːk] n Δανία.

denomination [dɪnɒmɪ'neɪʃən] n (name) ονομασία || (REL) δόγμα nt, θρήσκευμα nt.

denote [dɪ'nəut] vt δείχνω, εμφαίνω.

denounce [dɪ'nauns] vt καταγγέλλω.

dense [dɛns] a πυκνός || (stupid) βλάκας, αμαθής.

density ['dɛnsɪtɪ] n πυκνότητα.

dent [dɛnt] n κοίλωμα nt, βαθούλωμα nt ♦ vt κοιλαίνω, βαθουλώνω.

dental ['dɛntl] a (GRAM) οδοντόφωνος || ~ surgeon = dentist.

dentist ['dɛntɪst] n οδοντίατρος m/f || ~ry n οδοντιατρική.

denture ['dɛntʃə*] n οδοντοστοιχία, μασέλα.

deny [dɪ'naɪ] vt (declare untrue) διαψεύδω, αρνούμαι || (disown) απαρνιέμαι, ανακαλώ || (refuse) αρνούμαι.

deodorant [di:'əudərənt] *n* αποσμητικό.

depart [dɪ'pɑːt] *vi* αναχωρώ.

department [dɪ'pɑːtmənt] *n* τμήμα *nt*, υπηρεσία, κλάδος || *(UNIV, SCH)* τμήμα *nt* || *(POL)* διεύθυνση, γραφείο || *(US)* υπουργείο || ~ **store** *n* μεγάλο εμπορικό κατάστημα *nt*.

departure [dɪ'pɑːtʃə*] *n* αναχώρηση || **new** ~ *n* νέα τάση.

depend [dɪ'pɛnd] *vi*: **it** ~**s** εξαρτάται || **to** ~ **on** *vti* εξαρτώμαι από || ~**able** *a* αξιόπιστος || *(car, machine etc)* απολύτου ασφαλείας || ~**ent** *n (person)* προστατευόμενος ♦ *a (+ on)* εξαρτώμενος από || ~**ence** *n* εξάρτηση || *(trust)* εμπιστοσύνη.

depict [dɪ'pɪkt] *vt* περιγράφω, απεικονίζω.

depleted [dɪ'pliːtɪd] *a* εξαντλημένος.

deplorable [dɪ'plɔːrəbl] *a* θλιβερός, αξιοθρήνητος.

deplore [dɪ'plɔː*] *vt* αποδοκιμάζω, λυπούμαι πολύ.

deploy [dɪ'plɔɪ] *vt* αναπτύσσω.

depopulation ['diːpɔpju'leɪʃən] *n* ελάττωση πληθυσμού.

deport [dɪ'pɔːt] *vt* εκτοπίζω, απελαύνω || ~**ation** *n* απέλαση, εκτοπισμός || ~**ment** *n* συμπεριφορά.

depose [dɪ'pəuz] *vt* εκθρονίζω.

deposit [dɪ'pɔzɪt] *n* κατάθεση || *(down payment)* προκαταβολή, καπάρο || *(CHEM)* ίζημα *nt*, κατακάθι ♦ *vt (bank)* (παρα)καταθέτω, αποταμιεύω || *(place)* τοποθετώ, βάζω || ~ **account** *n* λογαριασμός καταθέσεως || ~**or** *n* καταθέτης.

depot ['dɛpəu] *n* αποθήκη || *(MIL)* βάση ανεφοδιασμού || *(US: for buses etc)* σταθμός.

depravity [dɪ'prævɪtɪ] *n* αχρειότητα, διαφθορά.

depreciate [dɪ'priːʃɪeɪt] *vt* υποτιμώ ♦ *vi* υποτιμούμαι, πέφτω.

depreciation [dɪpriːʃɪ'eɪʃən] *n* υποτίμηση, πέσιμο.

depress [dɪ'prɛs] *vt (make sad)* συντρίβω, αποθαρρύνω || *(press down)* καταπιέζω, κατεβάζω || ~**ed** *a (person)* μελαγχολικός, αποκαρδιωμένος || *(area)* φτωχός, υποανάπτυκτος || ~**ing** *a* καταθλιπτικός, αποθαρρυντικός || ~**ion** *n (ECON)* ύφεση, κρίση || *(hollow)* κοιλότητα, λακούβα || *(METEOROLOGY)* βαρομετρική ύφεση.

deprivation [dɛprɪ'veɪʃən] *n* στέρηση.

deprive [dɪ'praɪv] *vt (+ of)* στερώ του || ~**d** *a* στερημένος.

depth [dɛpθ] *n* βάθος *nt*, πυθμένας, βαθύτητα || **in the** ~**s of** στην καρδιά του.

deputation [dɛpju'teɪʃən] *n* αποστολή, επιτροπή.

deputize ['dɛpjutaɪz] *vi (+ for)* αναπληρώ, αντιπροσωπεύω.

deputy ['dɛpjutɪ] *a* αναπληρωτικός,

βοηθητικός ♦ *n* αναπληρωτής, αντικαταστάτης.

derail [dɪ'reɪl] *vt* εκτροχιάζω || ~**ment** *n* εκτροχίαση.

deranged [dɪ'reɪndʒd] *a* παράφρονας, στριμμένος.

derelict ['dɛrɪlɪkt] *a* εγκαταλελειμμένος.

deride [dɪ'raɪd] *vt* χλευάζω, εμπαίζω.

derision [dɪ'rɪʒən] *n* εμπαιγμός, χλευασμός.

derivative [dɪ'rɪvətɪv] *a* παράγωγος.

derive [dɪ'raɪv] *vt* παράγω, αποκομίζω ♦ *vi* κατάγομαι, παράγομαι.

dermatitis [dɜːmə'taɪtɪs] *n* δερματίτιδα.

derogatory [dɪ'rɔgətərɪ] *a* ξεφτελιστικός, δυσφημιστικός, μειωτικός.

derrick ['dɛrɪk] *n* γερανός || *(of oil well)* ικρίωμα *nt* γεωτρήσεως.

descend [dɪ'sɛnd] *vti* κατεβαίνω || *(rain etc)* πέφτω ♦ *vi*: **to** ~ **from** κατάγομαι || ~**ant** *n* απόγονος.

descent [dɪ'sɛnt] *n (coming down)* κάθοδος *f*, κατέβασμα *nt* || *(origin)* καταγωγή.

describe [dɪs'kraɪb] *vt* περιγράφω.

description [dɪs'krɪpʃən] *n* περιγραφή || *(kind, sort)* είδος *nt*, τύπος.

descriptive [dɪs'krɪptɪv] *a* περιγραφικός.

desecrate ['dɛsɪkreɪt] *vt* βεβηλώνω.

desert ['dɛzət] *n* έρημος *f* ♦ [dɪ'zɜːt] *vt* εγκαταλείπω ♦ *vi (MIL)* λιποτακτώ || ~**er** *n* λιποτάκτης || ~**ion** *n* λιποταξία.

deserve [dɪ'zɜːv] *vt* αξίζω.

deserving [dɪ'zɜːvɪŋ] *a* άξιος, αξιόλογος.

design [dɪ'zaɪn] *n (plan)* σχέδιο, σκοπός, επιδίωξη || *(drawing)* σχέδιο, τύπος || *(the art)* σχέδιο ♦ *vt (plan)* σχεδιάζω || *(purpose)* προορίζω || **to have** ~**s on** έχω βλέψεις σε.

designate ['dɛzɪgneɪt] *vt* (προ)ορίζω, διορίζω ♦ ['dɛzɪgnɪt] *a* εκλεγείς.

designation [dɛzɪg'neɪʃən] *n* ορισμός, τίτλος.

designer [dɪ'zaɪnə*] *n (TECH)* μελετητής || *(ART)* σχεδιαστής.

desirable [dɪ'zaɪərəbl] *a* επιθυμητός.

desire [dɪ'zaɪə*] *n* επιθυμία, πόθος ♦ *vt* επιθυμώ, ποθώ || *(ask for)* ζητώ.

desk [dɛsk] *n* γραφείο || *(of student)* θρανίο.

desolate ['dɛsəlɪt] *a (barren, dismal)* έρημος.

desolation [dɛsə'leɪʃən] *n* ερήμωση, καταστροφή.

despair [dɪs'pɛə*] *n* απόγνωση, απελπισία ♦ *vi (+ of)* απελπίζομαι για.

despatch [dɪs'pætʃ] = **dispatch.**

desperate ['dɛspərɪt] *a (hopeless)* απελπιστικός || *(reckless)* απεγνωσμένος, σκληρός.

desperation [dɛspə'reɪʃən] *n* απόγνωση.

despicable [dɪs'pɪkəbl] *a* απδής, σιχαμερός, αξιοκαταφρόνητος.

despise [dɪs'paɪz] vt περιφρονώ.
despite [dɪs'paɪt] prep παρά, σε πείσμα.
despondent [dɪs'pɒndənt] a απελπισμένος, συντριμμένος.
dessert [dɪ'zɜːt] n επιδόρπιο || **~spoon** n κουταλάκι του γλυκού.
destination [dɛstɪ'neɪʃən] n προορισμός.
destiny ['dɛstɪnɪ] n προορισμός || (fate) μοίρα.
destitute ['dɛstɪtjuːt] a άπορος.
destroy [dɪs'trɔɪ] vt καταστρέφω || **~er** n (NAUT) αντιτορπιλλικό.
destruction [dɪs'trʌkʃən] n καταστροφή.
destructive [dɪs'trʌktɪv] a καταστρεπτικός.
detach [dɪ'tætʃ] vt αποσπώ, αφαιρώ || **~able** a αφαιρούμενος, κινητός || **~ed** a (attitude) ανεπηρέαστος || **~ment** n (MIL) απόσπασμα nt || (fig) απόσπαση, αμερομψία.
detail ['diːteɪl] n λεπτομέρεια || (MIL) απόσπασμα nt ♦ vt εκθέτω λεπτομερώς || (MIL) ορίζω, αποσπώ || **in ~** λεπτομερώς.
detain [dɪ'teɪn] vt κρατώ, εμποδίζω || (imprison) φυλακίζω, κρατώ.
detect [dɪ'tɛkt] vt ανακαλύπτω, διακρίνω || **~ion** [dɪ'tɛkʃən] n ανακάλυψη || **~ive** n μυστικός αστυνομικός, ντετέκτιβ m inv|| **~ive story** n αστυνομικό μυθιστόρημα nt|| **~or** n ανιχνευτής.
detention [dɪ'tɛnʃən] n κράτηση.
deter [dɪ'tɜː*] vt αποτρέπω.
detergent [dɪ'tɜːdʒənt] n απορρυπαντικό, καθαρτικό.
deteriorate [dɪ'tɪərɪəreɪt] vi επιδεινούμαι, χειροτερεύω.
deterioration [dɪtɪərɪə'reɪʃən] n επιδείνωση.
determination [dɪtɜːmɪ'neɪʃən] n απόφαση, αποφασιστικότητα.
determine [dɪ'tɜːmɪn] vt (καθ)ορίζω, αποφασίζω || **~d** a αποφασιστικός, αποφασισμένος.
deterrent [dɪ'tɛrənt] n προληπτικό ♦ a αποτρεπτικός.
detest [dɪ'tɛst] vt απεχθάνομαι, αποστρέφομαι, σιχαίνομαι || **~able** a απεχθής, σιχαμένος.
detonate ['dɛtəneɪt] vti εκρηγνύω, εκπυροκροτώ.
detonator ['dɛtəneɪtə*] n επικρουστήρας, πυροκροτητής.
detour ['diːtuə*] n απόκλιση, στροφή, λοξοδρόμηση.
detract [dɪ'trækt] vi (+ from) δυσφημώ, μειώνω.
detriment ['dɛtrɪmənt] n: **to the ~ of** προς βλάβη του || **~al** a βλαβερός, επιζήμιος.
devaluation [dɪvælju'eɪʃən] n υποτίμηση.
devalue ['diː'væljuː] vt υποτιμώ.
devastate ['dɛvəsteɪt] vt ερημώνω, καταστρέφω.

devastating ['dɛvəsteɪtɪŋ] a εξολοθρευτικός.
develop [dɪ'vɛləp] vt (make grow) αναπτύσσω || (film) εμφανίζω ♦ vi (unfold) αναπτύσσομαι, εκδηλούμαι || (grow) αναπτύσσομαι || **~ing** a (country) αναπτυσσόμενη || **~ment** n ανάπτυξη.
deviate ['diːvɪeɪt] vi εκτρέπομαι, παρεκκλίνω.
deviation [diːvɪ'eɪʃən] n παρέκκλιση.
device [dɪ'vaɪs] n επινόημα nt, τέχνασμα nt.
devil ['dɛvl] n διά(β)ολος, δαίμονας || **~ish** a διαβολικός.
devious ['diːvɪəs] a (means) έμμεσος, παρεκκλίνων || (person) ύπουλος.
devise [dɪ'vaɪz] vt επινοώ, μηχανεύομαι.
devoid [dɪ'vɔɪd] a: **~ of** στερημένος, χωρίς...
devote [dɪ'vəut] vt αφιερώνω || **~d** a αφοσιωμένος || **~e** n λάτρης, οπαδός.
devotion [dɪ'vəuʃən] n αφοσίωση, λατρεία.
devour [dɪ'vauə*] vt καταβροχθίζω.
devout [dɪ'vaut] a ευσεβής, θρήσκος.
dew [djuː] n δρόσος, δροσιά.
dexterity [dɛks'tɛrɪtɪ] n επιδεξιότητα.
diabetes [daɪə'biːtɪz] n διαβήτητα.
diabetic [daɪə'bɛtɪk] a, n διαβητικός.
diagnose ['daɪəgnəuz] vt κάνω διάγνωση.
diagnosis [daɪəg'nəusɪs] n διάγνωση.
diagonal [daɪ'ægənl] a, n διαγώνιος.
diagram ['daɪəgræm] n διάγραμμα nt, σχέδιο.
dial ['daɪəl] n (esp TEL) δίσκος επιλογής, καντράν nt inv ♦ vt καλώ, παίρνω || **~ling tone** n ένδειξη ελεύθερης γραμμής.
dialect ['daɪəlɛkt] n διάλεκτος f.
dialogue ['daɪəlɒg] n διάλογος.
diameter [daɪ'æmɪtə*] n διάμετρος f.
diamond ['daɪəmənd] n διαμάντι || (CARDS) καρρό.
diapers ['daɪəpəz] npl (US) πάνες fpl.
diaphragm ['daɪəfræm] n διάφραγμα nt.
diarrhoea [daɪə'rɪə] n διάρροια.
diary ['daɪərɪ] n ημερολόγιο.
dice [daɪs] npl ζάρια ntpl ♦ vt (vegetables) κόβω σε κύβους.
Dictaphone ['dɪktəfəun] n (R) Dictaphone nt.
dictate [dɪk'teɪt] vt υπαγορεύω || (impose) επιβάλλω ♦ ['dɪkteɪt] n πρόσταγμα nt, διαταγή.
dictation [dɪk'teɪʃən] n υπαγόρευση.
dictator [dɪk'teɪtə*] n δικτάτορας.
dictatorship [dɪk'teɪtəʃɪp] n δικτατορία.
diction ['dɪkʃən] n ύφος λόγου, λεκτικό.
dictionary ['dɪkʃənrɪ] n λεξικό.
did [dɪd] pt of do || **~n't = did not** || see **do**.
die [daɪ] vi πεθαίνω, τα τινάζω || (end) σβήνω || **to ~ away** vi εξασθενίζω, σβήνω || **to ~ down** vi εξασθενίζω, πέφτω || **to ~ out** vi αποθνήσκω, σβήνω.

diesel ['di:zəl]: ~ **engine** n ντήζελ nt inv.

diet ['daɪət] n (food) (δια)τροφή || (special course) δίαιτα ♦ vi κάνω δίαιτα.

differ ['dɪfə*] vi διαφέρω, ξεχωρίζω || (disagree) διαφωνώ || ~**ence** n διαφορά || (disagreement) διαφωνία, διαφορά || ~**ent** a διάφορος, διαφορετικός || ~**ential** [dɪfə'renʃəl] n (AUT) διαφορικό || (wages) διαφορική || ~**entiate** vti διαφοροποιώ, ξεχωρίζω.

difficult ['dɪfɪkəlt] a δύσκολος || ~**y** n δυσκολία, δυσχέρεια.

diffidence ['dɪfɪdəns] n επιφυλακτικότητα, ντροπαλότητα.

diffident ['dɪfɪdənt] a διστακτικός, άτολμος.

diffuse [dɪ'fju:s] a διάχυτος ♦ [dɪ'fju:z] vt διαχέω, σκορπώ.

dig [dɪg] (irreg v) vt (hole, garden) σκάβω || (nails) χώνω || (delve into) ψάχνω, τρυπώ ♦ n (prod) κάρφωμα nt, πείραγμα nt || (ARCH) εκσκαφή || **to ~ up** vt εκσκάπτω, ξερριζώνω, ξεθάβω.

digest [daɪ'dʒest] vt χωνεύω || (work over) επεξεργάζομαι ♦ ['daɪdʒest] n περίληψη, σύνοψη || ~**ion** n χώνευση.

digit ['dɪdʒɪt] n (number) ψηφίο, αριθμός || (toe, finger) δάκτυλος.

dignified ['dɪgnɪfaɪd] a αξιοπρεπής.

dignity ['dɪgnɪtɪ] n αξιοπρέπεια.

digress [daɪ'gres] vi εκτρέπομαι, ξεφεύγω || ~**ion** n εκτροπή, παρέκβαση.

digs [dɪgz] npl (Brit col) δωμάτιο.

dilapidated [dɪ'læpɪdeɪtɪd] a σαραβαλιασμένος.

dilate [daɪ'leɪt] vti διαστέλλω, πλαταίνω, διαστέλλομαι.

dilemma [daɪ'lemə] n δίλημμα nt.

diligent ['dɪlɪdʒənt] a επιμελής.

dilute [daɪ'lu:t] vt αραιώνω, νερώνω ♦ a αραιός.

dim [dɪm] a αμυδρός, μουντός, σκοτεινός || (stupid) κουτός ♦ vt χαμηλώνω, θολώνω.

dime [daɪm] n (US) δέκατο του δολλαρίου.

dimension [dɪ'menʃən] n διάσταση, έκταση || ~**s** npl διαστάσεις fpl.

diminish [dɪ'mɪnɪʃ] vti ελαττώνω, ελαττώνομαι.

diminutive [dɪ'mɪnjutɪv] a υποκοριστικός ♦ n υποκοριστικό.

din [dɪn] n θόρυβος, πάταγος.

dine [daɪn] vi γευματίζω, τρώγω || ~**r** n τραπεζάρια τραίνου || (person) γευματίζων.

dinghy ['dɪŋgɪ] n μικρή βάρκα.

dingy ['dɪndʒɪ] a μαυρισμένος, βρώμικος.

dining car ['daɪnɪŋka:*] n βαγκόν-ρεστωράν nt inv.

dining room ['daɪnɪŋrum] n τραπεζαρία.

dinner ['dɪnə*] n γεύμα nt, φαΐ || (public) επίσημο γεύμα || ~ **jacket** n σμόκιν nt

inv || ~ **party** n τραπέζι || ~ **time** n ώρα φαγητού.

diocese ['daɪəsɪs] n επισκοπή.

dip [dɪp] n (slope) κλίση, πλαγιά || (bath) βουτιά ♦ vt εμβαπτίζω, βουτώ || (AUT) χαμηλώνω || (flag) κατεβάζω ♦ vi (slope) γέρνω, κατηφορίζω, χαμηλώνω.

diphtheria [dɪf'θɪərɪə] n διφθερίτιδα.

diphthong ['dɪfθɒŋ] n δίφθογγος f.

diploma [dɪ'pləumə] n δίπλωμα nt.

diplomacy [dɪ'pləuməsɪ] n διπλωματία.

diplomat ['dɪpləmæt] n διπλωμάτης || ~**ic** a διπλωματικός.

dipstick ['dɪpstɪk] n βυθομετρική ράβδος f.

dire [daɪə*] a καταστρεπτικός, τρομερός, έσχατος.

direct [daɪ'rekt] a (straight) ευθύς, ίσιος || (immediate) άμεσος ♦ vt (manage) διευθύνω, διοικώ || (aim) κατευθύνω, δείχνω.

direction [dɪ'rekʃən] n (control) διεύθυνση, διαχείριση || (of traffic) ρύθμιση || (of movement) κατεύθυνση, φορά || ~**s** npl (for use) οδηγίες fpl || ~**al** a κατά διεύθυνση.

directly [dɪ'rektlɪ] ad (in straight line) κατευθείαν, ίσια || (at once) αμέσως.

director [dɪ'rektə*] n διευθυντής/ρια m/f, ο γενικός.

directory [dɪ'rektərɪ] n (esp TEL) (τηλεφωνικός) κατάλογος || (COMPUT) κατάλογος.

dirt [də:t] n ακαθαρσία, βρωμιά, ρύπος nt || ~ **road** n (US) χωματόδρομος || ~**y** a ρυπαρός λερωμένος, ακάθαρτος || (mean) βρώμικος, πρόστυχος ♦ vt λερώνω, μουντζουρώνω.

disability [dɪsə'bɪlɪtɪ] n ανικανότητα || (physical) αναπηρία.

disabled [dɪs'eɪbld] a ανίκανος, σακατεμένος, ανάπηρος.

disadvantage [dɪsəd'va:ntɪdʒ] n μειονέκτημα nt, ελάττωμα nt || (sell at) ζημιά || ~**ous** [dɪsædvɑːn'teɪdʒəs] a ασύμφορος, δυσμενής.

disagree [dɪsə'gri:] vi διαφωνώ || **to ~ with** vt δεν ταιριάζω, δεν πηγαίνω || (food) πειράζω || ~**able** a δυσάρεστος, αντιπαθητικός || ~**ment** n διαφωνία, διάσταση, ασυμφωνία.

disallow ['dɪsə'lau] vt αρνούμαι, απορρίπτω, απαγορεύω.

disappear [dɪsə'pɪə*] vi εξαφανίζομαι || ~**ance** n εξαφάνιση.

disappoint [dɪsə'pɔɪnt] vt απογοητεύω, χαλώ, στενοχωρούμαι || ~**ing** a απογοητευτικός || ~**ment** n απογοήτευση, λύπη.

disapproval [dɪsə'pru:vəl] n αποδοκιμασία.

disapprove [dɪsə'pru:v] vi (+ of) αποδοκιμάζω, επικρίνω.

disarm [dɪs'a:m] vt αφοπλίζω || ~**ament** n αφοπλισμός.

disaster [dɪ'za:stə*] n συμφορά, δυστύχημα nt.

disastrous [dɪˈzɑːstrəs] a ολέθριος, καταστρεπτικός.

disband [dɪsˈbænd] vt απολύω, διαλύω.

disbelief [ˈdɪsbəˈliːf] n δυσπιστία.

disc [dɪsk] n δίσκος.

discard [dɪsˈkɑːd] vt απορρίπτω, αφήνω.

discern [dɪˈsɜːn] vt διακρίνω, ξεχωρίζω || ~ing a οξυδερκής, διακριτικός.

discharge [dɪsˈtʃɑːdʒ] vt (unload ship etc) ξεφορτώνω || (fire a gun) πυροβολώ || (dismiss) απολύω || (MIL) αποστρατεύω || (perform duties) εκτελώ, εκπληρώ ♦ n (MED) απέκκριμα nt || (MIL) αποστράτευση || (flow) εκκένωση.

disciple [dɪˈsaɪpl] n μαθητής/ήτρια m/f, οπαδός.

discipline [ˈdɪsɪplɪn] n πειθαρχία ♦ vt πειθαρχώ, τιμωρώ.

disclaim [dɪsˈkleɪm] vt απαρνούμαι.

disclose [dɪsˈkləuz] vt αποκαλύπτω.

disclosure [dɪsˈkləuʒə*] n αποκάλυψη, εκδήλωση.

disco [ˈdɪskəu] n abbr of discothèque.

discoloured [dɪsˈkʌləd] a ξεβαμμένο, ξεθωριασμένο.

discomfort [dɪsˈkʌmfət] n (uneasiness) δυσφορία, στενοχώρια || (lack of comfort) έλλειψη ανέσεως, κακουχία.

disconcert [dɪskənˈsɜːt] vt ταράσσω, συγχύζω.

disconnect [ˈdɪskəˈnɛkt] vt διασπώ, αποσυνδέω.

discontent [ˈdɪskənˈtɛnt] n δυσαρέσκεια || ~ed a δυσαρεστημένος.

discontinue [ˈdɪskənˈtɪnjuː] vti διακόπτω, καταργώ.

discord [ˈdɪskɔːd] n (quarrelling) διαφωνία, διχόνοια || (MUS) παραφωνία || ~ant a ασύμφωνος, παράφωνος.

discothèque [ˈdɪskəutek] n δισκοθήκη.

discount [ˈdɪskaunt] n έκπτωση, σκόντο || (bank) προεξόφληση, υφαίρεση ♦ [dɪsˈkaunt] vt (disbelieve) περιφρονώ, δεν πιστεύω.

discourage [dɪsˈkʌrɪdʒ] vt (take away confidence) αποθαρρύνω || (disapprove) αποδοκιμάζω, αποτρέπω.

discouraging [dɪsˈkʌrɪdʒɪŋ] a αποθαρρυντικός.

discourteous [dɪsˈkɜːtɪəs] a αγενής.

discover [dɪsˈkʌvə*] vt ανακαλύπτω || ~y n ανακάλυψη.

discredit [dɪsˈkredɪt] vt δυσπιστώ, υποτιμώ.

discreet [dɪsˈkriːt] a νουνεχής, διακριτικός.

discrepancy [dɪsˈkrepənsɪ] n διαφορά, ασυμφωνία.

discretion [dɪsˈkreʃən] n (prudence) φρόνηση, σύνεση || (right to decide) βούληση.

discriminate [dɪsˈkrɪmɪneɪt] vi κάνω διάκριση, ξεχωρίζω.

discriminating [dɪsˈkrɪmɪneɪtɪŋ] a διακριτικός, μεροληπτικός.

discrimination [dɪskrɪmɪˈneɪʃən] n διάκριση, ορθοφροσύνη.

discuss [dɪsˈkʌs] vt συζητώ || ~ion n συζήτηση.

disdain [dɪsˈdeɪn] vt περιφρονώ || n περιφρόνηση || ~ful a υπεροπτικός, περιφρονητικός.

disease [dɪˈziːz] n νόσημα nt, ασθένεια.

disembark [dɪsɪmˈbɑːk] vti αποβιβάζω, αποβιβάζομαι.

disengage [dɪsɪnˈgeɪdʒ] vt (AUT) αποσυμπλέκω.

disentangle [ˈdɪsɪnˈtæŋgl] vt διαχωρίζω, ξεμπλέκω.

disfigure [dɪsˈfɪgə*] vt παραμορφώνω.

disgrace [dɪsˈgreɪs] n (general) δυσμένεια || (thing) αίσχος nt, ντροπή ♦ vt ντροπιάζω, ξεφτελίζω || ~ful a επονείδιστος.

disgruntled [dɪsˈgrʌntld] a δυσαρεστημένος, κατουφιασμένος.

disguise [dɪsˈgaɪz] vt (change appearance) μεταμφιέζω || (hide) αποκρύπτω ♦ n μεταμφίεση, απόκρυψη.

disgust [dɪsˈgʌst] n απδία ♦ vt απδιάζω || ~ing a απδιαστικός, σιχαμερός.

dish [dɪʃ] n πιάτο || (meal) φαγητό || to ~ up vt παρουσιάζω, σερβίρω || ~ cloth n πιατόπανο.

dishearten [dɪsˈhɑːtn] vt αποθαρρύνω, απελπίζω.

dishevelled [dɪˈʃevəld] a ξεμαλλιασμένος, ανακατωμένος.

dishonest [dɪsˈɒnɪst] a ανέντιμος, κακοήθης || ~y n κακοήθεια, ατιμία.

dishonour [dɪsˈɒnə*] n αίσχος nt, ατιμία.

dishwasher [ˈdɪʃwɒʃə*] n πλυντήριο πιάτων.

disillusion [dɪsɪˈluːʒən] vt απογοητεύω.

disinfect [dɪsɪnˈfekt] vt απολυμαίνω || ~ant n απολυμαντικό.

disintegrate [dɪsˈɪntɪgreɪt] vi αποσυντίθεμαι, θρυμματίζομαι.

disinterested [dɪsˈɪntrɪstɪd] a αφιλοκερδής, αδιάφορος.

disjointed [dɪsˈdʒɔɪntɪd] a ασυνάρτητος, εξαρθρωμένος.

disk [dɪsk] n = disc.

diskette [dɪsˈket] n (COMPUT) δισκέτα.

dislike [dɪsˈlaɪk] n αντιπάθεια, αποστροφή ♦ vt αντιπαθώ, απεχθάνομαι.

dislocate [ˈdɪsləukeɪt] vt (bone) εξαρθρώνω, στραμπουλίζω || ξεχαρβαλώνω, χαλνώ.

dislodge [dɪsˈlɒdʒ] vt εκτοπίζω, εκδιώκω.

disloyal [dɪsˈlɔɪəl] a άπιστος.

dismal [ˈdɪzməl] a ζοφερός, μελαγχολικός.

dismantle [dɪsˈmæntl] vt παροπλίζω, λύω.

dismay [dɪsˈmeɪ] n κατάπληξη, φόβος ♦ vt (dishearten) πτοώ, φοβίζω, απογοητεύω.

dismiss [dɪsˈmɪs] vt (discharge) απολύω, παύω || (out of mind) διώχνω, βγάζω || (send away) απομακρύνω, διώχνω || (LAW)

απορρίπτω, απαλλάσσω || ~al n
απόλυση, παύση.
disobedience [dɪsəˈbiːdɪəns] n
ανυπακοή, παρακοή.
disobedient [dɪsəˈbiːdɪənt] a
ανυπάκουος, πεισματάρης.
disobey [ˈdɪsəˈbeɪ] vt παρακούω,
παραβαίνω.
disorder [dɪsˈɔːdə*] n (confusion)
ακαταστασία, αταξία || (commotion)
ταραχή, φασαρία || (MED) διαταραχή.
disorderly [dɪsˈɔːdəlɪ] a (untidy)
ακατάστατος || (unruly) άτακτος,
απείθαρχος.
disown [dɪsˈəun] vt απαρνούμαι,
αποκηρύττω.
disparaging [dɪsˈpærɪdʒɪŋ] a
δυσφημιστικό.
disparity [dɪsˈpærɪtɪ] n ανισότητα,
διαφορά.
dispatch [dɪsˈpætʃ] vt (goods) στέλνω,
διεκπεραιώνω ♦ n αποστολή,
διεκπεραίωση || (esp MIL) αναφορά,
μήνυμα nt.
dispel [dɪsˈpɛl] vt διασκορπίζω.
dispensary [dɪsˈpɛnsərɪ] n φαρμακείο.
dispense [dɪsˈpɛns] vt διανέμω, χορηγώ
|| **to ~ with** vt κάνω χωρίς.
disperse [dɪsˈpɜːs] vt διασκορπίζω ♦ vi
διασκορπίζομαι.
displace [dɪsˈpleɪs] vt εκτοπίζω || ~d
person n πρόσφυγας.
display [dɪsˈpleɪ] n (of goods) έκθεση,
επίδειξη || (of feeling) εκδήλωση || (MIL)
επίδειξη ♦ vt επιδεικνύω, εκθέτω.
displease [dɪsˈpliːz] vt δυσαρεστώ.
displeasure [dɪsˈplɛʒə*] n
δυσαρέσκεια.
disposal [dɪsˈpəuzəl] n (of property)
διάθεση || **at one's ~** στη διάθεση.
dispose [dɪsˈpəuz]: **to ~ of** vt
απαλλάσσομαι, ξεφορτώνομαι.
disposed [dɪsˈpəuzd] a διατεθειμένος.
disposition [dɪspəˈzɪʃən] n (character)
προδιάθεση, χαρακτήρας.
disproportionate [dɪsprəˈpɔːʃnɪt] a
δυσανάλογος.
disprove [dɪsˈpruːv] vt αναιρώ,
ανασκευάζω.
dispute [dɪsˈpjuːt] n αμφισβήτηση,
φιλονεικία ♦ vt αμφισβητώ, διεκδικώ.
disqualify [dɪsˈkwɒlɪfaɪ] vt καθιστώ
ακατάλληλο || (SPORT) αποκλείω.
disregard [ˈdɪsrɪˈgɑːd] vt παραβλέπω,
αγνοώ, περιφρονώ.
disreputable [dɪsˈrɛpjutəbl] a
ανυπόληπτος, κακόφημος.
disrespectful [dɪsrɪˈspɛktful] a ασεβής.
disrupt [dɪsˈrʌpt] vt διασπώ, διαλύω ||
~ion n διάσπαση.
dissatisfaction [ˈdɪssætɪsˈfækʃən] n
δυσαρέσκεια.
dissatisfied [ˈdɪsˈsætɪsfaɪd] a
δυσαρεστημένος.
dissect [dɪˈsɛkt] vt κατατέμνω,
διαμελίζω.

dissent [dɪˈsɛnt] n διχογνωμία,
διαφωνία ♦ vi διαφωνώ.
dissident [ˈdɪsɪdənt] a διϊστάμενος,
διαφωνών.
dissipate [ˈdɪsɪpeɪt] vt (waste) σπαταλώ,
ασωτεύω || (disperse) (δια)σκορπίζω.
dissociate [dɪˈsəuʃɪeɪt] vt αποσπώ,
διαχωρίζω, απομακρύνω.
dissolute [ˈdɪsəluːt] a άσωτος, έκλυτος.
dissolve [dɪˈzɒlv] vt διαλύω ♦ vi
διαλύομαι, λυώνω.
dissuade [dɪˈsweɪd] vt αποτρέπω,
μεταπείθω.
distance [ˈdɪstəns] n απόσταση,
διάστημα nt || **in the ~** μακρυά.
distant [ˈdɪstənt] a (far away) μακρυά,
μακρυνός || απομεμακρυσμένος,
επιφυλακτικός.
distaste [dɪsˈteɪst] n αποστροφή,
απέχθεια || ~ful a δυσάρεστος,
απεχθής.
distil [dɪsˈtɪl] vt αποστάζω, διϋλίζω ||
~lery n ποτοποιείο.
distinct [dɪsˈtɪŋkt] a (different)
διαφορετικός || (clear) ευδιάκριτος,
σαφής || ~ion n (difference) διαφορά ||
(honour etc) διάκριση, τιμή || (medal etc)
παράσημο || ~ive a διακριτικός,
χαρακτηριστικός || ~ly ad ευδιάκριτα,
καθαρά.
distinguish [dɪsˈtɪŋgwɪʃ] vt διακρίνω,
ξεχωρίζω, διαφοροποιώ || ~ed a
(eminent) διακεκριμένος || ~ing a
χαρακτηριστικός, διακριτικός.
distort [dɪsˈtɔːt] vt (out of shape)
διαστρέφω, στραβώνω || (fig)
διαστρεβλώνω, παραποιώ || ~ion n
παραμόρφωση, διαστρέβλωση.
distract [dɪsˈtrækt] vt αποσπώ, περισπώ
|| (drive mad) περιπλέκω, τρελλαίνω ||
~ion n (inattention) περίσπαση,
αφηρημάδα || (distress) διατάραξη,
αναστάτωση || (diversion) διασκέδαση.
distraught [dɪsˈtrɔːt] a ταραγμένος,
συγχυσμένος.
distress [dɪsˈtrɛs] n (grief) απελπισία,
αγωνία, πίκρα || (suffering) αθλιότητα,
δυστυχία || (difficulty) κίνδυνος, σε
δύσκολη θέση ♦ vt θλίβω, στενοχωρώ ||
~ing a δυσάρεστος, οδυνηρός || ~
signal n σήμα nt κινδύνου.
distribute [dɪsˈtrɪbjuːt] vt (give out)
διανέμω, μοιράζω || (spread) εξαπλώνω.
distribution [dɪstrɪˈbjuːʃən] n διανομή,
κατανομή.
distributor [dɪsˈtrɪbjutə*] n (COMM)
διανομέας, αντιπρόσωπος || (AUT etc)
διανομέας.
district [ˈdɪstrɪkt] n (of country) περιοχή,
περιφέρεια || (of town) συνοικία || ~
attorney n (US) εισαγγελέας || ~ **nurse**
n (Brit) επισκέπτρια νοσοκόμος.
distrust [dɪsˈtrʌst] n δυσπιστία, υποψία
♦ vt δυσπιστώ προς, υποπτεύομαι.
disturb [dɪsˈtɜːb] vt (upset) ταράσσω,
ενοχλώ || (agitate) ταράσσω, κλονίζω ||

~ance n διατάραξη, φασαρία || **~ing** a ενοχλητικός, ανησυχητικός.

disused ['dɪs'juːzd] a αχρησιμοποιημένος, απηρχαιωμένος.

ditch [dɪtʃ] n τάφρος f, χαντάκι.

ditto ['dɪtəu] n ομοίως.

divan [dɪ'væn] n (bed) ντιβάνι.

dive [daɪv] n (into water) βουτιά || (AVIAT) βύθιση ♦ vi βυθίζομαι, βουτώ || **~r** n (professional) δύτης.

diverge [daɪ'vɜːdʒ] vi δίίσταμαι, αποκλίνω.

diverse [daɪ'vɜːs] a διάφορος, ποικίλος.

diversify [daɪ'vɜːsɪfaɪ] vt διαφοροποιώ, ποικίλλω.

diversion [daɪ'vɜːʃən] n απόκλιση, λοξοδρομία || (of traffic) διοχέτευση || (pastime) διασκέδαση.

diversity [daɪ'vɜːsɪtɪ] n ανομοιότητα, ποικιλία.

divert [daɪ'vɜːt] vt αποσπώ, εκτρέπω || (entertain) διασκεδάζω.

divide [dɪ'vaɪd] vt διανέμω, (δια)μοιράζω, χωρίζω ♦ vi διαιρώ, χωρίζω.

dividend ['dɪvɪdɛnd] n μέρισμα nt, τοκομερίδιο (MATH) διαιρετέος.

divine [dɪ'vaɪn] a θείος, θεϊκός.

diving board ['daɪvɪŋbɔːd] n εξέδρα για βουτιές.

divinity [dɪ'vɪnɪtɪ] n θεότητα || (study) θεολογία.

division [dɪ'vɪʒən] a (dividing) διανομή, μοιρασιά || (MATH) διαίρεση || (MIL) μεραρχία || (part) τμήμα nt || (of opinion) διχόνοια, διαίρεση.

divorce [dɪ'vɔːs] n διαζύγιο, διάζευξη ♦ vt χωρίζω || **~d** a χωρισμένος.

divulge [daɪ'vʌldʒ] vt αποκαλύπτω, φανερώνω.

dizziness ['dɪzɪnɪs] n ίλιγγος, ζάλη.

dizzy ['dɪzɪ] a ζαλισμένος.

do [duː] (irreg v) vt κάνω, εκτελώ, εκπληρώ, τελειώνω, ταιριάζω, αρκώ ♦ vi (act, proceed) κάνω || (be suitable) ταιριάζω, κάνω ♦ n (party) πάρτυ nt inv.

docile ['dəusaɪl] a πειθήνιος, υπάκουος.

dock [dɒk] n (NAUT) νεοδόχος, δεξαμενή || (court) εδώλιο ♦ vi (NAUT) δεξαμενίζομαι || **~er** n φορτοεκφορτωτής, λιμενεργάτης.

docket ['dɒkɪt] n περιληπτική επιγραφή.

dockyard ['dɒkjɑːd] n ναύσταθμος.

doctor ['dɒktə*] n (MED) γιατρός m/f || (UNIV) διδάκτωρ m/f.

doctrine ['dɒktrɪn] n δόγμα nt, θεωρία.

document ['dɒkjumənt] n έγγραφο || **~ary** [dɒkju'mɛntərɪ] n (film) ντοκυμαντέρ nt inv.

dodge [dɒdʒ] n υπεκφυγή, τέχνασμα nt ♦ vt ξεφεύγω, αποφεύγω ♦ vi εκφεύγω, παραμερίζω, κάνω πλάι.

dog [dɒg] n σκυλί || (human) παλιάνθρωπος || **~ biscuit** n μπισκότο για σκύλους || **~ collar** n λαιμοδέτης (σκύλου) || (col) κολλάρο κληρικού.

dogged ['dɒgɪd] a ισχυρογνώμων, πεισματάρης.

dogma ['dɒgmə] n δόγμα nt || **~tic** [dɒg'mætɪk] a (stubborn) κατηγορηματικός, δογματικός.

doings ['duːɪŋz] npl (activities) πράξεις fpl, έργα ntpl.

doldrums ['dɒldrəmz] npl: **in the ~** άκεφος.

dole [dəul] n (Brit: for unemployed) επίδομα nt ανεργίας || **to be on the ~** παίρνω επίδομα ανεργίας || **to ~ out** vt διανέμω, μοιράζω.

doleful ['dəulful] a λυπητερός, πένθιμος.

doll [dɒl] n κούκλα ♦ vt: **to ~ o.s. up** στολίζομαι.

dollar ['dɒlə*] n δολλάριο, τάληρο.

dolphin ['dɒlfɪn] n δελφίνι.

dome [dəum] n θόλος, τρούλλος.

domestic [də'mɛstɪk] a (of the house) οικιακός, του σπιτιού || (of the country) εσωτερικός, εγχώριος || (tame: of animal) οικιακός || **~ated** a εξημερωμένος.

dominant ['dɒmɪnənt] a επικρατών, υπερισχύων.

dominate ['dɒmɪneɪt] vt δεσπόζω, κυριαρχώ.

domination [dɒmɪ'neɪʃən] n κυριαρχία.

domineering [dɒmɪ'nɪərɪŋ] a δεσποτικός, αυταρχικός.

dominion [də'mɪnɪən] n (rule) κυριαρχία, εξουσία || (land) κτήση (αποικία).

dominoes ['dɒmɪnəuz] npl ντόμινο.

donate [dəu'neɪt] vt δωρίζω.

donation [dəu'neɪʃən] n δωρεά.

done [dʌn] pp of **do**.

donkey ['dɒŋkɪ] n γάιδαρος, γαϊδούρι.

donor ['dəunə*] n δωρητής.

don't [dəunt] = **do not** || see **do**.

doom [duːm] n (fate) μοίρα || (death) θάνατος, καταστροφή ♦ vt: **to be ~ed** είμαι καταδικασμένος.

door [dɔː*] n πόρτα || **~bell** n κουδούνι (της πόρτας) || **~handle** n πόμολο, (χειρο)λαβή || **~man** n θυρωρός, πορτιέρης || **~mat** n ψάθα εξώπορτας || **~step** n σκαλοπάτι.

dope [dəup] n (drug) ναρκωτικό.

dopey ['dəupɪ] a (col) βλάκας || (doped) χασικλωμένος.

dormant ['dɔːmənt] a λανθάνων, κοιμώμενος.

dormitory ['dɔːmɪtrɪ] n υπνοθάλαμος.

dosage ['dəusɪdʒ] n δόση.

dose [dəus] n δόση ♦ vt δίνω φάρμακο.

dot [dɒt] n στιγμή || **on the ~** στη στιγμή, στην ώρα.

dote [dəut]: **to ~ on** vt αγαπώ τρελλά.

double ['dʌbl] a διπλός, διπλάσιος ♦ ad διπλά, διπλάσια, δύο-δύο ♦ n (match) σωσίας, ταίρι ♦ vt διπλασιάζω || (fold in two) διπλώνω ♦ vi διπλασιάζομαι, διπλώνομαι || **at the ~** τροχάδην || **~s** npl (TENNIS) διπλός (αγώνας) || **~ bass** n κοντραμπάσσο || **~ bed** n διπλό κρεββάτι || **~-breasted** a σταυρωτός || **~-cross** n προδοσία ♦ vt προδίδω,

εξαπατώ || ~-**decker** n διόροφο (λεωφορείο) || ~ **room** n δίκλινο.
doubly ['dʌblɪ] ad διπλάσια.
doubt [daut] n αμφιβολία ♦ vt αμφιβάλλω, αμφισβητώ || **without** ~ χωρίς καμμιά αμφιβολία || ~**ful** a αμφίβολος || ~**less** ad αναμφιβόλως.
dough [dəu] n ζυμάρι || ~**nut** n τηγανίτα, λουκουμάς.
dove [dʌv] n περιστέρι.
dovetail ['dʌvteɪl] n ψαλιδωτή ένωση ♦ vt ταιριάζω.
dowdy ['daudɪ] a άκομψος, κακοντυμένος.
down [daun] n (fluff) πούπουλο, χνούδι ♦ ad κάτω, χάμω ♦ prep πιο κάτω, προς τα κάτω, χαμηλότερα ♦ vt κατεβάζω, ρίχνω κάτω, νικώ || ~ **with** Χ! κάτω ο Χ || ~**-and-out** a κατεστραμμένος, στην ψάθα || αt-**heel** a μπατίρης || ~**cast** a κατηφής || ~**fall** n πτώση, παρακμή || ~**hearted** a αποθαρρημένος, κακόκεφος || ~**hill** ad κατηφορικώς, προς τα κάτω || ~**pour** n μπόρα || ~**right** a ευθύς, ειλικρινής, απόλυτος || ~**stairs** ad κάτω || a κάτω, στο κάτω πάτωμα || ~**stream** ad με το ρεύμα || ~**town** ad στην πόλη || ~**ward** a κατηφορικός, κατερχόμενος || ~**wards** ad προς τα κάτω, κάτω.
dowry ['dauri] n προίκα.
doz. abbr of **dozen.**
doze [dəuz] vi λαγοκοιμάμαι ♦ n υπνάκος.
dozen ['dʌzn] n δωδεκάδα.
Dr. abbr of **doctor** || abbr of **drive** (n).
drab [dræb] a (dull) μονότονος, ανιαρός.
drachma ['drækmə] n δραχμή.
draft [drɑ:ft] n (rough copy) (προ)σχέδιο || (ECON) γραμμάτιο, συναλλαγματική || (US MIL) στρατολογία ♦ vt συντάσσω, ετοιμάζω προσχέδιο || see **draught.**
drag [dræg] vt (pull) σέρνω || (NAUT) βυθοκορώ ♦ vi βραδυπορώ, σέρνομαι ♦ n (bore) φορτικός άνθρωπος || **to** ~ **on** vi συνεχίζω ανιαρά.
drain [dreɪn] n (lit) οχετός, αγωγός, αυλάκι || (fig) φυγή, διαρροή, εξάντληση ♦ vt (water) αποχετεύω || (fig) αδειάζω, απομυζώ ♦ vi (of water) στάζω, στραγγίζω || ~**age** n αποχέτευση, αποστράγγιση || ~**pipe** n σωλήνας αποχετεύσεως, υδρορρόη.
dram [dræm] n δράμι || (col) σταγόνα.
drama ['drɑ:mə] n δράμα nt || ~**tic** [drə'mætɪk] a δραματικός || ~**tist** n δραματουργός, δραματουργός.
drank [dræŋk] pt of **drink.**
drape [dreɪp] vt κοσμώ με ύφασμα, ντύνω || ~**s** npl (US) κουρτίνες fpl || ~**r** n υφασματέμπορος.
drastic ['dræstɪk] a δραστικός, αποφασιστικός.
draught [drɑ:ft] n (air) ρεύμα nt (αέρος) || (NAUT) βύθισμα nt || ~**s** n (game) ντάμα, νταμιέρα || (beer) **on** ~ (μπύρα) του βαρελιού || ~**board** n αβάκιο.

draughtsman ['drɑ:ftsmən] n σχεδιαστής.
draughty ['drɑ:ftɪ] a με πολλά ρεύματα.
draw [drɔ:] (irreg v) vt (pull) σέρνω, τραβώ, σηκώνω || (attract) ελκύω, τραβώ || (a picture) χαράσσω, σχεδιάζω, ζωγραφίζω || (take out) εξάγω, βγάζω, τραβάω ♦ vi (SPORT) έρχομαι ισόπαλος ♦ n (SPORT) ισοφάριση || (lottery) κλήρωση || **to** ~ **to a close** πλησιάζω στο τέλος || **to** ~ **out** vi (train) ξεκινώ || (lengthen) παρατείνω, τραβώ σε μάκρος ♦ vt (take out) αποσύρω, τραβώ || **to** ~ **up** vi (stop) φθάνω ♦ vt (document) συντάσσω, καταστρώνω || ~**back** n μειονέκτημα nt, ελάττωμα nt || ~**bridge** n κρεμαστή γέφυρα.
drawer [drɔ:*] n συρτάρι, ||
drawing ['drɔːɪŋ] n σχέδιο, σκίτσο || (art of drawing) σχέδιο || ~ **pin** n πινέζα || ~ **room** n σαλόνι, σάλα.
drawl [drɔ:l] n συρτή φωνή ♦ vi σέρνω τη φωνή.
dread [dred] n τρόμος, φόβος, ανησυχία ♦ vt φοβούμαι, τρέμω || ~**ful** a φοβερός, τρομερός.
dream [dri:m] (irreg v) n όνειρο || (fancy) ονειροπόληση ♦ vi ονειρεύομαι ♦ a ονειρώδης || ~**er** n ονειροπόλος || ~**y** a ονειροπόλος, φαντασιόπληκτος, θολός.
dreary ['drɪərɪ] a μονότονος, πληκτικός.
dredge [dredʒ] vt βυθοκορώ, εκβαθύνω || ~**r** n βυθοκόρος.
dregs [dregz] npl κατακάθι, μούργα.
drench [drentʃ] vt καταβρέχω, μουσκεύω.
dress [dres] n ενδυμασία, ρούχα ntpl, ντύσιμο || (esp woman's) φόρεμα nt, φουστάνι ♦ vt ντύνω, στολίζω || (a wound) επενδύω || (food) ετοιμάζω για μαγείρεμα || **to** ~ **up** vi ντύνομαι || ~ **circle** n πρώτος εξώστης || ~**er** n (person) που ντύνεται καλά || (US) κομψός || ~**ing** n (MED) επίδεση || (for food) ετοιμασία, σάλτσα || ~**ing gown** n ρόμπα || ~**ing room** n (THEAT) καμαρίνι || ~**ing table** n τουαλέττα (έπιπλο) || ~**maker** n ράφτρα, μοδίστρα || ~**making** n ραπτική || ~ **rehearsal** n τελευταία πρόβα, γενική δοκιμή.
drew [dru:] pt of **draw.**
dribble ['drɪbl] vi (trickle) στάζω ♦ vt (SPORT) κάνω τρίπλες.
dried [draɪd] a ξηρός, απεξηραμένος, στεγνός.
drift [drɪft] n (driven by tide etc) κατεύθυνση, απόκλιση, ταχύτητα || (mass of snow etc) χιονοστιβάδα, συσσώρευση || (meaning) έννοια, νόημα nt ♦ vi (off course) παρασύρομαι, ξεπέφτω || (aimlessly) περιφέρομαι άσκοπα || ~**wood** n ξύλο που επιπλάει.
drill [drɪl] n (tool) τρυπάνι, δράπανο || (MIL) γυμνάσια ntpl, άσκηση ♦ vt (bore) τρυπώ, ανοίγω || (exercise) εκπαιδεύω, γυμνάζω ♦ vi (+ for) κάνω γεώτρηση.
drink [drɪŋk] (irreg v) n (liquid) ποτό,

αναψυκτικό || *(alcoholic)* ποτό ♦ *vti (swallow liquid)* πίνω || ~**er** *n* πότης || ~**ing water** *n* πόσιμο νερό.

drip [drɪp] *n* στάξιμο, σταλαγματιά ♦ *vi* στάζω, σταλάζω || ~**ping** *n* στάξιμο || *(fat)* λίπος ψητού || ~**ping wet** *a* μουσκεμένος.

drive [draɪv] *(irreg v)* *n (trip in car)* κούρσα, διαδρομή || *(road)* δρόμος πάρκου || *(campaign)* καμπάνια, έρανος || *(energy)* ενεργητικότητα, δραστηριότητα || *(SPORT)* κτύπημα *nt* || *(COMPUT: also:* disk ~*)* μονάδα δίσκου ♦ *vt (car etc)* οδηγώ, σωφάρω || *(urge)* διώχνω, σπρώχνω || *(nail etc)* καρφώνω, μπάζω || *(operate)* κινώ, βάζω μπρος || *(force)* αναγκάζω, παρακινώ ♦ *vi (at controls)* οδηγώ, χειρίζομαι || *(travel)* πηγαίνω, τρέχω.

driver ['draɪvə*] *n* οδηγός || ~'**s license** *n (US)* άδεια οδηγού.

driving ['draɪvɪŋ] *a (rain)* νεροποντή || ~ **instructor** *n* δάσκαλος οδηγήσεως || ~ **lesson** *n* μάθημα οδηγήσεως || ~ **licence** *n (Brit)* άδεια οδηγού || ~ **school** *n* σχολή οδηγών || ~ **test** *n* εξέταση για άδεια οδηγού.

drizzle ['drɪzl] *n* ψιχάλισμα *nt* ♦ *vi* ψιχαλίζω.

droll ['drəʊl] *a* αστείος, κωμικός.

dromedary ['drɒmɪdərɪ] *n* κάμηλος *f* n δρομάς.

drone [drəʊn] *n (bee)* κηφήνας || *(sound)* βόμβος, βουητό ♦ *vi* σαλιαρίζω, μωρολογώ.

droop [druːp] *vi* πέφτω, γέρνω, σκύβω.

drop [drɒp] *n (of liquid)* σταγόνα, στάλα || *(fall)* πτώση, πέσιμο || *(MED)* σταγόνα ♦ *vt (let fall)* ρίχνω, αφήνω να πέσει || *(lower)* κατεβάζω, χαμηλώνω || *(cease)* εγκαταλείπω, παρατώ, αφήνω ♦ *vi (fall)* πέφτω || **to ~ off** *vi (sleep)* αποκοιμιέμαι || **to ~ out** *vi (withdraw)* αποσύρομαι.

dross [drɒs] *n* ακαθαρσίες *fpl*, απορρίμματα *ntpl*.

drought [draʊt] *n* ξηρασία.

drove [drəʊv] *pt of* drive ♦ *n (crowd)* πλήθος *nt* ανθρώπων, κοπάδι.

drown [draʊn] *vt* πνίγω || *(flood)* πλημμυρίζω ♦ *vi* πνίγομαι.

drowsy ['draʊzɪ] *a* νυσταλέος, νυσταγμένος.

drudgery ['drʌdʒərɪ] *n* μόχθος, αγγαρεία.

drug [drʌg] *n (MED)* φάρμακο || *(narcotic)* ναρκωτικό ♦ *vt* δίνω ναρκωτικό σε, ντοπάρω || ~ **addict** *n* τοξικομανής, πρεζάκιας || ~**gist** *n (US)* φαρμακοποιός *m/f* || ~**store** *n (US)* φαρμακείο.

drum [drʌm] *n (MUS)* τύμπανο, τούμπανο || *(barrel)* βαρέλι || ~**mer** *n* τυμπανιστής.

drunk [drʌŋk] *pp of* drink ♦ *n* μέθυσος, μπεκρής || *n* μεθύστακας || ~**en** *a* μεθυσμένος || ~**enness** *n* μέθη, μεθύσι.

dry [draɪ] *a (not wet)* ξηρός, ξερός || *(of well)* στερεμένος || *(rainless)* άνυδρος || *(uninteresting)* ξερός, κρύος || *(wine)* μπρούσκο ♦ *vt* ξηραίνω, στεγνώνω,

στίβω ♦ *vi* ξεραίνομαι, στεγνώνω || **to ~ up** *vi* ξεραίνομαι || *(of well)* στερεύω || ~-**cleaner** *n* καθαριστήριο || ~**er** *n* στεγνωτής, στεγνωτήριο || ~ **rot** *n* σαράκι.

dual ['djʊəl] *a* διπλός, δυϊκός || ~ **nationality** *n* διπλή υπηκοότητα || ~-**purpose** *a* διπλής χρήσεως.

dubbed [dʌbd] *a (CINE)* ντουμπλαρισμένο.

dubious ['djuːbɪəs] *a* αμφίβολος, αμφιβάλλων, αβέβαιος.

duchess ['dʌtʃɪs] *n* δούκισσα.

duck [dʌk] *n* πάπια ♦ *vt* βουτώ, σκύβω ♦ *vi* βουτώ || ~**ling** *n* παπάκι.

duct [dʌkt] *n* αγωγός, σωλήνας.

dud [dʌd] *n* μη εκραγείσα οβίδα ♦ *a* άχρηστος, τενεκές *m*, αποτυχημένος.

due [djuː] *a (owing)* οφειλόμενος, λήγων || *(deserved)* ανήκων, δίκαιος, ωστός || *(expected)* αναμενόμενος ♦ *ad* κατ'ευθείαν, ίσια προς || ~**s** *npl (debt)* τέλη *ntpl*, δασμός || *(balance)* οφειλόμενο, ανήκον || ~ **to** οφειλόμενο σε, λόγω.

duel ['djʊəl] *n* μονομαχία.

duet [djuː'et] *n* διωδία, ντουέτο.

dug [dʌg] *pt, pp of* dig.

duke [djuːk] *n* δούκας.

dull [dʌl] *a (person)* βραδύνους, κουτός || *(boring)* πληκτικός, ανιαρός || *(weather)* βαρύς, σκοτεινός ♦ *vt (soften, weaken)* εξασθενίζω, ξεθωριάζω.

duly ['djuːlɪ] *ad* δεόντως, εγκαίρως.

dumb [dʌm] *a (lit)* βουβός, μουγγός || *(stupid)* ανόητος, κουτός, πλίθιος.

dummy ['dʌmɪ] *n (model)* κούκλα, ανδρείκελο || *(substitute)* ομοίωμα *nt* || *(for baby)* πιπιλίστρα ♦ *a* πλαστός, ψεύτικος, εικονικός.

dump [dʌmp] *n* σκουπιδότοπος || *(storing place)* αποθήκη ♦ *vt* ξεφορτώνω, απορρίπτω || ~**ing** *n (COMM)* πουλώ φτηνά || *(rubbish)* ανατροπή, εκφόρτιση.

dumpling ['dʌmplɪŋ] *n* κομμάτι ζύμης βρασμένο με κρέας || *(pie)* πίτα.

dunce [dʌns] *n* αμαθής, ντουβάρι.

dune [djuːn] *n* αμμόλοφος.

dung [dʌŋ] *n* κοπριά.

dungarees [dʌŋgə'riːz] *npl* φόρμα εργάτη.

dungeon ['dʌndʒən] *n* μπουντρούμι, φυλακή.

dupe [djuːp] *n* θύμα *nt*, απάτη, κορόιδο ♦ *vt* εξαπατώ, κοροϊδεύω.

duplicate ['djuːplɪkɪt] *a* διπλός, διπλάσιος ♦ *n* διπλότυπο ♦ ['djuːplɪkeɪt] *vt* αντιγράφω || **in ~** εις διπλούν.

durable ['djʊərəbl] *a* ανθεκτικός, διαρκής.

duration [djʊə'reɪʃən] *n* διάρκεια.

during ['djʊərɪŋ] *prep* κατά τη διάρκεια.

dusk [dʌsk] *n* σούρουπο.

dust [dʌst] *n* σκόνη, κονιορτός, στάκτη ♦ *vt* ξεσκονίζω, πασπαλίζω || ~ **bin** *n (Brit)* τενεκές *nt* σκουπιδιών || ~**er** *n* ξεσκονόπανο || *(feather)* φτερό || ~**man**

n (Brit) οδοκαθαριστής, σκουπιδιάρης ||
~y α σκονισμένος.
Dutch [dʌtʃ] *α* ολλανδικός ♦ *n (LING)*
Ολλανδικά || **the** ~ *npl* οι Ολλανδοί ||
~**man** *n* Ολλανδέζος || ~**woman** *n*
Ολλανδέζα.
duty ['djuːtɪ] *n* καθήκον *nt* || *(job)*
καθήκον(τα), υποχρέωση || *(MIL)*
υπηρεσία || *(tax)* δασμός, φόρος || **on** ~
εν υπηρεσία || ~**-free** α αφορολόγητος
♦ *n* αφορολόγητα *ntpl*.
dwarf [dwɔːf] *n* νάνος.
dwell [dwel] *(irreg v) vi* διαμένω, κατοικώ
|| **to** ~ **on** *vt* εμμένω σε, επιμένω || ~**ing**
n κατοικία.
dwindle ['dwɪndl] *vi* ελαττώνομαι,
μικραίνω.
dye [daɪ] *n* βαφή, χρωματισμός ♦ *vt*
βάφω.
dying ['daɪɪŋ] *α (man)* ετοιμοθάνατος.
dynamic [daɪ'næmɪk] *α* δυναμικός || ~**s**
n δυναμική.
dynamite ['daɪnəmaɪt] *n* δυναμίτιδα.
dynamo ['daɪnəməʊ] *n* γεννήτρια,
δυναμό.
dynasty ['dɪnəstɪ] *n* δυναστεία.
dysentery ['dɪsntrɪ] *n* δυσεντερία.

E

each [iːtʃ] α καθένας, κάθε ♦ *pron* κάθε ||
~ **other** ο ένας τον άλλο, αλλήλους.
eager ['iːgə*] α* ένθερμος, ανυπόμονος,
πρόθυμος.
eagle ['iːgl] *n* αετός.
ear [ɪə*] n* αυτί || *(for music)* λεπτή ακοή ||
(of corn) στάχυ *nt* || ~**ache** *n* ωταλγία,
αυτόπονος || ~**drum** *n* τύμπανο.
earl [ɜːl] *n* κόμης, κόντες *m*.
early ['ɜːlɪ] α *(before the season)* πρώιμος,
πρόωρος || *(in the morning)* πρωινός ♦ *ad*
(in the morning) πρωί || *(in time)* ενωρίς.
earn [ɜːn] *vt* κερδίζω, βγάζω || *(acquire)*
αποκτώ, κατακτώ.
earnest ['ɜːnɪst] α σοβαρός || *(ardent)*
διάπυρος, ένθερμος || **in** ~ *ad* στα
σοβαρά.
earnings ['ɜːnɪŋz] *npl* απολαβές *fpl*,
αποδοχές *fpl* || *(of a firm)* κέρδη *ntpl*.
earphones ['ɪəfəʊnz] *npl* ακουστικά *ntpl*.
earring ['ɪərɪŋ] *n* σκουλαρίκι.
earth [ɜːθ] *n (planet)* γη, κόσμος || *(soil)*
γη, έδαφος, χώμα *nt* || *(ELEC)* γη,
προσγείωση ♦ *vt (ELEC)* προσγειώνω ||
~**enware** *n* πήλινα *ntpl* || ~**quake** *n*
σεισμός.
earwig ['ɪəwɪg] *n (insect)* φορφικούλη,
ψαλίδα.
ease [iːz] *n (facility)* ευχέρεια, ευκολία,
άνεση || *(comfort)* ανάπαυση, άνεση,
ξεκούραση ♦ *vt (reduce pain etc)*
ανακουφίζω, καταπραΰνω || *(remove
pressure)* χαλαρώνω, ξεφορτώνω || **at**
~! ανάπαυση! || **to** ~ **off** *or* **up** *vi*
ελαττώνω, εργάζομαι αργότερα.
easily ['iːzɪlɪ] *ad* ήρεμα, εύκολα.

east [iːst] *n (direction)* ανατολή || *(in
direction)* ανατολικά *ntpl* ♦ α ανατολικός
♦ *ad* προς ανατολάς, ανατολικά || **the**
E~ Ανατολή.
Easter ['iːstə*] n* Πάσχα *nt*, Λαμπρή.
eastern ['iːstən] α *(from, of the east)*
ανατολικός.
eastward(s) ['iːstwəd(z)] *ad* προς
ανατολάς.
easy ['iːzɪ] α *(not difficult)* ευχερής,
εύκολος || *(life)* ξεκούραστος, άνετος ||
(manner) άνετος, αβίαστος || *(yielding)*
καλόβολος ♦ *ad* εύκολα, ήρεμα, ήσυχα.
eat [iːt] *(irreg v) vt (swallow)* τρώγω || *(one's
words)* καταπίνω || *(consume)*
(κατα)τρώγω, υπονομεύω || **to** ~ **away**
vt κατατρώγω, προσβάλλω || ~**able** α
φαγώσιμος.
eavesdrop ['iːvzdrɒp] *vi (on)*
κρυφακούω.
ebb [eb] *n* άμπωτη || *(fig)* παρακμή,
πέσιμο ♦ *vi* κατεβαίνω, πέφτω.
ebony ['ebənɪ] *n* έβενος, αμπανός.
ebullient [ɪ'bʌlɪənt] α *(enthusiastic)*
εκδηλωτικός, ενθουσιώδης.
eccentric [ɪk'sentrɪk] α *(odd)*
εκκεντρικός, παράξενος ♦ *n (person)*
ιδιότροπος.
ecclesiastical [ɪkliːzɪ'æstɪkl] α
εκκλησιαστικός.
echo ['ekəʊ] *n* ηχώ *f*, αντήχηση,
αντίλαλος ♦ *vt* αντηχώ ♦ *vi* αντηχώ,
απηχώ, αντιλαλώ.
eclipse [ɪ'klɪps] *n* έκλειψη ♦ *vt* προκαλώ
έκλειψη || *(fig)* επισκιάζω.
economic [iːkə'nɒmɪk] α οικονομικός ||
~**al** α οικονομικός || *(of person)* φειδωλός
|| ~**s** *npl* οικονομικά *ntpl*.
economist [ɪ'kɒnəmɪst] *n*
οικονομολόγος *m/f*.
economize [ɪ'kɒnəmaɪz] *vi (+ on)*
οικονομώ, κάνω οικονομία σε.
economy [ɪ'kɒnəmɪ] *n* οικονομία.
ecstasy ['ekstəsɪ] *n* έκσταση, μάγεμα
nt.
ecstatic [ek'stætɪk] α εκστατικός.
ecumenical [iːkjuː'menɪkl] α
οικουμενικός.
eczema ['eksɪmə] *n* έκζεμα *nt*.
edge [edʒ] *n (boundary)* όχθη, παρυφή,
άκρη || *(of garment)* ούγια || *(brink)* ακμή,
χείλος, άκρη || *(of knife)* κόψη, ακμή || **on**
~ = **edgy**.
edgy ['edʒɪ] α εκνευρισμένος.
edible ['edɪbl] α φαγώσιμος.
edict ['iːdɪkt] *n* διάταγμα *nt*.
edifice ['edɪfɪs] *n* οικοδόμημα *nt*, κτίριο.
edit ['edɪt] *vt* εκδίδω, διευθύνω ||
(COMPUT) συντά σσω επιμελούμαι || ~**ion**
[ɪ'dɪʃən] *n* έκδοση || ~**or** *n (of newspaper)*
(αρχι)συντάκτης || *(of book)* εκδότης,
επιμελητής εκδόσεως || ~**orial** α
εκδοτικός, συντακτικός ♦ *n* (κύριο)
άρθρο.
educate ['edjukeɪt] *vt* εκπαιδεύω,
σπουδάζω, μαθαίνω.
education [edju'keɪʃən] *n (system)*

εκπαίδευση || *(schooling)* σπουδές *fpl*, εκπαίδευση, μόρφωση || ~**al** *a* εκπαιδευτικός, μορφωτικός.

EEC *n (abbr of European Economic Community)* Ε.Ο.Κ. *f* (ευρωπαϊκή οικονομική Κοινότητα).

eel [iːl] *n* χέλι.

eerie ['ɪərɪ] *a* μυστηριώδης, παράξενος, τρομακτικός.

effect [ɪ'fɛkt] *n (result)* ενέργεια, επίδραση, επιρροή, αποτέλεσμα *nt* || *(impression)* εντύπωση, αίσθηση ♦ *vt* πραγματοποιώ, επιτυγχάνω || ~**s** *npl (sound, visual)* σκηνικά *ntpl* εφφέ || **in** ~ πράγματι, πραγματικά || ~**ive** *a* αποτελεσματικός, ουσιαστικός.

effeminate [ɪ'fɛmɪnɪt] *a* θηλυπρεπής, γυναικωτός.

effervescent [ɛfə'vɛsnt] *a* (ανα)βράζων, αεριούχος || *(person)* ζωηρός.

efficiency [ɪ'fɪʃənsɪ] *n* αποτελεσματικότητα, δραστικότητα || *(of machine)* απόδοση.

efficient [ɪ'fɪʃənt] *a* αποτελεσματικός || *(person)* ικανός, επιδέξιος.

effigy ['ɛfɪdʒɪ] *n* ομοίωμα *nt*, εικόνα.

effort ['ɛfət] *n* προσπάθεια || ~**less** *a* χωρίς προσπάθεια, εύκολος.

effrontery [ɪ'frʌntərɪ] *n* αυθάδεια, αδιαντροπιά.

e.g. *ad (abbr of exempli gratia)* παραδείγματος χάρη, π.χ.

egalitarian [ɪgælɪ'tɛərɪən] *a* ισοπεδωτικός.

egg [ɛg] *n* αυγό || **to** ~ **on** *vt* εξωθώ, παρακινώ, σπρώχνω || ~**cup** *n* αυγοθήκη || ~**plant** *n* μελιτζανιά || ~**shell** *n* τσόφλι αυγού.

ego ['iːgəʊ] *n* το εγώ.

egotist ['ɛgəʊtɪst] *n* περιαυτολόγος.

Egypt ['iːdʒɪpt] *n* Αίγυπτος || ~**ian** [i:'dʒɪpʃən] *n* Αιγύπτιος ♦ *a* αιγυπτιακός.

eiderdown ['aɪdədaʊn] *n (quilt)* πουπουλένιο πάπλωμα *nt*.

eight [eɪt] *num* οκτώ, οχτώ || ~**een** *num* δέκα οκτώ || **eighth** *a* όγδοος || ~**y** *num* ογδόντα.

Eire ['ɛərə] *n* Ιρλανδία.

either ['aɪðə*] *a* εκάτερος, έκαστος, καθένας ♦ *pron* ο ένας ή ο άλλος, έκαστος || *cj* ή ... ή, είτε...είτε ♦ *ad* ούτε...ούτε.

eject [ɪ'dʒɛkt] *vt* εκβάλλω, βγάζω || *(throw out)* διώχνω, βγάζω έξω || ~**or seat** *n* εκτοξευόμενο κάθισμα *nt*.

elaborate [ɪ'læbərɪt] *a* επιμελημένος, εξονυχιστικός, περίπλοκος ♦ [ɪ'læbəreɪt] *vt* επεξεργάζομαι, δουλεύω, επιμελούμαι.

elapse [ɪ'læps] *vi* παρέρχομαι, περνώ.

elastic [ɪ'læstɪk] *n* ελαστικό, λάστιχο ♦ *a* ελαστικός, εύκαμπτος || ~ **band** *n* λαστιχάκι.

elated [ɪ'leɪtɪd] *a* συνεπαρμένος, έξαλλος.

elation [ɪ'leɪʃən] *n* έπαρση, χαρά, κέφι.

elbow ['ɛlbəʊ] *n* αγκώνας.

elder ['ɛldə*] *a* πρεσβύτερος, μεγαλύτερος ♦ *n* μεγαλύτερος || *(tree)* ακτή, σαμπούκος || ~**ly** *a* ηλικιωμένος.

elect [ɪ'lɛkt] *vt* εκλέγω ♦ *a* εκλεκτός || ~**ion** *n* εκλογή || ~**ioneering** *n* ψηφοθηρία || ~**or** *n* ψηφοφόρος *m/f* || ~**oral** *a* εκλογικός || ~**orate** *n* οι ψηφοφόροι *mpl*.

electric [ɪ'lɛktrɪk] *a (appliance)* ηλεκτρικός || ~**al** *a* ηλεκτρικός || ~ **blanket** *n* θερμοφόρα κουβέρτα || ~ **chair** *n (US)* ηλεκτρική καρέκλα || ~ **cooker** *n* η. κουζίνα, μάτι || ~ **current** *n* η. ρεύμα *nt* || ~ **fire** *n* ηλεκτρική σόμπα.

electrician [ɪlɛk'trɪʃən] *n* ηλεκτρολόγος.

electricity [ɪlɛk'trɪsɪtɪ] *n* ηλεκτρισμός.

electrify [ɪ'lɛktrɪfaɪ] *vt* (εξ)ηλεκτρίζω.

electrocute [ɪ'lɛktrəkjuːt] *vt* θανατώνω με ηλεκτρισμό, με ηλεκτροπληξία.

electron [ɪ'lɛktrɒn] *n* ηλεκτρόνιο.

electronic [ɪlɛk'trɒnɪk] *a* ηλεκτρονικός || ~**s** *n* ηλεκτρονική.

elegance ['ɛlɪgəns] *n* κομψότητα.

elegant ['ɛlɪgənt] *a* κομψός.

element ['ɛləmənt] *n (all senses)* στοιχείο || ~**ary** [ɛlɪ'mɛntərɪ] *a* στοιχειώδης.

elephant ['ɛlɪfənt] *n* ελέφαντας.

elevate ['ɛlɪveɪt] *vt* (αν)υψώνω.

elevation [ɛlɪ'veɪʃən] *n (height)* ύψος, ύψωμα *nt*.

elevator ['ɛlɪveɪtə*] *n* ανελκυστήρας, ασανσέρ *nt inv*.

eleven [ɪ'lɛvən] *a* έντεκα ♦ *n (team)* ομάδα έντεκα παικτών || ~**ses** *npl* κολατσό.

elf [ɛlf] *n* έλφα, αγερικό, ξωτικό.

elicit [ɪ'lɪsɪt] *vt* εξάγω, αποσπώ, βγάζω.

eligible ['ɛlɪdʒɪbl] *a* εκλέξιμος, κατάλληλος.

eliminate [ɪ'lɪmɪneɪt] *vt* αποβάλλω, διαγράφω || *(MATH)* εξαλείφω.

elimination [ɪlɪmɪ'neɪʃən] *n* αποκλεισμός, διαγραφή.

elite [ɪ'liːt] *n* εκλεκτή τάξη, αφρόκρεμα.

elm [ɛlm] *n* φτελιά.

elocution [ɛlə'kjuːʃən] *n* ευγλωττία, απαγγελία.

elongated ['iːlɒŋgeɪtɪd] *a* επιμήκης, μακρύς.

elope [ɪ'ləʊp] *vi* απάγομαι, φεύγω εκουσίως κλέβομαι || ~**ment** *n* εκουσία απαγωγή.

eloquence ['ɛləkwəns] *n* ευφράδεια.

eloquent ['ɛləkwənt] *a* ευφραδής, εύγλωττος.

else [ɛls] *ad* οποιοσδήποτε άλλος, επί πλέον, αλλού || *(otherwise)* άλλως, αλλοιώς || ~**where** *ad* αλλού.

elucidate [ɪ'luːsɪdeɪt] *vt* διευκρινίζω, δι ασαφηνίζω.

elude [ɪ'luːd] *vt* ξεφεύγω, διαφεύγω.

elusive [ɪ'luːsɪv] *a* άπιαστος, απατηλός.

emaciated [ɪ'meɪsɪeɪtɪd] *a* αδυνατισμένος, πετσί και κόκκαλο.

emanate ['ɛmǝneit] vi απορρέω, προέρχομαι, πηγάζω.

emancipate [i'mænsipeit] vt απελευθερώνω.

emancipation [imænsi'peiʃǝn] n χειραφέτηση, απελευθέρωση.

embalm [im'ba:m] vt ταριχεύω, βαλσαμώνω.

embankment [im'bæŋkmǝnt] n ανάχωμα nt.

embargo [im'ba:gǝu] n απαγόρευση, περιορισμός.

embark [im'ba:k] vt επιβιβάζω ♦ vi επιβιβάζομαι || **to ~ on** vt αρχίζω || **~ation** [emba:'keiʃǝn] n μπαρκάρισμα nt.

embarrass [im'bærǝs] vt φέρω σε αμηχανία, στενοχωρώ || **~ing** a (humiliating) ενοχλητικός, ξεφτελιστικός || **~ment** n στενοχώρια, αμηχανία, μπλέξιμο.

embassy ['embǝsi] n πρεσβεία.

embed [im'bed] vt χώνω, θάβω.

embellish [im'beliʃ] vt καλλωπίζω, στολίζω.

embers ['embǝz] npl θράκα.

embezzle [im'bezl] vt καταχρώμαι || **~ment** n κατάχρηση, σφετερισμός.

embitter [im'bitǝ*] vt πικραίνω.

emblem ['emblǝm] n (symbol) σύμβολο || (badge etc) έμβλημα nt.

embodiment [im'bɔdimǝnt] n ενσάρκωση, προσωποποίηση.

embody [im'bɔdi] vt (ideas) ενσαρκώνω, πραγματοποιώ || (new features) ενσωματώνω, περιλαμβάνω.

emboss [im'bɔs] vt αναγλύφω, χαράσσω αναγλύφως.

embrace [im'breis] vt (clasp) εναγκαλίζομαι, αγκαλιάζω || (include) περιλαμβάνω, περικλείω ♦ n εναγκαλισμός, ασπασμός.

embroider [im'brɔidǝ*] vt κεντώ, κάνω κέντημα || **~y** n κέντημα nt.

embryo ['embriǝu] n (fig) έμβρυο.

emerald ['emǝrld] n σμαράγδι.

emerge [i'mǝ:dʒ] vi αναδύομαι, (ξε)βγαίνω, ξεπροβάλλω.

emergence [i'mǝ:dʒǝns] n εμφάνιση.

emergency [i'mǝ:dʒǝnsi] n επείγουσα ανάγκη ♦ a (action) έκτακτος || **~ exit** n έξοδος f κινδύνου.

emery ['emǝri] n: **~ board** n γυαλόχαρτο || **~ paper** n σμυριδόχαρτο.

emetic [i'metik] n εμετικό.

emigrant ['emigrǝnt] n μετανάστης/ρια m/f ♦ a μεταναστευτικός.

emigrate ['emigreit] vi μεταναστεύω.

emigration [emi'greiʃǝn] n μετανάστευση.

eminence ['eminǝns] n (distinction) ανωτερότητα, διασημότητα || (ECCL) εξοχότητα.

eminent ['eminǝnt] a διακεκριμένος, έξοχος, διάσημος.

emission [i'miʃǝn] n (of gases) εκπομπή, αποβολή.

emit [i'mit] vt εκπέμπω, αναδίνω.

emotion [i'mǝuʃǝn] n συγκίνηση, (ψυχική) αναταραχή || **~al** a (person) ευσυγκίνητος, ευαίσθητος || (scene) συγκινητικός || **~ally** ad με συγκίνηση, συναισθηματικά.

emotive [i'mǝutiv] a συγκινητικός.

emperor ['empǝrǝ*] n αυτοκράτορας.

emphasis ['emfǝsis] n έμφαση.

emphasize ['emfǝsaiz] vt τονίζω, υπογραμμίζω.

emphatic [im'fætik] a εμφατικός.

empire ['empaiǝ*] n αυτοκρατορία.

empirical [em'pirikl] a εμπειρικός.

employ [em'plɔi] vt (use) χρησιμοποιώ, εφαρμόζω || (hire) απασχολώ, έχω || **~ee** n υπάλληλος m/f || **~er** n εργοδότης/ρια m/f || **~ment** n (job) απασχόληση, δουλειά, εργασία || (jobs collectively) χρήση, χρησιμοποίηση.

empress ['empris] n αυτοκράτειρα.

emptiness ['emptinis] n κενό.

empty ['empti] a κενός, άδειος ♦ vt (contents) κενώνω, αδειάζω || (container) αδειάζω || **~-handed** a με άδεια χέρια.

emulate ['emjuleit] vt αμιλλώμαι, μιμούμαι, ακολουθώ.

emulsion [e'mʌlʃǝn] n γαλάκτωμα nt.

enable [i'neibl] vt καθιστώ ικανό, διευκολύνω, επιτρέπω.

enamel [i'næml] n βερνίκι, σμάλτο, λάκα || (of teeth) σμάλτο.

enamoured [i'næmǝd] a (+ of) ερωτευμένος.

enchant [in'tʃa:nt] vt (bewitch) μαγεύω || (delight) γοητεύω || **~ing** a (delightful) γοητευτικός.

encircle [in'sǝ:kl] vt (peri)κυκλώνω, (περι)σφίγγω.

enclose [in'klǝuz] vt (shut in) περικλείω, (περι)μαντρώνω || (in a letter etc) εγκλείω, εσωκλείω.

enclosure [in'klǝuʒǝ*] n (space) φράκτης, μαντρότοιχος || (in a letter) συνημμένο, εσώκλειστο.

encore ['ɔŋkɔ:*] n πάλι, μπις.

encounter [in'kauntǝ*] n συνάντηση || (battle) σύγκρουση ♦ vt (meet) συναντώ.

encourage [in'kʌridʒ] vt ενθαρρύνω, δίνω κουράγιο || **~ment** n εμψύχωση, ενθάρρυνση.

encroach [in'krǝutʃ] vi (+ (up)on) καταπατώ.

encyclop(a)edia [ensaiklǝu'pi:diǝ] n εγκυκλοπαίδεια.

end [end] n (finish) τέρμα nt, τέλος nt || (of book, day, rope, street, queue) άκρη, τέλος nt, ουρά || (purpose) σκοπός, επιδίωξη ♦ a τελικός, ακραίος ♦ vt τερματίζω, τελειώνω ♦ vi τερματίζομαι, καταλήγω.

endanger [en'deindʒǝ*] vt διακινδυνεύω, (εκ)θέτω σε κίνδυνο.

endeavour [en'devǝ*] n προσπάθεια ♦ vi προσπαθώ, πασχίζω.

ending ['endiŋ] n τέλος nt, κατάληξη.

endless ['εndlιs] a ατελείωτος, απέραντος.

endorse [ιn'dɔːs] vt (cheque etc) οπισθογραφώ, θεωρώ || (approve) υποστηρίζω, εγκρίνω || ~**ment** n οπισθογράφηση || (of action) έγκριση.

endow [εn'dau] vt προικίζω || (equip) διωρίζω.

end product ['εndprɒdʌkt] n τελικό προϊόν.

endurance [εn'djuərəns] n αντοχή.

endure [εn'djuə*] vt υπομένω, ανέχομαι ♦ vi διαρκώ, αντέχω.

enemy ['εnəmι] n εχθρός ♦ a εχθρικός.

energetic [εnə'dʒεtιk] a ενεργητικός, δραστήριος.

energy ['εnədʒι] n (of person) ενέργεια, δύναμη || (PHYS) ενέργεια.

enforce [εn'fɔːs] vt επιβάλλω, εκτελώ, εφαρμόζω.

engage [εn'geιdʒ] vt (hire) προσλαμβάνω, παίρνω || (take part in) απασχολώ, επισύρω, τραβώ || (begin fight) επιτίθεμαι || (TECH) συνδέω, βάζω || ~**d** a (to marry) αρραβωνιασμένος || (TEL) κατειλημμένη, μιλάει || (in use) απησχολημένος, πιασμένος || (person) είμαι προσκεκλημένος, έχω κλείσει || ~**ment** n (appointment) δέσμευση, ραντεβού nt inv || (to marry) μνηστεία, αρραβώνιασμα nt || (MIL) συμπλοκή, σύγκρουση || ~**ment ring** n βέρα.

engaging [εn'geιdʒιη] a θελκτικός, που τραβάει.

engender [εn'dʒεndə*] vt γεννώ, προκαλώ.

engine ['εndʒιn] n (AUT) μηχανή, κινητήρας, μοτέρ nt inv || (RAIL) ατμομηχανή, ατμοτορίς || ~ **failure** or **trouble** n βλάβη μηχανής ή κινητήρα.

engineer [εndʒι'nιə*] n μηχανικός || (US RAIL) μηχανοδηγός.

engineering [εndʒι'nιərιη] n μηχανολογία.

England ['ιηglənd] n Αγγλία.

English ['ιηglιʃ] a αγγλικός ♦ n (LING) (τα) Αγγλικά || **the** ~ npl οι 'Αγγλοι mpl || **the** ~ **Channel** n n Μάγχη || ~**man** n 'Αγγλος, Εγγλέζος || ~**woman** n Αγγλίδα.

engrave [εn'greιv] vt χαράσσω.

engraving [εn'greιvιη] n χαρακτική.

engrossed [εn'grəust] a απορροφημένος.

engulf [εn'gʌlf] vt καταβροχθίζω, καταποντίζω.

enhance [εn'hɑːns] vt εξαίρω, ανυψώ, ανεβάζω.

enigma [ε'nιgmə] n a ίνιγμα nt || ~**tic** [εnιg'mætιk] a αινιγματικός, μυστηριώδης.

enjoy [εn'dʒɔι] vt μου αρέσει, χαίρομαι (κάτι) || (privileges etc) απολαμβάνω, κατέχω || ~**able** a απολαυστικός, ευχάριστος || ~**ment** n απόλαυση.

enlarge [εn'lɑːdʒ] vt μεγεθύνω, επεκτείνω || (PHOT) μεγεθύνω, μεγαλώνω || ~**ment** n μεγέθυνση.

enlighten [εn'laιtn] vt διαφωτίζω || ~**ed** a φωτισμένος || ~**ment** n διαφώτιση.

enlist [εn'lιst] vt στρατολογώ, προσλαμβάνω ♦ vi στρατολογούμαι, κατατάσσομαι.

enmity ['εnmιtι] n έχθρα, εχθρότητα.

enormity [ι'nɔːmιtι] n μέγεθος nt, τερατωδία.

enormous [ι'nɔːməs] a τεράστιος, πελώριος, κολοσσιαίος || ~**ly** ad πάρα πολύ, καταπληκτικά.

enough [ε'nʌf] n αρκ- ός, επαρκής, ικανός ♦ a αρκετός ~ ad αρκετά.

enquire [εn'kwaιə*] = **inquire**.

enrich [εn'rιtʃ] vt (εμ)πλουτίζω.

enrol [εn'rəul] vt (MIL) στρατολογώ ♦ vi εγγράφω, προσλαμβάνω, παίρνω || ~**ment** n στρατολογία || (SCH) αριθμός μαθητών.

ensign ['εnsaιn] n (flag) σημαία || (NAUT) σημαιοφόρος.

enslave [εn'sleιv] vt υποδουλώνω, σκλαβώνω.

ensue [εn'sjuː] vi έπομαι, επακολουθώ.

ensure [ιn'ʃuə*] vt (make certain) (εξ)ασφαλίζω.

entail [εn'teιl] vt συνεπάγομαι, επιφέρω.

enter ['εntə*] vt (go into) εισέρχομαι, μπαίνω || (join) εισέρχομαι, κατατάσσομαι, γίνομαι || (write in) εγγράφω, γράφω ♦ vi εισέρχομαι, μπαίνω || **to** ~ **for** vt εγγράφω || **to** ~ **into** vt (agreement) μπαίνω, συνάπτω, μετέχω || (argument) μπαίνω || **to** ~ **upon** vt αναλαμβάνω, αρχίζω.

enterprise ['εntəpraιz] n τόλμη, θάρρος nt || (COMM) επιχείρηση.

enterprising ['εntəpraιzιη] a τολμηρός.

entertain [εntə'teιn] vt (as guest) φιλοξενώ, περιποιούμαι || (amuse) διασκεδάζω || ~**er** n ντιζέρ m/f inv || ~**ing** a διασκεδαστικός || ~**ment** n (amusement) διασκέδαση || (show) θέαμα nt.

enthralled [ιn'θrɔːld] a γοητευμένος, κατακτημένος.

enthusiasm [ιn'θuːzιæzəm] n ενθουσιασμός.

enthusiast [ιn'θuːzιæst] n θαυμαστής/ρια m/f, λάτρης m/f || ~**ic** [ιnθuːzι'æstιk] a ενθουσιώδης, μανιώδης.

entice [ιn'taιs] vt (tempt) δελεάζω, ξεμυαλίζω.

entire [εn'taιə*] a ολόκληρος, ολάκαιρος, πλήρης || ~**ly** ad ακέραια, πλήρως || ~**ty** n: **in its** ~**ty** συνολικά.

entitle [εn'taιtl] vt (allow) εξουσιοδοτώ, δίνω το δικαίωμα, επιτρέπω || (name) τιτλοφορώ.

entrance ['εntrəns] n είσοδος f, μπάσιμο ♦ [εn'trɑːns] vt γοητεύω, μαγεύω || ~ **examination** n εισαγωγικές εξετάσεις fpl || ~ **fee** n τιμή εισιτηρίου, τιμή εγγραφής.

entrant ['entrant] n αρχάριος/α m/f, υποψήφιος/α m/f.
entrenched [in'trentʃt] a οχυρωμένος.
entrust [in'trʌst] vt (confide) εμπιστεύομαι || (put in charge) επιφορτίζω, αναθέτω.
entry ['entri] n (place) είσοδος f|| (act) είσοδος f, εμφάνιση || (in dictionary) εγγραφή, καταχώριση ||'no ~' 'απαγορεύεται η είσοδος' || ~ **form** n αίτηση εγγραφής, δελτίο εγγραφής.
enunciate [i'nʌnsieit] vt προφέρω.
envelop [in'veləp] vt (περι)καλύπτω, τυλίγω, σκεπάζω.
envelope ['enveləup] n φάκελλος.
envious ['enviəs] a ζηλόφθονος, φθονερός, ζηλιάρης.
environment [in'vaiərənmənt] n περιβάλλον || al α του περιβάλλοντός.
envoy ['envoi] n απεσταλμένος.
envy ['envi] n φθόνος, ζήλεια || (object of envy) αντικείμενο ζήλειας ♦ vt φθονώ, ζηλεύω.
enzyme ['enzaim] n ένζυμο.
ephemeral [i'femərəl] a εφήμερος.
epic ['epik] n έπος, επικό ποίημα ♦ a επικός.
epidemic [epi'demik] n επιδημία.
epilepsy ['epilepsi] n επιληψία.
epileptic [epi'leptik] a, n επιληπτικός.
epilogue ['epilog] n επίλογος.
episode ['episəud] n επεισόδειο.
epistle [i'pisl] n επιστολή, γράμμα nt.
epitome [i'pitəmi] n επιτομή, περίληψη, σύνοψη.
epitomize [i'pitəmaiz] vt συνοψίζω, κάνω περίληψη.
epoch ['iːpɔk] n εποχή.
equable ['ekwəbl] a ομοιόμορφος, ίσος.
equal ['iːkwl] a (same) ίσος || (qualified) αντάξιος, ανταποκρίνομαι προς ♦ n ίσος, ομότιμος, όμοιος ♦ vt ισούμαι, είμαι ίσος || ~ **to** αντάξιος, ανταποκρινόμενος || **without** ~ ασυναγώνιστος || ~ **ity** n ισότητα || ~ **ize** vt εξισώνω, αντισταθμίζω || ~ **izer** n εξισωτής, αντισταθμιστής || ~ **ly** ad εξ ίσου, ομοίως || ~ **(s) sign** n σημείο ισότητας.
equanimity [ekwə'nimiti] n γαλήνη, πρεμία.
equate [i'kweit] vt εξισώνω.
equation [i'kweiʒən] n εξίσωση.
equator [i'kweitə*] n ισημερινός || ~ **ial** [ekwə'tɔːriəl] a ισημερινός.
equilibrium [iːkwi'libriəm] n ισορροπία.
equinox ['iːkwinɔks] n ισημερία.
equip [i'kwip] vt εφοδιάζω, εξοπλίζω || ~ **ment** n εφόδια ntpl, εφοδιασμός, υλικά ntpl.
equitable ['ekwitəbl] a δίκαιος.
equity ['ekwiti] n δίκαιο, τιμιότητα.
equivalent [i'kwivələnt] a ισότιμος || (TECH) ισοδύναμος ♦ n αντίστοιχο.
equivocal [i'kwivɔkl] a (doubtful) διφορούμενος, αμφίβολος || (suspicious) ύποπτος.
era ['iərə] n εποχή.
eradicate [i'rædikeit] vt ξεριζώνω.
erase [i'reiz] vt εξαλείφω, σβήνω || (COMPUT) διαγράφω || ~ **r** n γομολάστιχα, γόμα.
erect [i'rekt] a ορθός, όρθιος, στητός, σηκωμένος ♦ vt υψώνω, αναγείρω, κτίζω.
erection [i'rekʃən] n όρθωση, σήκωμα nt, ανέργεση.
ermine ['ɜːmin] n ερμίνα.
erode [i'rəud] vt διαβρώνω, τρώγω.
erosion [i'rəuʒən] n διάβρωση.
erotic [i'rɔtik] a ερωτικός || ~ **ism** [i'rɔtisizəm] n ερωτισμός.
err [ɜː*] vi (make mistakes) σφάλλω, σφάλλομαι || (sin) πλανώμαι, αμαρτάνω.
errand ['erənd] n παραγγελία, αποστολή || ~ **boy** n ο μικρός.
erratic [i'rætik] a άτακτος, ακανόνιστος, εκκεντρικός.
erroneous [e'rəuniəs] a εσφαλμένος, λανθασμένος.
error ['erə*] n σφάλμα nt, λάθος nt.
erudite ['erjudait] a πολυμαθής, διαβασμένος.
erupt [i'rʌpt] vi κάνω έκρηξη || ~ **ion** n έκρηξη, ξέσπασμα nt.
escalate ['eskəleit] vt ανεβάζω ♦ vi ανεβαίνω.
escalator ['eskəleitə*] n κυλιόμενη κλίμακα.
escapade [eskə'peid] n ξέσκασμα nt, περιπέτεια.
escape [is'keip] n (getting away) (δια)φυγή, δραπέτευση, σκάσιμο || (leakage) εκφυγή, διαρροή ♦ vi (get free) δραπετεύω, (δια)σώζομαι || (unpunished) ξεφεύγω, γλυτώνω || (leak) διαφεύγω, διαρρέω, τρέχω ♦ vt (be forgotten) διαφεύγω, είμαι απαρατήρητος.
escort ['eskɔːt] n (MIL) συνοδεία, φρουρά || (of lady) συνοδός, καβαλιέρος ♦ [is'kɔːt] vt συνοδεύω.
Eskimo ['eskiməu] n Εσκιμώος/α m/f.
especially [is'peʃəli] ad ειδικώς, ιδιαιτέρως, κυρίως.
espionage ['espiənaːʒ] n κατασκοπεία.
esquire [is'kwaiə*] n (abbr **Esq.**): **J. Brown E~** Κύριο J. Brown.
essay ['esei] n (SCH) έκθεση || (LITER) δοκίμιο.
essence ['esns] n (quality) ουσία || (perfume) άρωμα nt, μυρουδιά.
essential [i'senʃl] a (necessary) ουσιώδης, ουσιαστικός || (basic) βασικός, απαραίτητος ♦ n ουσία, το απαραίτητο || ~ **ly** ad ουσιαστικά, κυρίως.
establish [es'tæbliʃ] vt (set up) ιδρύω, θεμελιώνω, εγκαθιστώ || (prove) στηρίζω, στερεώνω, αποδεικνύω || ~ **ment** n (setting up) ίδρυση, δημιουργία, επιβολή || (house of business) ίδρυμα nt, κατάστημα nt, οίκος || (MIL) σύνθεση (μονάδας) || **the E~ment** το Κατεστημένο.

estate [ɛs'teɪt] n (landed property) κτήμα nt, ακίνητο || (property left) κληρονομία || ~ **agent** n κτηματομεσίτης || ~ **car** n (Brit) στέισον-βάγκον nt inv.

esteem [ɛs'tiːm] n εκτίμηση.

estimate ['ɛstɪmɪt] n (opinion) εκτίμηση || (price quoted) (προ)υπολογισμός, τιμολόγιο ♦ ['ɛstɪmeɪt] vt εκτιμώ, υπολογίζω, λογαριάζω.

estimation [ɛstɪ'meɪʃən] n (judgment) κρίση, γνώμη || (esteem) εκτίμηση, υπόληψη.

estuary ['ɛstjʊərɪ] n εκβολή.

etching ['ɛtʃɪŋ] n χαλκογραφία.

eternal [ɪ'tɜːnl] a αιώνιος, ατελείωτος || ~**ly** ad αιωνίως.

eternity [ɪ'tɜːnɪtɪ] n αιωνιότητα.

ether ['iːθəˠ] n αιθέρας.

ethical ['ɛθɪkl] a ηθικός.

ethics ['ɛθɪks] npl ηθική.

ethnic ['ɛθnɪk] a εθνικός.

etiquette ['ɛtɪkɛt] n εθιμοτυπία, ετικέτα.

eulogy ['juːlədʒɪ] n εγκώμιο.

euphemism ['juːfəmɪzəm] n ευφημισμός.

euphoria [juː'fɔːr ɪə] n ευφορία.

Europe ['jʊərəp] n Ευρώπη || ~**an** a ευρωπαϊκός.

euthanasia [juːθə'neɪzɪə] n ευθανασία.

evacuate [ɪ'vækjueɪt] vt εκκενώνω, μεταφέρω.

evacuation [ɪnækjuː'eɪʃən] n εκκένωση, μεταφορά.

evade [ɪ'veɪd] vt αποφεύγω, ξεφεύγω, διαφεύγω.

evaluate [ɪ'væljueɪt] vt εκτιμώ, υπολογίζω.

evangelist [ɪ'vændʒəlɪst] n Ευαγγελιστής.

evaporate [ɪ'væpəreɪt] vi εξατμίζομαι, ξεθυμαίνω ♦ vt εξατμίζω || ~**d milk** n γάλα nt εβαπορέ.

evaporation [ɪvæpə'reɪʃən] n εξάτμιση.

evasion [ɪ'veɪʒən] n (avoiding question) υπεκφυγή, πρόφαση.

evasive [ɪ'veɪsɪv] a ασαφής, ακαθόριστος.

even ['iːvən] a ομαλός, επίπεδος, ίσιος || (score etc) ισόπαλος, πάτσι || (number) άρτιος, ζυγός ♦ vt σιάζω, ισώνω, εξισώνω ♦ ad ακόμη, και αν, ή ακόμη || (emphasis) και αν ακόμα || ~ **if** και αν || to ~ **out** or **up** vi πατσίζω, ανταποδίδω τα ίσα.

evening ['iːvnɪŋ] n (time) βράδυ nt || (event) εσπερίδα, βραδυνή συγκέντρωση || **in the** ~ το βράδυ || ~ **class** n βραδυνά μάθημα || ~ **dress** n (man's) φράκο || (woman's) βραδυνή τουαλέτα.

evenly ['iːvənlɪ] ad ομοιόμορφα, ομαλά, κανονικά.

event [ɪ'vɛnt] n (happening) γεγονός, περίπτωση, έκβαση || (SPORT) άθλημα nt, αγώνας, ματς nt inv || **in the** ~ **of** σε περίπτωση || ~**ful** a γεμάτος γεγονότα, αλησμόνητος.

eventual [ɪ'vɛntjʊəl] a (final) οριστικός, αναπόφευκτος, τελικός || ~**ity** n πιθανότητα || ~**ly** ad (at last) τελικά || (given time) πιθανώς.

ever ['ɛvəˠ] ad ποτέ, καμμιά φορά || (always) πάντα, πάντοτε || ~ **so big** τόσος δα || ~ **so many** τόσοι και τόσοι || ~**green** a αειθαλής || ~**lasting** a αιώνιος, διαρκής, άφθαρτος.

every ['ɛvrɪ] a καθένας, κάθε || ~ **other day** μέρα παρά μέρα || ~**body** pron όλοι, όλος ο κόσμος, καθένας || ~**day** a (daily) κάθε μέρα, καθημερινός || (commonplace) συνηθισμένος, κοινός || ~**one** = ~**body** || ~**thing** pron τα πάντα, όλα, κάθε τι || ~**where** ad παντού.

evict [ɪ'vɪkt] vt εκδιώκω, εξώνω, διώχνω || ~**ion** n έξωση, εκβολή.

evidence ['ɛvɪdəns] n (sign) σημάδι, σημείο, ένδειξη || (proof) απόδειξη, μαρτυρία || **in** ~ (obvious) διακρίνομαι, ξεχωρίζω.

evident ['ɛvɪdənt] a προφανής, κατάδηλος, φανερός || ~**ly** ad προφανώς, ολοφάνερα.

evil ['iːvɪl] a κακός ♦ n το κακό || (sin) κακία, αμαρτία.

evocative [ɪ'vɒkətɪv] a επικλητικός.

evoke [ɪ'vəʊk] vt επικαλούμαι, ξαναφέρνω στο νου.

evolution [iːvə'luːʃən] n εξέλιξη, ανέλιξη.

evolve [ɪ'vɒlv] vt αναπτύσσω, συνάγω ♦ vi εξελίσσομαι, απορρέω.

ewe [juː] n προβατίνα.

ex- [ɛks] a (former) πρώην, τέως.

exact [ɛg'zækt] a ακριβής, σωστός ♦ vt (obedience etc) απαιτώ, ζητώ || (payment) αποσπώ, παίρνω || ~**ing** a απαιτητικός, κουραστικός || ~**ly** ad ακριβώς, σωστά.

exaggerate [ɛg'zædʒəreɪt] vti υπερβάλλω, μεγαλοποιώ, (παρα)φουσκώνω.

exaggeration [ɛgzædʒə'reɪʃən] n υπερβολή, μεγαλοποίηση.

exalt [ɛg'zɔːlt] vt εξυμνώ, εκθειάζω, επαινώ.

exam [ɛg'zæm] n abbr of **examination**.

examination [ɛgzæmɪ'neɪʃən] n (SCH, UNIV) εξετάσεις fpl, διαγωνισμός || (MED) ιατρική εξέταση || (inquiry) ανάκριση, εξέταση || (CUSTOMS) έλεγχος, έρευνα.

examine [ɛg'zæmɪn] vt (MED, SCH) εξετάζω || (consider) εξετάζω, ερευνώ || (baggage) ερευνώ, ελέγχω || ~**r** n εξεταστής/ρια m/f, επιθεωρητής/ρια m/f.

example [ɪg'zɑːmpl] n δείγμα nt, παράδειγμα nt, υπόδειγμα nt || **for** ~ παραδείγματος χάριν, λόγου χάριν.

exasperate [ɛg'zɑːspəreɪt] vt εξάπτω, εξαγριώνω.

excavate ['ɛkskəveɪt] vt (hollow out) σκάπτω, ανοίγω, βαθαίνω || (unearth) ανασκάπτω, κάνω ανασκαφές.

excavation [ɛkskə'veɪʃən] n ανασκαφή.

excavator ['ɛkskəveɪtə*] n εκσκαφέας.

exceed [ɛk'siːd] vt (number) υπερβαίνω, (ξε)περνώ || (limit) υπερβαίνω || (powers) υπερβαίνω, εξέρχομαι || (hopes) υπερβάλλω || ~ingly ad υπερβολικά, πολύ.

excel [ɛk'sɛl] vi διακρίνομαι, διαπρέπω, ξεχωρίζω ♦ vt υπερέχω, υπερτερώ, ξεπερνώ.

excellence ['ɛksələns] n αξία, υπεροχή, αρετή.

Excellency ['ɛksələnsɪ] n: His ~ n Αυτού Εξοχότης.

excellent ['ɛksələnt] a εξαίρετος, θαυμάσιος, εξαίσιος.

except [ɛk'sɛpt] prep (also: ~ for) εκτός, έξω από, εξαιρουμένου του ♦ vt εξαιρώ, αποκλείω || ~ing prep= **except** || ~ion n εξαίρεση || to take ~ion to προσβάλλομαι, αντιλέγω || ~ional a εξαιρετικός, έξοχος, ασύγκριτος.

excerpt ['ɛksɜːpt] n απόσπασμα nt.

excess [ɛk'sɛs] n υπερβολή, πληθώρα ♦ a (fare, baggage) υπερβάλλων || ~ive a υπερβολικός.

exchange [ɛks'tʃeɪndʒ] n ανταλλαγή || (foreign money) συνάλλαγμα nt || (TEL) κέντρο ♦ vt (goods) ανταλλάσσω, αλλάζω || (greetings, blows) ανταλλάσσω || see **rate**.

exchequer [ɛks'tʃɛkə*] n δημόσιο ταμείο, θησαυροφυλάκιο.

excise [ɛk'saɪz] n φόρος ♦ [ɛk'saɪz] vt φορολογώ.

excitable [ɛk'saɪtəbl] a ευερέθιστος, ευέξαπτος.

excite [ɛk'saɪt] vt (ɛ)ερεθίζω, εξεγείρω, κεντρίζω || ~d a συγκινημένος, εκνευρισμένος || to get ~d εξάπτομαι || ~ment n έξαψη, αναστάτωση.

exciting [ɛk'saɪtɪŋ] a συναρπαστικός, συγκινητικός.

exclaim [ɛks'kleɪm] vi φωνάζω, αναφωνώ.

exclamation [ɛksklə'meɪʃən] n αναφώνηση, κραυγή || ~ **mark** n θαυμαστικό.

exclude [ɪks'kluːd] vt αποκλείω.

exclusion [ɪks'kluːʒən] n αποκλεισμός.

exclusive [ɪks'kluːsɪv] a (select) αποκλειστικός, περιορισμένος || (sole) αποκλειστικός, μοναδικός || (news etc) αποκλειστικός || ~ly ad αποκλειστικά, μόνο.

excommunicate [ɛkskə'mjuːnɪkeɪt] vt αφορίζω, αναθεματίζω.

excrement ['ɛkskrɪmənt] n αποπάτημα nt, σκατά ntpl.

excruciating [ɛks'kruːʃɪeɪtɪŋ] a φρικτός, ανυπόφορος.

excursion [ɛks'kɜːʃən] n εκδρομή.

excuse [ɛks'kjuːs] n δικαιολογία, πρόφαση ♦ [ɛks'kjuːz] vt (let off) απαλλάσσω, συγχωρώ || (overlook) δικαιολογώ || ~ me! συγγνώμη, με συγχωρείτε.

execute ['ɛksɪkjuːt] vt (perform) εκτελώ, εκπληρώ, ενεργώ || (put to death) εκτελώ, θανατώνω.

execution [ɛksɪ'kjuːʃən] n εκτέλεση || ~er n δήμιος, μπόγιας.

executive [ɛg'zɛkjutɪv] n (COMM) διευθυντής/ρια m/f|| (POL) εκτελεστική εξουσία ♦ a εκτελεστικός.

executor [ɛg'zɛkjutə*] n εκτελεστής.

exemplary [ɪg'zɛmplərɪ] a υποδειγματικός.

exemplify [ɪg'zɛmplɪfaɪ] vt παραδειγματίζω.

exempt [ɪg'zɛmpt] a απαλλαγμένος, εξαιρεμένος ♦ vt εξαιρώ, απαλλάσσω || ~ion n απαλλαγή.

exercise ['ɛksəsaɪz] n (of duties) άσκηση || (physical) γυμναστική || (SCH) σχολική άσκηση, γυμναστική || (MIL) άσκηση, γυμνάσια ntpl ♦ vt (muscle) εξασκώ, γυμνάζω || (power) εξασκώ || to ~ patience εξαντλώ υπομονή, κάνω υπομονή || ~ **book** n τετράδιο (μαθητού).

exhaust [ɪg'zɔːst] n (fumes) εξάτμιση, καυσαέρια ntpl || (pipe) σωλήνας εξαγωγής ♦ vt (weary) εξαντλώ, κατακουράζω || (use up) εξαντλώ, στειρεύω || ~ed a εξαντλημένος || ~ing a εξαντλητικός, κουραστικός || ~ion n εξάντληση, αποκάμωμα nt, τσάκισμα nt || ~ive a εξαντλητικός, πλήρης.

exhibit [ɪg'zɪbɪt] n (ART) έκθεμα nt, έκθεση || (LAW) τεκμήριο ♦ vt εκθέτω, παρουσιάζω, επιδεικνύω || ~ion [ɛksɪ'bɪʃən] n (ART) έκθεση || (of temper etc) επίδειξη, γελοιοποίηση || ~ionist n επιδειξίας || ~or n εκθέτης/ρια m/f.

exhilarating [ɪg'zɪləreɪtɪŋ] a φαιδρυντικός, ευχάριστος.

exhort [ɛg'zɔːt] vt προτρέπω, ενθαρρύνω.

exile ['ɛksaɪl] n εξορία || (person) εξόριστος.

exist [ɛg'zɪst] vi υπάρχω, υφίσταμαι, είμαι, ζω || ~ence n (state of being) ύπαρξη || (way of life) ζωή.

exit ['ɛksɪt] n έξοδος f.

exotic [ɪg'zɒtɪk] a εξωτικός.

expand [ɪks'pænd] vt (spread) διαστέλλω, ευρύνω, απλώνω || (operations) επεκτείνω, αναπτύσσω ♦ vi διαστέλλομαι, φουσκώνω.

expanse [ɛks'pæns] n έκταση.

expansion [ɪks'pænʃən] n επέκταση, ανάπτυξη || (PHYS) διαστολή, εκτόνωση.

expatriate [ɛks'pætrɪeɪt] vt εκπατρίζω, εκπατρίζομαι.

expect [ɪks'pɛkt] vt (anticipate) αναμένω, προσδοκώ, περιμένω || (require) απαιτώ, αναμένω || (suppose) σκέπτομαι, φρονώ, πιστεύω || (baby) περιμένω ♦ vi: to be ~ing περιμένω παιδί || ~ant a (hopeful) περιμένων, αναμένων || (mother) επίτοκος || ~ation [ɛkspɛk'teɪʃən] n (hope) προσδοκία, ελπίδα || ~ations npl ελπίδες fpl.

expedience [ɛks'piːdɪəns] n,

expediency [ɛksˈpiːdiənsi] n σκοπιμότητα, ωφελιμότητα.

expedient [ɛksˈpiːdiənt] a σκόπιμος, πρόσφορος, κατάλληλος ♦ n μέσο, τρόπος, τέχνασμα nt.

expedite [ˈɛkspɪdaɪt] vt επισπεύδω, επιταχύνω.

expedition [ɛkspɪˈdɪʃən] n (journey) αποστολή, εκστρατεία.

expel [ɛksˈpɛl] vt διώχνω, βγάζω || (alien) απελαύνω.

expend [ɛksˈpɛnd] vt (time) αφιερώνω, διαθέτω || (money) δαπανώ, ξοδεύω || (effort) δαπανώ, εξαντλώ || **~able** a αναλώσιμος || **~iture** n δαπάνη, κατανάλωση, έξοδα ntpl.

expense [ɛksˈpɛns] n (cost) δαπάνη, έξοδα ntpl || (high cost) βάρος, ακρίβεια || **~s** npl αποζημίωση, δαπάνες fpl || **at the ~ of** με τη θυσία του, εις βάρος του || **~ account** n έξοδα ntpl παραστάσεως.

expensive [ɛksˈpɛnsɪv] a πολυδάπανος, δαπανηρός, ακριβός.

experience [ɛksˈpɪərɪəns] n (happening) δοκιμασία, περιπέτεια || (knowledge) πείρα, εμπειρία ♦ vt δοκιμάζω, υφίσταμαι, αισθάνομαι || **~d** a πεπειραμένος, έμπειρος.

expert [ˈɛkspɜːt] n ειδικός, εμπειρογνώμων, πραγματογνώμων ♦ a έμπειρος, ειδικός || **~ise** n πραγματογνωμοσύνη.

expiration [ɛkspɪˈreɪʃən] n εκπνοή.

expire [ɛksˈpaɪə*] vi (end) εκπνέω, λήγω, τελειώνω || (die) αποθνήσκω, πεθαίνω || (ticket) λήγω.

expiry [ɛksˈpaɪərɪ] n εκπνοή, λήξη.

explain [ɛksˈpleɪn] vt (make clear) εξηγώ, λύω, ερμηνεύω || (account for) εξηγούμαι, δικαιολογούμαι || **to ~ away** vt εξηγώ, δικαιολογώ.

explanation [ɛkspləˈneɪʃən] n εξήγηση.

explanatory [ɛksˈplænətərɪ] a ερμηνευτικός, εξηγητικός.

explicit [ɛksˈplɪsɪt] a ρητός, σαφής, καθαρός, κατηγορηματικός.

explode [ɛksˈpləʊd] vi σκάω, ανατινάζομαι.

exploit [ˈɛksplɔɪt] n κατόρθωμα nt, ανδραγάθημα nt ♦ [ɪksˈplɔɪt] vt εκμεταλλεύομαι || **~ation** n εκμετάλλευση.

exploration [ɛkspləˈreɪʃən] n εξερεύνηση, έρευνα.

exploratory [ɛksˈplɔrətərɪ] a (fig) δοκιμαστικός.

explore [ɛksˈplɔː*] vt (for discovery) εξερευνώ || (examine) εξετάζω, (εξ)ερευνώ || **~r** n εξερευνητής.

explosion [ɛksˈpləʊʒən] n (lit) έκρηξη, εκτόνωση || (fig) ξεχείλισμα nt, ξέσπασμα nt.

explosive [ɛksˈpləʊzɪv] a εκρηκτικός ♦ n εκρηκτική ύλη.

exponent [ɛksˈpəʊnənt] n

ερμηνευτής/ρια m/f, υπέρμαχος || (MATH) εκθέτης.

export [ɛksˈpɔːt] vt εξάγω ♦ [ˈɛkspɔːt] n εξαγωγή ♦ a (trade) εξαγωγικός || **~ation** n εξαγωγή || **~er** n εξαγωγέας.

expose [ɛksˈpəʊz] vt (uncover) εκθέτω, αποκαλύπτω, ξεσκεπάζω || (leave unprotected) αφήνω απροστάτευτο, εκθέτω || (plot) αποκαλύπτω.

exposed [ɛksˈpəʊzd] a (position) εκτεθειμένος.

exposure [ɛksˈpəʊʒə*] n τράβηγμα nt, πόζα, φωτογραφία || (MED) έκθεση || **~ meter** n φωτόμετρο.

expound [ɛksˈpaʊnd] vt αναπτύσσω, εκθέτω, εξηγώ.

express [ɛksˈprɛs] a (clearly stated) σαφής, ρητός || (speedy) ταχύς ♦ n (fast train) ταχεία, εξπρές nt inv ♦ ad (speedily) γρήγορα, χωρίς σταθμό ♦ vt (idea) εκφράζω, διατυπώνω || (feeling) εκφράζω, εκδηλώνω || **to ~ o.s.** εκφράζομαι || **~ion** n (phrase) φράση, έκφραση, τρόπος εκφράσεως || (look on face) έκφραση || (showing) εκδήλωση || **~ive** a εκφραστικός || **~ly** ad ρητώς, επίτηδες.

expulsion [ɛksˈpʌlʃən] n απέλαση, αποβολή.

exquisite [ɛksˈkwɪzɪt] a άριστος, ευχάριστος, λεπτός.

extend [ɛksˈtɛnd] vt (visit) παρατείνω || (building) επεκτείνω, μεγαλώνω || (hand) τείνω, δίνω || **to ~ a welcome** εύχομαι, καλωσορίζω.

extension [ɛksˈtɛnʃən] n (general) έκταση, επέκταση, άπλωμα nt || (building) επέκταση, εύρυνση || (TEL) εσωτερική γραμμή.

extensive [ɛksˈtɛnsɪv] a εκτεταμένος, εκτενής, μεγάλος || **~ly** ad (travel) ευρέως || (use) εκτεταμένα.

extent [ɛksˈtɛnt] n έκταση, σημασία, μέγεθος nt.

exterior [ɛksˈtɪərɪə*] a εξωτερικός ♦ n εξωτερικό, έξω.

exterminate [ɛksˈtɜːmɪneɪt] vt εξοντώνω, εξολοθρεύω.

extermination [ɛkstɜːmɪˈneɪʃən] n εξολόθρευση, εκρίζωση.

external [ɛksˈtɜːnl] a εξωτερικός.

extinct [ɛksˈtɪŋkt] a (animal etc) εξαλειμμένος, εξαφανισμένος || **~ion** n εξαφάνιση, σβήσιμο.

extinguish [ɛksˈtɪŋgwɪʃ] vt σβήνω || **~er** n πυροσβεστήρας.

extort [ɪksˈtɔːt] vt (+ from) αποσπώ || **~ion** [ɪksˈtɔːʃən] n αναγκαστική είσπραξη, απόσπαση || **~ionate** a υπερβολικός.

extra [ˈɛkstrə] a πρόσθετος, έκτακτος, έξτρα ♦ ad πέρα από, εξαιρετικά, πολύ ♦ n συμπλήρωμα || (newspaper) έκτακτος έκδοση || (THEAT) κομπάρσος.

extract [ɛksˈtrækt] vt (distil) αποστάζω || (select) εξάγω, βγάζω, παίρνω ♦ [ˈɛkstrækt] n (LITER) απόσπασμα nt, εκλογή || (COOKING) εκκύλισμα nt || ~ion n εξαγωγή, βγάλσιμο || (origin) καταγωγή, προέλευση.

extradite ['ɛkstrədait] vt εκδίδω (εγκληματία).

extradition [ɛkstrə'diʃən] n έκδοση (εγκληματία).

extraneous [ɛks'treiniəs] a ξένος, άσχετος.

extraordinary [ɛks'trɔ:dnri] a έκτακτος, εξαιρετικός || (strange) παράξενος, αλλόκοτος.

extravagant [ɛks'trævəgənt] a (lavish) υπερβολικός, παράλογος || (wasteful) σπάταλος, άσωτος.

extreme [ɛks'tri:m] a (last) ακραίος, έσχατος, μακρυνός || (very great) υπερβολικός, μέγιστος || (not moderate) των άκρων εξτρεμιστικός ♦ n άκρο, άκρη || ~ly ad υπερβολικά, εις το έπακρο.

extremist [ɛks'tri:mist] a αδιάλλακτος, των άκρων ♦ n εξτρεμιστής/ρια m/f.

extremity [ɛks'trɛmiti] n (farthest end) άκρο, άκρη || (necessity) εσχάτη ανάγκη || **extremities** npl (ANAT) τα άκρα ntpl.

extricate ['ɛkstrikeit] vt εξάγω, βγάζω, ξεμπλέκω.

extrovert ['ɛkstrəvɜ:t] a, n εξωστρεφής.

exuberant [ig'zju:bərənt] a διαχυτικός, ζωηρός.

exude [ig'zju:d] vt εξιδρώ, εκκύνω.

exult [ig'zʌlt] vi χαίρομαι, αγάλλομαι, θριαμβεύω.

eye [ai] n (ANAT) οφθαλμός, μάτι || (of needle) μάτι, τρύπα || (for perception) καλό μάτι, μάτι ζωγράφου κτλ ♦ vt υποβλέπω, εποφθαλμιώ, κοιτάζω || **to keep an ~ on** προσέχω, επιβλέπω, παρακολουθώ || **in the ~s of** ενώπιο, στα μάτια || (**in the public ~**) διάσημος || **up to the ~s in** πνιγμένος στο, φορτωμένος με || ~**ball** n βολβός οφθαλμού || ~**brow** n φρύδι || ~**lash** n βλεφαρίδα, ματοτσίνουρο || ~**lid** n βλέφαρο || ~**-opener** n έκπληξη, αποκάλυψη || ~**shadow** n σκιά ματιών || ~**sight** n όραση || ~**sore** n ασχήμια || ~**witness** n αυτόπτης μάρτυρας.

F

F. abbr of **Fahrenheit**.

fable ['feibl] n μύθος, παραμύθι.

fabric ['fæbrik] n (cloth) ύφασμα nt, πανί.

fabulous ['fæbjuləs] a (imaginary) μυθικός, μυθώδης || (wonderful) μυθικός || (unbelievable) υπερβολικός.

facade [fə'sa:d] n πρόσοψη.

face [feis] n (ANAT) πρόσωπο, φάτσα, μούρη || (appearance) φυσιογνωμία || (grimace) μορφασμός || (front) όψη, εμφάνιση || (of clock) καντράν nt inv ♦ vt (look towards) αντικρύζω, γυρίζω || (bravely) αντιμετωπίζω || **in the ~ of** ενώπιο, μπρος από, σε || **to ~ up to** vt αντιμετωπίζω || ~ **cream** n κρέμα (του προσώπου).

facet ['fæsit] n (single part) μέρος, πλευρά || (of gem) έδρα διαμαντιού.

facetious [fə'si:ʃəs] a ευτράπελος, αστείος, περιπαικτικός || ~ly ad ευτράπελα, πειραχτά.

face to face ['feistu:'feis] ad πρόσωπο με πρόσωπο, φάτσα με φάτσα.

face value ['feis'vælju:] n ονομαστική αξία.

facial ['feiʃəl] a του προσώπου, καθάριση, μάσκα.

facile ['fæsail] a (US: easy) εύκολος.

facilitate [fə'siliteit] vt (δι)ευκολύνω.

facility [fə'siliti] n (ease) ευχέρεια, ευκολία || **facilities** npl ανέσεις fpl, ευκολίες fpl.

facsimile [fæk'simili] n πανομοιότυπο || (also: ~ **machine**) τηλεαντιγραφικό.

fact [fækt] n γεγονός nt, πραγματικότητα || see **matter**.

faction ['fækʃən] n φατρία, κόμμα nt.

factor ['fæktə*] n παράγων, συντελεστής.

factory ['fæktəri] n εργοστάσιο.

factual ['fæktjuəl] a πραγματικός.

faculty ['fækəlti] n (ability) ικανότητα, προσόν || (UNIV) σχολή || (US: teaching staff) διδακτικό προσωπικό.

fade [feid] vt (cause to fade) ξεθωριάζω, ξεβάφω ♦ vi (grow dim) εξασθενίζω, αδυνατίζω, πέφτω || (lose colour) ξασπρίζω ξεθωριάζω, ξεβάφω || (wither) μαραίνομαι.

fag [fæg] n αγγαρεία, μόχθος || (col: cigarette) τσιγάρο || ~**ged** a (exhausted) εξαντλημένος.

Fahrenheit ['færənhait] n Φαρενάιτ inv.

fail [feil] vt (exam) απορρίπτω, αποτυγχάνω ♦ vi (run short) λείπω || (lose power) εγκαταλείπω, χάνω, εξασθενίζω || (light) εξασθενίζω, πέφτω, σβήνω || (remedy) αποτυγχάνω || **to ~ to do sth** (neglect) παραλείπω κάνω κάτι || (be unable) αποτυγχάνω || **without** ~ χωρίς άλλο || ~**ing** n (shortcoming) ελάττωμα nt, αδυναμία ♦ prep ελλείψει || ~**ure** n (person) αποτυχημένος || (MECH) διακοπή, βλάβη.

faint [feint] a αδύνατος, ασθενής, αμυδρός, δειλός ♦ n λιποθυμία, αναισθησία ♦ vi λιποθυμώ || ~**hearted** a δειλός, μικρόψυχος, φοβιτσιάρης || ~**ly** ad ντροπαλά, αδύνατα, άτονα, μόλις || ~**ness** n (of voice) αδυναμία || (of light) αμυδρότητα.

fair [fɛə*] a (beautiful) ωραίος, όμορφος || (light) ξανθός, άσπρος || (weather) καλός καιρός, καλοκαιριά || (just, honest) δίκαιος, έντιμος, τίμιος || (tolerable) υποφερτός || (conditions) έτσι και έτσι || (sizeable) αρκετός, μεγάλος ♦ ad (play) τίμια, δίκαια, έντιμα ♦ n (COMM) πανήγυρις, έκθεση || (fun fair) λούνα-παρκ nt inv, πανηγύρι || ~**ly** ad έντιμα, δίκαια || (rather) αρκετά καλό, σχεδόν,

καλούτσικα || ~ness n τιμιότητα,
εντιμότητα.

fairy ['fɛərɪ] n νεράιδα || ~ **tale** n
παραμύθι.

faith [feɪθ] n (trust) εμπιστοσύνη, πίστη ||
(REL) πίστη, θρήσκευμα nt, θρησκεία || **in
good** ~ με καλή πίστη || ~**ful** a πιστός ||
~**fully** ad πιστά, έντιμα || (in letter)
υμέτερος.

fake [feɪk] n (thing) ψεύτικο είδος nt,
απομίμηση || (person) απατεώνας ♦ a
ψεύτικο, πλαστό ♦ vt παραποιώ,
πλαστογραφώ.

falcon ['fɔːlkən] n γεράκι.

fall [fɔːl] (irreg v) n πτώση, κατέβασμα nt ||
(drop) πτώση, πέσιμο || (of snow) πτώση ||
(US: autumn) φθινόπωρο ♦ vi πέφτω || ~**s**
npl (waterfall) καταρράκτης || **to** ~ **down**
vi (person) πέφτω κάτω || (building)
καταρρέω, γκρεμίζομαι || (fail)
αποτυγχάνω, πέφτω || **to** ~ **flat** vi πάω
χαμένο, πέφτω στα κούφια, πέφτω || **to**
~ **for** vt (trick) πιάνομαι κορόιδο, πέφτω
στην παγίδα || **to** ~ **off** vi (drop off)
πέφτω || (diminish) πέφτω, φθίνω,
μειούμαι, ολιγοστεύω || **to** ~ **out** vi
τσακώνομαι, τα χαλώ || **to** ~ **through** vi
αποτυγχάνω, γκρεμίζομαι || **to** ~ **under**
vi υπάγομαι σε.

fallacy ['fæləsɪ] n σόφισμα nt, πλάνη.

fallen ['fɔːlən] pp of **fall**.

fallible ['fæləbl] a σφαλερός.

fallout ['fɔːlaʊt] n ραδιενεργός σκόνη.

fallow ['fæləʊ] a χέρσος,
ακαλλιέργητος.

false [fɔːls] a (untrue) ψεύτικος,
λαθεμένος || (sham) πλαστός, τεχνητός,
κίβδηλος || **under** ~ **pretences** με
απάτη || ~ **alarm** n αδικαιολόγητος
φόβος || ~**ly** ad ψεύτικα, απατηλά || ~
teeth npl μασέλες fpl.

falter ['fɔːltə*] vi διστάζω, κοντοστέκω,
κομπιάζω || (in speech) τραυλίζω,
ψευδίζω || ~**ing** a διστακτικός, ασταθής.

fame [feɪm] n φήμη.

familiar [fə'mɪlɪə*] a (well-known)
γνωστός, γνώριμος || (intimate) οικείος,
στενός, φιλικός || **to be** ~ **with** ξέρω,
γνωρίζω || ~**ity** n οικειότητα, εξοικείωση
|| ~**ize** vt εξοικειούμαι με, συνηθίζω.

family ['fæmɪlɪ] n οικογένεια, φαμίλια ||
~ **allowance** n επίδομα nt οικογενείας
|| ~ **business** n οικογενειακή
επιχείρηση || ~ **doctor** n οικογενειακός
γιατρός || ~ **life** n οικογενειακή ζωή.

famine ['fæmɪn] n λιμός, πείνα.

famished ['fæmɪʃt] a πεινασμένος.

famous ['feɪməs] a διάσημος,
περίφημος, φημισμένος.

fan [fæn] n (folding) βεντάλια || (ELEC)
ανεμιστήρας || (SPORT etc) φανατικός
θαυμαστής/ρια m/f, λάτρης m/f ♦ vt
αερίζω, ανεμίζω || **to** ~ **out** vi
αναπτύσσω, απλώνω.

fanatic [fə'nætɪk] n φανατικός || ~**al** a
φανατικός.

fan belt ['fænbelt] n ιμάντας, ταινία,
λουρί.

fancied ['fænsɪd] a φανταστικός,
φαντασιώδης.

fanciful ['fænsɪfʊl] a (odd) παράξενος,
ιδιότροπος || (imaginative) φανταστικός.

fancy ['fænsɪ] n (liking) συμπάθεια,
αγάπη, τσίμπημα nt || (imagination)
φαντασία ♦ a φανταστικός,
φανταχτερός, φαντατζί ♦ vt (like)
συμπαθώ, μου αρέσει || (imagine)
φαντάζομαι, υποθέτω || (just) ~ (that)!
για φαντάσου! || ~ **dress** n μεταμφίεση ||
~**-dress ball** n χορός μεταμφιεσμένων,
μπάλ μασκέ nt inv.

fang [fæŋ] n δόντι || (of snake) φαρμακερό
δόντι.

fantastic [fæn'tæstɪk] a παράξενος,
φαντασιώδης, αλλόκοτος.

fantasy ['fæntəzɪ] n φαντασία,
καπρίτσιο.

far [fɑː*] a μακρινός, απώτερος ♦ ad
μακριά || (very much) κατά πολύ, τόσο
πολύ || ~ **away**, ~ **off** πολύ μακριά ||
by ~ ασυγκρίτως, κατά πολύ || **so** ~ ως
εδώ, μέχρι εδώ || ~ **away** a μακρινός ||
the F~ East Άπω Ανατολή.

farce [fɑːs] n κωμωδία, φάρσα.

farcical ['fɑːsɪkəl] a γελοίος, κωμικός,
σαν φάρσα.

fare [fɛə*] n εισιτήριο, ναύλα ntpl || (food)
φαΐ ♦ vi τα πάω, πηγαίνω || ~ **well** n
αποχαιρετισμός ♦ excl αντίο!, χαίρετε!,
γειά σου! ♦ a αποχαιρετιστήριος.

far-fetched ['fɑːfetʃt] a εξεζητημένος,
παρατραβηγμένος.

farm [fɑːm] n αγρόκτημα nt, φάρμα ♦ vt
καλλιεργώ || ~**er** n γεωργός m/f,
αγρότης/ισσα m/f, αγρομοδόρος ||
~**hand** n αγροτικός εργάτης || ~**house**
n αγροικία || ~**ing** n γεωργία,
καλλιέργεια || ~**land** n αγροτική έκταση
|| ~**yard** n περίβολος αγροικίας.

far-reaching ['fɑː'riːtʃɪŋ] a μεγάλης
εκτάσεως, μεγάλης σημασίας.

far-sighted ['fɑː'saɪtɪd] a προνοητικός,
διορατικός.

fart [fɑːt] (col) n πορδή ♦ vi πέρδομαι,
κλάνω.

farther ['fɑːðə*] a μακρυνότερος,
απώτερος ♦ ad μακρύτερα, περαιτέρω.

farthest ['fɑːðɪst] a απώτατος,
μακρυνότερος ♦ ad μακρύτατα, πιο
μακρυά.

fascinate ['fæsɪneɪt] vt γοητεύω,
μαγεύω.

fascinating ['fæsɪneɪtɪŋ] a γοητευτικός,
μαγευτικός.

fascination [fæsɪ'neɪʃən] n γοητεία,
μάγεμα nt.

fascism ['fæʃɪzəm] n φασισμός.

fascist ['fæʃɪst] n φασιστής,
φασίστας/ρια m/f ♦ a φασιστικός.

fashion ['fæʃən] n (custom) ράψιμο, μόδα
|| (manner) τρόπος, συνήθεια, μορφή ♦ vt
σχηματίζω, διαμορφώνω, πλάθω || **in** ~
της μόδας || **out of** ~ ντεμοντέ || **after**

a ~ όπως-όπως, έτσι κι έτσι || ~able a
(clothes) της μόδας, μοντέρνος || (place)
κοσμικός || ~ show n επίδειξη μόδας.

fast [fɑːst] a (swift) ταχύς, γρήγορος ||
(ahead of time) που τρέχει, που πάει
εμπρός || (steady, firm) σταθερός,
στερεός, σφικτός || (firmly fixed) στερεός,
γερός ♦ ad (rapidly) γρήγορα || (firmly)
στερεά, γερά ♦ n νηστεία ♦ vi νηστεύω.

fasten ['fɑːsn] vt (attach) στερεώνω,
σφίγγω || (with rope) δένω || (coat)
κουμπώνω ♦ vi δένομαι, κουμπώνομαι ||
~er n, ~ing n (on box) συνδετήρας,
ενδέτης || (on clothes) αγκράφα,
φερμουάρ nt inv.

fastidious [fæs'tıdıəs] a δύσκολος,
δύστροπος, στριφνός.

fat [fæt] a παχύς, χονδρός, εύσωμος ♦ n
(of person) ξύγγι, πάχος nt || (on meat)
λίπος nt, ξύγγι || (for cooking) λίπη nt,
λίπος nt || (ending in death) θανάσιμος
|| (disastrous) μοιραίος, καταστρεπτικός,
ολέθριος || ~ism n μοιρολατρεία,
φαταλισμός || ~ity n (road death etc)
θάνατος, θύμα nt || ~ly ad μοιραία,
αναπόφευκτα, θανάσιμα.

fate [feit] n (destiny) μοίρα, πεπρωμένο,
το γραφτό || (death) μοίρα, θάνατος ||
~ful a (prophetic) προφητικός ||
(important) υψίστης σημασίας,
αποφασιστικός.

father ['fɑːðə*] n (parent) πατέρας ||
(priest) πάτερ, πατήρ || (early leader)
πατέρας, δημιουργός || ~-in-law n
πεθερός || ~ly a πατρικός, σαν πατέρας.

fathom ['fæðəm] n οργυιά ♦ vt (sound)
βυθομετρώ || (understand) βολιδοσκοπώ,
καταλαβαίνω.

fatigue [fə'tiːg] n (weariness) κούραση,
κόπωση, κάματος ♦ vt κουράζω,
καταπονώ.

fatten ['fætn] vt παχαίνω, σιτεύω ♦ vi
παχαίνω, χοντραίνω.

fatty ['fæti] a (food) παχύς, λιπαρός.

fatuous ['fætjuəs] a ανόητος, ηλίθιος,
χαζός.

faucet ['fɔːsit] n (US) κάνουλα, βρύση.

fault [fɔːlt] n (offence) σφάλμα nt, λάθος
nt || (defect) ελάττωμα nt || (blame) λάθος
nt, φταίξιμο || (GEOL) ρήγμα nt, ρωγμή || at
~ σφάλλω, λαθεύω, είμαι φταίστης ||
~less a άψογος, τέλειος || ~y a
ελαττωματικός, λανθασμένος.

fauna ['fɔːnə] n πανίδα.

favour, (US) favor ['feivə*] n (approval)
εύνοια, συμπάθεια || (kindness) χάρη,
χατήρι || (plan) προτιμώ, υποστηρίζω,
μεροληπτώ || (in race) παίζω το φαβορί ||
in ~ of υπέρ || ~able a ευνοϊκός ||
~ably ad ευνοϊκά, συμπαθητικά || ~ite a
ευνοούμενος, αγαπητός ♦ n
ευνοούμενος || ~itism n ευνοιοκρατία,
ρουσφετολογία.

fawn [fɔːn] a, n (colour) πυρόξανθος.

fax [fæks] n (col) τηλεαντιγραφικό
έντυπο || (machine) τηλεαντιγραφικό ♦ vt
στέλλω με το τηλεαντιγραφικό.

fear [fiə*] n φόβος, τρόμος ♦ vt
φοβούμαι, τρέμω, ανησυχώ || no ~! μη
φοβάσαι!, δεν είναι πιθανό! || ~ful a
(timid) δειλός, φοβιτσιάρης || (terrible)
φοβερός, τρομερός || ~less a
ατρόμητος, άφοβος.

feasibility [fiːzə'bılıti] n (το)
πραγματοποιήσιμο.

feasible ['fiːzəbl] a δυνατός,
κατορθωτός.

feast [fiːst] n τραπέζι, φαγοπότι, γλέντι
♦ vi (+ on) απολαμβάνω, χορταίνω || ~
day n (REL) γιορτή.

feat [fiːt] n κατόρθωμα nt.

feather ['fɛðə*] n φτερό.

feature ['fiːtʃə*] n χαρακτηριστικό ||
(article) κύριο άρθρο || (film) κυρία ταινία
♦ vti χαρακτηρίζω, τονίζω, εμφανίζω ||
~less a ηλιόπληκτος, ασήμαντος.

February ['februəri] n Φεβρουάριος.

fed [fed] pt, pp of feed || to be ~ up vi
βαριέμαι, μπουχτώνω, αηδιάζω.

federal ['fedərəl] a ομόσπονδος,
ομοσπονδιακός.

federation [fedə'reiʃən] n ομοσπονδία,
συνασπισμός.

fee [fiː] n (payment) αμοιβή || (for entrance)
δίδακτρα ntpl, τέλος nt.

feeble ['fiːbl] a (person) φιλασθενής,
αρρωστιάρης || (excuse) αδύνατος,
αμφίβολος || ~-minded a διανοητικώς
ανεπαρκής.

feed [fiːd] (irreg v) n τροφή, τάισμα nt,
τροφοδότηση ♦ vt τρέφω, θρέφω ||
(machine etc) τροφοδοτώ || to ~ on vt
τρέφω με, τρέφομαι με || ~back n
ανάδραση.

feel [fiːl] (irreg v) n (touch) αφή, πιάσιμο ||
(feeling) αίσθηση, αίσθημα nt ♦ vt (touch)
αγγίζω || (examine) ψηλαφώ, ψαύω,
πιάνω || (be mentally aware of) αισθάνομαι,
νοιώθω || (think, believe) νοιώθω ♦ vi (give
impression) αισθάνομαι, νοιώθω || ~er n
βολιδοσκόπηση || ~ing n (sensation)
αφή, αίσθημα nt || (emotion) ευαισθησία,
συγκίνηση || (opinion) εντύπωση, γνώμη,
αίσθημα nt.

feet [fiːt] npl of foot.

feign [fein] vt προσποιούμαι,
υποκρίνομαι || ~ed a προσποιητός,
ψεύτικος.

feint [feint] n προσποίηση || (MIL)
ψευδεπίθεση.

fell [fel] pt of fall ♦ vt (tree) κόβω, ρίχνω
κάτω ♦ n (hill) βραχώδης λόφος.

fellow ['fɛləu] n (companion) σύντροφος,
συνάδελφος || (member of society)
εταίρος, μέλος || (man) άνθρωπος,
φουκαράς, τύπος || ~ citizen n
συμπολίτης/ρια m/f || ~ countryman n
συμπατριώτης || ~ feeling n
συναδελφοσύνη || ~ men npl
συνάνθρωποι || ~ship n (group)
(συν)αδελφότητα, εταιρεία ||
(friendliness) συντροφιά,
συντροφικότητα.

felony ['fɛləni] n κακούργημα nt.

felt [fɛlt] pt, pp of feel ♦ n πίλημα nt, τσόχα.

female ['fi:meɪl] n θηλυκό, γυναίκα ♦ a θηλυκός, γυναικείος.

feminine ['fɛmɪnɪn] a (GRAM) θηλυκό || (qualities) θηλυκός, γυναικείος.

feminist ['fɛmɪnɪst] n φεμινίστρια, φεμινίστρια m/f.

fence [fɛns] n φράγμα nt, φράχτης ♦ vt (also ~ in, ~ off) περιφράσσω, (περι) μαντρώνω ♦ vi ξιφομαχώ.

fencing ['fɛnsɪŋ] n (swordplay) ξιφασκία, ξιφομαχία || (fences) περίφραξη, φράκτης.

fend [fɛnd] vi: to ~ for o.s. φροντίζω, συντηρούμαι, καταφέρνω.

fender ['fɛndə*] n κυγκλίδωμα, πυρομάχος || (US: wing, mudguard) προφυλακτήρας.

fennel ['fɛnl] n μάραθο.

ferment [fə'mɛnt] vi ζημούμαι, βράζω ♦ ['fɜ:mɛnt] n ζύμωση, αναβρασμός || ~ation n ζύμωση, βράσιμο.

fern [fɜ:n] n φτέρη.

ferocious [fə'rəʊʃəs] a άγριος, θηριώδης.

ferry ['fɛrɪ] n (small) πέραμα nt, πορθμείο || (large: also ~boat) φέρρυ-μποτ nt inv ♦ vt διεκπεραιώ, διαπορθμεύω, περνώ.

fertile ['fɜ:taɪl] a (AGR) εύφορος, γόνιμος || (BIOL) γονιμοποιός.

fertility [fə'tɪlɪtɪ] n ευφορία, γονιμότητα.

fertilize ['fɜ:tɪlaɪz] vt γονιμοποιώ || ~r n λίπασμα nt.

fervent ['fɜ:vənt] a θερμός, φλογερός.

festival ['fɛstɪvəl] n (REL etc) γιορτή, πανηγύρι || (ART, MUS) φεστιβάλ nt inv.

festive ['fɛstɪv] a γιορταστικός, γιορτάσιμος || (person) εύθυμος, κεφάτος || the ~ season (Christmas) εποχή γιορτών.

fetch [fɛtʃ] vt πηγαίνω να φέρω || (a price) αποφέρω, πιάνω.

fetching ['fɛtʃɪŋ] a γοητευτικός, ελκυστικός.

fête [feɪt] n γιορτή, πανηγύρι.

fetters ['fɛtəz] npl δεσμά ntpl, αλυσίδες fpl.

fetus ['fi:təs] n (US) = foetus.

feud [fju:d] n έχθρα, έριδα, βεντέτα ♦ vi είμαι στα χέρια με || ~al a φεουδαλικός, τιμαριωτικός || ~alism n φεουδαλισμός.

fever ['fi:və*] n πυρετός, θέρμη || ~ish a (MED) πυρετώδης || ~ishly ad (fig) πυρετωδώς, με τα μούτρα.

few [fju:] a λίγοι, μερικοί || a ~ μερικοί, λίγοι || ~er λιγότεροι, σπανιότεροι || ~est ελάχιστοι, λιγότατοι.

fiancé [fɪ'ɑ̃:ŋseɪ] n μνηστήρας, αρραβωνιαστικός || ~e n αρραβωνιαστικιά.

fiasco [fɪ'æskəʊ] n φιάσκο, αποτυχία.

fib [fɪb] n ψεμματάκι, μπούρδα ♦ vi ψεύδομαι.

fibre, (US) fiber ['faɪbə*] n ίνα || ~glass n υαλοβάμβακας.

fickle ['fɪkl] a αλλοπρόσαλος, αλαφρομυαλός.

fiction ['fɪkʃən] n (invention) φαντασία || (novels) μυθιστορήματα ntpl || ~al a των μυθιστορημάτων.

fictitious [fɪk'tɪʃəs] a φανταστικός.

fiddle ['fɪdl] n (violin) βιολί || (swindle) κομπίνα ♦ vt (cheat) ξεγελώ ♦ vi παίζω, μαστορεύω, χάνω (το χρόνο) || to ~ with vt παίζω, μαστορεύω || ~r n βιολιστής/ρια m/f.

fidelity [fɪ'dɛlɪtɪ] n πίστη, αφοσίωση, πιστότητα.

fidget ['fɪdʒɪt] vi κάνω νευρικές κινήσεις || ~y a αεικίνητος, νευρικός, ανήσυχος.

field [fi:ld] n (land) χωράφι, κάμπος, περιοχή || (SPORT: ground) γήπεδο || (SPORT: in race) τα άλογα ntpl || (range) έκταση, πεδίο || (battleground) πεδίο || (COMPUT) πεδίο || ~ marshal n στρατάρχης || ~work n (MIL) έργο εκστρατείας.

fiend [fi:nd] n δαίμονας, τέρας nt || ~ish a διαβολικός.

fierce [fɪəs] a θηριώδης, μανιασμένος.

fiery ['faɪərɪ] a (of fire) φλογερός, καφτερός, φλεγόμενος || (person) ζωηρός, ορμητικός, ζωντανός.

fifteen [fɪf'ti:n] num δέκα πέντε.

fifth [fɪfθ] a πέμπτος.

fiftieth ['fɪftɪθ] a πεντηκοστός.

fifty ['fɪftɪ] num πενήντα.

fig [fɪg] n σύκο || (tree) συκιά.

fight [faɪt] (irreg v) n (between people) καυγάς, πιάσιμο || (campaign) μάχη, αγώνας, πάλη ♦ vt πολεμώ, μάχομαι ♦ vi (struggle against) μάχομαι, αγωνίζομαι, παλεύω || ~er n πολεμιστής, μαχητής || (AVIAT) καταδιωκτικό || ~ing n μάχη, καυγάς || (SPORT) πυγμαχία.

figurative ['fɪgərətɪv] a μεταφορικός, παραστατικός.

figure ['fɪgə*] n (shape) μορφή, σχήμα nt || (of person) παράστημα nt, κορμοστασιά, σιλουέτα || (picture) εικόνα, απεικόνιση || (person) πρόσωπο, (άνθρωπος) || προσωπικότητα || (MATH) σχήμα nt || (cipher) αριθμός, ψηφίο, νούμερο ♦ vt (US: imagine) υπολογίζω, λογαριάζω ♦ vi (appear) εμφανίζομαι, φαντάζομαι || to ~ out vt υπολογίζω, λογαριάζω || ~head n (NAUT) ξόανο, γοργόνα || (fig) διακοσμητικό πρόσωπο.

filament ['fɪləmənt] n νήμα nt.

file [faɪl] n (tool) ρίνη, λίμα || (dossier) φάκελλος, αρχείο || (folder) φάκελλος, ντοσιέ nt inv || (row) στοίχος, γραμμή, αράδα || (COMPUT) αρχείο ♦ vt (wood) λιμάρω || (nails) λιμάρω || (papers) ταξινομώ, αρχειοθετώ || (claim) καταθέτω, υποβάλλω ♦ vi: to ~ in/out μπαίνω/βγαίνω ένας-ένας || in single ~ σε μονή γραμμή.

filing ['faɪlɪŋ] n (of papers) ταξινόμηση, αρχειοθέτηση || ~s npl ρινίσματα ntpl, λιμαδούρα || ~ cabinet n δελτιοθήκη, αρχειοθήκη.

fill [fɪl] vt (make full) πληρώ, γεμίζω ||

(occupy completely) συμπληρώνω, γεμίζω
|| *(satisfy)* ικανοποιώ, χορταίνω || *(position etc)* κατέχω, γεμίζω ♦ *n* πλησμονή, κορεσμός, γέμισμα *nt* || **to ~ the bill** *(fig)* ανταποκρίνομαι || **to ~ in** *vt (hole)* γεμίζω, βουλώνω || *(form)* συμπληρώνω || **to ~ up** *vt (container)* γεμίζω τελείως || *(form)* συμπληρώνω.

fillet ['fɪlɪt] *n (food)* φιλέτο ♦ *vt* χωρίζω τα φιλέτα.

filling ['fɪlɪŋ] *n (for cakes, pies etc)* γέμισιν || *(for tooth)* σφράγισμα *nt*, βούλωμα *nt* || **~ station** *n* πρατήριο βενζίνης, βενζινάδικο.

fillip ['fɪlɪp] *n (reviver)* αναζωογόνηση, τόνωση.

film [fɪlm] *n (thin layer)* ελαφρό στρώμα *nt*, μεμβράνη || *(PHOT)* (φωτο)ταινία, φιλμ *nt inv*, (λήψις) || *(moving picture)* ταινία, φιλμ *nt inv* ♦ *vt (scene)* γυρίζω ταινία, φιλμάρω || **~ star** *n* αστέρας του κινηματογράφου.

filter ['fɪltə*] *n* φίλτρο || *(PHOT)* φίλτρο ♦ *vt* διυλίζω, φιλτράρω, λαμπικάρω ♦ *vi (fig)* διειοδύω, εισχωρώ || **~ tip** *n* επιστόμιο φίλτρου.

filth [fɪlθ] *n (lit)* ακαθαρσίες *fpl*, σκουπίδια *ntpl*, βρώμα || *(fig)* ηθική φθορά, βρωμιά, αισχρολογία || **~y** *a* ακάθαρτος, ρυπαρός, βρώμικος.

fin [fɪn] *n (fish)* πτερύγιο, φτερό.

final ['faɪnl] *a* τελικός, τελευταίος, οριστικός ♦ *n (SPORT)* τελικός (αγώνας) || **~s** *npl (UNIV)* απολυτήριοι εξετάσεις *fpl* || **~e** [fɪ'nɑːlɪ] *n (THEAT)* φινάλε *nt inv* || *(MUS)* φινάλε *nt inv* || **~ist** *n (SPORT)* φιναλιστής || **~ize** *vt* οριστικοποιώ || **~ly** *ad (lastly)* τελικά || *(eventually)* στο τέλος || *(irrevocably)* οριστικά, τελικά.

finance [faɪ'næns] *n* οικονομία ♦ *vt* χρηματοδοτώ || **~s** *npl* οικονομικά *ntpl*.

financial [faɪ'nænʃəl] *a (policy)* οικονομικό (πολιτική) || *(year)* οικονομικόν (έτος).

financier [faɪ'nænsɪə*] *n* κεφαλαιούχος, χρηματοδότης.

find [faɪnd] *(irreg v) vt (come across)* βρίσκω || *(discover, get)* ανακαλύπτω, βρίσκω || *(learn)* ανακαλύπτω, διαπιστώνω || *(declare)* αποφαίνομαι, κηρύσσω ♦ *n* ανακάλυψη, εύρημα *nt* || **to ~ out (about)** *vt* ανακαλύπτω, αναζητώ, πληροφορούμαι || **~ings** *npl (LAW)* απόφαση, ετυμηγορία || *(of report)* διαπίστωση, συμπέρασμα *nt*.

fine [faɪn] *a (thin, slender)* λεπτός, ψιλός, ψιλόλιγνος || *(delicate)* λεπτός, φίνος || *(handsome)* ωραίος, όμορφος || *(pure)* καθαρός || *(rainless)* ωραίος, καλός ♦ *ad (well)* θαυμάσια, περίφημα || *(small)* λεπτά, λεπτομερώς, ψιλά ♦ *n (LAW)* ποινική ρήτρα, πρόστιμο ♦ *vt (LAW)* επιβάλλω πρόστιμο || **~ arts** *n* καλές τέχνες *fpl*.

finery ['faɪnərɪ] *n* στολίδια *ntpl*, στόλισμα *nt*.

finesse [fɪ'nɛs] *n* τέχνασμα *nt*, πανουργία, φινέτσα.

finger ['fɪŋɡə*] *n* δάκτυλος, δάχτυλο ♦ *vt* ψαύω, ψηλαφώ, πιάνω || **~nail** *n* νύχι || **~print** *n* δακτυλικό αποτύπωμα || **~tip** *n* άκρη του δακτύλου.

finicky ['fɪnɪkɪ] *a* μικρολόγος, λεπτολόγος.

finish ['fɪnɪʃ] *n (end)* τέλος *nt* || *(SPORT)* τερματισμός, τέλος, τέρμα *nt* || *(completion)* τελείωμα *nt*, αποπεράτωση, συμπλήρωμα *nt* ♦ *vt (also:* **~ off, ~ up)** τερματίζω, τελειώνω, αποτελειώνω ♦ *vi (general)* τελειώνω, τερματίζομαι, λήγω || *(SPORT)* τερματίζω || **~ing line** *n* τέρμα *nt* || **~ing school** *n* σχολείο γενικής μορφώσεως.

finite ['faɪnaɪt] *a* πεπερασμένος, περιωρισμένος.

Finland ['fɪnlənd] *n* Φινλανδία.

Finn [fɪn] *n* Φινλανδός/n *m/f* || **~ish** *a* φινλανδικός ♦ *n (LING)* φιννική.

fiord [fjɔːd] *n* φιόρδ *nt inv*.

fir [fəː*] *n* έλατο.

fire [faɪə*] *n (element)* πύρ *nt* || *(in grate)* φωτιά || *(damaging)* πυρκαγιά || *(MIL)* πύρ *nt*, βολή ♦ *vt (cause to burn)* ανάβω, βάζω φωτιά || *(gun etc)* πυροδοτώ, βάλλω, ρίχνω || *(fig: imagination)* ενθουσιάζω, εξάπτω || *(col: dismiss)* απολύω, παύω, διώχνω ♦ *vi (gun)* πυροβολώ || **on ~** καίομαι, παίρνω φωτιά || **~ alarm** *n* σειρήνα πυρκαγιάς || **~ arm** *n* (πυροβόλο) όπλο || **~ brigade** *n* πυροσβεστική (υπηρεσία) || **~ engine** *n* πυροσβεστική αντλία || **~ escape** *n* σκάλα πυρκαγιάς || **~ extinguisher** *n* πυροσβεστήρος || **~ man** *n* πυροσβέστης || *(RAIL)* θερμαστής || **~ place** *n* τζάκι || **~side** *n* κοντά στο τζάκι || **~ station** *n* πυροσβεστικός σταθμός || **~wood** *n* καυσόξυλα *ntpl* || **~works** *npl (lit)* πυροτεχνήματα *ntpl*.

firing ['faɪərɪŋ] *n (MIL)* βολή, πυροβολισμός, πυρ *nt* || **~ squad** *n* εκτελεστικό απόσπασμα *nt*.

firm [fəːm] *a (solid)* στερεός, σφιχτός || *(determined)* αμετακίνητος, σταθερός ♦ *n* οίκος, εταιρεία, φίρμα || **~ly** *ad* σταθερά, στερεά, γερά.

first [fəːst] *a (time)* πρώτος || *(place)* πρώτος ♦ *ad (before others)* πρώτος || *(firstly = in the first place)* πρωτίστως, πρώτα-πρώτα || *(before time)* στην αρχή, μάλλον, καλύτερα ♦ *n (person: in race)* πρώτος || *(UNIV)* λίαν καλώς, άριστα || *(AUT)* πρώτη (ταχύτητα) || **at ~** κατά πρώτο, στην αρχή || **~ of all** πριν απ'όλα, κατ'αρχήν || **~-aid kit** *n* σακκίδιο πρώτων βοηθειών || **~-class** *a* πρώτης τάξης || **~-hand** *a* από πρώτο χέρι || **~ lady** *n (US)* πρώτη κυρία || **~ly** *ad* πρωτίστως, πρώτα-πρώτα || **~ name** *n* μικρό όνομα || **~ night** *n* πρώτη, πρεμιέρα || **~-rate** *a* πρώτης τάξεως.

fiscal ['fɪskəl] *a* οικονομικός.

fish [fɪʃ] *n* ψάρι ♦ *vt* ψαρεύω ♦ *vi* ψαρεύω

|| to go ~ing πάω για ψάρεμα || ~erman n ψαράς || ~ery n αλιεία, ψαρική || ~ing boat n ψαρόβαρκα || ~ing line n αρμίδι, πετονιά || ~ing rod n καλάμι || ~ market n ιχθυαγορά || ~monger n ιχθυοπώλης || ~y a (suspicious) ύποπτος, βρώμικος.

fission ['fɪʃən] n διάσπαση.

fissure ['fɪʃə*] n σχισμή, ρωγμή.

fist [fɪst] n πυγμή, γροθιά.

fit [fɪt] a (MED, SPORT) σε φόρμα, υγιής || (suitable) κατάλληλος, αρμόζων, καλός || (qualified, worthy) ικανός ♦ vt (suit) συμφωνώ, ταιριάζω || (insert, attach) πηγαίνω, μπαίνω ♦ vi (correspond) εφαρμόζω, πιάνω || (of clothes) πηγαίνω, έρχομαι ♦ n (of clothes) εφαρμογή, ταίριασμα nt || (MED: mild, of coughing) παροξυσμός || (MED: serious, epilepsy) προσβολή || (of anger) ξέσπασμα nt, έκρηξη || (of laughter) ξέσπασμα nt || to ~ in vi συμφωνώ, ταιριάζω ♦ vt ενώνω, συνδέω || to ~ out vt εξαρτίζω, εφοδιάζω, ντύνω || to ~ up vt εφαρμόζω, ταιριάζω, μοντάρω || ~fully, by ~s and starts ακανόνιστα, άστατα || ~ness n (suitability) ικανότητα, καταλληλότητα || (MED) υγεία || ~ter n εφαρμοστής || (of clothes) δοκιμαστής || ~ting a κατάλληλος, πρέπων, ταιριαστός ♦ n (of dress) πρόβα, προβάρισμα nt || (piece of equipment) εφαρμογή, μοντάρισμα nt || ~tings npl επιπλώσεις fpl, εξαρτήματα ntpl, σύνεργα ntpl.

five [faɪv] num πέντε || ~r n (Brit) πεντάρι (λίρες).

fix [fɪks] vt (fasten) τοποθετώ, στερεώνω, καρφώνω || (determine) καθορίζω, (προσδι)ορίζω, ρυθμίζω || (repair) επισκευάζω, επιδιορθώνω || (drink) ετοιμάζω, φτιάχνω ♦ n: in a ~ σε μπελάδες, σε μπλέξιμο, σε σκοτούρες || ~ed a σταθερός, αμετάβλητος, στερεωμένος || ~ture n ακινητοποιημένο έπιπλο, εξάρτημα nt.

fizz [fɪz] n σπίθισμα nt, άφρισμα ♦ vi σπιθίζω.

fizzle ['fɪzl] vi αφρίζω, τσιρίζω || to ~ out vi σθήνω, αποτυγχάνω.

fizzy ['fɪzɪ] a αεριούχος, αφρώδης.

fjord [fjɔːd] n = **fiord**.

flabbergasted ['flæbəgɑːstɪd] a κατάπληκτος, εμβρόντητος.

flabby ['flæbɪ] a πλαδαρός, άτονος.

flag [flæg] n (banner) σημαία || (also: ~stone) πλάκα, πλακόλιθος ♦ vi (strength) εξασθενίζω, χαλαρούμαι || (spirit) κάμπτομαι, πέφτω, σπάω || to ~ down vt σταματώ.

flagon ['flægən] n καράφα.

flagpole ['flægpəʊl] n κοντάρι.

flagrant ['fleɪgrənt] a κατάφωρος, καταφανής.

flair [flɛə*] n φυσική κλίση, ικανότητα.

flake [fleɪk] n (of rust) λέπι, τρίμα nt,

φύλλο || (of snow) νιφάδα, στούπα || (also: ~ off) ξελεπίζω, ξεφλουδίζομαι ♦ vi.

flame [fleɪm] n φλόγα.

flamingo [flə'mɪŋgəʊ] n φλαμίγκος.

flange [flændʒ] n φλάντζα.

flank [flæŋk] n (side) λαγόνα, πλαγιά || (MIL) πλευρά ♦ vt ευρίσκομαι πλάι.

flannel ['flænl] n φανέλα || ~s npl (trousers) φανελένιο πανταλόνι.

flap [flæp] n (of pocket) καπάκι (τσέπης) || (of envelope) κλείσιμο (φακέλλου) ♦ vt (of birds) φτερουγίζω ♦ vi (sail, flag) ανεμίζομαι, κυματίζω.

flare [flɛə*] n φωτοβολίδα || (in skirt etc) φάρδεμα nt || to ~ up vi (into flame) αστράφτω, ανάβω || (in anger) ανάβω, εξάπτομαι.

flash [flæʃ] n αναλαμπή, λάμψη || (news flash) τελευταία είδηση || (PHOT) φλας nt inv ♦ vt (light) κάνω να λάμψει, ρίχνω || (torch) ρίχνω, ανάβω || (message) μεταδίδω ♦ vi αστράφτω, γυαλίζω || in a ~ στη στιγμή || to ~ by or past vt περνώ σαν αστραπή || ~back n αναδρομή || ~ bulb n λάμπα φλας || ~er n (AUT) φανάρι του στόπ.

flashy ['flæʃɪ] a (pej) φανταχτερός, χτυπητός.

flask [flɑːsk] n τσότρα, φλασκί || (CHEM) φιάλη || (vacuum flask) θερμό.

flat [flæt] a (level) επίπεδος, ίσιος || (dull) χωρίς προοπτικές, θαμπό || (below pitch) σε ύφεση, μπεμόλ || (beer) ξεθυμασμένο || (tyre) ξεφουσκωμένο, πεσμένο ♦ n (rooms) διαμέρισμα nt || (MUS) ύφεση || (AUT) ξεφουσκωμένο λάστιχο || ~ broke a απένταρος, πατήρης || ~footed a με πλατειά πόδια || ~ly ad σαφώς, κατηγορηματικά || ~ten vt (also: ~ten out) επιπεδώνω, ισώνω.

flatter ['flætə*] vt κολακεύω || ~er n κόλακας || ~ing a κολακευτικός || ~y n κολακεία.

flaunt [flɔːnt] vt επιδεικνύω, δείχνω.

flavour, (US) flavor ['fleɪvə*] n γεύση ♦ vt καρικεύω, αρωματίζω || ~ing n καρίκευμα nt, άρωμα nt.

flaw [flɔː] n ελάττωμα nt || ~less a άψογος, τέλειος.

flax [flæks] n λινάρι || ~en a κατάξανθος.

flea [fliː] n ψύλλος.

fled [fled] pt, pp of **flee**.

flee [fliː] (irreg v) vi (κατα)φεύγω ♦ vt φεύγω.

fleece [fliːs] n δορά, δέρμα nt, τομάρι ♦ vt (rob) ληστεύω, γδέρνω, γδύνω.

fleet [fliːt] n (NAUT) στόλος || (of cars) συνοδεία, στολή.

fleeting ['fliːtɪŋ] a φευγαλέος, περαστικός.

Flemish ['flemɪʃ] a Φλαμανδικός ♦ n (LING) Φλαμανδική.

flesh [fleʃ] n σάρκα || (meat) κρέας nt || (of fruit) σάρκα.

flew [fluː] pt of **fly**.

flex [fleks] n εύκαμπτο καλώδιο ♦ vt

κάμπτομαι || ~ibility n ευκαμψία || ~ible a εύκαμπτος || (plans) ελαστικός.

flick [flɪk] vt κτυπώ ελαφρά.

flicker ['flɪkə*] n (of light) τρεμούλιασμα nt, παίξιμο ♦ vi τρέμω, τρεμοσβύνω.

flier ['flaɪə*] n ιπτάμενος, αεροπόρος.

flight [flaɪt] n (flying) πτήση, πέταμα nt || (of squadron) σμήνος nt || (journey) διαδρομή || (also: ~ of steps) σκαλοπάτια ntpl, κλίμακα || to take ~ τρέπομαι σε φυγή || to put to ~ τρέπω σε φυγή || ~ deck n κατάστρωμα nt απογειώσεως.

flimsy ['flɪmzɪ] a σαθρός, λεπτός, μικρής αντοχής || (weak) αδύνατος, ασθενής, πρόχειρος.

flinch [flɪntʃ] vi υποχωρώ, δειλιάζω.

fling [flɪŋ] (irreg v) vt ρίχνω, πετώ.

flint [flɪnt] n (in lighter) τσακμακόπετρα.

flip [flɪp] vt δίνω ελαφρό κτύπημα.

flippant ['flɪpənt] a ελαφρός, αφελής.

flirt [flɜ:t] vi φλερτάρω ♦ (woman) n φιλάρεσκη, κοκέτα || ~ation n φλερτ nt inv, φλερτάρισμα nt.

flit [flɪt] vi πηγαινοέρχομαι.

float [fləut] n πλωτήρας, φλοτέρ nt inv || (esp in procession) αποκριάτικο άρμα ♦ vi (swimming) κολυμπώ ανάσκελα || (in air) πλέω ♦ vt (company) ιδρύω || (loan) εκδίδω δάνειο || (rumour) διαδίδω, κυκλοφορώ || ~ing a (lit) επιπλέων || (fig: population) κινητός πληθυσμός.

flock [flɒk] n ποίμνιο, κοπάδι || (of people) πλήθος nt, κοπάδι.

flog [flɒg] vt μαστιγώνω, ραβδίζω.

flood [flʌd] n πλημμύρα, κατακλυσμός ♦ vt πλημμυρίζω, κατακλύζω || ~ing n πλημμύρισμα nt, ξεχείλισμα || ~light n προβολέας ♦ vt φωτίζω με προβολέα.

floor [flɔ:*] n (of room) δάπεδο, πάτωμα nt || (storey) όροφος, πάτωμα nt ♦ vt (person) ρίχνω κάτω || ground ~ (Brit), first ~ (US) ισόγειο || first ~ (Brit), second ~ (US) πρώτο πάτωμα || ~board n σανίδα || ~ show n νούμερα ntpl.

flop [flɒp] vi (fail) αποτυγχάνω, καταρρέω || (fall) κάνω πλάφ, σωριάζομαι.

floppy ['flɒpɪ] a πλαδαρός || (COMPUT: also: ~ disk) δισκέτα, εύκαμπτος (δίσκος).

flora ['flɔ:rə] npl χλωρίδα || ~l a ανθικός, λουλουδένιος.

florid ['flɒrɪd] a ανθηρός, γεμάτος στολίδια.

florist ['flɒrɪs] n ανθοπώλης || ~'s (shop) n ανθοπωλείο.

flounce [flauns] n βολάν ♦ vi: to ~ in / out μπαίνω/βγαίνω απότομα.

flounder ['flaundə*] vi παραπατώ, σπαρταρώ, τσαλαβουτώ.

flour ['flauə*] n αλεύρι.

flourish ['flʌrɪʃ] vi (thrive, prosper) προοδεύω, ανθώ, προκόβω ♦ vt κραδαίνω, κουνώ ♦ n (ornament)

στόλισμα nt, κόσμημα nt, τζίφρα || επίδειξις, φανφάρα || ~ing a (thriving) ακμαίος.

flout [flaut] vt αψηφώ, περιφρονώ.

flow [fləu] n (movement) ροή, ρεύμα nt || (stream: lit, fig) ρούς m, χύση, χείμαρρος || (of dress) χυτές γραμμές fpl, ντραπέ nt inv ♦ vi ρέω, χύνομαι || κυψώ || (traffic, supply) κυκλοφορώ, κινούμαι || (robes, hair) χύνομαι, πέφτω.

flower ['flauə*] n άνθος nt, λουλούδι ♦ vi ανθίζω || ~ bed n παρτέρι, βραγιά || ~pot n γλάστρα || ~y a πολυγαρνιρισμένος.

flowing ['fləuɪŋ] a (movement) ρέων || (hair) χυτός || (style) ρέων, άνετος.

flown [fləun] pp of fly.

flu [flu:] n γρίππη.

fluctuate ['flʌktjueɪt] vi κυμαίνομαι.

fluctuation [flʌktju'eɪʃən] n διακύμανση.

fluency ['flu:ənsɪ] n ευγλωττία, ευφράδεια.

fluent ['flu:ənt] a ευφράδης, στρωτός || ~ly ad ευχερώς, άνετα.

fluff [flʌf] n χνούδι || ~y a χνουδάτος.

fluid ['flu:ɪd] n ρευστό, υγρό ♦ a (lit) ρευστός, ρέων || (fig: plans) ρευστός, ευμετάβλητος.

fluke [flu:k] n (col: lucky stroke) κατά τύχη.

flung [flʌŋ] pt, pp of fling.

fluorescent [fluə'resnt] a φθορίζων.

fluoride ['fluəraɪd] n φθοριούχο.

flurry ['flʌrɪ] n (of activity) αναστάτωση, ταραχή.

flush [flʌʃ] n (blush) κοκκίνισμα nt, ερύθημα nt || (of excitement) ξέσπασμα nt || (CARDS) χρώμα nt, φλας nt inv ♦ vt ποτίζω, καθαρίζω, τραβώ (το καζανάκι) ♦ vi (blush) κοκκινίζω ♦ a επίπεδος, λείος, στην ίδια επιφάνεια || ~ed a (blushing) κόκκινος, ξαναμμένος || (with anger) κόκκινος.

fluster ['flʌstə*] n αναστάτωση || ~ed a ταραγμένος.

flute [flu:t] n φλογέρα, φλάουτο.

fluted ['flu:tɪd] a αυλακωτός.

flutter ['flʌtə*] n (of wings) φτερούγισμα nt || (of excitement) αναστάτωση, συγκίνηση ♦ vi (of birds) φτερουγίζω || τρέμω, ταράσσομαι.

flux [flʌks] n: in a state of ~ σε ρευστή κατάσταση.

fly [flaɪ] (irreg v) n (insect) μύγα || (on trousers: also: flies) μπροστινό άνοιγμα nt ♦ vt (plane) πετώ, πιλοτάρω || (passengers) μεταφέρω αεροπορικώς ♦ vi (travel by air) πετώ || (flee) φεύγω, τρέχω || (of flag) κυματίζω || ~er n = flier || ~ing n (activity) πτήση, αεροπορία ♦ a (rapid) γρήγορος, πεταχτός, σύντομος, βιαστικός || ~ing saucer n ιπτάμενος δίσκος || ~ing start n καλή αρχή, ταχύ ξεκίνημα nt || ~over n (Brit) εναέριος f διάβαση || n παρέλαση αεροπλάνων || ~wheel n σφόνδυλος, βολάν nt inv.

foal [fɔul] n πουλάρι.

foam [fɔum] n αφρός || (plastic etc) αφρολέξ nt inv ♦ vi αφρίζω.

fob [fɒb]: **to ~ off** vt πασσάρω, κοροϊδεύω.

focal [ˈfɔukɔl] a εστιακός.

focus [ˈfɔukɔs] n εστία ♦ vt συγκεντρώνω, ρυθμίζω || **in ~** ρυθμισμένος, ευκρινής || **out of ~** μη ρυθμισμένος, θαμπός.

fodder [ˈfɒdə*] n φορβή, χόρτο.

foe [fɔu] n εχθρός, αντίπαλος.

foetus [ˈfiːtɔs] n έμβρυο.

fog [fɒg] n ομίχλη ♦ vt (issue) θολώνω, περιπλέκω || **~gy** a ομιχλώδης.

foible [ˈfɔibl] n αδυναμία.

foil [fɔil] vt ανατρέπω, προλαμβάνω ♦ n (of metal) έλασμα nt, φύλλο || (person) αντίθεση || (fencing) ξίφος nt.

fold [fɔuld] n (bend, crease) πτυχή, ζάρα, δίπλα ♦ vt διπλώνω, πτυχώνω || **to ~ up** vi (map etc) τυλίγω, διπλώνω || (business) κλείνω το μαγαζί, χρεωκοπώ || **~er** n (pamphlet) διαφημιστικό φυλλάδιο || (portfolio) φάκελλος, ντοσιέ nt inv || **~ing** a (chair, bed etc) πτυσσόμενος, τσακιστός.

foliage [ˈfɔuliidʒ] n φυλλωσιά.

folio [ˈfɔuliɔu] n φύλλο.

folk [fɔuk] n άνθρωποι mpl ♦ a λαϊκός || **~s** npl άνθρωποι mpl, συγγενείς mpl, δικοί μου mpl || **~lore** n λαογραφία || **~song** n δημοτικό τραγούδι.

follow [ˈfɒlɔu] vt (come after) (παρ)ακολουθώ || (obey) ακολουθώ || (go along path) ακολουθώ, παίρνω || (profession) ακολουθώ, ασκώ || (understand) καταλαβαίνω, παρακολουθώ ♦ vi (after) ακολουθώ, συνοδεύω || (result) έπομαι, προκύπτω || **to ~ up** vt συνεχίζω, εκμεταλλεύομαι || **~er** n οπαδός || **~ing** a ακολουθών, επόμενος ♦ n οπαδοί mpl, ακολουθία.

folly [ˈfɒli] n ανοησία, τρέλλα.

fond [fɒnd] a: **to be ~ of** (person) είμαι αφοσιωμένος, συμπαθώ, αγαπώ || (thing) μου αρέσει, τρελλαίνομαι για || **~ness** n (+ for) αφοσίωση, συμπάθεια σε || αγάπη για τάση στο.

font [fɒnt] n κολυμβήθρα.

food [fuːd] n τροφή, τρόφιμα ntpl, φαΐ, φαγητό || **~ poisoning** n δηλητηρίαση || **~stuffs** npl είδη διατροφής.

fool [fuːl] n (silly person) ηλίθιος, βλάκας, κουτός, χαζός || (clown) παλιάτσος ♦ vt (deceive) εξαπατώ, ♦ vi (act like a fool) κάνω το βλάκα || **~hardy** a παράτολμος, απερίσκεπτος || **~ish** a παράλογος, γελοίος || **~proof** a (plan etc) αλάνθαστος.

foot [fut] n (of person) πόδι, ποδάρι || (of animal) πόδι || (base) πέλμα nt, πόδι, κάτω άκρο || (measure) αγγλικό πόδι (0.3μ) ♦ vt (bill) πληρώνω, κάνω τα έξοδα || **on ~** πεζή, με τα πόδια || **~ball** n (ball) μπάλα || (game) ποδόσφαιρο || **~baller** n ποδοσφαιριστής || **~brake** n

ποδόφρενο || **~bridge** n γέφυρα πεζών || **~hills** npl χαμηλοί λόφοι mpl || **~hold** n πάτημα nt, στήριγμα nt || **~ing** n (lit) σίγουρη θέση, πάτημα nt || (fig) θέση, κατάσταση || **~lights** npl ράμπα, προσκήνιο || **~man** n (servant) υπηρέτης, λακές m || **~-and-mouth (disease)** n αφθώδης πυρετός || **~note** n υποσημείωση || **~path** n μονοπάτι || **~sore** a με πονεμένα πόδια || **~step** n βήμα nt, πάτημα nt || (trace) ίχνος m, πατησιά || **~wear** n παπούτσι.

for [fɔ*] prep για || (in spite of) μόλο || cj διότι, γιατί || **what ~?** γιατί;, για ποιο λόγο;.

forage [ˈfɒridʒ] n βοσκή, χορτονομή, χόρτο || vi (col) ψάχνω για.

foray [ˈfɒrei] n επιδρομή, διαρπαγή.

forbearing [fɔːˈbɛəriŋ] a υπομονητικός, ανεκτικός.

forbid [fɔˈbid] (irreg v) vt απαγορεύω || **~den** a απαγορευμένος || **~ding** a αποκρουστικός, δυσάρεστος.

force [fɔːs] n (strength) δύναμη, ισχύς f || (compulsion) εξαναγκασμός, ζόρι || (body of men) δύναμη ♦ vt (compel) εξαναγκάζω, εκβιάζω || (break open) παραβιάζω || **to ~ into** vt πιέζω, σπρώχνω, μπάζω || **be in ~** ισχύω || **the F~s** npl οι δυνάμεις fpl || **~d** a (smile) προσποιητός, ψεύτικος || (landing) αναγκαστικός || **~ful** a αποφασιστικός, δραστήριος.

forcibly [ˈfɔːsəbli] ad με το ζόρι, αποφασιστικά.

ford [fɔːd] n πέραμα ♦ vt περνώ.

fore [fɔː*] n μπροστά, μπροστινός ♦ n: **to the ~** στο προσκήνιο, διαπρέπων.

forearm [ˈfɔːrɑːm] n αντιβράχιο.

foreboding [fɔːˈbɔudiŋ] n κακό προαίσθημα nt, κακός οιωνός.

forecast [ˈfɔːkɑːst] n πρόβλεψη, πρόγνωση ♦ vt προβλέπω.

forecourt [ˈfɔːkɔːt] n προαύλιο.

forefathers [ˈfɔːfɑːðɔz] npl πρόγονοι mpl.

forefinger [ˈfɔːfiŋgɔ*] n δείκτης.

forefront [ˈfɔːfrʌnt] n πρόσοψη || (fig) πρώτη σειρά.

forego [fɔːˈgɔu] vt προηγούμαι || **~ing** a προειρημένος || **~ne** [ˈfɔːgɒn] a (conclusion) προκαθορισμένος.

foreground [ˈfɔːgraund] n πρώτο πλάνο.

forehead [ˈfɒrid] n μέτωπο, κούτελο.

foreign [ˈfɒrin] a (country) ξένος, άσχετος || (trade) εξωτερικός || (accent) ξενικός || (body) ξένος || **~er** n ξένος, αλλοδαπός || **~ exchange** n συνάλλαγμα nt || **F~ Minister** n υπουργός εξωτερικών.

foreman [ˈfɔːmɔn] n προϊστάμενος, εργοδηγός.

foremost [ˈfɔːmɔust] a πρώτος, πρώτιστος, επί κεφαλής.

forensic [fɔˈrɛnsik] a: **~ medicine** n ιατροδικαστική.

forerunner ['fɔːrʌnə*] *n* πρόδρομος.

foresee [fɔː'siː] *vt* προβλέπω || ~**able** *a* δυνάμενος να προβλεφθεί.

foresight ['fɔːsaɪt] *n* πρόβλεψη, πρόνοια.

forest ['fɒrɪst] *n* δάσος *nt*, ρουμάνι.

forestall [fɔː'stɔːl] *vt* προλαμβάνω.

forestry ['fɒrɪstrɪ] *n* δασοκομία.

foretaste ['fɔːteɪst] *n* προαίσθηση.

foretell [fɔː'tel] *vt* προλέγω, προμηνύω.

forever [fə'revə*] *ad* παντοτεινά, για πάντα.

foreword ['fɔːwɜːd] *n* πρόλογος.

forfeit ['fɔːfɪt] *n* ποινική ρήτρα ♦ *vt* χάνω (δια κατασχέσεως), χάνω.

forge [fɔːdʒ] *n* καμίνι, σιδεράδικο ♦ *vt* (falsely) πλάθω, πλαστογραφώ || (shape) σφυρηλατώ || **to ~ ahead** *vi* προηγούμαι, προχωρώ || ~**r** *n* (criminal) πλαστογράφος, παραχαράκτης || ~**ry** *n* (activity) πλαστογράφηση || (article) πλαστός, κίβδηλο (αντικείμενο).

forget [fə'get] *vti* λησμονώ, ξεχνώ, παραλείπω || ~**ful** *a* ξεχασιάρης, απρόσεκτος || ~**fulness** *n* απερισκεψία, έλλειψη μνήμης.

forgive [fə'gɪv] *vt* συγχωρώ || ~**ness** *n* συγχώρηση.

forgo [fɔː'gəu] *vt* παραιτούμαι, αποφεύγω, κάνω χωρίς.

fork [fɔːk] *n* (for food) πηρούνι || (farm tool) δικράνα, δικάλα || (branch) διακλάδωση ♦ *vi* (road) διχάζομαι, χωρίζομαι || **to ~ out** *vti* (col: pay) πληρώνω || ~**ed** *a* διχαλωτός.

form [fɔːm] *n* (structure) μορφή, σχήμα *nt*, φόρμα || (class) τάξη || (bench) μπάγκος || (document) έντυπο, τύπος || (also: mental, physical condition) κατάσταση, φόρμα ♦ *vt* (shape) διαμορφώνω, σχηματίζω, φτιάνω || (make part of) συγκροτώ, σχηματίζω.

formal ['fɔːməl] *a* (according to rule) επίσημος, εθιμοτυπικός || (stiff) τυπικός || (dress) επίσημος || ~**ity** *n* (of occasion) τύπος, τυπικότητα || ~**ly** *ad* (ceremoniously) τυπικά, με διατυπώσεις || (officially) επίσημα, τυπικά.

format ['fɔːmæt] *n* σχήμα *nt* ♦ *vt* (COMPUT) τρόπος παρουσιάσεως.

formation [fɔː'meɪʃən] *n* διαμόρφωση, σχηματισμός || (forming) σχηματισμός, διάπλαση || (group) σχηματισμός, διάταξη, τάξη.

formative ['fɔːmətɪv] *a* (years) διαπλαστικός, μορφωτικός.

former ['fɔːmə*] *a* παλαιότερος, προγενέστερος, πρώην, τέως || (opposite of latter) πρώτος || ~**ly** *ad* άλλοτε, παλαιότερα.

formidable ['fɔːmɪdəbl] *a* φοβερός, τρομερός.

formula ['fɔːmjulə] *n* τύπος || (fig) τύπος, στερεοτυπία, κλισέ *nt inv* || (MATH) τύπος || ~**te** ['fɔːmjuleɪt] *vt* διατυπώνω.

forsake [fə'seɪk] (irreg v) *vt* εγκαταλείπω, αφήνω, αρνούμαι.

fort [fɔːt] *n* φρούριο.

forte ['fɔːtɪ] *n* δύναμη, φόρτε *nt inv*.

forth [fɔːθ] *ad* προς τα εμπρός, προς τα έξω || (in space) εμπρός, μπροστά || (in time) από τώρα και εμπρός || ~**coming** *a* (επ)ερχόμενος, προσεχής.

fortieth ['fɔːtɪɪθ] *a* τεσσαρακοστός.

fortification [fɔːtɪfɪ'keɪʃən] *n* (walls etc) οχύρωμα *nt*, οχύρωση.

fortify ['fɔːtɪfaɪ] *vt* (strengthen) ενισχύω, δυναμώνω, τονώνω || (protect) οχυρώνω.

fortnight ['fɔːtnaɪt] *n* δεκαπενθήμερο || ~**ly** *a* δεκαπενθήμερος ♦ *ad* κάθε δεκαπέντε.

fortress ['fɔːtrɪs] *n* φρούριο, κάστρο.

fortunate ['fɔːtʃənɪt] *a* ευτυχής, τυχερός, ευμενής || ~**ly** *ad* ευτυχώς.

fortune ['fɔːtʃən] *n* (chance) τύχη, σύμπτωση, καλοτυχία || (wealth) πλούτος, περιουσία || ~**teller** *n* μάντης, χαρτορίχτρα.

forty ['fɔːtɪ] *num* σαράντα.

forward ['fɔːwəd] *a* (lying ahead) πρόθιος, μπροστινός || (movement) κίνηση προστά, προοδευτικός || (advanced) με πρόωρο ♦ *ad* (προς τα) εμπρός, μπρος || (SPORT) κυνηγός ♦ *vt* (mail etc) αποστέλλω, διεκπεραιώνω || (help) προωθώ, ευνοώ, προάγω || ~**s** *ad* από τώρα και στο εξής.

fossil ['fɒsl] *n* απολίθωμα *nt*.

foster ['fɒstə*] *vt* καλλιεργώ, τρέφω || ~ **child** *n* θετό παιδί || ~ **mother** *n* θετή μητέρα, ψυχομάνα.

fought [fɔːt] *pt, pp of* **fight**.

foul [faul] *a* ακάθαρτος, ρυπαρός, βρωμερός, μολυσμένος || (language) βρωμολόχος, πρόστυχος, αισχρός || (weather) κακοκαιρίας ♦ *n* (SPORT) φάουλ *nt inv* ♦ *vt* (mechanism) φράσσω, μπλέκω, πιάνω || (SPORT) κάνω φάουλ.

found [faund] *pt, pp of* **find** ♦ *vt* (establish) ιδρύω, θεμελιώνω, κτίζω || ~**ation** *n* (act) ίδρυση, θεμελίωση, θεμέλιο *nt* || (fig) ίδρυμα *nt*, κληροδότημα *nt* || ~**ations** *npl* (building) θεμέλια *ntpl*.

founder ['faundə*] *n* ιδρυτής ♦ *vi* (NAUT) βυθίζομαι, βουλιάζω.

foundry ['faundrɪ] *n* χυτήριο.

fount [faunt] *n* (source) πηγή || ~**ain** *n* πηγή || (jet of water) συντριβάνι || ~**ain pen** *n* στυλογράφος, στυλό.

four [fɔː*] *num* τέσσερα || **on all ~s** με τα τέσσερα || ~**some** *n* διπλή παρτίδα || ~**teen** *num* δέκα τέσσερα || ~**teenth** *a* δέκατος τέταρτος || ~**th** *a* τέταρτος.

fowl [faul] *n* πουλί, πουλερικό.

fox [fɒks] *n* αλεπού *f*.

foyer ['fɔɪeɪ] *n* φουαγιέ *nt inv*.

fraction ['frækʃən] *n* (part) κομμάτι || (MATH) κλάσμα *nt*.

fracture ['fræktʃə*] *n* (of bone) κάταγμα *nt* ♦ *vt* θραύω, τσακίζω, προκαλώ κάταγμα.

fragile ['frædʒaɪl] *a* εύθραυστος.

fragment ['frægmənt] *n* θραύσμα *nt*, θρύμμα *nt*, σύντριμμα *nt* || (part) κομμάτι, απόκομμα nt, απόσπασμα nt|| ~ary a αποσπασματικός, τμηματικός.

fragrance ['freigrəns] n άρωμα nt, μυρωδιά.

fragrant ['freigrənt] a εύοσμος, μυρωδάτος.

frail [freil] a ευπαθής, ασθενικός.

frame [freim] n σκελετός, πλαίσιο || (border) πλαίσιο, κορνίζα ♦ vt (put into frame) πλαισιώνω, κορνιζάρω || (put together) καταστρώνω, διαμορφώνω, κατασκευάζω || (col: incriminate) μηχανορραφώ, σκηνοθετώ || ~ of mind n πνευματική κατάσταση, διάθεση || ~work n σκελετός, πλαίσιο.

France [fra:ns] n Γαλλία.

franchise ['fræntʃaiz] n προνόμιο.

frank [fræŋk] a ειλικρινής || ~ly ad ειλικρινά, ντόμπρα || ~ness n ειλικρίνεια.

frantic ['fræntik] a έξαλλος, μανιώδης || ~ally ad μανιασμένα, έξαλλα.

fraternal [frə'tə:nl] a αδελφικός.

fraternity [frə'tə:niti] n (club) οργάνωση || (spirit) αδελφότητα || (US SCH) φοιτητική οργάνωση.

fraternize ['frætənaiz] vi (with) συναδελφώνομαι με.

fraud [frɔːd] n (trickery) δόλος, απάτη || (trick) κόλπο, απάτη, παγίδα || (person) απατεώνας, κατεργάρης.

fraudulent ['frɔːdjulənt] a δόλιος, απατηλός.

fray [frei] n σύρραξη, καυγάς, σύγκρουση ♦ vt τρίβω, ταράζω, ξεφτίζω ♦ vi ξεφτίζομαι, τρίβομαι || ~ed a τριμμένος, φαγωμένος.

freak [fri:k] n ιδιοτροπία, καπρίτσιο || (col) τέρας nt ♦ a περίεργο φαινόμενο.

freckle ['frekl] n πανάδα.

free [fri:] a (at liberty) ανεξάρτητος, ελεύθερος || (loose) ελεύθερος || (not occupied) ελεύθερος || (gratis) δωρεάν, τζάμπα || (liberal) φιλελεύθερος, γενναιόφρων, ανοιχτός ♦ vt (set free) (απ)ελευθερώνω || (unblock) αποφράσσω, καθαρίζω || ~dom n ελευθερία, ανεξαρτησία || ~lance a ανεξάρτητος || ~ly ad ελεύθερα, αβίαστα || ~mason n μασώνος || ~trade n ελεύθερο εμπόριο || ~way n (US) αυτοκινητόδρομος || ~wheel vi πηγαίνω με ελεύθερο τροχό || ~will n ελευθέρα θέληση.

freeze [fri:z] (irreg v) vi (become ice) ψύχω, καταψύχω, παγώνω|| (feel cold) κρυώνω ♦ vt (lit) (κατα)ψύχω, παγώνω|| (fig) δεσμεύω, ακινητοποιώ ♦ n (lit) (κατά)ψυξη, παγωνιά || (fig, ECON) δέσμευση || ~r n καταψύκτης, ψυγείο καταψύξεως.

freezing ['fri:ziŋ] a: ~ cold a παγερό κρύο || ~ point n σημείο ψύξεως, πήξεως.

freight [freit] n (goods) φορτίο, εμπορεύματα ntpl|| (money charged) ναύλος || ~ car n (US) φορτηγό βαγόνι || ~er n (NAUT) φορτηγό.

French [frentʃ] a γαλλικός ♦ n (LING) (τα) Γαλλικά || the ~ npl οι Γάλλοι || ~ fried potatoes npl πατάτες τηγανιτές fpl|| ~man n Γάλλος || ~window n τζαμόπορτα || ~woman n Γαλλίδα.

frenzy ['frenzi] n φρενίτιδα, τρέλλα, παραλήρημα nt.

frequency ['fri:kwənsi] n συχνότητα, πυκνότητα || (PHYS) συχνότητα.

frequent ['fri:kwənt] a (happening often) συχνός, διαδεδομένος, συνηθισμένος || (numerous) άφθονος, πολυάριθμος ♦ [fri:'kwent] vt συχνάζω || ~ly ad συχνά.

fresco ['freskəu] n νωπογραφία, φρέσκο.

fresh [freʃ] a (new, additional) νέος, καινούριος, φρέσκος || (recent) νέος, πρωτότυπος || (not stale) νωπός, φρέσκος || (not tired) ρωμαλέος, ξεκούραστος, φρέσκος || (cool) καθαρός, δροσερός || (cheeky) αναιδής, ζωηρός || ~en (also: ~en up) vi φρεσκάρω, συνέρχομαι ♦ vt αναζωογονώ, φρεσκάρω || ~ly ad πρόσφατα, νεο-, φρεσκο- || ~ness n φρεσκάδα, δροσερότητα || ~water a του γλυκού νερού.

fret [fret] vi ταράσσομαι, ανησυχώ, στενοχωριέμαι.

friar ['fraiə*] n μοναχός, καλόγηρος.

friction ['frikʃən] n (resistance) τριβή, τρίψιμο || (disagreement) προστριβή, τσάκωμα nt.

Friday ['fraidi] n Παρασκευή || see good.

fridge [fridʒ] n ψυγείο.

fried [fraid] a τηγανισμένο.

friend [frend] n φίλος, γνωστός, γνώριμος || ~liness n φιλία || ~ly a (person) ευμενής, φιλικός || (attitude) φιλικός || ~ship n φιλία.

frieze [fri:z] n (ARCHIT) διάζωμα nt, ζωφόρος.

frigate ['frigit] n φρεγάτα.

fright [frait] n τρόμος, φόβος || (ugly) άσχημος, σκιάχτρο || ~en vt (κατα)τρομάζω, φοβίζω || ~ening a τρομακτικός, τρομερός || ~ful a (col) τρομερός, φρικτός || ~fully ad τρομερά, τρομακτικά.

frigid ['fridʒid] a ψυχρός, παγερός, κρύος.

frill [fril] n βολάν nt inv.

fringe [frindʒ] n (border) κροσσός, κρόσι || (fig) περιθώριο, παρυφή.

frisky ['friski] a παιχνιδιάρης, κεφάτος.

fritter ['fritə*] n τηγανίτα, σβίγγος || to ~ away vt σπαταλώ.

frivolity [fri'vɔliti] n επιπολαιότητα.

frivolous ['frivələs] a επιπόλαιος.

frizzy ['frizi] a σγουρός.

fro [frəu] see to.

frock [frɔk] n (of monk) ράσο || (of woman) φουστάνι.

frog [frɔg] n βάτραχος || ~man n βατραχάνθρωπος.

frolic ['frolɪk] n παιχνίδι, γλέντι ♦ vt διασκεδάζω, παιχνιδίζω.

from [from] prep από.

front [frʌnt] n (of house) πρόσοψη, μπροστινό, φάτσα || (MIL) μέτωπο || (POL) μέτωπο || (meteorology) μέτωπο || (fig: appearances) όψη, μούτρα ntpl, αναίδεια ♦ a (forward) πρόσθιος, μπροστινός || (first) μπροστινός, πρώτος || (door) κυρία είσοδος f, μπροστινή πόρτα || ~al a μετωνικός || ~ier n σύνορο, μεθόριος f|| ~-page a της πρώτης σελίδας || ~-wheel drive n κίνηση στους προσινούς τροχούς.

frost [frost] n παγετός, παγωνιά || ~bite n κρυοπάγημα nt|| ~ed a (glass) μάτ, αδιαφανής || ~y a παγερός, παγωμένος.

froth [froθ] n αφρός || (on beer) κολλάρο.

frown [fraun] n συνοφρύωση, κατσούφιασμα nt ♦ vi συνοφρυούμαι, σκυθρωπάζω || to ~ upon vt κάνω μούτρα σε.

froze [frəuz] pt of **freeze** || ~n pp of **freeze** || (COMM) παγωμένος || ~n food n κατεψυγμένος.

frugal ['fru:gəl] a λιτός, οικονομικός.

fruit [fru:t] n φρούτο, καρπός || ~s npl καρποί mpl, κέρδη ntpl|| ~ful a καρποφόρος, γόνιμος || ~ion [fru:'ɪʃən] n εκπλήρωση, απόλαυση.

frustrate [frʌs'treɪt] vt ματαιώνω, εξουδετερώνω, εμποδίζω || ~d a απογοητευμένος.

frustration [frʌs'treɪʃən] n ματαίωση, απογοήτευση.

fry [fraɪ] vt τηγανίζω || small ~ npl οι ανθρωπάκοι mpl|| ~ing pan n τηγάνι.

ft. abbr of **foot**, **feet**.

fuchsia ['fju:ʃə] n φούξια.

fudge [fʌdʒ] n ζαχαρωτό.

fuel [fjuəl] n (oil) καύσιμη ύλη, πετρέλαιο || (petrol) καύσιμα ntpl, βενζίνη || (wood) καυσόξυλα ntpl|| (coal) κάρβουνο || (gas) καύσιμο αέριο || ~ oil n (diesel fuel) ακάθαρτο πετρέλαιο || ~ tank n ντεπόζιτο βενζίνης.

fugitive ['fju:dʒɪtɪv] n φυγάδας, δραπέτης.

fulfil [ful'fɪl] vt (accomplish) εκπληρώνω || (obey) εκτελώ, εισακούω || ~ment n εκπλήρωση, εκτέλεση.

full [ful] a (box, bottle) πλήρης, γεμάτος || (vehicle) πλήρης, γεμάτος || (person: satisfied) χορτάτος, μπουκωμένος || (session) ολομέλεια || (complete) ολόκληρος || (moon) πανσέληνος || (price) ολόκληρος || (speed) ολοταχώς || (skirt) φαρδύς, μπουφάν || in ~ χωρίς έκπτωση, ολογράφως, στο ακέραιο || ~back n οπισθοφύλακας || ~ stop n τελεία || ~-time a (work) με πλήρες ωράριο ♦ ad ακριβώς, τελείως || ~y ad πλήρως, τελείως, απολύτως.

fumble ['fʌmbl] vti ψαχουλεύω, χειρίζομαι αδέξια.

fume [fju:m] vi (smoke) βγάζω καπνό, καπνίζω || (be furious) εξάπτομαι,

λυσσάζω || ~s npl ατμοί mpl, αναθυμιάσεις fpl, καπνιές fpl.

fumigate ['fju:mɪgeɪt] vt απολυμαίνω.

fun [fʌn] n διασκέδαση, κέφι, αστείο, χωρατό || to make ~ of κοροϊδεύω, περιπαίζω.

function ['fʌŋkʃən] n (use) λειτουργία, έργο, λειτούργημα nt|| (public occasion) τελετή, δεξίωση ♦ vi λειτουργώ || ~al a λειτουργικός || ~ key n (COMPUT) πλήκτρο λειτουργίας.

fund [fʌnd] n (capital) ταμείο, κεφάλαιο, παρακαταθήκη || (store) απόθεμα nt, πηγή.

fundamental [fʌndə'mentl] a θεμελιώδης || ~s npl στοιχεία ntpl, βασικές αρχές fpl|| ~ly ad ουσιαστικά, βασικά.

funeral ['fju:nərəl] n κηδεία ♦ a νεκρώσιμος, πένθιμος.

fun fair ['fʌnfɛə*] n λούνα-παρκ pl inv.

fungus ['fʌŋgəs] n μύκητας, μανιτάρι.

funnel ['fʌnl] n χωνί || (of ship) φουγάρο.

funny ['fʌnɪ] a (comical) αστείος, κωμικός || (strange) παράξενος, περίεργος.

fur [fɜ:*] n γούνα, γουναρικό || ~ coat n γούνινο παλτό.

furious ['fjuərɪəs] a μαινόμενος, λυσσαλέος, αγριεμένος || ~ly ad άγρια, με μανία.

furlong ['fɜ:lɒŋ] n = 220 υάρδες (201 μέτρα).

furlough ['fɜ:ləu] n (US) άδεια.

furnace ['fɜ:nɪs] n κλίβανος, κάμινος, φούρνος.

furnish ['fɜ:nɪʃ] vt (with furniture) επιπλώνω || (supply) παρέχω, προμηθεύω, προσφέρω || ~ings npl έπιπλα ntpl, επίπλωση.

furniture ['fɜ:nɪtʃə*] n έπιπλα ntpl.

furrow ['fʌrəu] n αυλακώνω.

furry ['fɜ:rɪ] a γούνινος.

further ['fɜ:ðə*] comp of **far** || a (additional) νέος, πρόσθετος, μεταγενέστερος || (more distant) μακρινότερος ♦ ad (more) περαιτέρω, περισσότερο || (moreover) άλλωστε, επί πλέον ♦ vt προάγω, υποστηρίζω || ~more ad εκτός απ'αυτό, εξάλλου.

furthest ['fɜ:ðɪst] superl of **far**.

furtive ['fɜ:tɪv] a λαθραίος, κρυμμένος, ύπουλος.

fury ['fjuərɪ] n οργή, θυμός, μανία.

fuse [fju:z] n (ELEC) ασφάλεια || (cord) φυτίλι ♦ vt τήκω, λειώνω ♦ vi (ELEC) τήκομαι, λυώνω || ~ box n κιβώτιο ασφαλειών.

fuselage ['fju:zəla:ʒ] n άτρακτος, σκελετός.

fusion ['fju:ʒən] n (union) συγχώνευση, σύμπραξη.

fuss [fʌs] n (dispute) φασαρία, θόρυβος, ταραχή || (bustle) φασαρία, αναστάτωση, || ~y λεπτολόγος, ιδιότροπος.

futile ['fju:taɪl] a (useless) φρούδος,

μάταιος || (unimportant) ασήμαντος, κούφιος.

futility [fjuːˈtɪlɪtɪ] n ματαιότητα.

future [ˈfjuːtʃəˈ] a μέλλων, μελλοντικός ♦ n μέλλον || in (the) ~ στο μέλλον.

futuristic [fjuːtʃəˈrɪstɪk] a φουτουριστικός.

fuze [fjuːz] (US) = fuse.

fuzzy [ˈfʌzɪ] a (indistinct) θαμπός || (from drink) σουρωμένος.

G

g. abbr of gram(s).

gabble [ˈgæbl] vi φλυαρώ.

gable [ˈgeɪbl] n αέτωμα nt.

gadget [ˈgædʒɪt] n μαραφέτι.

gag [gæg] n φίμωτρο || (funny phrase) αστείο, κασκαρίκα ♦ vt φιμώνω, αποστομώνω.

gaiety [ˈgeɪtɪ] n ευθυμία.

gaily [ˈgeɪlɪ] ad εύθυμα, χαρούμενα.

gain [geɪn] vt (obtain) αποκτώ, κερδίζω || (win over) κερδίζω, παίρνω || (make progress) προχωρώ, προηγούμαι ♦ vi (improve) κερδίζω, κατακτώ || (clock etc) τρέχω μπρος ♦ n κέρδος nt, αύξηση || ~ful a επικερδής.

gal. abbr of gallon.

gala [ˈgɑːlə] n γιορτή.

galaxy [ˈgæləksɪ] n (stars) γαλαξίας.

gale [geɪl] n θύελλα, φουρτούνα || ~ warning n αναγγελία θύελλας.

gallant [ˈgælənt] a (fine, brave) γενναίος, ηρωικός || (to women) γαλάντης, περιποιητικός || ~ry n γενναιότητα, λεβεντιά || (to women) περιποιητικότητα.

gall-bladder [ˈgɔːlblædəˈ] n χοληδόχος κύστη.

gallery [ˈgælərɪ] n (ART) πινακοθήκη || (THEAT) γαλαρία, εξώστης.

galley [ˈgælɪ] n (of ship) μαγειρείο || (vessel) γαλέρα.

gallon [ˈgælən] n γαλόνι (04.54 χλγρ.).

gallop [ˈgæləp] n καλπασμός, γκάλοπ nt inv ♦ vi καλπάζω.

gallows [ˈgæləuz] npl αγχόνη, κρεμάλα.

gallstone [ˈgɔːlstəun] n χολόλιθος.

gamble [ˈgæmbl] vi παίζω ♦ vt (risk) ριψοκινδυνεύω || n (τυχερό) παιχνίδι || ~r n (χαρτο)παίκτης.

gambling [ˈgæmblɪŋ] n παιχνίδι, παίξιμο.

game [geɪm] n (play) παιχνίδι, διασκέδαση || (animals) θήραμα nt, κυνήγι ♦ a θαρραλέος, τολμηρός || ~keeper n φύλακας κυνηγιού.

gammon [ˈgæmən] n οπίσθια μπούτια ntpl, χοιρομέρι.

gang [gæŋ] n συμμορία, σπείρα.

gangrene [ˈgæŋgriːn] n γάγγραινα.

gangster [ˈgæŋstəˈ] n γκάγκστερ m inv.

gangway [ˈgæŋweɪ] n (of ship) διαβάθρα, μαδέρι || (aisle) διάδρομος.

gaol [dʒeɪl] n = jail.

gap [gæp] n (opening) τρύπα, ρήγμα nt || (empty space) διάκενο.

gape [geɪp] vi χάσκω, χασμουριέμαι.

gaping [ˈgeɪpɪŋ] a χαίνων.

garage [ˈgærɑːʒ] n γκαράζ nt inv.

garbage [ˈgɑːbɪdʒ] n σκουπίδια ntpl || ~can n (US) σκουπιδοτενεκές m.

garbled [ˈgɑːbld] a (story) παραμορφωμένος, αλλοιωμένος.

garden [ˈgɑːdn] n κήπος, μπαξές m ♦ vi ασχολούμαι με κηπουρική || ~er n κηπουρός, περιβολάρης || ~ing n κηπουρική.

gargle [ˈgɑːgl] vi γαργαρίζω ♦ n γαργάρα.

gargoyle [ˈgɑːgɔɪl] n υδρορρόη.

garish [ˈgɛərɪʃ] a φανταχτερός, κακόγουστος.

garland [ˈgɑːlənd] n στέφανος, γιρλάντα.

garlic [ˈgɑːlɪk] n σκόρδο.

garment [ˈgɑːmənt] n φόρεμα nt.

garnish [ˈgɑːnɪʃ] vt (food) γαρνίρω ♦ n γαρνιτούρα.

garret [ˈgærɪt] n σοφίτα.

garrison [ˈgærɪsən] n φρουρά ♦ vt εγκαθιστώ φρουρά.

garrulous [ˈgærʊləs] a φλύαρος, πολυλογάς.

garter [ˈgɑːtəˈ] n καλτσοδέτα.

gas [gæs] n αέριο || (coal gas) φωταέριο, γκάζ nt inv || (MED) αναισθητικό || (US: gasoline) βενζίνη ♦ vt δηλητηριάζω με αέριο || ~ cooker n κουζίνα || ~ cylinder n φιάλη αερίου || ~ fire n σόμπα του γκαζιού.

gash [gæʃ] n εγκοπή, μαχαιριά ♦ vt κόβω, πληγώνω.

gasket [ˈgæskɪt] n (TECH) παρένθεμα nt.

gasmask [ˈgæsmɑːsk] n αντιασφυξιογόνα μάσκα.

gas meter [ˈgæsmiːtəˈ] n μετρητής του γκαζιού.

gasoline [ˈgæsəliːn] n (US) βενζίνη.

gasp [gɑːsp] vi ασθμαίνω, λαχανιάζω ♦ n κομμένη αναπνοή, ρόγχος.

gas ring [ˈgæsrɪŋ] n μάτι του γκαζιού.

gas station [ˈgæssteɪʃən] n (US) βενζινάδικο.

gas stove [ˈgæsˈstəuv] n κουζίνα του γκαζιού.

gassy [ˈgæsɪ] a (drink) αεριούχος.

gastric [ˈgæstrɪk] a γαστρικός.

gastronomy [gæsˈtrɒnəmɪ] n γαστρονομία.

gate [geɪt] n πύλη, πόρτα || (of estate etc) καγκελόπορτα, αυλόπορτα || ~crasher n (party) απρόσκλητος επισκέπτης, τζαμπατζής || ~way n πύλη, είσοδος f.

gather [ˈgæðəˈ] vt συλλέγω, μαζεύω || (gain) συμπεραίνω, συνάγω ♦ vi (assemble) συγκεντρούμαι, μαζεύομαι || ~ing n συγκέντρωση, μάζεμα nt.

gauche [gəuʃ] a χωρίς τακτ.

gaudy [ˈgɔːdɪ] a επιδεικτικός, φανταχτερός.

gauge [geɪdʒ] n (of metal) διάμετρος,

διαμέτρημα nt|| (RAIL) πλάτος,
μετατρόπιο || (measure) μετρητής,
(εν)δείκτης ♦ vt (δια)μετρώ, εκτιμώ.
gaunt [gɔːnt] a (lean) ισχνός,
κοκκαλιάρης || (grim) άγριος,
συντετριμμένος.
gauze [gɔːz] n γάζα.
gave [geɪv] pt of **give**.
gay [geɪ] a (merry) εύθυμος || (brightly
coloured) λαμπρός, ζωηρός || (homosexual)
ομοφυλόφιλος.
gaze [geɪz] n ατενές βλέμμα nt|| to ~ at
vt ατενίζω, καρφώνω.
gazelle [gəˈzɛl] n γαζέλα.
G.B. abbr see **great**.
G.C.E. n abbr of **General Certificate
of Education.**
gear [gɪə*] n (equipment) είδη ntpl|| (MECH)
μηχανισμός, οδοντωτός τροχός || (AUT)
ταχύτητα, κίνησις, στην
ταχύτητα || **out of** ~ νεκρό σημείο,
εκτός λειτουργίας || ~**box** n κιβώτιο
ταχυτήτων || ~**-lever**, (US) ~**shift** n
μοχλός ταχυτήτων.
geese [giːs] npl of **goose**.
gelatin(e) [ˈdʒɛlətiːn] n ζελατίνη, πηκτή.
gelignite [ˈdʒɛlɪgnaɪt] n ζελινίτης.
gem [dʒɛm] n πολύτιμος λίθος, πέτρα.
gender [ˈdʒɛndə*] n γένος nt.
general [ˈdʒɛnərəl] n ~ στρατηγός ♦ a
γενικός || ~ **election** n γενικές εκλογές
fpl|| ~**ization** n γενίκευση || ~**ize** vi
γενικεύω, εκλαΐκεύω || ~**ly** ad γενικά,
κατά κανόνα || ~ **practitioner (G.P.)** n
≈ γιατρός m/f παθολόγος.
generate [ˈdʒɛnəreɪt] vt παράγω,
(επι)φέρω προκαλώ || (ELEC) παράγω.
generation [dʒɛnəˈreɪʃən] n (into being)
γέννηση, γένεση || (descent in family)
γενεά, γενιά || (of same period) (σημερινή)
γενεά || (about 30 years) (μια) γενεά ||
third/fourth ~ a (COMPUT)
τρίτης/τέταρτης γενεάς.
generator [ˈdʒɛnəreɪtə*] n γεννήτρια.
generosity [dʒɛnəˈrɒsɪtɪ] n
γενναιοδωρία, γενναιοψυχία.
generous [ˈdʒɛnərəs] a γενναιόδωρος,
μεγαλόψυχος || (col) γενναίος, πλούσιος
|| ~**ly** ad γενναιόδωρα, μεγαλόψυχα.
genetics [dʒɪˈnɛtɪks] npl γενετική.
genial [ˈdʒiːnɪəl] a εύκρατος, ήπιος,
προσηνής.
genitals [ˈdʒɛnɪtlz] npl γεννητικά
όργανα ntpl.
genitive [ˈdʒɛnɪtɪv] n γενική (πτώση).
genius [ˈdʒiːnɪəs] n (person) ιδιοφυΐα,
μεγαλοφυΐα || (ability) πνεύμα nt.
genteel [dʒɛnˈtiːl] a ευγενής, κομψός.
gentile [ˈdʒɛntaɪl] n εθνικός, μη
Ιουδαίος.
gentle [ˈdʒɛntl] a ήπιος, μαλακός,
ευγενής.
gentleman [ˈdʒɛntlmən] n ευγενής,
κύριος, τζέντλεμαν m inv.
gentleness [ˈdʒɛntlnɪs] n λεπτότητα.
gently [ˈdʒɛntlɪ] ad ήρεμα, μαλακά.
gentry [ˈdʒɛntrɪ] n αρχοντολόι.

gents [dʒɛnts] n άνδρες mpl, κύριοι mpl.
genuine [ˈdʒɛnjuɪn] a γνήσιος,
αυθεντικός, αληθινός || ~**ly** ad ειλικρινά,
γνησίως.
geographical [dʒɪəˈgræfɪkəl] a
γεωγραφικός.
geography [dʒɪˈɒgrəfɪ] n γεωγραφία.
geological [dʒɪəˈlɒdʒɪkəl] a γεωλογικός.
geologist [dʒɪˈɒlədʒɪst] n γεωλόγος.
geology [dʒɪˈɒlədʒɪ] n γεωλογία.
geometric(al) [dʒɪəˈmɛtrɪk(əl)] a
γεωμετρικός.
geometry [dʒɪˈɒmɪtrɪ] n γεωμετρία.
geranium [dʒɪˈreɪnɪəm] n γεράνι.
germ [dʒɜːm] n (of disease) μικρόβιο ||
(bud or seed) σπέρμα nt|| (beginning)
σπέρμα nt.
German [ˈdʒɜːmən] a γερμανικός ♦ n
(person) Γερμανός || ~ **measles** n ερυθρά
|| (LING) γερμανός || (LING) Γερμανικά.
Germany [ˈdʒɜːmənɪ] n Γερμανία.
germination [dʒɜːmɪˈneɪʃən] n
βλάστηση, κύηση.
gesticulate [dʒɛsˈtɪkjuleɪt] vi
χειρονομώ.
gesture [ˈdʒɛstʃə*] n χειρονομία, νεύμα
nt.
get [gɛt] (irreg v) vt (fetch) (πηγαίνω να)
φέρω || (become) γίνομαι || (persuade)
πείθω, καταφέρνω || (catch)
(συλ)λαμβάνω, πιάνω ♦ vi (reach)
πηγαίνω, φθάνω, γίνομαι || **to** ~ **along**
vi (of people) πηγαίνω καλά || (depart)
προχωρώ, (ώρα) να φύγω || **to** ~ **at** vt
(facts) φθάνω, βρίσκω, πλησιάζω || **to** ~
away vi (leave) αναχωρώ, αποχωρώ ||
(escape) φεύγω, το σκάω || **to** ~ **down** vt
κατεβάζω, γράφω || **to** ~ **in** vi (train)
μπαίνω, πιάνω φιλίες || **to** ~ **on** vi (well,
badly etc) τα πάω καλά || **to** ~ **out** vi
βγάζω, αφαιρώ, βγαίνω || **to** ~ **over** vt
(illness) συνέρχομαι, τελειώνω || **to** ~ **up**
vi (in morning) σηκώνομαι || ~**away** n
φυγή, δραπέτευση.
geyser [ˈgiːzə*] n θερμοπίδακας,
γκάιζερ nt inv|| (heater) θερμοσίφωνας.
ghastly [ˈgɑːstlɪ] a φρικτός, τρομερός ||
(pale) ωχρός.
gherkin [ˈgɜːkɪn] n αγγουράκι.
ghetto [ˈgɛtəʊ] n γκέτο.
ghost [gəʊst] n φάντασμα nt|| ~**ly** a σαν
φάντασμα.
giant [ˈdʒaɪənt] n γίγαντας ♦ a
γιγαντιαίος.
gibberish [ˈdʒɪbərɪʃ] n αλαμπουρνέζικα
ntpl.
gibe [dʒaɪb] n σκώμμα nt, πείραγμα nt.
giblets [ˈdʒɪblɪts] npl εντόσθια ntpl
(πουλερικών).
giddiness [ˈgɪdɪnɪs] n ίλιγγος, ζάλη.
giddy [ˈgɪdɪ] a (dizzy) ζαλισμένος ||
(frivolous) επιπόλαιος.
gift [gɪft] n δώρο || (talent) προσόν,
ταλέντο || ~**ed** a προικισμένος, με
ταλέντο.
gigantic [dʒaɪˈgæntɪk] a γιγαντιαίος.
giggle [ˈgɪgl] vi χασκογελώ ♦ n νευρικό
γέλιο.

G

gild [gɪld] (irreg v) vt (επι)χρυσώνω.

gill [dʒɪl] n (measure = ¼ pint) ⅛ του λίτρου ♦ [gɪl] n (fish) βράγχιο, σπάραχνο.

gilt [gɪlt] pp of gild ♦ n επιχρύσωση, χρύσωμα nt ♦ a (επι)χρυσωμένος.

gin [dʒɪn] n (liquor) τζίν nt inv.

ginger ['dʒɪndʒə*] n πιπερόριζα || ~ beer n τζιτζιμπύρα || ~bread n μελόψωμο || ~-haired a κοκκινοτρίχης.

gingerly ['dʒɪndʒəlɪ] ad προσεκτικά, μαλακά.

gipsy ['dʒɪpsɪ] n τσιγγάνος, γύφτος.

giraffe [dʒɪ'rɑːf] n καμηλοπάρδαλη.

girder ['gɜːdə*] n δοκός f.

girdle ['gɜːdl] n ζωνάρι ♦ vt (περι)ζώνω.

girl [gɜːl] n (child) κορίτσάκι, κορίτσι || (young woman) νέα, κοπέλα || ~friend n (of girl) φιλενάδα || (of boy) φιλενάδα, φίλη || ~ish a κοριτσίστικος.

girth [gɜːθ] n (measurement) περιφέρεια, περίμετρος || (strap) έποχο, ίγγλα.

gist [dʒɪst] n ουσία, έννοια.

give [gɪv] (irreg v) vt (hand over) δίνω, χαρίζω || (supply) παρέχω, απονέμω ♦ vi (break) υποχωρώ, λυγίζω || to ~ away vt (give free) χαρίζω || (betray) καταδίδω, προδίδω || to ~ back vt αποδίδω, ξαναδίδω, γυρίζω || to ~ in vi (yield, agree) υποχωρώ, υποκύπτω ♦ vt (hand in) παραδίδω || to ~ up vi (surrender) παραδίδομαι ♦ vt (post, office) παραιτούμαι, εγκαταλείπω || to ~ way vi θραύομαι, υποχωρώ, αντικαθίσταμαι || ~r n δωρητής, δότης.

glacier ['glæsɪə*] n παγετώνας.

glad [glæd] a ευχαριστημένος, ευχάριστος || ~den vt χαροποιώ.

gladly ['glædlɪ] ad ευχαρίστως, με χαρά.

glamorous ['glæmərəs] a γοητευτικός, μαγευτικός.

glamour ['glæmə*] n γοητεία, μαγεία.

glance [glɑːns] n βλέμμα nt, ματιά ♦ vi (+ at) (look) ρίχνω ματιά || γλιστρώ πλαγίως.

glancing ['glɑːnsɪŋ] a (blow) πλάγιος.

gland [glænd] n αδένας || ~ular a αδενικός.

glare [glɛə*] n (light) εκτυφλωτική λάμψη || (fierce stare) άγριο βλέμμα nt ♦ vi απαστράπτω, λάμπω || (angrily) αγριοκοιτάζω.

glaring ['glɛərɪŋ] a (mistake) έκδηλος, ολοφάνερος.

glass [glɑːs] n (substance) γυαλί || (vessel) ποτήρι || (mirror) καθρέφτης || ~es npl γυαλιά ntpl || ~house n (AGR) θερμοκήπιο, σέρρα || ~ware n γυαλικά ntpl || ~y a (eye) σαν γυαλί, ανέκφραστος.

glaze [gleɪz] vt (furnish with glass) βάζω τζάμια || (finish) βερνικώνω, γυαλίζω ♦ n βερνίκι.

glazier ['gleɪzɪə*] n τζαμιτζής.

gleam [gliːm] n ακτίδα, λάμψη ♦ vi ακτινοβολώ, λάμπω || ~ing a αστραφτερός.

glee [gliː] n ευθυμία, χαρά || ~ful a εύθυμος, χαρούμενος.

glen [glen] n χαράδρα, δερβένι.

glib [glɪb] a εύγλωττος, επιπόλαιος || ~ly ad εύκολα, πονηρά.

glide [glaɪd] vi γλυστρώ, κυλώ ♦ n γλίστρημα || ~r n (AVIAT) ανεμόπτερο.

gliding ['glaɪdɪŋ] n ολίσθηση, ανεμοπορία.

glimmer ['glɪmə*] n αμυδρό φως nt.

glimpse [glɪmps] n γρήγορη ματιά ♦ vt βλέπω φευγαλέα.

glint [glɪnt] n λάμψη ♦ vi λάμπω, αστράφτω.

glisten ['glɪsn] vi απαστράπτω, σπιθίζω.

glitter ['glɪtə*] vi λάμπω, σπινθηροβολώ ♦ n λαμποκόπημα nt, γυάλισμα nt.

gloat [gləʊt] : to ~ over vt κοιτάζω με χαιρεκακία.

global ['gləʊbl] a παγκόσμιος.

globe [gləʊb] n (light) γλόμπος, λάμπα || (earth) σφαίρα, σφαίρα.

gloom [gluːm] n (also: ~iness) (darkness) σκότος nt, σκοτάδι || (depression) μελαγχολία, ακεφιά μελαγχολικά, σκυθρωπιά || ~y a σκοτεινός, βαρύς, μελαγχολικός.

glorify ['glɔːrɪfaɪ] vt εκθειάζω, εξυμνώ, δοξάζω.

glorious ['glɔːrɪəs] a ένδοξος, δοξασμένος, λαμπρός.

glory ['glɔːrɪ] n (splendour) δόξα, μεγαλείο || (fame) τιμή, φήμη, δόξα.

gloss [glɒs] n (shine) στιλπνότητα, λούστρο, γυαλάδα.

glossary ['glɒsərɪ] n λεξιλόγιο, γλωσσάριο.

glossy ['glɒsɪ] a (surface) στιλπνός, γυαλιστερός.

glove [glʌv] n γάντι.

glow [gləʊ] vi πυρακτούμαι, κοκκινίζω || (look hot) ζεσταίνομαι, ανάβω || (with emotion) αστράφτω, λάμπω ♦ n (heat) πυράκτωση || (colour) ροδαλότητα, κοκκινάδα || (feeling) σφρίγος nt, φλόγα.

glower ['glaʊə*] vi στραβοκοιτάζω.

glucose ['gluːkəʊs] n γλυκόζη.

glue [gluː] n κόλλα ♦ vt κολλώ.

glum [glʌm] a σκυθρωπός, κατσούφης.

glut [glʌt] n υπεραφθονία ♦ vt (ECON) πλημμυρίζω.

glutton ['glʌtn] n λαίμαργος, φαγάς || ~ous a αδηφάγος || ~y n λαιμαργία.

glycerin(e) ['glɪsəriːn] n γλυκερίνη.

gm, gms abbr of gram(s).

gnarled [nɑːld] a ροζιάρικος.

gnat [næt] n σκνίπα.

gnaw [nɔː] vt ροκανίζω, τραγανίζω.

gnome [nəʊm] n νάνος.

go [gəʊ] (irreg v) vi (travel) πηγαίνω, πάω || (progress) κινούμαι, πάω || (function) πάω, τρέχω, λειτουργώ || (depart) αναχωρώ, φεύγω || (disappear) χάνομαι || (be sold) (+ for) πουλιέμαι για || (fit, suit) πηγαίνω, ταιριάζω || (become) γίνομαι || (break etc) σπάζω, κόβομαι, πωλούμαι ♦ n (energy) δραστηριότητα, διάθεση || (attempt) δοκιμή, προσπάθεια, απόπειρα || to ~ ahead vi (proceed) προχωρώ, προοδεύω

|| to ~ **along with** vt (agree to support) συμφωνώ, ταιριάζω || to ~ **away** vi (depart) φεύγω || to ~ **back** vi (return) επιστρέφω || to ~ **back on** vt (promise) παραβαίνω, αθετώ || to ~ **by** vi (years, time) περνώ || to ~ **down** vi (sun) κατεβαίνω, γέρνω, πέφτω || to ~ **for** vt (fetch) πάω για || (like) συμπαθώ || to ~ **in** vi (enter) εισέρχομαι, μπαίνω || (fit) μπαίνω || to ~ **into** vt (enter) μπαίνω || (study) εξετάζω, μελετώ || to ~ **off** vi (depart) εξέρχομαι, φεύγω || (milk) ξυνίζω || (explode) εκπυρσοκροτώ ♦ vt (dislike) ξεθυμαίνω, αντιπαθώ || to ~ **on** vi (continue) συνεχίζω, εξακολουθώ || to ~ **out** vi (fire, light) σβήνω || (of house) βγαίνω || to ~ **over** vt (examine, check) εξετάζω, επαναλαμβάνω || to ~ **up** vi (price) ανεβαίνω || (explode) ανατινάσσομαι || to ~ **without** vt περνώ χωρίς.

goad [gəʊd] vt κεντρίζω, προκαλώ ♦ n βούκεντρο, κίνητρο.

go-ahead ['gəʊəhed] a δραστήριος.

goal [gəʊl] n (purpose) σκοπός || (on sports field) τέρμα nt || (score) γκωλ nt inv|| ~**keeper** n τερματοφύλακας || ~-**post** n δοκός f.

goat [gəʊt] n κατσίκα, γίδα.

gobble ['gɒbl] vt καταβροχθίζω.

go-between ['gəʊbɪtwiːn] n μεσάζων, μεσολαβητής.

god [gɒd] n θεός || G~ Θεός || ~**child** n βαφτιστικός || ~**dess** n θεά || ~**father** n νονός || ~**forsaken** a εγκαταλειμμένος, καταραμένος || ~**mother** n νουνά || ~**send** n θείο δώρο, κελεπούρι.

goggle ['gɒgl] vi γουρλώνω || ~**s** npl προστατευτικά γυαλιά ntpl.

going ['gəʊɪŋ] n (condition of ground) κατάσταση εδάφους ♦ a (rate) τρέχουσα (τιμή) || (concern) δραστήριος || ~**s-on** npl συμβάντα ntpl.

gold [gəʊld] n χρυσός, χρυσάφι || ~**en** a χρυσός, χρυσαφένιος || ~**fish** n χρυσόψαρο || ~ **mine** n χρυσορυχείο.

golf [gɒlf] n γκόλφ nt inv|| ~ **club** n (society) λέσχη του γκόλφ || (stick) κλόμπ nt inv|| ~ **course** n γήπεδο του γκόλφ || ~**er** n παίκτης του γκόλφ.

gondola ['gɒndələ] n γόνδολα.

gone [gɒn] pp of **go**.

gong [gɒŋ] n γκόγκ nt inv, κουδούνι.

good [gʊd] n (well-being) το καλό, όφελος || (goodness) αρετή, καλό ♦ a (well-behaved) καλός, έντιμος || (virtuous) τίμιος, αγαθός, καλός || (well-done) εξαιρετικός, καλός || (suitable) ταιριαστός, που πάει || (sound) σε καλή κατάσταση || ~**s** npl κινητά, αγαθά, είδη || a ~ **deal**, a ~ **many** αρκετός, πολύς || ~**bye!** αντίο! || γειά σου! || στο καλό! || G~ **Friday** n Μεγάλη Παρασκευή || ~-**looking** a όμορφος || ~ **morning!** καλημέρα! || ~**ness** n καλωσύνη, αρετή || ~**will** n καλή θέληση, κέφι.

goose [guːs] n χήνα.

gooseberry ['guzbərɪ] n φραγκοστάφυλο.

gooseflesh ['guːsfleʃ] n ανατριχίλα.

gore [gɔː*] vt κερατίζω ♦ n πηκτό αίμα nt.

gorge [gɔːdʒ] n στενό, φαράγγι ♦ vti παρατρώγω.

gorgeous ['gɔːdʒəs] a πολύχρωμος, εξαίσιος.

gorilla [gə'rɪlə] n γορίλλας.

gorse [gɔːs] n σπάρτο.

gory ['gɔːrɪ] a (details) αιματοβαφής.

go-slow ['gəʊ'sləʊ] n απεργία κωλυσιεργίας.

gospel ['gɒspəl] n ευαγγέλιο.

gossip ['gɒsɪp] n (idle talk) κουβεντολόι || (person) κουτσομπόλης ♦ vi κουτσομπολεύω, φλυαρώ.

got [gɒt] pt, pp of **get** || ~**ten** (US) pp of **get**.

gout [gaʊt] n αρθρίτιδα, ποδάγρα.

govern ['gʌvən] vt (general) κυβερνώ, διοικώ, διευθύνω || (GRAM) συντάσσομαι με.

governess ['gʌvənɪs] n γκουβερνάντα, νταντά.

governing ['gʌvənɪŋ] a διευθύνων, διοικών, κατευθυντήριος.

government ['gʌvnmənt] n κυβέρνηση || (management) διοίκηση || ~**al** a κυβερνητικός.

governor ['gʌvənə*] n κυβερνήτης, διοικητής.

Govt. abbr of **government**.

gown [gaʊn] n φόρεμα nt, φουστάνι || (of judge etc) τήβεννος.

G.P. n abbr see **general**.

grab [græb] vt αρπάζω, πιάνω ♦ n αρπαγή || (excavator) αρπάγη.

grace [greɪs] n (charm) χάρη || (favour, kindness) εύνοια, χατήρι || (God's blessing) θεία χάρη || (short prayer) προσευχή ♦ vt (honour) τιμώ || (adorn) στολίζω, ομορφαίνω || **5 days'** ~ 5 μέρες προθεσμία || ~**ful** a χαριτωμένος, κομψός || ~**fully** ad χαριτωμένα.

gracious ['greɪʃəs] a (kind, courteous) καλός, αγαθός, καλόβολος.

gradation [grə'deɪʃən] n διαβάθμιση.

grade [greɪd] n (degree, rank) βαθμός, τάξη, βαθμίδα || (slope) κλίση ♦ vt (classify) διαβαθμίζω, ταξινομώ || ~ **crossing** n (US) ισόπεδος διάβαση.

gradient ['greɪdɪənt] n κλίση.

gradual ['grædjʊəl] a βαθμιαίος || ~**ly** ad βαθμηδόν.

graduate ['grædjʊɪt] n πτυχιούχος ♦ ['grædjʊeɪt] vi αποφοιτώ.

graduation [grædjʊ'eɪʃən] n αποφοίτηση || (grade) διαβάθμιση.

graft [grɑːft] n (shoot) μπόλι, κεντρί || (on humans) μόσχευμα nt || (unfair means) δωροδοκία, ρεμούλα ♦ vt μπολιάζω || ~**ing** n μεταμόσχευση.

grain [greɪn] n (seed) κόκκος, σπυρί ||

(crop) δημητριακά *ntpl* || *(small particle)* ψήγμα *nt*, κόκκος || *(fibre)* κόκκος, υφή.

grammar ['græmə*] *n* γραμματική.

grammatical [grə'mætikəl] *a* γραμματικός.

gram(me) [græm] *n* γραμμάριο.

gramophone ['græməfəun] *n* γραμμόφωνο.

granary ['grænəri] *n* σιταποθήκη.

grand [grænd] *a (fine, splendid)* μεγάλος, μεγαλοπρεπής || *(final)* πλήρης, ολόκληρος || **~daughter** *n* εγγονή || **~eur** *n* μεγαλείο || **~father** *n* παππούς *m* || **~iose** *a (imposing)* μεγαλοπρεπής || *(pompous)* πομπώδης, φαντασμένος || **~mother** *n* γιαγιά || **~ piano** *n* πιάνο με ουρά || **~son** *n* έγγονος || **~stand** *n* εξέδρα.

granite ['grænit] *n* γρανίτης.

granny ['græni] *n (col)* γιαγιά, γρηούλα.

grant [graːnt] *vt (bestow)* απονέμω, δίνω || *(allow)* (απο)δέχομαι ♦ *n* δωρεά, επιχορήγηση.

granule ['grænjuːl] *n* κοκκίδιο, κοκκίο.

grape [greip] *n* σταφύλι, ρώγα.

grapefruit ['greipfruːt] *n* φράπα, γκρέιπ-φρουτ *nt inv.*

graph [graːf] *n* διάγραμμα *nt*, γραφική παράσταση || **~ic** *a (vivid)* ζωηρός, εκφραστικός || *(drawing, writing)* γραφικός.

grapple ['græpl] *vi (+ with)* πιάνομαι, έρχομαι στα χέρια.

grasp [graːsp] *vt* πιάνω, σφίγγω, αρπάζω || *(understand)* συλλαμβάνω, κατανοώ ♦ *n (handgrip)* λαβή, πιάσιμο, σφίξιμο || *(possession)* έλεγχος, εξουσία || *(understanding)* αντίληψη, γνώση || **~ing** *a* άπληστος, πλεονέκτης.

grass [graːs] *n* χορτάρι, γρασίδι || **~hopper** *n* ακρίδα || **~land** *n* λιβάδι || **~ snake** *n* νερόφιδο || **~y** *a* χορταριασμένος, πράσινος.

grate [greit] *n* σχάρα, κάγκελο ♦ *vi (scrape)* ξύνω || *(make harsh sound)* τρίζω || *(irritate)* ενοχλώ ♦ *vt (into small pieces)* τρίβω.

grateful ['greitful] *a* ευγνώμονας, ευχάριστος || **~ly** *ad* με ευγνωμοσύνη.

grater ['greitə*] *n* ξύστρα, τρίφτης.

gratify ['grætifai] *vt* ευχαριστώ, ικανοποιώ.

gratifying ['grætifaiiŋ] *a* ευχάριστος.

grating ['greitiŋ] *n (iron bars)* κιγκλίδωμα *nt*, κάγκελα *ntpl* ♦ *a (noise)* κακόηχος, στριγκός.

gratitude ['grætitjuːd] *n* ευγνωμοσύνη.

gratuity [grə'tjuːiti] *n* φιλοδώρημα *nt.*

grave [greiv] *n* τάφος ♦ *a* βαρύς, σοβαρός, δυσάρεστος || **~digger** *n* νεκροθάφτης.

gravel ['grævəl] *n* χαλίκι.

gravestone ['greivstəun] *n* επιτάφιος πλάκα.

graveyard ['greivjaːd] *n* νεκροταφείο.

gravitate ['græviteit] *vi* έλκομαι, ρέπω προς.

gravity ['græviti] *n* βαρύτητα, βάρος *nt* || *(seriousness)* σοβαρότητα.

gravy ['greivi] *n* είδος *nt* σάλτσας.

gray [grei] *a* = **grey.**

graze [greiz] *vi (feed)* βόσκω ♦ *vt (touch)* ψαύω, εγγίζω || *(scrape)* ξύνω ♦ *n (MED)* ξέγδαρμα *nt.*

grease [griːs] *n (fat)* λίπος *nt*, ξύγγι || *(lubricant)* γράσο, λάδι ♦ *vt* λαδώνω, γρασάρω || **~proof** *a* μη διαπερατός από λάδι.

greasy ['griːsi] *a* λιπαρός, λαδωμένος.

great [greit] *a (large)* μεγάλος || *(important)* σπουδαίος || *(distinguished)* μεγάλος || **G~ Britain (G.B.)** *n* Μεγάλη Βρεττανία || **~-grandfather** *n* πρόπαππος || **~-grandmother** *n* προμάμη || **~ness** *n* μεγαλείο, μέγεθος *nt.*

Greece [griːs] *n* Ελλάδα.

greed [griːd] *n (also:* **~iness)** απληστία, πλεονεξία || **~ily** *ad* άπληστα || **~y** *a* άπληστος, πλεονέκτης || *(gluttonous)* λαίμαργος, αδηφάγος.

Greek [griːk] *n (person)* Έλληνας/νίδα *m/f* || *(LING)* Ελληνικά *ntpl* ♦ *a* ελληνικός.

green [griːn] *a* πράσινος, άγουρος || *(inexperienced)* άπειρος || **~grocer** *n* μανάβης || **~house** *n* θερμοκήπιο.

greet [griːt] *vt* χαιρετίζω || **~ing** *n* χαιρετισμός || **~ings!** *excl* χαιρετισμούς! *mpl.*

gregarious [gri'gεəriəs] *a* κοινωνικός.

grenade [gri'neid] *n* (χειρο)βομβίδα.

grew [gruː] *pt of* **grow.**

grey [grei] *a* σταχτής, γκρίζος, ψαρός || *(dismal)* σκοτεινός || **~-haired** *a* γκριζομάλλης, ψαρομάλλης || **~hound** *n* λαγωνικό.

grid [grid] *n (of bars)* σχάρα, πλέγμα *nt* || *(network)* πλέγμα, δίκτυο || *(of map)* δικτυωτό, τετραγωνισμός || **~iron** *n* σχάρα.

grief [griːf] *n* θλίψη, λύπη, ατύχημα *nt.*

grievance ['griːvəns] *n* παράπονο.

grieve [griːv] *vi* λυπούμαι, θλίβομαι ♦ *vt* λυπώ, πικραίνω.

grill [gril] *n (on cooker)* σχάρα || *(of food)* της σχάρας ♦ *vt* ψήνω στη σχάρα || *(interrogate)* ανακρίνω.

grille [gril] *n (on car etc)* γρίλλιες *fpl.*

grim [grim] *a* φρικαλέος, απειλητικός, σκληρός.

grimace [gri'meis] *n* γκριμάτσα ♦ *vi* μορφάζω.

grime [graim] *n* ακαθαρσία, λέρα, φούμο.

grimly ['grimli] *ad* απαίσια, σκληρά, αυστηρά.

grimy ['graimi] *a* ακάθαρτος, βρώμικος.

grin [grin] *n* χαμόγελο, μειδίαμα *nt* ♦ *vi* χαμογελώ, μορφάζω.

grind [graind] *(irreg v) vt (crush)* τρίβω, αλέθω, κονιάζω || *(sharpen)* ακονίζω, τορνάρω, λειαίνω || *(teeth)* τρίζω ♦ *n (bore)* αγγαρεία, μαγγανοπήγαδο.

grip [grip] *n (firm hold)* σφίξιμο, πιάσιμο || *(handle)* λαβή || *(mastery)* πυγμή, γνώση, επιβολή || (suitcase) βαλιτσάκι ♦ vt πιάνω, σφίγγω.

gripes [graips] npl (bowel pains) κωλικόπονοι mpl.

gripping ['gripiŋ] a (exciting) συγκινητικός, συναρπαστικός.

grisly ['grizli] a φρικιαστικός, τρομακτικός.

gristle ['grisl] n χόνδρος, τραγανό.

grit [grit] n (sand) αμμόλιθος, ακαθαρσίες fpl || (courage) τόλμη, θάρρος nt ♦ vt (teeth) τρίζω.

groan [groun] n αναστεναγμός ♦ vi (ανα)στενάζω.

grocer ['grousə*] n μπακάλης || ~ies npl είδη μπακαλικής.

groggy ['grogi] a (dazed, staggering) κλονιζόμενος, σουρωμένος, ασταθής.

groin [groin] n βουβών m.

groom [gru:m] n ιπποκόμος || (bridegroom) γαμπρός ♦ vt (o.s.) ντύνομαι.

groove [gru:v] n αυλάκι, διάξυσμα nt|| (rut) ρουτίνα.

grope [group] vi ψηλαφώ, ψάχνω.

gross [grous] a (coarse) χονδροειδής, σωματώδης || (very bad) χοντρός, καταφανής || (total) ολικός, χονδρικός ♦ n γρόσσα, δώδεκα δωδεκάδες || ~ly ad χονδροειδώς, υπερβολικά.

grotesque [grou'tesk] a αλλόκοτος, παράλογος.

grotto ['grotəu] n σπηλιά, κρύπτη.

ground [graund] pt, pp of grind ♦ n (surface) έδαφος nt, γη, χώμα nt|| (piece of land) οικόπεδο, γη || (generally pl: reason) λόγος, αιτία, βάση || ~s npl (dregs) κατακάθι, ίζημα nt|| (land) περιοχή, κήποι mpl, πάρκο ♦ vt (run ashore) προσαράσσω, εξοκέλλω || (compel to stay) καθηλώνω || (instruct) διδάσκω εντατικά ♦ vi εξοκέλλω || ~ing n (instruction) οι βάσεις fpl || ~sheet n μουσαμάς εδάφους || ~work n θεμέλιος ntpl, βάσις.

group [gru:p] n ομάδα, παρέα ♦ vt συνδυάζω, συνδέω, συγκεντρώνω.

grouse [graus] n (bird) χαμωτίδα, αγριόγαλος || (complaint) γκρίνια ♦ vi (complain) γκρινιάζω.

grove [grouv] n άλσος nt, ασύλιο.

grovel ['grovl] vi (in fear) σέρνομαι, κυλίομαι || (abase o.s.) ταπεινώνομαι, πέφτω στα πόδια.

grow [grou] (irreg v) vi (in size) μεγαλώνω, αναπτύσσομαι || (be produced) φύομαι || (become) καθίσταμαι, γίνομαι ♦ vt (raise crops etc) καλλιεργώ || to ~ up vi μεγαλώνω || ~er n καλλιεργητής || ~ing a αυξανόμενος, που μεγαλώνει.

growl [graul] vi μουγγρίζω ♦ n μούγγρισμα nt, βρυχηθμός.

grown-up ['groun'ʌp] a ώριμος ♦ n ενήλικος.

growth [grouθ] n (development) ανάπτυξη || (increase) αύξηση, μεγάλωμα nt|| (what has grown) καλλιέργεια || (MED) σάρκωμα nt.

grub [grʌb] n (larva) σκουλίκι || (col: food) φαγητό || ~by a ακάθαρτος, βρώμικος.

grudge [grʌdʒ] n (μνησι)κακία, έχθρα ♦ vt ζηλεύω για, δείχνω απροθυμία || to bear a ~ κρατώ κακία για.

grudging ['grʌdʒiŋ] a απρόθυμος, φειδωλός.

gruelling ['gruəliŋ] a εξαντλητικός.

gruesome ['gru:səm] a φρικτός, απαίσιος.

gruff [grʌf] a τραχύς, απότομος.

grumble ['grʌmbl] vi γκρινιάζω, μουγγρίζω ♦ n μουγγρητό, γκρίνια.

grumpy ['grʌmpi] a κατσούφης, γκρινιάρης.

grunt [grʌnt] n γρύλλισμα nt ♦ vi γρυλλίζω.

guarantee [gærən'ti:] n (of goods) εγγύηση || (promise to pay) εγγύηση, ενέχυρο ♦ vt εγγυώμαι.

guard [gɑ:d] n (defence) φρουρά, προφύλαξη || (sentry) σκοπός || (official) φύλακας ♦ vt φυλάσσω, προστατεύω, φρουρώ || ~ed a υπό φρούρησιν || (words etc) επιφυλακτικός || ~ian n (keeper) φύλακας, προστάτης || (of child) κηδεμόνας.

guerilla [gə'rilə] n αντάρτης || ~ warfare n ανταρτοπόλεμος.

guess [ges] vti μαντεύω || (US) νομίζω ♦ n εικασία, γνώμη.

guest [gest] n καλεσμένος, ξένος || (of hotel) πελάτης || ~ house n πανσιόν f inv || ~ room n (in private house, for friends) δωμάτιο των ξένων.

guffaw [gʌ'fɔ:] n καγχασμός ♦ vi ξεσπώ στα γέλια.

guidance ['gaidəns] n (control) καθοδήγηση || (advice) συμβουλές fpl, οδηγίες fpl.

guide [gaid] n (person) οδηγός m/f, συνοδός m/f, ξεναγός m/f|| (book etc) οδηγός ♦ vt (καθ)οδηγώ || girl ~ n προσκοπίνα || ~book n οδηγός || ~d missile n κατευθυνόμενο βλήμα nt|| ~lines npl οδηγίες.

guild [gild] n (old: company) συντεχνία || (society) ένωση, σωματείο || ~hall n (Brit: town hall) δημαρχείο.

guile [gail] n τέχνασμα nt, δόλος || ~less a άδολος.

guillotine ['gilati:n] n λαιμητόμος f, γκιλοτίνα.

guilt [gilt] n ενοχή || ~y a ένοχος.

guise [gaiz] n (appearance) μορφή, εμφάνιση.

guitar [gi'ta:*] n κιθάρα || ~ist n κιθαριστής.

gulf [gʌlf] n κόλπος, κόρφος || (abyss) χάσμα nt.

gull [gʌl] n γλάρος.

gullet ['gʌlit] n οισοφάγος.

gullible ['gʌlibl] a εύπιστος, αφελής.

gully ['gʌli] n ρεματιά, στενό, υπόνομος.

gulp [gʌlp] vi (hastily) καταπίνω, καταβροχθίζω || (choke) κομπιάζομαι, πνίγομαι ♦ n ρουφηξιά, γουλιά.

gum [gʌm] n (of teeth) ούλο || (for sticking) γόμα, γόμμι || (for chewing) τσίχλα, μαστίχα ♦ vt κολλώ, αλείφω με γόμα || ~**boots** npl μπότες από καουτσούκ.

gun [gʌn] n (cannon) πυροβόλο, κανόνι || (rifle) τουφέκι || (revolver) πιστόλι || ~**fire** n βολή, πύρ nt, κανονιοβολισμός || ~**man** n ληστής, κακοποιός || ~**ner** n πυροβολητής || ~**powder** n πυρίτιδα, μπαρούτι || ~**shot** n τουφεκιά, κανονιά.

gurgle ['gɜːgl] n παφλασμός, κελάρισμα nt.

gush [gʌ] n εκροή, διάχυση, ξέσπασμα nt ♦ vi (out) εκχύνομαι, αναπηδώ || (be moved) συγκινούμαι, αναλύομαι σε.

gusset ['gʌsɪt] n (MECH) επένθεμα nt.

gust [gʌst] n ανεμοριπή, μπουρίνι.

gut [gʌt] n (intestine) έντερο, σπλάχνο || (string) χορδή || ~s npl θάρρος nt.

gutter ['gʌtə*] n (channel) λούκι, σούγγελο || (of street) ρείθρο, χαντάκι.

guttural ['gʌtərəl] a λαρυγγικός.

guy [gaɪ] n (NAUT) πρόδρομος, γκάγια f || (effigy) ανδρείκελο, σκιάχτρο || (man, fellow) τύπος, παιδί.

guzzle ['gʌzl] vi καταβροχθίζω, ρουφώ.

gym(nasium) [dʒɪm('neɪzɪəm)] n γυμναστήριο.

gymnast ['dʒɪmnæst] n γυμναστής || ~**ics** n γυμναστική.

gyn(a)ecologist [gaɪnɪ'kɒlədʒɪst] n γυναικολόγος.

gypsy ['dʒɪpsɪ] n = **gipsy**.

gyrate [dʒaɪ'reɪt] vi περιστρέφομαι.

H

habit ['hæbɪt] n συνήθεια, έθιμο || (dress) φόρεμα nt.

habitation [hæbɪ'teɪʃən] n κατοικία, διαμονή.

habitual [hə'bɪtjʊəl] a συνήθης, συνηθισμένος || ~**ly** ad συνήθως.

hack [hæk] vt κατακόβω, πετσοκόβω ♦ n άλογο που νοικιάζεται.

hackneyed ['hæknɪd] a ξεφτελισμένος, φθαρμένος.

had [hæd] pt, pp of **have**.

haddock ['hædək] n βακαλάος.

haemorrhage, hemorrhage (US) ['hemərɪdʒ] n αιμορραγία.

haemorrhoids, hemorrhoids (US) ['hemərɔɪdz] npl αιμορροΐδες fpl.

haggard ['hægəd] a κάτωχρος, χαμένος.

haggle ['hægl] vi κάνω παζάρι.

hail [heɪl] n (meteorology) χαλάζι ♦ vt (greet) χαιρετώ ♦ vi (meteorology) ρίχνει χαλάζι || to ~ from vt προέρχομαι από || ~**stone** n κόκκος χαλάζης.

hair [hɛə*] n (general) τρίχα, μαλλιά ntpl || (one hair) τρίχα || ~'**s breadth** n παρά τρίχα || ~**brush** n βούρτσα μαλλιών || ~**cut** n κούρεμα nt || ~**do** n κτένισμα nt || ~**dresser** n κομμωτής/ώτρια m/f, κουρέας || ~**drier** n στεγνωτήρας || ~**net** δίχτυ nt για τα μαλλιά || ~**oil** n

λάδι για τα μαλλιά || ~**pin** n (lit) φουρκέτα || (bend) απότομη στροφή || ~**raising** a τρομακτικός || ~**style** n κόμμωση, χτενισιά || ~**y** a τριχωτός, μαλλιαρός.

half [hɑːf] n μισό ♦ a μισός ♦ ad κατά το ήμισυ, μισό || ~**breed**, ~**caste** n μιγάδας || ~**hearted** a χλιαρός, με μισή καρδιά || ~**hour** n ημίωρο, μισή (ώρα) || ~**penny** n μισή πέννα || ~**price** μισή τιμή, μισό εισιτήριο || ~**way** ad στο ήμισυ της αποστάσεως, μισοστρατής.

halibut ['hælɪbət] n ιππόγλωσσος, είδος γλώσσας.

hall [hɔːl] n μεγάλη αίθουσα || (building, house) δημόσιο κτίριο || (dining) τραπεζαρία || (entrance) είσοδος f, χωλ nt inv.

hallo [hə'ləʊ] excl = **hello**.

hallucination [həluːsɪ'neɪʃən] n παραίσθηση, αυταπάτη.

halo ['heɪləʊ] n (of saint) φωτοστέφανος || (of sun, moon) άλως f, αλώνι.

halt [hɔːlt] n στάση, σταμάτημα nt ♦ vt σταματώ ♦ vi σταθμεύω, σταματώ.

halve [hɑːv] vt χωρίζω στα δύο, μοιράζω.

ham [hæm] n χοιρομέρι, ζαμπό nt inv.

hamburger ['hæmbɜːgə*] n μπιφτέκι από κιμά.

hamlet ['hæmlət] n χωριουδάκι.

hammer ['hæmə*] n σφυρί ♦ vt κτυπώ δυνατά, σφυρηλατώ.

hammock ['hæmək] n αμάκ nt inv, κούνια || (NAUT) αιώρα, μπράντα.

hamper ['hæmpə*] n καλάθι ♦ vt εμποδίζω, παρακωλύω.

hand [hænd] n χέρι || (of clock) δείκτης || (worker) εργάτης || (help) βοήθεια ♦ vt δίνω || βοηθώ || ~s npl (NAUT) πλήρωμα nt || to ~ down vt μεταβιβάζω || to ~ over vt παραδίδω || at ~ κοντά || in ~ στη διάθεσή μου || υπό τον έλεγχό μου || ~s up ψηλά τα χέρια || ~bag n τσάντα || ~book n εγχειρίδιο || (guide) οδηγός || ~brake n χειρόφρενο || ~cuffs npl χειροπέδες fpl || ~ful n φούχτα, φουχτιά.

handicap ['hændɪkæp] n εμπόδιο, μειονέκτημα nt || (SPORT) χάντικαπ nt inv ♦ vt παρεμποδίζω, δυσχεραίνω || (SPORT) βάζω χάντικαπ.

handicraft ['hændɪkrɑːft] n χειροτεχνία, τέχνη.

handkerchief ['hæŋkətʃɪf] n μαντήλι.

handle ['hændl] n (of door etc) πόμολο, (χειρο)λαβή || (of cup etc) χερούλι || (for winding) χειρολαβή, χερούλι ♦ vt (use, treat) μεταχειρίζομαι || (manipulate) χειρίζομαι || (touch) πιάνω, αγγίζω || (COMM) διεκπεραιώνω, διαχειρίζομαι.

hand-luggage ['hændlʌgɪdʒ] n αποσκευές fpl του χεριού.

handmade ['hændmeɪd] a χειροποίητος.

handsome ['hænsəm] a ωραίος,

handwriting ['hændraitiŋ] n γραφή, γράψιμο.

handy ['hændi] a επιδέξιος || (useful) βολικός, χρήσιμος.

handyman ['hændimən] n πολυτεχνίτης.

hang [hæŋ] (irreg v) vt αναρτώ, κρεμώ || (one's head) σκύβω || (wallpaper) κολλώ ♦ vi κρεμούμαι || **to ~ about** vi περιφέρομαι, τριγυρίζω, τεμπελιάζω.

hangar ['hæŋə°] n υπόστεγο.

hanger ['hæŋə°] n κρεμάστρα.

hanger-on ['hæŋər'ɒn] n κολλιτσίδα.

hangover ['hæŋəʊvə°] n (MED) πονοκέφαλος (από μεθύσι).

hanker ['hæŋkə°] vi: **to ~ after** ποθώ διακαώς, λαχταρώ.

haphazard [hæp'hæzəd] a στην τύχη, τυχαία.

happen ['hæpən] vi συμβαίνω, τυγχάνω || **~ing** n συμβάν, γεγονός.

happily ['hæpili] ad ευτυχώς.

happiness ['hæpinis] n ευτυχία.

happy ['hæpi] a ευτυχισμένος, τυχερός, επιτυχημένος || **~-go-lucky** a ξένοιαστος.

harass ['hærəs] vt παρενοχλώ, βασανίζω.

harbour, harbor (US) ['hɑːbə°] n λιμάνι, καταφύγιο ♦ vt στεγάζω, παρέχω άσυλο.

hard [hɑːd] a σκληρός, στερεός || (task) δύσκολος, δυσχερής || (person etc) αυστηρός, αλύπητος || (work) επίπονος, σκληρός ♦ ad δυνατά, σκληρά, δύσκολα || **~ by** κοντά || **~-boiled** a (egg) σφιχτό || (person) σκληρός || **~en** vi σκληραίνω || **~-hearted** a σκληρόκαρδος, αλύπητος.

hardly ['hɑːdli] ad μόλις.

hardship ['hɑːdʃip] n κακουχία, δοκιμασία, ταλαιπωρία.

hard-up [hɑːd'ʌp] a απένταρος.

hardware ['hɑːdwɛə°] n σιδηρικά ntpl, είδη ntpl, καγκελαρίας.

hardy ['hɑːdi] a σκληραγωγημένος || (brave) τολμηρός, θαρραλέος.

hare [hɛə°] n λαγός.

harem [hɑː'riːm] n χαρέμι.

harm [hɑːm] n κακό, βλάβη, ζημιά ♦ vt βλάπτω, θίγω || **~ful** a επιβλαβής, βλαβερός || **~less** a άκακος, αβλαβής, ακίνδυνος.

harmonica [hɑː'mɒnikə] n φυσαρμόνικα.

harmonious [hɑː'məʊniəs] a αρμονικός || (MUS) μελωδικός.

harmonize ['hɑːmənaiz] vt εναρμονίζω || (agree) συμφωνώ ♦ vi εναρμονίζομαι, ταιριάζω.

harmony ['hɑːməni] n (MUS) αρμονία || (agreement) συμφωνία.

harness ['hɑːnis] n σαγή, χάμουρα ntpl, χαμούρωμα nt ♦ vt (horse) χαμουρώνω.

harp [hɑːp] n άρπα || **~ist** n αρπιστής.

harpoon [hɑː'puːn] n καμάκι.

harrow ['hærəʊ] n βωλοκόπος, σβάρνα ♦ vt βωλοκοπώ.

harrowing ['hærəʊiŋ] a θλιβερός, σπαρακτικός.

harsh [hɑːʃ] a σκληρός, τραχύς || **~ly** ad σκληρά, απότομα || **~ness** n τραχύτητα, σκληρότητα || (of taste) ξινίλα.

harvest ['hɑːvist] n συγκομιδή, εσοδεία || (season) θέρος nt, εποχή θερισμού ♦ vt θερίζω, μαζεύω.

harvester ['hɑːvistə°] n θεριστική μηχανή.

has [hæz] see **have**.

hash [hæʃ] n κιμάς ♦ vt κατακόπτω, κάνω κιμά.

hashish ['hæʃiːʃ] n χασίς nt inv.

haste [heist] n βία, βιασύνη, γρηγοράδα || **~n** vt σπεύδω, επιταχύνω ♦ vi βιάζομαι, κάνω γρήγορα.

hastily ['heistili] ad βιαστικά.

hasty ['heisti] a βιαστικός, οξύθυμος.

hat [hæt] n καπέλλο.

hatch [hætʃ] n καταπακτή, μπουκαπόρτα ♦ vi εκκολάπτομαι, βγαίνω, σκάω ♦ vt κλωσώ.

hatchet ['hætʃit] n τσεκούρι.

hate [heit] vt μισώ ♦ n μίσος nt || **~ful** a μισητός.

hatred ['heitrid] n έχθρα, μίσος nt.

haughty ['hɔːti] a υπεροπτικός, αυθάδης.

haul [hɔːl] n τράβηγμα nt || (fish) δίχτυά ♦ vt έλκω, τραβώ, σύρω || **~age** n μεταφορά εμπορευμάτων.

haunch [hɔːntʃ] n ισχίο, γοφός.

haunt [hɔːnt] n λημέρι, στέκι ♦ vt συχνάζω σε || (of ghosts) στοιχειώνω.

have [hæv] (irreg v) vt έχω, κατέχω || (be obliged) αναγκάζω, έχω να, πρέπει να || (meal) λαμβάνω, παίρνω || (obtain) παίρνω || (children etc) γεννώ, κάνω || **to ~ on** vt φορώ.

haven ['heivən] n λιμάνι || (refuge) καταφύγιο, άσυλο.

haversack ['hævəsæk] n σακκίδιο || (MIL) γυλιός.

havoc ['hævək] n πανωλεθρία, καταστροφή.

hawk [hɔːk] n γεράκι.

hay [hei] n σανός, άχυρο || **~ fever** n αλλεργικό συνάχι || **~stack** n θημωνιά.

haywire ['heiwaiə°] a (col) **it's gone ~** δεν πάει καλά.

hazard ['hæzəd] n (chance) τύχη || (danger) κίνδυνος ♦ vt διακινδυνεύω, ριψοκινδυνεύω || **~ous** a ριψοκίνδυνος.

haze [heiz] n καταχνιά.

hazelnut ['heizlnʌt] n φουντούκι.

hazy ['heizi] a (weather) καταχνιασμένος || (vague) αμυδρός, αόριστος.

he [hiː] pron αυτός, εκείνος || αρσενικός.

head [hed] n (ANAT) κεφάλι || (leader) αρχηγός, προϊστάμενος, διευθυντής || (top) άκρο ♦ a πρωτεύων, κύριος ♦ vt ηγούμαι, διευθύνω, διοικώ || **to ~ for** vt κινούμαι προς, κατευθύνομαι || **~ache** n κεφαλόπονος, πονοκέφαλος || **~ing** n

επικεφαλίδα, τίτλος || ~**lamp** n
προβολέας, φανάρι || ~**land** n ακρωτήρι
|| ~**light** = ~**lamp** || ~**line** n
επικεφαλίδα, τίτλος || ~**long** ad με το
κεφάλι, απερίσκεπτος || ~**master** n
διευθυντής σχολείου || ~**mistress** n
διευθύντρια (σχολείου) || ~**-on** a κατά
μέτωπο || ~**quarters** (H.Q.) npl
αρχηγείο, στρατηγείο || ~**rest** n
προσκέφαλο || ~**strong** a
ισχυρογνώμονας, ξεροκέφαλος || ~
waiter n αρχισερβιτόρος, μαίτρ m inv ||
~**way** n πρόοδος f || ~**wind** n
αντίθετος άνεμος, αέρας κόντρα || ~**y** a
ορμητικός, φουριόζος || (drink etc) που
ζαλίζει, βαράει στο κεφάλι.
heal [hi:l] vt θεραπεύω, γιατρεύω ♦ vi
επουλώνομαι, γιατρεύομαι.
health [helθ] n υγεία || (toast) πρόποση ||
~**y** a υγιής, εύρωστος, γερός.
heap [hi:p] n σωρός || πλήθος nt ♦ vt
γεμίζω, συσσωρεύω.
hear [hiə*] (irreg v) vt ακούω || ακρόωμαι
|| (learn) ακούω, μαθαίνω || ~**ing** n (sense)
ακοή || ακρόαση || (LAW) (ακροαματική)
εξέταση μαρτύρων || ~**ing aid** n
ακουστικά ntpl βαρυκοΐας || ~**say** n
φήμη, διάδοση.
hearse [hɜ:s] n νεκροφόρα.
heart [ha:t] n (ANAT) καρδιά || (centre)
καρδιά || (courage) θάρρος nt || (emotion)
ψυχή || (tenderness) καρδιά, ψυχή ||
(CARDS) κούπα || ~ **attack** n καρδιακή
προσβολή || ~**beat** n παλμός καρδιάς ||
~**breaking** a θλιβερός, λυπηπερός ||
~**broken** a περίλυπος, θλιμμένος ||
~**burn** n καρδιαλγία, καούρα
(στομάχου) || ~**felt** a εγκάρδιος,
γκαρδιακός.
hearth [ha:θ] n τζάκι || πυροστιά.
heartily ['ha:tili] ad ειλικρινά, με όρεξη,
τελείως.
heartless ['ha:tlis] a άκαρδος.
hearty ['ha:ti] a εγκάρδιος || (healthy)
εύρωστος || (meal) πλούσιος, θρεπτικός.
heat [hi:t] n θερμότητα || (weather) ζέστη,
κάψα || (anger) έξαψη, οργή || (SPORT)
αγώνας δρόμου, κούρσα ♦ vt θερμαίνω,
ζεσταίνω || **to** ~ **up** vi ανάβω, (υπερι-)
θερμαίνομαι || ~**ed** a ζεστός,
θερμασμένος || ~**er** n θερμάστρα,
σόμπα.
heath [hi:θ] n (Brit) χέρσα γη, ρεικιά ||
ρείκη.
heathen ['hi:ðən] n ειδωλολάτρης,
εθνικός ♦ a ειδωλολατρικός.
heather ['heðə*] n (ε)ρείκι.
heating ['hi:tiŋ] n θέρμανση.
heatstroke ['hi:tstrəuk] n
θερμοπληξία.
heatwave ['hi:tweiv] n κύμα nt ζέστης,
καύσωνα.
heave [hi:v] (irreg v) vt σηκώνω,
ανυψώνω || (throw) ρίχνω ♦ vi ανυψούμαι
|| (NAUT) βιράρω ♦ n ανύψωση, σήκωμα
nt || φούσκωμα nt.
heaven ['hevən] n ουρανός || **for** ~'s

sake! για όνομα του Θεού! || **good** ~**s!**
Θεέ μου! || ~**ly** a ουράνιος || (col)
περίφημος.
heavily ['hevili] ad βαρειά, δυνατά.
heavy ['hevi] a βαρύς || (difficult)
δύσκολος, δύσβατος || (abundant)
άφθονος.
Hebrew ['hi:bru:] n (person) Εβραίος/α
m/f || (LING) Εβραϊκά ntpl ♦ a εβραϊκός.
heckle ['hekl] vt βομβαρδίζω με
ενοχλητικές ερωτήσεις.
hectic ['hektik] a πυρετώδης ||
ταραχώδης.
hedge [hedʒ] n φράχτης, φραγμός ♦ vt
(surround) περιφράσσω, φράσσω ♦ vi
υπεκφεύγω, μασώ τα λόγια μου.
hedgehog ['hedʒhɒg] n σκαντζόχοιρος.
heed [hi:d] vt προσέχω ♦ n προσοχή ||
~**less** a απρόσεκτος, αμέριμνος.
heel [hi:l] n φτέρνα || (of shoe) τακούνι ♦
vt (shoe) βάζω τακούνι σε.
hefty ['hefti] a δυνατός, ρωμαλέος.
heifer ['hefə*] n δαμάλι.
height [hait] n (of person) ανάστημα nt,
μπόι || (of object) ύψος nt, ύψωμα nt ||
ακμή || (of mountain) κορυφή || ~**en** vt
υψώνω, αυξάνω.
heir [εə*] n κληρονόμος || ~**ess** n n
κληρονόμος || ~**loom** n οικογενειακό
κειμήλιο.
held [held] pt, pp of **hold.**
helicopter ['helikɒptə*] n ελικόπτερο.
hell [hel] n κόλαση.
he'll [hi:l] = **he will, he shall** || see
will, shall.
hellish ['heliʃ] a απαίσιος, καταχθόνιος.
hello [hə'ləu] excl (greeting) γεια σου! ||
(TEL) αλλό! || (surprise) μπα, μπα!
helm [helm] n τιμόνι, δοιάκι.
helmet ['helmit] n κράνος nt, κάσκα ||
περικεφαλαία.
helmsman ['helmzmən] n
πηδαλιούχος.
help [help] n βοήθεια ♦ vt βοηθώ,
ενισχύω || (prevent) αποφεύγω, εμποδίζω
|| (serve food) σερβίρω || ~**er** n βοηθός
m/f || ~**ful** a χρήσιμος || ~**ing** n μερίδα ||
~**less** a αβοήθητος, σε αμηχανία.
hem [hem] n στρίφωμα nt || **to** ~ **in** vt
περικυκλώνω, στρυμώνω.
hemisphere ['hemisfiə*] n ημισφαίριο.
hemp [hemp] n κάνναβη, καννάβι.
hen [hen] n κότα, θηλυκό πουλί || ~**coop**
n κοτέτσι.
hence [hens] ad απ'εδώ, από τώρα ||
(therefore) απ'αυτό.
henchman ['hentʃmən] n πιστός
οπαδός, μπράβος.
her [hɜ:*] pron αυτή ♦ a δικός της.
herald ['herəld] n κήρυκας, πρόδρομος
♦ vt αναγγέλλω, προμηνύω,
προαγγέλλω.
heraldry ['herəldri] n οικοσημολογία.
herb [hɜ:b] n βότανο, χόρτο.
herd [hɜ:d] n (general) κοπάδι.
here [hiə*] ad εδώ ♦ n εδώ || ~! να! ||
come ~! έλα (δω)! || ~**after** ad στο

εξής ♦ n μέλλουσα ζωή || ~by ad μ'αυτό, διά του παρόντος.

hereditary [hɪ'redɪtrɪ] a κληρονομικός.

heredity [hɪ'redɪtɪ] n κληρονομικότητα.

heresy ['herɪsɪ] n αίρεση.

heretic ['herɪtɪk] n αιρετικός || ~al [hɪ'retɪkəl] a αιρετικός.

herewith ['hɪə'wɪð] ad με το παρόν, μ'αυτό.

heritage ['herɪtɪdʒ] n κληρονομία.

hermit ['hɜːmɪt] n ερημίτης.

hernia ['hɜːnɪə] n κήλη.

hero ['hɪərəʊ] n ήρωας, παληκάρι || (of a story) πρωταγωνιστής || ~ic a πρωϊκός.

heroin ['herəʊɪn] n ηρωίνη.

heroine ['herəʊɪn] n πρωϊδα, πρωταγωνίστρια.

heroism ['herəʊɪzm] n ηρωϊσμός.

heron ['herən] n ερωδιός, τσικνιάς.

herring ['herɪŋ] n ρέγγα.

hers [hɜːz] pron αυτής, δικός της.

herself [hɜː'self] pron n ίδια, τον εαυτό της.

he's [hiːz] = he is, he has || see be, have.

hesitant ['hezɪtənt] a διστακτικός.

hesitate ['hezɪteɪt] vi διστάζω.

hesitation [hezɪ'teɪʃən] n δισταγμός, ενδοιασμός.

het up ['het'ʌp] a θυμωμένος, στενοχωρημένος.

hew [hjuː] (irreg v) vt κατακόπτω, πελεκώ.

hexagon ['heksəgən] n εξάγωνο.

heyday ['heɪdeɪ] n ακμή, άνθος nt, καλές μέρες fpl.

hi [haɪ] excl ε!, ου! || (US) καλημέρα!, γεια σου!

hibernate ['haɪbəneɪt] vi διαχειμάζω.

hiccough, hiccup ['hɪkʌp] vi έχω λόξυγγα || ~s npl λόξυγγας.

hid [hɪd] pt of hide.

hidden ['hɪdn] pp of hide.

hide [haɪd] (irreg v) n δέρμα nt, πετσί, τομάρι ♦ vt (από) κρύβω ♦ vi κρύβομαι || ~-and-seek n κρυφτό.

hideous ['hɪdɪəs] a φρικτός, αποκρουστικός, άσχημος.

hiding ['haɪdɪŋ] n (beating) σπάσιμο στο ξύλο || in ~ (concealed) κρυμμένος || ~ place n κρυψώνας.

hierarchy ['haɪərɑːkɪ] n ιεραρχία.

high [haɪ] a (far up) ψηλός || (tall) ψηλός || (rank) ανώτερος, σπουδαίος || (class) ανώτερος || (price) μεγάλος, ψηλός || (pressure etc) ψηλός, μεγάλος || (opinion) μεγάλη εκτίμηση σε ♦ ad ψηλά, πλούσια || ~chair n ψηλό καρεκλάκι για μωρά || ~-handed a αυθαίρετα || ~-heeled a με ψηλά τακούνια || ~light n (fig) αποκορύφωμα nt, το μεγάλο νούμερο || ~ly ad εξαιρετικά, πάρα πολύ || ~ly strung a ευερέθιστος, νευρικός || H~ Mass n μεγάλη λειτουργία (των Καθολικών) || ~ness n (title) υψηλότητα || ~-pitched a (voice) διαπεραστικός, οξύς.

high school ['haɪskuːl] n γυμνάσιο.

highway ['haɪweɪ] n εθνική οδός f.

hijack ['haɪdʒæk] vt κάνω αεροπειρατία || ~er n (AVIAT) αεροπειρατής.

hike [haɪk] vi πεζοπορώ ♦ n πεζοπορία || ~r n πεζοπόρος.

hiking ['haɪkɪŋ] n πεζοπορία.

hilarious [hɪ'leərɪəs] a ιλαρός, εύθυμος.

hilarity [hɪ'lærɪtɪ] n ιλαρότητα, ευθυμία.

hill [hɪl] n λόφος || ~y a λοφώδης.

hilt [hɪlt] n λαβή (ξίφους) || up to the ~ τελείως.

him [hɪm] pron αυτόν, σ'αυτόν.

himself [hɪm'self] pron τον εαυτό του, (αυτός) ο ίδιος.

hind [haɪnd] a οπίσθιος ♦ n έλαφος f.

hinder ['hɪndə*] vt εμποδίζω, κωλύω.

hindrance ['hɪndrəns] n εμπόδιο.

Hindu ['hɪn'duː] n Ινδός/ή m/f.

hinge [hɪndʒ] n άρθρωση, μεντεσές m ♦ vt κρεμώ σε μεντεσέδες || vi (fig) εξαρτώμαι.

hint [hɪnt] n νύξη, υπαινιγμός ♦ vi υπαινίσσομαι.

hip [hɪp] n ισχίο, γοφός.

hippopotamus [hɪpə'pɒtəməs] n ιπποπόταμος.

hire ['haɪə*] n μίσθωση, ενοικίαση ♦ vt (worker) μισθώνω, πληρώνω, προσλαμβάνω || (rent) ενοικιάζω || (car) νοικιάζω || 'for ~' 'ελεύθερον', 'ενοικιάζεται' || ~ purchase (H.P.) n με δόσεις.

his [hɪz] pron δικός του ♦ a αυτού, (δικός) του.

hiss [hɪs] n σφύριγμα nt ♦ vi αποδοκιμάζω, σφυρίζω.

historian [hɪs'tɔːrɪən] n ιστορικός.

historic(al) [hɪs'tɒrɪk(əl)] a ιστορικός.

history ['hɪstərɪ] n ιστορία.

hit [hɪt] (irreg v) n κτύπημα nt || (success) επιτυχία ♦ vt κτυπάω, πλήττω || (target) ευστοχώ.

hitch [hɪtʃ] n τίναγμα nt, τράβηγμα nt || (bend) θηλειά || (fig) εμπόδιο ♦ vt δένω, προσδένω || (jerk) τραντάζω.

hitch-hike ['hɪtʃhaɪk] vi κάνω ωτοστόπ || ~r n αυτός που κάνει ωτοστόπ.

hive [haɪv] n κυψέλη.

H.M.S. abbr of His (Her) Majesty's Ship.

hoard [hɔːd] n θησαυρός, σωρός ♦ vt συσσωρεύω, θησαυρίζω, αποκρύπτω.

hoarding ['hɔːdɪŋ] n αποθησαυρισμός, απόκρυψη.

hoarse [hɔːs] a βραχνιασμένος.

hoax [həʊks] n αστείο, τέχνασμα nt, φάρσα.

hobble ['hɒbl] vi χωλαίνω, κουτσαίνω.

hobby ['hɒbɪ] n μεράκι, χόμπι nt inv.

hobo ['həʊbəʊ] n (US) αλήτης.

hock [hɒk] n (wine) άσπρο κρασί του Ρήνου.

hockey ['hɒkɪ] n χόκεϋ nt inv.

hoe [həʊ] n σκαλιστήρι ♦ vt σκαλίζω.

hog [hɒg] n γουρούνι.

hoist [hɔɪst] n ανελκυστήρας || τράβηγμα nt, σπρώξιμο nt ♦ vt ανυψώνω.

hold [hɔʊld] *(irreg v)* n λαβή, πιάσιμο || *(influence)* έχω επιρροή πάνω σε || *(NAUT)* αμπάρι ♦ *vt (grasp)* κρατώ || *(keep)* κρατώ, φέρω || *(contain)* περιέχω || *(keep back)* συγκρατώ, σταματώ || *(meeting etc)* συγκαλώ, κάνω || *(title)* κατέχω, έχω || to ~ **back** *vt* συγκρατώ || *(secret)* αποκρύβω || *(control)* αναχαιτίζω || to ~ **down** *vt* κρατώ || to ~ **out** *vt* εκτείνω || *(resist)* αντέχω || to ~ **up** *vt (support)* υποστηρίζω || *(display)* επιδεικνύω || *(stop)* σταματώ, καθυστερώ || *(rob)* ληστεύω ♦ *vi (withstand pressure)* αντέχω || ~**er** n κάτοχος *m/f* || *(handle)* λαβή, σφιγκτήρας || ~**ing** n *(share)* μετοχή || ~**up** n καθυστέρηση || *(robbery)* ληστεία.

hole [hɔʊl] n τρύπα ♦ *vt* τρυπώ, ανοίγω.

holiday ['hɔlɪdeɪ] n γιορτή, αργία || *(annual)* διακοπές *fpl* || ~-**maker** n παραθεριστής/ρια *m/f*.

holiness ['hɔʊlɪnɪs] n αγιότητα.

Holland ['hɔlənd] n Ολλανδία.

hollow ['hɔləʊ] a βαθουλός, κοίλος || *(empty)* κούφιος || *(false)* ψεύτικος ♦ n κοίλωμα nt, βαθούλωμα nt, γούβα || to ~ **out** *vt* βαθουλώνω, σκάβω.

holly ['hɔlɪ] n *(tree)* πουρνάρι.

holster ['hɔʊlstə*] n πιστολιοθήκη.

holy ['hɔʊlɪ] a άγιος, ιερός || *(divine)* θείος.

homage ['hɔmɪdʒ] n υποταγή.

home [həʊm] n σπίτι, κατοικία || *(native country)* πατρίδα || *(institution)* άσυλο ♦ a *(country)* πατρίδα || *(local)* εγχώριος, ντόπιος ♦ *ad* στο σπίτι, στην πατρίδα || **at** ~ στο σπίτι || *(at ease)* άνετα || ~**coming** n επάνοδος f, επαναπατρισμός || ~**less** a άστεγος || ~-**made** a σπιτίσιος, ντόπιος || ~-**sick** a νοσταλγός || ~-**ward(s)** *ad* προς το σπίτι || ~-**work** n κατ'οίκον εργασία.

homicide ['hɔmɪsaɪd] n *(US)* ανθρωποκτονία.

homogeneous [hɔmə'dʒiːnɪəs] a ομοιογενής.

homosexual ['hɔməʊ'sɛksjʊəl] a ομοφυλόφιλος ♦ n ομοφυλόφιλος, ανώμαλος.

honest ['ɔnɪst] a τίμιος, έντιμος, ευθύς || ~**ly** *ad* τίμια || ~**y** n εντιμότητα.

honey ['hʌnɪ] n μέλι || ~**comb** n κερήθρα || ~**moon** n μήνας του μέλιτος.

honk [hɔŋk] n *(AUT)* κορνάρισμα nt ♦ *vi* κορνάρω.

honor ['ɔnə*] *(US)* = **honour**.

honorary ['ɔnərərɪ] a τιμητικός || *(degree etc)* επίτιμος.

honour ['ɔnə*] n τιμή, υπόληψη ♦ *vt* τιμώ || *(bill)* εξοφλώ, πληρώνω || ~**s** *npl* *(UNIV)* τίτλος, τιμητική διάκριση || ~**able** a έντιμος || *(title)* εντιμότατος.

hood [hʊd] n κουκούλα, σκούφος || *(cover)* κάλυμμα nt || *(US AUT)* καπό || ~**wink** *vt* εξαπατώ, κοροϊδεύω.

hoof [huːf] n οπλή, πέλμα nt, νύχι.

hook [hʊk] n αγκίστρι, γάντζος ♦ *vt* αγκιστρώνω, γαντζώνω.

hooligan ['huːlɪgən] n ταραχοποιός.

hoop [huːp] n στεφάνι, τσέρκι.

hoot [huːt] n *(of owl)* σκούξιμο || *(AUT)* κορνάρισμα nt ♦ *vi* γιουχαΐζω, σφυρίζω || ~**er** n *(NAUT)* σειρήνα, σφυρίχτρα || *(AUT)* κλάξον nt inv, κόρνα.

hop [hɔp] n χοροπήδημα nt, πήδημα nt ♦ *vi* σκιρτώ, πηδώ, χοροπηδώ.

hope [həʊp] n ελπίδα ♦ *vt* ελπίζω || ~**ful** a γεμάτος ελπίδες, ελπιδοφόρος || ~**less** a *(without hope)* απελπισμένος || *(useless)* μάταιος.

hops [hɔps] *npl* λυκίσκος.

horde [hɔːd] n ορδή, στίφος.

horizon [hə'raɪzn] n ορίζοντας || ~**tal** [hɔrɪ'zɔntl] a οριζόντιος.

hormone ['hɔːməʊn] n ορμόνη.

horn [hɔːn] n κέρατο || *(insect)* κεραία || *(MUS)* κέρας nt, κόρνα || *(AUT)* κλάξον nt inv || ~**ed** a με κέρατα.

hornet ['hɔːnɪt] n σφήκα.

horny ['hɔːnɪ] a κεράτινος, σκληρός.

horoscope ['hɔrəskəʊp] n ωροσκόπιο.

horrible ['hɔrɪbl] a φρικτός, φρικώδης, απαίσιος.

horrid ['hɔrɪd] a φρικτός, αποτρόπαιος || *(col)* κακός.

horrify ['hɔrɪfaɪ] *vt* τρομάζω || *(shock)* σκανδαλίζω.

horror ['hɔrə*] n φρίκη, τρόμος.

hors d'oeuvres [ɔː'dɜːvr] *npl* ορεκτικά *ntpl*, μεζεδάκια *ntpl*, ορντέβρ nt inv.

horse [hɔːs] n άλογο || **on** ~-**back** καβάλα || ~-**chestnut** n αγριοκάστανο || ~-**drawn** a ιπποκίνητο || ~-**power** n *(h.p.)* ιπποδύναμη || ~-**racing** n ιπποδρομίες *fpl* || ~-**shoe** n πέταλο.

horticulture ['hɔːtɪkʌltʃə] n κηπουρική.

hose [həʊz] n *(water)* σωληνάκι ποτίσματος || ~-**pipe** n μάνικα, σωλήνας.

hosiery ['həʊʒərɪ] n πλεκτά είδη και κάλτσες *pl*.

hospitable [hɔs'pɪtəbl] a φιλόξενος.

hospital ['hɔspɪtl] n νοσοκομείο.

hospitality [hɔspɪ'tælɪtɪ] n φιλοξενία.

host [həʊst] n οικοδεσπότης || *(hotel)* ξενοδόχος, χανιτζής || *(large number)* πλήθος nt, στρατιά.

hostage ['hɔstɪdʒ] n όμηρος.

hostel ['hɔstəl] n οικοτροφείο, χάνι.

hostess ['həʊstɛs] n οικοδέσποινα.

hostile ['hɔstaɪl] a εχθρικός.

hostility [hɔs'tɪlɪtɪ] n εχθρότητα || **hostilities** *npl* εχθροπραξίες *fpl*.

hot [hɔt] a θερμός, ζεστός || *(fiery)* οξύθυμος, αναμμένος || ~ **dog** n λουκάνικο || ~-**water bottle** n θερμοφόρα.

hotel [həʊ'tɛl] n ξενοδοχείο || *(residential)* πανσιόν f inv.

hound [haʊnd] n σκυλί, λαγωνικό ♦ *vt* καταδιώκω, παροτρύνω.

hour ['aʊə*] n ώρα || ~**ly** a, *ad* κάθε ώρα.

house [haʊs] n σπίτι, κατοικία || *(PARL)* βουλή || *(THEAT)* ακροατήριο ♦ [haʊz] *vt* στεγάζω || *(store)* αποθηκεύω || ~-**boat** n πλωτό σπίτι || ~-**breaking** n διάρρηξη σπιτιού || ~**hold** n σπίτι || οικογένεια, σπιτικό || ~**keeper** n οικονόμος m/f|| ~**keeping** n νοικοκυριό || ~**wife** n νοικοκυρά || ~**work** n δουλειές του νοικοκυριού.

housing ['hauziŋ] n στέγαση.

hovel ['hɒvl] n καλύβα.

hover ['hɒvə*] vi μετεωρίζομαι, πλανώμαι || (between) διστάζω, ταλαντεύομαι || ~**craft** n χόβερκραφτ nt inv.

how [hau] ad πώς, με ποιο τρόπο || (extent) πόσο || **and ~!** (US) και βέβαια!, ασφαλώς!|| ~**ever** ad όπως κι αν || (much) οσοδήποτε, όσο κι αν || (yet) ωστόσο, κι όμως.

howl [haul] n ούρλιασμα nt, ουρλιαχτό ♦ vi ουρλιάζω, σκούζω.

howler ['haulə*] n ωρυόμενος || (mistake) γκάφα, χοντροκοπιά.

H.P., H.P. see **hire**, **horse**.

H.Q. abbr of **headquarters**.

hub [hʌb] n (of wheel) αφαλός || (of activity) κέντρο.

hubbub ['hʌbʌb] n φασαρία, θόρυβος, οχλαβοή.

huddle ['hʌdl] n σωρός, κουβάρι ♦ vi συσσωρεύω, μαζεύομαι, κουλουριάζομαι.

hue [hju:] n χροιά, χρώμα, απόχρωση.

huff [hʌf] n παραφορά, θυμός.

hug [hʌg] n αγκάλιασμα nt ♦ vt αγκαλιάζω, σφίγγω || (NAUT) **to ~ the shore** παραπλέω, πλέω πλάι-πλάι στην ακτή.

huge [hju:dʒ] a πελώριος, θεόρατος, τεράστιος.

hulk [hʌlk] n (NAUT) ξαρματωμένο πλοίο, σαπιοκάραβο || (person) μπατάλης, χοντράνθρωπος || ~**ing** a δυσκίνητος, χοντρός, βαρύς.

hull [hʌl] n σκάφος nt, κουφάρι πλοίου.

hullo [hə'ləu] excl = **hello**.

hum [hʌm] n βόμβος, βουητό, ψίθυρος ♦ vi βουίζω, ψιθυρίζω || μουρμουρίζω.

human ['hju:mən] a ανθρώπινος ♦ n άνθρωπος.

humane [hju:'mein] a ανθρωπιστικός, φιλάνθρωπος.

humanity [hju:'mænɪtɪ] n ανθρωπότητα || (kindness) φιλανθρωπιά.

humble ['hʌmbl] a ταπεινός, απλός || (unimportant) ασήμαντος ♦ vt ταπεινώνω, ξευτελίζω.

humbly ['hʌmblɪ] ad ταπεινά, απλά.

humdrum ['hʌmdrʌm] a μονότονος, ανιαρός, πληκτικός.

humid ['hju:mɪd] a υγρός, νοτερός || ~**ity** n υγρασία, υγρότητα nt.

humiliate [hju:'mɪlɪeɪt] vt ταπεινώνω, ξευτελίζω, κουρελιάζω.

humiliation [hju:mɪlɪ'eɪʃən] n ταπείνωση, κουρέλιασμα nt.

humility [hju:'mɪlɪtɪ] n ταπεινότητα, μετριοφροσύνη.

humor ['hju:mə*] (US) = **humour**.

humorist ['hju:mərɪst] n χιουμορίστας.

humorous ['hju:mərəs] a γεμάτος χιούμορ, εύθυμος.

humour ['hju:mə*] n χιούμορ nt inv, κέφι, διάθεση ♦ vt κάνω τα χατήρια, κάνω τα κέφια.

hump [hʌmp] n καμπούρα.

hunch [hʌntʃ] n ύβος, καμπούρα || (suspicion) υποψία ♦ vt κυρτώνω, καμπουριάζω || ~**back** n καμπούρης/α m/f.

hundred ['hʌndrɪd] num, n εκατό || ~**weight** n (weight = 112 pounds) στατήρας.

hung [hʌŋ] pt, pp of **hang**.

Hungarian [hʌŋ'gɛərɪən] a ουγγρικός ♦ n (person) Ούγγρος/Ουγγαρέζα m/f|| (LING) (τα) Ουγγρικά.

Hungary ['hʌŋgərɪ] n Ουγγαρία.

hunger ['hʌŋgə*] n πείνα || (desire) σφοδρή επιθυμία ♦ vi πεινώ λαχταρώ.

hungrily ['hʌŋgrɪlɪ] ad άπληστα, αχόρταγα, πεινασμένα.

hungry ['hʌŋgrɪ] a πεινασμένος.

hunt [hʌnt] n κυνήγι || (seeking) αναζήτηση ♦ vt κυνηγώ || (search) διώχνω ♦ vi κυνηγώ || (seek) ψάχνω || ~**er** n κυνηγός || ~**ing** n κυνήγι.

hurdle ['hɜ:dl] n (lit) φράκτης || (fig) εμπόδιο.

hurl [hɜ:l] vt εκσφενδονίζω, ρίχνω.

hurrah [hu'rɑ:] n, **hurray** [hu'reɪ] n ζητωκραυγή.

hurricane ['hʌrɪkən] n καταιγίδα, λαίλαπας.

hurried ['hʌrɪd] a βιαστικός || ~**ly** ad βιαστικά.

hurry ['hʌrɪ] n βία, βιασύνη ♦ vi βιάζομαι, είμαι βιαστικός ♦ vt επισπεύδω, βιάζω.

hurt [hɜ:t] (irreg v) n κακό || (wound) τραύμα nt, πληγή || (damage) βλάβη, ζημιά ♦ vt κτυπώ, τραυματίζω, πληγώνω || (insult) προσβάλλω, πειράζω ♦ vi πονώ, θίγομαι || ~**ful** a βλαβερός.

hurtle ['hɜ:tl] vt εκσφενδονίζω ♦ vi (rush) εφορμώ, ρίχνομαι.

husband ['hʌzbənd] n άνδρας, σύζυγος.

hush [hʌʃ] n σιωπή, σιγή ♦ vt (καθ)ησυχάζω ♦ vi σωπαίνω || ~**!** σιωπή!, σούτ!

husk [hʌsk] n φλοιός, φλούδα, τσόφλι.

husky ['hʌskɪ] a (voice) βραχνός || γεροδεμένος ♦ n σκύλος ελκύθρου.

hustle ['hʌsl] n σπουδή, βιασύνη || (push) σπρωξίδι ♦ vt (push) σπρώχνω || σκουντώ, βιάζω.

hut [hʌt] n καλύβα || (MIL) παράπηγμα nt.

hutch [hʌtʃ] n κλουβί.

hyacinth ['haɪəsɪnθ] n υάκινθος.

hybrid ['haɪbrɪd] n μιγάδας, μικτογενής, νόθος ♦ a νόθος, μπασταρδεμένος.

hydrant ['haɪdrənt] n σωλήνας πυρκαγιάς, στόμιο υδρολημψίας.

hydraulic [haɪ'drɔ:lɪk] a υδραυλικός.

hydroelectric ['haɪdrəuɪ'lektrɪk] a υδροηλεκτρικός.

hydrogen ['haɪdrədʒən] n υδρογόνο.

hyena [haɪˈiːnə] n ύαινα.
hygiene [ˈhaɪdʒiːn] n υγιεινή.
hygienic [haɪˈdʒiːnɪk] a υγιεινός.
hymn [hɪm] n ύμνος, υμνωδία.
hyphen [ˈhaɪfən] n ενωτικό σημείο.
hypnosis [hɪpˈnəʊsɪs] n ύπνωση.
hypnotism [ˈhɪpnətɪzəm] n υπνωτισμός.
hypnotist [ˈhɪpnətɪst] n υπνωτιστής.
hypnotize [ˈhɪpnətaɪz] vt υπνωτίζω.
hypocrisy [hɪˈpɒkrɪsɪ] n υποκρισία.
hypocrite [ˈhɪpəkrɪt] n υποκριτής.
hypocritical [hɪpəˈkrɪtɪkl] a
υποκριτικός.
hypothesis [haɪˈpɒθɪsɪs] n υπόθεση.
hypothetic(al) [haɪpəˈθetɪk(əl)] a
υποθετικός.
hysteria [hɪsˈtɪərɪə] n υστερία.
hysterical [hɪsˈterɪkl] a υστερικός.
hysterics [hɪsˈterɪks] npl υστερία.

I

I [aɪ] pron εγώ.
ice [aɪs] n πάγος || (refreshment) παγωτό ♦
vt (cake) γκλασάρω ♦ vi (also ~ up)
παγώνω || ~ **axe** n πέλεκυς m πάγου ||
~**berg** n παγόβουνο || ~**box** n (US)
ψυγείο || ~ **cream** n παγωτό || ~**-cold** a
παγερός, παγωμένος || ~ **hockey** n
χόκεϋ στον πάγο.
icicle [ˈaɪsɪkl] n σταλακτίτης πάγου.
icing [ˈaɪsɪŋ] n κρούστα για κέικ,
γκλασάρισμα nt.
icon [ˈaɪkɒn] n εικόνα.
icy [ˈaɪsɪ] a (slippery) γλιστερός || (frozen)
παγετώδης, παγωμένος.
I'd [aɪd] = **I would, I had** || see
would, have.
idea [aɪˈdɪə] n ιδέα || (plan) σκοπός, ιδέα.
ideal [aɪˈdɪəl] n ιδανικό, ιδεώδες nt ♦ a
ιδανικός, ιδεώδης || ~**ist** n ιδεαλιστής.
identical [aɪˈdentɪkəl] a όμοιος, ίδιος,
απαράλλακτος.
identification [aɪdentɪfɪˈkeɪʃən] n
εξακρίβωση ταυτότητας, συνταύτιση.
identify [aɪˈdentɪfaɪ] vt (person)
διαπιστώνω, εξακριβώνω || (regard as
same) ταυτίζω.
identity [aɪˈdentɪtɪ] n ταυτότητα.
ideology [aɪdɪˈɒlədʒɪ] n ιδεολογία.
idiocy [ˈɪdɪəsɪ] n ηλιθιότητα.
idiom [ˈɪdɪəm] n ιδίωμα nt || (dialect)
διάλεκτος.
idiosyncrasy [ɪdɪəˈsɪŋkrəsɪ] n
ιδιοσυγκρασία.
idiot [ˈɪdɪət] n ηλίθιος, ανόητος || ~**ic**
[ɪdɪˈɒtɪk] a ηλίθιος.
idle [ˈaɪdl] a αργός || (lazy) οκνηρός,
τεμπέλης || (useless) μάταιος, ανωφελής ||
~**ness** n αργία, τεμπελιά || ~**r** n
αργόσχολος.
idol [ˈaɪdl] n είδωλο || ~**ize** vt λατρεύω,
θαυμάζω.
idyllic [ɪˈdɪlɪk] a ειδυλλιακός.
i.e. ad (abbr of id est) δηλ. (δηλαδή).

if [ɪf] cj (condition) εάν, αν, όταν || (whether)
αν.
ignite [ɪgˈnaɪt] vt αναφλέγω, ανάβω.
ignition [ɪgˈnɪʃən] n ανάφλεξη || ~ **key** n
(AUT) κλειδί (ξεκινήσεως).
ignorance [ˈɪgnərəns] n άγνοια.
ignorant [ˈɪgnərənt] a αμαθής, αγνοών.
ignore [ɪgˈnɔː*] vt αγνοώ, αψηφώ.
I'll [aɪl] = **I will, I shall** || see **will,
shall.**
ill [ɪl] a άρρωστος || (evil) κακός ♦ n κακό,
ατυχία || ~**-advised** a ασύνετος,
απερίσκεπτος || ~**-at-ease** a
στενοχωρημένος, ανήσυχος.
illegal [ɪˈliːgəl] a παράνομος || ~**ly** ad
παράνομα.
illegible [ɪˈledʒəbl] a δυσανάγνωστος.
illegitimate [ɪlɪˈdʒɪtɪmɪt] a νόθος.
ill-fated [ˈɪlˈfeɪtɪd] a κακότυχος.
ill-feeling [ˈɪlˈfiːlɪŋ] n κακία, έχθρα.
illicit [ɪˈlɪsɪt] a παράνομος, αθέμιτος.
illiterate [ɪˈlɪtərɪt] a αγράμματος.
ill-mannered [ˈɪlˈmænəd] a
κακότροπος, κακομαθημένος.
illness [ˈɪlnɪs] n ασθένεια, αρρώστεια.
illogical [ɪˈlɒdʒɪkəl] a παράλογος.
ill-treat [ˈɪlˈtriːt] vt
κακομεταχειρίζομαι.
illuminate [ɪˈluːmɪneɪt] vt φωτίζω,
φωταγωγώ.
illumination [ɪluːmɪˈneɪʃən] n φωτισμός,
φωταγώγηση.
illusion [ɪˈluːʒən] n αυταπάτη, πλάνη.
illusive [ɪˈluːsɪv] a, **illusory** [ɪˈluːsərɪ] a
απατηλός.
illustrate [ˈɪləstreɪt] vt εικονογραφώ.
illustration [ɪləsˈtreɪʃən] n
εικονογράφηση, εικόνα.
illustrious [ɪˈlʌstrɪəs] a ένδοξος,
επιφανής.
ill will [ˈɪlˈwɪl] n κακοβουλία, κακία.
I'm [aɪm] = **I am** || see **be.**
image [ˈɪmɪdʒ] n (statue) εικόνα, είδωλο ||
(likeness) ομοίωμα nt, αναπαράσταση ||
(reflection) είδωλο || ~**ry** n ρητορικά
σχήματα ntpl.
imaginable [ɪˈmædʒɪnəbl] a διανοητός.
imaginary [ɪˈmædʒɪnərɪ] a φανταστικός.
imagination [ɪmædʒɪˈneɪʃən] n
φαντασία.
imaginative [ɪˈmædʒɪnətɪv] a
ευφάνταστος, επινοητικός.
imagine [ɪˈmædʒɪn] vt φαντάζομαι,
διανοούμαι.
imbalance [ɪmˈbæləns] n ανισότητα,
ανισορροπία.
imbecile [ˈɪmbəsiːl] n βλάκας, ηλίθιος.
imbue [ɪmˈbjuː] vt (εμ)ποτίζω,
διαποτίζω.
imitate [ˈɪmɪteɪt] vt μιμούμαι,
αντιγράφω.
imitation [ɪmɪˈteɪʃən] n (απο)μίμηση.
imitator [ˈɪmɪteɪtə*] n μιμητής.
immaculate [ɪˈmækjʊlɪt] a άσπιλος,
άψογος.
immaterial [ɪməˈtɪərɪəl] a ασήμαντος,
άυλος.

immature [ɪmə'tjuə*] a ανώριμος, άγουρος.

immediate [ɪ'miːdɪət] a (near) άμεσος, προσεχής || (present) επείγων, άμεσος || (not separated) πλησιέστερος || (instant) άμεσος, στιγμιαίος || ~ly ad (at once) αμέσως, στη στιγμή.

immense [ɪ'mɛns] a απέραντος, άπειρος || ~ly ad απέραντα.

immerse [ɪ'mɜːs] vt εμβαπτίζω, βυθίζω, βουτώ.

immigrant ['ɪmɪgrənt] n μετανάστης.

immigration [ɪmɪ'greɪʃən] n μετανάστευση.

imminent ['ɪmɪnənt] a επικείμενος, άμεσος.

immobilize [ɪ'məʊbɪlaɪz] vt ακινητοποιώ.

immoral [ɪ'mɒrəl] a ανήθικος, κακοήθης || ~ity [ɪmə'ræliti] n ανηθικότητα.

immortal [ɪ'mɔːtl] a αθάνατος, άφθαρτος ♦ n αθάνατος || ~ize vt αποθανατίζω.

immune [ɪ'mjuːn] a απρόσβλητος.

immunize ['ɪmjʊnaɪz] vt ανοσοποιώ.

impact ['ɪmpækt] n (lit) σύγκρουση, κτύπημα nt || (fig) επίδραση.

impair [ɪm'pɛə*] vt βλάπτω, εξασθενίζω.

impale [ɪm'peɪl] vt ανασκολοπίζω, παλουκώνω.

impartial [ɪm'pɑːʃəl] a αμερόληπτος || ~ity n αμεροληψία.

impassable [ɪm'pɑːsəbl] a αδιάβατος.

impatience [ɪm'peɪʃəns] n ανυπομονησία.

impatient [ɪm'peɪʃənt] a ανυπόμονος || ~ly ad ανυπόμονα, βιαστικά.

impeccable [ɪm'pɛkəbl] a άψογος, τέλειος.

impede [ɪm'piːd] vt εμποδίζω, παρακωλύω.

impediment [ɪm'pɛdɪmənt] n κώλυμα nt, εμπόδιο.

impending [ɪm'pɛndɪŋ] a επικείμενος.

imperative [ɪm'pɛrətɪv] a επιτακτικός ♦ n (GRAM) προστακτική.

imperceptible [ɪmpə'sɛptəbl] a ανεπαίσθητος, αδιόρατος.

imperfect [ɪm'pɜːfɪkt] a ελαττωματικός || (incomplete) ελλειπής || ~ion n ατέλεια, ελάττωμα nt.

imperial [ɪm'pɪərɪəl] a αυτοκρατορικός || (majestic) μεγαλοπρεπής.

impersonal [ɪm'pɜːsnl] a απρόσωπος.

impersonate [ɪm'pɜːsəneɪt] vt προσωποποιώ, υποδύομαι, παριστάνω.

impersonation [ɪmpɜːsə'neɪʃən] n προσωποποίηση, ενσάρκωση, μίμηση.

impertinent [ɪm'pɜːtɪnənt] a αυθάδης, άσχετος.

impervious [ɪm'pɜːvɪəs] a αδιαπέραστος, στεγανός, ανεπηρέαστος.

impetuous [ɪm'pɛtjʊəs] a ορμητικός, βίαιος.

impetus ['ɪmpɪtəs] n ώθηση, ορμή.

impinge [ɪm'pɪndʒ]: to ~ on vt συγκρούομαι, καταπατώ.

implausible [ɪm'plɔːzəbl] a απίθανος.

implement ['ɪmplɪmənt] n όργανο, εργαλείο, σύνεργο ♦ ['ɪmplɪmɛnt] vt εφαρμόζω.

implicate ['ɪmplɪkeɪt] vt εμπλέκω, αναμιγνύω.

implication [ɪmplɪ'keɪʃən] n ενοχοποίηση, υπαινιγμός.

implicit [ɪm'plɪsɪt] a υπονοούμενος, σιωπηρός || (complete) απόλυτος, αμέριστος.

implore [ɪm'plɔː*] vt ικετεύω, εκλιπαρώ.

imply [ɪm'plaɪ] vt υπονοώ, υπαινίσσομαι, προϋποθέτω.

impolite [ɪmpə'laɪt] a αγενής.

imponderable [ɪm'pɒndərəbl] a αναπολόγιστος, ανεκμύνιαστος.

import [ɪm'pɔːt] vt εισάγω ♦ ['ɪmpɔːt] n εισαγωγή || (meaning) σημασία.

importance [ɪm'pɔːtəns] n σπουδαιότητα, σοβαρότητα || (value) σημασία, αξία.

important [ɪm'pɔːtənt] a σημαντικός, σπουδαίος.

importer [ɪm'pɔːtə*] n εισαγωγέας.

impose [ɪm'pəʊz] vt επιβάλλω, επιτάσσω || (on s.o.) επωφελούμαι.

imposing [ɪm'pəʊzɪŋ] a επιβλητικός.

impossibility [ɪmpɒsə'bɪlɪti] n (το) αδύνατο.

impossible [ɪm'pɒsəbl] a αδύνατος, ακατόρθωτος, ανυπόφορος.

impostor [ɪm'pɒstə*] n αγύρτης, απατεώνας.

impotence ['ɪmpətəns] n (esp sexual) ανικανότητα.

impotent ['ɪmpətənt] a ανίκανος, ανίσχυρος.

impound [ɪm'paʊnd] vt κατάσχω.

impoverished [ɪm'pɒvərɪʃt] a πάμπτωχος, εξαντλημένος.

impracticable [ɪm'præktɪkəbl] a ακατόρθωτος, απραγματοποίητος.

impractical [ɪm'præktɪkəl] a μη πρακτικός.

impregnable [ɪm'prɛgnəbl] a απόρθητος.

impregnate ['ɪmprɛgneɪt] vt γονιμοποιώ, εμποτίζω.

impress [ɪm'prɛs] vt (influence) κάνω εντύπωση || (imprint) εντυπώνω, εγχαράσσω.

impression [ɪm'prɛʃən] n (mark) αποτύπωση, αποτύπωμα nt || (printed copy) έκδοση || (effect) εντύπωση, αίσθηση || (belief) ιδέα, εντύπωση, γνώμη || ~able a ευαίσθητος, ευσυγκίνητος || ~ist n ιμπρεσσιονιστής.

impressive [ɪm'prɛsɪv] a εντυπωσιακός, συγκινητικός.

imprison [ɪm'prɪzn] vt φυλακίζω || ~ment n φυλάκιση.

improbable [ɪm'prɒbəbl] a απίθανος.

impromptu [ɪm'prɒmptjuː] a

αυτοσχέδιος, εκ του προχείρου ♦ ad εκ του προχείρου.

improper [ɪm'prɒpə*] a (wrong) εσφαλμένος || (unsuitable) ανάρμοστος || (indecent) απρεπής.

impropriety [ɪmprə'praɪətɪ] n απρέπεια, ακαταλληλότητα.

improve [ɪm'pruːv] vt βελτιώνω, κάνω καλύτερο ♦ vi (become better) βελτιούμαι, καλυτερεύω || ~**ment** n βελτίωση, πρόοδος f.

improvisation [ɪmprəvaɪ'zeɪʃən] n αυτοσχεδιασμός.

improvise ['ɪmprəvaɪz] vi αυτοσχεδιάζω || vt κάνω εκ του προχείρου.

impudent ['ɪmpjudənt] a αναιδής, αναίσχυντος.

impulse ['ɪmpʌls] n (sudden desire) ορμή, ορμέμφυτο || ώθηση, αυθόρμητη διάθεση.

impulsive [ɪm'pʌlsɪv] a αυθόρμητος, ορμέμφυτος.

impunity [ɪm'pjuːnɪtɪ] n ατιμωρησία.

impure [ɪm'pjuə*] a ακάθαρτος || (bad) μιαρός, αισχρός.

impurity [ɪm'pjuərɪtɪ] n ακαθαρσία, ξένο σώμα nt.

in [ɪn] prep μέσα σε, εντός, σε || (made of) σε || (expressed in) σε, με || (dressed in) με ♦ ad εντός, μέσα || ~**s and outs** npl τα μέσα και τα έξω.

in., ins abbr of **inch(es)**.

inability [ɪnə'bɪlɪtɪ] n ανικανότητα, αδυναμία.

inaccessible [ɪnæk'sɛsəbl] a απρόσιτος, απλησίαστος.

inaccuracy [ɪn'ækjurəsɪ] n ανακρίβεια.

inaccurate [ɪn'ækjurɪt] a ανακριβής, εσφαλμένος.

inactivity [ɪnæk'tɪvɪtɪ] n αδράνεια, αργία.

inadequacy [ɪn'ædɪkwəsɪ] n ανεπάρκεια, ατέλεια.

inadequate [ɪn'ædɪkwɪt] a ανεπαρκής, ατελής.

inadvertently [ɪnəd'vɜːtəntlɪ] ad απρόσεκτα, από αμέλεια.

inadvisable [ɪnəd'vaɪzəbl] a ασύμφορος.

inane [ɪ'neɪn] a κενός, ανόητος.

inanimate [ɪn'ænɪmɪt] a άψυχος.

inappropriate [ɪnə'prəuprɪɪt] a ακατάλληλος, ανάρμοστος.

inapt [ɪn'æpt] a ανεπιτήδειος, αδέξιος || ~**itude** n ανικανότητα, αδεξιότητα.

inarticulate [ɪnɑː'tɪkjulɪt] a άναρθρος, βουβός, ασύνδετος.

inasmuch [ɪnəz'mʌtʃ]: ~ **as** ad επειδή, εφόσον.

inattention [ɪnə'tɛnʃən] n απροσεξία, αφηρημάδα.

inattentive [ɪnə'tɛntɪv] a απρόσεκτος, αμελής.

inaudible [ɪn'ɔːdəbl] a ανεπαίσθητος, ασθενής.

inaugural [ɪ'nɔːgjurəl] a εναρκτήριος.

inaugurate [ɪ'nɔːgjureɪt] vt εγκαινιάζω.

inauguration [ɪnɔːgju'reɪʃən] n εγκαινιασμός, εγκαίνια ntpl.

inborn ['ɪn'bɔːn] a έμφυτος.

inbred ['ɪn'brɛd] a έμφυτος, φυσικός.

Inc. abbr see **incorporated**.

incapability [ɪnkeɪpə'bɪlɪtɪ] n ανικανότητα.

incapable [ɪn'keɪpəbl] a ανίκανος.

incapacitate [ɪnkə'pæsɪteɪt] vt καθιστώ ανίκανο.

incarnate [ɪn'kɑːnɪt] a ενσαρκωμένος.

incarnation [ɪnkɑː'neɪʃən] n ενσάρκωση.

incendiary [ɪn'sɛndɪərɪ] a εμπρηστικός ♦ n εμπρηστής.

incense ['ɪnsɛns] n θυμίαμα nt, λιβάνι ♦ [ɪn'sɛns] vt εξοργίζω, εξαγριώνω.

incentive [ɪn'sɛntɪv] n κίνητρο, ελατήριο, τονωτικό.

incessant [ɪn'sɛsnt] a αδιάκοπος || ~**ly** ad αδιάκοπα.

incest ['ɪnsɛst] n αιμομιξία.

inch [ɪntʃ] n ίντσα (.0254 μ.).

incidence ['ɪnsɪdəns] n πρόσπτωση, περίπτωση.

incident ['ɪnsɪdənt] n επεισόδιο, περιπέτεια || ~**al** a τυχαίος, συμπτωματικός || ~**ally** ad παρεμπιπτόντως.

incinerator [ɪn'sɪnəreɪtə*] n αποτεφρωτήρας.

incision [ɪn'sɪʒən] n εντομή, χαραματιά.

incisive [ɪn'saɪsɪv] a κοφτερός || (cutting) δηκτικός.

incite [ɪn'saɪt] vt υποκινώ, παροτρύνω.

inclination [ɪnklɪ'neɪʃən] n κλίση, τάση, διάθεση.

incline ['ɪnklaɪn] n κλίση ♦ [ɪn'klaɪn] vi κλίνω, γέρνω || (be disposed) ρέπω, τείνω.

include [ɪn'kluːd] vt (συμ)περιλαμβάνω, περιέχω.

inclusion [ɪn'kluːʒən] n συμπερίληψη.

inclusive [ɪn'kluːsɪv] a συμπεριλαμβάνων, περιέχων.

incognito [ɪn'kɒgnɪtəu] ad ινκόγνιτο.

incoherent [ɪnkəu'hɪərənt] a ασυνάρτητος.

income ['ɪnkʌm] n εισόδημα nt || ~ **tax** n φόρος εισοδήματος.

incoming ['ɪnkʌmɪŋ] a (tide) ανερχόμενος, εισερχόμενος.

incompatible [ɪnkəm'pætəbl] a ασυμβίβαστος.

incompetence [ɪn'kɒmpɪtəns] n αναρμοδιότητα, ανικανότητα.

incompetent [ɪn'kɒmpɪtənt] a ανίκανος, αναρμόδιος.

incomplete [ɪnkəm'pliːt] a ατελής.

incomprehensible [ɪnkɒmprɪ'hɛnsəbl] a ακατανόητος, ακατάληπτος.

inconclusive [ɪnkən'kluːsɪv] a μη πειστικός.

incongruous [ɪn'kɒŋgruəs] a ασύμφωνος, ανάρμοστος.

inconsequential [ɪnkɒnsɪ'kwɛnʃəl] a ανακόλουθος, ασήμαντος.

inconsiderate [ɪnkən'sɪdərɪt] a απερίσκεπτος, αδιάκριτος.

inconsistent [ɪnkən'sɪstənt] a ασυνεπής, αντιφατικός.

inconspicuous [ɪnkən'spɪkjʊəs] a αφανής, απαρατήρητος.

inconstant [ɪn'kɒnstənt] a ευμετάβολος, ασταθής.

incontinent [ɪn'kɒntɪnənt] a ακρατής.

inconvenience [ɪnkən'viːnɪəns] n δυσκέρεια, ενόχληση, μπελάς.

inconvenient [ɪnkən'viːnɪənt] a στενόχωρος, ενοχλητικός, ακατάλληλος.

incorporate [ɪn'kɔːpəreɪt] vt ενσωματώνω, συγχωνεύω.

incorporated [ɪn'kɔːpəreɪtɪd] a ενσωματωμένος, συγχωνευμένος || ~ **company** *(US, abbr* **Inc.)** ανώνυμος (εταιρεία).

incorrect [ɪnkə'rekt] a εσφαλμένος, ανακριβής.

incorruptible [ɪnkə'rʌptəbl] a αδιάφθορος, ακέραιος, αδέκαστος.

increase ['ɪnkriːs] n αύξηση ♦ [ɪn'kriːs] vt αυξάνω, μεγαλώνω ♦ vi αυξάνομαι.

increasingly [ɪn'kriːsɪŋlɪ] ad διαρκώς περισσότερο.

incredible [ɪn'kredəbl] a απίστευτος.

incredulous [ɪn'kredjʊləs] a δύσπιστος.

increment ['ɪnkrɪmənt] n αύξηση.

incriminate [ɪn'krɪmɪneɪt] vt ενοχοποιώ.

incubation [ɪnkjʊ'beɪʃən] n επώαση, κλώσημα nt.

incubator ['ɪnkjubeɪtə*] n κλωσομηχανή.

incur [ɪn'kɜː*] vt υφίσταμαι, διατρέχω, προκαλώ.

incurable [ɪn'kjʊərəbl] a ανίατος, αγιάτρευτος.

incursion [ɪn'kɜːʃən] n επιδρομή.

indebted [ɪn'detɪd] a υποχρεωμένος, υπόχρεος.

indecent [ɪn'diːsnt] a απρεπής, άσεμνος.

indecision [ɪndɪ'sɪʒən] n αναποφασιστικότητα, αοριστία.

indecisive [ɪndɪ'saɪsɪv] a μή αποφασιστικός.

indeed [ɪn'diːd] ad πράγματι, πραγματικά, αληθινά.

indefinable [ɪndɪ'faɪnəbl] a απροσδιόριστος.

indefinite [ɪn'defɪnɪt] a αόριστος || ~**ly** ad επ'αόριστον.

indelible [ɪn'delɪbl] a ανεξίτηλος.

indemnify [ɪn'demnɪfaɪ] vt αποζημιώνω, εξασφαλίζω.

indentation [ɪnden'teɪʃən] n *(typing)* οδόντωση, χάραγμα nt.

independence [ɪndɪ'pendəns] n ανεξαρτησία.

independent [ɪndɪ'pendənt] a ανεξάρτητος.

indescribable [ɪndɪs'kraɪbəbl] a απερίγραπτος.

index ['ɪndeks] n ευρετήριο || ~ **finger** n δείκτης.

India ['ɪndɪə] n Ινδία || ~**n** n Ινδός/Ινδή m/f || *(of America)* ερυθρόδερμος ♦ a ινδικός, ινδιάνικος.

indicate ['ɪndɪkeɪt] vt δεικνύω, εμφαίνω, έδηλω.

indication [ɪndɪ'keɪʃən] n ενδειξη, σημείο.

indicative [ɪn'dɪkətɪv] a *(GRAM)* οριστική *(έγκλιση).*

indicator ['ɪndɪkeɪtə*] n *(sign)* δείκτης.

indict [ɪn'daɪt] vt μηνύω, ενάγω, καταγγέλλω || ~**able** a ενακτέος || ~**ment** n μήνυση, κατηγορία.

indifference [ɪn'dɪfrəns] n αδιαφορία.

indifferent [ɪn'dɪfrənt] a *(not caring)* αδιάφορος || *(unimportant)* αδιάφορος || *(neither good nor bad)* συνηθισμένος, έτσι κι έτσι || *(moderate)* μέτριος, ουδέτερος || *(impartial)* αμερόληπτος.

indigenous [ɪn'dɪdʒɪnəs] a γηγενής, ιθαγενής, ντόπιος.

indigestible [ɪndɪ'dʒestəbl] a δυσκολοχώνευτος.

indigestion [ɪndɪ'dʒestʃən] n δυσπεψία.

indignant [ɪn'dɪgnənt] a αγανακτισμένος.

indignation [ɪndɪg'neɪʃən] n αγανάκτηση.

indignity [ɪn'dɪgnɪtɪ] n προσβολή, ταπείνωση.

indirect [ɪndɪ'rekt] a πλάγιος, έμμεσος || ~**ly** ad έμμεσα.

indiscreet [ɪndɪs'kriːt] a αδιάκριτος, απρόσεκτος.

indiscretion [ɪndɪs'kreʃən] n αδιακρισία, ακριτομύθια.

indiscriminate [ɪndɪs'krɪmɪnɪt] a χωρίς διακρίσεις, τυφλός.

indispensable [ɪndɪs'pensəbl] a απαραίτητος.

indisposed [ɪndɪs'pəʊzd] a αδιάθετος, απρόθυμος.

indisputable [ɪndɪs'pjuːtəbl] a αναμφισβήτητος, αναμφίβολος.

indistinct [ɪndɪs'tɪŋkt] a αδιόρατος, συγκεχυμένος, αμυδρός.

individual [ɪndɪ'vɪdjʊəl] n άτομο, πρόσωπο ♦ a ιδιαίτερος, ατομικός || ~**ist** n ατομικιστής || ~**ity** n ατομικότητα, προσωπικότητα.

indoctrinate [ɪn'dɒktrɪneɪt] vt διδάσκω, κατηχώ, εμποτίζω.

indoctrination [ɪndɒktrɪ'neɪʃən] n εμποτισμός, διδασκαλία.

indolent ['ɪndələnt] a νωθρός, τεμπέλης.

Indonesia [ɪndəʊ'niːzɪə] n Ινδουνσία || ~**n** n Ινδούνσιος, ο ♦ a ινδουνσιακός.

indoor ['ɪndɔː*] a του σπιτιού, εσωτερικός || ~**s** ad μέσα στο κτίριο.

indubitable [ɪn'djuːbɪtəbl] a αναμφίβολος, βέβαιος.

induce [ɪn'djuːs] vt πείθω, προτρέπω, προκαλώ || ~**ment** n προτροπή, κίνητρο.

indulge [ɪn'dʌldʒ] vt ικανοποιώ || (allow pleasure) εντρυφώ, παραδίδομαι || **~nce** n επιείκια, διασκέδαση, εντρύφηση || **~nt** a επιεικής, συγκαταβατικός.

industrial [ɪn'dʌstrɪəl] a βιομηχανικός || **~ist** n βιομήχανος || **~ize** vt εκβιομηχανίζω.

industrious [ɪn'dʌstrɪəs] a φιλόπονος, επιμελής.

industry ['ɪndəstrɪ] n βιομηχανία || (diligence) φιλοπονία.

inebriated [ɪ'niːbrɪeɪtɪd] a μεθυσμένος.

inedible [ɪn'edɪbl] a μη φαγώσιμος.

ineffective [ɪnɪ'fektɪv] a, **ineffectual** [ɪnɪ'fektjuəl] a ατελέσφορος, μάταιος.

inefficiency [ɪnɪ'fɪʃənsɪ] n ανικανότητα, ανεπάρκεια.

inefficient [ɪnɪ'fɪʃənt] a ανίκανος, ατελέσφορος.

inelegant [ɪn'elɪgənt] a άκομψος, άγαρμπος.

ineligible [ɪn'elɪdʒəbl] a μη εκλέξιμος, ακατάλληλος.

inept [ɪ'nept] a άτοπος, ανόητος.

inequality [ɪnɪ'kwɒlɪtɪ] n ανισότητα.

ineradicable [ɪnɪ'rædɪkəbl] a αξερρίζωτος.

inert [ɪ'nɜːt] a αδρανής.

inertia [ɪ'nɜːʃə] n αδράνεια.

inescapable [ɪnɪs'keɪpəbl] a αναπόφευκτος.

inessential [ɪnɪ'senʃəl] a μη απαραίτητος.

inestimable [ɪn'estɪməbl] a ανεκτίμητος.

inevitable [ɪn'evɪtəbl] a αναπόφευκτος.

inexact [ɪnɪg'zækt] a ανακριβής.

inexhaustible [ɪnɪg'zɔːstəbl] a ανεξάντλητος.

inexorable [ɪn'eksərəbl] a αδυσώπητος, αμείλικτος.

inexpensive [ɪnɪks'pensɪv] a φθηνός, ανέξοδος.

inexperience [ɪnɪks'pɪərɪəns] n απειρία || **~d** a άπειρος.

inexplicable [ɪnɪks'plɪkəbl] a ανεξήγητος.

inextricable [ɪnɪks'trɪkəbl] a αδιέξοδος, άλυτος.

infallibility [ɪnfælə'bɪlɪtɪ] n (το) αλάνθαστο.

infallible [ɪn'fæləbl] a αλάνθαστος, σίγουρος.

infamous ['ɪnfəməs] a κακόφημος.

infamy ['ɪnfəmɪ] n ατιμία, κακόήθεια.

infancy ['ɪnfənsɪ] n νηπιακή ηλικία || (early stages) απαρχές fpl, πρώτη περίοδος.

infant ['ɪnfənt] n νήπιο, βρέφος nt || **~ile** a παιδικός, παιδιάστικος || **~ school** n κατώτερο δημοτικό σχολείο.

infantry ['ɪnfəntrɪ] n πεζικό || **~man** n στρατιώτης, φαντάρος.

infatuated [ɪn'fætjʊeɪtɪd] a ξεμυαλισμένος, συνεπαρμένος.

infatuation [ɪnfætjʊ'eɪʃən] n ξεμυάλισμα nt, τρέλα.

infect [ɪn'fekt] vt μολύνω, μιαίνω, βρωμίζω || (influence) επηρεάζω || **~ion** n μόλυνση, επίδραση || **~ious** a μολυσματικός, μεταδοτικός.

infer [ɪn'fɜː*] vt συνάγω, συμπεραίνω, υπονοώ || **~ence** ['ɪnfərəns] n συμπέρασμα nt, πόρισμα nt.

inferior [ɪn'fɪərɪə*] a κατώτερος, υποδεέστερος ♦ n κατώτερος, υφιστάμενος || **~ity** n κατωτερότητα, μειονεκτικότητα || **~ity complex** n (σύμ)πλεγμα nt κατωτερότητας.

infernal [ɪn'fɜːnl] a καταχθόνιος, διαβολικός, απαίσιος.

inferno [ɪn'fɜːnəʊ] n κόλαση.

infertile [ɪn'fɜːtaɪl] a άγονος, άκαρπος.

infertility [ɪnfɜː'tɪlɪtɪ] n (το) άγονο, στειρότητα.

infest [ɪn'fest] vt λυμαίνομαι, κατακλύζω.

infidelity [ɪnfɪ'delɪtɪ] n απιστία.

infiltrate ['ɪnfɪltreɪt] vti (δι)εισδύω, εισχωρώ.

infinite ['ɪnfɪnɪt] a άπειρος, απέραντος.

infinitive [ɪn'fɪnɪtɪv] n απαρέμφατο.

infinity [ɪn'fɪnɪtɪ] n άπειρο, απεραντοσύνη.

infirmary [ɪn'fɜːmərɪ] n νοσοκομείο, θεραπευτήριο.

infirmity [ɪn'fɜːmɪtɪ] n αδυναμία, αναπηρία.

inflame [ɪn'fleɪm] vt (excite) εξάπτω, ερεθίζω.

inflammable [ɪn'flæməbl] a εύφλεκτος.

inflammation [ɪnflə'meɪʃən] n φλόγωση, ερεθισμός.

inflate [ɪn'fleɪt] vt φουσκώνω || (ECON) προκαλώ πληθωρισμό.

inflation [ɪn'fleɪʃən] n πληθωρισμός.

inflexible [ɪn'fleksəbl] a άκαμπτος, αλύγιστος.

inflict [ɪn'flɪkt] vt καταφέρω, δίνω, επιβάλλω || **~ion** n επιβολή, βάρος nt, τιμωρία.

inflow ['ɪnfləʊ] n εισροή.

influence ['ɪnflʊəns] n επίδραση, επιρροή ♦ vt επηρεάζω, επιδρώ.

influential [ɪnflʊ'enʃəl] a σημαίνων, με επιρροή.

influenza [ɪnflʊ'enzə] n γρίππη.

influx ['ɪnflʌks] n εισροή, διείσδυση.

inform [ɪn'fɔːm] vt πληροφορώ, ειδοποιώ.

informal [ɪn'fɔːməl] a ανεπίσημος, παράτυπος || **~ity** n ανεπισημότητα.

information [ɪnfə'meɪʃən] n πληροφορίες fpl, είδηση.

informative [ɪn'fɔːmətɪv] a κατατοπιστικός, πληροφοριακός.

informer [ɪn'fɔːmə*] n καταδότης, χαφιές m inv.

infra-red [ɪnfrə'red] a υπέρυθρος.

infrequent [ɪn'friːkwənt] a σπάνιος.

infringe [ɪn'frɪndʒ] vt παραβαίνω, παραβιάζω ♦ vi καταπατώ || **~ment** n παράβαση.

infuriating [ɪn'fjʊərɪeɪtɪŋ] *a* εξοργιστικός.

ingenious [ɪn'dʒiːnɪəs] *a* οξύνους, πολυμήχανος.

ingenuity [ɪndʒɪ'njuːɪtɪ] *n* ευφυΐα, οξύνοια.

ingot ['ɪŋɡət] *n* ράβδος *f*, χελώνα.

ingratiate [ɪn'ɡreɪʃɪeɪt] *vt* αποκτώ εύνοια.

ingratitude [ɪn'ɡrætɪtjuːd] *n* αγνωμοσύνη.

ingredient [ɪn'ɡriːdɪənt] *n* συστατικό.

inhabit [ɪn'hæbɪt] *vt* κατοικώ, μένω || ~ant *n* κάτοικος *m/f*.

inhale [ɪn'heɪl] *vt* εισπνέω, ρουφώ.

inherent [ɪn'hɪərənt] *a* (+ *in*) συμφυής, έμφυτος.

inherit [ɪn'herɪt] *vt* κληρονομώ || ~ance *n* κληρονομία.

inhibit [ɪn'hɪbɪt] *vt* εμποδίζω, αναχαιτίζω, απαγορεύω || ~ion *n* απαγόρευση, αναχαίτιση.

inhospitable [ɪnhɒs'pɪtəbl] *a* αφιλόξενος.

inhuman [ɪn'hjuːmən] *a* απάνθρωπος.

inimitable [ɪ'nɪmɪtəbl] *a* αμίμητος.

iniquity [ɪ'nɪkwɪtɪ] *n* αδικία, κακοήθεια.

initial [ɪ'nɪʃəl] *a* αρχικός, πρώτος ♦ *n* αρχικό ♦ *vt* μονογράφω || ~ly *ad* αρχικά, κατ' αρχήν.

initiate [ɪ'nɪʃɪeɪt] *vt* αρχίζω, εισάγω || (*in a society*) μυώ.

initiation [ɪnɪʃɪ'eɪʃən] *n* μύηση.

initiative [ɪ'nɪʃɪətɪv] *n* πρωτοβουλία.

inject [ɪn'dʒekt] *vt* εγχέω, εισάγω, κάνω ένεση || ~ion *n* έγχυση, ένεση.

injure ['ɪndʒə*] *vt* βλάπτω, ζημιώνω, πληγώνω.

injury ['ɪndʒərɪ] *n* βλάβη, τραύμα *nt*, ζημιά.

injustice [ɪn'dʒʌstɪs] *n* αδικία.

ink [ɪŋk] *n* μελάνι.

inkling ['ɪŋklɪŋ] *n* υποψία, υπόνοια.

inlaid ['ɪn'leɪd] *a* εμπαιστός.

inland ['ɪnlænd] *a* εσωτερικός, μεσόγειος ♦ *ad* στο εσωτερικό, στα ενδότερα || ~ **revenue** *n* (*Brit*) Τμήμα Εσωτερικών Προσόδων.

in-laws ['ɪnlɔːz] *npl* πεθερικά *ntpl*.

inlet ['ɪnlɛt] *n* ορμίσκος, είσοδος *f*.

inmate ['ɪnmeɪt] *n* ένοικος/n *m/f*.

inn [ɪn] *n* πανδοχείο, ξενοδοχείο.

innate [ɪ'neɪt] *a* έμφυτος.

inner ['ɪnə*] *a* εσωτερικός.

innocence ['ɪnəsns] *n* αθωότητα, αφέλεια.

innocent ['ɪnəsnt] *a* αθώος, αγνός, αφελής.

innocuous [ɪ'nɒkjʊəs] *a* αβλαβής.

innovation [ɪnəʊ'veɪʃən] *n* καινοτομία, νεωτερισμός.

innuendo [ɪnjuˈɛndəʊ] *n* υπαινιγμός.

innumerable [ɪ'njuːmərəbl] *a* αναρίθμητος.

inoculation [ɪnɒkjʊ'leɪʃən] *n* μπόλιασμα *nt*.

inopportune [ɪn'ɒpətjuːn] *a* άκαιρος, άτοπος.

inordinately [ɪ'nɔːdɪnɪtlɪ] *ad* υπερβολικά.

inorganic [ɪnɔː'ɡænɪk] *a* ανόργανος.

in-patient ['ɪnpeɪʃənt] *n* εσωτερικός (ασθενής).

input ['ɪnpʊt] *n* εισαγωγή ♦ *vt* εισάγω, τροφοδοτώ.

inquest ['ɪnkwɛst] *n* ανάκριση, έρευνα.

inquire [ɪn'kwaɪə*] *vi* ρωτώ, ζητώ ♦ *vt* (*price*) ρωτώ την τιμή || **to ~ into** *vt* ερευνώ, εξετάζω.

inquiring [ɪn'kwaɪərɪŋ] *a* (*mind*) ερευνητικός.

inquiry [ɪn'kwaɪərɪ] *n* ερώτηση || (*search*) έρευνα, ανάκριση || ~ **office** *n* υπηρεσία πληροφοριών.

inquisitive [ɪn'kwɪzɪtɪv] *n* περίεργος, φιλοπερίεργος.

inroad ['ɪnrəʊd] *n* εισβολή, επιδρομή.

insane [ɪn'seɪn] *a* παράφρονας, τρελός.

insanitary [ɪn'sænɪtərɪ] *a* ανθυγιεινός.

insanity [ɪn'sænɪtɪ] *n* παραφροσύνη, τρέλα.

insatiable [ɪn'seɪʃəbl] *a* ακόρεστος, άπληστος.

inscription [ɪn'skrɪpʃən] *n* επιγραφή, αφιέρωση.

inscrutable [ɪn'skruːtəbl] *a* ανεξιχνίαστος, μυστηριώδης.

insect ['ɪnsɛkt] *n* έντομο, ζουζούνι || ~icide *n* εντομοκτόνο.

insecure [ɪnsɪ'kjʊə*] *a*, *a* επισφαλής.

insecurity [ɪnsɪ'kjʊərɪtɪ] *n* ανασφάλεια, (το) επισφαλές *nt*.

insensible [ɪn'sɛnsəbl] *a* αναπαίσθητος, αναίσθητος.

insensitive [ɪn'sɛnsɪtɪv] *a* αναίσθητος, χωρίς ντροπή.

inseparable [ɪn'sepərəbl] *a* αχώριστος, αναπόσπαστος.

insert [ɪn'sɜːt] *vt* παρεμβάλλω, καταχωρώ, εισάγω ♦ ['ɪnsɜːt] *n* παρεμβολή, ένθεμα *nt* || ~ion *n* παρεμβολή, καταχώρηση, βάλσιμο.

inshore ['ɪn'ʃɔː*] *a*, *ad* κοντά στην ακτή.

inside ['ɪn'saɪd] *n* (το) μέσα, εσωτερικό (μέρος) ♦ *a* εσωτερικός ♦ *ad* εσωτερικά, μέσα ♦ *prep* εντός, μέσα || ~-**forward** *n* (*SPORT*) μέσος κυνηγός || ~ **out** *ad* ανάποδα, το μέσα έξω || ~**r** *n* μεμυημένος, γνώστης.

insidious [ɪn'sɪdɪəs] *a* ύπουλος, δόλιος.

insight ['ɪnsaɪt] *n* διορατικότητα, οξύνοια.

insignificant [ɪnsɪɡ'nɪfɪkənt] *a* ασήμαντος, τιποτένιος.

insincere [ɪnsɪn'sɪə*] *a* ανειλικρινής.

insinuate [ɪn'sɪnjʊeɪt] *vt* αφήνω να εννοηθεί, υπαινίσσομαι.

insinuation [ɪnsɪnjʊ'eɪʃən] *n* υπαινιγμός.

insipid [ɪn'sɪpɪd] *a* ανούσιος, σαχλός.

insist [ɪn'sɪst] *vi* (+ *on*) επιμένω, εμμένω || ~ence *n* επιμονή || ~ent *a* επίμονος.

insolence ['ɪnsələns] *n* αναίδεια, θρασύτητα.

insolent ['ɪnsələnt] a αναιδής, θρασύς.

insoluble [ɪn'sɒljubl] a άλυτος, αδιάλυτος.

insolvent [ɪn'sɒlvənt] a αφερέγγυος, αναξιόχρεος.

insomnia [ɪn'sɒmnɪə] n αϋπνία.

inspect [ɪn'spekt] vt επιθεωρώ, επιτηρώ, επιβλέπω || ~**ion** n επιθεώρηση, επιτήρηση || ~**or** n επιθεωρητής/ήτρια m/f || (RAIL) επιστάτης/άτρια m/f, επόπτης/όπτρια m/f.

inspiration [ɪnspə'reɪʃən] n έμπνευση.

inspire [ɪn'spaɪə*] vt εμπνέω.

inspiring [ɪn'spaɪərɪŋ] a εμπνέων.

instability [ɪnstə'bɪlɪtɪ] n αστάθεια.

install [ɪn'stɔːl] vt εγκαθιστώ, μοντάρω || (in office) εγκαθιστώ || ~**ation** n εγκατάσταση, τοποθέτηση.

instalment, installment (US) [ɪn'stɔːlmənt] n δόση, παρτίδα.

instance ['ɪnstəns] n περίπτωση, παράδειγμα nt || **for** ~ παραδείγματος χάρη.

instant ['ɪnstənt] n στιγμή ♦ a άμεσος, επείγων || ~ **coffee** n στιγμιαίος καφές || ~**ly** ad αμέσως, στη στιγμή.

instead [ɪn'sted] ad αντί γι' αυτό || ~ **of** αντί.

instigation [ɪnstɪ'geɪʃən] n παρακίνηση, υποκίνηση.

instil [ɪn'stɪl] vt εμποτίζω, βάζω.

instinct ['ɪnstɪŋkt] n ένστικτο, ορμέμφυτο || ~**ive** a ενστικτώδης || ~**ively** ad ενστικτωδώς.

institute ['ɪnstɪtjuːt] n ίδρυμα nt, ινστιτούτο ♦ vt θεσπίζω, ιδρύω, εγκαθιστώ.

institution [ɪnstɪ'tjuːʃən] n (custom) θεσμός, θέσμιο || (organization) ίδρυμα nt, οργάνωση || (beginning) ίδρυση, σύσταση.

instruct [ɪn'strʌkt] vt (order) παραγγέλλω, διατάσσω || (teach) διδάσκω, μαθαίνω || ~**ion** n διδασκαλία || (direction) οδηγία || ~**ions** npl εντολές fpl, οδηγίες fpl || ~**ive** a διδακτικός, ενημερωτικός || ~**or** n δάσκαλος/άλα m/f, εκπαιδευτής/εύτρια m/f || (US) επιμελητής/ήτρια m/f.

instrument ['ɪnstrəmənt] n (implement) εργαλείο, όργανο || (MUS) όργανο || ~**al** a ενόργανος || (helpful) συντελεστικός, συμβάλλων || ~**alist** n οργανοπαίκτης || ~ **panel** n ταμπλό nt inv.

insubordinate [ɪnsə'bɔːdənɪt] a ανυπότακτος, ανυπάκουος.

insubordination ['ɪnsəbɔːdɪ'neɪʃən] n ανυπακοή, ανυποταξία.

insufferable [ɪn'sʌfərəbl] a ανυπόφορος, αφόρητος.

insufficient [ɪnsə'fɪʃənt] a ανεπαρκής, λειψός || ~**ly** ad ανεπαρκώς.

insular ['ɪnsjələ*] a (narrow-minded) με στενές αντιλήψεις.

insulate ['ɪnsjuleɪt] vt μονώνω || (set apart) απομονώνω.

insulating ['ɪnsjuleɪtɪŋ]: ~ **tape** n μονωτική ταινία.

insulation [ɪnsju'leɪʃən] n (ELEC) μόνωση.

insulin ['ɪnsjulɪn] n (for diabetic) ινσουλίνη.

insult ['ɪnsʌlt] n προσβολή, βρισιά ♦ [ɪn'sʌlt] vt βρίζω, προσβάλλω || ~**ing** a προσβλητικός.

insuperable [ɪn'suːpərəbl] a ανυπέρβλητος.

insurance [ɪn'ʃʊərəns] n ασφάλεια || ~ **agent** n πράκτορας ασφαλειών || ~ **policy** n ασφαλιστήριο.

insure [ɪn'ʃʊə*] vt (εξ)ασφαλίζω.

insurrection [ɪnsə'rekʃən] n επανάσταση, εξέγερση.

intact [ɪn'tækt] a άθικτος, απείραχτος.

intake ['ɪnteɪk] n (MECH) εισαγωγή.

intangible [ɪn'tændʒəbl] a ακαθόριστος.

integral ['ɪntɪgrəl] a (essential) αναπόσπαστος || (complete) ολοκληρωτικός.

integrate ['ɪntɪgreɪt] vti ολοκληρώνω.

integration [ɪntɪ'greɪʃən] n ολοκλήρωση.

integrity [ɪn'tegrɪtɪ] n ακεραιότητα, εντιμότητα.

intellect ['ɪntɪlekt] n διάνοια, νόηση, μυαλό || ~**ual** a διανοητικός, πνευματικός ♦ n διανοούμενος.

intelligence [ɪn'telɪdʒəns] n νοημοσύνη || (information) πληροφορία.

intelligent [ɪn'telɪdʒənt] a ευφυής, νοήμων, μυαλωμένος || ~**ly** ad ευφυώς, έξυπνα.

intelligible [ɪn'telɪdʒəbl] a (κατα)νοητός, καταληπτός.

intemperate [ɪn'tempərɪt] a ακρατής, μέθυσος.

intend [ɪn'tend] vt (mean) προτίθεμαι || **to** ~ **to do sth** σκοπεύω να κάνω κάτι.

intense [ɪn'tens] a έντονος, ισχυρός || ~**ly** ad υπερβολικά, έντονα.

intensify [ɪn'tensɪfaɪ] vt εντείνω, επιτείνω.

intensity [ɪn'tensɪtɪ] n ένταση, σφοδρότητα, ορμή.

intensive [ɪn'tensɪv] a εντατικός.

intent [ɪn'tent] n πρόθεση || **to all** ~**s and purposes** ουσιαστικά, πραγματικά.

intention [ɪn'tenʃən] n πρόθεση || (plan) σκοπός || ~**al** a σκόπιμος, εσκεμμένος || ~**ally** ad εσκεμμένα, σκόπιμα.

intently [ɪn'tentlɪ] ad προσεκτικά, έντονα.

inter [ɪn'tɜː*] vt ενταφιάζω, θάβω.

inter- ['ɪntə*] prefix διά-, μεσο(ο)-, μεταξύ.

interact [ɪntər'ækt] vi αλληλεπιδρώ || ~**ion** n αλληλεπίδραση.

intercede [ɪntə'siːd] vi επεμβαίνω, μεσολαβώ, μεσιτεύω.

intercept [ɪntə'sept] vt ανακόπτω, συλλαμβάνω, πιάνω || ~**ion** n σύλληψη, υποκλοπή.

interchange ['ɪntə'tʃeɪndʒ] n (exchange) ανταλλαγή || (roads) μεταλλαγή ♦

[ɪntə'tʃeɪndʒ] vt ανταλλάσσω || ~able a ανταλλάξιμος, εναλλάξιμος.

intercom ['ɪntəkɒm] n σύστημα εσωτερικής επικοινωνίας.

interconnect [ɪntəkə'nɛkt] vi αλληλοσυνδέω.

intercontinental [ɪntəkɒntɪ'nɛntl] a διηπειρωτικός.

intercourse ['ɪntəkɔ:s] n συναλλαγή, σχέσεις fpl || (sexual) συνουσία.

interest ['ɪntrɪst] n (curiosity) ενδιαφέρον nt|| (advantage) συμφέρον nt || (money paid) τόκος || (COMM: stake) συμφέροντα ntpl, συμμετοχή ♦ vt ενδιαφέρω, προσελκύω || ~ed a ενδιαφερόμενος || (attentive) με ενδιαφέρον || to be ~ed in ενδιαφέρομαι για || ~ing a ενδιαφέρων.

interface ['ɪntəfeɪs] n (COMPUT) θύρα, υπεδομή.

interfere [ɪntə'fɪə*] vi επεμβαίνω || (+ with) συγκρούομαι με, ανακατεύομαι || ~nce n (general) επέμβαση, ανάμιξη || (TV) παράσιτα ntpl.

interim ['ɪntərɪm] a προσωρινός ♦ n: in the ~ στο μεταξύ.

interior [ɪn'tɪərɪə*] n εσωτερικό || (inland) ενδοχώρα ♦ a εσωτερικός.

interjection [ɪntə'dʒɛkʃən] n (GRAM) επιφώνημα nt.

interlock [ɪntə'lɒk] vi συνδέομαι ♦ vt συνδέω, συμπλέκω.

interloper ['ɪntələupə*] n παρείσακτος.

interlude ['ɪntəlu:d] n διάλειμμα nt|| (THEAT) ιντερμέτζο.

intermarry ['ɪntə'mærɪ] vi επιμιγνύομαι.

intermediary [ɪntə'mi:dɪərɪ] n μεσάζων/άζουσα m/f, μεσίτης/ίτρια m/f.

intermediate [ɪntə'mi:dɪət] a μεσολαβών, ενδιάμεσος.

intermission [ɪntə'mɪʃən] n διάλειμμα nt, διακοπή.

intermittent [ɪntə'mɪtənt] a διαλείπων || ~ly ad διακεκομμένα.

intern [ɪn'tɜ:n] vt περιορίζω ♦ ['ɪntɜ:n] n (US) εσωτερικός γιατρός m/f.

internal [ɪn'tɜ:nl] a εσωτερικός || ~ly ad (MED) εσωτερικά || ~ revenue n (US) Τμήμα Εσωτερικών Προσόδων.

international [ɪntə'næʃnəl] a διεθνής ♦ n (SPORT) διεθνής (παίκτης).

internment [ɪn'tɜ:nmənt] n εγκάθειρξη, περιορισμός.

interplay ['ɪntəpleɪ] n αλληλεπίδραση.

interpret [ɪn'tɜ:prɪt] vt εξηγώ || (translate) μεταφράζω || (THEAT) ερμηνεύω || ~ation n ερμηνεία, εξήγηση || ~er n διερμηνέας m/f.

interrelated [ɪntərɪ'leɪtɪd] a αλληλένδετος.

interrogate [ɪn'tɛrəgeɪt] vt ερωτώ, ανακρίνω.

interrogation [ɪntɛrə'geɪʃən] n ανάκριση, εξέταση.

interrogative [ɪntə'rɒgətɪv] a ερωτηματικός.

interrogator [ɪn'tɛrəgeɪtə*] n ανακριτής.

interrupt [ɪntə'rʌpt] vt διακόπτω, εμποδίζω || ~ion n διακοπή.

intersect [ɪntə'sɛkt] vt τέμνω, διακόπτω, κόβω ♦ vi (roads) διασταυρώνομαι || ~ion n (roads) διασταύρωση, σταυροδρόμι.

intersperse [ɪntə'spɜ:s] vt διασπείρω, αναμιγνύω.

interval ['ɪntəvəl] n διάλειμμα nt, διάστημα nt|| (MUS) διάστημα nt|| at ~s κατά διαστήματα.

intervene [ɪntə'vi:n] vi μεσολαβώ, παρεμβαίνω, επεμβαίνω.

intervention [ɪntə'vɛnʃən] n μεσολάβηση, παρέμβαση.

interview ['ɪntəvju:] n (PRESS etc) συνέντευξη || (for job) συνάντηση, συνέντευξη ♦ vt παίρνω συνέντευξη || ~er n εκείνος που παίρνει συνέντευξη.

intestate [ɪn'tɛstɪt] a χωρίς διαθήκη.

intestine [ɪn'tɛstɪn] n έντερο.

intimacy ['ɪntɪməsɪ] n οικειότητα || (sexual) συνουσία.

intimate ['ɪntɪmɪt] a ενδόμυχος, ιδιαίτερος || (familiar) οικείος, στενός ♦ ['ɪntɪmeɪt] vt υποδηλώ, εκδηλώνω, υπαινίσσομαι || ~ly ad στενά, κατά βάθος.

intimidate [ɪn'tɪmɪdeɪt] vt (εκ)φοβίζω, φοβερίζω.

intimidation [ɪntɪmɪ'deɪʃən] n εκφοβισμός.

into ['ɪntu] prep (movement) σε, εντός, μέσα || (change) σε.

intolerable [ɪn'tɒlərəbl] a ανυπόφορος, αφόρητος.

intolerance [ɪn'tɒlərəns] n μισαλλοδοξία.

intolerant [ɪn'tɒlərənt] a μισαλλόδοξος, αδιάλλακτος.

intonation [ɪntəu'neɪʃən] n διακύμανση της φωνής.

intoxicate [ɪn'tɒksɪkeɪt] vt μεθώ, ζαλίζω || ~d a μεθυσμένος.

intoxication [ɪntɒksɪ'keɪʃən] n μέθυσι, παραζάλη.

intractable [ɪn'træktəbl] a ανυπάκουος, ατίθασος.

intransigent [ɪn'trænsɪdʒənt] a αδιάλλακτος.

intransitive [ɪn'trænsɪtɪv] a αμετάβατος.

intravenous [ɪntrə'vi:nəs] a ενδοφλέβιος.

intrepid [ɪn'trɛpɪd] a ατρόμητος, άφοβος.

intricacy ['ɪntrɪkəsɪ] n περιπλοκή, (το) περίπλοκο.

intricate ['ɪntrɪkɪt] a περίπλοκος || (of thoughts) συγκεχυμένος.

intrigue [ɪn'tri:g] n μηχανορραφία ♦ vt (make curious) διεγείρω την περιέργεια.

intriguing [ɪn'tri:gɪŋ] a (fascinating) περίεργος, μυστηριώδης.

intrinsic [ɪn'trɪnsɪk] a ουσιαστικός, πραγματικός.

introduce [ɪntrə'djuːs] vt *(person)* συνιστώ, συστήνω || *(sth new)* παρουσιάζω, μπάζω || *(subject)* εισάγω.

introduction [ɪntrə'dʌkʃən] n παρουσίαση, σύσταση || *(book)* εισαγωγή, πρόλογος.

introductory [ɪntrə'dʌktərɪ] a εισαγωγικός.

introspective [ɪntrəu'spɛktɪv] a ενδοσκοπικός.

introvert ['ɪntrəuvɜːt] a, n ενδόστροφος.

intrude [ɪn'truːd] vi (+ on) επιβάλλω, επεμβαίνω || ~r n παρείσακτος.

intrusion [ɪn'truːʒən] n επέμβαση, διείσδυση.

intuition [ɪntjuː'ɪʃən] n διαίσθηση, ενόραση.

intuitive [ɪn'tjuːɪtɪv] a διαισθητικός, ενστικτώδης.

inundate ['ɪnʌndeɪt] vt *(fig)* κατακλύζω, πλημμυρίζω.

invade [ɪn'veɪd] vt εισβάλλω, καταπατώ || ~r n επιδρομέας, εισβολέας.

invalid ['ɪnvəlɪd] n ασθενής m/f, ανάπηρος/n m/f ♦ [ɪn'vælɪd] a *(not valid)* άκυρος || ~ate vt ακυρώνω, αναιρώ.

invaluable [ɪn'væljuəbl] a ανεκτίμητος.

invariable [ɪn'vɛərɪəbl] a αμετάβλητος.

invasion [ɪn'veɪʒən] n εισβολή, επιδρομή.

invective [ɪn'vɛktɪv] n βρισιά, λοιδωρία.

invent [ɪn'vɛnt] vt εφευρίσκω || *(make up)* πλάθω || ~ion n εφεύρεση || ~ive a εφευρετικός, δημιουργικός || ~or n εφευρέτης.

inventory ['ɪnvəntrɪ] n απογραφή, κατάλογος.

inverse ['ɪn'vɜːs] n αντίστροφος, ανάστροφος.

invert [ɪn'vɜːt] vt αντιστρέφω || ~ed commas npl εισαγωγικά ntpl.

invertebrate [ɪn'vɜːtɪbrɪt] n ασπόνδυλο.

invest [ɪn'vɛst] vt *(ECON)* επενδύω || *(control)* παρέχω, αναθέτω.

investigate [ɪn'vɛstɪgeɪt] vt ερευνώ, εξετάζω.

investigation [ɪnvɛstɪ'geɪʃən] n έρευνα, εξέταση.

investigator [ɪn'vɛstɪgeɪtə*] n ερευνητής/ήτρια m/f, αναζητητής/ήτρια m/f.

investiture [ɪn'vɛstɪtʃə*] n τελετή απονομής αξιώματος.

investment [ɪn'vɛstmənt] n επένδυση.

investor [ɪn'vɛstə*] n κεφαλαιούχος m/f, επενδύτης m/f.

inveterate [ɪn'vɛtərɪt] a *(habitual)* φανατικός, αδιόρθωτος.

invigorating [ɪn'vɪgəreɪtɪŋ] a αναζωογονητικός, τονωτικός.

invincible [ɪn'vɪnsəbl] a αήττητος.

inviolate [ɪn'vaɪəlɪt] a απαραβίαστος, απαράβατος.

invisible [ɪn'vɪzəbl] a *(general)* αόρατος, αόπλος || *(ink)* συμπαθητική μελάνη.

invitation [ɪnvɪ'teɪʃən] n πρόσκληση.

invite [ɪn'vaɪt] vt *(προς)*καλώ || *(attract)* ελκύω, προκαλώ.

inviting [ɪn'vaɪtɪŋ] a δελεαστικός, ελκυστικός.

invoice ['ɪnvɔɪs] n τιμολόγιο ♦ vt τιμολογώ.

invoke [ɪn'vəuk] vt επικαλούμαι, απαιτώ.

involuntarily [ɪn'vɒləntərɪlɪ] ad ακουσίως, αθέλητα.

involuntary [ɪn'vɒləntərɪ] a ακούσιος, αθέλητος.

involve [ɪn'vɒlv] vt *(include)* συνεπάγομαι || *(entangle)* (περι)πλέκω, ανακατώνω || ~d a πλεγμένος || ~ment n ανάμιξη, μπλέξιμο.

invulnerable [ɪn'vʌlnərəbl] a άτρωτος.

inward ['ɪnwəd] a εσωτερικός, προς τα μέσα || ~(s) ad προς τα μέσα || ~ly ad εσωτερικά, μέσα.

iodine ['aɪədiːn] n ιώδιο.

iota [aɪ'əutə] n *(fig)* γιώτα nt, τίποτε, ελάχιστη ποσότητα.

I O U n *(abbr of I owe you)* γραμμάτιο.

I.Q. n *(abbr of intelligence quotient)* δείκτης ευφυΐας.

Iran [ɪ'rɑːn] n Ιράν nt inv, Περσία.

Iraq [ɪ'rɑːk] n Ιράκ nt inv.

irascible [ɪ'ræsɪbl] a ευέξαπτος, οξύθυμος.

irate [aɪ'reɪt] a θυμωμένος, εξαγριωμένος.

Ireland ['aɪələnd] n Ιρλανδία.

iris ['aɪrɪs] n *(ANAT)* ίριδα || *(BOT)* ίριδα, ρίδι.

Irish ['aɪrɪʃ] a ιρλανδικός || the ~ npl οι Ιρλανδοί || ~man n Ιρλανδός || ~woman n Ιρλανδή.

irk [ɜːk] vt ενοχλώ, στενοχωρώ.

iron ['aɪən] n σίδηρος || *(flat iron)* σίδερο || *(golf club)* ρόπαλο του γκολφ ♦ a σιδερένιος ♦ vt σιδερώνω || ~s npl *(chains)* αλυσίδες fpl, δεσμά ntpl || to ~ out vt *(crease)* σιδερώνω || *(difficulties)* εξομαλύνω || ~ curtain n σιδηρούν παραπέτασμα nt.

ironic(al) [aɪ'rɒnɪk(əl)] a ειρωνικός || ~ally ad ειρωνικά.

ironing ['aɪənɪŋ] n σιδέρωμα nt || ~ board n σανίδα σιδερώματος.

ironmonger ['aɪənmʌŋgə*] n σιδηροπώλης || ~'s (shop) n σιδηροπωλείο.

iron ore ['aɪənɔː*] n σιδηρομετάλλευμα nt.

ironworks ['aɪənwɜːks] n σιδηρουργείο.

irony ['aɪərənɪ] n ειρωνεία.

irrational [ɪ'ræʃənl] a παράλογος.

irreconcilable [ɪrɛkən'saɪləbl] a αδιάλλακτος, ασυμβίβαστος.

irredeemable [ɪrɪ'diːməbl] a *(COMM)* ανεξαγόραστος.

irrefutable [ɪrɪ'fjuːtəbl] a ακαταμάχητος, αδιάψευστος.

irregular [ı'regjulə*] a (not regular) ακανόνιστος, άτακτος || (not smooth) ανώμαλος || (against rule) αντικανονικός, αντίθετος || ~ity n ανωμαλία.
irrelevance [ı'relǝvǝns] n (το) άσχετο.
irrelevant [ı'relǝvǝnt] a άσχετος, ξεκάρφωτος.
irreparable [ı'repǝrǝbl] a ανεπανόρθωτος, αγιάτρευτος.
irreplaceable [ırı'pleısǝbl] a αναντικατάστατος.
irrepressible [ırı'presǝbl] a ακατάσχετος, ακάθεκτος.
irreproachable [ırı'prǝutʃǝbl] a άμεμπτος, άψογος.
irresistible [ırı'zıstǝbl] a ασυγκράτητος, ακαταμάχητος.
irresolute [ı'rezǝlu:t] a αναποφάσιστος, διστακτικός.
irrespective [ırı'spektıv] ~ of prep ανεξάρτητα από.
irresponsible [ırıs'pɔnsǝbl] a απερίσκεπτος, ελαφρόμυαλος.
irreverent [ı'revǝrǝnt] a ασεβής, ανευλαβής.
irrevocable [ı'revǝkǝbl] a αμετάκλητος, ανέκκλητος.
irrigate ['ırıgeıt] vt αρδεύω, ποτίζω.
irrigation [ırı'geıʃǝn] n άρδευση, πότισμα nt.
irritable ['ırıtǝbl] a οξύθυμος, ευέξαπτος.
irritate ['ırıteıt] vt (annoy) (εξ)ερεθίζω, εκνευρίζω || (skin etc) ερεθίζω.
irritation [ırı'teıʃǝn] n ερεθισμός, θυμός.
is [ız] see be.
Islam ['ızla:m] n Ισλάμ nt inv.
island ['aılǝnd] n νησί || ~er νησιώτης/ιώτισσα m/f.
isle [aıl] n νήσος f, νησάκι.
isn't ['ıznt] = is not || see be.
isolate ['aısǝleıt] vt (απο)μονώνω || ~d a απομονωμένος, απόμερος.
isolation [aısǝ'leıʃǝn] n απομόνωση.
isotope ['aısǝtǝup] n ισότοπο.
Israel ['ızreıl] n Ισραήλ m inv || ~i n Ισραηλινός/ή m/f || adj ισραηλινός.
issue ['ıʃu:] n (question) υπόθεση, ζήτημα nt || (giving out) έκδοση, διανομή, χορήγηση || (copy) τεύχος, φύλλο || (offspring) απόγονοι mpl ♦ vt (rations) διανέμω || (orders) εκδίδω, δημοσιεύω || (equipment) διανέμω, εκδίδω || at ~ υπό συζήτηση.
isthmus ['ısmǝs] n ισθμός.
it [ıt] pron τον, την, το, αυτό.
Italian [ı'tælıǝn] a ιταλικός ♦ n (person) Ιταλός/ίδα m/f || (LING) Ιταλικά ntpl.
italic [ı'tælık] a κυρτός, πλάγιος || ~s npl πλάγια γράφα.
Italy ['ıtǝlı] n Ιταλία.
itch [ıtʃ] n (fig) πόθος, όρεξη || (MED) φαγούρα, ψώρα ♦ vi έχω φαγούρα || ~ing n φαγούρα.
it'd ['ıtd] = it would, it had || see would, have.

item ['aıtǝm] n (on list) είδος nt, κονδύλι, εγγραφή || (in programme) νούμερο || (in agenda) θέμα nt || (in newspaper) είδηση || ~ize vt αναλύω.
itinerant [ı'tınǝrǝnt] a περιοδεύων.
itinerary [aı'tınǝrǝrı] n δρομολόγιο.
it'll ['ıtl] = it will, it shall || see will, shall.
its [ıts] poss a του || poss pron δικό του.
it's [ıts] = it is, it has || see be, have.
itself [ıt'self] pron τον εαυτό του.
I.T.V. n (abbr of Independent Television) Ανεξάρτητο Τηλεοπτικό Κανάλι.
I've [aıv] = I have || see have.
ivory ['aıvǝrı] n ελεφαντοστούν nt || ~ tower n (fig) τόπος μονώσεως.
ivy ['aıvı] n κισσός.

J

jab [dʒæb] vti κτυπώ, κεντώ, χώνω.
jabber ['dʒæbǝ*] vi φλυαρώ, τραυλίζω.
jack [dʒæk] n (MECH) γρύλλος || (CARDS) βαλές m, φάντης || to ~ up vt σηκώνω με γρύλλο.
jacket ['dʒækıt] n ζακέτα, σακάκι || (MECH) χιτώνιο, πουκάμισο.
jack-knife ['dʒæknaıf] n μεγάλος σουγιάς, κολοκοτρώνης.
jade [dʒeıd] n (stone) νεφρίτης.
jaded ['dʒeıdıd] a κουρασμένος, τσακισμένος.
jagged ['dʒægıd] a ανώμαλος, οδοντωτός, μυτερός.
jail [dʒeıl] n φυλακή || ~break n δραπέτευση || ~er n δεσμοφύλακας.
jam [dʒæm] n (fruit) μαρμελάδα || (stoppage) εμπλοκή, φρακάρισμα nt, στρίμωγμα nt ♦ vt σφηνώνω, σφίγγω, στριμώχνω ♦ vi σφίγγομαι, φρακάρω, κολλώ.
jangle ['dʒæŋgl] vti ηχώ κακόηχα, κουδουνίζω.
janitor ['dʒænıtǝ*] n (caretaker) θυρωρός m/f, επιστάτης/άτρια m/f.
January ['dʒænjuǝrı] n Ιανουάριος.
Japan [dʒǝ'pæn] n Ιαπωνία || ~ese n Ιαπωνικός ♦ n (LING) Ιαπωνικά ntpl.
jar [dʒa:*] n (glass) βάζο, λαγήνι, στάμνα ♦ vi τραντάζω, συγκρούομαι.
jargon ['dʒa:gǝn] n επαγγελματική φρασεολογία, αλαμπουρνέζικα ntpl.
jasmin(e) ['dʒæzmın] n γιασεμί.
jaundice ['dʒɔːndıs] n ίκτερος, χρυσή || ~d a (attitude) κακόβουλος, φθονερός.
jaunt [dʒɔːnt] n βόλτα, περίπατος || ~y a ζωηρός, ξένοιαστος.
javelin ['dʒævlın] n ακόντιο, κοντάρι.
jaw [dʒɔː] n σαγόνι, μασέλα.
jazz [dʒæz] n τζάζ f inv || to ~ up vt ζωηρεύω, επιταχύνω || ~ band n τζάζ-μπαντ f inv.
jealous ['dʒelǝs] a (envious) ζηλιάρης || (watchful) ζηλότυπος, προσεκτικός || ~ly ad ζηλότυπα, με επιμέλεια || ~y n ζήλεια.
jeans [dʒiːnz] npl ντρίλινο παντελόνι.

jeep [dʒi:p] n τζίπ nt inv.

jeer [dʒɪə*] vi (+ at) κοροϊδεύω, χλευάζω, γιουχαΐζω ♦ n εμπαιγμός, γιούχα.

jelly ['dʒelɪ] n ζελέ f || ~fish n μέδουσα, τσούχτρα.

jeopardize ['dʒepədaɪz] vt διακινδυνεύω.

jeopardy ['dʒepədɪ] n: in ~ σε κίνδυνο.

jerk [dʒɜːk] n τίναγμα nt, τράνταγμα nt || (US: idiot) χαζός ♦ vti τινάζω, τραντάζω.

jerkin ['dʒɜːkɪn] n πέτσινο σακκάκι.

jerky ['dʒɜːkɪ] a απότομος, κοφτός.

jersey ['dʒɜːzɪ] n φανέλα.

jest [dʒest] n χωρατό, αστείο ♦ vi κάνω αστεία, αστειεύομαι.

jet [dʒet] n (stream) πίδακας, αναπήδηση || (spout) στόμιο, μπεκ nt inv || (AVIAT) τζέτ nt inv || ~-black n κατάμαυρος || ~ engine n κινητήρας τζέτ.

jettison ['dʒetɪsn] vt απορρίπτω.

jetty ['dʒetɪ] n μώλος, αποβάθρα.

Jew [dʒu:] n Εβραίος.

jewel ['dʒu:əl] n κόσμημα nt || (fig) πολύτιμη, πέτρα || ~ler, (US) ~er n κοσμηματοπώλης || ~(l)er's (shop) n κοσμηματοπωλείο || ~(le)ry n κοσμήματα ntpl, διαμαντικά ntpl.

Jewess ['dʒu:ɪs] n Εβραία.

Jewish ['dʒu:ɪʃ] a εβραϊκός.

jib [dʒɪb] n (NAUT) αρτέμων inv, φλόκος ♦ vi αρνούμαι, κωλώνω, κλωτσώ.

jibe [dʒaɪb] n πείραγμα nt, αστείο.

jiffy ['dʒɪfɪ] n (col): in a ~ στη στιγμή, αμέσως.

jigsaw ['dʒɪgsɔ:] n (also: ~ puzzle) (παιχνίδι) συναρμολόγησης.

jilt [dʒɪlt] vt διώχνω, στρίβω.

jingle ['dʒɪŋgl] n κουδούνισμα nt, ♦ vti κουδουνίζω.

jinx [dʒɪŋks] n (col) γρουσούζης.

jitters ['dʒɪtəz] npl (col): to get the ~ τρέμω, φοβάμαι.

job [dʒɔb] n έργο, εργασία || (position) θέση, δουλειά || (difficult task) αγγαρεία || ~less a άνεργος.

jockey ['dʒɔkɪ] n τζόκεϋ m inv ♦ vi ελίσσομαι, μανουβράρω.

jocular ['dʒɔkjulə*] a αστείος, εύθυμος.

jog [dʒɔg] vt σπρώχνω, σκουντώ ♦ vi (move jerkily) κλυδωνίζω, τραντάζω.

join [dʒɔɪn] vt (fasten) ενώνω, συνδέω, ματίζω || (club) εγγράφομαι, γίνομαι μέλος ♦ vi (the army) κατατάσσομαι ♦ n ένωση, ραφή.

joiner ['dʒɔɪnə*] n μαραγκός || ~y n ξυλουργική.

joint [dʒɔɪnt] n (TECH) αρμός, άρθρωση || (of meat) κομμάτι κρέατος || (col: place) καταψύκτιο, τρώγλη || ~ly ad μαζί.

joist [dʒɔɪst] n δοκάρι, πατερό.

joke [dʒəʊk] n αστείο, χωρατό, καλαμπούρι ♦ vi αστειεύομαι || ~r n αστειολόγος || (CARDS) μπαλαντέρ m inv.

jolly ['dʒɔlɪ] a εύθυμος, χαρούμενος, κεφάτος ♦ ad (col) εξαιρετικά, πολύ.

jolt [dʒəʊlt] n τίναγμα nt, τράνταγμα nt || (col) ξάφνιασμα ♦ vt τινάζω, κουνώ.

jostle ['dʒɔsl] vt σπρώχνω.

jot [dʒɔt] n: not one ~ ούτε ίχνος, ούτε κατά κεραία || to ~ down vt σημειώνω, γράφω || ~ter n σημειωματάριο.

journal ['dʒɜːnl] n εφημερίδα, περιοδικό || ~ese n δημοσιογραφικό ύφος || ~ism n δημοσιογραφία || ~ist n δημοσιογράφος m/f.

journey ['dʒɜːnɪ] n ταξίδι, διαδρομή.

joy [dʒɔɪ] n χαρά, ευθυμία || ~ful a περιχαρής, χαρμόσυνος || ~ous a εύθυμος || ~ride n περίπατος με αυτοκίνητο.

Jr., Jun., Junr. abbr of **junior**.

jubilant ['dʒu:bɪlənt] a χαρούμενος, πανηγυρίζων.

jubilation [dʒu:bɪ'leɪʃən] n αγαλλίαση, χαρά.

jubilee ['dʒu:bɪli:] n γιορτή.

judge [dʒʌdʒ] n (in court) δικαστής ♦ vt δικάζω, κρίνω ♦ vi (estimate) υπολογίζω, θεωρώ || judg(e)ment n (sentence) δικαστική απόφαση || (opinion) κρίση, γνώμη.

judicial [dʒu:'dɪʃl] a (LAW) δικαστικός.

judicious [dʒu:'dɪʃəs] a συνετός, γνωστικός, φρόνιμος.

judo ['dʒu:dəʊ] n τζούντο nt inv.

jug [dʒʌg] n κανάτι, στάμνα.

juggle ['dʒʌgl] vi ταχυδακτυλουργώ, εξαπατώ || ~r n ταχυδακτυλουργός.

Jugoslav ['ju:gəʊ'slɑ:v] = **Yugoslav.**

juice [dʒu:s] n χυμός, ζουμί.

juicy ['dʒu:sɪ] a χυμώδης, ζουμερός.

jukebox ['dʒu:kbɒks] n τζουκ μποξ nt inv.

July [dʒu:'laɪ] n Ιούλιος.

jumble ['dʒʌmbl] n ανακάτεμα nt, κυκεώνας, μπέρδεμα nt ♦ vt (also: ~ up) ανακατεύω, μπερδεύω.

jumbo ['dʒʌmbəʊ] attr: ~ jet n τζάμπο τζετ nt inv.

jump [dʒʌmp] vi πηδώ ♦ vt πηδώ πάνω από, υπερπηδώ ♦ n πήδημα nt, άλμα nt || ~ed-up a (col) νεόπλουτος.

jumper ['dʒʌmpə*] n μπλούζα, ριχτή ζακέτα.

jumpy ['dʒʌmpɪ] a νευρικός.

junction ['dʒʌŋkʃən] n (road) διασταύρωση || (RAIL) διακλάδωση.

juncture ['dʒʌŋktʃə*] n: at this ~ στο σημείο αυτό.

June [dʒu:n] n Ιούνιος.

jungle ['dʒʌŋgl] n (tropical) ζούγκλα.

junior ['dʒu:nɪə*] a (in age) νεώτερος || (in rank) κατώτερος, υφιστάμενος ♦ n (US: school) πρωτελειόφοιτος/n m/f.

junk [dʒʌŋk] n (rubbish) σκουπίδια ntpl, παλιοπράγματα ntpl || (ship) τζόγκα || ~shop n παλιατζίδικο.

jurisdiction [dʒuərɪs'dɪkʃən] n δικαιοδοσία.

jurisprudence [dʒuərɪs'pru:dəns] n νομολογία, νομομάθεια.

juror ['dʒuərə*] n ένορκος m/f.

jury ['dʒuərɪ] n ένορκοι mpl || (of contest) κριτική επιτροπή || ~man n = **juror.**

just [dʒʌst] a *(fair, right)* δίκαιος, σωστός || *(exact)* ακριβής ♦ *ad (exactly)* ακριβώς || *(barely)* μόλις || ~ **as I arrived** μόλις έφθασα || **I have** ~ **arrived** μόλις ήλθα || ~ **a little** τόσο δα, λίγο || ~ **now** πριν λίγο, μόλις τώρα || ~ **you and me** εμεις μόνο συ κι εγώ.

justice ['dʒʌstɪs] n *(fairness)* δικαιοσύνη || *(magistrate)* δικαστικός, δικαστής.

justifiable [dʒʌstɪ'faɪəbl] a δικαιολογήσιμος, εύλογος.

justification [dʒʌstɪfɪ'keɪʃən] n δικαίωση, δικαιολογία.

justify ['dʒʌstɪfaɪ] vt *(prove right)* αιτιολογώ || *(defend etc)* δικαιώνω, δικαιολογώ.

justly ['dʒʌstlɪ] ad δίκαια, ορθά.

justness ['dʒʌstnɪs] n ορθότητα, το δίκαιο.

jut [dʒʌt] vi *(also:* ~ **out)** προεξέχω.

juvenile ['dʒuːvənaɪl] a νεανικός, παιδικός ♦ n νέος/α m/f.

juxtapose ['dʒʌkstəpəʊz] vt (αντι)παραθέτω.

K

K *(abbr of one thousand)* K.

kaleidoscope [kə'laɪdəskəʊp] n καλειδοσκόπιο.

kangaroo [kæŋgə'ruː] n καγκουρώ f inv.

keel [kiːl] n τρόπιδα, καρίνα.

keen [kiːn] a ζωηρός, επιμελής, θερμός || ~**ness** n ζήλος, ενθουσιασμός.

keep [kiːp] *(irreg v)* vt *(have)* έχω, κρατώ, συντηρώ || *(take care of)* φυλάω, συντηρώ, τρέφω || *(detain)* (κατα)κρατώ, καθυστερώ || *(be faithful)* τηρώ, σέβομαι, μένω πιστός σε ♦ vi *(continue)* συνεχίζω, εξακολουθώ || *(of food)* διατηρούμαι, κρατώ || *(remain: quiet etc)* μένω, στέκομαι ♦ n τροφή, συντήρηση, έξοδα ntpl συντηρήσεως || *(tower)* (ακρο) πύργος || **to** ~ **back** vti κρατώ, πίσω, απομακρύνομαι, κρύβω || **to** ~ **on** vi συνεχίζω, εξακολουθώ να φορώ || ~ '~ **out'** 'απαγορεύεται η είσοδος' || **to** ~ **up** vi (+ **with**) διατηρώ, καλλιεργώ || ~**ing** n *(care)* φύλαξη, συντήρηση || **in** ~**ing with** σύμφωνα με, ανάλογα με.

keg [keg] n βαρελάκι.

kennel ['kenl] n σπιτάκι σκύλου.

kept [kept] pt, pp of **keep**.

kerb(stone) ['kɜːb(stəʊn)] n κράσπεδο πεζοδρομίου.

kernel ['kɜːnl] n πυρήνας, κόκκος, ψύχα.

kerosene ['kerəsiːn] n φωτιστικό πετρέλαιο, παραφίνη.

ketchup ['ketʃəp] n κέτσαπ nt inv, σάλτσα τομάτας.

kettle ['ketl] n χύτρα.

key [kiː] n κλειδί || *(to problem)* κλείδα || *(set of answers)* κλείδα, λύση || *(lever)* πλήκτρο || *(MUS)* τόνος ♦ a *(position etc)* βασικός, καίριος || **to** ~ **in** vt πληκτρολογώ || ~**board** n πλήκτρο, κλαβιέ nt inv || *(of computer, typewriter)* πληκτρολόγιο ♦ vt *(COMPUT)* πληκτρολογώ || ~**hole** n κλειδαρότρυπα || ~**note** n κυρία ιδέα || ~ **ring** n κρίκος κλειδιών.

khaki ['kɑːkɪ] n, a χακί.

kick [kɪk] vt λακτίζω, κλωτσώ ♦ vi *(col)* παραπονιέμαι, αντιρώ ♦ n λάκτισμα nt, κλωτσιά || *(thrill)* συγκίνηση || **to** ~ **around** vi *(col)* σέρνομαι, χαζεύω || **to** ~ **off** vi *(SPORT)* δίνω την πρώτη κλωτσιά || ~**-off** n *(SPORT)* εναρκτήριο λάκτισμα.

kid [kɪd] n *(child)* πιτσιρίκος, παιδάκι || *(goat)* κατσικάκι, ρίφι || *(leather)* σεβρό.

kidnap ['kɪdnæp] vt απάγω, κλέβω || ~**per** n απαγωγέας || ~**ping** n απαγωγή.

kidney ['kɪdnɪ] n νεφρό.

kill [kɪl] vt *(murder)* φονεύω, σκοτώνω || *(destroy)* εξοριζώνω, αφανίζω ♦ n κυνήγι || ~**er** n φονιάς/φόνισσα m/f.

kiln [kɪln] n καμίνι, κλίβανος.

kilo ['kiːləʊ] n κιλό || ~**gramme**, ~**gram** *(US)* n χιλιόγραμμο || ~**metre**, ~**meter** *(US)* n χιλιόμετρο || ~**watt** n κιλοβάτ nt inv.

kilt [kɪlt] n φουστανέλα.

kimono [kɪ'məʊnəʊ] n κιμονό.

kin [kɪn] n συγγενείς mpl, συγγενολόι.

kind [kaɪnd] a καλός, καλοκάγαθος, καλόβολος ♦ n είδος nt || a ~ **of** ας το πούμε, κάποιος || **two of a** ~ του ιδίου φυράματος || **in** ~ *(merchandise)* σε είδος || *(same way)* με το ίδιο νόμισμα.

kindergarten ['kɪndəgɑːtn] n νηπιαγωγείο.

kindhearted ['kaɪnd'hɑːtɪd] a καλόκαρδος.

kindle ['kɪndl] vt ανάβω || *(rouse)* εξάπτω, προκαλώ.

kindly ['kaɪndlɪ] a καλός, ευγενικός ♦ ad ευγενικά, μαλακά, φιλικά.

kindness ['kaɪndnɪs] n αγαθότητα, καλωσύνη.

kindred ['kɪndrɪd] a συγγενής, συγγενικός.

king [kɪŋ] n βασιλιάς || *(CARDS)* ρήγας || ~**dom** n βασίλειο || ~**fisher** n ψαροφάγος, μπιρμπίλι.

kink [kɪŋk] n ζάρα, στράβωμα nt || ~**y** a *(fig)* ιδιότροπος || *(hair)* σγουρός.

kiosk ['kiːɒsk] n *(TEL)* θάλαμος || *(shop)* κιόσκι, περίπτερο.

kipper ['kɪpə*] n καπνιστή ρέγγα.

kiss [kɪs] n φιλί, φίλημα nt ♦ vt φιλώ nt ♦ vi: **they** ~**ed** φιλήθηκαν.

kit [kɪt] n σύνεργα ntpl, ατομικά είδη ntpl || ~**bag** n σάκκος.

kitchen ['kɪtʃɪn] n κουζίνα || ~ **garden** n λαχανόκηπος || ~ **sink** n νεροχύτης.

kite [kaɪt] n *(chart)* αετός || *(bird)* τσίφτης.

kitten ['kɪtn] n γατάκι.

kitty ['kɪtɪ] n *(pool of money)* κοινό ταμείο.

kleptomaniac [kleptəʊ'meɪnɪæk] n κλεπτομανής m/f.

knack [næk] n επιδεξιότητα, κόλπο.

knapsack ['næpsæk] n δισάκκι, γυλιός.

K

knead [niːd] vt ζυμώνω.

knee [niː] n γόνατο || ~**cap** n επιγονατίδα.

kneel [niːl] (irreg v) vi γονατίζω.

knell [nɛl] n καμπάνισμα nt, κωδωνοκρουσία.

knelt [nɛlt] pt, pp of **kneel**.

knew [njuː] pt of **know**.

knickers ['nɪkəz] npl κιλότα.

knife [naɪf] n μαχαίρι ♦ vt μαχαιρώνω.

knight [naɪt] n ιππότης || (CHESS) άλογο || ~**hood** n ιπποτισμός, ο τίτλος του ιππότη.

knit [nɪt] vt πλέκω ♦ vi συγκολλώ || ~**ting** n πλέξιμο, πλεκτική || ~**ting machine** n πλεκτομηχανή || ~**ting needle** n βελόνα (του πλεξίματος) || ~**wear** n πλεκτό, τρικό.

knives [naɪvz] npl of **knife**.

knob [nɒb] n (of door) πόμολο || (butter etc) κομμάτι.

knock [nɒk] vt (criticize) βρίζω, κακολογώ ♦ vi προσκρούω, χτυπώ ♦ n κτύπημα nt || **to ~ off** vi (finish) σταματώ || **to ~ out** vt βγάζω, τινάζω, || (SPORT) βγάζω νοκ-άουτ || ~**er** n (on door) κτυπητήρι || ~**-kneed** a στραβοπόδης, στραβοκάνης || ~**out** n (lit) νοκ-άουτ nt inv.

knot [nɒt] n (of rope etc) κόμπος, δεσμός || (of ribbon) κόμπος || (measure) κόμβος ♦ vt δένω κόμπο.

know [nəʊ] (irreg v) vti (be aware of) ξέρω || (recognize) γνωρίζω, διακρίνω, ξέρω || **to ~ how to do** ξέρω πώς || ~**-all** n παντογνώστης/τρια m/f|| ~**-how** n μέθοδος f, τέχνη || ~**ing** a έξυπνος, πονηρός || ~**ingly** ad σκόπιμος, πονηρά.

knowledge ['nɒlɪdʒ] n (what one knows) γνώση, μάθηση || (information) είδηση, πληροφορίες fpl|| ~**able** a καλά πληροφορημένος, μορφωμένος.

known [nəʊn] pp of **know**.

knuckle ['nʌkl] n φάλαγγα, κλείδωση.

K.O. n abbr of **knockout**.

koran [kɒˈrɑː] n κοράνιο.

L

l. abbr of **litre**.

lab [læb] n abbr of **laboratory**.

label ['leɪbl] n ετικέτα ♦ vt επιγράφω, κολλώ ετικέτα.

labor ['leɪbə*] n (US) = **labour**.

laboratory [ləˈbɒrətərɪ] n εργαστήριο.

laborious [ləˈbɔːrɪəs] a κοπιώδης, επίπονος.

labour ['leɪbə*] n εργασία, μόχθος || (workmen) εργάτες mpl|| ~**er** n εργάτης/τρια m/f|| **L~ Party** n εργατικό κόμμα.

lace [leɪs] n δαντέλα || (braid) σειρήτι || (cord) κορδόνι ♦ vt δένω, πλέκω, βάζω δαντέλες.

lack [læk] vt στερούμαι ♦ n έλλειψη || **for ~ of** λόγω ελλείψεως.

lackadaisical [lækəˈdeɪzɪkəl] a άτονος, νωθρός.

laconic [ləˈkɒnɪk] a λακωνικός.

lacquer ['lækə*] n βερνίκι, λάκα.

lad [læd] n (boy) αγόρι || (young man) παλληκάρι.

ladder ['lædə*] n (lit) σκάλα, ανεμόσκαλα || (fig) (κοινωνική) κλίμακα.

laden ['leɪdn] a φορτωμένος.

ladle ['leɪdl] n κουτάλα.

lady ['leɪdɪ] n κυρία || (title) λαίδη || '**Ladies**' (lavatory) 'Κυριών', 'Γυναικών' || ~**bird**, ~**bug** (US) n λαμπρίτσα, πασχαλίτσα || ~**-in-waiting** n Κυρία των Τιμών || ~**like** a αρχοντικός, ευγενικός.

lag [læg] n (delay) καθυστέρηση, επιβράδυνση ♦ vi (also: ~ **behind**) βραδυπορώ || ~ vt (pipes) επενδύω, φασκιώνω.

lager ['lɑːgə*] n ελαφρά μπύρα, λάγκερ f inv.

lagging ['lægɪŋ] n μονωτική επένδυση.

lagoon [ləˈguːn] n λιμνοθάλασσα.

laid [leɪd] pt, pp of **lay** || **to be ~ up** είμαι κρεβατωμένος.

lair [lɛə*] n φωλιά, άντρο.

lake [leɪk] n λίμνη.

lamb [læm] n αρνάκι || (meat) αρνί || ~ **chop** n παϊδάκι.

lame [leɪm] a κουτσός || (excuse) μη πειστικός.

lament [ləˈmɛnt] n θρήνος ♦ vt θρηνώ, οδύρομαι || ~**able** a αξιοθρήνητος.

laminated ['læmɪneɪtɪd] a φυλλωτός.

lamp [læmp] n λύχνος, λυχνάρι || (globe) λάμπα || (in street) φανάρι || ~**post** n φανοστάτης || ~**shade** n αμπαζούρ nt inv.

lance [lɑːns] n λόγχη ♦ vt εγχειρίζω, ανοίγω || ~ **corporal** n υποδεκανέας.

lancet ['lɑːnsɪt] n νυστέρι.

land [lænd] n γη, στερεά || (ground) γη, έδαφος nt || (country) γη, χώρα || (estate) κτήμα nt ♦ vi (from ship) αποβιβάζομαι || (AVIAT) προσγειούμαι || (fig: arrive, fall) πέφτω ♦ vt (obtain) πιάνω, λαμβάνω || (passengers, goods) αποβιβάζω, ξεφορτώνω || ~**ing** n απόβαση || (AVIAT) προσγείωση || (platform) πλατύσκαλο || ~**ing craft** n αποβατικό σκάφος || ~**ing stage** n αποβάθρα || ~**ing strip** n λωρίδα προσγειώσεως || ~**lady** n σπιτονοικοκυρά || ~**locked** a μεσόγειος || ~**lord** n σπιτονοικοκύρης || (innkeeper) ξενοδόχος || ~**lubber** n στεριανός || ~**mark** n ορόσημο || ~**owner** n γαιοκτήμονας.

landscape ['lændskeɪp] n τοπίο || (painting) ζωγραφική τοπίων.

landslide ['lændslaɪd] n (GEOG) (κατ)ολίσθηση || (POL) εντυπωσιακή στροφή.

lane [leɪn] n δρόμισκος, μονοπάτι || (of road) λωρίδα, διάδρομος || (SPORT) ατομική πίστα, λωρίδα.

language ['læŋgwɪdʒ] n γλώσσα ||

(national) γλώσσα, διάλεκτος *f* || *(style)* γλώσσα, ομιλία.

languid ['læŋgwid] *a* νωθρός, αδρανής.

languish ['læŋgwiʃ] *vi* λυώνω, μαραίνομαι.

lank [læŋk] *a* μακρυά και ίσια || ~**y** μακρύς και λεπτός.

lanolin ['lænəlin] *n* λανολίνη.

lantern ['læntən] *n* φανάρι.

lap [læp] *n* ποδιά, γόνατα *ntpl* || *(SPORT)* γύρος, βόλτα ♦ *vt* γλείφω ♦ *vi (of waves)* παφλάζω || ~**dog** *n* χαϊδεμένο σκυλάκι.

lapel [lə'pel] *n* πέτο.

lapse [læps] *n* σφάλμα *nt* || *(moral)* παράβαση || *(of time)* παρέλευση, εκπνοή.

larceny ['lɑːsəni] *n* κλοπή.

lard [lɑːd] *n* λαρδί.

larder ['lɑːdə*] *n* αποθήκη τροφίμων, κελλάρι.

large [lɑːdʒ] *a (broad)* ευρύχωρος, εκτενής || *(big, numerous)* μεγάλος || **at ~** *(free)* ελεύθερος || *(extensively)* γενικά || ~**ly** *ad* σε μεγάλο βαθμό || ~**-scale** *a* σε μεγάλη κλίμακα, μεγάλος.

lark [lɑːk] *n (bird)* κορυδαλός || *(joke)* αστείο, φάρσα || **to ~ about** *vi (col)* αστιεύομαι, κάνω φάρσες.

larva ['lɑːvə] *n* νύμφη.

laryngitis [lærin'dʒaitis] *n* λαρυγγίτιδα.

larynx ['læriŋks] *n* λάρυγγι.

lash [læʃ] *n (stroke)* καμτσικιά ♦ *vt (beat against)* δέρνω, ξεσπώ, κτυπώ || *(whip)* μαστιγώνω || *(bind)* (προς)δένω || **to ~ out** *vi (with fists)* επιτίθεμαι, εφορμώ || *(spend money)* κάνω σπατάλες.

lass [læs] *n* κορίτσι, κοπέλα.

lasso [læ'suː] *n* λάσσο ♦ *vt* πιάνω με λάσσο.

last [lɑːst] *a* τελευταίος, τελικός ♦ *ad* τελευταία ♦ *n (person or thing)* τελευταίος, ύστατος || *(for shoe)* καλαπόδι ♦ *vi (continue, hold out)* διαρκώ, παραμένω || *(remain)* συντηρούμαι, διατηρούμαι || **at ~** επί τέλους || ~ **night** χθες το βράδυ || ~ **week** την περασμένη βδομάδα || ~**ing** *a* διαρκείας, που κρατά || ~**-minute** *a* της τελευταίας στιγμής.

latch [lætʃ] *n* μάνταλο, σύρτης || *(yale lock)* λουκέτο || ~**key** *n* απλό κλειδί, αντικλείδι.

late [leit] *a* καθυστερημένος, αργοπορημένος || *(not early)* αργά || *(recent)* παλιός, πρώην, τέως || *(recently dead)* μακαρίτης ♦ *ad* καθυστερημένα, αργά || *(late hour)* αργά || **of ~** πρόσφατα || ~ **in the day** αργά το βραδάκι || ~**comer** *n* αργοπορημένος || ~**ly** *ad* πρόσφατα, τελευταία || ~**ness** *n (of person)* αργοπορία || *(of hour)* προχωρημένη ώρα.

latent ['leitənt] *a* αφανής, κρυφός.

later ['leitə*] *comp a, comp ad of* **late**.

lateral ['lætərəl] *a* πλάγιος, πλευρικός.

latest ['leitist] *sup a, sup ad of* **late** || *n (news)* το νεώτερο || **at the ~** το αργότερο.

lathe [leið] *n* τόρνος.

lather ['lɑːðə*] *n* σαπουνάδα ♦ *vt* σαπουνίζω ♦ *vi* κάνω αφρό.

Latin ['lætin] *n* Λατινική (γλώσσα) ♦ *a* λατινικός || ~**-America** *n* Λατινική Αμερική ~**-American** *a* λατινοαμερικανικός ♦ *n* Λατινοαμερικανός/ίδα *m/f*.

latitude ['lætitjuːd] *n* γεωγραφικό πλάτος *nt* || *(freedom)* ευρυχωρία, περιθώριο.

latrine [lə'triːn] *n* αποχωρητήριο, μέρος *nt*.

latter ['lætə*] *a (more recent)* ο δεύτερος, άλλος || *(later)* τελευταίος, πρόσφατος ♦ *n (opposite of former)* ο δεύτερος, άλλος || ~**ly** *ad* τώρα τελευταία, πρόσφατα.

lattice work ['lætiswɜːk] *n* δικτυωτό, καφάσι.

laudible ['lɔːdəbl] *a* αξιέπαινος.

laugh [lɑːf] *n* γέλιο ♦ *vi* γελώ || **to ~ at** *vt* διασκεδάζω, περιγελώ, γελώ για || **to ~ off** *vt* γελοιοποιώ || ~**able** *a* γελοίος, αστείος, διασκεδαστικός || ~**ing stock** *n* περίγελως, κορόιδο || ~**ter** *n* γέλιο.

launch [lɔːntʃ] *n (of ship)* καθέλκυση || *(of rocket)* εκτόξευση || *(ship)* άκατος || *(motor)* βενζινάκατος *f* ♦ *vt (ship)* καθελκύω || προβάλλω, βάζω εμπρός || ~**ing** *n* καθέλκυση, εκτόξευση || ~**(ing) pad** *n* πλατφόρμα εκτόξευσης.

launder ['lɔːndə*] *vt* πλένω και σιδερώνω || ~**ette** *n* πλυντήριο αυτοεξυπηρέτησης.

laundry ['lɔːndri] *n (place)* πλυντήριο || *(clothes)* ρούχα *ntpl* για πλύσιμο.

laureate ['lɔːriət] *a see* **poet**.

laurel ['lɒrəl] *n* δάφνη.

lava ['lɑːvə] *n* λάβα.

lavatory ['lævətri] *n* αποχωρητήριο, τουαλέτα.

lavender ['lævində*] *n* λεβάντα.

lavish ['læviʃ] *a* γενναιόδωρος, σπάταλος || *(abundant)* άφθονος, πλούσιος ♦ *vt* κατασπαταλώ, διασπαθίζω || ~**ly** *ad* άφθονα, σπάταλα.

law [lɔː] *n* νόμος, νομικά *ntpl* || *(system of laws)* δίκαιο || *(of game etc)* κανόνες *mpl* || ~**-abiding** *a* νομοταγής || ~**breaker** *n* παραβάτης του νόμου || ~ **court** *n* δικαστήριο || ~**ful** *a* νόμιμος || ~**less** *a* άνομος, παράνομος.

lawn [lɔːn] *n* πρασιά, γρασίδι || ~**mower** *n* χορτοκόπτης || ~ **tennis** *n* τέννις *nt inv*.

law school ['lɔːskuːl] *n* σχολή νομικής.

law student ['lɔːstjuːdənt] *n* φοιτητής/ήτρια *m/f* νομικής.

lawsuit ['lɔːsuːt] *n* δίκη.

lawyer ['lɔːjə*] *n* νομικός *m/f*, δικηγόρος *m/f*.

lax [læks] *a* χαλαρός || *(morals etc)* έκλυτος, άτακτος.

laxative ['læksətiv] *n* καθάρσιο.

laxity ['læksiti] *n* χαλαρότητα.

lay [lei] *(irreg v) pt of* **lie** || *a* λαϊκός, μη

ειδικός ♦ vt (put down) τοποθετώ, θέτω, βάζω || (lay low) ξαπλώνω, σωριάζω || (prepare) βάζω, στρώνω || (eggs) γεννώ, κάνω || to ~ aside vt θέτω κατά μέρος, βάζω || to ~ by vt αποταμιεύω, οικονομώ || to ~ down vt παραδίδω || (plan) σχεδιάζω || to ~ off vt (workers) απολύω || to ~ on vt επιβάλλω, επιθέτω || to ~ out vt απλώνω || (spend) ξοδεύω || (plan) σχεδιάζω || to ~ up vt (store) αποθηκεύω || (ship) παροπλίζω || ~-by n βοηθητική λωρίδα στάθμευσης.

layer ['leɪə*] n στρώμα nt.

layette [leɪ'et] n τα μωρουδιακά ntpl.

layman ['leɪmən] n λαϊκός.

layout ['leɪaʊt] n σχέδιο.

laze [leɪz] vi τεμπελιάζω, χασομερώ || **laziness** ['leɪzɪnɪs] n τεμπελιά, χάζεμα nt || **lazy** ['leɪzɪ] a οκνηρός, τεμπέλης.

lb. abbr. of **pound** (weight).

lead [led] n μόλυβδος || (of pencil) μολύβι, γραφίτης.

lead [liːd] (irreg v) n (front position) πρώτη θέση, αρχηγία || (distance, time ahead) προπορεία || (example) καθοδήγηση, παράδειγμα nt || (clue) υπαινιγμός || (THEAT) πρωταγωνιστής/ίστρια m/f ♦ vt οδηγώ, καθοδηγώ || (group etc) ηγούμαι, διευθύνω ♦ vi άγω, καταλήγω, πηγαίνω || to ~ astray vt παραπλανώ || to ~ away vt (παρα)σύρω || to ~ back vt επαναφέρω || to ~ on vt προτρέπω κεντρίζω || to ~ to vt (street) οδηγώ σε, πηγαίνω σε || (result in) καταλήγω || to ~ up to vt οδηγώ σε || ~er n αρχηγός, ηγέτης || (newspaper) κύριο άρθρο || ~ership n ηγεσία, αρχηγία || ~ing a κύριος, ηγετικός, σημαίνων || ~ing lady n (THEAT) πρωταγωνίστρια || ~ing light n (person) ηγετική φυσιογνωμία.

leaf [liːf] n φύλλο || (thin sheet) φύλλο || (table) φύλλο (τραπεζιού).

leaflet ['liːflɪt] n φυλλάδιο.

league [liːg] n σύνδεσμος, ένωση, συμμαχία || (measure) λεύγα.

leak [liːk] n διαφυγή, διαρροή || (hole) τρύπα ♦ vt (liquid etc) διαρρέω (δια)φεύγω || (NAUT) κάνω νερά ♦ vi (of pipe etc) διαρρέω, τρέχω || to ~ out vi (liquid etc) διαρρέω || (information) διαδίδομαι.

lean [liːn] (irreg v) a (thin) λιγνός || (meat) άπαχος || (poor) ισχνός, φτωχός ♦ n άπαχο κρέας nt ♦ vi κλίνω, γέρνω ♦ vt ακουμπώ, στηρίζομαι || to ~ back vi γέρνω προς τα πίσω || to ~ forward vi γέρνω προς τα εμπρός || to ~ on vt στηρίζομαι, ακουμπώ || to ~ over vi κύπτω || ~ing n κλίση, τάση || ~t [lent] pt, pp of lean || ~-to n υπόστεγο.

leap [liːp] (irreg v) n πήδημα nt ♦ vi πηδώ || by ~s and bounds αλματωδώς, καλπάζων || ~frog n καβάλες fpl, βαρελάκια ntpl || ~t [lept] pt, pp of leap || ~ year n δίσεκτος χρόνος.

learn [lɜːn] (irreg v) vti μαθαίνω || ~ed μορφωμένος, πολυμαθής || ~er n (also

AUT) μαθητευόμενος, αρχάριος || ~ing n (εκ)μάθηση, μόρφωση.

lease [liːs] n εκμίσθωση, ενοικίαση, συμβόλαιο ♦ vt εκμισθώνω, ενοικιάζω.

leash [liːʃ] n λουρί, αλυσίδα.

least [liːst] a ελάχιστος, μικρότατος, λιγότερος ♦ n (το) λιγότερο, (το) μικρότερο || at ~ τουλάχιστο || not in the ~ καθόλου, ποτέ.

leather ['leðə*] n δέρμα nt, πετσί ♦ a δερμάτινος, πέτσινος.

leave [liːv] (irreg v) vt (go away from) φεύγω, εγκαταλείπω || (go without taking) αφήνω || (let stay) αφήνω || (give by will) αφήνω ♦ vi (depart) φεύγω ♦ n άδεια || (MIL) άδεια || on ~ με άδεια || to take one's ~ of αποχαιρετώ, φεύγω || to ~ out vt παραλείπω.

leaves [liːvz] npl of **leaf**.

Lebanon ['lebənən]: the ~ ο Λίβανος.

lecherous ['letʃərəs] a λάγνος, ασελγής.

lecture ['lektʃə*] n διάλεξη, μάθημα nt ♦ vi κάνω διάλεξη, κάνω μάθημα || ~r n ομιλητής/ήτρια m/f, υφηγητής/ήτρια m/f.

led [led] pt, pp of **lead**.

ledge [ledʒ] n άκρο, χείλος nt, ράφι || (of rock) ύφαλος, ξέρα.

ledger ['ledʒə*] n καθολικό (κατάστιχο).

lee [liː] n (from wind) προκάλυμμα nt.

leek [liːk] n πράσο.

leer [lɪə*] vi στραβοκοιτάζω.

leeway ['liːweɪ] n (fig) χαμός χρόνου, περιθώριο.

left [left] pt, pp of **leave** ♦ a αριστερός ♦ n (το) αριστερό, η αριστερά || the L~ (POL) n αριστερά || ~-handed a αριστερόχειρας || ~-luggage (office) n γραφείο καταθέσεως αποσκευών || ~-overs npl πλεονάσματα ntpl, υπολείμματα ntpl || ~-wing n (POL) αριστερός.

leg [leg] n πόδι, γάμπα || (of table etc) πόδι || (on trouser etc) γάμπα.

legacy ['legəsɪ] n κληροδότημα nt || (from ancestors) κληρονομία.

legal ['liːgəl] a νομικός || (allowed) νόμιμος || ~ize vt νομιμοποιώ || ~ly ad νόμιμα, νομικώς || ~ tender n νόμισμα nt (υποχρεωτικά δεκτό).

legend ['ledʒənd] n θρύλος, μύθος || ~ary a θρυλικός, μυθικός.

legible ['ledʒɪbl] a ευανάγνωστος.

legion ['liːdʒən] n λεγεώνα ♦ a (countless) αναρίθμητος.

legislate ['ledʒɪsleɪt] vi νομοθετώ.

legislation [ledʒɪs'leɪʃən] n νομοθεσία.

legislative ['ledʒɪslətɪv] a νομοθετικός.

legislature ['ledʒɪslətʃə*] n νομοθετικό σώμα nt.

legitimacy [lɪ'dʒɪtɪməsɪ] n νομιμότητα, γνησιότητα.

legitimate [lɪ'dʒɪtɪmɪt] a νόμικός, λογικός.

leisure ['leʒə*] n σχόλη, άνεση, ελεύθερες ώρες fpl ♦ a της σχόλης, της αργίας || at ~ ελεύθερος, έχων καιρό || ~ly α αβίαστος, αργός, άνετος.

lemon ['lemən] n λεμόνι || (colour) λεμονής || ~**ade** n λεμονάδα.

lend [lend] (irreg v) vt δανείζω || (dignity etc) (προς)δίδω || **it ~s itself to** προσφέρεται, κάνει για || ~**er** n δανειστής/ίσρια m/f || ~**ing library** n δανειστική βιβλιοθήκη.

length [leŋθ] n μήκος nt, μάκρος nt || (of road, pipe etc) μήκος nt || (of material) κομμάτι || **at** ~ (finally) επί τέλους || (time) για πολλή ώρα || (extent) εν εκτάσει || ~**en** vt μακραίνω, επιμηκύνω ♦ vi επεκτείνομαι, παρατείνομαι || ~**ways** ad κατά μήκος, στο μάκρος || ~**y** a μακροσκελής, εκτενής.

leniency ['li:nɪənsɪ] n ηπιότητα, επιείκεια.

lenient ['li:nɪənt] a ήπιος, επιεικής.

lens [lenz] n φακός.

lent [lent] pt, pp vi **lend** || **L**~ n Σαρακοστή.

lentil ['lentl] n φακή.

leopard ['lepəd] n λεοπάρδαλη.

leper ['lepə*] n λεπρός/n m/f.

leprosy ['leprəsɪ] n λέπρα.

lesbian ['lezbɪən] a λεσβιακός ♦ n λεσβία.

less [les] a comp of **little** || λιγότερος ♦ ad λιγότερο ♦ n λιγότερο.

lessen ['lesn] vi μειούμαι, μικραίνω, λιγοστεύω ♦ vt μειώνω, ελαττώνω, μικραίνω.

lesson ['lesn] n μάθημα nt.

lest [lest] cj μήπως, μη τυχόν.

let [let] (irreg v) vt (allow) αφήνω, επιτρέπω || (lease) ενοικιάζω, εκμισθώνω ♦ n: **without** ~ **or hindrance** χωρίς εμπόδιο, ελεύθερα || ~'**s go** ας πάμε || 'to ~' 'ενοικιάζεται' || **to** ~ **down** vt κατεβάζω || (disappoint) απογοητεύω, εγκαταλείπω || **to** ~ **go** vti ελευθερώνω, χαλαρώνω || **to** ~ **off** vt απαλλάσσω, αφήνω, συγχωρώ, απολύω || **to** ~ **out** vt αφήνω || (garment) ανοίγω || (scream) αφήνω || **to** ~ **up** vi μειούμαι, ελαττούμαι.

lethal ['li:θəl] a θανατηφόρος.

lethargic [le'θɑːdʒɪk] a ληθαργικός, νυσταλέος.

lethargy ['leθədʒɪ] n λήθαργος, ατονία.

letter ['letə*] n (sign) γράμμα nt, στοιχείο || επιστολή, γράμμα || ~**box** n γραμματοκιβώτιο || ~**ing** n γράμματα ntpl, μαρκάρισμα nt.

lettuce ['letɪs] n μαρούλι.

let-up ['letʌp] n (col) μείωση, χαλάρωση.

leukaemia, leukemia (US) [luːˈkiːmɪə] n λευκαιμία.

level ['levl] a επίπεδος, οριζόντιος ♦ ad οριζόντιος ♦ n επίπεδο, επίπεδος επιφάνεια || (height) στάθμη ♦ vt ισοπεδώνω, οριζοντιώνω || **on the** ~ (lit) επίπεδος, στο αλφάδι || (fig: honest) τίμια, εντάξει || **to** ~ **off** or **out** vi εξισώνω || ~ **crossing** n επίπεδος

διάβαση || ~-**headed** a ισορροπημένος, ψύχραιμος.

lever ['liːvə*] n μοχλός ♦ vt κινώ μοχλό || ~**age** n ενέργεια μοχλού, μόχλευση.

levity ['levɪtɪ] n ελαφρότητα, έλλειψη σοβαρότητας.

levy ['levɪ] n (taxes) είσπραξη || (MIL) στρατολογία ♦ vt εισπράττω, επιβάλλω || (MIL) στρατολογώ.

lewd [luːd] a λάγνος, ασελγής.

liability [laɪəˈbɪlɪtɪ] n (being liable) ευθύνη, υποχρέωση || (debt) υποχρέωση, οφειλή || (disadvantage) προδιάθεση, τάση.

liable ['laɪəbl] a (responsible) υπεύθυνος || (likely) ενδεχόμενος.

liaison [liːˈeɪzɔn] n (coordination) σύνδεσμος.

liar ['laɪə*] n ψεύτης.

libel ['laɪbəl] n διαβολή, δυσφήμιση ♦ vt διασύρω, δυσφημώ.

liberal ['lɪbərəl] a (generous) γενναιόδωρος || (open-minded) φιλελεύθερος ♦ n φιλελεύθερος || **L**~ **Party** Φιλελεύθερο Κόμμα.

liberate ['lɪbəreɪt] vt απελευθερώνω.

liberation [lɪbəˈreɪʒən] n απελευθέρωση.

liberty ['lɪbətɪ] n ελευθερία || **at** ~ ελεύθερος, εύκαιρος.

librarian [laɪˈbreərɪən] n βιβλιοθηκάριος m/f.

library ['laɪbrərɪ] n βιβλιοθήκη.

libretto [lɪˈbretəʊ] n λιμπρέττο.

Libya ['lɪbɪə] n Λιβύη || ~n a λιβυκός ♦ n (person) Λίβυος/α m/f.

lice [laɪs] npl of **louse**.

licence, license (US) ['laɪsəns] n (permit) άδεια, έγκριση, προνόμιο || (lack of control) κατάχρηση || ~ **plate** n (US AUT) πινακίδα.

license ['laɪsəns] vt δίνω άδεια, παρέχω άδεια || ~**d** a (for alcohol: premises) με άδεια πωλήσεως ποτού || ~**e** n προνομιούχος.

licentious [laɪˈsenʃəs] a ακόλαστος.

lichen ['laɪkən] n λειχήνα.

lick [lɪk] vt γλείφω || (of flames etc) παίζω με, εγγίζω, καταβροχθίζω ♦ n γλείψιμο || (small amount) μικρή ποσότητα.

licorice ['lɪkərɪs] n γλυκόρριζα.

lid [lɪd] n κάλυμμα nt, καπάκι.

lido ['liːdəʊ] n (for swimming) δημόσια πισίνα.

lie [laɪ] (irreg v) n ψέμα nt ♦ vi (speak) λέω ψέματα || (rest) είμαι ξαπλωμένος, μένω || (of object: be situated) κείμαι, ευρίσκομαι.

lieu [luː] n: **in** ~ **of** αντί του, στη θέση του.

lieutenant [lefˈtenənt] n (army) υπολοχαγός || [luːˈtenənt] (US) υποσμηναγός.

life [laɪf] n (being alive) ζωή || (way of living) τρόπος ζωής, ζωή || (time of life) ζωή, διάρκεια ζωής, βίος || (story) βίος, βιογραφία || (energy, vigour) ζωηρότητα, ζωή, κίνηση || ~ **assurance** n ασφάλεια ζωής || ~**belt** n σωσίβιο || ~**boat** n ναυαγοσωστική λέμβος f|| ~guard n ναυαγοσώστης || ~ jacket n σωσίβιο || ~less a (dead) νεκρός || χωρίς ζωή, χωρίς κέφι || ~like a ρεαλιστικός, ζωντανός || ~line a (lit) σωσίβιο σχοινί || ~long a ισόβιος, ολόκληρης ζωής || ~-sized a φυσικού μεγέθους || ~ span n διάρκεια ζωής, μέσος όρος ζωής || ~ time n ζωή.

lift [lɪft] vt (αν)υψώνω, σηκώνω || (col: steal) κλέβω ♦ vi υψώνομαι, σηκώνομαι ♦ n ανύψωση, σήκωμα nt|| (AVIAT) άνωση || (machine, elevator) ανελκυστήρας, ασανσέρ nt inv|| (free ride) παίρνω στο αυτοκίνητο.

ligament ['lɪgəmənt] n σύνδεσμος.

light [laɪt] (irreg v) n φως nt|| (giving light) φως nt, φωτισμός || (for cigarette) φωτιά || (lamp) φως nt, λάμπα || (brightness) λάμψη || (of dawn) λάμψη || (information) διαφώτιση || (aspect) φως nt, όψη, άποψη ♦ vt ανάβω || (set burning) ανάβω || (brighten) φωτίζω, φέγγω ♦ a (bright) φωτεινός || (colour) ανοιχτόχρωμος, ξανθός || (not heavy) ελαφρός || (easy to do) εύκολος || (delicate) ελαφρός, απαλός || (cheerful) εύθυμος || to ~ up vi (lamps) ανάβω, φωτίζω || (face) αστράφτω, λάμπω ♦ vt (illuminate) (δια)φωτίζω || ~bulb n λάμπα, λαμπτήρας || ~en vi (brighten) φωτίζομαι || (flash lightning) αστράφτω ♦ vt (give light to) φωτίζω || (make less heavy) ελαφρώνω || ~er n (cigarette lighter) αναπτήρας || (boat) φορτηγίδα || ~-headed a ζαλισμένος || (thoughtless) επιπόλαιος, απερίσκεπτος || ~-hearted a εύθυμος, χαρούμενος || ~house n φάρος || ~ing n (on road) φωτισμός || (in theatre) φωτισμός || ~ly ad ελαφρώς, ελαφρά || ~ meter n (PHOT) μετρητής φωτός || ~ness n ελαφρότητα.

lightning ['laɪtnɪŋ] n αστραπή, κεραυνός || ~ conductor n αλεξικέραυνο.

light year ['laɪtjɪə*] n έτος φωτός.

like [laɪk] vt μου αρέσει, συμπαθώ, προτιμώ ♦ prep σαν, όπως, ως ♦ a (similar) όμοιος, ίδιος || (equal) ίσος, παρόμοιος ♦ ad όπως, σαν ♦ n όμοιος || ~able a ευχάριστος, συμπαθητικός.

likelihood ['laɪklɪhʊd] n πιθανότητα.

likely ['laɪklɪ] a πιθανός, που μπορεί να ♦ ad πιθανό, ίσως.

like-minded [laɪk'maɪndɪd] a με την αυτή γνώμη.

liken ['laɪkən] vt συγκρίνω, παρομοιάζω.

likewise ['laɪkwaɪz] ad ομοίως, επίσης, επί πλέον.

liking ['laɪkɪŋ] n κλίση, τάση, συμπάθεια, γούστο.

lilac ['laɪlæk] n πασχαλιά.

lily ['lɪlɪ] n κρίνο.

limb [lɪm] n μέλος nt, άκρο || (of tree) κλάδος.

limber ['lɪmbə*] : to ~ up vi γίνομαι ευλύγιστος.

limbo ['lɪmbəʊ] n: to be in ~ (fig) είμαι σε κατάσταση αβεβαιότητας.

lime [laɪm] n (tree) γλυκολεμονιά, κίτριο || φιλύρα || (fruit) γλυκολέμονο, κίτρο || (GEOL) ασβέστης.

limelight ['laɪmlaɪt] n (fig) το προσκήνιο, δημοσιότητα.

limestone ['laɪmstəʊn] n ασβεστόλιθος.

limit ['lɪmɪt] n όριο, σύνορο, πέρας nt ♦ vt περιορίζω || ~ation n περιορισμός, ανικανότητα || ~ed a περιωρισμένος, στενός || ~ed company (Ltd.) n εταιρεία περιωρισμένης ευθύνης.

limousine ['lɪməziːn] n λιμουζίνα.

limp [lɪmp] n χωλότητα ♦ vi χωλαίνω, κουτσαίνω ♦ a απαλός, πλαδαρός, μαλακός || (without energy) λυωμένος, τσακισμένος.

limpet ['lɪmpɪt] n πεταλίδα.

line [laɪn] n (cord, wire, string) σχοινί, γραμμή, σύρμα nt|| (narrow mark) γραμμή || (row, series) σειρά, γραμμή || (course, direction) κατεύθυνση, τρόπος, πορεία || (class of goods) σειρά, συλλογή, είδος || (poetry etc) στίχος, γραμμή ♦ vt (coat etc) φοδράρω || (border) χαράσσω || in ~ with σύμφωνα με || to ~ up vi μπαίνω στη γραμμή || σχηματίζομαι ουρά ♦ vt παρατάσσω, βάζω στη γραμμή.

linear ['lɪnɪə*] a (of length) του μήκους, γραμμική.

linen ['lɪnɪn] n λινό ύφασμα nt|| (articles) ασπρόρουχα ntpl.

liner ['laɪnə*] n πλοίο γραμμής.

linesman ['laɪnzmən] n (SPORT) λάινσμαν m inv.

line-up ['laɪnʌp] n παράταξη.

linger ['lɪŋgə*] vi (remain long) χρονοτριβώ, παρατείνομαι || (delay) αργοπορώ, βραδύνω.

lingerie ['lænʒəriː] n γυναικεία εσώρουχα ntpl.

lingering ['lɪŋgərɪŋ] a παρατεταμένος, βραδύς, αναιρός.

lingo ['lɪŋgəʊ] n (col) γλώσσα, διάλεκτος f.

linguist ['lɪŋgwɪst] n γλωσσολόγος m/f, γλωσσομαθής m/f.

linguistic [lɪŋ'gwɪstɪk] a γλωσσολογικός || ~s n γλωσσολογία.

lining ['laɪnɪŋ] n φόδρα.

link [lɪŋk] n (of chain) κρίκος || δεσμός σύνδεσμος ♦ vt συνδέω, ενώνω || ~s npl γήπεδο γκόλφ || ~-up n (communication) σύνδεση.

linoleum [lɪ'nəʊlɪəm] n μουσαμάς, δαπέδου.

lion ['laɪən] n λιοντάρι || ~ess n λέαινα.

lip [lɪp] n χείλι, χείλος nt|| to pay ~ service (+to) κάνω ψεύτικες υποσχέσεις || ~stick n κραγιόν nt inv.

liqueur [lɪ'kjʊə*] n λικέρ nt inv.

liquid ['lɪkwɪd] n υγρό ♦ a (substance) υγρός, ρευστός || (asset) ρευστός, διαθέσιμος || ~ate vt διαλύω,

ξεκαθαρίζω, χρεωκοπώ || ~ation n
διάλυση, εξόφληση, χρεωκόπηση..
liquor ['lıkə*] n (strong drink)
οινοπνευματώδες ποτό.
lisp [lısp] n τραυλισμός, ψεύδισμα nt.
list [lıst] n (of names etc) κατάλογος || (on
ship) κλίση || vt (write down)
εγγράφω, καταγράφω ♦ vi (of ship)
κλίνω, γέρνω.
listen ['lısn] vi ακούω, προσέχω || to ~
to vt ακούω || ~er n ακροατής/άτρια
m/f.
listless ['lıstlıs] a άτονος, νωθρός,
αδιάφορος.
lit [lıt] pt, pp of light.
litany ['lıtənı] n λιτανεία.
liter ['li:tə*] n (US) = litre.
literacy ['lıtərəsı] n βαθμός μόρφωσης.
literal ['lıtərəl] a (word for word) κατά
λέξη || (usual meaning) κατά κυριολεξία ||
~ly ad κυριολεκτικά.
literary ['lıtərərı] a λογοτεχνικός,
φιλολογικός.
literate ['lıtərıt] a εγγράμματος.
literature ['lıtərıtʃə*] n φιλολογία,
λογοτεχνία.
litre ['li:tə*] n λίτρο.
litter ['lıtə*] n (untidy bits) σκουπίδια ntpl
|| (young animals) γέννα, νεογνά ntpl ♦ vt
κάνω άνω-κάτω, βρωμίζω με σκουπίδια.
little ['lıtl] a (small) μικρός, λίγος, κοντός
|| (unimportant) ασήμαντος ♦ ad ελάχιστα,
λίγο ♦ n λίγο.
liturgy ['lıtədʒı] n λειτουργία.
live [lıv] vi ζω || (pass one's life) ζω || (last)
ζω, διαρκώ || (dwell) κατοικώ, διαμένω,
ζω || to ~ down vt κάνω να ξεχαστεί,
υπερνικώ || to ~ on vt τρέφομαι με,
συντηρούμαι με || to ~ up to vt
εφαρμόζω, τιμώ, εκπληρώνω.
live [laıv] a (living) ζωντανός || (burning)
αναμμένος || (wire) ηλεκτρισμένος με
ρεύμα || (broadcast) ζωντανό πρόγραμμα.
livelihood ['laıvlıhud] n τα προς το ζην.
lively ['laıvlı] a ζωηρός.
liver ['lıvə*] n (ANAT) συκώτι.
livery ['lıvərı] n στολή υπηρέτη.
lives [laıvz] npl of life.
livestock ['laıvstɒk] n ζώα ntpl, κτήνη
ntpl.
livid ['lıvıd] a (lit) πελιδνός, ωχρός ||
(furious) φουριόζος.
living ['lıvıŋ] n τα προς το ζην, βίος ♦ a
ζωντανός || (wage) βασικός μισθός || ~
room n σαλόνι.
lizard ['lızəd] n σαύρα.
load [ləud] n φορτίο, φόρτωμα nt ♦ vt
φορτώνω, γεμίζω.
loaf [ləuf] n καρβέλι ♦ vi χαζεύω,
τεμπελιάζω.
loan [ləun] n δάνειο, δανεισμός ♦ vt
δανείζω || on ~ απεσπασμένος.
loathe [ləuð] vt σιχαίνομαι.
loathing ['ləuðıŋ] n σιχαμός, απδία.
loaves [ləuvz] npl of loaf.
lobby ['lɒbı] n προθάλαμος, είσοδος f ♦
vt επηρεάζω βουλευτές.

lobe [ləub] n λοβός.
lobster ['lɒbstə*] n αστακός.
local ['ləukəl] a τοπικός, επιτόπιος ♦ n
(pub) ταβέρνα || the ~s npl ντόπιοι mpl ||
~ity n θέση, μέρος, τοποθεσία || ~ly ad
τοπικά, επίτοπα.
locate [ləu'keıt] vt εντοπίζω || (establish)
τοποθετώ.
location [ləu'keıʃən] n τοποθεσία.
loch [lɒx] n λίμνη.
lock [lɒk] n (of door) κλειδαριά || (of canal
etc) υδροφράκτης, φράγμα nt || (of hair)
βόστρυχος, μπούκλα ♦ vt κλειδώνω ||
σφίγγω, στερεώνω ♦ vi (door etc)
ασφαλίζομαι || (wheels) σφηνώνω,
μπλοκάρομαι.
locker ['lɒkə*] n αρμάρι, ντουλάπι,
αποθήκη.
locket ['lɒkıt] n μενταγιόν nt inv.
locomotive [ləukə'məutıv] n ατμάμαξα,
ατμομηχανή.
locust ['ləukəst] n ακρίδα.
lodge [lɒdʒ] n εξοχικό σπίτι || (at gate)
σπιτάκι του φύλακα || (meeting place)
στοά ♦ vi φιλοξενούμαι, διαμένω || (rent
a room) είμαι νοικάρης || (stick)
αφηνώνομαι, πιάνομαι ♦ vt καταθέτω,
υποβάλλω || ~r n ένοικος m/f.
lodgings ['lɒdʒıŋz] npl δωμάτια ntpl.
loft [lɒft] n υπερώο, σοφίτα.
lofty ['lɒftı] a ψηλός || (proud)
υπεροπτικός, αγέρωχος.
log [lɒg] n (of wood) κούτσουρο || (of ship
etc) ημερολόγιο.
logarithm ['lɒgərıθəm] n λογάριθμος.
logbook ['lɒgbuk] n ημερολόγιο
(πλοίου).
loggerheads ['lɒgəhedz] n: at ~
τσακωμένος, στα μαχαίρια.
logic ['lɒdʒık] n λογική || ~al a λογικός.
loin [lɔın] n πλευρό ntpl, λαγόνες mpl.
loiter ['lɔıtə*] vi χρονοτριβώ, χαζεύω.
loll [lɒl] vi ξαπλώνω, χουζουρεύω.
lollipop ['lɒlıpɒp] n γλειφιτζούρι.
London ['lʌndən] n Λονδίνο || ~er n
(person) Λονδρέζος/α m/f.
lone [ləun] a (solitary) μόνος, μοναχικός ||
~liness n μοναξιά, ερημιά || ~ly a (sad)
μελαγχολικός, έρημος, ακατοίκητος.
long [lɒŋ] a μακρύς, εκτενής || (length)
μάκρος ♦ ad (time) για πολλή ώρα ||
(during) όλη, σ όλη ♦ vi (+ for) ποθώ,
λαχταρώ || before ~ σύντομα || as ~ as
εφ' όσον || in the ~ run στο τέλος,
τελικά || ~-distance a (TEL)
υπεραστικός || (SPORT) μεγάλων
αποστάσεων || ~-haired a μακρυμάλλης
|| ~hand n κανονική γραφή || ~ing n
πόθος, μεγάλη επιθυμία, λαχτάρα.
longitude ['lɒŋgıtjuːd] n μήκος.
long: ~ jump n άλμα εις μήκος ||
~-lost a χαμένος προ πολλού || ~-
playing record (L.P.) n δίσκος μακράς
διαρκείας || ~-range a μεγάλης
διαρκείας, μεγάλης ακτίνας || ~-
sighted a πρεσβύωπας, οξύδερκής || ~-
standing a παλιός, μακροχρόνιος || ~-

suffering a υπομονητικός, μακρόθυμος || ~**-term** a μακροπρόθεσμος, μακροχρόνιος || ~ **wave** n μακρύ κύμα || ~**-winded** a ατελείωτος, φλύαρος.

loo [luː] n μέρος nt.

loofah [ˈluːfə] n (ελ)λύφι.

look [luk] vi (see) κοιτάζω, βλέπω || (seem) φαίνομαι || (face) βλέπω, αντικρύζω ♦ n βλέμμα nt, ματιά || ~**s** npl όψη, εμφάνιση || **to** ~ **after** vt φροντίζω για || **to** ~ **down on** vt (fig) περιφρονώ || **to** ~ **for** vt ψάχνω, ζητώ || (expect) προσδοκώ || **to** ~ **forward to** vt προσδοκώ || **to** ~ **out for** vt αναζητώ, ψάχνω, προσέχω || **to** ~ **to** vt φροντίζω για, βασίζομαι σε || **to** ~ **up** vt καλυτερεύω ♦ vt επισκέπτομαι, ψάχνω (σε βιβλίο) || **to** ~ **up to** vt σέβομαι || ~**out** n (watch) προσοχή || (view) θέα || (MIL) φρούρηση, φρουρός.

loom [luːm] n αργαλειός ♦ vi διαφαίνομαι, διακρίνομαι.

loop [luːp] n βρόχος, θηλιά ♦ vt κάνω θηλιά, δένω με θηλιά || ~**hole** n (for escape) υπεκφυγή, διέξοδος f.

loose [luːs] a χαλαρός || (free) ελεύθερος, λυμένος || (slack) απρόσεκτος, απαλός ♦ vt λύνω, λασκάρω, χαλαρώνω || **at a** ~ **end** χωρίς απασχόληση || ~**ly** ad χαλαρά, ασαφώς || ~**n** vt λύνω, λασκάρω.

loot [luːt] n λάφυρο, λεία, πλιάτσικο ♦ vt λαφυραγωγώ, λεηλατώ || ~**ing** n λεηλασία.

lop [lɔp] : **to** ~ **off** vt (απο)κόβω, κλαδεύω.

lop-sided [ˈlɔpˈsaidid] a ετεροβαρής, που γέρνει.

lord [lɔːd] n άρχοντας, αφέντης || (Brit) λόρδος || **the L** ~ ο Κύριος || ~**ly** a μεγαλοπρεπής, αγέρωχος || ~**ship** n (title) εξοχότητα.

lore [lɔː*] n ειδική γνώση, παραδόσεις fpl.

lorry [ˈlɔri] n φορτηγό (αυτοκίνητο), καμιόνι || ~ **driver** n οδηγός φορτηγού.

lose [luːz] (irreg v) vt (most senses) χάνω || (waste) σπαταλώ, χάνω || ♦ vi χάνω || ~**r** n νικημένος χαμένος.

loss [lɔs] n απώλεια, χάσιμο || (what is lost) απώλεια || (harm) ζημιά || **to be at a** ~ τα έχω χαμένα, βρίσκομαι σε αμηχανία.

lost [lɔst] pt, pp of **lose** ♦ a χαμένος || ~ **property** n (γραφείο) απολεσθέντων αντικειμένων.

lot [lɔt] n (large quantity) πολύ || (for prize) κλήρος || (group of objects) σύνολο, σε παρτίδες || **a** ~ **of** ένα σωρό, πολύ || ~**s of** πλήθος, ένα σωρό.

lotion [ˈləuʃən] n λοσιόν f inv.

lottery [ˈlɔtəri] n λαχείο.

loud [laud] a βροντερός, θορυβώδης, μεγαλόφωνος || (showy) κτυπητός ♦ ad δυνατά, μεγαλόφωνα || ~**ly** ad δυνατά, μεγαλόφωνα || ~**speaker** n μεγάφωνο.

lounge [laundʒ] n μικρό σαλόνι, χωλ nt inv ξενοδοχείου ♦ vi περιφέρομαι

άσκοπα, χαζεύω || ~ **suit** n καθημερινό κοστούμι.

louse [laus] n ψείρα.

lousy [ˈlauzi] a (lit) ψειριάρης || (fig) βρωμερός, άθλιος.

lout [laut] n άξεστος, ντουβάρι.

lovable [ˈlʌvəbl] a αξιαγάπητος.

love [lʌv] n αγάπη, έρωτας, στοργή || (person loved) αγαπημένος, ερωμένος || (SPORT) μηδέν ♦ vt (person) αγαπώ || (activity) λατρεύω, αγαπώ || **to** ~ **to do** μου αρέσει να κάνω || **to make** ~ κάνω έρωτα, φλερτάρω || ~ **affair** n ερωτική υπόθεση || ~ **letter** n ερωτικό γράμμα nt || ~ **life** n ερωτική ζωή.

lovely [ˈlʌvli] a ωραίος, χαριτωμένος, ευχάριστος.

lovemaking [ˈlʌvmeikiŋ] n ερωτοτροπία, κόρτε nt inv.

lover [ˈlʌvə*] n (general) φιλο- || (man) εραστής, φίλος.

lovesong [ˈlʌvsɒŋ] n ερωτικό τραγούδι.

loving [ˈlʌviŋ] a τρυφερός, στοργικός.

low [ləu] a (not tall) χαμηλός || (rank) ταπεινός, κατώτερος || (common) χυδαίος, άξεστος || (not loud) αδύνατος, χαμηλός || (weak) κακόκεφος || (tide) άμπωτη ♦ ad χαμηλά || (not loudly) χαμηλόφωνα, χαμηλά ♦ n (low point) ναδίρ nt inv || (meteorology) βαρομετρικό χαμηλό || ~**-cut** a (dress) ντεκολτέ.

lower [ˈləuə*] vt κατεβάζω, χαμηλώνω || (make less) ελαττώνω.

lowly [ˈləuli] a ταπεινός, μετριόφρονας.

loyal [ˈlɔiəl] a πιστός, αφοσιωμένος || ~**ty** n πίστη, αφοσίωση.

lozenge [ˈlɔzindʒ] n παστίλια.

L.P. n abbr see **long-playing record**.

Ltd. abbr see **limited**.

lubricant [ˈluːbrikənt] n λιπαντικό, γράσο.

lubricate [ˈluːbrikeit] vt λιπαίνω, λαδώνω, γρασάρω.

lucid [ˈluːsid] a σαφής, διαυγής || ~**ity** n σαφήνεια, διαύγεια.

luck [lʌk] n τύχη || ~**ily** ad ευτυχώς || ~**y** a τυχερός.

lucrative [ˈluːkrətiv] a επικερδής.

ludicrous [ˈluːdikrəs] a αλλόκοτος, γελοίος, αστείος.

lug [lʌg] vt σέρνω με δυσκολία.

luggage [ˈlʌgidʒ] n αποσκευές fpl || ~ **rack** n (in train etc) δίχτυ nt για βαλίτσες.

lukewarm [ˈluːkwɔːm] a χλιαρός || (indifferent) αδιάφορος.

lull [lʌl] n ανάπαυλα, κόπαση ♦ vt νανουρίζω || (calm) καθησυχάζω, καταπραΰνω.

lullaby [ˈlʌləbai] n νανούρισμα nt.

lumbago [lʌmˈbeigəu] n οσφυαλγία.

lumber [ˈlʌmbə*] n (old articles) παλιατσούρες fpl || (wood) ξυλεία || ~**jack** n ξυλοκόπος.

luminous [ˈluːminəs] a φωτεινός, φωτισμένος.

lump [lʌmp] n (σ)βώλος, μεγάλο κομμάτι || (swelling) εξόγκωμα nt, καρούμπαλο || *(of sugar)* κομμάτι ♦ *vt* σβωλιάζω, συσσωρεύω || a ~ sum στρογγυλό ποσό, ολική τιμή || ~y *a* σβωλιασμένος.

lunacy ['luːnəsɪ] *n* παραφροσύνη.

lunar ['luːnə*] *a* σεληνιακός.

lunatic ['luːnətɪk] *n* παράφρονας ♦ *a* παράφρονας, τρελός.

lunch [lʌntʃ] *n (also: ~eon)* γεύμα || ~time *n* μεσημβρινή διακοπή.

lung [lʌŋ] *n* πνεύμονας || ~ cancer *n* καρκίνος των πνευμόνων.

lunge [lʌndʒ] *vi* μηνίγω, κτυπώ ξαφνικά, εφορμώ.

lurch [ləːtʃ] *vi* τρικλίζω, ταλαντεύομαι ♦ *n* τρίκλισμα *nt*, μπότζι.

lure [ljuə*] *n* δέλεασμα *nt*, δόλωμα *nt*, έλξη ♦ *vt* δελεάζω, θέλγω.

lurid ['ljuərid] *a (shocking)* τρομερός.

lurk [ləːk] *vi* παραμονεύω, κρύβομαι.

luscious ['lʌʃəs] *a* γευστικός, χυμώδης, γλυκύτατος.

lush [lʌʃ] *a* γεμάτος χυμούς || *(countryside)* πλούσιος σε βλάστηση.

lust [lʌst] *n* σαρκική επιθυμία ♦ *vi (+ after)* εποφθαλμιώ, ορέγομαι || ~ful *a* λάγνος.

lustre, luster *(US)* ['lʌstə*] *n* λάμψη, στιλπνότητα.

lusty ['lʌstɪ] *a* εύρωστος, σφριγηλός.

lute [luːt] *n* λαούτο.

Luxembourg ['lʌksəmbɜːg] *n* Λουξεμβούργο.

luxuriant [lʌg'zjuərɪənt] *a* άφθονος, πλούσιος.

luxurious [lʌg'zjuərɪəs] *a* πολυτελής, πλούσιος.

luxury ['lʌkʃərɪ] *n* πολυτέλεια, λούσο.

lying ['laɪɪŋ] *n* κείμενος || *(not truthful)* ψευδόμενος ♦ *a* ψεύτικος.

lynch [lɪntʃ] *vt* λυντσάρω.

lyre ['laɪə*] *n* λύρα.

lyric ['lɪrɪk] *n* λόγια *ntpl* τραγουδιού ♦ *a* λυρικός || ~al *a (fig)* ενθουσιώδης, λυρικός.

M

M. *abbr of* **metre, mile, million.**

M. A. *abbr see* **master.**

mac [mæk] *n (raincoat)* αδιάβροχο.

macaroni [mækə'rəʊnɪ] *n* μακαρόνια *ntpl.*

mace [meɪs] *n (spice)* μοσχοκάρυδο.

machine [mə'ʃiːn] *n (general)* μηχανή, μηχάνημα *nt* ♦ *vt (dress etc)* επεξεργάζομαι, κατεργάζομαι || ~ gun *n* πολυβόλο || ~ry *n* μηχανές *fpl* || *(parts)* μηχανήματα *ntpl* || *(of government)* μηχανισμός.

machinist [mə'ʃiːnɪst] *n* μηχανουργός.

mackerel ['mækrəl] *n* σκουμπρί.

mackintosh ['mækɪntɒʃ] *n* αδιάβροχο.

mad [mæd] *a* παράφρονας, τρελός || *(foolish)* παράλογος.

madam ['mædəm] *n* κυρία.

madden ['mædn] *vt* τρελαίνω.

made [meɪd] *pt, pp of* **make** || ~-to-measure *a* κατά παραγγελία.

madly ['mædlɪ] *ad* τρελά, άγρια.

madman ['mædmən] *n (maniac)* φρενοβλαβής, τρελός.

madness ['mædnɪs] *n* παραφροσύνη, τρέλα.

Madonna [mə'dɒnə] *n* Παναγία.

magazine [mægə'ziːn] *n* περιοδικό.

maggot ['mægət] *n* σκουλήκι.

magic ['mædʒɪk] *n* μαγεία ♦ *a* μαγικός, μαγεμένος || ~al *a* μαγικός || ~ian *n* μάγος.

magistrate ['mædʒɪstreɪt] *n* ειρηνοδίκης.

magnanimous [mæg'nænɪməs] *a* μεγαλόψυχος.

magnate ['mægneɪt] *n* μεγιστάνας.

magnet ['mægnɪt] *n* μαγνήτης || ~ic *a* μαγνητικός || ~ism *n* μαγνητισμός.

magnification [mægnɪfɪ'keɪʃən] *n* μεγέθυνση.

magnificence [mæg'nɪfɪsəns] *n* μεγαλοπρέπεια.

magnificent [mæg'nɪfɪsənt] *a* μεγαλοπρεπής.

magnify ['mægnɪfaɪ] *vt* μεγεθύνω, υπερβάλλω || ~ing glass *n* μεγεθυντικός φακός.

magnitude ['mægnɪtjuːd] *n* μέγεθος *nt*, σπουδαιότητα.

magnolia [mæg'nəʊlɪə] *n* μανόλια.

magpie ['mægpaɪ] *n* καρακάξα.

mahogany [mə'hɒgənɪ] *n* μαόνι.

maid [meɪd] *n (servant)* υπηρέτρια.

maiden ['meɪdən] *n* κορίτσι, παρθένος *f* ♦ *a (lady)* άγαμος || ~ name *n* οικογενειακό όνομα || ~ speech *n* παρθενικός λόγος || ~ voyage *n* παρθενικό ταξίδι.

mail [meɪl] *n* επιστολές *fpl*, ταχυδρομείο || *(system)* ταχυδρομείο ♦ *vt (US)* ταχυδρομώ || ~box *n* γραμματοκιβώτιο || ~-order *n* ταχυδρομική εντολή.

maim [meɪm] *vt* ακρωτηριάζω, σακατεύω.

main [meɪn] *a* κύριος, πρωτεύων ♦ *n (pipe)* κεντρικός αγωγός || in the ~ γενικά, ως επί το πλείστο || ~frame (computer) *n* Η/Υ μεγάλου μεγέθους || ~land *n* στερεά, ηπειρωτική χώρα || ~road *n* κεντρική οδός *f* || ~stay *n (fig)* κύριο έρεισμα *nt*, στήριγμα *nt*.

maintain [meɪn'teɪn] *vt (machine)* διατηρώ, συντηρώ || *(support)* συντηρώ, τρέφω || *(traditions)* συντηρώ, συνεχίζω || *(an opinion)* υποστηρίζω.

maintenance ['meɪntɪnəns] *n (TECH)* συντήρηση.

maisonette [meɪzə'net] *n* διαμέρισμα *nt*, μονοκατοικία.

maize [meɪz] *n* αραποσίτι, καλαμπόκι.

majestic [mə'dʒestɪk] *a* μεγαλοπρεπής.

majesty ['mædʒɪstɪ] *n* μεγαλείο || His/Her M~ *n* Αυτού/Αυτή Μεγαλειότης.

M

major ['meɪdʒə*] n (MIL) ταγματάρχης ♦ a (MUS) μείζων.

majority [mə'dʒɒrɪtɪ] n πλειοψηφία || (number) πλειονότητα.

make [meɪk] (irreg v) vt (build, shape, produce) κάνω, φτιάχνω, δημιουργώ || (appoint) κάνω, ορίζω || (cause to do) αναγκάζω, κάνω, υποχρεώνω || (reach) φθάνω || (earn) κάνω, αποκτώ, κερδίζω, βγάζω || (do, perform) κάνω || (amount to) κάνω || (prepare) φτιάχνω ♦ n (style) κατασκευή, τύπος || (kind) μάρκα || **to ~ for** vt (place) κατευθύνομαι, πηγαίνω || **to ~ out** vi επιτυγχάνω, καταφέρνω ♦ vt (write out) συντάσσω, βγάζω, ετοιμάζω || (understand) καταλήγω, καταλαβαίνω || (pretend) προσποιούμαι, παριστάνω || **to ~ up** vt (make) συντάσσω, φτιάχνω, πλάθω || (face) βάφομαι, μακιγιάρομαι, φτιάχνομαι || (settle) ρυθμίζω, συμφιλιώνω, διευθετώ || **to ~ up for** vt ανακτώ, αναπληρώνω || **~-believe** n προσποίηση, υπόκριση ♦ a προσποιητός, ψεύτικος || **~r** n κατασκευαστής/άστρια m/f, δημιουργός m/f|| **~shift** a προσωρινή λύση || **~-up** n (cosmetics) μακιγιάζ nt inv || σύσταση || (THEAT) μακιγιάζ nt inv, βάψιμο.

making ['meɪkɪŋ] n: **in the ~** εν εξελίξει.

malaise [mæ'leɪz] n αδιαθεσία.

malaria [mə'lɛərɪə] n ελονοσία.

Malaysia [mə'leɪzɪə] n Μαλαισία.

male [meɪl] n άνδρας ♦ a αρσενικός.

malevolent [mə'levələnt] a κακόβουλος.

malfunction [mæl'fʌŋkʃən] vi λειτουργώ ελαττωματικά.

malice ['mælɪs] n κακεντρέχεια, έχθρα.

malicious [mə'lɪʃəs] a κακόβουλος, μοχθηρός.

malign [mə'laɪn] vt δυσφημίζω, κακολογώ.

malignant [mə'lɪgnənt] a (tumour) κακοήθης.

malleable ['mælɪəbl] a ελάσιμος, μαλακός.

mallet ['mælɪt] n ξύλινο σφυρί, κόπανος.

malnutrition [mælnju'trɪʃən] n υποσιτισμός.

malpractice [mæl'præktɪs] n αδίκημα nt, κατάχρηση.

malt [mɔːlt] n βύνη.

Malta ['mɔːltə] n Μάλτα.

maltreat [mæl'triːt] vt κακομεταχειρίζομαι.

mammal ['mæməl] n θηλαστικό, μαστοφόρο.

mammoth ['mæməθ] n γιγαντιαίος, πελώριος.

man [mæn] n άνθρωπος || (male) άνδρας || (race) ανθρωπότητα ♦ vt επανδρώνω.

manage ['mænɪdʒ] vi (succeed) καταφέρνω ♦ vt χειρίζομαι, διευθύνω, διοικώ || **~able** a ευχείριστος || (person) εύκολος || **~ment** n χειρισμός,

διαχείριση || (directors) διεύθυνση, διοίκηση || **~r** n διευθυντής || **~ress** n διευθύντρια || **~rial** a διευθυντικός, τεχνοκρατικός.

managing ['mænɪdʒɪŋ] a: **~ director** n γενικός διευθυντής.

mandarin ['mændərɪn] n (orange) μανταρίνι || (man) μανδαρίνος.

mandate ['mændeɪt] n (instruction) εντολή || (commission) εντολή.

mandatory ['mændətərɪ] a υποχρεωτικός.

mandolin(e) ['mændəlɪn] n μαντολίνο.

mane [meɪn] n χαίτη.

maneuver [mə'nuːvə*] (US) = **manoeuvre**.

manfully ['mænfəlɪ] ad παλληκαρίσια.

mangle ['mæŋgl] vt κατακρεουργώ, κατακόβω.

mango ['mæŋgəʊ] n μάγγο.

manhandle ['mænhændl] vt ξυλοφορτώνω, κακομεταχειρίζομαι.

manhole ['mænhəʊl] n ανθρωποθυρίδα, είσοδος f υπονόμου.

manhood ['mænhʊd] n ανδρικότητα, ανδρική ηλικία.

man-hour ['mæn'aʊə*] n ώρα εργασίας.

manhunt ['mænhʌnt] n ανθρωποκυνήγι.

mania ['meɪnɪə] n (craze) μανία, πάθος nt || (madness) τρέλα || **~c** n μανιακός.

manicure ['mænɪkjʊə*] n μανικιούρ nt inv ♦ vt φτιάχνω τα νύχια || **~ set** n κασετίνα του μανικιούρ.

manifest ['mænɪfest] vt επιδεικνύω, εκδηλώνω ♦ a έκδηλος, προφανής || **~ation** n εκδήλωση.

manifesto [mænɪ'festəʊ] n διακήρυξη, μανιφέστο.

manipulate [mə'nɪpjʊleɪt] vt χειρίζομαι, μανουβράρω.

mankind [mæn'kaɪnd] n ανθρωπότητα.

manly ['mænlɪ] a ανδρικός, ανδροπρεπής, αντρίκιος.

manner ['mænə*] n τρόπος || (custom) συμπεριφορά, είδος nt || **~s** npl συμπεριφορά, τρόποι mpl || **~ism** n (of person) ιδιορρυθμία, ιδιοτροπία.

manoeuvre [mə'nuːvə*] vti ελίσσομαι, μανουβράρω ♦ n (MIL) ελιγμός, άσκηση.

manor ['mænə*] n τιμάριο, κτήμα nt || **~ house** n αρχοντικό σπίτι.

manpower ['mænpaʊə*] n το εργατικό δυναμικό.

manservant ['mænsɜːvənt] n υπηρέτης, καμαριέρης.

mansion ['mænʃən] n μέγαρο.

manslaughter ['mænslɔːtə*] n ανθρωποκτονία.

mantelpiece ['mæntlpiːs] n γείσωμα nt τζακιού.

mantle ['mæntl] n μανδύας.

manual ['mænjʊəl] a χειρωνακτικός ♦ n εγχειρίδιο.

manufacture [mænju'fæktʃə*] vt κατασκευάζω, βιομηχανοποιώ ♦ n κατασκευή, βιομηχανία || ~r n βιομήχανος.

manure [mə'njuə*] n κοπριά, λίπασμα nt.

manuscript ['mænjuskrɪpt] n χειρόγραφο.

many ['menɪ] a πολλοί, αρκετοί ♦ n αρκετοί, πολλοί, όσοι.

map [mæp] n χάρτης ♦ vt χαρτογραφώ || to ~ out vt χαράσσω, καθορίζω, κανονίζω.

maple ['meɪpl] n σφεντάμι.

mar [maː*] vt βλάπτω, χαλώ, παραμορφώνω.

marathon ['mærəθən] n μαραθώνιος.

marauder [mə'rɔːdə*] n λεηλάτης, ληστής.

marble ['maːbl] n μάρμαρο || ~s n (game) βώλος, μπίλια.

March [maːtʃ] n Μάρτιος, Μάρτης.

march [maːtʃ] vi βαδίζω, βηματίζω, οδηγώ ♦ n (tune) εμβατήριο || (walk) πορεία, βάδισμα nt || ~-past n παρέλαση.

mare [mɛə*] n φοράδα.

margarine [maːdʒə'riːn] n μαργαρίνη.

margin ['maːdʒɪn] n (page) περιθώριο || (extra amount) περιθώριο || ~al a περιθωριακός.

marigold ['mærɪɡəuld] n κατιφές m.

marijuana [mærɪ'waːnə] n μαριχουάνα.

marina [mə'riːnə] n (for boats) μαρίνα.

marine [mə'riːn] a θαλάσσιος, ναυτικός || (MIL) πεζοναυτικός ♦ n (MIL) πεζοναύτης.

marital ['mærɪtl] a συζυγικός.

maritime ['mærɪtaɪm] a θαλασσινός, ναυτικός.

marjoram ['maːdʒərəm] n μαντζουράνα.

mark [maːk] n (coin) μάρκα || (scar etc) σημάδι, ίχνος, στίγμα nt || (sign) σημείο, ένδειξη || (target) στόχος, σημάδι || (grade) βαθμός ♦ vt (make a mark) μαρκάρω, σημαδεύω || (indicate) δεικνύω, εκδηλώνω, δείχνω || (watch etc) προσέχω, κοιτάζω || (exam) διορθώνω, βαθμολογώ || to ~ time κάνω βήμα σημειωτό || (make no progress) δεν προχωράω || to ~ out vt σημαδεύω || ~ed a έντονος, σαφής, φανερός, εμφανής || ~er n (sign) δείκτης.

market ['maːkɪt] n αγορά || (overseas) αγορά || (demand) ζήτηση ♦ vt (COMM: new product) πουλώ || (project) προβάλλω || ~ day n ημέρα αγοράς || ~ garden n (Brit) περιβόλι κηπουρικών || ~ing n αγορά, πώληση || ~ place n αγορά, παζάρι.

marksman ['maːksmən] n σκοπευτής || ~ship n σκοπευτική ικανότητα.

marmalade ['maːməleɪd] n μαρμελάδα.

maroon [mə'ruːn] vt (usually passive) εγκαταλείπω σε έρημη ακτή ♦ a (colour) ερυθρόφαιος.

marquee [maː'kiː] n μεγάλη τέντα.

marquess, marquis ['maːkwɪs] n μαρκήσιος.

marriage ['mærɪdʒ] n (institution) παντρειά || (wedding) γάμος.

married ['mærɪd] a (person, life) έγγαμος.

marrow ['mærəu] n μυελός, μεδούλι || (vegetable) κολοκύθι.

marry ['mærɪ] vt νυμφεύω, παντρεύω ♦ vi (also: get married) νυμφεύομαι, παντρεύομαι.

Mars [maːz] n Άρης.

marsh [maːʃ] n έλος nt, βάλτος.

marshal ['maːʃəl] n (US) σερίφης ♦ vt παρατάσσω, συγκεντρώνω || see field.

marshy ['maːʃɪ] a ελώδης.

martial ['maːʃəl] a πολεμικός, στρατιωτικός || ~ law n στρατιωτικός νόμος.

martyr ['maːtə*] n μάρτυρας || (fig) βασανιζόμενος || ~dom n μαρτύριο.

marvel ['maːvəl] n θαύμα nt ♦ vi (+ at) εκπλήσσομαι, θαυμάζω || ~lous, (US) ~ous a θαυμάσιος, καταπληκτικός.

Marxism ['maːksɪzəm] n μαρξισμός.

Marxist ['maːksɪst] n μαρξιστής.

mascara [mæs'kaːrə] n μάσκαρα.

mascot ['mæskət] n μασκότ nt inv.

masculine ['mæskjulɪn] a αρσενικός || (manly) ανδροπρεπής, ρωμαλέος || (GRAM) αρσενικός ♦ n το αρσενικό.

masculinity [mæskjʊ'lɪnɪtɪ] n αρρενότητα, ανδρικό ύφος.

mashed [mæʃt] a: ~ potatoes npl πατάτες fpl πουρέ.

mask [maːsk] n προσωπίδα, μάσκα || (pretence) προσωπείο ♦ vt καλύπτω, αποκρύπτω.

masochist ['mæsəukɪst] n μαζοχιστής.

mason ['meɪsn] n (stonemason) κτίστης || (freemason) τέκτονας || ~ic [mə'sɒnɪk] a τεκτονικός, μασονικός || ~ry ['meɪsnrɪ] n λιθοδομή, χτίσιμο.

masquerade [mæskə'reɪd] n μεταμφίεση ♦ vi μεταμφιέζομαι.

mass [mæs] n (PHYS) μάζα || (information, people) όγκος, μάζα, πλήθος nt || (majority) το μεγαλύτερο μέρος, η πλειοψηφία || (REL) λειτουργία ♦ vt συγκεντρώνω, αθροίζω, μαζεύω ♦ vi συγκεντρώνομαι, μαζεύομαι.

massacre ['mæsəkə*] n σφαγή, μακελειό ♦ vt σφάζω.

massage ['mæsaːʒ] n μάλαξη, μασσάζ nt inv ♦ vt μαλάσσω, κάνω μασσάζ.

masseur [mæ'sɜː*] n μασσέρ m inv.

masseuse [mæ'sɜːz] n μασέζ f inv.

massive ['mæsɪv] a ογκώδης, δυνατός.

mass media ['mæs'miːdɪə] npl μέσα ntpl μαζικής επικοινωνίας.

mass production ['mæsprə'dʌkʃən] n μαζική παραγωγή.

mast [maːst] n ιστός, κατάρτι || (pole) στήλη, στύλος.

master ['maːstə*] n κύριος, αφεντικό || (teacher) δάσκαλος, καθηγητής || (head) αρχηγός || (of ship) καπετάνιος || (artist) μεγάλος καλλιτέχνης ♦ vt εξουσιάζω, ελέγχω || (learn) μαθαίνω τέλεια || ~ly a έντεχνος, αριστοτεχνικός || ~ **mind** n εγκέφαλος ♦ vt συλλαμβάνω, πραγματοποιώ || **M~ of Arts (M.A.)** n ανώτερος πτυχιούχος θετικών επιστημών || ~ **piece** n αριστούργημα nt || ~ **stroke** n αριστοτεχνικό κτύπημα nt || ~ **y** n εξουσία, υπεροχή, μαεστρία.

masturbate ['mæstəbeɪt] vi μαλακίζομαι.

masturbation [mæstə'beɪʃən] n μαλακία.

mat [mæt] n ψάθα, χαλάκι || (material for table) στρωσίδι τραπεζιού || (tangled mass) μπλεγμένα νήματα ntpl κτλ ♦ vti μπλέκω, μπερδεύω.

match [mætʃ] n (matchstick) σπίρτο || (game) αγώνας || (equal) ταίρι || (marriage) συνοικέσιο ♦ vt (be like) εναρμονίζω, ταιριάζω || (equal strength etc) εξισούμαι με, φθάνω ♦ vi συμβιβάζομαι, συμφωνώ, ταιριάζω || ~ **box** n κουτί σπίρτα || ~ **ing** a προσαρμογή || ~ **less** a απαράμιλλος.

mate [meɪt] n σύντροφος, συνάδελφος || (husband, wife) σύζυγος, ταίρι || (NAUT) υποπλοίαρχος ♦ vi (chess) κάνω μάτ || (of animal) ζευγαρώνομαι.

material [mə'tɪərɪəl] n ύλη, υλικό ♦ a σημαντικός, ουσιώδης || (of matter) υλικός || (opposite of spirit) υλικός || ~ **s** npl υλικά ntpl, εφόδια ntpl || ~ **istic** a υλιστικός || ~ **ize** vi πραγματοποιούμαι, γίνομαι.

maternal [mə'tɜ:nl] a μητρικός || (relatives) από τη μητέρα.

maternity [mə'tɜ:nɪtɪ] n μητρότητα || ~ **dress** φόρεμα nt εγγύου || ~ **hospital** μαιευτήριο.

mathematical [mæθə'mætɪkəl] a μαθηματικός.

mathematician [mæθəmə'tɪʃən] n μαθηματικός m/f.

mathematics [mæθə'mætɪks] n, **maths** [mæθs] a μαθηματικά ntpl.

matinée ['mætɪneɪ] n παράσταση (απογευματινή).

mating ['meɪtɪŋ] n ζευγάρωμα nt, βάτεμα nt.

matriarchal [meɪtrɪ'ɑ:kl] a μητριαρχικός.

matrimonial [mætrɪ'məʊnɪəl] a γαμήλιος, συζυγικός.

matrimony ['mætrɪmənɪ] n γάμος, έγγαμη ζωή.

matron ['meɪtrən] n (MED) προϊσταμένη || (SCH) επιμελήτρια, οικονόμος f || ~ **ly** a σεβάσμιος, ατάραχος.

matt [mæt] a (paint) μουντός, μάτ.

matter ['mætə*] n ουσία, ύλη || (affair) υπόθεση, θέμα nt, πράγμα nt || (question, issue etc) ζήτημα nt || (discharge) πύο, έμπυο ♦ vi έχω σημασία, ενδιαφέρω || **what is the ~?** τι συμβαίνει; || **as a ~ of fact** στην πραγματικότητα || ~ **- of-fact** a πεζός, πρακτικός.

mattress ['mætrɪs] n στρώμα nt.

mature [mə'tjʊə*] a ώριμος ♦ vi ωριμάζω.

maturity [mə'tjʊərɪtɪ] n ωριμότητα.

maul [mɔ:l] vt κακοποιώ, κοπανίζω.

mauve [məʊv] a (colour) μώβ.

max. abbr of **maximum.**

maxim ['mæksɪm] n απόφθεγμα nt, γνωμικό.

maximum ['mæksɪməm] a ανώτατος, μεγαλύτερος ♦ n ανώτατο όριο, μάξιμουμ nt inv.

May [meɪ] n Μάιος.

may [meɪ] (irreg v) vi (be possible) ίσως να || (have permission) έχω την άδεια να, μπορώ να.

maybe ['meɪbi:] ad ίσως, πιθανώς.

May Day ['meɪdeɪ] n Πρωτομαγιά.

mayonnaise [meɪə'neɪz] n μαγιονέζα.

mayor [mɛə*] n δήμαρχος || ~ **ess** n (wife) κυρία δημάρχου || (lady mayor) n δήμαρχος.

maze [meɪz] n (network) λαβύρινθος, κυκεώνας.

me [mi:] pron (after prep) με, εμένα.

meadow ['medəʊ] n λειβάδι.

meagre, meager (US) ['mi:gə*] a ισχνός, πενιχρός.

meal [mi:l] n φαγητό || (grain) χοντράλευρο || ~ **time** n ώρα φαγητού.

mean [mi:n] (irreg v) a άθλιος, φτωχός, ταπεινός || (stingy) φιλάργυρος, τσιγκούνης || (average) μέσος, μεσαίος ♦ vt (signify) εννοώ, σημαίνω, θέλω να πω || (intend) προτίθεμαι, σκοπεύω || (be resolved) προορίζω ♦ n (average) μέσος όρος, μέσο || ~ **s** npl μέσα ntpl, τρόποι mpl || (wealth) πόροι mpl, μέσα ntpl, περιουσία || **by ~ s of** με τη βοήθεια του/της || **by all ~s** οπωσδήποτε.

meander [mɪ'ændə*] vi ελίσσομαι, σχηματίζω μαιάνδρους.

meaning ['mi:nɪŋ] n (intention) λόγος, σκοπός || (sense of word) έννοια, σημασία, νόημα nt || ~ **ful** a με σημασία, που λέει πολλά || ~ **less** a χωρίς νόημα.

meanness ['mi:nnɪs] n μικρότητα, μικροπρέπεια.

meant [ment] pt, pp of **mean.**

meantime ['mi:ntaɪm] ad, **meanwhile** ['mi:nwaɪl] ad εν τω μεταξύ, στο μεταξύ.

measles ['mi:zlz] n ιλαρά || **German ~** n ερυθρά.

measly ['mi:zli] a (col) ασήμαντος, ανάξιος, τιποτένιος.

measure ['mɛʒə*] vt (find size) μετρώ || (test) δοκιμάζω, αναμετρώμαι ♦ vi (be certain size) είναι, έχει διαστάσεις ♦ n (unit) μέτρο || (tape measure) μεζούρα, μέτρο || (plan) μέτρο, ενέργεια, πράξη || (a law) μέτρο || ~ **d** a μετρημένος || ~ **ment** n (way of measuring) μέτρηση, μέτρημα nt || (amount measured) μέτρα ntpl, διαστάσεις fpl.

meat [mi:t] n (flesh) κρέας nt || ~ **pie** n κρεατόπιτα || ~ **y** a (lit) σαρκώδης || (fig) ουσιαστικός, δεμένος, ζουμερός.

mechanic [mɪ'kænɪk] n τεχνίτης, μηχανικός || ~ **s** n μηχανική || ~ **al** a μηχανικός || (automatically) μηχανικός, αυτόματος.

mechanism ['mɛkənɪzəm] n μηχανισμός.

mechanization [mɛkənaɪ'zeɪʃən] n μηχανοποίηση.

medal ['mɛdl] n μετάλλιο || ~**lion** [mɪ'dæliən] n μενταγιό || ~**list**, ~**ist** (US) n κάτοχος μετάλλιου.

meddle ['mɛdl] vi (+ with) ανακατεύομαι, επεμβαίνω.

media ['mi:dɪə] npl (of communication) μέσα ntpl.

mediate ['mi:dɪeɪt] vi μεσολαβώ.

mediation [mi:dɪ'eɪʃən] n μεσολάβηση.

mediator ['mi:dɪeɪtə*] n μεσολαβητής.

medical ['mɛdɪkəl] a (science) ιατρικός || (student) (φοιτητής) ιατρικής.

medicated ['mɛdɪkeɪtɪd] a εμποτισμένος με φάρμακο.

medicinal [mɛ'dɪsɪnl] a φαρμακευτικός, ιατρικός, θεραπευτικός.

medicine ['mɛdsɪn] n ιατρική || (drugs) φάρμακο, γιατρικό || ~ **chest** n φαρμακείο.

medieval [mɛdɪ'i:vəl] a μεσαιωνικός.

mediocre [mi:dɪ'əʊkə*] a μέτριος, της αράδας.

mediocrity [mi:dɪ'ɒkrɪtɪ] n μετριότητα.

meditate ['mɛdɪteɪt] vi (+ on) μελετώ, σκέπτομαι, συλλογίζομαι.

meditation [mɛdɪ'teɪʃən] n συλλογισμός, διαλογισμός.

Mediterranean (Sea) [mɛdɪtə'reɪnɪən(si:)] n Μεσόγειος (θάλασσα).

medium ['mi:dɪəm] a μεσαίος, μέτριος ♦ n μέσο, μέσος όρος || (means) μέσο, όργανο.

medley ['mɛdlɪ] n σύμφυρμα nt, κυκεώνας, μίγμα nt.

meek [mi:k] a πράος, ήρεμος, πειθήνιος.

meet [mi:t] vt συναντώ, απαντώ, ανταμώνω || (come across) βρίσκω, απαντώ, διασταυρώνομαι || (go towards) προχωρώ, πηγαίνω || (pay, satisfy) εκπληρώνω, ανταποκρίνομαι, τιμώ ♦ vi (by arrangement) συναντώμαι, βλέπομαι || (fight) αντιμετωπίζω || (join) συναντώμαι, συναθροίζομαι, συνέρχομαι || **to ~ with** vt (problems) συναντώ, αντιμετωπίζω || (US: people) συναντώ, γνωρίζω || ~**ing** n συνάντηση, συνάθροιση, συνέλευση || ~ **ing place** n τόπος συναντήσεως.

megaphone ['mɛgəfəʊn] n μεγάφωνο.

melancholy ['mɛlənkəlɪ] n μελαγχολία, κατήφεια ♦ a μελαγχολικός.

mellow ['mɛləʊ] a ώριμος || (delicate) απαλός, γλυκός || (aged) απαλός ♦ vi ωριμάζω, απαλύνομαι.

melodious [mɪ'ləʊdɪəs] a μελωδικός.

melodrama ['mɛləʊdrɑ:mə] n μελόδραμα nt.

melody ['mɛlədɪ] n μελωδία.

melon ['mɛlən] n πεπόνι.

melt [mɛlt] vi τήκομαι, λυώνω || (disappear) χάνομαι, διαλύομαι ♦ vt τήκω, λυώνω || **to ~ away** vi λυώνω, διαλύομαι || **to ~ down** vt λυώνω, τήκω || ~**ing point** n σημείο τήξεως || ~**ing pot** n (fig) χωνευτήριο, ρευστή κατάσταση.

member ['mɛmbə*] n μέλος nt || M~ **of Parliament (M.P.)** n βουλευτής/ίνα m/f || ~**ship** n μέλη ntpl, αριθμός μελών.

membrane ['mɛmbreɪn] n μεμβράνη.

memento [mə'mɛntəʊ] n ενθύμιο, ενθύμηση.

memo ['mɛməʊ] n (COMM) υπόμνημα nt, σημείωση.

memoirs ['mɛmwɑ:z] npl απομνημονεύματα ntpl.

memorable ['mɛmərəbl] a αξιουνημόνευτος, αξέχαστος.

memorandum [mɛmə'rændəm] n (COMM) υπόμνημα nt, σημείωση.

memorial [mɪ'mɔ:rɪəl] n μνημείο ♦ a αναμνηστικός, επιμνημόσυνος.

memorize ['mɛməraɪz] vt αποστηθίζω, μαθαίνω απ' έξω.

memory ['mɛmərɪ] n μνήμη, μνημονικό, θυμητικό || (thing recalled) ανάμνηση, θύμηση || (COMPUT) μνήμη || **in ~ of** εις μνήμην του, εις ανάμνησιν του.

men [mɛn] npl of **man**.

menace ['mɛnɪs] n απειλή, φοβέρα ♦ vt απειλώ, φοβερίζω.

menacing ['mɛnɪsɪŋ] a απειλητικός.

menagerie [mɪ'nædʒərɪ] n θηριοτροφείο.

mend [mɛnd] vt (επι)διορθώνω, βελτιώνω ♦ vi αναρρώνω ♦ n επιδιόρθωση, επισκευή || **to be on the ~** συνέρχομαι, πάω καλύτερα.

menial ['mi:nɪəl] a ταπεινός, δουλοπρεπής.

meningitis [mɛnɪn'dʒaɪtɪs] n μηνιγγίτιδα.

menopause ['mɛnəʊpɔ:z] n εμμηνόπαυση.

menstruation [mɛnstrʊ'eɪʃən] n εμμηνόρροια, περίοδος f.

mental ['mɛntl] a διανοητικός, νοερός, πνευματικός || (col: abnormal) τρελός || ~**ity** n νοοτροπία.

mention ['mɛnʃən] n μνεία ♦ vt αναφέρω || **don't ~ it!** παρακαλώ!

menu ['mɛnju:] n (also COMPUT) μενού nt inv.

mercantile ['mɜ:kəntaɪl] a εμπορικός.

mercenary ['mɜ:sɪnərɪ] a φιλοχρήματος, πλεονέκτης ♦ n μισθοφόρος.

merchandise ['mɜ:tʃəndaɪz] n εμπορεύματα ntpl.

merchant ['mɜ:tʃənt] n έμπορος ♦ a εμπορικός || ~ **navy** n εμπορικό ναυτικό.

merciful ['mɜ:sɪful] a εύσπλαχνος.

merciless ['mɜ:sɪlɪs] a ανελέητος, άσπλαχνος.

mercury ['mɜ:kjʊrɪ] n υδράργυρος.

mercy ['mɜːsɪ] n ευσπλαχνία, έλεος nt|| (blessing) ευλογία || at the ~ of στο έλεος τού.
mere [mɪə*] a απλός, τίποτε άλλο από || ~ly ad απλώς, μόνο.
merge [mɜːdʒ] vt απορροφώ, συγχωνεύω || (COMPUT) αναμιγνύω ♦ vi (become absorbed) απορροφούμαι, συγχωνεύομαι || ~r n (COMM) συγχώνευση.
meridian [mə'rɪdɪən] n μεσημβρινός.
meringue [mə'ræŋ] n μαρέγγα.
merit ['merɪt] n αξία, προσόν ♦ vt αξίζω.
mermaid ['mɜːmeɪd] n γοργόνα.
merriment ['merɪmənt] n ευθυμία, διασκέδαση.
merry ['merɪ] a εύθυμος, φαιδρός, χαρωπός || (col: after drink) στο κέφι, πιωμένος.
mesh [meʃ] n θηλειά (δικτύου) ♦ vti (gears) εμπλέκω, εμπλέκομαι.
mesmerize ['mezməraɪz] vt μαγνητίζω, υπνωτίζω.
mess [mes] n σαλάτα, θάλασσα || (untidy state) ακαθαρσία, άνω-κάτω || (MIL) συσσίτιο, τραπέζι || (officers' mess) λέσχη αξιωματικών || to ~ about vi χασομερώ || to ~ about with vt πασπατεύω, σαχλαμαρίζω || to ~ up vt χαλώ, μπλέκω, περιπλέκω.
message ['mesɪdʒ] n μήνυμα nt, διάγγελμα nt, είδηση.
messenger ['mesɪndʒə*] n αγγελιαφόρος.
messy ['mesɪ] a ακάθαρτος, ακατάστατος.
met [met] pt, pp of meet.
metabolism [me'tæbəlɪzəm] n μεταβολισμός.
metal ['metl] n μέταλλο || ~lic a μεταλλικός || ~lurgy n μεταλλουργία.
metaphor ['metəfɔː*] n μεταφορά.
metaphysics [metə'fɪzɪks] n μεταφυσική.
meteor ['miːtɪə*] n μετέωρο || ~ic a μετεωρικός, λαμπρός || ~ological a μετεωρολογικός || ~ology n μετεωρολογία.
meter ['miːtə*] n (instrument) μετρητής || (US) = metre.
method ['meθəd] n μέθοδος f|| ~ical a μεθοδικός.
Methodist ['meθədɪst] a, n Μεθοδιστής.
methylated spirits ['meθɪleɪtɪd'spɪrɪts] n (also: meths) μεθυλικό οινόπνευμα nt.
meticulous [mɪ'tɪkjuləs] a λεπτολόγος, σχολαστικός.
metre ['miːtə*] n μέτρο.
metric ['metrɪk] a μετρικός.
metronome ['metrənəum] n μετρονόμος.
metropolis [mɪ'trɒpəlɪs] n μητρόπολη.
mews [mjuːz] n αδιέξοδο.
Mexican ['meksɪkən] a μεξικανικός ♦ n Μεξικανός/ίδα m/f.
Mexico ['meksɪkəu] n Μεξικό.

mezzanine ['mezəniːn] n ημιόροφος, μέτζο.
miaow [miːˈau] vi νιαουρίζω.
mice [maɪs] npl of mouse.
microbe ['maɪkrəub] n μικρόβιο.
microcomputer ['maɪkrəukəm'pjuːtə*] n μικροϋπολογιστής.
microfilm ['maɪkrəufɪlm] n μικροφίλμ nt inv.
microphone ['maɪkrəfəun] n μικρόφωνο.
microscope ['maɪkrəskəup] n μικροσκόπιο.
microscopic [maɪkrə'skɒpɪk] a μικροσκοπικός.
mid [mɪd] a μέσος, μεσαίος || in ~ course στο μέσο, στην ακμή.
midday ['mɪd'deɪ] n μεσημέρι.
middle ['mɪdl] n μέσο ♦ a μέσος, μεσαίος || ~-aged a μεσήλικας || the M~ Ages npl o Μεσαίωνας || ~ class n μεσαία τάξη, αστική τάξη || ~-class a αστικός || M~ East n Μέση Ανατολή || ~man n μεταπωλητής, μεσίτης || ~name n όνομα nt πατρός.
midge [mɪdʒ] n σκνίπα.
midget ['mɪdʒɪt] n νάνος, ανθρωπάκι ♦ a μικρός, μικροσκοπικός.
midnight ['mɪdnaɪt] n μεσάνυχτα ntpl.
midst [mɪdst] n: in the ~ of στο μέσο.
midsummer ['mɪd'sʌmə*] n μεσοκαλόκαιρο.
midway ['mɪd'weɪ] ad (+between) στο μέσο ♦ a μέσος.
midweek ['mɪd'wiːk] ad στα μέσα της εβδομάδος.
midwife ['mɪdwaɪf] n μαία, μαμμή || ~ry ['mɪdwɪfərɪ] n μαιευτική.
midwinter ['mɪd'wɪntə*] n στο μέσο του χειμώνα, μεσοχείμωνο.
might [maɪt] pt of may || n ισχύς, δύναμη || ~y a ισχυρός, δυνατός ♦ ad (col) πολύ, τρομερά.
migraine ['miːgreɪn] n ημικρανία.
migrant ['maɪgrənt] n μεταναστευτικός, περαστικός ♦ a αποδημητικός, μεταναστευτικός.
migrate [maɪ'greɪt] vi (birds) αποδημώ.
migration [maɪ'greɪʃən] n μετανάστευση.
mike [maɪk] n (microphone) μικρόφωνο.
mild [maɪld] a (rebuke) επιεικής, μαλακός || (warm) ήπιος, εύκρατος || (taste) ελαφρός || (slight) ελαφρός ♦ n (beer) ελαφριά μπύρα.
mildew ['mɪldjuː] n μούχλα, σείρηκας.
mildness ['maɪldnɪs] n ηπιότητα, γλύκα, επιείκεια.
mile [maɪl] n μίλι (1609 μ) || ~age n απόσταση σε μίλια || ~stone n μιλιοδείκτης || (fig) ιστορικός σταθμός.
militant ['mɪlɪtənt] n οπαδός της αμέσου δράσεως ♦ a μαχητικός.
military ['mɪlɪtərɪ] a στρατιωτικός ♦ n οι στρατιωτικοί mpl, στρατός.

militate ['mɪlɪteɪt] vi (+ against)
αντιστρατεύομαι, αντιμάχομαι.
militia [mɪ'lɪʃə] n εθνοφυλακή.
milk [mɪlk] n γάλα nt ♦ vt (cow) αρμέγω ||
(fig) εκμεταλλεύομαι, μαδώ || ~ **man** n
γαλατάς || **M~y Way** n Γαλαξίας.
mill [mɪl] n μύλος || (building) μύλος ||
(factory) εργοστάσιο ♦ vt (grind) αλέθω ♦
vi (move around) στριφογυρίζω.
millenium [mɪ'lenɪəm] n χιλιετηρίδα.
miller ['mɪlə*] n μυλωνάς.
millet ['mɪlɪt] n κεχρί, σόργο.
milligram(me) ['mɪlɪgræm] n
χιλιοστόγραμμο.
millilitre, milliliter (US) ['mɪlɪliːtə*] n
χιλιοστόλιτρο.
millimetre, millimeter (US)
['mɪlɪmiːtə*] n χιλιοστόμετρο.
milliner ['mɪlɪnə*] n καπελού f || ~**y** n
γυναικεία καπέλλα ntpl.
million ['mɪljən] n εκατομμύριο || ~**aire**
n εκατομμυριούχος.
mime [maɪm] n μίμος, μιμόδραμα nt ♦
vti μιμούμαι, παίζω με μιμική.
mimic ['mɪmɪk] n μίμος, μιμητής/ήτρια
m/f ♦ vti μιμούμαι, κοροϊδεύω,
αντιγράφω || ~**ry** n μίμηση, μιμική.
min. abbr of **minute(s), minimum.**
mince [mɪns] vt ψιλοκόβω, κάνω κιμά ||
(words) μασώ ♦ vi βαδίζω με προσποιητή
χάρη ♦ n (meat) κιμάς || ~**meat** n μείγμα
nt με φρούτα και σταφίδες || ~ **pie** n
πίτα σε φρούτα και σταφίδες,
κρεατόπιτα || ~**r** n κρεατομηχανή.
mind [maɪnd] n νούς m, μυαλό ||
(intelligence) σκέψη, γνώμη, ιδέα ||
(memory) μνήμη, ανάμνηση, θύμηση ♦
vti φροντίζω, προσέχω || (be careful)
προσέχω || (object to) έχω αντίρρηση,
ενοχλούμαι, πειράζομαι || **on my** ~ στη
σκέψη μου, ανησυχώ || **to my** ~ κατά τη
γνώμη μου || **out of one's** ~ τρελός ||
never ~! δεν πειράζει, άστο, μην
ανησυχείς || **to bear** or **keep in** ~ δεν
ξεχνώ, λαμβάνω υπόψη || **to make up**
one's ~ αποφασίζω || '~ **the step**'
'πρόσεκε το σκαλοπάτι' || ~**ful** a
προσεκτικός || ~**less** a απερίσκεπτος,
αδιάφορος, άμυαλος.
mine [maɪn] poss pron δικός μου, δική
μου, δικό μου ♦ n ορυχείο, μεταλλείο ||
(NAUT) νάρκη || (source) πηγή ♦ vt
εξορύσσω || (NAUT) ναρκοθετώ ♦ vi
εκμεταλλεύομαι || ~**field** n ναρκοπέδιο
|| ~**r** n μεταλλωρύχος, ανθρακωρύχος.
mineral ['mɪnərəl] a ορυκτός,
μεταλλευτικός ♦ n ορυκτό, μετάλλευμα
nt || ~ **water** n επιτραπέζιο νερό,
μεταλλικό νερό.
minesweeper ['maɪnswiːpə*] n
ναρκαλιευτικό.
mingle ['mɪŋgl] vt αναμιγνύω ♦ vi (+
with) αναμιγνύομαι.
mingy ['mɪndʒɪ] a (col) στριμμένος,
γύφτος, μίζερος.
miniature ['mɪnɪtʃə*] a μικρογραφικός

♦ n μικρογραφία, μινιατούρα || (model)
μακέτα || **in** ~ μικρού σχήματος.
minibus ['mɪnɪbʌs] n μικρό λεωφορείο.
minicab ['mɪnɪkæb] n μικρό ταξί.
minicomputer ['mɪnɪkəm'pjuːtə*] n
μικρο-υπολογιστής.
minimal ['mɪnɪml] a ελάχιστος.
minimize ['mɪnɪmaɪz] vt ελαττώνω,
μικραίνω, περιορίζω.
minimum ['mɪnɪməm] n ελάχιστο,
κατώτατο όριο, μίνιμουμ nt inv ♦ a
κατώτατος, ελάχιστος.
mining ['maɪnɪŋ] n εξόρυξη || (NAUT)
ναρκοθέτηση ♦ a μεταλλευτική,
ορυκτική.
miniskirt ['mɪnɪskɜːt] n κοντή φούστα,
μίνι.
minister ['mɪnɪstə*] n υπουργός m/f ||
(ECCL) ιερέας || ~**ial** [mɪnɪs'tɪərɪəl] a
υπουργικός, κυβερνητικός.
ministry ['mɪnɪstrɪ] n (government)
υπουργείο, κυβέρνηση || (ECCL) το
ιερατείο, κλήρος.
mink [mɪŋk] n είδος νιφίτσας ♦ a: ~
coat n παλτό από μινκ.
minor ['maɪnə*] a μικρότερος, μικρός ||
(MUS) ελάσσων ♦ n (under 18: Brit)
ανήλικος.
minority [maɪ'nɒrɪtɪ] n μειοψηφία,
μειονότητα.
minstrel ['mɪnstrəl] n ραψωδός,
τραγουδιστής.
mint [mɪnt] n (plant) δυόσμος || (sweet)
μέντα || (for coins) νομισματοκοπείο ♦ a
(condition) καινούργιος,
κατακαίνουργιος || ~ **sauce** n σάλτσα
με δυόσμο.
minuet [mɪnju'et] n μενουέτο.
minus ['maɪnəs] n σημείο του πλην ♦
prep πλην, μείον.
minute [maɪ'njuːt] a μικροσκοπικός,
ελάχιστος || (detailed) λεπτομερής ♦
['mɪnɪt] n λεπτό (της ώρας) || (moment)
στιγμή || ~**s** npl πρακτικά ntpl.
miracle ['mɪrəkl] n (esp REL) θαύμα nt.
miraculous [mɪ'rækjuləs] a
θαυματουργός, υπερφυσικός,
θαυμαστός.
mirage ['mɪrɑːʒ] n αντικατοπτρισμός,
οπτική απάτη.
mirror ['mɪrə*] n καθρέφτης, κάτοπτρο
♦ vt αντικατοπτρίζω, αντανακλώ.
mirth [mɜːθ] n ευθυμία, χαρά, κέφι.
misadventure [mɪsəd'ventʃə*] n
κακοτυχία, ατύχημα nt.
misapprehension ['mɪsæprɪ'henʃən] n
(misunderstanding) παρεξήγηση.
misbehave ['mɪsbɪ'heɪv] vi φέρομαι
άσχημα.
miscalculate ['mɪs'kælkjuleɪt] vt
υπολογίζω λανθασμένα.
miscalculation ['mɪskælkju'leɪʃən] n
λανθασμένος υπολογισμός.
miscarriage ['mɪskærɪdʒ] n αποτυχία ||
(of justice) δικαστικό λάθος || (MED)
αποβολή.

miscellaneous [mɪsɪ'leɪnɪɔs] a ποικίλος, ανάμικτος.

mischance [mɪs'tʃɑːns] n αποτυχία, ατύχημα nt.

mischievous ['mɪstʃɪvɔs] a κατεργάρης, σκανταλιάρης.

misconception ['mɪskɔn'sepʃɔn] n εσφαλμένη αντίληψη.

misconduct [mɪs'kɔndʌkt] n παράπτωμα nt, κακή διαγωγή.

miscount ['mɪs'kaʊnt] vt μετρώ λανθασμένα.

misdemeanour, misdemeanor (US) [mɪsdɪ'miːnɔ*] n (less important offence) παράπτωμα, πλημμέλημα nt.

misdirect ['mɪsdɪ'rekt] vt (person, letter) δίνω λανθασμένες οδηγίες, διευθύνω άσχημα.

miser ['maɪzɔ*] n φιλάργυρος, τσιγκούνης.

miserable ['mɪzɔrɔbl] a δυστυχισμένος, θλιβερός || (poor) άθλιος, ελεεινός, φτωχός.

miserly ['maɪzɔlɪ] a τσιγκούνικος.

misery ['mɪzɔrɪ] n δυστυχία, βάσανο || (poverty) αθλιότητα, φτώχια.

misfire ['mɪs'faɪɔ*] vi ρετάρω, παθαίνω αφλογιστία || (plan) πέφτω στο κενό.

misfit ['mɪsfɪt] n (person) απροσάρμοστος.

misfortune [mɪs'fɔːtʃɔn] n ατυχία, ατύχημα nt.

misgiving [mɪs'gɪvɪŋ] n (often pl) ανησυχία, αμφιβολία, φόβος.

misguided ['mɪs'gaɪdɪd] a πλανόμενος, παρασυρόμενος.

mishandle ['mɪs'hændl] vt (manage badly) κακομεταχειρίζομαι.

mishap ['mɪshæp] n ατυχία, αναποδιά.

mishear ['mɪs'hɪɔ*] vt (hear wrongly) παρακούω.

misinform ['mɪsɪn'fɔːm] vt πληροφορώ κακώς.

misinterpret ['mɪsɪn'tɜːprɪt] vt παρερμηνεύω.

misjudge ['mɪs'dʒʌdʒ] vt κρίνω λανθασμένα.

mislay [mɪs'leɪ] vt (misplace, lose) παραπετώ, χάνω.

mislead [mɪs'liːd] vt (deceive) παραπλανώ, εξαπατώ || ~ing a παραπλανητικός.

misnomer ['mɪs'nɔʊmɔ*] n λανθασμένη ονομασία.

misogynist [mɪ'sɔdʒɪnɪst] n μισογύνης.

misplace ['mɪs'pleɪs] vt (mislay) τοποθετώ κατά λάθος, χάνω.

misprint ['mɪsprɪnt] n τυπογραφικό λάθος.

misread ['mɪs'riːd] vt κακοδιαβάζω, παρερμηνεύω.

misrepresent ['mɪsreprɪ'zent] vt διαστρέφω, παραμορφώνω.

miss [mɪs] vt αστοχώ, αποτυγχάνω || (not notice) δε βλέπω, χάνω || (train etc) χάνω || (omit) παραλείπω || (regret absence) μού λείπει, αποζητώ ♦ vi αντιλαμβάνομαι ♦ n (fall short) αστοχία || (failure) αποτυχία.

Miss [mɪs] n: ~ X Δεσποινίδα Χ, Δεσποινίς Χ, Δις Χ || ~ Smith Δεσποινίδα Σμίθ, Δις Σμίθ.

misshapen ['mɪs'ʃeɪpɔn] a παραμορφωμένος.

missile ['mɪsaɪl] n (esp nuclear) βλήμα nt.

missing ['mɪsɪŋ] a (person) απών, αγνοούμενος || (thing) χαμένος.

mission ['mɪʃɔn] n αποστολή || (church) ιεραποστολή || ~ary n ιεραπόστολος.

misspent ['mɪs'spent] a (youth) χαμένα (νειάτα).

mist [mɪst] n ομίχλη, καταχνιά ♦ vi (also: ~ over, ~ up) σκεπάζω με ομίχλη, θαμπώνω.

mistake [mɪs'teɪk] n σφάλμα nt, λάθος nt ♦ vt παρανοώ, παρερμηνεύω || (for another) παίρνω για άλλο, παραγνωρίζω || ~n a (person) σφάλλω, κάνω λάθος || (identity) παραγνωρίζω.

mister ['mɪstɔ*] n (abbr Mr) κύριος (Κος) || see Mr.

mistletoe ['mɪsltɔʊ] n ιξός, γκί.

mistreat [mɪs'triːt] vt κακομεταχειρίζομαι.

mistress ['mɪstrɪs] n (teacher) δασκάλα || (of house) κυρία, οικοδέσποινα || (lover) ερωμένη, μαιτρέσσα || see Mrs.

mistrust [mɪs'trʌst] vt δυσπιστώ, υποπτεύομαι.

misty ['mɪstɪ] a ομιχλώδης, θαμπός, σκοτεινιασμένος.

misunderstand ['mɪsʌndɔ'stænd] vti παρανοώ, παρεξηγώ || ~ing n παρανόηση, παρεξήγηση.

misunderstood ['mɪsʌndɔ'stʊd] a (person) παρεξηγημένος.

misuse ['mɪs'juːs] n κακή χρήση ♦ ['mɪs'juːz] vt κάνω κατάχρηση, χρησιμοποιώ λανθασμένα.

miter ['maɪtɔ*] n (US) = mitre.

mitigate ['mɪtɪgeɪt] vt μετριάζω, καταπραΰνω.

mitre ['maɪtɔ*] n λοξή ένωση, ονυχωτή ένωση || (ECCL) μίτρα.

mitt(en) ['mɪt(n)] n είδος nt γαντιού.

mix [mɪks] vt αναμιγνύω, ανακατώνω ♦ vi αναμιγνύομαι, ταιριάζω ♦ n (mixture) μίξη, μίγμα nt || to ~ up vt ανακατεύω || (confuse) μπερδεύω || ~ed a (assorted) ανάμικτος || (school etc) μικτός || ~ed-up a (confused) συγχυσμένος, μπερδεμένος || ~r n (for food) μίξερ || (person) κοινωνικός || ~ture n (assortment) αμάλγαμα nt, ανακάτεμα nt || (MED) μίγμα nt || ~-up n (confusion) σύγχυση, ανακατωσούρα.

moan [mɔʊn] n (groan) γογγυσμός, βογγητό || (complaint) γκρίνια, μουρμουρητό ♦ vi στενάζω, βογγώ, γογγύζω.

moat [mɔʊt] n τάφρος f.

mob [mɔb] n όχλος, το πλήθος nt ♦ vt (star etc) πολιορκώ, κυκλώνω.

mobile ['məʊbaɪl] a ευκίνητος, κινητός, ευμετάβολος.

mobility [məʊ'bɪlɪtɪ] n ευκινησία, κινητικότητα.

mock [mɒk] vt εμπαίζω, κοροϊδεύω, περιπαίζω ♦ a ψεύτικος, φτιαστός || ~ery n (derision) εμπαιγμός, κοροϊδία || (object) περίγελος, κοροϊδο || ~ing a (tone) ειρωνικός, σαρκαστικός || ~-up n υπόδειγμα nt || (model) μακέτα.

model ['mɒdl] n ομοίωμα nt, μοντέλο || (example) πρότυπο, υπόδειγμα nt || (person) μοντέλο || (of clothes) μανεκέν nt inv ♦ vt (δια)πλάθω, διαμορφώνω, σχεδιάζω || (display clothes) κάνω επίδειξη (ρούχων) ♦ a (railway: toy) τρανάκι || (child) πρότυπο, ιδεώδης || ~ling, ~ing (US) n σχεδίασμα nt, πλάσιμο || (of styles) επίδειξη μόδας.

modem ['məʊdɛm] n (COMPUT) modem.

moderate ['mɒdərɪt] a μέτριος, μέσος || (fairly good) μέτριος, της σειράς ♦ n (POL) μετριοπαθής ♦ ['mɒdəreɪt] vi προΐσταμαι, προεδρεύω ♦ vt μετριάζω, περιορίζω || ~ly ad μετρημένα, συγκρατημένα, μέτρια.

moderation [mɒdə'reɪʃən] n μετριασμός, μετριοπάθεια.

modern ['mɒdən] a σύγχρονος, μοντέρνος || ~ization n (εκ)συγχρονισμός || ~ize vt συγχρονίζω, ανανεώνω.

modest ['mɒdɪst] a (attitude) μετριόφρων, σεμνός || (meal, home) ταπεινός, μέτριος || ~y n μετριοφροσύνη, σεμνότητα, ταπεινότητα.

modicum ['mɒdɪkəm] n: with a ~ of με ελάχιστο, με λίγο.

modification [mɒdɪfɪ'keɪʃən] n τροποποίηση, μετριασμός.

modify ['mɒdɪfaɪ] vt τροποποιώ, μετριάζω.

module ['mɒdjuːl] n (space) θαλαμίσκος.

mohair ['məʊhɛə*] n μαλλί μοχαίρ nt inv.

moist [mɔɪst] a υγρός, νοτισμένος || ~en vt υγραίνω, μουσκεύω || ~ure n υγρασία.

molar ['məʊlə*] n γομφίος, μυλίτης, τραπεζίτης.

mold [məʊld] (US) = mould.

mole [məʊl] n (spot) κρεατοελιά || (animal) τυφλοπόντικας || (pier) κυματοθραύστης, μώλος.

molecule ['mɒlɪkjuːl] n μόριο.

molest [məʊ'lɛst] vt (παρ)ενοχλώ, πειράζω.

molt [məʊlt] (US) = moult.

molten ['məʊltən] a χυτός, λυωμένος.

moment ['məʊmənt] n στιγμή || (importance) βαρύτητα, σπουδαιότητα || ~ary a στιγμιαίος, προσωρινός || ~ous a βαρυσήμαντος, σημαντικός.

momentum [məʊ'mɛntəm] n ορμή, φόρα.

monarch ['mɒnək] n μονάρχης || ~y n μοναρχία.

monastery ['mɒnəstrɪ] n μοναστήρι.

monastic [mə'næstɪk] a μοναχικός, μοναστικός.

Monday ['mʌndɪ] n Δευτέρα.

monetary ['mʌnɪtərɪ] a νομισματικός, χρηματικός.

money ['mʌnɪ] n χρήμα nt, νόμισμα nt, παράς || (wealth) χρήματα ntpl, πλούτη ntpl || ~lender n τοκιστής, τοκογλύφος || ~ order n ταχυδρομική επιταγή.

mongol ['mɒŋgəl] n (child) πάσχων εκ μογγολισμού ♦ a μογγολικός.

mongrel ['mʌŋgrəl] n μιγάδας ♦ a μιγαδικός, μιξιγενής.

monitor ['mɒnɪtə*] n παρεναίτης, επιμελητής || (television monitor) ελεγκτής || (COMPUT) οθόνη ♦ vt (broadcasts) ελέγχω.

monk [mʌŋk] n καλόγηρος, μοναχός.

monkey ['mʌŋkɪ] n πίθηκος, μαϊμού f || ~ nut n αραπεφύστικο || ~ wrench n γαλλικό κλειδί.

mono- ['mɒnəʊ] prefix μον(ο).

monochrome ['mɒnəkrəʊm] a (TV) μονόχρωμος.

monocle ['mɒnəkl] n μονύελο, μονόκλ nt inv.

monogram ['mɒnəgræm] n μονόγραμμα nt, μονογραφή.

monolithic [mɒnəʊ'lɪθɪk] a μονολιθικός.

monologue ['mɒnəlɒg] n μονόλογος.

monopoly [mə'nɒpəlɪ] n μονοπώλιο.

monorail ['mɒnəʊreɪl] n μονόραβδος f.

monosyllabic ['mɒnəʊsɪ'læbɪk] a (person) μονοσύλλαβικός.

monotone ['mɒnətəʊn] n μονοτονία ήχου, μονότονη ομιλία.

monotonous [mə'nɒtənəs] a μονότονος.

monotony [mə'nɒtənɪ] n μονοτονία.

monsoon [mɒn'suːn] n θερινός μουσώνας.

monster ['mɒnstə*] n (huge animal) τέρας nt, τερατούργημα nt || (wicked person) τέρας.

monstrosity [mɒns'trɒsɪtɪ] n τερατωδία, κτηνωδία.

monstrous ['mɒnstrəs] a τερατώδης, εκτρωματικός.

montage [mɒn'tɑːʒ] n (picture) μοντάζ nt inv, μοντάρισμα nt.

month [mʌnθ] n μήνας || ~ly a μηνιαίος, μηνιάτικος ♦ ad μηνιαίως, κάθε μήνα ♦ n (magazine) μηνιαίο περιοδικό.

monument ['mɒnjumənt] n μνημείο || ~al a μνημειακός || (work etc) μνημειώδης.

moo [muː] vi (cow) μηκώμαι, μουγκρίζω.

mood [muːd] n διάθεση, κέφι || (GRAM) έγκλιση || ~y a κακόκεφος, κατσούφης, σκυθρωπός, ιδιότροπος.

moon [muːn] n σελήνη, φεγγάρι || ~light n σελήνοφως nt, φεγγάρι || ~lit a φεγγαρόλουστος.

moor [mʊə*] n (Brit: heath) έλος nt, βάλτος, ρεικότοπος ♦ vt (ship) πρυμνοδετώ, δένω (πλοίο) ♦ vi πλευρίζω, πέφτω δίπλα.

moorings ['muərɪŋz] npl πρυμνήσια ntpl, πρυμάτσες fpl, ναύδετα ntpl.

moorland ['muələnd] n έλος nt, βάλτος, ρεικότοπος.

moose [mu:s] n άλκη n Αμερικανική.

mop [mɔp] n πατσαβούρα || (duster) ξεσκονιστήρι ♦ vt σφουγγαρίζω || ~ of hair n ξεντένιστα μαλλιά ntpl.

mope [məup] vi μελαγχολώ, πλήττω.

moral ['mɔrəl] a ηθικός, ψυχικός ♦ n επιμύθιο, ηθικό δίδαγμα nt|| ~s npl ήθη ntpl||~e n ηθικό || ~ity n ηθικότητα, ηθικό αίσθημα nt.

morass [mə'ræs] n έλος nt|| (fig) βόρβορος.

morbid ['mɔ:bid] a νοσηρός, αρρωστιάρικος.

more [mɔ:*] a περισσότερος ♦ ad περισσότερο, πιο πολύ || ~ or less σχεδόν, πάνω κάτω || ~ than ever περισσότερο παρά ποτέ.

moreover [mɔ:'rəuvə*] ad επί πλέον, εκτός τούτου.

morgue [mɔ:g] n νεκροτομείο.

moribund ['mɔribʌnd] a ετοιμοθάνατος.

morning ['mɔ:niŋ] n πρωί ♦ a πρωϊνός || in the ~ το πρωΐ.

Moroccan [mə'rɔkən] a, n Μαροκινός.

Morocco [mə'rɔkəu] n Μαρόκο.

moron ['mɔ:rɔn] n καθυστερημένος || (col) ηλίθιος, βλάκας || ~ic [mə'rɔnik] a ηλίθιος, βλακώδης.

morose [mə'rəus] a κακότροπος, σκυθρωπός.

morphine ['mɔ:fi:n] n μορφίνη.

Morse [mɔ:s] ~ code n μορσικός κώδικας.

morsel ['mɔ:sl] n (of food) μπουκιά, κομματάκι.

mortal ['mɔ:tl] a θνητός || (deadly) θανάσιμος, θανατηφόρος || (very great) τρομερός ♦ n (human being) θνητός (άνθρωπος) || ~ity n θνητότητα || (death rate) θνησιμότητα.

mortar ['mɔ:tə*] n ασβεστοκονίαμα nt, πηλός, λάσπη || (bowl) λάσπη || (weapon) όλμος.

mortgage ['mɔ:gidʒ] n υποθήκη.

mortuary ['mɔ:tjuəri] n νεκροθάλαμος.

mosaic [məu'zeiik] n μωσαϊκό, ψηφιδωτό.

Moscow ['mɔskəu] n Μόσχα.

Moslem ['mɔzləm] n Μουσουλμάνος/a m/f ♦ a μουσουλμανικός.

mosque [mɔsk] n τέμενος nt, τζαμί.

mosquito [mɔs'ki:təu] n κουνούπι.

moss [mɔs] n βρύο || ~y a βρυώδης, βρυόφυτος.

most [məust] a περισσότερος, πιο πολύς ♦ ad πιο, πιο πολύ ♦ n οι περισσότεροι || at the (very) ~ το πιο πολύ || to make the ~ of επωφελούμαι || ~ly ad ως επί το πλείστο, κυρίως, συνήθως.

M.O.T. n (abbr of Ministry of Transport):

the ~ (test) αναγκαστικός, ετήσιος τεχνικός έλεγχος οχημάτων.

motel [məu'tel] n μοτέλ nt inv.

moth [mɔθ] n βότριδα, σκώρος || ~ball n ναφθαλίνη (σε μπάλλες) || ~-eaten a σκωροφαγωμένος.

mother ['mʌðə*] n μητέρα, μάνα ♦ vt (spoil) χαϊδεύω, κανακεύω ♦ a (tongue, country) μητρική (γλώσσα) || ~hood n μητρότητα || ~-in-law n πεθερά || ~ly a μητρικά, σαν μάνα || ~-to-be n σε ενδιαφέρουσα.

motif [məu'ti:f] n μοτίφ nt inv, θέμα nt, μοτίβο.

motion ['məuʃən] n κίνηση || (proposal) πρόταση ♦ vi κάνω νόημα, νεύω || ~less a ακίνητος || ~ picture n ταινία, φιλμ nt inv.

motivated ['məutiveitid] a αιτιολογούμενος, κινητήριος.

motivation [məuti'veiʃən] n κίνητρο, ελατήριο.

motive ['məutiv] n κίνητρο, αίτιο, ελατήριο ♦ a κινητήριος.

motley ['mɔtli] a (heterogeneous) πολύχρωμος, ετερογενής.

motor ['məutə*] n κινητήρας, μηχανή || (automobile) αυτοκίνητο ♦ vi ταξιδεύω με αυτοκίνητο || ~bike n μοτοσυκλέτα || ~boat n βενζινάκατος f|| ~car n αυτοκίνητο || ~cycle n = ~bike || ~cyclist n μοτοσυκλετιστής || ~ing n χρήση του αυτοκινήτου, οδήγηση ♦ a του αυτοκινήτου, της οδηγήσεως || ~ist n αυτοκινητιστής || ~ oil n λάδι κινητήρων || ~ racing n αυτοκινητοδρομία || ~ scooter n σκούτερ nt inv, βέσπα || ~ vehicle n αυτοκίνητο || ~way n (Brit) αυτοκινητόδρομος.

mottled ['mɔtld] a διάστικτος, ποικιλόχρωμος.

motto ['mɔtəu] n ρητό, μόττο, αρχή.

mould [məuld] n τύπος, μήτρα, καλούπι || (shape) τύπωμα nt, πρότυπο || (mildew) μούχλα ♦ vt χύνω σε τύπους || (fig) διαπλάθω, διαμορφώνω || ~er vi (decay) σαπίζω, φθείρομαι || ~ing n (in plaster) τυποποιία, χυτό αντικείμενο || (in wood) κορνίζα || ~y a (food etc) μουχλιασμένος.

moult [məult] vi μαδώ.

mound [maund] n ανάχωμα nt, λοφίσκος, πρόχωμα nt.

mount [maunt] n (high hill) όρος nt, βουνό || (horse) άλογο || (for jewel etc) κορνίζα, υποστήριγμα nt, σκελετός ♦ vt (get on horse) ανεβάζω, ανεβαίνω στο || (put in setting) ανεβάζω, δένω, κορνιζάρω || (exhibition) ανεβάζω || (attack) οργανώνω επίθεση ♦ vi (also: ~ up) ανέρχομαι, ανεβαίνω.

mountain ['mauntin] n όρος nt, βουνό || (pile) σωρός, πλήθος nt|| ~eer n (climber) ορειβάτης || ~eering n ορειβασία || to go ~eering κάνω ορειβασία || ~ous a ορεινός || ~ side n πλευρά βουνού.

mourn [mɔ:n] vt πενθώ, θρηνώ ♦ vi
(+for) θρηνώ, κλαίω || ~er n πενθών,
πενθοφορών || ~ful a πένθιμος || ~ing
n πένθος nt||in ~ing (period etc) έχω
πένθος || (dress) πένθιμα ρούχα ntpl,
μαύρα ntpl.

mouse [maʊs] n ποντικός || (COMPUT)
ποντίκι || ~trap n ποντικοπαγίδα, φάκα.

moustache [məsˈtɑ:ʃ] n μουστάκι.

mouth [maʊθ] n (ANAT) στόμα nt||
(opening) στόμιο || (entrance) εκβολή,
στόμιο ♦ [maʊð] vt (words) ομιλώ με
στόμφο || ~ful n μπουκιά || ~ organ n
φυσαρμόνικα || ~piece n επιστόμιο ||
(speaker) όργανο, φερέφωνο,
εκπρόσωπος || ~wash n γαργάρα || ~-
watering a γαργαλιστικός.

movable [ˈmu:vəbl] a κινητός.

move [mu:v] n (movement) κίνηση || (in
game) κίνηση || (step) ενέργεια, βήμα nt||
(from house) μετακόμιση ♦ vt (meta)κινώ,
μετατοπίζω || (stir, rouse) συγκινώ,
γίνομαι (εξωφρενών κλ) ♦ vi (general)
κινούμαι, κουνιέμαι || (travel)
μετακινούμαι, φεύγω || (take action)
ενεργώ || (go elsewhere) μετακομίζω || to
get a ~ on σπεύδω, κάνω γρήγορα || to
~ house μετοικώ, μετακομίζω || to ~
about vi περιφέρομαι, τριγυρίζω || to ~
away vi απομακρύνομαι, φεύγω || to ~
back vi υποχωρώ, βαδίζω πίσω || to ~
forward vi προχωρώ ♦ vt κινώ προς
τα εμπρός || to ~ in vi (house)
μετακομίζω (στο νέο σπίτι),
εγκαθίσταμαι || to ~ on vi προχωρώ,
τραβώ το δρόμο μου ♦ vt κάνω να
κυκλοφορεί || to ~ out vi (house)
μετακομίζω (αλλού), αδειάζω || ~ment
n κίνηση, μετακίνηση || (social etc) κίνημα
nt, κίνηση || (MUS) μέρος nt.

movie [ˈmu:vi] n (film) φιλμ nt inv||the
~s (cinema) σινεμά nt inv|| ~ camera n
(amateur) κινηματογραφική μηχανή.

moving [ˈmu:vɪŋ] a (lit) κινούμενος,
κινητός || (stirring) συνταρακτικός,
συγκινητικός || (touching) συγκινητικός.

mow [məʊ] (irreg v) vt θερίζω || to ~
down vt θερίζω || ~er n (machine)
θεριστική μηχανή.

M.P. abbr see **member**.

m.p.g. (abbr of miles per gallon) ≈ x.α.λ.
(χιλιόμετρα ανά λίτρο).

m.p.h. (abbr of miles per hour) ≈ x.α.ω.
(χιλιόμετρα ανά ώρα).

Mr [ˈmɪstə*] n: ~ Smith Κύριος Σμιθ,
Κος Σμιθ.

Mrs [ˈmɪsɪz] n: ~ Smith Κυρία Σμιθ, Κα
Σμιθ.

much [mʌtʃ] a πολύς ♦ ad πολύ, συχνά,
σχεδόν ♦ n πολλά, πολύ || how ~ is it?
πόσο κάνει; || too ~ πάρα πολύ.

muck [mʌk] n (lit) κοπριά, βρωμιά || (fig)
σύγχυση, καταστροφή || to ~ about vi
(col) περιφέρομαι άσκοπα, χαζεύω ♦ vt
(col) λασπώνω, βρωμίζω || to ~ up vt
(col: ruin) χαλάω μια δουλειά || ~y a
(dirty) βρώμικος, βρομερός.

mud [mʌd] n λάσπη.

muddle [ˈmʌdl] n ακαταστασία, σαλάτα,
μπέρδεμα nt ♦ vt (also: ~ up) μπερδεύω,
κάνω άνω-κάτω || to ~ through vi
καταφέρνω κουτσά-στραβά.

muddy [ˈmʌdi] a λασπώδης,
λασπωμένος.

mudguard [ˈmʌdgɑ:d] n φτερό
(αυτοκινήτου).

mudpack [ˈmʌdpæk] n μάσκα (από
πηλό).

mud-slinging [ˈmʌdslɪŋɪŋ] n
συκοφαντία, κακολωγοσιά.

muffle [ˈmʌfl] vt πνίγω (ήχο) || (wrap up)
κουκουλώνω, σκεπάζω || ~d a
υπόκουφος, πνιγμένος.

mug [mʌg] n (cup) μεγάλο φλυτζάνι,
φλυτζάνα || (col: face) μούτρο, φάτσα ||
(col: dupe) κορόϊδο, κορόϊδα ♦ vt (assault)
κτυπώ από πίσω || ~ging n (assault)
επίθεση με ληστεία.

muggy [ˈmʌgi] a (weather) βαρύς
(καιρός), υγρός.

mule [mju:l] n η ημίονος, μουλάρι.

mull [mʌl]: to ~ over vt γυροφέρνω
στο μυαλό.

mulled [mʌld] a (wine) ζεστό κρασί με
κανέλλα.

multi [ˈmʌlti] prefix πολύ-.

multicoloured, multicolored (US)
[ˈmʌltiˈkʌləd] a πολύχρωμος.

multiple [ˈmʌltipl] n πολλαπλάσιο ♦ a
πολλαπλός || ~ store n κατάστημα nt με
πολλά υποκαταστήματα.

multiplication [mʌltipliˈkeiʃən] n
πολλαπλασιασμός.

multiply [ˈmʌltiplai] vt πολλαπλασιάζω
♦ vi πολλαπλασιάζομαι.

multitude [ˈmʌltitju:d] n πλήθος nt.

mum [mʌm] n (col) μαμά.

mumble [ˈmʌmbl] vti μουρμουρίζω,
μασώ ♦ n μπερδεμένα λόγια ntpl,
μουρμούρα.

mummy [ˈmʌmi] n μούμια || (col) μαμά.

mumps [mʌmps] n παρωτίτιδα
μαγουλαδες fpl.

munch [mʌntʃ] vti μασουλίζω,
τραγανίζω.

mundane [ˈmʌnˈdein] a εγκόσμιος,
γήινος.

municipal [mjuˈnisipəl] a δημοτικός.

munitions [mjuˈniʃənz] npl
πολεμοφόδια ntpl.

mural [ˈmjʊərəl] n τοιχογραφία.

murder [ˈmɜ:də*] n φόνος, δολοφονία
|| (fig: col) φονικό ♦ vt φονεύω, σκοτώνω,
δολοφονώ || ~er n φονιάς, δολοφόνος
|| ~erous a (δολο)φονικός || ~ess n
φόνισσα.

murky [ˈmɜ:ki] a σκοτεινός, ζοφερός.

murmur [ˈmɜ:mə*] n ψίθυρος,
μουρμουρητό ♦ vi ψιθυρίζω,
μουρμουρίζω, παραπονούμαι.

muscle [ˈmʌsl] n μυς m.

muscular [ˈmʌskjulə*] a μυϊκός,
γεροδεμένος.

Muse [mju:z] n Μούσα.

muse [mju:z] *vi* ρεμβάζω, ονειροπολώ.

museum [mju:'zɪəm] *n* μουσείο.

mush [mʌʃ] *n* πολτός.

mushroom['mʌʃrum] *n* μανιτάρι ♦ *vi* ξεφυτρώνω.

mushy ['mʌʃi] *a* πολτώδης, μαλακός.

music ['mju:zɪk] *n* μουσική || **to face the ~** ακούω εξάψαλμο || ~**al** *n* μουσική παράσταση ♦ *a* μουσικός, φιλόμουσος || ~**ian** *n* μουσικός *m/f*|| ~**stand** *n* αναλόγιο μουσικού.

muslin ['mʌzlɪn] *n* μουσελίνα.

mussel ['mʌl] *n* μύδι.

must [mʌst] *auxiliary v (obligation)* **I ~ do it** πρέπει να το κάνω || **I ~ not do it** δεν πρέπει να το κάνω || *(probability)* **he ~ be there by now** πρέπει να είναι εκεί τώρα ♦ *n* γλύκος, μούστος || **it is a ~** είναι αναγκαίο.

mustache ['mʌstæʃ] *n (US)* = **moustache**.

mustard ['mʌstəd] *n (condiment)* μουστάρδα.

mustn't ['mʌsnt] = **must not**.

musty ['mʌsti] *a* μουχλιασμένος || *(col)* παλιατσούρα, μπαγιάτικος.

mute [mju:t] *n* βουβός/ή *m/f*, μουγγός/ή *m/f*.

mutilate ['mju:tɪleɪt] *vt* ακρωτηριάζω, σακατεύω.

mutilation [mju:tɪ'leɪʃən] *n* ακρωτηριασμός, σακάτεμα *nt*.

mutinous ['mju:tɪnəs] *a* στασιαστικός, αντάρτικος.

mutiny ['mju:tɪni] *n* στάση, ανταρσία ♦ *vi* στασιάζω.

mutter ['mʌtə*] *vti* μουρμουρίζω.

mutton ['mʌtn] *n* αρνήσιο κρέας *nt*.

mutual ['mju:tjuəl] *a* αμοιβαίος, κοινός || ~**ly** *ad* αμοιβαίως.

muzzle ['mʌzl] *n (mouth and nose)* ρύγχος *nt*, μουσούδα || *(straps)* φίμωτρο || *(of gun)* στόμιο, στόμα *nt* ♦ *vt* φιμώνω.

my [maɪ] *poss a* δικός μου, μου.

myopic [maɪ'ɒpɪk] *a* μυωπικός.

myself [maɪ'self] *pron* εγώ ο ίδιος, τον εαυτό μου.

mysterious [mɪs'tɪərɪəs] *a* μυστηριώδης.

mystery ['mɪstəri] *n* μυστήριο.

mystic ['mɪstɪk] *n* μυστικός, μυστικιστής || ~**al** *a* μυστικιστικός, μυστηριώδης.

mystification [mɪstɪfɪ'keɪʃən] *n* αμηχανία, απάτη.

mystify ['mɪstɪfaɪ] *vt* προκαλώ έκπληξη.

myth [mɪθ] *n* μύθος || ~**ical** *a* μυθικός || ~**ological** *a* μυθολογικός || ~**ology** *n* μυθολογία.

N

nab [næb] *vt* αρπάζω, συλλαμβάνω.

nag [næg] *n (horse)* μικρό άλογο *(ιπποασίας)* || *(person)* γκρινιάρης, καυγατζής ♦ *vti* γκρινιάζω, καυγαδίζω || ~**ging** *n* καυγάς, φασαρία.

nail [neɪl] *n* νύχι || *(spike)* καρφί, πρόκα ♦ *vt* καρφώνω || **to ~ down** *vt (fig)* δεσμεύω || ~ **brush** *n* βούρτσα των νυχιών || ~ **file** *n* λίμα (για νύχια) || ~ **polish** *n* βερνίκι των νυχιών, μανό || ~ **scissors** *npl* ψαλιδάκι (για νύχια) || ~ **varnish** *n* βερνίκι για τα νύχια.

naïve [naɪ'i:v] *a* αφελής.

naked ['neɪkɪd] *a* γυμνός || *(uncovered)* εκτεθειμένος, καθαρός || ~**ness** *n* γυμνότητα.

name [neɪm] *n* όνομα *nt* || *(reputation)* φήμη, υπόληψη ♦ *vt* ονομάζω || *(call by name)* αναφέρω, κατονομάζω || *(appoint)* ορίζω, διορίζω || **in the ~ of** εξ ονόματός του || *(authority of)* εν ονόματι || ~**less** *a* άγνωστος, ανώνυμος || ~**ly** *ad* δηλαδή || ~**sake** *n* ομώνυμος, συνονόματος.

nanny ['næni] *n (for child)* νταντά.

nap [næp] *n (sleep)* υπνάκος || **to have a ~** τον παίρνω λιγάκι.

nape [neɪp] *n* αυχένας, σβέρκος.

napkin ['næpkɪn] *n* πετσέτα φαγητού || *(Brit)* χαρτοπετσέτα, πάνα (βρέφους).

nappy ['næpi] *n (for baby)* πάνα.

narcissus [naː'sɪsəs] *n* νάρκισσος.

narcotic [naː'kɒtɪk] *n* ναρκωτικό *nt*.

nark [naːk] *vt (col: annoy)* εξερεθίζω, εξαγριώνω.

narration [nə'reɪʃən] *n* διήγηση.

narrative ['nærətɪv] *n* διήγημα *nt*, αφήγηση ♦ *a* αφηγηματικός.

narrator [nə'reɪtə*] *n* αφηγητής.

narrow ['nærəu] *a* στενός, στενόχωρος ♦ *vi* στενεύω || **to ~ down** *vt* περιορίζω || ~**ly** *ad (miss)* μόλις, παρά λίγο || ~-**minded** *a* στενοκέφαλος.

nasal ['neɪzəl] *a* έρρινος, ρινικός, της μύτης.

nastiness ['naːstɪnɪs] *n* κακία, αχρειότητα, προστυχιά.

nasty ['naːsti] *a (mess)* δυσάρεστος, βρώμικος || *(business)* δύσκολος, επικίνδυνος, φοβερός || *(person)* πρόστυχος, ρεμάλι, κακός.

nation ['neɪʃən] *n* έθνος *nt* || ~**al** ['næʃənl] *a* εθνικός ♦ *n* υπήκοος *m/f*, πολίτης/ήτισσα *m/f* || ~**al anthem** *n* εθνικός ύμνος || ~**alism** *n* εθνικισμός || ~**alist** *a*, *n* εθνικιστής/ίστρια *m/f*, εθνικόφρων || ~**ality** *n* εθνικότητα || ~**alization** *n* εθνικοποίηση || ~**alize** *vt* εθνικοποιώ || ~**ally** *ad* από εθνικής άποψης || ~**wide** *a* πανεθνικό ♦ *ad* σ' ολόκληρη τη χώρα.

native ['neɪtɪv] *n* ντόπιος/ια *m/f* || *(non-European)* ιθαγενής *m/f* ♦ *a* εγχώριος || *(country etc)* γενέθλιος, μητρικός || *(inborn)* έμφυτος, φυσικός.

NATO [neɪtəu] *n* NATO (Οργανισμός Βορειοατλαντικού Συμφώνου).

natter ['nætə*] *vi (col: chat)* κουβεντιάζω.

natural ['nætʃrəl] *a* φυσικός || *(inborn)* έμφυτος, φυσικός || ~**ist** *n* φυσιοδίφης || ~**ize** *vt* πολιτογραφώ || *(plant etc)* εγκλιματίζω || **~ly** ad φυσικά, βέβαια || **~ness** n φυσικότητα.

nature ['neɪtʃə*] n φύση || (sort, kind) είδος nt, χαρακτήρας || **by ~** εκ φύσης.

naughty ['nɔːtɪ] a (child) άτακτος, κακός.

nausea ['nɔːsɪə] n ναυτία, αναγούλα || (disgust) απδία, αποστροφή || **~te** vt αηδιάζω (κάτι), προ ξενώ ναυτία.

nauseating ['nɔːsɪeɪtɪŋ] a αηδιαστικός, σιχαμερός.

nautical ['nɔːtɪkəl] a ναυτικός.

naval ['neɪvəl] a ναυτικός.

nave [neɪv] n κλίτος, νάρθηκας.

navel ['neɪvəl] n ομφαλός, αφαλός.

navigable ['nævɪgəbl] a πλωτός.

navigate ['nævɪgeɪt] vt (ship etc) κυβερνώ, διευθύνω ♦ vi ναυσιπλοώ, πλέω, ταξιδεύω.

navigation [nævɪ'geɪʃən] n γαυτιλία πλόευσις m, ναυσιπλοϊα m.

navigator ['nævɪgeɪtə*] n ναυτίλος, πλοηγός || (explorer) θαλασσοπόρος || (AVIAT) αεροναυτίλος.

navy ['neɪvɪ] n ναυτικό || **~ blue** a (colour) σκούρος μπλε, μπλε μαρίν.

nay [neɪ] ad (no) όχι || (also) τι λέω, ή καλύτερα.

Nazi ['nɑːtsɪ] n Ναζιστής.

neap tide ['niːp'taɪd] a άμπωτη.

near [nɪə*] a (close) εγγύς, κοντινός || (related) πλησίον, στενός ♦ ad (space) κοντά, πλησίον || (time) περί, εγγύς, κοντά ♦ prep (also: **~ to**) κοντά σε, παρά, || (space) παρά, κοντά || (time) περί, κοντά ♦ vt πλησιάζω || **~by** a κοντινός, πλαϊνός ♦ ad πολύ κοντά, εγγύτατα || **N~ East** n Εγγύς Ανατολή || **~ly** ad σχεδόν, περίπου || **I ~ miss** n λίγο έλειψε (να), παρά λίγο (να) || **~ness** n εγγύτητα, στενότητα || **~side** n (AUT) αριστερή πλευρά.

neat [niːt] a (tidy) καθαρός, καλοβαλμένος, κομψός || (clever) καλοβαλμένος, επιτυχής, κομψός || (pure) καθαρός, αγνός, χωρίς νερό.

nebulous ['nebjuləs] a νεφελώδης.

necessarily ['nesɪsərɪlɪ] ad απαραιτήτως, κατ' ανάγκη.

necessary ['nesɪsərɪ] a αναγκαίος, απαραίτητος.

necessitate [nɪ'sesɪteɪt] vt κάνω αναγκαίο, υποχρεώνω.

necessity [nɪ'sesɪtɪ] n ανάγκη.

neck [nek] n ανάγκη, αυχένας, τράχηλος, σβέρκος || (narrow part) λαιμός, στένωμα nt || **~ and ~** στα ίσια, ισόπαλος πλάι-πλάι.

necklace ['neklɪs] n περιδέραιο, κολιέ nt inv.

neckline n ['neklaɪn] λαιμός, ντεκολτέ nt inv.

necktie n ['nektaɪ] γραβάτα.

née [neɪ] a το γένος.

need [niːd] n ανάγκη, χρεία || (poverty) ένδεια, φτώχια ♦ vt (of person) χρειάζομαι || (of thing) απαιτώ, ζητώ (κάτι) || **to ~** to do έχω ανάγκη να κάνω.

needle ['niːdl] n βελόνι nt || (knitting) βελόνα f || (compass etc) βελόνη f.

needless ['niːdlɪs] a άχρηστος, περιττός.

needlework ['niːdlwɜːk] n εργόχειρο.

needy ['niːdɪ] a ενδεής, άπορος.

negation [nɪ'geɪʃən] n άρνηση.

negative ['negətɪv] n (PHOT) αρνητικό ♦ a αρνητικός.

neglect [nɪ'glekt] vt παραμελώ ♦ n αμέλεια, παραμέληση.

negligée ['neglɪʒeɪ] n νυχτικό.

negligence ['neglɪdʒəns] n αμέλεια.

negligent ['neglɪdʒənt] a αμελής, απρόσεκτος || **~ly** ad απρόσεκτα, αμελώς.

negligible ['neglɪdʒəbl] a αμελητέος.

negotiable [nɪ'gəʊʃɪəbl] a (cheque) εξαργυρώσιμος, μεταπρεπτός, μεταβιβάσιμος.

negotiate [nɪ'gəʊʃɪeɪt] vi διαπραγματεύομαι ♦ vt (treaty) διαπραγματεύομαι || (difficulty) διαβαίνω, ξεπερνώ.

negotiation [nɪgəʊʃɪ'eɪʃən] n διαπραγμάτευση.

negotiator [nɪ'gəʊʃɪeɪtə*] n διαπραγματευτής.

Negress ['niːgres] n νέγρα, μαύρη.

Negro ['niːgrəʊ] a νέγρος, μαύρος.

neighbour, neighbor (US) ['neɪbə*] n γείτονας/γειτόνισσα m/f || **~hood** n γειτονιά, περιοχή || **~ing** a γειτονικός || **~ly** a καλός γείτονας, γειτονικός.

neither ['naɪðə*] a ούτε ο ένας ούτε ο άλλος, κανένας || cj ούτε ... ούτε, ούτε (και) ♦ pron κανένας.

neo- ['niːəʊ] prefix νεο-.

neon ['niːɒn] n νέο || **~ light** n φως με νέο.

nephew ['nevjuː] n ανεψιός.

nerve [nɜːv] n νεύρο || (courage) σθένος nt, θάρρος nt || (impudence) θράσος nt || **~-racking** a εκνευριστικός.

nervous ['nɜːvəs] a νευρικός || (timid) ντροπαλός, νευρικός, δειλός || **~ breakdown** n νευρικός κλονισμός || **~ly** ad δειλά, φοβισμένα || **~ness** n νευρικότητα, δειλία.

nest [nest] n φωλιά.

nestle ['nesl] vi φωλιάζω, κουλουριάζομαι.

net [net] n δίκτυο, δίχτυ nt || (hair) φιλές m, δίχτυ nt ♦ a καθαρός.

Netherlands ['neðələndz] npl Ολλανδία.

netting ['netɪŋ] n δικτύωμα nt, πλέγμα nt.

network ['netwɜːk] n δίκτυο.

neurotic [njuə'rɒtɪk] a νευρωτικός ♦ n νευροπαθής.

neuter ['njuːtə*] a ουδέτερος ♦ n ουδέτερος.

neutral ['njuːtrəl] a ουδέτερος || **~ity** n ουδετερότητα.

never ['nevə*] ad ποτέ || **~-ending** a

N

ατελείωτος || ~**theless** ad εντούτοις, παρ' όλα αυτά.

new [nju:] a νέος, καινούργιος || (clothes etc) καινουργής, καινούργιος || (modern) σύγχρονος, μοντέρνος || (at work etc) αρχάριος, άπειρος || ~**born** a νεογέννητος || ~**comer** n φρεσκοφερμένος/νη m/f, νεοφερμένος/νη m/f || ~**ly** ad τελευταία, πρόσφατα || ~ **moon** n καινούργιο φεγγάρι || ~**ness** n νεότητα, φρεσκάδα.

news [nju:z] n νέα ntpl, ειδήσεις fpl || ~**agent** n πράκτορας εφημερίδων || ~**flash** n έκτακτη είδηση || ~**letter** n δελτίο ειδήσεων || ~**paper** n εφημερίδα || ~**reel** n ταινία επικαίρων.

New Year [nju:'jιə*] n Νέο Έτος || ~**'s Day** n Πρωτοχρονιά || ~**'s Eve** n παραμονή της Πρωτοχρονιάς.

New Zealand [nju:'zi:lənd] n Νέα Ζηλανδία.

next [nekst] a πλησιέστερος, γειτονικός, πλαϊνός || (in time) προσεχής, επόμενος ♦ ad έπειτα, κατόπιν, μετά ♦ prep: ~ to κοντά σε, σχεδόν || the ~ **day** την άλλη μέρα, την επομένη || ~ **year** επόμενο έτος nt, άλλος χρόνος, του χρόνου || ~ **of kin** n πλησιέστερος συγγενής.

N.H.S. abbr of National Health Service.

nibble ['nιbl] vt δαγκώνω, μασουλίζω, τρώγω σιγά-σιγά.

nice [naιs] a ευχάριστος, καλός, ωραίος || (exact) λεπτός, ευαίσθητος || ~-**looking** a ωραίος, όμορφος || ~**ly** ad ωραία, ευχάριστα.

nick [nιk] n (cut) χαραγή, εγκοπή || in the ~ of time στην κατάλληλη στιγμή.

nickel ['nιkl] n νικέλιο || (US) πεντάρα (5 σέντς).

nickname ['nιkneιm] n παρατσούκλι.

nicotine ['nιkəti:n] n νικοτίνη.

niece [ni:s] n ανεψιά.

niggling ['nιglιŋ] a ασημαντολόγος.

night [naιt] n νύχτα, βράδυ || **good** ~ καλή νύχτα || **at** or **by** ~ τη νύχτα || ~**cap** n (drink) νυκτερινό ρόφημα nt || ~**club** n νυκτερινό κέντρο || ~**dress** n νυχτικό || ~-**fall** n σούρουπο || ~ **life** n νυχτερινή ζωή || ~**ly** a νυχτερινός, βραδινός ♦ ad κάθε νύχτα, κάθε βράδυ || ~**mare** n εφιάλτης || ~ **school** n βραδινή σχολή || ~-**time** n νύχτα || ~ **watchman** n νυχτοφύλακας.

nightingale ['naιtιŋgeιl] n αηδόνι.

nil [nιl] n μηδέν, τίποτε.

nimble ['nιmbl] a εύστροφος, ευκίνητος.

nine [naιn] num εννέα, εννιά || ~**teen** num δεκαεννιά || ~**ty** num ενενήντα.

ninth [naιnθ] a ένατος.

nip [nιp] vt (pinch etc) τσιμπώ, δαγκώνω ♦ n τσίμπημα nt, δάγκωμα nt.

nipple ['nιpl] n (ANAT) θηλή, ρώγα.

nitrogen ['naιtrədʒən] n άζωτο.

no [nəυ] a κανείς, καθόλου ♦ ad όχι, καθόλου, μη ♦ n άρνηση, αρνητική ψήφος f.

nobility [nəυ'bιlιtι] n (social class) ευγενείς mpl.

noble ['nəυbl] a ευγενής, μεγαλοπρεπής ♦ n ευγενής, ευπατρίδης.

nobody ['nəυbədι] pron κανείς, κανένας, ♦ n (unimportant person) μηδαμινότητα, τιποτένιος.

nod [nɒd] vi νεύω, νέφω, κάνω νόημα || (droop with sleep) νυστάζω, κουτουλώ ♦ n νεύμα nt, νόημα nt, κουτούλισμα nt.

noise [nɒιz] n κρότος, βοή || (unpleasant) θόρυβος.

noisily ['nɒιzιlι] ad θορυβωδώς, με φασαρία.

noisy ['nɒιzι] a θορυβώδης.

nomad ['nəυmæd] n νομάδας || ~**ic** a νομαδικός.

nominal ['nɒmιnl] a ονομαστικός, εικονικός.

nominate ['nɒmιneιt] vt προτείνω, ονομάζω || (appoint) διορίζω.

nomination [nɒmι'neιʃən] n πρόταση, υποψηφιότητα, διορισμός.

nominee [nɒmι'ni:] n υποψήφιος/ήφια m/f.

non- [nɒn] prefix μη-, αντι-, αν-, α- || ~**alcoholic** a χωρίς οινόπνευμα.

nonchalant ['nɒnʃələnt] a ψύχραιμος, αδιάφορος.

nondescript ['nɒndιskrιpt] a ακαθόριστος, αχαρακτήριστος.

none [nʌn] a κανένας ♦ pron κανένας, καμμιά, κανένα ♦ ad καθόλου.

nonentity [nɒ'nentιtι] n μηδαμινότητα, ασήμαντος άνθρωπος.

nonplussed ['nɒn'plʌst] a (τα έχω) χαμένα, βρίσκομαι σε αμηχανία.

nonsense ['nɒnsəns] n ανοησία, παραλογισμός.

non-stop ['nɒn'stɒp] a χωρίς σταθμό.

noodles ['nu:dlz] npl φιδές m.

noon [nu:n] n μεσημέρι.

no one ['nəυwʌn] pron = nobody.

noose [nu:s] n βρόχος, θηλειά.

nor [nɔ:*] cj ούτε, μήτε.

norm [nɔ:m] n κανόνας, τύπος, μέτρο.

normal ['nɔ:məl] a κανονικός, συνηθισμένος, ομαλός || ~**ly** ad κανονικά.

north [nɔ:θ] n βορράς, βοριάς || (of country etc) τα βόρεια ♦ a βόρεια ♦ ad βορείως, προς βορρά || ~-**east** a βορειοανατολικός || ~**ern** a βόρειος, βορεινός || N~ **Pole** n Βόρειος Πόλος || N~ **Sea** n Βόρειος Θάλασσα || ~**ward(s)** ad προς βορρά || ~-**west** a βορειοδυτικός.

Norway ['nɔ:weι] n Νορβηγία.

Norwegian [nɔ:'wi:dʒən] a νορβηγικός ♦ n Νορβηγός/Νορβηγίδα m/f.

nose [nəυz] n μύτη || (smell) όσφρηση, μύτη || ~-**bleed** n ρινορραγία, μάτωμα nt της μύτης || ~-**dive** n κάθετη εφόρμηση || ~-**y** a περίεργος, αδιάκριτος.

nostalgia [nɒs'tældʒιə] n νοσταλγία.

nostalgic [nɒs'tældʒιk] a νοσταλγικός.

nostril ['nɒstrιl] n ρουθούνι.

not [nɒt] ad δεν, μη, όχι.

notable ['nəʊtəbl] a αξιοσημείωτος, σημαντικός.

notch [nɒtʃ] n εγκοπή, χαραγή, οδόντωση.

note [nəʊt] n νότα, τόνος, πλήκτρο || *(short letter)* γραμματάκι, σημείωμα nt || *(remark)* σημείωση, υπόμνημα nt || *(reputation)* φήμη διάκριση ♦ vt σημειώνω, παρατηρώ || *(write down)* σημειώνω, (κατα)γράφω ~**book** n σημειωματάριο, καρνέ nt inv || ~-**case** n πορτοφόλι || ~**d** a σημαίνων, διακεκριμένος, διάσημος || ~**paper** n χαρτί αλληλογραφίας.

nothing ['nʌθɪŋ] n μηδέν, τίποτε || *for ~ (free)* δωρεάν, τζάμπα.

notice ['nəʊtɪs] n *(announcement)* αγγελία, αναγγελία || *(attention)* προσοχή, παρατήρηση || *(warning)* ειδοποίηση, προειδοποίηση ♦ vt *(observe)* παρατηρώ, αντιλαμβάνομαι, προσέχω || ~**able** a αξιοσημείωτος, αξιοπρόσεκτος || ~ **board** n *(Brit)* ενοικιαστήριο, πίνακας ανακοινώσεων.

notification [nəʊtɪfɪ'keɪʃən] n (αν)αγγελία, ανακοίνωση, δήλωση, γνωστοποίηση.

notify ['nəʊtɪfaɪ] vt πληροφορώ, ειδοποιώ, γνωστοποιώ.

notion ['nəʊʃən] n αντίληψη, ιδέα || *(fancy)* γνώμη, ιδέα, σκέψη.

notorious [nəʊ'tɔːrɪəs] a περιβόητος, πασίγνωστος.

notwithstanding [nɒtwɪθ'stændɪŋ] ad παρ', όλα αυτά, εντούτοις, όμως.

nougat ['nuːgɑː] n μαντολάτο.

nought [nɔːt] n *(zero)* μηδέν || τίποτε, μηδέν.

noun [naʊn] n όνομα, ουσιαστικό.

nourish ['nʌrɪʃ] vt (δια)τρέφω || ~**ing** a θρεπτικός.

novel ['nɒvəl] n μυθιστόρημα nt ♦ a νέος, πρωτότυπος || ~**ist** n μυθιστοριογράφος m/f || ~**ty** n νεωτερισμός.

November [nəʊ'vembə*] n Νοέμβριος.

novice ['nɒvɪs] n αρχάριος, μαθητευόμενος.

now [naʊ] ad τώρα, λοιπόν || *right ~* αμέσως, στη στιγμή || ~ **and then** κάπου-κάπου, καμμιά φορά, || ~ **and again** κάθε τόσο, μερικές φορές, που και που || ~**adays** ad σήμερα.

nowhere ['nəʊwɛə*] ad πουθενά.

nozzle ['nɒzl] n στόμιο (σωλήνα), προφύσιο, ακροφύσιο.

nuclear ['njuːklɪə*] a *(energy etc)* πυρηνικός.

nucleus ['njuːklɪəs] n πυρήνας.

nude [njuːd] a γυμνός, γδυτός ♦ n *(ART)* γυμνό.

nudge [nʌdʒ] vt αγκωνίζω, σκουντώ.

nudist ['njuːdɪst] n γυμνιστής/ γυμνίστρια m/f.

nudity ['njuːdɪtɪ] n γυμνότητα.

nuisance ['njuːsns] n ενόχληση, μπελάς.

null [nʌl] a άκυρος.

numb [nʌm] a ναρκωμένος, μουδιασμένος ♦ vt ναρκώνω, μουδιάζω.

number ['nʌmbə*] n αριθμός, ψηφίο, νούμερο || *(sum)* αριθμός, σύνολο, άθροισμα nt || *(quantity)* πολλοί mpl, πλήθος nt || *(GRAM)* αριθμός || *(issue)* αριθμός (τεύχους) ♦ vt *(an)*αριθμώ, μετρώ || *(amount to)* ανέρχομαι, φθάνω, αριθμώ || ~ **plate** n *(Brit AUT)* πινακίδα κυκλοφορίας αυτοκινήτου.

numeral ['njuːmərəl] n αριθμός.

numerical [njuː'merɪkəl] a *(order)* αριθμητικός.

numerous ['njuːmərəs] a πολυάριθμος.

nun [nʌn] n μοναχή, καλόγρηα.

nurse [nɜːs] n νοσοκόμα, νοσοκόμα mmll || *(for children)* παραμάνα, τροφός f ♦ vt *(patient, invalid)* περιποιούμαι, νοσηλεύω || *(fig)* φροντίζω, επιμελούμαι, συγκρατώ.

nursery ['nɜːsərɪ] n παιδικός σταθμός, βρεφοκομείο || *(plants)* φυτώριο || ~ **rhyme** n παιδικό τραγουδάκι || ~ **school** n νηπιαγωγείο.

nursing ['nɜːsɪŋ] n *(profession)* επάγγελμα nt νοσοκόμου || ~ **home** n *(ιδιωτική)* κλινική.

nut [nʌt] n περικόχλιο, παξιμάδι || *(fruit)* καρύδι, ξηρός καρπός || ~**s** a *(col: crazy)* τρελός.

nutcracker ['nʌtkrækə*] n καρυοθραύστης.

nutmeg ['nʌtmeg] n μοσχοκάρυδο.

nutrient ['njuːtrɪənt] n θρεπτικό, τρόφιμο.

nutritious [njuː'trɪʃəs] a θρεπτικός.

nutshell ['nʌtʃel] n: *in a ~* σύντομος, με λίγα λόγια.

nylon ['naɪlɒn] a, n νάυλον nt inv.

O

oaf [əʊf] n αδέξιος, άξεστος.

oak [əʊk] n δρυς, βαλανιδιά ♦ a δρύινος.

O.A.P. abbr see **old.**

oar [ɔː*] n κώπη, κουπί.

oasis [əʊ'eɪsɪs] n όαση.

oath [əʊθ] n όρκος || *(swearword)* βλαστήμια.

oats [əʊts] npl βρώμη.

obedience [ə'biːdɪəns] n υπακοή, ευπείθεια.

obedient [ə'biːdɪənt] a υπάκουος.

obesity [əʊ'biːsɪtɪ] n παχυσαρκία.

obey [ə'beɪ] vti υπακούω.

obituary [ə'bɪtjʊərɪ] n νεκρολογία.

object ['ɒbdʒɪkt] n αντικείμενο || *(target)* στόχος, σκοπός, αντικείμενο || *(GRAM)* αντικείμενο ♦ [əb'dʒekt] vi *(+ to) (proposal)* αντιτίθεμαι, αποδοκιμάζω || *(a noise etc)* αποκρούω, επικρίνω || ~**ion** n αντίρρηση, αντιλογία || *(obstacle)* εμπόδιο, δυσκολία || ~**ionable** a απαράδεκτος, ανεπιθύμητος || ~ive n αντικειμενικός σκοπός ♦ a (impartial) αντικειμενικός || ~or n αντιρρησίας, αντιλέγων.

obligation [ɒblɪˈgeɪʃən] n υποχρέωση.

obligatory [ɒˈblɪgətərɪ] a υποχρεωτικός.

oblige [əˈblaɪdʒ] vt υποχρεώνω, επιβάλλω || (do a favour) εξυπηρετώ, υποχρεώνω.

obliging [əˈblaɪdʒɪŋ] a υποχρεωτικός, εξυπηρετικός.

oblique [əˈbliːk] a λοξός, πλάγιος.

obliterate [əˈblɪtəreɪt] vt εξαλείφω, σβήνω, καταστρέφω.

oblivious [əˈblɪvɪəs] a (+ of) επιλήσμων, ξεχασιάρης.

oblong [ˈɒblɒŋ] n επίμηκες σχήμα nt, ορθογώνιο ♦ a επιμήκης, μακρουλός.

obnoxious [əbˈnɒkʃəs] a απεχθής, δυσάρεστος.

oboe [ˈəʊbəʊ] n όμποε nt.

obscene [əbˈsiːn] a αισχρός, πρόστυχος.

obscenity [əbˈsenɪtɪ] n αισχρότητα, αχρειότητα.

obscure [əbˈskjʊə*] a σκοτεινός, σκούρος || (unnoticed) άσημος, ταπεινός ♦ vt συσκοτίζω, σκεπάζω.

obscurity [əbˈskjʊərɪtɪ] n σκοτάδι, αφάνεια.

obsequious [əbˈsiːkwɪəs] a δουλοπρεπής.

observance [əbˈzɜːvəns] n τήρηση, τύπος.

observant [əbˈzɜːvənt] a παρατηρητικός, προσεκτικός.

observation [ɒbzəˈveɪʃən] n παρατήρηση, παρακολούθηση.

observatory [əbˈzɜːvətrɪ] n αστεροσκοπείο.

observe [əbˈzɜːv] vt (the law etc) τηρώ, κρατώ || (study) παρατηρώ, κοιτάζω || (understand) διακρίνω, αντιλαμβάνομαι || ~r n παρατηρητής, τηρητής.

obsess [əbˈses] vt κατέχω, βασανίζω || ~ion n έμμονη ιδέα || ~ive a καταθλιπτικός, βασανιστικός.

obsolescence [ɒbsəˈlesns] n τάση προς αχρηστία, παλαίωμα nt.

obsolete [ˈɒbsəliːt] a απαρχαιωμένος.

obstacle [ˈɒbstəkl] n εμπόδιο, πρόσκομμα || ~ race n δρόμος μετ' εμποδίων.

obstetrics [ɒbˈstetrɪks] n μαιευτική.

obstinate [ˈɒbstɪnɪt] a επίμονος, πεισματάρης || ~ly ad επίμονα.

obstruct [əbˈstrʌkt] vt φράσσω, εμποδίζω || ~ion n κωλυσιεργία, εμπόδιο.

obtain [əbˈteɪn] vt παίρνω, αποκτώ, επιτυγχάνω || ~able a επιτευκτός, εφικτός.

obtrusive [əbˈtruːsɪv] a ενοχλητικός, φορτικός.

obvious [ˈɒbvɪəs] a προφανής, ευνόητος || ~ly ad προφανώς, φανερά.

occasion [əˈkeɪʒən] n (time) ευκαιρία,

φορά || (event) αφορμή, περίσταση || (reason) λόγος, αιτία ♦ vt προξενώ || ~al a σποραδικός, τυχαίος || (drink) που και που || ~ally ad κάπου-κάπου.

occult [ɒˈkʌlt] n: the ~ οι απόκρυφες επιστήμες.

occupant [ˈɒkjʊpənt] n κάτοχος m/f || (of house) ένοικος m/f.

occupation [ɒkjʊˈpeɪʃən] n απασχόληση, ασχολία, επάγγελμα nt || (of country) κατάληψη, κτήση || ~al a (hazard) επαγγελματικός.

occupier [ˈɒkjʊpaɪə*] n (of house) ένοικος/n m/f.

occupy [ˈɒkjʊpaɪ] vt (take possession) κατέχω, κατακτώ || (live in) κατοικώ || (hold) κατέχω || (employ) απασχολώ.

occur [əˈkɜː*] vi συμβαίνω, γίνομαι, λαμβάνω χώρα || (be found) συναντώμαι, εμφανίζομαι || (+ to) παρουσιάζεται στη σκέψη || it ~s to me μου έρχεται || ~rence n γεγονός nt, συμβάν nt.

ocean [ˈəʊʃən] n ωκεανός || ~-going a υπερωκεάνειος.

ochre [ˈəʊkə*] n ώχρα.

o'clock [əˈklɒk] ad: it is 5 ~ είναι πέντε n (ώρα).

octagonal [ɒkˈtægənl] a οκταγώνιος.

octane [ˈɒkteɪn] n οκτάνιο.

octave [ˈɒktɪv] n οκτάβα.

October [ɒkˈtəʊbə*] n Οκτώβριος.

octopus [ˈɒktəpəs] n χταπόδι.

odd [ɒd] a (number) περιττός, μονός || (not part of set) μονός, παράταιρος || (with some left over) αυτός που περισσεύει || (strange) περίεργος, παράξενος || (casual) τυχαίος || ~ity n παραδοξότητα || (person) παράξενος άνθρωπος || ~ly ad περίεργος, περίεργα || ~ments npl υπολείμματα ntpl || ~s npl ανισότητα, διαφορά || (advantage) πλεονέκτημα nt, πιθανότητες fpl || (chances) πιθανότητες fpl || (at racetrack) στοίχημα nt, ποντάρισμα nt || at ~s διαφωνώ, είμαι τσακωμένος || ~s and ends npl απομεινάρια ntpl, μικροπράγματα ntpl.

ode [əʊd] n ωδή.

odious [ˈəʊdɪəs] a απεχθής, μισητός.

odour, odor (US) [ˈəʊdə*] n οσμή, μυρουδιά || ~less a άοσμος.

of [ɒv, əv] prep από, περί, παρά.

off [ɒf] ad (absent) μακριά || (of switch) κλειστό || (milk) όχι φρέσκος, χαλασμένος ♦ prep από, μακριά από, λιγώτερο από.

offal [ˈɒfəl] n εντόσθια ntpl.

off-colour, off-color (US) [ˈɒfˈkʌlə*] a (ill) χλωμός.

offence [əˈfens] n (crime) παράπτωμα nt, αδίκημα nt || (insult) προσβολή.

offend [əˈfend] vt προσβάλλω || ~er n παραβάτης m/f || ~ing a προσβλητικός, πειρακτικός.

offense [əˈfens] n (US) = **offence**.

offensive [əˈfensɪv] a προσβλητικός, δυσάρεστος || (weapon) επιθετικός.

offer [ˈɒfə*] n προσφορά ♦ vt

προσφέρω, προτείνω || ~ing n (esp REL) θυσία, προσφορά.

offhand ['ɒf'hænd] a αυθόρμητος, απότομος ♦ ad στη στιγμή, απότομα.

office ['ɒfɪs] n (position) γραφείο || ~r n (MIL) αξιωματικός, αξιωματούχος || ~ work n εργασία γραφείου.

official [ə'fɪʃəl] a (authorized) επίσημος, υπηρεσιακός ♦ n υπάλληλος m/f (δημόσιος) || ~ly ad επίσημα.

officious [ə'fɪʃəs] a αυταρχικός, ενοχλητικός.

offing ['ɒfɪŋ] n: in the ~ εν όψει, στα ανοιχτά.

off line [ɒf'laɪn] a (COMPUT) έμμεση σύνδεση και προπέλαση || (switched off) αποσυνδεδεμένος.

off-season ['ɒfsɪːzn] a μη εποχιακός, εκτός εποχής, νεκρή εποχή.

offset ['ɒfset] vt αντιυσταθμίζω, αποζημιώνω.

offshore ['ɒf'ʃɔː*] ad στα ανοιχτά ♦ a χερσαίος, στεριανός.

offside ['ɒf'saɪd] a (AUT) έξω πλευρά, δεξιά πλευρά ♦ n (SPORT) οφσάϊντ.

offspring ['ɒfsprɪŋ] n απόγονος, βλαστός.

often ['ɒfən] ad συχνά, πολλές φορές.

oh [əʊ] excl ω!, αχ!

oil [ɔɪl] n πετρέλαιο, λάδι ♦ vt λαδώνω || ~can n λαδωτήρι || ~field n πετρελαιοφόρος περιοχή || ~-fired a καίων πετρέλαιο || ~ painting n ελαιογραφία || ~ refinery n διυλιστήριο || ~skins npl μουσαμάς || ~ tanker n δεξαμενόπλοιο || ~ well n πετρελαιοπηγή || ~y a ελαιώδης, λαδερός.

ointment ['ɔɪntmənt] n αλοιφή.

O.K., okay ['əʊ'keɪ] excl πολύ καλά, εντάξει ♦ a έγκριση ♦ vt εγκρίνω.

old [əʊld] a γέροντας, γέρος, ηλικιωμένος || (of age) της ηλικίας, χρονών || (worn) παλιός || (former) παλιός, πρώην, τέως || (friend) παλιός (σύντροφος) || ~ age n (βαθειά) γεράματα ntpl || ~ age pensioner (O.A.P.) n συνταξιούχος m/f || ~en a (old) παλιό, του παλιού || ~-fashioned a οπαδός του παλιού καιρού || (out of date) απαρχαιωμένος, παλιάς μόδας || ~ maid n γεροντοκόρη.

olive ['ɒlɪv] n (fruit) ελιά, ελαία ♦ a (colour) λαδής, ελαιόχρους || ~ oil n ελαιόλαδο, λάδι.

Olympic [əʊ'lɪmpɪk] a Ολυμπιακός || ~ Games npl (also: ~s) Ολυμπιακοί αγώνες mpl.

omelet(te) ['ɒmlɪt] n ομελέτα.

omen ['əʊmen] n οιωνός, σημάδι.

ominous ['ɒmɪnəs] a δυσοίωνος, δυσμενής.

omission [əʊ'mɪʃən] n παράλειψη, παραδρομή.

omit [əʊ'mɪt] vt παραλείπω.

on [ɒn] prep πάνω σε, σε, κατά, περί ♦ ad εμπρός, προς τα εμπρός, σε λειτουργία || ~ and off κάπου-κάπου || ~ the left αριστερά, στ, αριστερά || ~ Friday την Παρασκευή.

once [wʌns] ad μια φορά, άλλοτε, κάποτε || cj μόλις, από τη στιγμή που, μια και || at ~ αμέσως, στη στιγμή || (same time) ταυτόχρονα, σύγχρονα || all at ~ (suddenly) εντελώς ξαφνικά || (speaking etc) όλοι μαζί || ~ more ακόμη μια φορά || more than ~ πολλές φορές || ~ and for all μια και καλή || ~ upon a time μια φορά (και ένα καιρό).

oncoming ['ɒnkʌmɪŋ] a (traffic) επερχόμενος, προσεγγίζων.

one [wʌn] a ένας, μία, ένα || (only) μόνος, μοναδικός ♦ n ένα, ένας, μια ♦ pron ένας, αυτός, κανείς, τέτοιος || this ~ αυτός εδώ || that ~ αυτός εκεί || ~ by ~ ένας ένας || anοtπer πλλήλοug || ~-man a (business) (δουλειά) για έναν άνθρωπο || ~self pron εαυτό || ~-way a (street, traffic) μονής κατευθύνσεως.

onion ['ʌnjən] n κρεμμύδι.

on line [ɒn'laɪn] a (COMPUT) άμεση σύνδεση και προσπέλαση || (switched on) συνδεδεμένος.

onlooker ['ɒnlʊkə*] n θεατής.

only ['əʊnlɪ] ad μόνο ♦ a μόνος.

onset ['ɒnset] n (beginning) απαρχή.

onshore ['ɒnʃɔː*] a, ad προς την ακτή.

onslaught ['ɒnslɔːt] n εφόρμηση, επίθεση.

onto ['ɒntʊ] prep=on to.

onus ['əʊnəs] n βάρος nt, ευθύνη, καθήκον nt.

onwards ['ɒnwədz] ad (place) προς τα εμπρός, και πέρα || (time) και στο εξής.

ooze [uːz] vi (liquid) στάζω, εκρέω, διεισδύω.

opaque [əʊ'peɪk] a αδιαφανής, θαμπός.

open ['əʊpən] a ανοιχτός || (unlimited) ανοιχτός, απεριόριστος || (without cover) ακάλυπτος, ξέσκεπος || (clear) φανερός, έκδηλος || (question) φανερός, έκδηλος || (free) ελεύθερος, ανοιχτός || (sincere) ειλικρινής, απροκάλυπτος ♦ vt ανοίγω || (letter) αποσφραγίζω, ανοίγω || (box) λύνω, ανοίγω ♦ vi αρχίζω, ανοίγω || (shop) ανοίγω || (play) αρχίζω || to ~ out vt ανοίγω, ξεδιπλώνω || to ~ up vt (route) ανοίγω, χαράσσω, διανοίγω || ~-air a υπαίθριος || ~er n (for cans) ανοικτήρι || ~ing n άνοιγμα nt, ρωγμή || (beginning) έναρξη || (good chance) ευκαιρία || ~ly ad φανερά, ειλικρινά, δημόσια || ~-minded a απροκάλυπτος με ανοιχτό μυαλό || ~-necked a ανοιχτό || (φόρεμα) ντεκολτέ.

opera ['ɒpərə] n μελόδραμα nt, όπερα || ~ house n λυρική σκηνή, όπερα.

operate ['ɒpəreɪt] vt (machine) ενεργώ, κινώ, διευθύνω ♦ vi λειτουργώ, δρω, ενεργώ || (MED) (+ on) χειρουργώ, εγχειρίζω.

operation [ɒpə'reɪʃən] n λειτουργία, δράση || (MED) εγχείρηση || (MIL) επιχείρηση.

operative ['ɒprətɪv] a ενεργός, ισχύων, χειρουργικός.

operator ['ɒprəreɪtə*] n (of machine) χειριστής, οπερατέρ m inv || (TEL) τηλεφωνήτρια.

operetta [ɒpə'rɛtə] n οπερέττα.

opinion [ə'pɪnjən] n γνώμη, ιδέα, δοξασία.

opium ['əʊpɪəm] n όπιο.

opponent [ə'pəʊnənt] n αντίπαλος.

opportune ['ɒpətjuːn] a επίκαιρος, εύθετος, κατάλληλος.

opportunist [ɒpə'tjuːnɪst] n καιροσκόπος.

opportunity [ɒpə'tjuːnɪtɪ] n ευκαιρία.

oppose [ə'pəʊz] vt αντιτάσσω, αντικρούω, καταπολεμώ || ~d a (+ to) αντίθετος (προς), αντιτιθέμενος.

opposing [ə'pəʊzɪŋ] a (side) αντίθετος, αντίπαλος.

opposite ['ɒpəzɪt] a αντίθετος, αντικρυνός || (direction) αντίθετος ♦ ad απέναντι, αντίκρυ ♦ prep απέναντι ♦ n αντίστοιχο, αντίθετο || ~ number n (person) αντίστοιχος.

opposition [ɒpə'zɪʃən] n αντίσταση, αντίθεση || (party) αντιπολίτευση.

oppress [ə'prɛs] vt καταπιέζω, καταδυναστεύω || (heat etc) καταθλίβω, βασανίζω || ~ion n καταπίεση, στενοχώρια || ~ive a καταθλιπτικός, πνιγηρός.

opt [ɒpt] vi: to ~ for διαλέγω, επιλέγω.

optical ['ɒptɪkəl] n οπτικός.

optician [ɒp'tɪʃən] n οπτικός.

optimism ['ɒptɪmɪzəm] n αισιοδοξία.

optimist ['ɒptɪmɪst] n αισιόδοξος || ~ic a αισιόδοξος.

optimum ['ɒptɪməm] a ευνοϊκός, άριστος.

option ['ɒpʃən] n εκλογή || (right to choose) δικαίωμα nt εκλογής || ~al a προαιρετικός.

opulent ['ɒpjʊlənt] a πλούσιος, άφθονος.

or [ɔː*] cj ή.

oracle ['ɒrəkl] n χρησμός, μαντείο.

oral ['ɔːrəl] a προφορικός ♦ n (exam) προφορικές (εξετάσεις) fpl.

orange ['ɒrɪndʒ] n πορτοκάλι || (colour) πορτοκαλλί.

oration [ɔː'reɪʃən] n λόγος.

orbit ['ɔːbɪt] n τροχιά ♦ vt (earth) περιστρέφομαι.

orchard ['ɔːtʃəd] n οπωρόκηπος, περιβόλι.

orchestra ['ɔːkɪstrə] n ορχήστρα || ~l [ɔː'kɛstrəl] a ορχηστρικός.

orchid ['ɔːkɪd] n ορχεοειδές φυτό.

ordain [ɔː'deɪn] vt (προ)ορίζω, θεσπίζω διορίζω || (ECCL) χειροτονώ.

ordeal [ɔː'diːl] n βασανιστήριο.

order ['ɔːdə*] n (arrangement) τάξη, σειρά, διαδοχή || (instruction) διαταγή, εντολή, διάταγμα nt || (rank, class) τάξη || (ECCL) βαθμός ιερωσύνης || (MIL) τάγμα nt || (decoration) παράσημο || (COMM) επιταγή, παραγγελία ♦ vt διατάσσω || διευθετώ, ταξινομώ || (COMM) παραγγέλλω || ~ form n έντυπο εντολής || ~ly n αγγελιαφόρος, ορντινάντσα ♦ a φρόνιμος, τακτικός, ήσυχος || (tidy) συγυρισμένος, τακτικός.

ordinary ['ɔːdnrɪ] a συνήθης, συνηθισμένος || (commonplace) της αράδας, κοινός.

ore [ɔː*] n ορυκτό, μετάλλευμα nt.

organ ['ɔːgən] n (all senses) όργανο || ~ic [ɔː'gænɪk] a οργανικός, ενόργανος.

organism [ɔːgənɪzəm] n οργανισμός.

organist ['ɔːgənɪst] n οργανοπαίκτης.

organization [ɔːgənaɪ'zeɪʃən] n οργάνωση, οργανισμός.

organize ['ɔːgənaɪz] vt οργανώνω || ~r n (δι)οργανωτής.

orgasm ['ɔːgæzəm] n οργασμός, παροξυσμός.

orgy ['ɔːdʒɪ] n όργιο.

Orient ['ɔːrɪənt] n: the ~ Ανατολή, Άπω Ανατολή.

oriental [ɔːrɪ'ɛntəl] a ανατολικός, ασιατικός ♦ n Ασιάτης.

orientate ['ɔːrɪɛnteɪt] vt προσανατολίζω.

origin ['ɒrɪdʒɪn] n αρχή, γένεση, καταγωγή.

original [ə'rɪdʒɪnl] a (first) αρχικός || (new) πρωτότυπος || (individual) ιδιότυπος, πρωτότυπος ♦ n πρωτότυπο || ~ity [ərɪdʒɪ'nælɪtɪ] n πρωτοτυπία || ~ly ad αρχικά, εξ αρχής.

originate [ə'rɪdʒɪneɪt] vi κατάγομαι, προέρχομαι ♦ vt γεννώ, δημιουργώ.

originator [ə'rɪdʒɪneɪtə*] n δημιουργός, εγκαινιαστής.

ornament ['ɔːnəmənt] n κόσμημα nt, στολίδι || ~al a (δια)κοσμητικός.

ornate [ɔː'neɪt] a διακοσμημένος, φανταχτερός.

ornithology [ɔːnɪ'θɒlədʒɪ] n ορνιθολογία.

orphan ['ɔːfən] n ορφανός/ή m/f ♦ vt ορφανεύω || ~age n ορφανοτροφείο.

orthodox [ɔːθədɒks] a ορθόδοξος || (conventional) καθιερωμένος.

orthopaedic, orthopedic (US) [ɔːθəʊ'piːdɪk] a ορθοπεδικός.

ostensibly [ɒs'tɛnsəblɪ] ad κατά τα φαινόμενα, δήθεν.

ostentatious [ɒstɛn'teɪʃəs] a επιδεικτικός, φιγουρατζής, φανταχτερός.

ostracize ['ɒstrəsaɪz] vt εξοστρακίζω.

ostrich ['ɒstrɪtʃ] n στρουθοκάμηλος f.

other ['ʌðə*] a άλλος || (additional) άλλος, επιπρόσθετος || (opposite) άλλος, απέναντι ♦ pron άλλος ♦ ad: ~ than διαφορετικός από, εκτός από || ~wise ad αλλιώς, αλλιώτικα || (in other ways) κατά τα άλλα || (or else) διαφορετικά, αλλιώς, ειδάλλως.

otter ['ɒtə*] n ενυδρίδα.

ought [ɔːt] auxiliary v πρέπει, θα έπρεπε || **I ~ to do it** πρέπει να το κάνω || **you ~**

to go πρέπει να φύγεις || **he ~ to win** πρέπει να κερδίσει.

ounce [auns] n ουγγιά.

our [auə*] poss a δικός μας || **~s** poss pron δικός μας || **~selves** pron εμείς οι ίδιοι.

oust [aust] vt διώχνω, εκτοπίζω.

out [aut] ad έξω || (not indoors) εκτός || (not alight) σβηισμένος || (open) που βγήκε, βγαλμένος || (made known) γνωστός, που απεκαλύφθη || (in reckoning) σε λάθος, έξω || ~ **of** prep έξω από || (from among) από || (without) χωρίς || **made ~ of wood** καμωμένος από ξύλο || **~-of-bounds** a απαγορευμένος || **~-of-date** a ξεπερασμένος || **~ of doors** ad έξω, στο ύπαιθρο || **~ of order** a χαλασμένος || **~-of-the-way** a παράμερος, απόμερος || (unusual) ασυνήθης, ασυνήθιστος.

outboard (motor) ['autbɔːd('məutə*)] n εξωλέμβιος (κινητήρας).

outbreak ['autbreik] n έκρηξη, ξέσπασμα nt, έναρξη.

outburst ['autbɜːst] n έκρηξη, ξέσπασμα nt.

outcast ['autkɑːst] n απόβλητος.

outcome ['autkʌm] n έκβαση, πέρας nt.

outcry ['autkrai] n (κατα)κραυγή.

outdated ['aut'deitid] a παλιωμένος, ξεπερασμένος.

outdo [aut'duː] vt υπερβαίνω, υπερέχω.

outdoor ['autdɔː*] a υπαίθριος, εξωτερικός.

outdoors ['aut'dɔːz] ad στο ύπαιθρο.

outer ['autə*] a εξωτερικός || **~ space** n διάστημα nt.

outfit ['autfit] n εξοπλισμός, εργαλεία ntpl, απαιτούμενα ntpl.

outgoings ['autgəuiŋz] npl (expenses) έξοδα ntpl, πληρωμές fpl.

outgrow [aut'grəu] vt γίνομαι ψηλότερος από, ξεπερνώ.

outing ['autiŋ] n εκδρομή.

outlaw ['autlɔː] n ληστής, παράνομος ♦ vt βάζω εκτός νόμου.

outlay ['autlei] n δαπάνη, έξοδα ntpl.

outlet ['autlet] n διέξοδος f, άνοιγμα nt.

outline ['autlain] n περίμετρος f, περίγραμμα nt || (summary) περίληψη.

outlive [aut'liv] vt επιζώ.

outlook ['autluk] n (prospect) πρόβλεψη.

outlying ['autlaiiŋ] a απόκεντρος, απόμερος.

outmoded [aut'məudid] a ντεμοντέ.

outnumber [aut'nʌmbə*] vt υπερτερώ αριθμητικά.

outpatient ['autpeiʃənt] n εξωτερικός ασθενής m/f.

outpost ['autpəust] n (people, also place) προφυλακή, φυλάκιο.

output ['autput] n παραγωγή, απόδοση, προϊόν nt ♦ vt (COMPUT) εκτυπώνω.

outrage ['autreidʒ] n προσβολή, κατάφωρο αδίκημα nt ♦ vt προσβάλλω, πληγώνω, ταράζω || **~ous** a σκανδαλώδης, τερατώδης, αχρείος.

outright ['autrait] ad απερίφραστα,

ωμά, ξάστερα || (once and for all) τελείως, εντελώς ♦ a τέλειος, οριστικός.

outset ['autset] n αρχή, ξεκίνημα nt.

outside ['aut'said] n εξωτερικό ♦ a εξωτερικός, πιθανός ♦ ad απ' έξω, έξω ♦ prep έξω από, εκτός, από, πέραν του || **~r** n (in race etc) χωρίς πιθανότητες fpl || (independent) ξένος/n m/f, θεατής.

outsize ['autsaiz] a μεγάλων διαστάσεων.

outskirts ['autskɜːts] npl προάστια ntpl, περίχωρα ntpl.

outspoken [aut'spəukən] a ειλικρινής, ντόμπρος.

outstanding [aut'stændiŋ] a προέχων, κύριος, σημαντικός || (person) διακεκριμένος, σπουδαίος, διαπρεπής || (unsettled) εκκρεμής, απλήρωτος.

outstay [aut'stei] vt (welcome) μένω περισσότερο από.

outstretched ['autstretʃt] a (hand) απλωμένος, με ανοιχτές αγκάλες.

outward ['autwəd] a (sign) εξωτερικός || (journey) προς τα έξω, έξω || **~ly** ad εξωτερικά, φαινομενικά.

outwit [aut'wit] vt ξεγελώ.

oval ['əuvəl] a ωοειδής, ελλειψοειδής ♦ n ωοειδές σχήμα nt.

ovary ['əuvəri] n ωοθήκη.

ovation [əu'veiʃən] n επευφημία.

oven ['ʌvn] n κλίβανος, φούρνος.

over ['əuvə*] ad (above) από πάνω, πάνω από || (across) απέναντι, πέρα || (finished) περασμένος, τελειωμένος || (too much) πέραν του δέοντος, επί πλέον || (again) φορές (συνέχεια), πάλι ♦ prep (above) από πάνω, πάνω || (across) απέναντι || (in rank) υπεράνω, ανώτερος || (about) περί, για || **all ~** (everywhere) παντού, σ' όλο || (finished) τελειωμένος, περασμένος || **~ and ~** πολλές φορές, επανειλημμένα || **~ and above** πέρα από.

over- ['əuvə*] prefix υπέρ-, παρά-.

overall ['əuvərɔːl] n (Brit: for woman etc) ποδιά || **~s** npl (industrial etc) φόρμα.

overbalance [əuvə'bæləns] vi ανατρέπω, υπερέχω.

overbearing [əuvə'bɛəriŋ] a αυταρχικός, δεσποτικός, υπεροπτικός.

overboard ['əuvəbɔːd] ad στη θάλασσα (από πλοίο).

overcast ['əuvəkɑːst] a συννεφιασμένος, σκοτεινιασμένος.

overcharge [əuvə'tʃɑːdʒ] vt (price) παίρνω πολλά, πουλώ σε, υπερβολική τιμή.

overcoat ['əuvəkəut] n επανωφόρι, παλτό.

overcome [əuvə'kʌm] vt νικώ, καταβάλλω.

overcrowded [əuvə'kraudid] a υπερπλήρες, παραγεμισμένο.

overdo [əuvə'duː] vt (cook) παραψήνω || (exaggerate) υπερβάλλω, μεγαλοποιώ, παρακάνω.

overdose ['əuvədəus] n υπερβολική δόση.

overdraft ['əʊvədrɑ:ft] *n* ανάληψη χωρίς αντίκρισμα.

overdrawn [əʊvə'drɔ:n] *a (account) see* **overdraft.**

overdrive ['əʊvədraɪv] *n (AUT)* οβερντράϊβ.

overdue ['əʊvədju:] *a* καθυστερημένος, εκπρόθεσμος.

overestimate ['əʊvər'estɪmeɪt] *vt* υπερεκτιμώ, υπερτιμώ.

overexcited ['əʊvərɪk'saɪtɪd] *a* υπερδιεγειρόμενος.

overexpose ['əʊvərɪks'pəʊz] *vt (PHOT)* υπερεκθέτω, υπερφωτίζω.

overflow [əʊvə'fləʊ] *vi* ξεχειλίζω ♦ ['əʊvəfləʊ] *n* υπερχείλιση, ξεχείλισμα *nt.*

overgrown ['əʊvə'grəʊn] *a (garden)* κατάφυτος, γεμάτος από, σκεπασμένος με.

overhaul [əʊvə'hɔ:l] *vt (repair)* εξετάζω, επιθεωρώ, ελέγχω ♦ ['əʊvəhɔ:l] *n* προσεκτική εξέταση, επιθεώρηση, επισκευή.

overhead ['əʊvəhed] *a* εναέριος, γενικός ♦ ['əʊvə'hed] *ad* επάνω, υπεράνω, ψηλά || ~ **s** *npl* γενικά έξοδα *ntpl.*

overhear [əʊvə'hɪə*] *vt* ακούω τυχαία, κρυφακούω.

overjoyed [əʊvə'dʒɔɪd] *a* περιχαρής, γεμάτος χαρά.

overland ['əʊvəlænd] *a* χερσαίος, στεριανός ♦ [əʊvə'lænd] *ad (journey)* διά ξηράς.

overlap [əʊvə'læp] *vi* καβαλικεύω, σκεπάζω μερικώς ♦ ['əʊvəlæp] *n* επικάλυψη, καβαλίκεμα *nt.*

overleaf ['əʊvə'li:f] *ad* στο πίσω μέρος (της σελίδας).

overload ['əʊvə'ləʊd] *vt* παραφορτώνω, υπερφορτίζω.

overlook [əʊvə'lʊk] *vt* κοιτάζω πάνω από, δεσπόζω || *(not notice)* παραβλέπω, παραμελώ || *(pardon)* παραβλέπω, συγχωρώ.

overnight [əʊvə'naɪt] *a* ολονύκτιος, ξενυχτισμένος ♦ *ad* όλη τη νύκτα, ξενύχτι.

overpass ['əʊvəpɑ:s] *n (road)* ανυψωμένη διάβαση.

overpower [əʊvə'paʊə*] *vt* καταβάλλω, συντρίβω, καταπνίγω || ~**ing** *a* συντριπτικός, αποπνικτικός.

overrate ['əʊvə'reɪt] *vt* υπερτιμώ.

override [əʊvə'raɪd] *vt (invalidate)* υπερβαίνω, ανατρέπω.

overriding [əʊvə'raɪdɪŋ] *a* πρωταρχικός, δεσπόζων.

overrule [əʊvə'ru:l] *vt* ανατρέπω, αγνοώ, αναιρώ.

overseas ['əʊvə'si:z] *ad* στο εξωτερικό ♦ *a (trade)* εξωτερικός.

overshadow [əʊvə'ʃædəʊ] *vt* επισκιάζω.

overshoot ['əʊvə'ʃu:t] *vt (runway)* προσγειώνομαι μακριά.

oversight ['əʊvəsaɪt] *n* παράβλεψη, παραδρομή.

oversleep ['əʊvə'sli:p] *vi* παρακοιμάμαι.

overstate ['əʊvə'steɪt] *vt (case)* μεγαλοποιώ, υπερβάλλω || ~**ment** *n* υπερβολή, μεγαλοποίηση.

overt [əʊ'vɜ:t] *a* έκδηλος, καταφανής, φανερός.

overtake [əʊvə'teɪk] *vt* προσπερνώ, ξεπερνώ ♦ *vi* συμβαίνω σε, τυχαίνω σε.

overtaking [əʊvə'teɪkɪŋ] *n* ξεπέρασμα *nt.*

overthrow [əʊvə'θrəʊ] *vt* ανατρέπω || *(vanquish)* συντρίβω.

overtime ['əʊvətaɪm] *n* υπερωρία.

overture ['əʊvətjʊə*] *n (MUS)* εισαγωγή, ουβερτούρα.

overturn [əʊvə'tɜ:n] *vt* ανατρέπω, αναποδογυρίζω ♦ *vi* ανατρέπομαι.

overweight ['əʊvə'weɪt] *a* με βάρος ανώτερο του κανονικού.

overwhelm [əʊvə'welm] *vt* συντρίβω, κατακλύζω, καταβάλλω || ~**ing** *a* συντριπτικός, ακαταμάχητος.

overwork ['əʊvə'wɜ:k] *n* καταπόνηση, υπερκόπωση ♦ *vt* παραφορτώνω, παρακουράζω ♦ *vi* εργάζομαι υπερβολικά, παρακουράζομαι.

overwrought ['əʊvə'rɔ:t] *a* σε υπερένταση, παρακουρασμένος.

owe [əʊ] *vt* οφείλω, χρωστώ.

owing to ['əʊɪŋtu:] *prep* λόγω, ένεκα, συνεπεία, εξ αιτίας.

owl [aʊl] *n* κουκουβάγια.

own [əʊn] *vt (kat)*έχω, είμαι κύριος ♦ *a* δικός (μου) ♦ *n* δικός (μου), ιδιαίτερος || **all my** ~ μου ανήκει, όλο δικό μου || **on one's** ~ ανεξάρτητα, μόνος (μου) || **to** ~ **up** *vi (confess)* ομολογώ || ~**er** *n* ιδιοκτήτης/ήτρια *m/f*, κάτοχος/ία *m/f* || ~**ership** *n* κυριότητα, ιδιοκτησία.

ox [ɒks] *n* βόδι.

oxide ['ɒksaɪd] *n* οξείδιο.

oxygen ['ɒksɪdʒən] *n* οξυγόνο || ~ **mask** *n* μάσκα οξυγόνου || ~ **tent** *n* ασκός οξυγόνου.

oyster ['ɔɪstə*] *n* στρείδι.

oz. *abbr of* **ounce(s).**

ozone ['əʊzəʊn] *n* όζον *nt.*

P

p [pi:] *abbr of* **penny, pence.**

p.a. *abbr of* **per annum.**

pace [peɪs] *n* βήμα *nt*, βάδισμα *nt* || *(speed)* ταχύτητα ♦ *vi* βαδίζω, βηματίζω, περπατώ || **to keep** ~ **with** συμβαδίζω || ~**maker** *n* προπονητής || *(MED)* βηματοδότης.

Pacific (Ocean) [pə'sɪfɪk('əʊʃən)] *n* Ειρηνικός (Ωκεανός).

pacifist ['pæsɪfɪst] *n* ειρηνόφιλος/η *m/f.*

pacify ['pæsɪfaɪ] *vt* ειρηνεύω, καθησυχάζω.

pack [pæk] *n (bundle)* δέμα *nt*, πακέτο || *(wolves)* αγέλη, κοπάδι || *(cards)* δεσμίδα, τράπουλα || *(gang)* συμμορία ♦ *vt (case)*

συσκευάζω, πακετάρω, κάνω δέμα ||
(bags) μαζεύω (τα ρούχα μου).
package ['pækidʒ] *n* δέμα *nt*.
packet ['pækit] *n* δεματάκι, πακέτο.
pack ice ['pækaɪs] *n* σωρός πάγων,
ογκόπαγοι *mpl*.
packing ['pækɪŋ] *n (action)* πακετάρισμα
nt || *(material)* συσκευασία || ~ **case** *n*
κιβώτιο συσκευασίας, κασόνι.
pact [pækt] *n* συμφωνία, συνθήκη.
pad [pæd] *n (pillow)* μαξιλαράκι ||
(notebook) μπλόκ *nt inv* || *(for inking)*
ταμπόν *nt inv* ♦ *vt* (παρα)γεμίζω.
paddle ['pædl] *n (oar)* κουπί,
αναδευτήρας ♦ *vt (boat)* κωπηλατώ,
τραβώ κουπί ♦ *vi (in sea)* κωπηλατώ
ήρεμα, τσαλαβουτώ.
paddling pool ['pædlɪŋpuːl] *n* λιμνούλα
(για παιδιά).
paddock ['pædək] *n* περίβολος, μάντρα
(για άλογα).
paddy ['pædi] *n*: ~ **field** *n* ορυζοφυτεία.
padlock ['pædlɒk] *n* λουκέτο.
padre ['pɑːdrɪ] *n* παπάς.
paediatrics [piːdɪ'ætrɪks] *n* παιδιατρική.
pagan ['peɪgən] *a* ειδωλολατρικός.
page [peɪdʒ] *n (of book)* σελίδα || *(boy
servant)* νεαρός υπηρέτης, γκρούμ *m inv*
|| *(wedding)* ακόλουθος, παράνυμφος ♦
vt (in hotel etc) στέλνω μικρό να φωνάξει
(κάποιον).
pageant ['pædʒənt] *n* φαντασμαγορικό
θέαμα *nt*, επιβλητική πομπή.
paid [peɪd] *pt, pp of* **pay.**
pail [peɪl] *n* κάδος, κουβάς.
pain [peɪn] *n* πόνος || ~**s** *npl (efforts)*
κόπος || ~**ed** *a (expression)* θλιμμένος,
πικραμένος, πονεμένος || ~**ful** *a*
οδυνηρός || *(physically)* που πονεί ||
(difficult) επίπονος || ~**killing drug** *n*
ναυσίπονο || ~**less** *a* ανώδυνος ||
painstaking *a* φιλόπονος, προσεκτικός.
paint [peɪnt] *n* χρώμα *nt*, μπογιά ♦ *vt*
ζωγραφίζω, απεικονίζω || *(house etc)*
μπογιατίζω, χρωματίζω || ~**brush** *n*
χρωστήρας, πινέλο || ~**er** *n (ART)*
ζωγράφος *m/f* || *(decorator)* χρωματιστής,
μπογιατζής || ~**ing** *n (action)* ζωγραφική
|| *(picture)* πίνακας, ζωγραφιά.
pair [pɛə*] *n* ζευγάρι || *(of shoes)* ζεύγος *nt*
|| ~ **of scissors** *n* ψαλίδι || ~ **of
trousers** *n* πανταλόνι.
pajamas [pə'dʒɑːməz] *npl (US)* πυτζάμες
fpl.
pal [pæl] *n (col)* σύντροφος, φίλος.
palace ['pælɪs] *n* ανάκτορο, παλάτι.
palatable ['pælətəbl] *a* εύγευστος,
νόστιμος.
palate ['pælɪt] *n* υπερώα, ουρανίσκος ||
(taste) γεύση.
pale [peɪl] *a (face)* ωχρός, χλωμός ||
(colour) ανοιχτός.
palette ['pælɪt] *n* παλέτα.
palisade [pælɪ'seɪd] *n* φράκτης από
πασσάλους.
pall [pɔːl] *n (of smoke)* σύννεφο ♦ *vi*
κουράζω, βαριέμαι.

pally ['pælɪ] *a (col)* που πιάνει εύκολα
φιλίες.
palm [pɑːm] *n (tree)* φοίνικας || *(of hand)*
παλάμη || ~**ist** *n* χειρομάντης/ισσα *m/f* ||
P~ Sunday *n* Κυριακή των Βαΐων || ~
tree *n* φοινικιά, χουρμαδιά.
palpable ['pælpəbl] *a (obvious)* φανερός,
καταφανής.
palpitation [pælpɪ'teɪʃən] *n* παλμός,
σπαρτάρισμα *nt*.
paltry ['pɔːltrɪ] *a* μηδαμινός, τιποτένιος,
άθλιος.
pamper ['pæmpə*] *vt* (παρα)χαϊδεύω.
pamphlet ['pæmflɪt] *n* φυλλάδιο.
pan [pæn] *n* τηγάνι, κατσαρόλα ♦ *vi (+
out)* επιτυγχάνω, αποδίδω.
panacea [pænə'sɪə] *n (fig)* πανάκεια.
pancake ['pænkeɪk] *n* τηγανίτα.
panda ['pændə] *n* πάντα.
pandemonium [pændɪ'məʊnɪəm] *n*
πανδαιμόνιο.
pander ['pændə*] *vi (+ to)* κάνω το
ρουφιάνο, κολακεύω πρόστυχα.
pane [peɪn] *n* τζάμι.
panel ['pænl] *n (of wood)* φάτνωμα *nt*,
φύλλο || *(of people)* επιτροπή || ~**ling,**
~**ing** *(US) n* ξυλεπένδυση.
pang [pæŋ] *n* δυνατός πόνος || *(pain)*
αγωνία.
panic ['pænɪk] *n* πανικός ♦ *a (reaction)*
πανικόβλητος ♦ *vi* πανικοβάλλομαι ||
~**ky** *a (person)* πανικόβλητος, έντρομος,
φοβισμένος.
pannier ['pænɪə*] *n* κοφίνι, πανέρι.
panorama [pænə'rɑːmə] *n* πανόραμα
nt.
pansy ['pænzɪ] *n (flower)* πανσές *m*.
pant [pænt] *vi* λαχανιάζω.
panther ['pænθə*] *n* πάνθηρας.
panties ['pæntɪz] *npl (woman's)* κυλότα.
pantomime ['pæntəmaɪm] *n*
παντομίμα.
pantry ['pæntrɪ] *n* κελάρι || *(butler's)*
κάβα.
pants [pænts] *npl (woman's)* κυλότα ||
(man's) σώβρακο || *(US: trousers)*
παντελόνι.
papal ['peɪpəl] *a* παπικός.
paper ['peɪpə*] *n (material)* χαρτί ||
(newspaper) εφημερίδα || *(essay)* μελέτη,
διατριβή, υπόμνημα *nt* ♦ *a* χάρτινος ♦ *vt*
σκεπάζω με χαρτί, στολίζω με χαρτί ||
~**s** *npl (identity)* πιστοποιητικά *ntpl* ||
(documents) έγγραφα *ntpl* || ~**back** *n*
χαρτόδετο (βιβλίο) || ~ **bag** *n*
χαρτοσακούλα || ~ **clip** *n* συνδετήρας ||
~**weight** *n* πρες παπιέ *nt inv* || ~ **work**
n γραφική εργασία.
papier-mâché ['pæpɪeɪ'mæʃeɪ] *n*
πεπιεσμένο χαρτί.
par [pɑː*] *n (COMM)* ισοτιμία, άρτιο,
ισότητα || **on a ~ with** ίσος με, ίση αξία
με.
parable ['pærəbl] *n* παραβολή.
parachute ['pærəʃuːt] *n* αλεξίπτωτο ♦
vi πέφτω με αλεξίπτωτο.
parade [pə'reɪd] *n (procession)* παρέλαση

P

|| (review) παράταξη, παρέλαση ♦ vt επιδεικνύω, κάνω παρέλαση ♦ vi παρελαύνω.

paradise ['pærədaɪs] n παράδεισος.

paradox ['pærədɒks] n παράδοξο, παραδοξολογία || ~ical a παράδοξος.

paraffin ['pærəfɪn] n παραφίνη.

paragraph ['pærəgrɑːf] n παράγραφος f.

parallel ['pærəlel] a παράλληλος || (similar) όμοιος, παράλληλος, ανάλογος ♦ n παράλληλος.

paralysis [pə'rælɪsɪs] n παράλυση.

paralyze ['pærəlaɪz] vt παραλύω.

paramount ['pærəmaunt] a ύψιστος, υπέρτατος, εξαίρετος.

paranoia [pærə'nɔɪə] n παράνοια.

paraphernalia [pærəfə'neɪlɪə] n διάφορα ntpl, καλαμπαλίκια ntpl.

paraphrase ['pærəfreɪz] vt παραφράζω.

paraplegic [pærə'pliːdʒɪk] a παραπληγικός.

parasite ['pærəsaɪt] n παράσιτο.

parasol [pærə'sɒl] n ομπρέλα του ήλιου.

paratrooper ['pærətruːpə*] n αλεξιπτωτιστής.

parcel ['pɑːsl] n δέμα nt, πακέτο ♦ vt (also: ~ up) πακετάρω.

parch [pɑːtʃ] vt ξηραίνω, καψαλίζω, ψήνω || ~ed a ξηρός, στεγνός, άνυδρος.

parchment ['pɑːtʃmənt] n περγαμηνή.

pardon ['pɑːdn] n συγγνώμη, συγχώρηση ♦ vt (free from punishment) δίνω χάρη σε || ~! συγγνώμη! || ~ me! με συγχωρείτε! || I beg your ~! συγγνώμη! || I beg your ~? παρακαλώ;.

parent ['pɛərənt] n γονέας || ~al a πατρικός, μητρικός.

parenthesis [pə'renθɪsɪs] n παρένθεση.

parish ['pærɪʃ] n ενορία, κοινότητα || ~ioner n ενορίτης/ισσα m/f.

park [pɑːk] n πάρκο || (cars) χώρος σταθμεύσεως ♦ vti σταθμεύω, παρκάρω || ~ing n στάθμευση, παρκάρισμα nt, πάρκινγκ nt inv|| 'no ~ing' 'απαγορεύεται η στάθμευση' || ~ing lot n (US) χώρος σταθμεύσεως || ~ing meter n παρκόμετρο || ~ing place n θέση σταθμεύσεως.

parliament ['pɑːləmənt] n κοινοβούλιο || (in Britain) κοινοβούλιο, βουλή || ~ary a κοινοβουλευτικός.

parody ['pærədɪ] n παρωδία.

parole [pə'rəʊl] n: on ~ ελεύθερος (προσωρινά) επί λόγου.

parquet ['pɑːkeɪ] n παρκέτο.

parrot ['pærət] n παπαγάλος || ~ fashion ad (learn) παπαγαλίστικα.

parry ['pærɪ] vt αποκρούω, αποφεύγω, ξεφεύγω.

parsimonious [pɑːsɪ'məʊnɪəs] a φειδωλός, σφιχτός, τσιγγούνης || ~ly ad με φειδωλότητα, μετρημένα.

parsley ['pɑːslɪ] n μαϊντανός.

parsnip ['pɑːsnɪp] n δαυκί.

parson ['pɑːsn] n εφημέριος, παπάς.

part [pɑːt] n μέρος nt, κομμάτι || (in play) ρόλος || (of machine) τμήμα nt, μέρος nt, εξάρτημα nt, κομμάτι ♦ a μερικό, ημι-, μισο- ♦ ad =partly ♦ vt χωρίζω, διαιρώ, κόβω ♦ vi (people) χωρίζομαι || (roads) παρεκκλίνω, χωρίζομαι || for my ~ όσο για μένα || for the most ~ ως επί το πλείστον || to ~ with vt εγκαταλείπω, παραδίδω || ~ial ['pɑːʃəl] a μερικός || (favouring) μεροληπτικός || (+to) έχω συμπάθεια σε, έχω προτίμηση σε || ~ially ad μερικά, εν μέρει.

participate [pɑː'tɪsɪpeɪt] vi (+in) συμμετέχω, παίρνω μέρος.

participation [pɑːtɪsɪ'peɪʃən] n συμμετοχή.

participle ['pɑːtɪsɪpl] n μετοχή.

particular [pə'tɪkjʊlə*] a συγκεκριμένος || (single) ιδιαίτερος || (hard to please) ιδιότροπος, ακριβολόγος ♦ n λεπτομέρεια, ιδιομορφία || ~s npl (details) χαρακτηριστικά ntpl, περιγραφή || ~ly ad ιδιαίτερα, ειδικά, συγκεκριμένα.

parting ['pɑːtɪŋ] n (separation) αναχώρηση, χωρισμός || (of hair) χωρίστρα ♦ a ιδιωχωριστικός.

partisan [pɑːtɪ'zæn] n οπαδός, παρτιζάνος ♦ a μεροληπτικός.

partition [pɑːtɪʃən] n (wall) χώρισμα nt, μεσότοιχος.

partly ['pɑːtlɪ] ad εν μέρει.

partner ['pɑːtnə*] n εταίρος, συνέταιρος || (in dance etc) καβαλιέρος, ντάμα ♦ vt συνεταιρίζομαι, συμπράττω || ~ship n συνεταιρισμός, συνεργασία.

partridge ['pɑːtrɪdʒ] n πέρδικα.

part-time ['pɑːt'taɪm] ad για λίγες ώρες, μερικώς απασχολούμενος.

party ['pɑːtɪ] n (POL) κόμμα nt || (group) ομάδα, συντροφιά || (lawsuit) διάδικος || μέτοχος || (agreement) πρόσωπο || (celebration) πάρτυ nt inv ♦ a (dress) του πάρτυ, της διασκεδάσεως || (POL) του κόμματος, κομματικός.

pass [pɑːs] vt περνώ, διαβαίνω || (surpass) υπερβαίνω, ξεπερνώ, προσπερνώ || (move one to another) μεταβιβάζω, διαβιβάζω, δίνω || (spend time) περνώ || (be successful) επιτυγχάνω, περνώ || (approve) εγκρίνω ♦ vi μεταβαίνω, διαβαίνω, διέρχομαι ♦ n (passage) στενό, πέρασμα nt || (permission) άδεια || (success) περνώ || (SPORT) πάσα || to ~ away vi (die) πεθαίνω || (disappear) εξαφανίζομαι || to ~ by vi περνώ || παραμελώ || to ~ for vt περνώ για || to ~ out vi (faint) λιποθυμώ || ~able a διαβατός || (fairly good) υποφερτός, καλούτσικος.

passage ['pæsɪdʒ] n (corridor) διάδρομος || (part of book etc) απόσπασμα nt, κομμάτι || (crossing) διάβαση, δίοδος f, διάβα nt || ~way n δίοδος f, πέρασμα nt || (sidestreet) πάροδος f.

passenger ['pæsɪndʒə*] n επιβάτης/ρια m/f.

passer-by ['pɑːsə'baɪ] n διαβάτης, περαστικός.

passing ['pɑːsɪŋ] n (death) θάνατος ♦ a (car) διερχόμενος, διαβατικός || in ~ παρεμπιπτόντως.

passion ['pæʃən] n πάθος nt, θέρμη, μανία || (love) έρωτας, πάθος nt || ~ate a σφοδρός, φλογερός, βίαιος || ~ately ad παράφορα, θερμά.

passive ['pæsɪv] a (GRAM) παθητικός.

Passover ['pɑːsəʊvə*] n Λαμπρή, Πάσχα nt.

passport ['pɑːspɔːt] n διαβατήριο.

password ['pɑːswɜːd] n σύνθημα nt, παρασύνθημα nt.

past [pɑːst] ad, prep (beyond) πέρα, πέρα από || (with numbers) περασμένος || (with time) μετά, περασμένα ♦ a (years) περασμένος, τον παλιό καιρό || (president etc) τέως, πρώην.

paste [peɪst] n (for paper) κόλλα || (for cooking) πάστα, ζυμάρι.

pastel ['pæstəl] a (colour) παστέλ.

pasteurized ['pæstəraɪzd] a παστεριωμένος.

pastille ['pæstɪl] n παστίλια.

pastime ['pɑːstaɪm] n διασκέδαση, παιχνίδι.

pastor ['pɑːstə*] n πάστορας, παπάς.

pastry ['peɪstrɪ] n ζύμη, πάστα || (pies, tarts etc) γλυκό.

pasture ['pɑːstʃə*] n (ground) βοσκοτόπι.

pasty ['pæstɪ] n κρεατόπιτα ♦ ['peɪstɪ] a ζυμαρένιος, ωχρός.

pat [pæt] n ελαφρό κτύπημα nt, χάδι ♦ vt κτυπώ ελαφρά, χαϊδεύω.

patch [pætʃ] n μπάλωμα nt || (stain) λεκές m ♦ vt μπαλώνω || ~work n σύρραμα nt, συνονθύλευμα nt || ~y a (irregular) ανομοιόμορφος.

patent ['peɪtənt] n προνόμιο, πατέντα ♦ vt πατεντάρω ♦ a προφανής, απλός, προνομιακός, πρωτότυπος || ~ leather n λουστρίνι.

paternal [pə'tɜːnl] a πατρικός.

path [pɑːθ] n δρομάκος, μονοπάτι || (of sun etc) διαδρομή, πορεία γραμμή.

pathetic [pə'θetɪk] a συγκινητικός, αξιολύπητος || ~ally ad παθητικά, συγκινητικά.

pathologist [pə'θɒlədʒɪst] n παθολόγος.

pathology [pə'θɒlədʒɪ] n παθολογία.

pathos ['peɪθɒs] n πάθος nt, συγκίνηση.

pathway ['pɑːθweɪ] n μονοπάτι, πέρασμα nt.

patience ['peɪʃəns] n υπομονή.

patient ['peɪʃənt] n νοσηλευόμενος/n m/f, άρρωστος/n m/f ♦ a υπομονητικός.

patio ['pætɪəʊ] n πλακόστρωτη αυλή.

patriotic [pætrɪ'ɒtɪk] a πατριωτικός.

patrol [pə'trəʊl] n περίπολος f, περιπολία ♦ vti περιπολώ || on ~ σε περιπολία || ~ car n περιπολικό || ~man n (US) αστυφύλακας.

patron ['peɪtrən] n πάτρωνας, προστάτης/ρια m/f, υποστηρικτής/ίκτρια m/f || (COMM) τακτικός πελάτης || ~age ['pætrənɪdʒ] n προστασία, υποστήριξη || ~ize

['pætrənaɪz] vt υποστηρίζω || (manner) μεταχειρίζομαι συγκαταβατικά || ~izing a (attitude) συγκαταβατικός || ~ saint n προστάτης/ρια m/f, άγιος/a m/f.

patter ['pætə*] n (sound) ελαφρά συνεχή χτυπήματα ntpl || (sales talk) φλυαρία, κορακίστικα ntpl ♦ vi χτυπώ ελαφρά και συνεχώς.

pattern ['pætən] n υπόδειγμα nt, πρότυπο, μοντέλο || (design) σχέδιο, τύπος, μοντέλο.

paunch [pɔːntʃ] n κοιλιά.

pauper ['pɔːpə*] n άπορος/n m/f, πτωχός/ή m/f.

pause [pɔːz] n παύση, διακοπή, ανάπαυλα, διάλειμμα nt ♦ vi σταματώ, διστάζω, κοντοστέκομαι.

pave [peɪv] vt επιστρώνω || to ~ the way for ανοίγω το δρόμο, προετοιμάζω το έδαφος.

pavement ['peɪvmənt] n (Brit) πεζοδρόμιο.

pavilion [pə'vɪlɪən] n (building) περίπτερο, υπόστεγο.

paving ['peɪvɪŋ] n στρώσιμο.

paw [pɔː] n πέλμα nt ζώου, πόδι ♦ vt χτυπώ με το πόδι || (person) πασπατεύω.

pawn [pɔːn] n ενέχυρο ♦ vt ενεχυριάζω, βάζω ενέχυρο || ~broker n ενεχυροδανειστής || ~shop n ενεχυροδανειστήριο.

pay [peɪ] (irreg v) n πληρωμή, μισθός ♦ vt πληρώνω, καταβάλλω, ξοδεύω || (be profitable to) συμφέρω, αποδίδω ♦ vi πληρώνομαι, είναι συμφέρον || to ~ attention (to) προσέχω || to ~ for vt πληρώνω, κερνώ || to ~ up vi εξοφλώ || ~able a πληρωτέος || ~ day n μέρα πληρωμής || ~ee n δικαιούχος || ~ing a επικερδής, αποδοτικός || ~ment n πληρωμή || (compensation) αποζημίωση, ανταπόδοση || ~roll n μισθοδοτική κατάσταση.

p.c. abbr of per cent.

pea [piː] n (seed) μπιζέλι.

peace [piːs] n ειρήνη, ησυχία || ~ful a γαλήνιος, ήσυχος || ~ offering n δώρο συμφιλιώσεως.

peach [piːtʃ] n ροδάκινο.

peacock ['piːkɒk] n παγώνι.

peak [piːk] n κορυφή || (of cap) γείσος.

peal [piːl] n κωδωνοκρουσία, κτύπημα nt.

peanut ['piːnʌt] n αράπικο φυστίκι.

pear [peə*] n απίδι, αχλάδι.

pearl [pɜːl] n μαργαριτάρι.

peasant ['pezənt] n χωρικός/ή m/f, χωριάτης/ισσα m/f, αγρότης/ισσα m/f.

peat [piːt] n τύρφη, ποάνθρακας.

pebble ['pebl] n χαλίκι.

peck [pek] vti ραμφίζω, τσιμπώ ♦ n (with beak) ραμφισμός, τσίμπημα nt || (kiss) φιλάκι.

peckish ['pekɪʃ] a (col): to feel ~ νοιώθω το στομάχι άδειο.

peculiar [pɪ'kjuːlɪə*] a (interest) ειδικός, ιδιαίτερος || (+to) ιδιαίτερο χαρακτηριστικό, ιδιάζων || ~**ity** *n* ιδιομορφία, ιδιορρυθμία || *(oddness)* παραξενιά.

pedal ['pedl] *n* ποδωστήριο, πεντάλ *nt inv* ♦ *vti* χρησιμοποιώ πεντάλ, ποδηλατώ.

pedantic [pɪ'dæntɪk] *a* σχολαστικός.

peddle ['pedl] *vt* κάνω το μικροπωλητή, πουλώ στους δρόμους.

pedestal ['pedɪstl] *n* βάθρο, βάση αγάλματος.

pedestrian [pɪ'destrɪən] *n* πεζός, διαβάτης ♦ *a* με τα πόδια, πεζός || *(humdrum)* μονότονος, πεζός || ~ **crossing** *n* διάβαση πεζών.

pediatrics [piːdɪ'ætrɪks] *n (US)* = **paediatrics**.

pedigree ['pedɪgriː] *n* γενεαλογικό δέντρο, καταγωγή ♦ *a (animal)* καθαρόαιμος.

pee [piː] *(col)* η ούρα *ntpl* ♦ *vi* κατουρώ, κάνω πιπί.

peek [piːk] *n* ματιά ♦ *vi* κρυφοκοιτάζω, ξεπροβάλλω.

peel [piːl] *n* φλούδα ♦ *vi (paint etc)* ξεφλουδίζομαι, φεύγω.

peep [piːp] *n (look)* φευγαλέο βλέμμα *nt*, ματιά || *(sound)* τιτίβισμα *nt*, σκούξιμο, τσίριγμα *nt* ♦ *vi (look)* κρυφοκοιτάζω.

peer [pɪə*] *vi* κοιτάζω με προσοχή || (+ *at)* κοιτάζω προσεκτικά || *(peep)* κρυφοκοιτάζω ♦ *n (nobleman)* λόρδος, ευγενής || *(equal)* ισάξιος, ίσος, ταίρι || ~**age** *n* τάξη ευγενών || ~**less** *a* απαράμιλλος, ασύγκριτος.

peeve [piːv] *vt (col)* εκνευρίζω || ~**d** *a* εκνευρισμένος.

peevish ['piːvɪʃ] *a* ευερέθιστος, δύστροπος.

peg [peg] *n* γόμφος, πάσσαλος, κρεμάστρα || **to buy clothes off the** ~ αγοράζω έτοιμα ρούχα.

pekinese [piːkɪ'niːz] *n* πεκινουά *nt inv*.

pelican ['pelɪkən] *n* πελεκάνος.

pellet ['pelɪt] *n (of paper, bread etc)* σφαιρίδιο, οβλός || *(pill)* δισκίο.

pelt [pelt] *vt* πετροβολώ, πετώ, κτυπώ ♦ *vi (fall heavily)* πέφτω με δύναμη ♦ *n* δορά, δέρμα *nt*, προβειά.

pelvis ['pelvɪs] *n* λεκάνη.

pen [pen] *n (for writing)* γραφίδα, πένα, στυλό || *(for sheep)* μάντρα.

penal ['piːnl] *a* ποινικός || ~**ize** *vt* επιβάλλω ποινή σε, τιμωρώ || ~**ty** ['penltɪ] *n* ποινή, τιμωρία || ~**ty kick** *n* πέναλτυ *nt inv*.

penance ['penəns] *n* αυτοτιμωρία, μετάνοια.

pence [pens] *npl* πένες *fpl*.

pencil ['pensl] *n* μολύβι || *(of light)* δέσμη || ~ **sharpener** *n* ξύστρα.

pendant ['pendənt] *n* κρεμαστό κόσμημα *nt*.

pending ['pendɪŋ] *prep* κατά τη διάρκεια του, μέχρι ♦ *a* εκκρεμής.

pendulum ['pendjuləm] *n* εκκρεμές *nt*.

penetrate ['penɪtreɪt] *vt* εισχωρώ σε,

διεισδύω || *(pierce)* διαπερνώ, τρυπώ || **penetrating** *a* διαπεραστικός, οξύς.

penetration [penɪ'treɪʃən] *n (lit)* διείσδυση.

penfriend ['penfrend] *n* φίλος από αλληλογραφία.

penguin ['peŋgwɪn] *n* πιγκουίνος.

penicillin [penɪ'sɪlɪn] *n* πενικιλίνη.

peninsula [pɪ'nɪnsjulə] *n* χερσόνησος *f*.

penis ['piːnɪs] *n* πέος *nt*.

penitence ['penɪtəns] *n* μετάνοια.

penitent ['penɪtənt] *a* μετανοημένος.

penitentiary [penɪ'tenʃərɪ] *n (US)* σωφρονιστήριο.

penknife ['pennaɪf] *n* σουγιάς.

pen name ['penneɪm] *n* ψευδώνυμο *(φιλολογικό)*.

pennant ['penənt] *n* τριγωνικό σημαία.

penniless ['penɪlɪs] *a* απένταρος.

penny ['penɪ] *n* πένα.

pension ['penʃən] *n (from job)* σύνταξη || ~**er** *n* συνταξιούχος.

pensive ['pensɪv] *a* σκεπτικός, συλλογισμένος.

pentagon ['pentəgən] *n* πεντάγωνο.

Pentecost ['pentɪkɒst] *n* Πεντηκοστή.

penthouse ['penthaus] *n* ρετιρέ *nt inv*, υπόστεγο.

pent-up ['pentʌp] *a (feelings)* συγκρατημένη συγκίνηση.

people ['piːpl] *n* άνθρωποι *mpl*, κόσμος || *(nation)* λαός, έθνος *nt* ♦ *vt* κατοικώ, οικίζω.

pep [pep] *n (col)* κέφι, ζωή || **to** ~ **up** *vt* ενθαρρύνω, δίνω κέφι σε.

pepper ['pepə*] *n* πιπέρι || *(green)* πιπεριά ♦ *vt (pelt)* κοπανίζω, βομβαρδίζω || ~**mint** *n (plant)* δυόσμος, μέντα || *(sweet)* μέντα (καραμέλα).

per [pɜː*] *prep* κατά, διά || ~ **cent** τοις εκατό || ~ **annum** το χρόνο.

perceive [pə'siːv] *vt* διακρίνω, βλέπω || *(understand)* αντιλαμβάνομαι, καταλαβαίνω.

percentage [pə'sentɪdʒ] *n* ποσοστό, τοις εκατό.

perception [pə'sepʃən] *n* αντίληψη, αίσθηση.

perceptive [pə'septɪv] *a* αντιληπτικός.

perch [pɜːtʃ] *n* κούρνια, ξύλο || *(fish)* πέρκα ♦ *vi* κουρνιάζω, τοποθετώ ψηλά.

percolator ['pɜːkəleɪtə*] *n* καφετιέρα με φίλτρο.

percussion [pə'kʌʃən] *n (MUS)* κρουστά όργανα *ntpl*.

peremptory [pə'remptərɪ] *a* τελικός, αμετάκλητος, αποφασιστικός.

perennial [pə'renɪəl] *a* αιώνιος, μόνιμος, πολυετής ♦ *n* πολυετές φυτό.

perfect ['pɜːfɪkt] *a* τέλειος, πλήρης, τελειωμένος || *(GRAM)* τετελεσμένος ♦ *n (GRAM)* παρακείμενος ♦ [pə'fekt] *vt* τελειοποιώ, συμπληρώνω || ~**ion** [pə'fekʃən] *n* τελειότητα, εντέλεια, τελειοποίηση || ~**ly** *ad* εντελώς, τέλεια.

perforate ['pɜːfəreɪt] vt διατρυπώ, διαπερνώ || ~d a διάτρητος.

perforation [pɜːfə'reɪʃən] n διάτρηση, τρύπα.

perform [pə'fɔːm] vt εκτελώ, εκπληρώ, επιτελώ || (THEAT) παριστάνω, παίζω ♦ vi (THEAT) παίζω || ~ance n εκτέλεση, κατόρθωμα nt || (THEAT) παράσταση || ~er n εκτελεστής, ηθοποιός m/f || ~ing a (animal) γυμνασμένο (ζώο).

perfume ['pɜːfjuːm] n οσμή, μυρωδιά || (scent) άρωμα nt, μυρωδικό.

perhaps [pə'hæps] ad ίσως.

peril ['perɪl] n κίνδυνος || ~ous a επικίνδυνος || ~ously ad επικίνδυνα.

perimeter [pə'rɪmɪtə*] n περίμετρος f.

period ['pɪərɪəd] n εποχή, περίοδος f || (stop) τελεία || (MED) στάδιο, φάση, περίοδος f ♦ a (costume) της εποχής, || ~ic a περιοδικός || ~ical a περιοδικός ♦ n περιοδικό || ~ically ad κατά περιόδους.

peripheral [pə'rɪfərəl] a περιφερειακός, περιμετρικός ♦ n (COMPUT) περιφερειακή μονάδα.

periphery [pə'rɪfərɪ] n περιφέρεια, περίμετρος f.

periscope ['perɪskəup] n περισκόπιο.

perish ['perɪʃ] vi χάνομαι, αφανίζομαι, πεθαίνω || ~able a φθαρτός || ~ing a (col: cold) τρομερό κρύο.

perjury ['pɜːdʒərɪ] n επιορκία, ψευδομαρτυρία.

perk [pɜːk] to ~ up vi ξανακάνω κέφι, ξαναζωντανεύω || ~y a (cheerful) ζωηρός, εύθυμος.

perm [pɜːm] n περμανάντ f inv.

permanent ['pɜːmənənt] a μόνιμος, διαρκής || ~ly ad μόνιμα.

permissible [pə'mɪsəbl] a επιτρεπόμενος, ανεκτός.

permission [pə'mɪʃən] n άδεια, έγκριση.

permissive [pə'mɪsɪv] a επιτρεπτικός.

permit ['pɜːmɪt] n άδεια ♦ [pə'mɪt] vt επιτρέπω.

permutation [pɜːmjuː'teɪʃən] n (αντι)μετάθεση, αντιμετάταξη.

pernicious [pɜː'nɪʃəs] a ολέθριος, καταστρεπτικός.

perpendicular [pɜːpən'dɪkjulə*] a κάθετος, κατακόρυφος.

perpetrate ['pɜːpɪtreɪt] vt διαπράττω.

perpetual [pə'petjuəl] a αδιάκοπος, συνεχής, παντοτεινός.

perpetuate [pə'petjueɪt] vt διαιωνίζω, αποθανατίζω.

perplex [pə'pleks] vt περιπλέκω, φέρνω σε αμηχανία, μπερδεύω || ~ed a σε αμηχανία || ~ing a μπερδεμένος || ~ity n αμηχανία, παραζάλη, δίλημμα nt.

persecute ['pɜːsɪkjuːt] vt (oppress) καταδιώκω, διώκω.

persecution [pɜːsɪ'kjuːʃən] n διωγμός, καταδίωξη.

perseverance [pɜːsɪ'vɪərəns] n καρτερία, εμμονή, επιμονή.

persevere [pɜːsɪ'vɪə*] vi εμμένω, επιμένω.

Persia ['pɜːʃə] n Περσία || ~n a περσικός ♦ n (person) Πέρσης/ίδα m/f || (LING) Περσικά ntpl || ~n Gulf n Περσικός Κόλπος.

persist [pə'sɪst] vi επιμένω, μένω, σταθερός || (keep saying) επιμένω, εμμένω || ~ence n επιμονή, εμμονή || ~ent a επίμονος, διαρκής.

person ['pɜːsn] n πρόσωπο, άνθρωπος, άτομο || ~able a ευπαρουσίαστος, ωραίος || ~al a προσωπικός, ατομικός || (of body) σωματικός || ~ality n προσωπικότητα || ~ally ad προσωπικά || ~ify vt προσωποποιώ.

personnel [pɜːsə'nel] n προσωπικό || ~ manager n διευθυντής προσωπικού.

perspective [pə'spektɪv] n προοπτική || (view) άποψη, θέα.

perspex ['pɜːspeks] n (R) άθραυστο γυαλί, περσπέξ nt inv.

perspiration [pɜːspə'reɪʃən] n εφίδρωση, ιδρώτας.

perspire [pə'spaɪə*] vi ιδρώνω.

persuade [pə'sweɪd] vt πείθω, καταφέρνω.

persuasion [pə'sweɪʒən] n πειθώ f, πειστικότητα || (belief) πεποίθηση, θρήσκευμα nt.

persuasive [pə'sweɪsɪv] a πειστικός.

pert [pɜːt] a αναιδής, αυθάδης, τσαχπίνης.

pertaining [pɜː'teɪnɪŋ]: ~ to prep σχετικά με.

pertinent ['pɜːtɪnənt] a σχετικός, κατάλληλος, σωστός.

perturb [pə'tɜːb] vt διαταράσσω, προκαλώ ανησυχία.

perusal [pə'ruːzəl] n ανάγνωση, διάβασμα nt.

pervade [pɜː'veɪd] vt εμποτίζω, διαπερνώ, επικρατώ.

perverse [pə'vɜːs] a διεστραμμένος, κακότροπος.

perversion [pə'vɜːʃən] n διαστροφή, ανωμαλία.

pervert ['pɜːvɜːt] n διεστραμμένος, ανώμαλος τύπος, εκφυλισμένος ♦ [pə'vɜːt] vt διαστρέφω, στρεβλώνω, διαφθείρω.

pessimism ['pesɪmɪzəm] n απαισιοδοξία.

pessimist ['pesɪmɪst] n απαισιόδοξος/n nt || ~ic a απαισιόδοξος.

pest [pest] n επιβλαβές φυτό (ή έντομο) || (fig: person, thing) ενοχλητικός/ή m/f, πληγή.

pester ['pestə*] vt ενοχλώ, πειράζω.

pestle ['pesl] n κόπανος, γουδοχέρι.

pet [pet] n χαϊδεμένος/n m/f || (animal) ζώο του σπιτιού ♦ vt χαϊδεύω.

petal ['petl] n πέταλο.

peter ['piːtə*]: to ~ out vi εξαφανίζομαι, σβήνω.

petition [pə'tɪʃən] n αίτηση, αναφορά.

petrified ['petrɪfaɪd] a απολιθωμένος.

petrol ['petrəl] n (Brit) βενζίνη || ~ **engine** n βενζινομηχανή.

petroleum [pɪ'trəuliəm] n πετρέλαιο.

petrol: ~ **pump** n (in car) αντλία βενζίνης || ~ **station** n πρατήριο βενζίνης || ~ **tank** n δεξαμενή || (car) ρεζερβουάρ nt inv βενζίνης.

petticoat ['petɪkəut] n μεσοφόρι.

petty ['petɪ] a μικρός, ασήμαντος, κατώτερος || (mean) μικρόνους, στενοκέφαλος || ~ **cash** n μικροέξοδα ntpl, πρόχειρο ταμείο || ~ **officer** n υπαξιωματικός, υποκελευστής.

petulant ['petjulənt] a οξύθυμος, ευερέθιστος.

pew [pju:] n στασίδι.

pewter ['pju:tə*] n κράμα nt κασσιτέρου και μολύβδου.

phantom ['fæntəm] n φάντασμα nt.

Pharaoh ['fɛərəu] n Φαραώ m.

pharmacist ['fɑ:məsɪst] n φαρμακοποιός m/f.

pharmacy ['fɑ:məsɪ] n (shop) φαρμακείο || (science) φαρμακευτική.

phase [feɪz] n φάση.

Ph.D. (abbr = Doctor of Philosophy) = διδακτορικό δίπλωμα nt.

pheasant ['feznt] n φασιανός.

phenomenon [fɪ'nɒmɪnən] n φαινόμενο.

philanthropist [fɪ'lænθrəpɪst] n φιλάνθρωπος.

philately [fɪ'lætəlɪ] n φιλοτελισμός.

philosopher [fɪ'lɒsəfə*] n φιλόσοφος.

philosophical [fɪlə'sɒfɪkəl] a φιλοσοφικός.

philosophy [fɪ'lɒsəfɪ] n φιλοσοφία.

phlegm [flem] n φλέγμα nt.

phobia ['fəubɪə] n φοβία, φοβοπάθεια.

phone [fəun] (abbr of **telephone**) n τηλέφωνο ♦ vt τηλεφωνώ.

phonetics [fəu'netɪks] n φωνολογία, φωνητική.

phon(e)y ['fəunɪ] (col) a ψεύτικος ♦ n απατεώνας.

phosphate ['fɒsfeɪt] n φωσφορικό αλάτι.

phosphorus ['fɒsfərəs] n φωσφόρος.

photo ['fəutəu] n φωτογραφία.

photocopier ['fəutəu'kɒpɪə*] n φωτοτυπική μηχανή.

photocopy ['fəutəukɒpɪ] n φωτοαντίτυπο, φωτοτυπία ♦ vt κάνω φωτοτυπία.

photogenic [fəutəu'dʒenɪk] a φωτογενής.

photograph ['fəutəugræf] n φωτογραφία ♦ vt φωτογραφίζω, βγάζω φωτογραφίες || ~**er** [fə'tɒgrəfə*] n φωτογράφος || ~**ic** a φωτογραφικός || ~**y** n φωτογραφική τέχνη, φωτογράφιση.

photostat ['fəutəustæt] n φωτοστατικό αντίτυπο.

phrase [freɪz] n φράση ♦ vt διατυπώνω || ~ **book** n συλλογή εκφράσεων.

physical ['fɪzɪkəl] a φυσικός || (of the

body) σωματικός || ~**ly** ad φυσικά, σωματικά.

physician [fɪ'zɪʃən] n γιατρός m/f.

physicist ['fɪzɪsɪst] n φυσικός m/f.

physics ['fɪzɪks] n φυσική.

physiology [fɪzɪ'ɒlədʒɪ] n φυσιολογία.

physiotherapy [fɪzɪə'θerəpɪ] n φυσιοθεραπεία.

physique [fɪ'zi:k] n σωματική διάπλαση.

pianist ['pɪənɪst] n πιανίστας/ρια m/f.

piano ['pjɑ:nəu] n πιάνο.

pick [pɪk] n (tool) αξίνα, κασμάς, σκαπάνη || (choice) εκλογή || (best) ότι εκλεκτό, αφρόκρεμα ♦ vti μαζεύω, κόβω, συλλέγω || (choose) εκλέγω, διαλέγω || I ~ **a pocket** βουτώ από την τσέπη, κλέβω το πορτοφόλι || **to** ~ **out** vt διαλέγω || **to** ~ **up** vi (improve) βελτιώνομαι ♦ vt (arrest) συλλαμβάνω, πιάνω || (from ground) σηκώνω, μαζεύω || (in car etc) παίρνω || ~**axe** n σκαπάνη, κασμάς.

picket ['pɪkɪt] n (stake) πάσσαλος, παλούκι || (strikers) σκοπός απεργών ♦ vt βάζω σκοπούς.

pickle ['pɪkl] n (also: ~**s:** as condiment) τουρσί, άλμη ♦ vt διατηρώ σε άλμη, παστώνω.

pickpocket ['pɪkpɒkɪt] n πορτοφολάς.

pickup ['pɪkʌp] n (on record player) φωνολήπτης, πικάπ nt inv || (small truck) μικρό φορτηγό || (casual acquaintance) ψάρεμα nt, τσίμπημα nt πελάτου.

picnic ['pɪknɪk] n εκδρομή, πικνίκ nt inv ♦ vi τρώγω στην εξοχή || ~**ker** n εκδρομέας.

pictorial [pɪk'tɔ:rɪəl] a εικονογραφικός || (graphic) γραφικός || (illustrated) εικονογραφημένος.

picture ['pɪktʃə*] n εικόνα, ζωγραφιά, προσωποποίηση ♦ vt ζωγραφίζω, απεικονίζω, φαντάζομαι || **the** ~**s** npl κινηματογράφος || ~ **book** n βιβλίο με εικόνες.

picturesque [pɪktʃə'resk] a γραφικός.

pie [paɪ] n πίτα.

piece [pi:s] n κομμάτι || **in** ~**s** (broken) (σε) κομματάκια || (taken apart) σε κομμάτια || ~**meal** ad λίγο-λίγο, κομματιαστά || ~**work** n εργασία με το κομμάτι.

pier [pɪə*] n (landing place) προκυμαία, αποβάθρα.

pierce [pɪəs] vt τρυπώ, διεισδύω, εισχωρώ.

piercing ['pɪəsɪŋ] a (cry) διαπεραστικός.

piety ['paɪətɪ] n ευσέβεια, θρησκοληψία.

pig [pɪg] n γουρούνι || (person) παλιάνθρωπος, γουρούνι.

pigeon ['pɪdʒən] n περιστέρι || ~**hole** n (compartment) θυρίδα, γραμματοθήκη ♦ vt βάζω στο αρχείο.

piggy bank ['pɪgɪbæŋk] n κουμπαράς.

pigheaded ['pɪg'hedɪd] a πεισματάρης, ξεροκέφαλος.

piglet ['pɪglɪt] n γουρουνόπουλο.

pigment ['pɪgmənt] n χρώμα nt, βαφή.

pigmy ['pɪgmɪ] n = **pygmy.**

pigskin ['pɪgskɪn] n γουρουνόδερμα nt.

pigsty ['pɪgstaɪ] n χοιροστάσιο.

pigtail ['pɪgteɪl] n κοτσίδα.

pilchard ['pɪltʃəd] n μεγάλη σαρδέλα.

pile [paɪl] n (of books) σωρός, στοίβα || (in ground) πάσσαλος, παλούκι, κολώνα || (on carpet) τρίχα, χνούδι ♦ vti (also: ~ up) συσσωρεύω, στοιβάζω.

piles [paɪlz] npl αιμορροΐδες fpl, ζοχάδες fpl.

pilfer ['pɪlfə*] vt κλέβω, βουτώ, σουφρώνω.

pilgrim ['pɪlgrɪm] n προσκυνητής/ήτρια m/f || ~age n προσκύνημα nt.

pill [pɪl] n χάπι || **the P~** n χάπι αντισυλληπτικό.

pillage ['pɪlɪdʒ] vt λεηλατώ.

pillar ['pɪlə*] n κίονας, κολώνα, στύλος || (fig) στύλος || ~ **box** n (Brit) ταχυδρομικό κουτί.

pillion ['pɪljən] n πισινό κάθισμα nt.

pillory ['pɪlərɪ] vt διαπομπεύω, στηλιτεύω.

pillow ['pɪləʊ] n προσκέφαλο, μαξιλάρι || ~**case** n μαξιλαροθήκη.

pilot ['paɪlət] n πλοηγός, πιλότος || (AVIAT) χειριστής, πιλότος ♦ vt (AVIAT) οδηγώ, πιλοτάρω || ~ **light** n καυστήρας (θερμάστρας φωταερίου).

pimp [pɪmp] n μαστρωπός, ρουφιάνος.

pimple ['pɪmpl] n εξάνθημα nt, σπυρί.

pin [pɪn] n καρφίτσα || (peg) περόνη ♦ vt καρφιτσώνω || (hold fast) καρφώνω, πλακώνομαι || (on) ~**s and needles** στα κάρβουνα || **to ~ down** vt (fig: person) καθηλώνω.

pinafore ['pɪnəfɔː*] n ποδιά.

pincers ['pɪnsəz] npl τανάλια.

pinch [pɪntʃ] n μικρή ποσότητα, πρέζα || (nip) τσίμπημα nt, τσιμπιά ♦ vt (with fingers) τσιμπώ || (col: steal) αποσπώ, σουφρώνω, βουτώ ♦ vi (shoe) στενεύω, σφίγγω || **at a ~** στην ανάγκη, σε ώρα ανάγκης.

pincushion ['pɪnkʊʃən] n μαξιλαράκι για καρφίτσες.

pine [paɪn] n (also: ~ **tree**) πεύκο ♦ vi: **to ~ for** ποθώ, μαραζώνω.

pineapple ['paɪnæpl] n ανανάς.

ping [pɪŋ] n (noise) σφύριγμα nt, κουδούνισμα nt || ~-**pong** n πιγκ-πογκ nt inv.

pink [pɪŋk] n (plant) γαρουφαλιά || (pale red) ροζ ♦ a ροζ, ρόδινος.

pin money ['pɪnmʌnɪ] n χαρτζιλίκι.

pinnacle ['pɪnəkl] n (highest point) κορυφή, κολοφώνας.

pinpoint ['pɪnpɔɪnt] vi υποδεικνύω ακριβώς.

pint [paɪnt] n πίντα (.567 λ.).

pioneer [paɪəˈnɪə*] n πρωτοπόρος/α m/f.

pious ['paɪəs] a ευσεβής, θρήσκος.

pip [pɪp] n (seed) κουκούτσι || (on uniform) άστρο (επωμίδας).

pipe [paɪp] n σωλήνας, οχετός || (smoking) πίπα, τσιμπούκι || (instrument) αυλός || (of bird) κελάδημα nt || **to ~ down** vi (be quiet) το βουλώνω || ~ **dream** n μάταιη ελπίδα || ~**line** n αγωγός || ~**r** n αυλητής, παίκτης γκάιντας || ~ **tobacco** n καπνός πίπας.

piping ['paɪpɪŋ] ad: ~ **hot** καυτερός, ζεματιστός, αχνιστός.

piquant ['piːkənt] a πικάντικος.

pique [piːk] n μνησικακία, φούρκα.

piracy ['paɪərəsɪ] n πειρατεία.

pirate ['paɪərɪt] n πειρατής || ~ **radio** n πειρατικός σταθμός.

pirouette [pɪruˈet] n πιρουέτα ♦ vi κάνω πιρουέτες, περιστρέφομαι.

pissed [pɪst] a (col) μεθυσμένος.

pistol ['pɪstl] n πιστόλι.

piston ['pɪstən] n έμβολο, πιστόνι.

pit [pɪt] n λάκκος, ανθρακωρυχείο ♦ vt σπαδεύω, κόβω || (put to test) έχω κάποιον σαν αντίπαλο.

pitch [pɪtʃ] n (way of throwing) βολή, ριξιά || (ground) γήπεδο || (degree) βαθμός, κλίση || (of note) ύψος τόνου, διαπασών nt || (tar) πίσσα, κατράμι ♦ vt (throw) πετώ || (tent) στήνω (σκηνή) ♦ vi (fall headlong) πέφτω || (of ship) σκαμπανεβάζω || ~-**black** a μαύρος σαν κατράμι || ~**ed battle** n μάχη εκ του συστάδην.

pitcher ['pɪtʃə*] n στάμνα, κανάτα.

pitchfork ['pɪtʃfɔːk] n δίκρανο, τσουγκράνα, φούρκα ♦ vt φορτώνω με δικράνι.

pitfall ['pɪtfɔːl] n (trap) παγίδα.

pith [pɪθ] n (essence) ουσία, σθένος nt.

pithy ['pɪθɪ] a (concise) με ουσία, ουσιαστικός.

pitiable ['pɪtɪəbl] a αξιολύπητος, αξιοθρήνητος, οικτρός.

pitiful ['pɪtɪfʊl] a αξιολύπητος || (mean) ελεεινός || ~**ly** ad θλιβερά, ελεεινά.

pitiless ['pɪtɪlɪs] a ανελέητος, άσπλαχνος, άκαρδος || ~**ly** ad σκληρά, ανελέντα.

pittance ['pɪtəns] n εξευτελιστικός μισθός.

pity ['pɪtɪ] n έλεος, οίκτος, λύπηση || (of regret) κρίμα nt || **what a ~!** τι κρίμα!

pivot ['pɪvət] n άξονας, κέντρο περιστροφής, κεντρικό σημείο ♦ vi (turn) περιστρέφομαι.

pixie ['pɪksɪ] n ξωτικό, νεράιδα.

placard ['plækɑːd] n τοιχοκόλληση, ταμπέλα, πινακίδα.

placate [pləˈkeɪt] vi κατευνάζω.

place [pleɪs] n τόπος, μέρος nt, τοποθεσία || (position) σημείο, μέρος nt || (location) τοποθεσία || (town etc) τόπος || (employment, rank) θέση, υπηρεσία, βαθμός || (seat) θέση, κάθισμα nt ♦ vt (object) τοποθετώ, βάζω || (order) τοποθετώ, πουλώ || (in race) έρχομαι πλασέ || **in ~** στη σωστή θέση || **out of ~** άτοπος || **in the first ~** εν πρώτοις.

placid ['plæsɪd] a γαλήνιος, ήρεμος, ατάραχος.

plagiarism ['pleɪdʒərɪzəm] n λογοκλοπή, λογοκλοπία.

plague [pleɪg] n πληγή, μάστιγα, λοιμός, πανούκλα.

plaice [pleɪs] n γλώσσα (ψάρι).

plaid [plæd] n καρό ύφασμα nt.

plain [pleɪn] a (clear) σαφής, φανερός || (simple) απλός, λιτός || (not beautiful) κοινός, όχι ωραίος ♦ ad καθαρά, ευδιακρίτως, ειλικρινά ♦ n πεδιάδα, κάμπος || in ~ clothes (police) με πολιτικά || ~ly ad προφανώς, ολοφάνερα || (simply) απλά.

plaintiff ['pleɪntɪf] n ενάγων/ουσα m/f, μηνυτής/ύτρια m/f.

plait [plæt] n πλόκαμος, πλεξούδα ♦ vt πλέκω.

plan [plæn] n σχέδιο, προσχέδιο, πρόγραμμα nt || (of house etc) σχέδιο, πλάνο, σχεδιάγραμμα nt || (POL, ECON) σχέδιο ♦ vt (holiday etc) σχεδιάζω ♦ vi (make a plan) καταστρώνω, σχεδιαγραφώ.

plane [pleɪn] n (tree) πλάτανος || (tool) πλάνη, ροκάνι, πλάνια || (level) επίπεδο, επίπεδος (επιφάνεια) || (AVIAT) αεροπλάνο ♦ a επίπεδος ♦ vt (with tool) ροκανίζω, πλανίζω.

planet ['plænɪt] n πλανήτης.

plank [plæŋk] n σανίδα, μαδέρι.

planner ['plænə*] n προγραμματιστής m/f, σχεδιαστής/άστρια m/f.

planning ['plænɪŋ] n χάραξη (σχεδίου), κατάστρωση, προγραμματισμός.

plant [plɑːnt] n φυτό || (factory) εγκατάσταση, εργοστάσιο, μηχανήματα ntpl ♦ vt φυτεύω || (set firmly) καρφώνω, εγκαθιστώ.

plantation [plæn'teɪʃən] n φυτεία.

plaque [plæk] n (on wall) πλάκα (αναμνηστική) || (on teeth) πέτρα.

plasma ['plæzmə] n πλάσμα nt, πρωτόπλασμα nt.

plaster ['plɑːstə*] n σουβάς, κονίαμα nt, γύψος || (for wounds) έμπλαστρο, τσιρότο ♦ vt σοβατίζω || φορτώνω, σκεπάζω || in ~ (leg etc) σε γύψο || ~ed a (col) μεθυσμένος || ~er n σουβατζής.

plastic ['plæstɪk] n πλαστική ύλη ♦ a πλαστικός || (easily shaped) εύπλαστος || P~ine n (R) πλαστισίνη || ~ surgery n πλαστική εγχείρηση.

plate [pleɪt] n πιάτο, δίσκος || (table utensils) χρυσά ή αργυρά επιτραπέζια σκεύη ntpl, ασημικά ntpl || (flat sheet) πλάκα, λάμα, φύλλο.

plateau ['plætəʊ] n υψίπεδο, οροπέδιο.

plateful ['pleɪtful] n πιάτο γεμάτο.

plate glass ['pleɪt'glɑːs] n κρύσταλλο, υαλοπίνακας.

platform ['plætfɔːm] n (at meeting) εξέδρα, βήμα nt || (RAIL) αποβάθρα, εξέδρα.

platinum ['plætɪnəm] n λευκόχρυσος, πλατίνη.

platitude ['plætɪtjuːd] n κοινοτοπία.

platoon [plə'tuːn] n διμοιρία, ουλαμός.

platter ['plætə*] n πιατέλα.

plausible ['plɔːzəbl] a εύλογος, πιθανός.

play [pleɪ] n παιχνίδι, διασκέδαση || (stage) έργο || (of shadows etc) παίξιμο || (MECH) ανοχή, παίξιμο ♦ vt παίζω, διασκεδάζω || (trick) παιχνιδιάζω, κάνω αστείο || (part) παίζω, υποδύομαι ρόλο, ερμηνεύω || (instrument) παίζω ♦ vi (amuse o.s.) διασκεδάζω, παίζω || (of light etc) σπιθοβολώ, παίζω, χοροπηδώ || ~boy n γλεντζές m, έκλυτος νέος || ~ed-out a εξαντλημένος, αποκαμωμένος || ~er n παίκτης/ρια m/f, ηθοποιός m/f || ~ful a παιχνιδιάρικος, παιχνιδιάρης || ~ground n προαύλιο, τόπος διασκεδάσεως || ~ing card n τραπουλόχαρτο || ~ing field n γήπεδο || ~mate n συμπαίκτης, σύντροφος στο παιχνίδι || ~thing n παιχνίδι, παιχνιδάκι || ~wright n θεατρικός συγγραφέας m/f.

plea [pliː] n (LAW) έκκληση, αγωγή.

plead [pliːd] vt επικαλούμαι, προβάλλω ♦ vi παρακαλώ, ικετεύω || (LAW) υποστηρίζω, υπερασπίζω, απολογούμαι.

pleasant ['plɛznt] a ευχάριστος || ~ry n ευθυμία, κέφι, χιούμορ.

please [pliːz] vt αρέσω, ευχαριστώ || ~! παρακαλώ! || my bill, ~ το λογαριασμό, παρακαλώ || ~ yourself! κάνε το κέφι σου! || ~d a (happy, glad) ευχαριστημένος, ικανοποιημένος.

pleasing ['pliːzɪŋ] a ευχάριστος.

pleasurable ['plɛʒərəbl] a ευχάριστος, τερπνός.

pleasure ['plɛʒə*] n τέρψη, ευχαρίστηση, χαρά || (amusement) απολαύσεις fpl, ηδονές fpl, χαρές || it's a ~! χαίρομαι!, παρακαλώ!

pleat [pliːt] n πτυχή, πιέτα.

plebs [plɛbz] npl λαουτζίκος.

plectrum ['plɛktrəm] n πλήκτρο.

pledge [plɛdʒ] n ενέχυρο, δεσμευτική υπόσχεση, τεκμήριο ♦ vt δίνω το λόγο μου, υπόσχομαι.

plentiful ['plɛntɪful] a άφθονος, πλουσιοπάροχος.

plenty ['plɛntɪ] n αφθονία, πλήθος nt || (enough) αρκετό ♦ ad (col) πάρα πολύ || ~ of άφθονα, με το τσουβάλι.

plethora ['plɛθərə] n πληθώρα.

pleurisy ['plʊərɪsɪ] n πλευρίτιδα.

pliable ['plaɪəbl] a εύκαμπτος, ευλύγιστος.

pliers ['plaɪəz] npl τανάλια, λαβίδα.

plight [plaɪt] n κατάσταση, θέση.

plinth [plɪnθ] n πλίνθος, πλινθίο.

plod [plɒd] vi περπατώ βαρειά, σέρνομαι || ~der n φιλόπονος, ευσυνείδητος.

plot [plɒt] n (conspiracy) συνωμοσία || (of story) πλοκή, υπόθεση || (land) οικόπεδο, χωράφι ♦ vt χαράσσω, σχεδιάζω ♦ vt (plan secretly) συνωμοτώ, μηχανορραφώ.

plough, plow [plaʊ] n άροτρο, αλέτρι ♦ vt (earth) αροτριώ, αλετρίζω || (col: exam candidate) απορρίπτω (μαθητή) || to ~ back vt (COMM) επενδύω (τα

pluck στην ίδια επιχείρηση || **to ~ through** vt (book) διαβάζω με κόπο || **~ing** n άροση, αλέτρισμα nt.

pluck [plʌk] vt (fruit) κόβω || (feathers) μαδώ ♦ n (col) κουράγιο, θάρρος nt || **to ~ up courage** παίρνω κουράγιο || **~y** a θαρραλέος, παλικάρι.

plug [plʌg] n (for hole) πώμα nt, βούλωμα nt, τάπα || (wall socket) πρίζα || (col: publicity) διαφήμιση, προβολή || (AUT) μπουζί ♦ vt (hole) βουλώνω, ταπώνω || (col: advertise) διαφημίζω, προβάλλω.

plum [plʌm] n (fruit) δαμάσκηνο ♦ a (choice) εκλεκτό πράμα, καλύτερη θέση.

plumage ['plu:mɪdʒ] n φτέρωμα nt, φτερά ntpl.

plumb [plʌm] a κατακόρυφος || πλήρης, αληθής ♦ ad (exactly) ακριβώς || (wholly) τελείως ♦ vt βυθομετρώ, σταθμίζω.

plumber ['plʌmə*] n υδραυλικός

plumbing ['plʌmɪŋ] n (craft) υδραυλική τέχνη || (piping) σωληνώσεις fpl, υδραυλικά ntpl.

plume [plu:m] n λοφίο, φτερό.

plump [plʌmp] a στρογγυλός, παχουλός, αφράτος ♦ vi σωριάζομαι, πέφτω βαριά ♦ vt πετώ απότομα || **to ~ for** vt (col: choose) υποστηρίζω, ψηφίζω υπέρ.

plunder ['plʌndə*] n λεία, λεηλασία, πλιάτσικο ♦ vt λεηλατώ, λαφυραγωγώ.

plunge [plʌndʒ] n κατάδυση, βουτιά ♦ vt (κατα)βυθίζω, βουτώ, χώνω ♦ vi καταδύομαι, βουτώ.

plunging ['plʌndʒɪŋ] a (neckline) μεγάλο (ντεκολτέ).

pluperfect ['plu:'pɜ:fɪkt] n υπερσυντέλικος.

plural ['plʊərəl] a πληθυντικός, πολλαπλός ♦ n πληθυντικός.

plus [plʌs] prep πλέον, συν, μαζί με ♦ a θετικός.

plush [plʌʃ] a (col: luxurious) πολυτελής, πλούσιος.

ply [plaɪ] n (layer) φύλλο, φλοίωμα nt || **three~ wool** τρίκλωνο μαλλί ♦ vt (with questions) ταλαιπωρώ (με ερωτήσεις) || **to ~ a trade** ασκώ επάγγελμα ♦ vi ταξιδεύω, εκτελώ γραμμή || **~wood** n κοντραπλακέ nt inv.

P.M. abbr see **prime**.

p.m. ad (abbr of post meridiem) μ.μ. (μετά το μεσημέρι).

pneumatic [njuː'mætɪk] a πνευματικός, του πεπιεσμένου αέρα.

pneumonia [njuː'məʊnɪə] n πνευμονία.

P.O. abbr see **post office**.

poach [pəʊtʃ] vt (cook) βράζω ξεφλουδισμένο αυγό, ποσάρω || (steal) κλέβω ♦ vi λαθροθηρώ || **~ed** a (egg) (αυγό) ποσέ || **~er** n λαθροθήρας || **~ing** n λαθροθηρία, κλοπή.

pocket ['pɒkɪt] n τσέπη || (hollow) θύλακας, λάκκος || (of resistance) νησίδα αντιστάσεως ♦ vt τσεπώνω, βάζω στην τσέπη || **out of ~** ζημιωμένος, βγαίνω χαμένος || **~book** n (US: wallet)

πορτοφόλι || (notebook) σημειωματάριο (της τσέπης) || (small book) βιβλίο τσέπης || **~ful** n όσο χωρεί μια τσέπη || **~ knife** n σουγιάς (της τσέπης) || **~ money** n χαρτζιλίκι.

pod [pɒd] n περικάρπιο.

podgy ['pɒdʒɪ] a κοντόχονδρος, χοντρός.

poem ['pəʊɪm] n ποίημα nt.

poet ['pəʊɪt] n ποιητής/ήτρια m/f || **~ic** [pəʊ'etɪk] a ποιητικός || **~ laureate** n επίσημος ποιητής || **~ry** n ποίηση.

poignant ['pɔɪnjənt] a οξύς, δριμύς, τσουχτερός, δυνατός.

point [pɔɪnt] n (sharp end) ακίδα, άκρα, αιχμή, μύτη || (dot) στίξη, σημείο || (moment) στιγμή, σημείο || (detail) λεπτομέρεια, στοιχείο, σημείο || (railhead) αιρραντήριο || (RAIL) κλειδί, διασταύρωση || (of compass) ρόμβος πυξίδας, κάρτα || (degree) βαθμός, σημείο || (decimal point) κόμμα nt ♦ vt στρέφω, κατευθύνω, δείχνω || (gun etc) σκοπεύω με, σημαδεύω ♦ vi δείχνω, δακτυλοδεικτώ || **~s** npl κλειδί || **~ of view** n άποψη || **what's the ~?** τι το όφελος; || **to ~ out** vt δείχνω, επισύρω την προσοχή, υπογραμμίζω || **to ~ to** vt δείχνω, δακτυλοδεικτώ || **~-blank** ad κατ' ευθείαν, απερίστροφος || **~ duty** n υπηρεσία τροχαίας || **~ed** a (shape) αιχμηρός, μυτερός || (remark) δηκτικός, καυστικός, τσουχτερός || **~er** n δείκτης || **~less** a άσκοπος, μάταιος.

poise [pɔɪz] n παρουσιαστικό, κορμοστασιά ♦ vti ισορροπώ, σταθμίζω.

poison ['pɔɪzn] n δηλητήριο ♦ vt δηλητηριάζω, μολύνω || **~ous** a δηλητηριώδης, φαρμακερός.

poke [pəʊk] vt (stick into) κτυπώ, χώνω || (fire) συδαυλίζω, σκαλίζω ♦ n (jab) κτύπημα nt, σπρωξιά || **to ~ one's nose into** ανακατεύομαι σε || **to ~ about** vi ψηλαφώ, ψάχνω || **~r** n σκαλιστήρι || (CARDS) πόκερ nt inv.

poky ['pəʊkɪ] a μικρός, στενόχωρος.

Poland ['pəʊlənd] n Πολωνία.

polar ['pəʊlə*] a πολικός || **~ bear** n πολική άρκτος || **~ize** vt πολώνω ♦ vi πολούμαι.

pole [pəʊl] n (of wood) στύλος, ιστός, κοντάρι || (ELEC) στύλος || (GEOG) πόλος || **~-cat** n (US) είδος νυφίτσας || **~ star** n πολικό αστέρι || **~ vault** n άλμα nt επί κοντώ.

police [pə'liːs] n αστυνομία ♦ vt αστυνομεύω, ελέγχω, τηρώ (την τάξη) || **~ car** n αστυνομικό (αυτοκίνητο) || **~man** n αστυφύλακας, αστυνομικός, πολισμάνος || **~ state** n αστυνομικό κράτος nt || **~ station** n αστυνομικό τμήμα nt || **~woman** n n αστυνομικός, αστυνομικίνα.

policy ['pɒlɪsɪ] n πολιτική || (prudence) φρόνηση || (insurance) ασφαλιστήριο.

polio ['pəʊlɪəʊ] n πολυομυελίτιδα.

Polish ['pɒulɪʃ] a πολωνικός ♦ n (LING)
Πολωνικά ntpl.

polish ['pɒlɪʃ] n βερνίκι || (surface)
γυαλάδα, στιλπνότητα, λούστρο || (fig:
refinement) ευγένεια, καλοί τρόποι mpl ♦
vt στιλβώνω, γυαλίζω, λουστράρω ||
(refine) εξευγενίζω || **to ~ off** vt (work)
τελειώνω βιαστικά || (food) αδειάζω,
κατεβάζω, καθαρίζω || **~ed** a (fig)
ευγενικός, λεπτός || εκλεπτισμένος.

polite [pə'laɪt] a ευγενής, φιλόφρονας ||
~ness n ευγένεια, λεπτότητα.

politic ['pɒlɪtɪk] a (wise) συνετός,
προνοητικός || **~al** [pə'lɪtɪkəl] a
πολιτικός || **~ian** [pɒlɪ'tɪʃən] n πολιτικός,
πολιτικάντης || **~s** npl (n) πολιτική || (US)
πολιτικολογία.

polka [pɒlkə] n πόλκα || **~ dot** (φόρεμα)
με πίκες fpl, με βούλες fpl.

poll [pɒul] n ψηφοφορία, αριθμός
ψήφων ♦ vt συγκεντρώνω ψήφους,
ψηφίζω.

pollen ['pɒlən] n γύρη (λουλουδιού).

pollination [pɒlɪ'neɪʃən] n επικονίαση,
γονιμοποίηση.

polling booth ['pɒulɪŋbuːð] n
απομονωτήριο εκλογικού τμήματος.

polling day ['pɒulɪŋdeɪ] n μέρα
εκλογών.

polling station ['pɒulɪŋsteɪʃən] n
εκλογικό τμήμα nt.

pollute [pə'luːt] vt μολύνω, βρωμίζω.

pollution [pə'luːʃən] n μίανση, μόλυνση.

polo ['pɒulɒu] n πόλο nt inv.

poly- ['pɒlɪ] prefix πολυ-.

polygamy [pə'lɪgæmɪ] n πολυγαμία.

polytechnic [pɒlɪ'teknɪk] n
πολυτεχνείο.

polythene ['pɒlɪθiːn] n πολυθένιο.

pomegranate ['pɒmɪgrænɪt] n ρόδι.

pommel ['pʌml] vt γρονθοκοπώ,
κοπανίζω.

pomp [pɒmp] n λαμπρότητα, επίδειξη.

pompous ['pɒmpəs] a πομπώδης,
φανφαρόνος || **~ly** ad με
επιδεικτικότητα, με στόμφο.

ponce [pɒns] n (col) σωματέμπορος.

pond [pɒnd] n δεξαμενή, λιμνούλα.

ponder ['pɒndə*] vti ξανασκέφτομαι,
μελετώ, ζυγίζω || **~ous** a βαρύς, βραδύς,
ανιαρός.

pontificate [pɒn'tɪfɪkeɪt] vi (fig) μιλώ με
ύφος ποντιφικά.

pontoon [pɒn'tuːn] n πλωτό στήριγμα nt
γέφυρας || (CARDS) είκοσι ένα.

pony ['pɒunɪ] n αλογάκι || **~tail** n
αλογοουρά.

poodle ['puːdl] n σγουρόμαλλο σκυλάκι.

pool [puːl] n (of liquid) λιμνούλα,
νερόλακκος || (at cards) πόστα, πότ ||
(billiards) μπάτσικα || **~s** (football) προ-πο
nt inv ♦ vt (money etc) ενώνω,
συγκεντρώνω.

poor [puə*] a φτωχός, δυστυχισμένος ||
(feeble) αδύνατος, άθλιος || (pitied)
κακόμοιρος, αξιολύπητος ♦ n: **the ~** οι

φτωχοί mpl|| **~ly** ad φτωχικά, άθλια ♦ a
αδιάθετος.

pop [pɒp] n (noise) ξηρός κρότος || (MUS)
μουσική ποπ || (col US: father) μπαμπάς ♦
vt (put suddenly) θέτω απότομα ♦ vi
(explode) κάνω ποπ, κροτώ || (come
suddenly) μπαίνω ξαφνικά, βγαίνω || **~
concert** n λαϊκή συναυλία (ποπ) ||
~corn n ψημένο καλαμπόκι, ποπ-κορν
nt inv.

Pope [pɒup] n Πάπας.

poplar ['pɒplə*] n λεύκη.

poppy ['pɒpɪ] n παπαρούνα.

populace ['pɒpjuləs] n λαός, το πλήθος.

popular ['pɒpjulə*] a δημοφιλής,
κοσμοαγάπητος || (of the people) λαϊκός ||
~ity n δημοτικότητα, δημοφιλία || **~ize**
vt εκλαϊκεύω.

populate ['pɒpjuleɪt] vt (συν)οικίζω,
κατοικώ.

population [pɒpju'leɪʃən] n πληθυσμός.

porcelain ['pɔːslɪn] n πορσελάνη.

porch [pɔːtʃ] n προστέγασμα nt || (US)
βεράντα.

porcupine ['pɔːkjupaɪn] n
ακανθόχοιρος.

pore [pɔː*] n πόρος || **to ~ over** vt
προσηλώνομαι.

pork [pɔːk] n χοιρινό.

pornographic [pɔːnə'græfɪk] a
πορνογραφικός.

pornography [pɔː'nɒgrəfɪ] n
πορνογραφία.

porous ['pɔːrəs] a πορώδης.

porpoise ['pɔːpəs] n φώκαινα.

porridge ['pɒrɪdʒ] n χυλός (βρώμης).

port [pɔːt] n λιμένας, λιμάνι || (town)
πόρτο || (COMPUT) σύνδεση
εισόδου/εξόδου || (NAUT: left side)
αριστερή πλευρά || (wine) πορτό, οίνος
Πορτογαλίας.

portable ['pɔːtəbl] a φορητός.

portal ['pɔːtl] n είσοδος, πύλη.

portcullis [pɔːt'kʌlɪs] n καταραχτή
θύρα, καταραχτή.

portent ['pɔːtent] n κακός οιωνός ||
(good) θαυμάσιο πράγμα nt, οιωνός.

porter ['pɔːtə*] n αχθοφόρος, χαμάλης
|| (doorkeeper) θυρωρός.

porthole ['pɔːthɒul] n (NAUT) φινιστρίνι.

portion ['pɔːʃən] n μερίδα, μερίδιο.

portly ['pɔːtlɪ] a παχύς, επιβλητικός.

portrait ['pɔːtrɪt] n προσωπογραφία,
πορτραίτο.

portray [pɔː'treɪ] vt (describe)
περιγράφω || **~al** n απεικόνιση,
περιγραφή.

Portugal ['pɔːtjugəl] n Πορτογαλία.

Portuguese ['pɔːtju'giːz] a
πορτογαλικός ♦ n (person)
Πορτογάλος/ίδα m/f || (LING)
Πορτογαλικά ntpl.

pose [pɒuz] n (position) στάση ||
(affectation) προσποίηση, πόζα ♦ vi (take
up attitude) ποζάρω || (assume false pose)
εμφανίζομαι, παριστάνω ♦ vt (put

question) θέτω || ~r n (*problem*) δύσκολο πρόβλημα nt.

posh [pɒʃ] a (*col*) πλούσιος.

position [pə'zɪʃən] n θέση, στάση || (*place*) θέση, σειρά || (*location*) τοποθεσία || (*attitude*) θέση, πρόταση || (*rank*) θέση, βαθμός || (*job*) θέση, εργασία.

positive ['pɒzɪtɪv] a θετικός, καταφατικός || (*confident*) βέβαιος, σίγουρος || (*real*) πραγματικός, αληθινός || (*character*) θετικός.

posse ['pɒsɪ] n (*US*) απόσπασμα nt (αστυνομικών).

possess [pə'zɛs] vt (κατ)έχω, διατηρώ || ~ion n κατοχή, κτήμα nt || (*owning*) κατοχή || ~ive a κτητικός, παθολογικά στοργικός || (*GRAM*) κτητικό.

possibility [pɒsə'bɪlɪtɪ] n (*chance*) πιθανότητα || (*event*) δυνατότητα.

possible ['pɒsəbl] a δυνατός, ενδεχόμενος, λογικός || if ~ αν μπορώ, αν είναι δυνατό.

possibly ['pɒsəblɪ] ad κατά το δυνατό, πιθανό, ίσως.

post [pəʊst] n (*pole*) στύλος, πάσσαλος, κολώνα || (*mail*) ταχυδρομείο || (*man*) ταχυδρόμος || (*station*) θέση, φυλακή, πόστο || (*job*) θέση, πόστο ♦ vt (*notice*) τοιχοκολλώ || (*letters*) ταχυδρομώ || (*station*) εγκαθιστώ, τοποθετώ || ~age n ταχυδρομικά ntpl, γραμματόσημα ntpl || ~al a ταχυδρομικός || ~al order n ταχυδρομική επιταγή || ~box n ταχυδρομικό κουτί || ~card n καρτποστάλ f inv, κάρτα.

postdate ['pəʊst'deɪt] vt (*cheque*) μεταχρονολογώ, επιχρονολογώ.

poster ['pəʊstə*] n διαφήμιση, αφίσα.

poste restante [pəʊst'rɛstɑːnt] n ποστ-ρεστάντ.

posterior [pɒs'tɪərɪə*] n (*col*) ο πισινός, κώλος.

posterity [pɒs'tɛrɪtɪ] n (οι) μεταγενέστεροι.

postgraduate ['pəʊst'grædjuɪt] n μεταπτυχιακός σπουδαστής.

posthumous ['pɒstjuməs] a (*works*) κατάλοιπα ntpl.

postman ['pəʊstmən] n ταχυδρόμος.

postmark ['pəʊstmɑːk] n ταχυδρομική σφραγίδα.

postmaster ['pəʊstmɑːstə*] n διευθυντής ταχυδρομείου.

post-mortem ['pəʊst'mɔːtɛm] n (*examination*) νεκροψία.

post office ['pəʊstɒfɪs] n ταχυδρομείο || ~ box (P.O. Box) n ταχυδρομική θυρίδα (Τ.Θ.), ταχυδρομικό κιβώτιο.

postpone [pəʊst'pəʊn] vt αναβάλλω.

postscript ['pəʊsskrɪpt] n υστερόγραφο.

postulate ['pɒstjuleɪt] vt απαιτώ, αξιώνω.

posture ['pɒstʃə*] n στάση, θέση, κατάσταση ♦ vi τοποθετώ, στήνω, ποζάρω.

postwar ['pəʊst'wɔː*] a μεταπολεμικός.

posy ['pəʊzɪ] n μπουκέτο (από λουλούδια), ανθοδέσμη.

pot [pɒt] n (*for cooking*) χύτρα, δοχείο, γλάστρα || (*sl: marijuana*) ναρκωτικά ntpl ♦ vt (*plant*) βάζω σε γλάστρα, φυτεύω σε γλάστρα.

potash ['pɒtæʃ] n ποτάσσα.

potato [pə'teɪtəʊ] n πατάτα.

potent ['pəʊtənt] a ισχυρός, πειστικός.

potential [pəʊ'tɛnʃəl] a δυνητικός, λανθάνων, πιθανός, δυνατός ♦ n δυναμικό || ~ly ad ενδεχομένως, πιθανώς.

pothole ['pɒthəʊl] n πηγάδι, σπήλαιο || (*in road*) λακκούβα, λάκκος.

potholing ['pɒthəʊlɪŋ] n σπηλαιολογία.

potion ['pəʊʃən] n δόση (φαρμάκου).

potted ['pɒtɪd] a (*food*) διατηρημένος || (*plant*) στη γλάστρα, της γλάστρας.

potter ['pɒtə*] n κεραμοποιός, τσουκαλάς ♦ vi χασομερώ, ψευδοδουλεύω || ~y n αγγειοπλαστική, κεραμεική || (*place*) κεραμοποιείο.

potty ['pɒtɪ] a (*mad*) λοξός, τρελός ♦ n (*child's*) δοχείο (μωρού).

pouch [paʊtʃ] n (*ZOOL*) θύλακας || (*tobacco*) ταμπακιέρα.

poultice ['pəʊltɪs] n κατάπλασμα nt.

poultry ['pəʊltrɪ] n πουλερικά ntpl || ~farm n ορνιθοτροφείο.

pounce [paʊns] vi (+ on) εφορμώ, πηδώ πάνω σε, χυμώ ♦ n πήδημα nt, εφόρμηση.

pound [paʊnd] n (*weight*) λίμπρα (435 γρ), λίβρα, λίτρα || (*sterling*) λίρα (Αγγλίας) || (*area*) περίβολος, μάντρα ♦ vt κτυπώ, κοπανίζω || (*crush to powder*) λειοτριβώ, κονιοποιώ, κοπανίζω || ~ing n σφυροκόπημα nt.

pour [pɔː*] vt (*cause*) χύνω ♦ vi μπαίνω σαν ποτάμι, τρέχω, χύνομαι || to ~ away or off vt χύνω (έξω), ξεχύνομαι || to ~ in vi (*people*) μπαίνω κατά κύματα || ~ing rain n βροχή με το τουλούμι, καταρρακτώδης βροχή.

pout [paʊt] n κατσούφιασμα nt ♦ vi κατσουφιάζω, στραβομουριάζω.

poverty ['pɒvətɪ] n φτώχεια || ~-stricken a φτωχός, άπορος.

powder ['paʊdə*] n σκόνη || (*medicine*) σκόνη || (*cosmetic*) πούδρα ♦ vt (*make into powder*) κονιοποιώ, τρίβω || (*put on powder*) πουδράρω || to ~ one's nose πουδράρομαι || (*fig*) πάω στη τουαλέτα || ~ room n τουαλέτα || ~y a κονιώδης, σαν σκόνη.

power [paʊə*] n (*ability to act*) εξουσία, δύναμη, ικανότητα || (*strength*) δύναμη || (*mighty nation*) (μεγάλη) δύναμη || (*mental*) ικανότητα, ιδιοφυία, ταλέντο || (*ELEC*) ενέργεια, δύναμη || (*POL: of party or leader*) εξουσία, επιρροή, ισχύς ♦ vt παρέχω ενέργεια σε, κινώ || ~ cut n διακοπή ρεύματος || ~ful a (*person*) ρωμαλέος, μεγάλος, δυνατός || (*government*) ισχυρός || (*engine*) ισχυρός, αποδοτικός || ~less a ανίσχυρος, αδύναμος || ~ **line** n γραμμή μεταφοράς || ~ **station** n εργοστάσιο παραγωγής ρεύματος.

p.p. abbr: ~ P. Smith Δια τον κον Π. Σμιθ.

P.R. abbr of **public relations.**

practicable ['præktikəbl] a δυνατός, κατορθωτός, εφαρμόσιμος.

practical ['præktikəl] a πρακτικός, θετικός, εφαρμόσιμος || ~ **joke** n βαρύ αστείο, φάρσα || ~**ly** ad (almost) σχεδόν, ουσιαστικά.

practice ['præktis] n άσκηση, εξάσκηση || (habit) συνήθεια, έθιμο || (business) άσκηση, εξάσκηση || (clients) πελατεία || **in** ~ (in reality) στην πραγματικότητα || **to be out of** ~ (SPORT) ξεσυνηθίζω, δεν είμαι σε φόρμα.

practicing ['præktisiŋ] a (US) = **practising.**

practise, practice (US) ['præktis] vt ασκώ, εφαρμόζω, ακολουθώ, συνηθίζω || (SPORT) εκγυμνάζω || (piano) μελετώ, κάνω ασκήσεις || (profession) επαγγέλλομαι, (εξ)ασκώ.

practising ['præktisiŋ] a (Christian etc) που ασκεί τα θρησκευτικά του καθήκοντα.

practitioner [præk'tiʃənə*] n επαγγελματίας.

pragmatic [præg'mætik] a πρακτικός, πραγματικός.

prairie ['prεəri] n λιβάδι, κάμπος.

praise [preiz] n έπαινος, εγκώμιο ♦ vt επαινώ, εξυμνώ || (worship) δοξάζω || ~**worthy** a αξιέπαινος.

pram [præm] n καροτσάκι μωρού.

prance [prɑːns] vi ανασκιρτώ, αναπηδώ || (strut) κορδώνομαι, καμαρώνω.

prank [præŋk] n ζαβολιά, κατεργαριά, κόλπο.

prattle ['prætl] vi φλυαρώ.

prawn [prɔːn] n είδος nt γαρίδας.

pray [prei] vi προσεύχομαι, παρακαλώ || ~**er** n προσευχή || (praying) παράκληση || ~**er book** n ευχολόγιο, προσευχητήριο.

pre- [priː] prefix προ-.

preach [priːtʃ] vi κηρύσσω || ~**er** n ιεροκήρυκας.

preamble [priː'æmbl] n προοίμιο, εισαγωγή.

prearranged ['priːə'reindʒd] a προκαθορισμένος, συμφωνημένος από πριν.

precarious [pri'kεəriəs] a επισφαλής, επικίνδυνος, αβέβαιος.

precaution [pri'kɔːʃən] n προφύλαξη.

precede [pri'siːd] vti προηγούμαι, προπορεύομαι || ~**nt** ['presidənt] n προηγούμενο.

preceding [pri'siːdiŋ] a προηγούμενος.

precept ['priːsept] n κανόνας, δίδαγμα nt, διαταγή.

precinct ['priːsiŋkt] n περίβολος, περιοχή.

precious ['preʃəs] a πολύτιμος || (affected) επιτηδευμένος, προσποιητός.

precipice ['presipis] n γκρεμός.

precipitate [pri'sipitit] a (hasty) βιαστικός, εσπευσμένος || ~**ly** ad βιαστικά.

precipitous [pri'sipitəs] a (steep) κρημνώδης || ~**ly** ad απότομα.

precise [pri'sais] a ακριβής, ορισμένος, συγκεκριμένος || (careful) ακριβολόγος, τυπικός.

preclude [pri'kluːd] vt αποκλείω, προλαμβάνω.

precocious [pri'kəuʃəs] a πρόωρος.

preconceived ['priːkən'siːvd] a (idea) προκαταληπτικός.

precondition [priːkən'diʃən] n προϋπόθεση.

precursor [priː'kɜːsə*] n πρόδρομος.

predator ['predətə*] n ληστής, αρπακτικό || (animal) ζώο.

predecessor ['priːdisesə*] n προκάτοχος.

predestination [priːdesti'neiʃən] n προκαθορισμός.

predetermine ['priːdi'tɜːmin] vt προκαθορίζω, προαποφασίζω.

predicament [pri'dikəmənt] n δύσκολη θέση, δυσχέρεια.

predicate ['predikit] n βεβαιώνω, υποδηλώ.

predict [pri'dikt] vt προλέγω, προφητεύω || ~**ion** n πρόβλεψη, προφητεία.

predominance [pri'dominəns] n επικράτηση, υπεροχή.

predominant [pri'dominənt] a υπερισχύων, επικρατών.

predominate [pri'domineit] vi επικρατώ, υπερισχύω.

pre-eminent [priː'eminənt] a διαπρεπής, υπερέχων.

pre-empt [priː'empt] vt αποκτώ πρώτος.

preen [priːn] vt: **to** ~ **o.s.** στολίζομαι, καμαρώνω.

prefabricated ['priː'fæbrikeitid] a προκατασκευασμένος.

preface ['prefis] n πρόλογος, εισαγωγή, προοίμιο.

prefect ['priːfekt] n (of school) επιμελητής/ήτρια m/f.

prefer [pri'fɜː*] vt προτιμώ, υποβάλλω, προάγω || ~**able** ['prefərəbl] a (+to) προτιμότερος, καλύτερος (από) || ~**ence** n προτίμηση || ~**ential** a προνομιακός, προνομιούχος.

prefix ['priːfiks] n πρόθεμα nt.

pregnancy ['pregnənsi] n εγκυμοσύνη.

pregnant ['pregnənt] a έγκυος || (of ideas) γόνιμος (σε), γεμάτος συνέπειες.

prehistoric ['priːhis'tɒrik] a προϊστορικός.

prehistory ['priː'histəri] n προϊστορία.

prejudice ['predʒudis] n προκατάληψη, πρόληψη || (harm) ζημιά, βλάβη ♦ vt ζημιώνω, επηρεάζω || ~**d** a προκατειλημμένος, προδιατεθειμένος.

prelate ['prelit] n ιεράρχης.

preliminary [pri'liminəri] *a* προκαταρκτικός.

prelude ['prelju:d] *n* πρόλογος, προοίμιο || *(MUS)* προανάκρουσμα *nt*, πρελούντιο.

premarital ['pri:'mærɪtl] *a* προγαμιαίος.

premature ['prɛmətʃuə*] *a* πρόωρος || ~**ly** *ad* πρόωρα.

premeditated [pri:'mediteitid] *a* προεσκεμμένος, εκ προμελέτης.

premier ['prɛmiə*] *a* πρώτος, κύριος ♦ *n (head of country)* πρωθυπουργός *m/f* || ~**e** [prɛmi'ɛə*] *n* πρεμιέρα.

premise ['prɛmɪs] *n* πρόταση || ~**s** *npl* οίκημα *nt*, κτίριο.

premium ['pri:miəm] *n (insurance)* ασφάλιστρο.

premonition [pri:mə'nɪʃən] *n* προαίσθημα *nt*.

preoccupied [pri:'ɔkjupaid] *a* απορροφημένος, αφηρημένος.

prep [prɛp] *n (SCH: study)* βραδυνή, μελέτη.

preparation [prɛpə'reɪʃən] *n* προπαρασκευή, προετοιμασία.

preparatory [pri'pærətəri] *a (SCH)* προπαρασκευαστικός, προεισαγωγικός.

prepare [pri'pɛə*] *vt* προετοιμάζω, προπαρασκευάζω ♦ *vi* προετοιμάζομαι, προπαρασκευάζομαι || ~**d for** είμαι έτοιμος για || ~**d to** είμαι διατεθειμένος να.

preponderance [pri'pɔndərəns] *n* υπεροχή, επικράτηση.

preposition [prɛpə'zɪʃən] *n* πρόθεση.

preposterous [pri'pɔstərəs] *a* παράλογος, γελοίος.

prerequisite [pri:'rɛkwɪzɪt] *n* προϋπόθεση, αναγκαίος όρος.

prerogative [pri'rɔgətɪv] *n* προνόμιο.

Presbyterian [prɛzbi'tɪəriən] *a, n* Πρεσβυτεριανός.

preschool ['pri:'sku:l] *a* προσχολικός.

prescribe [pris'kraib] *vt* ορίζω, παραγγέλλω || *(medicine)* δίνω συνταγή.

prescription [pris'krɪpʃən] *n (for medicine)* συνταγή.

presence ['prɛzns] *n* παρουσία || *(bearing)* ύφος *nt*, παρουσιαστικό, εμφάνιση || ~ **of mind** ψυχραιμία, ετοιμότητα πνεύματος.

present ['prɛznt] *a* παρών || *(time)* σημερινός ♦ *n (time)* το παρόν, το σήμερα || *(gift)* δώρο || *(GRAM)* ενεστώτας ♦ [pri'zɛnt] *vt* παρουσιάζω, παρουσιάζομαι || *(introduce)* συστήνω, παρουσιάζω || *(offer, give)* καταθέτω, προσφέρω, δίνω || **at** ~ τώρα, προς το παρόν || ~**able** *a* παρουσιάσιμος || ~**ation** *n* παρουσίαση, παράσταση || ~-**day** *a* σημερινός || ~**ly** *ad (soon)* σε λίγο, αμέσως, σύντομα || *(at present)* τώρα.

preservation [prɛzə'veɪʃən] *n* διατήρηση, διαφύλαξη.

preservative [pri'zə:vətɪv] *n* συντηρητικό ♦ *a* α διατηρητικός.

preserve [pri'zə:v] *vt* διαφυλάσσω || *(keep up)* συντηρώ ♦ *n* μέρος *nt* διατηρήσεως ζώων || *(jam)* γλυκό κουταλιού, μαρμελάδα.

preside [pri'zaid] *vi* προεδρεύω.

presidency ['prɛzidənsi] *n* προεδρία.

president ['prɛzidənt] *n* πρόεδρος || *(of university)* πρύτανης || *(of a country)* πρόεδρος || ~**ial** *a* προεδρικός.

press [prɛs] *n (machine)* πιεστήριο, πρέσσα || *(printing house)* (τυπογραφικό) πιεστήριο, τυπογραφείο || *(newspapers)* τύπος, εφημερίδες *fpl* || *(journalists)* τύπος, δημοσιογράφοι *mpl* ♦ *vt* πιέζω, συνθλίβω || *(urge)* πιέζω, επιμένω || *(clothes)* σιδερώνω ♦ *vi* πιέζομαι, σφίγγομαι || **to be** ~**ed for** δεν έχω αρκετό, πιέζομαι για || **to** ~ **for** αξιώνω επιμένω σε, ασκώ πίεση για || **to** ~ **on** *vi* προωθώ, επισπεύδω, συνεχίζω || ~ **agency** *n* πρακτορείο ειδήσεων || ~ **conference** *n* δημοσιογραφική συνέντευξη || ~ **cutting** απόκομμα *nt* εφημερίδας || ~**ing** *a (urgent)* επείγων || *(persistent)* επίμονος, πιεστικός || ~ **stud** *n* κουμπί με πίεση.

pressure ['prɛʃə*] *n* πίεση || ~ **cooker** *n* χύτρα ταχύτητας, κατσαρόλα ταχύτητας || ~ **gauge** *n* θλιβόμετρο, πιεζόμετρο, μανόμετρο || ~ **group** *n* ομάδα με ισχυρή επιρροή.

pressurized ['prɛʃəraizd] *a* πιεζόμενος, υπό πίεσα.

prestige [prɛs'ti:ʒ] *n* γόητρο.

presumably [pri'zju:məbli] *ad* κατά το φαινόμενο, πιθανώς.

presume [pri'zju:m] *vti* υποθέτω, προϋποθέτω || *(venture)* τολμώ, παίρνω το θάρρος.

presumption [pri'zʌmpʃən] *n* υπόθεση, παραδοχή || *(impudence)* αναίδεια.

presuppose [pri:sə'pəuz] *vt* προϋποθέτω.

pretence [pri'tɛns] *n* προσποίηση || *(false excuse)* πρόσχημα *nt*, πρόφαση.

pretend [pri'tɛnd] *vt (feign)* προσποιούμαι, υποκρίνομαι ♦ *vi* προσποιούμαι.

pretense [pri'tɛns] *n (US)* = **pretence.**

pretension [pri'tɛnʃən] *n (claim to merit)* αξίωση, απαίτηση.

pretentious [pri'tɛnʃəs] *a* απαιτητικός, επιδεικτικός.

pretext ['pri:tɛkst] *n* πρόφαση, πρόσχημα *nt*.

pretty ['priti] *a* χαριτωμένος, ωραίος.

prevail [pri'veil] *vi* επικρατώ, υπερισχύω || *(succeed)* επιβάλλω, πείθω || ~**ing** *a (current)* επικρατών, ισχύων.

prevalent ['prɛvələnt] *a* διαδεδομένος, επικρατών.

prevent [pri'vɛnt] *vt* αποτρέπω, προλαμβάνω || *(hinder)* εμποδίζω, (παρα)κωλύω || ~**able** *a* αποφεύξιμος || ~**ative** *n* προληπτικό (φάρμακο) ||

~**ion** n πρόληψη, εμπόδιση || ~**ive** a
προληπτικός, προφυλακτικός.
preview ['pri:vju:] n προκαταρκτική
προβολή, δοκιμαστική προβολή.
previous ['pri:viəs] a προηγούμενος ||
~**ly** ad προηγουμένως, πρωτύτερα.
prewar ['pri:'wɔ:*] a προπολεμικός.
prey [prei] n λεία, βορά, θύμα nt|| to ~
on vt (chase) κυνηγώ || (eat) τρώγω ||
(mind) βασανίζω.
price [prais] n τιμή, τίμημα nt|| (value)
αξία ♦ vt διατιμώ, καθορίζω τιμή || ~**less**
a ανεκτίμητος.
prick [prik] n τσίμπημα nt ♦ vt τσιμπώ,
κεντρώ, τρυπώ.
prickle ['prikl] n αγκάθι.
prickly ['prikli] a (lit) αγκαθωτός,
τσουχτερός || (fig: person) δύσκολος.
pride [praid] n (self-respect) φιλότιμο ||
(something to be proud of) υπερηφάνεια,
καμάρι|| (conceit) αλαζονεία, υπεροψία ||
to ~ o.s. on sth υπερηφανεύομαι,
καμαρώνω για κάτι.
priest [pri:st] n ιερέας, παπάς || ~**ess** n
ιέρεια || ~**hood** n ιερωσύνη, ιερείς mpl.
prig [prig] n φαντασμένος, ξιπασμένος.
prim [prim] a ακριβής, τυπικός,
μαζεμένος.
primarily ['praimərili] ad πρωτίστως,
κυρίως || (at first) αρχικά, πρώτα-πρώτα.
primary ['praiməri] a πρώτος, αρχικός ||
(basic) βασικός || (first in importance)
πρωτεύων, κύριος, ουσιώδης ||
(education) στοιχειώδης || (election)
προκριματική εκλογή || ~ **colours** npl
πρωτεύοντα χρώματα ntpl|| ~ **school** n
δημοτικό σχολείο.
primate ['praimit] n αρχιεπίσκοπος,
πριμάτος || ['praimeit] (ZOOL) πρωτεύον
θηλαστικό.
prime [praim] a πρώτος, πρώτιστος,
κύριος || (excellent) εξαίρετος, πρώτης
ποιότητας ♦ vt κατηχώ, δασκαλεύω ||
(gun, pump) γεμίζω || ~ **minister** n
πρωθυπουργός m/f|| ~**r** n
αλφαβητάριο, πρώτον βιβλίο.
primeval [prai'mi:vəl] a πρωτόγονος,
αρχέγονος.
primitive ['primitiv] a πρωτόγονος.
primrose ['primrəuz] n πράνθεμο,
δακράκι, πασχαλούδα.
primula ['primjulə] n πριμούλη.
primus (stove) ['praiməs(stəuv)] n (R)
γκαζιέρα.
prince [prins] n (of royal family)
πρίγκηπας, βασιλόπουλο || ~**ss** n
πριγκήπισσα.
principal ['prinsipəl] a κύριος,
κυριότερος ♦ n (capital) κεφάλαιο || (of
school) προϊστάμενος/η m/f,
διευθυντής/ύντρια m/f|| ~**ly** ad κυρίως,
προπαντός, κατά το πλείστον.
principle ['prinsipl] n αρχή.
print [print] n σφραγίδα, τύπος ||
(fingerprint) αποτύπωμα nt|| (PHOT)
αντίτυπο, κόπια || (picture) εικόνα ||
(pattern) εμπριμέ nt inv ♦ vt τυπώνω,

εκτυπώνω || to ~ **out** (text) τυπώνω ||
~**ed matter** n έντυπα ntpl|| ~**er** n
τυπογράφος || ~**ing** n (εκ)τύπωση,
τυπογραφία || ~**ing press** n πιεστήριο
(τυπογραφείου).
prior ['praiə*] a προγενέστερος,
προηγούμενος ♦ n (ECCL) ηγούμενος.
priority [prai'ɒriti] n προτεραιότητα.
priory ['praiəri] n μοναστήρι, κοινόβιο.
prise [praiz] vt: to ~ **open** ανοίγω με
μοχλό.
prism ['prizəm] n πρίσμα nt.
prison ['prizn] n φυλακή || ~**er** n
φυλακισμένος/η m/f, υπόδικος/η m/f,
κατάδικος m/f|| (of war) αιχμάλωτος/η
m/f.
pristine ['pristain] a πρωτόγονος,
αρχικός.
privacy ['privəsi] n μοναξιά || (secrecy)
μυστικότητα.
private ['praivit] a ιδιωτικός, ιδιαίτερος
|| (secret) μυστικός ♦ n (MIL) φαντάρος ||
'~' (sign) 'ιδιωτικό', 'ιδιαίτερον' || in ~
ιδιαιτέρως, μυστικά || ~ **eye** n ιδιωτικός
αστυνομικός || ~**ly** ad ιδιωτικά || (in
confidence) εμπιστευτικά.
privet ['privit] n λιγούστρο,
αγριομυρτιά.
privilege ['privilidʒ] n προνόμιο || ~**d** a
προνομιούχος.
privy ['privi] a: ~ **council**
ανακτοβούλιο.
prize [praiz] n βραβείο, έπαθλο ♦ a
(example) λαμπρό υπόδειγμα || (idiot)
υπόδειγμα ηλιθίου ♦ vt εκτιμώ, τιμώ || ~
fight n πυγμαχικός αγώνας || ~ **giving** n
βράβευση || ~**winner** n βραβευμένος/η
m/f.
pro- [prəu] prefix (in favour) υπέρ-, αντί- ||
the pros and cons τα υπέρ και τα κατά.
pro [prəu] n (professional) επαγγελματίας.
probability [prɒbə'biliti] n πιθανότητα.
probable ['prɒbəbl] a ενδεχόμενος,
πιθανός.
probably ['prɒbəbli] ad πιθανώς,
πιθανόν.
probation [prə'beiʃən] n δοκιμασία || (in
court etc) αστυνομική επιτήρηση || **on** ~
υπό δοκιμασία || ~**er** n δόκιμος.
probe [prəub] n (MED) καθετήρας, μήλη ||
(enquiry) εξερεύνηση, διερεύνηση ♦ vti
(εξ)ερευνώ, διερευνώ.
probity ['prəubiti] n τιμιότητα,
ακεραιότητα.
problem ['prɒbləm] n πρόβλημα nt||
~**atic** a προβληματικός.
procedure [prə'si:dʒə*] n διαδικασία,
μέθοδος f.
proceed [prə'si:d] vi προχωρώ,
συνεχίζω || (begin) προβαίνω || ~**ings** npl
συζητήσεις fpl, πρακτικά ntpl|| (LAW)
δικαστική ενέργεια, δίκη || ~**s**
['prəusi:dz] npl εισπράξεις fpl.
process ['prəuses] n πορεία, εξέλιξη ||
(method) μέθοδος f, τρόπος ♦ vt
επεξεργάζω, κατεργάζω.
procession [prə'seʃən] n πομπή,

παρέλαση || *(orderly progress)* παράταξη, σειρά, συνοδεία.

proclaim [prə'kleɪm] *vt* κηρύσσω, ανακηρύσσω, αναγορεύω || *(show)* φανερώνω, δείχνω.

procure [prə'kjuə*] *vt* προμηθεύω, προμηθεύομαι.

prod [prɒd] *vt* σκαλίζω, κεντρίζω, εξάπτω ♦ *n (push, jab)* μπήξιμο, κέντρισμα *nt.*

prodigal ['prɒdɪɡəl] *a* άσωτος.

prodigious [prə'dɪdʒəs] *a* τεράστιος, καταπληκτικός.

prodigy ['prɒdɪdʒɪ] *n* φαινόμενο, θαύμα *nt.*

produce ['prɒdjuːs] *n (AGR)* προϊόν, καρπός ♦ [prə'djuːs] *vt (show)* παρουσιάζω, δείχνω || *(make)* παράγω, γεννώ, προξενώ || *(play)* ανεβάζω, παρουσιάζω || ~**r** *n* παραγωγός || *(THEAT)* σκηνοθέτης, παραγωγός.

product ['prɒdʌkt] *n* προϊόν || *(result)* αποτέλεσμα *nt.*

production [prə'dʌkʃən] *n* παραγωγή, κατασκευή || *(THEAT)* σκηνοθέτηση, παράσταση, ανέβασμα *nt* || ~ **line** *n* γραμμή παραγωγής.

productive [prə'dʌktɪv] *a* παραγωγικός || *(fertile)* γόνιμος.

productivity [prɒdʌk'tɪvɪtɪ] *n* παραγωγικότητα || *(fertility)* γονιμότητα.

profane [prə'feɪn] *a* βέβηλος || *(language)* βλάσφημος.

profess [prə'fɛs] *vt* διακηρύττω || *(confess)* ομολογώ || *(claim)* προσποιούμαι.

profession [prə'fɛʃən] *n* επάγγελμα *nt* || *(declaration)* ομολογία, διακήρυξη || ~**al** *n* επαγγελματίας ♦ *a* επαγγελματικός || ~**alism** *n* επαγγελματισμός.

professor [prə'fɛsə*] *n* καθηγητής/ήτρια *m/f.*

proficient [prə'fɪʃənt] *a* ικανός, ειδικός.

profile ['prəʊfaɪl] *n (of face)* κατατομή, προφίλ *nt inv* || *(fig report)* σύντομη βιογραφία.

profit ['prɒfɪt] *n* κέρδος *nt*, όφελος *nt*, ωφέλεια ♦ *vi* (+ *by, from)* ωφελούμαι (από) επωφελούμαι || ~**able** *a* επικερδής, επωφελής || ~**ably** *ad* επωφελώς, επικερδώς, ωφέλιμα.

profiteering [prɒfɪ'tɪərɪŋ] *n* κερδοσκοπία.

profound [prə'faʊnd] *a* βαθύς || *(mysterious)* μυστηριώδης.

profuse [prə'fjuːs] *a* άφθονος, γενναιόδωρος.

programing ['prəʊɡræmɪŋ] *n* = **programming.**

programme, program *(US, COMPUT)* ['prəʊɡræm] *n* πρόγραμμα *nt.*

programmer ['prəʊɡræmə*] *n* προγραμματιστής *m/f.*

programming ['prəʊɡræmɪŋ] *n* προγραμματισμός || ~ **language** *n* γλώσσα προγραμματισμού.

progress ['prəʊɡrɛs] *n* πρόοδος *f,*

εξέλιξη ♦ [prə'ɡrɛs] *vi* προοδεύω, προχωρώ, εξελίσσομαι || **to make** ~ σημειώνω πρόοδο, προκόβω || ~**ion** *n* πρόοδος *f* || ~**ive** *a* προοδευτικός.

prohibit [prə'hɪbɪt] *vt* απαγορεύω || ~**ion** *n* απαγόρευση || *(US: of alcohol)* ποταπαγόρευση || ~**ive** *a (price etc)* απαγορευτικός, απλησίαστος.

project ['prɒdʒɛkt] *n (plan)* σχέδιο || *(study)* μελέτη ♦ [prə'dʒɛkt] *vt (throw)* εκτοξεύω, εξακοντίζω || *(extend)* προεκτείνω || *(film etc)* προβάλλω ♦ *vi* (προ)εξέχω, προβάλλω.

projectile [prə'dʒɛktaɪl] *n* βλήμα *nt.*

projection [prə'dʒɛkʃən] *n* προεξοχή, προβολή.

projector [prə'dʒɛktə*] *n (film)* προβολέας, μηχάνημα *nt* προβολής.

proletariat [prəʊlɪ'tɛərɪət] *n* προλεταριάτο.

proliferate [prə'lɪfəreɪt] *vi* πολλαπλασιάζομαι.

prolific [prə'lɪfɪk] *a* γόνιμος || *(plentiful)* άφθονος.

prologue ['prəʊlɒɡ] *n* πρόλογος.

prolong [prə'lɒŋ] *vt* παρατείνω || *(extend)* προεκτείνω.

prom [prɒm] *n abbr of* promenade || *abbr of* promenade concert || *(US: college ball)* συναυλία με λαϊκές τιμές.

promenade [prɒmɪ'nɑːd] *n* περίπατος || *(place)* τόπος περιπάτου || ~ **concert** *n* συναυλία || ~ **deck** *n (NAUT)* κατάστρωμα *nt* περιπάτου.

prominent ['prɒmɪnənt] *a* περίφημος, διακεκριμένος.

promiscuity [prɒmɪs'kjuːɪtɪ] *n* σμίξιμο, ανακάτεμα *nt*, ελεύθερες ερωτικές σχέσεις.

promise ['prɒmɪs] *n* υπόσχεση, τάξιμο || *(hope)* υπόσχεση ♦ *vti* υπόσχομαι, δίνω υποσχέσεις, προμηνύω.

promising ['prɒmɪsɪŋ] *a* γεμάτος υποσχέσεις, ενθαρρυντικός.

promote [prə'məʊt] *vt* προάγω, προβιβάζω || *(support)* υποστηρίζω || ~**r** *n* υποστηρικτής, υποκινητής || *(organiser)* διοργανωτής.

promotion [prə'məʊʃən] *n (of sales etc)* διαφήμιση, προαγωγή || *(in rank)* προαγωγή, προβιβασμός.

prompt [prɒmpt] *a* άμεσος, σύντομος, πρόθυμος, ταχύς ♦ *ad (punctually)* στην ώρα ♦ *vt* παρακινώ || *(remind)* υποβάλλω || ~**er** *n (THEAT)* υποβολέας || ~**ness** *n* ταχύτητα, ετοιμότητα, προθυμία.

prone [prəʊn] *a* πρεσμένος μπρούμυτα || *(inclined)* (+ *to)* επιρρεπής (τιρος), αυτός που έχει τάση (τιρος).

prong [prɒŋ] *n* δόντι πηρουνιού, πηρούνα, δικάλα.

pronoun ['prəʊnaʊn] *n* αντωνυμία.

pronounce [prə'naʊns] *vt (GRAM)* προφέρω || *(LAW)* εκδίδω, επιβάλλω, γνωματεύω || ~**d** *a (marked)* έντονος, ζωηρός.

pronto ['prɒntəʊ] ad (col) αμέσως, γρήγορα.

pronunciation [prənʌnsɪ'eɪʃən] n προφορά.

proof [pru:f] n απόδειξη, τεκμήριο || (test) δοκιμή, δοκιμασία || (copy) δοκίμιο ♦ a αδιαπέραστος, στεγανός || (resistant) ανθεκτικός.

prop [prɒp] n στήριγμα nt, έρεισμα nt, υποστήριγμα nt || (THEAT) βοηθητικά ntpl, αξεσουάρ nt inv ♦ vt (also: ~ up) (υπο)στηρίζω, στηλώνω.

propaganda [prɒpə'gændə] n προπαγάνδα.

propagation [prɒpə'geɪʃən] n (of plants) αναπαραγωγή, πολλαπλασιασμός || (of knowledge) διάδοση.

propel [prə'pel] vt προωθώ || ~ler n έλικας, προπέλα.

proper ['prɒpə*] a πρέπων, αρμόζων || ~ly ad καλά, καταλλήλως, σωστά || ~ noun n κύριο όνομα nt.

property ['prɒpətɪ] n ιδιοκτησία, περιουσία || (quality) ιδιότητα, χαρακτηριστικό || (THEAT) βοηθητικό, αξεσουάρ nt inv || (land) κτήμα nt, ακίνητο || ~ owner n ιδιοκτήτης/ρια m/f.

prophecy ['prɒfɪsɪ] n (prediction) προφητεία.

prophesy ['prɒfɪsaɪ] vt προφητεύω, προλέγω.

prophet ['prɒfɪt] n προφήτης || ~ic a προφητικός.

proportion [prə'pɔːʃən] n σχέση, αναλογία || (share) μέρος, τμήμα nt ♦ vt ρυθμίζω, μοιράζω κατ' αναλογία || ~al a ανάλογος, συμμετρικός, αναλογικός || ~ate a ανάλογος.

proposal [prə'pəʊzl] n πρόταση, εισήγηση || (of marriage) πρόταση γάμου.

propose [prə'pəʊz] vt προτείνω, σκοπεύω ♦ vi (marriage) κάνω πρόταση γάμου.

proposition [prɒpə'zɪʃən] n πρόταση, σχέδιο, υπόθεση.

proprietary [prə'praɪətərɪ] a της ιδιοκτησίας, της κυριότητας.

proprietor [prə'praɪətə*] n ιδιοκτήτης/τρια m/f.

propulsion [prə'pʌlʃən] n (προ)ώθηση.

prorata [prəʊ'rɑːtə] ad κατ' αναλογία.

prosaic [prəʊ'zeɪɪk] a (ordinary) πεζός.

prose [prəʊz] n πεζός λόγος, πεζογραφία, πρόζα.

prosecute ['prɒsɪkjuːt] vt υποβάλλω μήνυση.

prosecution [prɒsɪ'kjuːʃən] n (ποινική) δίωξη || (people bringing action) κατηγορία, μηνυτής.

prosecutor ['prɒsɪkjuːtə*] n εισαγγελέας.

prospect ['prɒspekt] n (expectation) προσδοκία || (hope) ελπίδα || ~ing n (for minerals) αναζήτηση (μεταλλευμάτων) || ~ive a πιθανός, μελλοντικός || ~or n μεταλλοδίφης || (for gold) χρυσοθήρας.

prospectus [prə'spektəs] n αγγελία, πρόγραμμα nt.

prosper ['prɒspə*] vi ευδοκιμώ, ακμάζω, ευημερώ || ~ity n ευημερία, ευδαιμονία || ~ous a ευημερών, ακμάζων || (successful) επιτυχής.

prostitute ['prɒstɪtjuːt] n πόρνη, πουτάνα.

prostrate ['prɒstreɪt] a (lying flat) πρηνής, μπρούμυτος.

protagonist [prəʊ'tægənɪst] n πρωταγωνιστής/ίστρια m/f.

protect [prə'tekt] vt προστατεύω, προφυλάσσω, υπερασπίζω, καλύπτω || ~ion n προστασία, υπεράσπιση, άμυνα || (shelter) σκέπαστρο, προστατευτικό μέσο || ~ive a προστατευτικός || ~or n προστάτης, προφυλακτήρας.

protégé ['prɒteʒeɪ] n προστατευόμενος || ~e προστατευόμενη.

protein ['prəʊtiːn] n πρωτεΐνη.

protest ['prəʊtest] n διαμαρτυρία ♦ [prə'test] vi (+ against) διαμαρτύρομαι.

Protestant ['prɒtɪstənt] a, n Διαμαρτυρόμενος, Προτεστάντης.

protocol ['prəʊtəkɒl] n πρωτόκολλο.

prototype ['prəʊtəʊtaɪp] n πρωτότυπο.

protractor [prə'træktə*] n μοιρογνωμόνιο.

protrude [prə'truːd] vi προεξέχω, βγαίνω έξω.

proud [praʊd] a περήφανος || (snobbish) φαντασμένος || (condescending) ακατάδεκτος.

prove [pruːv] vt (show) αποδεικνύω, επαληθεύω || (turn out) δείχνομαι.

proverb ['prɒvɜːb] n παροιμία.

provide [prə'vaɪd] vt προμηθεύω, χορηγώ || ~d cj εφόσον, αρκεί να.

province ['prɒvɪns] n επαρχία || (fig) αρμοδιότητα.

provincial [prə'vɪnʃəl] a επαρχιακός.

provision [prə'vɪʒən] n (supply) προμήθεια || (condition) όρος || ~s npl (food) τρόφιμα ntpl || (equipment) εφόδια ntpl || ~al προσωρινός.

provocation [prɒvə'keɪʃən] n πρόκληση.

provocative [prə'vɒkətɪv] a προκλητικός, ερεθιστικός.

provoke [prə'vəʊk] vt προκαλώ, διεγείρω, εξερεθίζω.

prow [praʊ] n πρώρα, πλώρη.

prowess ['praʊɪs] n γενναιότητα || (bravery) ανδρεία, παλικαριά.

prowl [praʊl] vt (streets) περιφέρομαι, τριγυρίζω ♦ n: on the ~ ψάχνω διαρκώς || ~er n νυχτοπάτης, τριγυριστής.

proximity [prɒk'sɪmɪtɪ] n εγγύτητα, αμεσότητα.

proxy ['prɒksɪ] n πληρεξούσιος, αντιπρόσωπος || by ~ δι' αντιπροσώπου.

prudent ['pruːdənt] a συνετός, φρόνιμος.

prudish ['pruːdɪʃ] a σεμνότυφος || ~ness n σεμνοτυφία.

prune [pru:n] n ξερό δαμάσκηνο ♦ vt κλαδεύω.

pry [praɪ] vi (+ into) ψάχνω, χώνω τη μύτη (σε).

psalm [sɑ:m] n ψαλμός.

pseudo- ['sju:dəʊ] prefix ψεύτικος, κίβδηλος || (in compds) ψευδο-.

pseudonym ['sju:dənɪm] n ψευδώνυμο.

psyche ['saɪkɪ] n (soul, mind, intelligence) ψυχή.

psychiatric [saɪkɪ'ætrɪk] a ψυχιατρικός.

psychiatrist [saɪ'kaɪətrɪst] n ψυχίατρος m/f.

psychiatry [saɪ'kaɪətrɪ] n ψυχιατρική.

psychic(al) ['saɪkɪk(əl)] a ψυχικός.

psychoanalyst [saɪkəʊ'ænəlɪst] n ψυχαναλυτής/ύτρια m/f.

psychological [saɪkə'lɒdʒɪkəl] a ψυχολογικός || ~**ly** ad ψυχολογικά.

psychologist [saɪ'kɒlədʒɪst] n ψυχολόγος m/f.

psychology [saɪ'kɒlədʒɪ] n ψυχολογία.

psychopath ['saɪkəʊpæθ] n ψυχοπαθής m/f.

psychosomatic ['saɪkəʊsəʊ'mætɪk] a ψυχοσωματικός.

psychotherapy ['saɪkəʊ'θerəpɪ] n ψυχοθεραπεία.

psychotic [saɪ'kɒtɪk] a, n ψυχοτικός.

p.t.o. abbr of please turn over.

pub [pʌb] n (Brit) = **public house** || see **public**.

puberty ['pju:bətɪ] n ήβη, εφηβεία.

public ['pʌblɪk] a (generally known) πασίγνωστος ♦ n (also: **the general ~**) το κοινό || ~ **house** n ταβέρνα.

publican ['pʌblɪkən] n (innkeeper) ταβερνιάρης, κάπελας.

publication [pʌblɪ'keɪʃən] n (something published) δημοσίευση, έκδοση || (making known) κοινοποίηση, δημοσίευση.

publicity [pʌb'lɪsɪtɪ] n δημοσιότητα || (advertising) διαφήμιση.

publicly ['pʌblɪklɪ] ad δημόσια, ολοφάνερα.

public: ~ **opinion** n κοινή γνώμη || ~ **relations** n δημόσιες σχέσεις fpl || ~ **school** n (Brit) ιδιωτικό σχολείο (Αγγλίας) || ~**-spirited** a ενδιαφερόμενος για το κοινό καλό.

publish ['pʌblɪʃ] vt εκδίδω, δημοσιεύω || (figures etc) αναγγέλλω, δημοσιεύω || ~**er** n εκδότης/ρια m/f|| ~**ing** n έκδοση, δημοσίευση.

pucker ['pʌkə*] vt ζαρώνω.

pudding ['pʊdɪŋ] n πουτίγγα.

puddle ['pʌdl] n (pool) λακκούβα, λιμνούλα.

puff [pʌf] n ξεφύσημα nt, φύσημα nt ♦ vt ξεφυσώ, βγάζω καπνό ♦ vi φυσώ, λαχανιάζω || ~**ed** a (col: out of breath) λαχανιασμένος.

puff pastry ['pʌf'peɪstrɪ] n, **puff paste** (US) ['pʌf'peɪst] n γλύκισμα με φύλλο.

puffy ['pʌfɪ] a φουσκωμένος, φουσκωτός.

pull [pʊl] n (tug) έλξη, τράβηγμα nt || (fig) επιρροή, μέσο ♦ vt (trolley) σύρω, έλκω, τραβώ, σέρνω || (hair) τραβώ || (trigger) πατώ, τραβώ ♦ vi (on rope etc) τραβώ, σύρω || '~' (sign) 'σύρατε' || **to ~ a face** κάνω μούτρα, μορφάζω || **to ~ to pieces** τραβώ και κομματιάζω, κάνω κομμάτια || **to ~ o.s. together** συνέρχομαι || **to ~ apart** vt (break) σχίζω στα δύο, αποχωρίζω || (dismantle) λύω || **to ~ down** vt (house) κατεδαφίζω, γκρεμίζω || **to ~ in** vi (RAIL) μπαίνω (στο σταθμό) || **to ~ off** vt (deal etc) επιτυγχάνω (κάτι) || **to ~ out** vi φεύγω, ξεκινώ, αναχωρώ || (vehicle) βγαίνω από τη λωρίδα ♦ vt αφαιρώ, βγάζω, τραβώ || **to ~ round** or **through** vi συνέρχομαι, γλιτώνω || (from illness) αναρρώνω || **to ~ up** vi σταματώ.

pulley ['pʊlɪ] n τροχαλία.

pullover ['pʊləʊvə*] n πουλόβερ nt inv.

pulp [pʌlp] n πολτός, σάρκωμα nt.

pulpit ['pʊlpɪt] n άμβωνας.

pulsate [pʌl'seɪt] vi πάλλομαι, πάλλω, σφύζω.

pulse [pʌls] n σφυγμός, παλμός || (vegetable) όσπρια ntpl.

pulverize ['pʌlvəraɪz] vt κάνω σκόνη, κονιοποιώ.

pummel ['pʌml] vt γρονθοκοπώ.

pump [pʌmp] n αντλία || (bicycle) τρόμπα ♦ vt αντλώ || **to ~ up** vt (tyre) φουσκώνω (λάστιχο).

pumpkin ['pʌmpkɪn] n κολοκύθα.

pun [pʌn] n λογοπαίγνιο.

punch [pʌntʃ] n τρυπητήρι, ζουμπάς || (blow) γροθιά || (drink) πόντς nt inv, πόντσι ♦ vt γρονθοκοπώ, δίνω μια γροθιά || (a hole) τρυπώ, ανοίγω.

punctual ['pʌŋktjʊəl] a ακριβής.

punctuate ['pʌŋktjʊeɪt] vt στίζω || (fig) τονίζω, υπογραμμίζω.

punctuation [pʌŋktjʊ'eɪʃən] n στίξη.

puncture ['pʌŋktʃə*] n (παρα)κέντηση || (tyre) σκάσιμο, τρύπημα σε λάστιχο ♦ vt παρακεντώ, τρυπώ, σπάζω.

pungent ['pʌndʒənt] a δριμύς, σουβλερός, οξύς.

punish ['pʌnɪʃ] vt τιμωρώ, δέρνω || (in boxing etc) δίνω άγριο ξύλο, μαστιγώνω || ~**able** a αξιόποινος, τιμωρητέος || ~**ment** n τιμωρία.

punitive ['pju:nɪtɪv] a τιμωρητικός || (MIL) ~ **expedition** n εκστρατεία αντιποίνων.

punt [pʌnt] n πλοιάρι, ρηχή βάρκα.

punter ['pʌntə*] n (gambler) παίκτης.

puny ['pju:nɪ] a μικροκαμωμένος, αδύνατος, ασθματικός.

pup [pʌp] n σκυλάκι, κουτάβι.

pupil ['pju:pl] n μαθητής/ήτρια m/f|| (of eye) κόρη (οφθαλμού).

puppet ['pʌpɪt] n μαριονέτα || (person) ανδρείκελο.

puppy ['pʌpɪ] n σκυλάκι.

purchase ['pɜːtʃɪs] n ψώνισμα, ψώνιο || (buying) αγορά, ψώνισμα nt ♦ vt αγοράζω, ψωνίζω || ~r n αγοραστής.

pure [pjuə*] a καθαρός || (innocent) άδολος, αγνός || (unmixed) αμιγής, ανόθευτος.

purée ['pjuəreɪ] n πουρές m inv.

purge [pɜːdʒ] n κάθαρσιο || (POL) εκκαθάριση ♦ vt (εκ)καθαρίζω.

purify ['pjuərɪfaɪ] vt καθαρίζω, εξαγνίζω.

purist ['pjuərɪst] n: Greek language ~ καθαρευουσιάνος, καθαρολόγος.

puritan ['pjuərɪtən] n πουριτανός || ~ical a πουριτανικός.

purity ['pjuərɪtɪ] n καθαρότητα || (authenticity) γνησιότητα.

purl [pɜːl] n ανάποδη βελονιά ♦ vt πλέκω ανάποδες.

purple ['pɜːpl] (colour) a πορφυρός ♦ n πορφύρα, πορφυρό (χρώμα).

purpose ['pɜːpəs] n σκοπός, πρόθεση || on ~ σκόπιμα || ~ful a (προ)εσκεμμένος, σκόπιμος || ~ly ad επίτηδες, σκόπιμα.

purr [pɜː*] vi (of cat) ρουθουνίζω, κάνω ρονρό ♦ n γουργούρισμα.

purse [pɜːs] n πορτοφόλι ♦ vt ζαρώνω.

purser ['pɜːsə*] n λογιστής (πλοίου).

pursue [pə'sjuː] vt (κατα)διώκω, κυνηγώ || (carry on) συνεχίζω, ακολουθώ || ~r n διώκτης.

pursuit [pə'sjuːt] n (κατα)δίωξη, κυνήγημα nt || (occupation) επιδίωξη, επάγγελμα nt.

purveyor [pɜː'veɪə*] n προμηθευτής (τροφίμων).

pus [pʌs] n πύο.

push [puʃ] n ώθηση, σκούντημα nt, σπρωξιά || (MIL) προώθηση ♦ vt σπρώχνω, σκουντώ || (forward) προχωρώ, προοδεύω ♦ vi σπρώχνω, ωθώ, ασκώ πίεση || (make one's way) προχωρώ (με δυσκολία) || `~' (sign) 'ωθήσετε' || at a ~ (if necessary) στην ανάγκη || to ~ aside vt απωθώ, παραμερίζω || to ~ off vi (col) φεύγω, ξεκινώ || to ~ on vi (continue) προχωρώ, συνεχίζω, επισπεύδω || to ~ through vt (measure) περνώ (νομοσχέδιο κτλ) || ~ chair n καροτσάκι, παιδικό αμαξάκι || ~ing a δραστήριος, επίμονος || ~over n (col) εύκολο πράμα nt, εύκολη κατάκτηση.

puss [pus] n (also: pussy cat) γατάκι, ψιψίνα.

put [put] (irreg v) vt θέτω, τοποθετώ, βάζω || (express) εκφράζω, εξηγώ, υποβάλλω || to ~ about vi στρέφομαι, αναστρέφω ♦ vt διαδίδω, θέτω σε κυκλοφορία || to ~ across vt (succeed) επιτυγχάνω, βγάζω πέρα || (meaning) δίνω να καταλάβει || to ~ away vt (store) βάζω κατά μέρος, φυλάω || to ~ back vt (replace) βάζω πίσω || (postpone) αναβάλλω || to ~ by vt (money) αποταμιεύω || to ~ down vt (lit) κατεβάζω || (in writing) γράφω, σημειώνω || to ~ forward vt (idea) αναπτύσσω,

εισηγούμαι, προτείνω || (date) αναβάλλω || to ~ off vt (postpone) αναβάλλω || (discourage) μεταπείθω, εμποδίζω, αποθαρρύνω || to ~ on vt (clothes etc) φορώ || (light etc) ανάβω || (play etc) ανεβάζω || (brake) φρενάρω || (false air) προσποιούμαι || to ~ out vt (hand etc) εκτείνω, απλώνω || (news, rumour) διαδίδω || (light etc) σβήνω || (person: inconvenience) στενοχωρώ, ενοχλώ || to ~ up vt (raise) σηκώνω, υψώνω || (guest) φιλοξενώ || to ~ up with vt ανέχομαι.

putrid ['pjuːtrɪd] a σαπρός, σάπιος.

putt [pʌt] vt σέρνω (τη μπάλα) ♦ n συρτό χτύπημα nt, πάτινκ nt inv.

putty ['pʌtɪ] n στόκος.

put-up ['putʌp] a: ~ job δουλειά σκαρωμένη, στημένη μηχανή.

puzzle ['pʌzl] n αίνιγμα nt, δύσκολο πρόβλημα nt, μπέρδεμα nt || (toy) παιχνίδι συναρμολογήσεως, γρίφος ♦ vt (perplex) περιπλέκω, συγχίζω ♦ vi σπάζω το κεφάλι μου.

puzzling ['pʌzlɪŋ] a πολύπλοκος, δύσκολος, μπλεγμένος.

pygmy ['pɪgmɪ] n πυγμαίος.

pyjamas [pɪ'dʒɑːməz] npl πιζάμες fpl.

pylon ['paɪlən] n στύλος.

pyramid ['pɪrəmɪd] n πυραμίδα.

python ['paɪθən] n πύθωνας.

Q

quack [kwæk] n κραυγή πάπιας || (dishonest person) κομπογιαννίτης.

quad [kwɒd] n abbr of quadrangle, quadruple, quadruplet.

quadrangle ['kwɒdræŋgl] n (court) τετράγωνη αυλή.

quadruped ['kwɒdruped] n τετράποδο.

quadruple ['kwɒdrupl] a τετραπλός, τετραπλάσιος, τετράδιπλος ♦ [kwɒ'druːpl] vti τετραπλασιάζω, τετραπλασιάζομαι.

quadruplet [kwɒ'druːplɪt] n τετράδυμο.

quaint [kweɪnt] a παράξενος, αλλόκοτος.

quake [kweɪk] vi τρέμω, σείομαι || Q~r n Κουάκερος.

qualification [kwɒlɪfɪ'keɪʃən] n ικανότητα, προσόν nt || (reservation) επιφύλαξη, όρος, περιορισμός.

qualified ['kwɒlɪfaɪd] a έχων τα προσόντα, κατάλληλος || (reserved) επιφυλακτικός, περιωρισμένος, μετριασμένος.

qualify ['kwɒlɪfaɪ] vt καθιστώ κατάλληλο, αποκτώ τα προσόντα || (limit) τροποποιώ, προσδιορίζω ♦ vi (acquire degree) λαμβάνω δίπλωμα.

quality ['kwɒlɪtɪ] n (kind) ποιότητα || (of person) ιδιότητα, χαρακτηριστικό, ικανότητα ♦ a καλής ποιότητας.

qualm [kwɑːm] n (misgiving) τύψη, ενδοιασμός.

quandary ['kwɒndərɪ] n αμηχανία, δίλημμα nt.

quantity ['kwɒntɪtɪ] n ποσότητα || (large amount) μεγάλη ποσότητα, πολύ, με το σωρό.

quarantine ['kwɒrəntiːn] n καραντίνα.

quarrel ['kwɒrəl] n (argument) φιλονεικία, διένεξη, καυγάς, τσακωμός ♦ vi (argue) φιλονεικώ, τσακώνομαι || ~some a ευέξαπτος, καυγατζής.

quarry ['kwɒrɪ] n (of stone) λατομείο || (animal) θήραμα nt, κυνήγι.

quart [kwɔːt] n τέταρτο του γαλονιού.

quarter ['kwɔːtə*] n τέταρτο || (of year) τριμηνία ♦ vt κόβω στα τέσσερα || (MIL) στρατωνίζω || ~s npl (esp MIL) κατάλυμα nt, στρατώνας || (accommodation) στέγαση || ~ of an hour ένα τέταρτο (της ώρας) || ~ past three τρεις και τέταρτο || ~ to three τρεις παρά τέταρτο || ~-deck n πρυμναίο κατάστρωμα nt, κάσαρο || ~ly a τριμηνιαίος || ~master n (NAUT) υπονάυκληρος || (MIL) επιμελητής.

quartet(te) [kwɔː'tet] n τετραφωνία, κουαρτέτο.

quartz [kwɔːts] n χαλαζίας.

quash [kwɒʃ] vt (verdict) αναιρώ, ακυρώνω.

quasi ['kwɑːzɪ] a σαν, σχεδόν, τρόπον τινά.

quaver ['kweɪvə*] n (MUS) όγδοο ♦ vi τρέμω, κάνω τρίλιες.

quay [kiː] n αποβάθρα, προκυμαία.

queasy ['kwiːzɪ] a ευαίσθητος, απδιαστικός.

queen [kwiːn] n βασίλισσα || (CARDS) ντάμα || ~ mother n βασιλομήτωρ f.

queer [kwɪə*] a αλλόκοτος, παράξενος ♦ n (col: homosexual) 'τοιούτος'.

quell [kwel] vt καταπνίγω, καταβάλλω, κατευνάζω.

quench [kwentʃ] vt κόβω (τη δίψα μου), κατευνάζω || (fire etc) σβήνω.

query ['kwɪərɪ] n ερώτηση, ερώτημα nt ♦ vt ερωτώ, ερευνώ.

quest [kwest] n αναζήτηση, έρευνα.

question ['kwestʃən] n ερώτηση, ερώτημα nt || (problem) ζήτημα nt, θέμα nt || (doubt) αμφιβολία, αμφισβήτηση ♦ vt ρωτώ, εξετάζω || (doubt) αμφισβητώ || beyond ~ αναμφισβήτητα || out of the ~ εκτός συζητήσεως, απαράδεκτος || ~able a αμφίβολος, αμφισβητήσιμος || ~er n εξεταστής, ανακριτής || ~ing a ερώτηση, ανάκριση || ~ mark n ερωτηματικό.

questionnaire [kwestʃə'neə*] n ερωτηματολόγιο.

queue [kjuː] n (line) ουρά ♦ vi μπαίνω στην ουρά, σχηματίζω ουρά.

quibble ['kwɪbl] n (petty objection) υπεκφυγή.

quick [kwɪk] a (fast) ταχύς, γρήγορος, γοργός || (impatient) βιαστικός, ευέξαπτος || (keen) ζωηρός, ζωντανός, έξυπνος ♦ ad γρήγορα ♦ n (ANAT) ευαίσθητο σημείο, σάρκα, κρέας nt || (old:

the living) οι ζωντανοί || ~en vt (hasten) επιταχύνω || (rouse) (ανα)ζωογονώ, ζωντανεύω ♦ vi (ξανα)ζωντανεύω, αναζωπυρούμαι || ~ly ad γρήγορα || ~sand n κινητή άμμος f|| ~step n (MUSIC) ταχύς ρυθμός || ~-witted a ξύπνιος, ατσίδα.

quid [kwɪd] n (Brit col: £1) λίρα (Αγγλίας).

quiet ['kwaɪət] a (without noise) σιωπηλός, ήσυχος, αθόρυβος || (still) ήρεμος, γαλήνιος, ήσυχος || (peaceful) ήρεμος, ατάραχος ♦ n ησυχία, ηρεμία || ~en vti (also: ~en down) (καθ)ησυχάζω, καλμάρω || ~ly ad ήρεμα, απαλά, σιγαλά, σιωπηλά || ~ness n ηρεμία, γαλήνη, κάλμα.

quill [kwɪl] n (pen) πένα από φτερό.

quilt [kwɪlt] n πάπλωμα nt, εφάπλωμα nt.

quin [kwɪn] n abbr of quintuplet.

quinee [kwɪns] n κυδώνι.

quinine [kwɪ'niːn] n κινίνη.

quintet(te) [kwɪn'tet] n κουιντέτο.

quintuplet [kwɪn'tjuːplɪt] n πεντάδυμο.

quip [kwɪp] n ευφυολόγημα nt, πείραγμα nt, σαρκασμός ♦ vi ευφυολογώ.

quit [kwɪt] n (irreg v) vt εγκαταλείπω, φεύγω ♦ vi (give up) παραιτούμαι, εγκαταλείπω.

quite [kwaɪt] ad τελείως, εντελώς || (fairly) μάλλον, πολύ || ~ (so)! σωστά!, σύμφωνοι!

quits [kwɪts] ad στα ίσια, πάτσι.

quiver ['kwɪvə*] vi τρέμω, τρεμουλιάζω ♦ n (for arrows) φαρέτρα, σαϊτοθήκη.

quiz [kwɪz] n στραβοκοίταγμα nt || (test) προφορική εξέταση ♦ vt (question) εξετάζω || ~zical a αινιγματώδης, ερωτηματικός.

quorum ['kwɔːrəm] n απαρτία.

quota ['kwəʊtə] n ανάλογο μερίδιο, μερίδα.

quotation [kwəʊ'teɪʃən] n (from book) απόσπασμα nt || (price) προσφορά || ~ marks npl εισαγωγικά ntpl.

quote [kwəʊt] n (quotation) απόσπασμα nt ♦ vti (price) καθορίζω, δίνω τιμή || (cite) παραθέτω, αναφέρω.

quotient ['kwəʊʃənt] n πηλίκο nt.

R

rabbi ['ræbaɪ] n ραββίνος.

rabbit ['ræbɪt] n κουνέλι || ~ hutch n κλουβί κουνελιού.

rabble ['ræbl] n όχλος.

rabid ['ræbɪd] a (fig) μανιασμένος, αδιάλλακτος.

rabies ['reɪbiːz] n λύσσα.

R.A.C. abbr of Royal Automobile Club.

race [reɪs] n (people) ράτσα, φυλή || (generation) γενιά || (animals) ράτσα || (competition) αγώνας δρόμου || (rush) βία, γρηγοράδα ♦ vt κάνω αγώνα δρόμου ♦ vi τρέχω || (compete) συναγωνίζομαι || ~course n (for horses) ιππόδρομος || ~horse n άλογο ιπποδρομιών || ~

meeting n *(for horses)* ιπποδρομία || ~ **relations** npl φυλετικές σχέσεις fpl || ~**track** n *(for cars etc)* πίστα (αγώνων).

racial ['reıʃəl] a φυλετικός || ~**ism** n φυλετισμός, ρα(τ)σισμός || ~**ist** a ρα(τ)σιστικός.

racing ['reısıŋ] n αγώνες mpl, συμμετοχή σε αγώνες || ~ **car** n αυτοκίνητο αγώνων || ~ **driver** n οδηγός αυτοκινήτου αγώνων.

racist ['reısıst] a ρατσιστής.

rack [ræk] n *(clothes etc)* κρεμάστρα ♦ vt βασανίζω || ~ **and ruin** καταστροφή, κατά διαβόλου.

racket ['rækıt] n θόρυβος, φασαρία || *(dishonest scheme)* κομπίνα || *(for tennis)* ρακέτα.

racquet ['rækıt] n ρακέτα.

racy ['reısı] a *(spirited)* ζωηρός, κεφάτος.

radar ['reıda:*] n ραντάρ nt inv.

radiant ['reıdıənt] a λαμπερός || *(giving out rays)* ακτινοβόλος.

radiate ['reıdıeıt] vt *(of heat)* ακτινοβολώ, εκπέμπω ♦ vi *(lines)* εκτείνω ακτινοειδώς.

radiation [reıdı'eıʃən] n ακτινοβολία.

radiator ['reıdıeıtə*] n σώμα nt καλοριφέρ || *(AUT)* ψυγείο.

radical ['rædıkəl] a ριζικός || *(POL)* ριζοσπαστικός.

radio ['reıdıəυ] n ραδιόφωνο.

radio... ['reıdıəυ] prefix: ~**active** a ραδιενεργός || ~**activity** n ραδιενέργεια || ~**grapher** n ακτινογράφος || ~**telephone** n ασύρματο τηλέφωνο || ~ **telescope** n ραδιοτηλεσκόπιο || ~**therapist** n ακτινολόγος ιατρός.

radish ['rædıʃ] n ρεπανάκι.

radium ['reıdıəm] n ράδιο.

radius ['reıdıəs] n ακτίνα.

raffia ['ræfıə] n ραφία.

raffle ['ræfl] n λαχείο, λοταρία.

raft [ra:ft] n σχεδία.

rafter ['ra:ftə*] n δοκάρι, καδρόνι.

rag [ræg] n *(of cloth)* ράκος nt, κουρέλι || *(col: newspaper)* εφημερίδα ♦ vt κάνω φάρσα, κάνω καζούρα || ~**bag** n *(fig)* κακοντυμένη γυναίκα.

rage [reıdʒ] n *(fury)* λύσσα, μανία || *(fashion)* μανία της μόδας ♦ vi *(person)* μαίνομαι, είμαι έξω φρενών || *(storm)* μαίνομαι, είμαι αγριεμένος.

ragged ['rægıd] a *(edge)* τραχύς, απότομος.

raging ['reıdʒıŋ] a μαινόμενος, αγριεμένος.

raid [reıd] n *(MIL)* επιδρομή || *(invasion)* εισβολή || *(criminal)* επιδρομή, γιουρούσι || *(by police)* επιδρομή, μπλόκος ♦ vt εισβάλλω σε, κάνω μπλόκο || ~**er** n επιδρομέας.

rail [reıl] n *(on stair)* κάγκελο, κιγκλίδωμα nt || *(of ship)* κουπαστή, || *(RAIL)* σιδηροτροχιά, γραμμή || ~**s** npl *(RAIL)* τροχιά, γραμμές fpl || **by** ~ σιδηροδρομικώς, με τραίνο || ~**ings** npl κάγκελα ntpl, φράχτης || ~**road** n *(US)*,

~**way** n *(Brit)* σιδηρόδρομος, σιδηροδρομική γραμμή || ~**road** or ~**way station** n σιδηροδρομικός σταθμός.

rain [reın] n βροχή ♦ vti βρέχω || ~**bow** n ουράνιο τόξο || ~**coat** n αδιάβροχο || ~**drop** n σταγόνα βροχής || ~**storm** n καταιγίδα || *(flood)* κατακλυσμός || ~**y** a *(region)* βροχερός || *(day)* βροχερή (μέρα) || *(fig)* ώρα ανάγκης || *(season)* εποχή των βροχών.

raise [reız] n *(esp US: increase)* αύξηση (μισθού) ♦ vt *(build)* κτίζω, στήνω || *(lift)* σηκώνω, υψώνω, ανεβάζω || *(a question)* προβάλλω, θέτω || *(doubts)* προκαλώ, γεννώ || *(collect)* μαζεύω, συλλέγω || *(bring up)* ανατρέφω, τρέφω.

raisin ['reızən] n σταφίδα.

rake [reık] n τσουγκράνα || *(dissolute person)* έκλυτος, ακόλαστος ♦ vt *(AGR)* μαζεύω με τσουγκράνα, σκαλίζω || *(with shots)* γαζώνω || *(search keenly)* εξετάζω, ερευνώ || **to** ~ **in** or **together** etc vt μαζεύω.

rally ['rælı] n *(POL etc)* συγκέντρωση, συναγερμός || *(AUT)* ράλλυ nt inv || *(improvement)* ανάκτηση, βελτίωση ♦ vt συναθροίζω, συγκεντρώνω ♦ vi *(health)* συνέρχομαι, αναρρώνω || **to** ~ **round** vti συσπειρώνομαι.

ram [ræm] n κριάρι || *(beam)* έμβολο, κριός ♦ vt εμβολίζω, μπήγω || *(strike)* κτυπώ || *(stuff)* παραγεμίζω, χώνω.

ramble ['ræmbl] n περίπατος, περιπλάνηση ♦ vi κάνω βόλτες, περιφέρομαι || *(be delirious)* μιλώ ασυνάρτητα.

rambling ['ræmblıŋ] a *(plant)* αναρριχητικός || *(speech)* ασύνδετος, ασυνάρτητος.

ramification [ræmıfı'keıʃən] n διακλάδωση.

ramp [ræmp] n *(incline)* κεκλιμένο επίπεδο, ανωφέρεια.

rampage [ræm'peıdʒ] n: **to be on the** ~ vi *(also:* ~) συμπεριφέρομαι βίαια.

rampant ['ræmpənt] a *(unchecked)* αχαλίνωτος, ξαπλωμένος || *(on hind legs)* όρθιος.

rampart ['ræmpa:t] n έπαλξη, προμαχώνας, ντάπια.

ramshackle ['ræmʃækl] a ετοιμόρροπος, ερειπωμένος, ρημάδι.

ran [ræn] pt of **run**.

ranch [ra:ntʃ] n αγρόκτημα nt, ράντσο.

rancid ['rænsıd] a ταγγός, ταγκός.

rancour, rancor *(US)* ['ræŋkə*] n μνησικακία, έχθρα.

random ['rændəm] a τυχαίος ♦ n: **at** ~ στην τύχη, στα κουτουρού.

randy ['rændı] a *(col)* ασελγής, λάγνος.

rang [ræŋ] pt of **ring**.

range [reındʒ] n *(row, line)* σειρά, οροσειρά || *(extent, series)* έκταση, σειρά, περιοχή || *(of gun)* βεληνεκές nt, εμβέλεια || *(for shooting)* πεδίο βολής, σκοπευτήριο || *(cooking stove)* κουζίνα, μαγειρική συσκευή ♦ vt παρατάσσω, βάζω στη σειρά || (roam) περιπλανώμαι, περιφέρομαι ♦ vi (extend) εκτείνομαι, απλώνομαι || ~r n (of forest) δασάρχης, δασονόμος.

rank [ræŋk] n (row, line) στοίχος, γραμμή || (social position) (κοινωνική) τάξη || (high position) ανώτερη θέση, βαθμός ♦ a (of place) κατατάσσομαι, έρχομαι ♦ a (bad smelling) δύσοσμος, τσαγγός || (extreme) πλήρης, τέλειος, απόλυτος || the ~s npl (MIL) οι στρατιώτες, φαντάροι mpl || the ~ and file (fig) ο απλός λαός.

ransack ['rænsæk] vt λεηλατώ, κάνω άνω-κάτω, ψάχνω καλά.

ransom ['rænsəm] n λύτρα ntpl || to hold to ~ ζητώ λύτρα.

rant [rænt] vi κομπάζω || ~ing n στόμφος.

rap [ræp] n κτύπημα nt, κτύπος, κρότος ♦ vt κρούω, κτυπώ.

rape [reɪp] n βιασμός ♦ vt βιάζω.

rapid ['ræpɪd] a ταχύς, γρήγορος || ~s npl μικρός καταρράκτης || ~ly ad γρήγορα, γοργά.

rapist ['reɪpɪst] n βιαστής.

rapture ['ræptʃə*] n έκσταση, μεγάλη χαρά.

rapturous ['ræptʃərəs] a εκστατικός, ενθουσιασμένος.

rare [rɛə*] a σπάνιος, ασυνήθιστος || αραιός || (air) αραιός || (especially good) θαυμάσιος, σπουδαίος || (in cooking) μισοψημένος.

rarity ['rɛərɪtɪ] n σπάνιο πράγμα nt || (scarcity) σπανιότητα.

rascal ['rɑːskəl] n παλιάνθρωπος, μασκαράς.

rash [ræʃ] a παράτολμος, απερίσκεπτος ♦ n εξάνθημα nt.

rasher ['ræʃə*] n ψιλή φέτα μπέικον.

raspberry ['rɑːzbərɪ] n σμέουρο, φραμπουάζ nt inv, βατόμουρο.

rasping ['rɑːspɪŋ] a (noise) οξύς, στριγγός.

rat [ræt] n (animal) αρουραίος, μεγάλος ποντικός.

ratable ['reɪtəbl] a: ~ value φορολογήσιμο τεκμαρτό ενοίκιο (ακινήτου).

ratchet ['rætʃɪt] n οδοντωτός τροχός, καστάνια ntpl.

rate [reɪt] n (proportion) αναλογία, ανάλογο ποσό, ανάλογος αριθμός || (price) ποσοστό, τόκος || (speed) ρυθμός, ταχύτητα ♦ vt εκτιμώ, ταξινομώ || ~s npl (Brit) τοπικός φόρος || at any ~ οπωσδήποτε, εν πάσει περιπτώσει || at this ~ έτσι || ~ of exchange n τιμή συναλλάγματος || ~payer n φορολογούμενος || see first.

rather ['rɑːðə*] ad μάλλον, καλύτερα, παρά || (somewhat) λίγο, κάπως, μάλλον, σχετικά.

ratify ['rætɪfaɪ] vt επικυρώνω, εγκρίνω.

rating ['reɪtɪŋ] n (classification) εκτίμηση,

τάξη || (NAUT) μέλος πληρώματος, ειδικότητα.

ratio ['reɪʃɪəʊ] n λόγος, αναλογία.

ration ['ræʃən] n μερίδα || (usually pl, food) σιτηρέσιο, τρωμπ ♦ vt περιορίζω, επιβάλλω μερίδες.

rational ['ræʃənl] a λογικός || **rationale** [ræʃəˈnɑːl] n λογική εξήγηση, λογική βάση || ~ize vt ορθολογίζομαι, οργανώνω ορθολογικά.

rationing ['ræʃnɪŋ] n καθορισμός μερίδων, διανομή με δελτίο.

rattle ['rætl] n κρότος, κροταλισμός || (toy) ροκάνα, κρόταλο ♦ vi κροταλίζω, κροτώ || ~snake n κροταλίας.

raucous ['rɔːkəs] a βραχνός.

ravage ['rævɪdʒ] vt ερημώνω, αφανίζω, ρημάζω || ~s npl (of time etc) φθορά του χρόνου.

rave [reɪv] vi παραληρώ, παραμιλώ || (rage) μαίνομαι, ουρλιάζω.

raven ['reɪvn] n κοράκι, κόρακας.

ravenous ['rævənəs] a (hungry) πεινασμένος, λιμασμένος.

ravine [rəˈviːn] n φαράγγι.

raving ['reɪvɪŋ] a: ~ lunatic μανιακός, παράφρονας.

ravioli [rævɪˈəʊlɪ] n ραβιόλια ntpl.

ravish ['rævɪʃ] vt απάγω, κλέβω || (rape) βιάζω || ~ing a γοητευτικός, μαγευτικός.

raw [rɔː] a (uncooked) ωμός, άψητος || (not manufactured) ακατέργαστος || (tender) ευαίσθητος, ματωμένος || (inexperienced) άξεστος, ατζαμής || ~ material n πρώτες ύλες fpl.

ray [reɪ] n ακτίδα.

raze [reɪz] vt ισοπεδώνω, κατεδαφίζω, γκρεμίζω.

razor ['reɪzə*] n ξυράφι || ~ blade n ξυριστική λεπίδα.

Rd abbr of **road**.

re- [riː] prefix αντι-, ανά-, ξανά-.

reach [riːtʃ] n έκταση, άπλωμα nt, τέντωμα nt (χεριού) || (distance) εντός βολής, κοντά ♦ vt απλώνω, τεντώνω || (arrive at) φθάνω ♦ vi (επ)εκτείνομαι || to ~ out vi απλώνω (το χέρι).

react [riːˈækt] vi αντιδρώ || ~ion n αντίδραση || ~ionary a αντιδραστικός.

reactor [riːˈæktə*] n αντιδραστήρας.

read [riːd] (irreg v) n ανάγνωση, διάβασμα nt ♦ vti διαβάζω || (aloud) διαβάζω δυνατά || (understand) ερμηνεύω, δείχνω || (find in book) διαβάζομαι, (COMPUT) διαβάζω || ~able a αναγνώσιμος, που διαβάζεται || ~er n αναγνώστης/ρια m/f || (book) αναγνωστικό || ~ership n (of newspaper etc) αναγνωστικό κοινό.

readily ['redɪlɪ] ad πρόθυμα, αδίστακτα, εύκολα.

readiness ['redɪnɪs] n προθυμία || (being ready) ετοιμότητα.

reading ['riːdɪŋ] n ανάγνωση, διάβασμα nt || ~ lamp n λάμπα του τραπεζιού || ~ room n αναγνωστήριο.

readjust ['riːə'dʒʌst] vt αναπροσαρμόζω, διορθώνω, σιάζω.

ready ['redɪ] a έτοιμος || (willing) πρόθυμος, διατεθειμένος || (condition) έτοιμος || (quick, facile) γρήγορος, εύκολος || (available) πρόχειρος ♦ ad τελείως ♦ n: at the ~ έτοιμος || ~-made a έτοιμος.

real [rɪəl] a πραγματικός, αληθινός || ~ estate n ακίνητος περιουσία, οικόπεδα ntpl || ~ism n πραγματισμός, ρεαλισμός || ~ist n πραγματιστής, ρεαλιστής/ίστρια m/f || ~istic a ρεαλιστικός.

reality [riː'ælɪtɪ] n πραγματικότητα, αλήθεια || in ~ πράγματι, πραγματικά.

realization [rɪəlaɪ'zeɪʃən] n συνειδητοποίηση || (fulfilment) πραγματοποίηση.

realize ['rɪəlaɪz] vt (understand) κατανοώ, αντιλαμβάνομαι, καταλαβαίνω || (bring about) πραγματοποιώ.

really ['rɪəlɪ] ad πραγματικά, αληθινά, όχι δα.

realm [relm] n σφαίρα, δικαιοδοσία || (kingdom) βασίλειο.

reap [riːp] vt θερίζω || (harvest) συγκομίζω, μαζεύω || ~er n (machine) θεριστική μηχανή.

reappear ['riːə'pɪə*] vi επανεμφανίζομαι, ξαναφαίνομαι || ~ance n επανεμφάνιση, επάνοδος f.

reapply ['riːə'plaɪ] vi (+ to, for) ξαναυποβάλλω (αίτηση).

reappoint ['riːə'pɔɪnt] vt επαναδιορίζω.

rear [rɪə*] a οπίσθιος, πισινός ♦ n νώτα ntpl, οπίσθια ntpl, οπισθοφυλακή ♦ vt (bring up) (ανα)τρέφω ♦ vi ανορθούμαι, σηκώνομαι σούζα || ~guard n οπισθοφυλακή.

rearm [rɪ'ɑːm] vti επανεξοπλίζω, επανεξοπλίζομαι || ~ament n επανεξοπλισμός.

rearrange ['riːə'reɪndʒ] vt τακτοποιώ πάλι, αναδιαρρυθμίζω.

rear-view ['rɪəvjuː] a: ~ mirror καθρέφτης οδήγησης.

reason ['riːzn] n (cause) λόγος, αιτία || (ability to think) λογική, λογική || (judgment) κρίση ♦ vi σκέφτομαι, συλλογίζομαι, συμπεραίνω || ~able a λογικός || (fair) μετριοπαθής, μέτριος || ~ably ad λογικά || ~ed a (argument) αιτιολογημένος, δικαιολογημένος || ~ing n συλλογισμός, επιχείρημα nt.

reassert ['riːə'sɜːt] vt επαναβεβαιώνω.

reassure [riːə'ʃʊə*] vt ενθαρρύνω καθησυχάζω.

reassuring [riːə'ʃʊərɪŋ] a καθησυχαστικός || (encouraging) ενθαρρυντικός.

rebate ['riːbeɪt] n έκπτωση.

rebel ['rebl] n αντάρτης/ισσα m/f, επαναστάτης/ρια m/f ♦ a επαναστατημένος, αντάρτικός || ~lion [rɪ'beliən] n ανταρσία || ~lious a αντάρτικός, ανυπότακτος.

rebirth ['riː'bɜːθ] n αναγέννηση.

rebound [rɪ'baʊnd] vi αναπηδώ ♦ ['riːbaʊnd] n αναπήδηση.

rebuff [rɪ'bʌf] n απόκρουση, άρνηση ♦ vt αποκρούω, αρνούμαι.

rebuild [riː'bɪld] vt ανοικοδομώ || ~ing n ανοικοδόμηση.

rebuke [rɪ'bjuːk] n επίπληξη, μομφή ♦ vt επιπλήττω, επιτιμώ.

recalcitrant [rɪ'kælsɪtrənt] a ανυπάκουος, δύστροπος.

recall [rɪ'kɔːl] vt (call back) ανακαλώ || (remember) ξαναθυμίζω, ξαναθυμάμαι || (withdraw) ανακαλώ.

recant [rɪ'kænt] vi ανακαλώ, αναιρώ, αναθεωρώ.

recap ['riːkæp] vti ξαναβουλώνω.

recede [rɪ'siːd] vi αποσύρομαι, υποχωρώ, τραβιέμαι.

receipt [rɪ'siːt] n απόδειξη παραλαβής || (receiving) λήψη, παραλαβή || ~s npl εισπράξεις fpl, έσοδα ntpl.

receive [rɪ'siːv] vt λαμβάνω || (welcome) (υπο)δέχομαι || ~r n (TEL) ακουστικό.

recent ['riːsnt] a πρόσφατος, νέος || ~ly ad τελευταία, πρόσφατα.

receptacle [rɪ'septəkl] n δοχείο.

reception [rɪ'sepʃən] n (welcome) υποδοχή || (party) δεξίωση || (at hotel etc) γραφείο υποδοχής || ~ist n υπάλληλος m/f επί της υποδοχής.

receptive [rɪ'septɪv] a δεκτικός.

recess [rɪ'ses] n (interval) διακοπή, διάλειμμα nt || (in wall) εσοχή, βαθούλωμα nt || (inner place) μυστικό μέρος nt.

recharge ['riː'tʃɑːdʒ] vt (battery) αναφορτίζω, ξαναγεμίζω.

recipe ['resɪpɪ] n συνταγή.

recipient [rɪ'sɪpɪənt] n δέκτης, λήπτης, παραλήπτης.

reciprocal [rɪ'sɪprəkəl] a αμοιβαίος, αντίστροφος.

recital [rɪ'saɪtl] n (MUS) ρεσιτάλ nt inv.

recite [rɪ'saɪt] vt απαγγέλλω, αποστηθίζω || (tell one by one) εξιστορώ, απαριθμώ.

reckless ['reklɪs] a αδιάφορος, απρόσεκτος, απερίσκεπτος || ~ly ad απερίσκεπτα, παράτολμα.

reckon ['rekən] vt (count) υπολογίζω, λογαριάζω, μετρώ || (consider) εκτιμώ, λογαριάζω ♦ vi υπολογίζω || to ~ on vt στηρίζομαι σε, υπολογίζω σε || ~ing n υπολογισμός.

reclaim [rɪ'kleɪm] vi (land) εκχερσώνω, αποξηραίνω.

recline [rɪ'klaɪn] vi ξαπλώνω, πλαγιάζω, ακουμπώ.

reclining [rɪ'klaɪnɪŋ] a πλαγιαστός, ξαπλωμένος.

recluse [rɪ'kluːs] n ερημίτης.

recognition [rekəg'nɪʃən] n αναγνώριση.

recognize ['rekəgnaɪz] vt αναγνωρίζω || (admit) ομολογώ, παραδέχομαι.

recoil [rɪˈkɔɪl] *vi* οπισθοδρομώ, μαζεύομαι || *(spring)* αναπηδώ.

recollect [rekəˈlekt] *vt* θυμούμαι, αναπολώ || ~ion *n* ανάμνηση || *(memory)* μνημονικό.

recommend [rekəˈmend] *vt* συνιστώ || ~ation *n* σύσταση || *(qualification)* προσόν *nt*.

recompense [ˈrekəmpens] *n* ανταμοιβή, αποζημίωση ♦ *vt* ανταμείβω, αποζημιώνω.

reconcile [ˈrekənsaɪl] *vt (make agree)* συμβιβάζω || *(make friendly)* συμφιλιώνω.

reconciliation [rekənsɪlɪˈeɪʃən] *n* ουμφιλίωση, συμβιβασμός.

reconditioned [ˈriːkənˈdɪʃənd] a επισκευασμένος, ανακαινισθείς.

reconnoitre, reconnoiter *(US)* [rekəˈnɔɪtə*] *vti* κάνω αναγνώριση, εξερευνώ.

reconsider [ˈriːkənˈsɪdə*] *vti* αναθεωρώ, επανεξετάζω.

reconstitute [riːˈkɒnstɪtjuːt] *vt* επαναφέρω στη φυσική κατάσταση.

reconstruct [ˈriːkənˈstrʌkt] *vt* ανοικοδομώ, ανασυγκροτώ || ~ion *n* ανοικοδόμηση, ανασυγκρότηση.

record [ˈrekɔːd] *n* αναγραφή, καταγραφή, σημείωση || *(disc)* δίσκος, πλάκα || *(best performance)* πρωτάθλημα *nt*, ρεκόρ *nt inv*, επίδοση || *(COMPUT)* εγγραφή ♦ a *(time)* με μεγάλη ταχύτητα, σε διάστημα του σημειώνει ρεκόρ ♦ [rɪˈkɔːd] *vt (set down)* καταγράφω, αναγράφω || *(music etc)* ηχογραφώ, εγγράφω || ~ed a *(music)* ηχογραφημένος || ~er *n* μηχάνημα *nt* εγγραφής || *(tape recorder)* μαγνητόφωνο || ~ holder *n (SPORT)* πρωταθλητής/ήτρια *m/f* || ~ing *n (music)* ηχογράφηση || ~ player *n* πικάπ *nt inv*.

recount [rɪˈkaʊnt] *vt (tell in detail)* αφηγούμαι, εξιστορώ.

re-count [ˈriːkaʊnt] *n* νέα καταμέτρηση ♦ [riːˈkaʊnt] *vt* ξαναμετρώ.

recoup [rɪˈkuːp] *vt* αποζημιώνω, ξαναπέρνω.

recourse [rɪˈkɔːs] *n* καταφυγή, προσφυγή.

recover [rɪˈkʌvə*] *vt* ανακτώ, ξαναβρίσκω ♦ *vi* ανακτώ (την υγεία μου), θεραπεύομαι || ~y *n* ανάκτηση, ανεύρεση || *(from illness)* ανάρρωση.

recreation [rekrɪˈeɪʃən] *n* αναψυχή, διασκέδαση || ~al a διασκεδαστικός.

recrimination [rɪkrɪmɪˈneɪʃən] *n* αντέγκληση, αντικατηγορία.

recruit [rɪˈkruːt] *n* νεοσύλλεκτος ♦ *vt* στρατολογώ || ~ment *n* στρατολογία.

rectangle [ˈrektæŋgl] *n* ορθογώνιο.

rectangular [rekˈtæŋgjulə*] a ορθογώνιος.

rectify [ˈrektɪfaɪ] *vt* επανορθώνω, διορθώνω.

rectory [ˈrektərɪ] *n (ECCL)* πρεσβυτέριο, εφημερείο.

recuperate [rɪˈkuːpəreɪt] *vi* αναλαμβάνω, αναρρώνω.

recur [rɪˈkɜː*] *vi* επανέρχομαι, ξανασυμβαίνω || ~rence *n* επανάληψη.

red [red] *n (colour)* κόκκινο *n* || *(Communist)* κομουνιστής/ίστρια *m/f*, αριστερός/ή *m/f* ♦ a κόκκινος, ερυθρός || to be in the ~ έχω έλλειμα *nt* || R~ Cross *n* Ερυθρός Σταυρός || ~den *vti* κοκκινίζω || ~dish a κοκκινωπός.

redeem [rɪˈdiːm] *vt* αντισταθμίζω, εξοφλώ, εξαγοράζω.

red-haired [ˈredˈhɛəd] a κοκκινομάλλης.

red-handed [ˈredˈhændɪd] a επ' αυτοφώρω, στα πράσα.

redhead [ˈredhed] *n* κοκκινομάλλα.

red herring [ˈredˈhɛrɪŋ] *n (fig)* ξεγέλασμα *nt*, άσπετο θέμα *nt*.

red-hot [ˈredˈhɒt] a ερυθροπυρωμένος || *(fig)* φανατικός, ένθερμος.

redirect [riːdaɪˈrekt] *vt (mail)* απευθύνω σε νέα διεύθυνση.

rediscovery [ˈriːdɪsˈkʌvərɪ] *n* εκ νέου ανακάλυψη.

red-letter [ˈredˈletə*] a: ~ day μέρα ευτυχισμένων γεγονότων, αξιομνημόνευτη μέρα.

redness [ˈrednɪs] *n* κοκκινίλα, κοκκινάδα.

redo [ˈriːˈduː] *vt* ξανακάνω.

redouble [riːˈdʌbl] *vt* αναδιπλασιάζω.

red tape [ˈredˈteɪp] *n* γραφειοκρατία.

reduce [rɪˈdjuːs] *vt (decrease)* ελαττώνω, μικραίνω, περιορίζω || *(in strength)* αδυνατίζω || *(lower)* υποβιβάζω, κατεβάζω || *(change state)* μεταβάλλω || ~d a *(price)* μειωμένη (τιμή).

reduction [rɪˈdʌkʃən] *n* ελάττωση || *(in size)* σμίκρυνση || *(in price)* έκπτωση.

redundancy [rɪˈdʌndənsɪ] *n* περίσσευμα *nt*, πλεόνασμα *nt*.

redundant [rɪˈdʌndənt] a πλεονάζων, περιττός.

reed [riːd] *n* καλάμι || *(of clarinet etc)* γλωσσίδι.

reef [riːf] *n (at sea)* ύφαλος, ξέρα.

reek [riːk] *vi* αναδίδω κακή μυρωδιά, βρομάω.

reel [riːl] *n (for rope)* ανέμη || *(for cotton, film etc)* πηνίο, καρούλι, μασούρι || *(dance)* ζωηρός (σκωτικός) χορός ♦ *vt* τυλίγω || *(stagger)* τρικλίζω, ζαλίζομαι.

re-election [riːɪˈlekʃən] *n* επανεκλογή.

re-entry [riːˈentrɪ] *n* επάνοδος f, ξαναμπάσιμο.

re-examine [ˈriːɪgˈzæmɪn] *vt* επανεξετάζω.

ref [ref] *n (col: abbr of referee)* διαιτητής.

refectory [rɪˈfektərɪ] *n* τραπεζαρία μοναστηριού ή κολλεγίου.

refer [rɪˈfɜː*] *vt* παραπέμπω || to ~ to *vt* αναφέρομαι σε || *(consult)* συμβουλεύομαι.

referee [refəˈriː] *n* διαιτητής || *(for job application)* υπέγγυος, εγγυητής ♦ *vt* *(SPORT)* διαιτητεύω.

reference ['rɛfrəns] n αναφορά || (in book etc) παραπομπή || (of character) πιστοποιητικό, σύσταση || (person referred to) αυτός που δίνει τη σύσταση, ο εγγυητής || (allusion) μνεία, υπαινιγμός || ~ **book** n βιβλίο οδηγός, σύμβουλος.

referendum [rɛfə'rɛndəm] n δημοψήφισμα nt.

refill ['riːfil] n (for pen etc) ανταλλακτικό.

refine [rɪ'faɪn] vt καθαρίζω, διυλίζω, ραφινάρω || (make finer) εκλεπτύνω, εξευγενίζω || ~**d** a (person) λεπτός, καλλιεργημένος || ~**ment** n εξευγενισμός, λεπτή διάκριση || ~**ry** n διυλιστήριο.

reflect [rɪ'flɛkt] vt αντανακλώ ♦ vi (meditate) σκέφτομαι, συλλογίζομαι, μελετώ || ~**ion** n αντανάκλαση || (thought) σκέψη || ~**or** n ανακλαστήρας, καθρέφτης.

reflex ['riːflɛks] a (involuntary) αντανακλαστικός || ~**ive** a (GRAM) αυτοπαθής.

reform [rɪ'fɔːm] n μεταρρύθμιση, αποκατάσταση, ανασχηματισμός ♦ vt μεταρρυθμίζω, αποκαθιστώ, αναμορφώνω.

reformat [riː'fɔːmæt] vt (COMPUT) ανασχηματίζω.

refrain [rɪ'freɪn] vi (+ from) απέχω, συγκρατούμαι.

refresh [rɪ'frɛʃ] vt αναζωογονώ, δροσίζω, φρεσκάρω || ~**er course** n επανάληψη, μετεκπαίδευση || ~**ing** a ευχάριστος, ζωογόνος, δροσιστικός || ~**ments** npl (food, drink) αναψυκτικά ntpl.

refrigerator [rɪ'frɪdʒəreɪtə*] n ψυγείο.

refuel ['riːfjuəl] vti ανεφοδιάζομαι (με καύσιμα).

refuge ['rɛfjuːdʒ] n καταφύγιο, καταφυγή, προστασία || **refugee** [rɛfjuː'dʒiː] n πρόσφυγας.

refund ['riːfʌnd] n επιστροφή χρημάτων, απόδοση ♦ [rɪ'fʌnd] vt επιστρέφω (χρήματα).

refurbish [riː'fɜːbɪʃ] vt (decorate) ανακαινίζω, φρεσκάρω.

refusal [rɪ'fjuːzəl] n άρνηση.

refuse ['rɛfjuːs] n απορρίμματα ntpl, σκουπίδια ntpl ♦ [rɪ'fjuːz] vti αρνούμαι, απορρίπτω.

refute [rɪ'fjuːt] vt ανασκευάζω, ανατρέπω.

regain [rɪ'geɪn] vt επανακτώ.

regal ['riːgəl] a βασιλικός.

regard [rɪ'gɑːd] n (respect) εκτίμηση, σεβασμός ♦ vt (consider) θεωρώ || ~**s** npl (greetings) χαιρετισμοί mpl, χαιρετίσματα ntpl || ~**ing**, **as** ~**s** όσον αφορά, σχετικά με || **as** ~**s**, **with** ~ **to** ως προς, όσο για || ~**less** a (+ of) αδιάφορος, άσχετος ♦ ad αδιάφορος, αδιαφορώντας.

regatta [rɪ'gætə] n λεμβοδρομία.

régime [reɪ'ʒiːm] n καθεστώς nt.

regiment ['rɛdʒɪmənt] n σύνταγμα nt || ~**al** a του συντάγματος.

region ['riːdʒən] n περιοχή || ~**al** a τοπικός, περιφερειακός.

register ['rɛdʒɪstə*] n κατάλογος, ληξιαρχικό βιβλίο, μητρώο ♦ vt καταγράφω, εγγράφω || (write down) σημειώνω ♦ vi (at hotel) εγγράφομαι || (make impression) δείχνω || ~**ed** a (design) κατατεθειμένος || (letter) συστημένο γράμμα.

registrar [rɛdʒɪs'trɑː] n ληξίαρχος, γραμματέας m/f.

registration [rɛdʒɪs'treɪʃən] n (act) καταγραφή, εγγραφή || (number) αριθμός εγγραφής.

registry ['rɛdʒɪstrɪ] n ληξιαρχείο || ~ **office** n (for civil marriage) ληξιαρχείο.

regret [rɪ'grɛt] n λύπη, μεταμέλεια ♦ vt λυπούμαι, μετανοώ || ~**fully** ad με λύπη, με πόνο || ~**table** a δυσάρεστος, λυπηρός.

regular ['rɛgjulə*] a τακτικός, κανονικός, συνηθισμένος || (not varying) ομαλός ♦ n (client etc) τακτικός (πελάτης) || ~**ity** n κανονικότητα, ομαλότητα.

regulate ['rɛgjuleɪt] vt κανονίζω, τακτοποιώ, ρυθμίζω.

regulation [rɛgju'leɪʃən] n κανονισμός || (control) ρύθμιση.

rehabilitation ['riːəbɪlɪ'teɪʃən] n αποκατάσταση, παλινόρθωση.

rehash [riː'hæʃ] vt (col) ξαναδουλεύω, διασκευάζω.

rehearsal [rɪ'hɜːsəl] n δοκιμή, πρόβα.

rehearse [rɪ'hɜːs] vt (practise) κάνω δοκιμές, κάνω πρόβα.

reign [reɪn] n (period) βασιλεία ♦ vi βασιλεύω.

reimburse [riːɪm'bɜːs] vt επιστρέφω (χρήματα), αποζημιώνω.

rein [reɪn] n ηνία ntpl, χαλινάρι.

reindeer ['reɪndɪə*] n τάρανδος.

reinforce [riːɪn'fɔːs] vt ενισχύω, δυναμώνω || ~**d concrete** n μπετό αρμέ nt inv || ~**ment** n ενίσχυση || ~**ments** npl (MIL) ενισχύσεις fpl.

reinstate ['riːɪn'steɪt] vt επαναφέρω στη θέση του, αποκαθιστώ, επανεγκαθιστώ.

reiterate [riː'ɪtəreɪt] vt επαναλαμβάνω.

reject [rɪ'dʒɛkt] vt απορρίπτω, αποκρούω ♦ ['riːdʒɛkt] n απόρριμμα nt, σκάρτο || ~**ion** n απόρριψη.

rejoice [rɪ'dʒɔɪs] vi χαίρομαι, χαίρω.

relapse [rɪ'læps] n υποτροπή.

relate [rɪ'leɪt] vt διηγούμαι, εξιστορώ || (connect) συσχετίζω || ~**d** a (subjects) σχετιζόμενος, σχετικά με || (people) (+ to) συγγενής.

relating [rɪ'leɪtɪŋ] prep: ~ **to** σχετικός με, ότι αφορά.

relation [rɪ'leɪʃən] n (of family) συγγενής m/f || (connection) σχέση, συγγένεια || ~**ship** n συγγένεια, σχέση.

relative ['rɛlətɪv] n συγγενής m/f ♦ a αναφορικός, σχετικός || ~**ly** ad σχετικά || ~ **pronoun** n αναφορική αντωνυμία.

relax [rɪ'læks] vi χαλαρώνω, λασκάρω || (rest) ανακουφίζω ♦ vt χαλαρούμαι, αναπαύομαι, ξεκουράζομαι || ~**ation** n αναψυχή, διασκέδαση || ~**ed** a χαλαρός, λάσκος || ~**ing** a ξεκουραστικός.

relay ['riːleɪ] n (SPORT) σκυταλοδρομία ♦ vt (message) αναμεταδίδω.

release [rɪ'liːs] n (relief) απαλλαγή, απόλυση || (from prison) αποφυλάκιση || (device) διακόπτης ♦ vt απελευθερώνω || (prisoner) απολύω, αποφυλακίζω || (grip) χαλαρώνω, λασκάρω, απομπλέκω || (report, news) θέτω σε κυκλοφορία, επιτρέπω δημοσίευση.

relegate ['relɪgeɪt] vt (put down) υποβιβάζω.

relent [rɪ'lent] vi κάμπτομαι, μαλακώνω || ~**less** a αδιάλλακτος, αμείλικτος, ανελέητος.

relevant ['relɪvənt] a σχετικός.

reliable [rɪ'laɪəbl] a αξιόπιστος.

reliably [rɪ'laɪəblɪ] ad μ'εμπιστοσύνη, σίγουρα.

reliance [rɪ'laɪəns] n εμπιστοσύνη, πεποίθηση.

relic ['relɪk] n απομεινάρι, ενθύμιο || (of saint) λείψανο.

relief [rɪ'liːf] n (from pain etc) ανακούφιση, ξελάφρωμα nt || (help) βοήθεια || (from duty) αντικατάσταση, αλλαγή || (design) ανάγλυφο || (distinctness) προβολή, ευδιακρισία.

relieve [rɪ'liːv] vt (pain etc) ανακουφίζω, ξαλαφρώνω || (bring help) βοηθώ, περιθάλπω || (take place of) αντικαθιστώ, απαλλάσσω || **to ~ of** παίρνω, απαλλάσσω.

religion [rɪ'lɪdʒən] n θρησκεία, θρήσκευμα nt.

religious [rɪ'lɪdʒəs] a θρησκευτικός || (pious) ευσεβής.

relinquish [rɪ'lɪŋkwɪʃ] vt παραιτούμαι, εγκαταλείπω.

relish ['relɪʃ] n (sauce) καρύκευμα nt, σάλτσα ♦ vt απολαμβάνω, τρώγω ευχάριστα.

relive ['riː'lɪv] vt ξαναζώ.

reluctant [rɪ'lʌktənt] a απρόθυμος || ~**ly** ad με το ζόρι, με το σταλό.

rely [rɪ'laɪ]: **to ~ on** vt βασίζομαι, στηρίζομαι, εμπιστεύομαι.

remain [rɪ'meɪn] vi (be left) απομένω || (stay) παραμένω, μένω || ~**der** n υπόλοιπο || ~**ing** a υπόλοιπος || ~**s** npl υπολείμματα ntpl || (corpse) λείψανα ntpl.

remand [rɪ'mɑːnd] n : **on ~** παραπομπή (κατηγορούμενου) ♦ vt: **to ~ in custody** προφυλακίζω.

remark [rɪ'mɑːk] n παρατήρηση, σημείωση ♦ vt (say) λέγω || (notice) παρατηρώ || ~**able** a αξιοσημείωτος || (unusual) ασυνήθιστος || ~**ably** ad αξιόλογα, εξαιρετικά.

remarry ['riː'mærɪ] vi ξαναπαντρεύομαι.

remedial [rɪ'miːdɪəl] a θεραπευτικός.

remedy ['remədɪ] n θεραπεία || (MED) φάρμακο, γιατρικό ♦ vt θεραπεύω, διορθώνω.

remember [rɪ'membə*] vt θυμούμαι || (give regards) δίνω χαιρετισμούς σε.

remembrance [rɪ'membrəns] n ανάμνηση, μνήμη.

remind [rɪ'maɪnd] vt υπενθυμίζω, θυμίζω || ~**er** n κάτι που θυμίζει, ενθύμημα nt.

reminisce [remɪ'nɪs] vi αναπολώ, ξαναθυμάμαι.

reminiscences [remɪ'nɪsnsɪz] npl αναμνήσεις fpl, απομνημονεύματα ntpl.

reminiscent [remɪ'nɪsnt] a (+ of) που θυμίζει κάτι.

remission [rɪ'mɪʃən] n (from sins) άφεση, ελάττωση || (release) χάρη, μείωση (ποινής).

remit [rɪ'mɪt] vt (send money) εμβάζω, μεταβιβάζω || ~**tance** n έμβασμα nt (χρηματικό).

remnant ['remnənt] n υπόλειμμα nt.

remorse [rɪ'mɔːs] n τύψη, μεταμέλεια || ~**ful** a γεμάτος τύψεις, μετανοιωμένος || ~**less** a άσπλαγχνος, αμετανόητος.

remote [rɪ'məut] a μακρινός, απομακρυσμένος, απόμερος || (slight) αμυδρός, ελαφρός || (vague) αόριστος || ~ **control** n τηλερρυθμιστής || ~**ly** ad αόριστα, μακριά.

remould ['riː'məuld] vt (tyre) ξαναφορμάρω.

removable [rɪ'muːvəbl] a μεταθέσιμος, κινητός, φορητός.

removal [rɪ'muːvəl] n αφαίρεση, βγάλσιμο || (from house) μετακόμιση, μετακίνηση || (from office) απόλυση, ανάκληση || ~ **van** n φορτηγό μετακομίσεων.

remove [rɪ'muːv] vt αφαιρώ, βγάζω, μεταφέρω || (dismiss) απολύω, απομακρύνω || ~**r** (for paint etc) εξαλειπτικό μέσο || ~**rs** npl (company) εταιρεία μεταφορών οικοσκευών.

remuneration [rɪmjuːnə'reɪʃən] n αμοιβή, πληρωμή.

rend [rend] (irreg v) vt σχίζω, αποσπώ.

render ['rendə*] vt (make) καθιστώ, κάνω || (translate) μεταφράζω || ~**ing** n (MUS) ερμηνεία, απόδοση.

rendezvous ['rɒndɪvuː] n συνάντηση, ραντεβού nt inv.

renew [rɪ'njuː] vt (make new) ανανεώνω || (begin again) ανανσύβω, ξαναπιάνω || (negotiations) επαναλαμβάνω || ~**al** n ανανέωση, ανασύνδεση.

renounce [rɪ'nauns] vt (give up) εγκαταλείπω, αποκηρύσσω || (disown) αρνούμαι, αποποιούμαι.

renovate ['renəuveɪt] vt ανακαινίζω || (repair) επισκευάζω.

renovation [renəu'veɪʃən] n ανακαίνιση || (repair) επισκευή.

renown [rɪ'naun] n φήμη || ~**ed** a φημισμένος, ονομαστός.

rent [rent] n (of dwelling) ενοίκιο || (hiring) μίσθωμα, νοίκι ♦ vt ενοικιάζω || (hire) μισθώνω || (AUT etc) ενοικιάζω (αυτοκίνητο) || ~al n μίσθωμα, νοίκι.

renunciation [rɪnʌnsɪ'eɪʃən] n απάρνηση.

reorganize ['riː'ɔːgənaɪz] vt αναδιοργανώνω.

rep [rep] n (COMM: abbr of **representative**) αντιπρόσωπος || (THEAT: abbr of repertory) ρεπερτόριο.

repair [rɪ'pɛə*] n επισκευή, επιδιόρθωση || (in good condition) σε καλή κατάσταση ♦ vt επισκευάζω, επιδιορθώνω || ~ kit n σύνεργα ntpl επισκευή || ~man n επισκευαστής, επιδιορθωτής.

repartee [repɑː'tiː] n ετοιμολογία, εύστοχη απάντηση.

repay [riː'peɪ] vt (pay back) ανταποδίδω || (money) ξεπληρώνω || ~ment n ανταπόδοση.

repeal [rɪ'piːl] n ανάκληση, ακύρωση ♦ vt ανακαλώ, ακυρώνω.

repeat [rɪ'piːt] n (RAD, TV) επανάληψη ♦ vt επαναλαμβάνω || ~edly ad επανειλημμένα, πολλές φορές.

repel [rɪ'pel] vt αποκρούω, απωθώ || ~lent a αποκρουστικός, απωθητικός ♦ n: insect ~lent εντομοαπωθητική λοσιόν f inv.

repent [rɪ'pent] vi μετανοιώνω, μεταμελούμαι || ~ance n μετάνοια, μεταμέλεια.

repercussion [riːpə'kʌʃən] n (effect) αντίδραση, αντίκτυπος.

repertoire ['repətwɑː*] n δραματολόγιο, ρεπερτόριο.

repertory ['repətərɪ] n (THEAT) ρεπερτόριο.

repetition [repɪ'tɪʃən] n επανάληψη.

repetitive [rɪ'petɪtɪv] a επαναληπτικός.

replace [rɪ'pleɪs] vt αντικαθιστώ || (put back) ξαναβάζω || ~ment n αντικατάσταση || (person) αντικαταστάτης.

replenish [rɪ'plenɪʃ] vt ξαναγεμίζω, συμπληρώνω.

replica ['replɪkə] n πανομοιότυπο, αντίγραφο έργου τέχνης.

reply [rɪ'plaɪ] n απάντηση ♦ vi απαντώ, αποκρίνομαι.

report [rɪ'pɔːt] n (account) έκθεση, εξιστόρηση, αναφορά || (bang) κρότος, πυροβολισμός || vt αναφέρω || (give account of) εξιστορώ || (news) κάνω ρεπορτάζ ♦ vi (make a report) εκθέτω, αναφέρω, κάνω αναφορά || (present o.s.) παρουσιάζομαι || ~er n δημοσιογράφος.

reprehensible [reprɪ'hensɪbl] a αξιόμεμπτος.

represent [reprɪ'zent] vt (describe) παριστάνω, παρουσιάζω || (act) αντιπροσωπεύω || ~ation n παράσταση, αναπαράσταση || (in parliament) αντιπροσώπευση, αντιπροσωπεία || ~ative n αντιπρόσωπος ♦ a αντιπροσωπευτικός, παραστατικός.

repress [rɪ'pres] vt καταβάλλω, καταστέλλω, καταπνίγω || ~ion n καταστολή, κατάπνιξη || ~ive a κατασταλτικός, καταπιεστικός.

reprieve [rɪ'priːv] n αναστολή (θανατικής ποινής), αναβολή ♦ vt αναστέλλω, ανακουφίζω.

reprimand ['reprɪmɑːnd] n επιτίμηση, επίπληξη ♦ vt επιτιμώ, επιπλήττω.

reprint ['riːprɪnt] n ανατύπωση ♦ [riː'prɪnt] vt ανατυπώνω.

reprisal [rɪ'praɪzəl] n αντεκδίκηση, αντίποινο.

reproach [rɪ'prəʊtʃ] n επίπληξη, μομφή ♦ vt επιπλήττω, μέμφομαι, ψέγω.

reproduce [riːprə'djuːs] vt αναπαράγω || (make copy) ανατυπώνω ♦ vi αναπαράγομαι, πολλαπλασιάζομαι.

reproduction [riːprə'dʌkʃən] n (copy) αναπαράσταση, αντίγραφο || (breeding) αναπαραγωγή.

reproductive [riːprə'dʌktɪv] a αναπαραγωγικός.

reproving [rɪ'pruːvɪŋ] a επικριτικός, επιτιμητικός.

reptile ['reptaɪl] n ερπετό.

republic [rɪ'pʌblɪk] n δημοκρατία || ~an a δημοκρατικός || (party: US) ρεπουμπλικανικός ♦ n δημοκράτης || (US) ρεπουμπλικάνος.

repudiate [rɪ'pjuːdɪeɪt] vt απαρνούμαι, αποκρούω, αποκηρύσσω.

repugnant [rɪ'pʌgnənt] a απεχθής, απδιαστικός, σιχαμερός.

repulse [rɪ'pʌls] vt απωθώ, αποκρούω || (reject) αποκρούω, απορρίπτω.

repulsive [rɪ'pʌlsɪv] a αποκρουστικός, σιχαμερός.

reputable ['repjutəbl] a έντιμος, αξιοπρεπής.

reputation [repju'teɪʃən] n φήμη, υπόληψη || (good name) όνομα nt.

repute [rɪ'pjuːt] n εκτίμηση, υπόληψη || ~d a φημισμένος, υποτιθέμενος || ~dly ad κατά την κοινή γνώμη.

request [rɪ'kwest] n αίτηση, παράκληση || (demand) ζήτηση ♦ vt ζητώ, παρακαλώ.

requiem ['rekwiem] n μνημόσυνο.

require [rɪ'kwaɪə*] vt ζητώ, απαιτώ || (oblige) χρειάζομαι || ~ment n απαίτηση, ανάγκη.

requisite ['rekwɪzɪt] n απαιτούμενο πράγμα nt, προϋπόθεση ♦ a απαιτούμενος.

requisition [rekwɪ'zɪʃən] n επίταξη, απαίτηση ♦ vt απαιτώ, επιτάσσω.

reroute ['riː'ruːt] vt χαράσσω νέα πορεία, κάνω άλλο δρόμο.

resale ['riː'seɪl] n μεταπώληση, ξαναπούλημα nt.

rescue ['reskjuː] n διάσωση, απολύτρωση ♦ vt (save) σώζω, λυτρώνω || ~r n σωτήρας, λυτρωτής.

research [rɪ'sɜːtʃ] n έρευνα ♦ vi (+ into) κάνω έρευνα ♦ vt ερευνώ || ~er n ερευνητής.

resemblance [rɪ'zembləns] n ομοιότητα.

resemble [rɪ'zembl] vt μοιάζω.

resent [rɪ'zent] vt φέρω βαρέως, θίγομαι από || **~ful** a μνησίκακος, πειραγμένος || **~ment** n μνησικακία, έχθρα, πίκρα.

reservation [rezə'veɪʃən] n επιφύλαξη || (place) εξασφάλιση, κλείσιμο || (doubt) επιφύλαξη.

reserve [rɪ'zɜːv] n απόθεμα nt, αποθεματικό || (self-restraint) επιφύλαξη, συντηρητικότητα || (area of land) επιφυλασσόμενη περιοχή || (SPORT) εφεδρικός παίκτης ♦ vt (seats etc) κρατώ, αγκαζάρω, κλείνω || **~s** npl (MIL) εφεδρείες fpl || **in ~** κατά μέρος, για ρεζέρβα || **~d** a επιφυλακτικός, συγκρατημένος || **'~d'** (notice) 'κλεισμένος', 'κρατημένος'.

reservoir ['rezəvwɑː*] n δεξαμενή, ντεπόζιτο, ρεζερβουάρ nt inv || (store) απόθεμα nt.

reshape ['riː'ʃeɪp] vt μεταπλάθω, τροποποιώ, αναπλάθω.

reshuffle ['riː'ʃʌfl] n (POL) ανασχηματισμός.

reside [rɪ'zaɪd] vi διαμένω, ανήκω || **residence** ['rezɪdəns] n κατοικία, σπίτι || (living) διαμονή, παραμονή || **resident** n κάτοικος ♦ a εγκατεστημένος || **residential** a της μονίμου διαμονής, με ιδιωτικές κατοικίες.

residue ['rezɪdjuː] n υπόλοιπο, υπόλειμμα nt, κατάλοιπο.

resign [rɪ'zaɪn] vt παραιτούμαι || (submit) υποτάσσομαι, εγκαταλείπομαι || **resignation** [rezɪg'neɪʃən] n παραίτηση || (submission) υποταγή, υπομονή || **~ed** a ανεχόμενος, υποτακτικός.

resilient [rɪ'zɪlɪənt] a ελαστικός.

resin ['rezɪn] n ρητίνη, ρετσίνη.

resist [rɪ'zɪst] vt ανθίσταμαι σε, αντιδρώ κατά || **~ance** n αντίσταση.

resolute ['rezəluːt] a αποφασιστικός, σταθερός.

resolution [rezə'luːʃən] n αποφασιστικότητα || (decision) απόφαση.

resolve [rɪ'zɒlv] n απόφαση ♦ vt αναλύω, διαλύω, λύω ♦ vi διαλύομαι, αναλύομαι || (decide) αποφασίζω || **~d** a αποφασισμένος.

resonant ['rezənənt] a αντηχών, αντηχητικός.

resort [rɪ'zɔːt] n τόπος διαμονής, θέρετρο || (help) καταφυγή, μέσο, βοήθεια ♦ vi (+ to) προσφεύγω, καταφεύγω (σε) || **in the last ~** σαν τελευταία λύση.

resound [rɪ'zaʊnd] vi αντηχώ, απηχώ || **~ing** a απηχών, ηχηρός.

resource [rɪ'sɔːs] n καταφύγιο, μέσο, βοήθημα nt || **~s** npl (of fuel) πλούτος (σε καύσιμα) || (of a country etc) οι πόροι mpl, πλούτος || **~ful** a εφευρετικός.

respect [rɪs'pekt] n σεβασμός || (way) αναφορά ♦ vt σέβομαι || (treat with consideration) προσέχω || **~s** npl (greetings) σέβη ntpl, χαιρετίσματα ntpl ||

with ~ to όσον αφορά || **in ~ of** σχετικά με || **in this ~** ως προς αυτό το σημείο || **~able** a έντιμος, ευυπόληπτος || (fairly good) υποφερτός, αρκετά καλός || **~ed** a σεβαστός || **~ful** a γεμάτος σεβασμό || **~ive** a σχετικός, αμοιβαίος, αντίστοιχος || **~ively** ad αντιστοίχως.

respiration [respɪ'reɪʃən] n αναπνοή.

respite ['respaɪt] n ανάπαυλα, διακοπή.

resplendent [rɪs'plendənt] a (bright) λαμπρός || (magnificent) μεγαλοπρεπής.

respond [rɪs'pɒnd] vi απαντώ, αποκρίνομαι || (act in answer) ανταποκρίνομαι, ανταποδίδω.

response [rɪs'pɒns] n απάντηση, ανταπόκριση.

responsibility [rɪspɒnsə'bɪlɪtɪ] n ευθύνη.

responsible [rɪs'pɒnsəbl] a υπεύθυνος, υπόλογος || (reliable) αξιόπιστος.

responsive [rɪs'pɒnsɪv] a ευαίσθητος, που ανταποκρίνεται.

rest [rest] n ανάπαυση, ξεκούραση || (pause) πτώση, ανάπαυλα || (remainder) υπόλοιπο ♦ vi αναπαύομαι, ξεκουράζομαι || (be supported) στηρίζομαι, ακουμπώ || (remain) στηρίζομαι, βασίζομαι || **the ~ of them** οι υπόλοιποι.

restaurant ['restərɔ̃ːŋ] n εστιατόριο || **~ car** n βαγκόν-ρεστωράν nt inv.

rest cure ['restkjʊə*] n θεραπεία αναπαύσεως.

restful ['restful] a ξεκούραστος, ήσυχος, αναπαυτικός.

rest home ['resthəʊm] n πρεβαντόριο, αναρρωτήριο.

restive ['restɪv] a ατίθασος, ανήσυχος.

restless ['restlɪs] a ανήσυχος, αεικίνητος, άυπνος || **~ly** ad ανήσυχα, νευρικά, ταραγμένα.

restore [rɪs'tɔː*] vt επιστρέφω, αποκαθιστώ || (repair) επισκευάζω, αναστηλώνω.

restrain [rɪs'treɪn] vt συγκρατώ, συγκρατώ || **~ed** a (style etc) ήρεμος, συγκρατημένος, μετρημένος || **~t** n περιορισμός, περιστολή || (self-control) συγκράτηση.

restrict [rɪs'trɪkt] vt περιορίζω || **~ed** a περιορισμένος || **~ion** n περιορισμός || **~ive** a περιοριστικός.

rest room ['restrʊm] n (US) αποχωρητήριο, τουαλέτα.

result [rɪ'zʌlt] n αποτέλεσμα nt, συνέπεια || (of test) αποτελέσματα ntpl ♦ vi (+ in) καταλήγω, απολήγω.

resume [rɪ'zjuːm] vt επαναρχίζω, ξαναρχίζω.

résumé ['reɪzjuːmeɪ] n περίληψη.

resumption [rɪ'zʌmpʃən] n (επ)ανάληψη, συνέχιση.

resurgence [rɪ'sɜːdʒəns] n αναζωογόνηση, ανανέωση || (uprising) ξεσήκωμα nt.

resurrection [rezə'rekʃən] n ανάσταση, ανανέωση.

resuscitate [rɪ'sʌsɪteɪt] vt ανασταίνω, επαναφέρω στη ζωή.

resuscitation [rɪsʌsɪ'teɪʃən] n αναζωογόνηση, ανάσταση.

retail ['riːteɪl] n λιανική πώληση ♦ a λιανικός ♦ [riː'teɪl] vt πουλώ λιανικά || ~er n μεταπωλητής, λιανέμπορος || ~ price n τιμή λιανικής πωλήσεως.

retain [rɪ'teɪn] vt διατηρώ, συγκρατώ, κρατώ || ~er n υπηρέτης || (fee) προκαταβολή δικηγόρου.

retaliate [rɪ'tælɪeɪt] vi αντεκδικούμαι, ανταποδίδω.

retarded [rɪ'tɑːdɪd] a καθυστερημένος.

retention [rɪ'tenʃən] n διατήρηση, συγκράτηση.

retentive [rɪ'tentɪv] a συνεκτικός, ισχυρός.

rethink [riː'θɪŋk] vt ξανασκέπτομαι.

reticent ['retɪsənt] a λιγομίλητος, επιφυλακτικός.

retina ['retɪnə] n αμφιβληστροειδής (χιτών).

retinue ['retɪnjuː] n ακολουθία, συνοδεία.

retire [rɪ'taɪə*] vi αποχωρώ, γίνομαι συνταξιούχος || (withdraw, retreat) υποχωρώ, αποσύρομαι || (go to bed) πάω για ύπνο || ~d a (person) συνταξιούχος || ~ment n αποχώρηση, συνταξιοδότηση.

retiring [rɪ'taɪərɪŋ] a επιφυλακτικός, ακοινώνητος || (shy) ντροπαλός.

retort [rɪ'tɔːt] n (reply) οξεία απάντηση, έξυπνη απάντηση ♦ vi ανταπαντώ, αποκρίνομαι.

retrace [rɪ'treɪs] vt ανατρέχω, ξαναγυρίζω.

retract [rɪ'trækt] vti ανακαλώ, παίρνω πίσω || ~able a (aerial) εισελκόμενος.

retread [riː'tred] n (AUT: tyre) ανεπιστρώνω, ξαναφορμάρω.

retreat [rɪ'triːt] n υποχώρηση, οπισθοχώρηση || (escape) καταφύγιο ♦ vi υποχωρώ, οπισθοχωρώ.

retribution [retrɪ'bjuːʃən] n τιμωρία, ανταπόδοση, εκδίκηση.

retrieve [rɪ'triːv] vt επανακτώ, αποδίδω || (rescue) επανορθώνω, σώζω || ~r n κυνηγετικός σκύλος, ριτρίβερ.

retrograde ['retrəʊɡreɪd] a (step, action) οπισθοδρομικός, παλινδρομικός.

retrospect ['retrəʊspekt] n: in ~ σε ανασκόπηση, όταν το σκέφτομαι || ~ive a (LAW) αναδρομικός.

return [rɪ'tɜːn] n επιστροφή, επάνοδος f, γύρισμα || (arrival) ερχομός || (profits) κέρδος, εισπράξεις fpl || (rail ticket etc) εισιτήριο μετ' επιστροφής || (journey) ταξίδι επιστροφής || (match) αγώνας ανταποδόσεως || ~s npl (report) έκθεση, δήλωση || (statistics) στατιστική ♦ vi επιστρέφω, γυρίζω, επανέρχομαι ♦ vt (give back) επιστρέφω, δίνω πίσω, γυρίζω || (pay back) επιστρέφω, πληρώνω || (elect) εκλέγω || ~able a (bottle etc) επιστρεφόμενος, επιστρεπτός || ~ key n (COMPUT) πλήκτρο επαναφοράς.

reunion [riː'juːnjən] n συνάντηση, συγκέντρωση.

reunite ['riːjuː'naɪt] vt ξανασμίγω, συναντώμαι.

rev [rev] n (AUT) στροφές fpl ♦ vti (also: ~ up) φουλάρω.

reveal [rɪ'viːl] vt αποκαλύπτω, φανερώνω || ~ing a αποκαλυπτικός.

reveille [rɪ'vælɪ] n εγερτήριο σάλπισμα nt.

revel ['revl] vi (+ in) διασκεδάζω, γλεντώ.

revelation [revə'leɪʃən] n αποκάλυψη.

reveller ['revlə*] n γλεντζές m.

revelry ['revlrɪ] n διασκέδαση, γλέντι.

revenge [rɪ'vendʒ] n εκδίκηση ♦ vt εκδικούμαι.

revenue ['revənjuː] n πρόσοδος f, έσοδα ntpl, εισόδημα nt.

reverberate [rɪ'vɜːbəreɪt] vi αντηχώ, αντανακλώμαι.

revere [rɪ'vɪə*] vt σέβομαι, τιμώ || ~nce ['revərəns] n σέβας nt, σεβασμός || the R~nd Smith ο αιδεσιμώτατος Σμιθ || ~nt a ευσεβής.

reversal [rɪ'vɜːsəl] n αντιστροφή, αναστροφή.

reverse [rɪ'vɜːs] n αντίστροφο || (defeat) ήττα || (misfortune) ατυχία || (AUT: gear) όπισθεν f inv ♦ a (order, direction) αντίθετος, αντίστροφος ♦ vt (put upside down) αναστρέφω || (change) αντιστρέφω ♦ vi βάζω την όπισθεν.

revert [rɪ'vɜːt] vi επανέρχομαι, επιστρέφω.

review [rɪ'vjuː] n επιθεώρηση || (of critic) κριτική (βιβλίου) || (magazine) επιθεώρηση, περιοδικό ♦ vt (look back on) ανασκοπώ, εξετάζω || (troops) επιθεωρώ || (a book) γράφω κριτική || ~er n (critic) κριτικογράφος, κριτικός.

revise [rɪ'vaɪz] vt αναθεωρώ, ξανακοιτάζω || (correct) διορθώνω.

revision [rɪ'vɪʒən] n αναθεώρηση || (correct) επανεξέταση.

revitalize [riː'vaɪtəlaɪz] vt αναζωογονώ.

revival [rɪ'vaɪvəl] n αναγέννηση || (of play) επανάληψη.

revive [rɪ'vaɪv] vt αναζωογονώ, ανασταίνω, ξαναζωντανεύω ♦ vi αναζωογονούμαι, ξαναζωντανεύω, αναζωπυρούμαι.

revoke [rɪ'vəʊk] vt ανακαλώ, ακυρώνω.

revolt [rɪ'vəʊlt] n στάση, επανάσταση ♦ vi επαναστατώ || ~ing a αηδιαστικός, σκανδαλώδης.

revolution [revə'luːʃən] n (of wheel) περιστροφή || (change, POL) επανάσταση || ~ary a επαναστατικός, ανατρεπτικός ♦ n επανάσταση || ~ize vt αλλάζω οριστικά.

revolve [rɪ'vɒlv] vi περιστρέφομαι.

revolver [rɪ'vɒlvə*] n περίστροφο.

revue [rɪ'vjuː] n επιθεώρηση (θεατρική).

revulsion [rɪ'vʌlʃən] n μεταστροφή.

reward [rɪ'wɔːd] n (αντ)αμοιβή ♦ vt

ανταμείβω || ~ing a ανταμειπτικός || (fig) που αξίζει τον κόπο.

rewind ['ri:'waind] vt ξανατυλίγω, ξανακουρδίζω.

rewire ['ri:'waɪə*] vt (house) αλλάζω τα σύρματα (σπιτιού).

reword ['ri:'wɜːd] vt ανασυντάσσω, ξαναγράφω με άλλες λέξεις.

rewrite ['ri:'raɪt] vt ξαναγράφω.

rhapsody ['ræpsədi] n ραψωδία.

rhetoric ['retərɪk] n ρητορική, ρητορία || ~al a ρητορικός.

rheumatic [ru:'mætɪk] a ρευματικός.

rheumatism ['ru:mətɪzəm] n ρευματισμός.

rhinoceros [raɪ'nɒsərəs] n ρινόκερως m.

rhododendron [rəʊdə'dendrən] n ροδόδεντρο.

rhubarb ['ruːbɑːb] n ραβέντι, ρουμπάρμπαρο.

rhyme [raɪm] n ομοιοκαταληξία, ρίμα.

rhythm ['rɪðəm] n ρυθμός, μέτρο || ~ic(al) a ρυθμικός || ~ically ad ρυθμικά, με ρυθμό.

rib [rɪb] n πλευρά, πλευρό ♦ vt (mock) εμπαίζω, κοροϊδεύω.

ribald ['rɪbəld] a αισχρός, πρόστυχος, σόκιν.

ribbed [rɪbd] a ραβδωτός, με νευρώσεις.

ribbon ['rɪbən] n ταινία, κορδέλα.

rice [raɪs] n ρύζι || ~ pudding n ρυζόγαλο.

rich [rɪtʃ] a πλούσιος || (fertile) εύφορος, πλούσιος, γόνιμος || (splendid) πολυτελής, λαμπρός, υπέροχος || (of food) παχύς, από εκλεκτά συστατικά || the ~ οι πλούσιοι || ~es npl πλούτη ntpl, αφθονία || ~ly ad πλούσια || ~ness n πλούτος || (abundance) αφθονία.

rickety ['rɪkɪtɪ] a (unsteady) που τρέμει, σαθρός, σαραβαλιασμένος.

rickshaw ['rɪkʃɔː] n δίτροχη άμαξα συρόμενη από άνθρωπο.

ricochet ['rɪkəʃeɪ] n εποστρακισμός ♦ vi εποστρακίζω, αναπηδώ.

rid [rɪd] (irreg v) vt απαλλάσσω, ελευθερώνω || to get ~ of απαλλάσσομαι από || good riddance! καλά ξεκουμπίδια!, ας πάει στο καλό!

riddle ['rɪdl] n (puzzle) αίνιγμα nt ♦ vt (esp passive) κάνω κόσκινο.

ride [raɪd] (irreg v) n διαδρομή, περίπατος, ταξίδι ♦ vt τρέχω, διασχίζω || (horse, bicycle) καβαλικεύω ♦ vi πάω καβάλα, καβαλικεύω, πηγαίνω με αμάξι || (NAUT) είμαι αγκυροβολημένος || ~r ιππέας, καβαλάρης || (in contract etc) προσθήκη, παράρτημα nt, συμπληρωματική διάταξη.

ridge [rɪdʒ] n (hill) κορυφογραμμή, ράχη || (of roof) κολοφώνας, καβελαριά, κορφιάς || (narrow raised strip) πτυχή, ζάρα, προεξοχή.

ridicule ['rɪdɪkjuːl] n περίγελος, εμπαιγμός, κοροϊδία ♦ vt κοροϊδεύω, γελοποιώ.

ridiculous [rɪ'dɪkjʊləs] a γελοίος.

riding ['raɪdɪŋ] n: to go ~ πηγαίνω ιππασία || ~ school n σχολή ιππασίας.

rife [raɪf] a: ~ with μεστός, γεμάτος από.

riffraff ['rɪfræf] n αλητεία, σκυλολόι.

rifle ['raɪfl] n όπλο, τουφέκι ♦ vt (rob) αδειάζω, διαρπάζω || ~ range n πεδίο βολής, σκοπευτήριο.

rift [rɪft] n σχισμή, ρωγμή.

rig [rɪg] n (outfit) φορεσιά, στόλισμα nt || (oil rig) γεωτρύπανο ♦ vt (election etc) νοθεύω τις εκλογές || ~ging n ξάρτια ntpl || to ~ out vt ντύνω, στολίζω || to ~ up vt στήνω, μαντάρω.

right [raɪt] a (correct, proper) ορθός, σωστός, κανονικός || (just, good) ευθύς, δίκαιος, έντιμος || (on right side) στα δεξιά ♦ n (what is just or true) το δίκαιο, η δικαιοσύνη || (title, claim) δικαίωμα nt, προνόμιο || (not left) δεξιά (πλευρά), το δεξιό || (POL) n Δεξιά ♦ ad (straight) κατευθείαν, ίσια || (completely, thoroughly) ακριβώς, κατευθείαν, τελείως ♦ vt ανορθώνω, ισορροπώ, ξαναφέρνω στα ίσια ♦ excl σωστά!, σύμφωνοι!, έχεις δίκιο! || to be ~ έχω δίκαιο || all ~! εντάξει! || ~ now αμέσως || by ~s δικαιωματικά, νομίμως || on the ~ στα δεξιά || ~ angle n ορθή γωνία || ~eous a ευθύς, ηθικός || ~eousness n ορθότητα, τιμιότητα || ~ful a νόμιμος, δίκαιος || ~-hand drive a με δεξιό τιμόνι || ~-handed a δεξιόχειρας, δεξιόστροφος || ~-hand man n το δεξί χέρι || ~-hand side n τα δεξιά || ~ly ad δίκαια, ορθά || ~-minded a λογικός, ορθοφρονών || ~ of way n n προτεραιότητα || ~-winger n δεξιός.

rigid ['rɪdʒɪd] a άκαμπτος, αλύγιστος || (strict) αυστηρός || ~ity n ακαμψία, αλυγισία || ~ly ad άκαμπτα, αλύγιστα, αυστηρά.

rigmarole ['rɪgmərəʊl] n ασυναρτησίες fpl, κουραφέξαλα ntpl.

rigor ['rɪgə*] n (US) = rigour.

rigorous ['rɪgərəs] a αυστηρός, τραχύς.

rigour ['rɪgə*] n αυστηρότητα, δριμύτητα.

rim [rɪm] n στεφάνη, χείλος nt || (of wheel) στεφάνη, ζάντα || ~less a χωρίς σκελετό, χωρίς γείσο || ~med a με στεφάνη, με σκελετό.

rind [raɪnd] n φλοιός, φλούδα.

ring [rɪŋ] (irreg v) n δακτύλιος, δακτυλίδι || (of people) συντροφιά, φατρία, συμμορία || (arena) παλαίστρα, στίβος, πίστα, αρένα, ρινγκ nt inv || (TEL) τηλεφώνημα nt, κτύπημα nt τηλεφώνου ♦ vt κτυπώ το κουδούνι ♦ vi (TEL) (also: ~ up) τηλεφωνώ || (resound) αντηχώ, κτυπώ || (bell) κουδουνίζω || to ~ off vi διακόπτω τη συνομιλία, κλείνω το τηλέφωνο || ~leader n (of gang) αρχηγός συμμορίας.

ringlets ['rɪŋlɪts] npl (hair) μπούκλες fpl.

ring road ['rɪŋrəʊd] n περιφεριακή οδός f.

rink [rɪŋk] n πίστα πατινάζ.

rinse [rɪns] n ξέπλυμα nt ♦ vt ξεπλένω, ξεβγάζω.

riot ['raɪət] n στάση, οχλαγωγία ♦ vi οχλαγωγώ, θορυβώ || ~**ous** a ταραχώδης, οχλαγωγικός, οργιαστικός.

rip [rɪp] n σχισμή, σχίσιμο ♦ vti σχίζω, ξεσχίζω.

ripcord ['rɪpkɔːd] n σχοινί ανοίγματος.

ripe [raɪp] a ώριμος, γινομένος || ~**n** vti ωριμάζω, γίνομαι || ~**ness** n ωριμότητα.

ripple ['rɪpl] n κυματισμός, ρυτίδα ♦ vti κυματίζω, ρυτιδώνω.

rise [raɪz] (irreg v) n ύψωμα nt, ανήφορος, κλίση || (esp in wages) αύξηση, άνοδος f ♦ vi (from chair) σηκώνομαι όρθιος || (from bed) ξυπνώ, σηκώνομαι || (sun) ανατέλλω, βγαίνω || (smoke, prices) υψώνομαι, ανεβαίνω || (mountain) υψώνομαι || (ground) ανηφορίζω, υψώνομαι || (revolt) εξεγείρομαι, ξεσηκώνομαι, επαναστατώ || **to give ~ to** προκαλώ || **to ~ to the occasion** φαίνομαι αντάξιος των περιστάσεων.

risk [rɪsk] n κίνδυνος, ριψοκινδύνευση ♦ vt ριψοκινδυνεύω || ~**y** a επικίνδυνος, ριψοκίνδυνος.

risqué ['riːskeɪ] a τολμηρό.

rissole ['rɪsəʊl] n κεφτές m, κροκέτα.

rite [raɪt] n ιεροτελεστία, εκκλησιαστική τελετή.

ritual ['rɪtjʊəl] n τυπικό, λειτουργικό ♦ a τυπικός, καθιερωμένος.

rival ['raɪvəl] n, a αντίπαλος, αντίζηλος, ανταγωνιστής ♦ vt ανταγωνίζομαι, συναγωνίζομαι || ~**ry** n ανταγωνισμός, συναγωνισμός.

river ['rɪvə*] n ποταμός, ποτάμι || ~**bank** n όχθη (ποταμού) || ~**bed** n κοίτη ποταμού || ~**side** n όχθη ♦ a της όχθης.

rivet ['rɪvɪt] n καρφωμάτιο, καρφί ♦ vt καθηλώνω, καρφώνω || (fix) προσηλώνω, καρφώνω.

Riviera [rɪvɪˈɛərə] n: **the ~** n Ριβιέρα.

R.N. abbr of Royal Navy.

road [rəʊd] n οδός f, δρόμος || ~**block** n οδόφραγμα nt || ~**hog** n κακός οδηγός || ~**map** n οδικός χάρτης || ~**side** n άκρη του δρόμου, δίπλα στο δρόμο ♦ a στο δρόμο, του δρόμου || ~**sign** n πινακίδα δρόμου || ~**way** n αμαξιτή οδός || ~**worthy** a κατάλληλος για κυκλοφορία.

roam [rəʊm] vi περιπλανώμαι, περιφέρομαι ♦ vt διασχίζω, διατρέχω, τριγυρίζω.

roar [rɔː*] n βρυχηθμός, μουγγρητό ♦ vi βρυχώμαι, ωρύομαι || ~**ing** a (fire) γερή (φωτιά), δυνατή (φωτιά) || (trade) ακμάζον (εμπόριο), καλές (δουλειές).

roast [rəʊst] n ψητό κρέας nt, ψητό ♦ vt ψήνω || (coffee beans) καβουρντίζω.

rob [rɒb] vt κλέβω, ληστεύω, αποστερώ ||

~**ber** n ληστής, κλέφτης || ~**bery** n ληστεία.

robe [rəʊb] n ρόμπα, φόρεμα nt || (of office) στολή, τήβεννος ♦ vt περιβάλλω, ντύνω.

robin ['rɒbɪn] n κοκκινολαίμης, κομπογιάννης.

robot ['rəʊbɒt] n αυτόματο, ρομπότ nt inv.

robust [rəʊˈbʌst] a εύρωστος, ρωμαλέος.

rock [rɒk] n βράχος || (GEOL) πέτρωμα nt || (candy) είδος καραμέλας ♦ vti λικνίζω, κουνώ, κουνιέμαι || **on the ~s** (drink) με πάγο, χωρίς νερό || (ship) πέφτω στα βράχια || (marriage etc) υπό διάλυση, σε δύσκολη θέση || ~-**bottom** n (fig) κατώτερο σημείο || ~ **climber** n ορειβάτης βράχων || ~**ery** n τεχνητοί βράχοι mpl.

rocket ['rɒkɪt] n ρουκέτα, πύραυλος, βολίδα.

rock fall ['rɒkfɔːl] n πτώση βράχων.

rocking chair ['rɒkɪŋtʃɛə*] n κουνιστή πολυθρόνα.

rocking horse ['rɒkɪŋhɔːs] n αλογάκι (παιδικό).

rocky ['rɒkɪ] a βραχώδης.

rod [rɒd] n (bar) ράβδος f, βέργα.

rode [rəʊd] pt of ride.

rodent ['rəʊdənt] n τρωκτικό.

rodeo ['rəʊdɪəʊ] n διαγωνισμός (καουμπόϊδων).

roe [rəʊ] n (deer) δορκάδα, ζαρκάδι || (of fish) αυγά ntpl ψαριών.

rogue [rəʊg] n παλιάνθρωπος || (mischievous) κατεργάρης, πειραχτήριο, πονηρός.

roguish ['rəʊgɪʃ] a (playful) κατεργάρικος, τσαχπίνικος || (cheating) δόλιος, πανούργος.

role [rəʊl] n ρόλος.

roll [rəʊl] n (paper, meat etc) κύλινδρος, ρολό, τόπι || (bread) φραντζολάκι, κουλουράκι || (list) κατάλογος, λίστα || (of drum) συνεχής τυμπανοκρουσία ♦ vt (over) περιστρέφω, κυλώ || (wind round) τυλίγω, κάνω ρολό || (smooth out) ισοπεδώνω, πατώ, στρώνω ♦ vi (swing) στριφογυρίζω, κουνώ || (make deep sound) ηχώ, βροντώ || **to ~ by** vi (time) περνώ γρήγορα || **to ~ in** vi (mail) φθάνω σε μεγάλες ποσότητες || **to ~ over** vi ανατρέπομαι, κυλιέμαι || **to ~ up** vi (arrive) φθάνω, κουβαλιέμαι ♦ vt (carpet) τυλίγω || ~ **call** n ονομαστική κλήση, προσκλητήριο || ~**ed** a (umbrella) τυλιγμένος || ~**er** n κύλινδρος, τροχός || ~**er skates** npl πατίνια ntpl με ρόδες.

rolling ['rəʊlɪŋ] a (landscape) ανώμαλο έδαφος || ~ **pin** n πλάστης (για άνοιγμα φύλλου) || ~ **stock** n τροχαίο υλικό.

roly-poly ['rəʊlɪˈpəʊlɪ] n (pudding) πουτίγγα ρολό με φρούτα.

ROM abbr of read only memory μνήμη ROM, μνήμη που μόνο διαβάζεται.

Roman ['rəʊmən] a ρωμαϊκός ♦ n

Ρωμαίος || ~ **Catholic** a, n ρωμαιοκαθολικός.

romance [rəʊ'mæns] n ρομάντζο || (story) ρομαντική ιστορία ♦ vi υπερβάλλω, φαντασιολογώ.

Romanesque [rəʊmə'nɛsk] a ρωμανικός (ρυθμός).

romantic [rəʊ'mæntik] a ρομαντικός.

romp [rɒmp] n εύθυμο παιχνίδι, φασαρία ♦ vi (also: ~ about) θορυβώ, κάνω φασαρία, ατακτώ || ~**ers** npl μπλούζα, ποδιά παιδιού, φόρμα.

rondo ['rɒndəʊ] n (MUS) ροντώ nt inv, ρόντο nt inv.

roof [ruːf] n στέγη, σκεπή || (of car etc) σκεπή || (of mouth) ουρανίσκος ♦ vt στεγάζω, σκεπάζω || ~ **garden** n κήπος σε ταράτσα || ~**ing** n στέγαση, ταβάνωμα.

rook [rʊk] n (bird) κόρωνη, κουρούνα, χαβαρώνι || (thief) κλέφτης, λωποδύτης ♦ vt (cheat) κλέβω.

room [rʊm] n (in house) δωμάτιο, κάμαρα || (space) χώρος, τόπος || (opportunity) περιθώριο || ~**s** npl (flat) δωμάτια ntpl, διαμέρισμα nt || (lodgings) δωμάτια ntpl με φαγητό || ~**iness** n ευρυχωρία || ~**ing house** n οικία ενοικιάζουσα επιπλωμένα δωμάτια || ~**mate** n συγκάτοικος || ~ **service** n υπηρεσία || ~**y** a ευρύχωρος.

roost [ruːst] n κούρνια, κοτέτσι ♦ vi κουρνιάζω.

root [ruːt] n ρίζα || (source) πηγή, αιτία, ρίζα ♦ vt ριζώνω || **to** ~ **about** vi (fig) ψάχνω || **to** ~ **for** vt υποστηρίζω, ενθαρρύνω || **to** ~ **out** vt ξεριζώνω.

rope [rəʊp] n σχοινί ♦ vt δένω με σχοινί || **to** ~ **in** vt περικλείω, προσηλυτίζω, παρασύρω || **to know the** ~**s** ξέρω τη δουλειά μου, είμαι μπασμένος || ~ **ladder** n ανεμόσκαλα.

rosary ['rəʊzəri] n κομβολόι.

rose [rəʊz] pt of **rise** || (flower) n τριαντάφυλλο, ρόδο ♦ a ροδόχρους, ρόζ.

rosé ['rəʊzei] n (wine) κοκκινέλι.

rosebed ['rəʊzbed] n ροδωνιά, βραγιά με τριανταφυλλιές.

rosebud ['rəʊzbʌd] n μπουμπούκι τριανταφύλλου.

rosebush ['rəʊzbʊʃ] n τριανταφυλλιά.

rosemary ['rəʊzməri] n δενδρολίβανο.

rosette [rəʊ'zet] n ροζέττα.

roster ['rɒstə*] n κατάλογος, κατάσταση.

rostrum ['rɒstrəm] n άμβωνας, βήμα nt.

rosy ['rəʊzi] a (colour) ροδόχρους, ρόδινος, ρόζ || (hopeful) ρόδινα.

rot [rɒt] n σήψη, σαπίλα, σάπισμα nt || (nonsense) ανοησία, μπούρδα ♦ vti αποσυντίθεμαι, σαπίζω.

rota ['rəʊtə] n κατάλογος, πίνακας.

rotary ['rəʊtəri] a περιστροφικός.

rotate [rəʊ'teit] vt (two or more things in order) εναλλάσσω, εκτελώ εκ περιτροπής ♦ vi περιστρέφομαι, γυρίζω (γύρω από).

rotating [rəʊ'teitiŋ] a περιστρεφόμενος, περιστροφικός.

rotation [rəʊ'teiʃən] n περιστροφή.

rotor ['rəʊtə*] n στροφείο, ρώτωρ m inv, ρότορ m inv.

rotten ['rɒtn] a σαθρός, σάπιος, σαπισμένος || (dishonest) πρόστυχος, κακής ποιότητας.

rotund [rəʊ'tʌnd] a στρογγυλός, παχουλός.

rouble ['ruːbl] n ρούβλι.

rouge [ruː3] n κοκκινάδι, βαφή.

rough [rʌf] a (uneven) ανώμαλος, τραχύς || (violent, coarse) χονδροειδής, πρόστυχος, τραχύς, απότομος || (stormy, wild) άγριος, σφοδρός, τρικυμιώδης || (without comforts) πρόχειρος, στοιχειώδης || (unfinished drawing) πρόχειρος, πρωτόλειος || (stony) ακατέργαστος || (makeshift) βιαστικός, πρόχειρος || (approximate) κατά προσέγγιση ♦ n (uncut grass) ψηλό χορτάρι || (violent person) μάγκας, κουτσαβάκης ♦ vt to ~ **it** στερούμαι τις ανέσεις, αντιμετωπίζω δυσκολίες || **to play** ~ παίζω σκληρό παιχνίδι || **to** ~ **out** vt (draft) προσχεδιάζω, κάνω πρόχειρα || ~**en** vt τραχύνω || ~**ly** ad δυνατά || (draft) πρόχειρα || (approximately) περίπου || ~**ness** τραχύτητα, σκληρότητα.

roulette [ruː'let] n ρουλέτα.

Roumania [ruː'meiniə] n Ρουμανία || ~ **n** n (person) Ρουμάνος/α m/f ♦ a ρουμανικός.

round [raʊnd] a στρογγυλός, σφαιρικός, κυκλικός || (rough) στρογγυλός ♦ ad γύρω, τριγύρω ♦ prep γύρο από, περί ♦ n κύκλος, γύρος || (duty) γύρος, βόλτα, περιοδεία, καθημερινή δουλειά || (SPORT) γύρος ♦ vt (corner) κάμπτω, στρίβω, κάνω στροφή, παίρνω τη στροφή || **to** ~ **off** vt στρογγυλεύω, τελειώνω || **to** ~ **up** vt συγκεντρώνω, μαζεύω, πιάνω, περικυκλώνω || ~ **of ammunition** n φυσίγγι || ~ **of applause** n ομοβροντία χειροκροτημάτων || ~ **of drinks** n ένας γύρος ποτών || ~**about** n κυκλική διασταύρωση δρόμων || (merry-go-round) περιστρεφόμενα ξύλινα αλογάκια ntpl ♦ a κυκλικός, περιφερειακός || ~**ed** a στρογγυλεμένος || ~**ly** ad (fig) τέλεια, ολοσχερώς, πλήρως || ~**-shouldered** a με κυρτούς ώμους, σκυφτός || ~**up** n περίμαζεμα nt.

rouse [raʊz] vt σηκώνω || (stir up) προκαλώ, διεγείρω, ξεσηκώνω.

rousing ['raʊziŋ] a (welcome) θορυβώδης, ζωηρός.

rout [raʊt] n φυγή, άτακτη φυγή ♦ vt κατατροπώνω, τρέπω σε φυγή.

route [ruːt] n δρομολόγιο, δρόμος, πορεία || ~ **map** n οδικός χάρτης.

routine [ruː'tiːn] n ρουτίνα, στερεότυπη πορεία ♦ a κανονικός, τακτικός.

roving ['rəʊviŋ] a περιφερόμενος, περιπλανώμενος.

row [rəʊ] n (line) σειρά, στοίχος, γραμμή, αράδα || n (boat) κινώ με κουπί, μεταφέρω με τα κουπιά ♦ vi (in boat) κωπηλατώ, τραβώ κουπί ♦ [raʊ] n (noise) θόρυβος, φασαρία, σαματάς || (dispute) φιλονεικία, καυγάς, σκηνή || (scolding) επίπληξη, κατσάδα, λούσιμο ♦ vi φιλονεικώ, καυγαδίζω, αρπάζομαι.

rowdy ['raʊdɪ] a θορυβώδης, που κάνει σαματά ♦ n (person) θορυβοποιός, καυγατζής.

rowing ['rəʊɪŋ] n κωπηλασία, κουπί || ~ **boat** n βάρκα με κουπιά.

rowlock ['rɒlək] n σκαλμός.

royal ['rɔɪəl] a βασιλικός || ~**ist** n βασιλόφρων m, βασιλικός ♦ a βασιλικός.

royalty ['rɔɪəltɪ] n (royal family) βασιλική οικογένεια || (payment: to inventor) δικαιώματα ntpl εφευρέτου || (: to author) συγγραφικά δικαιώματα ntpl.

r.p.m. abbr (= revs per minute) στρ./λεπ., σ.α.λ. (στροφές ανά λεπτό).

R.S.V.P. abbr (= répondez s'il vous plaît) R.S.V.P.

Rt. Hon. abbr (= Right Honourable) Εντιμότατος.

rub [rʌb] n (polish, with cloth) τρίψιμο, σφούγγισμα nt ♦ vt τρίβω, επαλείφω, προστρίβω || (clean) στεγνώνω, σκουπίζω || **to ~ off** vi τρίβω, σβήνω.

rubber ['rʌbə*] n (substance) καουτσούκ nt inv || (Brit) γομμολάστιχα || ~ **band** n λάστιχο || ~ **plant** n εβέα, δέντρο καουτσούκ || ~ **stamp** n (lit) σφραγίδα || (fig) ο εγκρίνων τυφλά.

rubbish ['rʌbɪʃ] n σκουπίδια ntpl, απορρίμματα ntpl || (nonsense) ανοησίες fpl, κολοκύθια ntpl || ~ **dump** n τόπος απορρίψεως σκουπιδιών || ~**y** a άχρηστος, της πενταράς.

rubble ['rʌbl] n χαλίκι, σκύρο.

ruble ['ruːbl] n (US) = **rouble**.

ruby ['ruːbɪ] n ρουμπίνι ♦ a κόκκινο, ρουμπινί.

rucksack ['rʌksæk] n σακκίδιο.

rudder ['rʌdə*] n πηδάλιο, τιμόνι.

ruddy ['rʌdɪ] a (colour) ροδοκόκκινος, ερυθρωπός || (col: bloody) τρομερός.

rude [ruːd] a (vulgar) πρόστυχος || (impolite) βάναυσος, απολίτιστος, αγενής || (rough) τραχύς, πρωτόγονος || ~**ly** ad πρωτόγονα, απότομα || ~**ness** n χοντροκοπιά, αγένεια.

rudiment ['ruːdɪmənt] n στοιχείο, υποτυπώδης αρχή || ~**ary** a στοιχειώδης.

ruff [rʌf] n τραχηλιά.

ruffian ['rʌfɪən] n παλιάνθρωπος, κακούργος.

ruffle ['rʌfl] vt ρυτιδώνω, τσαλακώνω, ανακατεύω.

rug [rʌg] n τάπης, χαλί || (for knees) κουβέρτα, χράμι.

rugby ['rʌgbɪ] n ράγκμπυ nt inv.

rugged ['rʌgɪd] a τραχύς || (surface) ανώμαλος.

rugger ['rʌgə*] n ράγκμπυ nt inv.

ruin ['ruːɪn] n καταστροφή, συμφορά, αφανισμός ♦ vt καταστρέφω, αφανίζω || ~**s** npl ερείπια ntpl || ~**ation** n καταστροφή, όλεθρος, ρήμαγμα nt.

rule [ruːl] n (guide) κανόνας || (what is usual) συνήθεια, το κανονικό || (government) εξουσία, αρχή, κυριαρχία || (stick) κανόνας ♦ vt κυβερνώ, διοικώ || (pervade) διέπω || (lines) χαράκωνω || **as a ~** κατά κανόνα, συνήθως || ~**d** a (paper) ριγωτός, χαρακωμένος || ~**r** n κυβερνήτης, άρχοντας || (straight edge) χάρακας, ρίγα, μέτρο.

ruling ['ruːlɪŋ] a (party) άρχοντας, διευθύνων, κυβερνών || (class) άρχουσα (τάξη).

rum [rʌm] n ρούμι ♦ a (col) παράξενος, αλλόκοτος.

rumble ['rʌmbl] n υπόκωφος βοή, βροντή ♦ vi βροντώ, βουίζω, γουργουρίζω.

rummage ['rʌmɪdʒ] n έρευνα, ψάξιμο ♦ vt ερευνώ, ψάχνω.

rumour, rumor (US) ['ruːmə*] n φήμη, διάδοση ♦ vt: **it is ~ed that** λέγεται ότι, διαδίδεται ότι, φημολογείται ότι.

rump [rʌmp] n γλουτός, οπίσθια ntpl || ~**steak** n κόντρα φιλέτο.

rumpus ['rʌmpəs] n θόρυβος, ταραχή || (col) καυγάς, σαματάς.

run [rʌn] (irreg v) n (running) δρόμος, τρέξιμο || (AUT) διαδρομή, βόλτα || (series) σειρά, συνέχεια || (sudden demand) ζήτηση || (enclosed space) χώρος κλειστός || (ski run) πίστα του σκί, κατήφορος για σκι ♦ vt (cause to run) κατευθύνω, λειτουργώ || (train, bus) κυκλοφορώ, κάνω διαδρομή || (manage) διευθύνω || (compete in race) τρέχω σε αγώνα || (stand for election) βάζω υποψηφιότητα || (force) περνώ || (pass: hand, eye) περνώ || (COMPUT: program) τρέχω ♦ vi (move quickly) τρέχω, το βάζω στα πόδια || (in election) θέτω υποψηφιότητα || (in race) τρέχω σε αγώνες || (machine) λειτουργώ || (flow) ρέω, κυλώ, τρέχω || (colours) ξεβάφω, βγαίνω, τρέχω || **on the ~** σε φυγή || **to ~ riot** οργιάζω || **to ~ a risk** ριψοκινδυνεύω || **to ~ about** vi (children) τρέχω εδώ και κει || **to ~ across** vt (find) συναντώ τυχαία || **to ~ away** vi δραπετεύω || **to ~ down** vi (clock) ξεκουρδίζω ♦ vt (run over) κτυπώ, πατώ (κάποιον), πλακώνω || (talk against) δυσφημώ, κατηγορώ || **to be ~-down** είμαι εξαντλημένος, είμαι τσακισμένος || **to ~ off** vi φεύγω, τρέπομαι σε φυγή, το σκάω || **to ~ out** vi (person) βγαίνω τρέχοντας || (liquid) χύνομαι, τρέχω, στάζω || (lease) λήγω || (money) τελειώνω, εξαντλούμαι || **to ~ out of** vt εξαντλώ, τελειώνω, μένω από || **to ~ over** vt κτυπώ, πλακώνω, πατώ || (read) ρίχνω μια ματιά || **to ~ through** vt (instructions) διαβάζω γρήγορα, εξετάζω βιαστικά || **to ~ up** vt (debt) αφήνω να ανέβει, χρεώνομαι περισσότερα || (dress) ράβω γρήγορα-γρήγορα || **to ~ up against** vt

(difficulties) συναντώ, αντιμετωπίζω ||
~about n (small car) αυτοκίνητο δύο
θέσεων || ~away a (horse) αφηνιασμένο
(άλογο) || (person) ο δραπέτης.
rung [rʌŋ] pp of ring ♦ n βαθμίδα || (of
rope ladder) σκαλί ανεμόσκαλας.
runner ['rʌnə*] n (messenger)
αγγελιαφόρος || (of sleigh) πατίνι || ~-up
n ο επιλαχών, ο δεύτερος (νικητής).
running ['rʌnɪŋ] n (of business)
διεύθυνση || (of machine) λειτουργία,
κίνηση ♦ a (water) τρεχούμενος || ~
commentary n σύγχρονη περιγραφή,
(ραδιο) ρεπορτάζ nt inv.
run-of-the-mill ['rʌnəvðə'mɪl] a
κοινός, συνηθισμένος.
runt [rʌnt] n κοντοστούμπης.
run-through ['rʌnθruː] a γρήγορο
διάβασμα nt, γρήγορη επανάληψη.
runway ['rʌnweɪ] n διάδρομος
απογειώσεως.
rupture ['rʌptʃə*] n (MED) ρήξη,
διάρρηξη ♦ vt: to ~ o.s. πάσχω από
κήλη.
rural ['ruərəl] a αγροτικός, υπαίθριος.
ruse [ruːz] n τέχνασμα nt, πανουργία,
κόλπο.
rush [rʌʃ] n (dash) βιασύνη || (sudden
demand) μεγάλη ζήτηση || (current)
εκτόξευση, εισροή ♦ vt ορμώ, τρέχω
επειγόντως || (attack) κάνω έφοδο || (col:
overcharge) γδέρνω ♦ vi (dash) (εξ)ορμώ,
εφορμώ, σπεύδω, τρέχω || ~es npl (BOT)
βούρλο, σπάρτο || ~ hour n ώρα
συνωστισμού, ώρα πολλής δουλειάς.
rusk [rʌsk] n παξιμάδι.
Russia ['rʌʃə] n Ρωσία || ~n n
Ρώσος/ίδα m/f ♦ a ρωσικός, ρούσικος.
rust [rʌst] n σκωριά, σκουριά ♦ vi
σκουριάζω.
rustic ['rʌstɪk] a (of the country)
αγροτικός, χωριάτικος || (roughly made)
χοντροκαμωμένος.
rustle ['rʌsl] n ψίθυρος, τρίξιμο,
μουρμούρισμα nt ♦ vi θροΐζω,
μουρμουρίζω ♦ vt (US: animals) κλέβω,
είμαι ζωοκλέπτης.
rustproof ['rʌstpruːf] a ανοξείδωτος.
rusty ['rʌstɪ] a σκουριασμένος.
rut [rʌt] n (track) αυλάκι, τροχιά, ροδιά ||
(routine) ρουτίνα, μονοτονία.
ruthless ['ruːθlɪs] a ανελέητος,
άσπλαχνος, ωμός || ~ly ad χωρίς οίκτο,
αλύπητα || ~ness n ασπλαχνία,
σκληρότητα.
rye [raɪ] n σίκαλη || ~ **bread** n ψωμί από
σίκαλη.

S

sabbath ['sæbəθ] n (Jewish) Σάββατο ||
(Christian) Κυριακή.
sabbatical [sə'bætɪkəl] a: ~ **year** άδεια
ενός χρόνου (καθηγητού).
saber ['seɪbə*] n (US) = sabre.
sabotage ['sæbətɑːʒ] n σαμποτάζ nt inv.

sabre ['seɪbə*] n σπαθί.
saccharin(e) ['sækərɪn] n σακχαρίνη.
sack [sæk] n σάκος, τσουβάλι || (dismissal)
απόλυση ♦ vt απολύω || (town) λεηλατώ ||
~**ful** n σακιά, τσουβάλι || ~**ing** n
(material) σακόπανο || (dismissal)
απόλυση, παύση.
sacrament ['sækrəmənt] n μυστήριο,
μετάληψη.
sacred ['seɪkrɪd] a ιερός, άγιος || (duty
etc) απαραβίαστος.
sacrifice ['sækrɪfaɪs] n θυσία ♦ vt
θυσιάζω.
sacrilege ['sækrɪlɪdʒ] n ιεροσυλία ||
βεβήλωση.
sacrosanct ['sækrəusæŋkt] a ιερός και
απαραβίαστος.
sad [sæd] a λυπημένος, θλιμένος || (dull)
θλιβερός || ~**den** vt λυπώ, θλίβω.
saddle ['sædl] n σέλα ♦ vt (burden)
φορτώνω || ~**bag** n δισάκι.
sadism ['seɪdɪzəm] n σαδισμός.
sadist ['seɪdɪst] n σαδιστής/ίστρια m/f ||
~**ic** [sə'dɪstɪk] a σαδιστικός.
sadness ['sædnɪs] n θλίψη, μελαγχολία.
safari [sə'fɑːrɪ] n σαφάρι.
safe [seɪf] a ασφαλής, σώος || (cautious)
προσεκτικός, σίγουρος || (sure)
ασφαλής, ακίνδυνος ♦ n
χρηματοκιβώτιο || ~**guard** n
εξασφάλιση, προστασία ♦ vt
προστατεύω || ~**keeping** n ασφάλεια ||
~**ly** ad ασφαλώς, σίγουρα.
safety ['seɪftɪ] n ασφάλεια, σιγουριά || ~
belt n ζώνη ασφαλείας || ~ **curtain** n
αυλαία ασφαλείας || ~ **pin** n παραμάνα.
sag [sæg] vi κάμπτομαι, βουλιάζω.
sage [seɪdʒ] n (herb) φασκομηλιά,
αλιφασκιά || (man) σοφός.
sago ['seɪgəu] n (food) σάγος.
said [sed] pt, pp of say || a λεγόμενος,
λεχθείς.
sail [seɪl] n ιστίο, πανί || (trip) ταξίδι,
απόπλους ♦ vt κυβερνώ (πλοίο) ♦ vi
πλέω, πάω με το πανί || (depart) αποπλέω
|| (fig: cloud etc) τρέχω, περνώ || ~**boat** n
(US) βάρκα με πανί || ~**ing** n (SPORT)
ιστιοδρομία || **to go** ~**ing** κάνω
ιστιοδρομίες || ~**ing ship** n ιστιοφόρο
πλοίο || ~**or** n ναύτης, ναυτικός.
saint [seɪnt] n άγιος/α m/f.
sake [seɪk] n: **for the** ~ **of** για χάρη του
|| **for your** ~ για το καλό σου.
salad ['sæləd] n σαλάτα || ~ **dressing** n
είδος nt μαγιονέζας || ~ **oil** n λάδι για
σαλάτα.
salary ['sælərɪ] n μισθός.
sale [seɪl] n πώληση, πούλημα nt || (for
short periods) ξεπούλημα ntpl, εκπτώσεις
fpl || ~**room** n δημοπρατήριο ||
salesman n πωλητής || **saleswoman** n
πωλήτρια.
salient ['seɪlɪənt] a προεξέχων,
εντυπωσιακός.
saliva [sə'laɪvə] n σάλιο.
sallow ['sæləu] a ωχρός, χλωμός.
salmon ['sæmən] n σολομός.

S

salon ['sælɔ̃:ŋ] n κομμωτήριο.
saloon [sə'lu:n] n (AUT) κλειστό (αυτοκίνητο) || (ship's lounge) σαλόνι.
salt [sɔːlt] n άλας nt, αλάτι || (CHEM) άλας nt ♦ vt (cure) αλατίζω, παστώνω || (flavour) αλατίζω || ~-cellar n αλατιέρα || ~y α αλμυρός.
salutary ['sæljutərɪ] α ωφέλιμος, σωτήριος.
salute [sə'lu:t] n (MIL) χαιρετισμός ♦ vt (MIL) χαιρετίζω, αποδίδω χαιρετισμό.
salvage ['sælvɪdʒ] n διάσωση || (property saved) διασωθέν, υλικό ♦ vt διασώζω.
salvation [sæl'veɪʃən] n σωτηρία || S~ Army n ο Στρατός της Σωτηρίας.
salver ['sælvə*] n δίσκος.
salvo ['sælvəʊ] n κανονιοβολισμός, ομοβροντία.
same [seɪm] α ίδιος || all the ~ παρ' όλα αυτά.
sample ['sɑːmpl] n δείγμα nt ♦ vt (test) δοκιμάζω.
sanatorium [sænə'tɔːrɪəm] n σανατόριο.
sanctimonious [sæŋktɪ'məʊnɪəs] α ψευτοθεοφοβούμενος, υποκριτής.
sanction ['sæŋkʃən] n (POL, ECON) (επι)κύρωση.
sanctity ['sæŋktɪtɪ] n αγιότητα, αγιοσύνη || (sacredness) ιερότητα, το απαραβίαστο.
sanctuary ['sæŋktjʊərɪ] n ιερό, άδυτο || (for fugitive) άσυλο || (refuge) καταφύγιο.
sand [sænd] n άμμος f ♦ vt στρώνω με άμμο || ~s npl αμμουδιά.
sandal ['sændl] n σανδάλι, πέδιλο.
sandbag ['sændbæg] n σάκος άμμου.
sand dune ['sænddjuːn] n αμμόλοφος.
sandpaper ['sændpeɪpə*] n γυαλόχαρτο.
sandpit ['sændpɪt] n (for children) αμμόκοιτος.
sandstone ['sændstəʊn] n ψαμμίτης, ψαμμόλιθος.
sandwich ['sænwɪdʒ] n σάντουιτς ♦ vt παρεμβάλλω, στριμώχνω.
sandy ['sændɪ] α (with sand) αμμώδης, αμμουδερός || (colour) πυρόξανθος.
sane [seɪn] α συνετός || (sensible) λογικός.
sang [sæŋ] pt of sing.
sanitarium [sænɪ'tɛərɪəm] n (US) = sanatorium.
sanitary ['sænɪtərɪ] α υγιεινός || (protective) υγιεινομικός || ~ napkin (US), ~ towel n πετσέτα υγείας.
sanitation [sænɪ'teɪʃən] n υγιεινή.
sanity ['sænɪtɪ] n πνευματική υγεία, υγιής νους || (good sense) λογική.
sank [sæŋk] pt of sink.
Santa Claus [sæntə'klɔːz] n 'Αη Βασίλης.
sap [sæp] n (of plants) χυμός, οπός ♦ vt (wear away) υπονομεύω, υποσκάπτω.
sapling ['sæplɪŋ] n δενδρύλιο.
sapphire ['sæfaɪə*] n ο σάπφειρος.
sarcasm ['sɑːkæzəm] n σαρκασμός.
sarcastic [sɑː'kæstɪk] α σαρκαστικός.

sardine [sɑː'diːn] n σαρδέλα.
sash [sæʃ] n (MIL) ζώνη αξιωματικών.
sat [sæt] pt, pp of sit.
Satan ['seɪtn] n Σατανάς || ~ic [sə'tænɪk] α σατανικός.
satchel ['sætʃəl] n (SCH) τσάντα, σάκα.
satellite ['sætəlaɪt] n δορυφόρος ♦ α δορυφορικός.
satin ['sætɪn] n σατέν nt inv ♦ α σατινέ, από σατέν.
satire ['sætaɪə*] n σάτυρα.
satirical [sə'tɪrɪkəl] α σατυρικός.
satisfaction [sætɪs'fækʃən] n ικανοποίηση || ευχαρίστηση.
satisfactory [sætɪs'fæktərɪ] α ικανοποιητικός.
satisfy ['sætɪsfaɪ] vt ικανοποιώ || (convince) πείθω, διαβεβαιώ || ~ing α ικανοποιητικός.
saturate ['sætʃəreɪt] vt διαβρέχω, διαποτίζω, μουσκεύω.
Saturday ['sætədɪ] n Σάββατο.
sauce [sɔːs] n σάλτσα || ~pan n κατσαρόλα.
saucer ['sɔːsə*] n πιατάκι.
saucy ['sɔːsɪ] α αναιδής, αυθάδης.
saunter ['sɔːntə*] vi σουλατσάρω, περπατώ άσκοπα ♦ n βόλτα.
sausage ['sɒsɪdʒ] n λουκάνικο || ~ roll n λουκάνικο με ζύμη.
savage ['sævɪdʒ] α άγριος, θηριώδης || (uncivilized) απολίτιστος, βάρβαρος ♦ n άγριος ♦ vt (fig) επιτίθεμαι άγρια || ~ry n αγριότητα, βαρβαρότητα.
save [seɪv] vt σώζω, γλυτώνω || (store up) (εξ)οικονομώ, αποταμιεύω, μαζεύω || (avoid using up) αποφεύγω || (COMPUT) φυλάω ♦ prep, cj εκτός από εκτός, εξαιρουμένου.
saving ['seɪvɪŋ] α (redeeming) σωτήριος ♦ n οικονομία || ~s npl αποταμιεύσεις fpl, καταθέσεις fpl, οικονομίες fpl || ~s bank n ταμιευτήριο.
saviour ['seɪvjə*] n σωτήρας.
savour, savor (US) ['seɪvə*] n ουσία, γεύση, γούστο ♦ vt γεύομαι || (enjoy) απολαμβάνω || ~y α γευστικός, νόστιμος, ορεκτικός.
saw [sɔː] (irreg v) n (tool) πριόνι ♦ vt πριονίζω || pt of see || ~dust n πριονίδια ntpl || ~mill n πριονιστήριο.
saxophone ['sæksəfəʊn] n σαξόφωνο.
say [seɪ] (irreg v) n λόγος ♦ vt (tell) λέγω || (suppose) υποθέτω || ~ing n ρητό.
scab [skæb] n κάρκαδο || (pej: industry) απεργοσπάστης.
scabby ['skæbɪ] α ψωριάρης.
scaffold ['skæfəld] n ικρίωμα nt || ~ing n σκαλωσιά.
scald [skɔːld] n ζεμάτισμα nt ♦ vt ζεματίζω.
scale [skeɪl] n (of fish) λέπι || (MUS) κλίμακα, σκάλα || (for measuring) κλίμακα, διαβάθμιση || (on map) κλίμακα || (size) κλίμακα ♦ vt (climb) αναρριχώμαι, σκαρφαλώνω || ~s npl (balance) ζυγός, ζυγαριά || on a large ~ σε μεγάλη

κλίμακα || ~ **drawing** n σχέδιο υπό κλίμακα.

scallop ['skɒləp] n (shellfish) χτένι.

scalp [skælp] n τριχωτό δέρμα nt κεφαλής ♦ vt γδέρνω το κρανίο.

scalpel ['skælpəl] n νυστέρι.

scamper ['skæmpə*] vi τρέχω τρελά, το στρίβω.

scan [skæn] vt εξονυχίζω, διερευνώ || (POET) διαβάζω μετρικά.

scandal ['skændl] n σκάνδαλο || (gossip) κακολογία, κουτσομπολιό || ~**ize** vt σκανδαλίζω || ~**ous** a σκανδαλώδης.

Scandinavia [skændɪ'neɪvɪə] n Σκανδιναβία || ~**n** a σκανδιναβικός ♦ n Σκανδιναβός/ή m/f.

scant [skænt] a πενιχρός, ανεπαρκής, λιγοστός || ~**y** a ανεπαρκής, λιγοστός.

scapegoat ['skeɪpgəut] n αποδιοπομπαίος τράγος.

scar [skɑː*] n ουλή, σημάδι ♦ vt αφήνω σημάδι.

scarce [skɛəs] a σπάνιος || ~**ly** ad μόλις, σχεδόν καθόλου || ~**ness** n σπανιότητα έλλειψη.

scarcity ['skɛəsɪtɪ] n σπανιότητα, έλλειψη.

scare [skɛə*] n εκφόβιση, τρομάρα ♦ vt φοβίζω, τρομάζω || ~**crow** n σκιάχτρο.

scarf [skɑːf] n σάρπα, κασκόλ nt inv.

scarlet ['skɑːlɪt] a (colour) κατακόκκινος ♦ n κτυπητό κόκκινο || ~ **fever** n οστρακιά, σκαρλατίνα.

scarves [skɑːvz] npl of **scarf**.

scathing ['skeɪðɪŋ] a καυστικός, δηκτικός.

scatter ['skætə*] n διασπορά, σκόρπισμα nt ♦ vt (sprinkle) σκορπίζω || (an enemy) διασκορπίζω ♦ vi διαλύομαι, σκορπίζω || ~**brained** a άμυαλος, ξεμυαλισμένος || ~**ing** n μικρή ποσότητα, σκόρπισμα nt.

scavenger ['skævɪndʒə*] n (animal) ζώο που τρώει ψοφίμια.

scene [siːn] n (of accident etc) τόπος, θέατρο || (of play) σκηνή || (division of play) σκηνή || (view) τοπείο, άποψη, θέα || (fuss) σκηνή, φασαρία, επεισόδιο || (incident) σκηνή || **on the** ~ στον τόπο, επί σκηνής || ~**ry** n σκηνικό, σκηνογραφία, σκηνή || (view) τοπίο, θέα.

scenic ['siːnɪk] a σκηνικός, θεαματικός.

scent [sɛnt] n οσμή, άρωμα nt, μυρουδιά || (sense of smell) όσφρηση ♦ vt (make fragrant) αρωματίζω, μοσχοβολώ.

scepter ['sɛptə*] n (US) = **sceptre**.

sceptic ['skɛptɪk] n σκεπτικιστής || ~**al** a σκεπτικός, δύσπιστος || ~**ism** n σκεπτικισμός.

sceptre ['sɛptə*] n σκήπτρο.

schedule ['ʃɛdjuːl, (US) 'skɛdjuːl] n πρόγραμμα, πλάνο || (of trains) δρομολόγιο || (of prices) κατάλογος ♦ vt καταγράφω, προγραμματίζω || **on** ~ στην ώρα || σύμφωνα με το πρόγραμμα || **behind** ~ καθυστερημένος.

scheme [skiːm] n διάταξη || (plan)

σχέδιο || (plot) μηχανορραφία, δολοπλοκία ♦ vti (plot) μηχανορραφώ || (plan) σχεδιάζω.

scheming ['skiːmɪŋ] a δολοπλόκος, κομπιναδόρος.

schism ['sɪzəm] n σχίσμα nt.

schizophrenic [skɪtsəʊ'frɛnɪk] a σχιζοφρενικός.

scholar ['skɒlə*] n μελετητής, μορφωμένος || (with scholarship) υπότροφος || ~**ly** a μορφωμένος || ~**ship** n υποτροφία || (learning) μόρφωση.

school [skuːl] n σχολείο || (group) σχολή || (department) σχολή ♦ attr a σχολικό, του σχολείου ♦ vt διδάσκω, γυμνάζω, μορφώνω || ~**book** n σχολικό βιβλίο || ~**boy** n μαθητής || ~**days** npl σχολικά χρόνια ntpl || ~**girl** n μαθήτρια || ~**ing** n εκπαίδευση, μόρφωση || ~**master** n δάσκαλος, καθηγητής || ~**mistress** n δασκάλα, καθηγήτρια || ~**teacher** n δημοδιδάσκαλος/ισσα m/f.

schooner ['skuːnə*] n (ship) σκούνα || (glass for sherry etc) ποτηράκι.

sciatica [saɪ'ætɪkə] n ισχιαλγία.

science ['saɪəns] n επιστήμη.

scientific [saɪən'tɪfɪk] a επιστημονικός.

scientist ['saɪəntɪst] n επιστήμονας m/f.

scintillating ['sɪntɪleɪtɪŋ] a σπινθηροβόλος, αστραφτερός.

scissors ['sɪzəz] npl (also: **a pair of** ~) ψαλίδι.

scoff [skɒf] vt (eat) τρώγω, καταβροχθίζω ♦ vi (mock) (+at) σκόπτω, κοροϊδεύω.

scold [skəʊld] vt επιπλήττω, μαλώνω.

scone [skɒn] n είδος nt κέικ.

scoop [skuːp] n φτυάρι, σέσουλα ♦ vt: **to** ~ **out** αδειάζω || **to** ~ **up** vt βγάζω.

scooter ['skuːtə*] n (motorcycle) βέσπα || (child's toy) πατίνι.

scope [skəʊp] n αντίληψη, γνώση || (opportunity) ευκαιρία || (margin) περιθώριο.

scorch [skɔːtʃ] n καψάλισμα nt, κάψιμο ♦ vt καψαλίζω, τσουρουφλίζω || (wither) ψήνω, ξεραίνω || ~**ing** a καφτερός.

score [skɔː*] n (points) σκορ nt inv || (MUS) παρτιτούρα || (reason) σημείο || (twenty) εικοσάρα, εικοσάδα ♦ vt (win points) σημειώνω, κάνω πόντους || (mark) χαράσσω, χαρακώνω ♦ vi (keep record) κρατώ σκόρ || ~ n αριθμός των σκορ || ~**r** n (player) ο επιτυχών τέρμα || (recorder) μαρκαδόρος.

scorn ['skɔːn] n περιφρόνηση ♦ vt περιφρονώ.

scorpion ['skɔːpɪən] n σκορπιός.

Scot [skɒt] n Σκωτσέζος/α m/f || **Scotch** n (whisky) (σκωτσέζικο) ουίσκυ.

scotch [skɒtʃ] vt (terminate) αποτρέπω, καταπνίγω.

Scotland ['skɒtlənd] n Σκωτία.

Scots [skɒts] npl Σκωτσέζοι mpl ♦ a σκωτσέζος || ~**man** n Σκωτσέζος || ~**woman** n Σκωτίδα, Σκωτσέζα.

Scottish ['skɒtɪʃ] a σκωτικός, σκωτσέζικος.

scoundrel ['skaundrəl] n παλιάνθρωπος.

scour ['skauə*] vt (search) διατρέχω, ερευνώ || (clean) καθαρίζω || ~er n (for pans) σύρμα nt.

scourge [skɜːdʒ] n (plague) πληγή.

scout [skaut] n ανιχνευτής || (boy scout) πρόσκοπος ♦ vi (reconnoitre) ανιχνεύω, κάνω αναγνώριση.

scowl [skaul] n συνοφρύωση, σκυθρωπότητα ♦ vi συνοφρυούμαι, κατσουφιάζω.

scraggy ['skrægɪ] a ισχνός, κοκκαλιάρης.

scram [skræm] vi (col) στρίβω, το βάζω στα πόδια || ~! στρίβε!, δίνε του!

scramble ['skræmbl] n σκαρφάλωμα nt || (struggle) αγώνας, πάλη ♦ vi: to ~ for αγωνίζομαι || ~d eggs npl αυγά χτυπητά ntpl.

scrap [skræp] n κομματάκι, απόρριμμα nt, ψίχουλο || (fight) συμπλοκή, καυγάς || (scrap iron) παλιοσίδερα ntpl ♦ a για πέταμα, άχρηστος ♦ vt πετώ σαν άχρηστο, απορρίπτω ♦ vi (fight) πιάνομαι στα χέρια || ~s npl (waste) απομεινάρια ntpl, απορρίμματα ntpl || ~book n λεύκωμα nt αποκομμάτων.

scrape [skreɪp] n απόξεση, ξύσιμο || (awkward position) αμπχανία, μπελάς ♦ vt ξύνω, ξεγδέρνω || (clean) καθαρίζω, τρίβω ♦ vi ξύνω || ~r n ξύστρα, ξυστήρι.

scrap heap ['skræphiːp] n σωρός παλιοσιδερικών.

scrap merchant ['skræpmɜːtʃənt] n έμπορος παλιοσιδερικών.

scrappy ['skræpɪ] a ασύνδετος, ασυνάρτητος, ανακατεμένος.

scratch ['skrætʃ] n νυχιά, αμυχή, γρατσουνιά || (itch) ξύσιμο ♦ a πρόχειρος ♦ vt ξύνω, τρίβω || (wound) γρατσουνίζω, ξεγδέρνω ♦ vi (rub) ξύνομαι.

scrawl [skrɔːl] n ορνιθοσκαλίσματα ntpl ♦ vti κακογράφω, ορνιθοσκαλίζω.

scream [skriːm] n κραυγή, ξεφωνητό, στριγγλιά ♦ vi ξεφωνίζω || (speak loudly) στριγγλίζω.

screech [skriːtʃ] n κραυγή, στριγγλιά ♦ vi σκούζω, στριγγλίζω, ουρλιάζω.

screen [skriːn] n παραπέτασμα nt, προπέτασμα nt, παραβάν nt inv || (for films) οθόνη, πανί || (church) κιγκλίδωμα nt ♦ vt προφυλάσσω, προστατεύω || (film) κινηματογραφώ, γυρίζω.

screw [skruː] n κοχλίας, βίδα || (NAUT) έλικας, προπέλα ♦ vt βιδώνω, σφίγγω || (col) καταπιέζω || ~driver n κατσαβίδι || ~y a (col) μουρλός, ξεβιδωμένος.

scribble ['skrɪbl] n κακογραφία ♦ vt γράφω βιαστικά, ορνιθοσκαλίζω.

script [skrɪpt] n χειρόγραφο || (of play) κείμενο, σενάριο.

Scripture ['skrɪptʃə*] n n Αγία Γραφή.

scriptwriter ['skrɪptraɪtə*] n σεναριογράφος.

scroll [skrəul] n κύλινδρος, ρόλος (περγαμηνής) ♦ vt (COMPUT) μετακινώ το περιεχόμενα της οθόνης πάνω/κάτω.

scrounge [skraundʒ] vt (col) διακονεύω ♦ n: on the ~ πάω τσάρκα.

scrub [skrʌb] n (clean) τριβή, τρίψιμο, βούρτσισμα nt || (countryside) χαμόκλαδα ntpl, αγριμιά ♦ vt πλένω, βουρτσίζω, τρίβω || (erase) ακυρώνω, σβήνω.

scruff [skrʌf] n σβέρκο.

scrum(mage) ['skrʌm(ɪdʒ)] n συμπλοκή.

scruple ['skruːpl] n ενδοιασμός, δισταγμός της συνείδησης.

scrupulous ['skruːpjuləs] a ευσυνείδητος || ~ly ad ευσυνείδητα.

scrutinize ['skruːtɪnaɪz] vt εξετάζω προσεκτικά, διερευνώ.

scrutiny ['skruːtɪnɪ] n αυστηρός έλεγχος, διερεύνηση.

scuff [skʌf] vt (shoes) σέρνω.

scuffle ['skʌfl] n συμπλοκή, καυγάς.

scullery ['skʌlərɪ] n πλυντήριο μαγειρίου, λάντσα.

sculptor ['skʌlptə*] n γλύπτης/τρια n/f.

sculpture ['skʌlptʃə*] n γλυπτική || (statue) γλυπτό.

scum [skʌm] n βρώμικος αφρός, βρωμιά || (people) κατακάθια ntpl, αποβράσματα ntpl.

scurrilous ['skʌrɪləs] a υβριστικός, αχρείος, βρώμικος.

scurry ['skʌrɪ] vi τρέχω, σπεύδω.

scurvy ['skɜːvɪ] n σκορβούτο.

scuttle ['skʌtl] vt (plans) εγκαταλείπω, υποχωρώ ♦ vi (scamper) τρέχω βιαστικά, το στρίβω.

scythe [saɪð] n δρεπάνι.

sea [siː] n θάλασσα || (broad stretch) ωκεανός, θάλασσα ♦ a θαλασσινός, της θάλασσας || ~ bird n θαλασσοπούλι || ~board n ακτή, παραλία || ~ breeze n θαλασσινή αύρα, μπάτης || ~farer n θαλασσινός, θαλασσοπόρος || ~food n θαλασσινά ntpl || ~ front n παραλία, προκυμαία || ~going a ποντοπόρος || ~gull n γλάρος.

seal [siːl] n (animal) φώκια || (stamp) σφραγίδα, βούλα || (impression) σφραγίδα ♦ vt σφραγίζω || (close) κλείνω, σφραγίζω, βουλώνω.

sea level ['siːlevl] n η επιφάνεια της θάλασσας.

sealing wax ['siːlɪŋwæks] n βουλοκέρι.

sea lion ['siːlaɪən] n είδος φώκιας.

seam [siːm] n ραφή || (joining) ένωση, ραφή || (of coal etc) φλέβα.

seaman ['siːmən] n ναυτικός, ναύτης.

seamy ['siːmɪ] a ανάποδος, άσχημος.

seaport ['siːpɔːt] n λιμάνι.

search [sɜːtʃ] n έρευνα, αναζήτηση ♦ vt ερευνώ, αναζητώ || (COMPUT) διερευνώ || ~ing a ερευνητικός, προσεκτικός || ~light n προβολέας || ~ party n απόσπασμα nt έρευνας.

seashore ['siːʃɔː*] n ακτή, παραλία.

seasick ['si:sik] a αυτός που έχει ναυτία || ~**ness** n ναυτία.

seaside ['si:said] n παραλία, γιαλός.

season ['si:zn] n εποχή ♦ vt αρτύω, καρυκεύω || ~**al** a εποχιακός || ~**ing** n καρύκευμα, άρτυμα nt, μπαχαρικό || ~ **ticket** n διαρκές εισιτήριο.

seat [si:t] n κάθισμα nt, καρέκλα || (PARL etc) έδρα || (manner of sitting) κάθισμα nt, θέση || (bottom) πισινός, οπίσθια ntpl ♦ vt καθίζω || **it ~s 20 people** είναι 20 θέσεων || ~ **belt** n ζώνη ασφαλείας.

sea water ['si:wɔ:tə*] n θαλασσινό νερό.

seaweed ['si:wi:d] n φύκι, φύκια ntpl.

seaworthy ['si:wə:ði] a πλόιμος, ικανός να πλεύσει.

sec. abbr of **second(s)**.

secluded [si'klu:did] a παράμερος, απομονωμένος.

seclusion [si'klu:ʒən] n απομόνωση.

second ['sekənd] a δεύτερος ♦ ad (in second position) δεύτερος || (RAIL) δεύτερη (θέση) ♦ n (of time) δευτερόλεπτο || (COMM: imperfect) δεύτερο χέρι ♦ vt υποστηρίζω, βοηθώ || ~**ary** a δευτερεύων, ασήμαντος || ~**ary education** μέση εκπαίδευση || ~**ary school** n σχολείο μέσης εκπαιδεύσεως || ~**er** n υποστηρικτής/ίκτρια m/f || ~**hand** a μεταχειρισμένος, δεύτερο χέρι || (not original) μη πρωτότυπος || ~**ly** ad κατά δεύτερο λόγο || ~**-rate** a μέτριος, δεύτερος ποιότητας || ~ **thoughts** npl δεύτερες σκέψεις fpl.

secrecy ['si:krəsi] n μυστικότητα, εχεμύθεια.

secret ['si:krit] n μυστικό ♦ a μυστικός, κρυφός, απόρρητος.

secretariat [sekrə'teəriət] n γραμματεία.

secretary ['sekrətri] n γραμματέας m/f || (minister etc) υπουργός m/f.

secretive ['si:krətiv] a κρυψίνους.

sect [sekt] n αίρεση || ~**arian** a αιρετικός, στενοκέφαλος, κομματικός.

section ['sekʃən] n χωρισμός, κόψιμο || (piece) τμήμα nt, μέρος nt, τομή || ~**al** a τμηματικός, τοπικός.

sector ['sektə*] n (private or public sector) τομέας.

secular ['sekjulə*] a λαϊκός, κοσμικός.

secure [si'kjuə*] a βέβαιος, ακίνδυνος || (fixed) ασφαλής ♦ vt (fix) στερεώνω, σφίγγω || (obtain) εξασφαλίζω.

security [si'kjuəriti] n ασφάλεια, σιγουριά || (bond) εγγύηση, χρεώγραφο || (national security) ασφάλεια || see social.

sedate [si'deit] a ατάραχος, ήρεμος.

sedation [si'deiʃən] n (MED) καταπράυνση.

sedative ['sedətiv] n καταπραϋντικό ♦ a καταπραϋντικός.

sedentary ['sedntri] a αδρανής, καθιστικός.

sediment ['sedimənt] n κατακάθι, ίζημα.

seduce [si'dju:s] vt (general) δελεάζω, παρασύρω || (sexually) διαφθείρω, αποπλανώ.

seduction [si'dʌkʃən] n αποπλάνηση, δελεασμός.

seductive [si'dʌktiv] a γοητευτικός, αποπλανητικός.

see [si:] (irreg v) vt βλέπω || (find out) κοιτάζω || (understand) καταλαβαίνω || (make sure) φροντίζω || (accompany) συνοδεύω || (visit) πηγαίνω, βλέπω, επισκέπτομαι ♦ vi (understand) αντιλαμβάνομαι ♦ n (bishop's) επισκοπή || **to ~ through** vt φροντίζω μέχρι τέλους, παρακολουθώ || **to ~ to** vt φροντίζω για || **to ~ off** vt συνοδεύω, ξεπροβοδίζω.

seed [si:d] n σπόρος || (grain) κόκκος, σπειρί || ~**ling** n νεαρό φυτό || ~**y** a (ill) αδιάθετος, τσακισμένος || (shabby) κουρελιασμένος.

seeing ['si:iŋ] cj: ~ (**that**) εφόσον, αφού, δεδομένου ότι.

seek [si:k] (irreg v) vt αναζητώ, ψάχνω, ζητώ.

seem [si:m] vi φαίνομαι, μοιάζω || ~**ingly** ad φαινομενικά, κατά τα φαινόμενα.

seen [si:n] pp of **see**.

seep [si:p] vi διαρρέω, περνώ από.

seesaw ['si:sɔ:] n (plank) τραμπάλα.

seethe [si:ð] vi (be agitated) αναταράσσομαι, βράζω.

segment ['segmənt] n τμήμα nt.

segregate ['segrigeit] vt απομονώνω, χωρίζω.

segregation [segri'geiʃən] n απομόνωση, χωρισμός.

seismic ['saizmik] a σεισμικός.

seize [si:z] vt αρπάζω, πιάνω || (take possession) κατάσχω || (understand) αντιλαμβάνομα, συλλαμβάνω || **to ~ up** vi (MECH) σφηνώνομαι, μαγκώνω, κολλώ.

seizure ['si:ʒə*] n (illness) απότομη προσβολή.

seldom ['seldəm] ad σπανίως, σπάνια.

select [si'lekt] a εκλεκτός, διαλεχτός ♦ vt εκλέγω, διαλέγω || ~**ion** n εκλογή, διαλογή, επιλογή || ~**ive** a εκλεκτικός || ~**or** n (person) επιλογέας, εκλέκτωρ m || (TECH) επιλογέας.

self [self] n εαυτός, το πρόσωπο, το άτομο || ~**-appointed** a αυτοδιορισμένος || ~**-assured** a επηρμένος, γεμάτος αυτοπεποίθηση || ~**-confidence** n αυτοπεποίθηση || ~**-conscious** a δειλός, ενσυνείδητος || ~**-contained** a αυτοτελής, ανεξάρτητος || (reserved) επιφυλακτικός || ~**-defence** n αυτόμυνα || ~**-evident** a αυταπόδεικτος || ~**-indulgent** a αυτεντρύφηλος, τρυφηλός || ~**-interest** n ιδιοτέλεια || ~**-ish** a εγωιστικός, ιδιοτελής || ~**-ishness** n εγωισμός, ιδιοτέλεια || ~**-lessly** ad αλτρουϊστικά || ~**-portrait** n αυτοπροσωπογραφία || ~**-reliant** a ανεξάρτητος || ~-respect n αυτοσεβασμός || ~-righteous a υποκριτικός || ~-satisfied a αυτάρεσκος, ικανοποιημένος από τον εαυτό του || ~-service a αυτοσερβίρισμα || ~-sufficient a αυτάρκης || ~-supporting a (FIN) αυτοσυντήρητος, αυτάρκης.

sell [sεl] (irreg v) vt πουλώ ♦ vi (COMM) πωλούμαι || ~er n πωλητής/τρια m/f|| ~ing price n τιμή πωλήσεως.

selves [sεlvz] pl of **self.**

semaphore ['sεməfɔ:*] n (system) σηματοφόρος.

semi ['sεmi] prefix ημι– || ~circle n ημικύκλιο || ~colon n άνω τελεία || ~-conscious a ημιαναίσθητος || ~detached house n οριζόντιος ιδιοκατοικία || ~final n ημιτελικός.

seminar ['sεmina:*] n σεμινάριο.

semitone ['sεmitəun] n (MUS) ημιτόνιο.

semolina [sεmə'li:nə] n σιμιγδάλι.

senate ['sεnit] n σύγκλητος f|| (US) γερουσία.

senator ['sεnitə*] n γερουσιαστής.

send [sεnd] (irreg v) vt πέμπω, στέλνω, αποστέλλω || (col: inspire) ενθουσιάζω, τρελαίνω || to ~ away vt απολύω, διώχνω || to ~ back vt στέλνω πίσω, επιστρέφω || to ~ for vt στέλνω να φωνάξω, καλώ || to ~ off vt (goods) αποστέλλω, στέλνω || (player) αποβάλλω || to ~ out vi (invitation) στέλνω || to ~ up vt (general) ανεβάζω, στέλνω, ανυψώνω || ~er n αποστολέας || ~-off n αποχαιρετισμός.

senile ['si:nail] a γεροντικός.

senility [sι'nιliti] n γεράματα ntpl, ξεμωράματα ntpl.

senior ['si:niə*] a μεγαλύτερος, πρεσβύτερος || (rank) αρχαιότερος, ανώτερος ♦ n πρεσβύτερος, γηραιότερος, μεγαλύτερος || (US) τελειόφοιτος/n m/f|| ~ity n αρχαιότητα (βαθμού).

sensation [sεn'seifən] n αίσθηση, αίσθημα nt|| (state of excitement) αίσθηση, εντύπωση || ~al a εντυπωσιακός.

sense [sεns] n αίσθηση || (understanding) λογική, λογικό || (meaning) έννοια, νόημα nt|| (feeling) (συν)αίσθημα nt ♦ vt (δι)αισθάνομαι || ~less a ανόητος, παράλογος || (unconscious) αναίσθητος.

sensibility [sεnsι'bιliti] n ευαισθησία, ευπάθεια.

sensible ['sεnsəbl] a λογικός.

sensitive ['sεnsitιv] a (+ to) ευαίσθητος, ευπαθής || (easily hurt) ευσυγκίνητος, εύθικτος.

sensitivity [sεnsι'tιviti] n ευαισθησία, ευπάθεια.

sensual ['sεnsjuəl] a αισθησιακός, σαρκικός, φιλόδονος.

sensuous ['sεnsjuəs] a ηδυπαθής, αισθησιακός.

sent [sεnt] pt, pp of **send.**

sentence ['sεntəns] n (GRAM) πρόταση || (LAW) απόφαση, ποινή.

sentiment ['sεntimənt] n αίσθημα nt, αισθηματικότητα || (thought) γνώμη, άποψη || ~al a αισθηματικός || ~ality n αισθηματισμός.

sentry ['sεntri] n σκοπός, φρουρός.

separate ['sεprit] a χωριστός ♦ ['sεpəreit] vt χωρίζω, ξεχωρίζω || ~ly ad ξεχωριστά.

separation [sεpə'reifən] n χωρισμός, διαχώριση.

September [sεp'tεmbə*] n Σεπτέμβριος.

septic ['sεptik] a σηπτικός.

sequel ['si:kwəl] n συνέπεια, αποτέλεσμα nt|| (continuation) συνέχεια.

sequence ['si:kwəns] n διαδοχή, συνέχεια, ακολουθία.

sequin ['si:kwin] n πούλι nt.

serenade [sεrə'neid] n σερενάτα ♦ vt κάνω σερενάτα.

serene [sə'ri:n] a γαλήνιος, ατάραχος || ~ly ad ήρεμα, γαλήνια.

serenity [sι'rεniti] n γαλήνη, ηρεμία.

sergeant ['sa:dʒənt] n λοχίας || (police) ενωμοτάρχης.

serial ['siəriəl] n ιστορία σε συνέχειες || ~ number n αύξοντας αριθμός || ~ize vt δημοσιεύω σε συνεχείες.

series ['siəriz] n σειρά.

serious ['siəriəs] a σοβαρός || ~ly ad σοβαρά || ~ness n σοβαρότητα.

sermon ['sə:mən] n κήρυγμα nt, ομιλία.

serrated [sε'reitid] a οδοντωτός, πριονωτός.

serum ['siərəm] n ορός.

servant ['sə:vənt] n υπηρέτης/έτρια m/f || see civil.

serve [sə:v] vt υπηρετώ || (do work of) εξυπηρετώ, εκτελώ || (supply) προμηθεύω ♦ vi (be useful) χρησιμεύω για || (in army) υπηρετώ || (wait at table, tennis) σερβίρω ♦ n (tennis) σερβίρισμα nt|| it ~s him right καλά να πάθει || to ~ out or up vt (food) σερβίρω, διανέμω.

service ['sə:vis] n υπηρεσία || (work done) εξυπηρέτηση || (government department) υπηρεσία || (civil etc) υπηρεσία, εργασία || (help) διάθεση, χρησιμότητα || (REL) λειτουργία || (set of dishes) σερβίτσιο || (tennis) σερβίς nt inv || (AUT: maintenance) συντήρηση, επισκευή ♦ vt (AUT, MECH) συντηρώ, επισκευάζω || the S~s npl (armed forces) τα όπλα ntpl, οι ένοπλες δυνάμεις fpl || ~able a εύχρηστος, ανθεκτικός, χρήσιμος || ~men npl (soldier etc) άντρες των ενόπλων δυνάμεων || ~ station n γκαράζ nt inv.

serviette [sə:vi'εt] n πετσέτα (φαγητού).

servile ['sə:vail] a δουλικός, δουλοπρεπής.

session ['sεfən] n συνεδρίαση, συνεδρία.

set [sεt] (irreg v) n (of things) σειρά, συλλογή || (RAD, TV) συσκευή || (tennis) γύρος, σέτ nt inv|| (group of people) ομάδα, κατηγορία, συντροφιά, κόσμος || (CINE) συσκευή || (THEAT) διάκοσμος, σκηνικό ♦ a (specified) καθωρισμένος || (determined) αποφασισμένος ♦ vt θέτω, τοποθετώ, βάζω || (arrange) κανονίζω || (adjust) ρυθμίζω, βάζω, κανονίζω || (exam) δίδω τα θέματα ♦ vi (of sun) δύω, βασιλεύω || (fix) σκληρύνομαι, σφίγγω, πιάνω || to ~ on fire καίω, πυρπολώ, βάζω φωτιά || to ~ free ελευθερώνω || to ~ going ξεκινώ || to ~ sail αποπλέω || to ~ about vt (task) αρχίζω || to ~ aside vt ξεχωρίζω, βάζω κατά μέρος, απορρίπτω || to ~ back vt (in time) επιβραδύνω, καθυστερώ || (cost) κοστίζω || to ~ off vi ξεκινώ, φεύγω ♦ vt (explode) εκτοξεύω, ρίχνω, εκπηγνύω || (show up well) εξαίρω, αναδεικνύω, τονίζω, υπογραμμίζω || to ~ out vi ξεκινώ, φεύγω ♦ vt (arrange) ρυθμίζω, κανονίζω, σιάζω || (state) (καθ)ορίζω || to ~ up vt (organization) ιδρύω, οργανώνω || ~back n (reverse) αποτυχία, ατυχία, αναποδιά.

settee [sε'ti:] n καναπές m.

setting ['sεtiŋ] n (scenery) τοποθεσία, πλαίσιο || (MUS) μελοποίηση, μουσική τραγουδιού.

settle ['sεtl] vt (MED: calm) καθησυχάζω, καταπραΰνω || (pay) εξοφλώ, πληρώνω || (agree) ρυθμίζω κανονίζω ♦ vi (also: ~ down) εγκαθίσταμαι || (person) σοβαρεύομαι || ~ment n (payment) εξόφληση || (colony) εποικισμός || ~r n άποικος.

setup ['sεtʌp] n (arrangement) τοποθέτηση, οργάνωση || (situation) κατάσταση.

seven ['sεvn] num επτά || ~teen num δεκαεπτά || ~th α έβδομος || ~ty num εβδομήντα.

sever ['sεvə*] vt κόβω || (fig) διακόπτω.

several ['sεvrəl] a διάφορος, ξεχωριστός ♦ pron μερικοί.

severance ['sεvərəns] n διαχωρισμός || (fig) (δια)κοπή.

severe [si'viə*] a αυστηρός, σκληρός || (serious) σοβαρός || (hard, rigorous) δριμύς, σκληρός, άγριος || (unadorned) αυστηρός, απέριττος, λιτός || ~ly ad αυστηρά, σκληρά.

severity [si'vεriti] n αυστηρότητα, σκληρότητα, δριμύτητα.

sew [səu] (irreg v) vti ράβω || to ~ up vt ράβω.

sewage ['sju:idʒ] n ακαθαρσίες ftpl υπονόμων, βρωμόνερα ntpl.

sewer ['sjuə*] n οχετός, υπόνομος.

sewing ['səuiŋ]n ράψιμο || ~ machine n ραπτομηχανή.

sewn [səun] pp of sew.

sex [sεks] n φύλο, σέξ nt inv|| (activity) γενετήσια ορμή || ~ act n συνουσία.

sexual ['sεksjuəl] α γενετήσιος, σεξουαλικός || ~ly ad σεξουαλικά.

sexy ['sεksi] α ελκυστικός, σεξουαλικός.

shabby ['ʃæbi] α κουρελιασμένος,

σαραβαλιασμένος || (mean) μικροπρεπής, αχρείας.

shack [ʃæk] καλύβα.

shackles ['ʃæklz] npl δεσμά, χειροπέδες fpl.

shade [ʃeid] n σκιά, ίσκιος || (for lamp) αμπαζούρ nt inv || (of colour) απόχρωση || (small quantity) ίχνος m, μικρή ποσότητα ♦ vt σκιάζω.

shadow ['ʃædəu] n σκιά, σκοτάδι ♦ vt (follow) παρακολουθώ || ~y α σκιερός, σκιασμένος || (dim) ασαφής, θαμπός.

shady ['ʃeidi] α σκιερός || (dubious) ύποπτος.

shaft [ʃɑ:ft] n κοντάρι, στέλεχος, λαβή || (of mine) φρέαρ nt || (of machine) άξονας, άτρακτος f || (of light) αχτίδα.

shaggy ['ʃægi] α τραχύς, τριχωτός.

shake [ʃeik] (irreg v) vt σείω, κουνώ, τινάζω || (fist etc) απειλώ με τη γροθιά μου || (rock) (συγ)κλονίζω, κουνώ, τραντάζω || (weaken) κλονίζω || (alarm) συγκλονίζω, αναστατώνω ♦ vi τρέμω, κλονίζομαι, τραντάζομαι ♦ n τίναγμα nt, κούνημα nt, δόνηση || to ~ off vt τινάζω || (fig) απαλλάσσομαι από || to ~ up vt (lit) ταράζω, κουνώ || (fig) ξυπνώ || ~-up n πρόχειρο πράμα.

shaky ['ʃeiki] α ασταθής, τρεμουλιαστός || (weak) κλονισμένος, αδύνατος.

shall [ʃæl] auxiliary v: I ~ go θα φύγω, θα πάω || you ~ do it! θα το κάμεις.

shallot [ʃə'lɔt] n μικρό κρεμμύδι.

shallow ['ʃæləu] α (lit) ρηχός || (fig) επιπόλαιος.

sham [ʃæm] n προσποίηση, απομίμηση, ψευτιά ♦ a προσποιητός, ψεύτικος.

shambles ['ʃæmblz] n sing χάος nt.

shame [ʃeim] n ντροπή || (disgrace) αίσχος nt || (pity) ντροπή, αμαρτία, κρίμα nt ♦ vt (humiliate) ντροπιάζω || what a ~! τι κρίμα! || ~faced a ντροπιασμένος || ~ful a ντροπιασμένος || ~less a αναίσχυντος, αδιάντροπος.

shampoo [ʃæm'pu:] n σαμπουάν nt inv ♦ vt λούζω (τα μαλλία μου).

shamrock ['ʃæmrɔk] n τριφύλλι.

shandy ['ʃændi] n (beer and lemonade) μπύρα με λεμονάδα.

shan't [ʃɑ:nt] = shall not || see shall.

shanty ['ʃænti] n καλύβα, παράγγα || ~ town n παραγγούπολη.

shape [ʃeip] n σχήμα nt, μορφή, φόρμα, καλούπι ♦ vt σχηματίζω, διαμορφώνω, διαπλάθω || to take ~ διαμορφούμαι, παίρνω μορφή || ~less a άμορφος, ακανόνιστος || ~ly a καλοσχηματισμένος, όμορφος.

share [ʃεə*] n (thing received) μερίδιο || (contribution) μετοχή, μερίδιο || (FIN) μετοχή, τίτλος, αξία ♦ vt μοιράζω, διανέμω || (in common) (συμ)μετέχω || ~holder n μέτοχος.

shark [ʃɑ:k] n (fish) σκυλόψαρο, καρχαρίας.

sharp [ʃɑ:p] a (razor, knife) κοφτερός || (distinct) ξεχωριστός, έντονος, καθαρός ||

(biting) δριμύς, διαπεραστικός ||
(quick-witted) οξύνους, έξυπνος ||
(unscrupulous) πονηρός, κατεργάρης ♦ n
(MUS) δίεση ♦ ad ακριβώς, εντονα,
καθαρά || **look ~!** κάνε γρήγορα!,
κουνήσου! || **~en** vt ακονίζω, τροχίζω,
ξεμυτίζω || **~ener** n ξύστρα || **~-eyed** a
που κόβει το μάτι του || **~ness** n κόψη ||
~-witted a οξύνους, ευφυής.

shatter ['ʃætə*] vt θρυμματίζω, σπάζω,
κάνω κομμάτια || *(fig)* συντρίβω, κλονίζω
♦ vi συντρίβομαι, σπάω.

shave [ʃeɪv] *(irreg v)* n ξύρισμα nt ♦ vt
ξυρίζω || *(fig)* περνώ ξυστά ♦ vi ξυρίζομαι
|| **~r** n *(ELEC)* ξυριστική μηχανή.

shaving ['ʃeɪvɪŋ] n *(action)* ξύρισμα nt ||
~s npl *(of wood etc)* ροκανίδια ntpl,
ρινίσματα ntpl || **~ brush** n πινέλο του
ξυρίσματος || **~ cream** n κρέμα
ξυρίσματος.

shawl [ʃɔːl] n σάλι.

she [ʃiː] pron αυτή ♦ a θηλυκός.

sheaf [ʃiːf] n δέσμη, δεμάτι.

shear [ʃɪə*] *(irreg v)* vt *(sheep etc)*
κουρεύω || **to ~ off** vt κόβω || **~s** npl *(for
hedge)* ψαλίδα.

sheath [ʃiːθ] n θήκη, κολεός, θηκάρι.

shed [ʃed] *(irreg v)* n υπόστεγο ♦ vt
αποβάλλω, βγάζω || *(pour out)* χύνω.

she'd [ʃiːd] = **she had, she would** ||
see **have, would.**

sheep [ʃiːp] n πρόβατο || **~dog** n
τσοπανόσκυλο || **~ish** a δειλός,
ντροπαλός || **~skin** n προβιά.

sheer [ʃɪə*] a καθαρός πραγματικός,
γνήσιος || *(steep)* κατακόρυφος,
απότομος || *(almost transparent)*
διαφανής, λεπτός ♦ ad τελείως, πλήρως,
απολύτως.

sheet [ʃiːt] n σεντόνι || *(thin piece)* έλασμα
nt, φύλλο, λαμαρίνα || *(paper)* φύλλο
κόλλα.

sheik(h) [ʃeɪk] n σεΐχης.

shelf [ʃelf] n ράφι.

she'll [ʃiːl] = **she will, she shall** ||
see **will, shall.**

shell [ʃel] n κέλυφος nt, τσόφλι, φλοιός ||
(explosive) οβίδα, βλήμα nt || *(of building)*
σκελετός ♦ vt ξεφλουδίζω || *(MIL)*
βομβαρδίζω.

shellfish ['ʃelfɪʃ] n *(ZOOL)* οστρακοειδές
nt || *(as food)* θαλασσινά ntpl.

shelter ['ʃeltə*] n καταφύγιο ||
(protection) προστασία ♦ vt
προφυλάσσω, προστατεύω, στεγάζω ♦
vi προφυλάσσομαι, φυλάγομαι || **~ed** a
(life) αποτραβηγμένος, περιορισμένος ||
(spot) προφυλαγμένος,
προστατευμένος.

shelve [ʃelv] vt *(put aside)* βάζω στο ράφι
|| **~s** npl of **shelf.**

shepherd ['ʃepəd] n ποιμένας, βοσκός
♦ vt *(guide)* οδηγώ, συνοδεύω || **~ess** n
βοσκοπούλα || **~'s pie** n κιμάς
σκεπασμένος με πουρέ και ψημένος στο
φούρνο.

sheriff ['ʃerɪf] n σερίφης.

sherry ['ʃerɪ] n σέρυ nt inv.

she's [ʃiːz] = **she is, she has** || *see*
be, have.

shield [ʃiːld] n ασπίδα, σκουτάρι ||
(protection) προστατευτικό κάλυμμα nt ♦
vt προασπίζω, προστατεύω || καλύπτω.

shift [ʃɪft] n *(change)* αλλαγή || *(group of
workers, period)* βάρδια ♦ vt μετατοπίζω,
μεταθέτω, μετακινώ || *(remove)* αλλάζω,
μεταβάλλω ♦ vi μετακινούμαι,
μετατοπίζομαι || **~y** a πονηρός,
ύπουλος.

shilling ['ʃɪlɪŋ] n *(old)* σελίνι.

shimmer ['ʃɪmə*] n ανταύγεια,
μαρμαρυγή ♦ vi σπιθοβολώ, λαμπυρίζω,
γυαλίζω.

shin [ʃɪn] n αντικνήμιο, καλάμι *(ποδιού)*.

shine [ʃaɪn] *(irreg v)* n *(gleam)* γυάλισμα
nt, στιλπνότητα, γυαλάδα ♦ vt *(polish)*
στίλβω, λουστράρω, γυαλίζω || *(torch)*
ακτινοβολώ, λάμπω ♦ vi λάμπω,
αστράφτω, γυαλίζω || *(excel)*
διακρίνομαι, ξεπροβάλλω.

shingle ['ʃɪŋgl] n ξυλοκέραμος,
ταβανοσάνιδο || *(on beach)* βότσαλα ntpl,
κροκάλες fpl || **~s** npl *(MED)* έρπης,
ζωστήρ m.

shiny ['ʃaɪnɪ] a λαμπερός, γυαλιστερός.

ship [ʃɪp] n πλοίο, σκάφος nt ♦ vt
επιβιβάζω, μπαρκάρω || *(transport as
cargo)* φορτώνω, αποστέλλω ||
~building n ναυπηγική || **~ment** n
φόρτωση || *(goods)* φορτίο, εμπόρευμα nt
|| **~per** n *(sender)* αποστολέας || **~ping** n
(act) φόρτωση || *(ships)* πλοία ntpl,
ναυτιλία || *(ships of country)* εμπορική
ναυτιλία || **~shape** a περίφημος,
εξαιρετικός || **~wreck** n ναυάγιο ||
~yard n ναυπηγείο.

shire ['ʃaɪə*] n κομητεία.

shirk [ʃɜːk] vt αποφεύγω, ξεφεύγω,
φυγοπονώ.

shirt [ʃɜːt] n *(man's shirt)* πουκάμισο.

shiver ['ʃɪvə*] n ρίγος nt, τρεμούλα ♦ vi
(with cold) τρέμω, τουρτουρίζω.

shoal [ʃəʊl] n *(of fish)* κοπάδι *(ψαριών)*.

shock [ʃɒk] n δόνηση, σύγκρουση,
τίναγμα nt || *(ELEC)* ηλεκτρικό σοκ nt inv,
ηλεκτροπληξία || *(emotional)*
συγκλονισμός, ταραχή || *(MED)*
καταπληξία, σοκ ♦ vt σκανδαλίζω,
σοκάρω || **~ absorber** n αποσβεστήρας
κρούσεων, αμορτισέρ nt inv || **~ing** a
σκανδαλώδης || συγκλονιστικός ||
~proof a *(watch)* προφυλαγμένος από
δόνηση.

shod [ʃɒd] pt, pp of **shoe.**

shoddiness ['ʃɒdɪnɪs] n κακή ποιότητα.

shoddy ['ʃɒdɪ] a κακής ποιότητος, της
πεντάρας.

shoe [ʃuː] *(irreg v)* n υπόδημα nt,
παπούτσι || *(of horse)* πέταλο ♦ vt
πεταλώνω *(άλογο)* || **~brush** n βούρτσα
των παπουτσιών || **~horn** n κόκκαλο
των παπουτσιών || **~lace** n κορδόνι ||
~shop n παπουτσάδικο
υποδηματοποιείο.

shone [ʃɒn] pt, pp of **shine**.

shook [ʃʊk] pt of **shake**.

shoot [ʃuːt] (irreg v) n (branch) βλαστός, βλαστάρι ♦ vt (gun) πυροβολώ, εκκενώνω || (kill) σκοτώνω || (film) τραβώ, γυρίζω (ταινία) ♦ vi (move swiftly) (εξ)ορμώ, τρέχω, πετώ || (let off gun) πυροβολώ, κτυπώ || **to ~ down** vt (plane) καταρρίπτω || **~ing** n (shots) πυροβολισμός, πόλεμος || (hunting) κυνήγι || **~ing star** n διάττων αστέρας.

shop [ʃɒp] n κατάστημα nt, μαγαζί || (workshop) εργαστήριο, μαγαζί nt ♦ vi (also: **go ~ping**) ψωνίζω || **~ assistant** n υπάλληλος m/f καταστήματος || **~keeper** n καταστηματάρχης, μικρομέπορος || **~lifter** n κλέφτης καταστημάτων || **~lifting** n κλοπή καταστημάτων || **~per** n πελάτης/τρια m/f, αγοραστής/άστρια m/f || **~ping** n αγορές fpl, ψώνια ntpl || **~ping bag** n τσάντα για τα ψώνια || **~ping centre**, **~ping center** (US) n αγορά, εμπορικό κέντρο || **~soiled** a στραπατσαρισμένος || **~ steward** n (industry) αντιπρόσωπος του συνδικάτου || **~ window** n προθήκη, βιτρίνα || see talk.

shore [ʃɔː*] n (of sea, lake) ακτή, παραλία ♦ vt: **to ~ up** υποστηρίζω, στηλώνω.

shorn [ʃɔːn] pp of **shear**.

short [ʃɔːt] a βραχύς, κοντός || (not tall) κοντός || (soon finished) βραχύς, σύντομος || (curt) απότομος, κοφτός || (in measure) λιποβαρής, ελλειπής, λειψός || (ELEC: short-circuit) βραχύς (βραχυκύκλωμα nt) ♦ ad απότομα || **~ of** εκτός ♦ vti (ELEC) βραχυκυκλώνω, βραχυκυκλούμαι || **to cut ~** τερματίζω απότομα, συντομεύω, διακόπτω || **to fall ~** πέφτω κοντά, δεν πετυχαίνω || **to stop ~** σταματώ ξαφνικά || **~age** n ανεπάρκεια, έλλειψη || **~bread** n είδος nt κέικ || **~-circuit** n βραχυκύκλωμα nt ♦ vi βραχυκυκλούμαι || **~coming** n ελάττωμα nt, ατέλεια, μειονέκτημα nt || **~ cut** n συντομώτερος δρόμος || **~en** vt μικραίνω, κονταίνω || **~hand** n στενογραφία || **~hand typist** n στενοδακτυλογράφος m/f || **~-lived** a βραχύβιος, εφήμερος || **~ly** ad (soon) προσεχώς, σύντομα, σε λίγο || **~ness** n βραχύτητα, κοντία || **~-sighted** a (lit) μυωπικός || (fig) μη προνοητικός, κοντόφθαλμος || **~ story** n διήγημα nt || **~-tempered** a απότομος, ευέξαπτος || **~-term** a (FIN) βραχυπρόθεσμος || **~wave** n (RAD) βραχύ κύμα nt.

shot [ʃɒt] pt, pp of **shoot** ♦ n (firing etc) πυροβολισμός, τουφεκιά || (person) σκοπευτής || (attempt) δοκιμή, προσπάθεια, απόπειρα || (injection) ένεση || (PHOT) λήψη φωτογραφίας || **like a ~** (very readily) αμέσως, πρόθυμα || **~gun** n κυνηγετικό όπλο.

should [ʃʊd] auxiliary v: **I ~ go now** πρέπει να φύγω τώρα || **he ~ be there now** πρέπει να έχει φθάσει τώρα || **I ~ like** θα ήθελα.

shoulder [ˈʃəʊldə*] n ώμος ♦ vt επωμίζομαι || **~ blade** n ωμοπλάτη.

shouldn't [ˈʃʊdnt] = **should not** || see **should**.

shout [ʃaʊt] n κραυγή, φωνή ♦ vt κραυγάζω ♦ vi κραυγάζω, φωνάζω || **~ing** n φωνές fpl, κραυγές fpl.

shove [ʃʌv] n ώθηση, σπρωξιά, σπρώξιμο ♦ vt σπρώχνω || **to ~ off** vi (NAUT) απωθώ || (fig, col) φεύγω, ξεκινώ.

shovel [ˈʃʌvl] n φτυάρι ♦ vt φτυαρίζω.

show [ʃəʊ] (irreg v) n επίδειξη, προβολή || (appearance) εμφάνιση, όψη || (exhibition) έκθεση, θέαμα nt || (THEAT, CINE) θέατρο, σινεμά nt inv, παράσταση ♦ vt δείχνω, οδηγώ || (demonstrate) παρουσιάζω, αποδεικνύω || (explain) δείχνω, εξηγώ || (give) δείχνω ♦ vi (be visible) εμφανίζομαι, φαίνομαι, ξεπροβάλλω || **to ~ in** vi πες να μπει || **to ~ out** vi συνοδεύω στην έξοδο || **to ~ off** vi (pej) επιδεικνύομαι, καμαρώνω ♦ vt (display) επιδεικνύω, δείχνω, διαφημίζω || **to ~ up** vi (appear) εμφανίζομαι, παρουσιάζομαι ♦ vt δείχνω || **~down** n αναμέτρηση, διακήρυξη προθέσεων.

shower [ˈʃaʊə*] n μπόρα || (stones etc) βροχή από πέτρες κτλ || (shower bath) ντούς m inv ♦ vt (fig only) δίνω άφθονα || **~y** a (weather) βροχερός.

showing [ˈʃəʊiŋ] n (of film) εμφάνιση, προβολή.

shown [ʃəʊn] pp of **show**.

show-off [ˈʃəʊɒf] n (col: person) κορδωμένος.

showroom [ˈʃəʊruːm] n αίθουσα εκθέσεων.

shrank [ʃræŋk] pt of **shrink**.

shrapnel [ˈʃræpnl] n βολιδοφόρο βλήμα nt.

shred [ʃred] n (generally pl) κομμάτι, λουρίδα, κουρέλι ♦ vt κομματιάζω, σχίζω σε λουρίδες || **in ~s** ξεσχισμένος, κουρελιασμένος.

shrewd [ʃruːd] a διορατικός, επιδέξιος || **~ness** n ευφυΐα, εξυπνάδα.

shriek [ʃriːk] n ξεφωνητό, στριγγλιά ♦ vti ξεφωνίζω, στριγγλίζω.

shrill [ʃril] a οξύς, διαπεραστικός.

shrimp [ʃrimp] n γαρίδα.

shrine [ʃraɪn] n λειψανοθήκη, βωμός, ιερός τόπος.

shrink [ʃriŋk] (irreg v) vi συστέλλομαι, μαζεύομαι ♦ vt (make smaller) ζαρώνω, συστέλλω, κάνω να μαζέψει || **~age** n συστολή, ζάρωμα, μάζεμα nt.

shrivel [ˈʃrivl] vti (also: **~ up**) μαραίνομαι, ζαρώνομαι, ξεραίνομαι.

shroud [ʃraʊd] n σάβανο ♦ vt σκεπάζω, καλύπτω.

Shrove Tuesday [ˈʃrəʊvˈtjuːzdi] n Καθαρή Τρίτη.

shrub [ʃrʌb] n θάμνος, χαμόδεντρο || **~bery** n θαμνώνας, λόγγος.

shrug [ʃrʌg] n σήκωμα nt των ώμων || **to ~ off** vt αψηφώ, απορρίπτω.

shrunk [ʃrʌŋk] pp of **shrink**.

shudder ['ʃʌdə*] n ρίγος nt, φρικίαση, τρεμούλα ♦ vi τρέμω.

shuffle ['ʃʌfl] n (CARDS) ανακάτεμα nt (τράπουλας) ♦ vt ανακατεύω ♦ vi σέρνω τα πόδια.

shun [ʃʌn] vt αποφεύγω.

shush [ʃuʃ] excl (col) σουτ!

shut [ʃʌt] (irreg v) vt κλείνω ♦ vi κλείομαι, κλείνω || **to ~ down** vti κλείνω, σταματώ εργασίες || **to ~ off** vt (supply) διακόπτω, αποκόπτω, αποκλείω || **to ~ up** vi (keep quiet) σωπαίνω, βουλώνω ♦ vt (close) κλείνω καλά, κλειδώνω || (silence) αποστομώνω, κλείνω το στόμα || ~ **up!** σκασμός! || **~ter** n παραθυρόφυλλο, παντζούρι || (of camera) φωτοφράκτης.

shuttlecock ['ʃʌtlkɒk] n φτερωτή σφαίρα, βολάν nt inv.

shy [ʃaɪ] a ντροπαλός, δειλός || **~ly** ad ντροπαλά, δειλά || **~ness** n δειλία, ντροπαλότητα.

Siamese [saɪə'mi:z] a: **~ cat** Σιαμαία γάτα.

sick [sɪk] a ασθενής, άρρωστος || (inclined to vomit) έχω τάση προς εμετό || (disgusting) αηδιαστικός, σιχαμερός || **~ bay** n νοσοκομείο πλοίου || **~en** vt αρρωσταίνω, αηδιάζω ♦ vi αηδιάζω || **~ening** a (fig) αηδιαστικός.

sickle ['sɪkl] n δρεπάνι.

sick leave ['sɪkliːv] n αναρρωτική άδεια.

sickly ['sɪklɪ] a αρρωστιάρης, ωχρός, ασθενικός || (nauseating) που προκαλεί αναγούλα.

sickness ['sɪknɪs] n ασθένεια, αρρώστια, νόσος f || (vomiting) ναυτία, αναγούλα, εμετός.

sick pay ['sɪkpeɪ] n επίδομα nt ασθενείας.

side [saɪd] n πλευρά, πλευρό, μέρος nt, μεριά || (of body) πλευρά, μεριά || (of lake) όχθη || (aspect) πλευρά, όψη, άποψη ♦ a (door, entrance) πλαγία (είσοδος f), πλαϊνή (είσοδος f) ♦ vi: **to ~ with** πάω με, παίρνω το μέρος του || **by the ~ of** στο πλευρό του, σε σύγκριση με || **on all ~s** από παντού || **to take ~s (with)** υποστηρίζω, μεροληπτώ || **~board** n μπουφές m inv || **~boards, ~burns** npl (whiskers) φαβορίτες fpl || **~ effect** n (MED) παρενέργεια || **~light** n (AUT) πλευρικός φανός || **~line** n (RAIL) δευτερεύουσα γραμμή || (fig: hobby) πάρεργο || **~ road** n πάροδος f || **~ show** n δευτερεύον θέαμα nt || **~track** vt (fig) παραμερίζω || **~walk** n (US) πεζοδρόμιο || **~ways** ad πλάγια, λοξά.

siding ['saɪdɪŋ] n πλευρική διακλάδωση.

sidle ['saɪdl] vi: **to ~ up** πλησιάζω δειλά και πλάγια.

siege [si:dʒ] n πολιορκία.

sieve [sɪv] n κόσκινο ♦ vt κοσκινίζω.

sift [sɪft] vt κοσκινίζω || (examine) ξεχωρίζω, εξονυχίζω.

sigh [saɪ] n αναστεναγμός ♦ vi (ανα)στενάζω.

sight [saɪt] n όραση || (scene) θέα, θέαμα nt || (of rifle) κλισιοσκόπιο, στόχαστρο ♦ vt αντικρύζω, βλέπω, παρατηρώ || **in ~** φαίνομαι, γίνομαι ορατός || **out of ~** δε φαίνομαι || **~seeing** n επίσκεψη αξιοθεάτων || **to go ~seeing** επισκέπτομαι τα αξιοθέατα.

sign [saɪn] n (with hand) νεύμα nt, νόημα nt || (indication) ένδειξη, σημάδι || (notice, road etc) σήμα nt, ταμπέλα, πινακίδα || (written symbol) σημείο, σημάδι ♦ vt υπογράφω || **to ~ off** vi ξεμπαρκάρω || **to ~ up** vti (MIL) κατατάσσομαι.

signal ['sɪgnl] n σύνθημα nt, σημείο, σήμα nt ♦ vt σηματοδοτώ, στέλνω με σήματα.

signature ['sɪgnətʃə*] n υπογραφή.

significance [sɪg'nɪfɪkəns] n σημασία, έννοια, νόημα nt || (importance) σπουδαιότητα, σημαντικότητα.

significant [sɪg'nɪfɪkənt] a με σημασία, σημαντικός || (important) σημαντικός, σπουδαίος, σημαίνων || **~ly** ad με έννοια, με σημασία.

signify ['sɪgnɪfaɪ] vt σημαίνω, εννοώ || (express) είμαι ένδειξη, (εκ)δηλώνω.

sign language ['saɪnlæŋgwɪdʒ] n γλώσσα με νεύματα.

signpost ['saɪnpəʊst] n σήμα nt κυκλοφορίας, πινακίδα της τροχαίας.

silence ['saɪləns] n σιγή, σιωπή, ησυχία ♦ vt σωπαίνω, ησυχάζω || **~r** n σιγαστήρας, σιλανσιέ nt inv.

silent ['saɪlənt] a σιωπηλός, αθόρυβος, σιγαλός || (saying nothing) άφωνος, αμίλητος.

silhouette [sɪluː'et] n (outline) σιλουέτα ♦ vt διαγράφομαι σα σιλουέτα.

silk [sɪlk] n μετάξι ♦ a μεταξωτός || **~y** a μεταξένιος, απαλός, στιλπνός.

silliness ['sɪlɪnɪs] n μωρία, ανοησία, χαζομάρα.

silly ['sɪlɪ] a ανόητος, μωρός.

silt [sɪlt] n βόρβορος, λάσπη.

silver ['sɪlvə*] n άργυρος, ασήμι ntpl || (coins) αργυρά νομίσματα ntpl || (objects) ασημικά ntpl ♦ a αργυρός, ασημένιος || **~ paper** n ασημόχαρτο || **~-plated** a επάργυρος || **~smith** n αργυροχόος || **~y** a ασημένιος.

similar ['sɪmɪlə*] a (+ to) όμοιος (με) || **~ity** n ομοιότητα || **~ly** ad παρόμοια, όμοια.

simile ['sɪmɪlɪ] n παρομοίωση.

simmer ['sɪmə*] vi σιγοβράζω.

simple ['sɪmpl] a (easy) απλός, εύκολος || (natural) απλός, απλοϊκός || (plain) απλός, απλοϊκός || (of one kind) απλός || (weak-minded) αφελής, μωρόπιστος || **~-minded** a αφελής, απλοϊκός.

simplicity [sɪm'plɪsɪtɪ] n απλότητα.

simplify ['sɪmplɪfaɪ] vt απλουστεύω, απλοποιώ.

simulation [sɪmju'leɪʃən] n (imitation) απομίμηση, προσποίηση.

simultaneous [sɪməl'teɪnɪəs] a

ταυτόχρονος || ~ly ad ταυτόχρονα, σύγχρονα με.

sin [sɪn] n αμάρτημα nt, αμαρτία ♦ vi αμαρτάνω.

since [sɪns] ad έκτοτε, από τότε ♦ prep από ♦ cj (time) αφότου, από τότε που || (because) αφού, εφόσον.

sincere [sɪn'sɪə*] a ειλικρινής || ~ly ad ειλικρινά.

sincerity [sɪn'serɪtɪ] n ειλικρίνεια.

sinful ['sɪnful] a αμαρτωλός.

sing [sɪŋ] (irreg v) vt (song) τραγουδώ ♦ vi (gen) τραγουδώ || (bird) κελαηδώ || (ears) βουΐζω.

singe [sɪndʒ] vt τσουρουφλίζω, καψαλίζω.

singer ['sɪŋə*] n αοιδός m/f, τραγουδιστής/ίστρια m/f.

singing ['sɪŋɪŋ] n τραγούδι nt.

single ['sɪŋgl] a μόνος, μοναδικός || (bed, room) μονό (κρεββάτι, δωμάτιο) || (unmarried) άγαμος || (ticket) απλό (εισιτήριο) || (one part) απλός, ένας ♦ n (ticket) απλό εισιτήριο || ~s npl (tennis) απλό παιχνίδι, σίγκλ nt inv || to ~ out vt διαλέγω, επιλέγω, ξεχωρίζω || in ~ file κατ' άνδρα, στη γραμμή, ένας-ένας || ~-handed a ολομόναχος, αβοήθητος, μόνος || ~-minded a που έχει ένα μόνο σκοπό || ~-sided disk n (COMPUT) δίσκος μιας όψεως.

singlet ['sɪŋglɪt] n φανελίτσα.

singular ['sɪŋgjulə*] a ενικός || (odd) παράξενος, σπάνιος, μοναδικός ♦ n (GRAM) ενικός αριθμός.

sinister ['sɪnɪstə*] a απαίσιος, δυσοίωνος, μοχθηρός.

sink [sɪŋk] (irreg v) n νεροχύτης ♦ vt (put under) καταβυθίζω, βουλιάζω || (dig) σκάβω, ανοίγω ♦ vi (fall slowly) καταβυθίζομαι, βουλιάζω, καθίζω || to ~ in vi (news etc) χαράσσομαι στο μυαλό || with ~ing heart με σφιγμένη καρδιά.

sinner ['sɪnə*] n αμαρτωλός.

sinus ['saɪnəs] n (ANAT) κόλπος.

sip [sɪp] n ρουφηξιά, γουλιά ♦ vt πίνω γουλιά-γουλιά, ρουφώ.

siphon ['saɪfən] n σιφόνι || to ~ off vt αναρροφώ, σιφωνίζω.

sir [sɜː*] n κύριε || (title) κύριος || **yes S~** μάλιστα, κύριε.

siren ['saɪərən] n σειρήνα.

sirloin ['sɜːloɪn] n κόντρα φιλέτο.

sister ['sɪstə*] n αδελφή || (MED) αρχινοσοκόμος || (nun) μοναχή, καλογριά, αδελφή || ~-in-law n κουνιάδα, νύφη.

sit [sɪt] (irreg v) vi κάθομαι || (at session) συνεδριάζω ♦ vt (exam) δίνω εξετάσεις, εξετάζομαι || to ~ tight δεν το κουνώ, βάζω τα δυνατά μου || to ~ down vi καθόμαι || to ~ up vi (after lying) ανασηκώνομαι || (at night) αγρυπνώ, ξενυχτώ.

site [saɪt] n τοποθεσία, θέση ♦ vt τοποθετώ, εγκαθιστώ.

sit-in ['sɪtɪn] n (demonstration) καταλαμβάνω σαν ένδειξη διαμαρτυρίας.

sitting ['sɪtɪŋ] n συνεδρίαση || ~ room n σαλόνι.

situated ['sɪtjueɪtɪd] a κείμενος, ευρισκόμενος.

situation [sɪtju'eɪʃən] n (state of affairs) κατάσταση || (place) τοποθεσία, θέση || (post) θέση, εργασία, δουλειά.

six [sɪks] num έξι || ~teen num δεκαέξι || ~th a έκτος || ~ty num εξήντα.

size [saɪz] n μέγεθος, διάσταση, έκταση, όγκος || (glue) κόλλα || (of clothing) νούμερο || to ~ up vt (assess) εκτιμώ (το μέγεθος), σχηματίζω γνώμη για || ~able a αρκετά μεγάλος, μεγαλούτσικος.

sizzle ['sɪzl] n σφύριγμα nt, τσιτσίρισμα nt ♦ vi τσιτσιρίζω, σφυρίζω.

skate [skeɪt] n πέδιλο, πατίνι ♦ vi πατινάρω, παγοδρομώ || ~r n πατινέρ m/f inv, παγοδρόμος.

skating ['skeɪtɪŋ] n: to go ~ πηγαίνω για πατινάζ || ~ rink n παγοδρόμιο, αίθουσα πατινάζ.

skeleton ['skelɪtn] n σκελετός.

skeptic ['skeptɪk] n (US) = **sceptic**.

sketch [sketʃ] n σκαρίφημα nt, σκιαγραφία || (play) σκίτσο, σκέτς nt inv ♦ vt σκιαγραφώ, σκιτσάρω || ~book n σημειωματάριο || ~ pad n καρνέ nt inv για σκίτσα || ~y a ατελής, ασαφής, ακαθόριστος.

skewer ['skjuə*] n σούβλα.

ski [skiː] n σκι ♦ vi κάνω σκι || ~ boot n παπούτσι του σκι.

skid [skɪd] n (skid-pan) τροχοπέδη ♦ vi γλιστρώ πλαγίως, ντεραπάρω.

skidmark ['skɪdmɑːk] n ίχνη ntpl ντεραπαρίσματος.

skier ['skiːə*] n σκιέρ m/f inv.

skiing ['skiːɪŋ] n: to go ~ πάω για σκι.

skijump ['skiːdʒʌmp] n πήδημα nt με σκι.

skilful ['skɪlful] a ικανός, επιδέξιος, επιτήδειος.

skill [skɪl] n ικανότητα, επιδεξιότητα || ~ed a επιδέξιος || (trained) ειδικευμένος.

skim [skɪm] vt ξαφρίζω, βγάζω || (read) ξεφυλλίζω || (glide over) περνώ ξυστά.

skimp [skɪmp] vt τσιγγουνεύομαι || (do carelessly) εκτελώ γρήγορα και επιπόλαια || ~y a (work, dress) ανεπαρκής || (meal) φτωχός.

skin [skɪn] n δέρμα nt, πετσί, τομάρι || (peel, rind) φλούδι, φλούδα || (on milk) πέτσα ♦ vt γδέρνω, ξεφλουδίζω || ~-deep a επιπόλαιος, επιφανειακός || ~-diving n υποβρύχιο κολύμπι || ~ny a αδύνατος, κοκκαλιάρης, τσίρος || ~tight a (dress etc) (φόρεμα) εφαρμοστό.

skip [skɪp] n (ανα)πήδημα nt, σκίρτημα nt ♦ vi σκιρτώ, πηδώ, πετάγομαι ♦ vt παραλείπω, πηδώ.

ski pants ['skiːpænts] npl παντελόνι του σκι.

skipper ['skɪpə*] n (NAUT, SPORT) καπετάνιος.

skipping rope ['skɪpɪŋrəʊp] n σχοινάκι.

skirmish ['skɜːmɪʃ] n αψιμαχία.

skirt [skɜːt] n φούστα ♦ vt περιτρέχω, φέρνω βόλτα.

skit [skɪt] n ευθυμογράφημα nt, παρωδία, νούμερο.

skittle ['skɪtl] n (one pin) τσούνι || ~s n (game) τσούνια.

skull [skʌl] n κρανίο.

skunk [skʌŋk] n μεφίτη, είδος ασβού.

sky [skaɪ] n ουρανός || ~-blue a ανοιχτό μπλε || ~ blue n ουρανί (χρώμα) || ~light n φεγγίτης || ~scraper n ουρανοξύστης.

slab [slæb] n πλάκα.

slack [slæk] a χαλαρός, λάσκος || (slow, dull) πεσμένος, νεκρή (εποχή) || (careless) αμελής, αδρανής ♦ vi ατονώ, τεμπελιάζω ♦ n (in rope etc) χαλαρότητα || ~s npl σπορ πανταλόνι || ~en (also: ~en off) vi χαλαρούμαι, μειούμαι, πέφτω ♦ vt χαλαρώνω, μετριάζω, επιβραδύνω, λασκάρω.

slag [slæg] n σκουριά || ~ heap n σωρός σκουριάς.

slam [slæm] n κρότος, κτύπημα nt πόρτας ♦ vt (door) κλείνω απότομα, κτυπώ || (throw down) πετάω με δύναμη ♦ vi κλείνω με κρότο.

slander ['slɑːndə*] n κακολογία, διαβολή, συκοφαντία ♦ vt συκοφαντώ, κακολογώ, διαβάλλω || ~ous a συκοφαντικός.

slang [slæŋ] n μάγκικη γλώσσα, λαϊκό, ιδίωμα nt.

slant [slɑːnt] n (lit) κλίση, γέρσιμο || (fig) άποψη, αντίληψη ♦ vti κλίνω, γέρνω || ~ing a λοξός, πλάγιος.

slap [slæp] n κτύπημα nt, χαστούκι, μπάτσος, καρπαζιά ♦ vt ραπίζω, μπατσίζω, καρπαζώνω ♦ ad (directly) κατευθείαν || ~dash ad ξένοιαστα, απρόσεκτα || ~stick n (comedy) φάρσα.

slash [slæʃ] n δυνατό κτύπημα nt, σχίσιμο ♦ vt κόβω, σχίζω, πετσοκόβω.

slate [sleɪt] n σχιστόλιθος || (piece of slate) αβάκιο, πλάκα ♦ vt (criticize) επικρίνω, κουρελιάζω.

slaughter ['slɔːtə*] n σφαγή, σφάξιμο ♦ vt σφάζω.

Slav [slɑːv] n (person) Σλάβος/α m/f ♦ a σλαβικός.

slave [sleɪv] n σκλάβος, δούλος ♦ vi δουλεύω σκληρά, μοχθώ || ~ry n δουλεία, σκλαβιά.

slavish ['sleɪvɪʃ] a δουλικός || ~ly ad δουλικά.

sledge [sledʒ] n έλκηθρο || ~hammer n βαριά, μεγάλο σφυρί.

sleek [sliːk] a λείος, απαλός, προσποιητός.

sleep [sliːp] (irreg v) n ύπνος ♦ vi κοιμούμαι, πλαγιάζω || to go to ~ αποκοιμούμαι || to ~ in vi (late) ξυπνώ αργά || ~er n υπναράς || (RAIL)

κλινάμαξα || ~ily ad κοιμισμένα || ~iness n υπνηλία, νυσταγμός, νύστα ||~ing bag n σάκκος ύπνου || ~ing car n κλινάμαξα, βαγκόν-λι nt inv || ~ing pill n υπνωτικό χάπι || ~lessness n αϋπνία, αγρυπνία || ~walker n υπνοβάτης/άτρια m/f || ~y a νυσταλέος, νυσταγμένος.

sleet [sliːt] n χιονόνερο.

sleeve [sliːv] n μανίκι || ~less a (garment) χωρίς μανίκια.

sleigh [sleɪ] n έλκηθρο.

sleight [slaɪt] n: ~ of hand ταχυδακτυλουργία.

slender ['slendə*] a λεπτός, λιγνός || (small) ισχνός, ασθενής.

slept [slept] pt, pp of **sleep**.

slice [slaɪs] n (of bread) φέτα || (of cake, cheese etc) κομμάτι ♦ vt τεμαχίζω, κόβω σε φέτες.

slick [slɪk] a (smart) γλυστερός, δόλιος, επιτήδειος.

slid [slɪd] pt, pp of **slide**.

slide [slaɪd] (irreg v) n τσουλήθρα, ολισθητήριο, στίβος || (PHOT: transparency) διαφάνεια, σλάιντ nt inv || (brooch) τσιμπιδάκι || (fall in prices) πτώση τιμών ♦ vt παρακάμπτω, ξεφεύγω ♦ vi γλυστρώ.

sliding ['slaɪdɪŋ] a (door) συρτή (πόρτα).

slight [slaɪt] a λεπτός || (trivial) ελαφρός, ασήμαντος || (small) μικροκαμωμένος, μικρούλης ♦ n υποτίμηση, περιφρόνηση ♦ vt (offend) προσβάλλω, θίγω || ~ly ad ελαφρά, κάπως, λιγάκι.

slim [slɪm] a λεπτός, μικρός ♦ vi κάνω δίαιτα.

slime [slaɪm] n λάσπη, βούρκος.

slimming ['slɪmɪŋ] n αδυνάτισμα nt.

slimy ['slaɪmɪ] a βορβορώδης, γλοιώδης.

sling [slɪŋ] (irreg v) n (bandage) ανωμίτης, κρεμαστάρι ♦ vt εκσφενδονίζω, ρίχνω.

slip [slɪp] n (slipping) ολίσθημα nt, γλύστρημα nt || (petticoat) μισοφόρι || (of paper) φύλλο, χαρτί ♦ vt γλυστρώ αθόρυβα, μπαίνω || (escape from) ξεφεύγω από ♦ vi (lose balance) γλυστρώ || (move smoothly) κινούμαι αθόρυβα || (make mistake) κάνω γκάφα, σφάλλω || (decline) παρεκτρέπομαι, παραστρατώ || to ~ away vi γλυστρώ, φεύγω απαρατήρητα || to ~ in vt βάζω, χώνω || to ~ out vi βγαίνω (κρυφά).

slipper ['slɪpə*] n παντούφλα.

slippery ['slɪpərɪ] a ολισθηρός, γλυστερός || (tricky) πανούργος, πονηρός.

slipshod ['slɪpʃɒd] a ακατάστατος, απρόσεκτος.

slip-up ['slɪpʌp] n (mistake) σφάλμα nt, γκάφα.

slipway ['slɪpweɪ] n ναυπηγική κλίνη.

slit [slɪt] (irreg v) n σχίσιμο, σχισμή ♦ vt κόβω, σχίζω, σχίζομαι.

slither ['slɪðə*] vi σέρνομαι, γλιστρώ.

slob [slɒb] n (col: unpleasant person) ατζαμής.

slog [slɒg] n (great effort) αγγαρεία, βαρειά δουλειά ♦ vi (work hard) δουλεύω σκληρά.

slogan ['sləʊgən] n (catchword) σύνθημα nt.

slop [slɒp] vi ξεχειλίζω, χύνομαι ♦ vt χύνω.

slope [sləʊp] n κατηφοριά, πλαγιά || (slant) κλίση ♦ vi: to ~ down κατηφορίζω || to ~ up vi ανηφορίζω.

sloping ['sləʊpɪŋ] a λοξός, πλάγιος.

sloppy ['slɒpɪ] a λασπωμένος, λασπώδης || (untidy) πρόχειρος, ακατάστατος || (weak, silly) άτονος, σαχλός.

slot [slɒt] n σχισμή, χαραμάδα ♦ vt: to ~ in βάζω, τοποθετώ || ~ machine n αυτόματος πωλητής || μηχάνημα τυχερών παιχνιδιών.

slouch [slaʊtʃ] vi κινούμαι αδέξια.

slovenly ['slʌvnlɪ] a ακατάστατος, απρόσεκτος.

slow [sləʊ] a βραδύς, αργός || (of clock) πάω, πίσω || (stupid) βραδύνους, χοντροκέφαλος ♦ ad σιγά, αργά || '~' (roadsign) 'αργά' || to ~ down vi επιβραδύνω, μειώνω, κόβω (ταχύτητα) ♦ vt επιβραδύνω || to ~ up vi σταματώ, φρενάρω ♦ vt επιβραδύνω || ~ly ad σιγά, αργά || in ~ motion σε αργό ρυθμό, ρελαντί.

sludge [slʌdʒ] n λάσπη, βούρκος.

slug [slʌg] n γυμνοσάλιαγκας || (bullet) μικρή σφαίρα || ~gish a αδρανής, τεμπέλης, νωθρός || ~gishly ad νωθρά, τεμπέλικα || ~gishness n νωθρότητα, βραδύτητα.

sluice [sluːs] n υδροφράκτης, φράγμα nt.

slum [slʌm] n φτωχογειτονιά.

slumber ['slʌmbə*] n γαλήνιος ύπνος.

slump [slʌmp] n πτώση, ελάττωση ζητήσεως ♦ vi πέφτω απότομα.

slung [slʌŋ] pt, pp of sling.

slur [slɜː*] n βιαστική προφορά, τραύλισμα nt || (insult) στίγμα nt προσβολή ♦ vt (also: ~ over) κακοπροφέρω, τραυλίζω.

slush [slʌʃ] n λασπωμένο χιόνι || ~y a (lit) λασπωμένος || (fig: sentimental) σαχλός, γλυκανάλατος.

slut [slʌt] n τσούλα, παλιοθήλυκο.

sly [slaɪ] a πονηρός, πανούργος, ύπουλος.

smack [smæk] n (slap) κτύπημα nt, χαστούκι, μπάτσος ♦ vt (slap) ραπίζω, καρπαζώνω || to ~ one's lips κτυπώ τα χείλη.

small [smɔːl] a μικρός, λίγος || ~holding n μικρό κτήμα nt || ~ hours npl νυκτερινές ώρες fpl || ~ish a μάλλον μικρός, μικρούτσικος || ~pox n ευλογιά, βλογιά || ~ talk n φλυαρία.

smart [smɑːt] a (well-dressed) κομψός, μοντέρνος || (clever) έξυπνος, επιδέξιος ||

(sharp, quick) σβέλτος, γρήγορος, ζωηρός ♦ vi πονώ, τσούζω, υποφέρω || to ~en up vi ζωηρεύω, κάνω κέφι || κομψεύομαι ♦ vt επισπεύδω.

smash [smæʃ] n (collision) σύγκρουση ♦ vt τσακίζω, θρυμματίζω, κομματιάζω || (destroy) καταστρέφω, συντρίβω ♦ vi θραύομαι, κομματιάζομαι || ~ing a (col) σπουδαίος, περίφημος.

smattering ['smætərɪŋ] n επιπόλαια γνώση, πασάλειμα nt.

smear [smɪə*] n κηλίδα, λεκές m || επίχρισμα nt ♦ vt λερώνω, μουντζουρώνω.

smell [smɛl] (irreg v) n όσφρηση || (odour) οσμή, μυρωδιά ♦ vt (breathe in) μυρίζω vi μυρίζω, παίρνω μυρωδιά || (give out smell) μυρίζω, βρωμάω || ~y a (unpleasant) δύσοσμος, βρωμερός.

smile [smaɪl] n χαμόγελο ♦ vi χαμογελώ.

smiling ['smaɪlɪŋ] a χαμογελαστός, γελαστός.

smirk [smɜːk] n ψεύτικο χαμόγελο ♦ vi χαμογελώ ψεύτικα.

smith [smɪθ] n σιδηρουργός, σιδεράς || ~y ['smɪðɪ] n σιδηρουργείο, σιδεράδικο.

smock [smɒk] n μπλούζα, φόρμα.

smoke [sməʊk] n καπνός, καπνίλα || (tobacco) κάπνισμα nt, τσιγάρο ♦ vt (puff) καπνίζω || (dry food) καπνίζω ♦ vi αναδίδω καπνούς, καπνίζω || (of cigarette) καπνίζω || ~d a (bacon etc) καπνιστός || ~r n (person) καπνιστής || (RAIL) όχημα nt καπνιστών.

smoking ['sməʊkɪŋ] n κάπνισμα nt || 'no ~' (sign) 'απαγορεύεται το κάπνισμα'.

smoky ['sməʊkɪ] a γεμάτος καπνό, καπνισμένος.

smolder ['sməʊldə*] vi (US) = smoulder.

smooth [smuːð] a (in consistency) απαλός || (wine) γλυκόπιοτος || (movement) ομαλός, μαλακός, αθόρυβος || (person) γλυκομίλητος, γαλήφης ♦ vt (also: ~ out) λειαίνω, εξομαλύνω, ισιώνω.

smother ['smʌðə*] vt πνίγω, καταπνίγω.

smoulder ['sməʊldə*] vi σιγοκαίω, υποβόσκω.

smudge [smʌdʒ] n κηλίδα, λεκές m, βρωμιά ♦ vt λεκιάζω, λερώνω, βρωμίζω.

smug [smʌg] a αυτάρεσκος, καμαρωτός.

smuggle ['smʌgl] vt κάνω λαθρεμπόριο, περνώ λαθραία || ~r n λαθρέμπορος, κοντραμπαντζής.

smuggling ['smʌglɪŋ] n λαθρεμπόριο, κοντραμπάντο.

smutty ['smʌtɪ] a (fig: obscene) αισχρός, βρώμικος, πρόστυχος.

snack [snæk] n ελαφρό φαγητό, κολατσό || ~ bar n σνακ-μπαρ nt inv.

snag [snæg] n (obstacle) εμπόδιο, κώλυμα nt || (in stocking) τράβηγμα nt κλωστής.

snail [sneɪl] n σαλιγκάρι.

snake [sneɪk] n φίδι.

snap [snæp] n (sound) ψαλιδιά, κρακ nt inv, ξηρός κρότος || (photograph) στιγμιότυπο, ενσταντανέ nt inv, φωτογραφία ♦ a βιαστικός || (unexpected) απροσδόκητος ♦ vt (make sound) κροταλίζω || (break) θραύω, σπάζω, τσακίζω || (photograph) φωτογραφίζω, τραβώ, πέρνω ♦ vi (break) σπάω || to ~ off vt (break) σπάω || to ~ up vt αρπάζω, βουτώ || ~py a δηκτικός, απότομος, ζωηρός || ~shot n φωτογραφία ενσταντανέ.

snare [snɛə*] n παγίδα ♦ vt παγιδεύω, πιάνω.

snarl [snɑːl] n γρυλισμός, μούγγρισμα nt ♦ vi (also person) γρυλίζω.

snatch [snætʃ] n άρπαγμα nt || (small amount) κομμάτι ♦ vt αρπάζω, βουτώ.

sneak [sniːk] vi κινούμαι κρυφά.

sneer [snɪə*] n καγχασμός, σαρκασμός ♦ vi κοροϊδεύω, σαρκάζω, χλευάζω.

sneeze [sniːz] n φτέρνισμα nt ♦ vi φτερνίζομαι.

sniff [snɪf] n εισπνοή, ρούφηγμα nt ♦ vi ξεφυσώ, είμαι συναχωμένος ♦ vt (smell) μυρίζω, ρουφώ.

snigger ['snɪgə*] n πνιχτό γέλιο, πονηρό γέλιο ♦ vi κρυφογελώ, ξερογελώ.

snip [snɪp] n ψαλίδισμα nt, κομματάκι || (bargain) ευκαιρία, καλή δουλειά ♦ vt ψαλιδίζω, κόβω.

sniper ['snaɪpə*] n (marksman) ελεύθερος σκοπευτής.

snippet ['snɪpɪt] n κομματάκι, απόσπασμα nt.

snivelling ['snɪvlɪŋ] a (whimpering) κλαψιάρικος.

snob [snɒb] n σνόμπ m inv, ψωροπερήφανος/η m/f || ~bery n σνομπισμός || ~bish a σνόμπ, φαντασμένος, ποζάτος.

snooker ['snuːkə*] n είδος nt μπιλιάρδο.

snoop [snuːp] vi: to ~ about χώνω τη μύτη, παραφυλάω.

snooty ['snuːtɪ] a (col: snobbish) υπερόπτης, ψηλομύτης.

snooze [snuːz] n υπνάκος ♦ vi παίρνω έναν υπνάκο, μισοκοιμάμαι.

snore [snɔː*] vi ροχαλίζω.

snorkel ['snɔːkl] n αναπνευστικός σωλήνας.

snort [snɔːt] n φρίμασμα nt, ξεφύσημα nt, ρουθούνισμα nt ♦ vi ρουθουνίζω, φριμάζω, ξεφυσώ.

snout [snaut] n ρύγχος nt, μουσούδα, μύτη.

snow [snəu] n χιόνι ♦ vi χιονίζω, ρίχνω χιόνι || ~ball n μπάλα χιόνι, χιονόσφαιρα || ~bound a (απο)κλεισμένος από τα χιόνια || ~drift n χιονοστιβάδα || ~drop n γάλανθος ο χιονώδης || ~fall n χιονόπτωση || ~flake n νιφάδα || ~man n χιονάνθρωπος || ~plough, ~plow (US) n εκχιονιστήρας || ~storm n χιονοθύελλα.

snub [snʌb] vt αποκρούω, προσβάλλω, κόβω ♦ n επίπληξη, προσβολή, κατσάδα.

snuff [snʌf] n ταμπάκο, πρέζα.

snug [snʌg] a άνετος, βολικός, ζεστός, αναπαυτικός.

so [səu] ad (extent) τόσο(ν) || (in such manner) έτσι || (thus) μ' αυτόν τον τρόπο || (to such an extent) τόσο ♦ cj επομένως, γι αυτό, έτσι λοιπόν || or ~ περίπου, πάνω κάτω || ~ long! (goodbye) γεια σου!, αντίο!! || ~ many, ~ much τόσος || ~ that ούτως ώστε.

soak [səuk] vt διαβρέχω, μουσκεύω || (leave in liquid) διαποτίζω, μουσκεύω || to ~ in vi διεισδύω, διαποτίζω, ποτίζω.

soap [səup] n σαπούνι || ~flakes npl τριμμένο σαπούνι || ~powder n σαπούνι σε σκόνη || ~y a γεμάτος σαπούνι.

soar [sɔː*] vi πετώ ψηλά, ανυψώνομαι.

sob [sɒb] n λυγμός, αναφυλλητό ♦ vi κλαίω με αναφιλητά.

sober ['səubə*] a νηφάλιος, ξεμέθυστος || (calm) σοβαρός, εγκρατής, ήρεμος || to ~ up vi συνέρχομαι, ξεμεθώ.

Soc. abbr of **society**.

so-called ['səu'kɔːld] a δήθεν, λεγόμενος.

soccer ['sɒkə*] n ποδόσφαιρο.

sociable ['səuʃəbl] a κοινωνικός, φιλικός, ομιλητικός.

social ['səuʃəl] a κοινωνικός || ~ism n σοσιαλισμός || ~ist n σοσιαλιστής/ίστρια m/f ♦ a σοσιαλιστικός || ~ly ad κοινωνικώς || ~ science n κοινωνική επιστήμη || ~ security n κοινωνική ασφάλεια || ~ work n κοινωνική εργασία || ~ worker n κοινωνικός λειτουργός m/f.

society [sə'saɪətɪ] n (people and customs) κοινωνία || (club) εταιρεία || (fashionable life) κοσμική ζωή, καλός κόσμος.

sociologist [səusɪ'ɒlədʒɪst] n κοινωνιολόγος.

sociology [səusɪ'ɒlədʒɪ] n κοινωνιολογία.

sock [sɒk] n (κοντή) κάλτσα ♦ vt (hit) δίνω γροθιά.

socket ['sɒkɪt] n ντουί, ρίζα.

sod [sɒd] n (of earth) χορταριασμένο χώμα || (col: term of abuse) παλιάνθρωπος.

soda ['səudə] n (CHEM) νάτριο, σόδα || (drink) σόδα || ~ water n αεριούχο νερό, σόδα.

sodden ['sɒdn] a βρεγμένος, μουσκεμένος || (moist and heavy) λασπωμένος.

sofa ['səufə] n σοφάς, καναπές m.

soft [sɒft] a μαλακός, απαλός || (not loud) απαλός, γλυκός, ελαφρός || (kind) τρυφερός, καλός || (weak, silly) ανόητος, χαζός || ~ drink n αναψυκτικό || ~en vt μαλακώνω ♦ vi μαλακώνω, γίνομαι μαλακός || ~-hearted a ευαίσθητος, με τρυφερή καρδιά || ~ly ad απαλά, μαλακά, αθόρυβα || ~ness n μαλακότητα, απαλότητα.

soggy ['sɒgɪ] a υγρός, μουσκεμένος.

soil [sɔɪl] n (earth) έδαφος nt, χώμα nt ♦ vt

λερώνω|| ~ed a λερωμένος,
ακάθαρτος.
solar ['səʊlə*] a ηλιακός.
sold [səʊld] pt, pp of **sell**.
solder ['səʊldə*] vt (συγ)κολλώ ♦ n
συγκόλληση || (material) καλάι.
soldier ['səʊldʒə*] n στρατιώτης.
sole [səʊl] n πέλμα nt, πατούσα || (of shoe)
σόλα || (fish) γλώσσα ♦ a μόνος,
μοναδικός || ~ly ad (only) μόνο,
μοναδικά.
solemn ['sɒləm] a σοβαρός || (formal)
επίσημος, σεμνός.
solicitor [sə'lɪsɪtə*] n δικηγόρος m/f,
σύμβουλος, συνήγορος.
solid ['sɒlɪd] a στερεός, συμπαγής ||
(hard) στερεός, γερός, σκληρός ||
(reliable) σοβαρός, βάσιμος || (meal)
γερός, ολόκληρος ♦ n στερεό || ~arity
n ενότητα, αλληλεγγύη || ~ity [sə'lɪdɪtɪ]
vi στερεοποιούμαι, πήζω ♦ vt
στερεοποιώ, πήζω, παγιώνω || ~ity n
στερεότητα.
solitaire [sɒlɪ'tɛə*] n (game) πασιέντσα ||
(gem) μονό διαμάντι, μονόπετρο.
solitary ['sɒlɪtərɪ] a μόνος || (lonely)
ολομόναχος, μοναχικός.
solitude ['sɒlɪtjuːd] n μοναξιά, ερημιά.
solo ['səʊləʊ] n σόλο || ~ist n σολίστας
m, σολίστ m/f.
soluble ['sɒljʊbl] a διαλυτός,
ευδιάλυτος || (able to be solved)
επιδεικτικός λύσεως.
solution [sə'luːʃən] n λύση, λύσιμο ||
(explanation) λύση, εξήγηση || (in liquid)
διάλυση, διάλυμα nt.
solve [sɒlv] vt λύω, εξηγώ.
solvent ['sɒlvənt] a αξιόχρεος.
sombre, somber (US) ['sɒmbə*] a
σκοτεινός, μελαγχολικός || ~ly ad
μελαγχολικά.
some [sʌm] a (uncertain number) λίγος,
λίγοι, μερικοί || (indefinite) κάποιος ||
(remarkable) σπουδαίος, περίφημος ||
(partitive) μερικός ♦ pron μερικοί, κάτι ♦
ad περίπου || ~body pron κάποιος ♦ n
κάποιος || ~day ad (μιά) κάποια μέρα ||
~how ad κάπως, κατά κάποιο τρόπο ||
~one pron = somebody || ~place ad
(US) = somewhere.
somersault ['sʌməsɔːlt] n τούμπα,
κουτρουβάλα ♦ vi κάνω τούμπα.
something ['sʌmθɪŋ] pron κάτι,
οτιδήποτε.
sometime ['sʌmtaɪm] ad κάποτε || ~s
ad μερικές φορές, κάποτε-κάπου.
somewhat ['sʌmwɒt] ad κάπως.
somewhere ['sʌmwɛə*] ad κάπου.
son [sʌn] n γιός.
song [sɒŋ] n τραγούδι || ~writer n
(μουσικο)συνθέτης.
sonic ['sɒnɪk] a ηχητικός.
son-in-law ['sʌnɪnlɔː] n γαμπρός.
sonnet ['sɒnɪt] n σονέτο.
soon [suːn] ad γρήγορα || (early)
σύντομα, νωρίς || as ~ as possible το
συντομότερο δυνατό || ~er ad (time)

γρηγορότερα || (of preference) καλύτερα,
κάλιο.
soot [sʊt] n αιθάλη, φούμο, καπνιά.
soothe [suːð] vt καταπραϋνω,
παρηγορώ.
sophisticated [sə'fɪstɪkeɪtɪd] a (person)
κοσμικός, μοντέρνος || (machinery) πιο
σύγχρονος.
soporific [sɒpə'rɪfɪk] a υπνωτικός,
ναρκωτικός.
sopping ['sɒpɪŋ] a (very wet)
καταβρεγμένος, μουσκεμένος.
soppy ['sɒpɪ] a (col: sentimental)
δακρύβρεκτος, σαχλός.
soprano [sə'prɑːnəʊ] n υψίφωνος f,
σοπράνο f.
sordid ['sɔːdɪd] a ακάθαρτος, ρυπαρός ||
(mean) άθλιος, χυδαίος.
sore [sɔː*] n πονεμένος, ερεθισμένος nt
|| (offended) πειραγμένος, θυμωμένος ♦ n
πληγή, τραύμα || ~ly ad (tempted) βαθειά,
σοβαρά.
sorrow ['sɒrəʊ] n λύπη, θλίψη, μετάνοια
|| ~ful a θλιμμένος, λυπημένος.
sorry ['sɒrɪ] a λυπημένος, πονεμένος ||
(pitiable) άθλιος, αξιολύπητος.
sort [sɔːt] n είδος, τάξη ♦ vt (COMPUT)
ταξινομώ || (also: ~ out) (papers)
ταξινομώ, ξεκαθαρίζω || (problems)
τακτοποιώ, (ξε)χωρίζω.
so-so ['səʊsəʊ] ad έτσι κι έτσι.
soufflé ['suːfleɪ] n σουφλέ nt inv.
sought [sɔːt] pt, pp of **seek**.
soul [səʊl] n ψυχή || ~-destroying a
ψυχοφθόρος, αποκτηνωτικός || ~ful a
αισθηματικός, συγκινητικός || ~less a
άψυχος, άκαρδος.
sound [saʊnd] a (healthy) υγιής, γερός ||
(safe) στερεός, ασφαλής, σίγουρος ||
(reasonable) λογικός || (deep, hearty) γερός
♦ n (noise) ήχος, θόρυβος || (GEOG) στενό,
πορθμός ♦ vt (alarm) κτυπώ ♦ vi (find
depth) βυθομετρώ || (seem) φαίνομαι,
μοιάζω || to ~ out vt (opinions)
βολιδοσκοπώ || ~ barrier n φράγμα του
ήχου || ~ing n (NAUT etc) βυθομέτρηση,
βολιδοσκόπηση || ~ly ad (sleep) βαθειά,
καλά, ήσυχα || (beat) γερά, τελείως ||
~proof a (room) ηχομονωτικός ♦ vt
κάνω αδιαπέραστο από ήχο || ~track n
(of film) ηχητική ζώνη (ταινίας).
soup [suːp] n σούπα, ζωμός || in the ~
σε δύσκολη θέση || ~spoon n κουτάλι
της σούπας.
sour ['saʊə*] a ξυνός || (milk) ξυνός ||
(bad-tempered) στριφνός, γκρινιάρης.
source [sɔːs] n πηγή, προέλευση.
south [saʊθ] n νότος ♦ a νότιος ♦ ad
προς νότο, νοτίως || ~-east n το
νοτιοανατολικό || ~-easterly a
νοτιοανατολικός || ~ern a νότιος,
μεσημβρινός || S~ Pole n Νότιος Πόλος
|| ~ward(s) ad πρός νότο || ~-west n
το νοτιοδυτικό.
souvenir [suːvə'nɪə*] n ενθύμιο,
σουβενίρ nt inv.
sovereign ['sɒvrɪn] n μονάρχης

βασιλέας ♦ a (independent) κυρίαρχος ||
~ty n ηγεμονία, κυριαρχία.
soviet ['souviət] a σοβιετικός.
sow [sau] n γουρούνα || [sou] (irreg v) vt
σπέρνω || (spread abroad) ενσπείρω.
soya bean ['soiə'bi:n] n σόγια.
spa [spα:] n ιαματική πηγή || (place)
λουτρόπολη.
space [speis] n χώρος, τόπος || (distance)
απόσταση || (length of time) διάστημα nt ||
(universe) διάστημα nt || to ~ out vt
αραιώνω, τοποθετώ κατ' αποστάσεις ||
~craft n διαστημόπλοιο || ~man n
κοσμοναύτης.
spacing ['speisiŋ] n αραίωση.
spacious ['speiʃəs] a ευρύς, ευρύχωρος,
απλόχωρος.
spade [speid] n (tool) φτυάρι, τσάπα,
τσαπί || ~s npl (CARDS) μπαστούνι, πίκα.
spaghetti [spə'gεti] n σπαγέτο,
μακαρονάδα.
Spain [spein] n Ισπανία.
span [spæn] n (of arch) άνοιγμα nt,
απόσταση || (of time) διάρκεια (ζωής) ♦
vt συνδέω, καλύπτω.
Spaniard ['spænjəd] n Ισπανός.
spaniel ['spænjəl] n σπάνιελ nt inv.
Spanish ['spæniʃ] n (LING) Ισπανικά ntpl
♦ a ισπανικός.
spank [spæŋk] vt δέρνω (στον πισινό).
spanner ['spænə*] n κλειδί
(υδραυλικού).
spare [spεə*] a περίσσιος, λιτός, ισχνός ||
n = ~ part || vt (do without) οικονομώ,
φυλάγω || (save from hurt) λυπούμαι,
χαρίζω, φείδομαι || (lend, give)
περισσεύω, δίνω, παραχωρώ, διαθέτω ||
to ~ περισσεύω || ~ part n
ανταλλακτικό, εξάρτημα nt || ~ wheel n
ρεζέρβα || ~ time n ελεύθερες ώρες.
spark [spα:k] n σπινθήρας, σπίθα || (fig)
ίχνος, σπίθα || ~ plug n σπινθηριστής,
μπουζί nt inv.
sparkle ['spα:kl] n σπινθήρας, σπίθα,
λάμψη || (gaiety) σπιρτάδα ♦ vi
σπινθηρίζω, σπιθοβολώ, αστράφτω.
sparkling ['spα:kliŋ] a (lit)
αστραφτερός, σπινθηροβόλος || (wine)
αφρώδης || (conversation) πνευματώδης
(ομιλία).
sparrow ['spærəu] n σπουργίτης.
sparse [spα:s] a αραιός, σποραδικός.
spasm ['spæzəm] n σπασμός,
σπαρτάρισμα nt || (short spell) κρίση,
έξαψη || ~odic [-'mɔdik] a
σπασμωδικός, σπαστικός.
spastic ['spæstik] n σπαστικός.
spat [spæt] pt, pp of **spit**.
spate [speit] n (fig) πλημμύρα,
πλημμύρισμα nt || in ~ (river)
φουσκωμένος, πλημμυρισμένος.
spatter ['spætə*] n πιτσίλισμα nt,
ράντισμα nt ♦ vt πιτσιλίζω, ραντίζω ♦ vi
αναπηδώ, (ξε)πετιέμαι, στάζω.
spatula ['spætjulə] n σπάτουλα.
spawn [spɔ:n] vt αφήνω αυγά || (fig)
γεννώ.

speak [spi:k] (irreg v) vt λέγω, προφέρω,
εκφράζω || (truth) λέγω, λέω || (language)
μιλώ ♦ vi (+ to) μιλώ (σε) || μιλώ, συζητώ
|| (make speech) αγορεύω, μιλώ || to ~ for
vt συνηγορώ, μιλώ για || to ~ up vi
υψώνω τη φωνή μιλώ σε κάποιο || ~er n
ομιλητής/ήτρια m/f, συνομιλητής/ήτρια
m/f || (chairman) πρόεδρος || (loudspeaker:
on record player) μεγάφωνο.
spear [spiə*] n ακόντιο, δόρυ nt, κοντάρι
♦ vt τρυπώ με κοντάρι, πιάνω με
κοντάρι.
special ['speʃəl] a ειδικός, ίδιος ||
(particular kind) εξαιρετικός,
ασυνήθιστος || (particular purpose)
ιδιαίτερος, ξεχωριστός ♦ n (RAIL) ειδική
αμαξοστοιχία || (cooking) ειδικός,
ιδιαίτερος || ~ist n ειδικός || ~ity n
ειδικότητα || (food) σπεσιαλιτέ nt inv ||
~ize vi (+ in) ειδικεύομαι σε || ~ly ad
ειδικά, ιδιαίτερα, προ παντός, πάνω απ'
όλα.
species ['spi:ʃi:z] n είδος nt.
specific [spə'sifik] a ειδικός, ορισμένος,
ακριβής, σαφής || ~ally ad ειδικά,
συγκεκριμένα || ~ation [spesifi'keiʃən] n
περιγραφή, καθορισμός, προδιαγραφή.
specify ['spesifai] vt καθορίζω,
προσδιορίζω.
specimen ['spesimin] n δείγμα nt.
speck [spek] n κηλίδα, σταγόνα ||
(particle) κόκκος, μόριο.
speckled ['spekld] a διάστικτος,
πιτσιλισμένος.
specs [speks] npl (col) γυαλιά ntpl.
spectacle ['spektəkl] n θέαμα nt || ~s
npl ματογυάλια ntpl, γυαλιά ntpl.
spectacular [spek'tækjulə*] a
θεαματικός.
spectator [spek'teitə*] n θεατής.
spectre, (US) **specter** ['spektə*] n
φάντασμα nt, σκιάχτρο.
spectrum ['spektrəm] n φάσμα nt.
speculate ['spekjuleit] vi κάνω
υποθέσεις || (FIN) κερδοσκοπώ.
speculation [spekju'leiʃən] n (FIN)
κερδοσκοπία.
sped [sped] pt, pp of **speed**.
speech [spi:tʃ] n λόγος, λαλιά || (talk)
λόγος, αγόρευση, ομιλία || ~ day n (SCH)
απονομή των πτυχίων || ~less a άλαλος,
βουβός, άφωνος || ~ therapy n
θεραπευτική αγωγή λόγου.
speed [spi:d] (irreg v) n ταχύτητα,
σπουδή || (gear) ταχύτητα ♦ vi σπεύδω,
κάνω γρήγορα, τρέχω || to ~ up vi
επιταχύνω ♦ vt επισπεύδω, επιταχύνω ||
~boat n εξωλέμβιος || ~ily ad γρήγορα,
εσπευσμένα, βιαστικά || ~ing n
υπερβολική ταχύτητα || ~ limit n όριο
ταχύτητας || ~ometer n ταχύμετρο,
κοντέρ nt inv || ~way n
αυτοκινητόδρομος || ~y a ταχύς,
γρήγορος.
spell [spel] (irreg v) n (magic) γοητεία,
μαγεία, μάγια ntpl || (period of time)
διάστημα nt, χρονική περίοδος ♦ vt

ορθογραφώ || *(word)* συλλαβίζω || *(mean)* σημαίνω || **~bound** a γοητευμένος, μαγεμένος || **~ing** n συλλαβισμός, ορθογραφία.

spelt [spelt] pt, pp of **spell**.

spend [spɛnd] *(irreg v)* vt ξοδεύω, δαπανώ || *(use up)* εξαντλώ, χρησιμοποιώ.

spent [spɛnt] pt, pp of **spend ♦** a *(patience)* εξαντλημένος.

sperm [spɜːm] n *(BIOL)* σπέρμα nt.

spew [spjuː] vt ξερνώ, κάνω εμετό.

sphere [sfɪə*] n σφαίρα, υδρόγειος.

spherical ['sfɛrɪkəl] a σφαιρικός.

sphinx [sfɪŋks] n σφίγγα.

spice [spaɪs] n καρύκευμα nt, μπαχαρικό ♦ vt καρυκεύω.

spicy ['spaɪsɪ] a αρωματισμένος, πικάντικος.

spider ['spaɪdə*] n αράχνη || **~y** a αράχνινος.

spike [spaɪk] n αιχμή, καρφί, στάχυ nt, πάσσαλος.

spill [spɪl] *(irreg v)* vt *(upset)* ανατρέπω, αναποδογυρίζω || *(pour out)* χύνω ♦ vi *(flow over)* χύνομαι.

spin [spɪn] *(irreg v)* n *(revolution of wheel)* περιστροφή, στριφογύρισμα || *(trip in car)* περίπατος, βόλτα || *(AVIAT)* σπινάρισμα nt ♦ vt *(wool etc)* κλώθω, γνέθω || *(turn)* γυρίζω ♦ vi περιστρέφομαι, (στριφο)γυρίζω || **to ~ out** vi *(of money etc)* οικονομώ (τα λεφτά μου) ♦ vt παρατείνω, παρατραβώ.

spinach ['spɪnɪdʒ] n σπανάκι.

spinal ['spaɪnl] a νωτιαίος, ραχιαίος, σπονδυλικός || **~ cord** n νωτιαίος μυελός.

spindly ['spɪndlɪ] a λιγνός.

spin-drier ['spɪn'draɪə*] n στεγνωτήριο.

spine [spaɪn] n σπονδυλική στήλη, ραχοκοκκαλιά || *(thorn)* αγκάθι || **~less** a *(fig)* δειλός, άβολος.

spinning ['spɪnɪŋ] n *(of thread)* κλώσιμο, στρίψιμο || **~ wheel** n ροδάνι, ανέμη.

spinster ['spɪnstə*] n γεροντοκόρη.

spiral ['spaɪərəl] n σπείρα, έλικα ♦ a ελικοειδής, σπειροειδής ♦ vi κινούμαι σπειροειδώς || **~ staircase** n γυριστή σκάλα, στριφτή σκάλα.

spire ['spaɪə*] n κορυφή κωδωνοστασίου.

spirit ['spɪrɪt] n πνεύμα nt, ψυχή || *(ghost)* φάντασμα nt || *(humour, mood)* διάθεση, κέφι || *(courage)* κουράγιο, θάρρος nt || *(alcoholic)* οινοπνευματώδες ποτό, σπίρτο || **in good ~s** κεφάτος, καλόκεφος || **~ed** a ζωηρός, έντονος, θαρραλέος || **~ level** n αλφάδι.

spiritual ['spɪrɪtjuəl] a πνευματικός, ψυχικός ♦ n θρησκευτικό τραγούδι || **~ism** n πνευματισμός.

spit [spɪt] *(irreg v)* n *(for roasting)* σούβλα || *(saliva)* φτύσιμο, σάλιο ♦ vi φτύνω || *(of motor)* ρετάρω.

spite [spaɪt] n μίσος, έχθρα, κακία ♦ vt ενοχλώ, πεισμώνω, φουρκίζω || **in ~ of**

παρά το, παρ' όλα || **~ful** a μοχθηρός, εκδικητικός.

splash [splæʃ] n πιτσίλισμα nt, πλατσούλισμα nt, λεκές || *(of colour)* πολυχρωμία ♦ vti πλατσουλίζω, πιτσιλίζω.

spleen [spliːn] n σπλήνα.

splendid ['splɛndɪd] a λαμπρός, μεγαλοπρεπής || *(fine)* εξαίσιος, περίφημος.

splendour, *(US)* **splendor** ['splɛndə*] n λαμπρότητα, λάμψη || *(glory)* μεγαλοπρέπεια.

splint [splɪnt] n νάρθηκας.

splinter ['splɪntə*] n θραύσμα nt ♦ vi θραύομαι, σπάζω.

split [splɪt] *(irreg v)* n σχισμή, σχίσιμο, ρωγμή, διαίρεση ♦ vt σχίζω, θραύω, σπάζω ♦ vi *(divide)* διαιρείται || *(col. depart)* αναχωρώ || **to ~ up** vi διαιρούμαι ♦ vt διαιρώ, χωρίζω, διασπώ.

splutter ['splʌtə*] vi τραυλίζω || *(of motor)* ρετάρω.

spoil [spɔɪl] *(irreg v)* vt χαλώ || **~s** npl λεία, λάφυρα ntpl || **~sport** n αυτός που χαλάει το κέφι.

spoke [spəuk] n ακτίνα (τροχού) || pt of **speak** || **~n** pp of **speak** || **~sman** n εκπρόσωπος.

sponge [spʌndʒ] n σφουγγάρι ♦ vt πλένω, σφουγγίζω ♦ vi *(+ on)* ζω σε βάρος κάποιου || **~ bag** n σάκκος για σφουγγάρι || **~ cake** n παντεσπάνι.

spongy ['spʌndʒɪ] a σπογγώδης.

sponsor ['spɒnsə*] n ανάδοχος, εγγυητής/ήτρια m/f, εισηγητής/ήτρια m/f ♦ vt υποστηρίζω, εισηγούμαι || **~ship** n υποστήριξη.

spontaneous [spɒn'teɪnɪəs] a αυτόματος || *(natural)* αυθόρμητος.

spool [spuːl] n καρούλα, μασούρι.

spoon [spuːn] n κουτάλι || **~-feed** vt *(lit)* ταΐζω με το κουτάλι || *(fig)* επιχορηγώ || **~ful** n κουταλιά.

sporadic [spə'rædɪk] a σποραδικός.

sport [spɔːt] n *(games)* αθλητισμός, σπόρ nt inv || *(fun)* διασκέδαση, παιχνίδι || *(good-humoured person)* καλός άνθρωπος || **~ing** a *(fair)* τίμιος || **~s car** n αυτοκίνητο σπόρ || **~(s) coat** n, **~(s) jacket** n σακκάκι σπόρ || **~sman** n φίλαθλος, τίμιος παίκτης || **~smanship** n τιμιότητα στο σπορ || **~swear** n είδη ntpl αθλητισμού || **~swoman** n αθλήτρια.

spot [spɒt] n στίγμα nt, κηλίδα, λεκές m || *(place)* τόπος, μέρος nt, τοποθεσία || *(small amount)* στάλα, λίγο ♦ vt *(notice)* διακρίνω, σημειώνω || *(make spots on)* λεκιάζω || **~ check** n αιφνιδιαστικός έλεγχος || **~less** a άσπιλος, ακηλίδωτος, καθαρός || **~light** n προβολέας θεάτρου || *(position)* το προσκήνιο, κέντρο || **~ted** a διάστικτος, πιτσιλωτός || **~ty** a *(face)* με πανάδες, με σπειριά.

spouse [spauz] n σύζυγος m/f.

spout [spaut] n στόμιο, σωλήνας || *(jet)*

εκροή, πίδακας ♦ *vi* ξεπηδώ, αναπηδώ, ξεχύνομαι.

sprain [sprein] *n* διάστρεμμα *nt*, στραμπούλισμα *nt* ♦ *vt* στραμπουλίζω.

sprang [spræŋ] *pt of* **spring**.

sprawl [sprɔːl] *vi* εκτείνομαι, ξαπλώνομαι.

spray [sprei] *n (sprinkle)* πιτσιλίσματα *ntpl* || *(of sea)* αφρός || *(instrument)* ψεκαστήρας, βαποριζατέρ *nt inv* || *(branch)* κλωνάρι ♦ *vt* ψεκάζω, καταβρέχω.

spread [spred] *(irreg v) n (extent)* επέκταση, διάδοση || *(col)* τραπέζι, πλούσιο γεύμα *nt* ♦ *vt* απλώνω, στρώνω || *(scatter)* σκορπίζω, στρώνω, διαδίδω || *(smear)* αλείφω, χύνω.

spree [spriː] *n* διασκέδαση, ξεφάντωμα *nt*, γλέντι.

sprightly ['spraitli] *a* ζωηρός, κεφάτος.

spring [spriŋ] *(irreg v) n (leap)* πήδημα *nt* || *(of water)* πηγή || *(coil)* ελατήριο || *(season)* άνοιξη ♦ *vi (ανα)*πηδώ, ξεπετάγομαι || **to ~ up** *vi (problem)* δημιουργούμαι, εμφανίζομαι || **~board** *n* βατήρας, τραμπλέν *nt inv* || **~-clean** *n* γενικός καθαρισμός ♦ *vt* κάνω γενικό καθαρισμό || **~-cleaning** *n* γενικός καθαρισμός (ανοιξιάτικος) || **~iness** *n* ελαστικότητα || **~time** *n* άνοιξη || **~y** *a* ελαστικός, εύκαμπτος.

sprinkle ['spriŋkl] *n* ράντισμα *nt* ♦ *vt* ραντίζω, ραίνω.

sprint [sprint] *n* δρόμος ταχύτητας ♦ *vi* τρέχω σε δρόμο ταχύτητας || **~er** *n* δρομέας ταχύτητας.

sprite [sprait] *n* ξωτικό, στοιχειό.

sprout [spraut] *vi* βλαστάνω, φυτρώνω || *see* **Brussels sprout**.

spruce [spruːs] *n* έλατο ♦ *a* κομψός, περιποιημένος.

sprung [sprʌŋ] *pp of* **spring**.

spry [sprai] *a* ζωηρός, ενεργητικός.

spun [spʌn] *pt, pp of* **spin**.

spur [spɜː*] *n* σπηρούνι || *(fig)* κίνητρο, ελατήριο ♦ *vt (also:* **~ on)** κεντρίζω, παρακινώ || **on the ~ of the moment** χωρίς σκέψη, αυθόρμητα.

spurn [spɜːn] *vt* περιφρονώ, αποκρούω.

spurt [spɜːt] *n (effort)* σφίξιμο, φουλάρισμα *nt*, ξέσπασμα *nt* || *(jet)* ανάβλυση, πίδακας ♦ *vti* ξεχύνομαι, φουλάρω.

spy [spai] *n* κατάσκοπος *m/f* ♦ *vi* κατασκοπεύω ♦ *vt* διακρίνω, βλέπω, παρατηρώ || **~ing** *n (espionage)* κατασκοπεία.

sq. *(MATH),* **Sq.** *(in address) abbr of* **square**.

squabble ['skwɒbl] *n* φιλονεικία, καυγάς ♦ *vi* φιλονεικώ, καυγαδίζω, πιάνομαι (με).

squad [skwɒd] *n (MIL)* απόσπασμα *nt*, ουλαμός || *(police)* υπηρεσία διώξεως.

squadron ['skwɒdrən] *n* μοίρα.

squalid ['skwɒlid] *a* βρώμικος, βρωμερός, άθλιος.

squall [skwɔːl] *n (scream)* κραυγή, στριγγλιά.

squalor ['skwɒlə*] *n* ακαθαρσία, βρώμα, αθλιότητα.

squander ['skwɒndə*] *vt* σπαταλώ.

square [skwɛə*] *n (figure)* τετράγωνο || *(of town)* πλατεία || *(instrument)* γωνία, γνώμονας || *(product)* τετράγωνο || *(col: person)* ανιαρός, αταίριαστος ♦ *a* τετραγωνικός || *(honest)* τίμιος, καθαρός, δίκαιος || *(ample)* ικανοποιητικός, άφθονος ♦ *ad (exactly)* ακριβώς, κάθετα ♦ *vt (arrange)* ρυθμίζω, κανονίζω, τακτοποιώ || *(MATH)* τετραγωνίζω ♦ *vi (agree)* (+ **with**) συμφωνώ, συμβιβάζομαι || **all ~** στα ίσια, πάτσι || **2 metres ~** 4 τετραγωνικά μέτρα || **1 ~ metre** 1 τετραγωνικό μέτρο || **~ly** *ad* τίμια, ντόμπρα.

squash [skwɒʃ] *n (drink)* χυμός *(φρούτων)* ♦ *vt* συνθλίβω, ζουλώ, στύβω.

squat [skwɒt] *a* κοντόχοντρος ♦ *vi* κάθομαι σταυροπόδι || **~ter** *n* σφετεριστής γης.

squawk [skwɔːk] *n* κράξιμο, βραχνή κραυγή ♦ *vi* κράζω, φωνάζω, κραυγάζω.

squeak [skwiːk] *n* τσιριχτή φωνή, σκούξιμο ♦ *vi* σκούζω, τσιρίζω, τρίζω.

squeal [skwiːl] *n* διαπεραστικός ήχος, κραυγή, στριγγλιά ♦ *vi* στριγγλίζω, σκούζω.

squeamish ['skwiːmiʃ] *a* ευαίσθητος, με τάση στον εμετό || *(easily shocked)* σιχασιάρης, δύστροπος.

squeeze [skwiːz] *n (lit)* σύνθλιψη, σφίξιμο, στρίμωγμα *nt* || *(ECON)* πίεση ♦ *vt* συνθλίβω, σφίγγω, στύβω || **to ~ out** *vt* στύβω.

squid [skwid] *n* σουπιά.

squint [skwint] *n* αλλοιθωρισμός, στραβισμός ♦ *vi* αλλοιθωρίζω, στραβοκοιτάζω.

squirm [skwɜːm] *vi* συστρέφω το σώμα, στενοχωριέμαι, ντρέπομαι.

squirrel ['skwirəl] *n* σκίουρος.

squirt [skwɜːt] *n* εκτόξευση, πιτσίλισμα *nt*, ριπή ♦ *vi* αναβλύζω, πετάγομαι, εκτοξεύω.

Sr *abbr of* **senior**.

St *abbr of* **saint, street**.

stab [stæb] *n (blow)* κτύπημα *nt*, μπαμπεσιά || *(col: try)* **to have a ~** δοκιμάζω.

stability [stə'biliti] *n* σταθερότητα.

stabilize ['steibəlaiz] *vt* σταθεροποιώ || **~r** *n* ζυγοσταθμιστής, σταθεροποιητής.

stable ['steibl] *n* στάβλος ♦ *vt* σταβλίζω ♦ *a* σταθερός, μόνιμος.

stack [stæk] *n* θημωνιά, σωρός ♦ *vt* συσσωρεύω, στοιβάζω.

stadium ['steidiəm] *n* στάδιο.

staff [staːf] *n (stick)* ράβδος *f*, μπαστούνι, κοντάκι || *(people)* προσωπικό, επιτελείο ♦ *vt (with people)* καταρτίζω προσωπικό.

stag [stæg] *n* ελάφι.

stage [steidʒ] *n (theatre)* σκηνή || *(actors)*

θέατρο || (degree) στάδιο ♦ vt (play)
ανεβάζω, σκηνοθετώ || (demonstration)
οργανώνω, σκηνοθετώ || in ~s
βαθμηδόν, κατά στάδια || ~coach n
ταχυδρομική άμαξα || ~ door n είσοδος
f ηθοποιών || ~ manager n σκηνοθέτης.

stagger ['stægə*] vi κλονίζομαι,
τρικλίζω, παραπατώ ♦ vt (person) ζαλίζω,
συγκλονίζω, κάνω να τα χάσει || (hours)
κλιμακώνω (τις ώρες) || ~ing a (amazing)
καταπληκτικός, συγκλονιστικός.

stagnant ['stægnənt] a στάσιμος,
λιμνασμένος || (dull) αδρανής, άγονος.

stagnate [stæg'neit] vi είμαι στάσιμος,
αδρανώ.

staid [steid] a θετικός, σοβαρός.

stain [stein] n λεκές m, κηλίδα ||
(colouring) χρώμα nt, βαφή, μπογιά ♦ vt
λεκιάζω, λερώνω || ~ed glass n
χρωματιστό γυαλί || ~less a (steel)
ανοξείδωτος.

stair [stɛə*] n (one step) σκαλοπάτι, σκαλί
|| ~case n κλίμακα, σκάλα || ~s npl
σκάλα || ~way n σκάλα.

stake [steik] n πάσσαλος, παλούκι ||
(gambling) στοίχημα nt, μίζα, ποντάρισμα
nt ♦ vt ποντάρω || (fig) παίζω.

stalactite ['stæləktait] n σταλακτίτης.

stalagmite ['stæləgmait] n
σταλαγμίτης.

stale [steil] a μπαγιάτικος || ~mate n
αδιέξοδο.

stalk [stɔ:k] n κοτσάνι, στέλεχος nt,
μίσχος ♦ vt παρακολουθώ αθέατος ♦ vi
(walk stiffly) βαδίζω με μεγάλα βήματα.

stall [stɔ:l] n παράπηγμα nt στάβλου,
παχνί || (stand) μπάγκος, περίπτερο ♦ vt
(AUT) κολλώ, μπλοκάρω ♦ vi (AUT) κολλώ
|| (delay) αναβάλλω, χρονοτριβώ || ~s npl
(THEAT) καθίσματα ntpl (ορχήστρας).

stallion ['stæliən] n επιβήτορας,
βαρβάτο άλογο.

stalwart ['stɔ:lwət] a ρωμαλέος,
σταθερός ♦ n παλληκάρι.

stamina ['stæminə] n σφρίγος nt, ζωτική
δύναμη.

stammer ['stæmə*] n τραύλισμα nt,
τσέβδισμα nt ♦ vi τραυλίζω, ψευδίζω,
ψελλίζω.

stamp [stæmp] n (postage)
γραμματόσημο || (official) ένσημο || (of
foot) κτήπημα nt του ποδιού,
ποδοβολητό || (on document) σφραγίδα,
βούλα, στάμπα ♦ vi κτυπώ το πόδι,
περπατώ βαριά ♦ vt (make mark)
σφραγίζω, μαρκάρω, σταμπάρω || (fix
postage) κολλώ γραμματόσημο || ~
album n συλλογή γραμματοσήμων || ~
collecting n φιλοτελισμός.

stampede [stæm'pi:d] n εσπευσμένη
φυγή, πανικός.

stance [stæns] n (posture) στάση.

stand [stænd] (irreg v) n (position) στάση ||
(MIL) αντίσταση || (rest) υποστήριγμα nt,
πόδι, στήριγμα nt || (seats) εξέδρα ♦ vi
(erect) στέκομαι || (rise) σηκώνομαι ||
(place, set) κείμαι, βρίσκομαι, είμαι || (halt,
stop) σταματώ, στέκομαι ♦ vt (place)
τοποθετώ, βάζω, κουμπώ (όρθιο) ||
(endure) υποφέρω, αντέχω, υπομένω || to
make a ~ αντιστέκομαι, αντιτάσσομαι
|| it ~s to reason είναι λογικό || to ~
by vi (be ready) είμαι έτοιμος, είμαι σε
επιφυλακή ♦ vt (opinion) μένω πιστός σε
|| to ~ for vt (defend) υπερασπίζομαι,
υποστηρίζω || (signify) αντιπροσωπεύω ||
(permit, tolerate) υπομένω, ανέχομαι || to
~ in for vt αντικαθιστώ || to ~ out vi
(be prominent) (προ)εξέχω, ξεχωρίζω || to
~ up vi (rise) σηκώνομαι || to ~ up for
vt υποστηρίζω.

standard ['stændəd] n (measure)
υπόδειγμα nt, κανόνας, μέτρο || (flag)
σημαία, λάβαρο ♦ a (size etc) πρότυπος,
κανονικός, συνηθισμένος || ~ize vt
τυποποιώ || ~ of living n βιωτικό
επίπεδο.

standby ['stændbai] n (person)
αντικαταστάτης/τρια m/f.

stand-in ['stændin] n
αντικαταστάτης/τρια m/f,
αναπληρωτής/ώτρια m/f.

standing ['stændiŋ] a όρθιος || (lasting)
μόνιμος, διαρκής ♦ n διάρκεια ||
(reputation) κοινωνική θέση, υπόληψη ||
~ orders npl (MIL) μόνιμες διατάξεις fpl,
κανονισμοί mpl || ~ room only μόνο
όρθιοι.

stand-offish ['stænd'ɒfiʃ] a
υπεροπτικός.

standpoint ['stændpɔint] n άποψη,
σκοπιά.

standstill ['stændstil] n: at a ~
στασιμότητα, νεκρό σημείο || to come
to a ~ καταλήγω σε αδιέξοδο,
σταματώ.

stank [stæŋk] pt of stink.

stanza ['stænzə] n στροφή, στάντσα.

staple ['steipl] n άγκιστρο, συνδετήρας
|| (product) κύριο προϊόν ♦ a κύριος,
πρωτεύων ♦ vt στερεώνω, συνδέω || ~r
n συνδετήρας.

star [sta:*] n άστρο, αστέρι || (actor)
αστέρας, πρωταγωνιστής/ίστρια m/f,
στάρ m/f inv || (shape) αστέρι ♦ vi (in film)
πρωταγωνιστώ, παίζω σε ταινία ♦ vt (to
star an actor) παρουσιάζω σαν
πρωταγωνιστή.

starboard ['sta:bəd] n δεξιά πλευρά, ♦
a δεξιά.

starch [sta:tʃ] n άμυλο || ~ed a (collar)
κολλαριστός || ~y a αμυλώδης,
αμυλούχος || (formal) υπεροπτικός,
ποζάτος.

stardom ['sta:dəm] n θέση αστέρα.

stare [stɛə*] n ατενές βλέμμα nt,
καρφωτή ματιά ♦ vi (+ at) ατενίζω,
καρφώνω με το μάτι.

starfish ['sta:fiʃ] n αστερίας.

stark [sta:k] a ψυχρός, σκληρός ♦ ad: ~
naked ολόγυμνος, θεόγυμνος,
τσίτσιδος.

starlight ['sta:lait] n αστροφεγγιά.

starling ['sta:liŋ] n ψαρώνι, καραβέλι.

starry ['stɑːrɪ] a έναστρος, αστερόφεγγος, λαμπερός || ~-**eyed** a (innocent) ονειροπαρμένος αφελής.

start [stɑːt] n αρχή, σημείο εκκινήσεως, εκκίνηση || (beginning) αρχή, αρχίνισμα nt || (sudden movement) ξάφνιασμα nt, ανατίναγμα nt ♦ vt (set going) αρχίζω, ανοίγω, βγάζω ♦ vi (begin journey) αρχίζω, ξεκινώ || (make sudden movement) αναπηδώ, ξαφνιζομαι || **to ~ doing** αρχίζω με, πιάνομαι με || **to ~ off** vi (begin) αρχίζω, ξεκινώ || **to ~ up** vi βάζω μπρος || ~**er** n (AUT) εκκινητήρας, μίζα || (for race) αφέτης || ~**ing point** n αφετηρία, σημείο εκκινήσεως.

startle ['stɑːtl] vt ξαφνιάζω, φοβίζω, εκπλήσσω.

startling ['stɑːtlɪŋ] a καταπληκτικός, εντυπωσιακός, χτυπητός.

starvation [stɑːveɪʃən] n λιμός, λιμοκτονία, ασιτία, πείνα.

starve [stɑːv] vi (die of hunger) πεθαίνω από πείνα || (suffer from hunger) ψοφάω από της πείνας, πεινώ ♦ vt (keep without food) στερώ τροφής.

starving ['stɑːvɪŋ] a πεινασμένος, λιμασμένος, ψόφιος της πείνας.

state [steɪt] n κατάσταση, θέση || (government) κράτος nt, πολιτεία || (anxiety) αναστάτωση ♦ vt δηλώνω, λέγω, ανακοινώνω || ~**ly** a μεγαλοπρεπής, αξιοπρεπής || ~**ment** n δήλωση, έκθεση || ~**sman** n πολιτικός.

static ['stætɪk] n στατική ♦ a ακίνητος, αδρανής || (PHYS) στατικός || ~ **electricity** n στατικός ηλεκτρισμός.

station ['steɪʃən] n (RAIL) σταθμός || (post) σταθμός, θέση || (position in life) κοινωνική θέση, βαθμός ♦ vt τοποθετώ, βάζω.

stationary ['steɪʃənərɪ] a στάσιμος, ακίνητος.

stationer ['steɪʃənə*] n χαρτοπώλης || ~'**s** (shop) n χαρτοπωλείο || ~**y** n χαρτικά είδη ntpl.

station master ['steɪʃənmɑːstə*] n σταθμάρχης.

station wagon ['steɪʃənwægən] n (US AUT) στέισον-βάγκον nt inv.

statistic [stəˈtɪstɪk] n στατιστικό (στοιχείο) || ~**al** a στατιστικός || ~**s** npl στατιστική.

statue ['stætjuː] n άγαλμα nt.

stature ['stætʃə] n ανάστημα nt.

status ['steɪtəs] n θέση, κατάσταση || **the ~ quo** n καθεστώς nt, στάτους κβο nt inv.

statute ['stætjuːt] n νόμος, θέσπισμα nt.

statutory ['stætjutərɪ] a νομοθετημένος, θεσπισμένος.

staunch [stɔːntʃ] a αξιόπιστος, πιστός, δυνατός.

stave [steɪv] vt: **to ~ off** (attack) αποκρούω, απωθώ || (threat) αποτρέπω, αποφεύγω.

stay [steɪ] n διαμονή, παραμονή ♦ vi (παρα)μένω || (at place) διαμένω || **to ~**

put μένω στην ίδια θέση || **to ~ with friends** μένω με φίλους || **to ~ the night** μένω το βράδυ || **to ~ behind** vi παρακολουθώ από πίσω || μένω πίσω || **to ~ in** vi (at home) μένω (στο σπίτι) || **to ~ on** vi (continue) παραμένω || **to ~ out** vi (of house) μένω έξω, δεν επιστρέφω || **to ~ up** vi (at night) αγρυπνώ, ξενυχτώ.

STD n (abbr of Subscriber Trunk Dialling) τηλεφωνικός κώδικας (Τηλ. Κωδ.).

steadfast ['stedfəst] a σταθερός.

steadily ['stedɪlɪ] ad σταθερά.

steady ['stedɪ] a σταθερός, στερεός || (regular) κανονικός, συνεχής, σταθερός || (reliable) σταθερός, συνεπής, τακτικός ♦ vt σταθεροποιώ, στερεώνω || **to ~ o.s.** σταθεροποιούμαι, καθησυχάζω.

steak [steɪk] n (meat) μπριζόλα, μπιφτέκι || (fish) φέτα.

steal [stiːl] (irreg v) vt κλέβω, βουτώ, σουρφώνω ♦ vi φεύγω κλεφτά || ~**th** ['stelθ] n: **by ~th** κρυφά, κλεφτά, μυστικά || ~**thy** a κρυφός, φευγαλέος, προσεκτικός.

steam [stiːm] n ατμός ♦ vt βράζω στον ατμό ♦ vi αναδίνω ατμό, αχνίζω || (ship) κινούμαι, πλέω (με ατμό) || ~ **engine** n ατμομηχανή || ~**er** n ατμόπλοιο, βαπόρι || ~**roller** n οδοστρωτήρας || ~**y** a θολός, γεμάτος ατμούς.

steel [stiːl] n χάλυβας, ατσάλι ♦ a χαλύβδινος, ατσάλινος || ~**works** n χαλυβδουργείο.

steep [stiːp] a απότομος, απόκρημνος || (price) εξωφρενική ♦ vt διαποτίζω, μουσκεύω, βουτώ.

steeple ['stiːpl] n κωδωνοστάσιο || ~**chase** n ιπποδρομία με εμπόδια || ~**jack** n επιδιορθωτής καπνοδόχων.

steeply ['stiːplɪ] ad απότομα, κατηφορικά.

steepness ['stiːpnɪs] n το απότομο, το απόκρημνο.

steer [stɪə*] n μικρός ταύρος ♦ vt (car) οδηγώ || (boat) πηδαλιουχώ ♦ vi κατευθύνομαι, βάζω πλώρη για || ~**ing** n (AUT) σύστημα nt διεύθυνσης || ~**ing wheel** n βολάν nt inv, τιμόνι.

stem [stem] n στέλεχος nt, κορμός ♦ vt σταματώ, ανακόπτω || **to ~ from** vt προέρχομαι από.

stench [stentʃ] n δυσοσμία, δυσωδία.

stencil ['stensl] n μεμβράνη ♦ vt γράφω μεμβράνες, πολυγραφώ.

stenographer [steˈnɒgrəfə*] n στενογράφος m/f.

step [step] n βήμα nt, πάτημα nt || (stair) βαθμίδα, σκαλοπάτι, σκαλί || (action) διάβημα nt, ενέργεια || (sound) βήμα nt, βάδισμα nt ♦ vi βηματίζω, βαδίζω || ~**s** npl = **stepladder** || **to ~ down** vi (fig) παραιτούμαι || **to ~ up** vt αυξάνω, ανεβάζω || ~**brother** n ετεροθαλής αδελφός || ~**child** n προγονός, προγονή m/f || ~**father** n πατριός || ~**ladder** n σκάλα (φορητή) || ~**mother** n μητριά.

stepping stone ['stɛpɪŋstəʊn] n σκαλοπάτι, ενδιάμεσος σταθμός.

stereo ['stɪərɪəʊ] n (RAD) στερεοφωνικό ραδιόφωνο || ~phonic a στερεοφωνικό || ~type n στερεοτυπία ♦ vt τυπώνω διά στερεοτυπίας.

sterile ['stɛraɪl] a στείρος, άγονος, άκαρπος || (free from germs) αποστειρωμένος.

sterility [stɛ'rɪlɪtɪ] n στειρότητα, αγονία.

sterilization [stɛrɪlaɪ'zeɪʃən] n αποστείρωση.

sterilize ['stɛrɪlaɪz] vt στειρώνω || (from germs) αποστειρώνω.

sterling ['stɜːlɪŋ] a στερλίνα || (top quality) αμιγής, καλής ποιότητας.

stern [stɜːn] a αυστηρός, βλοσυρός ♦ n πρύμνη, πρύμη.

stethoscope ['stɛθəskəʊp] n στηθοσκόπιο.

stevedore ['stiːvɪdɔː*] n φορτοεκφορτωτής.

stew [stjuː] n κρέας nt με χορταρικά ♦ vt κάνω κρέας στην κατσαρόλα ♦ vi σιγοβράζω.

steward ['stjuːəd] n (AVIAT, NAUT, RAIL, in club etc) φροντιστής, οικονόμος, καμαρότος || ~ess n (AVIAT) αεροσυνοδός.

stick [stɪk] (irreg v) n βέργα, ράβδος f || (cane) μπαστούνι ♦ vt μπήγω, χώνω, καρφώνω || (gum) κολλώ || (col: tolerate) ανέχομαι, υποφέρω ♦ vi (stop) πιάνομαι, κολλώ, φρακάρω || (hold fast) κολλιέμαι, κολλώ || to ~ out vi (project) κρατώ μέχρι τέλους, επιμένω || to ~ up vi (project) υψώνομαι, στήνω || to ~ up for vt (defend) υπερασπίζομαι, παίρνω το μέρος || ~er n ετικέτα.

stickler ['stɪklə*] n (+ for) άκαμπτος, στενοκέφαλος (σε).

stick-up ['stɪkʌp] n (col: robbery) ληστεία.

sticky ['stɪkɪ] a κολλώδης, γλοιώδης.

stiff [stɪf] a δύσκαμπτος, σκληρός, άκαμπτος || (examination etc) δύσκολος || (paste) σκληρός, σφικτός || (formal) επιτηδευμένος, τυπικός, ψυχρός || (strong) ισχυρός, δυνατός || ~en vt σκληραίνω, δυναμώνω ♦ vi σκληραίνομαι, γίνομαι άκαμπτος || ~ness n σκληρότητα, πιάσιμο.

stifle ['staɪfl] vt (keep back) καταπνίγω, συγκρατώ.

stifling ['staɪflɪŋ] a (atmosphere) αποπνικτικός, ασφυκτικός.

stigma ['stɪgmə] n στίγμα nt, κηλίδα.

stile [staɪl] n στύλος.

still [stɪl] a ακίνητος, αθόρυβος, σιωπηλός ♦ ad (yet) ακόμη || (even) ακόμη (περισσότερα) || ~born a θνησιγενής || ~ life n νεκρή φύση.

stilt [stɪlt] n ξυλοπόδαρο.

stilted ['stɪltɪd] a άκαμπτος, τυπικός, τεχνητός.

stimulant ['stɪmjʊlənt] n διεγερτικό, τονωτικό.

stimulate ['stɪmjʊleɪt] vt διεγείρω, εξάπτω.

stimulating ['stɪmjʊleɪtɪŋ] a διεγερτικός, τονωτικός.

stimulation [stɪmjʊ'leɪʃən] n διέγερση, τόνωση.

stimulus ['stɪmjʊləs] n κίνητρο.

sting [stɪŋ] (irreg v) n δήγμα nt, κέντρισμα nt ♦ vt κεντρίζω, τσιμπώ.

stingy ['stɪndʒɪ] a φιλάργυρος, τσιγγούνης, σφιχτοχέρης.

stink [stɪŋk] (irreg v) n δυσοσμία, βρώμα ♦ vi βρωμώ, βρωμάω || ~ing a (fig) τρομερός.

stint [stɪnt] n όριο, καθήκον ♦ vt στερώ, περιορίζω.

stipend ['staɪpɛnd] n (to vicar etc) μισθός, επίδομα nt.

stipulate ['stɪpjʊleɪt] vt αποφαίνομαι, συμφωνώ, συνομολογώ.

stipulation [stɪpjʊ'leɪʃən] n όρος, διάταξη, συμφωνία.

stir [stɜː*] n ταραχή, σάλεμα nt, κούνημα nt, κίνηση ♦ vt (mix) ανακατώνω, αναδεύω ♦ vi (move) κουνιέμαι, σαλεύω || to ~ up vt υποκινώ, υποδαυλίζω || ~ring a συγκλονιστικός, συγκινητικός.

stirrup ['stɪrəp] n αναβολέας, σκάλα.

stitch [stɪtʃ] n βελονιά, ραφή || (sudden pain) σουβλιά πόνου, σουβλιά ♦ vt ράβω, κάνω βελονιές.

stock [stɒk] n (supply) απόθεμα nt, στοκ nt inv, προμήθεια || (trader's goods) εμπορεύματα ntpl, στοκ nt inv || (farm animals) κτήνη ntpl, ζώα ntpl || (liquid) ζωμός, κονσομέ nt inv || (ECON) χρεώγραφο, τίτλος, αξία ♦ a της σειράς, κανονικός, συνηθισμένος ♦ vt εφοδιάζω, έχω παρακαταθήκη από || to take ~ κάνω απογραφή || (+ of) κρίνω, εκτιμώ || to ~ up with vt αποθηκεύω.

stockade [stɒ'keɪd] n πασσαλόπηγμα nt, φράκτης.

stockbroker ['stɒkbrəʊkə*] n χρηματομεσίτης, χρηματιστής.

stock exchange ['stɒkɪkstʃeɪndʒ] n χρηματιστήριο.

stocking ['stɒkɪŋ] n κάλτσα.

stock market ['stɒkmɑːkɪt] n αγορά χρεωγράφων.

stockpile ['stɒkpaɪl] n αποθέματα ntpl ♦ vt δημιουργώ αποθέματα.

stocktaking ['stɒkteɪkɪŋ] n (COMM) απογραφή.

stocky ['stɒkɪ] a κοντόχοντρος.

stodgy ['stɒdʒɪ] a βαρύς, ανιαρός.

stoical ['stəʊɪkəl] n a στωικός.

stoke [stəʊk] vt τροφοδοτώ φωτιά, διατηρώ φωτιά.

stole [stəʊl] pt of **steal** ♦ n (fur) γούνα, σάρπα || ~n pp of **steal** ♦ a κλεμμένος.

stomach ['stʌmək] n στομάχι || (inclination) όρεξη, διάθεση ♦ vt ανέχομαι, χωνεύω || ~ ache n στομαχόπονος.

stone [stəʊn] n λίθος, πέτρα || (gem) πολύτιμος λίθος, πετράδι, κόσμημα nt ||

(of fruit) πυρήνας, κουκούτσι || (weight) βάρος 14 λιβρών ♦ a από λίθους, πέτρινος ♦ vt βγάζω κουκούτσια από || ~-**cold** a κρύος σαν μάρμαρο || ~-**deaf** a θεόκουφος || ~**work** n λιθοδομή.

stony ['stəʊnɪ] a πετρώδης, γεμάτος πέτρες.

stood [stʊd] pt, pp of **stand**.

stool [stu:l] n σκαμνί.

stoop [stu:p] vi σκύβω.

stop [stɒp] n στάση || (punctuation) σημείο στίξεως ♦ vt (prevent) σταματώ || (bring to end) διακόπτω, σταματώ ♦ vi (cease) παύω, σταματώ, διακόπτομαι || (remain) παραμένω, πηγαίνω || to ~ **doing sth** παύω να κάνω κάτι, σταματώ || ~ **it!** σταμάτα!, φτάνει! || to ~ **dead** vi σταματώ απότομα || to ~ **in** vi (at home) περνώ από, επισκέπτομαι || to ~ **off** vi κατεβαίνω, διακόπτω το ταξίδι μου ♦ vt (hole) φράζω, βουλώνω, κλείνω || ~**lights** npl (AUT) κόκκινα φανάρια ntpl, κόκκινα φώτα npl || ~**over** n (on journey) σταθμός, στάθμευση.

stoppage ['stɒpɪdʒ] n σταμάτημα nt, παύση, διακοπή.

stopper ['stɒpə*] n πώμα nt, βούλωμα nt.

stopwatch ['stɒpwɒtʃ] n χρονόμετρο.

storage ['stɔ:rɪdʒ] n (εν)αποθήκευση, αποθήκη.

store [stɔ:*] n παρακαταθήκη, εφόδιο || (place) αποθήκη || (large shop) κατάστημα nt, μαγαζί ♦ vt εφοδιάζω, αποθηκεύω || (COMPUT) αποθηκεύω || to ~ **up** vt συσσωρεύω, συγκεντρώνω, μαζεύω || ~**room** n αποθήκη, κελάρι.

storey ['stɔ:rɪ] n (Brit) όροφος, πάτωμα nt.

stork [stɔ:k] n πελαργός, λελέκι.

storm [stɔ:m] n θύελλα, καταιγίδα, φουρτούνα || (disturbance) θύελλα, καταιγισμός ♦ vi μαίνομαι ♦ vt (attack) εξαπολύω έφοδο || to take by ~ (lit) καταλαμβάνω με έφοδο || (fig) κατακτώ, παρασύρω || ~ **cloud** n μαύρο σύννεφο || ~y a (weather) θυελλώδης.

story ['stɔ:rɪ] n (account) ιστορία, αφήγηση, διήγημα nt || (lie) παραμύθι, ψέμα nt || (US: storey) όροφος, πάτωμα nt || ~**book** n βιβλίο διηγημάτων || ~**teller** n αφηγητής, παραμυθάς.

stout [staut] a (bold) δυνατός, γερός, θαρραλέος || (too fat) χονδρός, σωματώδης, παχύς ♦ n είδος μπύρας.

stove [stəʊv] n (for cooking) κουζίνα, συσκευή μαγειρεύματος || (for heating) θερμάστρα, σόμπα.

stow [stəʊ] vt στοιβάζω, αποθηκεύω || ~**away** n λαθρεπιβάτης.

straddle ['strædl] vt κάθομαι καβαλικευτά, καβαλικεύω.

straggle ['strægl] vi σκορπίζω, βραδυπορώ || ~r n παραπλανημένος, ο βραδυπορών.

straight [streɪt] a ευθύς, ευθύγραμμος, ίσιος || (honest) δίκαιος, ευθύς, τίμιος,

ντόμπρος || (in order) τακτικός, τακτοποιημένος, σιαγμένος ♦ ad ίσια, κατευθείαν, αμέσως || (drink) σκέτο ♦ n ευθεία || ~ **away** ad (at once) αμέσως || ~ **off** ad (without stopping) στη στιγμή, αυτοστιγμεί || ~**en** vt (also: ~ **out**) ισιώνω || (fig) τακτοποιώ || ~**forward** a (simple) χωρίς περιστροφές, ντόμπρος, ειλικρινής.

strain [streɪn] n (mental) ένταση, κούραση || (streak, trace) φυσική διάθεση, κλίση, τάση ♦ vt (stretch) εντείνω, τεντώνω || (filter) διυλίζω, φιλτράρω ♦ vi (make effort) μοχθώ, κοπιάζω, εντείνω || ~s npl (MUS) τόνος, ύφος nt || ~ed a (laugh) βιασμένος, ψεύτικος || (relations) τεταμένος || ~er n σουρωτήρι, φίλτρο, τρυπητό.

strait [streɪt] n (GEOG) στενό, πορθμός || ~ **jacket** n ζουρλομανδύας || ~-**laced** a ηθικολόγος, σεμνότυφος.

strand [strænd] n (thread) κλώνος, κλωνί, κλωστή ♦ vt εξοκέλλω || ~**ed** a εγκαταλειμμένος, αφισμένος πίσω.

strange [streɪndʒ] a ξένος || (unusual) ασυνήθιστος, παράξενος || ~**ness** n το περίεργο, παράξενο || ~r n ξένος/η m/f, άγνωστος/η m/f || (new to a place) νεοαφιχθείς/είσα m/f, καινούργιος/α m/f.

strangle ['stræŋgl] vt στραγγαλίζω, πνίγω, καταπνίγω.

strangulation [stræŋgjʊ'leɪʃən] n στραγγαλισμός.

strap [stræp] n λωρίδα, λουρί ♦ vt δένω με λουρί || (beat) δέρνω με λουρί || ~**ping** a γεροδεμένος.

strata ['stra:tə] npl of **stratum**.

stratagem ['strætɪdʒəm] n στρατήγημα nt, κόλπο.

strategic [strə'ti:dʒɪk] a στρατηγικός || ~**ally** ad στρατηγικά.

strategy ['strætɪdʒɪ] n στρατηγική, τέχνασμα nt.

stratum ['stra:təm] n στρώμα nt.

straw [strɔ:] n (AGR) άχυρο, ψάθα || (drinking straw) καλάμι, καλαμάκι ♦ a (hat, basket) ψάθινος, αχυρένιος.

strawberry ['strɔ:bərɪ] n φράουλα.

stray [streɪ] n χαμένος, ζώο που έχει ξεκόψει από το κοπάδι ♦ vi περιπλανώμαι, απομακρύνομαι ♦ a (animal) περιπλανώμενος, αδέσποτος || (thought) ξεκάρφωτος, σκόρπιος, ξεκόλλητος.

streak [stri:k] n γραμμή, λωρίδα, ρίγα || (strain) δόση ♦ vt χαράσσω, ριγώνω, σχηματίζω ραβδώσεις || ~y a ραβδωτός, γραμμωτός, ριγωτός.

stream [stri:m] n ποτάμι, ρυάκι, ρέμα nt || (flow) ροή, ρους, χείμαρρος || (crowd) κύματα ntpl, αδιάκοπη σειρά ♦ vi ρέω, τρέχω, κυλώ.

streamer ['stri:mə*] n σερπαντίνα, ταινία, σημαία.

streamlined ['stri:mlaɪnd] a αεροδυναμικός.

street [striːt] n οδός f, δρόμος || ~**car** n (US: tram) τράμ nt inv || ~ **lamp** n φανοστάτης.

strength [streŋθ] n (lit) δύναμη, ισχύς f || (fig) on the ~**of** βασιζόμενος σε, στηριζόμενος σε || ~**en** vt ενισχύω, δυναμώνω.

strenuous ['strenjυəs] a κουραστικός, δραστήριος || (requiring effort) επίπονος, σκληρός.

stress [stres] n (force, pressure) πίεση, καταναγκασμός || (mental strain) ένταση || (accent) τόνος ♦ vt τονίζω.

stretch [stretʃ] n (area) έκταση ♦ vt τεντώνω, απλώνω ♦ vi εκτείνομαι, πλαταίνω || at a ~ (continuously) χωρίς διακοπή || to ~ **out** vi επεκτείνομαι, αραιώνω ♦ vt τείνω, απλώνω || ~**er** n φορείο.

stricken ['strikən] a (person) χτυπημένος, λιμμένος || (city, country) χτυπημένος.

strict [strikt] a ακριβής, αυστηρός || δριμύς || ~**ly** ad αυστηρά, ακριβώς || ~**ly speaking** κυριολεκτικώς, για να πούμε την αλήθεια || ~**ness** n αυστηρότητα.

stride [straid] (irreg v) n μεγάλο βήμα nt, δρασκελιά ♦ vi δρασκελίζω, βηματίζω.

strident ['straidənt] a οξύς, στριγγός, στρίγγλικος.

strife [straif] n αγώνας, πάλη, σύγκρουση.

strike [straik] (irreg v) n απεργία || (discovery) ανακάλυψη, συνάντηση || (attack) επιχείρηση, πλήγμα nt ♦ vt κτυπώ, προσκρούω, σκουντώ || (come into mind) έρχομαι (στο μυαλό), μου φαίνεται || (find gold) ανακαλύπτω, βρίσκω ♦ vi (stop work) κηρύσσω απεργία, απεργώ || (attack) χτυπώ || (clock) ηχώ, χτυπώ, σημαίνω || to ~ **down** vt (lay low) ρίχνω χάμω || to ~ **out** vt (cross out) εξαλείφω, διαγράφω, σβήνω || to ~ **up** vt (music) αρχίζω (να παίζω) || (friendship) πιάνω φιλία || ~**r** n απεργός.

striking ['straikiŋ] a κτυπητός, ελκυστικός, ενδιαφέρων || ~**ly** ad εντυπωσιακά, χτυπητά.

string [striŋ] n σπάγγος, κορδόνι || (series) σειρά || (MUS) χορδή || (COMPUT) διατεταγμένη σειρά χαρακτήρων || ~ **bean** n φρέσκο φασολάκι.

stringent ['strindʒənt] a αυστηρός, στενός.

strip [strip] n λουρίδα, ταινία ♦ vt γυμνώνω, γδύνω, βγάζω || (machine etc) αποσυνδέω ♦ vi γδύνομαι, γυμνώνομαι || ~ **cartoon** n σειρά εύθυμων σκίτσων.

stripe [straip] n γραμμή, λουρίδα, ράβδωση || ~**d** a ραβδωτός, ριγωτός.

stripper ['stripə*] n στριπτηζέ f inv.

striptease ['striptiːz] n στριπτήζ nt inv.

strive [straiv] (irreg v) vi (+ for) αγωνίζομαι (για), προσπαθώ || ~**n** ['strivn] pp of strive.

strode [strəud] pt, pp of **stride**.

stroke [strəuk] n κτύπημα nt, πλήγμα nt ||

(TECH) κίνηση, διαδρομή, ρυθμός || (sudden attack) προσβολή || (caress) θωπεία, χάδι, χάιδεμα nt ♦ vt χαϊδεύω, τρίβω, σιάζω || at a ~ μ' ένα κτύπημα, με μιας || on the ~ of 5 στις 5 ακριβώς.

stroll [strəul] n περίπατος, βόλτα ♦ vi κάνω περίπατο, κάνω βόλτες.

strong [strɒŋ] a δυνατός, ισχυρός, γερός || (firm) στερεός, γερός || (flavour) δυνατός, έντονος || (protest) έντονος || (wind) ισχυρός, δυνατός || **they are 50** ~ δυνάμεως 50 ανδρών || ~**hold** n φρούριο, οχυρό, προπύργιο || ~**ly** ad δυνατά, γερά || ~**room** n αίθουσα χρηματοκιβωτίων.

strove [strəuv] pt of strive.

struck [strʌk] pt, pp of **strike**.

structural ['strʌktʃərəl] a δομικός.

structure ['strʌktʃə*] n κατασκευή, δομή || (building) οικοδόμημα nt, κτίριο, κτίσμα nt.

struggle ['strʌgl] n αγώνας, πάλη, σκληρή προσπάθεια ♦ vi (+ to) αγωνίζομαι, παλεύω.

strum [strʌm] vt (guitar) παίζω αδέξια, παίζω άτεχνα.

strut [strʌt] n (support) στήριγμα nt, υποστήριγμα nt ♦ vi περιφέρομαι καμαρωτός, κορδώνομαι.

stub [stʌb] n (cigarette etc) υπόλειμμα nt, γόπα.

stubble ['stʌbl] n καλαμιά, ρίζες fpl || (on face) γένια ntpl ημερών.

stubborn ['stʌbən] a επίμονος, πεισματάρης, ξεροκέφαλος || ~**ly** ad πεισματικά, επίμονα.

stubby ['stʌbi] a κοντόχοντρος.

stuck [stʌk] pt, pp of stick || ~-**up** a υπεροπτικός, φαντασμένος.

stud [stʌd] n πλατυκέφαλο καρφί || (of shirt) κουμπί, ξενόκουμπο || (of horses) στάβλος αλόγων, ιπποστάσιο ♦ vt διαστίζω, κοσμώ με καρφιά.

student ['stjuːdənt] n φοιτητής/ήτρια m/f, σπουδαστής/άστρια m/f, μελετητής.

studio ['stjuːdiəu] n εργαστήριο, ατελιέ nt inv || (also TV) στούντιο.

studious ['stjuːdiəs] a μελετηρός, φιλομαθής || (careful) προσεκτικός || ~**ly** ad (carefully) επιμελώς.

study ['stʌdi] n σπουδή, μελέτη || (something studied) μελέτη, έρευνα || (room) σπουδαστήριο, αναγνωστήριο ♦ vt σπουδάζω, μελετώ || (examine) μελετώ, παρατηρώ ♦ vi επιμελούμαι, μελετώ.

stuff [stʌf] n ύλη, υλικό, ουσία ♦ vt (παρα)γεμίζω || ~**ing** n παραγέμισμα nt, γέμιση || (of fowl etc) γέμισμα nt || ~**y** a (room) πνιγηρός, χωρίς αέρα || (ideas: old-fashioned) σεμνότυφος.

stumble ['stʌmbl] vt σκοντάφτω, προσκρούω || to ~ **on** vt ανακαλύπτω αναπάντεχα.

stumbling block ['stʌmbliŋblɒk] n εμπόδιο.

stump [stʌmp] n κούτσουρο, στέλεχος nt ♦ vt (puzzle) μπερδεύω, τα χάνω.

stun [stʌŋ] vt ζαλίζω, ταράζω.

stung [stʌŋ] pt, pp of sting.

stunk [stʌŋk] pp of stink.

stunning ['stʌnɪŋ] a εξαίσιος, καταπλικτικός.

stunt [stʌnt] n εκπληκτική παράσταση, άθλος ♦ vt περιστέλλω, εμποδίζω την ανάπτυξη || ~ed a κατοισασμένος.

stupefy ['stju:pɪfaɪ] vt καταπλήσσω.

stupendous [stju:'pɛndəs] a τεράστιος, πελώριος, καταπληκτικός || ~ly ad καταπληκτικά.

stupid ['stju:pɪd] a ηλίθιος, βλάκας, κουτός || ~ity n βλακεία, κουταμάρα || ~ly ad ηλίθια, βλακωδώς.

stupor ['stju:pə*] n νάρκη, λήθαργος, χαύνωση.

sturdy ['stɜ:dɪ] a δυνατός, σθεναρός, γεροδεμένος.

stutter ['stʌtə*] n ψέλλισμα nt, τραύλισμα nt ♦ vi τραυλίζω, τσεβδίζω.

sty [staɪ] n χοιροστάσιο, γουρνοστάσι.

stye [staɪ] n χαλάζιο, κριθαράκι.

style [staɪl] n στύλ nt inv, τεχνοτροπία, ύφος nt || (fashion) ρυθμός, στύλ nt inv, μόδα || (distinction) επιδεξιότητα, μεγαλοπρέπεια.

stylish ['staɪlɪʃ] a μοντέρνος, κομψός || ~ly ad κομψά, με σικ.

stylus ['staɪləs] n στύλος, γραφίδα.

suave [swɑ:v] a ευγενικός, απαλός, ευχάριστος.

sub- [sʌb] prefix υπο-.

subconscious ['sʌb'kɒnʃəs] a υποσυνείδητος ♦ n: the ~ το υποσυνείδητο.

subdivide ['sʌbdɪ'vaɪd] vt υποδιαιρώ.

subdivision ['sʌbdɪvɪʒən] n υποδιαίρεση.

subdue [səb'dju:] vt κατακτώ, υποτάσσω, μαλακώνω || ~d a συντριμμένος, μαλακωμένος.

subject ['sʌbdʒɪkt] n υπήκοος m/f || (theme) θέμα nt, αντικείμενο || (GRAM) υποκείμενο ♦ [səb'dʒɛkt] vt: to ~ s.o. to sth υποβάλλω κάποιον σε κάτι || to be ~ to υπόκειμαι σε, εξαρτώμαι από || ~ion n καθυπόταξη, υποταγή || ~ive a υποκειμενικός || ~ matter n θέμα nt, περιεχόμενο.

sublet ['sʌb'lɛt] vt υπενοικιάζω.

sublime [sə'blaɪm] a θείος, ανώτερος, υπέροχος, έξοχος.

submarine [sʌbmə'ri:n] n υποβρύχιο.

submerge [səb'mɜ:dʒ] vt βυθίζω, χώνω στο νερό ♦ vi καταδύομαι, βυθίζομαι, βουλιάζω.

submission [səb'mɪʃən] n υποταγή, υπακοή || (presentation) υποβολή.

submit [səb'mɪt] vt υποβάλλω ♦ vi υποτάσσομαι, υποβάλλομαι.

subnormal ['sʌb'nɔ:məl] a κάτω του κανονικού.

subordinate [sə'bɔ:dɪnɪt] a κατώτερος, εξαρτημένος ♦ n υφιστάμενος.

subpoena [səb'pi:nə] n κλήση

(μορτύρων) ♦ vt καλώ, αποστέλλω κλήση.

subscribe [səb'skraɪb] vi (pay contribution) εγγράφομαι, συνεισφέρω || (+ to) επιδοκιμάζω, αποδέχομαι, παραδέχομαι || ~ r n (to periodical, TEL) συνδρομητής/ήτρια m/f.

subscription [səb'skrɪpʃən] n συνεισφορά, συνδρομή.

subsequent ['sʌbsɪkwənt] a επακόλουθος, μεταγενέστερος || ~ly ad έπειτα, αργότερα.

subside [səb'saɪd] vi κατακαθίζω, υποχωρώ, κοπάζω || ~nce n καθίζηση, κόπαση.

subsidiary [səb'sɪdɪərɪ] a βοηθητικός, δευτερεύων ♦ n θυγατρική εταιρεία.

subsidize ['sʌbsɪdaɪz] vt επιχορηγώ, επιδοτώ.

subsidy ['sʌbsɪdɪ] n επιχορήγηση, βοήθημα nt, επίδομα nt.

subsistence [səb'sɪstəns] n ύπαρξη, συντήρηση, επιβίωση.

substance ['sʌbstəns] n ουσία || (wealth) περιουσία, αξία.

substandard ['sʌb'stændəd] a κάτω του μέσου όρου, κακής ποιότητας.

substantial [səb'stænʃəl] a (strong) στερεός, γερός || (important) σημαντικός, ουσιώδης || ~ly ad ουσιαστικά, πραγματικά.

substantiate [səb'stænʃɪeɪt] vt επαληθεύω, αποδεικνύω, αιτιολογώ.

substitute ['sʌbstɪtju:t] n αντικαταστάτης, υποκατάστατο ♦ vt υποκαθιστώ, αντικαθιστώ.

substitution [sʌbstɪ'tju:ʃən] n αντικατάσταση, υποκατάσταση.

subterfuge ['sʌbtəfju:dʒ] n υπεκφυγή, τέχνασμα nt, πρόφαση.

subterranean [sʌbtə'reɪnɪən] a υπόγειος.

subtitle ['sʌbtaɪtl] n (CINE) υπότιτλος.

subtle ['sʌtl] a (faint) λεπτός, διακριτικός || (clever, sly) έξυπνος, πανούργος || ~ty n λεπτότητα.

subtly ['sʌtlɪ] ad διακριτικά, με λεπτότητα.

subtract [səb'trækt] vt αφαιρώ || ~ion n αφαίρεση.

subtropical ['sʌb'trɒpɪkəl] a υποτροπικός.

suburb ['sʌbɜ:b] n προάστειο || ~an a των προαστείων.

subversive [sʌb'vɜ:sɪv] a ανατρεπτικός.

subway ['sʌbweɪ] n (US) υπόγειος σιδηρόδρομος.

succeed [sək'si:d] vi επιτυγχάνω, πετυχαίνω ♦ vt διαδέχομαι || ~ing a (following) επόμενος, μελλοντικός.

success [sək'sɛs] n επιτυχία, ευτυχής έκβαση || (person) επιτυχημένος άνθρωπος || ~ful a επιτυχής, επιτυχημένος || ~fully ad επιτυχώς, με επιτυχία.

succession [sək'sɛʃən] n διαδοχή.

successive [sək'sɛsiv] a διαδοχικός, συνεχής, αλλεπάλληλος.
successor [sək'sɛsə*] n διάδοχος.
succinct [sək'siŋkt] a σύντομος και σαφής.
succulent ['sʌkjulənt] a εύχυμος, ζουμερός, νόστιμος.
succumb [sə'kʌm] vi (+ to) υποκύπτω, υποτάσσομαι, ενδίδω.
such [sʌtʃ] a (of that kind) τέτοιος, τέτοιου είδους || (so great etc) τόσος ♦ pron αυτός, αυτοί, τέτοιος.
suck [sʌk] vt (toffee) πιπιλίζω || ~er n (col) κορόιδο.
suction ['sʌkʃən] n αναρρόφηση, άντληση.
sudden ['sʌdn] a ξαφνικός, αιφνίδιος || **all of a** ~ αιφνιδίως, ξαφνικά || ~ly ad ζωηρικά.
sue [su:] vt ενάγω, κάνω αγωγή.
suede [sweid] n καστόρι, σουέντ nt inv.
suet [suit] n λίπος nt, ξύγγι.
suffer ['sʌfə*] vt (death) θανατούμαι, εκτελούμαι || (permit) υποφέρω, ανέχομαι, δέχομαι ♦ vi υποφέρω, πάσχω || ~er n υποφέρων, πάσχων || ~ing n πόνος, βάσανα ntpl, πάθη ntpl.
suffice [sə'fais] vi (επ)αρκώ, φθάνω.
sufficient [sə'fiʃənt] a επαρκής, αρκετός || ~ly ad αρκετά.
suffix ['sʌfiks] n κατάληξη, πρόσφυμα nt.
suffocate ['sʌfəkeit] vi πνίγομαι, ασφυκτιώ.
suffocation [sʌfə'keiʃən] n ασφυξία, πνίξιμο.
sugar ['ʃugə*] n ζάχαρη ♦ vt ζαχαρώνω, βάζω ζάχαρη || ~ beet n ζαχαρότευτλο || ~ cane n ζαχαροκάλαμο || ~y a ζαχαρένιος, ζαχαρωμένος, γλυκύτατος.
suggest [sə'dʒɛst] vt εισηγούμαι, προτείνω || (show indirectly) υπαινίσσομαι, υπονοώ || (propose) προτείνω, υποβάλλω, υποδεικνύω || ~ion n πρόταση, υποβολή || ~ive a υπαινισσόμενος, υποβλητικός, με υπονοούμενα.
suicidal [sui'saidl] a της αυτοκτονίας.
suicide ['suisaid] n αυτοκτονία || (person) αυτόχειρας.
suit [su:t] n (of clothes) κοστούμι || (in cards) τα τέσσερα χρώματα ♦ vt ταιριάζω, πηγαίνω || (satisfy) ικανοποιώ, βολεύω || (adapt) προσαρμόζω || ~able a κατάλληλος, αρμόζων, ταιριαστός || ~ably ad καταλλήλως, όπως πρέπει.
suitcase ['su:tkeis] n βαλίτσα.
suite [swi:t] n (of rooms) διαμέρισμα nt, σουίτα || (MUS) σουίτα.
sulfur ['sʌlfə*] n (US) = **sulphur**.
sulk [sʌlk] vi κάνω μούτρα, κατσουφιάζω || ~y a κακόκεφος, κατσούφης.
sullen ['sʌlən] a (gloomy) κατηφής, μελαγχολικός || (bad-tempered) κακόκεφος, κατσούφης.
sulphur ['sʌlfə*] n θείο, θειάφι.

sultan ['sʌltən] n σουλτάνος || ~a n σουλτάνα || (raisin) σουλτανίνα.
sultry ['sʌltri] a αποπνικτικός, πνιγηρός.
sum [sʌm] n (total) σύνολο || (calculation) άθροισμα nt || (of money) ποσό (χρημάτων) || **to** ~ **up** vt συνοψίζω, ανακεφαλαιώνω ♦ vi κρίνω, εκτιμώ.
summarize ['sʌməraiz] vt συνοψίζω, συγκεφαλαιώνω.
summary ['sʌməri] n (συνοπτική) περίληψη, σύνοψη.
summer ['sʌmə*] n καλοκαίρι ♦ attr a (clothing) καλοκαιρινός || ~house n (in garden) περίπτερο κήπου || ~time n καλοκαίρι, θερινή ώρα.
summit ['sʌmit] n κορυφή || ~ conference n συνεδρίαση κορυφής.
summon ['sʌmən] vt (συγ)καλώ, προσκαλώ || (gather up) συγκεντρώνω, μαζεύω || ~s n κλήση ♦ vt κλητεύω, καλώ.
sump [sʌmp] n λεκάνη αποστραγγίσεως, κάρτερ nt inv.
sumptuous ['sʌmptjuəs] a πολυτελής, πολυδάπανος.
sun [sʌn] n ήλιος || (sunshine) λιακάδα || ~bathe vi κάνω ηλιοθεραπεία || ~burn n έγκαυμα nt από τον ήλιο || ~burnt a ηλιοκαμμένος, μαυρισμένος.
Sunday ['sʌndi] n Κυριακή.
sundial ['sʌndaiəl] n ηλιακό ρολόι.
sundry ['sʌndri] a διάφορος || **sundries** npl διάφορα είδη ntpl.
sunflower ['sʌnflauə*] n ήλιος, ηλίανθος.
sung [sʌŋ] pp of **sing**.
sunglasses ['sʌnglɑ:siz] npl γυαλιά ntpl του ηλίου.
sunk [sʌŋk] pp of **sink**.
sunlight ['sʌnlait] n ηλιακό φώς, λιακάδα.
sunlit ['sʌnlit] a ηλιόλουστος.
sunny ['sʌni] a ευήλιος, ηλιόλουστος || (cheerful) χαρωπός, γελαστός.
sunrise ['sʌnraiz] n ανατολή του ηλίου.
sunset ['sʌnsɛt] n ηλιοβασίλεμα nt.
sunshade ['sʌnʃeid] n (over table) αλεξήλιο, ομπρέλα του ηλίου.
sunshine ['sʌnʃain] n λιακάδα.
sunspot ['sʌnspɒt] n ηλιακή κηλίδα.
sunstroke ['sʌnstrəuk] n ηλίαση.
suntan ['sʌntæn] n μαύρισμα nt από τον ήλιο.
super ['su:pə*] a (col) υπέροχος, περίφημος, σπουδαίος || prefix υπερ-.
superannuation [su:pərænju'eiʃən] n συνταξιοδότηση.
superb [su:'pɜ:b] a υπέροχος, έξοχος, εξαίσιος || ~ly ad υπέροχα, έξοχα, λαμπρά.
supercilious [su:pə'siliəs] a αγέρωχος, υπεροπτικός.
superficial [su:pə'fiʃəl] a επιφανειακός || (shallow) επιπόλαιος, επιφανειακός.
superfluous [su'pɜ:fluəs] a περιττός.
superhuman [su:pə'hju:mən] a (effort) υπεράνθρωπος.

superimpose ['suːpərɪm'pəʊz] vt βάζω από πάνω, υπερθέτω.

superintendent [suːpərɪn'tendənt] n (police) αξιωματικός της αστυνομίας.

superior [su'pɪərɪə*] a ανώτερος, υπέρτερος, εξαιρετικός || (proud) υπεροπτικός, ακατάδεχτος ♦ n προϊστάμενος, ανώτερος || ~ity n υπεροχή, ανωτερότητα.

superlative [su'pɜːlətɪv] a ανώτατος, υπερθετικός ♦ n (το) υπερθετικό.

superman ['suːpəmæn] n υπεράνθρωπος.

supermarket ['suːpəmɑːkɪt] n σουπερμάρκετ f inv, υπεραγορά.

supernatural [suːpə'nætʃərəl] a υπερφυσικός.

superpower ['suːpəpaʊə*] n (POL) υπερδύναμη.

supersede [suːpə'siːd] vt αντικαθιστώ, παραμερίζω.

supersonic ['suːpə'sɒnɪk] a υπερηχητικός.

superstition [suːpə'stɪʃən] n δεισιδαιμονία, πρόληψη.

superstitious [suːpə'stɪʃəs] a δεισιδαίμονας, προληπτικός.

supertanker ['suːpətæŋkə*] n υπερδεξαμενόπλοιο.

supervise ['suːpəvaɪz] vt επιβλέπω, εποπτεύω, διευθύνω.

supervision [suːpə'vɪʒən] n εποπτεία, επιθεώρηση, διεύθυνση.

supervisor ['suːpəvaɪzə*] n επιθεωρητής/ήτρια m/f, επόπτης/όπτρια m/f, επιστάτης/άτρια m/f.

supper ['sʌpə*] n δείπνο.

supple ['sʌpl] a εύκαμπτος, ευλύγιστος, λυγερός.

supplement ['sʌplɪmənt] n συμπλήρωμα nt || (newspaper) παράρτημα nt ♦ [sʌplɪ'ment] vt συμπληρώνω || ~ary a συμπληρωματικός, πρόσθετος.

supplier [sə'plaɪə*] n προμηθευτής.

supply [sə'plaɪ] vt παρέχω, εφοδιάζω, προμηθεύω ♦ n εφόδιο, απόθεμα nt, προμήθεια || (supplying) εφοδιασμός, τροφοδότηση || **supplies** npl (food) τρόφιμα ntpl || (MIL) εφόδια ntpl || ~ **and demand** προσφορά και ζήτηση.

support [sə'pɔːt] n (moral, financial etc) υποστήριξη, ενίσχυση || (TECH) στήριγμα nt, υποστήριγμα nt, έρεισμα nt ♦ vt (υπο)στηρίζω, ενισχύω || (provide for) συντηρώ, κρατώ || (speak for) υποστηρίζω, ενισχύω || (endure) υπομένω, υποφέρω || ~er n (POL etc) οπαδός, υπερασπιστής/ίστρια m/f || (SPORT) οπαδός, υποστηρικτής/ίκτρια m/f || ~ing a (programme, role) βοηθητικός, δευτερεύων.

suppose [sə'pəʊz] vti υποθέτω, προϋποθέτω || (think, imagine) φαντάζομαι, νομίζω || ~ **he comes ...** αν έρθει ... || ~**dly** ad υποθετικά, δήθεν.

supposing [sə'pəʊzɪŋ] cj εάν, ας υποθέσουμε ότι.

supposition [sʌpə'zɪʃən] n υπόθεση, γνώμη.

suppress [sə'pres] vt καταπνίγω, καταστέλλω || (hold back) συγκρατώ, σκεπάζω || ~**ion** n κατάπνιξη, συγκράτηση, απόκρυψη.

supremacy [su'preməsɪ] n υπεροχή, ανώτατη εξουσία.

supreme [su'priːm] a υπέρτατος, ανώτατος, ύψιστος.

surcharge ['sɜːtʃɑːdʒ] n πρόσθετη επιβάρυνση.

sure [ʃʊə*] a βέβαιος, ασφαλής, σίγουρος ♦ ad βεβαίως, ασφαλώς || ~! (of course) βέβαια!, ασφαλώς! || **to make ~ of** βεβαιώνω || ~-**footed** a με σίγουρο πόδι || ~**ly** ad ασφαλώς, βεβαίως || (firmly) αναμφίβολα || (gladly) βεβαίως, μετά χαράς.

surf [sɜːf] n κύμα nt, αφρός.

surface ['sɜːfɪs] n (top side) επιφάνεια || (outward appearance) εξωτερικό, εμφάνιση ♦ vt (roadway) επιστρώνω, στρώνω ♦ vi βγαίνω στην επιφάνεια || ~ **mail** n τακτικό ταχυδρομείο.

surfboard ['sɜːfbɔːd] n σανίδα κυματοδρομίας, σέρφμπορντ nt inv.

surfeit ['sɜːfɪt] n υπεραφθονία, πληθώρα, κόρος.

surge [sɜːdʒ] n μεγάλο κύμα nt || (fig) μεγάλη αύξηση ♦ vi ορμώ, ξεχύνομαι.

surgeon ['sɜːdʒən] n χειρούργος.

surgery ['sɜːdʒərɪ] n χειρουργική || (room) ιατρείο, χειρουργείο.

surgical ['sɜːdʒɪkəl] a χειρουργικός.

surly ['sɜːlɪ] a αγροίκος, κατσούφης, αγενής.

surmise [sɜː'maɪz] vt εικάζω, υποθέτω, μαντεύω.

surmount [sɜː'maʊnt] vt (difficulty) υπερνικώ, ξεπερνώ.

surname ['sɜːneɪm] n επώνυμο.

surpass [sɜː'pɑːs] vt υπερτερώ, υπερβαίνω, ξεπερνώ.

surplus ['sɜːpləs] n περίσσευμα nt, πλεόνασμα nt ♦ a πλεονάζων, υπεράριθμος.

surprise [sə'praɪz] n έκπληξη, κατάπληξη, ξάφνισμα nt ♦ vt αιφνιδιάζω || (astonish) εκπλήσσω, καταπλήσσω, ξαφνίζω.

surprising [sə'praɪzɪŋ] a εκπληκτικός, καταπληκτικός.

surrender [sə'rendə*] n παράδοση, εγκατάλειψη ♦ vi παραδίδομαι, παραδίδω, παραχωρώ.

surreptitious [sʌrəp'tɪʃəs] a λαθραίος, κρυφός.

surround [sə'raʊnd] vt περιβάλλω, περικυκλώνω || ~**ing** a (countryside) περιβάλλων, εξοχικός || ~**ings** npl περιβάλλον, περίχωρα ntpl.

surveillance [sɜː'veɪləns] n (observation) επιτήρηση, εποπτεία.

survey ['sɜːveɪ] n (inquiry) επισκόπηση || (of land) χωρογράφηση, τοπογράφηση ♦ [sɜː'veɪ] vt επισκοπώ, εξετάζω || (measure *land*) χωρογραφώ, τοπογραφώ || ~**ing** *n* (*of land*) χωρογραφία, τοπογραφία || ~**or** *n* (*of land*) τοπογράφος.

survival [sə'vaɪvəl] *n* επιβίωση || (*from past*) υπόλειμμα, επιβίωμα *nt*.

survive [sə'vaɪv] *vi* επιζώ ♦ *vt* επιζώ || (*a shipwreck etc*) σώζομαι, γλυτώνω.

survivor [sə'vaɪvə*] *n* επιζών, διασωθείς.

susceptible [sə'sɛptəbl] *a* (+ *to*) επιδεκτικός, τρωτός.

suspect ['sʌspɛkt] *n* ύποπτος ♦ *a* ύποπτος ♦ [səs'pɛkt] *vt* υποπτεύομαι, υποψιάζομαι || (*think likely*) υποψιάζομαι, φαντάζομαι.

suspend [səs'pɛnd] *vt* αναστέλλω, διακόπτω || (*hang up*) αναρτώ, κρεμώ || ~**ers** *npl* καλτσοδέτες *fpl* || (*US*) τιράντες *fpl*.

suspense [səs'pɛns] *n* εκκρεμότητα, αντισυχία, αβεβαιότητα.

suspension [səs'pɛnʃən] *n* αναστολή, ανακοπή || (*being suspended*) απόλυση || (*AUT*) ανάρτηση || ~ **bridge** *n* κρεμαστή γέφυρα.

suspicion [səs'pɪʃən] *n* υποψία, υπόνοια || (*small amount*) μικρή δόση.

suspicious [səs'pɪʃəs] *a* ύποπτος, καχύποπτος || ~**ly** *ad* ύποπτα, δύσπιστα.

sustain [səs'teɪn] *vt* υποστηρίζω, στηρίζω, βαστάζω || (*confirm*) αποδέχομαι || (*injury*) υφίσταμαι, παθαίνω, δέχομαι || ~**ed** *a* (*effort*) επίμονος, συνεχής.

sustenance ['sʌstɪnəns] *n* συντήρηση, τροφή.

swab [swɒb] *n* (*pad*) ξέστρο.

swagger ['swægə*] *vi* περπατώ καμαρωτός, επιδεικνύομαι.

swallow ['swɒləʊ] *n* (*bird*) χελιδόνι || (*of food etc*) μπουκιά ♦ *vt* καταπίνω, χάφτω || **to ~ up** *vt* καταπίνω, καταβροχθίζω.

swam [swæm] *pt of* **swim.**

swamp [swɒmp] *n* έλος *nt*, βάλτος ♦ *vt* (*overwhelm*) συντρίβω, σαρώνω.

swan [swɒn] *n* κύκνος.

swap [swɒp] *n* (*exchange*) ανταλλαγή ♦ *vt* (+ *for*) ανταλλάσσω, αλλάζω.

swarm [swɔːm] *n* (*of bees*) σμήνος *nt*, πλήθος *nt* || (*of insects*) σύννεφο || (*of people*) μπουλούκι, τσούρμο ♦ *vt* (*crowd*) συρρέω, συγκεντρώνομαι.

swarthy ['swɔːðɪ] *a* μελαψός, μελαχροινός.

swastika ['swɒstɪkə] *n* αγκυλωτός σταυρός.

swat [swɒt] *vt* κτυπώ, βαρώ.

sway [sweɪ] *vi* ταλαντεύομαι, κουνιέμαι, τρικλίζω ♦ *vt* ταλαντεύω, κουνώ || (*influence*) διευθύνω, επηρεάζω, παρασύρω.

swear [swɛə*] (*irreg v*) *vi* ορκίζομαι || (*curse*) βλαστημώ, βρίζω || **to ~ to** ορκίζομαι σε, βεβαιώ || ~**word** *n* βλαστήμια, βρισιά.

sweat [swɛt] *n* ιδρώτας || (*MED*) ίδρωμα *nt* ♦ *vi* ιδρώνω || (*toil*) μοχθώ, σπάω στη δουλειά.

sweater ['swɛtə*] *n* πουλόβερ *nt inv.*

sweaty ['swɛtɪ] *a* ιδρωμένος.

Swede [swiːd] *n* Σουηδός/ή *m/f.*

swede [swiːd] *n* (*turnip*) ραπίτσα.

Sweden ['swiːdn] *n* Σουηδία.

Swedish ['swiːdɪʃ] *a* σουηδικός ♦ *n* (*LING*) Σουηδικά *ntpl*.

sweep [swiːp] (*irreg v*) *n* σκούπισμα *nt*, σάρωμα *nt* || (*wide curve*) κυκλική κίνηση, καμπή || (*range*) άνοιγμα *nt*, ευρύτητα || (*of chimney*) καπνοδοχοκαθαριστής ♦ *vt* σκουπίζω, καθαρίζω, σαρώνω ♦ *vi* (*move in curve*) εκτείνομαι, απλώνομαι || προχωρώ μεγαλόπρεπα || **to ~ away** *vt* σκουπίζω, σαρώνω || **to ~ past** *vi* περνώ γρήγορα || **to ~ up** *vi* φθάνω, ανεβαίνω ♦ *vt* σκουπίζω, μαζεύω || ~**ing** *a* (*gesture*) πλατειά (χειρονομία) || (*statement*) γενικός, ριζικός.

sweet [swiːt] *n* γλυκό || (*candy*) ζαχαρωτό, καραμέλα ♦ *a* γλυκός || (*fresh*) δροσερός, φρέσκος || (*charming, pretty*) χαριτωμένος, γλυκός, συμπαθητικός || ~**breads** *npl* γλυκάδια *ntpl* || ~**en** *vt* γλυκαίνω || ~**heart** *n* αγαπητικός, αγαπημένος || ~**ly** *ad* γλυκά, μελωδικά, ευχάριστα || ~**ness** *n* γλυκύτητα, γλύκα || ~ **pea** *n* λάθυρος, μοσχομπίζελο || ~ **tooth** *n* αδυναμία για γλυκά.

swell [swɛl] (*irreg v*) *n* (*wave*) μεγάλο κύμα *nt* ♦ *a* (*col: excellent*) εξαιρετικός, πρώτης τάξης ♦ *vt* (*numbers*) εξογκώνω, αυξάνω ♦ *vi* (*also:* ~ **up**) εξογκούμαι, φουσκώνω || (*become louder*) δυναμώνω || (*MED*) πρήζομαι || ~**ing** *n* εξόγκωση, πρήξιμο.

sweltering ['swɛltərɪŋ] *a* ιδρωμένος, αποπνικτικός.

swept [swɛpt] *pt, pp of* **sweep.**

swerve [swɜːv] *n* παρέκκλιση, παρατιμονιά ♦ *vti* παρεκκλίνω, παραστρατίζω, στρίβω.

swift [swɪft] *n* (*bird*) κλαδευτήρα, πετροχελίδονο ♦ *a* ταχύς, γρήγορος, άμεσος.

swig [swɪg] *n* (*col: of drink*) μεγάλη ρουφηξιά.

swill [swɪl] *n* (*for pigs*) τροφή χοίρων ♦ *vt* (*also:* ~ **out,** ~ **down**) ξεπλένω.

swim [swɪm] (*irreg v*) *n* κολύμπι ♦ *vi* (*person*) κολυμπώ || (*be flooded*) πλημμυρίζω, είμαι πλημμυρισμένος || (*feel dizzy*) ιλιγγιώ, ζαλίζομαι ♦ *vt* (*cross by swimming*) περνώ κολυμπώντας || ~**mer** *n* κολυμβητής/ήτρια *m/f* || ~**ming** *n* κολύμπι || **to go ~ming** πάω κολύμπι || ~**ming baths** *npl* κολυμβητικές δεξαμενές *fpl* || ~**ming cap** *n* σκουφί || ~**ming costume** *n* μαγιό || ~**ming pool** *n* πισίνα || ~**suit** *n* μαγιό.

swindle ['swɪndl] *n* απάτη ♦ *vt* (εξ)απατώ || ~**r** *n* απατεώνας, κατεργάρης.

swine [swaɪn] *n* χοίρος, γουρούνι || (*person*) γουρούνι, παλιάνθρωπος.

swing [swiŋ] (irreg v) n κούνια || (swinging) αιώρηση, ταλάντευση || (music) ρυθμός ♦ vt ταλαντεύω, κουνώ || (move round) περιστρέφω, στρέφω ♦ vi αιωρούμαι, κουνιέμαι || (move round) στρέφομαι, κάνω μεταβολή || in full ~ σε πλήρη δράση || ~ bridge n περιστρεφόμενη γέφυρα || ~ door n περιστρεφόμενη πόρτα.

swipe [swaip] n δυνατό κτύπημα nt ♦ vt (hit) κτυπώ δυνατά || (col: steal) κλέβω, βουτώ.

swish [swiʃ] a (col: smart) κομψός, μοντέρνος ♦ vt θροΐζω.

Swiss [swis] a ελβετικός ♦ n (person) Ελβετός/ίδα m/f.

switch [switʃ] n (for light, radio etc) διακόπτης || (change) αλλαγή ♦ vti διακόπτω || (turn) γυρίζω απότομα || to ~ off vt πραίνω που ανεβοκατεβαίνει διακόπτω, σβήνω || to ~ on vt ανάβω, ανοίγω || ~back n (at fair) σε λούνα παρκ || ~board n πίνακας διανομής, τηλεφωνικό κέντρο.

Switzerland ['switsələnd] n Ελβετία.

swivel ['swivl] vti (also: ~ round) (περι)στρέφομαι, στρέφω.

swollen ['swəʊlən] pp of swell ♦ a (ankle etc) πρησμένος, διογκωμένος.

swoon [swuːn] vi λιποθυμώ.

swoop [swuːp] n (esp by police) ξαφνική επίθεση, εφόρμηση ♦ vi (also: ~ down) εφορμώ, πέφτω.

swop [swɒp] = swap.

sword [sɔːd] n ξίφος nt, σπαθί || ~fish n ξιφίας.

swore [swɔː*] pt of swear.

sworn [swɔːn] pp of swear.

swum [swʌm] pp of swim.

swung [swʌŋ] pt, pp of swing.

sycamore ['sikəmɔː*] n συκομουριά.

syllable ['siləbl] n συλλαβή.

syllabus ['siləbəs] n διδακτέα ύλη.

symbol ['simbəl] n σύμβολο, σημείο || ~ic(al) [sim'bɒlik(əl)] a συμβολικός || ~ism n συμβολισμός || ~ize vt συμβολίζω, παριστάνω.

symmetrical [si'metrikəl] a συμμετρικός.

symmetry ['simitri] n συμμετρία.

sympathetic [simpə'θetik] a συμπαθητικός || (agreeing) ευνοϊκός με.

sympathize ['simpəθaiz] vi (+ with) συμπάσχω με, συμπονώ, συμπαθώ || ~r n οπαδός.

sympathy ['simpəθi] n συμπάθεια, συμπόνια.

symphony ['simfəni] n (composition) συμφωνία || ~ orchestra n συμφωνική ορχήστρα.

symposium [sim'pəʊziəm] n (meeting for discussion) συγκέντρωση, συμπόσιο.

symptom ['simptəm] n σύμπτωμα nt || ~atic a συμπτωματικός.

synagogue ['sinəgɒg] n συναγωγή.

synchronize ['siŋkrənaiz] vt

συγχρονίζω ♦ vi (+ with) γίνομαι ταυτοχρόνως.

syndicate ['sindikit] n συνδικάτο.

syndrome ['sindrəum] n (MED) σύνδρομο.

synonym ['sinənim] n συνώνυμο || ~ous [si'nɒniməs] a συνώνυμος.

synopsis [si'nɒpsis] n σύνοψη, περίληψη.

syntax ['sintæks] n σύνταξη, συντακτικό || ~ error n (COMPUT) συντακτικό λάθος nt.

synthesis ['sinθəsis] n σύνθεση.

synthetic [sin'θetik] a (artificial) συνθετικός.

syphilis ['sifilis] n σύφιλη.

syphon ['saifən] = siphon.

syringe [si'rindʒ] n σύριγγα.

syrup ['sirəp] n σιρόπι || ~y a σιροπασμένος.

system ['sistəm] n σύστημα nt || (railway etc) δίκτυο || (method) σύστημα nt, μέθοδος f || ~atic a συστηματικός, μεθοδικός.

T

tab [tæb] n θηλειά.

tabby ['tæbi] n (cat) γάτα.

table ['teibl] n τραπέζι || (list) πίνακας.

tablecloth ['teiblklɒθ] n τραπεζομάντηλο.

table d'hôte ['tɑːbl'dəut] a ταμπλ ν' τοτ.

table lamp ['teibllæmp] n πορτατίφ nt inv.

tablemat ['teiblmæt] n ψάθα για ζεστά πιάτα.

tablespoon ['teiblspuːn] n κουτάλι του σερβιρίσματος || ~ful n κουταλιά του σερβιρίσματος.

tablet ['tæblit] n πλάκα || (notebook) σημειωματάριο || (pellet) δισκίο, χάπι.

table tennis ['teibltenis] n πινγκ πονγκ nt inv.

table wine ['teiblwain] n επιτραπέζιο κρασί.

taboo [tə'buː] n ταμπού nt inv ♦ a απαγορευμένος, ταμπού.

tacit ['tæsit] a σιωπηρός, υπονοούμενος.

taciturn ['tæsitəːn] a σιωπηλός, λιγόλογος.

tack [tæk] n πινέζα || (stitch) μεγάλη βελονιά, τρύπωμα nt || (NAUT) αναστροφή, διαδρομή || (course) πορεία.

tackle ['tækl] n (for lifting) τροχαλία, παλάγκο || fishing ~ σύνεργα ψαρικής ♦ vt αντιμετωπίζω, καταπιάνομαι με || (a player) κάνω τάκελ.

tacky ['tæki] a κολλώδης.

tact [tækt] n τάκτ nt inv, λεπτότητα || ~ful a με τάκτ, διακριτικός.

tactical ['tæktikəl] a τακτικός.

tactics ['tæktiks] npl τακτική.

tactless ['tæktlıs] a στερούμενος τάκτ, αδέξιος.

tadpole ['tædpəʊl] n γυρίνος.

taffeta ['tæfıtə] n ταφτάς.

tag [tæg] n (label) ετικέτα.

tail [teıl] n ουρά || **to ~ off** vi (in size, quality etc) ελαττώνομαι, αραιώνομαι || **~ end** n τελευταίο τμήμα nt, ουρά, τέλος nt.

tailor ['teılə*] n ράφτης || **~ing** n ραπτική || **~-made** a καμωμένο ειδικά.

tailwind ['teılwınd] n ούριος άνεμος.

tainted ['teıntıd] a μολυσμένος, χαλασμένος.

take [teık] (irreg v) vt παίρνω, βγάζω || (seize) πιάνω, παίρνω, καταλαμβάνω || (require) απαιτώ, χρειάζομαι || (hire) παίρνω, νοικιάζω || (understand) δέχομαι, παραδέχομαι, συμπεραίνω || (choose) διαλέγω || (PHOT) φωτογραφίζω, φωτογραφίζομαι || **to ~ part in** συμμετέχω || **to ~ place** συμβαίνω || **to ~ after** vt μοιάζω || **to ~ back** vt (return) φέρνω πίσω, παίρνω πίσω || **to ~ down** vt κατεβάζω, ξεκρεμώ || (demolish) κατεδαφίζω || (write) σημειώνω καταγράφω || **to ~ in** vt (deceive) εξαπατώ, ξεγελώ || (understand) καταλαβαίνω, αντιλαμβάνομαι || (include) περιλαμβάνω || **to ~ off** vi (aeroplane) απογειούμαι, ξεκινώ ♦ vt (remove) αφαιρώ, βγάζω, παίρνω || (imitate) μιμούμαι, παρωδώ || **to ~ on** vt (undertake) αναλαμβάνω || (engage) μισθώνω, προσλαμβάνω || (accept as opponent) δέχομαι την πρόσκληση || **to ~ out** vt (licence etc) βγάζω, κάνω || (stain) βγάζω || **to ~ over** vt αναλαμβάνω || (succeed) διαδέχομαι || **to ~ to** vt (person) συμπαθώ || (sport, hobby) επιδίδομαι σε, μ' αρέσει να || **to ~ up** vt (raise) σηκώνω, μαζεύω || (occupy) καταλαμβάνω, πιάνω || (absorb) απορροφώ, τραβώ || (engage in) απασχολούμαι σε || **~-off** n (AVIAT) απογείωση || (imitation) μίμηση || **~over** n (COMM) ανάληψη επιχειρήσεως, κτήση.

takings ['teıkıŋz] npl (COMM) εισπράξεις fpl.

talc [tælk] n (also: **~um powder**) τάλκ nt inv.

tale [teıl] n αφήγηση, παραμύθι, ιστορία.

talent ['tælənt] n ταλέντο || **~ed** a με ταλέντο.

talk [tɔːk] n συζήτηση, συνομιλία, κουβέντα || (rumour) φλυαρία, διάδοση || (speech) λόγος, ομιλία || **to ~ shop** συζητώ για την εργασία μου || **to ~ over** vt συζητώ || **~ative** a φλύαρος.

tall [tɔːl] a ψηλός || **~boy** n (furniture) ψηλό κομμόδ, ψηλός καθρέφτης || **~ story** n μπούρδα, αρλούμπα.

tally ['tælı] n (account) λογαριασμός ♦ vi συμφωνώ, αντιστοιχώ.

tambourine [tæmbə'riːn] n ντέφι.

tame [teım] a ήμερος, δαμασμένος || (dull) άτονος || **~ness** n ημερότητα.

tamper ['tæmpə*] : **to ~ with** vt ανακατεύομαι με || (falsify) παραποιώ.

tan [tæn] n (colour) (also: **sun ~**) μελαχροινό χρώμα, μαύρισμα nt ♦ a (colour) φαιοκίτρινος, καφέ.

tandem ['tændəm] n διπλό ποδήλατο.

tang [tæŋ] n οξεία γεύση, δυνατή οσμή.

tangent ['tændʒənt] n εφαπτομένη.

tangerine [tændʒə'riːn] n μανταρίνι.

tangible ['tændʒəbl] a απτός, ψηλαφητός || (real) πραγματικός, αισθητός.

tangle ['tæŋgl] n μπέρδεμα nt, ανακάτωμα nt || (complication) περιπλοκή ♦ vti μπερδεύομαι || (complicate) περιπλέκω.

tango ['tæŋgəʊ] n ταγκό nt inv.

tank [tæŋk] n δεξαμενή, ντεπόζιτο || (MIL) τάνκ nt inv, άρμα μάχης.

tankard ['tæŋkəd] n κύπελλο, μαστραπάς.

tanker ['tæŋkə*] n (ship) δεξαμενόπλοιο, τάνκερ nt inv || (truck) βυτιοφόρο.

tankful ['tæŋkful] n γεμάτο δοχείο.

tantalizing ['tæntəlaızıŋ] a προκλητικός, βασανιστικός.

tantrum ['tæntrəm] n έκρηξη οργής, ξέσπασμα nt, παραφορά.

tap [tæp] n βρύση || (on barrel) κάνουλα || (gentle blow) ελαφρό κτύπημα nt ♦ vt (strike) κτυπώ ελαφρά || (supply) παίρνω, τροφοδοτώ, ανοίγω.

tap-dance ['tæpdɑːns] vi χορεύω με κλακέτες.

tape [teıp] n ταινία || **magnetic ~** μαγνητοταινία ♦ vt (to record) μαγνητογραφώ, ηχογραφώ || **measure** n μετρική ταινία, μέτρο.

taper ['teıpə*] n λαμπάδα, κερί ♦ vi λεπτύνομαι, λιγοστεύω.

tape recorder ['teıprıkɔːdə*] n μαγνητόφωνο.

tapestry ['tæpıstrı] n ταπέτο τοίχου, ταπετσαρία.

tar [tɑː*] n πίσσα.

tardy ['tɑːdı] a βραδύς, αργός.

target ['tɑːgıt] n στόχος.

tariff ['tærıf] n (list of charges) τιμολόγιο || (duty) δασμός, δασμολόγιο.

tarmac ['tɑːmæk] n (AVIAT) διάδρομος απογειώσεως.

tarnish ['tɑːnıʃ] vt (lit) θαμπώνω, σκοτεινιάζω || (fig) μαυρίζω, κηλιδώνω.

tarpaulin [tɑː'pɔːlın] n κηρόπανο, μουσαμάς.

tart [tɑːt] n (pie) τούρτα, τάρτα || (col: low woman) τσούλα ♦ a ξυνός, οξύς, δριμύς.

tartan ['tɑːtən] n σκωτσέζικο ύφασμα nt.

tartar ['tɑːtə*] n τρυγία, πουρί.

task [tɑːsk] n καθήκον, έργο, δουλειά, αποστολή.

tassel ['tæsəl] n θύσανος, φούντα.

taste [teıst] n γεύση, γούστο || (preference) προτίμηση ♦ vti γεύομαι, δοκιμάζω || **~ful** a κομψός, με γούστο, καλαίσθητος || **~less** a άγευστος, άνοστος || (bad taste) χωρίς γούστο, κακόγουστος.

tasty ['teisti] a γευστικός, νόστιμος.

tatters ['tætəz] npl: in ~ (also: tattered) κουρελιασμένος.

tattoo [tə'tu:] n (νυκτερινή) στρατιωτική επίδειξη || (on skin) δερματοστιξία, τατουάζ nt inv ♦ vt διαστίζω, τατουάρω.

tatty ['tæti] a (col: cheap, of poor quality) φτηνός, πρόστυχος.

taught [tɔːt] pt, pp of **teach**.

taunt [tɔːnt] n χλευασμός, λοιδορία, κοροϊδία ♦ vt χλευάζω, κοροϊδεύω.

taut [tɔːt] a τεντωμένος, τεταμένος.

tavern ['tævən] n ταβέρνα.

tawdry ['tɔːdrɪ] a φανταχτερός, φτηνός, τιποτένιος.

tawny ['tɔːnɪ] a φαιοκίτρινος.

tax [tæks] n ο φόρος ♦ vt φορολογώ || (burden) εξαντλώ, βάζω σε δοκιμασία || ~ation n φορολογία || ~ collector n εισπράκτορας φόρων || ~-free a αφορολόγητος.

taxi ['tæksɪ] n ταξί ♦ vi (AVIAT) τροχοδρομώ || ~ driver n οδηγός ταξί, ταξιτζής || ~ rank n, ~ stand n στάση ταξί, πιάτσα.

taxpayer ['tækspeɪə*] n φορολογούμενος.

T.B. abbr of **tuberculosis**.

tea [tiː] n τέιο, τσάι || (drink) τσάι || (meal) απογευματινό τσάι, γεύμα nt με τσάι || ~ bag n σακκουλάκι τσαγιού || ~ break n διάλειμμα nt για τσάι.

teach [tiːtʃ] (irreg v) vti διδάσκω, μαθαίνω || ~er n δάσκαλος/δασκάλα m/f || ~ing n διδασκαλία.

tea cosy ['tiːkəuzɪ] n σκέπασμα nt τσαγιέρας.

teacup ['tiːkʌp] n φλυτζάνι τσαγιού.

teak [tiːk] n τικ, τεκ ♦ a από τικ.

tea leaves ['tiːliːvz] npl φύλλα ntpl τσαγιού.

team [tiːm] n ομάδα, συνεργείο || (of animals) ζευγάρι || ~work n ομαδικό παίξιμο, συνεργασία.

tea party ['tiːpɑːtɪ] n δεξίωση με τσάι.

teapot ['tiːpɒt] n τσαγιέρα.

tear [tɛə*] n (rip) σχίσιμο, σχισμή δάκρυ nt ♦ (irreg v) vt ανοίγω τρύπα || (pull apart) σχίζω, σπαράσσω ♦ vi (become torn) σχίζομαι || (rush) τρέχω, ορμώ ♦ ['tɪə*] n (cry) δάκρυ || in ~s δακρυσμένος, βουτηγμένος στα δάκρυα || ~ful a δακρυσμένος, κλαμένος || ~ gas n δακρυγόνο αέριο.

tearoom ['tiːrum] n αίθουσα τεΐου.

tease [tiːz] n πειραχτήριο, πείραγμα nt ♦ vt πειράζω, κοροϊδεύω.

tea set ['tiːset] n σερβίτσιο τσαγιού.

teaspoon ['tiːspuːn] n κουταλάκι του τσαγιού || ~ful n κουταλιά του τσαγιού.

tea strainer ['tiːstreɪnə*] n σουρωτήρι του τσαγιού.

teat [tiːt] n θηλή, ρώγα.

teatime ['tiːtaɪm] n ώρα του τσαγιού.

technical ['tɛknɪkəl] a τεχνικός || ~ity n τεχνική λεπτομέρεια.

technician [tɛk'nɪʃən] n (craftsman) τεχνίτης, τεχνικός || (specialist) ειδικός.

technique [tɛk'niːk] n τεχνική, ειδική μέθοδος f.

technological [tɛknə'lɒdʒɪkəl] a τεχνολογικός.

technology [tɛk'nɒlədʒɪ] n τεχνολογία.

teddy (bear) ['tɛdɪ(bɛə*)] n αρκουδάκι (παιχνίδι).

tedious ['tiːdɪəs] a ανιαρός, βαρετός.

tedium ['tiːdɪəm] n ανιαρότητα, μονοτονία, ανία.

tee [tiː] n υψωματάκι, σωρός (άμμου).

teem [tiːm] vi βρίθω, αφθονώ || (pour) πέφτω καταρρακτωδώς.

teenage ['tiːneɪdʒ] a εφηβικός, μεταξύ 13 και 20 || ~r n έφηβος.

teens [tiːnz] npl ηλικία μεταξύ 13 και 20 χρονών.

teeth [tiːθ] npl of **tooth**.

teethe [tiːð] vi βγάζω δόντια.

teething ring ['tiːðɪŋrɪŋ] n ροδέλα μωρού (για οδοντοφυΐα).

teetotal ['tiː'təutl] a αντιαλκοολικός || ~ler, ~er (US) n απέχων από οινοπνευματωδών ποτά.

telecommunication ['tɛlɪkəmjuːnɪ'keɪʃən] n τηλεπικοινωνία.

telegram ['tɛlɪgræm] n τηλεγράφημα nt.

telegraph ['tɛlɪgrɑːf] n τηλέγραφος || ~ic a (address) τηλεγραφικός || ~ pole n τηλεγραφικός στύλος.

telepathic [tɛlɪ'pæθɪk] a τηλεπαθητικός.

telepathy [tɪ'lɛpəθɪ] n τηλεπάθεια.

telephone ['tɛlɪfəun] n τηλέφωνο ♦ vt τηλεφωνώ || ~ booth, ~ box n τηλεφωνικός θάλαμος || ~ call n τηλεφώνημα nt, κλήση || ~ directory n τηλεφωνικός κατάλογος || ~ exchange n κέντρο || ~ number n αριθμός τηλεφώνου.

telephonist [tɪ'lɛfənɪst] n τηλεφωνήτρια.

telephoto ['tɛlɪ'fəutəu] a: ~ lens τηλεφακός.

teleprinter ['tɛlɪprɪntə*] n τηλέτυπο.

telescope ['tɛlɪskəup] n τηλεσκόπιο ♦ vt (compress) συμπτύσσω.

telescopic [tɛlɪs'kɒpɪk] a τηλεσκοπικός.

televise ['tɛlɪvaɪz] vt μεταδίδω τηλεοπτικά.

television ['tɛlɪvɪʒən] n τηλεόραση || ~ set n δέκτης τηλεοράσεως.

telex ['tɛlɛks] n τέλεξ nt inv, τηλέτυπος ♦ vt στέλλω με τον τηλέτυπο.

tell [tɛl] (irreg v) vt λέγω, λέω || (make known) αφηγούμαι, γνωστοποιώ || (order) διατάσσω, παραγγέλλω, λέω σε || (person of sth) λέω κάτι, ανακοινώνω ♦ vi (have effect) αποφέρω, συνεπάγομαι, έχω || to ~ on vt (inform against) καταδίδω, προδίδω || to ~ off vt μαλώνω, κατσαδιάζω || ~er n (in bank) ταμίας ||

~ing a αποτελεσματικός || **~tale** a μαρτυριάρης, κουτσομπόλης.

telly ['tɛlɪ] n (col) abbr of **television**.

temerity [tɪ'mɛrɪtɪ] n θάρρος nt, τόλμη.

temper ['tɛmpə*] n (disposition) διάθεση, τεμπεραμέντο || (burst of anger) οργή, θυμός ♦ vt (moderate) απαλύνω, μαλακώνω, συγκρατώ.

temperament ['tɛmprəmənt] n διάθεση, ιδιοσυγκρασία, τεμπεραμέντο || **~al** a (moody) ιδιότροπος || (fig) γεμάτος βίδες.

temperance ['tɛmpərəns] n (in drinking) αποφυγή οινοπνευματωδών ποτών || (moderation) εγκράτεια, μετριοπάθεια.

temperate ['tɛmpərɪt] a μετριοπαθής, εύκρατος.

temperature ['tɛmprətʃə*] n θερμοκρασία.

tempered ['tɛmpəd] a (steel) εσκληρυμένος, βαμμένος.

tempest ['tɛmpɪst] n θύελλα, τρικυμία, φουρτούνα.

temple ['tɛmpl] n (building) ναός || (ANAT) κρόταφος, μηλίγγι.

tempo ['tɛmpəʊ] n ρυθμός, τέμπο || (of movement) ρυθμός, μέτρο.

temporal ['tɛmpərəl] a (of time) χρονικός, του χρόνου || (worldly) εγκόσμιος, κοσμικός.

temporarily ['tɛmpərərɪlɪ] ad προσωρινά, για λίγο.

temporary ['tɛmpərərɪ] a προσωρινός, πρόσκαιρος.

tempt [tɛmpt] vt (persuade) παροτρύνω, προτρέπω || (attract) δελεάζω || **~ation** n πειρασμός, δελεασμός || **~ing** a δελεαστικός.

ten [tɛn] num δέκα.

tenable ['tɛnəbl] a υπερασπίσιμος, υποστηρίξιμος, λογικός.

tenacious [tə'neɪʃəs] a εμμένων, επίμονος.

tenacity [tə'næsɪtɪ] n εμμονή, επιμονή.

tenancy ['tɛnənsɪ] n ενοικίαση, μίσθωση.

tenant ['tɛnənt] n ενοικιαστής/ ενοικιάστρια m/f, μισθωτής/ μισθώτρια m/f.

tend [tɛnd] vt (look after) περιποιούμαι ♦ vi τείνω, ρέπω, κλίνω.

tendency ['tɛndənsɪ] n τάση, κλίση, ροπή.

tender ['tɛndə*] a τρυφερός, μαλακός || (delicate) λεπτός, ευπαθής, τρυφερός || (loving) στοργικός, ευαίσθητος, πονετικός ♦ n (COMM: offer) προσφορά || **~ness** n τρυφερότητα, λεπτότητα, στοργικότητα.

tendon ['tɛndən] n τένων m.

tenement ['tɛnɪmənt] n λαϊκή πολυκατοικία.

tenet ['tɛnət] n αρχή, αξίωμα nt, δόγμα nt.

tennis ['tɛnɪs] n τένις nt inv, αντισφαίριση || **~ ball** n μπάλα του τένις

|| **~ court** n γήπεδο του τένις || **~ racket** n ρακέτα του τένις.

tenor ['tɛnə*] n (male voice) οξύφωνος, τενόρος || (singer) τενόρος.

tense [tɛns] a (fig) σε υπερένταση, τεταμένος || (taut) τεντωμένος ♦ n χρόνος || **~ness** n ένταση, τεταμένη κατάσταση.

tension ['tɛnʃən] n ένταση || (stretching) τάση, τέντωμα nt.

tent [tɛnt] n σκηνή, τέντα.

tentacle ['tɛntəkl] n κεραία, πλόκαμος.

tentative ['tɛntətɪv] a δοκιμαστικός, προσωρινός.

tenterhooks ['tɛntəhʊks] npl: **on ~** ανήσυχος, ανυπόμονος.

tenth [tɛnθ] a δέκατος, δέκατο.

tent peg ['tɛntpɛg] n πάσσαλος σκηνής.

tent pole ['tɛntpəʊl] n ορθοστάτης σκηνής.

tenuous ['tɛnjʊəs] a λεπτός, αραιός, ελαφρός.

tenure ['tɛnjʊə*] n κατοχή, κτήση.

tepid ['tɛpɪd] a χλιαρός.

term ['tɜːm] n όριο || (fixed time) περίοδος f, διάρκεια, χρόνος || (word) όρος, έκφραση, λέξη ♦ vt ονομάζω, καλώ || **~s** npl όροι mpl, διατάξεις fpl || (relationship) σχέσεις fpl.

terminal ['tɜːmɪnl] a τελικός, άκρος ♦ n (ELEC) ακροδέκτης, πόλος || (for oil, ore etc) ακραίος σταθμός || (COMPUT) τερματικό.

terminate ['tɜːmɪneɪt] vi (+ in) τερματίζω, τελειώνω.

termination [tɜːmɪ'neɪʃən] n τερματισμός, περάτωση, κατάληξη.

terminology [tɜːmɪ'nɒlədʒɪ] n ορολογία.

terminus ['tɜːmɪnəs] n ακραίος, σταθμός, τέρμα nt.

termite ['tɜːmaɪt] n τερμίτης.

terrace ['tɛrəs] n σειρά σπιτιών || (in garden etc) επιπέδωμα nt, ταράτσα || **~d** a (garden) σε βαθμίδες, κλιμακωτός || (house) ίδιου ρυθμού.

terrain [tɛ'reɪn] n έδαφος nt, πεδίο, έκταση.

terrible ['tɛrəbl] a (causing fear) τρομερός, τρομακτικός, φοβερός || (inferior) φοβερός, κατώτερος || (very great) απερίγραπτος, υπερβολικός.

terribly ['tɛrəblɪ] ad τρομερά, φρικτά, τρομακτικά.

terrier ['tɛrɪə*] n σκυλί τερριέ.

terrific [tə'rɪfɪk] a τρομερός, καταπληκτικός.

terrify ['tɛrɪfaɪ] vt τρομάζω, τρομοκρατώ.

territorial [tɛrɪ'tɔːrɪəl] a εδαφικός, τοπικός, κτηματικός.

territory ['tɛrɪtərɪ] n γη, περιοχή, έδαφος nt.

terror ['tɛrə*] n τρόμος, φρίκη, φόβος, τρομάρα || **~ism** n τρομοκρατία || **~ist** n τρομοκράτης || **~ize** vt τρομοκρατώ.

terse [tɜːs] a σύντομος, βραχύς || (concise) περιληπτικός.

test [tɛst] n δοκιμή, δοκιμασία || (examination) εξέταση, ανάλυση ♦ vt δοκιμάζω || (examine) εξετάζω.

testament ['tɛstəmənt] n διαθήκη.

testicle ['tɛstɪkl] n όρχις m, αρχίδι.

testify ['tɛstɪfaɪ] vi καταθέτω (ενόρκως).

testimonial [tɛstɪ'məʊnɪəl] n πιστοποιητικό, βεβαίωση || (gift) δώρο ευγνωμοσύνης.

testimony ['tɛstɪmənɪ] n μαρτυρία, κατάθεση || (proof) απόδειξη.

test match ['tɛstmætʃ] n (cricket, rugby) μεγάλη διεθνής συνάντηση.

test pilot ['tɛstpaɪlət] n πιλότος δοκιμών.

test tube ['tɛsttjuːb] n δοκιμαστικός σωλήνας.

testy ['tɛstɪ] a (short-tempered) ευέξαπτος, δύστροπος.

tetanus ['tɛtənəs] n τέτανος.

tether ['tɛðə*] vt δένω.

text [tɛkst] n κείμενο || ~**book** n εγχειρίδιο, διδακτικό βιβλίο.

textiles ['tɛkstaɪlz] npl υφαντά ntpl, υφάσματα ntpl.

texture ['tɛkstʃə*] n (of surface) υφή.

than [ðæn] prep, cj ή, παρά, από.

thank [θæŋk] vt ευχαριστώ || ~**ful** a ευγνώμων || ~**fully** ad με ευγνωμοσύνη || ~**less** a αχάριστος || ~**s** excl ευχαριστώ || (gratitude) ευγνωμοσύνη, ευχαριστίες fpl || T~**sgiving** n (US: festival) Ημέρα των Ευχαριστιών.

that [ðæt] a αυτός, εκείνος ♦ pron εκείνος, ο οποίος, που ♦ cj ότι, ώστε, διότι, να ♦ ad πόσο, έτσι.

thatched [θætʃt] a (cottage) αχυροστρωμένος.

thaw [θɔː] n τήξη, λυώσιμο ♦ vi τήκομαι, λυώνω.

the [ðiː, ðə] definite article ο, η, το || (pl) οι, τα.

theatre, theater (US) ['θɪətə*] n θέατρο || (drama) θεατρική τέχνη, δραματική τέχνη || (MED) αμφιθέατρο || ~**goer** n θεατρόφιλος.

theatrical [θɪ'ætrɪkəl] a θεατρικός, θεαματικός || (showy) θεατρινίστικος, προσποιητός.

theft [θɛft] n κλοπή, κλεψιά.

their [ðɛə*] poss a δικός τους, δική τους || ~**s** poss pron δικός τους, δικοί τους.

them [ðɛm, ðəm] pron αυτούς, αυτές, αυτά.

theme [θiːm] n θέμα nt, υπόθεση || (melody) θέμα, μοτίβο || ~ **song** n (of film etc) κύρια μελωδία.

themselves [ðəm'sɛlvz] pl pron τους εαυτούς τους || (they themselves) αυτοί οι ίδιοι.

then [ðɛn] ad τότε || (next) κατόπιν, έπειτα || cj λοιπόν, τότε, επί πλέον ♦ n τότε.

theological [θɪə'lɒdʒɪkəl] a θεολογικός.

theology [θɪ'ɒlədʒɪ] n θεολογία.

theorem ['θɪərəm] n θεώρημα nt.

theoretical [θɪə'rɛtɪkəl] a θεωρητικός.

theorize ['θɪəraɪz] vi κάνω θεωρίες.

theory ['θɪərɪ] n θεωρία || (idea) ιδέα.

therapeutic(al) [θɛrə'pjuːtɪk(l)] a θεραπευτικός.

therapist ['θɛrəpɪst] n θεραπευτής/ύτρια m/f.

therapy ['θɛrəpɪ] n θεραπεία.

there [ðɛə*] ad εκεί, να, έλα ♦ n εκείνος εκεί || (interj) να || (never mind) έλα, έλα || ~ **is** υπάρχει || ~ **are** υπάρχουν || ~**abouts** ad εκεί κοντά, περίπου || ~**after** ad έπειτα, κατόπιν || ~**fore** ad γι'αυτό το λόγο, επομένως || ~'s = there is, there has.

Thermos ['θɜːməs] n (R) (flask) θέρμο(ς).

thermostat ['θɜːməstæt] n θερμοστάτης.

thesaurus [θɪ'sɔːrəs] n θησαυρός, συλλογή λέξεων.

these [ðiːz] pl pron αυτοί, αυτές, αυτά.

thesis ['θiːsɪs] n θέμα, θέση || (UNIV) διατριβή.

they [ðeɪ] pl pron αυτοί, αυτές, αυτά.

thick [θɪk] a χοντρός, παχύς, πυκνός, πηκτός || (person: slow, stupid) κούτος, χοντροκέφαλος ♦ n: in the ~ of στη φούρια, στο οξύτερο σημείο || ~**en** vi (fog) πυκνώνω, γίνομαι πυκνώτερο ♦ vt (sauce etc) πήζω, πυκνώνω, δένω || ~**ness** n (of object) πάχος, πυκνότητα || (of voice) βραχνάδα || ~**set** a κοντόχοντρος || ~**skinned** a παχύδερμος, χοντρόπετσος.

thief [θiːf] n κλέφτης, λωποδύτης.

thieves [θiːvz] npl of thief.

thieving ['θiːvɪŋ] n κλοπή, κλεψιά.

thigh [θaɪ] n μηρός, μπούτι.

thimble ['θɪmbl] n δακτυλήθρα.

thin [θɪn] a λεπτός, ψιλός, αδύνατος || (not abundant) αραιός, διεσπαρμένος || (person) ισχνός, λιγνός, αδύνατος || (crowd) αραιός, λιγοστός.

thing [θɪŋ] n πράγμα nt, αντικείμενο.

think [θɪŋk] (irreg v) vi σκέπτομαι || (believe) νομίζω || (have in mind) σκοπεύω || to ~ over vt σκέπτομαι, συλλογίζομαι || to ~ up vt σκέπτομαι, καταστρώνω.

thinly ['θɪnlɪ] ad (disguised) μόλις.

thinness ['θɪnnɪs] n λεπτότητα, αδυναμία || (of liquids, crowds) αραιότητα.

third [θɜːd] a τρίτος ♦ n τρίτος, τρίτο || ~**ly** ad κατά τρίτο λόγο, τρίτο || ~**-party insurance** n ασφάλιση τρίτων || ~**-rate** a τρίτης τάξεως, κακής ποιότητας.

thirst [θɜːst] n δίψα || (strong desire) δυνατή επιθυμία, πόθος || ~**y** a διψασμένος.

thirteen [θɜː'tiːn] num δεκατρία.

thirty ['θɜːtɪ] num τριάντα.

this [ðɪs] pron, a αυτός, αυτή, αυτό || (this much) τόσος.

thistle ['θɪsl] n γαϊδουράγκαθο.

thorn [θɔːn] n αγκάθι || (plant) ακανθώδης θάμνος, αγκάθι || ~**y** a αγκαθωτός || (problem) ακανθώδης.

thorough ['θʌrə] a πλήρης, τέλειος || (accurate) λεπτομερής, εξονυχιστικός || ~**bred** n καθαρόαιμος, από ράτσα ♦ a καθαρόαιμος || ~**fare** n οδός f, διάβαση, αρτηρία || (main street) κεντρική λεωφόρος || ~**ly** ad τέλεια, πλήρως, κατά βάθος.

those [δəuz] pl pron αυτές, αυτοί, αυτά ♦ a τούτοι, εκείνοι.

though [δəu] cj ἀνκαι, μολονότι ♦ ad παρ' όλα αυτά, ωστόσο.

thought [θɔːt] n ιδέα, σκέψη || (thinking) σκέψη, συλλογισμός || pt, pp of **think** || ~**ful** a σοβαρός, σκεπτικός || (also kind) διακριτικός, ευγενικός || ~**less** a απερίσκεπτος, απρόσεκτος, αδιάκριτος.

thousand ['θauzənd] num χίλιοι, χίλιες, χίλια || ~**th** a χιλιοστός.

thresh [θreʃ] vt (lit) κτυπώ, δέρνω, ξυλοφορτώνω || (fig) νικώ.

thread [θred] n (of cotton, silk etc) νήμα nt, κλωστή || (of screw) σπείρωμα nt, βήμα nt || (of story) συνέχεια, ειρμός ♦ vt (needle) βάζω κλωστή σε, περνώ ♦ vi (pick one's way) περνώ με δυσκολία || ~**bare** a ξεφτισμένος, παλιός.

threat [θret] n φοβέρα, φοβέρισμα nt || (sign of danger) απειλή || ~**en** vti (person) απειλώ, φοβερίζω || (storm) απειλώ.

three [θriː] num τρεις, τρία || ~-**dimensional** a τρισδιάστατος || ~-**fold** a τριπλός, τρίδιπλος || ~-**piece suit** n (clothes) τρουαπιές nt inv || ~-**ply** a (wool) τρίκλωνος.

thresh [θreʃ] vt αλωνίζω.

threshold ['θreʃhəuld] n (beginning) κατώφλι, αρχή || (doorway) κατώφλι.

threw [θruː] pt of **throw**.

thrift [θrift] n (economy) οικονομία, αποταμίευση || ~**y** a οικονόμος, μετρημένος.

thrill [θril] n ρίγος nt, συγκίνηση, σύγκρυο, τρεμούλα ♦ vt προκαλώ ρίγος σε, συγκινώ, ηλεκτρίζω ♦ vi φρικιώ, ριγώ, τρέμω, αγωνιώ || ~**er** n μυθιστόρημα nt αγωνίας.

thrive [θraiv] vi (+ on) (plants) ευδοκιμώ || (business) ευημερώ || (children) αναπτύσσομαι.

thriving ['θraiviŋ] a ακμαίος, ρωμαλέος, ακμάζων || (successful) επιτυχής.

throat [θrəut] n λαιμός || (internal passages) φάρυγγας, λάρυγγας, λαρύγγι.

throb [θrɔb] n κτύπημα nt, παλμός, δόνηση ♦ vi κτυπώ, πάλλομαι.

throes [θrəuz] npl οδύνες fpl, πόνοι ntpl || in the ~ of αγωνιζόμενος με.

thrombosis [θrɔm'bəusis] n θρόμβωση.

throne [θrəun] n θρόνος.

throttle ['θrɔtl] n ρυθμιστική βαλβίδα μηχανής, δικλείδα ♦ vt (choke) στραγγαλίζω.

through [θruː] prep διαμέσου, καθ'όλην τη διάρκεια του || (because of) λόγω του, εξαιτίας του ♦ ad εξ ολοκλήρου, κατευθείαν, από την αρχή μέχρι το τέλος ♦ a (without a stop) κατευθείαν ||

(end to end) πέρα για πέρα || (ticket) ολοκλήρου διαδρομής (εισιτήριο) || (finished) τελειωμένος || ~**out** prep σε ολόκληρο, σ' όλο, παντού ♦ ad παντού, ολόκληρα.

throw [θrəu] (irreg v) n ρίψη, ρίξιμο, πέταγμα nt, βολή ♦ vt ρίχνω, πετώ || to ~ **out** vt (lit) πετώ έξω || (reject) απορρίπτω, αποκρούω || to ~ **up** vi (vomit) ξερνώ, κάνω εμετό || ~-**in** n (SPORT) δίνω επιπλέον.

thru [θruː] (US) = **through**.

thrush [θrʌʃ] n κίχλα, τσίχλα.

thrust [θrʌst] (irreg v) n (TECH) ώθηση, σπρωξιά ♦ vti σπρώχνω, μπήγω || (push one's way) διαπερνώ, διασχίζω, περνώ.

thud [θʌd] n γδούπος.

thug [θʌg] n γκάγκστερ m inv, μπράβος.

thumb [θʌm] n αντίχειρας ♦ vt (book) φυλλομετρώ || to ~ a **lift** κάνω ωτοστόπ || ~**tack** n (US) πινέζα.

thump [θʌmp] n βαρύ κτύπημα nt, γροθιά ♦ vti κτυπώ δυνατά, γρονθοκοπώ.

thunder ['θʌndə*] n βροντή ♦ vi βροντώ, βροντοφωνώ || ~**storm** n καταιγίδα, θύελλα || ~**struck** a εμβρόντητος, κατάπληκτος || ~**y** a (weather, sky) θυελλώδης.

Thursday ['θəːzdi] n Πέμπτη.

thus [δʌs] ad έτσι || (therefore) έτσι, λοιπόν.

thwart [θwɔːt] vt ματαιώνω, ανατρέπω, εμποδίζω.

thyme [taim] n θυμάρι.

thyroid ['θairɔid] n θυρεοειδής (αδένας).

tiara [ti'aːrə] n διάδημα nt, τιάρα.

tic [tik] n (nervous) τικ, σπάσμα nt, σπασμός.

tick [tik] n τικ (ρολογιού), λεπτό || (small mark) σημείο ελέγχου, τσεκάρισμα ♦ vi κτυπώ, κάνω τικ ♦ vt σημειώνω, τσεκάρω.

ticket ['tikit] n (for travel etc) εισιτήριο, δελτίο || (label) σημείωση, ετικέτα || ~ **collector** n ελεγκτής εισιτηρίων || ~ **holder** n κάτοχος εισιτηρίου || ~ **office** n γραφείο εκδόσεως εισιτηρίων.

tickle ['tikl] n γαργάλισμα nt ♦ vt γαργαλίζω, γαργαλώ || (amuse) διασκεδάζω.

ticklish ['tikliʃ] a που γαργαλιέται εύκολα || (difficult) λεπτός, δύσκολος.

tidal ['taidl] a παλιρροιακός.

tide [taid] n παλίρροια, ρεύμα nt || (season) εποχή.

tidiness ['taidinis] n τάξη, συγύρισμα.

tidy ['taidi] a συγυρισμένος, τακτοποιημένος, σιαγμένος ♦ vt τακτοποιώ, σιάζω, συγυρίζω.

tie [tai] n (necktie) γραβάτα, λαιμοδέτης || (connection) δεσμός || (SPORT) ισοπαλία || vt προσδένω, δένω || (into knot) δένω, κάνω κόμπο ♦ vi έρχομαι ισόπαλος, ισοψηφώ || to ~ **down** vt (lit) στερεώνω, δένω καλά || *(fig)* δεσμεύω || **to ~ up** *vt (dog)* προσδένω, δένω || *(boat)* δένω.

tier [tɪə*] *n* σειρά.

tiff [tɪf] *n* μικροτσακωμός, καυγαδάκι.

tiger ['taɪgə*] *n* τίγρη.

tight [taɪt] *a* σφικτός, στερεός || *(stretched)* τεντωμένος || *(close)* στεγανός, ερμητικός || *(col)* πιωμένος, σκνίπα || *(miserly)* τσιγγούνης || **~s** *npl* καλτσόν *nt inv* || **~en** *vti* σφίγγω, σφίγγομαι || **~-fisted** *a* σφιχτοχέρης, σπαγγοραμμένος || **~ly** *ad* σφιχτοκλεισμένα, σφιχτά, γερά || **~rope** *n* τεντωμένο σχοινί.

tile [taɪl] *n (in roof)* κεραμίδι || *(on wall or floor)* πλακάκι || **~d** *a (roof)* με κεραμίδια.

till [tɪl] *n* συρτάρι ταμείου ♦ *vt* καλλιεργώ ♦ *prep* ως, μέχρι ♦ *cj* έως ότου, ως που.

tilt [tɪlt] *vti* γέρνω, κλίνω.

timber ['tɪmbə*] *n* ξυλεία || *(trees)* δάσος *nt*, ψηλά δέντρα *ntpl*.

time [taɪm] *n* χρόνος || *(period)* καιρός || *(hour)* ώρα || *(point in time)* στιγμή, φορά || *(occasion)* καιρός, εποχή || *(rhythm, speed)* χρόνος, ρυθμός ♦ *vt* ρυθμίζω, χρονομετρώ || **in ~** έγκαιρα || *(MUS)* μέτρο, χρόνος || **on ~** στην ώρα || **five ~s** πέντε φορές || **local ~** τοπική ώρα || **what ~ is it?** τι ώρα είναι; || **~keeper** *n (SPORT)* χρονομετρητής || **~less** *a (beauty)* αιώνιος, άφθαρτος || **~ limit** *n* χρονικό όριο, προθεσμία || **~ly** *a* έγκαιρος, επίκαιρος || **~ switch** *n* χρονοδιακόπτης || **~table** *n (travel)* δρομολόγιο || *(schools)* ωρολόγιο πρόγραμμα *nt* || **~ zone** *n* άτρακτος χρόνου, ωριαία ζώνη.

timid ['tɪmɪd] *a* δειλός, φοβιτσιάρης.

timing ['taɪmɪŋ] *n* ρύθμιση, χρονισμός, χρονομέτρηση.

timpani ['tɪmpənɪ] *npl* τύμπανα *ntpl*.

tin [tɪn] *n* κασσίτερος, καλάι || *(container)* τενεκές *m*, κουτί κονσέρβας || **~foil** *n* ασημόχαρτο, αλουμινόχαρτο, χρυσόχαρτο.

tinge [tɪndʒ] *n* χροιά, απόχρωση, δόση ♦ *vt* χρωματίζω, βάφω.

tingle ['tɪŋgl] *n* τσούξιμο, έξαψη ♦ *vi* τσούζω, τσιμπώ.

tinker ['tɪŋkə*] *n* γανωματάς || **to ~ with** *vt* σκαλίζω, φτιάχνω αδέξια.

tinkle ['tɪŋkl] *vi* κουδουνίζω, πχώ.

tinned [tɪnd] *a (food)* κονσέρβα, του κουτιού.

tin opener ['tɪnəʊpnə*] *n* ανοιχτήρι.

tinsel ['tɪnsəl] *n* γυαλιστερές κορδέλες *fpl* μετάλλου, ασημένια βροχή.

tint [tɪnt] *n* χροιά, απόχρωση.

tiny ['taɪnɪ] *a* μικροσκοπικός, μικρούτσικος.

tip [tɪp] *n* άκρη, άκρο, μύτη || *(for protection)* σιδηρά άκρα *ntpl*, σίδερο, πετσάκι || *(of money)* φιλοδώρημα *nt*, πουρμπουάρ *nt inv* || *(useful hint)* υπαινιγμός, μυστική πληροφορία ♦ *vt (put end on)* προσθέτω άκρη σε || *(tip over)* γέρνω αναποδογυρίζω || *(waiter)* φιλοδωρώ, δίνω πουρμπουάρ || **~-off** *n*

(hint) πληροφορία, υπαινιγμός || **~ped** *a (cigarette)* με φίλτρο.

tipsy ['tɪpsɪ] *a* μεθυσμένος, πιωμένος.

tiptoe ['tɪptəʊ] *n*: **on ~** ακροποδητί, στα νύχια.

tiptop ['tɪp'tɒp] *a*: **in ~ condition** σε καλή φόρμα, πρώτης τάξεως.

tire ['taɪə*] *n (US)* = **tyre** ♦ *vti* κουράζω, εξαντλώ, κουράζομαι, βαριέμαι || **~d** *a* κουρασμένος, εξαντλημένος || **~d of** βαριέμαι || **~dness** *n* κόπωση, κούραση || **~less** *a* ακούραστος, ακαταπόνητος.

tiring ['taɪərɪŋ] *a* κουραστικός || *(boring)* πληκτικός, ανιαρός.

tissue ['tɪʃuː] *n* ιστός, υφή || *(paper handkerchief)* χαρτομάντηλο || **~ paper** *n* τσιγαρόχαρτο.

tit [tɪt] *n (bird)* αιγίθαλος, || *(col: breast)* βυζί, μαστός || **~ for tat** οφθαλμό αντί οφθαλμού.

titbit ['tɪtbɪt] *n* μεζές *m*.

title ['taɪtl] *n* τίτλος, επικεφαλίδα || *(rank etc)* τίτλος || *(legal)* τίτλος, δικαίωμα *nt* || *(SPORT)* (παγκόσμιος) τίτλος || **~ deed** *n* τίτλος κυριότητας, τίτλος ιδιοκτησίας || **~ role** *n* πρώτος ρόλος, ρόλος που δίνει το τίτλο του έργου.

titter ['tɪtə*] *vi* γελώ ανόητα, κρυφογελώ.

titular ['tɪtjʊlə*] *a* επίτιμος.

to [tuː, tə] *prep (towards)* προς, στο || *(as far as)* μέχρι || *(comparison)* προς το, έναντι || *(for infin)* για να || **~ and fro** πάνω κάτω, πηγαινοέλα, ανεβοκατέβασμα.

toad [təʊd] *n* φρύνος, βάτραχος || *(fig)* μπούφος || **~stool** *n* βωλίτης ο δηλητηριώδης (μανιτάρι).

toast [təʊst] *n* φρυγανιά || *(drink)* πρόποση ♦ *vt (drink)* κάνω πρόποση || *(brown)* ψήνω, φρυγανίζω || *(warm)* ζεσταίνω || **~er** *n* φρυγανιέρα.

tobacco [tə'bækəʊ] *n* καπνός || **~nist** *n* καπνοπώλης || **~nist's (shop)** *n* καπνοπωλείο.

toboggan [tə'bɒgən] *n* έλκηθρο, τόμπογκαν *nt inv*.

today [tə'deɪ] *n* το σήμερα ♦ *ad* σήμερα || *(present time)* σήμερα, τώρα.

toddy ['tɒdɪ] *n (warm, alcoholic drink)* ζεστό γκρόγκ *nt inv*.

toe [təʊ] *n* δάκτυλο του ποδιού ♦ *vt*: **to ~ the line** *(fig)* πακούω, υποτάσσομαι || **~nail** *n* νύχι του ποδιού.

toffee ['tɒfɪ] *n* καραμέλα με βούτυρο || **~ apple** *n* ζαχαρωμένο μήλο.

together [tə'geðə*] *ad* μαζί, μόνοι, ο ένας με τον άλλο || *(at the same time)* μαζί, συγχρόνως || **~ness** *n* πνεύμα συνεργασίας.

toggle switch ['tɒglswɪtʃ] *n (COMPUT)* διακόπτης με σκαλίσκο.

toil [tɔɪl] *n* μόχθος, κόπος, σκληρή δουλειά ♦ *vi* μοχθώ, εργάζομαι σκληρά.

toilet ['tɔɪlɪt] *n (lavatory)* αποχωρητήριο, μέρος *nt* ♦ *a* τουαλέτα || **~ paper** *n* χαρτί τουαλέτας, χάρτης υγείας || **~ries**

npl είδη *ntpl* τουαλέτας || ~ **roll** *n* ρολό χαρτιού τουαλέτας || ~ **water** *n* κολώνια.

token ['təʊkən] *n* ένδειξη, τεκμήριο, σημείο.

told [təʊld] *pt, pp of* **tell.**

tolerable ['tɒlərəbl] *a* ανεκτός, υποφερτός || *(moderate)* καλούτσικος.

tolerance ['tɒlərəns] *n* ανοχή, ανεκτικότητα || *(engineering)* ανοχή.

tolerant ['tɒlərənt] *a* ανεκτικός.

tolerate ['tɒləreɪt] *vt* ανέχομαι, υποφέρω.

toleration [tɒlə'reɪʃən] *n* ανοχή, ανεκτικότητα.

toll [təʊl] *n (tax, charge)* διόδια, φόρος ♦ *vi (bell)* κτυπώ (καμπάνα), καμπανίζω || ~**bridge** *n* γέφυρα με διόδια *ntpl.*

tomato [tə'mɑːtəʊ] *n* ντομάτα.

tomb [tuːm] *n* τύμβος, τάφος.

tomboy ['tɒmbɔɪ] *n* αγοροκόριτσο.

tombstone ['tuːmstəʊn] *n* επιτύμβιος λίθος.

tomcat ['tɒmkæt] *n* γάτος.

tomorrow [tə'mɒrəʊ] *n* αύριο, αυριανή μέρα ♦ *ad* αύριο.

ton [tʌn] *n* τόνος (2240 λίμπρες) || *(US)* τόνος (2000 λίμπρες) || ~**s of** *(col)* μεγάλη ποσότητα, πολλές φορές.

tone [təʊn] *n* τόνος, ήχος || *(character)* τόνος, πνεύμα *nt*, τάση || *(colour)* τόνος, απόχρωση ♦ *vi* συντονίζομαι, ταιριάζω ♦ *vt* τονίζω, τονώνω, ρυθμίζω || **to ~ down** *vt* απαλύνω, μαλακώνω, μετριάζω.

tongs [tɒŋz] *npl* λαβίδα, τσιμπίδα, μασιά.

tongue [tʌŋ] *n* γλώσσα || *(ox tongue: food)* βοδινή γλώσσα || **with ~ in cheek** ειρωνικά || ~**-tied** *a* άφωνος, βουβός (από κατάπληξη) || ~**-twister** *n* γλωσσοδέτης.

tonic ['tɒnɪk] *n* τονωτικό, δυναμωτικό || *(MUS)* τονική, βασική νότα || ~ **water** *n* τόνικ.

tonight [tə'naɪt] *n* σήμερα το βράδυ ♦ *ad* απόψε.

tonnage ['tʌnɪdʒ] *n* χωρητικότητα, τοννάζ *nt inv.*

tonsil ['tɒnsl] *n* αμυγδαλή || ~**litis** *n* αμυγδαλίτιδα.

too [tuː] *ad* πολύ, πάρα πολύ, υπερβολικά || *(also)* επίσης.

took [tʊk] *pt of* **take.**

tool [tuːl] *n* εργαλείο || ~**box** *n* κιβώτιο εργαλείων.

toot [tuːt] *n* κορνάρισμα *nt* ♦ *vi* κορνάρω.

tooth [tuːθ] *n* δόντι || *(on gearwheel)* δόντι || ~**ache** *n* πονόδοντος, οδοντόπονος || ~**brush** *n* οδοντόβουρτσα || ~**paste** *n* οδοντόπαστα || ~**pick** *n* οδοντογλυφίδα.

top [tɒp] *n* κορυφή, κορφή, απάνω (μέρος) || *(at school)* πρώτος, καλύτερος || *(spinning toy)* σβούρα ♦ *a* ανώτερος, ψηλότερος ♦ *vt (list)* είμαι επικεφαλής, είμαι πρώτος || **from ~ to toe** από την κορυφή ως τα νύχια || ~ **coat** *n* παλτό ||

~ **hat** *n* ψηλό καπέλο || ~**-heavy** *a* ασταθής, βαρύς στην κορυφή.

topic ['tɒpɪk] *n* θέμα *nt*, ζήτημα *nt* || ~**al** *a* επίκαιρος.

top-level ['tɒp'levl] *a* υψηλού επιπέδου.

topmost ['tɒpməʊst] *a* υψηλότερτος, κορυφαίος, ύψιστος.

topple ['tɒpl] *vti* κλονίζομαι, πέφτω || *(overturn)* αναποδογυρίζω.

topsy-turvy ['tɒpsɪ'tɜːvɪ] *a, ad* άνω κάτω.

torch [tɔːtʃ] *n (electric)* φακός, φανάρι || *(Olympic)* πυρσός, λαμπάδα, δαυλί.

tore ['tɔː*] *pt of* **tear.**

torment ['tɔːment] *n* βασανιστήριο, μαρτύριο ♦ [tɔː'ment] *vt* ενοχλώ, πειράζω || *(distress)* βασανίζω, τυραννώ.

torn [tɔːn] *pp of* **tear** || *a (undecided) (between)* ταλαντευόμενος, αναποφάσιστος.

tornado [tɔː'neɪdəʊ] *n* ανεμοστρόβιλος, λαίλαπα.

torpedo [tɔː'piːdəʊ] *n* τορπίλη.

torrent ['tɒrənt] *n* χείμαρρος || ~**ial** *a* χειμαρρώδης.

torso ['tɔːsəʊ] *n* κορμός, τόρσο.

tortoise ['tɔːtəs] *n* χελώνα.

tortuous ['tɔːtjʊəs] *a* ελικοειδής, στρεβλός || *(deceitful)* ανέντιμος, δόλιος.

torture ['tɔːtʃə*] *n* βασανιστήριο, βασανισμός, μαρτύριο ♦ *vt* βασανίζω.

Tory ['tɔːrɪ] *n* συντηρητικός ♦ *a* συντηρητικός.

toss [tɒs] *vt* πετώ, τραντάζω || *(in the air)* ρίχνω, πετώ ♦ *n (of coin to decide)* στρίψιμο || **to ~ a coin, to ~ up for** ρίχνω κορώνα-γράμματα.

tot [tɒt] *n* ποτηράκι, γουλιά || *(child)* παιδάκι, μωρό, μπέμπης.

total ['təʊtl] *n* σύνολο, όλο, άθροισμα *nt*, σούμα ♦ *a (συν)*ολικός, ολόκληρος, πλήρης ♦ *vt* προσθέτω, αθροίζω || *(amount to)* ανέρχομαι σε, φθάνω.

totem pole ['təʊtəmpəʊl] *n* στήλη του τότεμ.

totter ['tɒtə*] *vi* παραπατώ, τρικλίζω.

touch [tʌtʃ] *n* αφή, επαφή, άγγιγμα *nt* || *(sense)* επαφή, αφή || *(small amount)* μικρή δόση, ίχνος *nt*, υποψία || *(style)* πινελιά, μολυβιά, ύφος *nt* ♦ *vt* αγγίζω || *(come against)* εφάπτομαι, ακουμπώ || *(move)* θίγω, συγκινώ || **in ~ with** σ' επαφή με, διατηρώ επαφή || **to ~ on** *vt (topic)* θίγω (θέμα) || **to ~ up** *vt (paint)* ρετουσάρω, επισκευάζω || ~**-and-go** *a* επικίνδυνος, αβέβαιος, επισφαλής || ~**down** *n* προσγείωση || ~**ing** *a* συγκινητικός || ~**line** *n* γραμμή του τέρματος || ~**y** *a* ευαίσθητος, εύθικτος.

tough [tʌf] *a* σκληρός, στερεός || *(difficult)* δυσχερής, σκληρός, δύσκολος || *(meat)* σκληρός ♦ *n (gangster etc)* κακοποιός, μπράβος || ~**en** *vti* σκληραίνω, σκληρύνομαι || ~**ness** *n* σκληρότητα || *(resilience)* αντοχή.

toupee ['tuːpeɪ] *n (wig)* περούκα.

tour ['tuə*] n περιοδεία, περιήγηση ♦ vi περιηγούμαι, περιοδεύω || ~ing n περιοδεία.

tourism ['tuərɪzəm] n τουρισμός.

tourist ['tuərɪst] n τουρίστας/τουρίστρια m/f, περιηγητής/περιηγήτρια m/f || ~ office n τουριστικό γραφείο.

tournament ['tuənəmənt] n πρωτάθλημα nt, τουρνουά nt inv.

tousled ['tauzld] a (hair) αναστατωμένος, ξεχτένιστος.

tow [təu] n (pull) ρυμούλκηση ♦ vt (pull) ρυμουλκώ.

toward(s) [tə'wɔːd(z)] prep προς, κατά, για.

towel ['tauəl] n πετσέτα.

tower ['tauə*] n πύργος || ~ing a πανύψηλος || (rage) βίαιος, άγριος.

town [taun] n πόλη, πολιτεία, χώρα || ~ clerk n γραμματέας δημαρχίας || ~ hall n δημαρχείο || ~ planning n πολεοδομία.

towrope ['təurəup] n σχοινί ρυμούλκησης.

toxic ['tɒksɪk] a τοξικός.

toy [tɔɪ] n παιχνίδι, παιχνιδάκι || to ~ with vt παίζω με, σκέπτομαι να.

trace [treɪs] n ίχνος nt || (small amount) ίχνος nt, υπόλειμμα nt, τεκμήριο ♦ vt παρακολουθώ || (find out) ανιχνεύω, διακρίνω || (copy) χαράσσω, αντιγράφω, ξεσπκώνω.

track [træk] n ίχνη ntpl, πέρασμα nt, πατημασιές fpl || (path) μονοπάτι || (road) δρομάκος || (racing) διάδρομος αγώνων, στίβος, πίστα || (RAIL) (σιδηροδρομική) γραμμή ♦ vt παρακολουθώ || (persecute) καταδιώκω || to keep ~ of παρακολουθώ, βρίσκομαι σε επαφή με || to ~ down vt ανακαλύπτω, βρίσκω || ~er dog n κυνηγόσκυλο.

tract [trækt] n περιοχή, έκταση || (book) φυλλάδιο.

tractor ['træktə*] n ελκυστήρας, τρακτέρ nt inv.

trade [treɪd] n εμπόριο || (business) επάγγελμα nt, δουλειά || (people) συντεχνία, κλάδος ♦ vi (+ in) εμπορεύομαι, συναλλάσσομαι, κάνω δουλειές || ~mark n σήμα nt (κατατεθέν) || ~ name n εμπορική επωνυμία, φίρμα || ~r n έμπορος || ~sman n καταστηματάρχης, λιανέμπορος || (skilled workman) τεχνίτης || ~ union n εργατική ένωση, συνδικάτο.

trading ['treɪdɪŋ] n εμπόριο.

tradition [trə'dɪʃn] n παράδοση || ~al a παραδοσιακός, πατροπαράδοτος.

traffic ['træfɪk] n κίνηση, κυκλοφορία || (esp in drugs) εμπόριο, συναλλαγή ♦ vt (esp drugs) εμπορεύομαι (κάτι) || ~ circle n (US: roundabout) κυκλοφοριακός δρόμος || ~ jam n μποτιλιάρισμα || ~ lights npl φανάρια ntpl, φώτα ntpl κυκλοφορίας.

tragedy ['trædʒɪdɪ] n τραγωδία, δράμα nt.

tragic ['trædʒɪk] a τραγικός.

trail [treɪl] n ίχνος nt || (footsteps) πατήματα ntpl || (something trailing) γραμμή (καπνού), ουρά || (rough road) μονοπάτι ♦ vt (follow) σέρνομαι πίσω || (hang loosely) σέρνομαι, σέρνω || to ~ behind vi σέρνομαι πίσω || ~er n (truck) ρυμουλκούμενο όχημα nt || (film) απόσπασμα nt ταινίας || (US: caravan) τροχόσπιτο.

train [treɪn] n συρμός αμαξοστοιχίας, τραίνο || (of gown) ουρά || (series) σειρά, αλληλουχία, ειρμός ♦ vt εκπαιδεύω, διδάσκω, μαθαίνω || (plant) κατευθύνω, οδηγώ || (point gun) σκοπεύω ♦ vi (exercise) προπονώ, προγυμνάζω || ~ed a εκγυμνασμένος, εξασκημένος || ~ee n ασκούμενος μαθητής || ~er n εκπαιδευτής || (sport) προπονητής, γυμναστής/ γυμνάστρια m/f || ~ing n εκπαίδευση, εξάσκηση || (sport) προπόνηση || in ~ing σε φόρμα || ~ing college n παιδαγωγική ακαδημία.

traipse [treɪps] vi (wander) σέρνομαι εδώ και κει, τριγυρίζω κουρασμένα.

trait [treɪt] n χαρακτηριστικό.

traitor ['treɪtə*] n προδότης/τρια m/f.

tram(car) ['træm(kɑː*)] n τράμ nt inv.

tramp [træmp] n (vagabond) αλήτης/αλήτισσα m/f ♦ vi περπατώ βαρειά, βηματίζω βαρειά || (by foot) πεζοπορώ, πηγαίνω πεζή.

trample ['træmpl] vt ποδοπατώ, καταπατώ.

trampoline ['træmpəliːn] n τραμπολίνο.

trance [trɑːns] n έκσταση, ύπνωση, όραμα nt.

tranquil ['træŋkwɪl] a ήρεμος, ήσυχος || ~lity n πρεμία || ~lizer n (drug) καταπραϋντικό.

transact [træn'zækt] vt εκτελώ, διεξάγω, διεκπεραιώνω || ~ion n διεκπεραίωση, διεξαγωγή, συναλλαγή.

transatlantic ['trænzət'læntɪk] a υπερατλαντικός.

transcend [træn'send] vt υπερέχω, υπερβαίνω.

transcript ['trænskrɪpt] n αντίγραφο, αντιγραφή || ~ion n αντιγραφή, αντίγραφο.

transept ['trænsept] n πτέρυγα ναού, εγκάρσιο κλίτος nt.

transfer ['trænsfə*] n μεταφορά, (job) μετάθεση || (legal) μεταβίβαση, εκχώρηση, μεταγραφή || (design) χαλκομανία, στάμπα, αντιγραφή || (SPORT) μεταβίβαση, μεταφορά ♦ [trænsˈfɜː*] vt μεταφέρω, μεταθέτω, αλλάζω || ~able a μεταβιβάσιμος, μεταφερτός || 'not ~able' (on ticket) 'προσωπικό'.

transform [træns'fɔːm] vt μετασχηματίζω, μεταβάλλω, μεταμορφώνω || ~ation n μετασχηματισμός, μεταβολή, μεταμόρφωση || ~er n (ELEC) μετασχηματιστής.

transfusion [træns'fju:ʒən] n μετάγγιση.

transient ['trænzɪənt] a παροδικός.

transistor [træn'zɪstə*] n κρυσταλλικός πολλαπλασιαστής || (radio) τρανσίστορ nt inv, φορητό ραδιόφωνο.

transit ['trænzɪt] n: in ~ κατά τη μεταφορά, υπό μεταφορά.

transition [træn'zɪʃən] n μετάβαση, μεταβολή, αλλαγή || ~al a μεταβατικός.

transitive ['trænzɪtɪv] a μεταβατικό (ρήμα).

transitory ['trænzɪtəri] a παροδικός, βραχύς, εφήμερος.

translate [trænz'leɪt] vt μεταφράζω.

translation [trænz'leɪʃn] n μετάφραση.

translator [trænz'leɪtə*] n μεταφραστής/άστρια m/f.

transmission [trænz'mɪʃən] n (of information) μεταβίβαση, διαβίβαση || (AUT) μετάδοση || (RAD) εκπομπή, μετάδοση.

transmit [trænz'mɪt] vt μεταδίδω, μεταβιβάζω, διαβιβάζω || ~ter n πομπός.

transparency [træns'pɛərənsɪ] n (PHOT: slide) διαφάνεια, ολάντ nt inv.

transparent [træns'pɛərənt] a διαφανής, διαυγής || (clear) καθαρός.

transplant [træns'plɑːnt] vt μεταφυτεύω, μεταφέρω ♦ ['trænsplɑːnt] n (also MED) μεταφύτευση, μεταμόσχευση.

transport ['trænspɔːt] n μεταφορά ♦ [træns'pɔːt] vt μεταφέρω || ~able a μετακομιστός, φορητός || ~ation n μεταφορά.

transverse ['trænzvɜːs] a εγκάρσιος.

trap [træp] n (trick) παγίδα, απάτη || (snare) παγίδα, φάκα || (carriage) δίτροχη άμαξα || (col: mouth) στόμα nt ♦ vt παγιδεύω, πιάνω στην παγίδα || ~door n καταπακτή.

trapeze [trə'piːz] n τραπέζιο.

trappings ['træpɪŋz] npl διακόσμηση, στολίδια ntpl.

trash [træʃ] n σκουπίδια ntpl, χωρίς αξία || (nonsense) μπούρδες fpl, τρίχες fpl || ~ can n (US) σκουπιδοτενεκές m.

trauma ['trɔːmə] n τραύμα nt || ~tic a τραυματικός.

travel ['trævl] n ταξίδι, περιήγηση ♦ vi ταξιδεύω, κάνω ταξίδια ♦ vt (distance) πηγαίνω, βαδίζω, προχωρώ, μετακινούμαι || ~ler, ~er (US) n ταξιδιώτης/τισσα m/f || (salesman) πλασιέ m inv, αντιπρόσωπος || ~ler's cheque, ~er's check (US) n ταξιδιωτική επιταγή, τράβελερς τσεκ nt inv || ~ling, ~ing (US) n τα ταξίδια ♦ attr a ταξιδιωτικός, του ταξιδιού || ~ sickness n ναυτία.

traverse ['trævəs] vt διασχίζω, διαβαίνω, περνώ.

travesty ['trævɪstɪ] n διακωμώδηση, παρωδία.

trawler ['trɔːlə*] n αλιευτικό, τράτα.

tray [treɪ] n δίσκος.

treacherous ['tretʃərəs] a (person) δόλιος, ύπουλος || (road: dangerous, icy etc) επικίνδυνος, άστατος.

treachery ['tretʃəri] n δολιότητα, προδοσία, απιστία.

treacle ['triːkl] n μελάσσα, πετιμέζι.

tread [tred] (irreg v) n περπάτημα nt || (way of walking) βήμα nt, βηματισμός || (stair, tyre) βαθμίδα, πάτημα nt, πέλμα nt ελαστικού ♦ vi βαδίζω, περπατώ || to ~ on vt (πόδι)πατώ.

treason ['triːzn] n προδοσία.

treasure ['treʒə*] n θησαυρός ♦ vt αποθησαυρίζω || (value highly) εκτιμώ, θεωρώ πολύτιμο || ~ hunt n θησαυροθηρία || ~r n ταμίας.

treasury ['treʒəri] n θησαυροφυλάκειο, ταμείο.

treat [triːt] n ευχαρίστηση, απόλαυση ♦ vt μεταχειρίζομαι, φέρομαι || (entertain) κερνώ, προσφέρω.

treatise ['triːtɪz] n πραγματεία, διατριβή.

treatment ['triːtmənt] n μεταχείρηση, περιποίηση || (MED) κούρα, θεραπεία.

treaty ['triːtɪ] n συνθήκη.

treble ['trebl] a τριπλός, τριπλάσιος ♦ vt τριπλασιάζω ♦ n πρίμο || (voice) υψίφωνος, σοπράνο f inv.

tree [triː] n δέντρο || ~ trunk n κορμός δέντρου.

trek [trek] n ταξίδι, μετανάστευση ♦ vi (migrate) μετοικώ, μεταναστεύω.

trellis ['trelɪs] n δικτυωτό πλέγμα nt, καφασωτό πλαίσιο.

tremble ['trembl] vi τρέμω, δονούμαι.

trembling ['tremblɪŋ] n τρόμος, τρεμούλα ♦ a τρεμάμενος, τρεμουλιάρης.

tremendous [trə'mendəs] a (vast) πελώριος, τρομερός.

tremor ['tremə*] n τρεμούλιασμα nt.

trench [trentʃ] n τάφρος f, αυλάκι, χαντάκι || (of war) χαράκωμα nt.

trend [trend] n τάση, πορεία ♦ vi τείνω.

trepidation [trepɪ'deɪʃən] n φόβος, ανυσηχία, τρεμούλα.

trespass ['trespəs] vi καταπατώ.

tress [tres] n βόστρυχος, πλεξούδα, κοτσίδα, μπούκλα.

trestle ['tresl] n υπόβαθρο, υποστήριγμα nt, καβαλέτο || ~ table n τραπέζι σε καβαλέτο.

trial ['traɪəl] n (in court) δίκη, κρίση || (test) δοκιμή || (hardship) δοκιμασία, βάσανο || by ~ and error με τη μέθοδο της δοκιμής και πλάνης, εμπειρικά.

triangle ['traɪæŋgl] n τρίγωνο.

triangular [traɪ'æŋgjulə*] a τριγωνικός.

tribal ['traɪbəl] a φυλετικός.

tribe [traɪb] n φυλή || ~sman n μέλος m φυλής.

tribulation [trɪbjuˈleɪʃən] n δοκιμασία, συμφορά, πάθημα nt.
tribunal [traɪˈbjuːnl] n δικαστήριο.
tributary [ˈtrɪbjutərɪ] n παραπόταμος.
tribute [ˈtrɪbjuːt] n (respect) φόρος τιμής.
trice [traɪs] n: in a ~ στη στιγμή.
trick [trɪk] n τέχνασμα nt, κόλπο, κατεργαριά || (clever act) δεξιοτεχνία, ταχυδακτυλουργία || (habit) συνήθεια || (CARDS) κόλπο, πιάσιμο, λεβέ nt inv ♦ vt εξαπατώ || ~ery n απάτη, κοροϊδία.
trickle [ˈtrɪkl] n λεπτή ροή, στάξιμο, στάλα (νερού) ♦ vi σταλάζω, στάζω.
tricky [ˈtrɪkɪ] a (problem, situation) περίπλοκος, δύσκολος.
tricycle [ˈtraɪsɪkl] n τρίκυκλο.
trifle [ˈtraɪfl] n είδος nt τούρτας || (of little importance) μικροπράγματα ntpl, ασήμαντο γεγονός, μηδαμινό ποσό.
trifling [ˈtraɪflɪŋ] a ασήμαντος, τιποτένιος.
trigger [ˈtrɪgə*] n σκανδάλη.
trigonometry [trɪgəˈnɒmɪtrɪ] n τριγωνομετρία.
trim [trɪm] a κομψός, ευπρεπής ♦ n τάξη, φόρμα, ευπρεπής κατάσταση || (haircut etc) κόψιμο, φρεσκάρισμα nt (μαλλιών) ♦ vt κόβω, κουρεύω, κλαδεύω || (decorate) γαρνίρω || ~mings npl γαρνιτούρες fpl.
Trinity [ˈtrɪnɪtɪ] n: the ~ (REL) Αγία Τριάδα.
trinket [ˈtrɪŋkɪt] n μικρό κόσμημα nt, μπιμπελό nt inv.
trio [ˈtriːəʊ] n τριάδα || (MUS) τρίο.
trip [trɪp] n εκδρομή, ταξίδι || (stumble) παραπάτημα nt, τρικλοποδιά ♦ vi περπατώ ελαφρά, αλαφροπατώ || (stumble) σκοντάφτω, παραπατώ || to ~ up vi ανεβαίνω ελαφροπατώντας ♦ vt βάζω τρικλοποδιά σε.
tripe [traɪp] n (food) πατσάς || (rubbish) ανοησίες fpl, μπούρδες fpl.
triple [ˈtrɪpl] a τριπλός, τρίδιπλος.
triplets [ˈtrɪplɪts] npl τρίδυμα ntpl.
triplicate [ˈtrɪplɪkɪt] n: in ~ σε τριπλούν.
tripod [ˈtraɪpɒd] n τρίποδο.
trite [traɪt] a τριμμένος, κοινός, συνηθισμένος.
triumph [ˈtraɪʌmf] n θρίαμβος ♦ vi θριαμβεύω || ~ant a θριαμβευτικός.
trivial [ˈtrɪvɪəl] a ασήμαντος, τιποτένιος || ~ity n ασημαντότητα, κοινοτοπία.
trod [trɒd] pt of tread || ~den pp of tread.
trolley [ˈtrɒlɪ] n (small truck) καροτσάκι || ~ bus n τρόλλεϋ nt inv.
trombone [trɒmˈbəʊn] n τρομπόνι.
troop [truːp] n ομάδα, όμιλος || ~s npl στρατεύματα ntpl || to ~ in/out vi μπαίνω/βγαίνω ομαδικά || ~er n ιππέας, έφιππος αστυνομικός.
trophy [ˈtrəʊfɪ] n τρόπαιο, έπαθλο.
tropic [ˈtrɒpɪk] n τροπικός || ~al a τροπικός.

trot [trɒt] n τριποδισμός, ελαφρό τρέξιμο ♦ vi τρέχω σιγά.
trouble [ˈtrʌbl] n στενοχώρια, ανησυχία, σκοτούρα || (effort, care) κόπος ♦ vt ενοχλώ, ανησυχώ || ~d a ανήσυχος, ταραγμένος || ~-free a χωρίς σκοτούρες || ~maker n ταραχοποιός, ταραξίας || ~some a ενοχλητικός, δύσκολος.
trough [trɒf] n σκάφη, ποτίστρα || (channel) τάφρος f || (meteorology) σφήνα υφέσεως.
troupe [truːp] n θίασος.
trousers [ˈtraʊzəz] npl πανταλόνι.
trousseau [ˈtruːsəʊ] n προίκα (ασπρόρουχα και φορέματα).
trout [traʊt] n πέστροφα.
trowel [ˈtraʊəl] n μυστρί.
truant [ˈtrʊənt] n: to play ~ το σκάω, απουσιάζω αδικαιολόγητα.
truce [truːs] n ανακωχή.
truck [trʌk] n φορτηγό αμάξι, καμιόνι || (RAIL) φορείο || (barrow) χειράμαξα αχθοφόρου || ~ driver n οδηγός φορτηγού || ~ farm n (US) αγρόκτημα nt λαχανικών, περιβόλι.
truculent [ˈtrʌkjulənt] a βίαιος, άγριος, επιθετικός.
trudge [trʌdʒ] vi βαδίζω με δυσκολία, σέρνομαι.
true [truː] a αληθινός || (precise) ακριβής || (genuine) πραγματικός, αυθεντικός, γνήσιος || (friend) πιστός, τίμιος, αληθινός.
truffle [ˈtrʌfl] n τρούφα.
truly [ˈtruːlɪ] ad ειλικρινά, πιστά, αληθινά || (exactly) με ακρίβεια, ακριβώς, ορθά || yours ~ όλως υμέτερος.
trump [trʌmp] n (CARDS) ατού nt inv || ~ed-up a ψεύτικος, σκαρωμένος.
trumpet [ˈtrʌmpɪt] n σάλπιγγα, τρουμπέτα.
truncheon [ˈtrʌntʃən] n ρόπαλο, αστυνομικό γκλόμπ nt inv.
trundle [ˈtrʌndl] vti: to ~ along κυλώ, τρέχω, τσουλώ.
trunk [trʌŋk] n κορμός, κούτσουρο || (body) κορμός, τόρσο nt inv || (box) κιβώτιο, μπαούλο || (of elephant) προβοσκίδα || ~s npl μαγιό || ~ call n υπεραστική κλήση.
truss [trʌs] n (MED) κοιλεπίδεσμος, ζώνη.
trust [trʌst] n πίστη, εμπιστοσύνη || (property) καταπίστευμα nt ♦ vt εμπιστεύομαι σε || ~ed a έμπιστος, της εμπιστοσύνης || ~ee n επίτροπος, κηδεμόνας, έφορος || ~ful a γεμάτος εμπιστοσύνη, ευκολόπιστος || ~ing a πλήρης εμπιστοσύνης || ~worthy a αξιόπιστος || ~y a πιστός, αξιόπιστος.
truth [truːθ] n αλήθεια || ~ful a φιλαλήθης, αληθινός || ~fully ad αληθινά, ειλικρινά, πιστά || ~fulness n φιλαλήθεια, ειλικρίνεια.
try [traɪ] (irreg v) n προσπάθεια || (test) δοκιμή, απόπειρα ♦ vt δοκιμάζω, κάνω

δοκιμή || (in court) δικάζω || (strain)
κουράζω ♦ vi (attempt) προσπαθώ, ζητώ
να || to ~ on vt δοκιμάζω, προβάρω || to
~ out vt δοκιμάζω || ~ing a δύσκολος,
κουραστικός, σκληρός.

tsar [zɑːˠ] n τσάρος.

T-shirt [ˈtiːʃɜːt] n φανέλα (αθλητική).

tub [tʌb] n μεγάλη λεκάνη, σκάφη,
κάδος.

tuba [ˈtjuːbə] n μεγάλη κορνέτα,
κοντραμπάσο.

tubby [ˈtʌbi] a (fat) στρογγυλός σαν
βαρέλι, κοντοπίθαρος.

tube [tjuːb] n σωλήνας, αγωγός, αυλός ||
(also for toothpaste etc) σωληνάριο || (in
London) υπόγειος σιδηρόδρομος || (AUT:
for tyre) σαμπρέλα || ~less a (AUT) χωρίς
σαμπρέλα.

tuber [ˈtjuːbəˠ] n βολβός, γογγύλι.

tuberculosis [tjubɜːkjuˈləʊsɪs] n
φυματίωση.

tube station [ˈtjuːbsteɪʃən] n σταθμός
του υπόγειου τραίνου.

tubing [ˈtjuːbɪŋ] n σωλήν(ωση).

tubular [ˈtjuːbjʊləˠ] a (steel, furniture)
σωληνοειδής, σωληνωτός.

TUC n (abbr of Trades Union Congress)
Συμβούλιο Αγγλικών Εργατικών
Συνδικάτων.

tuck [tʌk] n (pleat) πιέτα, πτυχή ♦ vt
(gather) διπλώνω, μαζεύω || to ~ away
vt κρύνω || to ~ in vt μαζεύω, χώνω ♦ vi
(food) πέφτω με τα μούτρα στο φαΐ || to
~ up vt (child) σκεπάζω, τακτοποιώ.

Tuesday [ˈtjuːzdɪ] n Τρίτη.

tuft [tʌft] n θύσανος, φούντα.

tug [tʌg] n απότομο τράβηγμα nt ||
(steamship) ρυμουλκό (πλοίο) ♦ vti σύρω,
τραβώ δυνατά || ~-of-war n
διελκυστίνδα.

tuition [tjuˈɪʃən] n διδασκαλία || (fees)
δίδακτρα ntpl.

tulip [ˈtjuːlɪp] n τουλίπα.

tumble [ˈtʌmbl] n πέσιμο, τούμπα,
κουτρουβάλα ♦ vi πέφτω, τουμπάρω ||
(somersault) κάνω τούμπες,
αναποδογυρίζω ♦ vt (toss about)
κατρακυλώ, σωριάζομαι || to ~ to vt
συλλαμβάνω, αντιλαμβάνομαι || ~down
a ετοιμόρροπος, σαραβαλιασμένος ||
~r n (acrobat) ακροβάτης/τρια m/f ||
(glass) ποτήρι.

tummy [ˈtʌmi] n (col: stomach, belly)
στομάχι, κοιλιά.

tumour [ˈtjuːməˠ] n όγκος.

tumult [ˈtjuːmʌlt] n θόρυβος, σαματάς,
φασαρία || ~uous a θορυβώδης,
ταραχώδης, θυελλώδης.

tuna [ˈtjuːnə] n τόνος.

tune [tjuːn] n μελωδία, σκοπός || (pitch)
τόνος, συντονισμός ♦ vt κουρδίζω,
συντονίζω || (motorcar) ρυθμίζω,
εναρμονίζω, || in ~ μελωδικός,
συντονισμένος || out of ~ παραφωνία,
έξω από το τόνο || to ~ up vi (MUS)
συντονίζομαι, βρίσκω τον τόνο || ~ful a
μελωδικός, αρμονικός.

tunic [ˈtjuːnɪk] n χιτώνιο, αμπέχονο.

tuning [ˈtjuːnɪŋ] n (RAD) συντονισμός ||
(AUT) ρύθμιση.

Tunisia [tjuˈnɪzɪə] Τυνησία || ~n a
τψησιακός ♦ n Τυνήσιος.

tunnel [ˈtʌnl] n σήραγγα, τουνέλι ♦ vi
ανοίγω σήραγγα.

tunny [ˈtʌni] n τόνος.

turban [ˈtɜːbən] n σαρίκι, τουρμπάνι.

turbine [ˈtɜːbaɪn] n στρόβιλος,
τουρμπίνα.

turbulence [ˈtɜːbjʊləns] n (AVIAT)
στροβιλισμός, αναταραχή.

turbulent [ˈtɜːbjʊlənt] a ταραγμένος,
βίαιος, άτακτος.

turf [tɜːf] n χλόη, γρασίδι || (sod)
χορταριασμένος βώλος.

turgid [ˈtɜːdʒɪd] a (pompous) στομφώδης,
πομπώδης.

Turk [tɜːk] n Τούρκος.

turkey [ˈtɜːki] n γαλοπούλα, ινδιάνος ||
T~ n Τουρκία.

Turkish [ˈtɜːkɪʃ] a τουρκικός || (LING)
Τουρκική || ~ bath n χαμάμ nt inv.

turmoil [ˈtɜːmɔɪl] n αναταραχή,
αναστάτωση, πατιρντί.

turn [tɜːn] n περιστροφή, γύρισμα nt ||
(turning) στροφή || (performance) σειρά ||
(shape, manner) νοοτροπία, διάθεση ||
(chance) σειρά || (MED) κρίση ♦ vt
(peri)στρέφω, γυρίζω, στρίβω || (change
position) αλλάζω, γυρίζω || (of colour)
αλλάζω χρώμα nt ♦ vi περιστρέφομαι,
γυρίζω || (change direction) στρέφομαι,
στρίβω || (become sour) ξυνίζω || to ~
back vti γυρίζω πίσω || to ~ **down** vt
(refuse) απορρίπτω || (fold down) διπλώνω,
τσακίζω || to ~ **in** vi (go to bed) πάω για
ύπνο ♦ vt (fold) γυρίζω (μέσα), στριφώνω
|| to ~ **off** vi (from road) αλλάζω δρόμο,
στρίβω ♦ vt (light) κλείνω, σβήνω || (RAD)
κλείνω, σβήνω || to ~ **on** vt (light)
ανοίγω, ανάβω || (RAD) ανοίγω || to ~
out vt εξελίσσομαι, πάω || (extinguish)
κλείνω, σβήνω || to ~ **up** vi (person)
εμφανίζομαι, φθάνω ξαφνικά || (lost
object) ξαναβρίσκω ♦ vt (collar) σηκώνω,
ανασηκώνω || (RAD: increase volume)
ανεβάζω, δυναμώνω || ~ing n (in road)
καμπή, στροφή || ~ing point n κρίσιμο
σημείο, αποφασιστικό σημείο.

turnip [ˈtɜːnɪp] n γογγύλι.

turnout [ˈtɜːnaʊt] n συνάθροιση,
ακροατήριο.

turnover [ˈtɜːnəʊvəˠ] n τζίρος.

turnpike [ˈtɜːnpaɪk] n (US: toll highway)
οδός f με διόδια.

turnstile [ˈtɜːnstaɪl] n περιστροφική
είσοδος f.

turntable [ˈtɜːnteɪbl] n περιστροφική
εξέδρα, περιστροφική βάση.

turn-up [ˈtɜːnʌp] n (on trousers) ρεβέρ nt
inv.

turpentine [ˈtɜːpəntaɪn] n νέφτι.

turquoise [ˈtɜːkwɔɪz] n τουρκουάζ nt inv
♦ a (colour) κυανοπράσινος.

turret [ˈtʌrɪt] n πυργίσκος.

turtle ['tɜːtl] n χελώνα.

tusk [tʌsk] n χαυλιόδοντο.

tussle ['tʌsl] n τσακωμός, καυγάς.

tutor ['tjuːtə*] n ιδιαίτερος καθηγητής, οικοδιδάσκαλος || (at college) υφηγητής || ~ial n (UNIV) ιδιαίτερο μάθημα από καθηγητή.

TV [tiːˈviː] n (abbr of television) TV f, τηλεόραση.

twaddle ['twɒdl] n (col) μωρολογία, φλυαρία, μπούρδες fpl.

twang [twæŋ] n οξύς ήχος χορδής, ένρινος τόνος, σβούρισμα nt ♦ vti αφήνω τεντωμένη χορδή, αντηχώ, κρούω.

tweed [twiːd] n τουήντ nt inv.

tweezers ['twiːzəz] npl τσιμπίδα.

twelfth [twelfθ] a δωδέκατος || T~ Night η παραμονή των Φώτων.

twelve [twelv] num δώδεκα.

twentieth ['twentɪɪθ] a εικοστός.

twenty ['twentɪ] num είκοσι.

twerp [twɜːp] n (col: fool) βλάκας.

twice [twais] ad δύο φορές, διπλάσιος.

twig [twig] n κλαδί, κλωνάρι ♦ vt (understand, realize) αντιλαμβάνομαι, μπαίνω, πιάνω.

twilight ['twailait] n λυκόφως nt, λυκαυγές nt.

twin [twin] n δίδυμος ♦ a δίδυμος.

twine [twain] n σπάγγος, χοντρή κλωστή ♦ vi τυλίγομαι.

twinge [twindʒ] n δυνατός πόνος, σουβλιά.

twinkle ['twiŋkl] n σπινθηρισμός, σπίθισμα nt ♦ vi σπινθηροβολώ, σπιθίζω || (star) τρεμοσβήνω.

twirl [twɜːl] n περιστροφή, στρίψιμο ♦ vti περιστρέφω, στρίβω.

twist [twist] n συστροφή, στρίψιμο, στραμπούληγμα nt ♦ vt συστρέφω, πλέκω, στρίβω || (distort) στρεβλώνω, στραβώνω || (cheat) εξαπατώ ♦ vi συστρέφομαι, στρίβομαι || (curve) στρίβω.

twit [twit] n (col: fool) κορόιδο, βλάκας.

twitch [twitʃ] n σύσπαση, τίναγμα nt ♦ vi συσπώμαι νευρικά.

two [tuː] num δύο, δυο || ~-door a (AUT) με δύο πόρτες || ~-faced a (pej: person) διπρόσωπος || ~fold ad δύο φορές, διπλά ♦ a διπλός || ~-piece a (suit) ντεπιές || (swimsuit) κοστούμι μπάνιου ντεπιές || ~-seater n (plane) διθέσιο || (car) διθέσιο || ~some n ζευγάρι || ~-way n a (traffic) διπλής κυκλοφορίας.

tycoon [tai'kuːn] n μεγιστάνας των επιχειρήσεων.

type [taip] n τύπος || (example) είδος nt, τάξη || (printing) χαρακτήρες mpl, στοιχεία ntpl ♦ vt δακτυλογραφώ || ~-face n τύπος γραφής || ~script n δακτυλογραφημένο κείμενο || ~writer n γραφομηχανή || ~written a δακτυλογραφημένο.

typhoid ['taifɔid] n τυφοειδής.

typhoon [tai'fuːn] n τυφώνας.

typhus ['taifəs] n τύφος.

typical ['tipikəl] a τυπικός, χαρακτηριστικός.

typify ['tipifai] vt αντιπροσωπεύω, συμβολίζω.

typing ['taipiŋ] n δακτυλογράφηση.

typist ['taipist] n δακτυλογράφος m/f.

tyranny ['tirəni] n τυραννία.

tyrant ['tairənt] n τύραννος.

tyre ['taiə*] n (AUT) ρόδα, λάστιχο.

U

udder ['ʌdə*] n μαστός, μαστάρι.

UFO ['juːfəu] n (abbr of unidentified flying object) αντικείμενο αγνώστου ταυτότητας.

ugliness ['ʌglinis] n ασχήμια.

ugly ['ʌgli] a άσχημος, άσκημος || (bad) άσχημος, κακός || (dangerous) δυσάρεστος, επικίνδυνος, άσχημος.

UHF abbr of ultra-high frequency υπερηψηλή συχνότητα, UHF.

UK n abbr see united.

ulcer ['ʌlsə*] n (in mouth, stomach) έλκος nt.

ulterior [ʌl'tiəriə*] a (hidden) υστερόβουλος, κρυφός.

ultimate ['ʌltimit] a τελευταίος, τελικός, ύστατος, βασικός || ~ly ad τελικά, βασικά.

ultimatum [ʌlti'meitəm] n τελεσίγραφο.

ultraviolet ['ʌltrə'vaiəlit] a: ~ light υπεριώδες φώς nt.

umbilical [ʌmbi'laikəl] a: ~ cord ομφάλιος λώρος, ομφάλιος.

umbrella [ʌm'brelə] n ομπρέλα.

umpire ['ʌmpaiə*] n διαιτητής ♦ vti διαιτητεύω.

umpteen ['ʌmptiːn] num (col) ένα σωρό, δεν ξέρω πόσοι.

UN abbr see united.

unable [ʌn'eibl] a ανίκανος, μη δυνάμενος.

unaccompanied [ʌnə'kʌmpənid] a (child, lady) ασυνόδευτος, μόνος.

unaccountably [ʌnə'kauntəbli] ad ανεξήγητα.

unaccustomed [ʌnə'kʌstəmd] a ασυνήθιστος || (+ to) ασυνήθιστος (σε, να).

unaided [ʌn'eidid] a χωρίς βοήθεια, αβοήθητος.

unanimous [juː'næniməs] a ομόθυμος, ομόφωνος || ~ly ad ομόφωνα, παμψηφεί.

unattached [ʌnə'tætʃt] a (single) ελεύθερος, εργένης.

unattended [ʌnə'tendid] a χωρίς συνοδεία, παραμελυμένος.

unattractive [ʌnə'træktiv] a μη συμπαθητικός.

unauthorized [ʌn'ɔːθəraizd] a χωρίς άδεια, μη εξουσιοδοτημένος.

unavoidable [ʌnə'vɔɪdəbl] a αναπόφευκτος.

unaware [ʌnə'wɛə*] a ανίδεος, αγνοών || ~s ad ξαφνικά, χωρίς προειδοποίηση.

unbalanced [ʌn'bælənst] a μη ισορροπημένος, ανισόρροπος.

unbearable [ʌn'bɛərəbl] a ανυπόφορος, αφόρητος.

unbeatable [ʌn'biːtəbl] a (team) αήττητος, ακατανίκητος.

unbeaten [ʌn'biːtn] a (team, record) αήττητος, αχτύπητο ρεκόρ.

unbeknown [ʌnbɪ'nəʊn] ad (+ to) εν αγνοία του.

unbelievable [ʌnbɪ'liːvəbl] a απίστευτος.

unbend [ʌn'bend] vi ευθυγραμμίζομαι, σιάζω ♦ vt χαλαρώνω, ξετεντώνω.

unbounded [ʌn'baʊndɪd] a απεριόριστος, απέραντος.

unbreakable [ʌn'breɪkəbl] a άθραυστος.

unbridled [ʌn'braɪdld] a αχαλίνωτος, ασυγκράτητος.

unbroken [ʌn'brəʊkən] a (inviolate) άθραυστος, άσπαστος, || (undisturbed) απαράβατος, αδιατάρακτος.

unburden [ʌn'bɜːdn] vt: to ~ o.s. ανακουφίζω, ξαλαφρώνω.

unbutton [ʌn'bʌtn] vt ξεκουμπώνω.

uncalled-for [ʌn'kɔːldfɔː*] a άκαιρος, αδικαιολόγητος.

uncanny [ʌn'kænɪ] a παράξενος, αφύσικος, μυστηριώδης.

unceasing [ʌn'siːsɪŋ] a ακατάπαυστος.

uncertain [ʌn'sɜːtn] a αβέβαιος, αμφίβολος || (weather etc) ασταθής || (vague) ακαθόριστος || ~ty n αβεβαιότητα, αμφιβολία, αστάθεια.

unchanged [ʌn'tʃeɪndʒd] a αμετάβλητος.

uncharitable [ʌn'tʃærɪtəbl] a άσπλαχνος, αφιλάνθρωπος.

uncharted [ʌn'tʃɑːtɪd] a ανεξερεύνητος.

unchecked [ʌn'tʃekt] a (unhindered) ανεμπόδιστος, ασταμάτητος || (not confirmed) ανεξέλεγκτος.

uncivil [ʌn'sɪvɪl] a αγενής, άξεστος, κακότροπος.

uncle ['ʌŋkl] n θείος, μπάρμπας.

uncomfortable [ʌn'kʌmfətəbl] a (uneasy) ανήσυχος, δυσάρεστος.

unconscious [ʌn'kɒnʃəs] a ασυνείδητος || (not aware) αναίσθητος ♦ n: the ~ το ασυνείδητο || ~ly ad ασυνείδητα, χωρίς να το καταλάβω.

uncontrollable [ʌnkən'trəʊləbl] a αχαλίνωτος, ακατάσχετος, ασυγκράτητος.

uncouth [ʌn'kuːθ] a αδέξιος, άξεστος.

uncover [ʌn'kʌvə*] vt ξεσκεπάζω || (expose) αποκαλύπτω, εκθέτω.

undecided [ʌndɪ'saɪdɪd] a αναποφάσιστος || (pending) εκκρεμής.

undeniable [ʌndɪ'naɪəbl] a αναμφισβήτητος.

under ['ʌndə*] prep υπό, κάτω από || (in time of) επί, στην εποχή του ♦ ad κάτω, από κάτω || ~ age a ανήλικος || ~ repair υπό επισκευή.

undercarriage ['ʌndəkærɪdʒ] n, undercart ['ʌndəkɑːt] n σύστημα nt, προσγειώσεως.

underclothes ['ʌndəkləʊðz] npl εσώρουχα ntpl.

undercoat ['ʌndəkəʊt] n (paint) βασικό χρώμα nt.

undercover ['ʌndəkʌvə] a μυστικός, κρυφός.

undercurrent ['ʌndəkʌrənt] n ρεύμα nt, κάτω από την επιφάνεια.

undercut ['ʌndəkʌt] n (cooking) φιλέτο κρέατος ♦ vt πουλώ φθηνότερα από.

underdeveloped ['ʌndədɪ'veləpt] a (country) υποανάπτυκτος.

underdog ['ʌndədɒg] n ο πιο αδύνατος.

underdone [ʌndə'dʌn] a (cooking) μισοψημένος.

underestimate [ʌndər'estɪmeɪt] vt υποτιμώ.

underfed [ʌndə'fed] a υποσιτιζόμενος.

underfoot [ʌndə'fʊt] ad κάτω από τα πόδια.

undergo [ʌndə'gəʊ] vt υφίσταμαι, παθαίνω.

undergraduate [ʌndə'grædjuɪt] n φοιτητής/τήτρια m/f.

underground ['ʌndəgraʊnd] n υπόγειος σιδηρόδρομος ♦ a (press etc) μυστικός, κρυφός || (movement) της αντιστάσεως.

undergrowth ['ʌndəgrəʊθ] n θάμνοι mpl, χαμόκλαδα.

underhand ['ʌndəhænd] a πανούργος, ύπουλος.

underlie [ʌndə'laɪ] vt υπόκειμαι, είμαι η βάση.

underline [ʌndə'laɪn] vt υπογραμμίζω || (draw attention to) υπογραμμίζω, τονίζω.

underling ['ʌndəlɪŋ] n υφιστάμενος, παραγιός, υποτακτικός.

undermine [ʌndə'maɪn] vt υπονομεύω, υποσκάβω.

underneath [ʌndə'niːθ] ad κάτω από, από κάτω ♦ prep κάτω από, υπό.

underpaid [ʌndə'peɪd] a κακοπληρωμένος.

underpass [ʌndəpɑːs] n υπόγεια διάβαση.

underprivileged [ʌndə'prɪvɪlɪdʒd] a με μειωμένα προνόμια, αδικημένος.

underrate [ʌndə'reɪt] vt υποτιμώ.

underside ['ʌndəsaɪd] n κάτω πλευρά, το αποκάτω.

underskirt ['ʌndəskɜːt] n κομπιναιζόν nt inv, μεσοφόρι.

understand [ʌndə'stænd] vt αντιλαμβάνομαι || (know) γνωρίζω, καταλαβαίνω || (hear, believe) μαθαίνω, πιστεύω, νομίζω || (GRAM) υπονοώ || ~able a (κατα) νοητός, καταληπτός, ευνόητος || ~ing συνεννόηση, κατανόηση || (agreement) συμφωνία.

understatement ['ʌndəsteitmənt] n δήλωση κάτω από την πραγματικότητα.

understudy ['ʌndəstʌdi] n αντικαταστάτης/τρια m/f.

undertake [ʌndə'teik] vt αναλαμβάνω || ~r n εργολάβος κηδειών.

undertaking [ʌndə'teikiŋ] n επιχείρηση || (promise) δέσμευση, υποχρέωση.

underwater [ʌndə'wɔːtə*] ad υποβρυχίως ♦ a υποβρύχιος.

underwear ['ʌndəweə*] n εσώρουχα ntpl.

underweight [ʌndə'weit] a λιποβαρής, αδύνατος.

underworld ['ʌndəwɜːld] n (of crime) υπόκοσμος.

underwriter ['ʌndəraitə*] n (insurance) ασφαλιστής.

undesirable [ʌndi'zaiərəbl] a ανεπιθύμητος.

undies ['ʌndiz] npl (col) εσώρουχα (γυναικεία).

undisputed [ʌndis'pjuːtid] a αδιαφιλονίκητος, αδιαμφισβήτητος.

undo [ʌn'duː] vt λύνω, ξεκουμπώνω, ανοίγω || (work) καταστρέφω, χαλώ || ~ing n καταστροφή, αφανισμός.

undoubted [ʌn'dautid] a αναμφισβήτητος, αναμφίβολος || ~ly ad αναμφισβήτητα.

undress [ʌn'dres] vti γδύνομαι, γδύνω.

undue [ʌn'djuː] a υπερβολικός, αδικαιολόγητος.

undulating ['ʌndjuleitiŋ] a κυματούμενος, ταλαντευόμενος.

unduly [ʌn'djuːli] ad υπερβολικά, άπρεπα.

unearth [ʌn'ɜːθ] vt ξεθάβω, ανακαλύπτω || ~ly a υπερφυσικός, απόκοσμος.

uneasy [ʌn'iːzi] a ανήσυχος, στενοχωρημένος.

uneconomic(al) ['ʌniːkə'nɔmi(əl)] a ανοικονόμικος, σπάταλος, ασύμφορος.

uneducated [ʌn'edjukeitid] a ασπούδαστος, αμόρφωτος.

unemployed [ʌnim'plɔid] a άνεργος, αχρησιμοποίητος || npl: the ~ οι άνεργοι.

unemployment [ʌnim'plɔimənt] n ανεργία.

unending [ʌn'endiŋ] a ατελείωτος.

unerring [ʌn'ɜːriŋ] a αλάθαστος, ακριβής.

uneven [ʌn'iːvən] a (surface) ανώμαλος || (quality) άνισος, ακανόνιστος.

unfair [ʌn'fɛə*] a (unkind, unreasonable) άδικος || ~ly ad άδικα, άτιμα.

unfaithful [ʌn'feiθful] a (to spouse) άπιστος.

unfasten [ʌn'fɑːsn] vt λύνω || (clothes) ξεκουμπώνω || (open) ξεκλειδώνω.

unfavourable, (US) **unfavorable** [ʌn'feivərəbl] a δυσμενής, δυσοίωνος.

unfeeling [ʌn'fiːliŋ] a σκληρόκαρδος, αναίσθητος.

unfinished [ʌn'finiʃt] a ατέλειωτος, ασυμπλήρωτος.

unfit [ʌn'fit] a (in health) ανίκανος, ακατάλληλος || (+ for) ακατάλληλος (για).

unflagging [ʌn'flægiŋ] a ακλόνητος, ακατάπαυστος, αλύγιστος.

unfold [ʌn'fəuld] vt ξεδιπλώνω, ξετυλίγω, απλώνω || (reveal) αποκαλύπτω || (develop) αναπτύσσω || (explain) εξηγώ ♦ vi (develop) αναπτύσσομαι, εκτυλίσσομαι.

unforeseen ['ʌnfɔː'siːn] a απρόβλεπτος, απροσδόκητος.

unforgivable [ʌnfə'givəbl] a ασυγχώρητος.

unfortunate [ʌn'fɔːtʃnit] a άτυχος, κακότυχος || ~ly ad δυστυχώς.

unfounded [ʌn'faundid] a (rumour) αβάσιμος.

unfriendly [ʌn'frendli] a δυσμενής, εχθρικός.

unfurnished [ʌn'fɜːniʃt] a (flat) χωρίς έπιπλα.

ungainly [ʌn'geinli] a αδέξιος.

unhappiness [ʌn'hæpinis] n δυστυχία, στενοχώρια.

unhappy [ʌn'hæpi] a δυστυχισμένος, στενοχωρημένος.

unharmed [ʌn'hɑːmd] a σώος, αβλαβής, απείραχτος.

unhealthy [ʌn'helθi] a (lit) ανθυγιεινός, αρρωστιάρης || (fig) νοσηρός.

unheard-off [ʌn'hɜːdɒv] a πρωτάκουστος, ανήκουστος.

unhurt [ʌn'hɜːt] a χωρίς τραύμα, σώος και αβλαβής.

unidentified [ʌnai'dentifaid] a μη αναγνωρισθείς, άγνωστος.

uniform ['juːnifɔːm] n στολή ♦ a ομοιόμορφος, ίδιος || ~ity n ομοιομορφία.

unify ['juːnifai] vt ενοποιώ.

unilateral [juːni'lætərəl] a μονόπλευρος.

unintentional [ʌnin'tenʃənl] a ακούσιος, αθέλητος.

union ['juːnjən] n ένωση || (alliance) ένωση || (agreement) συμφωνία || (of workers) εργατικό σωματείο, συνδικάτο || **U~ Jack** n Αγγλική σημαία.

unique [juː'niːk] a μοναδικός, ιδιόρρυθμος, ασυνήθιστος.

unison ['juːnisn] n: in ~ ομόφωνα, από κοινού || (mus) αρμονία, μονοφωνία, ομοφωνία.

unit ['juːnit] n μονάδα || (team, squad) ομάδα, συγκρότημα nt.

unite [juː'nait] vt ενώνω ♦ vi ενώνομαι (με) || ~d a ενωμένος, συνδυασμένος || **U~d Kingdom (UK)** n Ηνωμένο Βασίλειο (Η.Β) || **U~d Nations (UN)** npl Ηνωμένα Έθνη (Ο.Η.Ε.) m || **U~d States (of America) (US, USA)** npl Ηνωμένες Πολιτείες (Αμερικής) (Η.Π.Α.) fpl.

unity ['juːniti] n ενότητα, αρμονία, σύμπνοια, μονάδα.

universal [juːni'vɜːsəl] *a* οικουμενικός, καθολικός || *(general)* γενικός || *(of the world)* παγκόσμιος.

universe ['juːnivɜːs] *n* σύμπαν *nt*, οικουμένη.

university [juːni'vɜːsiti] *n* πανεπιστήμιο.

unjust [ʌn'dʒʌst] *a* άδικος.

unkempt [ʌn'kempt] *a* ατημέλητος, ακτένιστος.

unkind [ʌn'kaind] *a* αγενής, άστοργος, σκληρός.

unknown [ʌn'nəʊn] *a* (+ *to*) άγνωστος (σε), αγνοούμενος από.

unladen [ʌn'leidn] *a* *(col: weight)* χωρίς φορτίο, κενός.

unleash [ʌn'liːʃ] *vt* λύνω, ελευθερώνω.

unless [ən'les] *cj* εκτός εάν, εκτός αν.

unlike [ʌn'laik] *a* ανόμοιός, διαφορετικός από.

unlimited [ʌn'limitid] *a* απεριόριστος.

unload [ʌn'ləʊd] *vt* εκφορτώνω, ξεφορτώνω.

unlock [ʌn'lɒk] *vt* ξεκλειδώνω.

unmarried [ʌn'mærid] *a* άγαμος.

unmask [ʌn'maːsk] *vt* *(expose)* αποκαλύπτω || αφαιρώ προσωπείο από.

unmistakable [ʌnmis'teikəbl] *a* αλάθητος, ολοφάνερος, σαφής.

unmitigated [ʌn'mitigeitid] *a* αμετρίαστος, απόλυτος.

unnecessary [ʌn'nesisəri] *a* περιττός, άσκοπος, μάταιος.

unobtainable [ʌnəb'teinəbl] *a* ανεπίτευκτος.

unoccupied [ʌn'ɒkjupaid] *a* *(seat etc)* ελεύθερος, διαθέσιμος.

unorthodox [ʌn'ɔːθədɒks] *a* ανορθόδοξος.

unpack [ʌn'pæk] *vti* ξεπακετάρω, βγάζω από βαλίτσας.

unparalleled [ʌn'pærəleld] *a* απαράμιλλος.

unpleasant [ʌn'pleznt] *a* δυσάρεστος.

unplug [ʌn'plʌg] *vt* ξεβουλώνω || *(ELEC)* βγάζω την πρίζα.

unpopular [ʌn'pɒpjulə*] *a* αντιδημοτικός.

unprecedented [ʌn'presidəntid] *a* χωρίς προηγούμενο.

unqualified [ʌn'kwɒlifaid] *a* αναρμόδιος, ακατάλληλος || *(success)* αμετρίαστος, απόλυτος.

unravel [ʌn'rævəl] *vt* ξεφτώ, ξηλώνω, ξετυλίγω || *(clarify)* διευκρινίζω || *(solve)* λύνω, διαλύω.

unreal [ʌn'riəl] *a* απατηλός, φανταστικός.

unreasonable [ʌn'riːznəbl] *a* *(unfair)* παράλογος.

unrelenting [ʌnri'lentiŋ] *a* αδυσώπητος, ανελέητος.

unrelieved [ʌnri'liːvd] *a* *(monotony)* χωρίς ποικιλία, μονότονος.

unrepeatable [ʌnri'piːtəbl] *a* *(offer)* που δεν επαναλαμβάνεται.

unrest [ʌn'rest] *n* *(discontent, trouble)* ανησυχία, ταραχή.

unroll [ʌn'rəʊl] *vt* ξετυλίγω.

unruly [ʌn'ruːli] *a* ανυπότακτος, ατίθασος, άτακτος.

unsafe [ʌn'seif] *a* επικίνδυνος, ανασφαλής.

unsaid [ʌn'sed] *a*: **to leave sth ~** αποσιωπώ κάτι.

unsatisfactory ['ʌnsætis'fæktəri] *a* μη ικανοποιητικός, ανεπαρκής.

unsavoury, *(US)* **unsavory** [ʌn'seivəri] *a* *(of bad character)* ύποπτος, σκοτεινός.

unscrew [ʌn'skruː] *vt* ξεβιδώνω.

unscrupulous [ʌn'skruːpjuləs] *a* ασυνείδητος, ανενδοίαστος.

unsettled [ʌn'setld] *a* ανήσυχος, αβέβαιος || *(weather)* ευμετάβλητος, αβέβαιος.

unshaven [ʌn'ʃeivn] *a* αξύριστος.

unsightly [ʌn'saitli] *a* άσχημος, δύσμορφος.

unskilled [ʌn'skild] *a* *(workman)* ανειδίκευτος.

unspeakable [ʌn'spiːkəbl] *a* απερίγραπτος, ανείπωτος, ανέκφραστος || *(very bad)* αποκρουστικός, απδιαστικός, σιχαμερός.

unstuck [ʌn'stʌk] *a*: **to come ~** ξεκολλώ || *(lit)* ξεκολλώ, ξεκολλιέμαι || *(fig)* καταρρέω, γκρεμίζομαι.

unsuitable [ʌn'suːtəbl] *a* ακατάλληλος.

unsuspecting [ʌnsəs'pektiŋ] *a* ανυποψίαστος.

unswerving [ʌn'swɜːviŋ] *a* *(loyalty)* σταθερός, πιστός.

untangle [ʌn'tæŋgl] *vt* ξεχωρίζω, ξεμπλέκω.

untapped [ʌn'tæpt] *a* *(resources)* ανεκμετάλλευτος.

unthinkable [ʌn'θiŋkəbl] *a* ασύλληπτος, πολύ απίθανος.

untidy [ʌn'taidi] *a* ακατάστατος.

untie [ʌn'tai] *vt* λύνω.

until [ən'til] *prep* μέχρι, έως || *cj* μέχρς ότου, έως ότου.

untimely [ʌn'taimli] *a* *(death)* πρόωρος.

untold [ʌn'təʊld] *a* *(countless)* αμέτρητος, ανυπολόγιστος.

untoward [ʌntə'wɔːd] *a* δυσάρεστος, δυσμενής.

unused [ʌn'juːzd] *a* αμεταχείριστος.

unusual [ʌn'juːʒuəl] *a* ασυνήθιστος, σπάνιος || **~ly** *ad* εξαιρετικά, αφάνταστα, ασυνήθιστα.

unveil [ʌn'veil] *vt* αποκαλύπτω, ξεσκεπάζω.

unwell [ʌn'wel] *a* αδιάθετος, άρρωστος.

unwieldy [ʌn'wiːldi] *a* δυσκίνητος, βαρύς, αδέξιος.

unwilling [ʌn'wiliŋ] *a* απρόθυμος, ακούσιος.

unwind [ʌn'waind] *vt* *(lit)* ξετυλίγω, ξεκουρδίζω ♦ *vi* *(relax)* χαλαρώνομαι.

unwitting [ʌn'wɪtɪŋ] a χωρίς πρόθεση, ακούσιος.

unwrap [ʌn'ræp] vt ξετυλίγω.

unwritten [ʌn'rɪtn] a (law) άγραφος, προφορικός.

up [ʌp] prep προς τα πάνω, αντίθετα με το ρεύμα ♦ ad επάνω, άνω, τελείως || ~ to you εξαρτάται από σένα || what is he ~ to? τι επιδιώκει; τι θέλει; || he is not ~ to it δεν έχει την ικανότητα (να) || ~-and-coming a εξαιρετικά δραστήριος, ανερχόμενος ♦ n: ~s and downs διακυμάνσεις fpl, μεταβολές fpl της τύχης.

upbringing ['ʌpbrɪŋɪŋ] n ανατροφή.

update [ʌp'deɪt] vt ενημερώνω, εκσυγχρονίζω.

upheaval [ʌp'hi:vəl] n (violent disturbance) αναστάτωση, αναταραχή.

uphill [ʌp'hɪl] a ανηφορικός ♦ ad προς τα άνω.

uphold [ʌp'həʊld] vt (maintain) υποστηρίζω.

upholstery [ʌp'həʊlstərɪ] n ταπετσαρία.

upkeep ['ʌpki:p] n συντήρηση, έξοδα ntpl συντηρήσεως.

upon [ə'pɒn] prep πάνω, σε.

upper ['ʌpə*] a ανώτερος, άνω, από πάνω || the ~ class n n ανωτέρα τάξη, η καλή κοινωνία || ~-class a της ανωτέρας τάξεως || ~most a υπέρτατος, ανώτατος.

upright ['ʌpraɪt] a όρθιος, κατακόρυφος, κάθετος || (honest) ευθύς, δίκαιος, τίμιος ♦ n ορθοστάτης.

uprising [ʌp'raɪzɪŋ] n εξέγερση, ξεσήκωμα nt.

uproar ['ʌprɔ:*] n θόρυβος, φασαρία, αναστάτωση.

uproot [ʌp'ru:t] vt ξεριζώνω.

upset ['ʌpset] n αναστάτωση, ανατροπή, αναποδογύρισμα nt ♦ [ʌp'set] vt (overturn) ανατρέπω, αναποδογυρίζω || (distress) ταράσσω, αναστατώνω.

upshot ['ʌpʃɒt] n αποτέλεσμα nt, έκβαση, κατάληξη.

upside ['ʌpsaɪd]: ~ down ad άνω-κάτω, ανάποδα, φύρδην-μίγδην.

upstairs ['ʌp'steəz] ad στο επάνω πάτωμα nt ♦ a (room) επάνω, του άνω ορόφου ♦ n επάνω.

upstart ['ʌpsta:t] n νεόπλουτος, αναιδής άνθρωπος.

upstream [ʌp'stri:m] ad αντίθετα με το ρεύμα.

uptake ['ʌpteɪk] n αντίληψη || to be quick, (slow) on the ~ (δεν) παίρνω, (δεν) αρπάζω.

up-to-date ['ʌptə'deɪt] a σύγχρονος, μοντέρνος || (fashionable) της μόδας.

upturn ['ʌptɜ:n] n (in luck) βελτίωση, άνοδος f.

upward ['ʌpwəd] a προς τα άνω || ~(s) ad προς τα άνω.

uranium [jʊə'reɪnɪəm] n ουράνιο.

urban ['ɜ:bən] a αστικός.

urbane [ɜ:'beɪn] a ευγενικός, αβρός, ραφιναρισμένος.

urchin ['ɜ:tʃɪn] n (boy) αλητάκι || sea ~ αχινός.

urge [ɜ:dʒ] n (desire) επίμονη επιθυμία, ώθηση ♦ vt (entreat) παροτρύνω.

urgency ['ɜ:dʒənsɪ] n επείγουσα ανάγκη, επιμονή, πίεση.

urgent ['ɜ:dʒənt] a επείγων, πιεστικός, άμεσος || ~ly ad επειγόντως.

urinal ['jʊərɪnl] n ουρητήριο.

urine ['jʊərɪn] n ούρα ntpl.

urn [ɜ:n] n υδρία, δοχείο, αγγείο || (teapot) σαμοβάρι.

us [ʌs] pron εμάς, μας.

US, USA n abbr see **united**.

usage ['ju:zɪdʒ] n μεταχείρηση, έθιμο, συνήθεια || (esp LING) χρήση.

use [ju:s] n χρήση || (custom) συνήθεια, έθιμο || (employment) χρήση, χρησιμοποίηση || (value) χρησιμότητα ♦ [ju:z] vt χρησιμοποιώ, μεταχειρίζομαι || (make most of) χρησιμεύω || in ~ εν χρήσει || out of ~ εν αχρηστία || ~d to συνηθίζω να || she ~d to do it συνήθιζε να το κάνει || to ~ up vt καταναλίσκω, εξαντλώ || ~d a (car) μεταχειρισμένος, δεύτερο χέρι || ~ful a χρήσιμος || ~less a άχρηστος || ~r n χρήστης.

usher ['ʌʃə*] n (at wedding) παράνυμφος || ~ette n (at cinema) ταξιθέτρια.

USSR n: the ~ Ε.Σ.Σ.Δ (Ένωση Σοσιαλιστικών Σοβιετικών Δημοκρατιών).

usual ['ju:ʒʊəl] a συνηθισμένος || ~ly ad συνήθως.

usurp [ju:'zɜ:p] vt σφετερίζομαι, αρπάζω.

utensil [ju:'tensl] n σκεύος nt, εργαλείο.

uterus ['ju:tərəs] n μήτρα.

utilitarian [ju:tɪlɪ'teərɪən] a κοινωφελής, ωφελιμιστικός.

utility [ju:'tɪlɪtɪ] n χρησιμότητα, ευχρηστία || (useful thing) χρήσιμο πράγμα nt || (also public utility: electricity supply industry) δημόσια υπηρεσία, κοινωφελής επιχείρηση.

utilize ['ju:tɪlaɪz] vt χρησιμοποιώ, εκμεταλλεύομαι.

utmost ['ʌtməʊst] a ακρότατος, απώτατος, έσχατος || n: to do one's ~ κάνω ότι μπορώ.

utter ['ʌtə*] a πλήρης, ολοσχερής ♦ vt αρθρώνω, εκστομίζω, προφέρω, λέω || ~ly ad τελείως, εξ ολοκλήρου.

U-turn ['ju:'tɜ:n] n (AUT) στροφή 180 μοιρών.

V

v. (abbr of verse) ποιητ. (ποιητικός) || abbr of **versus** || (abbr of vide) βλ (βλέπετε) || abbr of **volt**.

vacancy ['veɪkənsɪ] n κενό, κενή θέση || (room) δωμάτιο.

vacant ['veɪkənt] a κενός || (not occupied) άδειος, ελεύθερος || (stupid) αφηρημένος, ανέκφραστος || '~' (on door) 'δωμάτια'.

vacate [və'keɪt] vt εκκενώνω, αδειάζω, εγκαταλείπω.

vacation [və'keɪʃən] n διακοπή, αργία.

vaccinate ['væksɪneɪt] vt εμβολιάζω, μπολιάζω.

vaccination [væksɪ'neɪʃən] n εμβολιασμός, μπόλιασμα nt.

vaccine ['væksi:n] n εμβόλιο, βατσίνα.

vacuum ['vækjʊm] n κενό || ~ **bottle** n (US) φιάλη κενού, θερμός nt || ~ **cleaner** n ηλεκτρική σκούπα || ~ **flask** n (Brit) φιάλη κενού, θερμός nt.

vagina [və'dʒaɪnə] n κόλπος (γυναίκας).

vagrant ['veɪɡrənt] n περιπλανώμενος, αλήτης.

vague [veɪɡ] a ασαφής, αμυδρός, ακαθόριστος || ~**ly** ad αόριστα, ασαφώς.

vain [veɪn] a μάταιος, άκαρπος || (conceited) ματαιόδοξος || in ~ μάταια.

vale [veɪl] n κοιλάδα, λαγκαδιά.

valid ['vælɪd] a έγκυρος, βάσιμος, νόμιμος, λογικός || ~**ity** n εγκυρότητα, ισχύς f.

valise [və'li:z] n (suitcase) βαλίτσα.

valley ['vælɪ] n κοιλάδα, λαγκάδι.

valuable ['væljʊəbl] a πολύτιμος || ~**s** npl αντικείμενα αξίας ntpl.

valuation [vælju'eɪʃən] n εκτίμηση, αξία.

value ['vælju:] n αξία, τιμή, σημασία, έννοια ♦ vt εκτιμώ || ~ **added tax** (**VAT**) n Φόρος Προστιθέμενης Αξίας (Φ.Π.Α.) m || ~**d** a (appreciated) εκτιμώμενος.

valve [vælv] n βαλβίδα, δικλείδα, λυχνία.

vampire ['væmpaɪə*] n βρυκόλακας.

van [væn] n φορτηγό, σκευοφόρος.

vandal ['vændəl] n βάνδαλος || ~**ism** n βανδαλισμός.

vanilla [və'nɪlə] n βανίλια ♦ attr a (ice cream) παγωτό.

vanish ['vænɪʃ] vi εξαφανίζομαι, χάνομαι.

vanity ['vænɪtɪ] n ματαιοδοξία, εγωισμός || ~ **case** n γυναικείο τσαντάκι.

vantage ['vɑ:ntɪdʒ] n: ~ **point** (good viewpoint) πλεονεκτική θέση.

vapour, (US) **vapor** ['veɪpə*] n αχνός, πάχνη || (gas) ατμός, υδρατμός.

variable ['veərɪəbl] a μεταβλητός, ευμετάβλητος.

variance ['veərɪəns] n: at ~ σε διάσταση, σε διαφωνία.

variation [veərɪ'eɪʃən] n παραλλαγή, παρέκκλιση, μεταβολή.

varicose ['værɪkəʊs] a: ~ **veins** κιρσώδεις φλέβες fpl.

varied ['veərɪd] a διάφορος, ποικίλος, μεταβαλλόμενος.

variety [və'raɪɪtɪ] n ποικιλία, διαφορά || (varied collection) ποικιλία, πολλά και διάφορα || (kind) ποικιλία || ~ **show** n (THEAT) επιθεώρηση.

various ['veərɪəs] a ποικίλος, διάφορος.

varnish ['vɑ:nɪʃ] n βερνίκι, στιλβωμένη επιφάνεια ♦ vt βερνικώνω, στιλβώνω.

vary ['veərɪ] vt διαφοροποιώ, ποικίλω ♦ vi αλλάζω, μεταβάλλομαι, διαφέρω || ~**ing** a μεταβαλλόμενος, μεταβλητός, ποικίλος.

vase [vɑ:z] n βάζο, αγγείο.

vast [vɑ:st] a πελώριος, εκτεταμένος, απέραντος.

vat [væt] n κάδος, βούτα, δεξαμενή.

VAT [væt] n abbr see **value**.

Vatican ['vætɪkən] n: the ~ το Βατικανό.

vault [vɔ:lt] n θόλος, καμάρα || (cellar) υπόγειο || (tomb) θολωτός τάφος || (leap) πήδημα nt, άλμα nt ♦ vt πηδώ, κάνω άλμα επί κοντώ.

VD n abbr see **venereal**.

VDU n abbr see **visual**.

veal [vi:l] n μοσχάρι.

veer [vɪə*] vi στρέφω, αλλάζω κατεύθυνση, γυρίζω.

vegetable ['vedʒɪtəbl] n φυτό, λαχανικό, χορταρικό.

vegetarian [vedʒɪ'teərɪən] a, n (people) χορτοφάγος || (animal) φυτοφάγος.

vegetate ['vedʒɪteɪt] vi φυτοζωώ.

vegetation [vedʒɪ'teɪʃən] n βλάστηση.

vehement ['vi:ɪmənt] a βίαιος, ορμητικός.

vehicle ['vi:ɪkl] n όχημα nt, αμάξι.

veil [veɪl] n πέπλος, βέλο || (fig) κάλυμμα nt ♦ vt καλύπτω, κρύβω.

vein [veɪn] n φλέβα || (of ore) φλέβα, στρώμα nt || (streak) διάθεση, ταλέντο || (mood) πνεύμα nt, διάθεση, κέφι.

velocity [vɪ'lɒsɪtɪ] n ταχύτητα.

velvet ['velvɪt] n βελούδο.

vendetta [ven'detə] n βεντέτα, εκδίκηση.

vending machine ['vendɪŋməʃi:n] n μηχάνημα nt πωλήσεως.

vendor ['vendɔ:*] n πωλητής.

veneer [və'nɪə*] n (lit) καπλαμάς, επίστρωση, επένδυση || (fig) επίχρισμα nt, επίστρωμα nt || (lustre) λούστρο.

venerable ['venərəbl] a αξιοσέβαστος, σεβάσμιος.

venereal [vɪ'nɪərɪəl] a (disease) αφροδίσιος || ~ **disease** (**VD**) n αφροδίσιο νόσωμα.

venetian [vɪ'ni:ʃən] a: ~ **blind** παντζούρι.

vengeance ['vendʒəns] n εκδίκηση.

venison ['venɪsn] n κρέας nt ελαφιού.

venom ['venəm] n δηλητήριο, φαρμάκι || ~**ous** a φαρμακερός.

vent [vent] n τρύπα εξαερισμού, διέξοδος f, άνοιγμα nt ♦ vt ξεσπώ, ξεθυμαίνω.

ventilate ['ventɪleɪt] vt αερίζω.

ventilation [ventɪ'leɪʃən] n (εξ)αερισμός.

ventilator ['ventɪleɪtə*] n εξαεριστήρας, ανεμιστήρας.

ventriloquist [ven'trɪləkwɪst] n εγγαστρίμυθος.

V

venture ['ventʃə*] n τόλμημα nt, εγχείρημα nt|| (COMM) επιχείρηση ♦ vt ριψοκινδυνεύω, ρισκάρω ♦ vi αποτολμώ, τολμώ.

venue ['venjuː] n τόπος συναντήσεως, τόπος δίκης.

veranda(h) [və'rændə] n βεράντα.

verb [vɜːb] n ρήμα nt|| ~**al** a λεκτικός, προφορικός.

verbose [vɜː'bəus] a πολύλογος, μακροσκελής.

verdict ['vɜːdɪkt] n κρίση, γνώμη|| (of jury) ετυμηγορία, απόφαση.

verge [vɜːdʒ] n (of road) άκρη (του δρόμου)|| **on the** ~ **of doing** έτοιμος να ♦ vi: **to** ~ **on** πλησιάζω, τείνω προς.

verger ['vɜːdʒə*] n νεωκόρος.

verify ['verɪfaɪ] vt επιβεβαιώνω, αποδεικνύω.

vermin ['vɜːmɪn] npl βλαβερά ζωύφια ntpl.

vermouth ['vɜːməθ] n βερμούτ nt inv.

vernacular [və'nækjulə*] n τοπική διάλεκτος f, κοινή γλώσσα.

versatile ['vɜːsətaɪl] a πολύπλευρος, εύστροφος.

verse [vɜːs] n ποίηση, ποιήματα ntpl|| (line) στίχος || (of poem, song) στροφή || (of Bible) εδάφιο || ~**d** a (+ in) μυημένος, πεπειραμένος, μορφωμένος.

version ['vɜːʃən] n (account) έκδοση, ερμηνεία.

versus ['vɜːsəs] prep κατά, εναντίον.

vertebra ['vɜːtɪbrə] n σπόνδυλος, ραχοκόκκαλο.

vertebrate ['vɜːtɪbrɪt] a σπονδυλωτός.

vertical ['vɜːtɪkəl] a κάθετος, κατακόρυφος.

vertigo ['vɜːtɪgəu] n ίλιγγος, ζάλη.

very ['veri] ad πολύ || (precisely) ακριβώς ♦ a (identical) ίδιος || (mere) και μόνο.

vespers ['vespəz] npl εσπερινός.

vessel ['vesl] n πλοίο, σκάφος nt|| (container) αγγείο, σκεύος nt.

vest [vest] n φανελάκι || (US: waistcoat) γιλέκο ♦ vt περιβάλλω, παραχωρώ, παρέχω || ~**ed** a (interest) κεκτημένος.

vestibule ['vestɪbjuːl] n (of house) προθάλαμος, χώλ nt inv.

vestige ['vestɪdʒ] n υπόλειμμα nt, ίχνος nt.

vestry ['vestri] n ιεροφυλάκειο, σκευοφυλάκιο, βεστιάριο.

vet [vet] n (abbr of veterinary surgeon) κτηνίατρος ♦ vt εξετάζω.

veteran ['vetərən] n παλαίμαχος, βετεράνος ♦ a του παλαιμάχου, πεπειραμένος.

veterinary ['vetərɪnəri] a κτηνιατρικός || ~ **surgeon** n κτηνίατρος.

veto ['viːtəu] n δικαίωμα nt αρνησικυρίας, βέτο || (prohibition) απαγόρευση ♦ vt προβάλλω βέτο (σε).

vex [veks] vt ενοχλώ, ερεθίζω, ταράσσω || ~**ed** a θυμωμένος, πειραγμένος.

VHF n (abbr of very high frequency) πολύ υψηλή συχνότητα (Λ.Υ.Σ.).

via ['vaɪə] prep μέσω, διά μέσου.

viable ['vaɪəbl] a βιώσιμος.

viaduct ['vaɪədʌkt] n οδογέφυρα, αψιδωτή γέφυρα.

vibrate [vaɪ'breɪt] vi πάλλομαι, δονούμαι, ταλαντεύομαι || (resound) ηχώ.

vibration [vaɪ'breɪʃən] n ταλάντευση, δόνηση, κούνημα nt.

vicar ['vɪkə*] n εφημέριος || ~**age** n πρεσβυτέριο, οικία εφημερίου.

vice [vaɪs] n (evil) εκφυλισμός, ακολασία, αμάρτημα nt|| (TECH) μέγγενη.

vice- prefix αντί-, υπό || ~**chairman** n αντιπρόεδρος.

vice versa ['vaɪsɪ'vɜːsə] ad αντίστροφα.

vicinity [vɪ'sɪnɪti] n γειτονιά, εγγύτητα, περιοχή.

vicious ['vɪʃəs] a (also cruel) κακός, κακοήθης.

victim ['vɪktɪm] n θύμα nt|| ~**ization** n καταπίεση, αντίποινα ntpl|| ~**ize** vt κατατρέχω, μεταχειρίζομαι σαν θύμα.

victor ['vɪktə*] n νικητής/ήτρια m/f.

Victorian [vɪk'tɔːrɪən] a βικτωριανός.

victorious [vɪk'tɔːrɪəs] a νικηφόρος, θριαμβευτής.

victory ['vɪktəri] n νίκη.

video ['vɪdɪəu] n βίντεο.

vie [vaɪ] vi (compete) (+ with) αμιλλώμαι, ανταγωνίζομαι.

view [vjuː] n όψη, ματιά, βλέμμα nt|| (scene) θέα, προοπτική, όψη || (opinion) άποψη, έκθεση || (intention) πρόθεση, βλέψη, σκοπός ♦ vt (situation) επιθεωρώ, εξετάζω || ~**er** n (viewfinder) σκόπευτρο || (PHOT: small projector) μικρό μηχάνημα nt προβολής || (TV) θεατής || ~**finder** n σκόπευτρο, εικονοσκόπιο || ~**point** n σημείο με καλή θέα || (attitude) άποψη.

vigil ['vɪdʒɪl] n αγρυπνία, ξενύχτι, ολονυχτία || ~**ant** a άγρυπνος, προσεκτικός.

vigor ['vɪgə*] n (US) = **vigour**.

vigorous ['vɪgərəs] a ρωμαλέος, σθεναρός, ζωηρός || ~**ly** ad γερά, δυνατά.

vigour ['vɪgə*] n σθένος nt, σφρίγος nt, ζωτικότητα, ζωηρότητα.

vile [vaɪl] a ανήθικος, αχρείος, αισχρός || (foul) ακάθαρτος, βρωμερός, σιχαμερός.

villa ['vɪlə] n έπαυλη, βίλα.

village ['vɪlɪdʒ] n χωριό || ~**r** n χωριάτης/άτισσα m/f.

villain ['vɪlən] n ο κακός, παλιάνθρωπος.

vindicate ['vɪndɪkeɪt] vt δικαιώνω, υπερασπίζω.

vindictive [vɪn'dɪktɪv] a εκδικητικός.

vine [vaɪn] n αμπέλι, κλήμα nt.

vinegar ['vɪnɪgə*] n ξύδι.

vineyard ['vɪnjəd] n αμπελώνας, αμπέλι.

vintage ['vɪntɪdʒ] n (wine) κρασί ωρισμένου έτους || (gathering) τρυγητός, τρύγος.

vinyl ['vaɪnl] n βινύλιο.

viola [vɪ'əulə] n (MUS) βιόλα.

violate ['vaɪəleɪt] vt (break promise)

αθετώ, καταπατώ || *(disturb)* παραβιάζω || *(desecrate)* βεβηλώνω.

violation [vaɪə'leɪʃən] *n* παραβίαση, παράβαση, αθέτηση.

violence ['vaɪələns] *n* σφοδρότητα, ένταση || *(rough treatment)* βία, βιαιότητα.

violent ['vaɪələnt] *a* βίαιος, ορμητικός || *(extreme)* ζωηρός, έντονος, οξύς, ισχυρός || ~**ly** *ad* βίαια, απότομα, εξαιρετικά, πολύ.

violet ['vaɪəlɪt] *n* βιολέτα, μενεξές *m* ♦ *a* μενεξεδένιος, ιώβ.

violin [vaɪə'lɪn] *n* βιολί.

VIP *n (abbr of very important person)* ≈ Επίσημος/η *m/f*.

viper ['vaɪpə*] *n* έχιδνα, οχιά.

virgin ['vɜːdʒɪn] *n* παρθένα ♦ *a* παρθένος, παρθενικός, καθαρός || ~**ity** *n* παρθενία.

virile ['vɪraɪl] *a* ανδρικός, δυνατός, σθεναρός.

virility [vɪ'rɪlɪti] *n* ανδρισμός, ανδροπρέπεια, αρρενωπότητα.

virtually ['vɜːtjʊəlɪ] *ad (in fact)* ουσιαστικά || *(almost)* σχεδόν.

virtue ['vɜːtjuː] *n* αρετή || *(good quality)* ικανότητα, δραστικότητα || **by ~ of** δυνάμει, συνεπεία, λόγω, εξαιτίας.

virtuoso [vɜːtjʊ'əʊzəʊ] *n* δεξιοτέχνης μουσικός, βιρτουόζος.

virtuous ['vɜːtjʊəs] *a* ενάρετος.

virulent ['vɪrʊlənt] *a* τοξικός, θανατηφόρος || *(bitter)* εχθρικός, κακεντρεχής, φαρμακερός.

virus ['vaɪərəs] *n* ιός, μικρόβιο.

visa ['viːzə] *n* θεώρηση, βίζα.

vis-à-vis ['viːzəvɪ] *prep* απέναντι, αντίκρυ.

viscount ['vaɪkaʊnt] *n* υποκόμης.

visibility [vɪzɪ'bɪlɪti] *n* ορατότητα.

visible ['vɪzəbl] *a* ορατός, εμφανής, φαλερός || **visibly** *ad* καταφανώς, προφανώς, ολοφάνερα.

vision ['vɪʒən] *n* όραση || *(imagination)* διορατικότητα || *(dream)* όραμα *nt*, οπτασία || ~**ary** *n* οραματιστής, ονειροπόλος.

visit ['vɪzɪt] *n* επίσκεψη ♦ *vt* επισκέπτομαι || *(stay with)* κάνω βίζιτα, φιλοξενούμαι || ~**or** *n* επισκέπτης/ρια *m/f* || ~**ors' book** *n* βιβλίο επισκεπτών.

visor ['vaɪzə*] *n* προσωπίδα.

vista ['vɪstə] *n* θέα, άνοιγμα *nt*, προοπτική, άποψη.

visual ['vɪzjʊəl] *a* οπτικός, ορατός, πραγματικός || **~ display unit (VDU)** *n* μονάδα σφόνης βίντεο || ~**ize** *vt* φαντάζομαι, οραματίζομαι.

vital ['vaɪtl] *a* ουσιώδης, κεφαλαιώδης, ζωτικός || *(necessary to life)* ζωτικός, ουσιώδης || ~**ity** *n* ζωτικότητα, ανθεκτικότητα, ζωή.

vitamin ['vɪtəmɪn] *n* βιταμίνη.

vivacious [vɪ'veɪʃəs] *a* ζωηρός, εύθυμος, κεφάτος.

vivid ['vɪvɪd] *a* ζωντανός, ζωηρός || *(bright, clear)* ζωηρός, λαμπρός.

vivisection [vɪvɪ'sekʃən] *n* ζωοτομία.

vocabulary [vəʊ'kæbjʊləri] *n* λεξιλόγιο.

vocal ['vəʊkəl] *a* φωνητικός, πχητικός || **~ cord** *n* φωνητική χορδή || ~**ist** *n* αοιδός *m/f*, τραγουδιστής/ίστρια *m/f*.

vocation [vəʊ'keɪʃən] *n (calling)* προορισμός, κλήση || *(profession)* επάγγελμα *nt*, τέχνη.

vociferous [vəʊ'sɪfərəs] *a* κραυγαλέος, φωνακλάς.

vodka ['vɒdkə] *n* βότκα.

vogue [vəʊg] *n* μόδα || *(popularity)* δημοτικότητα.

voice [vɔɪs] *n* φωνή || *(right of opinion)* ψήφος, γνώμη || *(GRAM)* φωνή (του ρήματος) ♦ *vt* εκφράζω || **with one ~** ομόφωνα.

void [vɔɪd] *n* κενό ♦ *a (of meaning)* κενός, άδειος.

volatile ['vɒlətaɪl] *a* άστατος, ευμετάβολος, ασταθής || *(evaporating quickly)* πτητικός.

volcanic [vɒl'kænɪk] *a* ηφαιστειώδης, εκρυκτικός.

volcano [vɒl'keɪnəʊ] *n* ηφαίστειο.

volition [və'lɪʃən] *n*: **of one's own ~** με τη θέλησή μου.

volley ['vɒli] *n* ομοβροντία || *(shower)* καταιγισμός, θύελλα || *(TENNIS)* βολλέ *nt inv*, κατευθείαν κτύπημα *nt* || ~**ball** *n* χειροσφαίρηση, βόλλεϊ-μπωλ *nt inv*.

volt [vəʊlt] *n* βόλτ || ~**age** *n* τάση, βολτάζ *nt inv*.

volume ['vɒljuːm] *n* τόμος βιβλίων || *(amount)* μεγάλη ποσότητα || *(space)* όγκος || *(loudness of sound)* ένταση, όγκος.

voluntarily ['vɒləntərɪli] *ad* εκουσίως, αυθόρμητα, εθελοντικά.

voluntary ['vɒləntəri] *a* εθελοντικός, εκούσιος.

volunteer [vɒlən'tɪə*] *n* εθελοντής/όντρια *m/f* ♦ *vi* προσφέρομαι.

voluptuous [və'lʌptjʊəs] *a* φιλήδονος, ηδυπαθής.

vomit ['vɒmɪt] *n* εμετός, ξέρασμα *nt* ♦ *vti* κάνω εμετό, ξερνώ.

vote [vəʊt] *n* ψηφοφορία, ψήφος || *(right)* δικαίωμα *nt* ψήφου || *(result)* αποτέλεσμα *nt* ψηφοφορίας ♦ *vt* ψηφίζω, ♦ *vi* ψηφίζω || ~**r** *n* ψηφοφόρος *m/f*, εκλογέας.

voting ['vəʊtɪŋ] *n* ψηφοφορία.

vouch [vaʊtʃ]: **to ~ for** *vt* υποστηρίζω, εγγυώμαι για.

voucher ['vaʊtʃə*] *n* απόδειξη πληρωμής, δικαιολογητικό.

vow [vaʊ] *n* όρκος, τάξιμο, τάμα *nt* ♦ *vt* ορκίζομαι, διακηρύττω.

vowel ['vaʊəl] *n* φωνήεν *nt*.

voyage ['vɔɪdʒ] *n* ταξίδι.

vulgar ['vʌlgə*] *a* χυδαίος, πρόστυχος, άξεστος || *(of common people)* κοινός, λαϊκός || ~**ity** *n* χυδαιότητα, προστυχιά.

vulnerable ['vʌlnərəbl] *a* τρωτός, εύτρωτος, ευπρόσβλητος.

vulture ['vʌltʃə*] *n* γύπας, όρνιο.

W

wad [wɒd] n (bundle) δέσμη, μάτσο.

wade [weid] vi βαδίζω στο νερό.

wafer ['weifə*] n λεπτό μπισκότο.

waffle ['wɒfl] n (food) είδος nt τηγανίτα || (col: empty talk) φλυαρία ♦ vi (col) φλυαρώ.

waft [wɑːft] vti μεταφέρω, σκορπίζω.

wag [wæg] vti κινώ, κουνώ, κινούμαι.

wage [weidʒ] n ημερομίσθιο, μισθός, αμοιβή, μεροκάματο ♦ vt διεξάγω, διενεργώ || ~s npl μισθός || ~ **earner** n μισθωτός || ~ **freeze** n παγίωση μισθών.

wager ['weidʒə*] n στοίχημα nt.

waggle ['wægl] vti (tail) κουνώ, ταλαντεύομαι.

wag(g)on ['wægən] n (road, rail) άμαξα, βαγόνι.

wail [weil] n θρήνος, ολοφυρμός ♦ vi θρηνώ, κλαίω, ολοφύρομαι.

waist [weist] n μέση, ζώνη || ~**coat** n γιλέκο || ~**line** n μέση.

wait [weit] n αναμονή, στάση ♦ vi περιμένω, αναμένω, σερβίρω || to ~ **for** vt περιμένω, αναμένω, καρτερώ || ~**er** n σερβιτόρος, γκαρσόνι || ~**ing room** n αίθουσα αναμονής, προθάλαμος || ~**ress** n σερβιτόρα.

wake [weik] (irreg v) vt ξυπνώ ♦ vi αγρυπνώ, είμαι άυπνος ♦ n ξενύχτι νεκρού || ~ n vt αφυπνίζω, ξυπνώ.

Wales [weilz] n Ουαλία.

walk [wɔːk] n περπάτημα nt, βόλτα, περίπατος || (way of walking) βάδισμα nt, περπατησιά || (path, route) περίπατος, δρόμος, πεζοδρόμιο || (walk of life) επάγγελμα nt ♦ vi περπατώ, βαδίζω || ~**er** n πεζοπόρος/α m/f, περπατητής m/f || ~**ie-talkie** n φορητός ασύρματος || ~**ing** n πεζοπορία, περπάτημα nt ♦ attr a (holiday) με τα πόδια || ~**ing shoes** n παπούτσια ntpl πεζοπορίας || ~**ing stick** n μπαστούνι || ~**out** n (of workers) απεργία || ~**over** n (col) εύκολη νίκη, εύκολη δουλειά.

wall [wɔːl] n (of house) τοίχος || (of city) τείχος nt.

wallet ['wɒlit] n πορτοφόλι.

wallop ['wɒləp] n δυνατό χτύπημα.

wallow ['wɒləu] vi (+ in) κυλιέμαι (σε), πλέω (σε) || (in money) κολυμπώ στο χρήμα.

wallpaper ['wɔːlpeipə*] n τοιχόχαρτο, χαρτί ταπετσαρίας.

walnut ['wɔːlnʌt] n καρύδι || (tree) καρυδιά.

walrus ['wɔːlrəs] n θαλάσσιος ίππος.

waltz [wɔːlts] n βαλς nt inv ♦ vi χορεύω βαλς.

wand [wɒnd] n ράβδος f, ραβδί.

wander ['wɒndə*] vi περιπλανώμαι, περιφέρομαι, τριγυρίζω|| ~**ing** a πλανόδιος, περιπλανώμενος.

want [wɒnt] vt θέλω, επιθυμώ || (need)

χρειάζομαι, έχω ανάγκη ♦ n: for ~ of ελλείψει || ~s npl (needs) ανάγκες fpl.

wanton ['wɒntən] a ακόλαστος, λάγνος.

war [wɔː*] n πόλεμος.

ward [wɔːd] n (division) περιφέρεια, συνοικία || (hospital) θάλαμος ♦ vt: to ~ **off** αποκρούω, αποφεύγω.

warden ['wɔːdn] n διευθυντής, φύλακας.

warder ['wɔːdə*] n φύλακας, δεσμοφύλακας.

wardrobe ['wɔːdrəub] n ντουλάπα || (clothing) γκαρνταρόμπα, τα ρούχα ntpl.

warehouse ['wɛəhaus] n αποθήκη.

wares [wɛəz] npl εμπορεύματα ntpl.

warfare ['wɔːfɛə*] n πόλεμος.

warhead ['wɔːhed] n κώνος βλήματος.

warily ['wɛərili] ad προσεκτικά, επιφυλακτικά.

warlike ['wɔːlaik] a πολεμικός, πολεμοχαρής, φιλοπόλεμος.

warm [wɔːm] a θερμός || (fire) ζεστός || (welcome) θερμός, ζωηρός || to ~ **up** vti ζεσταίνω, ζωηρεύω, ενθουσιάζομαι || ~-**hearted** a με ζεστή καρδιά, συμπονετικός || ~**ly** ad θερμά, ενθουσιωδώς || ~**th** n θερμότητα, ζεστασιά, ενθουσιασμός.

warn [wɔːn] vt προειδοποιώ || ~**ing** n προειδοποίηση || (caution) ειδοποίηση.

warp [wɔːp] vt σκεβρώνω ♦ n παραμόρφωση || (in meaning) στημόνι.

warrant ['wɒrənt] n (police) ένταλμα nt.

warranty ['wɒrənti] n εξουσιοδότηση, εγγύηση.

warrior ['wɒriə*] n πολεμιστής.

warship ['wɔːʃip] n πολεμικό πλοίο.

wart [wɔːt] n κρεατοελιά.

wartime ['wɔːtaim] n πολεμική εποχή, πολεμική περίοδος f.

wary ['wɛəri] a προσεκτικός, πονηρός, επιφυλακτικός.

was [wɒz, wəz] pt of **be**.

wash [wɒʃ] n πλύση, πλύσιμο || (face, hands) νίψιμο || (clothes) μπουγάδα ♦ vt πλένω ♦ vi πλένομαι || to ~ **away** vt παρασύρω, παίρνω || ~**able** a που πλένεται || ~**basin** n λεκάνη (νιπτήρα) || ~**er** n ροδέλα || (person) πλύστρα || ~**ing** n (linen etc) ρούχα ntpl για πλύσιμο, πλύση, πλύσιμο || ~**ing machine** n πλυντήριο || ~**ing powder** n σκόνη πλυσίματος || ~**ing-up** n πλύσιμο των πιάτων || ~**out** n (col) αποτυχία, φιάσκο || ~**room** n τουαλέτα.

wasn't ['wɒznt] = **was not** || see **be**.

wasp [wɒsp] n σφήκα.

wastage ['weistidʒ] n σπατάλη.

waste [weist] n σπατάλη || (what is wasted) άχρηστα υλικά ntpl, σκουπίδια ntpl, απορρίμματα ntpl || (wilderness) έρημος f ♦ a άχρηστος || (land) χέρσος, ερημωμένος ♦ vt (object) σπαταλώ, καταστρέφω || (time) σπαταλώ, χάνω ♦ vi: to ~ **away** φθίνω, αδυνατίζω || ~**ful**

a σπάταλος || ~ **paper basket** n
κάλαθος αχρήστων.

watch [wɔtʃ] n επίβλεψη, επιτήρηση ||
(vigilance) επαγρύπνηση || (guard)
φυλακή, φρουρός || (NAUT) φυλακή,
βάρδια || (timepiece) ρολόι ♦ vt
παρατηρώ, παρακολουθώ ♦ vi αγρυπνώ,
προσέχω, φρουρώ || ~ **dog** n (fig)
επιστάτης/ρια m/f, φύλακας || ~ **ful** a
άγρυπνος, προσεκτικός || ~ **maker** n
ωρολογοποιός, ρολογάς || ~ **man**
(νυκτο)φύλακας || ~ **strap** n λουρίδα
ρολογιού.

water ['wɔːtə*] n νερό ♦ vt ποτίζω ||
(wet) βρέχω, καταβρέχω || (soak)
διαβρέχω || **to ~ down** vt απαλύνω
(έκφραση), εξασθενίζω || ~ **closet** n
αποχωρητήριο, απόπατος, μέρος nt ||
~ **colour**, (US) ~ **color** n πίνακας με
νερομπογιά, ακουαρέλα || (paint)
υδρόχρωμα nt, νερομπογιά || ~ **cress** n
νεροκάρδαμο || ~ **fall** n καταρράκτης ||
~ **hole** n νερόλακκος || ~ **ing can** n
ποτιστήρι || ~ **lily** n νούφαρο || ~ **line** n
ίσαλος (γραμμή) || ~ **logged** a
πλημμυρισμένος, διάβροχος,
μουσκεμένος || ~ **melon** n καρπούζι ||
~ **proof** a αδιάβροχος, υδατοστεγής ||
~ **shed** n γραμμή διαχωρισμού υδάτων ||
~ **-skiing** n θαλάσσιο σκί || ~ **tight** a
υδατοστεγής, στεγανός, αδιάβροχος ||
~ **works** nt μηχανοστάσιο υδρεύσεως
|| ~ **y** a (colour) ξεπλυμένος, άτονος.

watt [wɔt] n βάτ(τ) nt inv.

wave [weɪv] n κύμα nt || (of hand)
κούνημα nt του χεριού || (RAD) κύμα nt ||
(in hair) κυμάτωση, κατσάρωμα nt ♦ vt
(hand) χαιρετώ με το χέρι, κουνώ το χέρι
|| (shape in curves) κατσαρώνω ♦ vi (flag)
κυματίζω, ανεμίζω || ~ **length** n μήκος
nt, κύματος.

waver ['weɪvə*] vi ταλαντεύομαι,
κυμαίνομαι || (weaken) κλονίζομαι.

wavy ['weɪvi] a κυματώδης, κυματιστός.

wax [wæks] n κερί ♦ vt (floors) κερώνω,
παρκετάρω ♦ vi (moon) μεγαλώνω,
γίνομαι.

way [weɪ] n οδός f, δρόμος || (manner)
τρόπος || (direction) κατεύθυνση, δρόμος
|| (habit) τρόπος, συνήθεια, έθιμο || **in the**
~ φράζω, εμποδίζω, κόβω (το δρόμο) ||
by the ~ με την ευκαιρία || ' ~ **in**'
'είσοδος' || ' ~ **out**' 'έξοδος'.

waylay [weɪ'leɪ] vt ενεδρεύω,
καιροφυλακτώ.

wayward ['weɪwəd] a δύστροπος,
πεισματάρης.

W.C. ['dʌblju'siː] n τουαλέτα.

we [wiː] pl pron εμείς.

weak [wiːk] a αδύνατος, ασθενικός ||
(not powerful) ανίσχυρος || (diluted)
αδύνατος, ελαφρός || ~ **en** vti
εξασθενίζω, αδυνατίζω, εξασθενώ ||
~ **ling** n αδύνατος άνθρωπος, ασθενικό
πλάσμα nt || ~ **ness** n αδυναμία || (fault)
ελάττωμα nt || (fondness) προτίμηση,
αδυναμία.

wealth [wɛlθ] n πλούτος || (abundance)
αφθονία || (things having value) περιουσία
|| ~ **y** a πλούσιος.

wean [wiːn] vt απογαλακτίζω, αποκόβω.

weapon ['wɛpən] n όπλο.

wear [wɛə*] (irreg v) n ρούχα ntpl,
ρουχισμός, φόρεμα nt || (use) χρήση ||
(decay) φθορά ♦ vt φέρω, φορώ || (show)
δείχνω, κρατιέμαι || (use) φθείρω, λυώνω
♦ vi (last long) αντέχω, διατηρούμαι || ~
and tear n φθορά, χρήσεως || **to ~ away**
vti φθείρω, φθείρομαι, τρώγω, τρίβω || **to**
~ **down** vt φθείρω, τρώγω || **to ~ off** vi
εξαφανίζω, περνώ || **to ~ out** vt φθείρω,
τρίβω, λυώνω || ~ **er** n φορών.

weariness ['wɪərɪnɪs] n κόπωση,
κούρασιν.

weary ['wɪərɪ] a κουρασμένος,
αποκαμωμένος || (tiring) νευραστικός,
πληκτικός, ανιαρός ♦ vti κουράζω,
κουράζομαι.

weasel ['wiːzl] n νυφίτσα, κουνάβι.

weather ['wɛðə*] n καιρός ♦ vt
αντιμετωπίζω || (season) εκθέτω στον
καιρό || ~ **-beaten** a ανεμοδαρμένος,
ηλιοκαμμένος, μαυρισμένος || ~ **cock** n
ανεμοδείκτης || ~ **forecast** n πρόβλεψη
καιρού.

weave [wiːv] (irreg v) vt υφαίνω, πλέκω,
συνθέτω || ~ **r** n υφαντής/άντρια m/f.

weaving ['wiːvɪŋ] n ύφανση, πλέξιμο.

web [wɛb] n ύφασμα nt, μεμβράνη || (of
spider) ιστός αράχνης || ~ **bed** a
μεμβρανώδης || ~ **bing** n ύφασμα nt
λωρίδων || (for reinforcement) ενισχυτική
ταινία.

wed [wɛd] vt νυμφεύω, νυμφεύομαι,
παντρεύομαι.

we'd [wiːd] = **we had, we would** ||
see **have, would**.

wedding ['wɛdɪŋ] n γάμος, παντρειά ||
~ **day** n μέρα των γάμων, επέτειος f των
γάμων || ~ **present** n γαμήλιο δώρο || ~
ring n αρραβώνας, βέρα.

wedge [wɛdʒ] n σφήνα || vt ενσφηνώνω,
χώνω, μπήγω || (pack tightly) σφηνώνω,
στριμώχνω.

Wednesday ['wɛnzdɪ] n Τετάρτη.

wee [wiː] a (Scottish col) μικρούλης,
λιγάκι, τόσος δα.

weed [wiːd] n ζιζάνιο, αγριόχορτο ♦ vt
ξεχορταριάζω, σκαλίζω, βγάζω,
καθαρίζω || ~ **-killer** n ζιζανιοκτόνο.

week [wiːk] n βδομάδα || ~ **day**
καθημερινή || ~ **end** n Σαββατοκύριακο
|| ~ **ly** ad εβδομαδιαίως ♦ a
εβδομαδιαίος.

weep [wiːp] (irreg v) vi κλαίω, χύνω
δάκρυα, δακρύζω.

weigh [weɪ] vt σταθμίζω, ζυγίζω || (have
weight) ζυγίζω ♦ vi (be important) ζυγίζω ||
to ~ down n (υπερ)φορτώνω,
βαραίνω, πιέζω || **to ~ up** vt εκτιμώ,
ζυγίζω || ~ **bridge** n γεφυροπλάστιγγα.

weight [weɪt] n βαρύτητα || (something
used on scales) σταθμό, μέτρο, ζύγι || (load)
βάρος nt, φορτίο || (importance) κύρος nt,

W

επιρροή, αξία || ~ **lifting** n άρση βαρών || ~γ α βαρύς.

weir [wɪə*] n φράγμα nt ποταμού.

weird [wɪəd] a υπερφυσικός, παράξενος.

welcome ['wɛlkəm] n υποδοχή || (reception) δεξίωση ♦ vt καλωσορίζω, (υπο) δέχομαι.

welcoming ['wɛlkəmɪŋ] a καλής υποδοχής.

weld [wɛld] n συγκόλληση, κόλληση ♦ vt (συγ)κολλώ, ενώνω || ~**er** n συγκολλητής.

welfare ['wɛlfɛə*] n ευημερία, κοινωνική πρόνοια || ~ **state** n κράτος nt κοινωνικής πρόνοιας.

well [wɛl] n πηγάδι, πηγή, πετρελαιοπηγή ♦ ad καλά || (to considerable extent) αρκετά, σχεδόν || (thoroughly) καλά, τελείως ♦ a υγιής, καλά || (satisfactory) καλός, καλά || interj (beginning conversation) λοιπόν, ίσως, καλά || (surprise) αδύνατο, μπά || **as ~** (also) επίσης, ομοίως.

we'll [wiːl] = **we will, we shall** || see **will, shall**.

well-behaved ['wɛlbɪ'heɪvd] a φρόνιμος, πειθαρχημένος.

well-being ['wɛl'biːɪŋ] n ευημερία.

well-earned ['wɛl'ɜːnd] a (rest) δίκαιος, καλοκερδισμένος.

wellingtons ['wɛlɪŋtənz] npl ψηλές μπότες fpl.

well-known ['wɛl'nəʊn] a (person) πασίγνωστος, φημισμένος.

well-meaning ['wɛl'miːnɪŋ] a καλοπροαίρετος.

well-off ['wɛl'ɒf] a εύπορος, πλούσιος.

well-read ['wɛl'rɛd] a μορφωμένος, πολυδιαβασμένος.

well-to-do ['wɛltə'duː] a εύπορος.

well-wisher ['wɛlwɪʃə*] n καλοθελητής/ήτρα m/f.

Welsh [wɛlʃ] a ουαλικός ♦ n (LING) Ουαλικά || ~**man** n Ουαλός.

went [wɛnt] pt of **go**.

wept [wɛpt] pt, pp of **weep**.

were [wɜː*] pt, pl of **be**.

we're [wɪə*] = **we are** || see **be**.

weren't ['wɜːnt] = **were not** || see **be**.

west [wɛst] n δύση || (country) δύση, δυτικά ♦ a δυτικός ♦ ad δυτικά, προς δυσμάς || **the W~** n n Δύση || ~**erly** a δυτικός (άνεμος) || ~**ern** a δυτικός ♦ n (CINE) ταινία με καουμπόυς || **W~ Indies** npl Οι Αντίλλες || ~**ward(s)** ad προς τα δυτικά.

wet [wɛt] a υγρός, βρε(γ)μένος, μουσκεμένος || (rainy) βροχερός || '~ paint' 'προσοχή χρώμα' || ~ **blanket** n (fig) άνθρωπος που χαλάει το κέφι, κρύος.

we've [wiːv] = **we have** || see **have**.

whack [wæk] vt κτυπώ, δέρνω στα ψαχνά.

whale [weɪl] n φάλαινα.

wharf [wɔːf] n αποβάθρα, προκυμαία.

what [wɒt] a (relative) ότι, όσος || (quantity) όσος, πόσος || (interrogative) τι, πώς; ποιος || interj τι, πώς; || ~**ever** a όποιος...και, ο τι... και, οποιοσδήποτε.

wheat [wiːt] n σιτάρι, στάρι.

wheel [wiːl] n τροχός, ρόδα ♦ vt (περι)στρέφω, σπρώχνω ♦ vi περιστρέφομαι, γυρίζω γύρω-γύρω || ~**barrow** n χειράμαξα || ~**chair** n αναπηρική καρέκλα.

wheeze [wiːz] vi αναπνέω δύσκολα, ασθμαίνω, σφυρίζω.

when [wɛn] ad πότε || (relative) όταν || cj όταν, που || ~**ever** ad οποτεδήποτε.

where [wɛə*] ad τι || (relative) (εκεί) που, όπου || ~**abouts** ad πού; || (λοιπόν) || πού περίπου; ♦ n θέση, διαμονή, κατατόπια ntpl || ~**as** cj εφόσον, ενώ.

wherever [wɛə'rɛvə*] ad οπουδήποτε.

whet [wɛt] vt (appetite) διεγείρω, ανοίγω (την όρεξη).

whether ['wɛðə*] cj εάν, αν, είτε.

which [wɪtʃ] a ποιος ♦ pron (interrogative) ποιο || (relative) ο' οποίος, στο οποίο, του οποίου || ~**ever** a όποιος, απ' όπου ♦ pron οποσδήποτε.

whiff [wɪf] n πνοή, φύσημα nt, ρουφηξιά.

while [waɪl] n χρονική περίοδος f, καιρός, χρόνος || cj ενώ.

whim [wɪm] n παραξενιά, ιδιοτροπία, καπρίτσιο.

whimper ['wɪmpə*] vi κλαυθμηρίζω, βογγώ.

whimsical ['wɪmzɪkəl] a ιδιότροπος, παράξενος.

whine [waɪn] vi κλαυθμηρίζω, μεμψιμοιρώ.

whip [wɪp] n μαστίγιο, καμτσίκι || (PARL) κοινοβουλευτικός ηγέτης ♦ vt μαστιγώνω, δέρνω, κτυπώ || (snatch) κινώ απότομα, αρπάζω || ~-**round** n έρανος, συνεισφορά.

whirl [wɜːl] n στροβιλισμός, στριφογύρισμα nt, γύρισμα nt ♦ vti στροβιλίζω, στριφογυρίζω, περιστρέφομαι || ~**pool** n δίνη, ρουφήχτρα || ~**wind** n ανεμοστρόβιλος.

whirr [wɜː*] vi βουίζω, σβουρίζω.

whisk [wɪsk] n (for eggs) κτυπητήρι ♦ vt (cream etc) κτυπώ, ανακατεύω.

whisker ['wɪskə*] n φαβορίτα || (of cat) μουστάκι.

whisk(e)y ['wɪskɪ] n ουίσκυ.

whisper ['wɪspə*] n ψίθυρος, θρόισμα nt, ψιθύρισμα nt ♦ vi ψιθυρίζω, μουρμουρίζω ♦ vt (secretly) ψιθυρίζω, σφυρίζω.

whist [wɪst] n ουίστ nt inv.

whistle ['wɪsl] n σφύριγμα nt || (instrument) σφυρίχτρα ♦ vi σφυρίζω.

white [waɪt] n λευκό, άσπρο || (of egg, eye) λεύκακα nt, ασπράδι ♦ a λευκός, άσπρος || (with fear) άσπρος, χλωμός || ~-**collar worker** n υπάλληλος m/f σε γραφείο || ~ **lie** n αθώο ψέμα nt || ~**wash** n (paint) ασβεστόνερο,

ασβεστόχρωμα nt ♦ vt ασβεστώνω,
ασπρίζω || (fig) αποκαθιστώ, δικαιολογώ.
Whitsun ['wɪtsn] n (also Whit Sunday)
Πεντηκοστή.
whittle ['wɪtl] vt: to ~ **away** or **down**
ελαττώνω, περιορίζω.
whizz [wɪz] vi σφυρίζω, περνώ γρήγορα
|| ~ **sale** n χοντρική πώληση.
who [hu:] pron ποιος || (relative) όποιος,
που || ~**ever** pron οποιοσδήποτε,
οιοσδήποτε.
WHO n (abbr of World Health Organization)
Παγκόσμιος Οργανισμός Υγείας
(WHO).
whole [həʊl] a (complete) ολόκληρος,
όλος, πλήρης || (uninjured) αβλαβής,
σώος ♦ n σύνολο || (not broken) σύνολο,
ακέραιο || ~**hearted** a ολόψυχος ||
~**sale** n χοντρική πώληση,
χοντρεμπόριο || attr a (trade) χοντρικός ||
(destruction) ολοκληρωτικός || ~**saler** n
χοντρέμπορος, κατάστημα nt χοντρικής
πωλήσεως || ~**some** a υγιεινός, υγιής.
wholly ['həʊlɪ] ad πλήρως, τελείως.
whom [hu:m] pron (object) ποιον.
whooping cough ['hu:pɪŋkɒf] n
κοκκύτης.
whore [hɔ:*] n πόρνη, πουτάνα.
whose [hu:z] pron ποιου, τίνος ποιανού
|| (of whom) του οποίου.
why [waɪ] ad γιατί || (relative) που, γιατί ||
interj μπα || ε.
wick [wɪk] n φυτίλι.
wicked ['wɪkɪd] a κακός,
διεστραμμένος, κακοήθης.
wicker ['wɪkə*] n λυγαριά.
wicket ['wɪkɪt] n (cricket) φράκτης,
στυλίσκοι mpl του κρίκετ.
wide [waɪd] a ευρύς, πλατύς, φαρδύς,
εκτενής || (mouth) ορθάνοικτος || (in
firing) έξω (από το στόχο) άστοχος ♦ ad
(opening) διάπλατα || ~-**angle lens** n
ευρυγώνιος φακός || ~-**awake** a
εντελώς ξύπνιος || ~**ly** ad ευρύτατα,
πλατειά || ~ n vt (road) ευρύνω,
πλαταίνω, διευρύνω || ~ **open** a (lit)
ορθάνοιχτος, ακάλυπτος || ~**spread** a
εκτεταμένος || (rumour etc)
διαδεδομένος, γενικός.
widow ['wɪdəʊ] n χήρα || ~**ed** a
χηρεύσας, χηρεύσασα || ~**er** n χήρος.
width [wɪdθ] n εύρος nt, πλάτος nt,
φάρδος nt.
wield [wi:ld] vt χειρίζομαι, ελέγχω,
εξασκώ.
wife [waɪf] n η σύζυγος, γυναίκα.
wig [wɪg] n περούκα.
wiggle ['wɪgl] vti κινώ νευρικά, κουνώ,
κουνιέμαι.
wild [waɪld] a άγριος || (not cultivated) σε
άγρια κατάσταση || (excited) αχαλίνωτος,
ξετρελαμένος, τρελός || ~**erness**
['wɪldənɪs] n έρημος, αγριότοπος || ~-
goose chase n μάταιη αναζήτηση,
άσκοπη επιχείρηση || ~**life** n άγρια ζώα
ntpl || ~**ly** ad άγρια, σαν τρελός.
wilful ['wɪlful] a εσκεμμένος, εκ

προμελέτης || (obstinate) ξεροκέφαλος,
πεισματάρης.
will [wɪl] auxiliary v: he ~ come θα έρθει
|| I ~ do it! θα το κάνω! ♦ n βούληση,
θέληση || (purpose) απόφαση, βούληση,
θέλημα nt || (inheritance) διαθήκη ♦ vt
θέλω, αποφασίζω || ~**ing** a πρόθυμος.
willow ['wɪləʊ] n ιτιά.
will power ['wɪlpaʊə*] n θέληση,
αυτοέλεγχος.
wilt [wɪlt] vi μαραίνομαι.
wily ['waɪlɪ] a πανούργος.
win [wɪn] (irreg v) n νίκη, επιτυχία ♦ vt
νικώ, κερδίζω ♦ vi επιτυγχάνω || to ~
over vt κατακτώ, αποκτώ.
wince [wɪns] n σύσπαση, τρεμούλιασμα
nt ♦ vi μορφάζω, σφίγγομαι.
winch [wɪntʃ] n βαρούλκο, βίντσι.
wind [waɪnd] (irreg v) vt (wrap) τυλίγω ||
(tighten) σφίγγω, κουρδίζω ♦ vi στρέφω,
στρέφομαι, ελίσσομαι, τυλίγομαι || to ~
up vt (clock) κουρδίζω || (debate) κλείνω,
τερματίζω.
wind [wɪnd] n άνεμος, αέρας || (MED)
αέρια ntpl, τυμπανισμός || ~**fall** n (good
luck) κελεπούρι.
winding ['waɪndɪŋ] a (road)
ελισσόμενος, φιδίσιος, με κορδέλες,
στριφτός.
wind instrument ['wɪndɪnstrumənt] n
(MUS) πνευστό (όργανο).
windmill ['wɪndmɪl] n ανεμόμυλος.
window ['wɪndəʊ] n παράθυρο, βιτρίνα
|| (COMPUT) παράθυρο || ~ **box** n
κιβώτιο λουλουδιών || ~ **cleaner** n
(man) καθαριστής παραθύρων || ~
frame n πλαίσιο παραθύρου, κούφωμα
nt || ~ **ledge** n περβάζι παραθύρου || ~
pane n τζάμι || ~**sill** n περβάζι
παραθύρου.
windpipe ['wɪndpaɪp] n τραχεία,
λάρυγγι.
windscreen ['wɪndskri:n], (US)
windshield ['wɪndʃi:ld] n παρμπρίζ nt
inv || ~ **wiper** n υαλοκαθαριστήρας.
windswept ['wɪndswept] a
ανεμοδαρμένος.
windy ['wɪndɪ] a ανεμώδης,
εκτεθειμένος στους ανέμους.
wine [waɪn] n οίνος, κρασί || ~ **cellar** n
κάβα || ~**glass** n ποτήρι του κρασιού ||
~ **list** n κατάλογος κρασιών || ~
merchant n κρασέμπορος || ~ **tasting**
n δοκιμή κρασιών || ~ **waiter** n
σερβιτόρος για τα κρασιά.
wing [wɪŋ] n (of bird, plane) φτερούγα,
φτερό || (of building) πτέρυγα (κτιρίου) ||
(MIL) πτέρυγα || ~**s** npl (THEAT)
παρασκήνια ntpl.
wink [wɪŋk] n ανοιγοκλείσιμο του
ματιού, νεύμα nt ♦ vi κλείνω το μάτι,
νεύω.
winner ['wɪnə*] n νικητής/ήτρια m/f.
winning ['wɪnɪŋ] a (team) κερδίζων,
νικήτρια (ομάδα) || (goal) κερδίζων γκόλ
|| ~**s** npl κέρδη ntpl || ~ **post** n τέρμα nt.
winter ['wɪntə*] n χειμώνας ♦ attr a

(clothes) χειμωνιάτικα ♦ *vi* περνώ το χειμώνα (σε) || ~ **sports** *npl* χειμωνιάτικα σπόρ *nt inv.*

wintry ['wɪntrɪ] *a* χειμωνιάτικος, ψυχρός.

wipe [waɪp] *n* σκούπισμα *nt*, στέγνωμα *nt*, σφουγγισμα *nt* ♦ *vt* σκουπίζω, στεγνώνω, σφουγγίζω || **to ~ out** *vt* **(debt)** σβήνω, εξοφλώ || **(destroy)** εξολοθρεύω, σαρώνω.

wire ['waɪə*] *n* σύρμα *nt* || **(cable)** τηλεγράφημα *nt* ♦ *vt* ενώνω με σύρμα, τοποθετώ τα καλώδια.

wireless ['waɪəlɪs] *n* ασύρματος || **(radio)** ραδιόφωνο.

wiry ['waɪərɪ] *a* σαν σύρμα, νευρώδης, δυνατός.

wisdom ['wɪzdəm] *n* σοφία, φρόνηση || **(good judgment)** σωφροσύνη || **(prudence)** φρονιμάδα, γνώση || ~ **tooth** *n* φρονιμίτης.

wise [waɪz] *a* σοφός, φρόνιμος, συνετός || **-wise** *suffix* κατά κάποιο τρόπο, σαν || ~ **crack** *n* ευφυολόγημα *nt*, καλαμπούρι.

wish [wɪʃ] *n* **(desire)** επιθυμία, ευχή ♦ *vt* **(desire)** εύχομαι, επιθυμώ || **with best ~es** με τις καλύτερες ευχές || **to ~ good-bye** εύχομαι καλό ταξίδι || **to ~ to do** επιθυμώ, θέλω να || ~**ful thinking** *n* ευσεβείς πόθοι *mpl*.

wisp [wɪsp] *n* **(of hair)** τσουλούφι, τολύπη.

wistful ['wɪstful] *a* συλλογισμένος, πικραμένος.

wit [wɪt] *n* **(sense)** αντίληψη, κατανόηση, νους *m*, μυαλό || **(cleverness)** πνεύμα *nt*, ευφυΐα || **(person)** πνευματώδης άνθρωπος, ευφυής, σπίρτο || ~**s** *npl* μυαλό, εξυπνάδα.

witch [wɪtʃ] *n* μάγισσα || ~**craft** *n* μαγεία.

with [wɪð, wɪθ] *prep* μετά, μαζί, με || **(by means of)** με, από || **(concerning)** μαζί με, μετά || **(notwithstanding)** παρά, παρ' όλο.

withdraw [wɪð'drɔː] *vt* αποσύρω, σύρω, τραβώ, σέρνω ♦ *vi* αποσύρομαι, αποτραβιέμαι, τραβιέμαι || ~**al** *n* αποχώρηση, ανάκληση.

wither ['wɪðə*] *vi* μαραίνομαι, ξεραίνομαι || ~**ed** *a* μαραμένος.

withhold [wɪð'həuld] *vt* αναστέλλω, κατακρατώ.

within [wɪð'ɪn] *prep* εντός, μέσα σε.

without [wɪð'aut] *prep* εκτός, χωρίς, δίχως.

withstand [wɪð'stænd] *vt* αντιστέκομαι σε, αντέχω σε.

witness ['wɪtnɪs] *n* μαρτυρία || **(LAW)** μάρτυρας ♦ *vt* **(see)** παρίσταμαι μάρτυς, βλέπω || **(sign documents)** επικυρώνω, βεβαιώνω, υπογράφω || ~ **box,** **(US)** ~ **stand** *n* θέση του εξεταζόμενου μάρτυρα.

witticism ['wɪtɪsɪzəm] *n* ευφυολογία, ευφυολόγημα *nt*, εξυπνάδα, αστείο.

wittily ['wɪtɪlɪ] *ad* πνευματωδώς, έξυπνα, σπιρτόζικα.

witty ['wɪtɪ] *a* πνευματώδης, σπιρτόζικος, έξυπνος.

wives [waɪvz] *npl of* **wife**.

wizard ['wɪzəd] *n* μάγος.

wk *abbr of* **week**.

wobble ['wɒbl] *vi* παραπατώ, ταλαντεύομαι, τρέμω.

woe [wəu] *n* συμφορά, δυστυχία, λύπη, θλίψη.

woke [wəuk] *pt, pp of* **wake**.

wolf [wulf] *n* λύκος.

wolves [wulvz] *npl of* **wolf**.

woman ['wumən] *n* γυναίκα ♦ *attr a* **(doctor)** (n) γιατρός.

womb [wuːm] *n* μήτρα.

women ['wimin] *npl of* **woman**.

won [wʌn] *pt, pp of* **win**.

wonder ['wʌndə*] *n* θαύμα *nt* || **(feeling)** θαυμασμός, κατάπληξη ♦ *vi* **(want to know)** απορώ, διερωτώμαι || ~**ful** *a* θαυμάσιος, εκπληκτικός.

won't [wəunt] = **will not** | *see* **will**.

wood [wud] *n* ξύλο, ξυλεία || **(forest)** δάσος *nt*, δρυμός, άλσος *nt* || **(carving)** *n* ξυλογλυπτική || ~**en** *a* ξύλινος || **(stiff)** αδέξιος, άκαμπτος || ~**pecker** *n* δρυοκολάπτης || ~**wind** *n* ξύλινα πνευστά *ntpl* ~**work** *n* ξυλουργική || ~**worm** *n* σκουλήκι του ξύλου.

wool [wul] *n* μαλλί || **(material)** μάλλινο ύφασμα *nt* || ~**len,** **(US)** ~**en** *a* μάλλινος || **(industry)** υφαντουργική || ~**ly,** **(US)** ~**y** *a* σαν μαλλί, σκεπασμένος με μαλλί.

word [wɜːd] *n* λέξη || **(talk, speech)** λόγος, παρατήρηση || **(news)** είδηση, ειδοποίηση, μήνυμα *nt*, νέο || **(promise)** λόγος ♦ *vt* διατυπώνω, εκφράζω με λέξεις || ~**ing** *n* διατύπωση, φρασεολογία || ~ **processing** *n* επεξεργασία κειμένου || ~ **processor** *n* επεξεργαστής κειμένου.

wore [wɔː*] *pt of* **wear**.

work [wɜːk] *n* έργο || **(task)** εργασία, δουλειά, απασχόληση || **(ART, LITER)** έργο, προϊόν εργασίας ♦ *vi* εργάζομαι, δουλεύω || **(have occupation)** εργάζομαι, ασχολούμαι με, δουλεύω ♦ *vt* **(cause to act)** λειτουργώ, βάζω να λειτουργήσει || ~**s** *n* **(factory)** εργοστάσιο || **to ~ on** *vi* συνεχίζω || **(influence)** επηρεάζω || **to ~ out** *vi* **(sum)** υπολογίζομαι, ανέρχομαι σε ♦ *vt* **(problem)** λύνω, αναπτύσσω || **(plan)** επεξεργάζομαι || **to ~ up to** *vi* ανέρχομαι || **to get ~ed up** εξάπτομαι, θυμώνομαι || ~**able** *a* επεξεργάσιμος, εκμεταλλεύσιμος, εφαρμόσιμος || ~**er** *n* εργάτης/ρια *m/f*, εργαζόμενος/n *m/f* || ~**ing class** *n* εργατική τάξη, εργαζόμενοι *mpl* || ~**ing-class** *a* της εργατικής τάξη || ~**ing man** *n* εργάτης, δουλευτής || ~**man** *n* εργάτης, τεχνίτης || ~**manship** *n* εκτέλεση, δούλεμα *nt*, επεξεργασία || ~**shop** *n* εργαστήριο.

world [wɜːld] *n* σύμπαν *nt*, υφήλιος *f*, κόσμος || **(the earth)** γη, κόσμος || **(mankind)** κόσμος, ανθρωπότητα || **(society)** κοινωνία, κόσμος || **(sphere)**

κόσμος || *attr a (champion)* παγκόσμιος,
διεθνής || **out of this** ~ απίστευτος,
περίφημος || ~-**famous** *a* παγκοσμίου
φήμης || ~-**ly** *a* εγκόσμιος, του κόσμου ||
~-**wide** *a* παγκόσμιος, διεθνής.
worm [wɜːm] *n* σκουλήκι.
worn [wɔːn] *pp of* **wear** || a εφθαρμένος,
φορεμένος || ~-**out** *a (object)* τριμμένος,
φαγωμένος || *(person)* εξαντλημένος,
τσακισμένος.
worried ['wʌrɪd] *a* στενοχωρημένος,
ανήσυχος.
worry ['wʌrɪ] *n* ανησυχία, σκοτούρα ♦
vt βασανίζω, στενοχωρώ ♦ *vi* ανησυχώ,
στενοχωρούμαι || ~**ing** *a* ενοχλητικός,
βασανιστικός.
worse [wɜːs] *a comp of* **bad** ♦ *ad comp of*
badly ♦ *n* κάτι χειρότερο, πιο κακό || ~**n**
vt επιδεινώνω, χειροτερεύω ♦ *vi*
επιδεινούμαι.
worship ['wɜːʃɪp] *n* λατρεία,
προσκύνηση || *(religious service)* λατρεία,
εκκλησίασμα *nt* || *(title)* n αυτού
εντιμότης ♦ *vt* λατρεύω || *(adore)* αγαπώ,
λατρεύω.
worst [wɜːst] *a sup of* **bad** ♦ *ad sup of*
badly ♦ *n* ο χειρότερος, ο πιό κακός.
worsted ['wustɪd] *n* υφάσματα πενιέ,
μαλλί πενιέ.
worth [wɜːθ] *n* αξία ♦ *a* άξιος || ~**less** *a*
χωρίς αξία || *(useless)* άχρηστος || ~**while**
a αξιόλογος.
worthy ['wɜːðɪ] *a* άξιος || *(+ of)* αντάξιος.
would [wʊd] *auxiliary v.* she ~ come
ερχότανε || **if you asked he** ~ **come** άν
παρακαλούσες θα 'ρχότανε || ~ **you**
like a drink? θέλεις κανένα ποτό; || ~-
be a δήθεν || ~'t = ~ not.
wound [waund] *pt, pp of* **wind** ♦ [wuːnd]
n τραύμα *nt*, πληγή ♦ *vt* τραυματίζω,
πληγώνω.
wove [wəuv] *pt of* **weave** || ~**n** *pp of*
weave.
wpm *n (abbr of words per minute)*
λεξ/λεπ., λ.α.λ. (λέξεις ανά λεπτό).
wrangle ['ræŋgl] *n* καυγάς, τσακωμός,
λογομαχία ♦ *vi* καυγαδίζω, λογομαχώ,
τσακώνομαι.
wrap [ræp] *n* σκέπασμα *nt*, σάλι ♦ *vt (also:*
~ **up)** τυλίγω, περιβάλλω, καλύπτω ||
~**per** *n* περιτύλιγμα *nt*, κάλυμμα *nt* ||
(gown) ρόμπα || ~**ping paper** *n* χαρτί
περιτυλίγματος.
wreath [riːθ] *n* στεφάνι.
wreck [rɛk] *n* ερείπιο, καταστροφή ||
(NAUT) ναυάγιο || *(ruin)* καταστροφή ♦ *vt*
καταστρέφω || *(NAUT)* προκαλώ ναυάγιο ||
~**age** *n* ναυάγιο, συντρίμματα *ntpl.*
wren [rɛn] *n* τρόχιλος, τρυπποκαρύδα.
wrench [rɛntʃ] *n* (γαλλικό) κλειδί ||
(violent twist) βίαιη κίνηση στρέψεως,
στρέβλωση ♦ *vt* στρεβλώνω,
στραμπουλίζω.
wrestle ['rɛsl] *vi (+ with)* αγωνίζομαι ||
(SPORT) παλεύω.
wrestling ['rɛslɪŋ] *n* πάλη, πάλεμα *nt* ||
~ **match** *n* αγώνισμα *nt* πάλης.

wretched ['rɛtʃɪd] *a* πολύ
δυστυχισμένος άθλιος || *(bad, poor)*
άθλιος, θλιβερός, αξιοθρήνητος.
wriggle ['rɪgl] *n* συστροφή
στριφογύρισμα ♦ *vi* συστρέφομαι,
σπαρταρώ στριφογυρίζω, γλιστρώ.
wring [rɪŋ] *(irreg v) vt* συστρέφω,
στρίβω.
wrinkle ['rɪŋkl] *n (on face)* ρυτίδα || *(in
cloth)* πτυχή ♦ *vt* ρυτιδώνω, ζαρώνω ♦ *vi*
ρυτιδούμαι, ζαρώνω.
wrist [rɪst] *n* καρπός (του χεριού) || ~
watch *n* ρολόι του χεριού.
writ [rɪt] *n (LAW)* δικαστική πράξη,
ένταλμα *nt.*
write [raɪt] *(irreg v) vt* γράφω || *(book)*
συντάσσω, γράφω ♦ *vi (send letter)*
γράφω, στέλνω γράμμα || **to** ~ **down** *vt*
διατυπώνω, (κατα) γράφω, σημειώνω,
περιγράφω || **to** ~ **off** *vt (dismiss)*
ακυρώνω, διαγράφω, ξεγράφω || **to** ~
out *vt* καθαρογράφω, αντιγράφω,
συντάσσω || **to** ~ **up** *vt (report)*
συντάσσω, γράφω || ~-**off** *n (smashed
car)* τελείως κατεστραμμένο || ~**r** *n*
συγγραφέας, συντάκτης.
writing ['raɪtɪŋ] *n* γράψιμο, γραφή ||
(books etc) λογοτεχνικό έργο || ~ **paper**
n κόλλα, χαρτί γραψίματος.
written ['rɪtn] *pp of* **write.**
wrong [rɒŋ] *a* κακός, άδικος || *(incorrect)*
ανακριβής, λανθασμένος || *(to be
mistaken)* κάνω λάθος.
wrote [rəut] *pt of* **write.**
wrought [rɔːt] *a:* ~ **iron**
κατεργασμένος σίδηρος.
wrung [rʌŋ] *pt, pp of* **wring.**
wry [raɪ] *a* στρεβλός, στριμμένος,
στραβός.
wt. *abbr of* **weight.**

X

Xmas ['ɛksməs] *n (col: Christmas)*
Χριστούγεννα *ntpl.*
X-ray ['ɛks'reɪ] *n* ακτινογραφία,
ακτινοσκόπηση.
xylophone ['zaɪləfəun] *n* ξυλόφωνο.

Y

yacht [jɒt] *n* θαλαμηγός *f*, γιοτ *nt inv*,
κότερο || ~**ing** *n* ενασχόληση με γιωτ,
γιώτιγκ *nt inv* || ~**sman** *n* άνθρωπος
ασχολούμενος με γιώτ.
Yank [jæŋk] *n (col: American)*
Αμερικάνος, Γιάγκης.
yap [jæp] *vi (dog)* γαυγίζω.
yard [jɑːd] *n (of house etc)* αυλή,
προαύλιο, μάντρα || *(measure)* υάρδα
(0.914 μ).
yarn [jɑːn] *n* νήμα *nt*, κλωστή || *(tale)*
ιστορία φανταστική.
yawn [jɔːn] *n* χασμούρημα *nt*,
χασμουρητό ♦ *vi* χασμουριέμαι.

yd. *abbr of* yard(s).

year ['jiə*] n έτος nt, χρόνος || ~ly a
ετήσιος ♦ ad ετησίως, κάθε χρόνο.

yearn [jɜːn] vi (+ *for*) ποθώ, λαχταρώ ||
~ing n πόθος, λαχτάρα.

yeast [jiːst] n προζύμι, μαγιά.

yell [jel] n κραυγή, σκούξιμο ♦ vi
ωρύομαι, φωνάζω δυνατά, σκούζω.

yellow ['jeləu] a κίτρινος ♦ n κίτρινο.

yelp [jelp] vi γαυγίζω.

yes [jes] ad ναι, μάλιστα.

yesterday ['jestədei] ad χθες, χτες.

yet [jet] ad (*by now*) ακόμη, τώρα || (*still*)
ακόμη || (*by that time*) κι όμως, παρ' όλα
αυτά || cj κι όμως, εντούτοις.

yew [juː] n τάξος.

Yiddish ['jidiʃ] n (*LING*) γερμανοεβραϊκά.

yield [jiːld] n παραγωγή, απόδοση ♦ vt
αποδίδω, αποφέρω ♦ vi (*surrender*)
υποτάσσομαι, παραδίδομαι.

yodel ['jəudl] vi τραγουδώ (τυρολέζικα).

yoga ['jəugə] n γιόγκα nt inv.

yogurt ['jəugət] n γιαούρτι nt.

yoke [jəuk] n ζυγός, ζευγάρι || (*servitude*)
ζυγός.

yolk [jəuk] n κρόκος, κροκάδι.

you [juː] pron (ε)σείς, (ε)σύ.

you'd [juːd] = you had, you would
|| see have, would.

you'll [juːl] = you will, you shall ||
see will, shall.

young [jʌŋ] a νέος, νεαρός, μικρός || the
~ οι νέοι mpl, n νεολαία || ~ish a
μάλλον νέος, νεούτσικος || ~ster n
νεαρός, νέος, αγόρι.

your ['juə*] poss a σου, σας.

you're ['juə*] = you are || see be.

yours ['juəz] poss pron (δικός) σου,
(δικός) σας || ~ faithfully υμέτερος || ~
sincerely όλως υμέτερος.

yourself [jə'self] pron συ (ο ίδιος), τον
εαυτόν σας, χωρίς βοήθεια.

yourselves [jə'selvz] pron pl σεις (οι
ίδιοι), μόνοι σας.

youth [juːθ] n νεότητα, νιάτα, νιότη ||
(*young man*) νέος, νεαρός, έφηβος ||
(*young people*) νέοι mpl, νεολαία || ~ful a
νεανικός, νεαρός || ~ hostel n ξενώνας
νεότητας.

you've [juːv] = you have || see have.

Yugoslav ['juːgəu'slɑːv] a
γιουγκοσλαβικός ♦ n (*person*)
Γιουγκοσλάβος/α m/f || (*LING*)
Γιουγκοσλαβικά ntpl || ~ia n
Γιουγκοσλαβία.

Z

zany ['zeini] a ηλίθιος, βλάκας.

zeal [ziːl] n ζήλος || ~ous a γεμάτος
ζήλο.

zebra ['ziːbrə] n ζέβρα || ~ crossing n
διάβαση (πεζών).

zero ['ziərəu] n μηδέν nt, μηδενικό || ~
hour n ώρα μηδέν, ώρα (επιθέσεως).

zest [zest] n ζέση, ενθουσιασμός, όρεξη.

zigzag ['zigzæg] n ζιγκ-ζαγκ nt inv ♦ vi
κάνω ζιγκ-ζαγκ.

zinc [ziŋk] n ψευδάργυρος, τσίγκος.

Zionism ['zaiənizəm] n σιωνισμός.

zip [zip] n (*also:* ~ fastener, ~per)
φερμουάρ nt inv ♦ vt (*also:* ~ up) κλείνω
(με φερμουάρ).

zodiac ['zəudiæk] n ζωδιακός κύκλος.

zone [zəun] n ζώνη.

zoo [zuː] n ζωολογικός κήπος || ~logical
a ζωολογικός || ~logist n ζωολόγος ||
~logy n ζωολογία.

zoom [zuːm] vi βομβώ, βουίζω || ~ lens
n φακός μεταβλητής εστιακής
αποστάσεως, ζούμ nt inv.

ΑΓΓΛΙΚΑ ΑΝΩΜΑΛΑ ΡΗΜΑΤΑ

present	pt	pp	present	pt	pp
arise	arose	arisen	eat	ate	eaten
awake	awoke	awaked	fall	fell	fallen
be (am, is, are; being)	was, were	been	feed	fed	fed
			feel	felt	felt
			fight	fought	fought
bear	bore	born(e)	find	found	found
beat	beat	beaten	flee	fled	fled
become	became	become	fling	flung	flung
befall	befell	befallen	fly	flew	flown
begin	began	begun	forbid	forbade	forbidden
behold	beheld	beheld	forecast	forecast	forecast
bend	bent	bent	forget	forgot	forgotten
beset	beset	beset	forgive	forgave	forgiven
bet	bet, betted	bet, betted	forsake	forsook	forsaken
			freeze	froze	frozen
bid	bid	bid	get	got	got, (US) gotten
bind	bound	bound			
bite	bit	bitten	give	gave	given
bleed	bled	bled	go (goes)	went	gone
blow	blew	blown			
break	broke	broken	grind	ground	ground
breed	bred	bred	grow	grew	grown
bring	brought	brought	hang	hung, hanged	hung, hanged
build	built	built			
burn	burnt, burned	burnt, burned	have	had	had
			hear	heard	heard
burst	burst	burst	hide	hid	hidden
buy	bought	bought	hit	hit	hit
can	could	(been able)	hold	held	held
cast	cast	cast	hurt	hurt	hurt
catch	caught	caught	keep	kept	kept
choose	chose	chosen	kneel	knelt, kneeled	knelt, kneeled
cling	clung	clung			
come	came	come	know	knew	known
cost	cost	cost	lay	laid	laid
creep	crept	crept	lead	led	led
cut	cut	cut	lean	leant, leaned	leant, leaned
deal	dealt	dealt			
dig	dug	dug	leap	leapt, leaped	leapt, leaped
do (3rd person; he/she/it does)	did	done	learn	learnt, learned	learnt, learned
			leave	left	left
draw	drew	drawn	lend	lent	lent
dream	dreamed, dreamt	dreamed, dreamt	let	let	let
			lie (lying)	lay	lain
drink	drank	drunk	light	lit, lighted	lit, lighted
drive	drove	driven			
dwell	dwelt	dwelt			

Z

present	pt	pp	present	pt	pp
lose	lost	lost	speed	sped, speeded	sped, speeded
make	made	made			
may	might	—	spell	spelt, spelled	spelt, spelled
mean	meant	meant			
meet	met	met	spend	spent	spent
mistake	mistook	mistaken	spill	spilt, spilled	spilt, spilled
mow	mowed	mown, mowed			
			spin	spun	spun
must	(had to)	(had to)	spit	spat	spat
pay	paid	paid	split	split	split
put	put	put	spoil	spoiled, spoilt	spoiled, spoilt
quit	quit, quitted	quit, quitted			
			spread	spread	spread
read	read	read	spring	sprang	sprung
rend	rent	rent	stand	stood	stood
rid	rid	rid	steal	stole	stolen
ride	rode	ridden	stick	stuck	stuck
ring	rang	rung	sting	stung	stung
rise	rose	risen	stink	stank	stunk
run	ran	run	stride	strode	stridden
saw	sawed	sawn	strike	struck	struck, stricken
say	said	said			
see	saw	seen	strive	strove	striven
seek	sought	sought	swear	swore	sworn
sell	sold	sold	sweep	swept	swept
send	sent	sent	swell	swelled	swollen, swelled
set	set	set			
shake	shook	shaken	swim	swam	swum
shall	should	—	swing	swung	swung
shear	sheared	shorn, sheared	take	took	taken
			teach	taught	taught
shed	shed	shed			
shine	shone	shone	tear	tore	torn
shoot	shot	shot	tell	told	told
show	showed	shown	think	thought	thought
shrink	shrank	shrunk	throw	threw	thrown
shut	shut	shut	thrust	thrust	thrust
sing	sang	sung	tread	trod	trodden
sink	sank	sunk	wake	woke, waked	woken, waked
sit	sat	sat			
slay	slew	slain	wear	wore	worn
sleep	slept	slept	weave	wove, weaved	woven, weaved
slide	slid	slid			
sling	slung	slung	wed	wedded, wed	wedded, wed
slit	slit	slit			
smell	smelt, smelled	smelt, smelled	weep	wept	wept
			win	won	won
sow	sowed	sown, sowed	wind	wound	wound
			wring	wrung	wrung
speak	spoke	spoken	write	wrote	written

ΑΠΟΛΥΑ		CARDINAL NUMBERS
μηδέν	0	zero
ένας, μία (μια), ένα	1	one
δύο	2	two
τρεις, τρία	3	three
τέσσερις, τέσσερα	4	four
πέντε	5	five
έξι	6	six
επτά (εφτά)	7	seven
οκτώ (οχτώ)	8	eight
εννέα (εννιά)	9	nine
δέκα	10	ten
έντεκα	11	eleven
δώδεκα	12	twelve
δεκατρείς, δεκατρία	13	thirteen
δεκατέσσερις,		
δεκατέσσερα	14	fourteen
δεκαπέντε	15	fifteen
δεκαέξι	16	sixteen
δεκαεπτά (δεκαεφτά)	17	seventeen
δεκαοκτώ (δεκαοχτώ)	18	eighteen
δεκαεννέα (δεκαεννιά)	19	nineteen
είκοσι	20	twenty
είκοσι ένας, μία, ένα	21	twenty-one
είκοσι δύο	22	twenty-two
είκοσι τρεις, τρία	23	twenty-three
τριάντα	30	thirty
σαράντα	40	forty
πενήντα	50	fifty
εξήντα	60	sixty
εβδομήντα	70	seventy
ογδόντα	80	eighty
ενενήντα	90	ninety
εκατό	100	one hundred
εκατόν ένας, εκατό μία,		
εκατόν ένα	101	one hundred and one
εκατόν πενήντα έξι	156	one hundred and fifty-six
διακόσιοι,ες,α	200	two hundred
τριακόσιοι,ες,α	300	three hundred
τετρακόσιοι,ες,α	400	four hundred
πεντακόσιοι,ες,α	500	five hundred
εξακόσιοι,ες,α	600	six hundred
επτακόσιοι,ες,α		
(εφτακόσιοι,ες,α)	700	seven hundred
οκτακόσιοι,ες,α		
(οχτακόσιοι,ες,α)	800	eight hundred
εννιακόσιοι,ες,α	900	nine hundred
χίλιοι, χίλιες, χίλια	1,000	one thousand
δύο χιλιάδες	2,000	two thousand
τρεις χιλιάδες	3,000	three thousand
ένα εκατομμύριο	1,000,000	one million
ένα δισεκατομμύριο	1,000,000,000	one billion

211

TAKTIKA

ORDINAL NUMBERS

πρώτος, πρώτη, πρώτο	1st	first
δεύτερος	2nd	second
τρίτος	3rd	third
τέταρτος	4th	fourth
πέμπτος	5th	fifth
έκτος	6th	sixth
έβδομος	7th	seventh
όγδοος	8th	eighth
ένατος	9th	ninth
δέκατος	10th	tenth
ενδέκατος (εντέκατος)	11th	eleventh
δωδέκατος	12th	twelfth
δέκατος τρίτος	13th	thirteenth
δέκατος τέταρτος	14th	fourteenth
δέκατος πέμπτος	15th	fifteenth
δέκατος έκτος	16th	sixteenth
δέκατος έβδομος	17th	seventeenth
δέκατος όγδοος	18th	eighteenth
δέκατος ένατος	19th	nineteenth
εικοστός	20th	twentieth
εικοστός πρώτος	21st	twenty-first
εικοστός δεύτερος	22nd	twenty-second
εικοστός τρίτος	23rd	twenty-third
τριακοστός	30th	thirtieth
τεσσερακοστός	40th	fortieth
πεντηκοστός	50th	fiftieth
εξηκοστός	60th	sixtieth
εβδομηκοστός	70th	seventieth
ογδονκοστός	80th	eightieth
ενενηκοστός	90th	ninetieth
εκατοστός	100th	(one) hundredth
διακοσιοστός	200th	two hundredth
τριακοσιοστός	300th	three hundredth
τειρακοσιοστός	400th	four hundredth
πεντακοσιοστός	500th	five hundredth
εξακοσιοστός	600th	six hundredth
επτακοσιοστός (εφτακοσιοστός)	700th	seven hundredth
οκτακοσιοστός (οχτακοσιοστός)	800th	eight hundredth
εννιακοσιοστός	900th	nine hundredth
χιλιοστός	1,000th	(one) thousandth
εκατομμυριοστός	1,000,000th	millionth
δισεκατομμυριοστός	1,000,000,000th	billionth

THE TIME

what time is it?		τι ώρα είναι;
it is ...		είναι ...
at what time?		τι ώρα;
at 8		στις οκτώ
at midnight		τα μεσάνυχτα
at one p.m.		στη μία μετά το μεσημέρι

00.00	midnight	μεσάνυχτα, δώδεκα τα μεσάνυχτα
00.10	ten past midnight, ten past twelve a.m.	δώδεκα και δέκα μετά τα μεσάνυχτα
00.15	a quarter past midnight, twelve fifteen a.m.	δώδεκα και τέταρτο μετά τα μεσάνυχτα, δώδεκα και δεκαπέντε π.μ.
00.30	half past twelve, twelve thirty a.m.	δώδεκα και μισή, δώδεκα και τριάντα π.μ.
01.10	ten past one, one ten	μία (μια) και δέκα
01.15	a quarter past one, one fifteen	μία (μια) και τέταρτο, μία και δεκαπέντε
01.30	half past one, one thirty	μία (μια) και μισή, μία και τριάντα
01.45	a quarter to two, one forty-five	δύο παρά τέταρτο, μία και σαράντα πέντε
01.50	ten to two, one fifty	δύο παρά δέκα, μία και πενήντα
12.00	midday	μεσημέρι, δώδεκα το μεσημέρι
12.30	half past twelve, twelve thirty p.m.	δώδεκα και μισή, δώδεκα και τριάντα μ.μ.
13.00	one (o'clock) (in the afternoon), one p.m.	μία (μια) η ώρα (το απόγευμα ή μ.μ.)
19.00	seven (o'clock) (in the evening), seven p.m.	επτά η ώρα (το βράδυ ή μ.μ.)
21.30	nine thirty (p.m. or at night)	εννέα και μισή (μ.μ. ή το βράδυ)
23.45	a quarter to twelve, eleven forty-five p.m.	δώδεκα παρά τέταρτο, έντεκα και σαράντα πέντε μ.μ.

in 20 minutes	σε είκοσι λεπτά
20 minutes ago	πριν από είκοσι λεπτά
wake me up at 7	ξυπνήστε με στις επτά
20 km.p.h.	είκοσι χιλιόμετρα την ώρα

DATES AND NUMBERS

1. The date

what's the date today?	τι ημερομηνία είναι σήμερα;
it's the ...	είναι η ...
1st of February	πρώτη Φεβρουαρίου
2nd of February	δευτέρα Φεβρουαρίου
28th of February	εικοστή ογδόη Φεβρουαρίου
he's coming on the 7th of May	θα φθάσει στις επτά Μαΐου
I was born in 1945	γεννήθηκα το χίλια εννιακόσια σαράντα πέντε
I was born on the 15th of July 19 ...	γεννήθηκα στις δεκαπέντε Ιουλίου χίλια εννιακόσια...
during the sixties	στη δεκαετία του εξήντα
in the twentieth century	στον εικοστό αιώνα
in May	το Μάιο
on Monday (the 15th)	τη Δευτέρα (στις δεκαπέντε)
on Mondays	κάθε Δευτέρα
next/last Monday	την επόμενη/την περασμένη Δευτέρα
in 10 days' time	σε δέκα μέρες

2. Telephone numbers

I would like Athens 24 35 56

θα ήθελα Αθήνα είκοσι τέσσερα/ τριάντα πέντε/ πενήντα έξι

could you get me Athens 22 00 79, extension 2233

μπορείτε να μου πάρετε Αθήνα είκοσι δύο/ μηδέν μηδέν/ εβδομήντα εννέα, εσωτερική γραμμή είκοσι δύο/ τριάντα τρία

the Athens prefix is 01

ο κωδικός της Αθήνας είναι μηδέν ένα

3. Using numbers

he lives at number 10	μένει στον αριθμό δέκα
it's in chapter 7, on page 7	είναι στο έβδομο κεφάλαιο, στη σελίδα επτά
he lives on the 3rd floor	μένει στο τρίτο πάτωμα
he came in 4th	ήρθε τέταρτος
a share of one seventh	μερίδιο ένα έβδομο
scale 1:25,000	κλίμακα ένα στις είκοσι πέντε χιλιάδες